American Film History

D1560493

The Editors

Cynthia Lucia is Professor of English and Director of Film and Media Studies at Rider University. She is author of *Framing Female Lawyers: Women on Trial in Film* (2005) and writes for *Cineaste* film magazine, where she has served on the editorial board for more than two decades. Her most recent research includes essays that appear in *A Companion to Woody Allen* (Wiley-Blackwell, 2013), *Modern British Drama on Screen* (2014), and *Law, Culture and Visual Studies* (2014).

Roy Grundmann is Associate Professor of Film Studies at Boston University. He is the author of *Andy Warhol's Blow Job* (2003) and the editor of *A Companion to Michael Haneke* (Wiley-Blackwell, 2010). He is Contributing Editor of *Cineaste* and has published essays in a range of prestigious anthologies and journals, including *GLQ, Cineaste, Continuum, The Velvet Light Trap,* and *Millennium Film Journal.* He has curated retrospectives on Michael Haneke, Andy Warhol, and Matthias Müller.

Art Simon is Professor of Film Studies at Montclair State University. He is the author of *Dangerous Knowledge: The JFK Assassination in Art and Film* (2nd edition, 2013). He has curated two film exhibitions for the Solomon Guggenheim Museum in New York City and his work has been published in the edited collection *"Un-American" Hollywood: Politics and Film in the Blacklist Era* (2007) and in the journal *American Jewish History.*

Together they are the editors of the four-volume collection *The Wiley-Blackwell History of American Film* (2012) and *American Film History: Selected Readings, 1960 to the Present* (2016), both published by Wiley-Blackwell.

American Film History

Selected Readings, Origins to 1960

Edited by

Cynthia Lucia, Roy Grundmann, and Art Simon

WILEY Blackwell

This edition first published 2016

© 2016 John Wiley & Sons, Inc, except for Chapter 16 © 1999 University of Texas Press; Chapter 18 © 1989 James Naremore; and Chapter 26 © 1981 Cambridge University Press

Registered Office: John Wiley & Sons Ltd, The Atrium, Southern Gate, Chichester, West Sussex, PO19 8SQ, UK

Editorial Offices: 350 Main Street, Malden, MA 02148-5020, USA
9600 Garsington Road, Oxford, OX4 2DQ, UK
The Atrium, Southern Gate, Chichester, West Sussex, PO19 8SQ, UK

For details of our global editorial offices, for customer services, and for information about how to apply for permission to reuse the copyright material in this book please see our website at www.wiley.com/wiley-blackwell.

The right of Cynthia Lucia, Roy Grundmann, and Art Simon to be identified as the author of the editorial material in this work has been asserted in accordance with the UK Copyright, Designs and Patents Act 1988.

All rights reserved. No part of this publication may be reproduced, stored in a retrieval system, or transmitted, in any form or by any means, electronic, mechanical, photocopying, recording or otherwise, except as permitted by the UK Copyright, Designs and Patents Act 1988, without the prior permission of the publisher.

Wiley also publishes its books in a variety of electronic formats. Some content that appears in print may not be available in electronic books.

Designations used by companies to distinguish their products are often claimed as trademarks. All brand names and product names used in this book are trade names, service marks, trademarks or registered trademarks of their respective owners. The publisher is not associated with any product or vendor mentioned in this book.

Limit of Liability/Disclaimer of Warranty: While the publisher and authors have used their best efforts in preparing this book, they make no representations or warranties with respect to the accuracy or completeness of the contents of this book and specifically disclaim any implied warranties of merchantability or fitness for a particular purpose. It is sold on the understanding that the publisher is not engaged in rendering professional services and neither the publisher nor the author shall be liable for damages arising herefrom. If professional advice or other expert assistance is required, the services of a competent professional should be sought.

Library of Congress Cataloging-in-Publication Data

American film history : selected readings / edited by Cynthia Lucia, Roy Grundmann, Arthur Simon.
volume cm
Includes bibliographical references and index.
Contents: v. 1. Origins to 1960 –
ISBN 978-1-118-47513-3 (paperback)
1. Motion pictures–United States–History–20th century. I. Lucia, Cynthia A. Barto (Cynthia Anne Barto), editor. II. Grundmann, Roy, 1963- editor. III. Simon, Arthur, editor.
PN1993.5.U6A8656 2015
791.430973–dc23 2015015486

A catalogue record for this book is available from the British Library.

Cover image: Top: Clark Gable and Jean Harlow, *Red Dust*, 1932. Photo: Pictorial Press Ltd/Alamy.
Bottom: *Intolerance*, 1916. Photo: Wark Production Company/Album/akg-images.

Set in 10/12pt BemboStd by Aptara Inc., New Delhi, India

Printed in Singapore by C.O.S. Printers Pte Ltd

1 2016

Contents

Volume I: Origins to 1960

Part II 1929–1945

Also in the same series

Volume II: 1960 to the Present

Part III 1991 to the Present

Additional online resources such as sample syllabi, which include suggested readings and filmographies for both general and specialized courses, are available at www.wiley.com.

Acknowledgments

These volumes would not have been possible without the outstanding research and scholarship of our respected cinema and media colleagues whose essays appear on these pages. We thank them, along with other scholars whose advice has been invaluable along the way. We are deeply grateful to Wiley-Blackwell editor Jayne Fargnoli, who was instrumental in helping initiate this project and whose continued support and advice have been crucial. We also thank the highly professional and supportive Wiley-Blackwell editorial team, including Julia Kirk, Mary Hall, Mark Graney, Annie Jackson, Brigitte Lee Messenger, and so many others who have devoted their time and effort to designing these volumes. We also are grateful to Colin Root, Robert Ribera, Virginia Myhaver, and Nicholas Forster of Boston University who assisted in completing the four-volume hardcover edition from which this two-volume paperback edition is drawn. And there are so many others – both colleagues and students – at Rider University, Boston University, and Montclair State University to whom we owe our thanks. We also acknowledge the support of Rider University summer fellowships and research leaves that were instrumental in helping us complete both the hardcover and paperback editions.

We deeply appreciate the support of our families and friends through the years we've spent on this project, without whom we could not have sustained our efforts. We remain forever grateful to Barbara Berger, Isaac Simon, and Tillie Simon; Mark Hennessey; and Ray Lucia for their love, patience, and support.

We especially want to acknowledge Robert Sklar. Bob's contribution to these volumes goes well beyond the two essays that appear here. His mentorship, scholarship, and friendship meant so much to us over the years. It is with great respect and gratitude that we dedicate these volumes to his memory.

The Editors

Preface

In many ways, this project began in the classroom. When organizing American film history courses, often taught over two semesters, we encountered the recurring problem of how best to select readings for our students. A strong narrative history seemed essential and several of these are available. But because of their scope and synthesis, these texts do not have space for lengthy discussions of important events, film cycles, or artists. We wanted to create a collection of essays that would provide such in-depth discussions. We also wanted original treatments of "bread-and-butter topics" – the rise of the star system, the place of specific genres like the musical and gangster film, the operations of classical-era studios and their executives – as well as less frequently discussed topics. As a means of introducing new areas of inquiry into our courses and the larger field of film scholarship, we especially wanted essays that would cover film production on the margins, such as the avant-garde and documentary, and films made by and on topics associated with underrepresented groups – whether women, African-Americans, Asian-Americans, or gays and lesbians. Although we gladly reprinted several important essays, we mostly asked scholars to contribute new work, extending arguments they had made elsewhere or tackling entirely new areas. The result was *The Wiley-Blackwell History of American Film*, published in 2012, in four-volume hardback and online editions.

The book in front of you is part of a two-volume paperback collection of essays selected from the four-volume hardback/online edition. New material has been added, including expanded introductions and brief overviews of individual essays, designed to guide students by highlighting key concepts and separately listing "additional terms, names, and concepts" of importance. Overviews also reference related essays in the paperback and hardback/online editions,[1] encouraging readers to expand their understanding and further their research. Professors adopting this paperback volume(s) also will have access to pedagogically oriented materials online, including sample syllabi for survey courses in American film history and syllabi using these volumes to create more focused "special topics" courses.

With the classroom in mind, new and expanded introductions address historical time periods marked by each section division. These introductions, it must be noted however, do not pretend to be all-inclusive treatments of their particular periods nor do they systematically survey every essay within each volume – that task is performed by the overviews accompanying individual essays. Rather, the introductions function as a type of establishing long shot, a perspective on some of the more significant events, individuals, films, and developments in a given era, with collected essays providing closer, more detailed views. We also acknowledge that lines of demarcation from section to section, period to period, should always be understood as permeable, never rigid. As such, we do discuss films in the introductory essays that, from time to time, cross these flexible boundary lines.

As with every such collection, and with narrative accounts of film history, we were forced to make difficult decisions about those topics and essays from the 2012 edition that we would include or omit. Undoubtedly, readers will wonder about the inclusion of some subjects and the absence of others. This is perhaps particularly the case when it comes to individual artists. There are essays here devoted to Griffith, Capra, and Wilder but not to Ford, Hawks, and Hitchcock. All historians are painfully aware of who and what gets left out. Moreover, the essays focusing on individuals certainly favor directors over screenwriters or cinematographers. On the other hand, the critical importance of the star is addressed in several essays, many of which simultaneously take up the issue of genre. Our choices grew from the desire to create volumes that could most usefully be integrated into American film history courses as they typically are taught. Although our expanded introductions aim to fill in gaps, we acknowledge that more than a few gaps do, inevitably, remain.

Two approaches to American film history have guided the best work in the field over the past 30 years. The first is a cultural history approach offering an account that combines attention to the industry and its development with a focus on the political and cultural events central to US history in the late nineteenth, twentieth, and twenty-first centuries. A second approach undertakes a far more intensive study of the film industry's production, distribution, and exhibition strategies, tracing the emergence of a "classical" language and recording the shifting authorial forces within the industry. This has been accompanied by important work inside studio archives and with the professional/personal papers of key artists. In writing a history of American film, both approaches are indispensable.

With the 2012 *Wiley-Blackwell History of American Film* and this two-volume edition, we have sought to add a third, vital component – one that pays closer attention to the films themselves. Because the best narrative American film histories have limited space for elaborate, close readings of the films they reference,[2] we believe there is room in historical studies for attention to the relationship between representational or formal strategies of specific films and their narrative or thematic concerns. At the same time, we recognize that a call to include close reading in historical analysis is not without its problems. The wider historical picture can sometimes get lost in studies too focused on one film or a narrow selection of films. Furthermore, interpretive claims about a film do not lend themselves to the type of verification offered by work that draws significantly on archival sources. Still, we believe that close reading is an essential activity and makes a significant contribution. Although the essays published here adopt a "selected topics" approach, we believe they strike a rewarding balance between close readings that contribute to and those that complement the cultural history and history of industry approaches to American film history.

It is commonplace by now to understand cinema not as simple reflection but rather as a form of mediation that produces a perspective on, but by no means a transparent window onto, the world – a world it also simultaneously helps to construct. The relationship between the cinema and the world it represents travels a nuanced route that first passes through the conventions and pressures of the film industry itself. As Robert Sklar has argued in his seminal text *Movie-Made America: A Cultural History of American Movies*,

> We need to be wary of postulating a direct correspondence between society and cinema or condemning its absence. Film subjects and forms are as likely – more likely – to be determined by the institutional and cultural dynamics of motion picture production than by the most frenetic of social upheavals.[3]

With this in mind, we have found it useful to think in terms of groups or clusters of films, closely examining patterns or cycles that form a cinematic landscape. Such clusters or groupings, whether folk musicals of the 1930s and 1940s or comic Westerns of the 1960s, form a coherent field that past audiences had encountered over a relatively concentrated period of time. Essays built along such lines can serve the needs of scholars, students, and teachers who may have time to see or show only one film in class. The significance of that single film hopefully will be illuminated when placed in dialogue with other films with which it is grouped in any one of our essays.

Not all of the essays published here, however, cover clusters of films. Industry practices, significant moments of experimentation, and various modes of documentary and independent filmmaking also are considered, some as parts of larger cycles and some not. Indeed, the scope of these volumes and the larger 2012 collection permits us to place, side by side, a variety of approaches to American film history. We are pleased to showcase the varied methods employed and the range of material now being examined by film historians. We also are gratified to publish the work of so many people in our field, from senior, well-established scholars to those whose important work has garnered attention over the past several years.

Our hope is that, in moving through each volume in a relatively methodical fashion, students and scholars will discover a rich collage that will open new lines of inquiry and contribute to an ever-expanding knowledge of American film history.

The Editors

Notes

1. University libraries and individuals can get information about accessing the online edition at: http://onlinelibrary.wiley.com/book/10.1002/9780470671153

2. We do not mean so much the type of formal analysis of systems offered in a work like David Bordwell, Janet Staiger, and Kristen Thompson's *The Classical Hollywood Cinema* (1985) with its analysis that theorizes an entire mode of production, but, rather, historical writing that includes interpretive claims about the function of specific techniques – mise-en-scène, camerawork, lighting, editing, etc. – as deployed in a film or set of films.
3. Robert Sklar, *Movie-Made America: A Cultural History of American Movies*. Revised and updated. New York: Vintage Books (1994), p. 322.

Part I

Origins to 1928

1

Setting the Stage
American Film History, Origins to 1928

The origin of almost every important cultural form is a result of converging histories and rests at the intersection of intellectual, technological, and sociological changes. In the case of the American cinema, these origins are located toward the end of the nineteenth century and pivot around a series of developments in the economic, scientific, and artistic history of the nation: the tremendous growth of cities and the arrival of millions of immigrants between 1880 and 1920; the consolidation of business and manufacturing practices that maximized production and created a new means by which to advertise goods and services; the continuation, and in some cases culmination, of experiments devoted to combining photography and motion, most notably those of French scientist Étienne-Jules Marey and American photographer Eadweard Muybridge; and the emerging power of the United States and its place within the world economy.

This period is characterized by the remarkable penetration of cinema into the life of a nation. Between 1896 and 1928, the movies were the primary force behind a unifying transformation in the United States, turning people separated by region and class, educational and ethnic background, into a national audience that, by the late 1920s, consumed the same spectacles on the East Coast as the West, and in theaters in which every seat sold for one ticket price. To be sure, the cinema did not erase divisions of race and gender, and its democratizing impulse did not redraw the class boundaries in America. But one of the most remarkable aspects to the story of early American cinema is how it emerged at a moment when the nation could have drifted toward greater fragmentation, when the influx of immigrants from eastern and southern Europe could have created a disunited states, and how the cinema, and later radio as well, countered such forces. Indeed, it is perhaps the supreme irony of the movie industry that members of this very same immigrant population would be the ones to build and steer the industry through the first decades of the twentieth century and beyond. In the process, they, and the artists they employed, would produce a unifying set of myths that incorporated and rivaled the historical myths of the nation. Accompanied by its own icons and symbols, from movie stars to corporate logos of roaring lions and snow-capped mountains, and with its own version of holidays in the form of national premieres and award ceremonies, the movie industry created a visual language that transformed citizens into moviegoers. This language, rather quickly internalized by audiences, formed the scaffolding on which a genre-based mass medium developed. The consistent means by which time and space were organized on-screen was

American Film History: Selected Readings, Origins to 1960, First Edition. Edited by Cynthia Lucia, Roy Grundmann, and Art Simon.
© 2016 John Wiley & Sons, Inc. Published 2016 by John Wiley & Sons, Inc.

accompanied by a consistent array of settings and stories: legends of the Old West, urban crime, family melodramas, slapstick comedy, and, later, tales of horror and love stories set to song and dance.

This is not to suggest that in its early years all movies were the same or their tendencies conservative – far from it. While the movies functioned as a powerful tool of assimilation, they also presented a serious challenge to the prevailing values of the nineteenth century and the white Protestantism that was its anchor. The emerging cinema helped create and represent a new American cosmopolitan society, represented the working class and its struggles, contested nineteenth-century sexual mores, and helped dislodge the cultural officials of an earlier era. One need only think of the genius of Mack Sennett and his slapstick rendering of law enforcement to see the medium's potential for undermining authority. The nickelodeon opened its doors to women and offered business opportunities to new citizens. The larger movie houses to follow, and the content of their projections, as Richard Butsch argues in the hardcover/online edition, would be shaped by, but also contribute considerably to, the reshaping of the American middle class. And yet the history of the film industry over its initial 30 years is also remarkable for the stability it achieved, for its successful instituting of a shared set of conventions with respect to on-screen content and visual style, as well as production and exhibition methods. In this sense the movies reflected many of the wider patterns of American capitalism: modest experimentation so as to differentiate product, within a system of stability that maintained levels of output and consumer expectations while seeking to maximize profits.

The Nickelodeon Era

This period, beginning with film's rapid journey from Kinetoscope parlor to vaudeville house to nickelodeon, as outlined by Richard Abel in the hardcover/online edition, and ending with the changeover to talkies, is characterized by several overarching factors. The first has to do with developments in the machines of moving picture photography and projection. The years of intense experimentation with the production of moving images cover the last three decades of the nineteenth century and make up their own complex history. The name that for many years was most attached to the "invention" of the movies was Thomas Edison. But as early as the 1960s, historians began debunking the various myths around Edison's claim to be the father of the movies, setting the record straight as to how the Wizard of Menlo Park placed his name and his patent on devices and ideas, some produced under his employ, others purchased from beyond it, but all of which culminated in the most widely marketed moving picture machines. Specifically, credit has since been given to W. K. L. Dickson, who, working for Edison, developed the Kinetograph, a camera that drew film through the device at a stop-and-go speed appropriate for exposure using small perforations cut along its edges. Historians have noted that Edison's original intention was to use the movies to accompany his phonograph. Edison's first machine for watching movies was a stand-alone peep box, the Kinetoscope, which ran a 50-foot loop of film, and therefore first defined spectatorship as a solitary activity. Dickson's Kinetograph stood in stark contrast to the Cinématographe, the much lighter camera (that also functioned as a printer and projector) developed in France by the Lumière Brothers, and which may have convinced Edison that the future of the medium rested in projection. Indeed, it would be just two years between the appearance of the first Kinetoscope parlors in New York in April 1894 and the exhibition, in April 1896, of Edison's Vitascope movie projector, presumably a response to the Lumières' 1895 projection of movies in New York City. The Vitascope benefited from Edison's acquisition of a projection machine developed by C. Francis Jenkins and Thomas Armat and from the incorporation of what came to be known as the Latham Loop – developed by Woodville Latham and his sons – a technique whereby the film is pushed into a short arc before descending down past the projection bulb. The loop, which also arcs the film after projection on its way to the take-up reel, stabilizes the drag on the filmstrip to prevent it from breaking. In short, any account of the invention of the movies in America must be framed as a collaboration among individuals, some working together, some working far apart, a synthesis of ideas and experiments – with the recognition that stories about origins are often revised to fit the exigencies of history writing and of the marketplace.

The second overarching development has to do with the films themselves. In just one generation, the movies went from short actualities or simple stories, often screened as multifilm programs, to feature-length films running, in some cases, close to two hours. In the process, the film frame and the space within it became consolidated around the human figure, rather than around more abstract pursuits, and the properties of mise-en-scène (including set and costume design, lighting, and movement and behavior of characters), camerawork, and editing were integrated into the telling of legible and coherent narratives. Pioneer filmmakers such as Edwin S. Porter came to understand that the "basic signifying unit of film," to use David Cook's phrase, "the basic unit of cinematic meaning," was not the dramatic scene but rather the shot. In other words, a given scene could be presented across an unlimited number of shots (Cook 1996, 25). Charles Musser, in the hardcover/online edition, provides a detailed analysis of Porter's narrative innovations in such groundbreaking films as *The Execution of Czolgosz* (1901), *Jack and the Beanstalk* (1902), *The Great Train Robbery*, and *The Life of an American Fireman* (both 1903). Ordering of shots – to create the illusion of continuous action, to alternate the visual perspective on an action, or to create clear temporal markers for events unfolding on-screen – thus became the defining factor in telling a story on film. This essential concept of the shot could then be shaped by cinematographic elements such as lighting, camera angle, temporal duration, and the organization of the space within the frame. Filmmakers like D. W. Griffith, most notably, came to understand the relationship between the scale of a given shot – long, medium, or close-up – and access to the psychology of their fictional characters and thus the chains of identification between spectator and narrative action, as Charlie Keil points out in this volume. This simple insight, that greater visual intimacy was linked to understanding the emotions and motivations of the characters on-screen, opened the door to longer, more complex film narratives, complete with multiple locations and characters drawn over a longer period of time.

Over the course of hundreds of films made between 1908 and 1914, Griffith not only brought his characters closer to the camera, but also refined the use of parallel editing so as to clearly articulate the time frame of specific actions. As Tom Gunning has argued, the language by which Griffith advanced film narration developed within a specific context, responding to pressures from the emerging industry and the society into which his films were being released (1994, 7). Griffith advanced the language of storytelling while maintaining – one might even argue enhancing – the pleasure of the senses so attractive to the earliest moviegoers: "Griffith's films preserved a hedonistic experience, providing thrills that middle-class audiences learned to accept and desire" (Gunning 1994, 90). Griffith's experimentation culminated in his 1915 epic, *The Birth of a Nation*, a film in which his nineteenth-century racial politics collided with his twentieth-century cinematic artistry.

Prompted in part by the importation of European films running well over an hour, the American industry expanded to include the production of multireel features. During the mid-teens, producers, most notably perhaps Universal and the French company Pathé, created an in-between format, the serial, in which a story would be told through weekly installments two to three reels in length. In the late 1910s and into the 1920s, the industry moved increasingly toward feature production. With one reel consisting of approximately a thousand feet of film, a four-reel feature would run (at the silent speed of 16 frames per second) roughly 48 minutes. Four- and five-reel features thus allowed the industry to offer its growing middle-class audience stories with the scope and complexity approximating that which it had come to expect on the legitimate stage.

The development of the American film language was thoroughly enfolded with the methods of mass production created to meet the almost insatiable demand for new films during the first two decades of the twentieth century. Charles Musser has argued that the development of increasingly complex narratives must be attributed not only to the industry's desire to appease middle-class reformers, but even more to the demands of "standardization, narrative efficiency and maximization of profits" (1999, 272).

The factory system that evolved to full maturation in the 1910s came to rely increasingly on a detailed division of labor and came to recognize the need for real estate to hold studios, production facilities, and theaters; the need for the development or purchase of new technologies; and the need for vast amounts of capital to cover these and other expenses. Within two decades of the first film exhibition, the movies had become big business.

As a consequence, the early American film industry fell prey to the logic of that system, in particular the tendency toward combinations and monopoly. In 1908, the 10 largest film production companies, led by Edison and Biograph, formed the Motion Picture Patents Company (MPPC). Combining the patents they held on film technology with an exclusive deal with Eastman Kodak, the Trust, as it came to be known, sought to exert full control over the production and distribution of movies. Such control was short-lived, however, as a group of independent producers – Adolph Zukor, Carl Laemmle, and William Fox – successfully resisted MPPC control and gained a foothold in the industry. Indeed, these men, whose national and religious heritage set them starkly apart from the lords of the Trust, would ultimately not only surpass their rivals, but also go on to found the American movie business as it would come to be known thereafter – Hollywood. By the time the legality of the Trust and its trade practices came before US courts, it had already lost its dominance. But it would not be the last time the movie business would be challenged by fair trade laws, and the independents of one age would become the monopolists of another. Indeed, one of the recurring tropes of American film history is the drift toward market domination by a handful of companies or the conglomeration of the film industry by even still larger corporate enterprises.

In the 1910s, the center of film production shifted from the East Coast to southern California, taking advantage of its good climate, proximity to a variety of natural locations, and, perhaps most importantly, its inexpensive real estate and nonunion labor. By 1922, over 80 percent of film production was centered in or near Los Angeles. But in some ways the movies never left New York. The studios maintained their business offices in the nation's financial capital where, starting in the mid-teens, they had established important relationships with Wall Street and the giants of American banking. Well into the 1920s, producers continued to use production facilities in and around New York. D. W. Griffith would make important films, including *Way Down East* (1920) and *Orphans of the Storm* (1921), at his studio in Mamaroneck, just north of the city. And studio back lots frequently included a New York street, complete with tenements, front stoops, and shop windows (Koszarski 1994, 102).

Censorship Battles

If control over the production and distribution of movies became one recurring story for the history of American film, another would be the battle over their content and exhibition. From their earliest days, the movies were a site of struggle between filmmakers and the custodians of American morality. In December 1908, New York City Mayor George McClellan ordered all nickelodeons in the city closed. It was the most dramatic official response so far to a decade's-long chorus of concerns about the moral propriety of on-screen images, their violence and sexual content, and the conditions of their exhibition. While theater owners successfully challenged McClellan's actions, the industry as a whole sought to protect itself from future incursions by moving quickly to a strategy it would pursue, in one form or another, for decades – self-regulation. Seven years after the McClellan affair, the matter went before the United States Supreme Court. During that time the industry's National Board of Censorship had been established (its name subsequently changed to the National Board of Review) in order to certify the moral status of new films and defuse local censorship.

In *Mutual Film Corporation v. Industrial Commission of Ohio*, the court found in favor of the state and declared that Ohio's power to censor film content outweighed Mutual's claims to free speech or its argument that Ohio's regulating standards were inconsistent. (The Ohio censorship mechanism had, in fact, been established at the urging of the Ohio Exhibitors League.) But the court's ruling said as much about the status of the movies at this point in history as it did about the rights of state or local review boards. The movies were first and foremost a business, the court said, and do not function as "part of the press of the country or as organs of public opinion" (Sklar 1994, 128). Producers may well have understood their product in similar terms. Their opposition to censorship came less from aspirations toward art and its protection than from aspirations for profits and the threat posed by an unevenly applied set of regionally enforced moral standards.

The content of films troubled some in local communities, particularly after the trial of Fatty Arbuckle, indicted in 1921 for manslaughter in the death of a young woman at a Hollywood party. Despite his acquittal, the case scandalized the nation, but this and other sordid aspects of the movie business did not curtail its immense popularity. Between 1917 and 1928, the producers released an average of 600 films per year (Lewis 2008, 70). In the early teens, it was still commonplace for theaters to change their programs on a daily basis and even into the 1920s many exhibitors would have a new film playing every week. When, in 1922, the industry established its trade organization, the Motion Picture Producers and Distributors Association (MPPDA), it did so not only to respond to the Arbuckle scandal, but also to insure the continued flow of box office dollars. With Will Hays at the helm, the MPPDA convinced state and local censorship boards that it was serious about policing the moral content of movies. The MPPDA may have helped keep censors at bay, but filmmakers would largely ignore its code of movie conduct for another decade.

The Industry

Between 1915 and 1928, the major filmmaking companies of the studio era were established or stabilized. Loew's (MGM), Fox, Paramount, Universal, and Warner Bros. all emerged over the course of a fiercely competitive 15 years of mergers and acquisitions. The path to vertical integration, with studios acquiring their own theaters, also led in both directions. In response to what they took to be the unfair practices of block and blind booking – rental policies first enacted by Adolph Zukor at Paramount requiring independent-owned theaters to book entire groups or blocks of the studio's films without advance knowledge of their content – those owners united to form the First National Exhibitors Circuit. From there it was a quick step for First National to move into film production, facilitated by the signing on, in 1917, of Charlie Chaplin. Zukor, in turn, bankrolled by Wall Street powerhouse Kuhn, Loeb & Co., led Paramount on a mission to acquire first-run theaters – over 300 by 1921 (Koszarski 1994, 75).

During this period, movie theaters underwent not only changes in ownership but also a fundamental change in design. The nickelodeon era had witnessed a dramatic increase in the size of exhibition venues as theaters devoted exclusively to motion pictures moved rapidly from standing-space-only storefronts, in 1905, to theaters, less than a year later, seating several hundred as Richard Abel and Richard Butsch point out in the hardcover/online edition. In April 1914, The Strand, New York's first picture palace catering directly to the middle-class audience, opened with a seating capacity of 3,500. Many more palaces were to open across the country over the next decade, ushering in a long period of urban moviegoing amidst vast, ornately designed theaters with plush seating and sparkling chandeliers. Although not always profitable ventures for exhibitors, picture palaces survived in many cities into the 1970s, long past the time when movies were thought to need an elegant showcase.

In the same year as The Strand opened in New York City, a new mode of production became solidified in Hollywood. The central producer system, in which a detailed shooting script allowed for planning and budgeting well before a film went into production, replaced an earlier director-based approach. The director's work could now focus on approving the set design, shooting the film, and working with the editor in the assembling of a final cut. Overseeing virtually everything else – labor, props, set construction, wardrobe, players – was a producer who functioned like a general manager, someone also entrusted with the job of managing costs and estimating profits. Historians differ somewhat over the extent to which the central producer system dominated film production. Its primary phase ran from 1914 to 1931 and Thomas Ince is most often cited as the first to fully adapt these organizational practices to movie production (Staiger 1985, 136–137). Ince also was instrumental in foregrounding the importance of the script and writing of intertitles, as Torey Liepa points out in the hardcover/online edition of this series. Yet filmmakers such as D. W. Griffith, Erich von Stroheim, Cecil B. DeMille, and James Cruze, artists whose work transcended the run-of-the-mill films characterizing much of the industry's output, operated according to a method that still privileged the creative and managerial role of the director (Koszarski 1994, 110). Either way, by the mid-1920s, film production proceeded along a highly efficient path, with teams of artists and technicians working under the supervision of a handful of top executives at every studio. Those artists and executives included many women among their ranks. Indeed, the silent era is distinguished not only by the importance of women as moviegoers, but by the diverse roles women played within the industry as well. As Shelley Stamp points out in this volume and Jane M. Gaines and Victoria Sturtevant explain in the hardcover/online edition, the popular image of women as mere extras was contradicted by the facts. Screenwriters June Mathis and Anita Loos and directors Lois Weber and Ida May Park, to name just four, played crucial roles in shaping studio stars and product. While it is certainly true that individual executives made their mark on film production, the stability of the system was, in fact, certified by its very capacity to withstand changes in management personnel.

For audiences and moviemakers, the stability of the movies was also anchored to a codified method of story construction and editing, what has come to be known as the classical system. It prescribed that narrative events be organized according to a logic of cause and effect. The result would be a unified plot, despite whatever disparate ingredients it might contain, in which characters' actions are clearly motivated and the causal chain of scenes made legible. According to Kristin Thompson, this causal unity can be found in early one-reel films but would become increasingly necessary as films grew longer and their narratives more complex (Thompson 1985, 174–175). To present the classical narrative, there emerged a consistent method for linking shots together, one that could handle the myriad temporal and spatial variables that came with telling stories through multishot films. Needless to say, these variables grew exponentially as the industry turned toward feature film production. As Thompson concludes, "The continuity rules that filmmakers devised were not natural outgrowths of cutting, but means of taming and unifying it. In a sense, what the psychological character was in the unification of the longer narrative, the continuity rules were in the unification of time and space" (Thompson 1985, 162). Those rules would come to dictate such practices as shot-reverse shot editing, the eyeline match, the match cut, and respect for the 180-degree axis of action. These techniques were implemented so as to minimize any possible disorientation introduced by cutting from one shot to another, thereby permitting the viewer's attention to remain focused on the story being told.

Genres and Stars

What also achieved a remarkable stability were the subject categories into which most film production fell. Action-adventure pictures, Westerns, melodramas, and comedies dominated the silent era. Despite recurring declarations by industry analysts that Americans were tiring of cowboys on-screen, the Western remained the most popular genre of the era. In 1910, 21 percent of all American-made films were Westerns and in 1926, that figure came close to 30 percent (Buscombe 1988, 24, 427). Undoubtedly, most of these were B-films, but in the 1920s, the genre was enhanced by several epic productions – *The Covered Wagon* (1923), *The Iron Horse* (1927), a film Nicholas Baer discusses in depth in the hardcover/online edition – predecessors to a number of A-Westerns made in the next decade, such as *Cimarron* (1931), *The Big Trail* (1930), and *Union Pacific* (1939). More than any other genre, at least up to the coming of sound, the Western marked Hollywood's greatest contribution to national myth. Yet the heroic Westerner was hardly a singular character. William S. Hart's stoic, dirt-stained loner contrasted sharply with Tom Mix's clean-clad hero, but the cowboy nonetheless functioned as an exemplary figure for the celebration of white expansion into and across Western and American Indian lands.

The melodrama, and more particularly the maternal melodrama, were staples of the era. The very earliest film melodramas typically revolve around physical peril and a last-minute rescue, as in Porter's *Life of an American Fireman* and *Rescued from an Eagle's Nest* (1907) and in Griffith's shorts – including *The Adventures of Dollie* (1908) in which the title character, as a baby, is kidnapped by gypsies. Such plots, as Gerald Mast and Bruce Kawin point out, clearly were influenced by the theatrical productions of David Belasco, in which "good miraculously won out in the last 15 minutes" of plays lasting more than two hours: "Melodrama was a world of pathos, not of tragedy, of fears and tears, not of ideas" (2003, 31). But with feature-length films like Griffith's *Broken Blossoms* (a.k.a. *Broken Blossoms or The Yellow Man and the Girl*, 1919) melodrama took on much greater sophistication, in terms of both narrative complexity and richly textured visual style, albeit with a damsel generally remaining in distress. The young girl Lucy (Lillian Gish), in *Broken Blossoms*, lives with her violently abusive alcoholic father, prizefighter Battling Burrows (Donald Crisp), and is rescued by a Chinese shopkeeper, Cheng Huan (Richard Barthelmess), when she collapses on the street after her father has brutally

Figure 1.1 Lillian Gish as the poor, vulnerable Lucy in D. W. Griffith's *Broken Blossoms or The Yellow Man and the Girl* (1919, produced by D. W. Griffith Productions).

beaten her. These two outsiders – defined as such by race, in Cheng's case, and by gender and impoverishment, in Lucy's case – develop an affectionate, Platonic bond based on past misfortunes and present vulnerabilities, with Cheng Huan nurturing and caring for Lucy until Burrows and his henchmen discover her. In this case, the last-minute rescue fails, and Lucy suffers a fatal beating. The otherwise gentle Cheng Huan obtains some measure of revenge by shooting Burrows before stabbing himself, yet his actions attest to the very fragility of tenderness and beauty in a harsh urban world. Griffith's *Way Down East* (1920) is most known, perhaps, for its iconic image of Lillian Gish lying unconscious on an ice floe as it dangerously approaches a waterfall before she is rescued. In both films parallel editing heightens suspense and creates nuanced relationships among sympathetically connected characters. Griffith's precisely calculated close-ups imbue the films with a powerful pathos so central to the genre.

Way Down East further exemplifies aspects of the maternal melodrama, a subgenre popular during the silent and early sound era, as Lea Jacobs points out in the hardcover/online edition of this series. Generally revolving around women who are banished from their homes and from their children when they are suspected of adultery, such films are of particular interest for their representations of motherhood and maternal suffering, and in their appeal and address to female viewers of the period (Jacobs 2012, 398). The many remakes of *Madame X* (1916), for instance, attest to an appeal that has spanned the decades (with much updating, of course) through versions in 1920, 1929, 1937, 1952, 1966, and 1994, along with several in the new millennium – as does *Stella Dallas* (1925), with its iconic 1937 remake starring Barbara Stanwyck. Another variation of the maternal melodrama, in a more updated form, centers on an erotic triangle involving a mother, her love interest or second husband, and her late-teen/early twenties daughter, as in Ernst Lubitsch's *Three Women* (1924). These variations represent a few of the many melodramatic tropes on the silent screen, almost all of which, ultimately, depend upon the stabilizing force of a good man or a male-enforced legal system to restore order in response to imagined or actual moral transgressions.

In sharp contrast to the melodrama, no genre, perhaps, is more thoroughly associated with the silent era than comedy. To be sure, the rise of the star was a defining aspect of the movies during their first 30 years, becoming an inseparable part of genre production. As players became associated with a given genre – Douglas Fairbanks and adventure, Tom Mix and the Western, Lillian Gish and melodrama – studios recast them again and again in familiar stories, constructing on-screen personas that only fed the formula. But in the case of silent comedy, star and authorship often were combined. A film with Charlie Chaplin or Buster Keaton was also a film by Charlie Chaplin or Buster Keaton. And while Gish and Fairbanks, or Lon Chaney and Gloria Swanson might have returned frequently to similar roles, the stars of silent comedy appeared to carry the same character from film to film, story to story, as Charles J. Maland points out in this volume. Whether he was an immigrant or a pawnshop assistant, a waiter or a boxer, Chaplin was, in the dozens of films he made during the teens, the tramp.

What does it tell us about an era that its most beloved figure was a man of such little means? It seems just as remarkable that this hero, and here one can add Keaton as well, should be of diminutive stature. In the classic films of silent comedy, grace was privileged over strength, underdog ingenuity over rugged machismo. But it was more than outwitting bigger rivals or escaping hostile authorities. In the films of Chaplin, Keaton, and Harold Lloyd, there was something funny about merely surviving. This often took the form of perilous encounters with the most profound factor of the early twentieth century – mechanized life. Whether it was dodging fast cars, scaling the walls of a tall building, or working on the assembly line, silent comics kept their balance and drew laughs from anxiety in the effort to coexist with modern times.

The acrobatics of Keaton and the dance hall physicality of Chaplin point, in fact, to a quality that defined much of silent cinema – its fascination with the body. To a great extent this would characterize the cinema throughout its history. From its athleticism, like the horseback riding of Westerns or the dueling of adventure films, to its more precise movements through dance or the far subtler but no less important gestures of smiling and posture, the body was the star of silent cinema in an era not yet overwhelmed by the voice. This was, to be more precise, a cinematic body, set to the rhythms of editing and photographed within a precise calculation of light, costume, and makeup.

What exactly makes a star performer attractive to moviegoers is one of those inestimable matters that ultimately cannot be adduced from polls. Talent, physical appeal, high-quality supporting artists and material certainly help, as does good timing. But while the list of most popular stars might have been reshuffled every few years, the economic centrality of the star was an industry fact by 1910, as Mark Lynn Anderson details in this volume. Filmmakers could solicit brand reliance by featuring stars in film after film. In turn, the professional power of the star grew tremendously. In 1916, for example, Adolph Zukor created Artcraft to handle productions starring Mary Pickford, whose career Victoria Sturtevant examines at length in the hardcover/online edition. The actress was making $10,000 per week and taking 50 percent of the profits (Koszarski 1994, 266). Chaplin's contract with Mutual paid him $12,884 a week and when, in 1917, he moved to First National, he became his own producer with the company advancing him $125,000 for each film of an eight-two-reelers-in-one-year deal. After the recuperation of all costs for advertising, prints, and distribution, Chaplin would get 50 percent of the net profits (Robinson 1985, 223). Stars were even more essential as box office attractions, given the frequency with which theaters changed programs. While some special features enjoyed runs of several weeks, perhaps even months, it was common throughout this period for theaters to exhibit a film for only a week before moving on to another. Thus, stars were often the only form of reliable advertising, that is, the only aspect of a film with which audiences might be familiar before going to see it (Koszarski 1994, 35–36). Although the interests of the stars and the demands of the studios often would collide in subsequent years, the star would remain fixed as the centerpiece of virtually every quality production.

Figure 1.2 In Charlie Chaplin's *The Immigrant* (1917, producers John Jasper, Charlie Chaplin, and Henry P. Caulfield), Charlie and Edna Purviance are roped off immediately upon arriving in "the land of liberty."

Hollywood and World Cinema

The rise of the silent film star coincided with the emergence of American film on the world market. While the industry's expansion onto foreign screens did not get underway until after the domestic market was consolidated by the MPPC in 1908, it took less than a decade for American movie companies to gain a major foothold in that market. As Kristin Thompson has detailed, World War I threw the Western world into turmoil, ultimately permitting the American film industry to take over international markets previously controlled by European suppliers such as Italy and France (Thompson 1985, 71). While foreign buyers were lured by the quality of American films, especially once US production turned to more costly feature films, the domination of the world market really depended on the construction of an exporting infrastructure. As with the domestic business, power over the global market depended on controlling distribution. During the war, London ceased to function as the center of foreign distribution, and American film companies moved aggressively to deal directly with overseas markets. This meant establishing offices throughout the world and, in some cases, sending representatives to negotiate deals for specific pictures. The opening of subsidiary offices in non-European countries would be particularly important to the postwar domination exerted by American companies. In turn, major South American exchanges set up offices in New York. As World War I boosted the economies of North America, Japan, and various South American countries, these countries could better afford the importation of American goods, films included. During the 1920s, American filmmakers continued to enjoy a dominant role in the exhibition of movies throughout the world. Several countries, most notably Germany, would secure its domestic market from American domination, as well as build a healthy exportation business. And cooperation between European countries would prevent their national cinemas from being totally overwhelmed. But the changes brought about by sound and, then, the rise of fascism in Europe, would present new obstacles, as well as opportunities, for the American industry in its efforts to exploit overseas markets.

While American films were being sent overseas for exhibition on international screens, the talent of international cinemas slowly made its way to Hollywood and its impact would be felt throughout the studio era. Even before the consolidation of production in southern California, French film artists, such as directors Maurice Tourneur and George Archainbaud, went to work for the World Film Corporation, an American production and distribution company (Koszarski 1994, 66). From Germany came F. W. Murnau and Ernst Lubitsch, the latter surviving and succeeding well into the sound era. Joseph von Sternberg got his start in American movies. In the late 1920s, he briefly returned to his native Germany to make films for UFA, before returning to Hollywood, with Marlene Dietrich in tow. Victor Sjöström had been a prolific director in Sweden before directing films in Hollywood beginning in 1924. Several European actors also became immensely popular during the 1920s. As Diane Negra details in the hardcover/online edition of this series, Pola Negri had worked in the Polish and German film industries before becoming a star in Hollywood. Greta Garbo, who, unlike Negri, survived the talkie revolution to continue as one of MGM's biggest stars, arrived from Sweden to make her first American film in 1926. The exoticism of foreign stars was matched by the exoticism of films built around foreign subjects. Rex Ingram would direct a number of these films, including *The Four Horsemen of the Apocalypse* (1921), *The Prisoner of Zenda* (1922), *The Arab* (1924), and *The Garden of Allah* (1927) – the first of which featured Rudolph Valentino, a star whose immense popularity grew into something of a national cult. Whether placed in Argentina, Spain, or the Sahara desert, Valentino's characters projected a sexual magnetism inseparable from their foreign identity. In *The Sheik* (1921), Valentino plays Ahmed Ben Hassan, a European-born Arabian prince who woos and seduces Lady Diana Mayo (Agnes Ayres). As in many of his films, the allure of Valentino's Sheik is wrapped, quite literally, in the garments of exoticism – in this case flowing robes and headdresses. In this film, in particular, he seems inseparable from the mise-en-scène of costume and layered curtains.

The Jazz Age On-Screen – Inside and Outside of Hollywood

While the silent cinema looked overseas for exotic locales, to America's West for stories of cowboys on the range, and to the sentiments of nineteenth-century melodrama, it registered, as well, the contours of its age – the Jazz Age. Indeed, in its formal rhythms and inherent voyeuristic appeal, in its fabrication of star personas, and its urban settings (whether on location or in the studio), the movies contributed to the transformation undergone by the nation, from genteel agrarianism to cosmopolitan renaissance. No doubt American film remained wedded, at points, to an earlier era. Griffith's cinema, for example, while modern in its editing, often remained tied to his Victorian roots. But the rise of mass culture, with the movies in the lead, now appears inseparable from the era of scandal sheets and speakeasies, the Scopes Trial that debated teaching Darwin's theory of evolution in public schools, and the victory for women's voting rights in 1920. Indeed, the New Morality of the period – leisure, consumption, and sexual independence – found expression in many films of the era.

The migration from country to city that characterized the 1920s, and the harsh realities of that movement, were represented in King Vidor's *The Crowd* (1928), which tells the story of John Sims who comes to New York to achieve success but finds struggle, heartbreak, and tragedy instead. Vidor's montage of bustling streets captures the dynamic rhythms of urban dwellers at work and at play, as David A. Gerstner details in the hardcover/online edition. Vidor's mobile camera, influenced perhaps by the stylistic breakthroughs of Murnau in Germany, appears to climb the side of a skyscraper and then glide over a giant office filled with two hundred workers at their desks. Combining melodrama with realism to present the individual buffeted by mass culture, Vidor's film illustrates how, within the Hollywood mode, the mobility of cinema could trace the dimensions of city life, its pace and scope.

So, too, in *The Big Parade* (1925), *What Price Glory?* (1926), and *Wings* (1927), did Hollywood present a sober encounter with World War I. The movies also found a partner in another burgeoning Jazz-Age pastime – sports. An enthusiasm for boxing, fueled by the stardom of Jack Dempsey (who would himself appear in several films and marry screen star Estelle Taylor), found its way into such films as Famous Players-Lasky's *The World's Champion* (1925), Buster Keaton's *Battling Butler* (1926), and Tay Garnett's *Celebrity* (1928). Baseball, too, provided material for films from this period, most notably in *The Busher* (1919) and *Headin' Home* (1920), the latter starring Babe Ruth.

The period crystallizes most clearly perhaps in Frank Urson's *Chicago* (1927) – a narrative continually remade for screen and restaged for Broadway over the decades to follow, extending into the new millennium. Originally adapted to screen at the end of the silent era from a Broadway play based on actual events, *Chicago* is both a product and a satire of its age. The film is rife with scandal-hungry journalists, crimes of passion, a greedy criminal mouthpiece, a career-driven District Attorney, policemen happy to be in on the action, and, at the center, a sexually independent married woman. Released at the end of 1927, the film's story of Roxie Hart (Phyllis Haver), a less than moral flapper who murders her lover and is then acquitted by a leering and gullible all-male jury, is played mostly for laughs. But it carries a sophisticated sting in satirizing a gossip-crazed public manipulated by truth-bending tabloid reporters. Registering the power of mass culture and its place within a novelty-seeking era, in love with both profits and self-promotion, *Chicago* represented the kinship that then existed and would remain between the movies and the newspaper world. The thorough reciprocity between Hollywood and publishing, in the form of fan magazines, film reviews, and gossip columns, would only be strengthened with the coming of sound and the migration of writers from Eastern and Midwestern cities to the movie colony.

While the fictional narrative dominated production throughout this period, three other categories of filmmaking also got their start during the silent era. Two of these came from within the industry – newsreels and animation. The third, a less well-defined category that, at times, worked in the animation and documentary modes, emerged from outside the studios – experimental film. But before turning to these, at least one significant figure working in an independent mode needs to be acknowledged – Oscar Micheaux. The child of parents who had been slaves, Micheaux was drawn to the cinema while struggling to be a writer. He made his first film in 1919 from a position totally outside the white-dominated commercial industry and would, over the next 30 years, become the most prolific producer/director of feature films aimed at a black audience, as Paula J. Massood observes in the volume, most notably perhaps his *Body and Soul* (1925) that marked the film debut of Paul Robeson, as a bit of a shyster, but nonetheless charismatic, preacher.

Newsreels

The ancestry of the weekly newsreel dates back to the Kinetoscope when the Edison Company staged prizefights at its Black Maria studio. Edison-era actualities and films of the Spanish–American War, many of them staged for the camera, established in the minds of moviegoers the sense that the cinema could provide more than theatrical entertainment. In 1900, camera operators arrived in Galveston, Texas within days of a hurricane that leveled the city and killed 5,000 people. Six years later, in the aftermath of the San Francisco earthquake, cameramen from Edison and Vitagraph were on the scene to photograph the devastation. In addition to events such as these, and the more modest tragedies of daily life, silent news films also covered the affairs of state, with Teddy Roosevelt a particularly frequent figure before the cameras.

American moviemakers were relatively slow in turning to weekly news films, and the first newsreels exhibited in the United States were the product of French producer Charles Pathé, who introduced an American edition of his newsreel in 1911 (Fielding 1972, 70). During the teens a variety of production companies tried their hand at the genre, some in association with major news organizations such as the Hearst press and the *Chicago Tribune*. By the middle of the decade, Universal, Selig, and Vitagraph had established themselves as fixtures. Then, in 1919, Fox entered newsreel production and, with its cameramen stationed around the globe and a state-of-the-art laboratory in New York, quickly emerged as a leader in the field.

Newsreel production in the 1920s was characterized by aggressive competition. Exclusive rights to photographing sporting events were often undermined by undercover competitors, and the race was always on to bring events to screen as quickly as possible. To meet the demand for regular programs, newsreel producers frequently turned to the reenactment of news, and at times, the staging of events exclusively for filming. Still, the newsreel cameraman, glorified in the popular press, was often on scene recording spectacular events, frequently risking life and limb in the process. In 1927, both Paramount and MGM entered the newsreel business just in time for the conversion to sound, and in a short time *Paramount News* took a leading role. But it was Fox's *Movietone News* that recorded the first important sound-on-film events – the takeoff of Charles Lindbergh's pioneering transatlantic flight from Long Island on May 20, 1927 and the ceremonies welcoming his safe return on June 27. Fox premiered the first regular all-sound newsreel at the Roxy in New York in October 1927.

Animation

Animation for the screen would not approach anything close to maturity until after sound came to cinema. But certain essential technical advances were achieved during this time, establishing the means by which the medium would enter into its golden age. Winsor McCay pioneered animation with *Little Nemo* (1911) and *Gertie the Dinosaur* (1914). Billed in *Little Nemo* – a film about the artist and his process – as "The Famous Cartoonist of the *N.Y. Herald Tribune*," McCay relied upon hand drawing thousands of cartoons set before the Vitagraph camera. The impracticality of this method for mass production is clear, but it would not be long before Earl Hurd and J. R. Bray, working separately, would develop the means by which to animate specific sections of the frame against a background that did not require movement. Hurd's cels, which could be layered, allowed the artist to animate only those parts of a drawing that needed motion, thus drastically reducing labor time and making the animated film amenable to the industry's mode of production (Koszarski 1994, 170).

While several popular newspaper cartoon characters found their way into animated shorts – and the later "star," Felix the Cat, debuted during this time – perhaps the most significant films reflexively featured the animation process itself. The plot of *Little Nemo* revolves directly around McCay's efforts to impress his colleagues by bringing his drawings to life. McCay is also on-screen at the beginning of *Gertie* and his voice is heard throughout, via intertitles, instructing his dinosaur to do tricks for the audience. A similar reflexivity characterizes the early work of Max Fleischer, who would go on to be among the most important of sound-era animators and the creator of Betty Boop. Fleischer's "Out of the Inkwell" series typically began with a shot of the artist's hands opening his ink bottle, and in *Cartoon Factory* (1925), he appears in the frame in live-action next to his animated Koko the Clown.

In its infancy then, American animation frequently broke the frame of illusion and foregrounded itself as the main attraction. In *Cartoon Factory* and *Gertie the Dinosaur*, animated figures break free from or disregard the orders of their creators. As such, they point toward an irreverence that would characterize many of the most accomplished animated shorts of the sound era, in particular those created by Warner Bros. In exposing their means of production and in their direct address to the spectator, early animators signaled how their genre, more than any other within the Hollywood mode, would joyfully challenge the conventions of illusion. The arrival of sound on film provided a boost to animation because it eventually brought to an end the live stage presentation that often preceded the projection of a feature. As a theater's film program became standardized, a permanent place was created for the animated sound short.

Walt and Roy Disney founded their animation studio in Hollywood in October of 1923. Like the Fleischers, Disney's early work combined animation with live-action, as Kirsten Moana Thompson points out in this volume, and in the first of his silent *Alice* cartoons from 1923, Disney and his collaborators are featured in the frame alongside their drawings that come to life. Disney's first star, Mickey Mouse, was introduced in *Plane Crazy* (1928), but it would not be released as a sound cartoon until after the success of the better-known *Steamboat Willie* (1928). Like so many Disney cartoons to follow, character and music seem inseparable. We meet Mickey at the wheel of the steamboat, whistling and tapping his foot, and for the next eight minutes virtually everything within Mickey's reach becomes a musical instrument – bull's teeth become a xylophone, pots and a washboard a percussion section. The bodies of objects and creatures undergo amazing transformations in a space where nothing seems permanent. As Robert Sklar has written of Disney's 1920s and early 1930s animation, it created a world in which "there is no fixed order of things: the world is plastic to imagination and will" (1994, 200).

The First Avant-Garde

While the canon of early avant-garde filmmaking has been located firmly within European borders, the 1920s witnessed the emergence of a widespread experimental movement in the United States as well. As Jan-Christopher Horak has demonstrated in this volume and elsewhere, the professionalized avant-garde of post–World War II America supported by university teaching positions and foundation grants had been preceded by a self-identified "amateur" movement two decades earlier. During the 1920s, a far-ranging network of filmmakers, art house theaters, and publications was established. By 1927, according to Horak, there were roughly 30,000 amateur filmmakers in the United States and a year later, more than 100 film clubs (1995, 19).

This is a cinema of remarkable variation, much of it lost to history. Unlike Hollywood, experimental filmmakers often chose not to privilege the human figure within the frame. Rather, their films frequently pivoted around lyrical editing, abstract compositions, and psychological expressionism. They often functioned as personal records. Some of what survives from this period, and certainly that which is most often screened today, reveals a fascination with modern urban life and the rich visual patterns of the cityscape. Like their European counterparts – Walter Ruttmann (*Berlin: Symphony of a Great City*, 1927), Dziga Vertov (*Man with a Movie Camera*, 1929), and Joris Ivens (*Rain*, 1929) – filmmakers such as Charles Sheeler, Paul Strand, Herman Weinberg, and Robert Flaherty pursued a nonnarrative cinema that combined documentary and poetic impulses.

In *Manhatta* (1921), Sheeler and Strand's cinematic transposition of Walt Whitman, the skyscraper "iron beauties" of the city are offered as monumental sculptures, combining art and industry. In Flaherty's *The 24 Dollar Island* (1927), the camera is liberated from framing the human form so that the "mountains of steel and stone" are captured in all their patchwork density through extreme long shots. Flaherty orchestrates an interframe montage that combines the fixity of stone structures like the Brooklyn Bridge with the mobility of cars, tugs, and ships in the harbor. In short, the poetic potential of nonnarrative filmmaking was no less significant for American filmmakers as for their European counterparts.

But the early American avant-garde did far more than document cities. Like its European influence, it frequently used the frame not for verisimilitude but for abstraction, preferring the symbolic rather than the indexical potential of the medium. In *The Life and Death of 9413—A Hollywood Extra* (1928), Robert Florey and Slavko Vorkapich satirize the movie business, depicting a man whose dreams of stardom turn nightmarish when he is transformed into a numbered, mechanized Hollywood extra. Shot by Gregg Toland, the film intercuts expressionist iconography, miniatures, and images of the real Hollywood. A sequence, in which editing prevents the man from successfully ascending a set of stairs, echoes a similar pattern in *Ballet Mécanique* (Fernand Léger and Dudley Murphy, 1924), also an experimental film that hinges on abstracting everyday objects and body parts – bowls, whisks, necklaces, numbers, eyes, and lips. Montages of close-ups and interiors with pitch-black backgrounds create a hallucinatory space in *The Life and Death of 9413*. This antirealist impulse, eager to explore the subjective, perceptual realm, would remain an important component of alternative cinema. In fact, while the economics of film production in the United States permitted the commercial industry to define the medium for most moviegoers, experimental filmmakers of the 1920s initiated an avant-garde that would consistently challenge that definition throughout the twentieth century.

The Coming of Sound to the Cinema

The period covered by this section is punctuated by the rise of the talkies. The silent cinema had, of course, rarely been silent and live musical accompaniment had almost always been part of the moviegoing experience. But because sound synchronized with the image – either on disk or on the film itself – would arrive in the late 1920s to forever change the industry as well as the art form, it continues to make sense to periodize the history of cinema at this juncture. Over the past 30 years, considerable scholarship has been focused on the coming of sound. That work has successfully overthrown the myths of an earlier era – that *The Jazz Singer* (1927) revolutionized the industry virtually overnight, throwing studios into a panic, and that Warner Bros., on the brink of collapse, single-handedly pioneered a new film form. But that does not mean a singular interpretation of this period has emerged, as Paul Young points out in this volume. Douglas Gomery has consistently argued that the transition to sound was thoroughly planned, the result of cooperation and consolidation within and between filmmaking companies and the giants of the recording, electric, and telephone industries (Gomery 2005). Donald Crafton has argued that the changeover to sound was "partly rational, partly confused," that the studios' master plan, enacted to maximize profits, was accompanied by regular improvisation to deal with the unanticipated problems posed by the application of new technologies (Crafton 1997, 4). For David Bordwell and Janet Staiger, the introduction of synchronized sound can hardly be understood as a revolution. Rather, it exemplifies the flexibility of the system, "a typical case of how the Hollywood mode of production could accommodate technological change" (Bordwell & Staiger 1985, 247).

What is clear is that sound came to cinema over a protracted period of experimentation, first outside the movie industry and then also within it, and it did so over the course of expanding applications before and after the October 1927 premiere of *The Jazz Singer*. In 1926, the Vitaphone (sound-on-disk) presentations of *Don Juan* (1926) and *The Better 'Ole* (1926) offered musical scores to accompany each feature. During 1927, the sound-on-film system that Fox labeled Movietone was used for newsreels and the filming of shorts capturing vaudeville performers. During the 1929–1930 season, the studios released silent and sound versions of all their films, with sound-on-film technology rapidly becoming the standard. Finally, all-sound production became standard practice starting with the 1930–1931 season (Gomery 2005, 2). What is also clear is that sound film was enormously profitable, handsomely returning studio investments in new theaters and sound equipment. As Gomery has suggested, it was not so much *The Jazz Singer* as it was Jolson's next film, *The Singing Fool* (1928), with its record-breaking revenues, that convinced the industry of the box office potential of synchronized sound.

The transition to sound may have been smoothly accommodated by the Hollywood mode of production and it certainly secured rather than destabilized the major studios' domination of the domestic and world markets, but it changed forever what audiences expected and got every time they went to the movies. Synchronized sound gave filmmakers a new and powerful tool to advance realism – the ricochet of bullets, the screeching of tires, the tapping of dancing feet – and restored to acting the volume and inflections of voice. It also provided a new source of anxiety for those who worried about the influence of the movies – the sounds of passion, the potential crudities of language – as the medium moved toward a more faithful representation of the world beyond the screen.

As quickly as the audience took to the movies, it took to their new incarnation with sound, bringing to a close a remarkable period in the history of American culture. The golden age of silent film was giving way to what would become another golden age, the years during which the movies came into full kinship with the American stage, in its Broadway and vaudeville traditions, and the increasingly popular form of radio. Few could know, in 1927, how truly prophetic were Al Jolson's words in *The Jazz Singer*: "You ain't heard nothin' yet."

References

Bordwell, David, & Staiger, Janet. (1985). "Technology, Style and Mode of Production." In David Bordwell, Janet Staiger, & Kristin Thompson (eds), *The Classical Hollywood Cinema* (pp. 243–261). New York: Columbia University Press.

Bordwell, David, Staiger, Janet, & Thompson, Kristin. (1985). *The Classical Hollywood Cinema: Film Style and Mode of Production to 1960*. New York: Columbia University Press.

Buscombe, Edward (ed.). (1988). *The BFI Companion to the Western*. London: BFI Publishing.

Cook, David. (1996). *A History of Narrative Film*. New York: W. W. Norton.

Crafton, Donald. (1997). *The Talkies: American Cinema's Transition to Sound 1926–1931*. New York: Charles Scribner's Sons.

Fielding, Raymond. (1972). *The American Newsreel 1911–1967*. Norman: University of Oklahoma Press.

Gomery, Douglas. (2005). *The Coming of Sound*. New York: Routledge.

Gunning, Tom. (1994). *D. W. Griffith and the Origins of American Narrative Film*. Urbana: University of Illinois Press.

Horak, Jan-Christopher. (1995). *The First American Film Avant-Garde, 1919–1945*. Madison: University of Wisconsin Press.

Jacobs, Lea. (2012). "Unsophisticated Lady: The Vicissitudes of the Maternal Melodrama in Hollywood." In Cynthia Lucia, Roy Grundmann, & Art Simon (eds.), *The Wiley-Blackwell History of American Film. Vol. 1: Origins to 1928* (pp. 397–416). Oxford: Wiley-Blackwell.

Koszarski, Richard. (1994). *An Evening's Entertainment: The Age of the Silent Feature Picture, 1915–1928*. Berkeley: University of California Press.

Lewis, Jon. (2008). *American Film: A History*. New York: W. W. Norton.

Mast, Gerald, & Kawin, Bruce F. (2003). *A Short History of the Movies*. 8th edn. New York: Pearson Longman.

Musser, Charles. (1999). "The Nickelodeon Era Begins Establishing the Framework for Hollywood's Mode of Representation." In Thomas Elsaesser (ed.), *Early Cinema: Space, Frame, Narrative* (pp. 256–273). London: British Film Institute.

Robinson, David. (1985). *Chaplin: His Life and Art*. New York: McGraw-Hill.

Sklar, Robert. (1994). *Movie-Made America: A Cultural History of American Movies*. Revised and updated. New York: Vintage Books.

Staiger, Janet. (1985). "The Central Producer System: Centralized Management after 1914." In David Bordwell, Janet Staiger, & Kristin Thompson (eds), *The Classical Hollywood Cinema* (pp. 128–141). New York: Columbia University Press.

Thompson, Kristin. (1985). *Exporting Entertainment: America in the World Film Market 1907–1934*. London: British Film Institute.

2

D. W. Griffith and the Development of American Narrative Cinema

Charlie Keil
Professor, University of Toronto, Canada

Few American directors have received as much attention by historians and scholars over the past 20 years as **D. W. Griffith**. Charlie Keil focuses on Griffith's work during the transitional period in American cinema, approximately 1908–1913, asking whether Griffith should be understood as representative of his era or as a highly innovative aberration. Griffith's emergence at **Biograph** is situated at a point of transformation, not just for the studio but also for the fledgling industry as it sought to meet growing demand, produce an enhanced **narrative language** that could appeal to **middle-class audiences**, and respond to the era's call for a cinema of serious **moral uplift**. Keil traces Griffith's development of narrative strategies over three phases, emphasizing Griffith's experimentation with the individual shot. Keil's essay shares ground with Gaylyn Studlar on Stroheim/DeMille in this volume and with Charles Musser on Edwin S. Porter and Torey Liepa on Thomas Ince in the hardcover/online edition.

Additional terms, names, and concepts: Motion Picture Patents Company (MPPC or Trust), editing patterns, space, place, and all elements of mise-en-scène

The first and arguably most significant phase of D. W. Griffith's film directing career began in 1908 and ended in 1913, the years when he was the most important filmmaker at the preeminent film production company in America. That Griffith's tenure at Biograph coincides almost to the year with the tumultuous period of industrial and formal change typically referred to as "the transitional era" is but one of many reasons that historians view the director as central to the period's developments. But what role did Griffith ultimately play in the American film industry's adoption of a storytelling approach that brought together the resources of performance and decor, framing and composition, and, most crucially, editing, in producing thousands of one-reel narratives for a growing audience of moviegoers in the post-nickelodeon marketplace? Some have questioned the tendency to attribute the period's change in narrational strategies to the singular achievements of Griffith, no matter how impressive those achievements may have been.

American Film History: Selected Readings, Origins to 1960, First Edition. Edited by Cynthia Lucia, Roy Grundmann, and Art Simon.
© 2016 John Wiley & Sons, Inc. Published 2016 by John Wiley & Sons, Inc.

Opposition to understanding Griffith as a key transitional figure derives less from any hesitation about his talent and more from the distinctiveness of his output. The debate focuses on whether we should label Griffith as a representative director of this period: While he may be the era's most celebrated filmmaker, does he actually define that era? Close attention to the formal qualities of Griffith's Biograph films can certainly help us to assess more precisely his contribution to the developing norms of the transitional period; but beyond such study, we also need to consider his films in relation to those of his competitors. Only then can we establish with any certainty whether Griffith stood apart from the rest of the industry during the Biograph years, or whether he merely realized the aims of the era more proficiently, albeit also more idiosyncratically, than any other filmmaker at this time.

Properly contextualizing Griffith's contribution to the transitional period becomes even more vexed when one factors in the complications that history introduces. Past historical accounts have tended to privilege him to the point of describing him as the "most revered and influential movie creator of his day, and perhaps of all motion picture history" (Jacobs 1968, 95). Aside from erroneously ascribing to Griffith the invention of all manner of formal devices that predated his first film, these histories improperly imagine how film production operated during these years, casting Griffith as the only notable filmmaker in existence, and his work as the sole laboratory of experimentation. If historians tended to inflate Griffith's role as an innovator, they were doubtless influenced by an advertisement that Griffith himself took out in 1913, on the heels of his departure from Biograph. In this ad, published in the *New York Dramatic Mirror*, the director boldly proclaimed himself responsible for "revolutionizing Motion Picture drama and founding the modern technique of the art," taking credit for a range of stylistic features, from the close-up to crosscutting to the fade-out. Moreover, Griffith actively contributed to the formation of his own authorial legend by asserting his unassailable influence on other filmmakers of the day: The ad argues that all of the innovations that Griffith introduced are "now generally followed by the most advanced producers." With all other companies (and the filmmakers under their hire) relegated to the position of impressionable imitators, Griffith found his reputation for genius reinforced by the accounts historians devised in the subsequent decades, accounts informed more by the recollections of Griffith and his coworkers than a careful and broad-based examination of films from the period.

If Griffith's campaign of self-promotion exerted considerable influence on seminal histories of the development of American narrative cinema, an unforeseeable accident of preservation provided the additional textual evidence needed to uphold the argument for his superiority as a cinematic storyteller. Empire Trust, the primary investor in Biograph at the time Griffith joined the company, preserved virtually all of the nitrate negatives for the films made during the director's tenure there (Bowser 2009, 62–63). Eventually, these films were acquired and preserved by the Museum of Modern Art; this retention of Griffith's filmmaking legacy promoted intensive study of his oeuvre at the same time as it further marginalized the work of his competition, whose films had largely disappeared.[1]

Griffith's status as the preeminent figure of the transitional era has been fortified by commanding works of scholarship devoted exclusively or primarily to his Biograph period, themselves fueled by the relative ease of access to large swaths of the director's oeuvre.[2] Sustained engagement with his work from these years culminated in the ambitious research initiative entitled *The Griffith Project*, a multivolume publication from the British Film Institute that coincided with the screening of every extant Griffith film at the Giornate del Cinema Muto, in a massive retrospective that spanned a decade. Dozens of early cinema scholars contributed descriptions of the Griffith canon, with seven of the series' 12 volumes devoted to the Biograph period. One can now say with certainty that every film Griffith directed during these years has at this point received some degree of scholarly attention, even the few that have not survived.

In contrast, we still have only piecemeal textual records of the films made at Vitagraph, Lubin, Selig, Kalem, Essanay, Solax, Thanhouser, and a host of other companies, all of which contributed to the changes that mark this endlessly inventive period in American filmmaking. Whereas Griffith's extant films from this period number in the hundreds, those of his peers, when they can be attributed, run in the double digits at best. Not surprisingly, comparatively little scholarly attention has been devoted to the work of Biograph's competitors, though investigation of the broader underpinnings of transitional style and narration continues apace. If, ultimately, the survival rate of Griffith's films will always favor the director in any assessment of the transitional period, this lopsided textual record can still prove instructive: In its entirety, the mammoth Biograph oeuvre provides illuminating evidence of how the grueling release schedules of the day affected film production. Viewing Griffith's output in its totality, we might be much more inclined to echo an assessment put forward by Griffith scholar Russell Merritt, who notes that Griffith's aesthetic development was hardly one of "uninterrupted creative evolution [but rather] more erratic: sporadic bursts of experimentation were often followed by periods of backsliding, or weeks and even months of coasting" (1999, 177). If the analysis of Griffith's Biograph period provided in this essay errs on the side of privileging the director's aesthetic high-water marks, acknowledgment of Merritt's insight always underwrites the long view of Griffith's achievement. If we keep in mind that the overall arc of Griffith's time at Biograph embraced convention in equal measure with innovation, and that every impressive experiment was counterbalanced by efforts that did little to challenge developing stylistic or narrational norms, we move closer to separating the working director from the retrospectively created myth.

Griffith's Move to Biograph: An Industry in Flux

Accounts of Griffith's career before he began making films tend to emphasize his limited success as a playwright and his modest talents as an actor. One wonders how he was able to translate this largely undistinguished résumé into an indisputably impressive career as a novice director of films. One possible explanation, rooted in the moment Griffith entered the American film industry, suggests itself: Because narrative filmmaking was undergoing a profound shift, and filmmakers now had to tackle more involved stories at the same time that they needed to devise new ways of rendering their stories comprehensible and engaging, no obvious skill set ensured success. Enthusiasm, drive, and a willingness to try untested approaches probably counted as much as any demonstrated facility in directing actors or staging dramatic action. Griffith was fortunate to have the abilities of two veteran cameramen, Arthur Marvin and Billy Bitzer, to rely on when he started making films at Biograph. And, in a medium that often employed the young and inexperienced, Griffith's relative maturity when he assumed the post of director conferred upon him an authority that allowed him to control completely the productions that he oversaw. While the phrase "the right place at the right time" often signals the desperate move of a historian who cannot summon up any convincing causal argument, in this instance invoking it seems justified.

When Griffith arrived at Biograph at the end of 1907, he encountered a company redefining itself at the same time that the American film industry was experiencing its own transformation. Earlier that year, J. J. Kennedy from Empire Trust had taken over Biograph's management, and he appears to have been instrumental in charting the company's aggressive course of action when confronted by legal challenges in 1908. Biograph was subject to mounting pressure to concede control of domestic production to the Edison Film Combine throughout the year. By using a legal decision that found the Warwick camera in violation of the Edison company's camera patent, Edison had coerced most of its domestic competition to join forces as part of a licensed combine. Standing almost alone in opposition to the Edison Film Combine, Biograph pursued its own patent-based suits in the courts, inviting further counterclaims from Edison. Emboldened by its success in turning the tables on Edison, Biograph began issuing licenses to numerous importers in a bid to quickly increase production. Eventually Edison and Biograph would call a truce and pool their patents to create the Motion Picture Patents Company (MPPC), or the Trust, late in 1908.

As much as Edison wished to gain sole control of the domestic marketplace, the company shared certain objectives with Biograph: to expand its production capacity to keep pace with vaulting demand, and to improve the quality of its films while aiming for a reliably comprehensible final product with each release. A more centralized form of production could help to insure the latter, while a monopolistic industry structure was viewed as a way to promote the former. Companies also had to contend with the constant calls for evidence of social uplift in the cinema, spurring manufacturers to develop scenarios that featured more complicated dramatic narratives.

By producing serious dramas, the industry hoped that it might placate fears that film exerted a negative influence on its working-class audience; at the same time such films were also designed to appeal to a middle-class audience still largely resistant to the medium. But crafting comprehensible dramatic narratives of a limited running time brought its own problems. Initially, solutions arose at the level of the exhibitor, as supports to the film text in the form of lecturers and actors voicing parts behind the screen were enlisted to render such films intelligible to their audiences (Musser 1983). But for an industry aiming to expand its output and to manufacture films according to principles of rational management and dependability, solving the problem of comprehension had to take place at the level of production. In short, the solution had to be text-centered. Investing the director function with the power to control the elements that contributed to the telling of a story represented one step in the problem-solving process; looking to the theater for creative talent was another. D. W. Griffith, a refugee from the theatrical world eager to exercise his creative prerogative, even in the degraded arena of film production, arrived at Biograph at an opportune time.

Storytelling Challenges and Stylistic Strategies

Any filmmaker starting out in 1908 would have found the prospect of directing a dramatic film daunting. Few models existed for crafting a compelling and comprehensible narrative of under 20 minutes. While the theater and the short story might provide material for adaptation and even general principles of narrative construction, nothing could prepare filmmakers of the era for the challenge of how to translate the scenarios they were assigned into short films that audiences could easily grasp and find involving. Up to this point, most early films had expended little effort in establishing temporal relations among shots, nor had they attempted to invest characters with psychological motivations or molded the depicted action to elicit suspense or sympathy. If dramatic material of some complexity were to succeed with audiences, these aims would have to be realized. The central question was how. There is a danger when setting out the situation in these terms that it might be misconstrued as implying that filmmakers were merely trying to "find their way" to the classical system of narration and that they slowly fumbled around until they perfected that system. Clearly, filmmakers did not know what would work until they tried it, and they did not have a firm set of linked objectives in mind as they formulated different experiments in storytelling over the course of the transitional period. Even so, preferred practices did emerge, and effective solutions to key problems often found favor in the trade press; if easily emulated, these quickly spread across the field of production.

As I have outlined elsewhere, filmmakers were guided by certain broad principles, many of them promulgated within the pages of influential trade journals of the day, including *Moving Picture World* and the *New York Dramatic Mirror*. Foremost among these principles was film's obligation to provide a believable fictional world, preserving a sense of verisimilitude while actively soliciting emotional investment from the viewer. As I have noted, audience belief and emotional investment became the twin hallmarks of a commendable film (Keil 2001, 35). Where earlier cinema had traded primarily in the presentation of visually arresting material, transitional-era films were charged with the responsibility of generating drama from the varied resources of the medium. Whether it be the actors' performances or the sets and the costumes, the distance of the camera from the filmed action or the positioning of the camera, the staging of the action within the confines of the playing space or the arrangement of the shots themselves, filmmakers turned to cinema's formal dimensions to devise ways of rendering their narratives intelligible and emotionally compelling. Eventually, they would settle on selected approaches that became codified and led to the establishment of the classical system of narration, but in 1908, the formal possibilities must have seemed both exciting for their boundlessness and overwhelming in their very indeterminacy.

Though a particularly limited number of films has survived from the key years of 1908–1910, we can say on the basis of what is available for viewing that Griffith proved comparatively adept at discerning how his newly chosen medium might be harnessed for its storytelling potential. If Griffith was not in the vanguard of every new practice that helped usher in a changed approach to narration during this time, he certainly seems to have found the potential in a significant number of important storytelling techniques.

Moreover, Griffith continued to develop these techniques in arresting ways over the course of his time at Biograph. Though he was reportedly frustrated by the limitations imposed by the one-reel format near the end of his stint at the company, some of his most accomplished efforts emerged in 1912–1913. And while Griffith has always been acknowledged for his facility with crosscutting, his narrational skills were not limited only to the domain of editing. He experimented with a panoply of devices involving mise-en-scène and cinematographic properties, displaying a stylistic range that definitely marks him as one of the period's foremost filmmakers.

Tracing Griffith's accomplishments chronologically invites certain problems, not the least of which is an implicit suggestion that Griffith's style evolved toward a satisfying point of maturation that prepared him for feature filmmaking. But such an approach allows the analyst to link the changes in Griffith's storytelling practices to changes in the industry, while also acknowledging concurrent developments at other companies. Moreover, analyzing Griffith's films in their totality allows us to investigate his style as a system of interlocking devices, in which elements of the mise-en-scène, cinematographic properties, and editing work in concert to shape his distinct narrational approach. In tying Griffith's stylistic development to his role in shaping the narrational norms of the transitional period, I am broadening the basic project Tom Gunning established in his landmark work on the director, *D. W. Griffith and the Origins of American Narrative Film*. Concentrating on the formative years of 1908–1909, Gunning shows how the director employed style to create a more psychologically rich vein of characterization, to articulate spatiotemporal relationships among shots, and to adopt a moral perspective on the dramatic action. Collectively, a variety of devices – performance style, shot scale, and crosscutting the most celebrated among them – provided cinema with an arsenal of storytelling strategies that achieved the desired effect of delivering more complex and engaging stories. Gunning (1991) labels Griffith's distinct approach to storytelling "the narrator system," and argues that the director helped usher in a new order of narrativization distinct from that evident in the previous period. In what follows, I will trace out that narrator system by dividing Griffith's Biograph career into three periods, each lasting approximately two years and each marking a stage of his development as a storyteller.[3] For each period, I will analyze a handful of representative Biograph films, buttressed by invocations of trends evident in films from competing companies. In this way, I hope to show not only how Griffith's approach to narration shifted over time, but also how his efforts related to those of his competitors during the transitional period.

1908–1909: Shaping a Story

The first six months of Griffith's time as a director at Biograph found him working on a range of story material, from adaptations of literature and theater (Shakespeare, Molnar, and Jack London, among other sources) to farcical comedy (*A Calamitous Elopement*). He learned how to work within the constraints of studio sets for certain films (*For Love of Gold*), but took full advantage of exteriors for others (*Where the Breakers Roar*). While becoming accustomed to the demands of a punishing production schedule, Griffith began to develop certain strengths, most obviously in the crafting of dramas of imperilment. Films such as *The Fatal Hour*, *The Guerilla*, and *An Awful Moment* gained attention in part for how they deployed editing to create more dynamic action and suspense. But at the same time that Griffith appeared to recognize that the distinct tempos of crosscutting could energize these scenarios of threat and rescue, his conception of screen space underwent a concomitant transformation. One begins to sense a progressive grasp of the potential of the discrete shot that has two obvious outcomes: First, a film becomes not merely an aggregate of completed short scenes, but a product of the interplay among shots; second, the resources of an individual shot, be they graphic, tonal, or expressive, can be exploited and then built upon as a film's narrative progresses.

Of course such potential can only be glimpsed in the Biographs of 1908, many of which are rushed, somewhat perfunctory affairs. And yet one sees in particular moments an attentiveness to the capacities of mise-en-scène, whether it be the emphatic diagonals dominating the frame in the opening shot of *Where the Breakers Roar*, the joyous dancing in the background space at the outset of *Call of the Wild*, or the layered staging of the introductory courtroom scene in *An Awful Moment*. The latter instance epitomizes what will become one of Griffith's specialties: The highlighting of discrete bits of business within a crowded composition, both to convey a sense of social interaction and to invite the viewer to engage with the drama about to unfold. As one of the observers of the trial consistently turns back to a woman behind her, for instance, she reveals her face to us in the process; this act of confiding in her friend creates a focal point at the foreground of the composition at the same time that it evokes verisimilitude, encouraging us to imagine that we are observing action already in progress. Because Griffith created a stock company of skilled actors, those not deployed for principal roles could fill out the ranks of the background players, allowing for particularly rich pools of ancillary action, which the director would come to stage with increasing care.

Griffith's vaunted experiments with cutting in 1908 resulted in prefigurations of more assured work the following year: *The Guerilla* anticipates *The Lonely Villa*'s three-pronged last-minute rescue while the moralizing contrast editing in *Song of the Shirt* prepares for *A Corner in Wheat* (Gunning 1991, 134). But perhaps his most celebrated instance of realizing the narrational potential of editing emerged in *After Many Years*, Griffith's first version of Tennyson's *Enoch Arden*, a film the director later remade in 1911. When a shipwreck separates a husband and wife, leaving the man stranded on a remote island, he and his wife are still connected by strategic cuts. The most striking of these cuts occurs at the moment the husband kisses a locket containing his wife's image, giving way to a shot of his wife reaching out her arms as if welcoming his embrace. Through the agency of the cut, the narration forges a connection that not only intensifies the couple's desire but bespeaks a knowledge that outstrips that belonging to any character. As Tom Gunning succinctly expresses it: "The narrator system affirms [the couple's] gestures of devotion, creating an omniscience that allows this paradoxical embrace" (1991, 113). As Gunning goes on to point out, the fact that the cut interrupts the action of the kiss further underscores the power of editing to signal the presence of a storyteller: By switching from the husband to the wife at a crucial moment, the edit shapes our understanding of their relationship, cementing the bond between the two, but also intensifying our emotional investment in the characters and the strain that the husband's absence creates for both of them. Griffith would continue to find ways to deepen the viewer's connection to character, relying on editing in combination with performance style and other elements within the mise-en-scène.

By 1909, Griffith's apprenticeship was largely complete, and his next 12 months at Biograph represent one of his most fruitful periods. Three of the most well-known transitional-era one-reelers were released during this year, including *The Lonely Villa, The Country Doctor*, and *A Corner in Wheat*. Tellingly, each of these canonical works reveals a key facet of Griffith the storyteller: the master of the rescue scenario; the sensitive poet of pastoral lyricism; and the socially engaged moralist. What unites them all is their distinct sense of space, articulated both at the level of the shot and in the relationships among shots. Beyond that, each plays a variation on one of Griffith's favored narrative situations – the family structure under siege.

The Lonely Villa, in concert with *The Lonedale Operator* (1911), has enshrined Griffith's reputation for perfecting the last-minute rescue. Derived from an oft-adapted play in the Grand Guignol tradition, André de Lorde's *Au Téléphone, The Lonely Villa* employs a familiar situation as the spur for its crosscutting: Left alone in their well-appointed home, a mother and her three daughters face imminent danger from intruders while the father races back to save them. Griffith invests this simple tale with particular urgency by carefully defining the interior spaces of the home so that the viewer clearly understands the distance separating besieged family members from menacing thieves. The systematic layout of the domestic space renders its eventual violation by the intruders both immediately comprehensible and palpably disturbing. Here, more than in any other Biograph to date, Griffith relies on the principle of repetition to reinforce spatial relations. While the taut crosscutting alternating between adjacent spaces represents this principle at its most refined, repeated spaces permeate the film's entire structure. As Gunning has pointed out, *The Lonely Villa* possesses the greatest number of shots of any Biograph film up to this time (52), but only 12 different camera positions, with four of them used only once (1999a, 143). This translates into eight separate camera positions employed across 48 shots, allowing for multiple returns to the same setup. This is an approach that Griffith will employ time and again, insistently returning to established spaces to measure change over time or to reinforce the spatial relationship of one space to another.

Were the editing patterns in *The Lonely Villa* engineered only to articulate proximate spatial relationships, that alone would demonstrate Griffith's growing confidence in molding the integrity of the shot to the transformative qualities of cutting. But *The Lonely Villa* introduces a third strand of action distinct from that unfolding within the home. Once the father has been separated from his family, editing introduces the space he occupies into the circuitry of shots, linking him back to the home through the instrument of the telephone. (His wife calls him to alert him to the danger she and her daughters face.) As Gunning notes, the film expends more cuts on the telephone exchange between husband and wife (seven instances of intercutting) than to the subsequent race to the rescue that the husband undertakes once the robbers cut the phone line (only two instances). Parallel placement of the husband and wife within separate frames, with each standing to the right holding the phone in the left hand, connects them across spaces as surely as the technology of the telephone carries one's voice to the other (1999a, 143). More than one commentator has noted that the telephone operates as both salvation and threat in this scenario, no less so than its formal equivalent, parallel editing. Tying together invaders, victims, and rescuer with one device, Griffith demonstrates the potential of crosscutting for disturbance while also exhibiting its role in resolution. The myriad uses he will devise for editing will only increase during his remaining years at Biograph.

The family comes under threat once more in *The Country Doctor*, but in this instance, death claims the sole child of the titular physician, the ironic outcome of his choice to stay at the home of an ailing young neighbor rather than rush back to his daughter, also felled by illness. Griffith employs parallel editing again in this film, though less for the purposes of engineering a timely rescue than to derive suspense from the doctor's moral predicament: He must choose between staying to tend a sick stranger and abandoning her to help his own child. The editing possesses distinct narrational force, as the comparison of the two cases of illness points up the impossibility of the doctor's situation. Griffith buttresses the implied parallelism through manipulation of the mise-en-scène, positioning each of the sickbeds in similar portions of the frame. This strategy reveals illness as an equalizer – more starkly conveyed through the contrast between the doctor's comfortably bourgeois home and the more Spartan surroundings of the country family's cabin. The doctor's decision to uphold his duty to a patient elicits no cosmic reward, and the narrative comes to a close with the bereaved father clutching his dead child's limp body.

Tellingly, the film does not end with this shot, but instead closes with a variation on the opening pan across the surrounding countryside. This forceful camera movement serves multiple narrational functions: First, the atmospheric quality of the pan deepens the emotional tenor of the story's bleak conclusion; second, this shot, empty of characters, asserts the primacy of nature, the final arbiter; third, by mimicking the film's opening shot, a pan moving in the opposite direction, this final camera movement provides symmetry, ending the story as it began. Yet the formal unity scarcely provides release from the pall of death in the previous shot; instead, the rhyming pans measure the loss experienced over the course of the narrative. The opening pan begins by capturing a peaceful haven, identified as the Valley of Stillwater by an accompanying intertitle. The camera movement then gradually sweeps over a pastoral landscape to reveal the doctor's happy family emerging from their home. In the corresponding final pan, the point of departure for the camera movement is the closed door of the house, death having cut short any subsequent familial sojourns. In the words of Tom Gunning, with this evocative pairing of contrasting pans, "Griffith has discovered the power of a cinematic gesture and structure to express emotion, beyond the actor's craft. The camera's narrative role in introducing the film here becomes an emotionally loaded withdrawal from the scene of grief across a landscape which, no longer merely pictorial, resonates with grief and loss" (1999b, 165–166).

Griffith echoes a film's opening in its concluding shot once again in *A Corner in Wheat*, a film released near the end of 1909, and in many ways the culmination of much that he had been developing over the past 18 months. Typically characterized as the crowning achievement of Griffith's early period, *A Corner in Wheat* fuses the director's increasingly authoritative use of editing with his penchant for social protest, resulting in a film that the *New York Dramatic Mirror* labeled "an editorial," doubtless because it weaves together three narrative strands, linked only by broad-based economic causes as opposed to character interaction. *A Corner in Wheat* may stand as Griffith's most abstract employment of editing until the ambitious experiment of *Intolerance*: Cuts draw parallels emphasizing the nature of social relations, most pointedly in the alternation between shots of the Wheat King's feast and those of the starving masses at the bakery. Griffith's approach to composition mirrors his use of editing, insofar as a number of the shots are self-consciously posed, not only the second and final shots of farmers sowing wheat in their field (modeled after Millet's painting *The Sower*) and the famous tableau of the bread line in the bakery, but also the first shot in the Wheat King's office, where his lackeys stand virtually rooted in place while he issues orders. Other shots are studies in controlled arrangement of complex activity, particularly the mounting frenzy of the trading pit, where one can still distinguish key narrative developments, and the Wheat King's lavish dinner party, featuring one of the deeper interior compositions to be found in an early Biograph single-reeler.

The studied approach to both editing and composition underscores Griffith's pretensions to self-conscious artistry, partly a response to repeated calls for morally uplifting drama during this period, but equally a sign of the director's increasing aesthetic confidence. The pictorialism that marks *A Corner in Wheat*, coupled with its commitment to social commentary, sets this work apart from most of Griffith's films of the period, and certainly from those of his contemporaries. Another notable example of this tendency from 1909 is *Pippa Passes; or, The Song of Conscience*, an adaptation of Browning's poem that uses recurrent images of the titular figure and carefully crafted lighting effects to emulate dawn and the dimming of the day. The film's visual distinctiveness prompted the *New York Times* to compare its lighting effects to "those obtained by the Secessionist Photographers" (quoted in Schickel 1984, 142). Griffith also experimented with lighting effects in *A Drunkard's Reformation*, a temperance drama made in the spring of 1909, and mined the atmospheric effects of location shooting in his moody seashore drama, *Lines of White on a Sullen Sea*. In addition, the latter film employs a fade to render the image of its heroine looking out across the water as a silhouette; the technique also designates a passage of time when followed by an intertitle stating: "Six years later, sick unto death with waiting." As Kristin Thompson points out, the technique "combines an objective passage of time and a subjective suggestion that [her] continued vigil is a sort of suspended existence where the empty sea has overwhelmed her life on land" (1999, 80–81).

Were other filmmakers attempting equally ambitious experiments with style and narration at this time? It is difficult to say with any certainty, given the relatively small number of films that survive from competing companies in the 1908–1909 period. What does become clear, however, is that some companies were experimenting in areas that Griffith did not seem particularly interested in developing. By 1909, Vitagraph, for example, began employing a noticeably closer shot scale by virtue of adopting the "nine-foot line," wherein its actors were positioned nearer to the camera than was the industry norm. At around the same time, Vitagraph also initiated a staging practice of having actors turn their backs to the camera when placed in the foreground, promoting the kind of naturalistic interaction Griffith was pursuing through other means. And while Griffith did exhibit some interest in the capacity of the moving camera, he appears to have been outstripped in this regard by a number of companies, most prominently Laemmle's Independent Moving Picture Company (IMP) and Lubin. Finally, while Griffith was developing a particular approach to the representation of depicted space that saw him dependably return to the exact camera setup multiple times, other companies altered the camera's perspective on a repeated space. This last divergence between Griffith's preferred practice and tendencies at other companies points to the way in which aspects of the director's narrational approach would become identifiably his own, especially in the later Biograph years.

1910–1911: An Increasingly Confident Style

The American industry of 1910 was a considerably changed entity from what Griffith had encountered when he first starting working in films in late 1907. The monopolistic efforts of the MPPC had imposed numerous reforms on the distribution system, including the elimination of duping, the introduction of a regularized release schedule, and higher rental prices. Trust producers benefited from these new policies, primarily in the form of increased revenues; these, in turn, translated into elevated production values as evident in the progressively more well-appointed interior sets and varied costumes on display in Griffith's films. By 1910, as the MPPC attempted to extend its control over distributors by absorbing affiliated exchanges into the Trust-controlled General Film Company, opposition to its policies only increased. Rival companies excluded from the MPPC took advantage of the expanding marketplace and the Independent movement ultimately flourished, matching the Trust in size and even in achievement by the time Griffith left Biograph in 1913. But in 1910, Biograph was securely positioned as an industry leader (along with Vitagraph); Griffith's cameraman, Billy Bitzer, recalled that "the little independent companies would quickly copy anything we did that the public seemed to favor" (1973, 52). If the first phase of Griffith's career at Biograph was foundational, these middle years represented a time of deepening engagement with aspects of style that would further his narrational goals of communicating the psychological dimensions of the stories on-screen while creating increasingly more complex spatiotemporal relationships.

Distinct changes to production practices at Biograph altered the routine established at the company for the previous 18 months: First, an additional unit, headed by former leading man Frank Powell, began turning out its own films, primarily comedies; second, Biograph sent Griffith and 50 other employees to the West Coast to film in California for four months (Olsson 2000, 20). The director took full advantage of the new surroundings, incorporating the varied topography of the region into a wide range of stories, from a revenge drama set in the desert (*Over Silent Paths*) to romance in a garden (*Love Among the Roses*) to a seaside tone poem (*The Unchanging Sea*). *The Unchanging Sea*, a loose adaptation of the Charles Kingsley poem "The Three Fishers," combines aspects of various Biograph films from the previous year: Its setting and scenario of a devoted woman waiting for the return of a man gone to sea recall *Lines of White on a Sullen Sea*; the deliberately recurrent imagery designed to mirror the cadences of its source poem resembles the approach of *Pippa Passes*; and the posed, near-frozen compositions bring to mind a similar tendency toward tableau in *A Corner in Wheat*. What renders *The Unchanging Sea* distinctive is its striking economy of means. Of the 30 shots employed, 17 are devoted to just two locales, the exterior of the couple's home and the point on the shore where the wife awaits her husband's return. The two spaces are almost always paired, such that an appearance of the home triggers a recurrence of the shore. The insistent return to these two spaces marks them as touchstones for the film, and indeed, they chart the progression of the wife's narrative as the years pass without her husband having come back to her. The first time we see the spot on the shore that will become exclusively associated with the wife (and the strong bond she feels for her husband), the couple frolics together, running close to the waves before heading back toward the camera. In subsequent shots, we will see the wife go back to the spot, first with other women searching for their men, then through the stages of her daughter's growth, until she is finally reunited with her husband. The constancy of the backdrop matches the steadfast devotion of the wife, even as other aspects of her life change. The fixed perspective used for each shot of the space on the shore reinforces the interweaving of repetition and variation. Thus, when the wife is approached by a suitor in shot number 18, she signals her rejection of him by pointing out to the sea, turning herself toward the waves as she has done several times before. Yet, accompanied by her young daughter, she is no longer alone: The child now gambols near the waves as the husband and wife had done many years before.

Later, when a young man proposes to the grown daughter, the situation mirrors that of the shot featuring the wife's suitor. Now, of course, the child has assumed the place of her mother, as the latter sits impassively, her back to the camera and to the young lovers whose relationship she is unable to see as it blossoms behind her. Griffith trusts that the evocative power of the California seascape will charge this simple tale of a wife's devotion with emotional resonance, but that power also finds its proper channeling through the director's reliance on a system of editing that makes a virtue of repetition.

Repetition and alternation defined not only Griffith's development of editing strategies, but also on occasion his treatment of story material. The later Biograph years are dotted with loose reworkings of earlier films: *After Many Years* begets *Enoch Arden* (1911), *A Drunkard's Reformation* would become *Brutality* (1912), and *Where the Breakers Roar* (1908) leads to *The House of Darkness* (1913). Griffith waited only six months to transform one of his most highly regarded films, *A Corner in Wheat*, into a similarly themed cautionary parable, *The Usurer* (1910).

Figure 2.1 A recurrent atmospheric image from D. W. Griffith's *The Unchanging Sea* (1910, producer Biograph Company).

Though the films share no more than a few details, principally a compositional sameness in their depiction of the protagonists' lavish banquets, they tell similar stories of capitalism's devastating effects on the poor and powerless, with retribution coming in the form of suffocation for the rapacious figure responsible for the suffering of others. Unlike the earlier film, *The Usurer* fails to link the moneylender's actions to broader economic patterns and abandons any framing device that would contrast the depredations of the wealthy with the purity of nature.[4]

Still, the localized nature of the moneylender's negative influence lends *The Usurer* a structural leanness that differentiates it from its predecessor. The film breaks down into two sections, equal in duration, with the first contrasting the self-indulgent lifestyle of the title character to the dire circumstances of those who owe him money. As in *A Corner in Wheat*, the alternation between the moneylender's feast and the shots of his victims' suffering creates a causal relationship. But the editing also serves to highlight the gulf separating the respective lifestyles of the usurer and his victims: In the shots of the banquet, Griffith fills the image to its edges, with characters in the foreground, their backs to the camera, seated at a table that stretches to the back recesses of the frame, as celebrants crowd around both sides; conversely, the homes of the indebted appear stripped down even before the usurer's minions carry out the removal of their furnishings. In one particularly striking instance of parallelism, the usurer adorns the neck of his wife with elaborate jewelry, while in the next shot the debt collectors strip the meager belongings from the tabletop of one of the families owing money. Ultimately, the debtors will be totally bereft, left standing alone in their bare rooms.

The first section culminates in a masterful sequence of six shots, which Tom Gunning has pointed to as exemplifying Griffith's ability to combine the "contrast pattern with the practice of suspending the outcome of an action by an edit" (1981, 19). The tail end of the sequence's first shot shows a female debtor (Kate Bruce), standing at the right of the frame, her daughter seated in a chair beside her. With most of the room's furniture now removed, it bears a striking resemblance to the space of the subsequent shot, occupied by the other depicted debtor (Henry B. Walthall). The sparse mise-en-scène of the two spaces draws attention to the features that they share – a similarly positioned window, a chair to the left of the door, and a single article of clothing hanging on the wall above the chair. The characters, standing in virtually the same spot in each of their respective shots, render the combination of the two images a graphic match. Yet while Bruce's character raises her arms in a beseeching manner, Walthall's grabs a gun concealed behind his hat: If the woman seems to be pleading for divine intervention, the man has already conceded defeat. At the moment Walthall wields the gun, Griffith cuts back to the usurer's banquet. As the moneylender rises to drink a toast, his positioning in the frame, coupled with his raised arm, transforms the shot into a rhyming complement to its two predecessors. A subsequent cut returns us to Walthall: His act of shooting himself elided by the cut, he now collapses onto the floor. The final shot shows the usurer completing the toast before leaving the banquet room.

As Gunning has pointed out, Griffith's deliberate interruption of Walthall's act of suicide elevates narrational contrast to the level of causality; but beyond that, the edit ties the guilt deriving from the debtor's death to the ignorant moneylender (1981, 19). The associative power of the cut illustrates what an earlier title had already declared, that the usurer drinks "blood-distilled wine." (Conveniently, the cut also displaces a potentially offensive act, thereby avoiding the displeasure of those monitoring the cinema for disturbing imagery.) Later, when the moneylender lies suffocating in his safe, Griffith will draw on a graphic parallel one more time by cutting back to an image of Walthall's outstretched body. The force of the cut in this instance demonstrates how the director employs editing as narrational commentary, passing judgment on the usurer.

The events leading up to the usurer's demise constitute the film's second section, and the emphasis of the editing shifts from contrasting the moneylender and his victims to creating a tight spatial relationship predicated on contiguity. If the first section stressed how the usurer benefited from the pain of others by surrounding him with adoring admirers, the restricted spatial schema of the second part isolates him from all else but his wealth, which proves useless in keeping him from death. Thus, when the Bruce character inadvertently locks the usurer within his own safe, no one realizes he is there, neatly inverting his ignorance of the plight of those he had undone earlier. Cutting back and forth between the adjacent spaces of the moneylender's office and the safe promotes the irony of his predicament – though within arm's reach of his office, the mechanisms he has devised to preserve his wealth insure his destruction. While Griffith's crosscutting typically serves the last-minute rescue scenario, here it only reinforces the hopelessness of the usurer's situation, demonstrating how the director continued to ring variations on trusted devices.

Griffith also returned to familiar narrative material in the series of films he made about the Civil War and its aftermath. Perhaps because the fiftieth anniversary of that war led to widespread commemorative projects, Biograph released its heaviest concentration of films on the subject during the 1910–1911 period. In 1910, the company produced *In the Border States*, *The House with Closed Shutters*, and *The Fugitive*, followed by *His Trust*, *His Trust Fulfilled*, *Swords and Hearts*, and *The Battle* in 1911. As a subject, the Civil War also appealed to Griffith on a number of levels: It touched on his family history, as his father had served for its duration as a Confederate officer; it possessed a long-standing heritage of representation on stage, dependent on the conventions of theatrical melodrama (Mayer 2001, 112); and it permitted a dramatic intertwining of the personal and the epic, of bravery tested on the field of battle and loyalty demonstrated within the walls of the family home. Though each of the Civil War films of 1910–1911 approaches its topic in a distinct fashion, one can still find echoes among them as a body of work, either on the level of recurrent characters and situations (the loyal slave who proves the financial salvation of his masters in *His Trust*, *His Trust Fulfilled*, and *Swords and Hearts*; the plucky heroine who masquerades as a man to aid the cause in *Swords* and *The House with Closed*

Shutters; the cowardly son who finds himself overwhelmed by battle in *House* and *The Battle*; the home providing refuge for a pursued soldier in *The Fugitive* and *In the Border States*) or on the level of dominant themes (the testing of familial bonds, the strength of maternal love, the preservation of honor).

More than one commentator has noted that Civil War subject matter "brought out [Griffith's] ambitious best" (Simmon 2009, 40), whether it is mining the emotional cost of war's strain on the family – most pointedly expressed in *House* and *The Fugitive* – or staging large-scale action on the battlefield, as he does spectacularly in *House* and *The Battle*. Certainly Griffith's command of large masses of extras, staged legibly in expansive exterior long shots, demonstrates his increased dexterity in rendering wartime combat in epic terms. Skirmishes and chases emerge as dynamic incidents, aided by the director's kinetic editing and sensitivity to the distinct qualities that the locations (most often in New Jersey) afforded. And Griffith's attentiveness to the resources of mise-en-scène persist: He stages the Confederate officer's return to his burnt-out family home in *Swords* so that the actor's back remains turned to the camera, using restraint to signal emotional devastation; he has the brave sister in *House* snip off a lock of her hair as a sign of her affection for a suitor about to head off to war, prefiguring her decision to shear off all of her tresses once she elects to impersonate her brother in battle; he uses the fallen son's army jacket as a touchstone for his mother's undying devotion in *The Fugitive*, consecrated in the final shot when she places a strand of lilies of the valley in the coat's pocket. Grace notes such as these offer ample evidence that Griffith maintained Biograph's reputation as the preeminent American film producer through attention to all of the particulars of storytelling.

But other companies also put effort into enhancing their profiles through stylistic innovation. The sets of chief competitors Edison and Vitagraph rivaled and often surpassed those of Biograph for the detail of their decor elements and the depth achieved. Vitagraph also appears to have been an industry leader in experiments with atmospheric lighting effects, though by 1910–1911 many companies were engaging in the deployment of such techniques as the "open-door shot," where light pours in from the outside, often illuminating a character standing in the doorway. These lighting effects helped to establish tone or create dramatic emphasis, supplying their own narrational valence. In the realm of performance, Vitagraph became progressively more reliant on what Roberta Pearson (1992) has labeled the "verisimilar" style of acting, where actors rely on muted gesturing, facial reactions, and interaction with props to convey a character's thoughts and emotions. (Biograph was engaged in the pursuit of a similar approach to performance during this time as well.) The deployment of a closer shot scale aided in rendering the verisimilar style more legible, and by 1911, numerous companies began using occasional cut-ins to more closely scaled shots of actors in order to emphasize reactions. Griffith used just such framings to highlight Blanche Sweet's responses in *The Battle*. But the director's experiments with rapid cutting completely outstripped those of his rivals, such that the average number of shots in a 1910 Biograph was more than double that of other companies in 1910 and almost triple the number of its rivals in 1911. The next two years would see Griffith pursue distinct narrational strategies to an even greater degree, at the same time that the American film industry, as a whole, accelerated changes in its general approach to storytelling.

1912–1913: Refinement and Reconfiguration

By 1912, the one-reel format had become the entrenched story form for American filmmakers, and many filmmakers demonstrated increased ease with the demands of crafting narratives to fit its duration. For his part, Griffith had now directed hundreds of 1,000-foot films over the previous three and one-half years and the shorts he made during his last 18 months at the company continue to reveal a filmmaker who found new challenges in matching style to narrative. The result is a form of narration that never ceases to surprise. Despite the high caliber of many of the films Griffith would direct from early 1912 until mid-1913, the status of the so-called late Biographs remains a point of dispute among scholars. When I first wrote about these works in the late 1980s, they tended to be disregarded relative to key films from the period of discovery (Keil 1989, 22). Gradually, critical appraisal of this phase in Griffith's time at Biograph has shifted to the point where Paolo Cherchi Usai, general editor of *The Griffith Project*, can declare that there is "widespread consensus on the view that 1912 is the first 'golden year' in the career of D. W. Griffith" (2002, vii), and that "in its first six months, the year 1913 ... appears to be one of the best known in the context of his creative trajectory" (2003, vi). Even so, there are dissenters, including Scott Simmon, who argues that "for all [the] pleasures of the late Biographs, it sometimes seems as though Griffith's great years may have been back in 1910 and 1911, after which comes a certain narrowing of interest, of narrative drive, of ensemble discovery, of verve ... For all the formal sophistication of the late Biographs, Griffith may have had less to say in them" (1993, 60).[5]

Simmon's criticism presupposes that one can separate Griffith's method of representation from the content of his films. But this runs antithetical to the premises built into Gunning's concept of the narrator system. As Gunning says, "if the filmic narrator exists only in the way it highlights and intensifies the story, if it is visible only through its storytelling, we can also say that the story is visible only through the filmic discourse that tells it" (1991, 286). And Griffith's storytelling approach continued to develop during this late period, especially apparent in how he handles performance style, staging of background action, and intra-scene editing, elements that further guide the viewer to perceive the story as though it were emerging directly from the depicted action.[6] However, these tendencies continued to be counterbalanced by more overt narrational moments when the self-consciousness of Griffith's storytelling technique asserted itself.

Many commentators have noted how Griffith showcased his actors in a number of the late Biographs, creating ample opportunity for demonstrations of the verisimilar style of performance. Occasionally this would result in bravura moments, such as those supplied by Claire McDowell in *The Female of the Species* (1912), Lillian Gish in *The Mothering Heart* (1913), or Blanche Sweet in *The Painted Lady* (1913).[7] But the verisimilar style is sufficiently pervasive to inform performances in films not obviously designed to highlight acting. In *The Girl and Her Trust* (1912), for example, a film typically remarked upon for its rapid editing and extensive tracking shots, Dorothy Bernard expresses flirtatiousness and innocence through a series of small-scale gestures involving a bottle of soda pop and a straw. Whether swirling the bottle to create bubbles or touching her fingers to her lips after an erstwhile suitor has foregone her offer of sharing a drink in order to steal a kiss, Bernard sustains a mood of spirited romantic engagement, relying primarily on facial expression and diegetically motivated props.

Griffith also evinces care in having his background players engage in bits of business to create the illusion of a self-contained story world. The range of activities contained in a single busy composition crammed with extras nearly overwhelms the eye. In films such as *Friends* (1912), *One is Business; the Other Crime* (1912), and *The Musketeers of Pig Alley* (1912), these compositions are built upon multiple pools of action, channeled along a narrow corridor. In the latter film in particular, Griffith consistently accentuates the depth of such images by telescoping the contents of the shot; this approach results in an inverted cone where the action in the foreground spreads out in direct contrast to the more compressed activity in the background.

If compositions such as these tend to create a ricocheting effect, amplified by the host of unreciprocated glances cast by so many characters massed together yet engaged in diverse activities, Griffith's increasingly refined editing strategies aim for spatial analysis and spectatorial guidance. One notes more instances of intra-scene editing, which contributes to the high shot counts of films such as *The Girl and Her Trust* and *The Lady and the Mouse* (1913), both of which feature extended sequences of intricate actions, analyzed by a breakdown of space into more legible sectors. But Griffith would also gravitate toward cut-ins to isolate reactions, such as the numerous shots of Mary Pickford on the staircase in *Friends*. (Obviously, the employment of a closer shot scale also insured that the verisimilar performance style would register its effects more readily.) In fact, analytical editing represents one aspect of narrational development in which one can see Griffith still experimenting with options. In *The Burglar's Dilemma* (1912), for example, when the director wishes to register the moral struggle Henry Walthall's character undergoes, he first frames Walthall, positioned in the shot's mid-ground, in the exact space opened up between the shoulders of the two actors standing closer to the camera. Later, during the same scene, Griffith will opt for separate shots of Walthall instead. Where the first option presents us with Walthall's struggle as a function of the men flanking him (one is the burglar whom Walthall has

Figure 2.2 A typically dense and deep composition in D. W. Griffith's *The Musketeers of Pig Alley* (1912, producer Biograph Company).

falsely accused of a crime that he himself has committed; the other a detective), the second registers his dilemma through performance all the more clearly.

One could argue that the second option seems more "natural" to contemporary eyes, in part because the compositional manipulation required for the first option shows marks of an intrusive storyteller. At this point in the development of Griffith's narrator system, such moments of narrational intervention are still fairly easy to identify. One thinks of the deliberate and startling moves of characters toward the camera in both *The House of Darkness* and *Musketeers*, the carefully composed shots that privilege mood over transmission of narrative information in *House* and *The Sands of Dee* (1912), or the overt parallelism of the opening of *One is Business*. If the aim of classical narration is to suppress narrational self-consciousness in order to encourage the sense that the story is telling itself, Griffith never embraced such an approach, even if his films exhibit a narrational dexterity. As I have expressed elsewhere, to fully understand Griffith as an exemplary transitional director, one must take into account his significant contributions to the period's developments while also acknowledging how idiosyncratic some of those contributions are. Only during the transitional period could a director as distinctive as Griffith still be as pertinent (Keil 2008, 4).

As one final demonstration of the distinctiveness of Griffith's narrational range during the late Biograph period, I will offer a somewhat more extended analysis of a significant film from 1913, *Death's Marathon*.[8] The film is notable for featuring an unsuccessful last-minute rescue, with the inevitability of its failure signaled by the suggestive title, which fuses the stasis of mortality and the endurance of a race, just as the film's centerpiece of parallel editing arrests the rapidity of the intercutting with lingering shots of death and its aftermath. By 1913, Griffith had proved sufficiently adept at the various permutations of the last-minute rescue that setting himself the task of thwarting its expected outcome became the ultimate version of reworking this familiar device.

The fatalism of the title casts a pall over the entirety of the last-minute rescue, which employs roughly half of the film's shots and takes up one-third of its running time. (Its shot total of 112 is just a few shy of the highest for a Griffith single-reeler produced this year.) Perhaps because the rescue's outcome is preordained, Griffith devotes no time to tracing out in advance the route that the erstwhile rescuer (Walter Miller) will use when speeding toward the office where his partner (Henry Walthall) is threatening to kill himself. By this time viewers may have become accustomed to understanding that each successive shot of the rescuer's car should be read as bringing it progressively closer to its intended destination, but more to the point, the refusal to underscore increasing proximity reinforces the futility of the rescue attempt. Ironically, when Miller finally reaches his destination (in a shot whose mise-en-scène does confirm the locale as the exterior of the office building), it is already too late. While I am not ruling out the possibility that Griffith designed the sequence to encourage suspense, the suspense comes cloaked in the dread of inevitability. Rather than having the viewer speculate whether the agent of salvation will arrive in time to prevent wrongdoing, Griffith employed his standard battery of rapid cuts and precise alternation of specified spaces to keep the spectator guessing about when death will finally intervene to thwart the efforts of the rescuer.

As Tom Gunning has pointed out, placing a threatened suicide at the center of the film's last-minute rescue converts the terms of the rescue's representation (2003, 63). Unlike the standard version, where the rescue line of action speeds toward the space of the imperiled party, even as the forces of imperilment move ever closer, here victim and assailant reside within the same space (and, indeed, the same body). The retardatory function of editing within the rescue scenario, where delay proves essential for the perpetuation of suspense and where interruption renders the ultimate act of salvation all the more gratifying, becomes almost sadistically obvious in *Death's Marathon*. All that stands between the suicide and death are the delaying tactics of his wife (Blanche Sweet) on the other end of the phone. Griffith cuts methodically between shots of the two parties, alternating between closely scaled shots of Walthall, who never moves from his seated position at his desk, and Sweet, framed at a slightly greater distance from the camera, and allowed one moment of mobility when she runs off to another room to enlist the persuasive powers of the couple's baby. (Such is the pessimism of *Death's Marathon* that even the innocence of an infant cannot dissuade the suicide from pursuing self-destruction.) The intense spatial restriction of this series of alternating shots is interrupted only by the methodical insertion of shots detailing Miller's progress. As we might expect, the speed and movement embodied in these shots of Miller's automobile rushing from one side of the screen to the other stand in direct contrast to the largely static and intimate shots of the couple linked by the telephone. But near metronomic timing of these interjections proves to be their most distinctive feature. Once the spatial coordinates for the husband and wife are fixed, six shots are devoted to Miller in his car, from the moment that he arrives at the couple's home to the moment when he finally reaches the office, and the intervals separating each of their appearances create a remarkably symmetrical pattern: nine shots (50 seconds), two shots (10 seconds), nine shots (51 seconds), nine shots (34 seconds), five shots (31 seconds). Recurring with such predictability, these shots of Miller's ride to the rescue assume an inevitability that renders the fruitlessness of his attempt all the more poignant. Never has a rescue been presented with such machine-like precision yet failed so abysmally.

The shots of the rescue attempt also operate as strategically positioned structuring devices, carving the interaction of husband and wife into discrete narrative segments. Gunning's analysis carefully details this justly celebrated aspect of the film, reminding us that the extended telephone conversation relies on the strength of the performances of Walthall and Sweet, despite the brevity of most of the shots (2003, 64–65). If attention has properly focused on the bravura depiction of resignation and barely controlled mania conveyed by the former – and Roberta Pearson provides a concise account of its power – Sweet's achievement emerges as no less remarkable (1992, 110–111).

Particularly striking is the moment of Walthall's actual death, registered by Sweet's reaction rather than depiction of the shooting itself. Unlike Walthall, who uses the gun throughout as a prop to telegraph the fluctuations in his emotions, Sweet is left largely to her own devices. The horror of Walthall's death is played out on her face. Up until this point, the give-and-take of action and reaction has sustained the wife's ploy of keeping her husband on the line, while also motivating the constant alternation of shots between the two parties. Seeing the husband's death performed through the wife's reactions simultaneously registers the chill of recognition that she is now alone. The intensity of Sweet's focused performance conveys the finality of her husband's decision, as does the extended duration of the two shots devoted to her expression of shock and grief, both noticeably longer than any of the shots leading up to this moment. The phone line no longer connects her to her spouse, nor does it hold forth the prospect of his salvation. When Miller finally picks up the receiver and confirms the obvious, we might be tempted to read the succession of shots as laying the groundwork for the creation of a new couple, as Miller assumes the husband's role. But Griffith tempers this impression by sustaining the action past the moment the phone call ends, to include a shot of Sweet stumbling aimlessly to the adjoining room, only to collapse. With this image of physical and emotional exhaustion ends the most unorthodox last-minute rescue that Griffith would ever film.

If *Death's Marathon* provided us with nothing else than this shockingly downbeat challenge to the last-minute rescue's conventions, it would warrant attention. But the latter half also gains power from the way Griffith initiates numerous parallels and image patterns in the early sections that then resonate throughout the rest of the film. The film's fascination with floral imagery and smoking, initiated in the opening sequences of courtship, persists throughout. While Walthall's penchant for smoking conveys his self-confidence, Miller's appropriating the same habit only underscores his loneliness. Griffith compounds this impression by placing the shot of Miller shown smoking alone at the gentlemen's club directly after the sole sequence devoted to portraying Sweet and Walthall's brief period of domestic bliss. Later, when a delivery boy grabs a puff of a cigarette, exhaling emphatically before completing his errand in the adjoining office (and then picking up the temporarily abandoned butt before exiting the offices altogether), it seems little more than an incidental bit of business given to Bobby Harron to inject a walk-on role with some interest. But the message Harron delivers leads Miller to discover that Walthall has embezzled invested funds to support his gambling. And the blast of smoke emitted by his cigarette will later be reproduced by the gun that takes Walthall's life, as the cockiness that Walthall displayed earlier proves his undoing. The meanings generated by such imagery twist and turn as the film's tone darkens and the characters find that they can neither control nor predict what life has in store for them. Accordingly, flowers, so closely associated with Sweet as a natural outgrowth of love at the outset, come to signify a failed marriage, and the various bouquets appointing the home she and Walthall share eventually stand as a mockery of their past happiness. By the film's final shot, the slate is wiped clean, with Sweet (in a composition reminiscent of the fourth shot that introduced her) clad in widow's weeds, and all flowers in her home removed. The bittersweet tone of the film's conclusion arises from Miller's final gesture. He brings her a bouquet of roses and then leaves. Though her half-smile suggests the possibility of a new life, it could equally imply a rueful recognition of her changed status.

Death's Marathon is a film all but bursting with directorial inventiveness. It becomes even more suggestive when viewed in combination with *The Mothering Heart*, the Biograph film likely produced directly afterward, as the later film rings variations on the former. Both films feature wives neglected by husbands lured away from the home; both employ floral imagery to convey the failing fortunes of the marriage; both employ infants at critical junctures in attempts to strengthen the weakened bonds between husband and wife. But viewing the films in combination is also instructive because it shows us that, by 1913, Griffith was not only toying with his own formulae but borrowing from trends developing around him. Experimenting with the depiction of subjective states, exploring the depth of sets with extensive background space, exploiting the emotional and visual potential of offscreen space, arranging characters around tables so that some have their backs to the camera, showing characters reflected in mirrors – one finds Griffith trying out all of these approaches, though none is strongly associated with his filmmaking style at this time. As the pressure increased to find ways to render narratives that were psychologically dense and emotionally compelling, that were visually resonant and narrationally inventive, Griffith employed an array of approaches to provide solutions to the problems posed by his chosen scenario. In this he differs little from other filmmakers of the period, though few would experiment so insistently in a single film. In my first published essay on Griffith (and on transitional cinema), I identified a productive tension between the demands of style and narrative as the salient trait of the late Griffith-era Biographs (Keil 1989). I see little reason to amend that assessment now, more than 20 years later, except to add that in Griffith the tension often seems even more palpable and the works emerging out of that tension the most satisfying the period has to offer. Griffith's Biograph films offer no evidence that we should bracket him off from central tendencies of transitional-era production, but they do force us to continue rethinking its conceptual boundaries.

Notes

1. Even so, one can overstate the availability of the Griffith Biograph oeuvre. Near-total preservation has not translated into the availability of all titles as viewable prints. (For one account of the archival status of many of Griffith's films from this period, see Usai 2001, vii.)
2. Primary among these would be Jesionowski 1987, Gunning 1991, Pearson 1992, and Simmon 1993.
3. I have assigned dates to films based on the time of their release rather than when they were made. Typically, only a few months separated the time of production from the time of release.
4. The analysis of *The Usurer* is an edited and revised version of the one that appears in Keil 2000, 153–156.
5. Russell Merritt disagrees, saying "as Griffith became more self-assured, his best narratives had become simpler and less moralistic, with undertones more intricate than ever" (2002, 160).
6. As Kristin Thompson has said of transitional narration generally, it "found ways of motivating the telling process so that it seemed for the most part to come from within the action of the scene" (1997, 432).
7. Aside from Pearson's book-length study (1992), Russell Merritt's influential essay on *The Painted Lady* (1976) provides an exacting analysis of late-era Biograph performance style.
8. The analysis of *Death's Marathon* is an edited and revised version of the one that appears as part of Keil 2008, 5–9.

References

Bitzer, Billy. (1973). *His Story: The Autobiography of D. W. Griffith's Master Cameraman.* New York: Farrar, Straus & Giroux.

Bowser, Eileen. (2009). "Movies and the Stability of the Institution." In Charlie Keil & Ben Singer (eds), *American Cinema of the 1910s: Themes and Variations* (pp. 48–68). New Brunswick: Rutgers University Press.

Gunning, Tom. (1981). "Weaving a Narrative: Style and Economic Background in Griffith's Biograph Films." *Quarterly Review of Film Studies*, 6.1, 11–25.

Gunning, Tom. (1991). *D. W. Griffith and the Origins of American Narrative Film: The Early Years at Biograph.* Urbana: University of Illinois Press.

Gunning, Tom. (1999a). "The *Lonely Villa.*" In Paolo Cherchi Usai (ed.), *The Griffith Project*, vol. 2 (pp. 139–144). London: British Film Institute.

Gunning, Tom. (1999b). "The *Country Doctor.*" In Paolo Cherchi Usai (ed.), *The Griffith Project*, vol. 2 (pp. 162–166). London: British Film Institute.

Gunning, Tom. (2003). "*Death's Marathon.*" In Paolo Cherchi Usai (ed.), *The Griffith Project*, vol. 7 (pp. 58–66). London: British Film Institute.

Jacobs, Louis. (1968). *The Rise of the American Film: A Critical History.* New York: Teachers College Press.

Jesionowski, Joyce. (1987). *Thinking in Pictures: Dramatic Structure in D. W. Griffith's Biograph Films.* Berkeley: University of California Press.

Keil, Charlie. (1989). "Transition through Tension: Stylistic Diversity in the Late Griffith Biographs." *Cinema Journal*, 28.3, 22–40.

Keil, Charlie. (2000). "*The Usurer.*" In Paolo Cherchi Usai (ed.), *The Griffith Project*, vol. 4 (pp. 58–66). London: British Film Institute.

Keil, Charlie. (2001). *Early American Cinema in Transition: Story, Style, and Filmmaking, 1907–1913.* Madison: University of Wisconsin Press.

Keil, Charlie. (2008). "D. W. Griffith as a Transitional Filmmaker." In Paolo Cherchi Usai (ed.), *The Griffith Project*, vol. 12 (pp. 1–10). London: British Film Institute.

Mayer, David. (2001). "*Swords and Hearts.*" In Paolo Cherchi Usai (ed.), *The Griffith Project*, vol. 5 (pp. 110–114). London: British Film Institute.

Merritt, Russell. (1976). "Mr. Griffith, *The Painted Lady*, and the Distractive Frame." *Image*, 19.4, 26–30.

Merritt, Russell. (1999). "*The Helping Hand.*" In Paolo Cherchi Usai (ed.), *The Griffith Project*, vol. 1 (pp. 176–177). London: British Film Institute.

Merritt, Russell. (2002). "*The Musketeers of Pig Alley.*" In Paolo Cherchi Usai (ed.), *The Griffith Project*, vol. 6 (pp. 158–165). London: British Film Institute.

Musser, Charles. (1983). "The Nickelodeon Era Begins: Establishing the Framework for Hollywood's Mode of Representation." *Framework*, 22/23, 4–11.

Olsson, Jan. (2000). "*The Thread of Destiny*." In Paolo Cherchi Usai (ed.), *The Griffith Project*, vol. 4 (pp. 19–25). London: British Film Institute.

Pearson, Roberta. (1992). *Eloquent Gestures: The Transformation of Performance Style in the Griffith Biograph Films*. Berkeley: University of California Press.

Schickel, Richard. (1984). *D. W. Griffith: An American Life*. New York: Simon & Schuster.

Simmon, Scott. (1993). *The Films of D. W. Griffith*. Cambridge: Cambridge University Press.

Simmon, Scott. (2009). "Movies, Reform, and New Women." In Charlie Keil & Ben Singer (eds), *American Cinema of the 1910s: Themes and Variations* (pp. 26–47). New Brunswick: Rutgers University Press.

Thompson, Kristin. (1997). "Narration Early in the Transition to Classical Filmmaking: Three Vitagraph Shorts." *Film History*, 9.4, 410–434.

Thompson, Kristin. (1999). "*Lines of White on a Sullen Sea*." In Paolo Cherchi Usai (ed.), *The Griffith Project*, vol. 3 (pp. 79–81). London: British Film Institute.

Usai, Paolo Cherchi. (2001). "Foreword." In Paolo Cherchi Usai (ed.), *The Griffith Project*, vol. 5 (pp. vii–ix). London: British Film Institute.

Usai, Paolo Cherchi. (2002). "Foreword." In Paolo Cherchi Usai (ed.), *The Griffith Project*, vol. 6 (pp. vii–ix). London: British Film Institute.

Usai, Paolo Cherchi. (2003). "Foreword." In Paolo Cherchi Usai (ed.), *The Griffith Project*, vol. 7 (pp. vi–viii). London: British Film Institute.

3

Women and the Silent Screen

Shelley Stamp
Professor, University of California, Santa Cruz, United States

The role of women in early American film history has been underplayed, at best, and, at worst, all but forgotten in many conventional film histories. Shelley Stamp illustrates the crucial roles women played as filmmakers, producers, screenwriters, editors, set and costume designers, actors, exhibitors, film critics, and columnists – all playing important advocacy roles in support of **women's suffrage**, **legalized contraception**, and other **Progressive-era reforms** at a time when the audience demographic was dominated by women whom the industry aggressively courted. Women also were central figures on both sides of the **censorship** battle. Stamp's essay shares ground with Mark Lynn Anderson on the star system and Veronica Pravadelli on cinema and the modern woman in this volume, with Lucy Fischer on feminism and film in Volume II of this series, and with Jane M. Gaines on women in the silent film industry, Victoria Sturtevant on Mary Pickford, Diane Negra on Pola Negri, and Lea Jacobs on the maternal melodrama in the hardcover/online edition.

Additional terms, names, and concepts: "movie-struck girl," "extra girl," "casting couch," Hollywood Studio Club, Central Casting Bureau, Screen Writers Guild, National Board of Censorship

Women were more engaged in movie culture at the height of the silent era than they have been at any other time since. Female filmgoers dominated at the box office; the most powerful stars were women, and fan culture catered almost exclusively to female fans; writers shaping film culture through the growing art of movie reviewing, celebrity profiles, and gossip items were likely to be women; and women's clubs and organizations, along with mass-circulation magazines, played a signature role in efforts to reform the movies at the height of their early success. In Hollywood women were active at all levels of the industry: The top screenwriters were women; the highest-paid director at one point was a woman; and women held key leadership roles in the studios as executives and heads of departments like photography, editing, and

American Film History: Selected Readings, Origins to 1960, First Edition. Edited by Cynthia Lucia, Roy Grundmann, and Art Simon.
© 2016 John Wiley & Sons, Inc. Published 2016 by John Wiley & Sons, Inc.

screenwriting. Outside Hollywood women ran movie theaters, screened films in libraries and classrooms, and helped to establish venues for nonfiction filmmaking. Looking at the extraordinary scope of women's participation in early movie culture – indeed, the way women *built* that movie culture – helps us rethink conventional ideas about authorship and the archive, drawing in a broader range of players and sources. As Antonia Lant reminds us, the binary notion of women working on "both sides of the camera" needs to be significantly complicated and expanded in order to accommodate all of the ways in which women engaged with and produced early film culture (2006, 548–549).

Exhibitors, Moviegoers, and Fans: "Remember the 83%!"

Women were prized moviegoers early on. Exhibitors began aggressively courting female patronage in the early 1910s, hoping that by cultivating white, middle-class women in particular they might elevate cinema's cultural cachet. As the primary consumers in many families, women were also presumed to be in a position to influence the entertainment choices of others. Matinee screenings, commodious service, and theater redecorating schemes invited women to integrate cinemagoing into their daily routines of shopping, socializing, childrearing, and work, while contests, prize giveaways, and merchandising tie-ins with local storeowners framed cinemagoing in an analogous relationship with shopping. In fact, many of the design modifications recommended to theater owners – improved lighting and ventilation, mirrored common areas, perfumed deodorizers, and uniformed attendants – borrowed heavily from department store interiors, spaces already associated with women's leisure (Stamp 2000, 20). In some cases the gentility associated with feminine accommodations and female patronage extended to theater owners themselves, and there are a few examples of female exhibitors during these years. Alta M. Davis, manager of the Empire Theater in Los Angeles, believed the movie business was a "great field" for women, particularly those "of the progressive type who are not satisfied to let the masculine element of every community dominate, plan, manage, and originate everything" (2006, 674).

The campaign to woo female filmgoers paid off and by the early 1920s women constituted an unmistakable majority of movie patrons. Audience estimates vary widely and are notoriously unverifiable, but the pattern is clear: One 1920 assessment suggested that 60 percent of audiences were women, another calculated the figure was closer to 75 percent, and in 1927, *Moving Picture World* determined that 83 percent of moviegoers were female (Studlar 1996, 263; Koszarski 1990, 30). Young working women stopped into the movies on their way home, visiting theaters clustered along shopping streets and trolley lines in urban centers; mothers came with their families in the evenings; black women in Chicago could hear jazz in their neighborhood theaters; small-town women might attend a movie theater fashion show sponsored by one of their local merchants; Mexicana women gathered at Spanish-language theaters in Los Angeles' growing Mexican entertainment district; and young women everywhere escaped to the movies with their beaus as moviegoing became thoroughly integrated into the country's dating culture. At the movies women saw serial heroines exhibiting feats of athleticism and bravery, "flapper" stars like Clara Bow and Joan Crawford embodying daring new modes of femininity, European stars like Pola Negri and Greta Garbo importing an exoticized sexuality, matinee idols like Rudolph Valentino and Ramón Novarro challenging traditional masculine norms, and they watched scandalous "sex comedies" and radical films on feminist causes like contraception and suffrage, finding entertainment in the era's shifting sexual and political mores. A highly participatory fan culture, geared almost exclusively to women, extended the moviegoing experience well beyond the theater through contests, letters, fan clubs, scrapbooking, and souvenir-gathering (Studlar 1996, 268).

Women were also increasingly visible working in theaters as ticket sellers, pianists, and ushers, particularly in sumptuous movie palaces staffed by vast armies of employees. "Roxy" Rothapfel calculated that "over 350 persons" were "connected with the active operation" of his Capitol Theater in Chicago, many in positions that might have been filled by women, including restroom attendants, ushers, cashiers, clerks, musicians, "wardrobe women," and cleaners (2002, 101). Despite the diversity of job opportunities, commentary about women who worked in movie theaters was largely devoted to "those whose bodies and

Figure 3.1 *Photoplay*, January 1920.

personalities are put to the task of 'luring them in,'" Ina Rae Hark has found, the archetypal example being the "girl in the box office" (2002, 147). Yet the use of female employees as "added attractions" at the theater required a delicate hand. "The ticket seller should be a bright and attractive young lady, neatly dressed and wide-awake," the *Motion Picture Handbook* suggested in 1916, adding that "many a theater loses business it might otherwise get simply because of an untidy looking ticket office presided over by an unprepossessing, gum-chewing girl." At the same time, exhibitors were cautioned not to let ushers and accompanists inside the theater compete with the entertainment on-screen; ushers should be "attractive, but not too pretty," and facilities should be provided to partially obscure pianists from view (quoted in Stamp 2000, 32).

It is evident from descriptions of both patrons and theater employees that some anxiety surrounded women's presence in the feminized sphere of movie houses. Would comely employees do more than attract patrons? Would finely dressed moviegoers distract others from the show? The caricatured "movie-struck girl," whose profound love of the movies could only be understood as a desire to appear on-screen herself, condensed many of these anxieties. As I've argued elsewhere, this stereotype not only infantilized female viewers, it also obscured the extraordinary range of work women performed in the early movie industry as screenwriters, directors, editors, designers, tastemakers, and photographers, as well as outside the industry as journalists, educators, activists, and exhibitors.

Filmmakers, Stars, and Extras: Women at Work in Early Hollywood

"The film business offers to a young girl many opportunities, from the highest skilled art to the lowest unskilled manual labor," noted *The Girl and the Job* (Hoerle & Saltzberg 1919, 235), a comprehensive 1919 guide to vocations for women. Moving quickly beyond the idea that young women ought to pursue acting careers, the authors directed readers toward an array of options open to women in motion picture work, noting that many conventional occupations, like stenographer and seamstress, were needed in the new industry and often commanded higher-than-average wages, while also pointing out new opportunities available for women in this still-evolving field. Scenario departments were usually equally staffed by women and men, they noted, while many women were employed as film cutters, editors, title writers, and publicists. "In this, as in perhaps no other line, is ability recognized and advancement offered," they concluded (Hoerle & Saltzberg 1919, 242). Of all the Western cities benefiting from westward migration in the first decades of the twentieth century, only Los Angeles attracted more women than men (Hallett 2013). Indeed, there is good reason to presume that many ambitious women traveled there with the aim of living rather unconventional lives – outside of marriage, free from their families, economically self-sufficient, and creatively employed. Two such "Girl Picture Magnates" were profiled in *Photoplay*

(Jordan 1922). Unmarried and self-supporting, they had immigrated to Los Angeles separately in 1915, then pooled their financial and artistic resources, setting up house together and establishing their own production company.

Despite an abundance of opportunities, the most prevalent image of women working in Hollywood was that of the "extra girl" seeking work at the studios in the hope that she might someday become a star. *Woman's Home Companion* of June 1918 (Page 1918) described a "pathetic breadline of waiting actresses anxious for 'extra' work" lined up outside studio gates each morning. One observer reported that "tens of thousands of film aspirants" flocked to Hollywood each year, "ranging from the fourteen-year-old school girl in love with a certain film hero to the grandmother of fifty-odd who has suddenly discovered her histrionic talent" (quoted in Stamp 2004, 332). Helen G. Smith warned *Photoplay* readers: "The reason that they are called 'extra' girls is because of the extra amount of work that one has to do. The only thing that isn't extra is the pay" (quoted in Stamp 2004, 341). Concerns about moral and sexual transgressions amongst "extra girls" were common. The long hours and "easy camaraderie" of movie sets, some felt, could lead to sexual exploitation, fears that became more pronounced after several "casting couch" scandals in the teens, and that escalated still further when Roscoe "Fatty" Arbuckle became implicated in the death of would-be starlet Virginia Rappe. Anxieties sometimes took on racist overtones as well, with one 1921 newspaper report suggesting that "10,000 girls" moved to Hollywood each year in search of work in an industry controlled by "morally degenerate" and "un-American" Jews (quoted in Hallett 2013).

Soon fan magazines were publishing exposés of extra work, warning women not to make the journey out to Los Angeles. With the city's Welfare League kept busy looking after women who had not found success looking for movie work, the YWCA established a "Studio Club" in Los Angeles in 1916, providing residents with social and educational opportunities, including visits with industry notables like actress Geraldine Farrar and filmmaker Lois Weber. When the YWCA embarked on a national fund-raising campaign to expand the Studio Club in 1923, the Motion Picture Producers and Distributors Association (MPPDA) lent its support and the wives of several prominent studio executives and filmmakers signed onto the campaign. Thanks to their efforts, a new Hollywood Studio Club, designed by noted architect Julia Morgan, opened in 1926. As Heidi Kenaga demonstrates, through its involvement with the Studio Club, the MPPDA succeeded in refiguring the "extra girl" as the "Studio Girl," "a respectable, middle-class emblem of decorous femininity" (2006, 131, 137). Alongside the Studio Club, the MPPDA was also involved in efforts to regulate the employment of extras on movie sets, engaging Mary van Kleeck, a top industrial sociologist with the Russell Sage Foundation, to conduct a study of Hollywood extras in 1924. While van Kleeck found little evidence that female extras were deliberately exploited, she criticized the industry for "neglecting its employment problems" and the MPPDA took action (quoted in Kenaga 2006, 132). In early 1926, the Central Casting Bureau was established with a women's division headed by former assistant secretary of the California Industrial Welfare Commission Marion Mel, who had led that organization's investigation into the working conditions of women and child extras. Central Casting thus had the dual effect, according to Kenaga, of controlling unfavorable publicity about the exploitation of movie-struck girls, while at the same time taming and containing the least powerful members of the labor force through "a *de facto* company union" (2006, 132).

Elsewhere (Stamp 2004) I have made the point that the persistent image of young women waiting outside studio gates in Hollywood, denied access to the riches inside, created an impression that women were shut out of the industry and that appearing on-screen was the sum total of women's engagement with the cinema – an image that belied the state of the field during a period when so many women worked at all levels of the industry, many in positions of creative or executive control. In no other field were women as powerful as they were in screenwriting. Women wrote at least half of all silent films and writers like Frances Marion, June Mathis, Anita Loos, Bess Meredyth, and Jeanie Macpherson were the highest-paid and most-respected writers of their day. As Anthony Slide remarks, "How many male screen-writers from the silent era are remembered today?" (1977, 10). Their influence was profound: Women were responsible for crafting many of the era's landmark screen personalities (Mary Pickford, Rudolph Valentino, Douglas Fairbanks, Clara Bow, and Gloria Swanson), as well as some of its definitive filmmaking modes – social problem films, sex comedies, and historical epics. Working alongside these high-profile screenwriters were a host of other women involved at all levels of the writing process in studio writing departments that employed clerks, manuscript readers, story editors, continuity writers, and title writers. By the 1920s, women held at least half of all positions in the writing departments at most of the major studios, described by one commentator as a "manless Eden" (Holliday 1995, 114–115; MacMahon 1920, 140).

This was an era when women's voices were particularly valued. If audiences were primarily female, many felt, women were better able to "determine and understand women's likes and dislikes, and thus be able to give them the kind of pictures they enjoy," as Frances Marion once put it (quoted in Lant 2006, 552). "Remember the 83%!" cried screenwriter and journalist Beth Brown in 1927, exhorting studio executives to cater to the female majority (Brown 2006). Screenwriting also suited women, as Anne Morey points out, for it provided work that could be completed almost anywhere, could be tucked around other domestic routines if necessary, and did not particularly threaten traditional conceptions of femininity (2003, 48).

June Mathis was, without question, the top screenwriter of the 1920s, author of well over 100 titles in her 12-year career. Appointed head of the scenario department at Metro in 1918 when she was only 27 years old, Mathis was the first woman to occupy such an executive rank. In that capacity she influenced the studio to cast unknown Rudolph Valentino in her script for *The Four Horsemen of the Apocalypse* (1921); the film launched Valentino's stardom and became one of the top-grossing pictures of the decade. Mathis then became story division director at Goldwyn where she worked on several of Alla Nazimova's films and wrote other iconic roles for Valentino in *Camille* (1921) and *Blood and Sand* (1922). As Thomas Slater (2010) notes, these roles helped not only to shape Valentino's screen persona, but also to redefine masculine norms in the aftermath of World War I. Mathis later became production executive at Goldwyn where she was instrumental in the formation of Metro-Goldwyn-Mayer, helped rewrite and reedit Erich von Stroheim's monumental *Greed* (1925), and adapted the screenplay for *Ben-Hur* (1926). Mathis was not alone in helping to shape the signature screen personalities and film trends of the era. Jeanie Macpherson wrote virtually all of Cecil B. DeMille's best-known early work, including his groundbreaking sex comedies, his iconic biblical epics, and formative roles for Gloria Swanson. Their creative partnership lasted for three decades, ending only with her death. As one contemporary put it, "from her brain has sprung the Big Ideas for all the Cecil B. De Mille features: from her hand has come the completed scenarios replete with original business for the picture dramas that have stood, each one of them, as milestones in the photoplay's progress" (Beach 1921). Screenwriter Frances Marion was largely responsible for crafting Mary Pickford's persona, writing principal roles for her in three 1917 pictures – *Poor Little Rich Girl*, *Rebecca of Sunnybrook Farm*, and *The Little Princess* – along with many others that followed. Anita Loos helped define Douglas Fairbanks's unique brand of upbeat athleticism in her screenplays for five early films that made him a star, including *His Picture in the Papers* (1916) and *Wild and Woolly* (1917).

Screenwriters like these often wielded considerable influence at different stages of production, consulting with wardrobe mistresses, property masters, and set constructors during preproduction, directors, actors, and script girls during shooting, then title writers and editors during postproduction (Holliday 1995, 156). Observers noted, for instance, how Mathis sat at the side of director Rex Ingram throughout the shooting of *The Four Horsemen of the Apocalypse* in 1921 (Holliday 1995, 170). Screenwriting also sometimes led women to positions of creative control in studio management, as Mathis's career demonstrates. Other notable examples include Marguerite Bertsch, who became head of Vitagraph's scenario department in 1916, only three years after she joined the studio, and Kate Corbaley, who became a story editor at MGM, working closely with Irving Thalberg and Louis B. Mayer (Slide 1996, 62; Morey 2003, 93).

If women were imagined as idealized scenario writers, they also became instrumental in the evolving professionalization of screenwriting through university instruction. Beginning in 1917 and continuing well into the 1930s, Frances Taylor Patterson taught classes on "Photoplay Composition" through Columbia University Extension. Guest lecturers included prominent Hollywood women, like Clara Beranger and Eve Unsell; a transcript of Unsell's

Figure 3.2 Lois Weber (right) directing *Too Wise Wives* (1921, producer Lois Weber Productions). (Courtesy of Academy of Motion Pictures Arts and Sciences.)

1919 talk was included in Patterson's 1920 book *Cinema Craftsmanship*. Patterson also appears to have taken screenwriting instruction well into the realm of film analysis, for she successfully lobbied Columbia to install analytical projectors so that she could screen and analyze films in class (Polan 2007, 56–61). At USC Beranger was one of the founding faculty members in the School of Cinematic Arts when it began in 1929, as a collaboration between the campus and the Academy of Motion Picture Arts and Sciences. Beranger would teach screenwriting there for several decades. Many Hollywood screenwriters began authoring their own writing guides as well, including Marguerite Bertsch, who published *How to Write for Moving Pictures* in 1917, and Anita Loos, who coauthored a series of columns with John Emerson for *Photoplay* in 1918 subsequently published as *How to Write Photoplays* (1920). Many correspondence schools also offered instruction in scenario writing; the best known and most comprehensive of these was the Palmer Photoplay Corporation founded in 1918. As Anne Morey notes, Palmer literature reached out to women "with a particularly welcoming tone" (2003, 106). Board members included women prominent in the industry, such as Lois Weber and Jeanie Macpherson; Weber's script *For Husbands Only* (1919) was one of those included in the curriculum for students to analyze; Macpherson authored a manual on *The Necessity and Value of Theme in the Photoplay* (1920); Kate Corbaley, former story editor at MGM, headed the company's sales department; and successful female graduates, who purportedly outsold their male rivals, were touted in Palmer promotions.

Alongside well-known screenwriters and aspiring amateurs, women were also active directing pictures in the late 1910s and early 1920s, perhaps more so than any other period since. Lois Weber was the best-known and most prolific female filmmaker of this period, responsible for writing, directing, and sometimes acting in hundreds of shorts made between 1911 and 1916, and at least 44 feature films from 1914 through 1934, including *The Merchant of Venice* (1914), the first American feature directed by a woman. Weber wrote and directed a series of high-profile films on social issues of the day, including religious hypocrisy in *Hypocrites* (1915), capital punishment in *The People vs. John Doe* (1916), drug addiction in *Hop, the Devil's Brew* (1916), poverty in *Shoes* (1916), and contraception in *Where Are My Children?* (1916) and *The Hand That Rocks the Cradle* (1917). Her name was routinely mentioned alongside contemporaries like Griffith and DeMille as one of the top talents in Hollywood. In 1916, she became the first and only woman elected to the Motion Picture Directors Association, a solitary honor she would retain for decades (Stamp 2011).

Though Weber was the most prominent woman directing pictures in the silent era, she was by no means alone: Pioneering filmmaker Alice Guy Blaché continued to direct features in the late teens and early 1920s, including *The Ocean Waif* (1916); comedienne Mabel Normand began directing many of her Keystone shorts after 1914 and released her first feature, *Mickey*, in 1918; Alla Nazimova directed several features, including an adaptation of Oscar Wilde's *Salome* in 1923; and editor Dorothy Arzner began directing as well, with *Fashions for Women* in 1927. Some studio environments yielded particularly fruitful opportunities for women, most notably Universal where, alongside Weber, many women directed in the late teens, including Cleo Madison, Ida May Park, Lule Warrenton, Ruth Stonehouse, Elsie Jane Wilson, Grace Cunard, and a young Jeanie Macpherson (Cooper 2010). Several of these women had acted under Weber's direction, and it is likely either that she explicitly helped them in their move from acting to directing, or that, at the very least, she provided them with inspiration. Elsewhere many prominent performers, such as Lillian Gish, Mrs Sidney Drew, and Margery Wilson, also pursued opportunities to direct. Through a combination of acting, writing, directing, and producing, Nell Shipman embodied a series of athletic, independent, outdoorsy heroines in films such as *Back to God's Country* (1919) and *Something New* (1920). Working largely outside the industry, Shipman crafted a model of active feminism on- and offscreen (Armatage 2003). So rich was the field that a 1920 guide to *Careers for Women* included a chapter on "The Film Director," written by Ida May Park.

Still, when searching for models of female authorship in early Hollywood, it is important to look beyond the title "director" or "screenwriter," for many women assumed positions of creative control in other capacities. Many female stars, for instance, formed independent production companies in the late 1910s, seeking to have more input over the projects in which they were involved and resulting in what one observer described as a "her-own-company epidemic" (quoted in Mahar 2006, 155). Mary Pickford, unquestionably the top star of the late 1910s and early 1920s, provides a particularly compelling case in point because her girlish on-screen persona belied the substantial authorial control she exercised behind the scenes. At the height of her fame, Pickford successfully negotiated a series of contracts that not only insured she would retain a greater percentage of the profits from her films, but also, more importantly, gave her measurable creative control. In 1916, she demanded (and got) a salary equivalent to Charlie Chaplin's, noting that she, not he, was the bigger star. That same year she formed her own production unit within Famous Players, the Pickford Film Corporation, insuring that she had a voice in selecting her own projects, assigning directors, casting roles, and designing publicity. When she signed with First National in 1918, Pickford's contract guaranteed her complete creative control from script to final cut. Although often uncredited, Pickford also produced many of her own films. Long after her acting career ended, in fact, Pickford continued her work as producer. Pickford was also instrumental in establishing significant Hollywood institutions, beginning in 1919 when she cofounded United Artists with Chaplin, Griffith, and Fairbanks. In 1926, she became one of the founding members of the Academy of Motion Picture Arts and Sciences. Finally, demonstrating a prescient interest in preserving and insuring her historical legacy, Pickford purchased most of her early films back from the Biograph Company in 1925.

If Pickford exerted authorial control largely out of view, Dorothy Davenport Reid provides a more visible example of the varied contexts for female authorship in early Hollywood, as Mark Lynn Anderson has shown. When her husband, matinee idol Wallace Reid, died from a drug overdose in 1923, Davenport Reid reinvented herself as an authority on social issues. She returned to the screen to star in *Human Wreckage* (1923) about the illegal narcotics trade, and under the banner of "Mrs. Wallace Reid Productions" helped make two additional social problem films, *Broken Laws* (1924) about juvenile delinquency and *The Red Kimona* [*sic*] (1925) about prostitution. Although the exact nature of her contribution to these productions remains unclear, each film features a brief prologue in which she speaks directly to the audience about the topic at hand, advocating for particular policies and changes in popular attitude. According to Anderson, "Davenport Reid's ability to become a 'film author' rested, in part, on her ability to speak from the sometimes contradictory positions of Hollywood producer, actress, widow, mother, and social reformer" (Anderson 2011). In other words, her feminine experience and voice were central to her authority on these subjects.

Like Davenport Reid, Elinor Glyn exerted authorial control in an unconventional manner that has sometimes obscured her contributions to early Hollywood. Glyn arrived in Hollywood in 1920, having already achieved fame as a romance novelist. As Anne Morey argues, "Glyn was ultimately more successful as a branded article than she was as a screenwriter" (2006, 110). Positioning herself as an expert on all things European, Glyn marketed not only her texts but also her extratextual knowledge about the tastes and habits of wealthy nobility, and a sophisticated, "continental" approach to sexuality, penning articles for fan magazines on such topics as "How to Get a Man and Hold Him" and "Sex and the Photoplay." Also known for coaching actors behind the scenes, Glyn was said to have "remade" Gloria Swanson in 1921, transforming her from a young, rather asexual woman with curly hair and frilly dresses into a mature sex symbol with slicked-back hair and tight, slinky gowns – an image Swanson would retain throughout the decade. Alongside June Mathis, Glyn also played a considerable role in shaping Rudolph Valentino's persona, apparently ghostwriting some of his fan magazine "autobiographies." Though Glyn did not receive official screenwriting credit on many screen adaptations of her fiction, the projects were described as having been "made under her personal supervision" and she offered her services as a consultant on manners, dress, and mise-en-scène, sometimes even appearing in on-screen cameos, most famously in the 1927 production of *It*. As one reviewer remarked of *Three Weeks* (1924), "The whole picture carried a suggestion of her constant supervision" (quoted in Morey 2006, 112).

Outside Hollywood, women were active in crafting alternative forms of production in documentary and the avant-garde. Husband-and-wife teams Martin and Osa Johnson and Carl and Mary Jobe Akeley made "adventure genre" and naturalist pictures with footage shot on location in Africa and other locales (Griffiths 2002, 248). Photographer Frances Hubbard Flaherty collaborated with her husband, Robert, on ethnographic documentaries such as *Nanook of the North* (1922), and would later chronicle their efforts in her book *The Odyssey of a Filmmaker* (Griffiths 2002, 142). Because these women worked alongside their husbands, the historical record has sometimes obscured the exact nature of their collaboration. Antonia Lant, for instance, finds evidence that a photograph of Osa Johnson filming in Africa was subsequently altered for the cover of the couple's book, *Camera Trails in Africa*, to show Osa "helping" her husband Martin, who is thus reconfigured as the primary filmmaker (2006, 264–267).

Less visible, but no less important, were women working behind the scenes in professions like editing, costume design, and art direction – all fields in which women had been traditionally employed and which were beginning to achieve professional respect and recognition. Women had worked as negative cutters and film splicers from the earliest days of motion pictures, performing the menial tasks of preparing prints for distribution. As the field evolved into a creative practice critical to feature-length storytelling, several women rose to prominence. Dorothy Arzner, later better known as a director, first worked in the 1920s as a highly respected editor at Paramount's Realart, where she eventually became chief editor. Arzner recalled that alongside her own editing work, she also "supervised the negative cutting and trained the girls who cut negative and spliced film by hand. I set up the film filing system and supervised the art work on the titles" (quoted in Mayne 1994, 25). Arzner's work editing *Blood and Sand* (1922), Valentino's first star vehicle, established her reputation, for she was able to integrate stock footage and new material together in the film's bullfighting sequences. Jane Loring, a friend of Arzner's, began as an assistant editor at Paramount in 1927, launching a very successful career, particularly renowned for her ability to cut image and sound together during the transition to sound film in the late 1920s. A lesbian like Arzner, Loring cut quite a figure at the studio. "She used to wear slacks and overcoats and men's hats," one observer remembered (Mann 2006, 239). As their craft evolved, editors were often given considerable autonomy in shaping films. Describing her early days working on pictures directed by Clarence Brown, celebrated editor Margaret Booth recalled, "I cut a number of his pictures and never saw him in the cutting room" (quoted in Rosenblum & Karen 1986, 62). Other directors, recognizing the importance of a well-assembled film, worked closely with editors and maintained career-long partnerships with favored collaborators. Anne Bauchens, for instance, served as DeMille's editor for most of his career, beginning as coeditor on *Carmen* in 1915, his third year as a director (Lewis 2006).

If Jazz-Age stars like Gloria Swanson, Norma Talmadge, and Clara Bow embodied Hollywood's evolving glamour culture, women working behind the scenes also played a considerable role in shaping and circulating their modern look. Clare West, one of the first costume designers employed by the studios, helped elevate the traditional position of "head of wardrobe" – responsible for purchasing ready-made clothes and tailoring them to fit – to that of a "studio designer" charged with implementing a unique creative vision. By the mid-1920s, most studios employed such a person and by the end of the decade all studios had a costume department headed by a noted designer. West began her career on *Intolerance* (1916), helping to create costumes for the multiple historical epochs depicted in the film. She was hired by DeMille two years later to oversee costumes at Famous Players-Lasky. Early to recognize the centrality of costuming to production design, DeMille knew West's work could "make people gasp." Edith Head began her celebrated, decades-long career at Paramount in 1924, when she was hired as a costume sketch artist. She began designing costumes for the studio the following year, rising to become one of Hollywood's most admired designers by the early 1930s. Unlike many of her male counterparts, Head consulted extensively with the women she clothed ("International History of Costume Design" and Landis & Kirkham 2002, 247–251). Natacha Rambova's set and costume designs also added considerably to Hollywood's glamour culture, particularly its association with an exoticized "East." After working on four DeMille pictures, including *Why Change Your Wife?* (1920) with Gloria Swanson, Rambova worked with Alla Nazimova as costume designer and art director on Nazimova's failed project *Aphrodite*, as well as *Billions* (1920) and *Salomé* (1923), considered Rambova's most daring work. Rambova also designed costumes for several of her husband Rudolph Valentino's films – *Camille* (1921), *The Young Rajah* (1922), and *Monsieur Beaucaire* (1924) – helping to shape his unconventional image.

Perhaps more important than images of stars onscreen were still photographs that circulated in and around films, were published in newspapers, magazines, and press books, and offered to fans as souvenirs. Ruth Harriet Louise, MGM's chief portrait photographer between 1925 and 1929, crafted incandescent images of the studio's top players, particularly its women, among them Joan Crawford, Greta Garbo, and Norma Shearer. As Robert Dance and Bruce Robertson maintain, Louise's photographs were "not merely a byproduct of the movies" but "critical to their success" (2002, 2). Louise Brooks, Garbo's contemporary, put it best: "When you think of it, what people remember of those stars is not from films, but one essential photograph … When I think of Garbo, I do not see her moving in any particular film … She is a still picture – unchangeable" (quoted in Dance & Robertson 2002, 2). The image locked in Brooks's imagination was more than likely taken by Ruth Harriet Louise.

An extensive network of social and professional connections, both formal and informal, bolstered these collaborative working relationships. One example might be the social events Frances Marion hosted for Hollywood's most powerful women, allowing stars to mingle with screenwriters, producers, and directors, as well as wives of influential male filmmakers and studio executives. Dubbed "hen parties" by the press, they were, in fact, signature elements of women's culture in early Hollywood. A photograph of one such gathering shows actors like the Talmadge sisters, Colleen Moore, and Theda Bara alongside Dorothy Davenport Reid, journalist Adela Rogers St Johns, and Marion herself, among a host of others (Beauchamp 1998, 231). Women working on the lower rungs of the industry also socialized together at residences like the Hollywood Studio Club and at more informal gathering spots like the corner of Hollywood Boulevard and Cahuenga in Hollywood (Stamp 2004, 334). Many of these women formed lasting friendships that in some cases yielded professional collaborations. Marion and Pickford, close friends, worked together for years, as Marion became both Pickford's main screenwriter and the ghostwriter for her "Daily Talks" newspaper columns. Marion also remained close friends with Lois Weber after the director aided Marion early in her career. Screenwriter Bebe Daniels remembered spending many nights sitting with her friend Dorothy Arzner in the editing room, an experience that, she recalled, "taught me more about writing for the motion pictures than anything in the world could have taught me" (quoted in Mayne 1994, 25).

In other instances, professional guilds and clubs helped to build personal and professional relationships amongst women. The Screen Writers Guild, founded in 1920, was open to both men and women and through its social arm, the Writers' Club, hosted many events at its clubhouse on Sunset Boulevard. As Holliday observed, "the boundaries of work and play were fluid," allowing women to participate in "behind-the-scenes deal-making, intrigue, and story conferences" (1995, 177–178). Female journalists swapped "shop talk" at regular weekly meetings of the Hollywood Women's Press Club, formed in 1928. The group included founder Louella Parsons, who first hosted meetings in her apartment before they moved to the famed Brown Derby restaurant, *Photoplay* editor Ruth Biery, Regina Carewe, film writer for the Hearst syndicate, along with many of the well-known feature writers for *Motion Picture* and *Motion Picture Classic* (Barbas 2006, 124–125). These writers, as I will demonstrate, created a rich intertextual discourse on the movies, America's moviegoing habits, and its favorite movie stars, shaping early motion picture culture through a feminine eye.

Critics, Writers, and Tastemakers: Film Culture as a Feminine Sphere

By 1915, writing about the cinema comprised a key element of film culture. Daily newspapers began regular movie reviewing in the mid-1910s, fostering a critical discourse about performance techniques, preferred plot lines, and cinematic style. Reviews were published alongside a growing body of film journalism that included profiles of movie stars' homes, wardrobes, and family lives, advice for those hoping to work in the industry, and commentary on cinema's cultural value and its industry practices. Moviegoing culture thus extended well beyond theater boundaries to encompass a wide range of discourses on stardom, personality, art, industry, gender, race, and ethnicity published in an array of sources including daily newspapers, mass-circulation monthlies, fan magazines, trade papers, and other publications. Women were central authors of this discourse, the principal celebrities profiled within it, and often its primary audience as well, demonstrating that far from being a marginal adjunct to mainstream movie culture, women sat at its heart.

Prominent early film journalists included Grace Kingsley at the *Los Angeles Times*, syndicated columnist Gertrude Price, and Irene Thirer who introduced her influential three-star ratings system to *New York Daily News* readers in 1928. Myra Nye, society columnist for the *Los Angeles Times* between 1915 and 1935, also wrote frequently on movie stars in a feature she called "Society of Cinemaland." Others remained anonymous, identified only by initials or pseudonyms, the most famous being "Mae Tinee," the feminine *nom de plume* used by staff writers at the *Chicago Tribune*.

The *Los Angeles Times* was the first newspaper to take an active interest in the motion picture business, assigning Grace Kingsley to be a movie columnist in 1913 and creating a section called "The Preview" to feature writing on the industry, its stars, and its projects (Goodman 1961, 149; Gottlieb & Wolt 1977, 148). Recent sources sometimes refer to Kingsley as a "gossip columnist," but her writing furnished detailed portraits of Hollywood's major players, including many of its women. For instance, Kingsley chronicled Dorothy Arzner's move into directing in 1927 with a piece entitled "Leave Sex Out, Says Director" (Mayne 1994, 194). Like Kingsley, L.A.-based nationally syndicated columnist Gertrude Price helped promote women's work at all levels of the film industry, and in doing so, fostered a keen female fan base for the movies, as Richard Abel documents. By his calculation, some two-thirds of Price's articles were focused on women in the industry – performers, directors, and screenwriters alike (Abel 2006, 140–153). Mabel Condon, West Coast correspondent for the *New York Dramatic Mirror*, was one of several women writing for industry trade papers, though these forums remained largely male-oriented as the wider discourse on cinema shifted to a decisively feminine address. Still, on the pages of *Moving Picture World* Margaret I. MacDonald drew attention to women working in Hollywood and reminded exhibitors and tradesmen about the importance of their female clientele.

Film coverage in daily newspapers also played a notable role in helping to define cinema's growing impact on society, particularly for young women caught up in its fan culture and middle-class women active in the reform movement. L.A.'s largest Spanish-language newspaper, *La opínion*, published a regular cinema page featuring Spanish translations of columns by Louella Parsons and publicity items on many female stars including Latina actresses like Dolores del Río and Lupe Vélez. The paper reported on films it considered offensive to Mexicans and chronicled the influence of American mores on Mexicano moviegoers, especially the controversy surrounding "*las pelonas*" (the bobbed-hair girls) influenced by Hollywood's flapper culture (Monroy 1999, 173–187; Gunckel 2008, 325–330). African-American newspapers, such as the *Chicago Defender* and the *New York Age*, shaped responses to the cinema in black communities by circulating reports of films and industry practices they considered racist, promoting the educational and cultural value of cinema for black audiences, and publicizing African-American filmmakers and stars like Edna Morton, dubbed "Our Mary Pickford" (Everett 2001, 159–177; Stewart 2005, 114–154).

Mass-circulation women's magazines targeted female readers even more directly, positioning women as the primary audience for the movies, as well as an important influence on moviegoing tastes and habits in others. Women's monthlies devoted considerable coverage to the movies beginning at least as early as 1912 when *Ladies' World* published the first serialized fiction tie-in with the movie serial *What Happened to Mary?*. The trend continued in the late teens and early 1920s as publications like *Ladies' Home Journal*, *Good Housekeeping*, and *Woman's Home Companion* – all with circulations over one million – published profiles of women working in Hollywood, analyses of the "movie-struck girl" phenomenon, and tips about how to get screenplays sold, all the while exhorting readers to take an active role in advocating for "better films" in their communities. A steady stream of ads featured female movie stars promoting beauty products, clothing, and accessories.

While journalists contributed to an evolving critical commentary on movies and movie culture, a growing fan culture provided movie aficionados with intimate details about their favored players. Romances, marriages, divorces, childhoods, and children all became targets of increased curiosity, as did homes, kitchens, closets, and dressing tables. Fan culture increasingly tailored its appeal to women, by catering to supposedly "feminine" preoccupations with romance, beauty, decorating, and family life, rather than the technical and scientific details that had colored much of the earliest film publicity (Studlar 1996; Fuller 1996, 115–132). Women authored much of this early fan discourse, forming its "backbone," according to Anthony Slide (1992, 6). A quick survey of fan magazine writing in the late 1910s and 1920s reveals that at least half of the featured pieces in each volume were written by women. Adele Whitely Fletcher, Gladys Hall, Fritzi Remont, Pearl Gaddis, and Aline Carter, among many others, were all regular contributors to *Motion Picture*. At *Photoplay* the majority of writers were women, the best known being Ruth Waterbury, Elizabeth Peltret, Mabel Condon, Agnes Smith, and Frances Denton. Well-known journalist Adela Rogers St Johns also contributed to *Photoplay* in the 1920s, bringing her distinctive, emotional style to tales of life in Hollywood in both factual pieces and fiction, most notably a serialized novella dubbing Hollywood the "port of missing girls." In some cases, the prominent role played by female writers translated into positions of editorial leadership: Florence M. Osborne became editor of *Motion Picture* in 1925, and Ruth Biery served as West Coast editor for *Photoplay* where editorial assistant Kathryn Dougherty also made important editorial decisions and eventually took over the editorship in 1932 (Barbas 2006, 125; Barbas 2002, 71; Lant 2006, 563).

Alongside fawning portraits of stars' homes, careers, wardrobes, and families, fan culture also spawned a gossip industry reporting on the sometimes less-than-savory aspects of Hollywood life in items with which neither studio publicists nor the stars themselves were complicit. Gossip, perhaps even more than fan magazine reporting, helped female fans negotiate and assimilate rapidly changing gender norms and shifting sexual mores, a view only confirmed by a survey of the era's signal scandals: Mary Pickford's "quickie" divorce and marriage to Douglas Fairbanks in 1920; the star scandals of 1921 and 1922, all of which involved questions of feminine propriety; Charlie Chaplin's marriage to a pregnant and 16-year-old Lita Grey in 1924, after having divorced his similarly teenaged bride, Mildred Harris; and Rudolph Valentino's "unconventional" marriage to Natacha Rambova. Chief among early gossip columnists was Louella Parsons, best known for her daily column "Flickerings from Film Land," syndicated between 1926 and 1965 in hundreds of Hearst newspapers nationwide with a readership estimated at six million. Parsons positioned herself *within* Hollywood, becoming a regular at the Cocoanut Grove night club and parties held at San Simeon and Pickfair, evolving into a kind of celebrity herself, providing readers with a unique and privileged window on Hollywood culture (Barbas 2002, 91–96).

Writers famous in other fields contributed to the evolving discourse on cinema, publishing pieces on everything from moviegoing habits to Hollywood trends. Janet Flanner, Paris correspondent for the *New Yorker* in the 1920s and 1930s, began her career as a movie reporter for her local paper, the *Indianapolis Star*, in 1916. Before setting up shop in Paris, she wrote pieces for *Filmplay Journal* describing her experiences watching movies abroad in the early 1920s, including one particularly trenchant piece about the impact of Islamic practices of sex segregation on cinemagoing habits in Turkey. Noted fiction writer Katherine Anne Porter published items in *Motion Picture Magazine* and novelist and playwright Mary Roberts Rinehart wrote for *Photoplay*, contributing a particularly biting commentary on Hollywood's cult of the "new" (Rinehart 1992, 59–60; Flanner 1992).

While oftentimes dismissed as mere purveyors of gossip, it is clear that female journalists writing for daily newspapers, popular magazines, industry trade papers, and fan publications were much more than that. They helped pioneer the art of movie reviewing, helped draw attention to the many women, not just high-profile stars, working in the new industry, and helped to foster a critical distance from Hollywood trends, all the while – yes – providing privileged access to the medium's ethereal celebrities and crafting a fan culture by, about, and for women.

Censors, Reformers, and Educators: "Ultimately a Woman's Responsibility"

If female journalists and women's magazines helped shape an evolving critical and cultural discourse about popular cinema, female reformers and educators took an equally active role in evaluating, monitoring, and attempting to regulate cinema and cinemagoing. An industry that had invested so much energy into courting female patronage now found those patrons discerning, critical, and always vocal. As Anne Morey remarks, "women used filmgoing to advance their own influence, parlaying their role as consumer into a more obviously political function as the arbiters of their own and others' consumption" (2002, 333). On the one hand, women's activism drew upon an outmoded view of middle-class women extending a maternal hand into the public sphere, taking care of "less fortunate" working-class and immigrant communities; on the other hand, it also drew upon newly radicalized women's organizations recently successful in their campaigns for women's suffrage and Prohibition, both ratified in 1920.

Positioned as gatekeepers of culture and morality, women had been a visible force in regulating cinema early on. As narrative features began to dominate the market after 1915, reformers turned their attention to the content of films, rather than theater conditions that had been their primary concern initially. The National Board of Censorship was staffed largely by middle-class women who volunteered to evaluate films prior to their release. By 1915, 100 out of 115 volunteers were female (Grieveson 2004, 101). Less is known about personnel who screened films at many of the state film censorship boards, but it is likely that many were also women active in progressive reform movements. When Chicago replaced its police censorship board with a 10-person commission of salaried civilians in 1914, for instance, women occupied half of the seats (Hallett 2013).

Among the many prominent women's organizations taking an active interest in cinema was the Women's Christian Temperance Union (WCTU), which stepped up its scrutiny of the movies after the successful passage of Prohibition. WCTU members visited local cinemas to rate the appropriateness of current offerings, sending appreciative letters to companies that produced "wholesome" pictures and protesting to mayors and police chiefs about pictures they considered "vulgar." Particularly concerned about the effects of filmgoing on the very young, local chapters published statistics on children's movie attendance and sent literature on the hazards of moving picture shows to all new mothers in their area. WCTU groups sponsored screenings of educational films in churches and community halls and influenced local politics, successfully preventing the showing of Sunday movies in several states through special elections (Parker 1996, 75–83; Parker 1997, 213–216). Recognizing cinema's new prominence in the cultural domain, the WCTU would proclaim, "motion pictures are having a far more injurious effect upon public morals in general than the saloon ever had" (quoted in Parker 1996, 87).

A more moderate strain of activism was centered in the Better Films Movement, a grassroots campaign to promote "quality" pictures coordinated largely through women's magazines and clubs. By the mid-1920s, most members of the National Federation of Women's Clubs had established their own Better Films department. The all-woman International Federation of Catholic Alumnae (IFCA) reviewed up to 11,000 films annually, then circulated lists of recommended titles to Catholic schools across the country. The National Congress of Parents and Teachers, comprised largely of women, circulated a pamphlet on "Endorsed Films" to parent–teacher organizations nationwide. Popular magazines like *Woman's Home Companion* and *Ladies' World* also encouraged readers to exercise their civic "duty" and advocate for quality pictures in their communities by helping to spread the word about recommended titles and demanding better fare from local exhibitors. Through its Good Citizenship Bureau *Woman's Home Companion* ran a Better Films Service that published lists of recommended films for its readership, coordinated by Bureau director Anna Steese Richardson (Lant 2006, 271–273; Stamp 2000, 13). For African-American women, cinema's potential to uplift was particularly profound. Writing in *Half-Century Magazine*, a monthly geared toward upwardly mobile black women, Jean Voltaire Smith argued against the black church's traditional opposition to popular amusements, suggesting that cinema might be a medium that could not only educate African-Americans, but also help to bridge the gap between the less educated and the elite. "Would it not be better then, to encourage more of our people to produce pictures – films of the clean, helpful sort, that will uplift; urge them to build class moving pictures theaters, rather than discourage them from attending picture shows?" she wrote (quoted in Everett 2001, 157). Though women's magazines and industry sponsors alike often characterized the Better Films Movement as a group of mothers simply advocating wholesome entertainment for their families and their communities, many women active in the movement had long track records of public activism and social service. Catheryne Cooke Gilman, who led the Better Films Movement in Minneapolis before assuming a position of national leadership, had been a schoolteacher and a settlement worker at Chicago's famed Hull House, and had also been active in campaigns for women's suffrage, sex education, and children's welfare. As Cynthia Hanson points out, Gilman's interest in motion pictures also manifested a decidedly progressive attitude to the project of reform – a belief that if social problems were documented, publicized, and discussed, society would respond because all Americans shared a common standard of morality (1989, 204–205). This view was severely tested as Gilman came to realize that neither the filmgoing public nor Hollywood producers necessarily shared her own sense of propriety. After many years espousing the belief that "better" films would triumph if women simply guided audience tastes and Hollywood proclivities, Gilman ended up an advocate for federal regulation of the motion picture industry.

Ultimately, early efforts by women to evaluate, review, and critique films had a lasting impact on movie culture, according to Richard Koszarski, who argues that the Better Films Movement was "ambitious, well-organized, and certainly the earliest national effort to promote film as a medium of social and artistic importance" (1990, 208). Through their interest in promoting quality cinema, some Better Films activists became involved in the "little theater" movement that sought to expand the distribution of European art films in the United States. Mrs Regge Doran founded one such example, Hollywood's long-standing Filmarte Theater, in 1928. That same year New York's Little Picture House was opened by a group of society women (Horak 1998, 22; Guzman 2005). They planned to offer programs of films and educational talks aimed at schoolchildren and "women who go to lectures, who go on shopping expeditions, and many who go nowhere and are bored" (quoted in Lant 2006, 582).

When Will Hays assumed leadership of the MPPDA in 1922, he wasted no time in cultivating women's groups that had been critical of Hollywood. Hoping to gain their support in his efforts to ward off federal censorship, Hays publicly supported the Better Films Movement and efforts to promote children's matinees, spoke regularly to women's organizations, and cultivated relationships with prominent activists like Catheryne Cooke Gilman. When the MPPDA stepped up industry self-regulation in 1927, forming a Studio Relations Committee to evaluate scripts and completed films, representatives from major women's organizations, including the General Federation of Women's Clubs, the IFCA, and library groups, were invited to preview prerelease prints in a special Hollywood screening room (Morey 2003, 110–111; Wheeler 2007, 81–83). The following year Hays invited clubwomen to elect a designate to serve on the Studio Relations Committee itself. They chose Alice Ames Winter, past president of the General Federation of Women's Clubs, to be, as one observer described, an ambassador for "the feelings and wishes of womanhood" (quoted in Wheeler 2007, 83).

Hays's efforts to woo female reformers were not always successful, however, as several of his allies became disillusioned with the MPPDA's efforts to police the industry from within. Gilman ultimately distanced herself from Hays following the star scandals of 1921 and 1922, particularly outraged that Hays did not object when Fatty Arbuckle returned to work after Virginia Rappe's death (Hanson 1989, 207). Maude Aldrich, director of the WCTU's motion picture department, refused Hays's offer to serve on the MPPDA's public relations council, choosing instead to continue advocating for federal control of motion pictures. Both women joined the Federal Motion Picture Council, formed in 1925, which sought to create an independent commission, similar to the recently established Federal Trade Commission, that would supervise the film industry, inspecting and modifying, if necessary, films containing "sex, white slavery, illicit love, nudity, crime, gambling, or excessive drinking" (quoted in Wheeler 2007, 79). Women remained the public face of the group's campaign: The Council proposed that at least four of the commissions' nine seats would be occupied by women, and Gilman was elected president in 1928 after the Council's board of directors decided motion picture reform was "ultimately a woman's responsibility" (quoted in Wheeler 2007, 81).

While reformers and clubwomen focused attention on regulating the movie industry, others saw cinema's educational potential, especially in film titles and distribution outlets that circumvented the control increasingly exerted by Hollywood's commercial interests. As both arbiters of culture and targets of reform, women were instrumental in promoting, screening, and watching films in nontheatrical settings like churches, schools, libraries, museums, clubs, workplaces, and community centers. New publications like *Educational Film Magazine* and *Educational Screen* provided information to educators, social workers, librarians, and clergy, while books like *Motion Pictures for Community Needs: A Practical Manual of Information and Suggestion for Educational, Religious and Social Work*, coauthored by Gladys and Henry Bollman in 1922, furnished practical tips on how to book films from exchanges and how to equip and run a screening facility. Many of the 100 film programs suggested by the Bollmans were specifically targeted for female audiences at YWCAs, girls' reformatories, women's clubs, and settlement houses. The Educational Films Corporation, founded in 1915 by Katherine F. Carter, furnished motion picture "entertainments" for "clubs, hotels and private residences," also offering to equip "schools, churches and educational institutions with the necessities of moving picture projection" (MacDonald 1915). Before forming her own company, Carter had been in charge of General Film's educational division, a situation not uncommon at other commercial studios and exchanges that ran educational divisions headed by women. Elizabeth Richey Dessez, director of the educational department at Pathé Exchange, for instance, had had a long association with the Better Films Movement prior to her appointment.

The introduction of 16mm technology in 1923 further aided the circulation of films outside commercial exhibition circuits – one estimate calculated that some 15,000 churches, schools, and clubs were screening films that year alone. By 1927, that number had nearly doubled (Maltby 1990, 190). The new gauge particularly helped to spur a "visual instruction" movement amongst schoolteachers, and the female teacher as projectionist soon figured in accounts of the modern classroom (Waller 2011). Anna Verona Dorris, author of *Visual Instruction in the Public Schools* (1928), the first such comprehensive guide, was particularly concerned to help women feel at home using 16mm technology in the classroom. "Anyone who is capable of operating an automobile can learn to operate any type of motion-picture projector," she wrote (quoted in Waller 2011). Librarians, most of whom were women, were also instrumental in supporting nontheatrical screenings and cultivating an educated film culture amongst their patrons, as Jennifer Horne (2011) has documented. Librarians suggested books that might be read in conjunction with screenings at local movie houses, hosted matinee screenings alongside children's story hours, and programmed groups of travelogues, newsreels, and historical dramas together around particular themes. Libraries also began to acquire films for in-house screenings and circulating film collections, becoming major supporters of educational and documentary filmmaking. Recognizing cinema's potential as an instrument of progressive social change, feminist Charlotte Perkins Gilman imagined the construction of free public film libraries across the nation, financed, she speculated, with the help of noted library benefactor Andrew Carnegie.

If women could master the projector in classrooms and libraries, surely they could do so at home too. Ads targeting affluent female consumers promoted 16mm as a "domestic" gauge that allowed women to become both purveyors of healthy entertainment for their families and amateur filmmakers themselves. Department stores like Macy's and Gimbel's began renting 16mm projectors to their customers, while *Ladies' Home Journal* featured advertisements for 16mm "home theater" systems showing women programming "healthy, edifying, and safe family fare" in their homes (Wasson 2007). Bell and Howell's advertisements for amateur 16mm cameras circulated images of women filming their children at home or in nature, suggesting the equipment's ease of operation, as well as its seamless integration into middle-class family life. In 1928, the company even introduced a flat, lightweight camera, the Filmo 75, designed to fit into a woman's pocket or purse (Zimmermann 1995, 61–62).

Cinema's educational potential was not lost on more radical groups as well; many early feminist organizations produced films to garner support for their causes. If one strand of female activism focused on policing cinema during these years, another recognized its extraordinary persuasive authority and the importance of visual rhetoric in any feminist campaign. Women's suffrage groups, among the earliest to grasp cinema's powers of influence, released features including *Eighty Million Women Want —?* (1913) and *Your Girl and Mine* (1914), using theaters to mobilize supporters after screenings (Stamp 2000, 168–176). The fight to legalize birth contraception, or "voluntary motherhood," was dramatized in several films, including *Where Are My Children?* (1916) and *The Hand That Rocks the Cradle* (1917), both written and directed by Lois Weber. In *Birth Control* (1917) activist Margaret Sanger reenacted scenes from her storied career on-screen, then toured the country with the film promoting her cause (Sloan 1988, 86–87; Norden 2004). Activists like Sanger and the suffragists saw moviegoers not as innocents in need of moral protection and "betterment," but as potential fellow radicals who might be marshaled for action.

Whether monitoring films at their local cinemas, screening films in classrooms, libraries, and settlement houses, opening alternative theaters and exhibition outlets, or producing advocacy pictures, women stood at the heart of dual efforts in the Progressive era to reform American politics, classrooms, and workplaces through the use of moving pictures and to reform cinema itself. A history of cinema that recognizes this work of advocacy and activism moves women from the margins to the center, assigning this labor its rightful place alongside filmmaking, screenwriting, and journalism in shaping film culture during the silent era.

Conclusion: "History Has Not Been Kind"

A stand-alone essay on women and the silent screen implies that women occupied an ancillary relation to early film culture – the conjunction suggests a summative relationship between women and cinema rather than the fundamental interconnectedness I have outlined above. At the same time, such an essay is clearly necessary, since women have been repeatedly and routinely written out of conventional histories of the field, a process that began in the 1920s and early 1930s and continues to this day: Women, apart from big-name stars, were largely absent from the earliest film histories written by Terry Ramsaye, Benjamin Hampton, and Lewis Jacobs; and when women did begin to appear, as they did in Andrew Sarris's influential taxonomy of American directors, they amounted to "little more than a ladies' auxiliary" (1996, 216). As recently as 2009, one introductory film text informed readers that there had been a "brief vogue" for women in Hollywood during the silent era, under the heading of "feminine mystique" (Gianetti & Eyman 2009, 45). A recent spate of scholarship has begun to amplify and complicate this reductive history, not only by including and celebrating the work of early filmmakers like Lois Weber and early screenwriters like June Mathis, but also by working to broaden the very terms under which women's extraordinary contributions to early film culture are understood. What I hope to have demonstrated here is the absolutely central role that women played in defining silent cinema – that a history of this era simply cannot be told without accounting for women at its center. Women were instrumental in defining early film culture: as the majority of filmgoers and stars; as critics, journalists, and tastemakers commenting on films, filmgoing habits, and the new celebrity culture; as reformers and educators eager to adapt the medium for progressive aims; as screenwriters, filmmakers, and creative artists responsible for defining not only the era's most memorable screen personas but also its dominant genres. As Anthony Slide concludes, "never again would such women shape the tastes of a generation" (Slide 1977, 10).

References

Abel, Richard. (2006). "Fan Discourse in the Heartland: The Early 1910s." *Film History*, 18.2, 140–153.

Anderson, Mark Lynn. (2011). "Dorothy Davenport Reid." In Jane Gaines, Radha Vatsal, & Monica Dall'Asta (eds), *Women Film Pioneers Project*. New York: Center for Digital Research and Scholarship, Columbia University Libraries.

Armatage, Kay. (2003). *The Girl From God's Country: Nell Shipman and the Silent Cinema*. Toronto: University of Toronto Press.

Barbas, Samantha. (2002). *Movie Crazy: Fans, Stars, and the Cult of Celebrity*. London: Palgrave Macmillan.

Barbas, Samantha. (2006). *The First Lady of Hollywood: A Biography of Louella Parsons*. Berkeley: University of California Press.

Beach, Barbara. (1921). "The Literary Dynamo." *Taylorology*, 70, at http://www.public.asu.edu/~bruce/Taylor70.txt (accessed March 2015).

Beauchamp, Cari. (1998). *Without Lying Down: Frances Marion and the Powerful Women of Early Hollywood*. Berkeley: University of California Press.

Bertsch, Marguerite. (1917). *How to Write for Moving Pictures: A Manual of Instruction and Information*. New York: George H. Doran Co.

Bollman, Gladys, & Bollman, Henry. (1922). *Motion Pictures for Community Needs: A Practical Manual of Information and Suggestion for Educational, Religious and Social Work*. New York: Henry Holt.

Brown, Beth. (2006). "Making Movies for Women." In Antonia Lant (ed.), *The Red Velvet Seat: Women's Writing on the First Fifty Years of Cinema* (p. 488). London: Verso. (Original work published 1927.)

Cooper, Mark Garrett. (2010). *Universal Women: Filmmaking and Institutional Change in Early Hollywood*. Urbana-Champaign: University of Illinois Press.

Dance, Robert, & Robertson, Bruce. (2002). *Ruth Harriet Louise and Hollywood Glamour Photography*. Berkeley: University of California Press.

Davis, Alta M. (2006). "Great Field for Women: Lady Manager of Theater Writes to Balboa Company." In Antonia Lant (ed.), *The Red Velvet Seat: Women's Writing on the First Fifty Years of Cinema* (p. 674). London: Verso. (Original work published 1917.)

Everett, Anna. (2001). *Returning the Gaze: A Genealogy of Black Film Criticism, 1909–1949*. Raleigh, NC: Duke University Press.

Filene, Catherine. (1920). *Careers for Women*. New York: Houghton, Mifflin Co.

Flanner, Janet. (1992). "The Turkish Fez and the Films." In Anthony Slide (ed.), *They Also Wrote for the Fan Magazines: Film Articles by Literary Giants from e. e. cummings to Eleanor Roosevelt, 1920–1939* (pp. 60–63). Jefferson, NC: McFarland. (Original work published 1922.)

Fuller, Kathryn H. (1996). *At the Picture Show: Small-Town Audiences and the Creation of Movie Fan Culture*. Washington, DC: Smithsonian Institution Press.

Gianetti, Louis, & Eyman, Scott. (2009). *Flashback: A Brief Film History*. 6th edn. Boston: Allyn & Bacon.

Goodman, Ezra. (1961). *The Fifty-Year Decline and Fall of Hollywood*. New York: Simon & Schuster.

Gottlieb, Robert, & Wolt, Irene. (1977). *Thinking Big: The Story of the Los Angeles Times, Its Publishers, and their Influence on Southern California*. New York: Putnam.

Grieveson, Lee. (2004). *Policing Cinema: Movies and Censorship in Early-Twentieth-Century America*. Berkeley: University of California Press.

Griffiths, Alison. (2002). *Wondrous Difference: Cinema, Anthropology and Turn-of-the-Century Visual Culture*. New York: Columbia University Press.

Gunckel, Colin. (2008). "The War of the Accents: Spanish Language Hollywood Films in Mexican Los Angeles." *Film History*, 20.3, 325–343.

Guzman, Tony. (2005). "The Little Theater Movement: The Institutionalization of the European Art Film in America." *Film History*, 17.2/3, 261–284.

Hallett, Hilary. (2013). *Go West, Young Women! The Rise of Early Hollywood*. Berkeley: University of California Press.

Hanson, Cynthia A. (1989). "Catheryne Cooke Gilman and the Minneapolis Better Movie Movement." *Minnesota History*, 51.6, 202–216.

Hark, Ina Rae. (2002). "The 'Theater Man' and 'The Girl in the Box Office'." In Ina Rae Hark (ed.), *Exhibition: The Film Reader* (pp. 143–154). New York: Routledge.

Hoerle, Helen Christene, & Saltzberg, Florence B. (1919). *The Girl and the Job*. New York: Henry Holt.

Holliday, Wendy. (1995). "Hollywood's Modern Woman: Screenwriting, Work Culture, and Feminism, 1910–1940." PhD dissertation, New York University.

Horak, Jan-Christopher. (1998). *Lovers of Cinema: The First American Film Avant-Garde, 1919–1945*. Madison: University of Wisconsin Press.

Horne, Jennifer. (2011). "A History Long Overdue: The Public Library and Motion Pictures." In Charles Acland & Haidee Wasson (eds), *Useful Cinema*. Raleigh, NC: Duke University Press.

"International History of Costume Design." (n.d.). At http://www.filmreference.com/encyclopedia/Academy-Awards-Crime-Films/Costume-INTERNATIONAL-HISTORY-OFCOSTUME-DESIGN.html (accessed March 2015).

Jordan, Joan. (1922). "The Girl Picture Magnates." *Photoplay*, August 22–23, 111.

Kenaga, Heidi. (2006). "Making the 'Studio Girl': The Hollywood Studio Club and Industry Regulation of Female Labour." *Film History*, 18.2, 129–139.

Koszarski, Richard. (1990). *An Evening's Entertainment: The Age of the Silent Feature Picture, 1915–1928*. Vol. 3 of *History of the American Cinema*, ed. Charles Harpole. New York: Scribner's.

Landis, Deborah Nadoolman, & Kirkham, Pat. (2002). "Designing Hollywood: Women Costume and Production Designers." In Pat Kirkham (ed.), *Women Designers in the USA, 1900–2000: Diversity and Difference* (pp. 247–267). New Haven: Yale University Press.

Lant, Antonia (ed.). (2006). *The Red Velvet Seat: Women's Writing on the First Fifty Years of Cinema*. London: Verso.

Lewis, Kevin. (2006). "The Moviola Mavens and the Moguls: Three Pioneering Women Editors Who Had the Respect of Early Hollywood's Power-Brokers." *Editors' Guild Magazine*, 27.2, at http://www.editorsguild.com/v2/magazine/archives/0306/cover_story.htm (accessed March 2015).

Loos, Anita, & Emerson, John. (1920). *How to Write Photoplays*. New York: James A. McCann.

MacDonald, Margaret I. (1915). "Educational Films Corporation of America." *Moving Picture World*, July 31, 803.

MacMahon, Henry E. (1920). "Women Directors of Plays and Pictures." *Ladies' Home Journal*, December 20, 12–13, 140, 143–144.

Macpherson, Jeanie. (1920). *The Necessity and Value of Theme in the Photoplay*. Los Angeles: Palmer Photoplay Co.

Mahar, Karen Ward. (2006). *Women Filmmakers in Early Hollywood*. Baltimore: Johns Hopkins University Press.

Maltby, Richard. (1990). "*The King of Kings* and the Czar of all Rushes: The Propriety of the Christ Story." *Screen*, 31.2, 188–213.

Mann, William J. (2006). *Kate: The Woman Who Was Hepburn*. New York: Henry Holt.

Mayne, Judith. (1994). *Directed by Dorothy Arzner*. Bloomington: Indiana University Press.

Monroy, Douglas. (1999). *Rebirth: Mexican Los Angeles from the Great Migration to the Great Depression*. Berkeley: University of California Press.

Morey, Anne. (2002). "'So real as to seem like life itself': The *Photoplay* Fiction of Adela Rogers St Johns." In Jennifer Bean & Diane Negra (eds), *A Feminist Reader in Early Cinema* (pp. 333–346). Raleigh, NC: Duke University Press.

Morey, Anne. (2003). *Hollywood Outsiders: The Adaptation of the Film Industry, 1913–34*. Minneapolis: University of Minnesota Press.

Morey, Anne. (2006). "Elinor Glyn as Hollywood Labourer." *Film History*, 18.2, 110–118.

Norden, Martin F. (2004). "Revisionist History, Restricted Cinema: The Strange Case of Margaret Sanger and *Birth Control*." In Lester D. Friedman (ed.), *Cultural Sutures: Medicine and Media* (pp. 263–279). Raleigh, NC: Duke University Press.

Page, William A. (1918). "The Movie-Struck Girl." *Woman's Home Companion*, June, 18.

Parker, Alison M. (1996). "Mothering the Movies: Women Reformers and Popular Culture." In Francis G. Couvares (ed.), *Movie Censorship and American Culture* (pp. 73–96). Washington, DC: Smithsonian Institution Press.

Parker, Alison M. (1997). *Purifying America: Women's Cultural Reform and Pro-Censorship, 1873–1933*. Urbana-Champaign: University of Illinois Press.

Patterson, Frances Taylor. (1921). *Cinema Craftsmanship: A Book for Photoplaywrights*. 2nd edn. New York: Harcourt, Brace & Co.

Polan, Dana. (2007). *Scenes of Instruction: The Beginnings of the U.S. Study of Film*. Berkeley: University of California Press.

Rinehart, Mary Roberts. (1992). "Face and Brains." In Anthony Slide (ed.), *They Also Wrote for the Fan Magazines: Film Articles by Literary Giants from e. e. cummings to Eleanor Roosevelt, 1920–1939* (pp. 123–128). Jefferson, NC: McFarland. (Original work published 1922.)

Rosenblum, Ralph, & Karen, Robert. (1986). *When the Shooting Stops, the Cutting Begins: A Film Editor's Story*. New York: Da Capo.

Rothapfel, Samuel L. ("Roxy"). (2002). "Picture Theater." In Gregory A. Waller (ed.), *Moviegoing in America: A Sourcebook in the History of Film Exhibition* (pp. 100–102). Oxford: Blackwell. (Original work published 1925.)

Sarris, Andrew. (1996). *The American Cinema: Directors and Directions, 1929–68*. New York: Da Capo. (Original work published 1968.)

Slater, Thomas J. (2010). "June Mathis's Valentino Scripts: Images of Male 'Becoming' after the Great War." *Cinema Journal*, 50.1, 99–120.

Slide, Anthony. (1977). *Early Women Directors: Their Role in the Development of the Silent Cinema*. New York: A. S. Barnes.

Slide, Anthony (ed.). (1992). *They Also Wrote for the Fan Magazines: Film Articles by Literary Giants from e. e. cummings to Eleanor Roosevelt, 1920–1939*. Jefferson, NC: McFarland.

Slide, Anthony. (1996). *The Silent Feminists: America's First Women Directors*. Lanham, MD: Scarecrow Press.

Sloan, Kay. (1988). *The Loud Silents: Origins of the Social Problem Film*. Urbana: University of Illinois Press.

Stamp, Shelley. (2000). *Movie-Struck Girls: Women and Motion Picture Culture after the Nickelodeon*. Berkeley: University of California Press.

Stamp, Shelley. (2004). "'It's a Long Way to Filmland': Starlets, Screen Hopefuls and Extras in Early Hollywood." In Charlie Keil & Shelley Stamp (eds), *American Cinema's Transitional Era: Audiences, Institutions, Practices* (pp. 332–352). Berkeley: University of California Press.

Stamp, Shelley. (2011). "Lois Weber." In Jane Gaines, Radha Vatsal, & Monica Dall'Asta (eds), *Women Film Pioneers Project*. New York: Center for Digital Research and Scholarship, Columbia University Libraries.

Stewart, Jacqueline Najuma. (2005). *Migrating to the Movies: Cinema and Black Urban Modernity*. Berkeley: University of California Press.

Studlar, Gaylyn. (1996). "The Perils of Pleasure? Fan Magazine Discourse as Women's Commodified Culture in the 1920s." In Richard Abel (ed.), *Silent Film* (pp. 263–298). New Brunswick: Rutgers University Press. (Original work published 1991.)

Waller, Gregory A. (2011). "Projecting the Promise of 16mm, 1935–45." In Charles Acland & Haidee Wasson (eds), *Useful Cinema*. Raleigh, NC: Duke University Press.

Wasson, Haidee. (2007). "The Reel of the Month Club: 16mm Projectors, Home Theaters and Film Libraries in the 1920s." In Richard Maltby, Melvyn Stokes, & Robert C. Allen (eds), *Going to the Movies: Hollywood and the Social Experience of Cinema* (pp. 217–234). Exeter: University of Exeter Press.

Wheeler, Leigh Ann. (2007). *Against Obscenity: Reform and the Politics of Womanhood, 1873–1935*. Baltimore: Johns Hopkins University Press.

Zimmermann, Patricia R. (1995). *Reel Families: A Social History of Amateur Film*. Bloomington: Indiana University Press.

4

African-Americans and Silent Films

Paula J. Massood
Professor, Brooklyn College, City University of New York, United States

Paula J. Massood provides an overview of African-American filmmakers, producers, actors, and characters as represented in movies of the silent era – many responding, in part, to **D. W. Griffith's *The Birth of a Nation*** and to images of African-Americans in earlier print, vaudeville, and screen sources. Notably, however, the first black-directed, black-cast motion picture, ***The Railroad Porter*** (1912), predated Griffith's film and was produced by the black-owned **Foster Photoplay Company**, formed to create comedies that would entertain without degrading their African-American characters. Through the work of such key figures as **Oscar Micheaux**, **Noble Johnson**, and **Lawrence Chenault**, Massood explores **entertainment** and **uplift** as the two key focal points of early African-American cinema. Massood also examines exhibition practices targeting black audiences and the impact of the coming of sound on black filmmakers and audiences. Her essay shares ground with Charlie Keil on D. W. Griffith in this volume and with Alex Lykidis and Janet K. Cutler on black independent film in Volume II of this series, and with Ed Guerrero on Blaxploitation and Keith Harris on black crossover cinema in the hardcover/online version.

Additional terms, names, and concepts: National Association for the Advancement of Colored People (NAACP), blackface, minstrelsy, the New Negro

Histories of African-American participation in American silent film often cite D. W. Griffith's *The Birth of a Nation* (1915) as the defining moment in black cinematic representation. The film's myths of black inferiority and the sanctity of white nationhood seemed almost nostalgic at a moment of national growth and change, of which the new film technology was a part. At the same time, its images of black brutes lasciviously chasing innocent white women and a congressional hall filled with barefoot, chicken-eating black coons solidified a number of myths that appealed to a young nation furiously attempting to define itself in the face of increasing immigration from abroad, the massive growth of urban industrial areas (and the

American Film History: Selected Readings, Origins to 1960, First Edition. Edited by Cynthia Lucia, Roy Grundmann, and Art Simon.
© 2016 John Wiley & Sons, Inc. Published 2016 by John Wiley & Sons, Inc.

attendant loss of an agrarian culture), and the threat of world war.

While Griffith's film is responsible for sparking African-American protest movements on the local level through churches and civic groups and on the national level through the efforts of the National Association for the Advancement of Colored People (NAACP), it is inaccurate to suggest that its depictions of African-American characters were novel. In fact, besides the relatively new depiction of Gus's lust-filled, violent black brute, many of the black character types included in the film were drawn, like the narrative itself, from older representations of black people from the page, stage, and screen.[1] Therefore, in order to fully understand the relationship between American silent cinema and African-American representation, we must first briefly consider earlier moments in the history of silent cinema, for the preceding decades of filmmaking set the stage for the representational and political issues raised in *The Birth of a Nation* and that were further examined, especially by black independent filmmakers, throughout the remainder of the silent period.

Early Background: Vaudeville, Blackface Minstrelsy, and Film

African-American participation in American silent cinema, whether in front of or behind the camera, roughly follows two trajectories: entertainment and uplift. The former path draws on early cinema's roots in carnivals, vaudeville acts, and the minstrel stage, often borrowing from popular and familiar forms of stereotype and caricature, particularly blackface minstrelsy, for comic relief and overall entertainment. In a number of ways this transition was to be expected because many of the actors and skits from vaudeville appeared in early American film, the new medium providing a novel presentation of what was essentially carnival and sideshow material. The latter path, uplift, grew out of more explicit political goals that sought to counter demeaning white stereotypes of African-Americans with images of black strivers and professionals. Both entertainment and uplift films have complex histories that deserve further exploration.

As early as 1894, Thomas Edison's company was incorporating minstrel subject matter and performers, many of them African-American, into its first films. For example, *The Pickaninny Dance – From the "Passing Show"* (1894), *James Grundy, no. 1/Buck and Wing Dance* (1895), and *James Grundy, no. 2/Cake Walk* (1895) feature popular acts from the vaudeville circuit. Other Edison titles, such as *A Watermelon Contest* (1895), *Sambo and Jemima* (1900), *Bally-Hoo Cake Walk* (1901), and *The Gator and the Pickaninny* (1903), drew upon familiar character types and comic scenarios from the stage. In these early examples, we can see cinema's inherent contradictions taking shape: The shorts capture actual, but often identified, black minstrel performers engaged in acts of fiction that were frequently taken to represent or mimic real life. The only roles open to black performers, these character types became the norm and were read as such by early film audiences.

The early films were most often single-shot, one-reel depictions of characters or short events. Over the next decade, however, the development of story films extended the complexity of cinematic narrative, and white actors in blackface increasingly supplanted African-American performers, shifting theatrical performance practices to the screen. Some films, like *What Happened in the Tunnel* (Edison, 1903) and *A Bucket of Cream Ale* (American Mutoscope, 1904), are set in unspecified locations, but the majority of films from this time are located in the rural South in a series of celluloid plantation dramas inspired by Plantation School novels, most notably *Uncle Tom's Cabin* (Edison, 1902), which was repeatedly remade during the silent era.[2] Other examples include *The Chicken Thief* (American Mutoscope, 1904), *A Nigger in the Woodpile* (Edison, 1904), and *The Watermelon Patch* (Edison, 1905). Like their literary and visual precursors, many of the story films (especially those detailing black subservience and/or criminality) were, according to Jacqueline Stewart, a means of "disavow[ing], via mass culture, Black agency and progress" by presenting black subjects as backward, uncivilized, or as comic buffoons to both white *and* black audiences, since they were available to all viewers (Stewart 2005, 34).

There's no doubt that Griffith, a Southerner by birth and a stage actor by training, was familiar with these character types and narratives. From roughly 1897 until his film career began in 1908, Griffith supported himself on the stage as a member of various touring companies that performed legitimate theater, including Thomas Dixon, Jr's antisocialist *The One*

Woman (based on his novel of the same name), in which he had a role in New York between 1906 and 1907. During his early time at Biograph, Griffith directed a number of Civil War narratives, including *In Old Kentucky* (1909), *His Trust* (1911), *His Trust Fulfilled* (1911), and *The Informer* (1912) (Lang 1994, 29). Many of the themes of these early films would be developed in *The Birth of a Nation*, including a sympathetic rendering of the Southern slave system and the use of white performers in blackface.

While major film companies were expanding and moving to the West Coast, African-American showmen saw the new medium's potential as a viable profit-making opportunity as well as a means of presenting alternative versions of black life to audiences. The companies they began could be found throughout the country, though many were located in areas with large African-American populations. In 1912, for example, vaudeville showman William Foster established the Foster Photoplay Company in Chicago with the intention of making, as he announced in the *Indianapolis Freeman*, "non-degrading Black-cast comedies" for black audiences. The company's first film, *The Railroad Porter* (1912), starring "former members of the Pekin Stock Company," is considered to be the first black-directed motion picture (Sampson 1995, 174).[3] The film's narrative of a Pullman porter who learns that his wife is carrying on an affair with another man is filled with comic antics and suggests the appeal of the comedic form for black as well as white filmmakers. Yet Foster viewed film as a means of displaying African-American talents to the world along with being a tool to "offset so many insults to the race" (quoted in Everett 2001, 54). For Foster, then, film could be entertaining, profitable, and political.

Soon other race film companies were established in Foster's wake; for example, in 1913, the Afro-American Film Company was founded in New York by white investors and with African-American businessman Hunter C. Haynes as head of production. The Afro-American Film Company, like Foster's Photoplay Company, initially produced short comedies featuring popular black vaudevillians, again demonstrating the strong links between the stage and the screen. Unlike Foster's company, however, the Afro-American Film Company was white-owned, having been incorporated by A. W. Burg and G. K. and F. A. Wade for $10,000. Given the cost of capitalization, many companies producing films for black audiences – and it should be noted that audiences were often segregated in both the North and the South at this time – had white financing. In the case of the Afro-American Film Company, Haynes's role in the company's decision-making remains unclear (Walton 1914, 6). In fact, he may have been nothing more than the company's black face, a common organizational strategy for white owners looking to gain legitimacy with black audiences.

The Afro-American Film Company released two films in 1914, *Lovie Joe's Romance* and *One Large Evening*. While reviews were initially neutral, the company's films soon became the target of criticism in the black press over their inclusion of demeaning stereotypes. For example, Henry T. Sampson suggests that despite the use of black stars, *Lovie Joe's Romance* and *One Large Evening* were received poorly by "black theatre owners and managers [who] refused to book the films because they contained many of the same derogatory racial-stereotype characterizations of blacks in films released by the major companies" (1995, 178).[4] The theater managers' reluctance to show the films prompted Haynes to publish an appeal in black newspapers for increased community support for black films. In it he focused on the ways in which Afro-American films differed from those being released by mainstream companies:

> There has been so much trash put out by film companies representing the colored man … that it has almost disgusted him, and he is very suspicious when he sees a colored film advertised. But he can rest assured that any film advertised by the Afro-American Film Co. cannot but meet his approval. (Quoted in Sampson 1995, 178)[5]

For its part, the black press was willing to forgive Haynes for what it viewed as the sins of the company's white backers. Lester Walton, for example, observed in the *New York Age* that when

> *One Large Evening* was shown at the Lafayette Theatre [in Harlem] there were some who were disposed to criticize Hunter C. Haynes … for putting the picture on the market. But it is said that "his voice did not have any sound to it" when the advisability of producing *One Large Evening* was discussed.… Perhaps it is the same old story – the colored man furnishing the idea, but shut out from partnership when the proposition materializes. (Walton 1914, 6)

Shortly afterward, and perhaps due to such criticism coupled with a desire to make different films, Haynes left Afro-American to form his own Harlem-based company, the Haynes Photoplay Company. The company produced one short comedy, *Uncle Remus' First Visit to New York* (1914), a play on the familiar narrative of a pair of country bumpkins in the big city. According to Stewart, even though the film's humor comes at the expense of the unsophisticated rubes from the South, the critical response to *Uncle Remus* acknowledged the increasing modernity and urbanization of black audiences; for example, a reviewer for the *Indianapolis Freeman* suggested that the film is a "faithful portrait that contrasts the new Negro with the old and forges a chain of circumstances that vividly point out the progress the race has made in his fifty years of freedom" (quoted in Stewart 2005, 194). Haynes also produced a newsreel focusing on elite blacks in New York and Boston, which featured the popular boxers Sam Langford and Joe Walcott. This film was also reviewed favorably by the black press, which described it in 1914 as "by far the most meritorious picture of its kind ever thrown upon the screen" (quoted in Sampson 1995, 179).

Meanwhile, major film companies continued borrowing from popular vaudeville themes, most often for comic effect. Del Henderson, Griffith's colleague at Biograph, produced a number of single-reel comedies during the early teens. Many of these films, including *Black and White* (1913) and *Rag-Time Romance* (1913), feature white actors in blackface. Another company, New York's Crystal Films, also produced single-reel comedies with similar race themes. One title in particular, *A Change of Complexion* (Phillips Smalley, 1914), plays on the idea of mistaken identity through the comic construct of a white middle-class couple being "darkened" by a maid who had been chastened previously for associating with a vaudeville performer.[6] Like *What Happened in a Tunnel*, an Edison film in which the comedy is centered on an identity switch between a white woman and her black maid (to the horror of the white woman's suitor), these longer narratives played on the comic and sometimes threatening possibilities of white people suddenly turning black.

After the release of *The Birth of a Nation* in 1916, Biograph released *A Natural Born Gambler*, starring popular *Ziegfeld Follies* and vaudeville star Bert Williams, who is also credited as writer and director. The film, set in a bar with an illegal gambling space in the back, depicts Williams's character, "Jonah Man," and his cronies (none of whom are in blackface) as drinkers and gamblers engaged in many of the behaviors that had become rote for African-American characters in American film. And yet *A Natural Born Gambler* is interesting in that it features Williams, a West Indian blackface performer, in the lead role, implying that the entertainer had a strong enough popular following to carry a film intended for white audiences. In fact, Williams received the equivalent of top billing at the time, with his name appearing before the title of the film: This placement is perhaps a reflection of his fame and also the autonomy he enjoyed with his Biograph contract.

While the depiction of the group of men, the "Independent Order of Calcimine Artists of America," is played for comic effect, *A Natural Born Gambler* manages, however slightly, to offer alternatives to the more familiar black buffoons and fools normally showcased in Biograph products. First, almost the entire black cast (excluding Williams) performs without blackface makeup. They are relatively well dressed and educated, the latter suggested by various scenes in which the characters read newspapers, write reports, and calculate bar tabs and club dues. Additionally, Williams plays his character with a subtlety and complexity lacking in most cinematic blackface renditions of the time. Originally part of the Williams and Walker comedy duo, Williams rose to fame as a blackface performer who often, especially with George Walker, pushed the limits of blackface performance on stage, using what had become a demeaning stage convention as a conscious performative strategy. In this film, Williams is the center of attention both within and outside of the narrative: The characters look to him to carry the narrative forward just as the audience follows and even identifies with his character through story and framing (for example, his expressions are readable through close-up shots of his face). That Williams also plays his role, despite the blackface and the use of stereotypical dialect in title cards, with dignity and humanity, moves his minstrel character beyond sheer stereotype. In the end, Williams succeeds in manufacturing audience identification and empathy, perhaps a first for a black film performer in American film.

Story Films, Melodrama, and Uplift

As the responses to the Afro-American Company films suggest, black critics and audiences approached film with a critical eye even before *The Birth of a Nation* was released. However, even though it incorporated familiar racial tropes, Griffith's film was different in that it presented, through the use of sophisticated formal techniques and multiple reels, American history on an epic scale. Moreover, and perhaps more important, *The Birth of a Nation* depicted fictional events as though they were real, often presenting tableaux as if directly from historical documents. For Griffith, the "motion picture approaches more closely real life" than theater, and the camera "doesn't lie" (quoted in Rogin 1994, 259). In a sense, then, the power of *The Birth of a Nation* wasn't that it extended black caricatures, but that it argued – repeatedly through plot details and form – that these caricatures were true.

In addition to state and national protests and censorship battles, the African-American response to Griffith's film was cinematic. Most immediately, the Birth of a Race Photoplay Corporation was established in 1917, with the stated purpose of presenting "the true story of the Negro, his life in Africa, his transportation to America, his enslavement, his freedom, his achievements, together with his past, present and future relations with his white neighbor" (quoted in Sampson 1995, 208). Initially produced by Emmett J. Scott and Booker T. Washington (the narrative was based on Washington's *Up From Slavery*), the film eventually had the involvement of the NAACP and Universal Studios. Funding problems and the demands of attempting to fulfill various producers' visions unfortunately changed the scope of the film, and what was originally meant to highlight black American accomplishment became a presentation of Judeo-Christian history from the pages of the Bible. *The Birth of a Race* opened nearly two years after production began, was a critical and financial failure, and served as a cautionary tale for black filmmakers about white interference.

While *The Birth of a Race* was intended to be a direct response to Griffith's film, other race film companies were established in the late teens that resulted from the convergence of a number of social, political, and economic factors. As the earlier discussion points out, at the beginning of the twentieth century there already was an interest in the production of films featuring black characters and stories for African-American audiences. The release of *Birth* helped fuel the desire to create positive representations of blacks, a desire that was also closely aligned with the black elite's project to define a "New Negro" in the twentieth century. At the same time, the nation's African-American population was becoming more urban as Northern industrial cities opened their factories to an influx of Southern, formerly agrarian, workers. This Great Migration resulted in an African-American population that was increasingly urban and one for whom antebellum melodramas, such as Griffith's, were outmoded. Film, in this environment, was seen as an important tool for educating the newly arrived migrants, especially by the black middle class who took a progressive and pedagogical approach to the new technology.

While a number of race film companies were established in the late teens and the early 1920s, arguably the most influential African-American outfits were the Lincoln Motion Picture Company, established by George and Noble Johnson in 1916, and the Micheaux Book and Film Company, founded by Oscar Micheaux in 1918. Noble Johnson was a versatile character actor who played a variety of roles in Hollywood films from 1915 onward. Not long after beginning his career in film, Johnson founded, with his brother George, the Lincoln Motion Picture Company, aiming to provide black audiences with dramatic stories of African-American accomplishment. Firmly ensconced in the uplift ideology embraced by W. E. B. Du Bois's "Talented Tenth," the company was celebrated in the black press for its "dedication to technical merits and thematic integrity in depicting black life and culture" (Everett 2001, 117). In his capacity as top talent for the company, Noble Johnson appeared in three releases, *The Realization of a Negro's Ambition* (1916), *A Trooper of Troop K* (1917), and *The Law of Nature* (1917), before he left in 1918. He often used the money he earned from his work in studio films, along with other sources, to bankroll Lincoln's operations. His resignation from the company was rumored to be the result of an ultimatum set by Universal Studios, which had a contract with the actor (Bogle 2006, 23).

While there remain no extant prints of the Lincoln films, descriptions of their narratives provide insight into their uplift strategies: "to make positive family films, each structured around a black hero's struggle to accomplish some admirable ambition" (Berry 2001, 50). *The Realization of a Negro's Ambition*, for example, narrates the story of a recent Tuskegee graduate with an engineering degree who returns to the family farm after failing to find employment in a discriminatory oil industry. Through a series of plot twists, which lead him to Los Angeles and an oil job (after he's saved the life of a white executive's daughter), the young man manages to find oil on the family farm, marry his long-time sweetheart, and live happily ever after. The film's hero is presented as an upright citizen who is college educated, hard working, and ambitious. His success at the film's end provided an alternative embodiment of black masculinity to the image of black masculinity projected by most films of the time, which presented black men as lazy, dumb, and uneducated.

Through narratives that dramatized the concerns and ambitions of the black middle class, the Lincoln films offered a further alternative to the films typically being produced by both black and white film companies. This was not lost on the black press, whose readership was made up of the black bourgeoisie. The Los Angeles-based *California Eagle* was especially supportive of the company's endeavors, covering the premiere of *The Realization of a Negro's Ambition* and praising the final product. According to Everett, Lincoln's

> commitment to serious dramas as opposed to the cheaply made ribald comedies of its competitors prompted the *Eagle* to conclude that Lincoln not only represented a significant advance for black incursions into the influential medium of film but, more importantly, symbolized a giant step in the black community's quest for building black institutions. (2001, 110)

But the company also struggled to stay afloat while facing competition from more established studios, including Universal, which held Noble's contract. George Johnson continued Lincoln's mission for a few more years following the departure of his brother Noble in 1918, but the company went out of business in 1923, after releasing one more film, *By Right of Birth* (1921).

Lincoln's most serious competitor was the Micheaux Book and Film Company. A former railroad porter, homesteader, and novelist, Oscar Micheaux was also an entrepreneur, a provocateur, and a race man who symbolizes the two, often competing, facets of African-American silent filmmaking – entertainment and uplift. Micheaux moved into filmmaking after George and Noble Johnson refused his request to direct the Lincoln adaptation of his novel, *The Homesteader* (the Johnsons had attempted to purchase the rights to the novel after its publication in 1917).[7] Micheaux had no prior filmmaking experience before establishing the Micheaux Book and Film Company in Chicago in 1918, but he went on to direct the adaptation and release *The Homesteader* in February 1919. The director's first film, a semi-autobiographical story about a homesteader in South Dakota, was a critical success upon release, with the *Half-Century Magazine*, for example, suggesting that *The Homesteader* ranked "in power and workmanship with the greatest of white western productions" (quoted in McGilligan 2007, 131).

The Homesteader also introduced many of the stylistic patterns that would continue to appear throughout Micheaux's filmmaking career, one that extended from the silent to the sound era and included over 40 films. Characteristic of Micheaux, also, was his skill at marketing. Prior to *The Homesteader*'s release, Micheaux was a relative unknown in Chicago, and – even though the interiors were shot in the city and the director cast members of the popular Lafayette Players (who had opened up a satellite troupe in Chicago in 1918) in a number of roles in the film – there was little press coverage of the production. Micheaux booked an 8,000-seat theater in the city for the film's premiere and took out half-page advertisements in local black newspapers announcing his "Mammoth Photoplay ... destined to mark a new epoch in the achievements of the darker races." The ads called upon the community's race pride by exclaiming:

> Every Race man and woman should cast aside their skepticism regarding the Negro's ability as a motion picture star and go and see [the film], not only for the absorbing interest obtaining herein, but as an appreciation of those finer arts which no race can ignore and hope to obtain a higher plane of thought and action. (Quoted in McGilligan 2007, 129)

Micheaux, like Foster, saw that uplift didn't have to come at the expense of profit. More important, he never questioned his or other black filmmakers' ability and right to make a film.

While he may have been extolling race pride and accomplishment, the black middle class never fully accepted Micheaux or his films. Part of this resulted from his personality, which had George and Noble Johnson referring to him as "a rough Negro who got his hands on some cash" (quoted in Cripps 1993, 184). Part may also have been due to his commitment to the self-help ideals of Booker T. Washington at a time when W. E. B. Du Bois was at the forefront of modern African-American political life. And part also resulted from the subject matter of his films, which included such controversial content as racially motivated violence (including lynching scenes), miscegenation, black urban criminality, and the hypocrisy of the black church. *The Homesteader*, for example, may have opened to enthusiastic reviews, but its premiere run was short-lived. After receiving complaints from members of the black clergy claiming that the film vilified black preachers, the Chicago Censorship Board banned future screenings of the film in the city because of its "tendency to disturb the public peace" (quoted in McGilligan 2007, 130). The ban was overturned a few days later, but it was just one of many similar incidents in Micheaux's career. The upside of such controversy, however, was that the director drew upon such press for subsequent advertising campaigns.

After *The Homesteader*, Micheaux quickly began work on his next film, *Within Our Gates* (1919), which presents a much more powerful and controversial rejoinder to *The Birth of a Nation* than the earlier *The Birth of a Race*. The film, one of the few surviving examples of Micheaux's silent work, is basically an uplift melodrama focusing on a young, educated woman named Sylvia Landry. After a failed romance, Sylvia moves from the North to take a teaching position in an all-black school in the South. When the school experiences financial troubles, she heads back north in search of a possible patron. Through a variety of plot twists, Sylvia finds a patron for the school and meets and falls in love with a young, handsome Doctor Vivian. But Sylvia has a past: Near the end of the film a flashback reveals that she is the product of a mixed-race marriage and that her adoptive parents (the reasons for her adoption remain unclear) were victims of a violent lynching. Despite this history, Sylvia and Doctor Vivian marry and live happily ever after.

In its story of African-American accomplishment and success, *Within Our Gates* offered an uplifting narrative of the New Negro. Yet the film also contains a number of controversial elements that troubled the black establishment in places like Chicago and New York. As noted, Micheaux's film offers an answer to a number of the more demeaning moments in *The Birth of a Nation*. Most important, it suggests that violence, such as lynching, which was on the rise in the late teens, was not the result of black depravity as represented when a lust-filled black brute chases an innocent white woman in *The Birth of a Nation*. Rather, it stemmed from white greed, lust, and desire for power. In *Within Our Gates*, for example, Sylvia is nearly raped by a white man who, it turns out, is actually her father. Also, her adopted family is lynched because the educated Sylvia determines that the white plantation owner has been cheating her sharecropper father. Moreover, rather than simply imply the lynching, Micheaux showed most of the action, including shots of the parents being captured and hanged by a white mob.

Like *The Homesteader*, *Within Our Gates* proved to be highly controversial, especially in Chicago, which had experienced a wave of race riots in its predominantly black South Side neighborhoods the previous summer. The violence was initiated when a young black man was stoned to death for swimming on the wrong side of a segregated city beach. Race relations were already strained in the city, the result of a burgeoning black population that was moving beyond the borders of the overcrowded South Side into other neighborhoods. Black Chicago erupted at news of the murder and the authorities' lack of response to the community's cries for justice. The violence was responsible for 38 deaths and hundreds of injuries. In such an environment, it was feared that Micheaux's film would incite a new wave of riots, a fear that was shared equally by the city's black and white communities.[8] Both black and white social and religious leaders protested the film and called for its more offensive scenes of lynching and attempted rape to be cut, with which the director had no choice but to comply. Micheaux's experiences in Chicago were replicated in other cities with large black communities and suggested the expectations and the limits black leaders often placed on the content of films meant for their constituencies.

Micheaux had a prolific film career, directing over 20 films during the silent era. Of these, in addition to *Within Our Gates*, only two prints exist: *The Symbol*

Figure 4.1 The moment before the lynching in *Within Our Gates* (1919, director and producer Oscar Micheaux).

of the Unconquered (1920) and *Body and Soul* (1925). The former, the first film made after Micheaux relocated to Harlem in the early 1920s (where he had no better luck connecting with the black elite), continued his revisionist interpretation of Griffith's *The Birth of a Nation* by returning to the themes of miscegenation and racial violence. The film is another version of a homesteading tale, focusing on a young woman who inherits a farm claim in the West. She becomes an object of the wrath of a local white property owner who tries to scare her off with the help of the Ku Klux Klan, who are presented as largely motivated by greed. The latter film, *Body and Soul*, marked Paul Robeson's screen debut in dual roles as a dishonest preacher (and rapist) and a young, upstanding inventor, both of whom vie for the hand of a young woman. Both films were controversial, but the latter especially, which again sparked the wrath of the black church.

These films, in combination with Micheaux's other, now-missing, silents, suggest the filmmaker's interest in creating controversy. More important, however, they signify his sophisticated grasp of race politics of the time. Controversial, and often lacking in production values, the Micheaux Book and Film Company's silent films were also exclusively black-financed, a rarity for black film at this time and, as we have seen with Hunter Haynes's experiences with the Afro-American Film Company, a guarantee that what was being filmed was not the result of compromise. As far as we can tell from the documentary evidence that survives, many of the films, for example his adaptations of Thomas Stribling's *Birthright* (1924) and Charles Chestnutt's *The House Behind the Cedars* (1924/1925) and *The Conjure Woman* (1926), focus on black identity and ambition. Others, like *The Brute* (1920) and *The Devil's Disciple* (1926), offer moral lessons regarding the temptations of urban life, a popular theme among the black bourgeoisie and both black and white progressives. Whether focusing on the black middle class or the underworld, preachers or teachers, Micheaux's silent films examine the complexities of increasingly modernized and urbanized African-American life.

White-Owned Race Film Companies: Competition and Collaboration

In addition to black-owned and operated production companies, there were a number of white-owned companies making films during the 1920s, and three that were well respected at the time stand out for their uplift films: The Norman Film Manufacturing Company of Florida, Reol Productions of New York, and the Colored Players Film Company of Philadelphia. Richard Norman from Jacksonville established the Norman Company in 1912. The company briefly made films with white casts before shifting into the production of black-cast melodramas, Westerns, mysteries, and flying films. The Westerns, *The Bull Dogger* (1921) and *The Crimson Skull* (1922), headlined well-known African-American cowboy Bill Pickett and were shot in the all-black town of Boley, Oklahoma. Both films also starred Anita Bush, who founded the Lafayette Players (originally the Anita Bush Stock Company) and was known as the "Little Mother of Colored Drama." *The Crimson Skull* was described as "a typical picture of the old swash-buckling west, with the added attraction of a cast composed of our actors and actresses who could ride and shoot in true Western style" (quoted in Klotman 2001, 168–169). Besides the Westerns, Norman also produced a shipwreck story, *Regeneration* (1923), and *The Flying Ace* (1926), the latter a well-received aviation film described in its posters as "The Greatest Airplane Thriller Ever Produced."

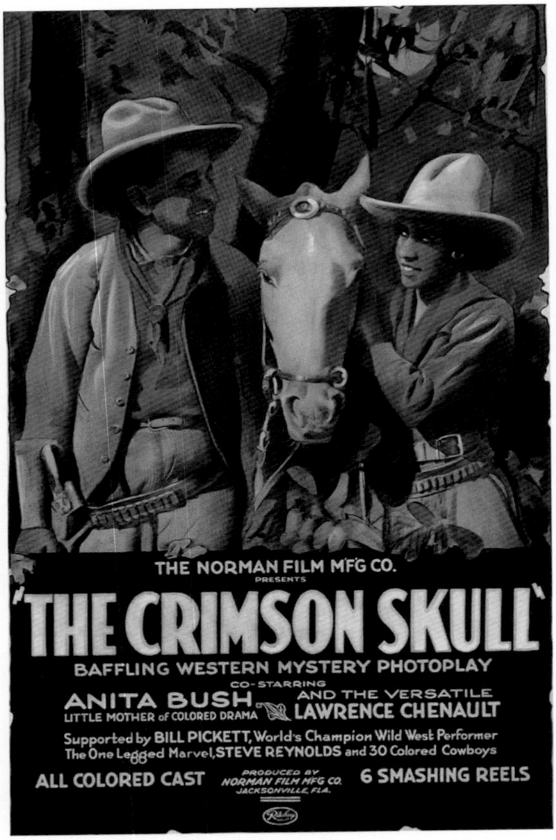

Figure 4.2 Poster for Richard E. Norman's *The Crimson Skull* (1922, producer Norman Film Manufacturing Company).

The Norman Company, like the Lincoln Company, did not survive the transition to sound. Richard Norman continued his involvement in the film business, distributing other companies' films into the 1930s. Among the films he distributed were a few of Micheaux's sound titles. According to Phyllis Klotman, the pair established a relationship in the 1920s, perhaps a result of their combined interests and the fact that the race film circuit was relatively small (Norman also shared correspondence with George Noble of the Lincoln Company). This early communication and Norman's continuing connections with the race film distribution circuit may have prompted Micheaux to work with him later in his career (Klotman 2001, 172).

Another of Lincoln's and Micheaux's competitors was Reol Productions, a New York-based production company that made race films from 1920 until approximately 1924. Reol was founded by Robert Levy, an experienced theater and film man, who had previously worked in the Los Angeles offices of the Éclair Film Company and also was the former owner of the Quality Amusement Corporation, operators of race theaters (including Harlem's Lafayette Theatre). Through this latter connection, Levy enjoyed a direct line to some of Harlem's, and the Lafayette's, most popular talents, including Lawrence Chenault, who also appeared in a number of Oscar Micheaux's productions, and Edna Morton, considered by the black press to be the "Colored Mary Pickford." Reol produced a number of feature-length uplift dramas during its short life span, along with two newsreels (focusing on Booker T. Washington and Tuskegee) and three comedies (two shorts and one feature): *The Jazz Hounds* (1921), *The Simp* (1921), and *Easy Money* (1922). *The Jazz Hounds* drew its subject matter from a series of popular black Sherlock Holmes films produced by another white-owned race film company, Ebony Film Corporation, during the teens (Petersen 2008, 310),[9] while the next two comedies starred popular stage comedian and theater owner Sherman H. Dudley, who later worked with the Colored Players Film Corporation.

Reol's uplift films followed a similar pattern as their main black and white competitors in their focus on black heroes and heroines of accomplishment or those striving for success; for example, *Secret Sorrow* (1921) includes a successful district attorney, while *The Burden of Race* (1921) focuses on a young university student. Additionally, Reol adapted a number of narratives from popular literature of the time, including Paul Laurence Dunbar's 1902 migration novel, *The Sport of Gods* (1921), its debut film, and Aubrey Bowser's serialized passing story, "The Man Who Would Be White," as its second feature, titled *The Call of His People* (1921). The films explored popular themes from the time – migration, passing, and achievement – and did so by depicting "exemplary African Americans rising to middle-class status" (Petersen 2008, 311). Despite their subject matter, their popularity with the black press, and Levy's connections to the black theater circuit, Reol Productions went out of business in 1924. According to Levy, "Negro amusement buyers are fickle and possessed of a peculiar psychic complex, and they prefer to patronize the galleries of white theatres [rather] than theirs" (quoted in Sampson 1995, 215), a common lament among race film producers.

The Colored Players Film Corporation of Philadelphia had similar roots as Reol; David Starkman established it in 1926 with Louis Groner and Roy Calnek (the latter of whom also directed three of the company's four releases). Starkman came from the film world, having owned a film exchange and a theater catering to black patrons. Calnek was an experienced director who had made at least three race films (for Superior Art Motion Pictures, Inc., another Philadelphia-based company) by the time he joined Starkman (Musser 2001, 180). The company drew its acting talent and technical personnel from the Philadelphia area and often combined professionals like Calnek and Lawrence Chenault (who appeared in all of the company's films) with unknowns.

According to a number of scholars, including Henry T. Sampson and Charles Musser, Starkman was the Jewish equivalent of Oscar Micheaux in that he was the primary power behind the Colored Players, creating the majority of its promotion and advertising himself (Sampson 1995, 218; Musser 2001, 181).[10] Starkman, like Micheaux, also believed in making uplifting films that were free of demeaning stereotypes. Rather than form an alliance, however, such as the one Micheaux worked out with Richard Norman, the Colored Players Film Corporation and the Micheaux Book and Film Company were competitors for the comparatively small box office enjoyed by race film productions in contrast to the more mainstream product coming from what was increasingly a standardized industry based in Hollywood. The rival companies' films often opened in the same cities at the same time, and just as often the companies poached each other's stars. Lawrence Chenault, for example, first worked in Micheaux films before appearing in Colored Players features, and Shingzie Howard, a Micheaux discovery, appeared in at least two of the company's productions. One of the primary differences between the two companies, however, was in their reception by the black press. Whereas Micheaux's films often were controversial and the subject of censorship battles, the Colored Players' productions received high marks from assorted newspapers; the company's debut, *A Prince of His Race* (1926), for instance, was described as "a decided step forward in the field of cinema art as it pertains to the Negro" by the *Philadelphia Tribune* (quoted in Musser 2001, 185).

Despite differences in reception and production values (the Colored Players productions had more generous budgets and the films often looked better), Starkman and the Colored Players personnel engaged with similar subject matter as most of the black-owned companies: Their films focused on educated and ambitious black heroes and heroines trying to better themselves in the twentieth century. *Ten Nights in a Barroom* (1926), the company's second feature, provides a good example of these concerns. Starring the respected black stage actor Charles S. Gilpin in his first and only screen role (prior to this he had most famously starred on the stage in Eugene O'Neill's *The Emperor Jones*) and Lawrence Chenault in a supporting role, the film is an adaptation of Timothy Shay Arthur's nineteenth-century temperance tale of the same title, in which a man loses everything because of his drinking. Gilpin's performance was well received and the film as a whole was described in the *Chicago Defender* as "of a very high standard" and "presented in a manner which holds intense interest, being actually exciting and melodramatic in spots. It is a Racial novelty and one which carries a deep moral" (quoted in Sampson 1995, 341).

The Scar of Shame (1927), the company's last film and the only one that has survived almost intact, was equally well received. The film narrates the story of an ill-fated marriage between two individuals who meet in a Philadelphia boarding house. Alvin Hillyard, an aspiring composer, meets Louise Howard while rescuing her from a beating by her stepfather, an alcoholic underworld figure named Strike. After delivering her from two more attacks, Alvin marries Louise and the resulting union pairs his bourgeois blood and ambitions with her less admirable family tree. Through a variety of plot twists and misunderstandings that result in the pair's separation – Alvin mistakenly wounds Louise with a gun, is sent to prison, and eventually escapes – Alvin resumes his middle-class life as a music teacher while Louise, the child of the underworld, ends up a prostitute and eventually commits suicide.

The Scar of Shame's class dynamics, which include Alvin's eventual engagement to a woman of similar class background and Louise's convenient demise, have been discussed in detail by a number of film scholars.[11] The film's narrative, casting, and mise-en-scène work toward what Thomas Cripps describes as "the finer things, the higher hopes, and higher aims" (1997, 55). The film presents a world in which these "higher ideals" are embodied by Alvin and a few of the boarding house residents. The world outside the boarding house is presented as dangerous for those striving for a better life: It is where Louise's father spends his time, along with another boarding house resident, who is Alvin's chief competitor for Louise's attentions. And yet, while *The Scar of Shame* embodies the ideology of the bourgeoisie, its narrative of uplift fails to extend to Louise. A child of the lower class (she was employed by the boarding house), she cannot escape her class status through marriage to Alvin. Her demise clears the way for his rightful coupling with a woman more of his social caste.

Despite, or perhaps because of this class bias, *The Scar of Shame* fared well with reviewers who focused on its production values and narrative. A reviewer for the *New York Amsterdam News*, for example, asserted that the film "sets a new standard of excellence," and Cripps suggests that *The Scar of Shame* "exemplified the highest hope of the black generation of the 1920s who placed faith in individual aspiration as the path to group emancipation" (1997, 57). The film was the result of the partnership between Starkman and Sherman H. Dudley, with Starkman as the general manager of the reorganized company and Dudley serving as the president. Dudley, who had become interested in race films with his involvement in Reol's *The Simp*, was a vocal supporter of the industry, even arguing in the *Chicago Defender*: "We need them [race films]. I don't believe any manager lost a dime on a Race picture regardless of how rotten the picture was. If that be the case, why can't they make money with good pictures with good Race scenarios written carefully around Race atmosphere. I think we should write about ourselves and stop trying to ape the white man" (quoted in Musser 2001, 182). Unfortunately, the Colored Players, like many race film companies invested in rewriting African-American representations, failed financially, and *The Scar of Shame* was the last film produced by the company.

The Minors: Lesser-Known Race Film Companies

The Lincoln, Micheaux, Norman, Reol, and Colored Players companies were the most visible and successful race film producers of the silent era, but a number of lesser-known companies, incorporated during the 1920s, also were scattered across the country. Some managed to make a film or two before ceasing operations while others failed to produce anything before disappearing. The more noteworthy examples include the Detroit-based Maurice Film Company, founded in 1920 by Richard Maurice. Maurice made two films almost 10 years apart, *Nobody's Children* (1920) and *Eleven P.M.* (1928). The latter film, which is extant, is considered to be one of the earliest (if not the first) experimental films made by an African-American filmmaker. The film contains an innovative visual style – employing superimpositions and split screens along with a complicated narrative structure, including dream sequences and flashbacks – to tell an uplift tale about a young writer who must finish a magazine story by the appointed hour of the title. He falls asleep and dreams of a musician whose life is ruined by living on the street. The musician is reincarnated as a dog that then returns to exact vengeance on the people who ruined his family. The young writer eventually wakes up and uses his dream as inspiration to successfully complete his own narrative.

At least eight black-owned and operated film production companies incorporated between 1914 and 1928 in New York, and one in New Jersey, the Frederick Douglass Film Company. Of these, half were involved exclusively in newsreel production (Haynes Photoplay Company, Toussaint Motion Picture Exchange/Whipper Reel Negro News, the Downing Film Company, BEJAC Film Company, Douglass). Of the remaining companies, three made fiction films (Seminole Film Producing, Colored Feature Photoplay, Inc., and Paragon Pictures Corporation), and one never produced a film (the Eureka Film Co., Inc.). Little is known about most of the films released by the companies; however, Paragon's *The Crimson Fog* (1928) starred well-known actors Inez Clough and Lawrence Chenault, suggesting that the company enjoyed access to many of the same performers as the larger firms.[12]

In Chicago, Peter Jones established the Peter P. Jones Photoplay Company in 1914 before moving to Harlem in 1922 (where he founded Seminole); the Unique Film Company was established in 1916 and made one film, *Shadowed by the Devil* (1916), before going out of business; and the Royal Gardens Motion Picture Company was founded in 1919 by a former Ebony Film Company actor, Sam T. Jacks, and made one film, *In the Depths of Our Hearts* (1919) (Sampson 1995, 188). Elsewhere, companies appeared in Los Angeles (Booker T. Film Company, est. 1921, and the Rosebud Film Corporation, est. 1927), Massachusetts (Peacock Photoplay, est. 1921), St Louis (the Eagle Film Company, est. 1922), Kansas City (the Western Picture Producing Company, est. 1922), and Washington, DC (Monumental Pictures Corporation, est. 1921). The dates of the various companies suggest that 1920–1922 was the high point in race film production, with only some of the larger companies, like Micheaux, producing throughout the decade, especially once the industry transitioned to sound after 1927.

Judging from what little evidence exists, there were fewer white-controlled race film companies established during the early part of the 1920s, suggesting that the rapidly professionalizing mainstream industry held greater appeal and profit potential for white entrepreneurs looking to make films (though a number of small companies continued making films in the New York area, using the facilities left behind by larger filmmaking concerns). It also highlights the persistence of the industry's discriminatory practices, which disallowed black technical personnel or performers from achieving any positions of power in Hollywood.

In addition to the firms already discussed, most of the white independent production companies, like the black-owned companies, were located around the country. Some white companies, such as the Al Bartlett Film Manufacturing Company of Atlanta (est. 1913), the Ebony Film Corporation of Chicago (est. 1917), and the Harris Dickson Film Company of Mississippi (est. 1921), made comedies with subject matter drawn from popular vaudeville scenarios or, as in the last example, from a series of popular *Saturday Evening Post* plantation stories (Sampson 1995, 212). Others, like the Democracy Film Corporation of Los Angeles (est. 1917) and the Dunbar Film Corporation of New York (est. 1928), produced dramas, many of which were uplift narratives and featured accomplished and intelligent protagonists. The Democracy Film Corporation, for example, released *Injustice* in 1919, a controversial film that was advertised as an answer to Dixon's *The Clansman*. Also, the Dunbar Film Corporation, who employed Oscar Micheaux's brother Swan Micheaux as its vice president, successfully released the detective film *Midnight Ace* (1928) before going out of business.[13]

While the race film industry experienced a number of changes during the late teens through the mid-1920s, the mainstream American film industry was taking the shape that it still retains. From the early teens onward many Eastern companies began moving west – following the lead of the Selig Polyscope Film Company, the Christie Film Company, Carl Laemmle's Independent Moving Picture Company (IMP), and others – lured by the promise of fine weather, cheap land, and a continent's distance away from the East Coast's restrictive business practices (for example, those practiced by the Motion Picture Patents Company). By the mid-1920s most of the major film studios were established on the West Coast, with Warner Bros., Paramount (formerly Famous Players-Lasky), RKO (formerly Mutual Film Corporation), Metro-Goldwyn-Mayer (formerly Louis B. Mayer Picture and Metro Pictures), and Fox Film Corporation making up the "big five" studios. Minor studios included Columbia Pictures, United Artists, and Universal Studios, the largest among numerous smaller producers.

Even though the West Coast studios developed into a modern, vertically integrated, profit-making industry, they continued to rely on a number of conventions from film's earliest Eastern iterations, including a narrative focus on melodrama and comedy and a practice of typecasting by race, ethnicity, and gender. During the 1920s, as noted, there was little or no hope for African-American technical personnel seeking jobs in Hollywood; the industry remained as segregated as it was on the East Coast. Roles in front of the camera promised little more and often took the form of uncredited bit parts as domestic help or other background players (such as slaves in plantation dramas as *In Old Kentucky* or *Topsy and Eva*, both from 1927). The use of blackface decreased onscreen during the later silent era, as did the more demeaning types (the sexualized brutes, for instance) of Griffith's *The Birth of a Nation*, but no new images filled the gap, and there remained few opportunities for African-American dramatic performers to sustain a career in Hollywood. Actors such as Evelyn Preer and Charles Gilpin, stars of the black stage and screen, were virtually invisible in Hollywood productions; Preer appeared in very small roles in early sound films and Gilpin was fired from Universal's version of *Uncle Tom's Cabin* in 1927 for being uncooperative.[14] Lawrence Chenault, perhaps the most ubiquitous male star of race films, never appeared in a major studio release.

The performers who managed to work regularly during the 1920s did so either by playing a number of different ethnicities rather than African-American characters or by accepting variations of the same stereotypes drawn from vaudeville and the early screen. In the former category is Noble Johnson, founder and president of the Lincoln Motion Picture Company, who enjoyed a Hollywood career that spanned from 1915 to 1950 (and who used his Hollywood earnings to support Lincoln, as noted). Johnson was a versatile character actor who played a variety of roles in Hollywood film, though few of them were identifiably "black." Instead, the light-skinned Johnson was cast in brown-skinned or exotic roles, playing Native Americans, Asians, and Pacific Islanders in a number of prestige pictures, including Rex Ingram's *The Four Men of the Apocalypse* (1921), Cecil B. DeMille's *The Ten Commandments* (1923) and *The King of Kings* (1927), and Raoul Walsh's *The Thief of Bagdad* (1924). Throughout this time, the black press functioned as boosters, overlooking the racial mismarking and reading Johnson's work experiences as a sign of black achievement.

More often than not, however, black performers were expected to play roles of the pickaninny or the comic buffoon. Donald Bogle argues, for example, that the most visible black performers in Hollywood during the early 1920s were children associated with the "Our Gang" series, including Ernest Morrison (Sunshine Sammy), Eugene Jackson (Pineapple), Billie Thomas (Buckwheat), Allen Clayton Hoskins (Farina), and Matthew Beard (Stymie) (2006, 41). Of these performers, Ernest Morrison has the distinction of being one of the first black actors to sign with a studio (Hal Roach in 1919). In his early work with the studio, Morrison acted as sidekick to comedians Harold Lloyd and Sam Pollard, most famously in *Haunted Spooks* (1920) as a flour-covered pickaninny opposite Lloyd. In 1921 Morrison was cast as the lead in *The Pickaninny*, the first in a planned series of short films featuring his Sunshine Sammy character. The series never materialized because exhibitors informed Roach "that mainstream theatres would not show shorts featuring a colored star" (Bogle 2006, 33). Morrison's role in the "Our Gang" series followed the next year, in which he played the only black child amidst an ensemble cast of children (though Allen "Farina" Hoskins was soon added to the mix). Morrison left the series in 1924 and was replaced by a succession of black child actors playing similar roles. He later returned to the screen in the "East Side Kids" series.

These examples suggest that the more satisfying, though less lucrative, roles for African-American actors and comedians tended to be in the race film industry. Most of the major producers, including Lincoln, Micheaux, and the Colored Players, drew from established theatrical troupes for their players, and many launched the relatively long careers of actors in race films; for example, Lawrence Chenault, a Lafayette Player, appeared in race film productions for virtually all the major companies, including Norman, Micheaux, and the Colored Players, and continued working with Micheaux after the transition to sound. And Evelyn Preer, as noted, had a much more successful career with Micheaux than she ever experienced during her short stay in Hollywood. However, the practice of casting dramatic performers, along with the types of roles available to them, would change, like much of the race film industry, with the transition to sound in 1927.

The End: The Coming of Sound

The release of *The Jazz Singer* in 1927 marked an important and strange moment in American film history, one that underscores the *Fort/Da* relationship that Hollywood has had with African-Americans throughout its history. On the one hand, when popular vaudevillian Al Jolson performed, in blackface, the first few spoken words in a feature-length film, he transferred the nation's almost naturalized minstrel aesthetic from silent to sound film. On the other hand, the film launched a new moment in African-American participation in the industry as blackface Jolsons, Eddie Cantors, and other white stage performers translated a variety of new African-American performative modes, especially jazz, to audiences. It wasn't long before Hollywood started casting black singers and dancers; the new sound technology, it was believed, was especially well suited for black voices.[15] Popular cabaret performers like Bessie Smith and Ethel Waters were cast in musical intervals within longer narratives or in the all-black musicals, such as *Hearts in Dixie* (1929) and *Hallelujah!* (1929), released by studios at the end of the decade. The Hollywood vogue for African-American performers was relatively short-lived, however, and soon the demeaning roles – domestics (the mammy of Louise Beavers), comic buffoons (Stepin Fetchit), or "atmospheric furniture" (Cripps 1993, 127) – again became the norm.

What may have been an opportunity for performers such as Waters, Nina Mae McKinney, Noble Sissle, and Eubie Blake, among others, was initially devastating for the race film industry. Many companies were undercapitalized and lacked the financial resources to adapt to sound filmmaking. Likewise, theaters that catered to black patrons, sometimes the only venue for race films, could not afford to equip their facilities with sound equipment. African-American audiences, as mentioned, were historically drawn to Hollywood's production values, and sound film made the difference in quality all the more obvious. That they could see big-name African-American performers in featured roles – at least in black-cast musicals – was an added bonus. All of these factors, coupled with the fact that many race film stars, such as Evelyn Preer, Spencer Williams, and Clarence Brooks, were drawn to Hollywood's higher pay and superior sound and image, put all production companies, but especially those that were black-owned (which were often in an even more financially precarious position), at an even greater disadvantage. By the late 1920s, most black-owned companies, with the exception of Oscar Micheaux's, had gone out of business, and Micheaux only survived by declaring bankruptcy in early 1928 and reorganizing in 1929 as the Micheaux Film Corporation, with money from (white) theater owners and managers Leo Brecher and Frank Schiffman.[16]

In addition to Micheaux's newly organized company, a few other production companies appeared on the periphery of the larger industry, mostly in New York and Los Angeles, and all of them showed the demands that sound had placed on the industry. First, they were all composed of mixed-race personnel, with whites serving in financial and technical roles behind the cameras while the black talent largely remained in front, with some, nevertheless, in powerful positions. In the 1930s and 1940s, for example, Ralph Cooper, Herb Jeffries, and Spencer Williams would remain influential in their respective companies.[17] Second, most companies switched from explicit uplift content and started producing popular genre films – gangster films, musicals, sports films, and Westerns – in order to more effectively and directly compete with Hollywood. At the end of the decade, and with the advent of sound, race cinema's more reformist phase passed, and a new industry emerged.

Notes

1. *The Birth of a Nation* was based on two novels written by Thomas Dixon, Jr, *The Leopard's Spots* (1902) and *The Clansman* (1905), the latter of which was adapted into a stage play before being made into the film.
2. The number of silent film versions of Harriet Beecher Stowe's *Uncle Tom's Cabin* resulted from the novel's massive readership (in serial or novel form) and the popularity of traveling stage adaptations ("Tom shows"). In almost all the silent adaptations, a white actor in blackface was cast as Uncle Tom. It wasn't until 1914 that the story was adapted to the screen with a black stage actor, Sam Lucas, in the role of Uncle Tom. And no version, including the 1927 *Uncle Tom's Cabin*, ever featured an African-American performer in the part of Topsy.
3. The Pekin Players were formed in Chicago in 1906. They staged serious plays along with "refined white comedies," which included actors in whiteface (Haskins, quoted in Curtis 1998, 41).
4. The company's marketing practices, which geared different advertising toward different audiences, may not have helped *One Large Evening*. According to Thomas Cripps, the film was called *One Large Evening* "in the ghetto and *A Night in Coontown* in white exhibition houses," a change that was noted by Lester Walton in the *New York Age* in his discussion of the Chicago Censorship Board's decision not to show the film (Cripps 1993, 42; see also Walton 1914).
5. Haynes's appeal appeared in the *Indianapolis Freeman* on March 14, 1914.
6. Phillips Smalley was married to Lois Weber, an early American filmmaker, who often produced shorts with reformist themes.
7. Micheaux's novels include *The Conquest* (1913), *The Homesteader* (1917), and *The Forged Note* (1918), among others.
8. For more on this subject, see also Gaines 2001; Stewart 2005, 226–244; and Massood 2003, 47–57.
9. The Ebony Film Corporation was based in Chicago and operated 1916–1919. It produced two-reel comedy films featuring a black detective character. According to Sampson, the films were "well-received in white theaters," perhaps because of their use of demeaning stereotypes of foolish blacks, and "were heavily criticized by the black press in Chicago" for the same reasons (1995, 204).
10. However, Micheaux's correspondence with Norman suggests that he wasn't fond of Starkman. For more on their rivalry, see Klotman 2001.
11. See also Gaines 1997.
12. Clough was a popular stage and screen performer, who had appeared in Reol's *Ties of Blood* (1921), *The Simp* (1921), *The Secret Sorrow* (1921), and *Easy Money* (1922), as well as Micheaux's *The Gunsaulus Mystery* (1921). She also appeared in numerous Broadway productions, including *Three Plays for a Negro Theater* (1917), *The Chocolate Dandies* (1924), and *Harlem* (1928), among other productions.
13. Swan Micheaux was employed as the secretary-treasurer of the Micheaux Book and Film Company until 1927, when he left after one too many disagreements with his older brother (McGilligan 2007, 230).
14. The reasons behind Gilpin's dismissal remain unclear. Universal cited Gilpin's demanding stage schedule, while rumors also circulated suggesting that the studio felt he was too "aggressive" for the role (Cripps 1993, 159).
15. This view was popular among both white and black cultural critics. One of the strongest voices of African-American aesthetics in the 1920s, Alain Locke, for example, commented on the almost natural synergy between sound film and black voices in which sound technology had the potential to reveal the "realism" of African-American culture rather than the "hackneyed caricatures" of motion picture representation (Locke & Brown 1975, 26).
16. According to Patrick McGilligan, the pair "controlled Harlem's five largest theaters [Odeon, the Roosevelt, the Douglas, the Lafayette, and the Renaissance theaters], offering movies and live entertainment to a combined capacity of 6,700 people (2007, 256). While the partnership with Micheaux didn't last long, it guaranteed, in the short term, exhibition spaces for his films.
17. Cooper, former emcee of the Apollo Theater, along with George Randol, founded Cooper-Randol Pictures in 1937. The company faced financial difficulties while making their first film, *Dark Manhattan* (1937), and joined with producers Jack and Bert Goldberg's Million Dollar Productions. Popular singer Herb Jeffries worked with Sack Amusement Enterprises to produce a series of Westerns in the late 1930s. Spencer Williams directed a number of popular race films in the 1940s.

References

Berry, S. Torriano, with Berry, Venise T. (2001). *The 50 Most Influential Black Films: A Celebration of African-American Talent, Determination, and Creativity*. New York: Citadel Press.

Bogle, Donald. (2006). *Bright Boulevards, Bold Dreams: The Story of Black Hollywood*. New York: One World/Ballantine Books.

Cripps, Thomas. (1993). *Slow Fade to Black: The Negro in American Film, 1900–1942*. New York: Oxford University Press.

Cripps, Thomas. (1997). "'Race Movies' as Voices of the Black Bourgeoisie: *The Scar of Shame*." In Valerie Smith (ed.), *Representing Blackness: Issues in Film and Video* (pp. 47–60). New Brunswick: Rutgers University Press.

Curtis, Susan. (1998). *The First Black Actors on the Great White Way*. Columbia: University of Mississippi Press.

Everett, Anna. (2001). *Returning the Gaze: A Genealogy of Black Film Criticism, 1909–1949*. Durham, NC: Duke University Press.

Gaines, Jane. (1997). "*The Scar of Shame*: Skin Color and Caste in Black Silent Melodrama." In Valerie Smith (ed.), *Representing Blackness: Issues in Film and Video* (pp. 61–82). New Brunswick: Rutgers University Press.

Gaines, Jane. (2001). *Fire & Desire: Mixed-Race Movies in the Silent Era*. Chicago: University of Chicago Press.

Klotman, Phyllis. (2001). "Planes, Trains, and Automobiles: *The Flying Ace*, the Norman Company, and the Micheaux Connection." In Pearl Bowser, Jane Gaines, & Charles Musser (eds), *Oscar Micheaux and His Circle: African-American Filmmaking and Race Cinema of the Silent Era* (pp. 161–177). Bloomington: Indiana University Press.

Lang, Robert. (1994). "Biographical Sketch." In Robert Lang (ed.), *The Birth of a Nation* (pp. 25–33). New Brunswick: Rutgers University Press.

Locke, Alain, & Brown, Sterling. (1975). "Folk Values in a New Medium." In Lindsay Patterson (ed.), *Black Films and Filmmakers* (pp. 25–29). New York: Dodd Mead & Company.

McGilligan, Patrick. (2007). *Oscar Micheaux: The Great and Only*. New York: Harper Perennial.

Massood, Paula J. (2003). *Black City Cinema: African American Urban Experiences in Film*. Philadelphia: Temple University Press.

Musser, Charles. (2001). "Colored Players Film Corporation: An Alternative to Micheaux." In Pearl Bowser, Jane Gaines, & Charles Musser (eds), *Oscar Micheaux and His Circle: African-American Filmmaking and Race Cinema of the Silent Era* (pp. 178–187). Bloomington: Indiana University Press.

Petersen, Christina. (2008). "The 'Reol' Story: Race Authorship and Consciousness in Robert Levy's Reol Productions, 1921–1926." *Film History*, 20.3, 308–324.

Rogin, Michael. (1994). "'The Sword Became a Flashing Vision': D. W. Griffith's *The Birth of a Nation*." In Robert Lang (ed.), *The Birth of a Nation* (pp. 250–293). New Brunswick: Rutgers University Press.

Sampson, Henry T. (1995). *Blacks and Black and White: A Source Book on Black Films*. 2nd edn. Lanham, MD: Scarecrow Press.

Stewart, Jacqueline Najuma. (2005). *Migrating to the Movies: Cinema and Black Urban Modernity*. Berkeley: University of California Press.

Walton, Lester. (1914). "Chicago Censor Board Rejects *One Large Evening*." *New York Age*, April 23, 6.

5

Chaplin and Silent Film Comedy

Charles J. Maland
Professor, University of Tennessee, United States

Perhaps no genre is more closely associated with the silent era than **comedy**. Charles J. Maland surveys the work and careers of its three most important practitioners – **Charlie Chaplin**, **Harold Lloyd**, and **Buster Keaton**. Each, in his own way, stabilized the genre in its passage from the antic chaos of **Mack Sennett** to complex narratives built around a single persona. Maland outlines the apprenticeship period for each comic **auteur**, illustrating how the defining and now recognizable **persona** of each was the product of sustained refinement. Maland's essay also suggests the expansive appetite for comedy during the 1920s, with tastes diverse enough to embrace **Chaplin's tramp**, **Lloyd's middle-class man in the glasses**, and **Keaton's stoic everyman**. Maland pays close attention to production conditions and the degree to which changes in the industry, most notably the coming of sound, shaped the careers of these three seminal figures. His essay shares ground with Gaylyn Studlar on Stroheim/DeMille and Mark Lynn Anderson on the star system in this volume, and with Victoria Sturtevant on Mary Pickford in the hardcover/online edition.

Additional terms, names, and concepts: Keystone Studios, United Artists, First National Exhibitors' Circuit, Hal Roach, Roscoe "Fatty" Arbuckle

On May 12, 1913, Keystone movie producer Mack Sennett sent a telegram to Alf Reeves, the manager of a touring British music hall company, performing at the Nixon Theater in Philadelphia. It read: "IS THERE A MAN NAMED CHAFFIN IN YOUR COMPANY OR SOMETHING LIKE THAT STOP IF SO WILL HE COMMUNICATE WITH KESSEL AND BAUMAN 24 LONGACRE BUILDING BROADWAY NEW YORK." Reeves showed the telegram to a featured comedian, Charles Chaplin, whom Sennett, although he had forgotten the name, had seen perform at the American Music Hall in 1911. Chaplin had no experience in the movies but agreed to try after Sennett offered him $150 weekly – twice his music hall salary (Chaplin 1964, 137–139).

American Film History: Selected Readings, Origins to 1960, First Edition. Edited by Cynthia Lucia, Roy Grundmann, and Art Simon.
© 2016 John Wiley & Sons, Inc. Published 2016 by John Wiley & Sons, Inc.

It was a fortunate choice. Chaplin arrived unheralded at Keystone in December 1913, but within two years his movie character – the tramp, or Charlie – was enormously popular, and the contours of American silent film comedy were beginning to be sketched out. From that point until the talkies arrived, silent film comedies, particularly those revolving around a central comic persona, became one of the most popular film genres in the movie business.

This chapter examines the flowering of silent film comedy from Chaplin's arrival at Keystone through a pinnacle of silent film comedy – Chaplin's *City Lights*, which appeared in 1931, well after the talkies were established. This chapter also examines Chaplin's career, as well as the careers of Buster Keaton and Harold Lloyd – including the films and the comic personas they developed through a body of films.

During this era the most famous and accomplished of the film comedians – Chaplin, Lloyd, and Keaton, all of whom had roots in the music hall, the stage, or vaudeville – began making one- or two-reel comic shorts and then gradually moved to feature-length narratives. Through his tramp comedies from 1914 on, Chaplin was a central figure in establishing the boundaries, conventions, and narrative structure of silent film persona comedy. Yet once those narrative conventions in Chaplin's film comedies were being employed by other filmmakers, Lloyd and Keaton also created their own distinctive characters and made their own singular marks on silent film comedy.

Of course, film comedies were not invented by Keystone and Chaplin. One of the very first movies made by the Lumière Brothers in 1895, a one-shot classic called *L'Arroseur arrosé* (*The Waterer Watered*), showed an impish boy stepping on the water hose and then stepping off when a perplexed gardener looks at the end of the hose. As narrative began to expand in the movies between 1903 and 1907, comedies became more popular: Eileen Bowser has estimated that before 1908, 70 percent or more of fiction films were comedies (1990, 178–179). However, the industry's push around 1908–1909 to attract a larger middle-class audience, in part by making movies "respectable," led to a temporary decline in production of film comedy: Kalton Lahue opens his study of silent-era comic shorts by writing, "In 1910 the American silent motion picture comedy was in a sorry state" (1966, 3).

Mack Sennett, Chaplin's first boss, was a key figure in reinvigorating comedy when, in 1912, he left Biograph to establish Keystone Studios, though he did so not by producing movies that appealed to genteel viewers but, rather, by making those that mocked respectability. Born of Canadian parents both of Irish descent in 1880, Sennett moved to Connecticut in 1897 and worked as an iron mill boilermaker before making his way to New York at age 20. There he appeared briefly in burlesque and on Broadway before acting and directing at Biograph from 1908 on. After his Biograph apprenticeship, Sennett moved to Keystone and began specializing in irreverent comedies that quickly became popular. By April 1913, the Keystone Cops – soon to be a Keystone trademark – appeared for the first time in *The Bangville Police*. Sennett headed Keystone until 1917, when he established Mack Sennett Comedies, a company he maintained through the silent era. Over the span of his career, Sennett hired many who became popular film comedians in the 1910s and 1920s, including not only Chaplin, Lloyd, Roscoe "Fatty" Arbuckle, and Harry Langdon but also Mabel Normand, Chester Conklin, Mack Swain, Ben Turpin, and Oliver Hardy. Although they may have started with Sennett, many of these performers parlayed their popularity into higher salaries and, often, greater creative control at other studios.

A 2009 study of Keystone argues that the studio played an important cultural role during its half-decade of existence: Although the movie industry was seeking respectability to expand its middle-class audience when Sennett established the studio in 1912, "Keystone's filmmakers unabashedly rejected such refinements, reviving 'low' traditions of broad slapstick derived from the popular culture of America's workers" (King 2009, 2). Keystone comedies often mocked authority figures and made respectable citizens the butt of humor. Predictably, genteel elites often criticized the Keystones as vulgar and beneath serious attention, even as the films drew large and appreciative urban audiences, many of whom were working-class and/or immigrant patrons.

The genteel culture these films so enthusiastically mocked, however, was itself in the midst of crumbling, as cultural historians like Henry May have demonstrated – a crumbling to which silent comedy in the 1910s probably contributed. As the studio system began to establish itself, as more movie palaces began to be built, and as American society became more urban and consumer-oriented in the 1920s, film historians have demonstrated that the middle-class portion of the movie audience did indeed grow (Sklar 1994; Ross 1998). As it did, the shape of American film comedy evolved from comedy centering on slapstick in one- and two-reel shorts to feature-film comedy that blended slapstick with other forms of comedy and more conventional modes of sustained feature-film storytelling. And Charlie Chaplin, Buster Keaton, and Harold Lloyd played key roles in the establishment and evolution of American silent film comedy.

The Tramp and Chaplin's Rise to Stardom

Appropriately, Chaplin (1889–1977) got his start at Keystone. Born Charles Spencer Chaplin in London to two English music hall singers, Chaplin endured a short, unstable, and troubled childhood. After his parents separated, his mother lost her singing voice and his father died of alcoholism. At age 10, Chaplin was already working as a professional entertainer, and, by 1908, he signed on as a pantomime comedian for a Fred Karno music hall troupe, where he became a featured comedian in skits like "The Inebriate." He toured with Karno in US and Canadian vaudeville houses in 1910–1911, when Sennett first saw him, then again in 1912–1913, when he accepted the Keystone offer.

When Chaplin arrived at the studio in late 1913, Keystone employees were working at a furious pace, each unit turning out approximately one comedy a week. Chaplin began working at that pace, appearing in 36 films between *Making a Living* (February 1914) and *His Prehistoric Past* (December 1914). By the time of his second film, *Kid Auto Races at Venice*, Chaplin had already cobbled together his trademark tramp costume – tight coat, baggy pants, floppy shoes, narrow brush moustache, derby hat, and cane. Chaplin argued with Sennett, however, that he wanted to develop his tramp character with more complexity than was possible in the midst of Keystone frenzy; by his twelfth film, *Caught in a Cabaret*, he had persuaded Sennett to allow him to codirect with female lead Mabel Normand. From then on he codirected or directed 20 of his last 23 films at Keystone. In most of the films, Chaplin honed his tramp persona, with the costume that was clearly becoming a trademark: In the last Keystone film, *His Prehistoric Past*, Chaplin sported his derby and cane but wore only caveman's skins, suggesting that his face, derby, and cane were recognizable enough to audiences to identify his character.

As 1914 waned, the popularity of Chaplin and his tramp waxed, and Chaplin's career trajectory established a paradigm that Lloyd and Keaton, to a greater or lesser extent, would follow later in the decade and into the 1920s: Because his films were so popular, Chaplin was able to negotiate increasingly favorable contracts with higher salaries and greater creative control. As he gained more control, Chaplin surrounded himself with a stable group of collaborators like cinematographer Rollie Totheroh and actors Edna Purviance and Eric Campbell, who worked with him efficiently from film to film. As his popularity and aesthetic aspirations grew (and as the studio system and the conventions of classical Hollywood narrative became more firmly established), Chaplin was able to work at a slower pace, and his films expanded from one-reelers to two-reelers and eventually to feature-length films. More than any of the other silent film comedians – Lloyd is the only filmmaker who later approached Chaplin's degree of creative and financial independence – Chaplin came to control his art and means of production by directing and writing all of his films. Eventually building his own movie studio and distributing his films through United Artists, a company he coestablished with director D. W. Griffith and actors Mary Pickford and Douglas Fairbanks, Chaplin liberated himself from the whims of movie executives.

The rise to fame was stunning. In 1915, Chaplin signed with Essanay at a salary of $1,250 a week, plus a $10,000 signing bonus: That year he made 14 two-reeler films. After the first seven were released within three months, Chaplin slowed his working pace and devoted about a month to each of the last seven films, two of which, *The Tramp* and *The Bank*, broadened his comic narrative to include a romance with the Edna Purviance character and to evoke a feeling of pathos for the tramp when the romance seemed to have failed. The craze for Chaplin films and the tramp character that year became so pronounced that Charles McGuirk (1915) suggested that the country had a case of "Chaplinitis."

From Essanay, Chaplin moved on to Mutual, where he signed for a salary of $10,000 a week and a $150,000 bonus to make 12 two-reelers, all released between May 1916 and October 1917. The Mutual films include *One A.M.* (1916), which drew on the drunken music hall routine Chaplin made famous with Karno. In it, the Charlie character comes home drunk at night and tries to make it to the second floor of his home, and then into an uncooperative Murphy bed to get some sleep. Chaplin also further refined his Charlie character and honed his blend of comedy, romance, and pathos in memorable films like *The Vagabond* (1916), *Easy Street* (1917), and *The Immigrant* (1917). He later recalled this creative and productive stretch as "the happiest period of my career" (1964, 188).

The Mutual films proved so popular that other companies again clamored for Chaplin's services when his contract was about to expire, and in early 1918, Chaplin signed with First National Exhibitors' Circuit. The contract called for him to make eight two-reel comedies for a million dollars, granting him complete creative control. First National paid Chaplin a $75,000 signing bonus and advanced $125,000 for each two-reel film to cover salary and production costs. First National paid for prints and advertising, and their distribution fee was 30 percent of the total rentals. First National and Chaplin divided the remaining net profits, and after five years, the rights to the films reverted to Chaplin (Vance 2003, 85). His fortune growing, Chaplin decided to build his own movie studio on four acres of land near Sunset Boulevard and Du Longpre Avenue in Hollywood. Early in 1919, as noted, he joined with Mary Pickford, Douglas Fairbanks, and D. W. Griffith to establish United Artists (UA), a distribution company that would release their independently produced films. All of Chaplin's films from *A Woman of Paris* (1923) through *Limelight* (1952) were released through UA.

Although he had hoped to honor his First National contract in a year or two, Chaplin began working even more slowly as he became drawn to longer films. Of the eight films he made for First National, some – like *The Idle Class* (1921) – were two-reelers. Some, however, were longer, including his World War I comedy, *Shoulder Arms* (1918, three reels); his satire on small towns and religion, *The Pilgrim* (1922, nearly four reels); and most notably, *The Kid* (1921, five reels), described by the opening title as "A picture with a smile – and perhaps, a tear." The story of the poor but kind-hearted Charlie raising a son (Jackie Coogan) who had been abandoned at birth engrossed audiences in 1921 and garnered ecstatic reviews. In *New Republic* Francis Hackett called the film a "triumph" and added that Chaplin's "wisdom, his sincerity, his integrity ... should go some way to revolutionize motion picture production in this country. From an industry *The Kid* raises production to an art" (1921, 137). Similar reviews and impressive box office receipts encouraged Chaplin to move completely into feature films once he began making his United Artists films late in 1922.

Between his first appearance at Keystone in 1914 and the last of his First National films in 1923, Chaplin's tramp character evolved, although one constant feature was his working-class or marginalized social position. Sometimes the tramp has no visible means of support, as in *The Vagabond* (1916), but often he has a working-class job – as a baker in *Dough and Dynamite* (1914), a custodian in *The Bank* (1915), and a waiter in *The Rink* (1916). In the early Keystone films the tramp tends to be meaner and more disruptive, drawing from the studio ethos encouraged, and even cultivated, by Sennett. In *Mabel at the Wheel* (1914), for example, he sticks a pin into Mabel's thigh. As a dentist's handyman in *Laughing Gas* (1914), he hits a patient in the mouth with a brick, knocking out a mouthful of teeth. Responding, in part, to negative reaction to such "vulgarity" from genteel quarters, Chaplin softened the tramp's mean streak when he began experimenting with romance and pathos in the Essanay and Mutual films. The focus on romance and pathos became more prominent as he moved toward feature films, culminating in *City Lights* (1931).

Another interesting shift occurs in *The Idle Class*, in which Chaplin plays two roles: the tramp and an elegant but unhappy member of the upper class. This duality is interesting in part because of Chaplin's own unusual class position: During the unstable years of his early childhood, he experienced first-hand both genuine poverty and the strains of a marginalized social life. Once established in the entertainment world, he found his way out of financial destitution, however, and his rapid rise to stardom in the middle 1910s led Chaplin to such celebrity status that it became impossible for him to lead a normal middle-class life. Although an obsessive worker when in the midst of a film production, Chaplin interacted more often with social and economic elites from the early 1920s on, and *The Idle Class* provided him one opportunity to look at the two extremes of the economic spectrum. While Chaplin would not always play both roles, the feature-length films that he wrote and directed commonly included both the tramp and an antagonist who was wealthy and powerful, including the ringmaster in *The Circus* (1928), the millionaire in *City Lights*, the factory owner in *Modern Times* (1936), and Hynkel in *The Great Dictator* (1940). The roots of this evolution can be traced back to films like *The Idle Class*.

Chaplin's first United Artists feature was *A Woman of Paris* (1923), a melodrama that he wrote and directed but did not star in. The film featured Edna Purviance and, while it may have enhanced Chaplin's reputation as a director, it did not do particularly well at the box office, prompting him to return to the tramp and to comedy. His next two feature comedies starred the tramp before talkies came to dominate the film industry: *The Gold Rush* (1925), in which the tramp goes to the Klondike in 1898 to seek his fortune, and *The Circus*, in which he gets work in a circus while falling in love with a beautiful woman who does a bareback horse-riding routine. *The Gold Rush* was the most expensive comedy made up to that time – its budget exceeded $920,000 – yet it eventually brought in over $6 million and was second only to *The Big Parade* as the highest-grossing film of 1925 (Robinson 1985, 358).

The Gold Rush solidified the conventions of a Chaplin feature-length comedy: (1) Charlie as working-class or marginalized protagonist; (2) a female lead that attracts Charlie's ardor (here Georgia – played by Georgia Hale); (3) effective comic pantomime, as in the Thanksgiving shoe dinner with Big Jim (Mack Swain) and the New Year's Eve Dance of the Rolls sequence; (4) the use of pathos, as when Charlie, alone, stares longingly into the Monte Carlo Dance Hall on New Year's Eve; and (5) antagonists (here, natural forces like snowstorms and characters like Black Larsen and Jack) that make it difficult for Charlie to achieve his goals. Although none of Chaplin's peers, except perhaps Harry Langdon, so consciously aimed for pathos in their films, the other Chaplin conventions worked their way into many of the feature-length comedies of Lloyd and Keaton.

In *The Circus* the vagabond Charlie finds work at a circus run by a cruel ringmaster (Allen Garcia). The ringmaster's daughter Merna (Merna Kennedy), a bareback rider, and Rex (Harry Crocker), a tightrope walker, are his two star performers. Infatuated with Merna, Charlie mistakenly comes to believe that she loves him rather than Rex, the true object of her affection. By accident Charlie becomes a successful clown in the troupe, and one of the film's climactic comic scenes comes when Charlie tries to impress Merna and show up Rex by doing a tightrope walk himself, which becomes funnier (and more suspenseful) when monkeys start climbing all over him. Yet Charlie eventually realizes that Merna loves and will marry Rex, and in the final melancholy scene, the circus wagons drive off to their next destination without Charlie, who shuffles away from the camera in the opposite direction, shoulders slumped, until he shakes his body and walks on, reinvigorated, with an air of resilience. Chaplin had to interrupt the production for about eight months at the start of 1927 because of tax problems and divorce proceedings filed by his wife Lita Grey; his associations with the film were apparently so unpleasant that he hardly mentions the movie in his autobiography. Nevertheless, it is another fine example of a silent film comic feature, with the tightrope/monkey scene and the scene of Charlie imitating a mechanical comic figure outside the funhouse among the film's most hilarious, while the scene in which he overhears Merna say that she's in love with Rex, not Charlie, provides a powerful moment of pathos. As the film was nearing release, Chaplin began work on *City Lights*, to which we shall return at the end of this essay.

From Willie Work to the Glasses Character: Harold Lloyd

Chaplin's remarkable success from 1914 on cast a long shadow on comic filmmaking and set a high bar for competing comedians. About the time Chaplin signed his Essanay contract and began making films for them in 1915, film comics made up to look like the tramp figure began to appear, with Billy Ritchie and Billy West two of the most prominent (Lahue 1966, 55–56, 102–108). Although neither enjoyed great success as a Chaplin look-alike, another actor who started out his career as a film comedian by imitating Chaplin later achieved major stardom through a distinctively different character. The actor was Harold Lloyd.

Figure 5.1 In *The Circus* (1928, director and producer Charlie Chaplin), Charlie, despondent, overhears that the bareback rider Merna is in love with Rex.

Lloyd (1893–1971), unlike Chaplin or Keaton, never achieved acclaim as a comedian in vaudeville or the music hall before entering the movies. Born in Burchard, Nebraska, Lloyd was early drawn to the stage and even got an occasional small part in plays after his family moved to Omaha in 1906, where Lloyd met an actor named John Lane Connor. In 1911, Lloyd moved with his father to San Diego, where Connor had established a dramatic school, and immersed himself in theater activities while he finished high school (Merton 2007, 18). After moving with his father to Los Angeles, Lloyd tried to get into the movies and scraped along as an occasional extra at Universal and Keystone. During this period he met and befriended another extra named Hal Roach.

Roach, who aspired to be a producer, thought that Lloyd showed some promise as a film comic. They first worked together in 1914, after Roach hired Lloyd, who created a short-lived character named Willie Work, but the venture failed when Pathé canceled its distributor contract after seeing several films and not finding them funny. Going their separate ways, the pair reunited in 1915, when Roach offered Lloyd $50 a week to act in comic shorts. This time Lloyd created a character named Lonesome Luke that made Lloyd, indirectly at least, just one more of the many Chaplin imitators. As Lloyd put it in his autobiography, *An American Comedy*, "Chaplin was going great guns, his success such that unless you wore funny clothes and otherwise aped him you were not a comedian. Exhibitors who could not get the original demanded imitations" (1928, 91). Lloyd tried to reverse Charlie's costume: "All his clothes were too large, mine all too small. My shoes were funny, but different; my mustache funny, but different" (1928, 92). For the next two years, Lloyd served his apprenticeship in comedy, working furiously: From July 1915, when Chaplin was making his Mutual films, to December 1917, Lloyd appeared in 54 Lonesome Luke one-reelers and 14 two-reelers. At a time when Chaplin was making a two-reeler every five or six weeks, Lloyd was churning out a reel a week through January 1916, then a one-reeler every week or 10 days. In some ways, the Lonesome Luke films resemble Chaplin's films at Keystone – as Roach told an interviewer, he would take Harold, a girl, and perhaps a policeman to a setting like a park, then improvise a story, climaxing with a chase (Vance et al. 2002, 23). The films were modestly successful at a time when exhibitors were desperate for Chaplin comedies (or, failing that, films with Chaplin imitators), and Lloyd recalls getting his salary up to $100 a week – Chaplin, at the time, was earning $10,000 weekly.

Fortunately for Lloyd, he began to feel that he had taken Lonesome Luke as far as he could. Around September 1917 he tried out a new character with eyeglasses as a trademark that would "At the same time suggest the character – quiet, normal, boyish, clean, sympathetic, not impossible to romance" (Lloyd 1928, 102). This "Glasses" character – sometimes just called "the boy," sometimes Harold – first appeared in *Over the Fence* (September 1917), and for several months Lloyd alternated between making a Lonesome Luke two-reeler one week and a Glasses one-reeler the next week. Jeffrey Vance describes the change Lloyd was going through during the period as from the "resourceful but callously aggressive Luke to the gentler, cleverer, and kinder Glass Character, whose personality eventually caused romance to become a part of the films" (Vance et al. 2002, 33). By early December 1917, Roach and Lloyd committed themselves fully to the Glasses character: From then until July 1919, Lloyd appeared in 83 one-reel Glasses films, shifting to two-reelers in November 1919 with *Bumping into Broadway*. After nine two-reelers – and after Chaplin had already completed slightly longer films, like the three-reel *Shoulder Arms*, released in November 1918, and was in production with *The Kid*, a five-reeler released in January 1921 – Lloyd also started to experiment with three-reel narratives in *Now or Never*, which came out in July 1921, and *Never Weaken*, in October 1921. A four-reeler (*Sailor Made Man*, 1921) and five-reeler (*Grandma's Boy*, 1922) followed and did well. Lloyd kept busy for the rest of the silent era making nine more feature films through 1928 featuring his Glasses character, among them *Safety Last!* in 1923, *The Freshman* in 1925, *The Kid Brother* in 1927, and *Speedy* in 1928.

Lloyd became rich, famous, and successful via his Glasses character: His November 1921 contract paid him $1,000 a week and an 80 percent share of company profits. This success came partly because Lloyd, in collaboration with his writers and directors, was imaginative in constructing and executing gags within the structure of a tight narrative, one prerequisite of successful silent feature-film comedy. One trademark of Lloyd's comic process, which appeared in what he called his "thrill" films, generated both comedy and suspense by putting Harold in dangerous high places. This was most famously true in the climax of *Safety Last!*, where Harold hangs from a large clock at the top of a tall building, but it also is central in his shorts *High and Dizzy* (1920) and, even more effectively, *Never Weaken*. Other gag sequences in the features are wonderfully constructed: Harold's capture of the tramp in *Grandma's Boy*; the tackling dummy scene, as well as the scenes in which Speedy's suit comes apart and Speedy becomes a football hero in *The Freshman*; and the scene on the boat in *The Kid Brother* in which Harold tries to take back the money and elude his captors. In the last of these, Lloyd uses a monkey even more effectively than Chaplin did in *The Circus*: In one particularly amusing sequence, Harold slips a pair of much-too-large shoes on a little monkey who walks one floor above a villain, distracting him enough so that Harold can elude his potential captors.

Although Lloyd is certainly remembered for these comic or thrilling sequences, his comic persona was grounded in a different kind of class address than was Chaplin's. As we have seen, Chaplin most often played a lower- or working-class character at the social margins, even if his behavior, costume, and aspirations were characterized by a frayed gentility and resilience. Lloyd's character owed more to the Horatio Alger success myth of the late nineteenth century. From his first feature, *Grandma's Boy*, and onward his character early in the film is often a shy or insecure middle-class youth who is seeking the approval of others and must learn to act decisively to overcome the antagonist and win the affections of the girl (and in Lloyd's films, she's often called just that – "the girl"). In *Grandma's Boy* he captures the tramp and wins the support of the townspeople after his Granny tells him about the exploits

Figure 5.2 Harold recovers from a tough football practice in Andrew Bergman's *The Freshman* (1925, producer Harold Lloyd).

of his grandfather in the Civil War. In *The Freshman* Harold tries too hard to become the Big Man on Campus, earning scorn from the "in-crowd," until Peggy, the coat check girl at the hotel, tells him to be himself rather than what he believes others would most admire. He follows Peggy's advice and even, through a fortunate set of circumstances, becomes the hero of the big football showdown against Union State. In *The Kid Brother* Lloyd plays Harold Hickory, the son of the burly town sheriff, Jim Hickory. His father depends on the work of his two older, bigger, and stronger brothers, Olin and Leo, while in the absence of a mother Harold is relegated to domestic tasks like doing the laundry. Harold falls in love with Mary Powers (Jobyna Ralston), who has taken over the medicine show that her recently deceased father operated. When two scoundrels who work in the show steal money that Sheriff Hickory is holding for the community to build a dam, the sheriff sends his older sons to find them. Harold, despondent about being passed over for the job, tells Mary he's a pretender and a failure. Mary refuses to accept that, however, and tells Harold, "you can be what I think you are – without pretending." Energized, he tracks down the culprits in a large boat on the river, recaptures the money and one of the culprits, and returns both to town just as a mob is threatening his father. By retrieving the money, Harold calms the townsmen and wins his father's approval. In the last shot Harold and Mary, united, walk happily down the road together.

Lloyd's middle-class success stories played particularly well in the 1920s, an era when a pro-business ethos encouraged the notion that hard work and determination necessarily lead to success. Sinclair Lewis may have satirized that ethos in *Babbitt* (1922), but Lloyd's films tended to reinforce the success myth, one reason why they were so popular. If the Keystone Cops undermined the attempts of some in the movie industry to broaden the audience by making movies more "respectable" in the early and middle 1910s, Lloyd's comic narratives flourished at a time when the movie audience had expanded and the studio system had helped to solidify the production mode and the narrative conventions of what Bordwell, Staiger, and Thompson have called the "classical Hollywood cinema" (1985, esp. chs 15–17). And flourish they did: *Grandma's Boy* cost approximately $86,000 to make, while grossing over $975,000, setting a pattern – the gross of a Lloyd feature comedy was sometimes nearly 10 times the production costs. *The Freshman* was the third highest-grossing film of 1925, right behind *The Gold Rush*. With production costs of just over $300,000, it grossed over $2.65 million. *The Kid Brother*, Lloyd's penultimate silent comic feature, grossed over $2.4 million (Lloyd 2004, 128, 119, 166, 107, 185). As Richard Koszarski has pointed out, Lloyd "far outgrossed Buster Keaton (whose best films … sometimes lost money) and surpassed even Chaplin over the long run, since there was always at least one new Lloyd feature every year" (1990, 304). In terms of ticket sales, Lloyd was the most popular of the film comedians in the 1920s. One list of wealthy entertainers in the decade estimated Lloyd's net worth at over $15 million (Vance et al. 2002, 45). Clearly, the cheerful and persevering Glasses character had a special appeal to movie audiences in the 1920s.

A Calm Demeanor Beneath a Porkpie Hat: Buster Keaton

In March 1917 – a couple of months after Chaplin released *Easy Street* and six months before Harold Lloyd first introduced his Glasses character – a 21-year-old vaudevillian named Buster Keaton (1895–1966) visited Fatty Arbuckle's movie studio in Manhattan and – to his surprise and delight – started his movie career. Born Joseph Frank Keaton in Piqua, Kansas, to two medicine-show entertainers, Buster picked up his nickname early on when the escape artist Harry Houdini, after watching the child take a tumble down a flight of stairs without injury, tagged him "Buster." By the age of five Buster joined the family's knockabout comedy routine, and "The Three Keatons," as they billed themselves, soon became a successful vaudeville act. Besides perfecting his skills at acrobatic pratfalls, Buster learned to affect a deadpan expression during the act: Both would later become key elements in his movie persona. As Keaton moved toward adulthood, his father's alcoholism strained both the family and the act, and Keaton decided to set out on his own. He quickly found a job in a musical comedy review in New York, and his visit to Arbuckle (who was familiar with Keaton's vaudeville act) took place just before rehearsals were about to begin.

After Arbuckle showed him around his studio, he invited Keaton to appear in a two-reel comedy he was making. In the film he wore the flat porkpie hat that would become as familiar a trademark as Chaplin's derby and Lloyd's glasses. Released as *The Butcher Boy* (1917), the film testified to Keaton's natural gift for visual comedy, as his character enters the general store, fiddles with some brooms, gets his foot stuck in spilled molasses, and participates in an accelerating food fight that ends with pies in faces and flour bags exploding. Arbuckle quickly offered him $40 a week to appear in his two-reel comedies. Whereas Chaplin entered the movies because Keystone doubled his music hall salary, Keaton, intrigued by the movies, accepted a significant salary cut – from $250 a week. As he told Arthur Friedman, "One of the first things I did was tear a motion picture camera practically to pieces and find out about the lenses and the splicing of film and how to get it on the projector … this fascinated me" (1958, 9). Quickly, he was hooked.

Thus began a magnificent career. Thereafter, Keaton created a body of work that has held up even better than Lloyd's, with his reputation now rivaling Chaplin's as the greatest of the silent comic filmmakers. Arriving as an already gifted comic performer, Keaton luckily fell into a situation that allowed him to work with little interference from movie executives throughout most of the silent period, thus enabling him to do what he did best – create cinematically imaginative and taut comic narratives that made audiences laugh, think, and identify with his unique comic persona.

Keaton served his movie apprenticeship with Arbuckle but never had to work at the frenzied pace of Chaplin at Keystone or Lloyd making the Lonesome Lukes. When Keaton joined him, Arbuckle – who had learned the ropes at Keystone starting in

1913 – was already well established, taking seven or eight weeks to make a two-reeler. From March 1917 on, Keaton worked closely with Arbuckle's Comique Film Corporation. Over the next 15 months they completed 12 films, first in New York, then in California, until Keaton was drafted in June 1918. Keaton left for France in August and was back home by April 1919, returning to make three more films with Arbuckle, including his final film with Arbuckle, *The Garage* (released in 1920). That year Comique President Joe Schenck sold Arbuckle's contract to Paramount to make feature films and promoted Keaton to star in his own two-reel comedies at $1,000 a week, 25 percent of the films' profits, and complete creative control. After loaning Keaton to Metro to appear in a feature film, *The Saphead* (1920), which helped establish him as a star, Schenck gave Keaton free rein creatively, to which he responded with 19 remarkable shorts between 1920 and 1923. The first eight of these two-reelers were released through Metro, whereupon Schenck worked out a distribution deal with First National, which released the last 11. The films were strong and profitable, in part because Keaton's working pace slowed to a film every six weeks or so.

Keaton also assembled a stable team of collaborators. "The greatest thing about working in a small studio like ours," Keaton later recalled, "was having the same bunch of men going with me as a team on each new movie" (Keaton & Samuels 1960, 129). Eddie Cline codirected most of the shorts, working with studio manager Lou Anger and cameraman Elgin Lessley. Buster and Cline did the stories and gags at first, and they were joined in 1921 by Joseph Mitchell and Clyde Bruckman. Though no formal scripts existed, Buster supervised the overall creative effort. Starting out most often with Buster, a girl, and a villain at the core of the films, along with a relatively defined set or location (a house under construction, a boat, a downtown area, a haunted house, and so on), the creative team worked their magic (Keaton et al. 2001, 64–65). As Gabriella Oldham has demonstrated, the 19 films show considerable variety, but they also exhibit preoccupations that define Keaton's comic world: "His dream-mind; his thoughtful perceptions of Machine, Woman, Nature, and Self; his wry humor and mesmerizing agility" (1996, 332–333). Among the finest are *One Week* (1920), *The Play House* (1921), *Cops* (1922), and *The Love Nest* (1923).

By the time Keaton finished his last two-reeler, both Chaplin and Lloyd were finding success with feature films – Chaplin most prominently with *The Kid* and Lloyd with *Grandma's Boy* and *Safety Last!*. Keaton was eager to follow. When the head of Metro asked Schenck to have Keaton make feature films, Schenck agreed and doubled Keaton's salary to $2,000 a week plus 25 percent of the profits to make two feature films a year, one for spring release and one for fall. Starting with a parody of Griffith's *Intolerance* called *Three Ages* (codirected with Edward F. Cline in 1923), in the same vein as his 1922 two-reel parody of cowboy star William S. Hart, *The Frozen North*, Keaton made nine more features with Buster Keaton Productions, including *Our Hospitality* (1923), *Sherlock Jr.* (1924), *Seven Chances* (1925), *The General* (1926), and *Steamboat Bill, Jr.* (1928).

At this point, with talking films already on the horizon, Keaton accepted Schenck's advice to produce his films through MGM. The move was a mistake. Although two more silent comedies emerged – *The Cameraman* (1928) and *Spite Marriage* (1929), which contained a synchronized musical score and sound effects – Keaton was now forced to work more closely with a script and endured more interference from above, a situation that stifled his creative juices.

In contrast, the period of the pre-MGM features was prolific and inventive, even if the movies were not especially profitable, as compared with the films of Chaplin and Lloyd. Some of the movies were genre parodies – *Sherlock Jr.*, for example, drew on detective film conventions, and *Go West* (1925) parodied the Western. *College* (1927) was an attempt to cash in on the box office success of Harold Lloyd's *The Freshman*. *The Navigator* (1924) and *Steamboat Bill, Jr.* made good use of the confined settings of a ship and a riverboat, respectively, while *Our Hospitality* and *The General* were set in the Old South and depended heavily on trains. Although Keaton later told interviewers that his features usually grossed between $1 and $1.5 million, he was exaggerating. MGM studio records list the following grosses for Keaton features: *Three Ages* ($448,000), *Our Hospitality* ($537,000), *Sherlock Jr.* ($448,000), and *The Navigator* ($680,000). Even Keaton's most famous film struggled at the box office: *The General* was Keaton's most expensive film to date at $415,000, yet the domestic gross was only $474,000, $300,000 less than *Battling Butler* (1926), his previous film (Dardis 1979, 113, 145). As the silent period waned, Keaton was forced to pare production costs, although when he moved to MGM in 1928, he had enough clout to obtain a two-year contract for $3,000 per week and 25 percent of the net profits his company received from MGM (Keaton et al. 2001, 164).

If Chaplin's comic persona tended to be a lower-class or socially marginalized character and Lloyd's an energetic middle-class youth striving for success, Keaton's was more variable. In the comic shorts with Arbuckle, he played working-class or middle-class roles like a delivery boy, a stagehand, a bellboy, a sheriff, a vaudeville artist, and a manager of a general store. In his own comic shorts, he played such roles as a mechanic/fireman, a prisoner, a farmhand, a bank clerk, a generic role ("the boy"), and, in *The Play House*, all roles in the film. In his first feature film, *The Saphead*, he plays Bertie Van Alstyne, the spoiled son of a rich silver mine owner. In other feature films he plays such roles as a movie projectionist, a rich socialite, a struggling financial broker who will inherit a fortune if he can marry quickly, a jobless small-town man who goes west and becomes a cowboy, a young man who pretends to be a champion boxer, a bookish college student, a snobbish son of a riverboat captain, a documentary cameraman, and a star-struck worker in a dry cleaning business. Keaton's comic persona is not associated with a particular social class so much as with his ability to interact successfully, ingeniously, and comically with his environment – often featuring machines – to achieve his goals.

The General and *Sherlock Jr.* offer striking examples of Keaton's achievements. In *Sherlock Jr.*, he plays "the Boy," a shy movie projectionist who dreams of becoming a famous and confident detective. Following the model of Chaplin's narrative structure, Keaton's character is drawn to "the Girl" and is obstructed by his rival, "the Cad," who implicates Buster in the theft of a pocket watch belonging to the Girl's father. Keaton develops wonderful gags early in the film, as when he searches for some money in a pile of trash he's swept up by the entrance to the movie theater or when he "shadows" the Cad by walking step-by-step, just inches behind him. But the film takes a striking turn in the middle when Buster falls asleep in the projection booth, and his figure – a dreamy superimposition – separates from Buster, walks down into the darkened theater, and steps up into the movie screen (a device Woody Allen borrows in *The Purple Rose of Cairo*, 1985).

At first the bewildered Buster is caught by surprise as montage patterns in this film-within-the-film force him, in a split second, to negotiate his movements and behavior in radically different settings – a bench by a brick fence, a city street, a mountain precipice, a jungle, a desert, a beach, snowy woods, then back to the bench and brick fence – using graphic matches to join the locations. For example, Buster jumps off a rock into the water and, after a cut, lands in a pile of snow. Finally, the Boy becomes a famous detective – Sherlock Jr – and in the long subjective dream sequence, he attempts to solve a crime amidst a variety of characters that resemble the Cad, the Girl, and her father, all playing wealthier and more elegantly dressed people than they are in "real" life. Two scenes are particularly striking in the dream sequence: a pool-table scene in which the audience fears that the detective will hit an 8-ball filled with explosives and a chase sequence in which Buster rides on the handlebars of a motorcycle, unaware that no one else is steering. In the wish-fulfillment dream sequence Sherlock Jr vanquishes the Cad and saves the Girl, only to awaken in the projection booth, realizing that it was only a dream. But Keaton does not end there. In a magnificent final scene that asks us to reflect upon the relationship between moviegoers and the movies they attend, the Boy is reconciled with the Girl in the projection room after she discovers that the Cad, not Buster, is the thief. Buster wants to express his affection but, in his awkward shyness, doesn't know how. He learns, though, by looking through the projection booth window to the movie's final scene, where the romantic hero serves as his model, cuing him into how he should grasp the hands of the Girl, kiss them, place a ring on her finger, then kiss her on the lips, "teaching" the Boy how to exhibit the confidence and romantic acumen he wishes he possessed. Through its tight narrative construction, clever gags that rely on Keaton's acrobatic skills and deadpan expression, and a skillful use of the film medium, *Sherlock Jr.* reflexively meditates on film form itself, and on the ways in which viewers use the movies and learn from them.

While *Sherlock Jr.* runs only 44 minutes, *The General* is, at 75 minutes, a more ambitious film. This epic Civil War comedy, based on the actual theft of

Figure 5.3 The projectionist separates from his sleeping self and heads for the movie screen in Buster Keaton's *Sherlock Jr.* (1924, producers Buster Keaton and Joseph M. Schenck).

a Confederate train in Georgia in 1863, focuses on the efforts of a Southern train engineer, Johnnie Gray, to contribute to the war effort after he's been turned down while trying to enlist in the Confederate army and is spurned by his sweetheart Annabelle. (Although he doesn't know it, the army's officers believe Johnnie is more valuable as an engineer.) The bulk of the story traces Johnnie's trip toward Tennessee to recover his stolen train, *The General*, and to return it safely to Georgia and Confederate territory. The film is notable in part for its authentic Civil War feel and look – critics have often compared it to the photographs of Matthew Brady – propelled by the use of authentic narrow-gauge train engines and a substantial budget. The film cost about $415,000 to make, a substantial budget for that time, and it's likely that Schenck approved such a large budget because he had just taken over as president of United Artists, which was short of product, and he planned to add *The General* to the list of UA releases (Dardis 1979, 137, 145). When Keaton discovered that locations in Georgia and Tennessee lacked narrow-gauge railroad tracks, he moved the production near Cottage Grove, Oregon, where the terrain could pass for the North Georgia foothills and where narrow-gauge tracks were plentiful because of the surrounding timber industry (Dardis, 1979, 140). Keaton insisted on authentic costumes and, to lend the film its epic scope, at one point made use of 500 extras, sometimes in Confederate gray, sometimes in Union blue (Pratt 2007, 45–46).

More than many silent film comedies, the film makes extensive use of suspense, as when Johnnie hides under a dining room table and overhears the strategy of Union officers. As often true of Keaton films, its humor elicits gasps of amazement as much as outright laughter from viewers, as when Johnnie sits at the front of a train engine and dexterously uses a railroad tie to knock another tie off the track in order to keep the engine from derailing. Even more stunning is the shot of an actual bridge blowing up, catapulting the actual locomotive (*The Texas*) to the river below. Refusing to use miniatures to achieve the effect, Keaton sacrificed an entire locomotive and the full-size bridge that his set designer built, even though a miniature would have been the more common practice in film productions in the 1920s. By using the real thing, Keaton gave viewers then and now a feeling of stunned amazement, a feeling elicited more by Keaton than by any other film comedian in the era. Sadly, the film got mixed reviews at best and was a box office disappointment, grossing just over $474,000. As a result, Keaton was pressured to make a less expensive film, *College*, that Schenck hoped would capitalize on the success of Lloyd's *The Freshman* (Dardis 1979, 145). Despite the relative failure of *The General* in 1926, however, it plays well to contemporary audiences, and its reputation has grown. The agile, athletic Keaton, his stone face topped by a porkpie hat, has an indisputable place in the pantheon of American comic filmmakers.

City Lights: A Farewell to Silent Film Comedy

Having begun making *City Lights* in December 1927, about a year after the release of *The General* and even before *The Circus* had its premiere, Chaplin was faced with what would become a troubled production history for two primary reasons – one financial and the other aesthetic. Chaplin had been forced to delay the production of *The Circus* for eight months in 1927 because of highly publicized divorce proceedings initiated by his second wife, Lita Grey. Shortly after Grey filed for divorce, the Bureau of Internal Revenue brought legal action against Chaplin, seeking back taxes. By the time the divorce, legal fees, and tax claims were settled in early 1928, Chaplin owed some $3.5 million. Add to that the crash of the stock market in October 1929, while the film was still early in production, and one can understand why Chaplin experienced serious financial pressures.

This financial difficulty was accentuated by the shift to sound within the film industry. The transition came to completion while Chaplin was making the film, yet he remained committed to making a non-talkie that relied on the universal language of pantomime. Although he knew he was taking a risk, Chaplin surmised that the appeal of the tramp, combined with the synchronized musical score he planned to compose and record, would make a successful "silent" film comedy possible, even in the talkie era (Maland 2007, sec. 4–10).

Despite the troubled production history, the completed film, in Alistair Cooke's apt phrase, flows "like water over pebbles, smooth and simple for all to see" (Maland 2007, 36). Chaplin again plays Charlie, a marginalized and homeless tramp in an unfriendly city, as the film opens. Following the opening scene, in which Charlie is abruptly awakened when a statue he's been sleeping on is uncovered at a public dedication ceremony, the narrative alternates between two plots. In the romantic plot, Charlie falls in love with a blind flower girl who believes him to be a wealthy man. In the second plot, Charlie talks a drunken, despondent millionaire out of committing suicide, and through the rest of the film the millionaire treats Charlie as his best friend when he's drunk, while, when sober, he doesn't even recognize the tramp. By shuttling Charlie between these two worlds, Chaplin contrasts the world of flowers, romance, and kindness with the world of money, material plenitude, and frequent despair. When Charlie learns about a new cure for blindness, he tries to earn money to pay for the flower girl's surgery but, failing that, gets the money from the drunken millionaire. After taking the money to her, Charlie is thrown in jail for theft once the millionaire sobers up. In the film's famous final scene, the bedraggled tramp, just released from prison, encounters the flower girl at her prospering flower shop, her sight now restored. She at first seems amused at his appearance and response but then beckons him to the sidewalk outside her store, offering him a rose and a coin. As she offers him both and touches his hands, she realizes that he is her benefactor. He acknowledges his identity; she acknowledges she now can see. In alternating close-ups, we see the flower girl experience a welter of complex emotions at her shock of recognition, while the tramp communicates his anxiety, his hope, and his joy. The final shot – a close-up of Charlie smiling – leaves the viewer hanging about the outcome of the romantic relationship.

Just as the film conveys a thematic richness and complexity in the character relationships, particularly between Charlie and the flower girl, it also skillfully blends comedy, romance, and pathos. The film includes a number of hilarious scenes, among them Charlie's attempts to climb off the statue while the city elites harass him in the opening scene; his exploits when he accompanies the millionaire to a cabaret; and the ingeniously choreographed boxing match, in which Charlie tries to raise money for the blind girl by boxing a much tougher fighter – a scene that shifts rapidly to a powerful note of pathos, when we discover that Charlie loses the fight and the money. That sudden and effective shift of tone occurs often in the film, as when Charlie first meets the flower girl. He's immediately and clearly smitten with her beauty, in love at first sight. At the end of the scene, he tip-toes back toward her and sits next to a small fountain. As he gazes longingly at her, she fills a vase at the fountain to rinse it out, swirls the water around, then flings the water out of the vase, unknowingly soaking Charlie. Comedy here undercuts the romance, just as pathos undercuts comedy in the previous example. Chaplin's orchestration of the film's dominant emotions – humor, the desire for romance, and pathos – demonstrates how fully he is in control of his material.

By the time Chaplin was ready to release his film early in 1931, the US economy was swirling downward into a Great Depression, and Chaplin's socially marginalized tramp caught the temper of the times more than Lloyd's go-getting Glasses character or Keaton's imperturbable, unflappable Buster. The coming of sound, in fact, essentially ended the careers of Lloyd and Keaton as stars in Hollywood; Chaplin, because he owned his movie studio, was able to continue as a silent pantomime comedian through *Modern Times* in 1936, and his first talkie as a writer/director/actor – *The Great Dictator* (1940) – was also the largest-grossing film of his career, not least because of its timely and biting satirical attack on Hitler and the Nazis. Although less overtly political than either of those films, *City Lights* seems in many ways Chaplin's farewell to the 1920s from a perspective tinged by the growing strains of the Depression era.

Chaplin's gamble in *City Lights* paid off in a fitting culmination of the era of silent film comedy. The film cost a little over $1.5 million to produce, and despite the fact that it was distributed, both in the United States and abroad, during a declining economic environment, it brought in over $3 million to Chaplin's studio. It also garnered generally positive and sometimes rapturous reviews – in the *New Republic* Gilbert Seldes wrote that the film "is magnificently organized, deeply thought out and felt, and communicated with an unflagging energy and a masterly technique" (1931, 46). Its reputation has grown over time: In "Comedy's Greatest Era," Agee wrote that the final scene constitutes "the highest moment in the movies" (1958, 10). Moreover, when, in 2007, the American Film Institute named its 10th-Anniversary list of top 100 American films, *City Lights* ranked eleventh, having moved up from seventy-sixth in 1997.

Two other silent film comedies made the list: Keaton's *The General* at eighteenth and *The Gold Rush* at fifty-eighth. These three films also appear on the National Film Registry, along with five silent comic shorts (Arbuckle's *Tintype Tangle*, 1915; *The Immigrant*, *One Week*, *Cops*, and the Charley Chase *Mighty Like a Moose*, 1926), and six additional silent comic features (*Safety Last!*, *Sherlock Jr.*, *The Freshman*, Frank Capra's *The Strong Man*, 1926, W. C. Fields's *So's Your Old Man*, 1926, and *The Cameraman*). If it is true that film genres combine familiar formal conventions with inventiveness and originality within that conventional framework, American film comedy represents one of the most successful film genres in the silent era. These comedies entertained millions of filmgoers around the world in the 1910s and 1920s; the best of them also offered shrewd insights into human social experience and relationships, and sometimes inventively used the medium of cinema to amuse and amaze audiences through the stories they told. To understand the achievements of American film in the silent era, one must certainly explore the work of Keaton, Lloyd, and Charles Spencer Chaplin – the artist who, happily, started it all by responding to Mack Sennett's telegram in 1913.

References

Agee, James. (1958). *Agee on Film*, vol. 1. New York: Putnam.

Bordwell, David, Staiger, Janet, & Thompson, Kristin. (1985). *The Classical Hollywood Cinema: Film Style and Mode of Production to 1960*. New York: Columbia University Press.

Bowser, Eileen. (1990). *The Transformation of the Cinema, 1907–1915*. New York: Scribner's.

Chaplin, Charlie. (1964). *My Autobiography*. New York: Simon & Schuster.

Dardis, Tom. (1979). *Keaton: The Man Who Wouldn't Lie Down*. New York: Scribner's.

Friedman, Arthur. (1958). *Interview with Buster Keaton*. Tape interview. Los Angeles: UCLA Library.

Hackett, Francis. (1921). Review of *The Kid*. *New Republic*, 26, 136–137.

Keaton, Buster, & Samuels, Charles. (1960). *My Wonderful World of Slapstick*. With a new introduction by Dwight Macdonald and a new filmography compiled by Raymond Rohauer. Garden City, NY: Doubleday.

Keaton, Eleanor et al. (2001). *Buster Keaton Remembered*. Afterword by Kevin Brownlow. New York: Harry N. Abrams.

King, Rob. (2009). *The Fun Factory: The Keystone Film Company and the Emergence of Mass Culture*. Berkeley: University of California Press.

Koszarski, Richard. (1990). *An Evening's Entertainment: The Age of the Silent Feature Picture, 1915–1928*. Vol. 3 of *History of the American Cinema*, ed. Charles Harpole. New York: Scribner's.

Lahue, Kalton C. (1966). *World of Laughter: The Motion Picture Comedy Short, 1910–1930*. Norman: University of Oklahoma Press.

Lloyd, Annette D'Agostino. (2004). *The Harold Lloyd Encyclopedia*. Jefferson, NC: McFarland.

Lloyd, Harold. (1928). *An American Comedy*. Acted by Harold Lloyd. Dir. Wesley W. Stout. New York: B. Blom.

McGuirk, Charles. (1915). "Chaplinitis." *Motion Picture Magazine*, 9.6, 85–89.

Maland, Charles. (2007). *City Lights*. London: British Film Institute.

May, Henry. (1959). *The End of American Innocence: A Study of the First Years of Our Time, 1912–1917*. New York: Knopf.

Merton, Paul. (2007). *Silent Comedy*. London: Random House.

Oldham, Gabriella. (1996). *Keaton's Silent Shorts: Beyond the Laughter*. Carbondale: Southern Illinois University Press.

Pratt, George C. (2007). "'Anything Could Happen – And Generally Did': Buster Keaton on His Silent-Film Career." In Kevin W. Sweeney (ed.), *Buster Keaton: Interviews* (pp. 32–47). Jackson: University Press of Mississippi.

Robinson, David. (1985). *Chaplin, His Life and Art*. New York: McGraw-Hill.

Ross, Steven J. (1998). *Working-Class Hollywood: Silent Film and the Shaping of Class in America*. Princeton: Princeton University Press.

Seldes, Gilbert. (1931). "A Comic Masterpiece." *New Republic*, 66, February 25, 46–47.

Sklar, Robert. (1994). *Movie-Made America: A Cultural History of American Movies*. New York: Vintage Books.

Vance, Jeffrey. (2003). *Chaplin: Genius of the Cinema*. Introduction by David Robinson. New York: Harry N. Abrams.

Vance, Jeffrey, Lloyd, Suzanne, & Bowman, Manoah (photographic ed.). (2002). *Harold Lloyd: Master Comedian*. Introduction by Kevin Brownlow. New York: Harry N. Abrams.

6

Erich von Stroheim and Cecil B. DeMille

Early Hollywood and the Discourse of Directorial "Genius"

Gaylyn Studlar

Professor, Washington University in St. Louis, United States

Erich von Stroheim and **Cecil B. DeMille** are among the most significant of early feature filmmakers, having made movies that, to differing degrees, challenged cultural norms. Whereas the Austrian-born von Stroheim fought vigorously to exert his artistic vision, often resulting in cost overruns and a growing reputation as temperamental, DeMille submitted to multiple pressures, producing commercially viable films and extending his career well into the sound era. Gaylyn Studlar explores their work, divergent career trajectories, and both critical and box office reception as emblematic of early industry operations. Exploring the **film-as-commercially-viable-entertainment** versus **film-as-art-for-art's-sake** division that shaped perceptions of "**directorial genius**," Studlar casts von Stroheim as a talented artist victimized by Hollywood and DeMille as a Hollywood success adept at negotiating the commercially driven workings of the industry. Studlar's essay shares ground with Charlie Keil on D. W. Griffith and Charles J. Maland on silent comedies in this volume, and with Charles Musser on Edwin S. Porter and Torey Liepa on Thomas Ince in the hardcover/online edition.

Additional terms, names, and concepts: parallelism, Jazz Age, Famous Players-Lasky, stock company approach, analytic editing, visual detail, internal optics

Two Directors and the Rise of the Feature Film

Cecil B. DeMille and Erich von Stroheim were two of the most important filmmakers to emerge in the early years of Hollywood feature film production. Their legacies now are perceived – rightfully – as having been of a radically different order. DeMille has come to epitomize the commercially savvy studio director who cultivated the public persona of an American "showman." Over a career that spanned five decades, his name recognition revolved around

American Film History: Selected Readings, Origins to 1960, First Edition. Edited by Cynthia Lucia, Roy Grundmann, and Art Simon.
© 2016 John Wiley & Sons, Inc. Published 2016 by John Wiley & Sons, Inc.

a legacy of popularity and longevity. Rather than retaining recognition as a motion picture innovator and visual artist of the silent era, DeMille is now remembered almost exclusively as the director of entertaining, star-studded film spectacles of the sound era that commercially exploited low- and medium-brow tastes. By way of contrast, von Stroheim has grown to become one of the central referents in discussions of Hollywood's victimization of artists. An uncompromising perfectionist and proponent of naturalism, von Stroheim saw his vision thwarted by the industry. Through their triumph over him, producers consolidated their power in a move that would define the studio system for the next 40 years. For von Stroheim, that milestone was a tragic one that led writer Jim Tully to call the director, "the first man of genius and original talent to break his heart against the stone wall of cinema imbecility" (Tully 1927, 71).

In spite of these perceived and real differences, the careers of DeMille and von Stroheim and the public discourse about them overlapped in the late 1910s and 1920s: Popular and industry press used the two men as touchstones for the creation of a director-centered cinema that might legitimize American cinema as art and solidify the interest of middle-class audiences in the feature film as a culturally legitimate – if frequently controversial – entertainment. Both von Stroheim and DeMille were characterized in the popular press, in trade industry sources, and in studio promotion in the late 1910s and the 1920s as directors who possessed "genius," who advanced the art of film, and who served as important brands for selling films to the public. Although recognized as artistic innovators who drew heightened attention to the motion picture director as a figure aligned with aesthetic quality, they also came to be associated with moral controversy and, by the end of the 1920s, with profligate spending and flawed artistry.

Cecil B. DeMille: The Genius of Jazz-Age Hokum

As the son of one playwright and brother of another, Cecil B. DeMille seemed destined for a theatrical career, but success as a playwright and as an actor eluded him. He abandoned a modest stage career to become one of the cofounders of the Jesse L. Lasky Feature Play Company. As "director-general" for Lasky, he codirected the first feature film shot in Hollywood, *The Squaw Man* (1914), a successful adaptation of a stage play that was followed by several more so-called "pictorialized plays." Influenced by David Belasco's stage melodramas and Italian film superspectacles, DeMille was at the center of the rise of the American feature film; through enhanced screen realism and more complex stylistic and narrative elements, his productions helped solidify the perception that the multireel feature was a superior mode of storytelling to the one- and two-reelers that had dominated nickelodeon screens. During this period, DeMille often filmed preexisting stage plays and novels adapted for film by screenwriters, like Jeanie Macpherson, who were handpicked by the director (and worked frequently with him).

DeMille's name attained the "above the title" position of a star because Lasky and DeMille realized the value of the director as a focus for the industry's marketing of feature films. The goal was to bring the coveted middle-class demographic into the regular motion-picture-going audience. As a model for the industry's cultivation of a director-centered cinema, studio advertisements for DeMille's films often prominently featured his image as well as his name, thus displacing the actor as the chief marketing tool of Hollywood. After the merger of the Lasky company with Adolph Zukor's Famous Players in 1916, DeMille was well established as one of the industry's top directorial talents, as well as a "star" of the new Famous Players-Lasky. In May 1921 in *Ladies' Home Journal*, the Paramount Picture division of the studio advertised its lineup of forthcoming pictures "founded on the work of the world's great authors" ("Greatest Living Authors" 1921, 30). The full-page advertisement uses an illustration of a DeMille look-alike. Standing in front of a camera on the right side of the advertisement, the DeMille look-alike is posed with a bespectacled author (with script in hand). In back and to the left is a typical DeMille set: A grand staircase is filled with ladies and gentlemen in fine dress. In mid-background, a soft-focus image, semi-nude figures embrace in a dance-influenced pose, recalling the poses characters often assume in the exotic fantasy/flashback sequences that characterize DeMille films (sometimes graced by the presence of dancer Theodore Kosloff). The advertisement implies that DeMille is the exemplar of the Paramount director working with major authors to bring quality to the screen. "Genius" is the term reserved in the advertisement for the artists who create literary works and plays that have "the power of showing us ourselves and our neighbors"; although film directors are not mentioned, "artistic achievement" is attributed to Paramount as an organization that "has assembled, and maintains . . . perfection and completeness of personnel and mechanical equipment." Such an organization can take great literature and plays beyond "the cold limitations of the printed page" ("Greatest Living Authors" 1921, 30).

In another register of DeMille's star status as a director, an advertisement in the same magazine for *Adam's Rib* in April 1923 shows DeMille's name in huge letters above the film's title, with the names of actors appearing in very small print below the title. A picture of DeMille posed in a dynamic stance, as he studies a script or notes, appears in the lower half of the advertisement. He is clothed in his established work attire of white shirt and jodhpurs. Framed copy positioned beside his picture declares: "Cecil B. DeMille Director of Directors! – whose screen record literally glitters with successes . . . who places his art before anything else" ("*Adam's Rib*" 1923, 47). Whether used anonymously, to represent the artistic resources of Paramount the corporation, as in the "Greatest Living Authors" advertisement, or named and individualized as an artist, as in this publicity for *Adam's Rib*, DeMille had attained the visible status of a Hollywood icon. He was part of a well-oiled machine bringing high art to film and to a better class of audience that included middle-class women, who were believed to be all-important in bringing that audience into the movie theater.

DeMille's films occasionally proved instrumental in advancing top star personalities (notably Gloria Swanson and Wallace Reid), but otherwise depended upon players of varying popularity who were contracted with the studio. Echoing D. W. Griffith's approach to casting, a recognizable stock company emerged from DeMille's repeated use of players who included Elliott Dexter, Theodore Roberts, Wanda Hawley, Raymond Hatton, Charles de Roche, Julia Faye, Rod La Rocque, Bebe Daniels, Leatrice Joy, Robert Edeson, and Theodore Kosloff. The 1916 merger between the Lasky studio and Zukor's Famous Players did give DeMille the opportunity to direct Zukor-contracted superstar Mary Pickford in two 1917 films, *A Romance of the Redwoods* and *The Little American*. There was no doubt that the primary box office draw of these two films was Pickford, whose name replaced DeMille's above the title. Nevertheless, at least one critic pointed – indirectly – to the director/producer's contribution: "It is the most wonderful five-reel picture that ever has been shown and it does not depend on the charms of our Mary for its success, either" ("*The Little American*" 1917, n.p.).

In spite of the box office drawing power of top stars like Pickford, studios – including Famous Players-Lasky – were economically motivated to look for other means of securing the loyalty of motion picture audiences. DeMille's fame, as well as his stock company, saved Lasky the cost of rapidly inflating star salaries, which were the subject of industry criticism in the mid-1910s. More than advertising was needed, however, to secure audience loyalty, especially to a director. Publicity and promotion might make DeMille into a visually identifiable persona, but audience expectations of a predictably enjoyable moviegoing experience depended upon his establishing a solid record of favorably received films. DeMille had that record of films that received acclaim and for which reviewers singled him out for praise.

As a result of films like *The Golden Chance* (1915), *The Cheat* (1915), and *Carmen* (1915), in the mid-1910s DeMille's name represented innovation and artistry. *The Golden Chance* is a rather downbeat Cinderella story about a genteel young woman (Cleo Madison) who marries badly. Forced to hire out as a seamstress to keep from starving, she agrees to masquerade as a high society debutante so that her wealthy employer can successfully entertain a young millionaire (Wallace Reid). Clearly influenced by D. W. Griffith's use of parallelism, DeMille focuses on this married heroine as the unhappy mediator between the worlds of the rich and the poor; she experiences the refined living and the social snobbery of the rich who use her for their convenience, as well as the demoralizing effects of poverty and the ire of an abusive husband. The millionaire proposes to her, and her husband is subsequently killed while committing a crime, but the ending leaves the question of her future happiness unresolved. The *New York Dramatic Mirror* critic praised "the master hand of Cecil DeMille" for making *The Golden Chance* a picture that could "be favorably compared to anything that either the stage or the screen has brought forth" ("*The Golden*

Chance" 1915, 50). W. Stephen Bush went even further, calling attention to the film's admirable visual qualities: "If the paintings in a Rembrandt gallery or a set of Titians or Tintorettos were to come to life . . . the effect could not have been more startling" (Bush 1916, 255). *The Golden Chance* provided evidence of DeMille's artistic use of expressive visual techniques that began with his work with cinematographer Warren Buckland and continued through his multifilm collaboration with Alvin Wyckoff. The studio marketed these signature lighting effects as "Lasky lighting" or "Rembrandt lighting." DeMille, speaking in less artistically evocative language, sometimes called his approach "contrasty lighting."

In 1915, DeMille's fame was extended worldwide by *The Cheat*, a daring melodrama that offered audiences the taboo appeal of interracial attraction: An American society matron, Edith Hardy (Fannie Ward), forms a flirtatious friendship with a wealthy Japanese visitor, Hishuru Tori (Sessue Hayakawa). To finance her self-indulgent lifestyle, Edith embezzles from a charity organization, and, fearing that her crime will be discovered, she borrows money from Tori to replace the funds. When her husband's business ventures finally succeed, she offers Tori repayment. He refuses, declaring his sexual ownership of her by branding her back with a hot iron and threatening her with rape. She shoots and wounds him. Her husband (Jack Dean) nobly takes responsibility for the shooting and is jailed. In the last moments of his trial, Edith speaks the truth and – shockingly – reveals her branding to the packed courtroom. A near riot against Tori ensues. Reviews again drew attention to the dramatic efficacy of DeMille's lighting; they also praised his talent for visually energizing the movement of masses in the melodramatically overwrought ending. In *Motion Picture News* William Ressman Andrews declared that "in staging *The Cheat*, [the director's] genius reached a climax" (1915, 127). The film was an international box office sensation and critical success.

Also released in 1915, DeMille's screen adaptation of Mérimée's "Carmen," with opera star Geraldine Farrar in the title role, demonstrated other avenues for DeMille's contribution to the technical and cultural maturation of the feature film. With Farrar's high art credentials as a star of Bizet's *Carmen* at the Metropolitan Opera and source material that had served as the basis of that opera, DeMille's movie version appealed to middle-class viewers who could embrace it as respectable, "high-class" entertainment, in spite of the low-class behaviors of the story's heroine. Here, DeMille applied his strong pictorial talents to a production that ventured well beyond the intimate domestic scale of melodramas like *The Golden Chance* and *The Cheat*. In *Carmen*, he demonstrated his ability to give an emotionally approachable, human dimension to epic-scaled mise-en-scène. Another spectacle with a patriotic theme, *Joan the Woman* (1916), starring Farrar as the Maid of Orleans, drew DeMille deeper into identification with spectacle.

Once again, visual effects and DeMille's handling of masses drew praise. While criticizing the miscasting of the "rampageous Geraldine Farrar" in a role that he said demanded the "spiritual beauty" of a Mae Marsh, Alexander Woollcott nevertheless offered praise for the film: "The beautiful and exalted pageantry of the coronation is the sort of spectacle that takes the breath away and lingers in the memory" (1917, 2). Writing in *Photoplay*, Julian Johnson brought attention to the visual effects of the film in language that linked DeMille to high art tradition: "Joan pleads for soldiers to save France . . . figures of great knights in armour . . . plunge over them all . . . This is more than double photography, it is handling a camera as Michelangelo handled his chisel" (1917, 114). Even though the film seemed to cover all the bases by blending war propaganda, pageantry, spiritual uplift, and even romance, *Joan the Woman* failed to inspire box office boffo. Nevertheless, these signature strengths of early DeMille productions would move to the foreground in the 1920s to become central in sustaining his career after the arrival of talking pictures.

DeMille applied many of these elements to a spectacular reproduction of the sinking of the *Lusitania* in the propaganda-oriented Pickford vehicle *The Little American* (1917). Nevertheless, Lasky suggested that DeMille turn from film spectacles to focus on "modern stories of great human interest" (Higashi 1994, 145). The result was *Old Wives for New* (1918), the film that initiated DeMille's notorious high society sex comedies of the late 1910s and early 1920s. These films, with screenplays written by frequent collaborator Jeanie Macpherson or by Cecil's brother William, based their appeal on sexually daring content and the depiction of luxurious upper-class lifestyles. DeMille, however, was always careful to wrap sensuality and sin

Figure 6.1 DeMille directing the spectacular *Joan the Woman* (1916, producers Jesse L. Lasky and Cecil B. DeMille). (From the author's private collection.)

in the cloak of moralizing affirmations of monogamy and marriage.

Old Wives for New nevertheless *was* sexually scandalous, so much so that Famous Players-Lasky, which heavily promoted their Paramount Pictures brand as family friendly, initially hesitated to release the film, especially without significant censorship cuts (DeMille 1959, 214–215; Higashi 1994, 160). Adapted from a novel by David Graham Phillips, the film told the story of a husband who divorces his wife because she has grown fat and unkempt. Both husband and wife find other partners. One exhibitor characterized *Old Wives for New* as "objectionable . . . [but] very artistic" ("Exhibitor to Exhibitor" 1918, 3400). The film was attacked by the Pennsylvania State Censorship Board for its depiction of prostitutes. One critic bristled at the "scenes of disgusting debauchery" and condemned DeMille's apparent desire "to revel in the most immoral episodes" (Smith 1918, 45). In spite (or because) of its stirring of controversy, the immense popularity of *Old Wives for New* inspired similarly themed DeMille films – *Why Change Your Husband?* (1919), *Why Change Your Wife?* (1920), and *The Affairs of Anatol* (1921), along with numerous copycat films from other studios.

Credited with bringing Jazz-Age sexual morality and a heightened emphasis on consumerism to film audiences, DeMille's films of this type, which critic Burns Mantle labeled "the society sex film" (1920, 64–65) and Adela Rogers St Johns called "sex pictures" (DeMille 1920b, 28), responded to popular tastes by mixing highly stylized consumer-oriented spectacle with a somewhat ambiguous take on the cultural debate raging around changing sexual norms in the United States. More specifically, the films focused on childless, companionate marriage and the benefits of divorce. In one fan magazine interview, DeMille was declared to be "the film's greatest authority on matrimonial problems," while the director lends moral justification to his controversial films: "I believe I have a message to give ... I believe I can do more to prevent divorce, that I am doing more to prevent divorce than any minister or anti-divorce league in the world" (DeMille 1920b, 28).

This justification is echoed in DeMille's films, which were accused by critics of cynically offering up moral commentary to audiences in order to avoid censorship. In keeping with this, Burns Mantle, writing in *Photoplay*, reacted against *Why Change Your Wife?* by stating: "Mr. DeMille and his studio associates know that the 'moral' they have tacked on to this picture ... is not true of normal husbands anywhere in the world" (1920, 64–65). Intertitles laced this and other DeMille films of the period with moral didacticism, but in keeping the films "clean" in spite of their theme, sexual discontent and experimentation were sometimes rendered so ambiguous as to make plots, like that of DeMille's adaptation of Schnitzler's *The Affairs of Anatol*, almost nonsensical. In another apparent strategy with similar motives, open displays of lust were moved to the distant past through DeMille's signature use of flashbacks as fantasy sequences, as in *Male and Female* (1919), adapted from James Barrie's play *The Admirable Crichton*.

Male and Female, one of DeMille's most successful films of this period, was not focused on divorce but on a cross-class attraction between an upright butler, Crichton (Thomas Meighan), and Lady Mary Lasenby (Gloria Swanson), the spoiled daughter of the aristocratic British family. When the Lasenby family and its servants are shipwrecked, Crichton rescues Lady Mary. In a highly sensual shot, photographed in silhouette, he is shown emerging out of the sea, carrying her limp body in his arms. By virtue of his survival skills, Crichton rises to the position of "king" of the marooned group, and Lady Mary falls in love with him. A fantasy/flashback to ancient Babylon provides the excuse for a sensationally sadomasochistic scene in which Lady Mary appears as a Christian slave who refuses to become the king's (Crichton's) concubine. The king sends her to the lions' den, where, dressed in a spectacular and revealing costume, she is last seen collapsed (dead?) on the floor, her beautifully posed body literally under the paws of a roaring lion.

By the early 1920s, critics had begun to make fun of DeMille's over-the-top excesses such as those in *Male and Female*: the melodrama, outrageously overstyled mise-en-scène, sensuous displays of female flesh, and gratuitous flashbacks and fantasy sequences with exotic spectacle and titillating sexual behaviors. In a review of *Why Change Your Wife?* Burns Mantle quipped: "The Sennetts and the Sunshine boys may outdo Mr. DeMille as masters of the lower limb displays, but he completely distances them in the technique of the torso" (1920, 65). In spite of naming *Male and Female* as one of the 20 best films of the year, Frederick James Smith took the director to task in a slightly more serious tone: "DeMille is running rife in boudoir negligee. His dramas are as intimate as a department store window" (1920, 44). Reacting somewhat defensively, DeMille was quoted in the same year: "I believe I have had an obvious effect on American life. I have brought a certain sense of beauty and luxury into everyday existence, all jokes about ornate bathrooms and deluxe boudoirs aside" (1920a, 194–195). By 1922, Smith declared that DeMille was "fast slipping from his luxuriously upholstered seat as one of our foremost directors" (1922, 92).

In this marked slide in critical opinion, DeMille's films were increasingly affiliated with "hokum" (or "hoke"), a term that film scholar Lea Jacobs says was used in critical discourse of the 1920s to indicate an overreliance on qualities that appealed to naïve or unsophisticated viewers. Jacobs says of DeMille: "I can think of few directors who better deserve the term" (2008, 90). As she explains, the sexually sensational subject matter of DeMille's films might have made them seem sophisticated, but this was only one of the ways in which sophistication was understood. Numerous letters to the editors of fan magazines as well as film reviews of the era provide evidence to support Jacobs's assertion that sophistication also referred to more refined, restrained techniques of acting, storytelling, visual style, and tone. Jacobs cites DeMille's use of bombastic intertitles and "big effects at the levels of both spectacle and plot" as among those unsophisticated elements of his films that appealed to naïve tastes (2008, 90). A review in *Wid's Daily* referring to *Why Change Your Wife?* supports Jacobs's view of the bifurcated nature of DeMille's appeal: "Its spice, its gorgeous displays of clothes and of extravagance in setting ... will bring it success in such [Broadway or big city] houses." The review went on to assert that "DeMille is capable of better things than this. At times herein he insults intelligence while catering to the supposed mob demand for the exotic and the sensuous and the forbidden" ("*Why Change Your Wife?*" 1920, 31). Reviewing *Adam's Rib* in 1923, Laurence Reid of *Motion Picture Classic* not only labeled this film "hokum" (1923, 93), but also echoed the disdain of Frederick James Smith who, writing in the same fan magazine, had dismissed DeMille's *Fool's Paradise* (1922) as "a mess of piffle" (Smith 1922, 92).[1]

With his reputation in decline, unequivocally positive box office and critical reception largely eluded DeMille in the 1920s. His biggest box office success, *The Ten Commandments* (1923), elicited mixed critical reactions in response to the particularly interesting structure of the film, which combined a biblical story (the so-called "prelude") with a modern story of two brothers, one extremely good and the other deity-defying and obviously very bad. *Variety* dismissed the modern plot in *The Ten Commandments* as "ordinary... hoke" ("*The Ten Commandments*" 1923, n.p.). In contrast, committed DeMille-basher Robert E. Sherwood found himself liking the modern story so much that he compared its display of DeMille's "directorial genius" to that of Chaplin and *A Woman of Paris* (2006a, 28). A *New York Times* review pointed to both the genius and hokum of DeMille and this film, saying that "no more wonderful spectacle has ever been put before the shadowform than the greatly heralded prelude to Cecil B. DeMille's costly film... All this [the Israelites leaving Egypt] was obviously directed by a genius." The critic goes on to observe, however, that "as soon as he swept on to his modern drama he is back to the ordinary and certainly uninspired movie, one in which the direction at times had 'business' apparently intended to appeal to the very young" ("The Screen" 1923, 8).

The Ten Commandments also marked increasing tensions in DeMille's relationship with Famous Players-Lasky. Although DeMille was regarded as the ultimate "company" director, the production of this film supposedly led one studio executive to tell Jesse Lasky: "You've got a crazy man on that [production]. Look at the cost" (Higashi 1994, 199). Production costs in the film industry were generally on the rise. Universal's Paul Kohner would use the tremendous production costs of von Stroheim's *Foolish Wives* in a publicity campaign that would sell the film as the first "one million dollar picture." Released the following year, the production costs of *The Ten Commandments* were said to have topped $1.5 million, causing a financial crisis at Famous Players-Lasky. Staff members were forced into layoffs and the studio was closed for 10 weeks (Higashi 1994, 199–200). After an expensive publicity campaign, the film made up its costs and much, much more, but DeMille was no longer the studio's golden boy. Famous Players-Lasky and DeMille would part ways over *The Ten Commandments*. In particular, Zukor was determined to curb costs on DeMille's subsequent productions and to renegotiate the director's new contract at terms less favorable to DeMille. DeMille refused to renew his contract and started his own independent studio, but this plan would prove to be a financial disaster for him.

With the release of *King of Kings* in 1927, DeMille's critical reputation was restored to luster, but his independently produced biblical spectacle cost a reported $2 million. When it did not earn back its costs, DeMille's studio was financially ruined; in the wake of this, he signed a contract to direct for MGM, where, ironically, von Stroheim had recently directed *The Merry Widow*, which became a phenomenal box office hit. By the end of the 1920s and into the 1930s, DeMille alternated between historical spectacles and sex comedies, but his survival in the sound era depended on the former rather than the latter. He went back to Famous Players-Lasky (renamed Paramount Publix) in 1932. There, the biblical epic *The Sign of the Cross* (1932) brought him back to box office success with a "hoke" formula of sex and sin, righteousness and religion. Like DeMille films of the late 1910s, it drew both crowds and calls for censorship. DeMille continued the same successful formula for decades, with films like *Samson and Delilah* (1949) and the last film he directed before his death in 1959, *The Ten Commandments* (1956), a loose remake of the prelude section of his silent version of the film. In this star-studded, VistaVision, Technicolor spectacle, the youthful Moses (Charlton Heston) was part of a steamy love triangle among Egyptian royalty. Still recalling the old DeMille combination of genius and hokum in the silent era, this version of *The Ten Commandments* became the biggest box office draw of the 1950s and a symbol of the American film industry's "last stand" against the threat of television and runaway productions. After missteps in the 1920s, DeMille had ultimately learned to obey the system's economic demands to become less of an artistic "genius," perhaps, but more of a "success" as defined by Hollywood standards – "hokum" notwithstanding.

Erich von Stroheim: The Genius Hollywood Loved to Hate

By way of contrast, von Stroheim has come to be understood as the epitome of the artist-director who threw himself against a system that destroyed first his films, and then his career. Von Stroheim has been represented throughout film history as a genius whose obsession with details and with using film to tell novelistic character-centered stories led to his filming dozens of takes and hours upon hours of footage that extended shooting to 20-hour working days and long beyond anticipated production schedules. For reasons that are still largely unexplained, studios allowed him to shoot the unusually large amount of footage that could never reasonably be accommodated into a standard feature-length film of one to two hours.

When von Stroheim, after editing this footage – sometimes for months – presented studio executives feature films that were two, three, or four times longer than the standard feature, they demanded draconian cuts. This was in keeping with the conventional opinion that exhibitors would rebel against any film that altered standard showing times, limited the turnover of audiences, and, thus, cut into profits. Yet some considered feature films of much greater length as viable. In 1915, D. W. Griffith wrote: "The day will come when … the long picture, so long that it cannot be shown in a day, will be regarded as the masterpiece, and people will see it in installments, just as they read a book a chapter at a time" (quoted in Lenning 2000, 78).

Although his first two films came in after reasonable shooting schedules and without outrageous cost overruns, von Stroheim's third film, *Foolish Wives* (1922), would become a watershed in changing the relationship between the studio system, the director, and public discourse on the latter. Starting with *Foolish Wives*, more often than not studios shut down von Stroheim's shooting, submitted his films to drastic cutting before (and even after) release, or pulled him from the production and handed over filming to another director. In the notorious case of his fourth film, *The Merry-Go-Round* (1923), Irving Thalberg, then head of production for Universal, fired von Stroheim and turned the filming of von Stroheim's screenplay over to Rupert Julian ("Production Shut Down" 1923, 2225–2226). *Foolish Wives* and *Greed*

Figure 6.2 Erich von Stroheim poses with his *Foolish Wives* footage (1922, producers Irving Thalberg and Carl Laemmle). (From the author's private collection.)

(1924) were taken away from him in the editing process. The former was released by Universal in a version some 40 percent shorter in running time than von Stroheim wanted. *Greed* was cut by MGM to 10 reels from Stroheim's 42-reel version that the director had hoped would be shown to audiences in two installments of 10 reels (Koszarski 2001, 164–167). Von Stroheim was fired in early 1929 from Gloria Swanson's self-produced star vehicle *Queen Kelly* (1931), a film condemned to failure, in part, by the transition to talkies. In 1931, Fox studio hired von Stroheim to direct *Walking Down Broadway*, then took the production away from him. He would never direct another film before his death in 1957.

Even after being mutilated by studios, von Stroheim's films were recuperated years later by critics who elevated films like *Foolish Wives*, *Greed*, and *The Wedding March* (1928) into masterpieces of film art in spite of their existence as only partial remnants of von Stroheim's original vision. At the time of their original release, however, von Stroheim's films were condemned as frequently as they were praised. Yet even those condemnations often acknowledged the director's passion for perfection and his directorial talent – what studio promotion never hesitated to label his "genius"? In response to *Foolish Wives*, for example, *Photoplay* offered a special full-page negative commentary: "At times startlingly beautiful, at other times repulsively ugly, it is an amazing hodgepodge.... An unworthy theme, the ugly amours of a pseudo-count from Russia, it has been produced with consummate care and unceasing imagination ... That he could give to it his admitted genius for detail and artistic talents is nothing short of incredible" ("*Foolish Wives*" 1922, 70). After the release of *Greed*, Robert E. Sherwood quipped that von Stroheim was "a genius ... badly in need of a stopwatch" (2006b, 29). But to von Stroheim, the loss of his films as he imagined them was no joke. With understandable bitterness, von Stroheim once remarked: "I have made only one real picture in my life and nobody ever saw that.... The poor, mangled, mutilated remains were shown as *Greed*" (quoted in Weinberg 1973, 10).

Those who see von Stroheim first and foremost as a victim of Hollywood consider him a casualty of the industry's rigid economic model, but also as a victim of US xenophobia in the age of "100% Americanism" (Staiger 1992, 125–131). Von Stroheim was met with a generally hostile response – considered to be an arrogant upstart, a foreigner from an enemy empire, clearly ungrateful for the chance that the American film industry afforded him. In the press, he was regularly vilified for the difficulty of his distinctly "foreign" or "Teutonic" personality, the degeneracy of his films' subject matter, and the desultory effect his films had on the financial health of any studio foolish enough to succumb to the lure of hiring him.

Von Stroheim emigrated to the United States from Austria in 1909. He claimed (falsely) throughout his life to have aristocratic origins and a service record as an officer in an elite corps of the Austrian army. Establishing himself as a technical expert on military matters in Hollywood, he served as a directorial assistant to John Emerson, Allan Dwan, and D. W. Griffith. He also used his falsified biography as a "Count" to bolster his acting career. During World War I, von Stroheim (actually the son of a Viennese-Jewish hat merchant) was typecast as the sadistic Hun in several propagandistic feature films, including Griffith's *Hearts of the World* (1918), Alan Crosland's *The Unbeliever* (1918), and, most notoriously, Universal's *The Heart of Humanity* (1919). In the latter, his character hurls a wailing baby out of a window to get it out of the way so he can rape its mother. These stereotyped portrayals of the "Hated Hun" led to his being called "The Man You Love to Hate," a moniker that registers an ambivalence toward von Stroheim's brand of constructed foreignness not unlike that used to elicit public interest in Theda Bara as a film vamp in the mid-1910s.

In von Stroheim's case, that teeter-totter structuring of public fascination and repulsion continued to be stoked by Hollywood publicity when he made the leap from character actor to director about the same time that DeMille's first high society sex comedy was being released. As the desire for character actors specializing in "Huns" waned after World War I, von Stroheim pitched his story "The Pinnacle" to Universal Studio head Carl Laemmle. Laemmle took a chance on bringing the story to the screen with von Stroheim as screenwriter, director, and star of the film.

The plot of "The Pinnacle" revolved around von Stroheim's character, Lieutenant von Steuben, an indiscriminate seducer of women. One reviewer remarked of this more charming version of von Stroheim's established screen villain: "His appearance is repulsive and his morals appalling. But his technique with women is perfect" (*Photo-Play Journal*, 1920, n.p., quoted in Lenning 2000, 107). The film not only exploited audience familiarity with von Stroheim's established screen persona but also played on popular notions of the clash between American values and European sexual mores. Lieutenant von Steuben attempts to seduce an American woman vacationing with her doctor husband in the Alps. The lieutenant is a man perfectly mannered in public, but so godless that he tries to make love to Mrs Armstrong (Francella Billington) under the shadow of three roadside crucifixes.

"The Pinnacle," released in 1919 as *Blind Husbands*, relied on a melodramatic plot but was also visually arresting and startlingly frank in its depiction of lustful male sexuality as well as female sexual passivity. As Arthur Lenning has pointed out, the film is quite bold in suggesting that the seducer and the wife are not the only ones to be blamed for the latter's sexual vulnerability (2000, 106). An intertitle clearly articulates a modern rather than a moralizing perspective on the situation: " ... the husband in his self-complacency forgets the wooing wiles of his pre-nuptial days . . . Guilty! Says the world condemning 'the other man.' . . . But what of the husband?" The last-reel confrontation between husband and would-be seducer occurs on a mountain peak, "the pinnacle," referenced in von Stroheim's original title. Contrary to the advertising copy declaring the film offered "the glorious surprise that sends you away in a glow of happiness," the actual "happy ending" is pitched at a tone of hope rather than celebration. Mr and Mrs Armstrong leave their vacation retreat in a scene that is virtually wordless; the acting is restrained so that forgiveness and reconciliation are affirmed primarily through the sensitive visual treatment. Camera placement and cutting emphasize the beauty of the landscape and an exchange of looks between the Armstrongs and a younger couple who, earlier, commented on the former's apparently sexless marriage.

Blind Husbands was a huge critical and box office hit for Universal Pictures. Von Stroheim followed it with *The Devil's Passkey*, a film about American expatriots in Paris and one that he did not write, made quickly, and that also achieved profitability.

Running counter to the public discourse surrounding DeMille's films in the 1920s, von Stroheim's films, even those with familiar melodramatic origins, like *Blind Husbands*, are truly "sophisticated," and refuse easy categorization. Reviewers noticed and appreciated that film's unusual qualities, especially its sense of reality and sober, mature tone that did not speak down to audiences. *Variety* remarked of *Blind Husbands*: "This former Griffith heavy has written, directed and acted in a feature that makes others shown on Broadway seem like a novel by Chambers besides a masterpiece by Sudermann and Schnitzler" ("*Blind Husbands*" 1919, 46).

Influenced by both naturalism and an obsessive interest in the habits of Austro-Hungarian aristocracy, *Blind Husbands* established a pattern followed in almost all of von Stroheim's silent films, with the notable exception of *Greed*. Von Stroheim's films would return again and again – in *Merry-Go-Round*, *The Merry Widow*, *The Wedding March*, and *Queen Kelly* – to the cultural, geographical, and sexual terrain of the Austro-Hungarian empire or its "Ruritanian," fictional equivalent. Von Stroheim came to be regarded as *the* interpreter of the complexities in the clash between American and European sexual values, often through the trope of the prince or aristocrat who falls in love with a commoner, as in *Queen Kelly*, *The Wedding March*, and *Merry-Go-Round*, or in the sexual tensions created in the meeting of Americans abroad with Continental sophisticates, as in *Blind Husbands*, *The Devil's Passkey*, *Foolish Wives*, and *The Merry Widow*.

Genius, originality, and authorship were attributed to von Stroheim in studio marketing and by the discourses of reception from the beginning of his directorial career in 1918, even in Universal's prerelease promotion for *Blind Husbands*. But this discourse of artistic authorship was complicated by the ways in which Universal Pictures and later studio employers of von Stroheim (including MGM) featured him in advertisements for his films, often in illustrations that, through costuming and demeanor, conflated his directorial persona with that of the characters he played on-screen. One advertisement for *Blind Husbands* appearing in *Photoplay* featured a large portrait of a bemonocled von Stroheim (then referred to just as "Stroheim" by the nervous studio), slightly smiling, and looking obliquely and rather menacingly at the camera. "Ask your Theatre When you can see it," declared the copy of what was proclaimed to be "The Picture You'll Never Forget." As with many publicity materials that followed, it is difficult to discern whether this is a picture by von Stroheim the director or featuring von Stroheim as actor/character. Why should the two be separated, the studio seemed to ask, if conflation tweaked audience interest?

In fact, Universal seized on this conflation to produce an advertisement for *The Devil's Passkey* that shows director von Stroheim (who wasn't cast in the picture) surrounded by complete darkness, lit from below, and looking up into the camera. The visual effects turn him into the disturbing equivalent of Nosferatu from Murnau's recently released film of the same name (reproduced in Koszarski 2001, 56). A poster for *Foolish Wives* depicts von Stroheim, in uniform, wielding a whip that is raised behind his head. The copy reads: "He's going to make you hate him even if it takes a million dollars of our money to do it!!" (reproduced in Koszarski 2001, 84).

As with DeMille, the marketing of von Stroheim was changing conventional star-centered strategies into a director-centered discourse. In this instance, however, von Stroheim and Universal exploited the duality of the director-as-star and the notoriety of von Stroheim's villainous screen persona rather than completely displacing the actor-centered model with a positive "director-as-artist" model that operated in the DeMille publicity. Von Stroheim's films, while also depending – like DeMille's – upon a stock company approach to the use of actors and key technicians, were distinguished by the director's assuming the role of screenwriter, and often of leading actor as well. In the earliest stage of von Stroheim's career, the studio saw the monetary benefit of using the public's familiarity with him as an actor to increase audience interest in his films. In the wake of the huge cost overruns on *Foolish Wives* and his other films, the industry realized the dangers in this strategy as applied to the director. James R. Quirk of *Photoplay* remarked: "Von always prefers to act [in his films] because then ... they can't fire him, because he's part of the picture ... He can direct. He is a great actor. But to date he has not made that genius usable – he has wasted so much money and so much time that no one could afford his services" (Quirk 1925b, 27).

Almost immediately after the release of his first directorial effort, von Stroheim differentiated himself from the usual motion-picture-director-as-studio-employee by publishing "A Protest to the Trade" in *Motion Picture News*. In it, he blasted Carl Laemmle for changing the name of "the film from the original story" that, declared von Stroheim, was "part of *myself*." The title change to *Blind Husbands*, "a name which is the absolute essence of commercialism ... [but with] no sense of the artistic," was, said von Stroheim, "a direct slap at the feelings of the Author – or Director" (1919, 2678). In his published reply, Laemmle proclaimed that commercialism must trump art in the picture business because of the need for "Money to pay for the *art*!" (1919, 2678).

The published "protest" by von Stroheim shows one dimension of the director's defining his films as extensions of his personal vision. That vision demanded an absolute control over his films that he never achieved. While this particular published exchange may have been part of a studio ploy to generate controversy and interest in *Blind Husbands*, it became the opening salvo in what would become an all too sincere and tragic battle between von Stroheim as "author" of his films and entrenched studio interests. Indeed, this could be seen as a major difference between von Stroheim and DeMille. Unlike DeMille, von Stroheim never stopped fighting against a "culture industry" that demanded, as Adorno and Horkheimer have argued, "enthusiastic obedience to the rhythm of the iron system" (1969, 30). For the film industry, that system involved satisfying, first of all, the commercial interests of exhibitors, distributors, and producers. DeMille learned to submit to those interests; von Stroheim could submit – as he proved with *The Merry Widow* – but he chose not to. He did not want to make "hokum." Published interviews suggest that he self-consciously sought to model his films after the literary approaches of Zola and Balzac.

At the center of the praise *and* the condemnation of von Stroheim's films were often issues of morality and realism. At the same time as von Stroheim's films were regarded as more realistic and more intellectually and emotionally challenging than the usual product of the American film industry, they were also condemned as lacking in entertainment and commercial value, and as inappropriate for family audiences. Many reviews of *Foolish Wives* suggested that von Stroheim had insulted Americans, women, and children. *Moving Picture World*'s review called the film "a studied and flippant slam at all things American" (Tidden 1922, 316). *Photoplay* condemned *Foolish Wives* as "a story you could never permit children or even adolescents to see ... an insult to every American in the audience ... not good, wholesome entertainment" ("*Foolish Wives*" 1922, 70). Yet, as one letter to the editor in the same fan magazine suggested, why should every film be expected to be for children (Arnold 1922, 116)?

Foolish Wives inspired heated debates and generated calls for censorship with its plot that bore certain similarities to that of *Blind Husbands*. The film depicts an American couple whose marriage is threatened by a sexual interloper who is European and is played by von Stroheim. On a country outing with the wife of the American diplomat newly assigned to Monaco, von Stroheim's Count Karamzin pretends they are lost so that he can maneuver her into an isolated hut. The arrival of a monk seeking shelter from the storm outside prevents this counterfeiter and false Russian count from forcing himself on the sleeping woman. In the end, Mrs Hughes's virtue and her marriage are saved, but not necessarily by the strength of her resistance to the seductive ways of European "aristocracy." Count Karamzin is killed by a criminal associate and is unceremoniously stuffed down a sewer drain. An editorial in *Photoplay* declared the film to be alternately beautiful and repugnant, a "gruesome, morbid, unhealthy tale" that is an insult "to American ideals and womanhood" as well as a "waste of one million dollars" ("*Foolish Wives*" 1922, 70). Audiences, as if seeking to be shocked, descended upon movie theaters in droves and made the film a success.

Reviews of von Stroheim's films also often regarded them, like DeMille's, as censorable and sexually bold, but at the same time they were regarded as moving in a distinctly opposite direction than those of DeMille. In reviewing von Stroheim's *Greed*, an adaptation of Frank Norris's naturalist novel, Iris Barry seemed to have DeMille's films in mind when she wrote that the negative audience reaction to von Stroheim's most ambitious project suggested that "the majority [of filmgoers] . . . frankly prefer the usual type of film, with its . . . gilded boudoirs and ballrooms, its false but flattering psychology, and its soothing 'happy ending.'" In contrast to such fare, she noted, von Stroheim's *Greed* was for those "who appreciate a degree of realism, of imagination, or of wit" (Barry 1925, 402). The reviewer for *Exceptional Photoplays* dismissed the idea that *Greed* should be judged by normal standards for the usual audience: "There have already been many criticisms of its brutality, its stark realism, its sordidness. But the point is that it was never intended to be a pleasant picture. . . . [it is] for just those adults who have been complaining most about the sickening sentimentality of the average film" ("*Greed*" 1982, 37–38).

Throughout his career, von Stroheim was determined to make serious (though never humorless) works of art for adults. It was obvious that such films would likely be appreciated best by educated sophisticates in the major cities looking for serious drama, but the complete break these films made with expected Hollywood fare endangered their appeal even to this audience. The *Variety* review of *Greed* declared of von Stroheim's film that "nothing more morbid and senseless, from a commercial picture standpoint, has been seen on the screen in a long, long time. . . . Never has there been a more out-and-out box office flop . . . than this picture" ("*Greed*" 1924, 34). Yet, after one of von Stroheim's severest critics, James R. Quirk, watched the uncut, six-hour version of *Greed*, he admitted that he could not help but admire von Stroheim's desire to make films that were not in the service of commercialism, but purely "art for art's sake" (1925a, 27). Harry Carr, who later collaborated as a screenwriter with von Stroheim, called the original cut of *Greed* "a magnificent piece of work" and noted that the director pleaded with Goldwyn executives to show the film in two installments (1924, 76). He would later defend von Stroheim as Hollywood's "one real genius" and favorably compare him to DeMille, remarking slyly that the latter was "an adroit and skillful mixer of certain theatrical lotions – and notions" (Carr 1928, 39).

Von Stroheim was working in territory far removed from the "lotions and notions" and high-styled "hokum" of DeMille. He did not trade in commercially minded products that would automatically appeal to the masses within the conventional terms of Hollywood entertainment. This extends even to his combination of American and European film influences. As Barry Salt observes, von Stroheim's lighting was influenced by Maurice Tourneur and deviated from some established Hollywood conventions (1983, 146, 189). Yet von Stroheim's visual techniques, or what I call his "optics," adhered rather closely to Hollywood principles of micro-organization, especially in his heavy dependence on shot-reverse shot sequences as fundamental coordinates in the structuring of vision. Stylistically, von Stroheim's films suggest something quite a bit more complicated than Bazin suggested, when he talked about von Stroheim's style as a precursor to the deep focus, long take composition practiced by Orson Welles (Bazin 1967, 23–28). Von Stroheim was a realist, but as particularly evident in *The Merry Widow* and *The Wedding March*, he was quite capable not only of offering, but also of emphasizing a heady and almost dreamlike combination of realism and fantasy. Many critics, even those who denounced his films, called attention to the remarkable juxtaposition of the sacred and the profane, the grotesque and the beautiful in his work. His films were anything but simplistically committed to the long shot long take, and to limited editing. In fact, quite the reverse was true. Learning lessons from Griffith and influenced by the cinematography of Maurice Tourneur's films, he defied Hollywood convention in his visual style. This defiance is manifested not only in the deep focus compositions sometimes found in his films, his penchant for building up details associated with verisimilitude, or his bringing themes associated with realism (and naturalism) to the screen, but also in his sophisticated visual style that depends on well-motivated changes of camera perspective and analytical editing. His visual style established the underlying emotional significance of visual phenomena as fundamental coordinates to the audience's understanding of relations between characters, events, and the filmmaker's attitude. Von Stroheim's visual style did not achieve "realism" merely through an excess of visual detail, both diachronically inscribed across shots and synchronically in single shots, but through an emphasis on what Francesco Casetti refers to as the gaze "as a form of action" (1998, 127).

That is, von Stroheim's genius – or whatever we may label the driving aesthetic and structural force of vision created inside the film frame – is not just a matter of the accumulation of detail, but relies on a construction of the internal optics that foregrounds the inclusion of the film's spectator. *The Wedding March*, a film regarded by Herman Weinberg as the "other" Stroheimian masterpiece apart from *Greed*, perfectly illustrates this idea, since vision becomes a central theme in the film. It functions quite self-consciously in *The Wedding March*, in contrast to other Hollywood films of the period that develop it less explicitly or with less complexity. *The Wedding March* creates a spectatorial presence through its remarkably powerful style that positions the very act of looking as central to its main thematic concern – the exchange value of people. Vision here is narrativized as the act of constructing optical relations that privilege the act of seeing, through the eyes of characters who participate in a system of sexually oppressive exchanges – manifestations of a society based on the dominance of spectacle as commodity production. Von Stroheim carefully separates spectacle in its broader scope from more intimate moments, as in the scene in which a bored, cynical member of the Austrian nobility, Prince Nicki, played by von Stroheim, and a commoner, Mitzi (Fay Wray), are drawn into a flirtation that evolved into a bond of great emotional intensity.

With *The Merry Widow*, von Stroheim would prove that he could, like DeMille, make a commercially focused, star-centered success. Yet even this film is distinctly his, with the von Stroheimian theme of Old World debauchery and decadence turning Franz Lehar's opera into something it was not. This Metro-Goldwyn release was von Stroheim's last wholesale accommodation to the Hollywood system. Its success was undermined by his next directorial effort, *The Wedding March*. With radical cost overruns and massive amounts of footage becoming an industry joke, Paramount took the film away from von Stroheim and cut it from 55 to 14 reels (Koszarski 2001, 240–244). *The Wedding March* flopped at the box office and was followed by the debacle of *Queen Kelly*. After his aborted involvement with *Walking Down Broadway*, von Stroheim struggled in Hollywood as a low-paid staff writer, technical adviser, and script doctor until he left for Europe in 1936. He would return to the United States only as an actor.

Von Stroheim became the legendary example of the talented if temperamental director "destroyed" by the Hollywood system. In a sickening confirmation of the destruction of von Stroheim's authorial ambition and of industrial injustice, he was forced, by economic necessity, to embody on-screen a fictionalized version of himself. In *Sunset Boulevard* (1950), Billy Wilder's corrosive indictment of Hollywood, von Stroheim, who had not been allowed to direct a film in almost 20 years, played the character of Max von Mayerling, a once prominent silent film director who works in humiliating circumstances as the butler for his former wife and star, Norma Desmond (Gloria Swanson). Von Stroheim despised the role.[2] Ironically, Cecil B. DeMille, playing himself, would appear in this same film as what he was – a still vital and respected director, busily engaged in working on his latest feature film (*Samson and Delilah*) at Paramount. The two "geniuses" of early feature film would be brought together in Wilder's film – one in humiliation and the other in triumph. One bittersweet moment, however, brings the two directors together in another, more disturbing and richer way. At the end of the film, it is von Stroheim's character who snaps into a mode of authority and directs the newsreel photographers as they record Norma Desmond's last, mad walk before the cameras. Norma, however, imagines that she has just been directed by Cecil B. DeMille.

Notes

1. Lea Jacobs 2008, 90, says that she did not find an actual reference to DeMille's films as "hoke" or "hokum" even though, for her, his work well deserves the term.
2. See Lenning 2000, 444–449, and Koszarski 2001, 333–334, on von Stroheim's reluctant involvement in *Sunset Boulevard*.

References

"*Adam's Rib*." (1923). Advertisement. *Ladies' Home Journal*, April, 47.

Adorno, Theodor W., & Horkheimer, Max. (1969). "The Culture Industry." In *Dialectic of Enlightenment* (pp. 120–167), trans. John Cummings. New York: Continuum.

Andrews, William Ressman. (1915). "*The Cheat*." *Motion Picture News*, December 25, 127.

Arnold, Alexander. (1922). "Separate Theaters for Children?" In "Brickbats and Bouquets." Letters to the editor. *Photoplay*, 22.7 (December), 116.

Barry, Iris. (1925). "*Greed* – A Film of Realism." *Spectator*, March 14, 402.

Bazin, André. (1967). "The Evolution of the Language of Cinema." *What Is Cinema?*, vol. 1, trans. Hugh Gray. Berkeley: University of California Press.

"*Blind Husbands*." (1919). *Variety*, December 12, 46.

Bush, W. Stephen. (1916). "*The Golden Chance*." *Moving Picture World*, January 8, 255.

Carr, Harry. (1924). "On the Camera Coast." *Motion Picture Magazine*, April, 76.

Carr, Harry. (1928). "Hollywood's One Real Genius – Von." *Photoplay*, 33.6 (May), 39, 138–139.

Casetti, Francesco. (1998). *Inside the Gaze: The Fiction Film and Its Spectator*, trans. Nell Andrew with Charles O'Brien. Bloomington: Indiana University Press.

DeMille, Cecil B. (1920a). "The Heart and Soul of Motion Pictures." *New York Daily Mirror*, June 12, 194–195.

DeMille, Cecil B. (1920b). "What Does Marriage Mean?" As told to Adela Rogers St Johns. *Photoplay*, 19.1 (December), 28–31.

DeMille, Cecil B. (1959). *The Autobiography of Cecil B. DeMille*, ed. Donald Hayne. Englewood Cliffs, NJ: Prentice Hall.

"Exhibitor to Exhibitor Review Service." (1918). *Motion Picture News*, June 8, 3400.

Fletcher, Adele Whitely. (1922). "Sans Mask." *Motion Picture Magazine*, July, 28–29, 88.

"*Foolish Wives*." (1922). *Photoplay*, 21.4 (March), 70.

"*The Golden Chance*." (1915). *New York Daily Mirror*, January 29, 50.

"The Greatest Living Authors Are Now Working With Paramount." (1921). Advertisement for Paramount Pictures. *Ladies' Home Journal*, May, 30.

"*Greed*." (1924). *Variety*, December 19, 34.

"*Greed*." (1982). *Exceptional Photoplays*, December 1924–January 1925. Reprinted in Stanley Hochman (ed.), *From Quasimodo to Scarlett O'Hara: A National Board of Review Anthology, 1920–1940* (pp. 37–38). New York: F. Ungar.

Higashi, Sumiko. (1994). *Cecil B. DeMille and American Culture: The Silent Era*. Berkeley: University of California Press.

Jacobs, Lea. (2008). *The Decline of Sentiment*. Berkeley: University of California Press.

Johnson, Julian. (1917). "*Joan of Arc*." *Photoplay*, 11.4 (March), 113–116.

Koszarski, Richard. (2001). *Von: The Life and Films of Erich von Stroheim*. New York: Limelight.

Laemmle, Carl. (1919). "Response [to von Stroheim]." *Motion Picture News*, October 4, 2678.

Lenning, Arthur. (2000). *Stroheim*. Lexington: University of Kentucky Press.

"*The Little American*." (1917). Review. *Variety*, July 6, n.p.

Mantle, Burns. (1920). "The Shadow Stage." *Photoplay*, 17.6 (May), 64–65.

"*Production Shut Down*." (1923). *Motion Picture News*, November 10, 2225–2226.

Quirk, James R. (1925a). "My Estimate of Erich von Stroheim." *Photoplay*, 27.2 (January), 27.

Quirk, James R. (1925b). "Speaking of Pictures." *Photoplay*, 28.5 (October), 27.

Reid, Laurence. (1923). "The Celluloid Critic." *Motion Picture Classic*, May, 93.

Salt, Barry. (1983). *Film Style and Technology: History and Analysis*. London: Starword.

"The Screen: Remarkable Spectacle, *The Ten Commandments*." (1923). *New York Times*, December 22, 8.

Sherwood, Robert E. (2006a). "*The Ten Commandments*." In Phillip Lopate (ed.), *American Movie Critics: An Anthology from the Silents until Now* (pp. 27–29). New York: Library of America. (Original work published 1923.)

Sherwood, Robert E. (2006b). "*Greed*." In Phillip Lopate (ed.), *American Movie Critics: An Anthology from the Silents until Now* (pp. 29–30). New York: Library of America. (Original work published 1925.)

Smith, Frederick James. (1918). "The Celluloid Critic." Review of *Old Wives for New*. *Motion Picture Classic*, August, 45.

Smith, Frederick James. (1920). "The Screen Year in Review." *Motion Picture Classic*, August, 44.

Smith, Frederick James. (1922). "The Celluloid Critic." Review of *Fool's Paradise*. *Motion Picture Classic*, 92.

Staiger, Janet. (1992). *Interpreting Films: Studies in the Historical Reception of American Cinema*. Princeton: Princeton University Press.

Stroheim, Erich von. (1919). "A Protest to the Trade." *Motion Picture News*, October 4, 2678.

"*The Ten Commandments*." (1923). Review. *Variety*, December 27, n.p.

Tidden, Fritz. (1922). "*Foolish Wives*." *Moving Picture World*, 54, January 21, 316.

Tully, Jim. (1927). "Irving Thalberg." *Vanity Fair*, 29.2 (October), 71, 98.

Weinberg, Herman G. (1973). *The Complete "Greed" of Erich von Stroheim*. New York: E. P. Dutton.

"*Why Change Your Wife?*" (1920). Review. *Wid's Daily*, May 2, 31.

Woollcott, Alexander. (1917). "Second Thoughts on First Nights." *New York Times*, February 25, 3.2.

7

The Star System

Mark Lynn Anderson

Associate Professor, University of Pittsburgh, United States

Public fascination with "picture personalities" first emerged in 1909–1910, and took hold in the mid-teens as feature film production intensified and the concept of the "**movie star**" was born. Mark Lynn Anderson details the workings of the **star system** – from the manufacture and marketing of stars, to voracious popular press consumption of the public- and private-life stories of iconic figures **Mary Pickford**, **Rudolph Valentino**, **Theda Bara**, and **Clara Bow**. With comic actor **"Fatty" Arbuckle**'s notorious trial on murder charges came an intensified public fascination – now with **star scandals** in the 1920s. As some groups rallied for tighter industry supervision and censorship control, others were titillated by fantasies of a glamorously sinful Hollywood Babylon. Anderson studies industry maneuverings of these newly discovered profit-makers and actors' attempts to assert their own control. His essay shares ground with Shelley Stamp in this volume and Jane M. Gaines on women in silent film, Victoria Sturtevant on Mary Pickford, and Diane Negra on Pola Negri in the hardcover/online edition.

Additional terms, names, and concepts: Adolph Zukor, Famous Players-Lasky, the Arbuckle case, "the picture personality"

In the summer of 1918, after failing to negotiate a new contract with his most important star, Adolph Zukor offered Mary Pickford a quarter of a million dollars to leave the motion picture business.[1] Given the meagerness of this sum as compared with Pickford's enormous earning capacity at that moment, one might well conclude that Zukor was merely joking. Yet, might this have been a genuine bribe? The Famous Players-Lasky's chief executive had built his empire upon the exploitation of movie stars like Pickford, and historians of the studio system have long commented upon Zukor's keen involvement in the parallel development of both the feature-length motion picture and the star system during the late transitional period of 1912 to 1915. In the subsequent period of industrial consolidation, however, Zukor apparently sought to turn his back on the star performer as a business strategy, while he instead

American Film History: Selected Readings, Origins to 1960, First Edition. Edited by Cynthia Lucia, Roy Grundmann, and Art Simon.

© 2016 John Wiley & Sons, Inc. Published 2016 by John Wiley & Sons, Inc.

Figure 7.1 Even a motion picture star known as a decadent *féministe* could represent the industry and the interests of the nation. Theda Bara appeals to the public in New York City during the Second Liberty Loan Drive in the autumn of 1917. (Courtesy of George Eastman House.)

pursued theater ownership, the promotion of famous authors, and the production of multiple-star specials that sought to effectively short-circuit the authority of the individual star. When Zukor proposed that Pickford stop working in 1918, she and scores of other Hollywood stars were preparing to participate in the fourth Liberty Loan campaign, where their extraordinary earning power would be once again put on display as beneficial to the American troops overseas, to the nation, and ultimately, to the fate of the entire world.

Zukor, too, was serving on the War Cooperation Committee, on which executives from several studios aided the nation's war effort by placing film industry resources and talent at the service of the US Treasury Department (DeBauche 1997, 116–122). So what exactly was Zukor attempting to buy by proposing that America's Sweetheart simply disappear from view?

Federal agents certainly did not consider this unusual proposition a laughing matter. In 1923, during the Federal Trade Commission (FTC) investigation into Famous Players-Lasky's business practices, government attorneys questioned Pickford about her previous negotiations with Zukor, concluding that his offer to pay the star for leaving the business in 1918 might, indeed, constitute an instance of bribery – one of many ethically questionable and potentially illegal actions that might be traced to Zukor himself and not just to the corporation that he headed. The FTC reached this conclusion despite the fact that Pickford herself fairly dismissed his offer as unreasonable, if not irrational. As she testified at a federal hearing, "Right away I said, 'Mr. Zukor, I am a young girl. Why should I retire at this time of life?' I wanted to go ahead and make bigger and better pictures." When an FTC attorney then asked whether Zukor had given the actress any reason for such an unusual proposal, she simply replied, "No reason."[2]

Immediately following this hearing, Pickford made complaints to the press about Famous Players-Lasky's growing national control over motion picture distribution. Because the federal hearings had been closed to the public and to the press, allegations about Zukor's previous attempt to end Pickford's screen career did not make it into the nation's newspapers, while those comments that Pickford made about monopoly control of distribution did. Interestingly, her complaints against Famous Players-Lasky took the form of a threat to quit the motion picture business because, as she was widely quoted as saying, "I have to worry so much about distribution under the present conditions that my ability as an actress is constantly impaired" ("Mary Pickford Threatens" 1923, 1).

Pickford's testimony at the federal hearing and her comments to the press afterwards sought to pose an increasingly familiar conflict between art and commerce in the film industry, with the latter stifling the former. In this conflict, Pickford presented herself and other powerful film stars as protectors of the original Hollywood dream in which industry and art, work and leisure, production and consumption, magically coalesced to produce a democratic art for the modern age. Pickford herself had turned producer under Zukor's seemingly generous contract of 1916, taking on the responsibility of budgeting each of her productions. She then became a full-fledged studio executive by founding United Artists in 1919, along with Douglas Fairbanks, Charles Chaplin, and the renowned director David Wark Griffith. This move by the stars into studio ownership and film distribution was widely portrayed in the fan magazines and trade journals as an attempt to improve the quality of American motion pictures by placing the creative artists of the cinema in financial control.

When Pickford publicly complained in 1923 about her mounting difficulties with film distribution and exhibition, she claimed that the callous business interests and ruthless practices of the major firms were cheating the public out of its New Jerusalem, derailing a dream of a new era that had been made manifest by the founding of a colony known as Hollywood. Heroic defenders of art, the movie stars apparently were being abandoned by the very industry they had made possible, and now they remained stars only because of their continuing faith in themselves, their cause, and the moviegoing public they served. By this point in 1923, however, such appeals, even by Pickford, were relatively unconvincing, if they were not received as outright bathos.

This is not an unusual or unfamiliar story. The period from 1920 to 1923 represents a moment of perceived crisis in the Hollywood star system, as well as a moment in its transformation. Although the prominent star scandals that erupted during this period often have been cited as the most significant factors in this crisis, star identity was, in fact, already being subjected to corporate pressures working to dissociate the stars from easy identification with the motion picture industry. While the popular appeal of the earlier stars had served to valorize the entire motion picture industry as a uniquely modern institution capable of providing an important new experience of personality within mass society, the subsequent separation of film stars from such intimate proximity with the industry sought to protect the business interests of producers by defining the stars in terms of the various obligations they were required to fulfill, both to their employers and to the filmgoing public. In 1921, the introduction of morality clauses into the standard contract for actors was one of the most visible signs of this sea change. By either denying or making incoherent the stars' previous status as organic representatives of the motion picture enterprise, industry-directed discourse and business practices began emphasizing the contractual nature of motion picture star identity – as an employee now publicly marked as subject to continual managerial evaluation and popular approval. While the sensational star scandals of the early 1920s were the immediate determining instance for this change – since they obviously produced an urgent public relations need for the studios to quickly sever connections with disgraced actors and actresses – the move toward dissociating the star from the studio had preceded the various scandals of 1921 through 1923.

Even though the star system had been integrated into the production process by 1915, stars presented a peculiar problem for the full rationalization of film production, and some sort of solution was required if the studios were to fully consolidate and assume their post–World War I position of globally dominant corporations. This problem of the star sometimes manifested itself in press coverage of the exorbitant salaries motion picture stars began earning in the mid-1910s, a discourse that also underwent a series of transformations during the silent era and through which it is possible to track the changing nature of star identity. The core of the problem that early stars posed to the formation of the studio system, however, was their unique status as "personal monopolies," to borrow a phrase from Paul McDonald. Stars were, first and foremost, employees of the studios, and, as skilled workers, they occupied a place in the technical division of labor within the industry. Yet, film stars were also products of the industry given the prominent consideration they received in almost every aspect of the production process, from the planning of production schedules to the advertising of completed motion pictures. In many ways, by the mid-teens, what Hollywood was selling for the price of a movie ticket was an experience in which the star was most often the principal attraction. Because the star was seen as possessing a popular and appealing personality – a unique identity that was observable in the many public appearances of the star both on-screen and off – she or he owned an important portion of the studio's capital assets, namely, the star's image and the personality associated with that image. McDonald observes that the studios had to "deal with stars as both labor and capital, defining relationships over not only the star as a particular category of worker, but also the star as property and product that can be exploited for commercial purposes in image markets" (2000, 12).

Of course, it is the contract that determines the rights of use and ownership of the star's labor and image for a specified period of time, with the money spent by the firm on the star as both working capital and investment capital. If the star's value appreciated during the term of a contract, the producing company could only realize that appreciation on its investment by renegotiating for the continued use of its asset at a higher cost. This is why standard contracts for stars often gave the studio options for retaining the star for subsequent years at specified higher rates. If, at the end of a contract, the producers calculated that the retention of the star at a higher rate was not economically worthwhile (whether that rate was for a new contract or for exercising an option to renew), they also had to factor in the additional losses that would result from a competing firm subsequently acquiring their asset and the already constituted market for an exclusive product, that is, the star's paying public. If Zukor was genuinely offering a bribe to Pickford in 1918, it was likely offered in order to prevent these additional losses to the studio. Such a motivation would also explain the relatively low amount offered in the bribe since it would have been calculated by the studio as a cost solely in relation to an anticipated loss of market share to a competitor such as First National, and not in relation to Pickford's potential earnings over the next several years. In other words, Famous Players-Lasky figured that Pickford's continued appearances in the motion pictures of another firm would amount to losses somewhat greater than the sum Zukor offered Pickford to quit the business, somewhat greater than a quarter of a million dollars if her testimony in 1923 is to be believed. Whether or not Zukor's offer to Pickford constituted bribery, it nevertheless shows that by 1918 studio executives understood the star system as a unique commodities market through which a firm might well profit by severely restricting the availability of that commodity, even to the point of making that commodity entirely unavailable to a purchasing public. In other words, long before the scandals began in 1921, the Hollywood star system was already subjected to processes of monopolistic control that resulted in calculated attempts to keep particular stars out of public view.[3]

Larger-than-Life Figures

Attempts at rationally calculating the market value of a star were not only the prerogative of the studio executive; they were also a prominent part of the public discourse about stars from the mid-teens on. A star's reported earnings were, of course, part of the star's prestige. At a moment when the star system was being integrated into the production process, the stars themselves had already become ubiquitous figures in the public sphere, their names and images appearing on posters, magazine covers, advertisements, various gift items, and in entertainment sections of the nation's newspapers. Pickford herself wrote an advice column that was nationally syndicated in 1916 and 1917 (Beauchamp 1997, 61; Whitfield 1997, 152–153). As Richard deCordova has observed, by 1914, stars were rather quickly becoming the chief means of experiencing the cinema outside of the movie theater, with fan magazine coverage of the stars' private lives outstripping publication of fictional works based on narratives of already-released films. *Motion Picture Story Magazine*, which first appeared in February of 1911, changed its name to *Motion Picture Magazine* in March 1914. But it was over a year later that the most popular stars began using their unusual status as capital assets to negotiate ever greater compensation, a situation that, as numerous historians have pointed out, manifested itself in their conspicuous consumption of luxurious goods and services (Lowenthal 1961; May 1980). Coverage of the stars' hobbies, homes, and material possessions revealed utterly charmed lives, a condition of grace expressing the unique personalities upon which that very grace was premised. The stars led tautologically beautiful lives because they were beautiful people, and it was the film industry that had brought them all together in one place, making it possible for a vast audience to participate in an exploration of modern personality. Nevertheless, consumption was not the first or even principal context for divulging the inflated incomes of movie stars. Initial fan magazine coverage of star salaries compared their weekly earnings and bonuses to those of the most popular stars of the stage in order to explain how such enormous sums could be justified, as well as to associate film stardom with the prestige of the most esteemed sectors of the legitimate theater. In the pages of *Photoplay* in 1915, for instance, *New York World* columnist Karl Kitchen compared Mary Pickford's salary of $2,000 a week with the same amount paid to Maude Adams by the late Charles Frohman just before the impresario's death earlier that year. The salaries of both stars were further justified by the equally large profits realized by their respective employers (Kitchen

1915, 138–139). Similarly, in early 1916, Alfred Cohn defended Chaplin's salary and the numerous bonuses he received at Essanay on the basis that his films purportedly had earned that company more than $2 million (Cohn 1916, 28).[4] At the same time, readers were also warned that reports of inflated star salaries were often only so much ballyhoo, with Kitchen offering a formula for arriving at the actual income of a given film star – take the announced salary, "divide it by two and then subtract a third of the quotient" (Kitchen 1915, 139).

The largest salaries reported during this period were paid by motion picture concerns to stars from the legitimate stage who had accepted offers to appear in one or more pictures. Cohn reported that the highest price ever paid to a performer for a single picture went to Ziegfeld star Billie Burke, who contracted to make *Peggy* for $40,000, though he also mentions Metropolitan Opera soprano Geraldine Farrar's having earned $5,000 a week from the Lasky Company, as well as the comic stage actor DeWolf Hopper's lucrative contract with Triangle at a salary comparable to Douglas Fairbanks's "similar arrangement" with that company. Despite the relatively short or sporadic careers in motion pictures enjoyed by most of the headliners imported from the theatrical world of New York, such crossover stars helped establish the first iterations of that geographical imaginary known as "Hollywood." As the *Los Angeles Times* reported at the beginning of 1916, "The transplanted Broadwayites dwell for the most part in Hollywood where several motion-picture studios are located. They live in bungalows, motoring back and forth to their work" ("Movie Stars Who Scintillate" 1916, 71). When complaints were mounted about the inflated salaries of motion picture performers during this period, they, more often than not, focused on salaries earned by theatrical personalities appearing in motion pictures – as when *Photoplay* editor James Quirk blamed the rapid disappearance of both older and smaller producing firms in 1916 on the "swollen salaries" paid to stage performers "step[ping] before the camera for the first time" ("The Motion-Picture Crisis" 1916, 64). Of course, another group of small producing outfits headed by individual stars would appear within a couple of years, as the studios increasingly passed production oversight to their top performers – just as Zukor had done with Pickford in 1916, transforming the star into a producer of sorts, albeit one closely tethered to the budget and contractual arrangements of the parent company (Mahar 2006, 154–178; Whitfield 1997, 144–145). The rise and relatively short heyday of the star-run studio at the end of the 1910s correlated with a transformation in the discourse on star salaries from a justification of six-figure incomes as an index of the star's worth and a function of market supply and demand to a portrayal of the star as both an entrepreneur and a commercial enterprise – with the star's large salary now presented as commensurate with the new managerial position of the star. The salary was further represented as investment capital for the star's productions, with the most important product being the star him- or herself. By 1918, for example, Hector Ames could explain to readers of *Motion Picture Magazine* "that a big salary means big expenses" and "that a good part of a star's salary must go right back into his business as an investment for the future." Ames went on to describe that the stars do not simply buy extravagant clothes as much as invest in wardrobes. He also indicated that movie stars needed at least two secretaries to manage all sorts of sundry business and social obligations and that they would also often employ various consultants and trainers to acquire those skills necessary to their work in motion pictures and publicity appearances (Ames 1918, 73–75). Far from idols of consumption, what we have here are idols of business acumen who are presented to the public as models for self-fashioning.[5]

It was obvious to all that the stars commanded enormous salaries and, while the stars became "idols of consumption," they were not made glamorous solely because they were enviable in their ability to consume. The stars were compelling because the lives they lived in public view, however constructed those lives may have been, posed another possibility for American mass society, the possibility of living beyond the traditional social divisions central to capitalist social formation: the divisions between work and leisure, public and private, industry and art, employer and worker. In the early 1920s, Pickford presented herself to the public as a defender of these earlier halcyon days of the star system. By then, though, Pickford and other first-generation movie stars were already becoming film history, and the massive salaries enjoyed by many of the stars were no longer promoted as part of the miracle of a newly emerged culture industry. A common explanation for the perceived excesses of star behaviors in the early 1920s was that the industry had developed far too rapidly, leaving some individuals ill-prepared for the sudden wealth of stardom. According to this discourse, the escalating success of the industry produced unforeseen conditions for a small number of its workers, allowing them to pursue self-indulgent and self-destructive lifestyles. The "excessive" weekly star paycheck was seen as a dangerous influence on the star's moral behavior and on the continuing viability of the film industry. This was essentially a problem of industrial growth, the remedy for which was reinscription of a proper managerial division of labor at the level of film industrial culture.

Reinventing the Star System

After World War I, many of the earliest American movie stars who had, only a few years before, garnered both national and international fame were publicly remembered as already long forgotten. As a newspaper editorialist put it in 1921, "The moving picture stars of yesteryear, who were on the lips of every theatre-goer throughout the country, have practically all faded into oblivion, and the memory of their entertaining talents are [*sic*] as remote from that same enthusiastic movie patronage, as though they had never occupied a place in screendom" ("Fading Film Stars" 1921, 45). The writer continues by briefly recalling the careers of first-generation stars, such as Bronco Billy Anderson, Francis X. Bushman, Maurice Costello, J. Warren Kerrigan, Edith Storey, and Lillian Walker, for a newspaper readership presumed to be completely unfamiliar with these names. A typical explanation for this rapid descent into oblivion was the natural aging of the first popular screen performers whose now middle-aged countenances could no longer meet the requirements of those youthful romances or adventures that were becoming staples of feature film production and popular tastes. In January 1922, for instance, the *Literary Digest* reported on an article that had appeared in the Los Angeles publication *Camera* describing an imminent crisis faced by the film industry, a crisis resulting from a generation of skilled motion picture actors now too old to convincingly portray youthful screen characters, and another group of performers who "suffer from a startlingly uneven mental combination which renders their knowledge of art and its inseparable complement, realism, entirely negligible, while lending them an overamount of that reprehensible affectation, commonly termed worldly wisdom" ("The Trouble with the Movie Face" 1922, 28). The former were considered, then, to be genuine screen artists who had had their day in the sun, with exceptions granted to veteran star performers Mary Pickford and Charles Ray, who remained "truly young in spirit," while the latter constituted a group of undeserving screen celebrities whose talents ran principally toward stereotypical posturing. Such "manufactured stars" would typically include outdated older performers like Theda Bara, as well as newcomers like Rudolph Valentino. The *Camera* article argued that the solution to this crisis was a fresh injection of "genuine youth" into the movies, championing those screen talents who successfully projected a youthful élan, such as May McAvoy, Richard Barthelmess, and the by-then late Bobby Harron.[6] Hollywood would, as is well known, answer the call of youth in the mid-1920s by promoting stars like Colleen Moore, Bill Haines, and Clara Bow and by producing film scripts that would help define the era's preoccupation with jazz dancing, college life, automobiles, and flappers. But in the early 1920s, Hollywood's promotion of America's new youth culture had yet to be established, and the film industry was quite often described through metaphors of stagnation and morbidity.

A significant part of this impasse was how to regenerate an ailing and malfunctioning star system. The rhetoric of "out with the old and in with the new" could not simply be imposed by the studios, since many older stars remained incredibly powerful and profitable. Throughout 1923, the public discussion on the excesses of stars' salaries escalated significantly. This was also the year during which Rudolph Valentino was absent from the screen as a result of contract disputes with Famous Players-Lasky, an absence weighted with enormous significance by the fan press and generally viewed as the catalyst for the industry's importation of several new stars to fill the void created by Valentino's departure. *Photoplay* praised Ramón Novarro, one of the most important and successful of the "Valentino replacements," for the financial skills he reportedly exhibited in contract negotiations with Marcus Loew, favorably comparing the dashing young Latin star to John D. Rockefeller (Howe 1923, 104). These new star personalities were more easily represented as difficult, as having domestic problems, and as walking out on their contracts. While the leaders of the industry could question the Hollywood credentials of the new stars in ways they could never question, say, Pickford, Fairbanks, or Chaplin, these new contract players also could be championed as the future of Hollywood, masters of contract negotiation and the business deal, rather than crafters of a false dream about eternal youth and undying beauty.

Making Stars Pay

The success and continuation of this strategy that insisted upon the entrepreneurial identity of the film star can be seen at work in the protracted public dispute that unfolded between Valentino and Famous Players-Lasky during the final months of 1922 and throughout 1923. After several years of performing for the camera in various supporting roles, Valentino's rise to stardom had been fairly meteoric after he appeared as a suave Argentinean gaucho in Metro's prestige production of *The Four Horsemen of the Apocalypse*, released early in 1921. Perhaps more than any other film star of the period, Valentino represented a new brand of film celebrity, one whose fame rested principally upon the affections of an adoring and somewhat irrational audience rather than upon any intrinsic ability or talent possessed by the star himself and whose popular success then might be credited to the film industry's ability to locate, develop, and authorize star quality. Indeed, Valentino's "discovery" was continually attributed in the fan press to a single industrial insider, screenwriter June Mathis, a woman who would remain Valentino's loyal advocate throughout most of his short career (Slater 1995, 135). According to this particular narrative, it was Mathis's personal insight into Valentino's potential for popular appeal, as well as her obstinate promotion of him against more skeptical powers at Metro, that eventually launched a screen performance powerful enough to create a spontaneous cult around the star that continues to this day. Rather than being the product of an industrial system dedicated to the production of popular art and to the refinement of star personalities, Valentino would henceforth live under the charge of being a "woman-made man" (Studlar 1996, 150–198). He seemingly belonged to the public more than to any studio.

A second film that contributed greatly to the formation of the cult of Valentino was *The Sheik*, the first picture he made for Famous Players-Lasky late in 1921, and the first picture in which he donned the apparel of a Bedouin Arab, a costume that would quickly become iconic in the star's popular image. In January 1922, Valentino signed a long-term contract with the studio in which he was to receive $1,250 per week for one year, with an option of $2,000 per week for a second year, and $3,000 per week for a third. After a succession of four rapidly produced pictures in 1922, Valentino walked out on his contract in August, claiming that the studio had seriously breached its agreement with him and misrepresented the terms of the original contract. Famous Players-Lasky responded by obtaining a legal injunction to prevent the star from performing for any other motion picture concern or from taking any speaking roles on the theatrical stage. Valentino used the occasion of his unemployment to lambaste the studio system as inherently hostile to both motion picture arts and artists because the major producers pursued financial profits with little regard for anything else.

Without substantially harming the star's popularity, Famous Players-Lasky responded by attempting to represent Valentino as narcissistically misguided and, ultimately, ridiculous – a fairly successful strategy that helped defuse the charges that Valentino and other stars were making about corporate greed. Indeed, it was during the early 1920s that fallout from the full implementation of the central producer system in the studios gave rise to a new type of popular motion picture celebrity, the star or other creative talent who was slightly out-of-touch with reality and who railed against the oppressive restrictions placed upon his or her artistic genius. Corporate discipline was then positioned as a necessary and beneficial constraint upon exceptional but impractical individuals who were made to appear that much more interesting and "sensitive" for their unusual suffering and sacrifices.[7] Such individuals were typically Europeans or Americans who affected European sensibilities.

While more extensive and sensational than that of the monthly fan publications such as *Photoplay*, *Movie Weekly*'s coverage of Valentino's contract dispute is indicative of a new popular interest in star complaints about all aspects of the industry. After the studio had won an injunction against the actor in September, *Movie Weekly* serialized portions of the affidavit that

Valentino filed in the Superior Court of New York State in response to the suit brought against the star by Famous Players-Lasky Corporation. The titles of these installments sought to capitalize on the star's indignity about the manner in which he had been treated by the studio. Titles such as "They Tried to Discipline Me," "'Friends Insulted,' Declares Valentino," and "Valentino Swears, '*Blood and Sand* Mutilated'" sought to portray the film star as an outraged defender of art whose refined sensibilities had been offended by the studio's coarse and dehumanizing production practices. In the first of these extended excerpts from the legal briefs, Valentino complains at length about how studio executives refused to provide him with an adequate dressing room – one suitable to his position as a major star. The star describes how he was forced to occupy one of the smaller rooms in a building some distance from the set, where "actors and actresses who have less arduous work to do" are asked to share quarters without "convenient sanitary facilities." He also complains about the even more unacceptable lack of accommodation provided while shooting *Blood and Sand* on location at the Lasky ranch, where he was humiliated by having to make frequent costume changes "under a scorching sun" and "in full sight of everyone" ("Valentino Says" 1922, 19, 29). Subsequent coverage of the affidavit in *Movie Weekly* presented Valentino's claims that the studio systematically refused or ignored his ideas and suggestions about the films in which he was required to perform, and he further described how he was repeatedly denied various privileges enjoyed by most other employees of the studio, such as having friends or business associates visit him on the set.

In essence, Valentino was alleging these actions were malicious and were intended as punishments for even contemplating that he might be allowed to have some say in the production of his motion pictures. According to the affidavit, when Valentino complained about the deletion of a scene from *Blood and Sand* that both he and June Mathis had requested be retained in the final release version as crucial to the narrative, Jesse Lasky replied that studio executives "knew more about their business than [he] did." Simultaneous with its coverage of the legal dispute, *Movie Weekly* also published a lengthy message from Valentino (or one ghostwritten for the star) in which he brandishes his knowledge of modern business by describing, in some detail, the centralized organization of the Famous Players-Lasky Corporation, its production schedule, its recent aggressive move toward vertical integration through theater takeovers, its practice of block-booking pictures, the history of the studio's organization through important mergers, its current total assets, its liabilities in terms of preferred and common stocks, and the dividends these stocks have paid – in short, everything that was of interest to the ongoing investigation of the Federal Trade Commission. The star's purpose in explaining to the public the political economy of the studio system was to counter the corporation's claim that his premature departure caused significant financial harm to the studio by disrupting production. According to the star, "This business has been built up by its regular merchandise methods of merchandising bills in which a regular supply of average pictures is depended upon and not a reliance upon any given star of [any] given production" ("Came East to See Wife" 1922, 31). Here was a star claiming that stars were of little relevance to the practical operation of the studio system.

Movie Weekly also published, in response to the star's allegations, depositions from several Famous Players-Lasky executives and employees, including the affidavits of general studio manager Charles Eyton, acting general manager Victor Clarke, film editor Frank Woods, and corporation president Adolph Zukor. Each of these affidavits, with the possible exception of Zukor's, methodically counters Valentino's claims in the dispassionate voice of the reasonable and knowledgeable businessman. In the most contentious response by the firm, Zukor claims that Valentino only "deserted" the studio in order to seek an inflated salary of $5,000 a week, and he insists on Valentino's utter duplicity in this matter, even casting aspersions upon the star's masculinity when he contends that Valentino "boasts of his physical prowess, and then complains about the alleged inconveniences and discomforts which no red-blooded man would notice." Yet, the most significant instance of the star's dissembling cited by Zukor had to do with Valentino's refusal of entrepreneurial identity: "He pleads his ignorance … of business affairs and the business aspects of motion pictures[,] and presents a mass of alleged facts and figures which would indicate that he possessed all of the existing knowledge on the subject, and had negotiated and signed many contracts prior to the one in controversy" ("'Charges Absolutely False!'" 1922, 13). While Valentino's associations with exoticism, European decadence, and ethnic indeterminacy were certainly a result of studio packaging, the star's own self-presentation, as well as his cultural investments in romantic notions of artistic culture, contributed significantly to the apparent artificiality of his identity. His relentless posturing supported various camp and queer receptions of the star during the decade and beyond, and these fabulously failed attempts at sincerity resulted from the dissonance between Valentino's performed earnestness and the success of the new corporate strategy of the producers that insisted upon both the commodity nature of the film star and the utter falseness of any claim by the star that she or he was anything more than a talented but self-interested business person with whom the studio had a contract. The larger significance of these protracted disputes was that the film industry could expand its ongoing distancing of the stars from any easy overidentification with the corporate firm, in part by inviting public interest in labor disputes between well-paid stars and the studios. What was true for the star was not necessarily true for the studio, and this was an extremely important message to convey to the public during the period of the star scandals.

Coming to Know the Stars

For the last 20 years, the work of Richard deCordova has been centrally important to the historical study of stars and the star system. By shifting our critical attention away from some of the more established issues – such as whether the early star system can be said to have resulted from a rapidly mounting popular interest in particular performers that occurred during 1909 and early 1910, or whether it might be more accurately considered an industrial innovation aimed at further stabilizing production while controlling reception through product differentiation – deCordova emphasized the discursive qualities of the star system as a formal means of communication, one that articulated and continually rearticulated the relations between the audience and the star. In other words, from a position that sees knowledge as bound to the material terms of its expression, deCordova posed new questions about how we know stars and how we come to know them. Stars do not simply appear. The very conditions of their appearance have first to be secured, and deCordova asks us to understand stardom as a set of specific signifying practices about particular bodies and particular personalities, a set of practices that cohere as a discourse. He points out that any historically emergent interest in the motion picture star would depend upon the notion of a performer whose regular work was to play in fictional filmed stories and who was readily identifiable from picture to picture, identifiable in such a way that previous appearances would contribute to the meanings and pleasures of each new role. This precondition of the motion picture star deCordova terms "the picture personality," whose appearance he dates around the time that most histories locate the first movie stars, approximately 1910. The picture personality is itself a complex entity that only becomes known through the alignment of specific developments in production practices, exhibition practices, early trade paper and newspaper review practices, the emerging fan press, and, of course, the pictures that regularly featured the performer as a personality. All these disparate signifying practices reinscribed the picture personality in such a way that the personality became an object of the filmgoing public's attention.

For deCordova, the appearance of the picture personality likewise depended upon a previous discourse on acting that would finally make the bodies on the screen legible as performing the work of acting, rather than, say, as simply posing before the camera. Both the discourse on acting and the emergence of the picture personality appeared prior to the emergence of the star, prior in the chronological sense, as well as discursively antecedent. His analyses of the rudiments of the early star are borne out in the column, "Observations by Our Man About Town," from the November 20, 1909 edition of *Moving Picture World*:

> Up-to-date moving picture places have adopted the ancient custom of regular playhouses in placing in the lobbies of the theater large frames containing photographs of the leading people in various film subjects. It is making quite a hit and the film manufacturers are being besieged for photographs. The patrons of the picture houses have at last become convinced that the pictures are made from posing regular actors and actresses and that they are reproductions of regular performers. This has led to the bringing forward of personal identity of the people engaged in the productions. Regular patrons of the house have their favorites and are quick to recognize them on screen. (714)

Whether or not a viewing public had to be persuaded by exhibitors to see those who appeared in films as possessing acting talent, it is clear that a process of coming to know film actors and actresses as particular personalities was contingent upon the material practices of the cinema as an institution.

The importance of this earlier period to the subsequent appearance of film stars after 1914 has to do with the way a process of elaboration was established for the reception of picture personalities. As deCordova pointed out, each new film appearance by a favored performer promised to reveal some further aspect of his or her personality, thereby adding to the overall pleasure one could take in both the performer and the performance. The early fan press and the trade magazines alerted audiences to upcoming pictures of the performers, while discussing the merits of their past screen appearances. For deCordova, the increasing intertextuality of the picture personality established a hermeneutic of continual investigation and discovery, one in which the experience of each new picture in which a favorite performer appeared was enhanced by learning about that performer's career in the fan press or in the entertainment section of the newspapers, as well as by viewing photographs and posters of the performer in the lobbies of motion picture houses. In essence, the picture personality became the key term in a search for information that would lead audiences from the motion picture theater to the newsstands and back again in a continuous route. The economic benefits to the industry were obvious.

This continual elaboration of the picture personality at multiple sites led to a transformation in the object of popular investigation when, during the period of late 1913 and 1914, coverage of the private lives of the more popular performers became possible and was quickly accepted as a regular feature in both studio promotions and news coverage of the industry. Not coincidentally, this was the moment in which star income became a prevalent part of the coverage, since the question of star salaries as investment capital or take-home pay nicely represented the indeterminacy of the line dividing work and leisure in the lives of stars. For deCordova, this expansion of attention to the performer's time spent at home or in activities away from the studio constituted the star proper, since it was now possible to appreciate the entire life and lifestyle of the performer as pertinent to an interest in the cinema, a situation that continues to define stardom today. Besides expanding the types of information that could be part of the ongoing appreciation of a performer, new information about the personal lives of popular players allowed the film industry to promote its differences from the theater in terms of the stability and normality of the home lives of its personnel, even as it exploited some of the theater's biggest celebrities. Unlike the fairly disorganized and unsettled lives that were presumably led by most stage actors and actresses who were required to spend much of their time away from family when traveling from town to town in theatrical circuits, the fan magazines emphasized the genial stability of studio work that allowed the motion picture stars to return each evening to the same home in the same community. Early coverage of the lives of the stars also emphasized the wholesomeness of their hobbies, their fairly conventional opinions about the world, their recognizable living situations, their homes, their automobiles, and their romantic and matrimonial relations. While such information certainly increased popular interest in the movies by offering depictions of the stars' lives to which large numbers of people might relate (or to which they might aspire), it also helped to promote the cinema as a respectable, responsible, and even socially beneficial institution. As these fascinating and familiar performers increasingly relocated to the production centers in southern California, this emphasis on the stability, charm, and integration of the stars' domestic and professional lives was arguably the first iteration of what would quickly become the myth of Hollywood – that ideal modern community of pioneering industrial artists whose charter Pickford was defending in 1923 when she protested monopoly distribution practices, that very Hollywood to which Valentino sought to claim himself heir in his contract disputes with Famous Players-Lasky. The utopian myth of Hollywood, however, had grown rather stale in less than a decade. By the early 1920s, many stars would be complaining that corporate growth was stifling screen art, while the major studios pursued a strategy to promote the real value of motion pictures as equivalent to the sound business organization and practices that allowed for their efficient manufacture, distribution, and enjoyment by the public.

The Public's Loyalties

In many ways, what was happening in the early 1920s was an attempt by the industry to return to an insistence upon the manufacture's brand name as the principal selling point of motion pictures to both the exhibitor and the public, a marketing situation that had existed during the transitional era of American cinema but one that was rapidly eclipsed by the nascent star system (Bowser 1990, 103–119). The real difference between brand name promotion during the transitional era and that of the major studios in the 1920s was the latter's widespread deployment of emotional appeals to the consumer whose very happiness and health were figured as significantly enhanced by the uniformity of experience guaranteed by the trusted name-brand. As corporate public relations developed during and immediately after World War I, large companies looked to the visual and narrative appeal of the movies for models of mass address that could effectively produce emotional attachments to their products by emphasizing affect over reason, psychological appeal over rational argument, and images over texts – in other words, those strategies that quickly became the very basis of modern advertising (Ewen 1996). More importantly, the most effective public relations strategies pursued by the larger corporations sought to establish emotional attachments to the company name by suggesting that the company's products or services helped make interpersonal relationships possible, thereby quelling much of the antitrust sentiment that was still lingering from the Progressive era. The rise in importance of public relations during this era is clearly evident in those advertising practices that integrated the corporate name or logo with images of everyday life in such a way that products bearing that name became, more or less, one of the family. Of course, not only was the popularity of Hollywood movies and movie stars an object lesson for public relations experts, but the studios themselves became important innovators in using advertising to shape public opinion toward accepting what would eventually become "corporate America."

Consider the Famous Players-Lasky's advertising campaign of 1921. The company placed regular, full-page advertisements in several large-circulation, general interest magazines such as the *Saturday Evening Post* and *Good Housekeeping*. They usually mentioned popular stars like Wallace Reid or Gloria Swanson, but only in the small type used for sidebars that announced current releases; the far more prominent advertising copy discussed the value of "Paramount Pictures," the well-known name of the distribution and exhibition wings of Famous Players-Lasky. These high-profile spots typically featured sentimental images of couples or families who were either at home preparing to go to the movies, in the street in front of a theater showing a Paramount release, or in the lobby of a theater purchasing tickets. One that appeared in the February 19 issue of the *Saturday Evening Post* featured a boy and a man looking at a poster displayed outside a downtown picture palace that read, "It's a Paramount Picture." The accompanying text explained, "The idea of shopping for their photoplay is gradually taking hold of people. Just the way they shop for suits, rugs or motor cars. It may seem strange to shop for such a romantic thing as a motion picture but good business methods turn out as well in buying entertainment as in buying anything else." Such promotions sought to link the family to the corporation by demonstrating how the dependability of a name-brand can create familial consensus. An advertisement placed in the November issue of the *Ladies' Home Companion* featured the image of a young couple preparing to leave their small children in the care of a maid for the evening. The copy addressed similarly blessed young couples, explaining how "your evenings out together are precious. Keep them up. Once or twice a week you parents deserve a great show." The advertisement then proclaimed the corporation's vast geographical reach as a guarantee to providing authentic domestic fulfillment through entertainment. "More than 11,200 theaters possess the Paramount Franchise of Romance to show Paramount Pictures. Surely your home is not outside this charmed circle." Here, the routine linking of the home to the motion picture house sought to transfer onto the corporation those affective attachments to moviegoing and movie products that had been made possible by the star system. While this Paramount promotion campaign literally marginalized the stars by reducing their names to so much information about scheduled releases, it also sought to appropriate some of the ways in which star discourse had been able to construct lasting, intimate connections between the ordinary moviegoer and the extraordinary motion picture star. In large measure, these connections had been sustained by those continual revelations about the health and normality of the stars' domestic lives, habits, and interpersonal relations, and it was those felt connections that quickly became the impetus for movie star endorsements of various consumer products. In the early 1920s, Famous Players-Lasky and other large studios attempted to persuade the public that the corporation was the authentic source for those cinematic pleasures of identity and repetition that had defined the early star system. As the September 1921 ad in the *Ladies' Home Journal* put it, "Each Paramount Picture that you see gives birth to a desire to see the next – an endless chain of happy evenings."

The Compulsion to Repeat

The star scandals of the early 1920s, particularly those that involved protracted criminal investigations or criminal trials, expanded coverage of the stars' daily lives and habits from the advice, style, and entertainment sections of daily papers to their front pages. Two of the most prominent of the star scandals that stayed in the headlines the longest and became ensconced in the popular memory of the period were the arrest and subsequent trials of Roscoe "Fatty" Arbuckle for the rape and murder of actress Virginia Rappe and the unsolved murder of film director William Desmond Taylor, an event that revealed his intimate and morally questionable relations with a pair of younger star actresses who, at one time or another, were also considered suspects in the homicide investigation. Even though other sectors of American society, such as professional sports and politics, were being rocked by sensational scandals during this era, the considerable media attention devoted to the star scandals of the early 1920s demonstrated the uniqueness of the cinema as an institution, as well as the failure of the industry to fully distinguish itself from those famous individuals it employed. Yet, intentionally or not, the industry had been preparing to protect itself from the possibilities of such scandals through an organized consolidation of industry-aligned theater owners, who sought to present a unified front against the screen exploitation of notorious individuals by small-time producers and renegade exhibitors (Anderson 2007), and through the discursive positioning of the motion picture star as an autonomous and self-interested business person. Nevertheless, the Arbuckle case produced widespread attacks on the film industry from reformers, women's groups, the clergy, and politicians at all levels of government. While many of these voices had long been critical of the motion picture industry, the Arbuckle scandal allowed reformers to augment their demand for more stringent censorship of immoral and harmful pictures with a similar call to ban from the screen all immoral and harmful performers. Almost overnight, Arbuckle, who had been an internationally beloved screen comedian, perhaps second in popularity only to Chaplin, was turned into a hedonistic monster, a perception that has forever stuck to the rotund comedian despite his eventual acquittal in the spring of 1922. The three criminal trials that dragged on for over eight months provided the daily papers with seemingly endless testimony about the sensual living of some Hollywood stars, and with exposé reports of the allegedly hidden underbelly of the film colony, coverage that dramatically widened once the Taylor murder investigation began in February 1922.

As deCordova has pointed out, the star scandals can be considered just another extension of the star system rather than evidence of its radical rupture. Those processes of investigating the identity of the star that had been established earlier now readily lent themselves to the sorts of pleasures to be gained in locating the truth of the individual through the revelation of deeply guarded secrets. Michel Foucault defined the interrogation of the individual in order to establish hidden truth as an operation of disciplinary power that would become the principal form of knowledge production in the West after the nineteenth century. For Foucault, sexuality had provided modern society with an "incitement to discourse" that increasingly multiplied the sites of sexuality and specified the ways that sex might be talked about, identified, tested, and ultimately regulated. As such, the discourse on sexuality as a way of knowing extended far beyond the means of any particular institution or organization to control or contain its permutations or effects. Indeed, such organizations and institutions were more or less structured by the very discourses they deployed. Accordingly, deCordova has proposed that the star system came to be defined by that same or by very similar epistemological pursuits, only to likewise arrive at those truths about the individual that could be

October 1, 1921 MOVING PICTURE WORLD 513

The Arbuckle Case

Enclosed in the Following Space Is Our Idea What Should Be Said by Everybody in the Moving Picture Business About the Arbuckle Case from Now Forth Until the Entire Matter Is Settled

MOVING PICTURE WORLD

Figure 7.2 Wishful thinking on the part of the editors at *Moving Picture World*.

revealed and interpreted by the modern human sciences: "The sexual scandal is the primal scene of all star discourse, the only scenario that offers the promise of a full and satisfying disclosure of the star's identity" (1990, 141). As the imagined scene of violent and fatal sexual violation attached itself to the identity of Arbuckle, the industry was well aware of its inability to control the discursive implications of such a revelation, despite the widespread bans immediately placed on his films by exhibitor organizations, and despite Famous Players-Lasky's attempt to radically distance itself from Arbuckle by refusing to publicly defend one of its top stars. Within weeks of Arbuckle's arrest, the *Moving Picture World* correctly predicted that continued public attention to the incident would create a situation making it impossible for Arbuckle to resurrect his screen career, whatever the outcome of the legal proceedings against him. Yet, the editorialist was far more concerned about the inevitable harm such publicity would cause the entire industry due to "the sensational retelling in the daily newspaper of all the sickening details of the death and its causes" (James 1921, 383). This was more than just an acknowledgment that the scandal would provide ammunition for Hollywood's many critics, but a lament that the industry could not effectively hide from view that which it had continuously made amenable to public revelations, the perpetually fascinating personality of the star. Movie stars were increasingly discussed and represented within institutional contexts that were unaligned with Hollywood, such as the courts and the tabloid press, and the industry's inability to effectively distance itself from the discursive imperatives of the star system was poignantly captured by another editorial that appeared in *Moving Picture World* a week later.

The startling sense of waste and inefficiency conveyed by encountering this empty frame within the usually crowded pages of the trade journal is a haunting reminder of the star system's resistance to complete industrial rationalization. At the same time, and despite the caption's insistence upon maintaining silence about the scandal – a policy of discretion to which the fan magazines of the era meticulously subscribed – the negative space prompts the reader to fill it up with some sort of imagined truth about the affair. This command to silence is, in effect, an invitation to discourse, demonstrating the Foucauldian insight that silences are rarely outside of discourse but constitutive of them.

If the star scandals did not ultimately constitute a discursive break in the star system, they did mark a fairly thorough cleaving of star identity, separating the star's work for a company and the star's personal life apart from the studio – a separation that also became a legacy for film history. The pursuit of debauched lifestyles by film stars was widely seen as facilitated by their unusually large paychecks and their unchecked consumption, a somewhat constricted perspective on star salaries that was drowning out industry efforts to also represent such large sums as capital investment. Studies of the star system have predominantly documented the former understanding of star pay and lifestyles as subtending Hollywood's role in promoting consumer culture in the United States and abroad. Yet, the star system also provided an important vision of the star as a model of production, someone in the business of producing a relative new commodity – the media personality. It is now difficult for us to appreciate how the early movie stars embodied the seamless integration of work and leisure that made them the unique and privileged representatives of the entire industry prior to the scandal period. After the scandals, from both popular and corporate points of view, Arbuckle could be seen as a poor manager of his own affairs, although these two perspectives defining poor management were not the same. Whether understood as a bad man or a bad businessman, however, Arbuckle would no longer be considered the proximate instance of the larger corporation itself, and, thus, he could no longer be all that bad for business.

Notes

1. This is according to Pickford's testimony at a Federal Trade Commission hearing in Los Angeles on November 10, 1923. Eileen Whitfield cites an anonymous story claiming the bribe to have been $750,000 a year for a five-year cessation of motion picture work (1997, 187).
2. See direct examination of Pickford by W. H. Fuller on November 10, 1923. FTC. Box 440 at 6837.
3. Rob King reports that, by late spring of 1915, Charles Baumann, vice president of New York Motion Picture Company, was urging Mack Sennett to bring Chaplin back to Keystone in order to attenuate the comedian's appearances before the public. "We are all of the opinion here that if we have to pay him $3,000 a week and he

doesn't even appear in pictures, we have accomplished a great deal by getting him away from a competing Company, thereby leaving no competition in the field for Keystone film" (Baumann, quoted in King 2009, 96).

4. Cohn also reported that Chaplin "netted something like $175,000 during that time, his salary of $1,500 a week having been augmented by a bonus of $10,000 at the completion of each picture. It is said that Chaplin made more than $2,000,000 from the Chaplin pictures alone, so that the amount does not seem so large in proportion" (1916, 28).
5. Hollywood's promotion of self-fashioning technologies during this period has been finely documented by scholars such as Anne Morey, whose work on juvenile literature and photoplay correspondence schools demonstrates how the film industry as a cultural institution was an important vector in disseminating the corporate logics of the market psychology and marketability to a mass audience. Also important is Mark Garrett Cooper's work on Hollywood's mobilization of the romance narrative in the 1920s as a strategy for establishing the effectiveness and necessity of embracing corporate forms of subjectivity.
6. Harron had died somewhat mysteriously at the height of his career in 1920 from a self-inflicted gunshot wound that was presumed to be accidental, though rumors persisted that his death was a suicide.
7. Masochism was an important component of Valentino's stardom. See Hansen 1991, 269–294.

References

Ames, Hector. (1918). "Spending a Star's Money." *Motion Picture Magazine*, 14.2, January.

Anderson, Mark Lynn. (2007). "Tempting Fate: Clara Smith Hamon, or, The Secretary as Producer." In Jon Lewis & Eric Smoodin (eds), *Looking Past the Screen: Case Studies in American Film History and Method*. Durham, NC: Duke University Press.

Beauchamp, Cari. (1997). *Without Lying Down: Frances Marion and the Powerful Women of Early Hollywood*. Berkeley: University of California Press.

Bowser, Eileen. (1990). *The Transformation of Cinema, 1907–1915*. New York: Scribner's.

"Came East to See Wife, Declares Valentino." (1922). *Movie Weekly*, 11.47, December 30.

"'Charges Absolutely False!' Replies Zukor." (1922). *Movie Weekly*, 43, December 2.

Cohn, Alfred A. (1916). "What They Really Get – NOW!" *Photoplay*, 9.4, March.

Cooper, Mark Garrett. (2003). *Love Rules: Silent Hollywood and the Rise of the Managerial Class*. Minneapolis: University of Minnesota Press.

DeBauche, Leslie Midkiff. (1997). *Reel Patriotism: The Movies and World War I*. Madison: University of Wisconsin Press.

deCordova, Richard. (1990). *Picture Personalities: The Emergence of the Star System in America*. Urbana: University of Illinois Press.

Ewen, Stuart. (1996). *PR! A Social History of Spin*. New York: Basic Books.

"Fading Film Stars." (1921). *New York Clipper*, December 21.

Federal Trade Commission (FTC). (1915–1936). Investigation of Famous Players-Lasky. FTC Docketed Case Files 835. National Archives II, College Park, MD.

Foucault, Michel. (1980). *The History of Sexuality. Vol. 1: An Introduction*, trans. Robert Hurley. New York: Random House.

"'Friends Insulted,' Declares Valentino." (1922). *Movie Weekly*, 2.44, December 9.

Hansen, Miriam. (1991). *Babel and Babylon: Spectatorship in American Silent Cinema*. Cambridge, MA: Harvard University Press.

Howe, Herbert. (1923). "What Are Matinee Idols Made Of?" *Photoplay*, 23.5, April.

James, Arthur. (1921). "The Sordid Arbuckle Tragedy." *Moving Picture World*, 24, September.

King, Rob. (2009). *The Fun Factory: The Keystone Film Company and the Emergence of Mass Culture*. Berkeley: University of California Press.

Kitchen, Karl K. (1915). "What They Really Get." *Photoplay*, 8.5 (October), 138–141.

Lowenthal, Leo. (1961). "The Triumph of the Mass Idol." In *Literature, Popular Culture and Society*. Englewood Cliffs, NJ: Prentice Hall.

McDonald, Paul. (2000). *The Star System: Hollywood's Production of Popular Identities*. London: Wallflower.

Mahar, Karen Ward. (2006). *Women Filmmakers in Early Hollywood*. Baltimore: Johns Hopkins University Press.

"Mary Pickford Threatens to Retire from Screen." (1923). *Salt Lake Tribune*, November 11, 1.

May, Lary. (1980). *Screening Out the Past: The Birth of Mass Culture and the Motion Picture Industry*. New York: Oxford University Press.

Morey, Anne. (2003). *Hollywood Outsiders: The Adaptation of the Film Industry, 1913–1934*. Minneapolis: University of Minnesota Press.

"The Motion-Picture Crisis." (1916). *Photoplay*, 10.6, November.

"Movie Stars Who Scintillate in Los Angeles." (1916). *Los Angeles Times*, January 1, III.

"Observations by Our Man About Town: Public Interest in Film Actors." (1909). *Moving Picture World*, November 20, 714.

Slater, Thomas J. (1995). "June Mathis: A Woman Who Spoke Through Silents." *Griffithiana*, 53, May.

Studlar, Gaylyn. (1996). *This Mad Masquerade: Stardom and Masculinity in the Jazz Age*. New York: Columbia University Press.

"The Trouble with the Movie Face." (1922). *Literary Digest*, 72.2, January 14.

"Valentino Says, 'They Tried to Discipline Me.'" (1922). *Movie Weekly*, 2.43, December 2.

"Valentino Swears, '*Blood and Sand* Mutilated.'" (1922). *Movie Weekly*, 2.45, December 16.

Whitfield, Eileen. (1997). *Pickford: The Woman Who Made Hollywood*. Lexington: University of Kentucky Press.

8

Synchronized Sound Comes to the Cinema

Paul Young
Associate Professor, Dartmouth College, United States

As Paul Young points out, the coming of sound to the cinema emerged from sometimes conflicting conditions at the convergence of commerce, technology, exhibition, and audience desire and demand. Film sound posed difficulties, including the dismissal of movie theater musicians, the search for actors with workable voices, and the fact that early, synchronized sound drew attention to the **artificiality** rather than the **realism** of stories on-screen. Young outlines industry maneuverings in the first **Vitaphone sound-on-disk** program (*Don Juan*, 1926) and delves into the racial complications of **Al Jolson**, **Eddie Cantor**, and others' reassuming vaudeville-inspired **blackface** in early on-screen musical performances. From intersecting artistic, technological, and economic perspectives, **standardization** of sound recording and projection methods was essential to the industry's rapid and smooth conversion. Young's essay shares ground with Paula J. Massood on African-American silent films in this volume and with Torey Leipa on Thomas Ince and Rick Altman on silent film sound in the hardcover/online edition.

Additional terms, names, and concepts: De Forest Phonofilm Corporation, Western Electric, Movietone (sound-on-film), Electrical Research Products Incorporated (ERPI), Photophone (sound-on-film), photoelectric recording, Five-Cornered Agreement, scale-matching, backstage musical, integrated musical

By 1926, Hollywood had established conventions for staging, filming, and editing silent pictures that told stories efficiently and enjoyably while emphasizing the glamour and pathos of their stars. But in that same year Warner Bros. threatened the stability of these conventions by releasing *Don Juan* (directed by Alan Crosland), the first major-studio feature film distributed with synchronized musical accompaniment. Even more radical was the prologue Warners distributed with *Don Juan* to the few theaters equipped to project it with sound: a gaggle of short films featuring fully synchronized speeches, orchestral music,

American Film History: Selected Readings, Origins to 1960, First Edition. Edited by Cynthia Lucia, Roy Grundmann, and Art Simon.
© 2016 John Wiley & Sons, Inc. Published 2016 by John Wiley & Sons, Inc.

opera singers, and jazz. Warners' breakthrough is a documented fact; how the studio system managed the breakthrough, however, is a matter of some debate. One influential account, Alexander Walker's 1978 book *The Shattered Silents*, suggests that *Don Juan*'s release was the first step toward an industry-wide panic that came to a head with Warners' release of the first "part-talking" picture, *The Jazz Singer*, the following year. Suddenly, Walker reports, industry leaders foresaw talking pictures taking over the film industry, but had no clue how to harness or even survive the upheaval a full transition to sync sound would undoubtedly wreak on this "silent" industry (Walker 1986, 40–41, 62–68).

Whether one views the transition as a full-scale crisis, however, depends on the degree to which one accepts the press hype as a transparent assessment of the situation. From the perspective of economic history, as Douglas Gomery has demonstrated, Hollywood studios absorbed the technological innovation as smoothly as could be expected of any established industry. They survived the transition by rapidly reconciling the necessary shifts in capital investment, labor organization, patent management, manufacturing, marketing, and distribution with their existing business model (Gomery 2005a, xvii–xxi, 1–6; see O'Brien 2005, ch. 2, for an illuminating taxonomy of different historiographic approaches to the conversion to sound). But Walker's book doesn't entirely misrepresent the transition, either. Demographics within the industry – actors with voices that recorded poorly being foremost among them – did indeed experience the transition as a crisis, as Walker's eyewitness testimonies demonstrate. Both the producers who shepherded the transition and the exhibitors who alternately suffered and gained from it had their share of choices to make that seemed more like high-stakes bets than everyday business decisions. Indeed, working in production or postproduction units in the years between 1926 – when Warner Bros. employed giant phonograph records to accompany its static-looking talking pictures – and 1933 – when films like RKO's action picture *King Kong* (directed by Merian C. Cooper and Ernest B. Schoedsack) were distributed with multitrack mixes of synchronized music, dialogue, and sound effects recorded on the filmstrip itself – must have resembled being awakened every other morning by an erupting volcano and having to pretend it was all business as usual: You never knew which actor, technician, or standardized practice (such as image editing, made nearly impossible by the necessity of recording image and phonographic sound simultaneously) would get flash-fried next. Exhibitors in particular, even those working for a big studio chain, found their ability to turn a profit suddenly up for grabs: Could they afford the installation of new projectors and amplified speaker systems? Would the studios subsidize these expensive upgrades? Or would exhibitors have to raise ticket prices and pray that the novelty of the talkies would precipitate a box office boom, or at least help them retain their current patrons rather than drive them away?

What follows is an account of the coming of sound that describes the dramatic changes that took place, while distinguishing the very different experiences of the transition encountered by studio executives, production and postproduction crews, exhibitors, and audiences. The development of sound was driven not by inevitable progress toward a more fully realistic cinematic experience, but by the tension between multiple, often contradictory impulses – market competition, patent control, exhibition pressures, and, as Donald Crafton reminds us, audience response. For when asking questions like these about the industry's history, we cannot neglect the experience of the spectators who completed Hollywood's circuit between production, exhibition, and future production practices (Crafton 1997, 5–6). From the perspective of Hollywood's audiences, the transition consisted of a series of surprises – some exciting, some curious, some funny, and some downright awful. Moving picture fans, long attached to the stars and storytelling strategies of the silent era, found "talking" short films and newsreels astonishing, and they enjoyed the music that accompanied the features. But they also endured disappointments ranging from poor sound reproduction and the revelation that silent matinee idols didn't sound as glamorous as they looked, to missing out on sound cinema altogether during the sluggish installation of theater sound systems outside metropolitan markets. Unable to bank on sound's novelty alone, producers considering sound had to figure out how to make each sound film as pleasurable and unique as the films of the silent era had been, or risk losing their audience altogether.

Warner Bros.' Gambit: The Vitaphone

Our historical imagination about the conversion to sound usually focuses on production: Hollywood studios innovated, implemented, and perfected technologies for recording sound and synchronizing it with the moving image. But using the terms "production" or "Hollywood" to represent the entire film industry during this time (or any other) oversimplifies the causes, and thereby the complexity, of the conversion. At the time of the transition, three distinct businesses revolved around film as commodity: production, distribution, and exhibition. Transforming the commodity at the center of this orbit as dramatically as sound did meant drastic changes to all three. Synchronized sound required synchronization during both print production and projection; it required distributing not only films but also their soundtracks, using whatever media a studio's chosen format necessitated, and it required providing theaters with compatible equipment for playing back that soundtrack, and doing so at an adequate volume. As a consequence, the decisions leading to the conversion were not made lightly, nor were they driven by the simple force of technological progress. Profit potential drove the conversion, but the essential conservatism of industry – the impulse to innovate for competition's sake, but to innovate *within* existing systems of production and distribution in order to keep overhead expenses low – tempered both the rapidity of the transition and the level of innovation it fostered.

Hollywood in the late 1920s would have been much quieter had not one small studio, Warner Bros., decided to innovate a bit beyond these conservative limits. This is not to say that American producers before Warners had never considered sound film. At the Edison laboratories, which developed key sound media of the late nineteenth century (the telephone and the gramophone) as well as the first moving picture camera in the United States, W. K. Laurie Dickson experimented with synchronizing gramophone to moving-picture projector already in the mid-1890s (Altman 2004, 78–79). Independent inventors followed Edison's lead for three decades, attempting everything from synchronizing phonographs with projectors and positioning actors behind the screen to speak characters' lines, to broadcasting live sound to multiple theaters simultaneously.[1] These experiments garnered little attention from the powerful production studios that emerged during the 1910s. One reason for their tepid response was that the studios lacked a primary incentive the movie business needed to develop sound film into a viable commodity: the promise of profits grand enough to justify the reorganization of their already-successful practices.

But Warner Bros. gambled that technological novelty would secure them a seat at the big table. Synchronized sound, produced by the studio and distributed with film rentals, would make cinema-as-usual obsolete if it succeeded, thereby catapulting the Warners to the head of their field. At that time, phonography must have seemed the only way to realize this ideal. No other medium rivaled the phonograph record in reproduction quality or ease of recording and playback, and technicians could easily be hired away from (or subcontracted through) the recording industry. But projecting a film and playing sound in tandem posed difficulties, not least of which was synchronizing two separate mechanisms, the projector and the record player, without one rushing ahead of or falling behind the other. To regulate synchronization, hand-cranked cameras (and projectors) would have to be replaced with electric ones running at a uniform speed (24 frames per second became the industry standard, still in use today). Quality control of fidelity and amplification would be extremely difficult to achieve across diverse exhibition spaces. And perhaps most daunting of all, recording the sounds of actors performing for the camera meant rethinking the entire production process. Silent films could be shot amid the noise of shouted stage directions, other movies filming on adjacent sets, and the grinding sound of the camera itself. Now that cacophony would have to be mediated somehow for the microphone's sake, or eliminated altogether.

Even the most integral storytelling conventions of the medium would be affected, perhaps most noticeably at the postproduction level. Silent editing patterns that focused spectators' attention on story elements – establishing shots cutting in to closer shots, eyeline matches and point-of-view shot sequences, matches on action, shot-reverse shot series and so forth – would have to be tabled in favor of long takes and expensive multiple-camera shooting setups, at least until soundtracks could be edited more easily to accompany image tracks. For the time being, phonograph records seemed like the quickest fix, but sound cannot be edited if the only medium involved is the phonograph record itself; sound had to be recorded live from beginning to end of the record, during shooting in most cases, and could only "cut" at the end of a film reel. Some of these difficulties could conceivably have been overcome five years earlier had independent developers like Lee de Forest possessed the business clout to partner with studios (rather than selling or leasing patents, neither of which guaranteed long-term profit). De Forest, inventor of the first radio amplification tube, had been working since 1918 on a nonphonographic recording process he eventually called Phonofilm. Phonofilm used modulated electric light to record sound directly on the filmstrip in the form of a variable-density pattern running parallel to the image track. When perfected, such "sound-on-film" processes would provide more reliable synchronization than any sound-on-disk system could achieve. Eager to get the attention of Hollywood, in 1923–1924 De Forest demonstrated a number of sync-sound short films, including performance films by lower-tier vaudeville stars, presaging what would become a staple for Warner Bros. shortly thereafter. While these tests were not exactly triumphs, they did prove that De Forest was on to something, particularly where newsworthy events such as political speeches were concerned (Gomery 2005a, 30–32; Crafton 1997, 30–34, 63–70). Without powerful partners, however, small businesses (even those with important-sounding names like the De Forest Phonofilm Corporation) could not assimilate their inventions into the cinema mainstream.

Warner Bros. needed an experienced partner to implement the unfamiliar technologies involved, and found that partner in Western Electric. As the manufacturing arm of telephone monopoly AT&T, which had decades of experience in transmitting and amplifying sound signals, Western Electric was already equipped to innovate this technology, and better prepared than the De Forests of the world to fight the patent challenges and other legal battles that such a momentous change as sound would certainly bring.[2] Already by 1925, Western Electric had developed a working synchronized sound film system, and hoped eventually to supply all the studios with their sound film equipment by selling or leasing licenses and equipment to studios and their theater chains while still controlling its own patents. The 1925 deal that Western Electric struck with Warner Bros. gave birth to the Vitaphone Corporation, a joint venture company that would market, license, distribute, and install what was now officially called the Vitaphone system.

It should be clear from this discussion that the transition to synchronized sound was not the result of a perception by studios or audiences that something was "missing" from the silent cinema. (Maxim Gorky, the Russian author, was not alone in criticizing the earliest silent films as uncanny in their voicelessness, but innovations in characterization and storytelling methods within the cinema's first couple of decades compensated for that.)[3] For one thing, exhibitors in the 1920s rarely screened films without accompanying them with anything from a piano to a full orchestra, depending on the fortunes of the theater. For another, silent cinema had gained recognition among both mainstream critics and more culturally revered observers – psychologist Hugo Münsterberg, poet Vachel Lindsay, European art critic Rudolf Arnheim, and poet and critic Béla Balàzs, to name a few – as a visual art complete unto itself. Western Electric's goal was neither to improve the silent cinema nor to invent the all-talking, all-singing feature film, but rather to expand its own markets. If sound cinema succeeded, AT&T stood to gain a big slice of the Hollywood pie, especially if it could salt its licensing agreements with shares of the profits of individual films.

For Vitaphone, in fact, the option of producing "talkies" – feature films in which characters spoke or sang from start to finish – wasn't even on the table. As Warners and Western Electric foresaw it, sound cinema would be less a talking-singing phenomenon than a means of transmitting clear music and intelligible vocals where needed, with sound reproduced by the best-amplified phonograph system yet designed. To market film sound, Western Electric took advantage of Americans' fascination with how electricity had transformed everyday life and communication over the preceding decades by paralleling the Vitaphone to a device synonymous with the AT&T/Bell brand: the telephone (Crafton 1997, 34–38). The Vitaphone system worked better than any other process then under development. Once the Vitaphone Corporation had perfected a system linking the phonograph platter motor to the film camera (and projector), thus insuring relatively close synchronization, it exploited the phonograph industry's high-fidelity recording and playback technology as well. Thanks to AT&T's electronic amplification system, the system could fill even the largest picture palace with music.

The competition did not have much to put up against this juggernaut. Phonofilm's fidelity could not match that of the 16-inch Vitaphone records, and without patent or even license rights to his own Audion radio tube – which De Forest had sold to AT&T some time before, and which was now the key to Vitaphone's high-quality amplification – he could barely make the Phonofilm audible. De Forest also ran afoul of his one-time collaborators, Case Laboratories, when he falsely took credit for significant improvements that Theodore Case had made to Phonofilm. Having bested De Forest in the subsequent legal battle, Case formed a business relationship with William Fox – head of another small studio hoping to ride sound film all the way to the Hollywood winner's circle – and began developing another sound-on-film system, Movietone, the patents to which Fox would control jointly with Case (Crafton 1997, 89–100; Gomery 2005a, 47–54).

In the meantime, Vitaphone and Warner Bros. ruled the sound revolution. The first Vitaphone program hit theaters for the first time in New York City on August 6, 1926. It consisted of six short, fully synchronized musical performance films and *Don Juan*, the first feature-length film with a prerecorded music and sound effects track. An early attempt at a Warners prestige picture, *Don Juan* starred the well-respected actor John Barrymore, another investment in Warner Bros.' future growth. It contained no dialogue, only music and a few not-quite-synchronized sound effects (a church bell motif, a few door-knocks, and a scant few others). Vitaphone's promotional literature and industry reports alike made it explicit that the Vitaphone was, first and foremost, a machine for producing musical accompaniment (Crafton 1997, 71–72). The score, performed by the "Vitaphone Orchestra," was synchronized to amplify dramatic tension and mood on a scene-by-scene (and sometimes shot-by-shot) basis and occasionally even to "mickey-mouse" (that is, sonically imitate) movement on the screen – just as the written musical scores that producers distributed to theaters along with silent film prints had been engineered to do. Similar effects were achieved by Vitaphone's second feature, *The First Auto* (directed by Roy Del Ruth, 1927), though the soundtrack did contain a single word – "Bob!" – addressed to the hero just before an intertitle displayed the same word (see illustration in Crafton 1997, 172). Jim Lastra has argued that this spoken word, isolated as it is, functions not as dialogue *per se* but as another sound effect akin to *The First Auto*'s sporadic horn-honking (Lastra 2000, 120). The emphasis on music rather than speech – one of many early precedents that would determine the scope and type of future innovations in film sound – brings us to another incentive behind Warner Bros.' spearheading the transition: the elimination of live musicians from theater-chain payrolls. Though the musicians' unions fought Hollywood on this issue for a few years, the Vitaphone sounded the death-knell for live music in a majority of theaters, especially once the Great Depression hit in 1929 and theater chains made even deeper spending cuts (Hubbard 1985, 429–441; Crafton 1997, 219–221, 223–224). Another benefit Warners and its competitors gained by banning live acts from its theaters was control: the power to dictate nearly everything about how their films were presented to audiences, even if the theater in question wasn't owned by a major studio. By the early 1930s, poor musicianship and "creative" scoring decisions that distracted spectators from the story would be things of the past. Along with them, however, would go the neighborhood theater as a spot where the music on offer reflected the culture, tastes, and interests of its particular audience.

Early Sound Cinema: A Multimedia Distraction

By calling on the discourses of phonography, telephony, and radio to sell sound film to audiences, companies with sync-sound systems under development (the foremost being Western Electric/AT&T and the Radio Corporation of America, or RCA) could present sync sound as familiar rather than alienating or distracting (Crafton 1997, 23–51). That familiarity, however, could not diminish the degree to which sound film called attention to the technology of motion pictures – the fact of the movies' artificiality. This was not good news for the industry, which had worked since at least the early 1910s to eliminate any such distractions from the film experience and to focus spectators on stories and characters instead. Warner Bros. diminished this self-reflexive potential

Figure 8.1 Will Hays's speech introducing the first Vitaphone program, which preceded the synched-music feature Alan Crosland's *Don Juan* (1926, producer Warner Bros. Entertainment). (Author's collection.)

somewhat by dividing its Vitaphone products into two categories: silent-style narrative films with music only, thus retaining both a historically successful form and (with luck) an attentive, absorbed audience; and the aforementioned short performance films that featured sound recorded live on the set. These Vitaphone shorts functioned as what Donald Crafton has called "virtual Broadway" – performances delivered by famous performers and seemingly "transmitted" from the Vitaphone stages Warners had set up in the old Vitagraph studio in New York to (theoretically) any picture palace in the country (Crafton 1997, 63–88).

Crude as the Vitaphone shorts seem today, the *Don Juan* shorts program epitomized the story of complementary media that Western Electric used to market its sound-on-disk system. The program consisted of both highbrow and lowbrow fare: the New York Philharmonic performing the overture to Wagner's opera *Tannhäuser*, tenor Giovanni Martinelli singing "Vesti la giubba" from the opera *I Pagliacci*, a Spanish dance featuring a performance by a soprano from the Metropolitan Opera, a violin solo, a guitar performance, and a soprano aria by Marion Talley, another Met diva. The whole program, as heterogeneous as a day's worth of radio broadcasting, was kicked off by a short in which Motion Picture Producers and Distributors of America president Will Hays addressed the camera, delivering a celebration of the Vitaphone that doubled as a valediction for silent cinema.

Gesticulating broadly and looking from side to side as if addressing a live audience, Hays offered a singsong homily praising the Vitaphone for disseminating "good music" to those small-town and rural locations that apparently needed it in order to become properly acculturated. I don't make this comment altogether sarcastically, for one intention behind Hays's remarks was to pitch sound cinema as a medium of social uplift, and he was particularly appropriate to this task. Hays had recently been imported to Los Angeles from Washington, DC (where he was President Hoover's Postmaster General) to head Hollywood's self-censorship efforts and thereby to rehabilitate the moral reputation of the industry, which had recently weathered scandals involving illicit sex, adultery, drug abuse, and suspicious deaths. Hays's "good music" promise echoed Vitaphone's often-repeated pronouncement that its shorts prologues would nurture the nation's taste for high art (Crafton 1997, 73–74).

Vitaphone had no monopoly on the rhetoric of uplift, however, any more than it monopolized sound film. William Fox entered a partnership with Case in 1926, after the Vitaphone hit theaters (though it hit cautiously; Warners did not release *Don Juan* widely until the year after its premiere, and a large percentage of theaters nationwide screened it as a silent), in hopes of turning Fox theaters into sources for news, information, and education. In the deal, Fox purchased the patents to Case's Movietone sound-on-film process, which he used to produce virtual Broadway shorts of his own. By 1927, the Fox Movietone Newsreel series ushered the voices as well as images of George Bernard Shaw, Benito Mussolini, Charles Lindbergh, and scores of other renowned (and notorious) figures to Fox's theater chain. Now the dominos of business transformation really began to tumble. Movietone, like De Forest's Photophone, lacked reliable amplification, a snag that in 1927 impelled Fox to turn to Western Electric for assistance. That year, Western Electric had caught on to how dramatically its exclusive partnership with Warner Bros. curtailed its potential profits; its response was to set up an entirely distinct subsidiary, Electrical Research Products Incorporated (ERPI), that could supply Fox and other studios without breaking their contract with Warner Bros. (though not without raising the brothers' collective blood pressure a few points). To complicate the field further, RCA threw its hat into the sync-sound ring the very same year. Promising a superior sound-on-film process called Photophone, RCA wasted little time in advertising its contribution as the filmed equivalent of broadcast radio, the medium that had made its fortune. Since roughly 1920, RCA and other champions of broadcasting praised radio as a wondrous machine for transforming the United States into a community united by electronic media, similar to what Marshall McLuhan would tout in the 1960s as a global village (McLuhan 1964). "King Radio," as it was dubbed by a doggerel poet of the time, was expected to unite Americans more or less automatically by disbursing loftier tastes, informed opinions, and better understanding of foreign peoples (Marvin 1988, 194; Douglas 1987, 60; Young 2006, 54). According to RCA, sound cinema was the progeny of radio in that it, too, was a "product of electrical science" (Crafton 1997, 28), and like broadcasting it would export audiovisual entertainment from New York and Los Angeles to the so-called hinterlands (that is, nonmetropolitan communities) of the United States, fulfilling Will Hays's promise of a cinema of cultural uplift, powered by sound.[4]

Cinema-as-radio rhetoric manifests in subtle ways in the first "part-talkie," Warner Bros.' *The Jazz Singer*, released in 1927. Though the importance of this film as a "first" for talking pictures has been overstated – to the point where Janet Bergstrom has touted the necessity of "saving" film historians' study of 1927 "from *The Jazz Singer*" (2005, 163) – Broadway sensation and recording artist Al Jolson's screen debut provides a glimpse into Hollywood's tentative plans for future sync-sound features, in which the *Don Juan* model of sync music would fuse with the Vitaphone shorts format into a kind of hybrid of silent film, musical phonograph recordings, and broadcasting. *The Jazz Singer* starred Jolson as Jakie Rabinowitz, a child of Jewish immigrants who transforms himself into Jack Robin, a blackface minstrel performer desperate to break into show business. Against the will of his father, who wants Jack to follow in his footsteps as a cantor in the local synagogue, Jack blacks his face with burnt cork and sings such "plantation" songs as "My Mammy" to adoring crowds of Jews and Gentiles alike.

Michael Rogin's influential interpretation of the film casts it as a reflection of how many European Jews (like the Warner brothers themselves, for instance) Americanized themselves by entering the field of mass culture. In *The Jazz Singer*'s case, the mass cultural "medium" of choice is minstrelsy, a theatrical form dating back to the early nineteenth century in which white performers stereotyped and appropriated the speech patterns and music of black slaves; for Rogin, Jack Robin's appropriation of black music to reach the height of stardom is a wishful allegory for Warner Bros.' exploitation of (Jolson's) blackface vocal performance to position itself in the firmament of cinematic culture (Rogin 1996, 73–120). Whatever cultural messages viewers took from *The Jazz Singer*, however, it seems clear that they employed their knowledge of other sound media to define their encounter with the film. One reviewer's description, quoted by Crafton, suggests the degree to which the film succeeded in characterizing sync-sound film as a medium primarily for music and performance, not dialogue: "*The Jazz Singer* is scarcely a motion picture. It should be more properly labeled an enlarged Vitaphone record of Al Jolson in half a dozen songs" (Crafton 1997, 110). And so it was. *The Jazz Singer* was not an all-talking feature but a largely silent melodrama with synched music, peppered with several synchronized scenes of Jolson singing, chatting with audiences within the film, and delighting his character's mother with ad-libbed jokes and a song. Charles Wolfe has shown how the film capitalizes on the Vitaphone shorts' format of singular, unconnected, highly theatricalized performances, only scantly developing the format to fit the exigencies of a feature-length narrative (Wolfe 1990). Crafton suggests further that in the beginning the Vitaphone system was packaged, marketed, and exhibited as nothing more than a channel for distributing high- and middlebrow musical performance, "not an art in its own right." As he provocatively puts it, "the culture proposed to be spread by Vitaphone *was not film*," at least not in the sense that silent film was a distinct and unique form of art (Crafton 1997, 74).

What the Vitaphone *was*, at least in the media imaginary of *The Jazz Singer* and its parlor serenade scene in particular, seems linked to the American imaginary of broadcasting during this "golden age" of radio. For Crafton, the Vitaphone was a musical, quasi-theatrical medium first and foremost, its effects merely supported and supplemented by the cinematic image; hence the possibility that a part-talkie like *The Jazz Singer* could be experienced as an illustrated phonograph record – or an illustrated radio broadcast, considering especially the "live" aesthetics (long takes, direct address to the camera) of the Vitaphone shorts and the sync segments of *The Jazz Singer.* As a medium that ushered the biggest musical stars of the moment into private living rooms and addressed its listeners directly all day long, radio allowed listeners to become (virtually) intimate with faraway people whose very presence on the radio made them important. One could not talk back to those radio personalities, of course, but the radio's installation in the home rather than in public venues like movie theaters nudged listeners to experience broadcast listening as an interactive event, as if the wireless telegraphy craze that preceded the rise of broadcasting had simply switched models, from a postal model of delivering private messages between users to a mass communication model that brought the same entertainment to millions.[5] Ensconced as he is in Mother Rabinowitz's parlor, his dialogue spoken in low, affectionate tones as we invisibly "listen in" (a popular term for radio listening at the time), Jack flirts with his beloved mother in what seems less like an attempt to weld moving pictures onto phonograph records than an attempt at building a species of visual radio, thereby making good on RCA's predictions (though in a film with sound provided by RCA's competitors Western Electric and AT&T; Young 2006, 90–92).

But there was an insidious side to this ideal of radio-generated intimacy, and it cast an ideological shadow on sound films as well. Early broadcasting discourse stressed how the new medium would foster intimacy between home listeners and (welcome) strangers – its direct address to the listener, the close-miked sound that dominated its vocal aesthetic (McCracken 2001, 111–112), its emphasis on live performance, and the reports, short stories, and poems published in RCA's fan magazine *Radio Age.*[6] This being the case, however, radio might also allow more ostensibly threatening presences into white middle-class homes, specifically the African-American musicians who introduced the most controversial – and probably the most popular – musical genre of its time, jazz, to America. Throughout the 1920s, religious leaders and other watchdogs condemned jazz for its sly eroticism and purportedly deleterious effects on the tastes of the nation, especially when broadcasting opened wide the virtual doors of every home to this lurking threat.

The Jazz Singer participates in this debate by generating avatars for these anxieties, then resolving them through a combination of cinema-as-radio fantasy and strict organization of performance spaces. In a long take running several minutes, Jack's parlor serenade telegraphs a fascinating, embarrassing, quasi-incestuous intimacy barely mitigated by filial piety, but his self-infantilization, the jaunty optimism of "Blue Skies," the number he sings for his mother, and above all his *whiteness* function to inoculate the scene against any hints of impropriety. In other synched performance scenes (and significantly not in this one), Jolson's blackface makes jazz "safe" by characterizing blackness as a mere masquerade to be put on or taken off by brilliant white performers – in public.[7] By covering his features in burnt cork soot and singing minstrel songs in a dialect that blacks spoke only in racist fantasies, Jolson cleansed these songs of the raw eroticism and hyperkinetic syncopation of a Bessie Smith or a Louis Armstrong. Like Paul Whiteman and other white musicians who made jazz acceptable to white listeners on both radio and records, *The Jazz Singer* offered a fantasy of "democratizing" a uniquely American form of music by "cleaning" it up, infantilizing its African-American inventors, and drawing a sharp boundary between public space as the proper place for musical blackness (if overseen by whites) and private space as the bastion of "wholesome" entertainment conducive to (white) domestic affection.

The Technical Demands of Sound

Many things changed in Hollywood in the months before and after *The Jazz Singer*'s release. Indeed, things had to change dramatically if Warner Bros. or anyone else was to profit from sound. Equipping theaters with new projectors and amplification systems required time and money. Times were flush in the 1920s until the Great Depression hit, but neither Warners nor anyone else stood to profit very quickly from aggressive conversion of those same hinterland theaters with which the Vitaphone was to civilize the masses. Thus the first major sound pictures, such as Fox's 1927 sync-music melodrama *Sunrise*, made by German director F. W. Murnau and touted by studio publicity as a piece of timeless high art, were rarely seen outside large cities like Pittsburgh, New

York, Los Angeles, or Chicago. Warner Bros. distributed silent versions of *Don Juan* and *The Jazz Singer* to rural and small-town theaters rather than distress its budget by wiring such small houses immediately.[8] And then there was the more fundamental problem of making sound work properly. Records delivered the clearest sound and broadest frequency range by far of any medium then available, but they had a habit of scratching or breaking, thus rendering synchronization a moot issue. Paramount and Loew's/MGM bided their time before making their own licensing deals with ERPI; Paramount in particular profited quite nicely from silents and a few sync-sound features that used Vitaphone equipment (see the discussion of the Five-Cornered Agreement, below; see also Gomery 2005a, 69–76; Gomery 2005b). By the time Paramount made its deal, in 1928, many of the most difficult production problems had been resolved by others.

Solving these problems required a good deal of seat-of-the-pants experimentation. In 1927 Warners was just figuring out how to soundproof their cameras using blimps – camera-sized sound-dampening chambers – and how to inject continuity editing into synched scenes. But the phonographic element of the Vitaphone gave producers a continuous headache. Because a phonograph record can't be edited, the sound for a sync scene had to be recorded on a master record "live," while the image track was filmed. Any nondiegetic music had to be played off-camera and recorded then and there; nothing could be mixed into the soundtrack in postproduction. If an actor flubbed a line or the cinematographer coughed during a long take of a dialogue scene, it meant thousands of feet of wasted negative. Mixing a soundtrack out of multiple recordings could only be accomplished by playing multiple phonograph recordings simultaneously and recording the result, a process that inevitably introduced (new) synchronization problems and (further) distortion (Belton 1999, 231–232; Lastra 2000, 200).

But Warners' technicians did determine how to put a reasonable facsimile of unrestricted editing on the screen, by shooting scenes with multiple cameras.[9] They could thereby reproduce the varied angles and camera distances that the silent single-camera shooting schedules offered to editors, who could then begin scenes with establishing shots and cut in reactions and close-ups as they had before the microphones and blimps arrived on the set. Compared to silent-era raw footage, however, talking footage was expensive. Shooting longer takes with multiple cameras meant that two to six times the negative stock used to shoot silent scenes got eaten up in a flash – and more if the footage had to be junked. This shooting style also deprived directors and cinematographers of the minute, shot-by-shot control over such elements as lighting and performance that they had enjoyed when shooting silent, and forced them to extend the length of the average shot compared to the laconically efficient shots of late silent features (Salt 1992, 214–216). It is little wonder that Paramount chief Adolph Zukor wasn't terribly eager to produce all-talking, feature-length films. Paramount released its epic film *Wings* (directed by William A. Wellman, 1927), the first winner of the Academy Award for Best Picture in 1929, with both phonographic and sound-on-film options featuring a musical score only, no dialogue. But part-talkies like *The Jazz Singer* made clear that there was interest in at least brief interludes of speech and singing in features, though *The Jazz Singer* didn't fare as well with critics and audiences as Hollywood mythology has led us to believe. Indeed, the film was released in both part-talking and silent versions, and the combined profits for both versions place it squarely in the range of other successful but not blockbuster films of the season (Crafton 1997, 524–531). But the incredible box office generated by Warners' next Jolson vehicle, *The Singing Fool* (directed by Lloyd Bacon, 1928), made it clear that the public was indeed interested in hearing the stars sing and talk.

Fine-Tuning: Sound-on-Film Processes and Theories of Sound Recording

The full exploitation of sync sound seemed unlikely unless something could be done about the clumsiness of the Vitaphone system. Photoelectric recording, which uses beams of light to record a soundtrack to a strip of photographic film, promised greater editing flexibility and fewer mechanical headaches during exhibition. Already in 1927, Movietone and RCA had independently solved many of the fidelity, distortion, and noise problems associated with photoelectric recording. That same year, RCA head David

Sarnoff made overtures to the most powerful Hollywood studios – MGM, Paramount-Famous Lasky, Film Booking Office (FBO), and First National (later to merge with Warners) – to win them away from potential ERPI contracts. When Sarnoff failed to convince them to switch over to his Photophone optical (sound-on-film) process, he began to organize a new studio of his very own. RCA gained control of FBO and merged it with the Keith-Albee-Orpheum vaudeville theater chain to form the Radio Pictures studio, more formally known as RKO (Radio-Keith-Orpheum). RKO immediately joined the ranks of the major studios thanks to its immense capital pool and the strength of its exhibition chain (see Gomery 2005a, 77–85). In effect, Sarnoff had built his own dream factory just to exploit Photophone. Fox, too, planned to build a production empire atop its sound-on-film patents. Frustrated with phonographic recording and looking to market his own proprietary system, Fox went behind Warners' back to make a cross-licensing deal between Fox/Movietone and Western Electric. In the process, Fox facilitated an arrangement between RCA and AT&T that undermined his own position in the sound technology market. This arrangement allowed the two companies to reap profits from both their respective sound systems – RCA's Photophone and Western Electric's amplification system – via joint licensing fees and profit-percentage agreements.

By 1928, it was only a matter of time before the 16-inch, 33-1/3 revolutions-per-minute Vitaphone record went extinct, though it was phased out gradually, film by film and theater by theater. By 1930, "Vitaphone" had been changed from the name of a sound-on-disk process into a brand. Warner Bros. still employed Western Electric technology for recording and amplification, but the majority of its films bore variable-area optical soundtracks. Image and sound could now share a single medium that was pulled through the projector via a single motor. Sound was read by an optical pickup lens that read variances in the amount of light beamed through the soundtrack portion of the filmstrip, translated the variances of the beam back into an electrical signal that roughly matched the one created by microphones during the recording process, and finally amplified that signal for playback.

However complicated the switch from silent to sound and the subsequent switch from sound-on-disk to sound-on-film were for Warner Bros. and Fox, the overall benefits of sound conversion eventually outweighed the costs. But the more established producers would not be rushed. In 1927, the same year Sarnoff was organizing RKO, the heads of MGM, Paramount Famous-Lasky, Universal, First National, and Producers Distributing Company (PDC) signed what the trade press nicknamed "the Five-Cornered Agreement," in which the signers agreed to delay choosing a permanent sound format for a year while a joint committee weighed options for future standardization (and while, as Crafton notes, AT&T and RCA competed with each other for the producers' affections by polishing their systems and undercutting the other's prices; see Crafton 1997, 129–131; Gomery 2005a, 68–76). Having struck out on their own already, Fox, Warner Bros., and FBO all skipped the meeting (thus aborting a more complicated eight-cornered agreement), but the implications of the Agreement affected them all regarding an issue that threatened to slow sound cinema's development just as it hampered that of the video recorder half a century later: compatibility. In the end, would it profit studios and their theater chains more to cling to their proprietary sound formats, or to adopt a standardized, industry-wide format?

Following the path of the Agreement's signers, the industry decided to take the latter route. Compatibility would mean that studio-owned theater chains could rent some films from rival studios, while independent chains no longer had to choose only one studio's format and thereby deprive their venues of hit films from multiple studios. The path of least resistance to compatibility was for the studios to adopt sound-on-film technologies, meaning that any projector with an optical pickup could project any film produced using either the variable-area or variable-density recording/playback formats. No longer would projectionists with sound-on-disk machines chew their nails waiting for the stylus to hit a scratch on a worn-out record, wreck the synchronization, and thereby destroy the illusionism of a scene.[10] Not even a missing image frame could undermine synchronization now, for such a breach would eliminate a frame's worth of sound as well, insuring that in projection, synchronization would correct itself in a matter of seconds.[11] Most important from the perspective of film production, studios could now manipulate sound as easily as they had manipulated images by the end of the silent era. They could edit the soundtrack to *accompany* the image track, rather than subordinating the image to the recorded sound. Multiple recordings could even be mixed together at different volumes to allow filmmakers to modulate background and foreground sounds, clarity of dialogue, nondiegetic music, and so forth, without the synchronization headaches caused by attempts to mix sound using multiple record players.

To be sure, the establishment of a standard sound-on-film format did not in itself smooth over the institutional and aesthetic bumps of sync sound.[12] But production teams now had the luxury of experimenting with standards and practices that would best serve the new era of speech, music, and noise. One panic-borne practice that Hollywood quickly reconsidered was hiring Broadway actors to replace silent film actors whose squeaky voices, poor memorization skills, and other "defects" rendered them useless for talking pictures. As it turned out, the London-by-way-of-Broadway accents and over-enunciation of many stage performers spelled ticket trouble for films pitched to the broadest possible American audience (Walker 1986, 51, 129–130; Crafton 1997, 497–509, 455–456). The studios had also unwittingly complicated the behind-the-scenes labor of production by importing sound technicians from the recording and radio industries. Some technicians, such as RKO sound engineer (and former radio engineer) Carl Dreher, insisted that the volume of a given sound should match the source's distance from the camera. This theory, which Lastra refers to as the "scale-matching" or fidelity model of sync sound recording, offers listeners sounds as they might have sounded to a listener within the scene space; for example, a recording or broadcast of a symphony concert should reproduce what the music sounded like from a (very good) seat in a concert hall, and dialogue volume should diminish or increase depending on camera distance as well as movements of actors within the frame. Other technicians proposed a theory of maximum intelligibility, in which clear and audible dialogue (and any other sounds important to the film's story) took priority at all times; this model mandated adjusting the volume levels only slightly to accompany different camera distances, and stressed *storytelling* – not faithful reproduction of what and how an "invisible auditor" standing near the camera would hear a shot's dialogue and noise – as sync sound's true calling (see Lastra 2000, esp. 159–179). The intelligibility model (which drove a shift to what Crafton 1997 calls the "modulated," or less noisy and distracting, soundtrack by the early 1930s; 269) was well on its way to becoming an industry standard as early as 1928. As late as 1931, even as Dreher doggedly lobbied for the fidelity model, he warned that extreme differences in loudness between, say, a long shot and a close-up should be reduced "if the action of the play requires it" (Dreher 1931, 757, quoted in Lastra 2000, 214–215; see also Altman 1980).

This debate among studio sound engineers helps to demonstrate the degree to which human negotiation – not machinery – determines the uses of new film technologies. By 1928, the question of whether sync sound could be naturalized – that is, whether it would ever seem like anything but an add-on that drew attention to the technology involved and away from its role as storyteller and conjurer of dreams – still stood in the way of the development of sound cinema from an "illustrated" musical medium into another animal entirely: talking pictures. Another nontechnical obstacle, or so it seemed, was Hollywood's reluctance to phase out silent filmmaking. The all-talking features released before 1929 had made clear that audiences preferred them to part-talking features, but industry executives weren't ready to announce their intentions to get out of the silent film business altogether. Though studios protested to the Hollywood press as late as 1928–1929 that silent and sound films would coexist so long as there remained "good" stories to tell in both formats, Crafton shows that they were hedging against audience and exhibitor disapproval rather than announcing actual plans (Crafton 1997, 169–171, 177–179, 311). By that time all the studios had undertaken serious all-talking film experimentation and were beginning to attain the level of box office success enjoyed by Warners Bros.' biggest hits.

By the time Warner Bros. released *The Singing Fool* and the all-talking crime drama *The Lights of New York* (directed by Bryan Foy, 1928), the industry was still tentative about making speech a feature-film staple. But these two films helped tip the scale toward talkies. *The Lights of New York* drew razzes from critics then and seems even more hilarious now, brimming as it is with potted dialogue and microphones "hidden" in stage props toward which its performers perpetually lean. But *Lights* shocked the doubters by returning its paltry $23,000 production costs nearly five times over. Its success apparently shocked Warner Bros., too, for the studio had interspersed expository intertitles throughout the film, as if to keep spectators mindful of silent film narration strategies in case the all-talking experiment tanked. By twenty-first-century standards (not to mention the standards of 1930), *The Lights of New York* is a dull film with wooden performances, stagey blocking, overly loud nondiegetic music, and an overabundance of single-shot scenes. Together with the equally stunning box office of *The Singing Fool*, however, it proved that feature films could sustain a more radio-like emphasis on speech, whether it be overtly presentational – Jolson's long scene addressing the audience in the club early in *The Singing Fool*, for example – or representational – as in the intimate, if stilted, conversations between the hero of *The Lights of New York* and his mother as she fails to dissuade him from investing in a barber shop/bootlegging scheme in faraway New York.

Despite their remarkable progress in a few short years, however, producers had yet to discover a successful formula for injecting song and dance into feature-length films. Several attempted full-length musical variety-show films like MGM's *Hollywood Revue of 1929* (directed by Charles Reisner), Warners' *The Show of Shows* (directed by John G. Adolfi, 1929), or Universal's *The King of Jazz* (directed by John Murray Anderson, 1929), but with little box office or critical success. The stilted dialogue exchanges and the seemingly endless number of distinct voices that characterize these films foreground sync sound as a curiosity just when Warner Bros. was trying to downplay its novelty, particularly in the Vitaphone full-length fiction talkies. Indeed, Warners' *The Lights of New York* and its second "all-talking" feature, *Tenderloin* (directed by Michael Curtiz, 1928), presented sync sound not as a fascinating element in itself but as simply another means of selling a story to the viewer.

But how to include singing – one of the most exciting promises of sound – in features without overplaying the novelty card? Paramount's answer was to assimilate songs into stories while bringing presound techniques of visual storytelling out of retirement. Although its all-talking musical *Applause*, overseen by stage director Rouben Mamoulian in 1929, did not fare well at the box office, it did convince critics and filmmakers that reintroducing such silent film techniques as tracking shots and montage sequences was a viable and exciting alternative to the conservatism forced upon them by sound-on-disk. Mamoulian's film also displayed important possibilities for integrating instrumental music (whether diegetic or nondiegetic) and singing, as well as speech, into feature-length narratives. *Applause*, which charts the decline of an aging burlesque star and the vibrant maturation of her prim yet modern daughter, flaunts some of the most inventive uses of sync sound any studio had attempted up to that point, and signals the return of the camera to its pre-Vitaphone role as a motile storyteller. In the final scene, upbeat music coming from the stage provides ambient context for the backstage reconciliation of the daughter and her beau. At the same time this music – like nondiegetic silent film accompaniment, except here supplied by the world of the film itself – heightens the irony of the burlesque queen's death, about which the daughter remains ignorant as the film concludes. While in most talkies up to this point the camera is kept static in an effort to simplify the sound recording and mixing processes, in *Applause* the camera roams frequently and with clear narrational intent, as when it tracks in and tilts up to end the film on the face of the dead mother, smiling in effigy from a huge poster on the wall behind the young lovers.[13]

A very few years later, musical experiments like Mamoulian's *Love Me Tonight* (Paramount, 1932), in which French theater star Maurice Chevalier bursts into happy-go-lucky song whenever the mood takes him, began a trend toward what Jane Feuer and others have called "integrated musicals," in which musical performance occurs spontaneously, rather than being motivated by a theatrical setting (see Feuer 1981 and Schatz 1981; see also Altman 1988). This same trend sparked RKO's most successful film cycle, a series of song-and-dance musicals starring Fred Astaire and Ginger Rogers, beginning with *Flying Down to Rio* (directed by Thornton Freeland, 1933). Warners' backstage musical *42nd Street* (directed by Lloyd Bacon, 1933) kicked off a series of similarly entertainment-themed films from Warners, as well as imitations produced by Paramount, MGM, and others. These musicals allowed audiences symbolically to have their radio and the cinema too: They supplied exciting musical performances by big stars of radio, sound recording, and screen without sacrificing the narrative flow and character psychology that had made silent Hollywood narrative so successful. It is worth speculating whether the reason *Applause* tanked with audiences in 1929 was not that it narrativized stage

Figure 8.2 Young lovers reconcile before an image of the dead burlesque queen as a bouncy show tune fills the soundtrack in Rouben Mamoulian's *Applause* (1929, producer Paramount Pictures). (Author's collection.)

performances in ways that look and sound crude to viewers today, but rather that it mourned too openly the demise of live vaudeville and burlesque at the cost of downplaying its romance plot, the very element that had cemented the popularity of the feature-length silent film during the preceding decade.

Conclusion: The Lost Futures of Sync Sound

As I've remarked, none of the changes precipitated by the coming of sound was inevitable. Like the transition itself, the shape of these changes depended upon a complex of forces that ranged from business plans executed by Warner Bros., Fox, Western Electric, and others, to the precedents set by the phonograph and the radio, both as audio technologies and as culturally meaningful artifacts in themselves. One reminder of how local and national history determined the shape of Hollywood's transition is the different approaches taken to sync sound by other national cinemas. Film historians have assumed for too long that Hollywood sound practices exercised the same near-total influence on European practices as had its conventions of visual storytelling. As Charles O'Brien has demonstrated, however, the French cinema developed a distinct sound aesthetic influenced heavily by music hall performance. This aesthetic thrived through the late 1930s, and vestiges of it survived for decades in the form of greater average camera distances and longer average shot lengths than those of Hollywood talkies from the same decade (O'Brien 2005, 44–81 and *passim*).

In the Soviet Union, where Hollywood cinema was both championed for its kineticism and condemned for its middle-class values, the groundbreaking filmmakers Sergei Eisenstein, Vsevolod Pudovkin, and Grigori Alexandrov issued a "statement" on sound in 1928 in which they urged other national film industries to avoid using sound merely to accompany the image (Eisenstein et al. 1999, 361). To do so would ignore the possibilities sound offered for radical experimentation with film as an art medium. Instead of foregrounding dialogue and downplaying the technology of sound, these giants of avant-garde cinema warned, filmmakers ought to explore sound as counterpoint to the image, the better to startle audiences out of their narrative-drenched complacency and forcing them to analyze unexpected juxtapositions of image with sound.

As much as Hollywood respected Eisenstein and his colleagues' artistry, the chances that 1920s and 1930s Hollywood would heed the Soviets' warning stood somewhere between slim and none. The robustness of classical fiction-film production depended in no small part upon the invisibility of the technological and stylistic maneuvers underwriting it. Hollywood's only global concern regarding sound was the problem of exporting sound films produced in English. Whereas in the silent era all the studios had to do was reedit films to adhere to the cultural and censorship imperatives of the host country and replace English intertitles with translations, now films would either have to be postdubbed in other languages (difficult, though not impossible, during the sound-on-disk phase) or reshot entirely. Following the latter path at least for a while, Hollywood studios collaborated with companies in Europe, sharing actors and reducing their own export and distribution costs by filming "remakes" of American films on location in France and Germany. There was little chance of radical experimentation, especially after the stock market crash of 1929 sent ticket sales into a nosedive and hit the newest "big" studio, RKO, with the first in a series of financial crises from which it would never entirely recover.

By that time, William Fox, who had released *Sunrise* to great acclaim but poor box office just two years earlier, had lost his studio. Energized by the success of his Movietone newsreels, he organized a takeover of MGM, which its resident moguls aggressively and successfully countermanded. The failed bid, together with the onset of the Great Depression, forced Fox into the courtroom in a desperate attempt to save the studio he already had. All he had to show for it in the end was a bribery conviction – for attempting to pay off a jury, no less.[14] When the Twentieth Century company purchased Fox's former material assets and incorporated under the name Twentieth Century-Fox, at its helm stood one of the very moguls Fox had faced in court.

By closing this chapter on a story about one studio's failed gamble on sound, I hope to drive home once again how closely the development of sound film was tied to the history of the business of American film, rather than to technological determinism or consumer desire. Hollywood was indeed a very different place after the coming of sound, but the transition could have turned out very differently. Talking pictures did not lie dormant within the silent cinema, waiting for Warners and *The Jazz Singer* to manifest them at last. Nor were they the cause of Hollywood's upheaval in the mid-1920s so much as they were a symptom of continuing attempts by studios to expand their own markets. Had Warner Bros. and Fox not determined to take larger market shares for themselves, or Western Electric and RCA not determined to expand their own markets to include the film industry at just that moment, sound cinema simply would not have developed in quite the way it did, and it might look and sound subtly (or perhaps drastically) different from how it does in the twenty-first century. Even in the few years between *Don Juan* and *King Kong*, filmmakers in Hollywood had many opportunities to make of sync-sound film an experimental medium unto itself, not at all wed to the storytelling imperatives that had established American silent film as the world's most powerful entertainment institution.

Notes

1. On pre-1926 sound film experiments, see Gomery 2005a, 24–29, and Altman 1992, 113–125. For an international perspective on the numerous attempts to synchronize sound mechanically or otherwise before 1925, see the special issue of *Film History*, 11.4 (1999) edited by Richard Abel and Rick Altman, and the slightly different set of essays collected in Abel and Altman 2001, which track historical experiments with mechanical, live, and audience-generated film sound from the 1890s through 1915's *The Birth of a Nation*. For a focused account of the development of sound and music accompaniment practices in the United States through the early 1920s, see Altman 2004.
2. The film industry had weathered such battles at its inception regarding basic technology: cameras,

projectors, and even filmstrip gauge and sprocket-hold placement. See Musser 1990, chs 3 and 4.

3. Gorky in 1896 (trans. Jay Leyda), quoted in Gunning 1999, 821–822.
4. AT&T countered RCA's technological/cultural claim to sound cinema by promoting its own sound system as an outgrowth of the telephone. For a superb account of this publicity war over sync sound's "electric affinities" and the ideology of technological determinism that spawns such claims, see Crafton 1997, 23–62; on the notion of sound "cinema as radio" in the late 1920s beyond the claims of these corporations, see also Altman 1992, 118–120.
5. On the amateur wireless craze of 1906–1912 and the period's fascination with its two-way capabilities, see Douglas 1987, 187–215.
6. On the perceived threat of broadcast African-American voices and hot jazz entering the unsuspecting middle-class home, and the function of radio minstrel acts and "sweet" jazz in mitigating this threat, see Hilmes 1997, 46–49, 76–96.
7. Here I am paraphrasing and expanding Rogin's argument (Rogin 1996). In a corollary argument to Rogin's, Alice Maurice argues that early sound film's focus on actual African-American voices as ideal voices for sound recording also acted as a racial control mechanism: "Claims that African American performers' voices could be reproduced more faithfully than others essentially promised that these voices would be 'in sync' with their bodies – and with audience expectations about what should emanate from those bodies," that is, "the image or stereotype of the 'Negro' long produced and exploited by Hollywood" (2002, 33–34).
8. By July 1929, according to a survey conducted by the trade journal *Film Daily*, only 5,251 theaters in the United States had been converted to synchronized sound, fewer than 25 percent of all theaters nationwide. Nevertheless, "sound films were *within driving distance* for most middle-class people by the end of 1929" (Crafton 1997, 253, 254, emphasis in original).
9. See Bordwell et al. 1985, 305–308; Bordwell and Thompson 1994, 216–219; Crafton 1997, 244–249; Lastra 2000, ch. 6. The limitations that synchronization placed on image-track editing made the Vitaphone's early emphasis on vaudeville and musical performance expedient if not inevitable. Indeed, editing these "stage" performances too much might have undermined the illusion of live performance that the Vitaphone shorts programs worked to cultivate.
10. See the musical *Singin' in the Rain* (Gene Kelly and Stanley Donen, 1951), set in Hollywood during the transition, where a test screening of the newly sonorized film-within-the-film turns disastrous for exactly this reason. More frequent than synchronization disasters were fidelity problems, particularly regarding actors speaking the letter "s," scratches and recording noise on the soundtrack, and complaints of uneven or altogether poor amplification. See, for example, Crafton 1997, 258–261.
11. On a 35mm strip of film the optical soundtrack runs 21 frames after the frame with which it is synchronized; thus the playback pickup is located at a different spot on projectors from the gate where the projector lamp shines through individual frames of film.
12. Spadoni 2007 argues that Universal's *Dracula* (1931) stresses the uncanniness of filmed bodies that talk by reanimating the stagey aesthetics that characterized the first couple of years of sync-sound shorts and features. While this mode served *Dracula* very well, judging by the positive box office returns and contemporary reviews, Spadoni speculates that it couldn't become an effective horror-film convention because the experience of the first sound films faded from viewers' memories as sync-sound conventions became regularized.
13. See Fischer 1985 for an examination of *Applause*'s unique approach to representing sound space. *Applause* may be considered a precursor to what Rick Altman calls the "backstage" musical – a musical in which rehearsals and performances motivate most of the singing and dancing, of which Warner Bros.' *42nd Street* (Lloyd Bacon, 1933) and *Gold Diggers of 1933* (Mervin LeRoy, 1933) are more accepted early examples – as opposed to the integrated musical, in which song and dance arise spontaneously whenever and wherever characters feel the urge. One must take care not to overstate *Applause* as an origin, however, considering its modest success and the (however few) years intervening between it and the highly successful Warner Bros. musicals of the mid-1930s. See Schatz 1981, ch. 7, esp. 186–196; Altman 1988, 204–206. See also Feuer 1981.
14. See Gomery 2005a, 52–54; Crafton 1997, 201–202. For Fox's side of the story as told to an unlikely sympathizer, the muckraker and novelist Upton Sinclair (*The Jungle*, 1906), see Sinclair 1933.

References

Abel, Richard, & Altman, Rick (eds). (2001). *The Sounds of Early Cinema*. Bloomington: Indiana University Press.

Altman, Rick. (1980). "Moving Lips: Cinema as Ventriloquism." *Yale French Studies*, 60, 67–79.

Altman, Rick. (1988). *The American Film Musical*. Bloomington: Indiana University Press.

Altman, Rick (ed.). (1992). *Sound Theory/Sound Practice*. New York: Routledge.

Altman, Rick. (2004). *Silent Film Sound*. New York: Columbia University Press.

Arnheim, Rudolf. (1957). *Film as Art*. Berkeley: University of California Press. (Original work published 1933.)

Balàzs, Béla. (1970). *Theory of the Film: Character and Growth of a New Art*, trans. Edith Bone. New York: Dover Publications. (Original work published 1952.)

Belton, John. (1999). "Awkward Transitions: Hitchcock's *Blackmail* and the Dynamics of Early Film Sound." *Musical Quarterly*, 83.2, 227–246.

Bergstrom, Janet. (2005). "Introduction: The Year 1927." *Film History*, 17.2/3, 163–167.

Bordwell, David. (1985). "The Introduction of Sound." In David Bordwell, Janet Staiger, & Kristin Thompson, *The Classical Hollywood Cinema: Film Style and Mode of Production to 1960* (pp. 298–308). New York: Columbia University Press.

Bordwell, David, & Thompson, Kristin. (1994). *Film History: An Introduction*. New York: McGraw-Hill.

Bordwell, David, Staiger, Janet, & Thompson, Kristin. (1985). *The Classical Hollywood Cinema: Film Style and Mode of Production to 1960*. New York: Columbia University Press.

Crafton, Donald. (1997). *The Talkies: American Cinema's Transition to Sound, 1926–1931*. Berkeley: University of California Press.

Douglas, Susan. (1987). *Inventing American Broadcasting, 1899–1922*. Baltimore: Johns Hopkins University Press.

Dreher, Carl. (1931). "Recording, Re-Recording, and Editing of Sound." *Journal of the Society of Motion Picture Engineers*, 16.6, 756–765.

Eisenstein, Sergei, Pudovkin, Vsevolod, & Alexandrov, Grigori. (1999). "Statement on Sound." In Leo Braudy & Marshall Cohen (eds), *Film Theory and Criticism* (pp. 360–362). 5th edn. New York: Oxford University Press. (Original work published 1928.)

Feuer, Jane. (1981). "The Self-Reflective Musical and the Myth of Entertainment." In Rick Altman (ed.), *Genre: The Musical* (pp. 159–174). London: Routledge. (Original work published 1977.)

Fischer, Lucy. (1985). "*Applause*: The Visual and Acoustic Landscape." In Elisabeth Weis & John Belton (eds), *Film Sound* (pp. 232–246). New York: Columbia University Press.

Gomery, Douglas. (2005a). *The Coming of Sound: A History*. New York: Routledge.

Gomery, Douglas. (2005b). "What Was Adolph Zukor Doing in 1927?" *Film History*, 17.2/3, 205–216.

Gunning, Tom. (1999). "An Aesthetic of Astonishment: Early Film and the (In)credulous Spectator." In Leo Braudy & Marshall Cohen (eds), *Film Theory and Criticism* (pp. 818–832). 5th edn. New York: Oxford University Press. (Original work published 1989.)

Hilmes, Michele. (1997). *Radio Voices: American Broadcasting, 1922–1952*. Minneapolis: University of Minnesota Press.

Hubbard, Preston J. (1985). "Synchronized Sound and Movie-House Musicians." *American Music*, 3.4, 429–441.

Lastra, James. (2000). *Sound Technology and the American Cinema: Perception, Representation, Modernity*. New York: Columbia University Press.

Lindsay, Vachel. (1915). *The Art of the Moving Picture*. New York: Macmillan.

McCracken, Allison. (2001). "Real Men Don't Sing Ballads: The Radio Crooner in Hollywood, 1929–1933." In Pamela Robertson Wojcik & Arthur Knight (eds), *Soundtrack Available: Essays on Film and Popular Music* (pp. 105–133). Durham, NC: Duke University Press.

McLuhan, Marshall. (1964). *Understanding Media: The Extensions of Man*. New York: McGraw-Hill.

Marvin, Carolyn. (1988). *When Old Technologies Were New: Thinking about Electric Communication in the Late Nineteenth Century*. New York: Oxford University Press.

Maurice, Alice. (2002). "'Cinema at its Source': Synchronizing Race and Sound in the Early Talkies." *Camera Obscura*, 17.1, 30–71.

Münsterberg, Hugo. (2001). *Hugo Münsterberg on Film: The Photoplay: A Psychological Study and Other Writings*. New York: Routledge. (Original work published 1916.)

Musser, Charles. (1990). *The Emergence of Cinema: The American Screen to 1907*. Berkeley: University of California Press.

O'Brien, Charles. (2005). *Cinema's Conversion to Sound: Technology and Film Style in France and the US*. Bloomington: Indiana University Press.

Rogin, Michael. (1996). *Blackface, White Noise: Jewish Immigrants in the Hollywood Melting Pot*. Berkeley: University of California Press.

Salt, Barry. (1992). *Film Style and Technology: History and Analysis*. 2nd edn. London: Starword.

Schatz, Thomas. (1981). *Hollywood Genres: Formulas, Filmmaking, and the Studio System*. Boston: McGraw-Hill.

Sinclair, Upton. (1933). *Upton Sinclair Presents William Fox*. Los Angeles: Author (self-published).

Spadoni, Robert. (2007). *Uncanny Bodies: The Coming of Sound Film and the Origins of the Horror Genre*. Berkeley: University of California Press.

Walker, Alexander. (1986). *The Shattered Silents: How the Talkies Came to Stay*. London: Harrap. (Original work published 1978.)

Wolfe, Charles. (1990). "Vitaphone Shorts and *The Jazz Singer*." *Wide Angle*, 12.3, 58–78.

Young, Paul. (2006). *The Cinema Dreams Its Rivals: Media Fantasy Films from Radio to the Internet*. Minneapolis: University of Minnesota Press.

Part II

1929–1945

9

Setting the Stage

American Film History, 1929–1945

In 1941, Harcourt, Brace published *Hollywood: The Movie Colony, The Movie Makers*, Leo Rosten's anthropological study of the film industry. The book came with a paper jacket illustrated with a 1937 painting by Thomas Hart Benton titled *Hollywood*. Benton's painting takes us inside the studio, combining into one canvas the sets on which at least three movies are being shot. Populated by the curvy, long-limbed figures that were his signature, Benton's painting presents the factory system at work – camera operators, sound engineers, actors being made up, and extras sitting around. For this most American of artists, Hollywood is not a glamorous still but an active site of labor, another regional locale, like the Midwest of his murals, woven into the fabric of national life. Benton's painting was a brilliant choice for a book that would argue Hollywood was not some anomaly on the West Coast, "no more screwy," in Rosten's words, "than other and less conspicuous parts of our society." In fact, Rosten claimed, "a study of Hollywood can cast the profile of American society into sharper relief" (1941, 5).

Rosten understood full well that moviemakers had been characterized over the years as corrupters of youth, as foreign-born agents who "were not drawn from the supposedly far-sighted ranks of American business." But he used his book to recast their identity, telling readers that the moguls "had the virtues and failings of pioneers." They were of the people, showmen who did "not cater to small, cultivated circles." Rather, they had "brains, confidence and a phenomenal capacity for work" (1941, 68). Movies, and the people who made them, Rosten suggested, could now be understood as firmly within the American grain.

Indeed, by the end of World War II, it would be impossible to consider the era without thinking about the role movies had played in helping steer the nation through two major crises – the Great Depression and World War II. Moreover, between 1929 and 1945, the movies solidified their role as the dominant force in American mass culture, influencing in complex and profound ways how the population thought about gender and race, romance and government, foreign countries and the nation's own history. Along with radio, and often in partnership with it, the cinema became the prevailing industry of culture – mass-producing stories, promoting fashions, and popularizing songs. And while Hollywood did not shy away from hard times – whether the plight of chain gangs or people in search of their daily bread – it also provided hour upon hour of escape from social realities through Wild West adventures, the song and dance of Shirley Temple, and the dizzying choreography

American Film History: Selected Readings, Origins to 1960, First Edition. Edited by Cynthia Lucia, Roy Grundmann, and Art Simon.
© 2016 John Wiley & Sons, Inc. Published 2016 by John Wiley & Sons, Inc.

of Busby Berkeley. Outside Hollywood, filmmakers documented bread lines and sit-down strikes, the flooded Mississippi delta, and the parched lands of the Dust Bowl. When war came calling, the studios lent their talent to the battlefield and the bond drive, telling the nation why we fight in both fictional and nonfictional voices and holding a mirror to the home front.

Perhaps no period in American film history has attracted greater attention than this one, from scholars and casual movie fans alike. It has been dubbed the golden age and many have seen fit to call it classical. Contemporary historians have been as awe-inspired as their predecessors in celebrating Hollywood's output during this time. Tino Balio begins his history of Hollywood during the 1930s with the claim that in 1939 "Hollywood turned out more 'classics' ... than [in] any other year in the decade" (1995, 1). In his survey of American film, Jon Lewis labels 1939–1941 "the last best years" (2008, 149). This was, indeed, a remarkable period, one that produced *Mr. Smith Goes to Washington* (1939) and *Gone With the Wind* (1939), *Stagecoach* (1939) and *Wuthering Heights* (1939), *The Wizard of Oz* (1939) and *Citizen Kane* (1941). But one can point to any number of periods in which Hollywood turned out an impressive catalog of films. Between 1953 and 1955, for example, the industry released *The Band Wagon* (1953), *Shane* (1953), *Rear Window* (1954), *On the Waterfront* (1954), *Night of the Hunter* (1955), and *Marty* (1955), though few have labeled this a golden period.

The Studio Industry

The era that runs from the first all-talkies through World War II can, in fact, be framed as classical, not because better movies were made during this time – such judgments are too idiosyncratic – but because of the way in which both industrial and social-political factors coalesced. Historians who find this period artistically appealing ultimately define its classicism not on aesthetic grounds but because this was the era in which the industry worked at maximum efficiency, an era in which talent – not only stars, but writers, directors, and below-the-line artists – was tied through long-term contracts to one company and as a result produced recognizable studio styles. There was, in other words, a division of artistic labor that effectively mobilized those with expertise in particular genres working in a system that manufactured a consistently coherent product. Once advances in sound technology were fully integrated, a range of genres could be produced, with the musical, talking comedy, horror, and mature gangster film added to the already established melodrama, Western, and adventure picture.

Indeed, the classical studio system was remarkable for the coherence of its storytelling methods that readily accommodated such diversity of subject matter. The recognizable plot structures, the repetition of scenarios in which characters confronted and overcame obstacles, the reliable resolutions at the end of so many stories – these hardly created a one-dimensional cinema. Rather, they supported an array of genres, settings, and emotional tones. From the bleak world of *I Am a Fugitive from a Chain Gang* (1932) to the utopian energies of a Garland and Rooney musical, from the theater-revue structure of Eddie Cantor's *Whoopee!* (1930) to the bizarre horrorscape of *Frankenstein* (1931), the classical system adapted itself to representing a multiplicity of worlds, all of them ultimately amenable to its star-centered narrative conventions.

The efficiency of this system was anchored by a business structure defined by vertical integration, that is, the control by a handful of companies, often acting collusively, over film production, distribution, and exhibition. During this period, five major corporations – Loew's MGM, Paramount, Warner Bros., Twentieth Century-Fox, and RKO – dominated the industry, as Matthew H. Bernstein points out in this volume, not only or primarily because they were responsible for most of the A-films produced at this time, but also because they owned the most profitable theaters in the country. While such theaters composed only one-fifth of the nation's total venues, they made up 80 percent of the first-run and most successful subsequent-run screens (Balio 1995, 7). The grand picture palaces of urban America and the vast theater chains spread across the most widely populated regions of the country were company assets of far greater value than the movie stars held under contract. Those theaters, and the thousands of independent screens nationwide, exhibited the output of the Big Five and also the films of what came to be known as the Little Three – Universal, Columbia, and United Artists, the last solely a distribution company. As a corporate oligarchy, these companies set the terms for the American picture business. Those terms included trade practices such as block booking, the insistence that theaters not affiliated with the five majors rent a season's schedule in a block rather than on a film-by-film basis. These unaffiliated theaters were forced to commit to a slate of films not yet in production and also to accept a given studio's short subjects. The problem was not that theaters were forced to rent films they did not need – as earlier noted, they needed films to fill their robust exhibition schedules. It was, rather, that independent theater owners lost all power of discrimination, obliged to accept poor films if they wanted to show a studio's best product, and, moreover, that their studio-affiliated counterparts were not held to this same all-or-nothing standard (Balio 1995, 20). Vertical integration and a set of highly advantageous trade practices were the foundation, then, for this classical era, remarkable for its level of stable production and profits. David Cook reports that between 1930 and 1945 the studios produced 7,500 features, a figure that does not include hundreds of live and animated shorts or newsreels (1996, 285).

But the stability of this era was only achieved after the industry coped with the turmoil of the early 1930s and had its great profitability underwritten by America's involvement in World War II. The movies were hardly immune to the collapse of the economy, although its full effects would not hit the industry for about two years after the crash of 1929. It was not simply that fewer Americans could afford to go to the movies or go as often as they had in the preceding decade. The Depression began at a point at which the studios were particularly vulnerable, having extended themselves through investments in sound production and the acquisition and wiring of thousands of theaters. With box office dollars greatly reduced, what companies owed far outweighed what was coming in. Warner Bros., for example, was among several studios posting losses in 1931, in that case about $8 million. In 1932, Paramount's losses were $21 million (Balio 1995, 15). Whether a studio fell into bankruptcy, like Paramount, or into some form of receivership, like RKO, or was forced to sell off theater holdings, like Universal, it meant several years lost to reorganization and delay on the road back to fiscal health. But it was also a period in which those with a stake in the profitability of movies learned that the future of the industry belonged to moviemakers and not to the professional financiers from Wall Street who tried, but failed, to steer the industry through hard times.

In 1931, studios began reorganizing their production hierarchies, replacing the central producer system with unit production, a structure in which perhaps half a dozen producers were made responsible for six to eight pictures per year. The industry trade press heralded the change as a cost-saving method in advancing the cause of individual artistry. A producer assigned to only a few films, it was argued, could keep a closer watch on budgets and efficiency, and with multiple producers managing units each concentrating on a given genre, a studio's total output would be less likely to carry the homogenized personality of one central producer. The year 1931 also saw exhibitors introducing the double bill, lengthening their program with a second feature in an effort to provide more entertainment for the dollar.

The industry's economic horizon began to brighten in 1934 with an uptick in box office receipts. A year later several companies had wiped debt off their books (Balio 1995, 30). The recovery appears to have been the product of several factors. First, the nation had passed through the most painful stage of the crisis (although the Depression was by no means over) to the point that weekly attendance at the movies increased steadily after 1934. Second, as Robert Sklar has pointed out, a new generation assumed the reins of studio management – Irving Thalberg, Darryl F. Zanuck, and David O. Selznick most importantly – men who largely turned away from contentious social issues, instead frequently adapting literary sources, either the classics or best-selling novels, and who embraced projects that preserved, to use Sklar's words, "the basic moral, social and economic tenets of traditional American culture" (1994, 175).[1] Thalberg's impact on the Marx Brothers is a suggestive case in point. After five anarchic comedies at Paramount in which they attacked social propriety, the upper classes, higher learning, and higher office, not to mention the conventions of Hollywood storytelling, the brothers found themselves at MGM after the box office disappointment of their masterpiece, *Duck Soup* (1933). Under Thalberg's supervision, the brothers' comedy was tamed and their outrageous personas integrated into more conventional plots. Frequently, despite top billing, they found themselves supporting romantic leads toward courtship and marriage.

The Production Code

The year 1934 was also the year in which the Motion Picture Production Code was reinforced. While it has become commonplace to refer to Hollywood's pre- and post-Code eras, it is not the case that industry self-regulation began at this point, either in response to some dramatic change of heart by producers or as a strategy to attract moviegoers back to theaters with a morally reformed cinema. The Code had its roots in various efforts by the Motion Picture Producers and Distributors of America (MPPDA) during the 1920s to contend with local censorship boards and standards. As Richard Maltby has pointed out in this volume and elsewhere, before the publication of the Production Code in 1930, the Studio Relations Committee of the MPPDA only functioned in an advisory role, recommending cuts in potentially offensive material. But the early years of sound made it far more difficult to cut objectionable material without disrupting image-to-sound synchronization. Sound also presented the challenge of monitoring suggestive or crude language and audio effects to accompany on-screen violence or passion (Maltby 1995, 45). Once the Code was published, with its list of strictures against sympathetic representations of crime and what might be interpreted as sinful or immoral sexuality, studio cooperation was inconsistent. With the 1931 release and success of *Dracula* and *Little Caesar*, the latter spearheading a cycle of gangster films, criticism of the movie industry from religious and civic organizations grew more intense. As a result, the MPPDA required studios to submit scripts and final prints for approval. But pressure, much of it generated by lay leadership of the Catholic Church, including Joseph Breen working within the MPPDA, continued to mount. With the industry's economic crisis at its apex in 1933 and widespread worry over how President Franklin Roosevelt would restructure business – the movies included – Will Hays made the case to studio executives that reinforcing the Production Code was essential to their survival. Vulnerable to proposed boycotts by the Church and looking to deflect government antagonism toward their trade practices, studio executives came around to greater cooperation. In June 1934, the Studio Relations Committee was renamed the Production Code Administration (PCA) and Breen was named its director.

The PCA had the authority to refuse its seal of approval to release prints of films and, while its official role was defined as advisory, it had enormous influence over the production of all films. Any MPPDA studio, and of course this included the Big Five and Little Three, that released a film without PCA approval was subject to a $25,000 fine. Breen's office met with studio executives at every step along the production process – story planning, scriptwriting, shooting – and then reviewed the finished product to make sure no offending dialogue or scenes had slipped through. No detail was too small for negotiation, and release schedules could be delayed until the seal of approval had been assigned. The Production Code also proved amendable and over the next two decades, as new film cycles troubled the PCA or emerging social issues found their way into scripts, new categories for prohibition were added.

During the shift from the "golden age of turbulence" to the "golden age of order" (Sklar 1994, 175), no single causal factor underwrites the change. Did the tastes of American moviegoers shift in 1934 and drive the studios away from the vaudeville aesthetic of the Marx Brothers and Mae West to the reassuring romances of screwball comedy? Did a change in national temperament signal to filmmakers that it was time to abandon cynical dramas like *Five Star Final* (1931) and *I Am a Fugitive from a Chain Gang* in favor of the affirmation found in *Snow White and the Seven Dwarfs* (1937) and *Mr. Smith Goes to Washington*? To be sure, the 1930s do not break so neatly in two, and – as several historians have pointed out – the common pre-Code, post-Code binary homogenizes the studio's output on both sides of the divide (Maltby 1995, 38–40). Moreover, any interpretation pivoting around the notion that moviemakers were simply following mass tastes simplifies both Hollywood's power to create the audience menu and the complex pressures on the industry in the early 1930s. From the threat posed by Christian leadership, several of whom, like Breen, were hardly circumspect about their anti-Semitism, to the view from the economic abyss in 1932–1933, to the looming shadow of New Deal regulators, the men behind the movies had ample motivation to adjust the direction of their industry and set a new course for reconciliation.

In retrospect, the price for adopting the Production Code appears to have been paid by writers and directors far more than by the studio executives who initially worried over its limitations on popular subject matter. Dealing with the Breen office became just another step in the production process. But this is not to say the movies were unaffected by the power of the PCA. To a substantial degree, the subject matter of pre-Code production differed markedly from that of the post-Code era, as Ruth Vasey points out in the case of the gangster film in this volume. Frank presentations of sexuality and the exposure of the (mostly female) body, depictions of business corruption and the plight of individuals often pitted against a brutal social world are on display in pre-Code films in ways they never would be again during the studio era. In response to Code restrictions, screenwriters and directors perfected the art of inference and post-Code Hollywood was hardly shorn of violence or allusions to sexuality. After 1934, however, the bitterness and cynicism to be found in a Warner's drama or a W. C. Fields short would be, for many moviegoers, an increasingly rare pleasure.

The Hollywood studios emerged from the worst of the Depression with their essential business structure intact. In 1933, following guidelines established by the National Industrial Recovery Act (NIRA), industry executives and the unions that represented their workers agreed to the Code of Fair Competition. The code permitted the continuation of block booking, with minimal changes, and did not challenge the vertical integration studio majors enjoyed. After an intense lobbying effort by independent theater owners, Fair Competition permitted the continuation of double features that had begun in 1931. Another long-term effect of New Deal legislation resulted from section 7A of the NIRA, the now famous granting of workers' rights to organize and bargain collectively. Throughout the 1930s, studio executives and their most expensive talent battled over wages and work conditions, but by the end of the decade virtually all of the industry's labor force was unionized. The various craft professionals were represented by IATSE, the International Alliance of Theatrical Stage Employees. The Screen Actors Guild won recognition in 1937, the Screen Writers Guild in 1938, and the Screen Directors Guild in 1939, as Larry Ceplair details in the hardcover/online edition.

B-Films

The increased demand for films needed to fill out a double bill accelerated the production of low-budget pictures (a relative term given, say, the difference between MGM and Warners) and what came to be known as B-films. B-pictures were budgeted far below the $350,000 average of A-films, were usually shot in less than a month, and never featured studio stars. While the well-known studios produced their share of B fare, so-called Poverty Row companies such as Monogram and Republic devoted their schedule entirely to such films, producing approximately 300 annually. According to Brian Taves, B-pictures made up roughly half the production schedule at the major studios and comprised 75 percent, or over 4,000 films, of all films made during the 1930s (1995, 314). In between the A- and B-film were productions that have come to be known as programmers. These were films that could play at the top or bottom of a double bill, could be budgeted as high as $200,000, and, unlike a standard B, might have a running time of over 70 minutes. Perhaps the best-known programmers were film series like the Charlie Chan pictures made first at Fox and later by Monogram.

The genres exploited by B production were familiar to audiences of prestige pictures, but their budgets and shooting schedules demanded an economy of production values with respect to sets, scripting, and rehearsal time. Crime dramas were popular but perhaps no genre would become more associated with B-films than the Western. B-Western stars such as Harry Carey, Hoot Gibson, Ken Maynard, and, initially, John Wayne rode through hundreds of films, many of them quickies with budgets of $8,000 or less. Among the most profitable and enduring stars was Gene Autry, whose success with *Tumblin' Tumbleweeds* in 1935 spurred the production of additional singing cowboy pictures.

Studio House Styles, Genres, and Auteurs

B-films and programmers supplied a steady product for exhibitors, kept many studios operating at full capacity, and, due to rentals based on a fixed rate rather than a percentage, could be budgeted to maintain consistent profits. But the studios defined themselves by A- and prestige pictures between 1929 and 1945, with both budgets and contracted talent contributing to the particular house styles each company established. MGM, for example, the wealthiest of the studios, spent an average of $500,000 for its prestige films during this time. Perhaps more than any other studio, it would attach its long list of stars – Greta Garbo, Clark Gable, Spencer Tracy, Jean Harlow, Wallace Beery, Norma Shearer – to adaptations of critically acclaimed plays such as Eugene O'Neill's *Anna Christie* (1930) and *Strange Interlude* (1932), Noel Coward's *Private Lives* (1931), and George S. Kaufman and Edna Ferber's *Dinner at Eight* (1933), or of best-selling books like *Grand Hotel* (1932), *Little Women* (1933), and *Mutiny on the Bounty* (1935). But the signature of a studio was based on more than its stars, and in the case of MGM, art director Cedric Gibbons was the central figure. The range of Gibbons's vision can be measured by the span from the art deco design of *Grand Hotel* to the Technicolor dreamscape of *The Wizard of Oz*.

Far more cost-conscious but with no less recognizable a style was Warner Bros., as Richard Maltby points out in this volume. While the studio's prestige pictures were its adventure films featuring Errol Flynn and its biopics, many directed by William Dieterle, Warners' profile came to be defined even more by its backstage musicals, gangster, and social problem dramas. With James Cagney and Edward G. Robinson, Barbara Stanwyck and Bette Davis as contract players, the studio became associated with an urban realism as stark and menacing as the hard times in which its films were set. Even after Code reinforcement, Warner Bros. continued to tackle troubling subjects like racial and ethnic hatred in *Black Legion* (1937), vigilante justice in *They Won't Forget* (1937), and organized crime in *Marked Woman* (1937).

Perhaps no genre cut a wider swath across the industry than the musical, as Desirée J. Garcia points out in this volume. Unlike, say, the Western, virtually every studio boasted a list of recognizable musicals or musical talent – at RKO, Ginger Rogers and Fred Astaire; at Universal, Deanna Durbin; and at Fox, Shirley Temple. Paramount featured Maurice Chevalier and, perhaps the studio era's biggest star, Bing Crosby. The Warner Bros. musical was often of the backstage variety, centering the story on a theatrical production, and at the height of the Depression it scored hits with *42nd Street* (1933), *Footlight Parade* (1933), and *Gold Diggers of 1933* (1933), all choreographed by Busby Berkeley. Each presented professional song and dance as the result of hard work and as vehicles for resilience during hard times. At MGM, films that teamed Judy Garland and Mickey Rooney also pivoted around putting on a show, but for many of the characters they played, staging a musical marked the passage from adolescent to adult, amateur to professional. In *Babes in Arms* (1939), directed by Berkeley, Mickey Moran (Rooney) and Patsy Barton (Garland) not only move a show from backyard to Broadway, they reinvigorate musical theater altogether, continuing the legacy of their veteran vaudeville parents. In the Garland–Rooney films, song and dance appeared a natural outgrowth of their youthful energies and the product of small-town America rather than eastern European immigrants.

It should be clear that studio styles emerged as collaborative products, the result in some cases of genre preferences – Universal and horror, for example – or the combination of actor and genre. But the auteurism first promoted in the United States by critic Andrew Sarris, in which the director emerges as the key figure in Hollywood authorship, has given way to a more holistic understanding of the creative impulses behind any single film. Thomas Schatz has argued that "the chief architects of a studio's style were its executives," that Thalberg, Zanuck, and Selznick held definitive power over shaping the films produced at their respective studios (1996, 7). Studio-era authorship might best be understood on the basis of production teams, a consistent combination of the creative departments at any given studio. And while it is the case that studio producers often assigned a single project to multiple writers, this should not erase the screenwriter from consideration. Consider the cases of John Ford and Frank Capra – as do Nicholas Baer and Vito Zagarrio, respectively, in the hardcover/online edition. Both directors maintained intensely collaborative relationships with a single writer during important points in their careers. Between 1934 and 1939, Ford collaborated with screenwriter Dudley Nichols on eight films, including *The Lost Patrol* (1934), *The Informer* (1935), and *Stagecoach* (1939). Between 1948 and 1950, he collaborated with Frank Nugent on four Westerns, including *Fort Apache* (1948), *She Wore a Yellow Ribbon*

(1949), and *Wagon Master* (1950) – all A-Westerns, an industry production strategy Kevin L. Stoehr discusses at length in the hardcover/online edition. Between 1932 and 1938, Frank Capra worked with screenwriter Robert Riskin on seven films, including *It Happened One Night* (1934), *Mr. Deeds Goes to Town* (1936), and *You Can't Take It With You* (1938). From the current vantage point, the vast majority of films from this period appear more recognizable on the basis of studio rather than directorial imprint. Thus, the lack of auteur status assigned to such essential 1930s-era directors as Lloyd Bacon, Clarence Brown, Roy Del Ruth, and even Michael Curtiz. As Schatz, among others, has argued, enhanced creative freedom for the director, indeed, the director-producer, as marketing tool and authorial force, would not emerge until the 1940s.

One director who was granted considerable freedom but then subsequently subjected to savage studio interference was, of course, Orson Welles. Responsible for *Citizen Kane* (1941), a film that has maintained its fascination for each subsequent generation, Welles, as both artist and individual, combined, to a remarkable degree, tendencies that looked both backward and forward. Like many who shaped the first decade of the sound era, he brought experience in both theater and radio. He came to political maturation during the Popular Front, a movement that had shaped documentary production and informed the antifascist cause, which would get full expression during wartime Hollywood. The breakthroughs of technique – in sound, staging, and adaptation – that distinguished his pre-Hollywood career were genuinely avant-garde. But as James Naremore points out in this volume and elsewhere, Welles's aesthetic tastes also looked to the past, to Gothic themes and imagery, as well as the expressionism that had informed the 1920s and would reemerge in postwar Hollywood. The creative freedom he received at RKO was due not only to his tremendous reputation, but also to his arrival "at a particular movie studio at a particular historical moment." Signed and shielded by studio boss George Schaefer, Welles's latitude at RKO lasted only, however, as long as he had an ally in charge (Naremore 1989, 52). Welles's experience, while in many ways unique, was not wholly uncharacteristic for the Hollywood mode. That is, rather than a monolithic system of production, as it has frequently been defined, the industry often functioned as a series of alliances and negotiations between artists and executives. For some – Howard Hawks, Ernst Lubitsch – this resulted in a degree of creative or professional independence not granted to many working within the system. For Welles after 1941, the studio system would present a series of violations and restrictions, raising the great unanswered question of the golden age: What might Welles, and the movies, have been were he to have maintained his autonomy after *Citizen Kane*?

Although Howard Hawks directed several features during the silent era – most notably *A Girl in Every Port* (1928), which first presented the theme of male bonding that would become so central to his later work, and *The Air Circus* (1928), the first of several aviation films he later would direct – it is in the sound film that Hawks would truly take flight. He relished equally the rat-a-tat-tat of machine gun fire in *Scarface* (1932) and of quick-fire dialogue in *Twentieth Century* (1934), often credited as a model for the many screwball comedies to follow – including his own *Bringing Up Baby* (1938), *His Girl Friday* (1940), and *Ball of Fire* (1941). Language is the very subject of *Ball of Fire*, as Gary Cooper's ivory tower linguist needs to learn something about American slang from Barbara Stanwyck's Sugarpuss O'Shea in order to contribute to an encyclopedia. Although Hawks depended on talented writers like Ben Hecht and Charles Brackett to supply sometimes ethnically colored and frequently witty dialogue, he actively worked with his screenwriters (Cook 1996, 320), and – sometimes credited and sometimes not – was producer of many of his own films. While not widely regarded as a "visual stylist," as David Cook claims, Hawks worked with such accomplished cinematographers as Gregg Toland and James Wong Howe, establishing himself as "a great visual storyteller with an urbane wit and a nearly existential concern with the condition of men in extreme situations" (1996, 322).

Among his consistent themes were those grounded in the historical moment – "America's mood as the Wall Street panic morphed into the Great Depression and the Hoover administration stood idly by" as in *Scarface*, as William Rothman observes in his essay in the hardcover/online edition (2012, 228), and the historical record, as in *The Road to Glory* (1936) and the award-winning *Sergeant York* (1941). Other Hawksian themes appear in his work across several genres: masculine codes of honor, friendship, and professionalism as in aviation and adventure films like

Only Angels Have Wings (1939) and Westerns like *Red River* (1948); and the complications of romance, marriage, and remarriage, sometimes colored by social class differences, as in his screwball comedies. These same themes pervade Hawks's later film noir (*The Big Sleep*, 1946), which, like the screwball comedies, features strong female characters who are equally skillful talkers, holding their own when sparring verbally with their male counterparts. Paradoxically, Hawks's celebration of male camaraderie is more welcoming to female characters than many other films of the period, usually casting the woman as, proverbially, one of the boys, as true of Jean Arthur in *Only Angels Have Wings*, Katharine Hepburn in *Bringing Up Baby*, and Lauren Bacall in *The Big Sleep*. Although in some cases powerful Hawksian women are a source of male anxiety, unlike in Hitchcock and so many films noir, this anxiety often becomes a source of comedy.

Hawks's *Scarface* is an especially significant film of the early 1930s. Along with the other two most prominent gangster films of the time, *Little Caesar* and *The Public Enemy* (both 1931), its violence intensified ongoing censorship battles resulting, ultimately, in stringent enforcement of the newly revised Production Code, as noted. Shot in 1930, the film was held from release for two years as producer Howard Hughes argued over content with the Hays Office. When it finally was released, some scenes had been eliminated and others of a highly didactic nature were added, preaching the disgrace and degradation of crime in civilized society. Similar messages appear in written admonitions framing the film, and the film's title itself was changed to *Scarface, Shame of a Nation*. But such high-minded messages could not dampen the engagingly buoyant, if sometimes frenetic (and at moments comically unhinged) appeal of Paul Muni as Chicago gangster Tony Camonte (loosely based on the real-life Al Capone), who both inelegantly and ruthlessly rises to the top of the mob. Driven by the desire to have it all – as ironically signaled by a travel agency billboard that captures his attention and imagination, announcing that "The World is Yours" – Tony also is driven by psychosexual demons, centered on an incestuous obsession with his sister Cesca (Ann Dvorak) and on obtaining the approval and unconditional love of his mother (Inez Palange). Lee Garmes's cinematography captures the shadowy, unstable psyche of the gangster, with lighting effects that echo the film's "X" motif – foreshadowing and marking Tony's victims but also reflecting his own outsider status, whether in his family or as a criminal ultimately defeated by the law.

Hawks thus adds a unique psychological complexity to his character, uncommon in other gangster films of the period, while at the same time avoiding any clear sociological explanation for gang violence, very much in keeping with those films. As Robert Sklar has pointed out, gangster films of the time did, however, illustrate that "their heroes' chaotic lives were more than matched by the chaos in society around them" (1994, 181) – in contrast with later screwball comedies, like Hawks's *Twentieth Century*, in which "improbability and incongruity were never allowed to disturb the social order but, rather, to show how well it worked" (1994, 188). Hawks's significant contributions to both genres support Cook's conclusion, quoting French film historian Henri Langlois, that Hawks is best described as an "American" with work that "'anticipates his time'" and "'enables us to better and more fully identify with it [America], both in admiration and criticism'" (1996, 323).

Among the most important of émigré directors was Ernst Lubitsch, who arrived in Hollywood in 1922 after earning critical praise directing films in his native Germany. In his move across the Atlantic, Lubitsch hardly missed a beat, directing a series of well-regarded silent comedies (*The Marriage Circle*, 1924; *Lady Windermere's Fan*, 1925) at Warner Bros. He would find even greater success, commercial as well as critical, in the new sound era – first with a string of stylish musicals that featured the talents of Maurice Chevalier or Jeanette MacDonald and then with sophisticated comedies that enjoyed the permissiveness of the pre-Code era, in particular *Trouble in Paradise* (1932) and *Design for Living* (1933), centered on the romantic entanglements of the privileged class.

The Lubitsch touch, as it came to be called, was joined with political satire in his masterpieces *Ninotchka* (1939) and *To Be or Not to Be* (1942). *Ninotchka* skewers the cold and doctrinaire official Soviet personality when the title character, played by Greta Garbo, is seduced by the pleasures, both material and romantic, of the West in the form of the charming Leon played by Melvyn Douglas. Scripted by Charles Brackett and Billy Wilder, the latter Lubitsch's most important protégé, *Ninotchka* draws on the brilliant comic work of Sig Ruman, Felix Bressart, and Alexander Granach – three of

Figure 9.1 Greta Garbo in Ernst Lubitsch's *Ninotchka* (1939, producers Sidney Franklin and Ernst Lubitsch) embraces her trio of comrades Iranoff (Sig Ruman), Buljanoff (Felix Bressart), and Kopalski (Alexander Granach) outside the Soviet Union.

Hollywood's most gifted character actors. Ruman and Bressart would join major stars Carole Lombard and Jack Benny in the even more daring *To Be or Not to Be*. The film's title refers not only to the staging of *Hamlet* by a small theater troupe, but also to the very survival of Polish citizens under the Nazi boot. Drawing on their skills as actors, the troupe is forced, through historical necessity, to become agents of resistance. Political theater and the theater of war merge in the tour de force sequence in which stage lights are used to track down Nazi spy Professor Siletsky in the theater where he is trapped and killed. *To Be or Not to Be* brought together two of the greatest comic talents of the era, Carole Lombard (*Twentieth Century*, 1934; *My Man Godfrey*, 1936; *Nothing Sacred*, 1937), whose career would be cut short in a tragic plane crash when *To Be or Not to Be* was in postproduction, and Jack Benny, whose greatest work would be produced for radio. Lubitsch, too, would die young, at the age of 55, leaving an irreparable gap in Hollywood comedy at mid-century.

Fritz Lang was central among those émigré directors who came to Hollywood somewhat later, fleeing the rising tide of fascism in Europe. Lang's earlier films included highly acclaimed German Expressionist classics, among them *Siegfried* (1924), *Metropolis* (1927), *M* (1931), and *The Testament of Dr. Mabuse* (1933) – the last three, films that infuse Expressionist stylization with realism of location and action. His first US film, *Fury* (1936), is a statement against mob violence and also, indirectly, a statement against both fascism and lynching in the American South. Wrongly accused of a kidnapping as he travels through a small town, Joe Wilson (Spencer Tracy) is arrested and later assumed dead when an angry mob of townspeople set fire to the jail that holds him. Taking "justice" into its own hands, this mob echoes the underworld mob in *M* that captures child murderer Hans Beckert (Peter Lorre), intending to seek retribution outside the justice system, which likely would take Beckert's mental illness into account. Although the criminal is victimized in *M*, in *Fury* Joe, at first an innocent victim, becomes as callous as the mob in seeking his own revenge. Unbeknownst even to his fiancée, Joe has survived the fire and, with the help of his brothers, sees to it that key members of the mob are placed on trial for his murder. As true of Lang's later film, *The Big Heat* (1953), the brutality of those surrounding the protagonist transforms him into an obsessively dissolute figure who has fallen away from his sense of self and his values. Lang's dark critique of human fallibility extends to legal and government institutions, often shown as ineffectual at their best or as deeply corrupt at their worst.

In *You Only Live Once* (1937) – the first of several films to be based on the story of the infamous criminal duo, Bonnie Parker and Clyde Barrow, though in this case very loosely so – dark twists of fate make it impossible for ex-convict Eddie Taylor (Henry Fonda) to live the life he longs to share with his new, pregnant wife Joan (Sylvia Sidney). Wrongly accused of a bank robbery in which several people are killed, he manages to escape death row just before his execution. He shoots a priest – sadly, the one prison official who truly believes in him – unaware that, minutes earlier, he had been exonerated when the identity of the true murderer was discovered. But Eddie now *is* guilty of murder. He and Joan flee, living a punishing life on the road – forced to steal cars and food along the way – until discovered and shot by authorities. As in *Fury* and *You Only Live Once*, Lang's morally complex narratives actively challenge viewers to think beyond good/evil binaries, eliciting sympathy for characters caught in circumstances beyond their control. Maze-like networks of hallways and city streets, as well as cluttered, claustrophobic rooms, often literalize this sense of entrapment, no more dramatically than in the chiaroscuro pattern of light and shadow cast on the floor by the bars of Eddie's prison cell, extending eerily in all directions.

Understandably less morally ambiguous although no less complex, however, are Lang's most overtly antifascist films – *Man Hunt* (1941), *Hangmen Also Die!* (1943), and *Ministry of Fear* (1944). The title of *Man Hunt*, alone, announces a theme running through many of Lang's films, this time centered on Captain Thorndike (Walter Pidgeon), a big-game hunter and would-be assassin of Adolf Hitler. Thorndike is tortured, miraculously survives an assassination attempt, and is pursued by the Nazis. The film's clearly antifascist stance, during America's isolationist period before entering the war, prompted restrictions from the Hays Office and producer Darryl F. Zanuck. *Hangmen Also Die!* is the product of a very brief collaboration between Lang and playwright Bertolt Brecht, who together developed the story, based loosely on the assassination of Reinhard Heydrich, a high-ranking Third Reich official known as "The Hangman of Prague." According to Lang biographer Patrick McGilligan, although Lang helped bring Brecht to the United States from Finland, where he was in hiding, Brecht neither warmed up to Hollywood and writing for movies, nor to Lang's calculated attention to what audiences would or would not accept in a film (McGilligan 2009). In the movie Heydrich is killed by Dr. Franticek Svoboda (Brian Donlevy), a member of the Czech resistance with Communist Party ties (in reality it was British resistance fighters who carried out the mission). When they cannot ferret out Svoboda, Nazi officials initiate a plan to execute 400 citizens – in groups of 40 – in order to pressure the assassin to surrender. The resistance, however, is able to ensnare a Nazi sympathizer as the supposed assassin – a key figure also in orchestrating the planned executions. As in *Fury*, which features the courtroom screening of a film as evidence of mob violence, *Hangmen* registers Lang's ongoing interest in the media and in surveillance technology, with the Gestapo secretly listening in on Czech citizens. Set in England at the height of German bombings, *Ministry of Fear*, adapted from a Graham Greene novel, anticipates film noir with its labyrinthine plot of paranoid deception involving an undercover ring of Nazi spies with whom Stephen Neale (Ray Milland) unsuspectingly becomes involved. Recently released from a short sentence in an asylum – for having planned to euthanize his terminally ill wife, who ultimately committed suicide – Neale is wracked with guilt and his own stability is called into question, adding layers of complexity to this dark, paranoid thriller. Lang would go on to direct a number of films noir with similar tropes in the postwar period.

In contrast with Lang, Preston Sturges, perhaps like no other director, offered a respite from wartime worries. Among the golden age's most gifted writers, Sturges parlayed Broadway success into an invitation to Hollywood at the very beginning of the sound era. Few screenwriters gained the financial and critical success of Sturges, who was able to convince Paramount to let him direct his own script for *The Great McGinty* in 1940. His status as an auteur was solidified over the next decade as he used such films as *The Lady Eve* (1941), *The Palm Beach Story* (1942), *Hail the Conquering Hero* (1944), and *The Miracle of Morgan's Creek* (1944) to puncture the aura of society's most cherished institutions, most notably marriage and patriotism. In a time when Gary Cooper and John Wayne represented an ideal American male, Sturges countered with Eddie Bracken and his befuddled and innocent comic persona. A master at combining zaniness with smart satire, Sturges often mocked the privileged class and celebrated the little guy, often worrying the PCA in the process. Despite the sophistication imbued in his films, Sturges celebrated popular entertainment, a philosophy rendered most clearly in *Sullivan's Travels* (1941) when Hollywood director John L. Sullivan (Joel McCrea) decides to hit the road in the spirit of many Depression-era artists to live amidst "the people." What he learns by film's end is that the masses do not crave social commentary but laughs, that the disenfranchised are nourished best by the kind of entertainment that was Hollywood's bread and butter.

As crucial to the emotional tone of Hollywood films, but often overlooked given the attention paid to the cinematic image, is the music scored and orchestrated by industry composers and conductors. The music of Max Steiner made an essential contribution to the Warner Bros. catalog of films such as *Jezebel* (1938), *Dark Victory* (1939), *Casablanca* (1942), *Now, Voyager* (1942), and *Mildred Pierce* (1945). In 1939, he was loaned to David Selznick in order to compose the score for *Gone With the Wind*. Bernard Herrmann began his career with scores for Orson Welles (*Citizen Kane* and *The Magnificent Ambersons*) and later gave pulsating life to several Hitchcock thrillers.

Such entertainment during the classical era, however, was the product primarily of men. While women were very much a part of the silent film industry on both sides of the camera, as Shelley Stamp points out in this volume, many of these women were since written out of mainstream film histories, as Jane M. Gaines explains in the hardcover/online edition. As cinema transitioned from the silent to the sound eras, opportunities for women in the industry quickly evaporated. Although actress Ida Lupino directed seven films from the late 1940s through the mid-1950s, including *Never Fear* (1949), *Outrage* (1950), *Hard, Fast and Beautiful* (1951), *The Hitch-Hiker* (1953), and *The Bigamist* (1953), her work as a director from the mid-1950s through 1968 was limited to television episodes.

Some 20 years Lupino's senior, Dorothy Arzner began her career as a highly regarded film editor during the silent era. Her editing of *Blood and Sand* (1922), starring Rudolph Valentino, is regarded as one of her greatest accomplishments. Having directed 19 films from 1927 through 1943, most notably *Fashions for Women* (1927, her first feature), *Manhattan Cocktail* (1928), *Sarah and Son* (1930), *Merrily We Go to Hell* (1932), *Christopher Strong* (1933), *Nana* (1934), *Craig's Wife* (1936), *Dance, Girl, Dance* (1940), and two other films on which she is not credited (*Behind the Make-Up*, 1930; *The Last of Mrs. Cheyney*, 1937), Arzner's body of work far exceeds that of any other female filmmaker, whether during the studio era or beyond.

Arzner began her career at Paramount and then went on to work independently for several studios. As influential as many male directors of her time, she introduced three major stars into the movies: Katharine Hepburn in *Christopher Strong*; Rosalind Russell in *Craig's Wife*; and Lucille Ball in *Dance, Girl, Dance*. As a female director, she typically was assigned to direct melodramas with female-centric characters and themes, and "although many of her films reflect stereotypical Hollywood conventions regarding the representation of women," as Judith Mayne argues, "there is also in Arzner's work a sense of women's independence and a stylistic vision to go along with it" (1994, 1).

In *Christopher Strong* (adapted from a Gilbert Frankau novel), Hepburn plays a self-possessed aviator – the kind of woman she would come to play in many films to follow, including those of Hawks. Yet the independence of Hepburn's Cynthia Darrington is compromised by an affair with the title character, a married man whose child she will carry until deliberately ending her life in a plane crash. In *Craig's Wife* (adapted from a George Kelly play), Russell's Harriet Craig is largely understood by those around her to be cold and unfeeling. In the end she is left alone and isolated in her house – itself a barricade she has constructed to stave off meaningful human contact. While these stories would seem to reflect the typical Hollywood treatment that punishes or isolates women for their perceived flaws or indiscretions, Arzner revised the original sources in order to "stress the complexity of women's lives," as Theresa L. Geller argues (2003). Both films reveal heterosexual romance and marriage as a "'bargain' that 'shackles' women," further revealing "the limits imposed upon women under patriarchy," if only in understated terms (Geller 2003). Arzner's maternal melodrama *Sarah and Son* adds complexity to this subgenre so popular during the early sound era, one that Lea Jacobs defines in the hardcover/online edition as evoking sentimentalized images of mother-love and home. Although she is a mother who suffers deeply the loss of her son after her estranged husband has given the infant to a wealthy family, Ruth Chatterton's Sarah creates a self-sustaining, independent life for herself, rising to become a successful opera singer, while never relenting in her attempt to reunite with her son. This film attests to Arzner's subtle efforts to produce films ever-so-slightly against the grain of the studio system in which she worked – if even as an independent.

Although a box office and critical disappointment at the time of its release, Arzner's *Dance, Girl, Dance* underwent significant reassessment with the rise of feminist film criticism in the 1970s to become her best-known and most widely examined work. Although the story of two dancers – Judy O'Brien (Maureen O'Hara), with aspirations to become a ballerina, and Bubbles/Tiger Lily White (Lucille Ball), a success in the burlesque hall – would seem to represent high/low, artistic/marketplace, middle/working class, sexually innocent/sexually experienced, good/bad girl binaries, Arzner refuses such clear-cut dichotomies, allowing each woman her admirable qualities and her flaws. Of greatest interest to feminist critics is the way in which the film interrogates what Laura Mulvey would famously define as the dominant male gaze of mainstream narrative cinema, relegating female bodies as objects of male viewing pleasure (and anxiety). In the dance hall setting women perform for male (and female) spectators, a dynamic of voyeuristic desire that Arzner undermines when Judy addresses a rowdy audience, in effect returning the voyeuristic gaze – extending to film audiences. Arzner's work, in general, has become a means for feminist and queer theorists to examine the gender ambiguities and multiple other ambiguities beneath the dynamics of desire in cinema, with her films expressing some measure of resistance to mainstream aesthetics and themes. A lesbian often noted for the mannish suit and tie worn on her movie sets, Arzner both set herself apart and, ironically, blended in with the predominantly male filmmakers of her era. In her films Arzner deconstructs and challenges the heterosexist dynamic at the core of Mulvey's theory – years before Mulvey would articulate and later revise it.

Often overlooked in the discussion of classical-era genres is the extent to which so many addressed historical subjects. Indeed, films set in the past or recent past and that took part in the writing of history, from *Gone With the Wind* to *Robin Hood* (1922 and 1938), from the biopics of "great men" to stories of westward expansion, compose, perhaps, the fullest catalog of studio-era production. While the sweep of these films might prevent assigning them to a single genre – often having resulted in simple dismissal of Hollywood as historian – their centrality to the Hollywood mode has attracted the attention of historians within and outside of film studies. As J. E. Smyth argues in this volume, studio screenwriters were frequently dedicated to serious research and understood well the historiographic terrain over which they were crossing. Moreover, unlike many academic historians of the time, Hollywood challenged the male-centered account of the nation's past. In films like *Cimarron* (1931) and *Show Boat* (1936), Hollywood made the case that "women drove the course of American history."

Innovations in Film Technology

The classical period also is one of remarkable innovation in film technology, and while individual directors and cinematographers would deploy these advances in their own ways, such developments were shared across the entire industry. Arzner herself is credited with having rigged a fishing pole with a microphone to afford her actors greater mobility in her first sound film, *The Wild Party* (1920) – a device anticipating the development of the boom. The introduction of sound ushered in a brief period during which films were shot with multiple cameras operating simultaneously. But when cameras were quieted and directional microphones developed, most productions returned to the one-camera shooting method that had been standard during the silent era. The return of single camera filming opened the way for the invention of new devices to increase its mobility: During the early 1930s, cameras were set on carriages or boom arms and then eventually cranes that offered seating for cinematographers and the capacity to rise as high as 30 feet into the air. Rear projection, a technique that located characters in front of a screen on which any number of backgrounds could be projected, became standard throughout the industry in the mid-1930s, and it would be put to use in almost every genre for the next 30 years.

Two technological developments in particular would have a long-term aesthetic impact – color and deep focus photography. While Technicolor sequences were used in several epics of the 1920s – *The Ten Commandments* (1923), *Ben-Hur* (1925) – and its widespread use would not come until the 1940s, important 1930s films such as *Trail of the Lonesome Pine* (1936), *A Star is Born* (1937), and *Gone With the Wind* (1939) pointed toward its future success. In 1932, its three-color process was developed in which a specially designed camera used a prism to split the light onto three different strips of film. These strips, each with a primary aspect (red, green, or blue), were then developed to negatives. Projecting through these negatives onto a specially prepared film stock, positive relief images were created in a hardened gelatin. These three gelatin reliefs were then used as printing matrices, capable of absorbing dye that could be transferred to yet another filmstrip. Once this final strip had absorbed dye from all three color-transfers, it became the final print ready to be projected. The engineers behind this process were confident the three-strip process could, in the words of J. A. Ball, Vice President and Technical Director of Technicolor, "reproduce whatever is placed in front of the camera, not only as to color but also as to light and shade" (Ball 1935, 130).

Ball's reference to light and shade underscores the thorough interconnection of film technologies, the enfolded relationship between cameras, film stock, and lighting, as well as the impact of these elements on set design and construction. Thus, developments in cinematography such as deep focus must be framed next to improvements in the speed of film stock, the quieting of cameras, the enhancing of powerful arc lamps, as well as their location on the set, and chemical developments for the coating of lenses. All of these factors contributed in the late 1930s to efforts by some cinematographers, most notably Gregg Toland and James Wong Howe, to move away from the soft focus style of the late silent era toward sharper photography composed in depth. Orson Welles's *Citizen Kane* is, of course, the paradigmatic film here, but Toland's work on William Wyler's *Dead End* (1937) and *Wuthering Heights* (1939) and on John Ford's *The Grapes of Wrath* (1940) exemplifies his innovations while working alongside three strong directors. Filmmakers of an earlier era had practiced shooting in depth, but the 1940s saw renewed experiments with deep focus, energizing film space, expanding the action from one or perhaps two planes into three planes of depth. This is not to suggest that all films from the late 1930s on were photographed in deep focus, far from it, but as the classical era unfolded, directors saw their creative options expand with respect to staging and the sharpness of the image.

William Wyler is an especially interesting example in that a close look at his career makes clear that his use of deep space and the long take notably predates the late 1930s, when the practice emerged in a number of high-profile films. *Dodsworth* (1936), Wyler's adaptation of the Sinclair Lewis novel about a middle-aged American couple whose marriage falls apart on a trip to Europe, undermines the standard historical narrative suggesting that Hollywood cinematography of the 1930s largely was centered on a shallow image with a soft focus background. *Dodsworth* is a significant example of Wyler's long-standing ambition to use depth of field cinematography to explore how the American middle class is defined by materialism. *Dodsworth*'s cinematography by Rudolph Maté deftly juxtaposes the material comfort of the protagonists' Midwestern living room with the bustling surface detail of the ocean liner on which the couple journeys. Particularly in the closing scene, in which Dodsworth tells his wife he will not return to her, a spectacle of surface details expresses the male protagonist's determination to start a new life. Their conversation takes place amidst the hustle and bustle of an entrance lobby crowded with freshly boarded passengers ready to begin their journey, forming a stream of elegantly coutured bodies that Dodsworth must move against as he gets up to leave his wife. He disembarks the ship by a large hatch through which another anchored ocean liner is visible.

Wyler's use of deep space becomes more darkly analytical in *The Little Foxes* (1941), an adaptation of the Lillian Hellman play that features Bette Davis as the ruthlessly ambitious matron of a Southern middle-class family. Wyler, along with Toland, here skillfully uses deep focus to accentuate the physical distance between the family members as they scheme against each other in their bourgeois parlor. The film's climactic scene, however, in which Davis's character refuses to give the necessary medicine to her husband suffering a heart attack, uses deep space in a more differentiated manner. The background action, with her husband trying to crawl up the stairs, remains blurry, giving just enough a sense of what is happening without distracting from Davis's tense and determined posture in the foreground, on which the camera focuses.

In Wyler's landmark, Oscar-decorated returning war veteran drama, *The Best Years of Our Lives* (1946), his and Toland's creative use of deep focus is apparent in almost every scene. It ranges from the realistic shots of airport terminals overcrowded with GIs (who are given secondary treatment to rich American tourists) and airfields cluttered with planes whose wings are clipped (a symbol of the emasculated state of returning veterans), to dramatic aerial views shot from inside a bomber over the shoulders of the three main protagonists, who, on their domestic journey back to their families, look out of the plane's front window onto an America that seems like foreign territory. Wyler continued to make landmark films in the 1950s, such as the Audrey Hepburn romance *Roman Holiday* (1953) and the 1959 remake of *Ben-Hur*, but it is his 1930s and 1940s work that identifies his pioneering role as a visual stylist and that has inspired film theorists of cinematic realism from Siegfried Kracauer to André Bazin.

Documentary Filmmaking

The classical era also witnessed the maturing of the American documentary. Sound helped newsreels secure a regular spot in theatrical programs, and by 1937, newsreels were being produced by most of the major studios. Fox led the way with *Movietone*, with virtually all of its crews recording sound on the spot by 1934. Unlike its major competitors *Pathé News*, Hearst's *News of the Day*, and *Paramount News*, Fox *Movietone* followed a rigid structure – news, novelty, fashion, and sports (Fielding 1972, 191). *The March of Time*, Time Inc.'s once-a-month, 20-minute documentaries, engaged both domestic and global political issues much more directly than did studio newsreels. It eschewed the multistory newspaper approach, preferring to focus an entire film around one issue and frequently employing dramatic recreations of news events.

But it was documentary filmmakers working outside the industry who recorded the great crises of the era, their work originating from two sources: a network of left-wing filmmakers and the federal government. Left-wing filmmakers, some with direct ties to the Communist Party, produced work throughout the decade that would be screened in union halls, art cinemas, or, in some cities, friendly schools like the New School for Social Research in New York City (Wolfe 1995, 358). The Workers' Film and Photo League (later just the Film and Photo League or FPL), established in 1930, was committed to documenting the myriad social protests erupting in response to the Great Depression. Several of the League's most important films were made at the Depression's depths in 1932. *National Hunger March* (1932) recorded a march in Detroit in which police brutally attacked demonstrators, and *Hunger 1932* documented a march from New York to the nation's capital. Sit-down strikes, Scottsboro protests, and Hoovervilles were also subjects for FPL cameras. These were silent films in which the filmmakers – Samuel Brody, Leo Seltzer, and Lester Balog, among others – resisted the detached position of commercial newsreels in order to capture events as participant observers.

In 1935, Leo Hurwitz, Ralph Steiner, and Irving Lerner, hoping to expand their aesthetic repertoire while still making films from a radical-critical posture, left the FPL to found Nykino. Two years later, this growing collection of filmmakers and their sponsors became Frontier Films. Joined by a host of important filmmakers, including Jay Leyda, Paul Strand, and Willard Van Dyke, Frontier would make the essential documentaries of the Popular Front. *People of the Cumberland* (1937) documented the Highlander Folk School in Tennessee. *The Spanish Earth* (1937), directed by Joris Ivens and screened for FDR in the White House, was one of several films dedicated to advancing the loyalist cause in the Spanish Civil War. When Frontier dissolved in 1942, it brought to a close one of the most remarkable periods of radical filmmaking in the United States.

The federal government sponsored two of the most important New Deal films, both directed by Pare Lorentz – *The Plow that Broke the Plains* (1936) and *The River* (1938). Lorentz was working as a film critic when asked by Rexford Tugwell, head of the Resettlement Administration, to make a film advocating Roosevelt's agriculture policy. In need of experienced assistants, Lorentz turned to Hurwitz, Strand, and Steiner of Frontier Films, and together they made a 28-minute film about the Dust Bowl. Lorentz's on-screen success with this film was matched by his success in having it exhibited. After being denied distribution by the Hollywood studios, Lorentz won praise from several influential film critics and ultimately secured a booking at the Rialto on Broadway in New York City. From there it was on to independent theaters throughout the Midwest, a run successful enough to earn Lorentz a second, even larger project under Tugwell.

Lorentz's second film, *The River*, combined Whitmanesque narration, a rhythmic montage of Mississippi River towns, and dramatic footage of flooding to create an argument on behalf of the Tennessee Valley Authority (TVA). But beyond its advocacy of the TVA, *The River* made a case for federal action, asserting that collective blame for land mismanagement – "We cut the top off Minnesota and sent it down the river/We built a hundred cities and a thousand towns, but at what a cost?" – should be redressed by collective action. As Paula Rabinowitz points out in the hardcover/online edition, the work of 1930s documentarians is best understood within a wider context of social action by artists. Indeed, this remarkable period in cultural production, from proletarian novels and the workers' theater to the publication of Works Progress/Projects Administration (WPA) guides, was underwritten by a powerful impulse to leave urban centers in order to understand the regional life of the nation. In books such as *Let Us Now Praise Famous Men*, by James Agee, and *The People Talk*, by Benjamin Appel, or the work of numerous photographers cited by Rabinowitz, American artists sought to take full measure of the social crisis. Indeed, the cinematic contribution of the FPL, Frontier Films, and New Deal documentaries makes up an essential component of the 1930s cultural front.

The Film Avant-Garde

Like documentary practice, the American film avant-garde flowered during this period, building on the important experiments of the 1920s. And like the documentary movement with which it shared some artists and venues, the avant-garde survived on a combination of alternative distribution networks, cinema clubs, small arts journals, and little theaters. The city film, pioneered in its American incarnation by Charles Sheeler, Paul Strand, and Robert Flaherty, carried over into the 1930s in the work of Lewis Jacobs, Herman Weinberg, and Rudy Burkhardt. Whereas the city symphonies of the 1920s were composed on a giant scale, the rectangular geometry of the cityscape dominating the frame, in the 1930s there was often a more subjective rendering of city life. Jay Leyda's lyrical evocation of a Bronx neighborhood restored the human figure to city streets. Children playing, shoppers on their morning rounds, and local vendors populate *A Bronx Morning* (1931). As Jan-Christopher Horak demonstrates in this volume, numerous figures of the American avant-garde, including Mary Ellen Bute and Ralph Steiner, brought to their work a strong abstract impulse. For these filmmakers, the artistic potential of the medium turned on its ability to transform material objects and natural forms into patterns of light and movement.

Unlike the commercial cinema, with its genre foundations and formal conventions, and to a great extent consciously positioned against the dominant mode, the experimental cinema was characterized by its multiple aesthetic contours. In fact, the avant-garde has consistently challenged the historian's ability to fix it with a precise taxonomy. Perhaps no single film from the period combines the abstract impulse and a dialogue with the Hollywood mode more precisely than Joseph Cornell's *Rose Hobart* (1936). Cornell took *East of Borneo*, a 1931 run-of-the-mill Laemmle adventure film, and recut it into a 19-minute collage. Gone are the narrative development and editing continuity. Originally projected through a blue-tinted pane of glass and set to the music of Nestor Amaral, the result is a meditation on the actress Rose Hobart as her gestures and reaction shots are stitched side by side. Torn from the story, circular patterns of movement and the repetitions of performance begin to

Figure 9.2 In Maya Deren and Alexander Hammid's avant-garde *Meshes of the Afternoon* (1943, producer Maya Deren), the filmmakers create a vertiginous staircase in a home that is imagined as threatening and entrapping.

emerge. Moreover, Cornell invests his film with personal emotion and detached humor as the Hollywood film floats between fetishized icon and mass-produced image, as Horak and Jared Rapfogel discuss in this volume.

Finally, the early work of Maya Deren belongs to this period, and her most acclaimed film, *Meshes of the Afternoon* (1943), is also positioned between an American surrealism and the shadows of Hollywood. *Meshes*, shot in the movie capital in 1943 by Deren and her husband Alexander Hammid, redefines the domestic home front as a dangerous place. Deren's philosophy that the camera should function not to record reality but to present the subjective experience of reality found form through her use of montage, canted angles, and spatial discontinuity. The central figure, played by Deren, encounters her multiple selves and sexual violence as she struggles throughout to achieve some balance in virtually every room in her home. Deren's work has often been used to mark the beginning of the mature, postwar experimental cinema, but recent studies of the avant-garde of the 1930s and 1940s reveal continuities between her work and that of her predecessors, casting her less as a point of origin than a key figure working during a period of historical transition.

Animation

In the early 1930s, the arrival of sound ushered in a new era in animation. Of the studios and independent producers that made cartoons, three stand out: the Fleischer Studio, Disney, and Warner Bros. The Fleischer Studio, with Max Fleischer as producer and Dave Fleischer as director, successfully made the transition from silent to sound, and their cartoons, distributed by Paramount, were among the most innovative of the period. The Fleischers had great success with Popeye the Sailor, who had first met the public through newspapers, but would become most famously associated with their star Betty Boop. Between 1930 and 1939, Betty appeared in 122 films, singing, dancing, and strutting her figure for maximum sex appeal. As Kirsten Moana Thompson points out in this volume, the work of the Fleischer brothers was "brashly urban, with stories set in factories, skyscrapers, nightclubs, and bars." Even after the Production Code raised her neckline, Betty continued to offer a rhythmic, short-skirted alternative to the family-oriented fare of the Disney studios.

Disney was the undisputed king of animation during the 1930s, making hundreds of short cartoons with Mickey Mouse and Donald Duck, as well as his Silly Symphonies. Even more than Fleischer's Betty Boop, Disney's films were structured around music. In some cases, as in *The Band Concert* (1935) with Mickey and Donald, the story revolves entirely around musical performance. In other cases, as in *The Three Little Pigs* (1933), musical performance is integrated into a plot centered elsewhere. The rhythm and pace of Disney's shorts, indeed, the entire world of these cartoons, is synchronized to melodies drawn from every genre, from classical to traditional American to jazz. Disney's animation also pioneered the brilliant use of Technicolor well before it became a fixture of feature filmmaking. In 1937, Disney produced *Snow White and the Seven Dwarfs*. Released through RKO, it was the first animated feature and, to the surprise of the industry, became one of the most successful films of the decade. Disney would follow it with *Pinocchio* (1940), *Fantasia* (1940), and *Bambi* (1942).

Warner Bros., which had pioneered the conversion to sound, looked to animation to further exploit the new technology. It hired producer Leon Schlesinger and over the next three decades the studio would go on to produce some of the most popular and iconic animated shorts in the history of film. As Krin Gabbard details in the online/hardcover edition, its Merrie Melodies and Looney Tunes series made stars of Bugs Bunny, Porky Pig, Elmer Fudd, and Daffy Duck, all products of one of Hollywood's most creative ensemble of artists – animator-directors Tex Avery, Chuck Jones, Friz Freleng, Robert McKimson, Bob Clampett, Frank Tashlin – working with the musical composer Carl Stalling and the voice of Mel Blanc. Warners' wartime cartoons mocked the Axis Powers as in *Herr Meets Hare* (1945) in which Göring and Hitler turn out to be no match for the Brooklyn-accented Bugs. Like the Fleischer cartoons of a decade before, Warners' animation was frequently reflexive, exposing the artifice of cinema and often poking fun at the "serious" side of the studio's output.

Hollywood and World War II

A decade's worth of negotiation between the industry and the government over a range of issues was punctuated in July 1938, well before America entered the war, when the US Justice Department filed suit charging the major studios with restraint of free trade. The Paramount Case, as it came to be known, brought before the courts a review of those trade practices that had been at the heart of the major studios' power and profits. Consent decrees signed in 1940 minimized block booking and ended blind booking. It would not be long, however, before the studios and the government entered into a very different relationship, one defined largely by partnership, as the nation prepared for, and then entered, World War II.

Hollywood's relationship with international audiences had been one of popularity and profits. While few foreign films, with the exception of British imports, made it onto American screens beyond New York City, American films dominated overseas markets. Throughout Europe, the major studios constructed dubbing facilities that permitted its stars to play on movie screens throughout the world. But as the 1930s progressed, the politics of war slowly eroded the presence of American films overseas. The Spanish Civil War, begun in 1936, and the annexation of Austria in 1938, curtailed the distribution of American films to both countries. Exportation to Germany ended in 1937.

Warner Bros. was the first studio to take up the antifascist cause, releasing *Confessions of a Nazi Spy* in 1939, although it was the Three Stooges who first satirized Hitler with their Yiddish-inflected comic short *You Nazty Spy!*, released in January 1940. (Chaplin's *The Great Dictator*, begun in 1938, did not get released until October 1940.) The coalition of left-wing and liberal forces that came to be known as the Popular Front – with its ardent combination of antifascist, pro-labor, and pro–civil rights politics – had an active constituency in the movie capital, as Saverio Giovacchini explains in this volume. The Hollywood Anti-Nazi League, founded in 1936, with a membership at its height of some 3,000 members, raised awareness about Hitler's threat, provided economic support to émigrés, and sought to pressure the studios into making topical pictures.

But what had been the concerted effort of some in Hollywood became the war effort of the entire industry after the attack on Pearl Harbor on December 7, 1941. Like every other industry, Hollywood was swept up by war mobilization. The government did not move to seize control of moviemaking or demand that all production be devoted to training or propaganda films, however. While Hollywood executives certainly found ways to integrate the war into every genre, Franklin Roosevelt declared that producers should retain the power to entertain the domestic audience, as well as the troops overseas, as they saw fit. Still, as the war progressed, Washington would play an increasingly significant oversight role. When the Office of War Information was established in 1942, its Bureau of Motion Pictures became the primary liaison with Hollywood, and after 1943, through the Office of Censorship, it would exert considerable influence over Hollywood's representation of the enemy and the allies, theaters of battle, and the home front.

On-screen, Hollywood fought the war on every front – on Wake Island, at Bataan and Guadalcanal, on submarines in the Pacific in *Destination Tokyo* (1943), in tanks in *Sahara* (1943), and on foot in the Italian countryside in *A Walk in the Sun* (1945). In any number of combat films, screenwriters insisted the American fighting force was a diverse population fighting to create a world that could be home to all. In *Pride of the Marines* (1945), blinded hero Al Schmidt and his buddy Lee Diamond are on board a train bringing Al home to Philadelphia. When Al resentfully expresses his fear that no employer will want to hire a blind veteran, Lee's response, that he might be denied work because his name is Diamond instead of Jones, because he celebrates Passover instead of Easter, is summarized by his declaration, "You and me, we need the same kind of a world, we need a country to live in where nobody gets booted around for any reason."

Musicals and comedies were immensely popular during the war and their stars – Abbott and Costello, Betty Grable, Bing Crosby, and Bob Hope – were consistently cited by polls as among the audience's favorite stars. Even a film as seemingly far from the war as *Pride of the Yankees* (1942), in which Gary Cooper plays baseball legend Lou Gehrig, resonated with the war in its prologue: "He faced death with that same valor and fortitude that has been displayed by thousands of young Americans on far-flung fields of battle." On those far-flung fields, soldiers were treated to the latest releases, in some cases before they were exhibited on the home front. Hollywood's War Activities Committee, cooperating with the War Department, shipped thousands of shorts and features, in 16mm format, to troops all over the world. But Hollywood's war effort went well beyond compelling illusions. At its peak in late 1944, the number of industry employees giving wartime service, many in combat, climbed to over 6,000 (Schatz 1997, 142). This included some of the industry's most important artists. Between 1942 and 1945, Frank Capra produced his seven-part documentary *Why We Fight*, instructing the nation on every aspect of the war effort, at home and abroad, as Charles Wolfe details in this volume. John Ford, John Huston, and William Wyler all produced combat reports from either the Pacific or European fronts. The Hollywood Victory Committee organized a massive USO effort such that by 1944, 80 units were touring with live performances overseas (Schatz 1997, 147). At home, the Hollywood Canteen, romanticized by Warner Bros. in its 1944 film, catered to soldiers with free food and entertainment hosted by some of the biggest stars in the business.

The wartime period was tremendously profitable for the movie industry. Total profits for 1941 amounted to $34 million, and during the last three years of the war that figure ballooned to near $60 million. As revenues increased, the total number of films produced by the majors decreased. Between 1940 and 1942, the five majors released 694 pictures, but between 1943 and 1945 that number fell to 432. During this time, more money was spent, on average, for each picture, and the average length of shooting time also increased (Schatz 1997, 172–173). The profits generated during this period motivated many artists to move toward independence. Producers, producer-directors, and stars went from being tethered to one studio via long-term contract to working on a picture-by-picture basis, each film financed through a corporation established for that film alone. While this approach offered greater creative freedom, even more attractive perhaps were the financial advantages. The single-film package permitted artists to shift their tax burden from income to capital gains, a money-saving tactic for stars and producers alike.

As the war came to an end, the film industry shared both the nation's sense of triumph and its apprehension about the future. It had played a vital role in sustaining morale and projecting ideological support for battle against the Axis Powers. It enjoyed unparalleled profits. But the antitrust issue had not gone away and the threat of court-ordered reorganization still loomed. Industry labor relations would perhaps be even more of a problem. In fact, as the war was ending, Hollywood's wartime luster was tarnished when set decorators at MGM struck in protest over the studio's failure to recognize the Conference of Studio Unions (CSU), the union alternative to IATSE. Months of picketing erupted into occasional violent episodes, most fiercely outside the Warner Bros. studio on October 5, 1945. As Larry Ceplair discusses in the hardcover/online edition, while the CSU was ultimately recognized in this go-around as the bargaining agent for the set decorators, its battle with IATSE, and the industry's wider labor trouble, would spill over into the postwar era.

Hollywood and Postwar Challenges

While the end of the war can function for the purposes of periodization, it would be inaccurate to see 1945 as marking a decisive break from the so-called golden era. Undoubtedly, the end of the war brought changes to the industry, but many of the vital postwar events were reactions to or continuations of struggles experienced during the 1930s and wartime period. The political inquisition in Hollywood, highlighted by House Un-American Activities Committee (HUAC) hearings in 1947, really looked back to the radical 1930s, the Popular Front, the New Deal, and wartime contributions of artists on the left. The Paramount Case, finally resolved in 1948, had its origins in the 1930s, as did the labor strife that would also trouble the postwar era. And while the war might have ended in 1945, screen time devoted to the plight of the returning veteran, from World War II, and later from Korea and Vietnam, would be a recurring trope for the next period of American cinema.

In 1946, Sam Goldwyn released *The Best Years of Our Lives*, William Wyler's sprawling drama about the return home of three soldiers. It announced the industry's intention to explore the painful consequences of victory and, along with *Pride of the Marines*, its intention to represent the nation's concerns over returning veterans. In fact, between 1945 and 1947, the movie industry presented its best picture award to three films far more solemn than celebratory. *The Lost Weekend* (1945), *The Best Years of Our Lives*, and *Gentleman's Agreement* (1947) offered stark images of alcoholism, veterans damaged both physically and emotionally, and anti-Semitism. And although each would conclude with what might be termed a Hollywood happy ending, none could fully mask the anxiety provoked as America looked to the future.

Note

1. Thalberg was the first of the three to enter the picture business, joining Carl Laemmle in 1918. Zanuck would enter the industry in the early 1920s and Selznick the mid-1920s. In *The Genius of the System*, Thomas Schatz adds Hal Wallis to this threesome, referring to them as "Hollywood's second-generation of moguls," who entered "filmmaking with a feel for the business and with a certain cinematic literacy" (1996, 50).

References

Balio, Tino. (1995). *Grand Design: Hollywood as a Modern Business Enterprise, 1930–1939*. First paperback printing. Berkeley: University of California Press.

Ball, J. A. (1935). "The Technicolor Process of Three-Color Cinematography." *Journal of Motion Picture Engineers*, 25.2 (August), 127–138.

Cook, David. (1996). *A History of Narrative Film*. New York: W. W. Norton.

Fielding, Raymond. (1972). *The American Newsreel 1911–1967*. Norman: University of Oklahoma Press.

Geller, Theresa L. (2003). "Dorothy Arzner." *Senses of Cinema*, 26 (May), at http://sensesofcinema.com/2003/great-directors/arzner/ (accessed March 2015).

Lewis, Jon. (2008). *American Film: A History*. New York: W. W. Norton.

McGilligan, Patrick. (2009). "Hangmen Also Die: The Short-Lived Alliance of Fritz Lang and Bertolt Brecht," at http://www.focusfeatures.com/article/hangmen_also_die__the_short_lived_alliance_of_fritz_lang_and_b (accessed March 2015).

Maltby, Richard. (1995). "The Production Code and the Hays Office." In Tino Balio, *Grand Design* (pp. 37–72). Berkeley: University of California Press.

Mayne, Judith. (1994). *Directed by Dorothy Arzner*. Bloomington: Indiana University Press.

Naremore, James. (1989). *The Magic World of Orson Welles*. Dallas: Southern Methodist University Press. (Originally published 1978.)

Rosten, Leo. (1941). *Hollywood: The Movie Colony, The Movie Makers*. New York: Harcourt, Brace and Company.

Rothman, William. (2012). "The Screwball Comedy." In Cynthia Lucia, Roy Grundmann, & Art Simon (eds), *The Wiley-Blackwell History of American Film. Vol. 2: 1929 to 1945* (pp. 226–246). Oxford: Wiley-Blackwell.

Schatz, Thomas. (1997). *Boom and Bust: American Cinema in the 1940s*. Berkeley: University of California Press.

Schatz, Thomas. (1996). *The Genius of the System: Hollywood Filmmaking in the Studio Era*. New York: Henry Holt.

Sklar, Robert. (1994). *Movie-Made America: A Cultural History of American Movies*. Revised and updated. New York: Vintage Books.

Taves, Brian. (1995). "The B Film: Hollywood's Other Half," in Tino Balio, *Grand Design* (pp. 313–350). Berkeley: University of California Press.

Wolfe, Charles. (1995). "The Poetics and Politics of Nonfiction: Documentary Film." In Tino Balio, *Grand Design* (pp. 351–386). Berkeley: University of California Press.

10

Era of the Moguls
The Studio System

Matthew H. Bernstein
Professor, Emory University, United States

Matthew H. Bernstein outlines a valuable schema for understanding the work of studio executives, frequently referred to as "**moguls**." Setting aside personal profiles central to biographers and industry mythmakers, Bernstein looks at studio executives in the context of historical, industrial, corporate, and aesthetic forces. In this framework, the mogul is a figure responding to demands on multiple fronts: **corporate offices in New York**; the **Production Code Administration**; historical events like the **Depression** and **World War II**; and, of course, the tastes of audiences, which would, in part, influence the **acquisition of story properties** and the **hiring and assignment of talent** including screenwriters, directors, and stars. Bernstein identifies all major players during the **classical Hollywood** era, following them, often through a dizzying display of executive musical chairs, from studio to studio. He further characterizes **studio styles** that dominated the moviemaking and theater ownership landscape. Bernstein's essay shares ground with Richard Maltby on studio realism and Ruth Vasey on the gangster film in this volume, and with Larry Ceplair on Hollywood unions and the blacklist in the hardcover/online edition.

Additional terms, names, and concepts: 1940 consent decree, vertical integration, Big Five, Little Three, independent production

Since Hollywood has long been a vehicle for mythmaking about America, it should not surprise us that American popular culture is rife with mythologizing of the film industry itself. If America is allegedly the place where anyone can become rich and famous (see Horatio Alger or *American Idol*), Hollywood is a special setting for that transformation (the myth holds that Lana Turner, a glamorous star from the late 1930s through the 1960s, was discovered at a lunch counter; she was not).

The process of mythologizing works in multiple ways. Countless magazines and books have hyped the film industry and particularly its creative personnel. Movie stars, because of our endless fascination with both their performances and what they are "really like" as people, are exhibit A in this process.

American Film History: Selected Readings, Origins to 1960, First Edition. Edited by Cynthia Lucia, Roy Grundmann, and Art Simon.
© 2016 John Wiley & Sons, Inc. Published 2016 by John Wiley & Sons, Inc.

Interviews, advertising, publicity, and fan magazine articles (*Photoplay* was the movie version of *People* magazine) all helped promote the movie star, making larger-than-life figures out of the appealing personalities on larger-than-life movie screens (deCordova 2001; Dyer 2008). Yet the promotion of Hollywood encompassed other creative personnel in the industry – screenwriters and directors, for example, even before the diffusion of the so-called "auteur theory" in the early 1960s.

The movie moguls of classical Hollywood cinema – such as Harry Cohn (Columbia Pictures), Samuel Goldwyn (Goldwyn Pictures), Louis B. Mayer and Irving Thalberg (MGM), David O. Selznick (Selznick International Productions), Jack Warner and Hal Wallis (Warner Bros.), and Darryl F. Zanuck (Warner Bros. and Twentieth Century-Fox) have enjoyed a schizophrenic mythology of their own in the now more than 10 decades of ink spilled about the American film industry. (A point of terminology: "Moguls" have been variously identified as studio founders, production executives, and studio producers. These categories are not always distinct – Louis B. Mayer was a studio founder, an official production executive, and he oversaw the making of particular films even after he hired Irving Thalberg at MGM. In this essay, I will focus primarily on the heads of production and their subordinates at major studios and at semi-independent companies.) These men have been lionized ever since Hollywood histories began to be published in the early decades of the twentieth century (Allen & Gomery 1985).

The most enduring instance of mythologizing the mogul, of course, occurred in F. Scott Fitzgerald's posthumously published 1941 novel *The Last Tycoon*, which focused on the aptly named studio production head Monroe Stahr. Fitzgerald is widely acknowledged to have based Stahr on Irving Thalberg, for whom the writer had worked on several scripts in the 1930s. More often, however, moguls were condemned and derided by reporters and unhappy screenwriters as vulgarians (Ben Hecht compared studio executives to Coney Island pinhead clowns). Auteurists continued in this vein, denouncing studio executives and studio producers as the primary reason great directors could not realize their visions onscreen (Schatz 1988, 5–6; Bernstein 2000, xiv–xv). Both versions of the mogul have their basis in fact – but they are facile versions of a more complex reality.

The mythology of the mogul flourished because, on the one hand, studio heads were on the ground in Hollywood, closer to the "magic" of moviemaking than their too often overlooked corporate masters in New York (about whom more below). The studio production executives were the authorities to whom writers, directors, and stars would most often answer; their power made them objects of fear and loathing, and more rarely, admiration, but their authority also gave them an aura that has compelled our fascination. (To take a recent example: In fall 2010, Turner Classic Movies showed a new multipart documentary series entitled *Hollywood: A History of Moguls and Movie Stars*.) Paradoxically, the studio executive's work as a manager did not conform to more traditional definitions of creativity. Indeed, few people understood what a studio production chief actually did, whereas even casual observers knew that writers wrote, actors acted, and directors directed. It was easier to define a producer by his personality (and from 1929 to 1945, it was, with very rare exceptions, a "he") rather than by the work he was doing.

Scholarship dating from the mid-1980s (in particular Janet Staiger in Bordwell et al. 1985, on the Hollywood studios' mode of production, and Thomas Schatz 1988) has provided a more precise and measured assessment of the production executive's role in Hollywood. Schatz, in fact, took inspiration from Fitzgerald's characterization of Stahr as one of the few people who could "keep the whole equation of pictures in their heads," to argue persuasively that the studio executive was the linchpin of Hollywood's industrial system, the studio's form of collaborative creativity, and "the most misunderstood and undervalued figure in American film history" (1988, 8). Such scholarship is based on Staiger's model of how movies were made in Hollywood but also on the examination of previously unexamined studio archival documents that help us understand what the production executive and even the producer's creative contribution to a studio's films could be.

That contribution in fact varied from studio to studio, depending upon its production policies, working ethos, and, not least, the personality of the producer in question (some studio honchos and film producers *were* clueless, but many were enlightened). Still, the producer's influence on Hollywood filmmaking was strongest from the 1920s through 1945. After 1945, and particularly after 1948, the studios and the studio

Figure 10.1 Two producers with contrasting approaches to work: the hands-off, semi-independent Walter F. Wanger on the left and the highly creative Twentieth Century-Fox studio chief Darryl F. Zanuck on the right. They talk with Wendell Willkie at a lunch he facilitated in 1942, at which Walter White, leader of the National Association for the Advancement of Colored People (NAACP), exhorted studio heads to rethink their reductive depictions of African-Americans in studio films. Willkie was a third-party presidential candidate in 1940, the industry's defending attorney against Senate accusations of warmongering in 1941, and served on Twentieth Century-Fox's board of directors. (Photo courtesy of the Wisconsin Center for Film and Theater Research.)

production heads began to lose their creative authority; as directors became producer-directors and stars continued to form their own production companies, the studio executive became less imposing, while the talent agent's ascent to greater creative and managerial power continued unabated (Kemper 2010).

The Historical Context

One can best appreciate the work of the studio production executive and the film producer within several contexts – historical, industrial, corporate, and aesthetic. The American film industry faced some of its greatest challenges and enjoyed some of its greatest triumphs during the period from 1929 to 1945. There had been no more turbulent and wrenching period in Hollywood's history to that time, marked as it was by the Great Depression, the late-decade recession and rumblings of war, the surprise attack on Pearl Harbor in 1941, and the Allied struggle against the Axis Powers.

These worldwide historical events had a powerful impact on the movie business that went beyond the need to adjust to the technical dislocations caused by the advent of sound – mythologized as misplaced microphones among other headaches in the 1952 *Singin' in the Rain* (Crafton 1997, 2–3). While accounting for all such developments would fill a book in itself, we can briefly summarize key developments here. The major film corporations had to learn how to accommodate and exploit the growing popularity of radio broadcasting, eventually developing, among other strategies, cross-media promotional strategies and placing radio performers under contract (Hilmes 1999). They had to address the crisis of declining ticket sales in the Depression largely by tolerating, then producing, films for the double-feature format and introducing more sensational subject matter into their films. They had to endure their slide into red balance sheets and corporate receivership, which resulted in major changes in corporate leadership and studio executive personnel. Fortunately for the major film corporations, the federal government's National Recovery Act helped to insure their industrial dominance from 1933 through 1935. Yet the most powerful companies still had to address sociological studies that denounced the movies as a debilitating influence on viewers and the largely Catholic threat of boycotts against "immoral" films that peaked in 1933–1934, while being constantly on the lookout for possible federal censorship bills: As a result the film companies began enforcing more vigorously the Production Code adopted in 1930. The most profitable firms also had to defend against the antitrust case brought by the Roosevelt administration's Department of Justice in 1938; this resulted, among other things, in a consent decree in 1940 that allowed the vertically integrated studios to force only blocks of five films, rather than their entire annual slate, upon independent exhibitors. The major companies had to find strategies to compensate for the loss of foreign distribution and exhibition as war broke out in Europe and Asia; one policy involved developing South American markets.

During the war, although they launched into making combat films and other projects that supported the effort, the studios had to parry attempts by the Office of War Information to influence filmmaking and had to compensate for the enlistment of major male stars while also overcoming homefront rationing of major resources, which limited the studios' ability, among other things, to create sets, to light them, and to costume performers. When the war ended in 1945, the major Hollywood corporations would face studio strikes, the renewal of the antitrust case against them, declining audiences domestically, restricted markets abroad, and an increased trend toward semi-independent production by successful talents. Indeed, Schatz argues that "World War II marked an extended, dramatic and most welcome interval in a decade-long period of industry decline" (1999, 2). Through 1945, however, the industry was able to reap the benefits of a wartime economy in which Americans spent their leisure time and hard-earned dollars at the movies.

The Industrial Context

In spite of all this, and except for a few troubled years, the commercial mainstream American film industry managed not only to survive but to thrive, creating so much of what we think of as classical Hollywood filmmaking in a wrenching period of profound change at home and abroad. Yet, when we consider the industrial context of studio work, this should come as no surprise. The formation and development of the major studios by their visionary founders (former exhibitors, most of them) minimized risk. In particular, Paramount leader Adolph Zukor pioneered the strategy of vertical integration (corporate ownership of production, distribution, and exhibition of films) in 1919, and set the template for the other companies to follow through the 1920s. This resulted in an oligopoly in which a few firms dominated the industry – the "Big Five," namely Fox Films (later Twentieth Century-Fox), Loew's/MGM, Paramount, Warner Bros., and to a lesser extent RKO, supplemented by the "Little Three": Universal, Columbia, and United Artists. Vertical integration also minimized challenges to the profitability of the eight majors – even those unforeseen events such as the Wall Street Crash and World War II. As economist Mae Dana Huettig wrote in 1944, "the most important present day characteristics of the industry were already indicated by 1923. Further development merely gave substance to the skeleton structure" (1944, 39).

While filmmaking remained a highly risky venture – no one could predict with precision what audiences would pay to see – production executives and producers at the Big Five worked from 1929 to

1945 with the knowledge that any film they produced would get shown in many theaters, chief among them the first-run theaters in which they shared ownership or owned outright. The major studios were also diversified with numerous subsidiaries (film laboratories, music companies) and different kinds of filmmaking (animation, short subjects, newsreels) that contributed to the evening's entertainment in a first-run theater. Yet the biggest portion of their assets lay not in the studio facilities but in the theaters: nine-tenths of the invested capital, two-thirds of the industry's total assets, and the source of two-thirds of the industry's income. It is crucial to remember the point that "the production of films by the major companies is not really an end in itself, on the success or failure of which the company's existence depends," as Huettig wrote:

> it is ... domination of the theater market. This does not mean that there is no attempt to make successful films or that film production is itself unprofitable ... it means simply that the principal concern of ... the major companies is their theaters. (1944, 69)

Moreover, the integrated Big Five companies did not need to own or control *all* the first-run theaters to dominate the market. As Huettig noted, the majors owned or controlled "the operations of 126 of 163 first-run theaters in the 25 largest cities in the country," and "the rentals in these theaters could account for anywhere from 50–80% of the rentals on a film" (1944, 77, 79). Furthermore, the majors' theaters, whether fully or partially owned, ranged across the country: Paramount theaters were concentrated in the South, New England, and the upper Midwest; Fox's strength was on the West Coast; RKO's and Loew's theaters were located primarily in New York, New Jersey, and Ohio; Warner Bros.' theaters lay primarily in the mid-Atlantic states. Yet the major studios also had joint ownership or pooling arrangements in other regions, and they played each other's films to everyone's benefit. The chief rivalry of the Big Five resided in selling their films to the best of the non-affiliated theaters (Gomery 2005, 5; Gomery 1992, 57–82).

The Big Five also guaranteed that their films would play in those theaters they did not own or control, which could also be first- (or second- or third-) run in major cities, or small houses in rural areas. Through the practice of block booking, unaffiliated exhibitors had to book and pay for an entire season of films from a studio sight unseen in order to get the best films with the biggest stars (Balio 1985, 258). The Little Three who owned no theaters but maintained national distribution exchanges were able, often with great difficulty, to book their films into affiliated first-run houses and more often catered to smaller theaters in lesser markets. Filmmakers who were not among the Big Eight (Poverty Row studios, race filmmakers, and others) had to struggle mightily to get their films rented. These other independent companies (with the exception of the low-budget Republic and Monogram) came and went, lasting for varied but limited durations; as Douglas Gomery notes, "after 1930, only eight studios collected 95 per cent of the revenues" (2005, 2).

Vertical integration and the oligopoly structure of the film industry did not make the studios immune to losses, however. The transition to sound, which historian Donald Crafton has characterized as "partly rational, partly confused" (1997, 4–5), was a great challenge to the industry's profitability because of technology wars and the uncertainty of how to implement the new machinery. Yet by early 1929, all the majors were creating all-talking films using Fox's Movietone sound-on-film system. Moreover, sound films helped postpone the impact on the film industry's coffers of the Wall Street Crash of October 1929. The industry only began to feel the crunch in May 1931, when making and showing sound films had become the norm. The Great Depression was another challenge: By 1932, estimated audience attendance dropped from 90 million to 75 million viewers weekly (Brown 1995, 99, 103). Fox, Paramount, RKO, and Warner Bros. all went into receivership as a result of the financing required for their previous expansion, and this had consequences for the executives in charge of production. Still, by 1935, all but Paramount and Universal were making profits again, in good part because of the Roosevelt administration-endorsed National Recovery Act, which reinforced monopolistic industry practices as a means of speeding the country's economic recovery (Gomery 1982).

In terms of filmmaking itself, the corporate structure of each of the Big Five – in Huettig's memorable image, "a large inverted pyramid, top-heavy with real estate and theaters, resting on a narrow base of the intangibles which constitute films" (1944, 54) – provided the business foundation of the standardized yet supple classical Hollywood cinema. This consisted, first, of a variable yet stable film style designed to be, in David Bordwell's memorable phrase, "an excessively obvious cinema," in which the viewer's ability to follow the story was of the greatest concern (Bordwell et al. 1985, 3). These films simultaneously were standardized (via narrative and cinematic conventions) and differentiated from one another (Staiger in Bordwell et al. 1985, 96–112). The latter was accomplished primarily by genre – star combinations, as stars were, in effect, monopolies on personalities: Humphrey Bogart or James Cagney in a Warner Bros. crime film; Gary Cooper in a Paramount or Goldwyn Western or comedy; Joan Crawford or Bette Davis in an MGM or Warner Bros. romantic melodrama; Cary Grant in a Columbia light comedy; or Betty Grable in a Twentieth Century-Fox musical. During World War II, many of these stars would increasingly appear in films noir, a production trend diametrically opposed to war films (Schatz 1999, 3; Neale 2000). Classical Hollywood style, the star system, and the creation and extension of film genres all fulfilled principles of production and marketing that each of the major companies adhered to: The making of films varied enough to lure audiences back to the theaters repeatedly, out of routine habit and for the sheer pleasure of going and seeing well-crafted variations on formulas realized by artists who honed their skills on an ambitious yearly slate of production.

Owning the house at the casino that was the movie business did not in and of itself, however, guarantee the making of classical Hollywood genre films. It is here that corporate managers, particularly the studio executives, came into play – insuring that the right directors, writers, actors, and set and costume designers at each studio played variations on these preexisting formulas, many of them established in literature and on the stage, to muster box office success.

The Corporate Context

As Tino Balio has put it, "The thirties transformed the American film industry into a modern business enterprise. No longer run by their founders as family businesses, motion picture companies were managed by hierarchies of salaried executives who rationalized operations to ensure long-term stability and profits" (1996a, 8). Most significantly, the mythologized producers did their work within budgetary frameworks set by their corporate superiors – the presidents and vice presidents of exhibition and distribution who were based in New York. As Douglas Gomery has put it, "[Louis B.] Mayer and his like took their orders from corporate leaders … in Mayer's case Nicholas Schenck, who oversaw general operations as the head of Loews, the parent company of MGM. It was Schenck, not Mayer, who had the final say and planned the whole corporate strategy, of which filmmaking was just a part" (2005, 2).

Schenck and his counterparts at other companies were experts in corporate finance and managing the real estate of movie theaters, and they were assisted by experts in advertising, sales, and promotion, with film bookings arranged from the home office in New York. The logic for this hierarchy was not just the assets invested, but also the belief that film distributors and exhibitors had a better understanding of audience tastes than did the artists, even though they may have had no experience in filmmaking.

Hence, every year, between January and April, the filmmaking corporation's president, the executive in charge of distribution, and the executive in charge of exhibition – all located in the Manhattan home office – set the parameters of a yearly production budget for the studio production executives. At Paramount in the late 1920s and early 1930s, for example, president Adolph Zukor, vice president Sidney Kent (head of distribution), and vice president Sam Katz (head of exhibition) announced the number of films Paramount would make, based on sales force calculations – how many films in different budget categories they estimated they could sell to the theaters and the audience (Staiger in Bordwell et al. 1985, 143–144). From the West Coast, the studio heads at Paramount – vice president in charge of production Jesse Lasky and managing director of production Ben P. Schulberg – and their management teams would present arguments for what they thought the program should be, but the New York office had the upper hand in such discussions. The production team then decided on the annual program of films, based on the story properties and stars they had in house or that they needed on loanout from other companies.

Every film on a studio's production slate was grouped into some variant of a "special" (an "A" film featuring its leading stars) or a "program" film. The names and numbers of production categories changed over time, and films in the "B" category could change status while in distribution (Jacobs 1992). Still, at this stage of formulating the slate, no specific titles, stars, or properties were involved. As Schulberg's late 1920s executive assistant David O. Selznick later described it, the pictures' "cost was predetermined, their gross was predetermined. You knew that you could make *x* dollars of profits on each picture you made for *x* dollars" (Brownlow 1976, 434).

The production executives would then set up a release schedule for the first half of the season and a less definite schedule for the remainder of the year: Unlike today, in the classical Hollywood heyday, the box office in the fall and spring was weak, the summer was weakest, and the winter was the strongest (Lewis 1933, 44).

For 1931–1932, Ben P. Schulberg, then managing director of production at Paramount's West Coast Studio (and incidentally the father of screenwriter/novelist Budd Schulberg), mapped out a tentative production schedule that listed 15 specials, including Josef von Sternberg's *American Tragedy* (eventually released August 22, 1931); a second "Von Sternberg Special" (which turned out to be *Shanghai Express*, released on February 12, 1932); the Marx Brothers in *Monkey Business* (released September 12, 1931); an Anna Mae Wong vehicle (with Warner Oland and Sessue Hayakawa entitled *Daughter of the Dragon*, released September 5); and *The Lives of a Bengal Lancer* (not actually produced and released until 1935). On the list there were also a number of star productions featuring such studio talents as George Bancroft, Ruth Chatterton, and others. It was in Schulberg's portfolio to assign associate producers to oversee the realization of these films from development through postproduction, though creative authority at Paramount at this time typically resided with the directors.

While making plans for the upcoming season, the head of production also oversaw the studio's acquisition of properties (stories purchased or commissioned), hired screenwriters, and placed under contract performing talent to maximize the studio's options for putting films into production. Every studio's production department stood by to help producers of individual titles plan films by coordinating different facets of filmmaking: costumes, sets, cinematography, editing, and sound recording and dubbing, for example. Significantly, beginning in the early 1930s, the studios shifted their approach to production management. Where a central producer overseeing all production had been the norm, after the diffusion of sound, many studios shifted to a unit-producer system. Here, a number of producers supervised cadres of filmmaking talents that formed around particular stars and directors, turning out anywhere from three to eight films per year. This shift was believed to allow for greater quality control and diversity of studio output, particularly for A-films. This tendency grew more pronounced in the 1940s, providing a management structure that prefigured a shift in industry structure: the advent of more semi-independent firms, not just at United Artists but at the major studios as well (Bordwell et al. 1985, 320–329; Schatz 1999, 44–45).

Censorship and Self-Regulation

The moguls also had to negotiate with Hollywood's self-censorship agencies, which operated as a division of the industry's trade association, the Motion Picture Producers and Distributors Association (MPPDA), founded in 1922. The first such fully formed office was called the Studio Relations Committee (SRC). Created in 1927 and operating through 1934, the SRC took as its brief the 1927 guidelines – "The Don'ts and Be Carefuls" – that the MPPDA had compiled from a long list of city and state censor complaints about improper content in the movies (such as drug trafficking, sex perversion, sex hygiene and venereal disease, and profanity). The rationale of the SRC was to demonstrate that the film industry could keep its own house in order and that there would be no need for federal censorship of the movies or for the creation of additional city or state censoring bodies. Even more important, however, was protecting the majors' oligopoly from federal dismantling.

Negotiating with SRC chiefs Colonel Jason Joy and James Wingate (the former head of New York State's Censor Board) became part of a mogul's job description. Through 1934, Joy and Wingate proved susceptible to producers' arguments for the inclusion of sensational material; alternately, the "Hollywood Jury" of producing peers would override the SRC's judgments (Jacobs 1997, 110). Irving Thalberg and Ernst Lubitsch, to take just two examples, were able to persuade the SRC to allow them to show racy subjects and scenes on the basis of their reputation for handling such matters with good taste. The result was the production of films like MGM's *Red-Headed Woman* (1931), Paramount (and Lubitsch's) *Trouble in Paradise* (1932), *Design for Living* (1933), and countless other films (Mae West and Marx Brothers comedies also from Paramount and violent gangster films from virtually all the studios, but especially from Warner Bros. in the early 1930s). As Lea Jacobs has shown in detail, the SRC strove to have filmmakers cut potentially offensive material, and those cuts quite often backfired. As historian Gregory Black describes, "Although reformers had favoured cooperation with Hays in 1922, by the end of the decade they were convinced that Hays was ineffective and that federal intervention was necessary to control Hollywood" (1989, 169).

Hollywood's Production Code was actually adopted by the industry in March 1930. This was yet another move by the industry to fend off more drastic censorship. Drafted by Father Daniel Lord, a Jesuit priest who also taught drama at St Louis University, the Code also had the input of a number of Catholic laymen who had foremost in mind the effect of movies on young and impressionable audiences. The writers of the Code, as Black has put it, had one fundamental idea: "No picture should lower the moral standards of those who see it" (1989, 172). Crime had to be punished, no sympathy was to be given to characters involved in immoral behavior, violence could not be too detailed; society's institutions had to be depicted positively: The Code's guidelines were extensive and comprehensive.

At Catholic layman Joseph I. Breen and Hays's behest, the Production Code Administration (PCA) officially replaced the SRC in 1934, and Breen replaced Joy and Wingate. A $25,000 fine was imposed on any exhibitor who showed a film without a PCA seal of approval. ("Pre-Code" films such as *Red-Headed Woman* and *Trouble in Paradise* could be more accurately described as "Pre-Breen.") Breen and the PCA were skeptical of studio heads and their arguments for inclusion of racy materials in a film (Doherty 2009). They were far more thoroughgoing in reviewing film projects at every stage – as purchased properties, script treatments, screenplay drafts, song lyrics, costume designs, set designs, and – most important of all – the finished film. Moreover, Breen, in reinterpreting the Code, was attentive to tone and narrative arc and worked with producers to devise ways of creating ambiguity in questionable scenes (Jacobs 1997, 106–149). In addition, the PCA became mindful of what was called "industry policy," those potentially offensive elements not covered by the Code – the depiction of social themes, politics, professions, and foreign nationals that could be viewed as insensitive or even insulting (Vasey 1997, 194–224). Where the portrayal of sexy, violent, or otherwise unseemly material could sell tickets in the short run, the eight majors' dominance of the industry, their incredible cultural power and their freedom from more extensive, external censorship, and their oligopoly cash flow remained long-term goals.

Breen, the PCA, and their predecessors could prevent certain actions and sensibilities from reaching the screen. The moguls' arguments with them could be fierce. At the same time, Breen and his team most often engaged in negotiation with filmmakers. As Lea Jacobs has written, "The utopian ideal of self-regulation was to forestall criticism while at the same time allowing the producer maximal use of his original material … Thus censorship did not simply reflect social pressures; it articulated a strategic response to them … censorship … helped to shape film form and narrative" (1997, 23). The fundamental fact was that Breen worked for the very studios with whom he negotiated film content. Should a producer publicly criticize the Code, as Walter F. Wanger did on the occasion of the 1939 premiere of the now classic Western *Stagecoach*, he was, as one of Breen's assistants put it, "criticizing himself" (Bernstein 2000, 142).

Ironically, the PCA had prepared the ground for Roosevelt's Office of War Information (OWI), which, from June 1942 until August 1945, sought to insure that studio movies appropriately supported the war effort and American ideals in their depiction of the home front, United States' allies, and even its enemies. The OWI thus functioned as a kind of federal regulating body of motion picture content. Hollywood initially bristled at this outside imposition of guidelines for filmmaking consisting of proper themes and subjects, but Clayton Koppes and Gregory Black characterize this three-year operation as ultimately "compatible" with Hollywood style and content (1987, 321; 1999, 130–156). At the same time, they acknowledge, the OWI's Hollywood operation was "the most comprehensive and sustained government attempt to change the content of a mass medium in American history" (1987, 324).

These, then, were the historic, industrial, corporate, and regulatory contexts in which the studio mogul operated. There were many guidelines and limitations on the mogul's work and different studio production executives defined their jobs differently. When it comes down to actual films made, production heads and their subordinates made specific decisions that would determine a studio's overall success across an entire year, while, on the other hand, the work of individual directors, stars, screenwriters, and craftspeople would determine the achievements of a given set of films. As Leo Rosten wrote in his study of Hollywood in 1941:

> each studio's product shows special emphases and values. … the sum total of a studio's personality … may be traced to its producers … who establish the preferences, the prejudices, and the predispositions of the organization and, therefore, of the movies which it turns out. (242–243)

As we shall see, not all studios' personalities were determined by a single individual, and not every studio had a consistent personality.

Fox and Twentieth Century-Fox

The Fox company had been a major, vertically integrated company since the 1920s, producing films by directors on their way to becoming major figures in the industry, including Raoul Walsh (action films), Frank Borzage (romantic melodramas), Howard Hawks (comedies), and John Ford (Westerns, along with an assortment of other genres). Founder William Fox had ambitions to dominate the industry, at one point engineering an ultimately failed merger with Loew's/MGM, and he was technically adventurous, insisting that his studio develop the sound-on-film system Movietone and experiment with a wide film format in 1930. Building upon its theater holdings on the West Coast, Fox was able to buy the newly built and palatial Roxy Theater as a showcase in New York City. Yet Fox himself suffered a series of financial setbacks and by 1930 had been kicked out of the company; in 1936 he was forced to declare bankruptcy.

During the transitional period through 1934, Paramount's former distribution manager Sidney R. Kent was perhaps the most experienced studio head in Fox's revolving door; but the studio production chief remained Winfield Sheehan, who in late 1931 placed Sol Wurtzel and former Paramount executive Jesse L. Lasky as unit producers (Bordwell et al. 1985, 326). The studio relied on the popularity of the waif-like Janet Gaynor, and the beefy George O'Brien and Charles Farrell, as well as the more elegant Warner Baxter, to carry studio features through the sound transition. Beginning in 1929, the string of 21 sound films starring folksy, shrewd columnist, radio host, and star Will Rogers proved him one of the era's most popular box office stars, until his death in a plane crash in August 1935. The company enjoyed a few major critical successes, such as a 1933 Oscar-winning adaptation of Noël Coward's *Cavalcade*, but Coward was an atypical story source at the studio; more often, Sheehan insured Fox's emphasis on more sentimental, less sophisticated fare.

In late spring 1933, Fox merged with Darryl F. Zanuck's independent company. Twentieth Century Pictures had itself been formed with then-United Artists (UA) president Joseph Schenck in Spring 1933. Through 1935, Zanuck produced 18 films for UA release; according to studio historian Aubrey Solomon, only one of these did not make a profit (1988, 17). Now at Twentieth Century-Fox, Zanuck initially was able to thrive with completed Will Rogers productions ready for release and the advent of astonishing child star Shirley Temple. Indeed, Temple's series of family musical comedies, some set in the Old South – such as *The Little Colonel* and *The Littlest Rebel*, both in 1935 and costarring entertainer Bill "Bojangles" Robinson – likewise became number one box office attractions in the mid-1930s. To such inherited stars on the studio roster, Zanuck would add Tyrone Power as the studio's heartthrob and Norwegian skater Sonja Henie. One major coup Zanuck achieved in the late 1930s was signing Henry Fonda to a studio contract; Fonda was a signature star at the studio in the late 1930s and early 1940s, beginning his association with John Ford in *Young Mr. Lincoln* and the Technicolor historical drama *Drums Along the Mohawk* (both 1939). Even as Abraham Lincoln, Fonda excelled at portraying ordinary Americans. His collaboration with Ford reached its peak in 1940 with the critically acclaimed *The Grapes of Wrath* (1940), and Ford continued his winning streak the following year with *How Green Was My Valley* (1941), the latter winning Academy Awards for Best Picture, Best Director, Cinematography, Art Direction, and Best Supporting Actor (Donald Crisp). During World War II, while Zanuck served in the Signal Corps, theater head Spyros P. Skouras took over production; during this period, the studio added additional stars to its stable and built up those already under contract – Dana Andrews, Linda Darnell, singer Alice Faye, Gene Tierney, Don Ameche, and Victor Mature among them.

The war years aside, Zanuck personally dominated Twentieth Century-Fox through the mid-1950s, operating with a central producer system that put him at the core of all the studio's production operations. Beyond the broad managerial aspects that were part of his job description as head of production, Zanuck's routine was comparable only to that of Irving Thalberg in his prime. Zanuck sat in on script conferences, dictating story lines, character profiles, and even creating whole scenes for his screenwriters to employ. He closely viewed daily production rushes, consistently urging the filmmakers to pick up the pace, and personally participated in the cutting of studio films, insuring that their tempo did not become too slow (Behlmer 1993). Nunnally Johnson, one of Fox's leading screenwriters, best known for *The Grapes of Wrath*, went so far as to call Zanuck "the best cutter" of films in Hollywood (quoted in Bernstein 2000, 396). The film's director John Ford, by 1935 a veteran whose work at Fox began in the 1920s, was perhaps the only director Zanuck could not push around. Screenwriter Philip Dunne also praised Zanuck for knowing "which writer or director best responded to iron discipline, which to sweet persuasion" (quoted in Bernstein 2000, 300). Certainly Zanuck relied heavily on a stable of loyal screenwriters (Dunne, Johnson, Lamar Trotti), directors (Henry King and, through 1945, John Ford), and associate producers who answered to him to realize his annual program.

Pre-Zanuck Fox had specialized in sentimental melodramas; Zanuck continued this trend, but initially produced adaptations of classic novels and added to the mix a slew of biopics. According to biographer George Custen, one quarter of the company's scripts were set between 1865 and 1920, playing upon the nostalgic appeal of imagined small-town life to provide reassuring entertainment for a mass audience (1997, 200). As Leo Rosten put it, Fox "uses formula plots with clever variations – the characters are stereotyped; the motivations are shallow; the movement is swift and economic; the conflicts are unsubtle and the denouements are 'pat'" (1941, 244). Leavened with combat films and musicals, this was the studio's winning formula through 1945; 1940 was the only year when the studio did not record a profit, an outstanding business performance record.

Zanuck's production program through the early 1940s was in complete opposition to the gritty Warner Bros. films that had made his reputation earlier in the decade. *The Grapes of Wrath* aside, Zanuck would not return to making social problem films until after the war, when Twentieth Century-Fox would lead the industry in producing protest films against anti-Semitism and racism.

MGM

Loew's/MGM survived the Great Depression without going into debt or receivership; it produced high-quality films from 1924 onward under the supervision of vice president and general manager in charge of production Louis B. Mayer, and under him, second vice president and supervisor of production Irving Thalberg. Willingness to spend money on production was one reason for MGM's glossy house style: Huettig estimated Loew's annual production budget at $28 million, well above the other majors: Paramount, RKO, and Twentieth Century-Fox spent anywhere from $23–$25 million, with Universal spending $11.6 million and Columbia $8.8 million (1944, 89).

Much like Zanuck, Thalberg – until his devastating heart attack in late 1932 – was a central producer with a team of producer assistants whose work he would closely oversee from preparation through preproduction to postproduction. According to biographer Mark Vieira, Thalberg's routine involved assigning "a battery of big-name writers working simultaneously to create one script; a series of story conferences to distil the best of each draft; negotiations with the SRC to satisfy the censors; a producer to tailor the material to its star; a preview to test the film's effectiveness; and retakes to fix whatever was wrong" (2009, 159). Thalberg was in charge of the studio's prestige productions, such as the multistar 1932 Oscar winner for Best Picture, *Grand Hotel*, and the star vehicles for his wife Norma Shearer, such as *The Barretts of Wimpole Street* (1934) and *Marie Antoinette* (1937).

The producers working under Thalberg each had their specialties. Paul Bern was assigned to oversee many of Jean Harlow's films. Albert Lewin, who held a doctorate from Columbia University and would briefly become a director in the mid-1940s, was associated with cultured films, especially stage adaptations like those of Noël Coward plays and *The Guardsman* (1931) – the one film in which Thalberg persuaded stage legends Alfred Lunt and Lynn Fontanne to appear.

Eddie Mannix was a specialist in action movies, such as *Trader Horn* (1931) and the Clark Gable/Jean Harlow vehicle *Red Dust* (1932). Harry Rapf was most often associated with the films starring MGM's most popular stars, particularly Joan Crawford, whom he had discovered. Hunt Stromberg produced the *Thin Man* films. Each of these men would report to Thalberg on the progress of their productions before 1932; they continued to seek his advice thereafter.

Returning to MGM after a European vacation in early 1933, Thalberg found that Mayer had arranged with the New York office to have Thalberg's status diminished. Mayer's motivations here were mixed: He was jealous of the accolades Thalberg earned for the high-quality films he oversaw, but he also realized MGM could not continue with a central producer in frail health. Mayer opted for a shift toward producer units, in keeping with the trend throughout the industry. Mayer hired David O. Selznick from RKO and former Paramount executive Walter F. Wanger among others to supervise a smaller group of films more closely according to their own preoccupations. Selznick, for example, emulated Thalberg's big-budget, star-studded approach in *Dinner at Eight* (1933) and pursued his penchant for literary adaptations, as with *David Copperfield* (1935). Wanger took over the supervision of the Greta Garbo–Rouben Mamoulian 1933 film *Queen Christina*; he also affiliated with William Randolph Hearst's on-the-lot studio, Cosmopolitan Pictures, to realize the politically charged *Gabriel Over the White House* (1933), which gave the SRC no end of trouble. He also worked on the Marion Davies Civil War spy melodrama *Operator 13* (1934) (Schatz 1988, 161–172; Bernstein 2000, 81–90). Eventually, MGM refined this organization of management into a team of executive producers.

MGM was most famous for the development of its star roster. Thalberg and Mayer groomed and promoted Clark Gable (who modeled himself after director Vincent Fleming), Wallace Beery, Joan Crawford, Greta Garbo, Spencer Tracy, William Powell, and Myrna Loy (in the *Thin Man* series among other films). In the later 1930s, Mayer developed Judy Garland and Mickey Rooney and continued a star-making process into the war years with such new performers as singer-dancer Gene Kelly and the Anglo-Irish Oscar-winning star Greer Garson (in William Wyler's 1942 film *Mrs. Miniver*). When she was let go by RKO after *Bringing Up Baby* (1938), Katharine Hepburn chose MGM to mount her 1940 production of Philip Barry's play *The Philadelphia Story*. She came under contract as well, and began her series of romantic comedies opposite Spencer Tracy during World War II, as the studio also ventured into combat films in support of the war effort.

Taking its cue from Thalberg, MGM became associated primarily with the polished set designs from its art department led by Cedric Gibbons, but like every studio, it produced a varied slate. Thalberg, in particular, supported "experiments" such as King Vidor's all-black cast *Hallelujah!* (1929) and Tod Browning's *Freaks* (1932), the former to capitalize on the new sound technology and the latter as a means of competing with Universal's new and very successful horror series. Marie Dressler's films, most prominently *Min and Bill* (1930), likewise depicted a lower-class milieu that was exceptional but was of definite importance on the studio's production slate given Dressler's popularity (Sturtevant 2009). After Thalberg's death, the studio was less experimental but continued its considerable success, with teenage star Mickey Rooney (in the Andy Hardy series initiated by Mayer), and the production unit organized around Arthur Freed beginning with *Meet Me in St. Louis* (1944) (Fordin 1984).

Paramount Pictures

Paramount had a strong, if shifting, studio identity in the 1930s, in spite of the corporation's financial difficulties; the company filed for bankruptcy and went into receivership in 1933. Through 1936, a revolving door of executives led the studio: "factory manager" Ben P. Schulberg on the West Coast; executive Walter F. Wanger and Monta Bell in the Astoria, Long Island, studio through 1931 (Koszarski 2008, 179–227); former newsreel producer and editor Emanuel Cohen; master director Ernst Lubitsch; William LeBaron; and finally, Y. Frank Freeman beginning in 1936. Even here, however, Freeman relied on other executives (Buddy De Sylva and Henry Ginsburg chief among them) to supervise the studio's films. Most strikingly, where MGM was known as a producers' studio, Paramount gave directors greater autonomy. As noted, Schulberg, through 1931, had associate producers in an advisory capacity to directors. With LeBaron, producing directors had their own units, while more producer-based units realized other films (Bordwell et al. 1985, 328). However organized, the studio relied on volume production through the 1930s.

In the early 1930s, the studio specialized in making several different kinds of films whose formulas, style, and sensibility owe more to the studio's creative workers than to the production heads. Among them were the witty, sophisticated, "European"-style musicals and the comedies about sexual infidelity, typified by the work of influential director Ernst Lubitsch: *The Love Parade* (1929), *Monte Carlo* (1930), *One Hour with You* (1932), *Trouble in Paradise* (1932), and *Design for Living* (1933), all featuring such contracted male stars as Maurice Chevalier and Gary Cooper opposite Jeanette MacDonald, Miriam Hopkins, and others. Another prominent production strand was Josef von Sternberg's series of visually dense, highly stylized, sensual romantic melodramas starring the mysterious and alluring Marlene Dietrich: *The Blue Angel* and *Morocco* (both 1930), *Dishonored* (1931), *Shanghai Express* and *Blonde Venus* (both 1932), *The Scarlet Empress* (1934), and *The Devil is a Woman* (1935). Yet another filmmaking policy supported the outlandish, anarchic, and blissfully vulgar vaudeville-style comedies starring the Marx Brothers and supervised by Herman Mankiewicz: *The Coconuts* (1929), *Animal Crackers* (1930), *Horsefeathers* (1932), and *Duck Soup* (1933). Alongside these were the sexually aware burlesque films of Mae West – *Night after Night* (1932), *She Done Him Wrong* (1933), *I'm No Angel* and *Belle of the Nineties* (both 1934), and, to a lesser extent, *Goin' to Town* (1935). Indeed, West, whose films were supervised by William LeBaron, is commonly credited with providing a major source of income to Paramount in the early Depression years until the PCA decisively reigned in their overt sexual tone with *Klondike Annie* (1936) (Curry 1991). Certainly her films, as well as those of the Marx Brothers and von Sternberg, required extensive negotiations with the SRC and the PCA.

Both Mae West and the Marx Brothers were imports from vaudeville and the stage. Paramount also drafted radio talents for its films, most notably Bing Crosby, who, beginning in 1939, was teamed up with radio comedian Bob Hope for a popular series of "road" films (though Crosby had been under contract since the early 1930s). New production head Freeman and his associate producers put Hope to work in multiple film comedies, while Bing Crosby was one of Hollywood's biggest stars from year to year, culminating in his lead performance in Leo McCarey's 1944 Oscar-winning *Going My Way*. The studio's strategy of synergistically building on stars in other entertainment media paid off handsomely.

Likewise, Preston Sturges, who more than any single filmmaker maintained Paramount's reputation for outrageous comedy during the early 1940s, was a former playwright employed by many studios throughout the 1930s. Sturges enjoyed a period of astonishing creativity and invention as a writer-director in 1940 with *The Great McGinty*, and continued with a run of unconventional, parodic romantic comedies featuring weak men overwhelmed by strong but often wrong-headed women: *Christmas in July* (1940), *The Lady Eve* (1941), and *The Palm Beach Story* (1942). Sturges also created *Sullivan's Travels* (1941), a landmark lampooning of Hollywood, and two social satires on America's war craze: *The Miracle of Morgan's Creek* and *Hail the Conquering Hero* (both 1944). Inspired by Sturges's example, German expatriate screenwriter Billy Wilder moved into directing his own scripts with *The Major and the Minor* (1942), a comedy of disguise starring Ginger Rogers and Paramount contractee Ray Milland. Wilder brought to his films an affectionate but critically clear-eyed European attitude toward America, which he reframed in the classic film noir *Double Indemnity* (1944) and the Oscar-winning portrait of alcoholism, *The Lost Weekend* (1945), also starring Milland. Wilder also schooled himself in Lubitsch's comedies of mistaken identities and indirect style, carrying on a foundational tradition at the studio. Indeed, one motivation for Wilder's shift into directing was his dissatisfaction with the handling of his scripts by Mitchell

Leisen, another highly successful house director who specialized in sophisticated romantic comedy.

Paramount always nurtured talents under contract, drawing heavily from the stage: Performers included, besides the Marx Brothers and Mae West, stars such as Jeanne Eagels, Claudette Colbert, Fredric March, and Cary Grant, as well as studio directors, most famously, George Cukor and Rouben Mamoulian. Many of the studio's silent-era stars, such as W. C. Fields, Harold Lloyd, or William Powell, thrived well into the sound era, joined by new faces such as gangster icon George Raft and the vulnerable, waiflike Sylvia Sidney. Claudette Colbert headlined romantic comedies and costume films. While the studio eventually lost Gary Cooper, the prototype of the strong silent hero, to Samuel Goldwyn, many of its contracted stars remained in place. In the 1940s, the studio developed new talents such as Alan Ladd, whose breakthrough was his role as a contract killer in *This Gun for Hire* (1942) alongside wartime heartthrob Veronica Lake; Ladd's career would continue well into the 1960s, while Lake's was remarkably short. Longer-lived than any Paramount talent was studio cofounder Cecil B. DeMille, who shifted from early 1930s epic spectaculars (*The Sign of the Cross*, 1932; *Cleopatra*, 1934; *The Crusades*, 1935) to Westerns (*The Plainsman*, 1936; *Union Pacific*, 1939; *Northwest Mounted Police*, 1940) and sailing adventure films (*The Buccaneer*, 1938; *Reap the Wild Wind*, 1942).

In contrast to Twentieth Century-Fox or MGM, then, it is not possible to speak of a dominant personality at Paramount arising from its production executives. Directors and writers, not studio heads, maintained many of the studio's distinctive traditions into the war years and initiated new production strategies. Still, with the exception of the 1932–1935 period of receivership and bankruptcy, Paramount showed a profit every year in the period under discussion, peaking with $39 million in 1946, the greatest profit since it had netted $25 million in 1930 (Gomery 1985, 34). This, as Douglas Gomery notes, was a tribute to Barney Balaban's corporate leadership, as well as to the popularity of the studio's films in the first half of the 1940s (Gomery 2005, 81–93).

RKO

An "instant major" created in October 1928, RKO never achieved the stability of the other vertically integrated studios. Radio Corporation of America (RCA) president David Sarnoff was determined to have RCA's Photophone sound-on-film system adopted in Hollywood, and with Joseph P. Kennedy he oversaw the amalgamation of RCA, the B studio Film Booking Office of America, Inc. (FBO), and the Radio-Keith-Orpheum vaudeville theater circuit (its radio tower antenna logo remains iconic). Yet three years later, the company was in bankruptcy; in 1935, RCA sold half its holdings in the company to the Atlas Corporation (led by Floyd Odlum) and Lehman Brothers. Though its flagship was Radio City Music Hall (which opened its doors in 1933), RKO's theater chain remained the smallest among the majors and had a minor presence in major markets. This limited its income (Gomery 1989, 39).

Like Paramount, RKO experienced frequent shifts in production management. In Richard Jewell's words, however, RKO was "less stable" than the other majors and "never discovered its real identity," resulting in "films [that] tended to reflect the personality of the individual in charge of the studio at any given time – and since this time was always short … the pictures never evolved into an overall style unique to the studio" (1985, 10). These studio heads were William LeBaron (1928–1931), David O. Selznick (1931–1933), Merian C. Cooper (1933–1935), Sam Briskin (1935–1937), and Pandro S. Berman (1937–1939). LeBaron came from Paramount and oversaw the production of two big-screen adaptations of major stage musicals, Florenz Ziegfeld's *Rio Rita* (1929) and *Hit the Deck* (1930), as well as the Oscar-winning Western *Cimarron* (1931), with its spectacular land rush sequence. Selznick, the most forceful executive, had also been at Paramount; he signed up Fred Astaire, Lucille Ball, and Katharine Hepburn to add to RKO's existing meager roster of stars, including Joel McCrea and Irene Dunne; he also put into production some major adaptations, such as *A Bill of Divorcement* (1932), Hepburn's film debut, and *What Price Hollywood?* (1932), the first incarnation of the Hollywood classic *A Star is Born* (1937) (remade in 1954 and 1976).

Continuing Selznick's production policies, Cooper oversaw more Hepburn vehicles, including the 1933 adaptation of *Little Women*, and the first film to feature the performing dance duo of Fred Astaire and Ginger Rogers, *Flying Down to Rio* (1933). There was also Cooper's pet project, the iconic horror film *King Kong* (1933), which Cooper coproduced and codirected with Ernest B. Schoedsack. Cooper also oversaw John Ford's Oscar-winning adaptation of *The Informer* (1934).

Under the production heads, RKO relied on producer units, sometimes involving directors, as at Paramount (Bordwell et al. 1985, 328). In house, the most consistent and successful production cycle at RKO in the 1930s was the Astaire–Rogers musical series (eight films in all), from *The Gay Divorcee* in 1934 through *The Story of Vernon and Irene Castle* in 1939. American audiences embraced the star duo's romantic comedies that played on studio art director Van Nest Polglase's celebrated "big white" art deco sets. From late 1934 until late 1936, four of the top 10 box office films were Astaire and Rogers musicals. These were Pandro Berman's productions; Berman, along with Selznick, was the closest the studio came to a central producer production head in the mold of Irving Thalberg. Berman, however, preferred supervising individual films and in fact oversaw most of the studio's outstanding films each year: *Of Human Bondage* (1934, directed by John Cromwell), *Stage Door* (1938, Gregory LaCava), *Gunga Din* (1939, George Stevens), *Love Affair* (1939, Leo McCarey), and *The Hunchback of Notre Dame* (1939, William Dieterle). As this list suggests, RKO's yearly production slate was enlivened with films by strong directors, often outside talents: George Cukor (the early Hepburn films, as well as *Sylvia Scarlet*, 1936), John Ford, and Howard Hawks (Jewell 1995). Indeed, as Richard Jewell argues, managerial instability allowed the studio to support the creation of outstanding films in various genres (1985). Yet the lack of major stars on the roster (aside from Ginger Rogers) by the early 1940s also hampered the studio's fortunes.

In 1939, Berman left RKO permanently to join MGM. His successor was George J. Schaefer, former head of United Artists, who was also the company's president. It was Schaefer who lured Orson Welles to the studio with an exceptional contract that allowed him considerable creative freedom (including the right of final cut) for two films. The result was Welles's extraordinary film debut as cowriter-star-director-producer in *Citizen Kane* (1941), which also benefited from the remarkable cinematography of Gregg Toland, the inventive, cost-cutting set designs of Perry Ferguson, and the moving music of Bernard Herrmann (in his first Hollywood film score). As is well known, Welles's working relationship with RKO went south quickly, after the shooting of *The Magnificent Ambersons* (1942), and this also cost Schaefer his own job. Robert Carringer, in his meticulous study of the making of *Citizen Kane*, writes: "it should be stated unequivocally for the historical record that without Schaefer's gamble and continued trust in his own instincts on Welles, *Citizen Kane* would never have been possible" (1996, 3).

Yet even after Schaefer departed, the studio was able to thrive during World War II with Alfred Hitchcock productions packaged by David O. Selznick (*Suspicion*, 1941; *Spellbound*, 1945), and films made by International Pictures (the management team of former RKO president Leo Spitz and Twentieth Century-Fox's interim studio head William Goetz), such as *The Woman in the Window* (1944), directed by Fritz Lang and starring Edward G. Robinson and Joan Bennett. As Douglas Gomery has noted, "United Artists is remembered as the distributor of independent producers, but during the 1940s, RKO ranked with UA as a home for independent producers" (Gomery 1985, 146). Indeed, RKO scored a coup when it lured Walt Disney away from United Artists in 1936 and reaped the benefits of distributing Disney's dazzling first feature film, *Snow White and the Seven Dwarfs*, in 1937, followed by *Pinocchio* in 1940, and several other features. Samuel Goldwyn followed Disney in 1941, shoring up the company's release schedule with Goldwyn's independently produced productions (*Ball of Fire* and *The Pride of the Yankees*, both 1941; the Bob Hope comedy *The Princess and the Pirate*, 1944; and many more).

But RKO's best-remembered homegrown product during the war years was the series of low-budget films produced by former Selznick story-editor-turned-unit-producer Val Lewton. Teaming with directors Jacques Tourneur, Mark Robson, and Robert Wise, along with writers DeWitt Bodeen and Ardel Wray, among others, Lewton's unit turned out *Cat People* (1942), *I Walked with a Zombie* (1943), *The Leopard Man* (1943), *The Seventh Victim* (1943), and continued through 1946 with *Bedlam*, all of which were enormously successful, in part because of the ability of Lewton and his creative team to turn the budgetary restrictions imposed by the studio and the wartime government into an evocative, distinctive, and suggestive low-key style.

After a takeover by Howard Hughes in the late 1940s and into the mid-1950s, RKO would sputter, restart, and finally collapse, its studio facilities famously bought by Desi Arnaz and Lucille Ball, renamed Desilu Studios, and used to shoot the groundbreaking TV sitcom *I Love Lucy* (1951–1957).

Warner Bros.

By 1929, the company founded by the Warner brothers (Harry, deceased in 1927; Albert, Sam, and Jack) was firmly established as a major Hollywood player. They had gone into serious debt using loans from Goldman, Sachs and Catchings to finance the takeover of the silent-era giant Vitagraph, instantly giving them a sizable number of distribution exchanges. In 1926, they inaugurated Vitaphone, their sound-on-disk system, which they envisioned as replacing stage shows prior to the film program in nonurban markets. Vitaphone worked on signing up major performing artists of the day – from the stage, the concert hall, and vaudeville. *Don Juan* (1926), *The Jazz Singer* (1927), and especially the all-talking *Lights of New York* (1928), among other films, demonstrated that sound also boosted the box office performance of feature films and that it was not a passing fad. Even earlier, Warner Bros. was able to use the proceeds from the studio's sound film venture to further build up their theater chain and become one of the Big Five – acquiring the Philadelphia-based Stanley Theater chain and the First National production company to expand production. As Douglas Gomery notes, Warner Bros. had $5 million in assets in 1925; they had $230 million in assets by 1930 (Gomery 1985, 250).

Through the early 1930s, the studio relied heavily on the production guidance of Darryl F. Zanuck, who had begun his career there in the 1920s writing scripts and stories for Rin-Tin-Tin movies, among many others, and rose to the position of production supervisor. Though Jack Warner was the nominal executive in charge of production, it was Zanuck who oversaw the making of many of the studio's notable classics of the period: the fast-paced social problem films, such as *I Am a Fugitive from a Chain Gang* (1932); the revitalized gangster genre films, such as *Public Enemy* (1931) and *Little Caesar* (1932); the Busby Berkeley musicals *42nd Street* (1933) and *Gold Diggers of 1933* (1933), typically starring Ruby Keeler and Dick Powell. In the early 1930s, the studio was built around stage-trained, hard-edged stars with an urban ethos – Joan Blondell, James Cagney, Bette Davis, Paul Muni, and Edward G. Robinson. Among these genres and performers, the studio developed a "proletarian" style that also arose from the brothers' restricted budget allocations (the average negative cost of a Warner Bros. film from this period was $200,000, less than half of MGM's), from its low-lit handling of its films' urban milieu, from the assignment of accomplished and efficient directors like William Wellman, Mervyn LeRoy, and Michael Curtiz, and from fast-paced cutting. Warner Bros. was equally famous in the industry for constantly remaking its own films under new titles – the 1932 production *I Am a Fugitive from a Chain Gang* became *Road Gang* in 1936.

Zanuck left Warner Bros. in early 1933 (ostensibly in protest over the studio's refusal to reverse austerity cuts in personnel salary) to form his new independent company, Twentieth Century Pictures. Warner Bros. production continued under Jack Warner, who reconfigured the studio for unit production (Bordwell et al. 1985, 326). Hal Wallis, now associate executive in charge of production, for example, oversaw the making of several prestigious films: Max Reinhardt's *A Midsummer Night's Dream* (1935) and more lavish productions like the Bette Davis–William Wyler Southern belle melodrama *Jezebel* (1938), which would not have been out of place as an MGM release. Bryan Foy supervised B-films. Henry Blanke was in charge of biopics such as the Oscar-winning Paul Muni vehicle *The Life of Emile Zola* (1937) and of the Errol Flynn swashbucklers, most memorably, *The Adventures of Robin Hood* (1938), costarring Olivia de Havilland and directed in Technicolor by contractee Michael Curtiz (Behlmer 1986).

With Jack Warner's encouragement, the studio was more politically minded than any other of the late 1930s, openly supportive of Franklin D. Roosevelt's administration – his image and the insignia of the National Recovery Act appear in an overhead shot of a dance number in Berkeley's 1933 *Footlight Parade*. In the late 1930s, Warner Bros. also produced one of the earliest Hollywood films to dramatize the rise of Hitlerism (*Confessions of a Nazi Spy*, 1939) and the need for American involvement in the worldwide conflict (*Sergeant York*, 1941, personally produced by Jesse L. Lasky). The culmination of this trend was *Casablanca* (1942), a film often regarded not only as a quintessential prowar film, but also as a perfect illustration of the strength of the studio system for the way in which casting, scripting, and direction – here under Wallis's guidance – came together (Schatz 1988, 297–298, 314–319; Harmetz 1992).

The war years also saw the rise of Humphrey Bogart, who starred in films scripted (*High Sierra*, 1941) and directed (*The Maltese Falcon*, 1941) by studio-based John Huston, as well as by freelancing veteran director Howard Hawks. Huston and Hawks (Hawks with the influential combat film *Air Force*, 1943, in particular), along with the Bogart–Lauren Bacall hits *To Have and Have Not* (1944) and *The Big Sleep* (1946), helped to recast Warner Bros.' "proletarian" aesthetic as a blueprint for its films noir, typically hard-boiled crime and detective stories. The studio, now with the assistance of producer Jerry Wald (Hal Wallis left the company when Jack Warner denied him credit at the Academy Awards for *Casablanca*), produced yet another important entry in the film noir canon when MGM did not renew Joan Crawford's contract near the end of the war. Warner Bros. and Wald scored a triumph with Crawford's Oscar-winning performance in *Mildred Pierce* in 1945, a signal achievement as the studio transitioned into the postwar era under Jack Warner's overall production leadership.

Columbia Pictures Corporation

Founded by former Universal Pictures employees Jack and Harry Cohn in 1919, Columbia Pictures Corporation (named CBC until early 1924) was, as one of the Little Three, a threadbare operation through the 1920s and much of the 1930s. The year 1927 was a crucial one: The studio made its first public offering, and Harry Cohn, who remained the company's president *and* executive in charge of production through the 1950s, hired former film comic Harry Langdon's director Frank Capra.

Gaining increasing independence from Cohn, Capra was Columbia's top director, making an array of comedies, action films, and melodramas (the latter including several starring Barbara Stanwyck, such as *Ladies of Leisure*, 1930; *The Miracle Woman*, 1931; and *Forbidden*, 1932). Capra, working with his own unit, consolidated his and the studio's reputation, however, with the 1933 adaptation of Damon Runyon's *Lady for a Day*, and raised Columbia to previously-thought-impossible recognition with the unprecedented 1934 romantic comedy smash hit *It Happened One Night*, which starred MGM's leading man Clark Gable and Paramount's Claudette Colbert. As the ambitious Cohn had cultivated Louis B. Mayer for years and aspired to equal MGM someday, the film's box office success and its sweep of the Academy Awards (Best Picture, Director, Adapted Screenplay, Best Actor, Best Actress) was an extraordinary achievement.

Capra famously specialized in uplifting stories of Americans overcoming class divisions (*It Happened One Night*), urban/rural divides (*Mr. Deeds Goes to Town*, 1936, starring laconic star Gary Cooper), American eccentrics (*You Can't Take It With You*, 1938), and government corruption (*Mr. Smith Goes to Washington*, 1939, with James Stewart, another MGM loanout). He won two more Best Director Academy Awards and enjoyed an incredible run of success, with the exception of his big-budgeted 1937 adaptation of James Hilton's *Lost Horizon*. Cohn further seasoned the Columbia annual schedule with films from major directors who floated among studios and thus were not entitled to annual salaries: Frank Borzage with *A Man's Castle* (1933); John Ford with the mistaken-identity comedy *The Whole Town's Talking* (1935), starring Edward G. Robinson; George Cukor with the 1938 remake of *Holiday*; Howard Hawks with *Twentieth Century* (1934), *Only Angels Have Wings* (1939), and *His Girl Friday* (1940); and Leo McCarey's 1937 directing triumph *The Awful Truth*. These all featured major stars such as Carole Lombard, Cary Grant, and Irene Dunne. Most of these films, as well as the Claudette Colbert vehicle *She Married Her Boss* (1935) and the Irene Dunne title *Theodora Goes Wild* (1936), were screwball comedies, a production predilection at the studio that Capra inspired (Balio 1996b, 431).

Combined with Capra's films, these one-off films fit perfectly into Harry Cohn's production policy, which was to make dozens of cheap films (B-Westerns, series films such as Blondie, Boston Blackie, Buck Jones) with just a few high-budget productions to keep exhibitors interested in the studio's output (Bernstein 2000, 75; Dick 1993). The outstanding films of 1939, for example, were *Golden Boy*, *Mr. Smith Goes to Washington*, and *Only Angels Have Wings* – just three out of 29 total releases.

Cohn's cost-cutting ways also entailed placing few stars under contract through the 1930s: Barbara Stanwyck and Carole Lombard in the early 1930s, opera singer Grace Moore at mid-decade, Rosalind

Russell beginning in 1936, Jean Arthur through 1944, and Cary Grant, who also had a working arrangement with RKO (Hirschorn 1989, 12). In the 1940s, while continuing his overall production policy, Cohn began developing studio stars in earnest. Rita Hayworth had been on the lot since mid-decade, and had a featured role in Hawks's *Only Angels Have Wings*, but she became a star in a series of musicals in the early 1940s: *You'll Never Get Rich* (1941) and *You Were Never Lovelier* (1942), both costarring Fred Astaire, and *Cover Girl* with Gene Kelly in 1944 – only the studio's second film in Technicolor. Hayworth famously became a film noir femme fatale in the postwar era (McLean 2004). Glenn Ford, by contrast, appeared in a series of low-budget films before coming to prominence and breaking through opposite Hayworth in the iconic *Gilda* (1946).

Columbia took advantage of wartime demand for movies and began to increase the budgets of its best films, and even to make more A-films during the 1940s: the Humphrey Bogart combat film *Sahara* (1943), the comedy fantasy *Here Comes Mr. Jordan* (1941), and a trio of George Stevens films – the melodrama *Penny Serenade* (1941), the comedy *The Talk of the Town* (1942), both starring Cary Grant, and the romantic comedy *The More the Merrier* (1943). The studio's greatest box office triumph of the period, however, was *The Jolson Story* (1945), a nostalgic portrayal of the life of the star of Warner Bros.' groundbreaking 1927 film, *The Jazz Singer.* Columbia's ability to thrive – not just survive – through 1945 owed a great deal to Cohn's management skills and his feel for popular entertainment – but much of this he learned from Frank Capra's tenure at his studio.

Universal Pictures Corporation

Universal was initially the most solid member of the "Little Three" companies; it remains the longest lived. The studio, created in 1913, started out strong, particularly after the March 1915 opening of Universal City. From *Traffic in Souls* in 1913 through John Ford's 1917 *Straight Shooting* with Western star Harry Carey, Erich von Stroheim's lavishly produced tales of European decadence and American innocence from *Blind Husbands* (1919) through *Foolish Wives* (1922), and Lon Chaney vehicles such as *The Hunchback of Notre Dame* (1923) and *The Phantom of the Opera* (1925), Carl Laemmle's studio had the makings of a dominating presence in Hollywood. Yet because it only briefly owned theaters (from 1928 to 1933) and found itself excluded from the most profitable markets, Universal could only collect a limited amount of revenue (Gomery 1985, 150; Dick 1997).

Production policy also limited what Universal could accomplish under Laemmle's leadership. The von Stroheim and Lon Chaney titles of the 1920s notwithstanding, Universal made mostly B-films that could not compete with the top-of-the-line output of the Big Five, instead finding their audiences in small and rural markets. The production schedule looked to change when Carl Laemmle, Jr became head of production in 1930, especially with that year's extraordinary if star-bereft Oscar-winning adaptation of Erich Maria Remarque's novel *All Quiet on the Western Front* – a condemnation of World War I from a German perspective – which boasted the company's largest budget in its history and earned its first Academy Award. Laemmle, Jr also initiated the famous horror cycle (*Dracula*, 1930; *Frankenstein*, 1931; *The Mummy*, 1932; *The Invisible Man*, 1933) that helped maintain some income during the Depression years. Universal's biggest box office attraction in the 1930s, however, was singing teen Deanna Durbin, whose modestly budgeted musicals (produced by a unit overseen by Joe Pasternak) proved box office gold. Subsequent head of production Charles Rogers continued in this vein. Nonetheless, the company showed few profitable years through the late 1930s; even when in the black, what profits Universal earned were minuscule.

In 1938, new president Nathan J. Blumberg appointed Clifford Work as head of production (both had worked as exhibition executives at RKO). This inaugurated a shift into more A-features, using unit production and semi-independents (Bordwell et al. 1985, 327). By 1940, the studio was in the black again. In 1941, the comedy team of Bud Abbott and Lou Costello earned an unexpected ranking as the second most popular box office stars in the industry (Gary Cooper was first), not only because of their comedic talents honed and popularized on national radio, but also because they were workhorses, making four films in one year.

Since the 1940 consent decree outlawing block booking, and after Pearl Harbor, films enjoyed longer runs among a growing domestic audience with disposable income. Universal embarked upon a new production policy that involved spending more on individual films featuring major directors, stars, and producers. Alfred Hitchcock made *Saboteur* in 1942 and *Shadow of a Doubt* in 1943; Ernst Lubitsch created *That Uncertain Feeling* (1941); and Gregory LaCava (who had realized the studio's 1936 smash screwball comedy *My Man Godfrey* with loanout stars William Powell and Carole Lombard) directed two films starring Irene Dunne, *Unfinished Business* in 1941 and *Lady in a Jam* in 1942. Beginning in 1942, Walter F. Wanger produced a series of war films, escapist comedies, and melodramas (his *Arabian Nights* proved the biggest moneymaker for the company in 1943). J. Arthur Rank also began distributing quality British films (albeit to indifferent box office) through Universal. By 1945, the company looked to create greater prestige pictures, exemplified by Fritz Lang's controversial *Scarlet Street* (Bernstein 1986).

In 1946, the studio merged with the thriving semi-independent company International Pictures (previously releasing through RKO). Universal, now Universal-International, was at this point well positioned to survive the struggles of the postwar era (Gomery 2005, 198–225).

United Artists and Hollywood's Semi-Independent Producers

Formed in 1919 by the artistic powerhouses Charlie Chaplin, Douglas Fairbanks, D. W. Griffith, and Mary Pickford, United Artists was created as a distribution and marketing company only. The four founders had so much capital at the time that they could rent or build their own studios and control their production costs. They wanted to reap the profits of their incredibly successful films (particularly in the case of the three stars) without profit-sharing arrangements with already established distributors, and they wanted to maintain creative autonomy. Indeed, this was their chief motivation in creating UA.

"Independent production" in Hollywood then, as now, was a slippery term. The UA founders fit the general description: They had no corporate ties to (or financing loans from) the other filmmaking corporations. Others who joined UA later had a similar status. Samuel Goldwyn, who was bought out at the creation of Loew's/MGM (the G stood for Goldwyn), owned his own studio facilities, held stars and technicians under contract, and enjoyed complete control over his films. The same was true of David O. Selznick and his Selznick International Pictures. Yet they all functioned as adjuncts of the major studios – getting stars on loanout and producing films that could be shown in the Big Five theaters – and can therefore be thought of more accurately as semi-independents (Bernstein 1993). UA also distributed the films of producers with corporate ties to other companies: Walter F. Wanger, who signed on with UA in 1936, financed his films through bank loans guaranteed by the distributor; UA had representation on the board of directors of Wanger's company, and actually had budget and approval power over his filmmaking. Though he too had stars under contract (including at one time Joan Bennett, Charles Boyer, Madeleine Carroll, and Henry Fonda, among others), Wanger was beholden to UA at every turn, and left in 1941 when UA refused to finance a pet project (Bernstein 2000, 129–194).

In 1919, UA's founders had a bold, ambitious plan, and it began well, with D. W. Griffith's *Orphans of the Storm* and Mary Pickford's *Tess of the Storm Country* highlighting a year of 11 releases in 1922. Pickford and Fairbanks were good for at least one film per year, and Griffith produced two films in 1924. Still, a slate of 11 films annually could not keep UA competitive with the other studios. Several of the UA founders had contractual obligations elsewhere to dispose of first. Griffith stopped producing films for UA in 1924 (and his career ended after *The Struggle*, 1931). Pickford retired after *Secrets* (1933), and Fairbanks did not produce again for UA distribution after *Mr. Robinson Crusoe* (1932). Of the four, only Chaplin continued to produce films, but these appeared only once every four or five years: *City Lights* in 1931, *Modern Times* in 1936, and *The Great Dictator* in 1940.

Moreover, one cannot speak of a United Artists production policy *per se*, since UA was not a studio. Under board chair Joseph Schenck, made a partner in 1924, UA did venture into funding production with its Art Finance Corporation and into filmmaking with its short-lived Art Cinema Corporation. There were successes in the 1920s, such as several Buster Keaton comedies, Talmadge sister melodramas, and Rudolph Valentino's *The Son of the Sheik* (1926). Many of these Schenck himself produced. Yet these, although top-quality features, did not constitute a consistent UA house style. Indeed, the very concept of a house style is inimical to UA's rationale for existing and its

Figure 10.2 The lineup at United Artists in 1936. From left, back row: Douglas Fairbanks, Jr, Samuel Goldwyn, "Jock" Whitney, David O. Selznick (Whitney was Selznick's financier), Jesse L. Lasky, and Douglas Fairbanks, Sr. Front row from left: Charles Chaplin, Mary Pickford, Walter F. Wanger, and Roy Disney. (Photo courtesy of the Wisconsin Center for Film and Theater Research.)

function solely as a distributor of others' films (Balio 1976).

In this struggle for product, Schenck was able to enhance the company's roster by signing Samuel Goldwyn in 1926, Walt Disney from 1932 to 1936 (producing Mickey Mouse and Silly Symphony shorts), and Darryl F. Zanuck's Twentieth Century Pictures in 1933. Zanuck was especially prolific during his two years at UA: He produced biopics such as *The House of Rothschild* (1934) and *Cardinal Richelieu* (1935), as well as literary adaptations such as *Les Misérables* and *Call of the Wild* (both in 1935). Goldwyn likewise supplied a steady stream of literary adaptations: Sinclair Lewis's *Arrowsmith* in a 1932 John Ford production, William Wyler's film of Lillian Hellman's *These Three* and Lewis's *Dodsworth*, both in 1936, and Emily Brontë's *Wuthering Heights* in 1939. Goldwyn also adapted popular fiction (*Stella Dallas*, 1925, remade with Barbara Stanwyck in 1937, and *Bulldog Drummond*, 1929), Eddie Cantor musical comedies (from *Whoopee!*, 1930, to *Strike Me Pink*, 1936), and adventure films. Howard Hughes contributed several silent features, and, most famously, Lewis Milestone's dynamic 1931 adaptation of Ben Hecht and Charles MacArthur's *The Front Page*, as well as Howard Hawks's 1932 gangster classic *Scarface*. Yet another major source of films for UA were British imports such as Alexander Korda's *The Private Life of Henry VIII* (1933), *The Scarlet Pimpernel* (1935), and Gabriel Pascal's 1941 adaptation of George Bernard

Shaw's *Major Barbara*. Korda in fact became a regular UA producer in the late 1930s and into the early 1940s, providing Technicolor fantasy adventure films, such as a live version of *The Jungle Book* (1941) and, the year before, *The Thief of Bagdad*, a property Fairbanks had made for UA release in 1924.

Selznick International Productions also augmented the 1930s and 1940s lineup with a number of literary adaptations, such as *Little Lord Fauntleroy*, *The Garden of Allah* (both 1936), *The Adventures of Tom Sawyer* (1938), and perhaps the best remembered, Alfred Hitchcock's Academy Award-winning *Rebecca* (1940). Selznick returned to UA distribution in the mid-1940s via his new company, Vanguard Productions, with the 1944 homefront epic *Since You Went Away* and the romantic *I'll Be Seeing You*, and Hitchcock's 1945 psychoanalytic mystery *Spellbound*. Moreover, Selznick produced several films in Technicolor in the late 1930s, a time when few studios would make such an investment (Behlmer 1972; Thomson 1992).

Second only to Irving Thalberg in mogul mythology, Selznick was a hands-on, creative producer who could keep in mind (and agonized daily over) thousands of details as he personally supervised major projects. Selznick was, for example, one of the few filmmakers to take advantage of George Gallup's audience research (Ohmer 2006). His greatest achievement was his 1939 blockbuster *Gone With the Wind*, not only the most expensive film made in Hollywood to date but the most successful at the box office. Ironically, he was compelled by Louis B. Mayer to grant Loew's the distribution rights to his landmark film in exchange for the loanout of Clark Gable for the role of Rhett Butler. In fact Loew's was able to distribute this road-shown epic far more effectively than United Artists could have done. UA was not pleased with Selznick's choice of distributor – but was powerless to intervene.

One blow the founders could have avoided some years earlier involved Zanuck's Twentieth Century Pictures. They refused to allow Zanuck to become a stockholder (Goldwyn, Korda, and Selznick were). That eventually also cost the company Joseph Schenck's invaluable leadership (which insured decent bookings for UA films in major theaters and had even extended UA to a limited investment in theaters of their own). Except in the case of its top films, UA, at least by the late 1930s, with a revolving door of presidents, could not bid competitively for play dates in the best houses, particularly as its sales force booked films individually, not in blocks as the other companies did. UA's producers became disheartened. Of the 17 films Walter F. Wanger produced over a period of five years, only three were significantly profitable (*Algiers* and *Trade Winds*, both 1938, and especially John Ford's 1939 landmark Western *Stagecoach*). Wanger blamed UA for this poor performance. He left UA in 1941 to produce for Universal. Samuel Goldwyn left the same year to have his films distributed through RKO (Balio 1976).

Semi-independent production became more prevalent during World War II and after, as punishing income tax rates for the war effort encouraged talents (producers, directors, and stars) to incorporate to finance a film or a series of films and dissolve the company in order to generate capital gains, which were taxed at lower rates. At this time, UA's biggest name aside from Chaplin was James Cagney, who tried this system in search of non-gangster roles when he was finally able to leave Warner Bros. (Hagopian 1986). William Cagney Productions was short-lived, however; by 1949, Cagney was back at Warner Bros. making another gangster film, *White Heat*. Moreover, UA's renewed attempt to finance production during the early 1940s (creating United Artists Productions out of the assets of the Wanger company) rarely resulted in box office success.

UA, not surprisingly, was the only major Hollywood corporation to show losses throughout the war years (Gomery 2005, 167). The company's fortunes would decline steadily until 1950, when the founders agreed to be bought out by a new set of managers. This group (led by attorneys Arthur Krim and Robert Benjamin) revived UA with a new model of production packaging, financing, and distribution, which had been pioneered by talent agents (Balio 1976; Kemper 2010). It was then, particularly after the 1948 Paramount decision, that UA could take advantage of the growth of semi-independent production.

Conclusion

As this survey suggests, the dominance of the movie mogul from 1929 to 1945 was circumscribed by historical, corporate, industrial, artistic, and personal conditions. All the major companies defined their filmmaking management in similar ways – the post of vice president in charge of production, head of studio operations, or just plain "producer." At different times, each studio employed a central producer system with a team of associates or a producer unit system – or some combination of the two. Those most consistently exemplifying the central producer system were Irving Thalberg and Louis B. Mayer at MGM, Jack Warner and Hal Wallis at Warner Bros., Darryl F. Zanuck at Twentieth Century-Fox, Harry Cohn at Columbia, the producing founders of UA, and, to a certain extent, semi-independents Walt Disney, Samuel Goldwyn, Alexander Korda, and David O. Selznick. They oversaw all studio productions, keeping an eye on the work of their subordinates' units, and personally producing prestige productions. Producers performed the same function at their studio units, in addition to insuring that the films were completed on time. These production models resulted in the output of the classical Hollywood cinema, both the B-films and the A-line films, the canonic films, and the films forgotten today. Yet it is important to remember that their management was a matter of responding to public taste as they saw it. As Tino Balio has noted, "production had to be tailored first and foremost to their perceptions of the paying public. Producing films to suit the personal tastes of studio moguls, boards of directors, or financiers would have ruined a company" (1996b, 420).

Thomas Schatz has argued persuasively that the "quality and artistry" of classical Hollywood's best films "were the product not simply of individual human expression, but of a melding of institutional forces" (1988, 6). Moreover, classical filmmaking relied on the collaboration of the many talents involved – screenwriters, directors, stars, art directors, cinematographers, costume designers – who made, in Robert Carringer's words, "a distinguishable contribution to a film" (1996, x). The mogul was the first among these collaborators, the individual at the nexus of the institutional forces that shaped a studio's output. Their work was far more complex and constructive than the myth has allowed.

References

Allen, Robert, & Gomery, Douglas. (1985). *Film History: Theory and Practice*. New York: McGraw-Hill.

Balio, Tino. (1976). *United Artists: The Company Built by the Stars*. Madison: University of Wisconsin Press.

Balio, Tino. (1985). *The American Film Industry*. 2nd edn. Madison: University of Wisconsin Press.

Balio, Tino. (1996a). *Grand Design: Hollywood as a Modern Business Enterprise, 1930–1939*. Berkeley: University of California Press.

Balio, Tino. (1996b). "Columbia Pictures: The Making of a Motion Picture Major, 1930–1943." In David Bordwell & Noel Carroll (eds), *Post-Theory: Reconstructing Film Studies* (pp. 419–433). Madison: University of Wisconsin Press.

Behlmer, Rudy. (1972). *Memo from David O. Selznick*. New York: Grove Press.

Behlmer, Rudy. (1986). *Inside Warner Bros*. New York: Viking Penguin.

Behlmer, Rudy. (1993). *Memo from Darryl F. Zanuck: The Golden Years at Twentieth Century Fox*. New York: Grove Press.

Bernstein, Matthew. (1986). "Fritz Lang, Incorporated." *The Velvet Light Trap*, 22, 33–52.

Bernstein, Matthew. (1993). "Semi-Independent Production." *Cinema Journal*, 35.1 (Spring), 41–54.

Bernstein, Matthew. (2000). *Walter Wanger, Hollywood Independent*. Minneapolis: University of Minnesota Press. (Original work published 1994.)

Black, Gregory. (1989). "Hollywood Censored: The Production Code Administration and the Hollywood Film Industry, 1930–1940." *Film History*, 3, 167–189.

Bordwell, David, Staiger, Janet, & Thompson, Kristin. (1985). *The Classical Hollywood Cinema: Film Style and Mode of Production to 1960*. New York: Columbia University Press.

Brown, Gene. (1995). *Movie Time: A Chronology of Hollywood and the Movie Industry from its Beginnings to the Present*. New York: Macmillan.

Brownlow, Kevin. (1976). *The Parade's Gone By*. Berkeley: University of California Press.

Carringer, Robert. (1996). *The Making of Citizen Kane*. Revised edn. Berkeley: University of California Press. (Original work published 1985.)

Crafton, Donald. (1997). *The Talkies: American Cinema's Transition to Sound, 1926–1931*. New York: Charles Scribner's Sons.

Curry, Ramona. (1991). "Mae West as Censored Commodity: The Case of *Klondike Annie*." *Cinema Journal*, 31.1, 57–84.

Custen, George. (1997). *Twentieth Century's Fox: Darryl F. Zanuck and the Culture of Hollywood*. New York: Basic Books.

deCordova, Richard. (2001). *Picture Personalities: The Emergence of the Star System in America*. Urbana: University of Illinois Press. (Original work published 1990.)

Dick, Bernard F. (1993). *The Merchant Prince of Poverty Row: Harry Cohn of Columbia Pictures*. Lexington: University Press of Kentucky.

Dick, Bernard F. (1997). *City of Dreams: The Making and Remaking of Universal Pictures*. Lexington: University Press of Kentucky.

Doherty, Thomas. (2009). *Hollywood's Censor: Joseph I. Breen and the Production Code Administration*. New York: Columbia University Press.

Dyer, Richard. (2008). *Stars*. London: British Film Institute.

Fordin, Hugh. (1984). *The World of Entertainment! Hollywood's Greatest Musicals*. New York: Doubleday. (Original work published 1975.)

Gomery, Douglas. (1982). "Hollywood, the National Recovery Administration, and the Question of Monopoly Power." In Gorham Kindem (ed.), *The American Movie Industry: The Business of Motion Pictures* (pp. 205–214). Carbondale: Southern Illinois University Press. (Original work published 1979.)

Gomery, Douglas. (1985). *The Hollywood Studio System*. New York: St Martin's Press.

Gomery, Douglas. (1989). "Orson Welles and the Hollywood Industry." *Persistence of Vision*, 7, 39–43.

Gomery, Douglas. (1992). *Shared Pleasures: A History of Movie Presentation in the United States*. Madison: University of Wisconsin Press.

Gomery, Douglas. (2005). *The Hollywood Studio System: A History*. Revised and expanded. London: British Film Institute.

Hagopian, Kevin. (1986). "Declarations of Independence: A History of Cagney Productions." *The Velvet Light Trap*, 22, 16–32.

Harmetz, Aljean. (1992). *Round Up the Usual Suspects: The Making of Casablanca: Bogart, Bergman and World War II*. New York: Hyperion Books.

Hilmes, Michele. (1999). *Hollywood and Broadcasting: From Radio to Cable*. Champaign: University of Illinois Press.

Hirschorn, Clive. (1989). *The Columbia Story*. New York: Crown.

Huettig, Mae Dana. (1944). *Economic Control of the Motion Picture Industry*. Philadelphia: University of Pennsylvania Press. Reprinted by Jerome S. Ozer, 1971.

Jacobs, Lea. (1992). "The B Film and the Problem of Cultural Distinction." *Screen*, 33.1, 1–13.

Jacobs, Lea. (1997). *The Wages of Sin: Censorship and the Fallen Woman Film, 1928–1942*. Berkeley: University of California Press.

Jewell, Richard B. (1995). "How Howard Hawks Brought *Baby* Up: An *Apologia* for The Studio System." In Janet Staiger (ed.), *The Studio System* (pp. 39–49). New Brunswick: Rutgers University Press. (Original work published 1984.)

Jewell, Richard, with Harbin, Vernon. (1985). *The RKO Story*. New York: Crown.

Kemper, Tom. (2010). *Hidden Talent: The Emergence of Hollywood Agents*. Berkeley: University of California Press.

Koppes, Clayton R., & Black, Gregory D. (1987). *Hollywood Goes to War: How Politics, Profits and Propaganda Shaped World War II Movies*. New York: Basic Books.

Koppes, Clayton R., & Black, Gregory D. (1999). "Blacks, Loyalty, and Motion Picture Propaganda in World War II." In Matthew Bernstein (ed.), *Controlling Hollywood: Censorship and Regulation in the Studio Era* (pp. 130–156). New Brunswick: Rutgers University Press. (Original work published 1986.)

Koszarski, Richard. (2008). *Hollywood on the Hudson: Film and Television in New York from Griffith to Sarnoff*. New Brunswick: Rutgers University Press.

Lewis, Howard T. (1933). *The Motion Picture Industry*. New York: D. Van Nostrand Co.

McLean, Adrienne. (2004). *Being Rita Hayworth: Labor, Identity, and Hollywood Stardom*. New Brunswick: Rutgers University Press.

Neale, Steve. (2000). *Genre and Hollywood*. New York: Routledge.

Ohmer, Susan. (2006). *George Gallup in Hollywood*. New York: Columbia University Press.

Rosten, Leo C. (1941). *Hollywood: The Movie Colony, The Movie Makers*. New York: Harcourt, Brace & Company.

Schatz, Thomas. (1988). *The Genius of the System: Hollywood Filmmaking in the Studio Era*. New York: Pantheon.

Schatz, Thomas. (1999). *Boom and Bust: American Cinema in the 1940s*. Berkeley: University of California Press. (Original work published 1997.)

Solomon, Aubrey. (1988). *Twentieth Century-Fox: A Corporate and Financial History*. New York: Scarecrow Press.

Sturtevant, Victoria. (2009). *A Great Big Girl Like Me: The Films of Marie Dressler*. Urbana: University of Illinois Press.

Thomson, David. (1992). *Showman: The Life of David O. Selznick*. New York: Borzoi.

Vasey, Ruth. (1997). *The World According to Hollywood: 1918–1939*. Madison: University of Wisconsin Press.

Vieira, Mark. (2009). *Irving Thalberg: Boy Wonder to Producer Prince*. Berkeley: University of California Press.

11

"As Close to Real Life as Hollywood Ever Gets"

Headline Pictures, Topical Movies, Editorial Cinema, and Studio Realism in the 1930s

Richard Maltby
Professor, Flinders University, Australia

Although Hollywood's Depression-era social realist films often are regarded as sober institutional indictments, Richard Maltby argues that such "raw," "gruesome" **topical stories** were produced as "**escapist** representations of the **crisis of capitalism**" intended for a comfortable, if "jittery," middle-class audience. Box office profitability, rather than social **consciousness-raising**, was of paramount concern in Hollywood's protagonist-driven narratives. Cost-effective, hard-boiled productions made **headline currency** a marketing tool, as true of the 1932 Warner Bros. sensation ***I Am a Fugitive from a Chain Gang***. Maltby examines ideological compromises the **Studio Relations Committee** demanded of this and other **social problem films**, while also noting critical responses from the left. Tracing negotiations between Warner Bros. and the **Production Code Administration** over ***Black Legion*** (1937), a film about an actual, KKK-related organization, Maltby illustrates ongoing industry debates concerning **entertainment**, **propaganda**, and **social responsibility** at a time when productions openly critical of **fascism** were contested. Maltby's essay shares ground with Ruth Vasey on the gangster film and Saverio Giovacchini on the Hollywood Left and World War II in this volume.

Additional terms, names, and concepts: Darryl F. Zanuck and Warner Bros. "house style," editorializing, gangster cycle, fallen woman cycle, Burbanking, Popular Front coalition, personality film

On November 11, 1932, three days after Franklin Roosevelt's landslide victory in the presidential election, New Yorkers and the citizens of more than 200 other cities could celebrate the defeat of Herbert Hoover, the "Great Engineer" of the previous decade, by going to the opening performance of a Warner Bros. movie about the rise and fall of another engineer in the 1920s, *I Am a Fugitive from a Chain Gang*.[1] Critics and historians have identified *Fugitive* as particularly emblematic of the nadir of the Depression, an icon of both Warner Bros.' social consciousness and Hollywood's "Golden Age of Turbulence"

American Film History: Selected Readings, Origins to 1960, First Edition. Edited by Cynthia Lucia, Roy Grundmann, and Art Simon.
© 2016 John Wiley & Sons, Inc. Published 2016 by John Wiley & Sons, Inc.

Figure 11.1 Paul Muni as icon of the early Depression in Mervyn LeRoy's *I Am a Fugitive from a Chain Gang* (1932, producer Hal. B. Wallis). "But how do you live?" – "I steal."

(Sklar 1978, 175). In his book *The Great Depression*, for example, Robert McElvaine argues that *Fugitive*'s protagonist, James Allen, "symbolizes all Depression victims," and that the movie "was the perfect expression of the national mood in 1932: despair, suffering, hopelessness" (1984, 208, 213).

From a sufficient historical perspective, the resonance of *Fugitive*'s release date seems unavoidable, allowing us to view it simultaneously as a remarkable piece of studio realism, a representative text of the early Depression, and "a crushing indictment of American society" (Shindler 1996, 18). Despite the fact that the movie is set in the 1920s, the Depression is not its subject matter and its only explicit reference to a social context wider than Allen's personal story is in a final newspaper headline asking whether Allen is "another Forgotten Man." *Fugitive* nevertheless shares an iconography with contemporary images of the unemployed and the "forgotten men" of the Bonus Army who had marched on Washington that summer. *I Am a Fugitive from a Chain Gang* represents 1932 in the way that Morris Dickstein suggests that we "read *The Grapes of Wrath* today,"

> or look at the photographs of Dorothea Lange, or listen to songs like "Brother Can you Spare a Dime?" not so much to document the Depression but to experience it, to understand the feelings and touch the human tragedy, full of shock, hope, pain, and plaintive longing. (2009, xix)

If, as these commentaries suggest, *Fugitive* is a representation of the crisis of capitalism, it is so by allusion rather than by explicit statement, and the timing of its production and release was incidental to the metaphorical responsibilities that subsequent interpretations have thrust upon it. Warners certainly aimed to produce a topical movie, but its topicality lay in its adaptation of a current best-selling book rather than in its allusion to broader events in the culture, and nowhere in the surviving documentation of the movie's production and distribution is there any evidence that its makers intended that it provide a definitive expression of the national mood in 1932 or, whatever their later claims, to reform the penal system. The movie that most conspicuously engaged with the immediate political and economic circumstances of Roosevelt's election was not *Fugitive* but *Prosperity*, an MGM comedy starring Marie Dressler as the mother of a small-town banker steering her community through the Depression. Released on the same day as *Fugitive* and distributed to comparable success by the same highly unusual release strategy that had both movies playing in 200 theaters across the country within a week of their New York opening, *Prosperity* was promoted with the claim that "*Prosperity* is Positively Not around the Corner! ... It's Here Right Now! ... in *Prosperity*, the Greatest Comedy Ever Made!"[2] Its adverts enthusiastically proclaimed: "Give America *Prosperity* Mr. Roosevelt, Hooray for our new President!" Yet while *Fugitive* has been canonized as a foundational text of Hollywood's social realism (Bergman 1972, 10), *Prosperity*, along with Dressler's other movies, has been entirely ignored by film historians despite her being ranked by the *Motion Picture Herald* as the "Biggest Money Making Star" of the 1931–1932 and 1932–1933 production seasons.

Many early 1930s movies display symptoms of an economic and cultural crisis, and a significant number provide accounts of the events of the previous decade, reflecting on how those events had led to the Crash. Almost invariably, however, the movies confronted these issues obliquely, displacing fears of economic dislocation onto other settings or other registers by, for example, representing the crisis of industrial capitalism as a crisis within the patriarchal family (Hark 2007, 2). *Prosperity*, like Frank Capra's *American Madness* (released by Columbia in August 1932), sought to represent the crisis of capitalism entertainingly, incorporating it into the familiar generic conventions of family drama and sentimental slapstick comedy.[3] Victoria Sturtevant has argued that in her movies Dressler, "the nation's adored surrogate mother," addressed her audiences' "ideological need for answers" to the circumstances in which they found themselves, as well as their "affective need for escape" (2009, 93, 63).

Sturtevant's is one of several recent arguments to suggest that some of the most popular pictures of the early 1930s were more closely engaged with contemporary political circumstances than their subsequent critical neglect would imply. Lary May argues that Will Rogers, the top male box office attraction of the early 1930s, purveyed a left-wing populism, a "radicalism of tradition" that "appealed to the minorities of the city and the poor of the countryside" (2000, 14, 17). Other critics have interpreted depictions of ethnic and sexual minorities in movies of the early 1930s as subversive representations of social disorder (Lugowski 1999, 12–15). It is possible to find a range of responses to the economic and social crisis, from the Marx Brothers' surrealist "hymn to anarchy and whole-hearted revolt" (Artaud 1958, 142) in *Animal Crackers* (1930) to the vigilantism of Cecil B. DeMille's *This Day and Age* or the quasi-fascism of *Gabriel Over the White House*, released within a month of Roosevelt's 1933 inaugural commitment "to wage war against the emergency," and described by Walter Lippmann as a "dramatization" of newspaper tycoon William Randolph Hearst's editorials (quoted in Bergman 1972, 115). Whether these movies were interpreted as commentaries on current circumstances by their diverse and disparate audiences, or whether, as industry trade association president Will Hays claimed in March 1934, "the movies literally laughed the big bad wolf of the depression out of the public mind," is a more difficult question to resolve.[4] Some pictures in the fallen woman cycle that dominated the woman's film early in the decade provided more or less explicit histories of the previous decade – *Baby Face* (1933) or *The Crash* (1932), for example – while the heroines of *The Easiest Way* (1931), *Blonde Venus* (1932), and *Faithless* (1932) were compelled by circumstance to sin in order to save their families. Although it would certainly have been possible for viewers to understand these narratives as melodramatic allegories of contemporary conditions, their representations were subject to the fashions of audience taste, and hardly any cycles lasted more than two annual production seasons.[5] Should we understand the decline of the fallen woman cycle by the end of 1932 as a reflection of the changing national mood or merely an effect of the cycle's box office saturation?

The movies that have entered the historical record as symptoms of national sentiment have done so largely through critical claims for their aesthetic merit and perceived social relevance, usually articulated around a loose concept of realism. As is surprisingly typical of movies commonly interpreted as being metaphors for their times, it is *Fugitive*'s challenge to conventions of representation rather than its conformity that has underpinned its claim to historical resonance. Every account of the movie, in particular, dwells on its distinctive ending, in which the possibility of romantic stability is denied and Allen, responding to the question "How do you live?," retreats into the darkness from where he replies, "I steal."

The question that lay behind many of the internal discussions of Hollywood's representation in the early 1930s was: How could the motion picture industry represent the crisis of capitalism entertainingly? *Fugitive* is one instance among many in this period in which the documentation of discussions within the studio and between the studio and the trade association officials responsible for implementing the Production Code explicitly deal with this issue, if not in quite those words. It is important to remember that the majority audience that Hollywood addressed were not themselves unemployed. They were, rather, predominantly the urban middle class, still able to afford admission to the first-run theaters, still with something to lose and something to worry about losing. Peter Baxter argues that the movies of the early 1930s did not address working-class anger or despair so much as middle-class fear: The anxiety that they "might be plunged into unemployment and penury, placed in the same position as ... the veterans in Washington" or Paul Muni's James Allen (1993, 148). So we can, perhaps, state Hollywood's problem in the early 1930s more precisely as being how to entertain a jittery middle-class audience with escapist representations of the crisis of capitalism.

Realism and Editorial Cinema

To a significant extent American sound cinema inherited key aspects of its understanding of realism from the Broadway theater of the late 1920s. What critic Benjamin deCasseres called "flat Realism" sought "to put before an audience an exact reproduction of a New York street, a city-room in a newspaper office [or] a front-line dug out." It was epitomized in productions such as *Street Scene*, *The Front Page*, *Journey's End*, and *The Trial of Mary Dugan*, all of which were adapted to the screen between 1929 and 1931. Although this version of realism had literary parallels in the work of Sinclair Lewis and Theodore Dreiser, deCasseres identified its sources as residing primarily in the content of newspapers and magazines.[6] His was one of many voices deploring Broadway's becoming "a three-dimensional supplement to the picture tabloid," assaulting the audience with a "compelling literalism" that left playgoers "battered and torn as if by an actual experience."[7]

This form of realism, involving the dramatization of topical events, had obvious appeal to Hollywood, especially when it was combined with aspects of what industry representatives called "realism in the raw" or "sordid realism" in what were euphemistically known as "social problem" pictures.[8] These terms referred either to an overly explicit representation of sex or to what the Production Code called "gruesomeness" in the presentation of crime or other forms of violence. Intertwined with these tabloid, "hard-boiled" connotations was a potentially more radical conception of social realism that signaled a desire among some writers and performers to confront their audiences with the worst realities of contemporary American life (Giovacchini 2001, 2, 37, 39). But as Robert Sklar has argued, the realism of the early sound era was most fundamentally shaped by "the crassest expediency" in employing "whatever forms of shock or titillation would lure audiences into theatres as economic conditions worsened and patronage began to fall away" (1978, 176). Particularly for a budget-conscious studio like Warner Bros., topical stories carried fewer production costs, and "ideas in the public domain cost nothing" (Custen 1997, 156).

More than any other individual, Darryl F. Zanuck, head of production at Warner Bros., created the hard-boiled, tabloid style of headline and editorial pictures, by orchestrating the process by which the studio's stable of writers, technicians, and performers took "a news headline or magazine piece, a recent novel or Broadway hit, and transpose[d] it to the screen quickly enough to exploit its social currency" (Schatz 1988, 141). In 1934, Alva Johnston described Zanuck as "primarily a great journalist using the screen instead of the printing press."[9] Appropriating the New York-based journalistic culture of the 1920s, Warners' headline pictures blended information and entertainment to create "the most distinctive house style in Hollywood" (Custen 1997, 157). Constantly reminding viewers of their topicality, these pictures repeatedly used inserts of newspaper headlines to attach themselves to traditions of muckraking journalism and offer evidence of their stories' newsworthiness, to telegraph the delivery of their narratives, and not incidentally to eliminate the need for expensive sets. Editorial comment was also an inherent component of Warners' tabloid style, most vividly seen in its contributions to the gangster cycle of 1930–1931.

The gangster cycle, which took off with the success of *The Doorway to Hell* in late 1930, took its content from the tabloid headlines and its rhetoric from contemporary press editorials demanding an end to "the reign of gangdom." The cycle appeared at a moment when the spectacle of gangsterdom had ceased to be the acceptable price of Prohibition and the public image of criminal celebrities such as Al Capone was changing rapidly from that of "fascinating middleman" to scapegoat for the excesses of the previous decade and the turbulence of the early Depression (Lacey 1991, 88). Released in April 1931, *The Public Enemy* begins with an explicit statement of authorial intent:

> It is the intention of the authors of *The Public Enemy* to honestly depict an environment that exists today in a certain strata [*sic*] of American life, rather than to glorify the hoodlum or the criminal.

The movie ends with the editorial comment that "'The Public Enemy' is not a man, nor is it a character – it is a problem that sooner or later, WE, the public, must solve."[10] While this "rhetoric of civic responsibility" has frequently been dismissed as a cynical gesture intended to appease critics concerned at the movies' socially destabilizing effects, contemporary reviews took the movie's claim to be "something of a sociological document" more seriously, debating the value of its contribution to solving the problem of urban crime.[11] Zanuck's motives were, of course, primarily commercial: Arguing that "if we can sell the idea that ... only by the betterment of environment and education for the masses can we overcome the widespread tendency toward lawbreaking – we have then punched over a moral that should do a lot toward protecting us," he established a way of promoting the movie that would earn the endorsement of at least some contributors to public debate and insure that protests against it would enhance its box office performance rather than damage it.[12] His approach integrated several aspects of "realism" in what its publicity claimed was "the finest film document" of its subject yet produced. The movie's authenticity was asserted by its claim to historical and factual accuracy, its rejection of the "sentimental, preachy type" of plot, and its representation of an environmental account of the causes of criminality, which echoed the conclusions of the most recent sociological research.[13] Expressed in its opening and closing titles and the claim that its dramatization stripped the criminal of "every shred of false heroism that might influence young people," the picture's environmentalist stance provided a defense for its "vigorous and brutal assault upon the nerves."[14]

The device of the editorial subsequently became more generally used as a way of justifying contentious content by claiming a social purpose, which was most commonly articulated as informing the public of a situation through its picturization. RKO's chain gang picture *Hell's Highway* (1932) proclaimed itself "Dedicated to an early end of the conditions portrayed herein – which, though a throw-back to the Middle Ages, actually exist today." *Cabin in the Cotton* (1932) opened with a title presenting the sharecropping system as an "endless dispute between the rich landowners, known as planters, and the poor cotton-pickers," before declining to "take sides ... on the rights and wrongs of both parties" and limiting the movie's responsibilities to "an effort to picturize conditions" (Roffman & Purdy 1981, 122). While the movies themselves commonly avoided laying claim to any more explicit political or social purpose beyond drawing attention to the existence of a problem, both their press books and reviewers far more frequently suggested that the movie presented an "indictment" of the conditions it described: MGM publicity for *Fury* (1936) repeatedly described it as an "indictment" of lynching, while in his review of Warner Bros.' *Massacre* (1934) in the *New York Evening Post*, Thornton Delahanty described it as "an unsparing indictment of social injustice; honest, powerful and impassioned in its presentation of the blight wrought on the Indians at Government reservations through the maladministration and corruptive greed of the petty officials":

> *Massacre* is an appeal for a New Deal for the American Indian, and its pleading rests on a logical and well-documented story. It is as if the authorities behind the production of this picture, namely the executives of First National, bore the conviction that *Massacre* has a high office to perform; that it was to play a significant part in the reshaping of national affairs. In doing so the picture may come under the head of propaganda, but if that is true then the motion picture industry in this country has reason to be proud of itself.[15]

In 1938, the press book for *Angels with Dirty Faces* went one stage further, including an "Editorial" that could be inserted into a cooperative local newspaper:

> It is not our purpose in this column to review the picture, but only to urge that its message be heard and heeded. That the children of the slums for whom it pleads so eloquently be given the helping hand that will spell for them the difference between a good life and a life of crime. That these potential "enemies of society" be given a chance to become, instead, its friends. This is the message that *Angels with Dirty Faces* brings to the nation's screens, and it is a message that must not be ignored.

Warners' definition of topical pictures was, however, much broader than has been recognized in critical assessments of studio realism or "social consciousness," and included movies about recent murder cases or media events. In November 1932, while Fox ran adverts in the trade press claiming that "the news that's important" to exhibitors was not Roosevelt's victory or a prison riot, but Clara Bow's comeback in *Call Her Savage*, Warners claimed that their policy of "timeliness" in selecting "news-value pictures" such as *Public Enemy*, *Blessed Event* (1932), and *The Crash* had had a "tremendous influence ... on the upturn of picture business."[16] Among their forthcoming "giant" productions for 1933 – "every one backed by the tidal power of flaming Public Interest!" – they included *I Am a Fugitive from a Chain Gang*, declaring that "this very minute headlines are screaming the sensational facts bared in this national best-seller which made its author front-page news. Every newspaper in the country has helped to sell this show!" In the same trade advert they declared *20,000 Years in Sing Sing* (1932) would be "front-page news when America's foremost warden discloses what really goes on behind prison walls." Lewis Lawes's book had been the May 1932 Book-of-the-Month-Club selection, serialized in newspapers nationwide, and had "built up public interest for a box-office killing."[17] With *The Match King*, based on the life of Swedish financier and industrialist Ivar Kreuger who committed suicide in March 1932, ahead of the exposure of his financial empire's fraudulent basis, Warners offered exhibitors "the *first* cash-in on this front-page sensation of the year! ... thrones tottered, kingdoms fell when the headlines told how the world's greatest international swindler took a run-out powder on thousands of investors." But the advert also mentioned *Grand Slam*, starring Paul Lukas and Loretta Young: "Millions tuned in their radios to follow the card-by-card reports of the tournament of the bridge giants. *Grand Slam*, an absolute novelty will give you a direct screen tie-up with this famous contest and America's second greatest indoor sport!"[18]

In a December 1932 article in *Hollywood Reporter*, Darryl Zanuck argued that "the producer of pictures today, in searching for entertainment, finds himself in a position very similar to that of the editor of a metropolitan newspaper," and enlarged on his concept of the "'headline' type of screen story." Not to be "confused with the gangster or underworld cycle of productions," it was defined by having "the punch and smash that would entitle it to be a headline on the front page of any successful metropolitan daily":

> Sometimes the story is a biography or an autobiography, like *I Am a Fugitive from a Chain Gang*. Sometimes the story is that of a fictitious character, based on headline incidents from the life of a real character, such as *The Match King* ... retaining enough of the original story matter so that the average picture-goer easily grasps the identity of the notorious personality that is being exploited. Sometimes the story is of an exposé nature, like *Grand Slam*, which endeavors to tear the lid off the contract bridge racket. In this case we use a formula that calls for a mixture of drama and comedy, bordering slightly on satire. (Behlmer 1986, 9–10)

Listing *Little Caesar*, *Smart Money*, *Five Star Final*, *Life Begins* (a 1932 drama set in a maternity ward), and *Silver Dollar* (1932, depicting "the spectacular rise and fall of Colorado's most famous silver mining character," Horace A. W. Tabor), as "headline" pictures, Zanuck extended the category to include *42nd Street* and *Frisco Jenny*, "based on the life of a very notorious San Francisco Barbary Coast hostess." Even romances could be "headline material," and Zanuck cited *Baby Face* and *Ex-Lady*, both then in production, as examples.[19]

Zanuck's classification was obviously in large part driven by the obligation to publicize his current production slate, but it is also clear that "headline" or topical pictures constituted an identifiable and understood category of production at Warners, and one that endured beyond Zanuck's period at the studio. Promoting their plans for the coming production season in June 1936, Warners announced that it would make seven headline pictures, "developed from important news stories of the last several years" and demonstrating, as its Publicity Office declared, "that actuality can beat fiction at its own game of providing excitement." The subject matter of these headline pictures was as diverse as Zanuck's earlier list. As well as *Black Legion*, which I discuss in more detail below, the seven pictures included *China Clipper* (1936), based on the history of Pan American Airlines, *Over the Wall* (1938), a prison drama based on another story by Lewis Lawes, *Draegerman Courage* (1937), about a Canadian mine rescue, *Mountain Justice* (1937), based on the trial of a Kentucky girl for the murder of her father, and a horseracing movie called *Sergeant Murphy* (1938) starring Ronald Reagan. "Anything worth newspaper space is worth a picture," Warner producer Lou Edelman told *Fortune* in 1937, and the magazine's profile of the studio noted that even *The Prince and the Pauper*, "the lavender romance by Mark Twain, came out with a big coronation sequence just in time to collar the crowds who couldn't go to London" for the coronation of King George VI, which took place a week after the movie's New York opening.[20]

While Warners emphasized the topical component in their production schedule, it was by no means unique to them, any more than it was limited to "social problem" pictures. Topicality was, to an extent, a promotional quality engineered into any movie with a contemporary setting, and topical pictures constituted a production trend comparable to and often overlapping with other production-based categories such as the woman's film.[21] Like other production trends, the content of topicals was largely governed by cycles, so that newspaper pictures or movies about politics, for example, tended to occur in relatively shortlived batches over one or two production seasons, usually beginning with the imitation of a commercial success and lasting until the specific content or formula had been played out.[22] Almost invariably falling in the lower production budget bands of "specials" or "programmers," topical pictures operated within the constraints of these categories' planning cycles, marketing strategies, and distribution patterns.

When Zanuck left Warners in 1933, he took the concept with him to Twentieth Century Productions, but his company's merger with Fox in 1935 led the studio to concentrate on a different line of product aimed more squarely at Fox's first-run theater holdings on the West Coast with more biography, spectacle, and literary respectability than would play well in Warners' metropolitan theaters in the Northeast. While all the studios made headline and topical pictures, and other studios inaugurated cycles – MGM's *The Big House* (1930) and *Fury* (1936), or Fox's production of *The Man Who Dared* (1933), a biography of assassinated Chicago mayor Anton Cermak, which was announced four days after Cermak's death, would be cases in point – Warners' reputation as "The Ford of the Movies" meant that it assembled and maintained the assets that this mode of production required: a stable of writers with experience in journalism and a stock company of working-class character actors such as Allen Jenkins and Barton MacLane, who provided a solid platform for the leading performers. Although at one level this house style amounted to a form of brand differentiation comparable to RKO's Art Moderne styling or MGM's design *largesse*, it also demarcated Warners pictures as being, in *Fortune* magazine's words, "as close to real life as Hollywood ever gets":

> except for MGM with its one brave picture *Fury*, Warner is the only major studio that seems to know or care what is going on in America besides pearl-handled gunplay, sexual dalliance, and the giving of topcoats to comedy butlers.[23]

Fugitive

However wide Zanuck might have thrown his "headline" net for publicity purposes, *I Am a Fugitive from a Chain Gang* clearly belonged at the center of the topical grouping. As I have suggested, the production of *Fugitive* was more precisely topical than is suggested by its conventional allegorical interpretation, and more exactly located in Zanuck's enthusiasm for exploiting a subject of current interest. In the face of public opposition to the volume of gangster pictures, the Association of Motion Picture Producers had passed a resolution in September 1931 prohibiting their members from the further production of motion pictures with a gangster theme.[24] Having abandoned one generic territory in which they had represented disorder as criminality, they began looking for others in topical subject matter, and found one in the

Southern chain gang system. This provided a variation on the prison cycle of the two previous production seasons, from which it borrowed its basic narrative formula of the excessive punishment of an innocent or almost innocent character.

In early 1932, there were two literary properties dealing with chain gangs available for purchase. Both Warner Bros. and MGM were interested in Robert Burns's autobiography, *I Am a Fugitive from a Georgia Chain Gang!*, which had been serialized in *True Detective Mysteries* from January to June 1931 ahead of its book publication in January 1932 (Schatz 1988, 143). Burns's account was a sensational contribution to a body of literature condemning the chain gang as a remnant of Southern barbarism. Reviewed by the *New York Times* as "a breath-taking and heart-wrenching book" that "shocks and horrifies the reader," it became a best seller, and Warners secured the film rights for $12,500 in February.[25] *Fugitive* was a typical Warner Bros. Special, budgeted at around $200,000 and designed from the outset as a star vehicle for Paul Muni, for whom it was the first production in a four-picture contract with the studio. A month later, Universal bought the rights to *Laughter in Hell*, a novel set on a chain gang by former hobo and prizefighter Jim Tully. At about the same time, David O. Selznick, head of production at RKO, initiated a project variously called *Chains*, *Chain Gang*, *Liberty Road*, and eventually *Hell's Highway*.

A World War I veteran from New Jersey, Robert Burns had been arrested in Atlanta in 1922 and sentenced to 10 years' imprisonment for his part in an armed robbery. A few months into his sentence, he escaped the chain gang and settled in Chicago, where he became the successful editor and publisher of a real estate trade journal, the *Greater Chicago Magazine*. Betrayed to the Georgia authorities by his estranged wife, Burns was arrested in Chicago and extradited to Georgia in 1929. His story had been front-page news when, in 1930, he again escaped from the Troup County chain gang after having been denied parole.[26]

By the time of *Fugitive*'s release, the story had, if anything, become even more topical, as conditions on the chain gang had become a focus of media attention. In June 1932, a 22-year-old white prisoner named Arthur Maillefert, also from New Jersey, had been strangled to death while being punished in a "sweatbox" in the Sunbeam prison camp in Duval County, Florida. The incident occasioned considerable press coverage, particularly in October, just before the movie opened, during the trial of the two guards held responsible.[27] In September, John L. Spivak, "America's Greatest reporter," published his novel *Georgia Nigger*, based on his undercover investigations into conditions on Georgia chain gangs during the previous two years. The novel included an appendix containing photographs of shackled and tortured prisoners and copies of "whipping reports" as visual evidence of the veracity of his account.[28] Serialized in several newspapers in the final months of 1932 and credited with "the weight and authority of a sociological investigation" by its *New York Times* reviewer, Spivak's novel fueled the press controversy created by the "sweatbox" trial and encouraged a number of periodicals including *Harper's* and *New Republic* to launch a campaign for the abolition of the chain gang.[29]

Concerned that the chain gang pictures might "create another censorship problem of major proportions" as the gangster cycle had done, Jason Joy, Director of the Studio Relations Committee (SRC), the body then responsible for administering the Production Code, tried unsuccessfully to dissuade each of the three companies from developing their projects.[30] Selznick, convinced that there would probably be only one successful movie in this cycle, pressed ahead to bring *Hell's Highway* to market as far ahead of *Fugitive* as possible, while Zanuck maintained that he owned "the only legitimate chain gang story on the market and, incidentally, the property that started the interest."[31] Universal was, however, persuaded to set *Laughter in Hell* in 1880, "removing the suggestion that [the brutality of the chain gang system] is a current problem."[32]

For the SRC, the chain gang pictures presented three main difficulties. The first was what Joy called the "oversensitivity" of Southerners "on all matters pertaining to their manners and customs," and the related issue of industry policy as to "whether we are willing to incur the anger of any large section by turning our medium of entertainment to anything which may be regarded as a wholesale indictment" of a state, a region, or its legal practices.[33] Joy's second concern was with the "gruesomeness" with which the chain gang was depicted, while the third centered around balancing the dramatic requirement that the protagonist appear sympathetic, and therefore innocent, against the political obligation to minimize the movies' criticism of state authority as dishonest and vengeful.

In dealing with the hostile representation of the South and the brutality of the chain gang, the burden of the SRC's work lay in insuring that the movies conformed to conventions of inexplicitness and imprecision. Gruesomeness was straightforwardly handled, by informing the studios of what state censor boards were likely to delete: "The censors will not permit you to show a whipping in a two-shot, and I doubt if they will permit you to show the lash actually striking the men's bodies."[34] In *Fugitive*'s final shooting script, a number of details of the chain gang, including the sweatbox, were removed, and in October the SRC reported to Will Hays that "the element of brutality has been handled fairly well" in *Fugitive*, "with the exception of the lashing sequence which can be trimmed to suit local taste."[35] Within both Warners and RKO, there were debates about whether what Warners' director Roy Del Ruth called the movie's "morbid" tone should be relieved by more obvious box office appeal.[36] After previews in August, RKO hastily lightened *Hell's Highway* with several comedy scenes and a less pessimistic ending.[37] The trade reviews found these ameliorations had failed to "lift the story out of the slough" created by its central character being unsympathetic to a general audience because he was a convicted bank robber.[38] The unenthusiastic response to *Hell's Highway* may well have helped Zanuck in his insistence on not diluting *Fugitive*'s brutal sequences.

In representing the South so as to minimize offensiveness to Southern white sensibilities, the principal strategy was imprecision. In all three movies Joy drew the producers' attention to the importance of avoiding "any distinguishing feature that might be identified, even with a stretch of the imagination, as belonging to any one state."[39] In the light of the publicity given to the "sweatbox" trial, Joy assumed that "the average motion picture fan will probably think" *Fugitive* was set in Florida, but he correctly anticipated that such vagueness would not appease the officials of Georgia.[40]

The third problem was, however, intransigent. It was a Production Code requirement that if Allen was to remain unpunished at the end of the movie, he be innocent, and as *Variety*'s critique of *Hell's Highway* suggested, innocence was also conventionally necessary to secure audience sympathy. Moreover, since the story was allegedly true and the author's veracity relied on his innocence, Allen had to be represented as an innocent victim. But because the story was allegedly true, the fictional option adopted in *Laughter in Hell*, of making the protagonist the victim of a malign individual, could not be followed lest some individual Georgia prison official took litigious objection to his misrepresentation as a figure of evil. While the movie's press book and advertising campaign sought to stage *Fugitive* as the escape of truth – "They can't let me go now! I've seen too much! And I've dared to tell the whole hideous truth about it! … They've got to shut me up because they know I've lifted the lid off hell!" – the SRC offered an alternative interpretation to state censor boards considering banning or cutting the movie, presenting it not as "a preachment against the chain gang system in general, but a strongly individualized story of one man's personal experiences arising from one particular miscarriage of justice," made "with a proper consideration for the requirements of entertainment."[41]

As *Variety* suggested, *Fugitive*'s simultaneous nationwide release was intended to capitalize on the media attention given to "the current chain gang abolition activity." Nevertheless, the trade paper initially thought that "its chances of getting into the important money are slim," while the *Hollywood Filmograph* was convinced that "the public would never want to see such a picture – that people wanted escape from depressing things" (Jacobs 1939, 522). Against the nervous expectations of the Warner Bros.' Sales Department about the marketability of a movie with an evident lack of "femme appeal" and enough "gruesomeness" to cause walkouts at the preview, *Fugitive* was a resounding financial success. In the week after its release, Zanuck triumphantly circulated to production staff the texts of two telegrams received from Charles Einfield, head of Sales:

> Fugitive biggest Broadway sensation in last three years. … must admit you people were right when we asked you to cut down on blood and brutal sequences and you refused. Audiences throughout America have vindicated your decision. (Quoted in O'Connor & Balio 1981, 37)

Fugitive's advertising makes it clear that it was directed at a male or male-led audience. The press book advocated: "Sell the picture as a big show … showing a stark realism that it took a lot of guts to make! ... Because of the topic, and the facts revealed, the picture will arouse the sympathy of all for 'the Fugitive,' and will have a great appeal for the women." *Variety*'s review observed that it was "a man's picture"; the unexpected ending was "a shocker for the average fan," and women in the audience would "shudder at its gruesome realism but they'll not be bored." Even with "its shortcomings on the romantic angle" and the lack of a happy ending, it "should get some big grosses."[42] *Fugitive*'s narrative trajectory shares with the gangster cycle of 1930–1931 and the fallen woman cycle problems of resolution emanating from the moral status of their protagonists. *Fugitive* seems "bleaker" (the adjective used most often by critics) in its ending than the gangster movies because it incorporates the fallen woman cycle's structure of sympathy into a male melodrama. While *Fugitive* was a commercial success, the exercise proved difficult to repeat, since the protagonist-as-victim was not easily integrated into audience expectations of masculine narrative assertiveness. It was by far the most successful topical picture of the decade, and earned much of its cultural currency from that fact.

Burbanking

Ironically, the very element that gave *Fugitive* its emotional power – its capacity to arouse sympathy for its protagonist – was also the component that occasioned most criticism of its social effectiveness, at least from the left. Critic Harry Alan Potamkin, who described *Fugitive* as "probably the best film in a long time from Hollywood," argued that it nevertheless remained a "personality film" rather than offering an explanation for "the existence of a medievalism like the chain gang." A "complete chain gang picture," he thought, would require a combination of *Hell's Highway*'s initial social analysis and *Fugitive*'s characterization of "the state as nemesis," together with its "inspired conclusion" (1977, 203, 207).

Potamkin gave particularly articulate voice to a persistent concern of left intellectuals inside and outside Hollywood, at the time and since: Hollywood's protagonist-driven movies were "hopelessly individualist," unable to frame issues except as personal conflicts, since the "social" or the "historical" frame "must never compete with Paul Muni."[43] Like the prison pictures before it, *Fugitive* redirected anger at the conditions that created the chain gang into "indignation against the unjust treatment of the innocent hero" (Roffman & Purdy 1981, 28). As Jason Joy's interpretation of the movie to state censor boards suggested, this narrative strategy of focusing a movie's exposé of a social problem on an individual provided a way of accommodating the Production Code's insistence that the conditions from which the problem emanated be represented not as endemic but as the result of the actions of bad individuals, and therefore remediable through a fantastical act of benevolence. Any fundamental criticism of the social and economic order lay buried, as Matthew Bernstein has argued, "under the contingencies of individual personality" (1994, 78). Although the archetypal expression of this narrative occurred in Zanuck's 1934 production of "Victor Hugo's *Les Misérables*" (which Zanuck described as "I'm a Fugitive from a Chain Gang in costume"),[44] *Variety* named the strategy "Burbanking" after the location of the Warner Bros. studio where it was most extensively practiced.[45] In Nick Roddick's interpretation of the *Variety* term, to "Burbank" was to remove "the potentially dangerous implications of a contemporary subject ... by a deft manipulation of the narrative and a suitable 'melodramatisation' of motives" (1983, 252). Burbanking explained why intellectuals on the left "considered Hollywood as embodying the possibility, rather than the actuality, of progressive cinema": Topical movies might engage their audiences through their initial exposition of a social problem, but the problem was then individualized and resolved without the movie ever proposing a wider solution (Giovacchini 2001, 52).

For the rest of the decade, left-wing critics and screenwriters debated the limitations and possibilities of Classical Hollywood's "personality film" as they returned to the question of whether studio-produced pictures could "simultaneously display the people's world accurately, give audiences what they wanted to see, and move the masses to action."[46] Against Peter Ellis's criticism in *New Masses* that Warners' *Black Fury* (1935) depiction of a mining strike was "a calculated attack on the rank and file movement" intended "to confuse millions of workers," *New Republic*'s critic Otis Ferguson argued that however much its message had been softened, it was still "the most powerful strike picture that has yet been made," because its characters "are so cleverly worked into a pattern of cause and result, environment and hopes, that they were neither block symbols nor foreigners, but people you knew."[47] Movies, he insisted,

> don't go over with the popular audience unless they are built to move and enlist people's belief by means of characters sustained through their make-believe problems, conflicts, joys, what-not. So much of a film's production is taken up with building these qualities tightly in, that when you have to turn about and spend most of the time sketching a wide historic or economic background – well, trouble.

He encouraged his fellow critics on the left to "stop demanding a ten-reel feature on the Rise of Western Imperialism and look around to see what *can* be done with pictures" (1971, 166–167). In her 1939 book *America at the Movies*, Margaret Thorp observed that "when it can be done without boring the others who are more important because more numerous, the industry delights to win the approval of the 'class' audience, the 'intellectuals,' as it politely calls them, who want 'art' in their movies and 'content' as well as escape and excitement and glamour" (1946, 24). While the intellectuals might debate the ideological vices and virtues of Burbanking, the studios remained as committed to its aesthetic strategy as they were to avoiding political controversy. They recognized clearly that editorial cinema, in which "the express purpose of the producer [was] to make a picture that will attract public thought and criticism to the problem presented ... presages difficulties" for the industry's public relations.[48] These difficulties were most succinctly explained by the MPPDA's Canadian representative, Colonel John Cooper, reporting on Canadian censors' criticisms of RKO's 1932 juvenile delinquency picture *Are These Our Children?*:

> They reasoned that if we say our pictures are intended for entertainment and not for education, we cannot depart from this argument on occasion to ask that a picture be passed for its educational value. In other words, they tell us that we cannot have our pie and eat it.[49]

Nevertheless, Peter Roffman and Jim Purdy argue that regardless of these constraints, by early 1934, the studios had developed a narrative formula within which contemporary events could safely be represented: No matter what viewpoint the films took, that of conservative populism or liberal New Dealism, the trouble was always the same – shysterism. And in both cases, a hero-redeemer, whether the populist country crusader bearing the strength of the pioneers or the liberal New Dealer representing a strong federal government, was ready to protect the "little people," the masses of innocent victims, from all manner of social parasites and selfish profiteers (1981, 87–88). The recovery of federal authority resolved the tension between the attempt to address causes and the desire to avoid blaming the government or official agencies implicit in the industry's earlier representations of the topical. Warners in particular responded to the implementation of Roosevelt's New Deal policies in a cycle of topical pictures that presented federal authority as a *deus ex machina* resolution of its protagonists' problems, in *Heroes for Sale* (released in July 1933), *Wild Boys of the Road* (released in October 1933), and *Massacre* (released in January 1934), for example. Nick Roddick has called *Massacre* "the New Deal picture *par excellence*," charting its central character's progress from an initial violent response to the discovery of an injustice to a recognition of the federal government's benevolent authority as it rights the wrongs perpetrated by previous administrations (1983, 150). The movie was part of a short-lived cycle of pictures sympathetic to Native Americans released in the first half of 1934, coinciding with the passage of the Indian Reorganization Act, which sought to establish self-determination and cultural plurality among Native American communities, but despite the industry's belief that public opinion was in sympathy with the pictures' criticism, all three pictures in the cycle failed badly at the box office.[50]

Once positive representations of ameliorative solutions had become possible, the environmentalist thesis articulated by *Public Enemy* and the Chicago school of sociology could return to the fold of Hollywood's justificatory plot devices. In 1937, Samuel Goldwyn's "gorgeous" production of Sidney Kingsley's Broadway success *Dead End* was strongly promoted as a social document, declaring in its press book that "*Dead End* cries aloud to America to suffocate its criminals in the cradle. It beseeches Society to do something to alleviate the disease-breeding tenements in which its future citizens are asked to grow strong."[51] Its advertising featured endorsements from civic leaders as well as journalists, and a review in the *New York Post* declared it "the finest social drama of which the screen has record ... a masterpiece of propagandist cinematographic art," which should have been shown to the Congressional committees that "crippled the Wagner housing act" in the most recent session of Congress: "Best of all, it will be seen by all classes and kinds of people, seen by the millions who ought to have this story presented to them. They will be entertained and troubled and made to think. No drama could do more."[52]

Writing in 1939, Margaret Thorp argued that the issues taken up in movies of social comment tended to be "causes in which 'everybody' believes," like "the importance of preventing crime ... or the necessity for better housing," and that their proposed remedies – "a little more understanding and charity on the part of the rich" – were placebos. The intellectuals, she declared, "were encouraged by the beginnings of these films, but not by their fade-outs" (1946, 165). Environmentalism provided a generalized cause that could be invoked without targeting specific individuals or institutions. A reformist social agenda was an integral element of the late 1930s cycle of juvenile crime movies, evident not only in the movies' publicity but woven firmly and in detail into their structure. Nevertheless, *Angels with Dirty Faces* presented Cagney as "both a pariah and a role model to aspire to," and the movie's press book seemed to revel in these contradictions, simultaneously editorializing its "strong social message" that "the children of the slums ... be given the helping hand that will spell for them the difference between a good life and a life of crime" and advertising its unmatched depiction of the "glamour of gangsterism."[53]

However ideologically compromised *Dead End* or *Angels with Dirty Faces* might have been by their glamour lighting, set design, and concluding sentiments, their self-contradictory representations constituted a commercial response to a perceived audience demand. They also embodied what Saverio Giovacchini has called Hollywood's "realistic paradigm" (2001, 132), in which contradictory notions of "realism" and "social value" could cohabit in an aesthetic coalition as broad and as imprecisely defined as the "complex, contradictory, and discordant *ensemble*" of social forces that traveled under the banner of the Popular Front.[54] It provided a middle ground for the interaction of an assortment of artistic, political, and commercial motives to interact in "creative, and often expedient, misunderstandings ... a realm of constant invention, which was just as constantly presented as convention."[55] One of the shared assumptions of this middle ground was what Eric Smoodin has called a "popular-front sensibility about the possibilities for film to build better, more-informed, and enlightened citizens" (2004, 80), which motivated the film appreciation programs that progressive educationalists introduced into schools in increasing numbers in the second half of the decade. According to the textbook for one of these programs, "the most important question of all" for students to ask, before any consideration of aesthetic merit, was: "Does the [photo] play have any social value? Does it leave some part of its meaning in the minds of those who saw it, and will it govern their thoughts and actions after they have left the theater?"[56]

Film reviewers similarly regarded social criticism as a key criterion for critical praise. In reviewing Warners' *They Won't Forget* (1937), based on the 1915 lynching of Leo Frank in Georgia, the Brooklyn *Daily Eagle*'s critic drew parallels with the then-current Scottsboro case and stated that the picture "should be seen by every citizen of the United States ... it teaches a lesson that can be taken to heart by people in every section of the country" (quoted in Bernstein 2009, 115). The movie's publicity sought to position it "somewhere between fact and fiction," comparing it to *Fugitive* and describing it as "a dramatic, uncompromising indictment of the legal and social system which can railroad an innocent man to his death solely on the strength of circumstantial evidence."[57] In explanation of the movie's lack of well-known actors, the press book "quoted" director Mervyn LeRoy as claiming:

> *They Won't Forget* is such a powerful human story and so true to actual life, that I want people seeing it to believe they are watching life move before their eyes. If they see actors who look to them just like people on the street, rather than actors they have seen in a number of different pictures, they will believe the story, feel it more convincingly.

Hollywood's Popular Front

Hollywood's engagement with social and political issues in the second half of the 1930s was the product of a matrix of intersecting factors. The opportunities presented by the introduction of sound had drawn many liberal and radical writers and performers to Hollywood, seeking to address a national audience. From mid-decade, they were augmented by European émigrés escaping Nazism. Hollywood was a significant center of Popular Front activity, both in the form of direct political activity and as expressions, however compromised and negotiated, in popular culture. By mid-decade, left intellectuals writing on film in the United States had largely abandoned their commitment to Soviet montage theory and moved to a "less formulated, more inductive approach" that looked to redeploy Hollywood's conventions of emotional identification, character development, and linear narrative to progressive ends, acknowledging the importance of an "emotional platform" to appeal to audiences, and accepting the proposition that "progressive content could entertain as well as generate thought" (Robé 2010, 31–32, 11; Giovacchini 2001, 70). As Giovacchini suggests, the filmmakers who coalesced around the Hollywood Anti-Nazi League were "trying to make the Hollywood film more responsive to the issues of the day, while maintaining its ability to engage the masses," recognizing that the value of Walter Wanger's *Blockade* (1938) "was its popularity, which was, in turn, predicated upon its staying close to the Hollywood formula" (2001, 86).

Just as it is naïve to accept *Our Daily Bread* (1934) or *The Grapes of Wrath* (1940) as documentary realism, so is it also too simplistic to dismiss Hollywood's engagement with the Depression as merely escapism or Burbanking. As at all other times, people in the 1930s went to the movies for a heightened but contained emotional experience. They expected not only to be taken on a journey but also returned safely to their point of departure. Catharsis was not what they were after; at least, not every Friday night. Expressing her concern at what she called "the horror of realism," Thorp acknowledged that "people ought to be aware of the cruelties practised on mankind by man," but then asked: "how often is it good for an audience to spend an evening in a chain gang? Surely not so often as once a week" (1946, 170). As David Eldridge has argued, "ostensibly happy or unrealistic endings could not totally undercut the dark and often threatening images and situations that preceded them" (2008, 81). Lawrence Levine cautions against assuming that audiences in the 1930s unthinkingly accepted Hollywood's "happy endings," and posits the possibility "that audiences were able to learn from the main thrust of the films they saw, even while they derived comfort and pleasure from the formulaic endings" (1993, 253).

This contradiction was articulated in the distance between Thorp's assertion in 1939 that "audiences wanted to be cheered up when they went to the movies; they had no desire to see on the screen the squalor and misery of which there was too much at home" (1946, 17), and Darryl Zanuck's claim, the same year, that "when times are hard" audiences wanted "dramas, heavy stuff. They don't want anyone up there on the screen being just too gay for words when the factory's closing down next week."[58] It also manifested itself in productions. At the end of the decade, the contradiction was staged in *Sullivan's Travels* (1941), which simultaneously debunks its protagonist's Popular Front desire to employ film as a "sociological and artistic medium" and "draws the viewer into just the kind of 'social problem' movie that Sullivan's producers say it is impossible to get people to watch," before finally disavowing any responsibility for providing its audience with anything other than entertainment (Eldridge 2008, 82–83).

Some Popular Front organizations sought to mobilize consumer demand for progressive films by emulating and countering the activities of conservative pressure groups such as the Legion of Decency. Created in March 1937, the Associated Film Audiences (AFA) represented church, social, labor, and educational groups and aimed to encourage Hollywood "to produce films that give a true and socially useful portrayal of the contemporary scene" and "better the understanding between racial and religious groups." Advocates maintained that "constant agitation by audience organizations for better films" had led to the production of movies such as *The Life of Emile Zola*, *Fury*, *Black Legion*, and *Dead End*.[59] These audience organizations were in part an outgrowth of the Better Films Movement organized by civic and women's groups since the early 1920s, which had alternated between bouts of cooperation with the industry and condemnation of it. Although frequently derided for their complaints about the movies' emphasis on sex and violence, many of the movement's members were political liberals who had consistently argued for a more socially aware cinema from Hollywood. Some producers cooperated with the AFA in much the same way that they dealt with the Legion of Decency; MGM's publicity director Howard Dietz declared, "We do not care what their political views may be if they can help us put people in line at box offices" (quoted in Robé 2010, 17–18). Nevertheless, the studios ignored the AFA's opposition to "militarist" films, welcoming federal government "inspiration and assistance" in the production of a cycle of pictures built around the armed services such as *Submarine D-1*, *Annapolis Salute*, and *Wings over Honolulu* (all 1937) (quoted in Beard & Beard 1939, 597).

Black Legion

One of the topical pictures that Warner Bros. announced in June 1936, *Black Legion*, was quite literally ripped from the headlines. Its production was announced less than a month after the main events in its story took place, and less than two weeks after the central character in them confessed to the murder that is the central event in the story; two weeks later, Warners submitted a treatment to the Production Code Administration. The studio's speed was in part driven by knowledge that Columbia was also developing a story from the same incidents, which became *Legion of Terror*, released at the beginning of November 1936, two months ahead of *Black Legion*.[60]

The Black Legion was a secret organization founded in Ohio in the mid-1920s as an offshoot of the Ku Klux Klan. In the revived form in which it existed in the early 1920s, the Klan was a large and politically significant nativist organization active across much of the country, particularly the South and Midwest, with at least three million members at its height in 1924, a figure indicating that one of every three or four white, adult, Protestant American males in those regions was a Klansman. As firmly anti-Catholic and anti-Semitic as it was anti-Negro, the Klan collapsed rapidly in the later 1920s, after the passage of anti-immigration legislation and after its leadership was revealed to be corruptly profiteering from the membership. Its disintegration gave rise to a number of comparable organizations, of which the Black Legion, with a membership of perhaps 100,000 in the four Midwest states of Michigan, Indiana, Ohio, and Illinois, was one of the most prominent and exotic.

Its members were mainly working-class Anglo-Saxon men, most of them poorly educated migrants from the South working in unskilled jobs in steel or automobile assembly plants, their nativism exaggerated by the economic conditions of the Depression and their fears of losing their jobs to immigrant labor. Like the KKK, the Black Legion was notionally dedicated to upholding "Protestantism, Americanism, and Womanhood," while in reality it operated as a protective organization finding and preserving its members' jobs. Like its costumes, its rituals were even more bizarre than the Klan's and read, according to the *New York Times*, "as if they had been composed by Tom Sawyer to impress Huck Finn and Indian Joe."[61] But the Black Legion engaged in a variety of acts of nativist vigilantism and terrorism, including crimes often described as lynchings.[62] It was involved in the antiunion violence perpetrated by Ford and General Motors in Detroit, and between 1933 and 1935, the Black Legion bombed or burned a number of left-wing bookstores and meeting halls and shot two communist labor organizers, all without police interference.

Some of the more extravagant plans of which its members boasted included a plot to kill one million Jews by planting mustard gas bombs in every American synagogue during Yom Kippur, another plot to kill Jews in Detroit by putting typhoid germs in milk, and very vague plans to storm every Army arsenal in the country on a given signal. There was no real evidence that these were ever anything more than fantasies by the Black Legion's leadership, but together with the secret rituals and paraphernalia they gave rise to blood-curdling newspaper headlines for much of the summer of 1936, when one of their actual crimes, the murder of Charles Poole, a Catholic married to a Protestant, was investigated. The chief suspect quickly confessed, and he and 10 others were tried, convicted, and sentenced to life imprisonment in September, four months after the murder.

Two events earlier in 1936, both involving MGM, provide an industrial context for the story of *Black Legion*. In February 1936, MGM purchased the screen rights to the Nobel Prize-winning author Sinclair Lewis's novel *It Can't Happen Here*, about a fascist takeover of the United States, and then decided not to produce a film version of it, allegedly as a result of pressure from the Hays Office, the Republican Party, and the German and Italian governments. While

MGM insisted that they had made a purely business decision based on the likely expense of the production, Lewis protested that the industry's political timidity meant that "a film cannot be made showing the horrors of fascism and extolling the advantages of Liberal Democracy because Hitler and Mussolini might ban other Hollywood films from their countries." In response, Terry Ramsaye, editor of *Motion Picture Herald*, suggested that MGM's decision "has all of the vast significance that would attach to a decision by ... Armour and Company to discontinue a brand of ham." Accurately predicting that Lewis's eminence would lead to the story's being inscribed into Hollywood's history, Ramsaye observed that while discontented readers directed their indignation at the authors of what they read,

> the motion picture spectator, when he is annoyed, is annoyed with "the damned movies" and likely as not the theatre where he saw the annoying picture. ... If his publishers were continuously on a battlefront defending the book business from attempts at punitive taxation, from measures of censorship, from measures addressed at nationalization of their industry, they would perhaps at times weigh the possible effect of product of political implication and influence.[63]

Within the discourse of the industry, this was an economic and not an ideological consideration, but throughout the 1930s the industry voiced a public commitment to what Will Hays called "'pure entertainment' – entertainment unadulterated, unsullied by any infiltration of 'propaganda.'" In 1938, Hays declared it "pleasant to report that American motion pictures continue to be free from any but the highest possible entertainment purpose. ... Propaganda disguised as entertainment would be neither honest salesmanship nor honest showmanship." The distinction between entertainment and propaganda could only be determined, he claimed, "through the process of common sense" (quoted in Thorp 1946, 160), embodied for the industry in the Production Code Administration (PCA). Its head, Joseph Breen, insisted that:

> the members of the Production Code Administration are regarded by producers, directors, and their staffs, as "participants in the processes of production" ... The studios have come, in recent years, to look to us for sound guidance on matters of political censorship.[64]

Regarding the PCA as representing a national consensus on political issues as well as moral ones, Breen denied that there was anything "sinister" in his rejecting material "in which police officials are shown to be dishonest; or ... in which lawyers, or doctors, or bankers, are indicted as a class":

> Surely the organized motion picture industry is performing a useful public service when spokesmen for the Association insist that screen material involving racial conflicts between whites and blacks be handled in such a way as to avoid fanning the flame of race prejudice. The film *Fury* proves conclusively that there is a way to handle satisfactorily and with tremendous dramatic power the heinous crime of lynching without including the racial angle.[65]

Fury, directed by Fritz Lang and starring Spencer Tracy, was released on June 5, at the height of newspaper coverage of the Black Legion case and the day after Warners' announcement. In a laudatory review in the *New York Times* on June 6, film reviewer Frank Nugent drew parallels between the mob violence in the movie and the activities of "Detroit's Black Legion and kindred '100 per cent American'" societies (1936, 21).

As Breen pointed out, however, *Fury* discussed lynching without mentioning race, and he recommended the same policy to the makers of *Black Legion*. Robert Lord's original treatment emphasized the Black Legion's religious bigotry, redbaiting, and anti-Semitism. On June 18, Breen wrote to Jack Warner that "certain elements in the material submitted to us" made the story, in its present form, not acceptable from the point of view of the Production Code, because "it has been our policy not to approve stories which raise and deal with the provocative and inflammatory subjects of racial and religious prejudice."[66] Breen was by no means alone in these views. Jewish organizations frequently expressed the view that the endemic presence of anti-Semitism in at least some parts of American society suggested that it was wiser to avoid overt condemnations of Nazism or overt defenses of Jewry on American film screens, in case they provoked a hostile reaction. "There are times," argued Rabbi William H. Fineshriber, who claimed to have persuaded MGM not to make *It Can't Happen Here*, "when to say nothing is better than to say something favorable" (Herman 2001, 15).

Black Legion's producer, Robert Lord, nevertheless persuaded Breen to let him develop a script that would "treat the subject as broadly and strongly as he wished, so that we might test out the limit of the acceptability of the treatment of such subjects as religious and racial prejudices."[67] Initially, Lord and studio head Hal Wallis planned *Black Legion* as a major production, possibly starring Edward G. Robinson, and suggesting strong parallels both to the rise of Nazism in Germany and to the possible emergence of a native American fascism depicted in *It Can't Happen Here*. The movie itself was no more than ambivalent in its expression of the ethnic and religious prejudice underpinning the Legion's activities. The Legion members did not inflame the audience's prejudices by explicitly naming any religious or ethnic group. One of their victims was evidently Irish, but not identified as Catholic, although the churches mentioned several times in the picture were identified as Protestant. And in a typically inventive Hollywood circumlocution, some of the characters disparaged others as "Huniaks," a term of ethnic derision either fictional or so obscure as to be fictional in effect.[68]

From a conventional historical perspective, *Black Legion* appears as evasive as every other piece of Burbanking in its articulation of political controversy. But it is arguable that "the limit of acceptability" in the movie's treatment of religious or racial prejudice actually lay not in its textual features but in the contradictions inherent in its intertextual engagements. Warners' publicity emphasized the factual origins of the story and distributed stories suggesting that the ending was rewritten from newspaper reports on the day the verdict was returned in Detroit. The press book encouraged exhibitors to connect the movie to the issues raised by the actual events by recruiting editorials in the local newspaper and soliciting "civic-minded individuals and groups" to give talks. At the same time, the movie conventionally declared itself to be fictitious, and a number of changes were made late in the production to comply with the legal department's concerns to protect the studio from possible libel suits. *Motion Picture Herald* played with the contradictions of the movie's claims to be simultaneously fictional and based on actual events:

> It is not possible, you see, to say that the film closely parallels the facts because the film pointedly declares that it does not. And it isn't possible to say that it does not, you see, because it does. ... Probably it is possible, of course, to say to showmen that, if you would like a picture that is what you would expect this picture to be if you weren't told what it isn't, then this is the picture you would like.[69]

Most reviews were, however, much less equivocal, emphasizing what Frank Nugent called "one of the most courageous, forthright and bitter editorials the screen has written ... editorial cinema at its best – ruthless, direct, uncompromising ... a quasi-documentary record":

> For this is the unforgettable, the horrible thing about "Black Legion" – it did happen here! Thousands of our illustrious Midwestern citizens did ... don their childish regalia with its skull-and-cross-bones insignia, they did hold their secret conclaves and choose their victims. And homes were burned and shops destroyed and men flogged and lynched as a consequence. ... "Black Legion" will not stay in its place as a cinema fiction. It strikes too hard, too deep and too close to the mark. ... I hope the Midwest can take it. (1937, 21)

The movie's final trial scene confronted its audience with what Graham Greene called "the real horror" of its story, the knowledge that the Legion's robes and hoods "hide the weak and commonplace faces you have met over the counter and minding the next machine."[70] Echoing the trial scenes in *Fury*, shots of the convicted killers and their families confronted at least some members of its audience with images of themselves and their own history. Nobody watching *Black Legion* when it opened in Michigan in January 1937, in the middle of the United Auto Workers' Flint sit-down strike, would not have known what it depicted, from the newspaper and radio reports, the lurid descriptions of the Legion in *True Detective* and *Official Detective Stories*, and other media accounts.[71] Nobody listening to the movie's rabble-rousing speech about "poisonous vipers" clinging "tenaciously to their alien doctrines, foreign faiths, and un-American morals" would be in any doubt about the religious and ethnic identity of the "Hunyaks" who were the Legion's victims.

Whether the Midwest could "take it" was another question. Exhibitor comments in the trade press suggested that despite the movie's accolades from the National Board of Review and comparisons to *I Am a Fugitive from a Chain Gang*, it did not draw well,

Figure 11.2 In the final scene in Raoul Walsh's *Black Legion* (1937, producer Robert Lord), images of the convicted killers and their families confront those members of its audience who had belonged to the Ku Klux Klan with representations of themselves and their own history.

most likely because the "gruesome" advertisements had kept audiences away. One Detroit exhibitor commented, "Could not ask for a better picturization of the Black Legion, but apparently our customers have had enough of the Black Legion from the papers."[72] While Warners remained wedded to its commercial strategy of serving up topical material "ripped from the headlines," this piece of editorial cinema may have confronted at least some of its audiences with too recognizable and too antagonistic a representation of themselves, masquerading as commercial entertainment.

Although alienating the audience was unlikely to be a commercially viable strategy, avoiding direct confrontation was not necessarily always a gesture of political evasion or ideological timidity. While *Fury* was criticized, both at the time and subsequently, for its representation of lynching without mentioning race, Amy Louise Wood emphasizes that prominent antilynching campaigners strongly endorsed the movie for that very reason.[73] Walter White and Roi Otley, then leading the National Association for the Advancement of Colored People (NAACP) campaign to pass the Costigan-Wagner federal antilynching bill through Congress, insisted that *Fury* would have "a wider and more sympathetic audience," and thus contribute more effectively to the fight against lynching, precisely because the victim was white (Wood 2009, 255). *Fury* provided a spectacular representation of the antilynching movement's rhetoric, which had consciously sought to deflect public attention away from questions of racism and black suffering to present lynching as "a barbaric abomination to American ideals":

> If lynching opponents of the 1930s rhetorically posited white society and the white psyche to be the primary victim of lynching, antilynching films made them literally so … depict[ing] lynching through the experiences of the victim, the individual unjustly accused and punished without due process. (Wood 2009, 226, 232)

Wood argues that *Fury*'s deployment of Classical Hollywood's rhetoric of emotional engagement allowed viewers to identify with the victims of lynching, and "impelled white southern viewers to support law and civility without directly attacking their regional pride or their notions of white supremacy." Unlike the rhetoric of campaign propaganda, the movies "allowed viewers to adopt an antilynching position comfortably and quietly, as entertainment" (2009, 259). In a comparable argument, Alex Lichtenstein suggests that *Fugitive* was more effective in bringing the barbarities of Georgia's penal system to public attention than Spivak's *Georgia Nigger* "precisely because it did not ask Americans to confront their racial caste system that made the chain gang possible" (1995, 654).

However persuasive such justifications may have been, the movies' representations were also occasioned by the need to compromise with the studios' commercial strategies and the requirements of the Production Code. Breen's initial response to the script for *They Won't Forget* was that it was "both in basic theme and in detail … in violation of the Production Code and … utterly impossible" because "no political censor, anywhere, would allow such a picture to be publicly exhibited."[74] But Breen's approach, and the idea of entertainment unsullied by propaganda, was beginning to come under question, even within the MPPDA, principally because it exposed the industry to accusations of political censorship.

Conclusion: "An Official Welcome to Ideas"?

Although Walter Wanger's Spanish Civil War picture *Blockade*, released in June 1938, scrupulously avoided naming either party to the conflict, it provoked extensive and sometimes violent protests by Catholic organizations accusing Hollywood of communist propaganda, and denunciations by liberal groups who complained that "the Hays Office … sometimes performs its work so zealously as to make films not only safe but insipid."[75] Wanger, the producer most publicly critical of the Production Code and lauded by *Time* magazine and Popular Front organizations for being "in the forefront of Hollywood's crusade for social consciousness" (Bernstein 1994, 129), defended *Blockade*'s compromises by arguing that it represented an initial step toward creating more explicitly political pictures in Hollywood. Speaking at a July 1938 Conference on Freedom of the Screen, he declared that "it is not *Blockade* reactionaries are fighting against but against the fact that, if *Blockade* is a success, a flood of stronger and stronger films will appear and the films will not only talk but say something. … the time has come for Hollywood to strike back" (quoted in Bernstein 1994, 137).

While Hays might have shrugged off accusations that the industry was unprepared to experiment "with less popular themes aimed at smaller, more specific audiences" when they came from the liberal intelligentsia, the federal government's increasing concern to restrain the industry's oligopolistic trade practices made this much more serious. The antitrust suit filed by the Department of Justice in July 1938 implicated the PCA in the majors' restrictive practices. It alleged that the majors used the Code to exercise a practical censorship over the entire industry, restricting the production of pictures treating controversial subjects, hindering innovations by companies seeking to challenge their market control, and denying any opportunity "for new forms of artistic expression which are not approved by those in control of the major companies, even though there exist communities which would support them."[76] Over Breen's vociferous protests, an internal MPPDA investigation in 1938 recommended that some categories of picture, including newsreels, advertising, sponsored and government films, be regarded as falling outside the authority of the PCA, as should all issues other than a film's conformity "to standards of decency, morality and fairness embodied in the Production Code":

> If the film deals with a controversial subject, but is free from that which offends decency or is listed in the Code as morally objectionable, then the sole remaining question to be decided by the PCA should not be whether

> the film is "desirable" but whether the presentation deals fairly and honestly, and without deliberate deception, with the subject matter.[77]

The federal government's redefinition of what constituted unreasonable restraint of trade in the Paramount suit created a practical political need for the industry to encourage, or at least acquiesce in, the use of politically more controversial content as a way of demonstrating that the "freedom of the screen" was not hampered by the operations of the PCA. Like the imposition of stricter self-regulation earlier in the decade, this change was not occasioned by any clear public demand, but in order to maintain a political quiescence that would protect its oligopoly structure.

Instead of emphasizing the value of entertainment unsullied by propaganda in his 1939 Annual Report, Hays claimed that "The increasing number of pictures ... which treat honestly and dramatically many current themes proves that there is nothing incompatible between the best interests of the box-office and the kind of entertainment that raises the level of audience appreciation whatever the subject treated." Margaret Thorp identified Hays's changed tone as marking "the day the motion picture industry extended an official welcome to ideas" (1946, 160). This was in part the result of Hollywood's Popular Front coalition of liberals and radicals pressing for greater freedom of expression, and in part a recognition that a section of the audience wanted popular cinema to engage with issues of national importance (Smoodin 2004, 152). But it was also a pragmatic response to the industry's immediate political and legal situation, as the MPPDA sought to head off the federal government's challenge to its oligopoly structure. If Hays's rhetoric in 1939 echoed that of Sinclair Lewis in 1936, it did so for quite different reasons, as part of a campaign to persuade the government to recognize the "special significance and peculiarly difficult problems" of the film industry's international situation, a line of argument that would allow the MPPDA to gain government acceptance as an "essential industry" during the war (Wolfe 1990, 304).

The immediate beneficiaries of this change in policy were two explicitly anti-Nazi pictures then in production at Warner Bros. The Paul Muni biopic *Juarez*, released in June 1939, was part of Hollywood's contribution to Roosevelt's Good Neighbor policy of seeking to improve US relations with Latin America, but it was also intended by producer Wolfgang Reinhart to draw parallels to contemporary events in Europe, in a manner so explicit that "every child must recognize that Napoleon in his intervention in Mexico is no one other than Mussolini plus Hitler in their adventure in Spain" (quoted in Vasey 1997, 156). More directly, Hollywood's first explicitly anti-Nazi propaganda feature, *Confessions of a Nazi Spy* (1939), resisted the neutering that earlier interpretations of the PCA's authority would have imposed. Despite his profound concerns at the apparent acceptance of what publisher Martin Quigley called "the idea of radical propaganda on the screen," and his conviction that the industry should not "sponsor a motion picture dealing with so highly controversial a subject," Breen found himself obliged to write to studio head Jack Warner that "the Production Code Administration has neither the authority, nor responsibility, to pass upon a question of this kind."[78]

Although low-budget spy melodramas such as *Crack-Up* (1936), *Cipher Bureau* (1938), and *South of the Border* (1939) had made increasingly less ambiguous references to German espionage activities, *Confessions* was both a far more prestigious production and far more directly denunciatory than any picture that had preceded it. As the Burlington, North Carolina *Times-News* said, "*Confessions* lets the bars down. Germany is called Germany, bluntly; and all the secret menace, the insidious war of propaganda, [its] organization and nation-wide espionage designed to destroy democracy [is shown]."[79] In the movie's press book, Warner declared that "With this picture, I hope to do for the persecuted victims of Germany – Jews and Catholics – what we did for law and order with *Public Enemy*. The immediate result of that picture was to arouse the public to the horrors of gangsterdom and put Al Capone behind bars." Despite being simultaneously released to 100 first-run theaters nationwide and heavily promoted, however, *Confessions*, like *Juarez*, was not a commercial success. Although William Dieterle, the director of *Blockade* and *Juarez* and a leading member of the Hollywood Anti-Nazi League, told the readers of *Liberty* magazine in 1940 that he did not believe that progressive pictures ever lost money, and appealed to an audience that otherwise never attended Hollywood films, *Time* magazine reported that 19 separate Gallup surveys had established "that only New York audiences seem to want pictures with political content involving Hitler and the Nazis."[80] Margaret Thorp noted that *Confessions* and *Juarez* had "very nearly succeeded in satisfying the intellectuals," but while she personally applauded "this desire for films with content," she suspected that it was no more than "one of those unaccountable public whims which will fade out eventually like the craze for spectacular musicals or the enthusiasm for Marlene Dietrich" (1946, 174).

As the decade progressed, *I Am a Fugitive from a Chain Gang* became ensconced as the inescapable reference point for critics reviewing movies of social comment, however poorly the actual history of its reception and influence was remembered.[81] Kenneth Fearing's review of *Fury* in *New Masses*, for example, began by asking his readers, "How many of you can remember as far back as *Fugitive from a Chain Gang?* ... *Fury* is just like it, only better."[82] In the literature on film appreciation, *Fugitive* was invariably cited along with *All Quiet on the Western Front* (1930) as an exemplar of Hollywood's occasional "public responsibility": a Study Guide to the picture produced by the Progressive Education Association provided questions for school classes to debate, dealing "not only with the particular problems or situations portrayed in the film, but with related subjects," including the purpose of the prison system.[83] What had perhaps most embedded *Fugitive* in public critical memory, however, was its remarkable commercial success. Topical pictures, whatever their particular content, were almost invariably modestly budgeted program fare intended to fill distribution schedules, feed "the maw of exhibition," and avoid offense. Although political circumstances affecting the industry at the end of the decade relaxed the "restrictions on what the American screen shall show and say" (Wanger 1939, 46), the boundaries of Hollywood's expression remained constrained by the commercial realism that governed the studios' decisions.

Notes

1. For a discussion of the image of Hoover as heroic engineer, see Tichi 1987, 169–170.
2. *Motion Picture Herald*, November 5, 1932, 26; November 12, 1932, 39. United Artists used the slogan "Prosperity is Just Around the Corner" in trade advertisements for *Mr. Robinson Crusoe* during the election campaign. *Variety*, September 27, 1932, 15.
3. Banker A. H. Giannini, on whom the protagonist of *American Madness* was allegedly based, declared in Columbia's publicity that the picture "will do more than any other single agency to stop runs on banks which are started by false or malicious rumours." Letter, from A. H. Giannini (Chairman, General Executive Committee, Bank of America, L.A.) to Harry Cohn, 5-28-32, Production Code Administration Archive, Margaret Herrick Library, Academy of Motion Picture Arts and Sciences, Beverly Hills, California (hereafter PCA), *American Madness* file. In a letter to Harry Cohn about the script for *American Madness* on March 21, Jason Joy commented that "There is, of course, a real obligation on us to make certain that confidence in banking institutions at this time is not impaired." Four days later he advised Hays that "The bank stories I think are all right from a policy standpoint and will even do good by helping rebuild confidence in banking institutions. ... There is a realization in the studios of a responsibility not to impair confidence in banks and I foresee no danger of their doing so." PCA *American Madness* file.
4. Hays, Annual Report to the Motion Picture Producers and Distributors Association (MPPDA), March 31, 1934, quoted in Bergman 1972, 31.
5. While *Variety* reported that "every infant torn from a sobbing mother brought a happy smile to the box office" in 1931, the fallen woman cycle had waned considerably in quantity and popularity by the 1932–1933 production season (quoted in Balio 1993, 236).
6. Benjamin deCasseres, "Does Stage Realism Really Reflect Life?" *Theatre Magazine*, July 1929, 14–15.
7. John Anderson, "And This Is Realism," *Theatre Magazine*, April 1930, 18–19, 62.
8. Hays, President's Report to the MPPDA, April 11, 1932, 22; Memo, Wingate, November 30, 1932; Report, Wingate to Hays, December 2, 1932. PCA *She Done Him Wrong* file.
9. Alva Johnston, "The Wahoo Boy," *New Yorker*, November 10, 1934, 25, quoted in Custen 1997, 128.
10. See Richard Maltby, "The Spectacle of Criminality," in J. David Slocum (ed.), *Violence and American Cinema* (New York: Routledge, 2001), 117–152.
11. Jonathan Munby, *Public Enemies, Public Heroes: Screening the Gangster from Little Caesar to Touch of Evil* (Chicago: University of Chicago Press, 1999), 51; James Shelley Hamilton, "Some Gangster Films," *National Board of Review Magazine* (May 1931), reprinted in Stanley Hochman (ed.), *From Quasimodo to Scarlett: A National Board of Review Anthology, 1920–1940* (New York: Ungar, 1982), 144.
12. Zanuck to Joy, January 6, 1931, PCA *Public Enemy* file. Typography in original. Warners bought the story, "Beer and Blood," on December 1, 1930. The Final

Screenplay by Harvey Thew was dated January 18, 1931, and shooting began in February.

13. Warner Bros. press book for *The Public Enemy*.
14. *Variety* review of *The Public Enemy*, April 29, 1931; Will Hays, Annual Report of the President of the Motion Picture Producers and Distributors of America, Inc., March 30, 1931. Motion Picture Producers and Distributors of America, Inc. Archive (hereafter MPPDA), 1931, Meetings file. For an extended discussion, see Richard Maltby, "Why Boys Go Wrong: Gangsters, Hoodlums and the Natural History of Delinquent Careers," in Lee Grieveson, Esther Sonnet, and Peter Stanfield (eds), *Mob Culture: Hidden Histories of the American Gangster Film* (New Brunswick: Rutgers University Press, 2005), 41–66.
15. Thornton Delahanty, *New York Evening Post*, January 18, 1934.
16. *Motion Picture Herald*, November 26, 1932; October 15, 1932.
17. As well as being a prominent penal reformer, Lawes was a media personality in the early 1930s: He had been on the cover of *Time* magazine and began a six-year-long weekly radio series called *20,000 Years in Sing Sing* in early 1933. The series featured Lawes narrating dramatizations of the criminal careers of inmates, with a concluding moral.
18. *Grand Slam* was based on the novel *Grand Slam: The Rise and Fall of a Bridge Wizard* by Benjamin Russell Herts (New York, 1932). *Motion Picture Herald*, October 15, 1932.
19. Final draft of an article by Darryl F. Zanuck for the "Holiday Number" of *The Hollywood Reporter*, December 1932, in Behlmer 1986, 9–10.
20. "Warner Bros.," *Fortune*, December 1937, reprinted in Behlmer 1986, 56.
21. Production trends are analyzed in Balio 1993, 179–312.
22. For example, *Washington Masquerade*, *Washington Merry-Go-Round*, *The President Vanishes*, and *The Dark Horse* were all released during the 1932 election campaign (Balio 1993, 310).
23. "Warner Bros.," *Fortune*, December 1937, reprinted in Behlmer 1986, 55.
24. For further discussion of this decision, see Richard Maltby, "Tragic Heroes? Al Capone and the Spectacle of Criminality, 1948–1931," in John Benson, Ken Berryman, and Wayne Levy (eds), *Screening the Past: VI Australian History and Film Conference Papers* (Melbourne: La Trobe University Press, 1995), 112–119.
25. *New York Times*, January 31, 1932; Matthew J. Mancini, "Foreword" to Burns 1997, xii; Isaac Herman Schwarz, "Welcome to Our Chain Gang," *New Republic*, April 8, 1931, 200–202.
26. In most respects, the movie is a noticeably faithful adaptation of Robert Burns's autobiography, but one of the changes it does make is to the protagonist's career. No production documentation discusses the decision to make James Allen an engineer; while it obviously provided more photogenic opportunities, the symbolic force of those images of bridges being built and blown up derived in part from the cultural resonance that had accrued to the figure of the engineer in the 1920s, a resonance that had been politically charged by the Republicans' deployment of its connotations. The change was made in the first draft of the script. It is conceivable that this change was politically motivated, since the first draft also contains some early scenes critical of businessmen who had profited from the war. See O'Connor and Balio 1981, 21–23. Burns was, however, working as a dynamiter in a New Jersey copper refinery in December 1932, when he was rearrested (Burns 1997, xiv).
27. "Florida sweat box," *Time*, October 24, 1932. *Hell's Highway* opens with a montage of newspaper headlines from the *Seattle Post-Intelligencer* referring to the Maillefert case: "Prison Guards Accused of Murder as Tortured Youth Dies in Sweat Box."
28. John L. Spivak, *Georgia Nigger* (New York: Brewer, Warren & Putnam, 1932); Spivak also published a pamphlet documenting conditions on the chain gang: *On the Chain Gang* (New York: International Pamphlets, 1932); "Dictators dissected," *Time*, May 25, 1936.
29. "Miss Latimer's Stories and Other Recent Works of Fiction," *New York Times*, October 16, 1932.
30. Interoffice memo from Lamar Trotti, March 31, 1932, PCA *Laughter in Hell* file.
31. Letter, Darryl Zanuck to Joy, March 30, 1932, PCA *I Am a Fugitive from a Chain Gang* file.
32. Interoffice memo from Lamar Trotti, March 31, 1932, PCA *Laughter in Hell* file.
33. Joy to Irving Thalberg and Darryl Zanuck, February 26, 1932, PCA *I Am a Fugitive from a Chain Gang* file. Joy's argument was echoed by both Warner Bros.' legal and story departments, which had recommended not purchasing *Fugitive* because "all the strong and vivid points in the story are certain to be eliminated" by censor boards. Memo from Warner Bros. story department, February 19, 1932, quoted in Schatz 1988, 143.
34. Joy to Laemmle, August 30, 1932, PCA *Laughter in Hell* file.
35. James Wingate to Hays, October 21, 1932, PCA *I Am a Fugitive from a Chain Gang* file.
36. Warner Bros. Interoffice memo, Roy Del Ruth to Hal Wallis (n.d., probably May or June 1932), Warner Bros. Production File, *I Am a Fugitive from a Chain Gang*.

37. August 18, 1932, David O. Selznick to B. B. Kahane; August 19, Kahane to Ned Depinet, RKO Production File, *Hell's Highway*.
38. *Variety*, September 27, 1932, 21. Mordaunt Hall in the *New York Times* concurred that the producers had failed "by being overeager to horrify audiences," while Richard Dix in the lead role was "vehement without being really effective"; his preaching about "the torturing of the felons ... would be all very well if it came from an upstanding character, and not, as it does, from a bank robber" (*New York Times*, September 26, 1932). One consequence of this widely held view is that so many innocent men go to prison in Classical Hollywood movies, in order that they can be exonerated in the last reel.
39. June 13, 1932, Selznick to C. D. White, RKO Production File, *Hell's Highway*.
40. Joy to Zanuck, July 26, 1932, PCA *I Am a Fugitive from a Chain Gang* file. The press book for the movie explicitly advised exhibitors that "the picture also affords a timely tie-up with the recent Maillefert trial in Florida."
41. Joy to censor boards in Chicago, Toronto, New York, October 17, 1932, PCA *I Am a Fugitive from a Chain Gang* file.
42. *Variety*, November 15, 1932, 19.
43. Lincoln Kerstein, "Film Problems of the Quarter," *Films*, 1 (Spring 1940), 24–25; quoted in Giovacchini 2001, 48.
44. Zanuck quoted in Alva Johnston, "The Wahoo Boy – II," *New Yorker*, November 17, 1934, 26. Zanuck explained that he was making *Les Misérables* in 1934 because "it is the story of a normal, family-loving man that found himself balked on every hand, a man that was persecuted, a man that was beaten – and a man that would steal a loaf of bread, if he had to, to feed his children. It's the theme of today" (R. P. White, "The Miracle Man of Hollywood," *Los Angeles Times Magazine*, November 4, 1934). Both quoted in Custen 1997, 189.
45. Nick Roddick, who calls the conclusion to his book *A New Deal in Entertainment: Warner Brothers in the 1930s* "The Burbanking of America," cites *Variety*'s critic Abel Green's review of *Black Fury* (1935) as his source: "*Black Fury* is basic box office. ... Provocative and attuned to a day and age where the administrative 'new deal' lends added significance to the story, *Black Fury* is something which the exploitive boys can go to town about ... Disturbing chiefly by inference, possibly left-wing radical by innuendo, canny Burbanking evidences studio wisdom in pruning, motivating and editing in just the right degrees" (quoted in Roddick 1983, 174).
46. Moran and Rogin 2000, 107. Sidney Kaufman, "America at the Movies," *Films* (Spring 1940), 78–80; and Sawyer Falk, "Towards a New Ethical Base," *Films* (November 1939), 5.
47. Peter Ellis, "The Movies," *New Masses*, April 23, 1935, 29; Otis Ferguson, review of *Black Fury*, April 24, 1935, in Ferguson 1971, 73; Otis Ferguson, "Life Goes to the Pictures," *Films*, 1 (Spring 1940), 24–25, quoted in Giovacchini 2001, 48.
48. March 18, 1933, Wingate to Julia Kelly, PCA *The Mayor of Hell* file.
49. Col. John Cooper, head of the MPPDA office in Canada, to Col. Joy, June 24, 1932, PCA *Are These Our Children?* file.
50. Wingate to W. D. Kelly of MGM, New York, April 12, 1934, PCA *Laughing Boy* file.
51. *Dead End* press book; Allen Larsen, "1937: Movies and New Constructions of the Star," in Hark 2007, 183.
52. "Out of Hollywood," *New York Post*, August 31, 1937.
53. Fran Mason, *American Gangster Cinema: From Little Caesar to Pulp Fiction* (London: Palgrave, 2002), 45; "Editorial," in *Angels with Dirty Faces* press book (1938). The press book told exhibitors to sell the picture "as a powerful human document," encouraging them to enlist "co-operation from leaders in welfare work, heads of organizations interested in youth uplift work, women's clubs, civic clubs, PTAs, Boy Scouts, Big Brothers and city officials."
54. Robé 2010, 22, is quoting Antonio Gramsci, *Selections from the Prison Notebooks*, ed. and trans. Quintin Hoare and Geoffrey Nowell Smith (New York: International Publishers, 1971), 366.
55. Richard White, *The Middle Ground: Indians, Empires, and Republics in the Great Lakes Region, 1650–1815* (New York: Cambridge University Press, 1991), x, 52. White's description is of the cultural interactions between Europeans and Native Americans in the Great Lakes region during the eighteenth century, and is concerned with the face-to-face interactions of the frontier. Yet he does provide a powerfully suggestive model of how what he calls the "search for accommodation and common meaning" between cultures takes place, and his model has much broader applicability than the case he considers.
56. Sarah McLean Mullen, *How to Judge Motion Pictures*, quoted in Smoodin 2004, 9.
57. One publicity department memo suggested that the use of newsreel type for the titles in the trailer "is to get over the inference that the story is an actual news event without saying so."
58. J. P. McEvoy, "He's Got Something," *Saturday Evening Post*, July 1, 1939, 67.

59. David Platt, "Progressive Films Take Over Silver Screen of Hollywood," *Daily Worker*, August 29, 1937, 10.
60. A third movie based on the same events, *Nation Aflame*, written by Thomas Dixon, author of *The Birth of a Nation*, appeared from the independent production company Treasure Pictures in April 1937.
61. *New York Times* Editorial, May 27, 1936.
62. Newspaper reports suggested that its members may have been responsible for as many as 57 murders, although members were only tried for five. More than 50 members of the Michigan Black Legion were convicted of various crimes, including arson, kidnapping, flogging, plotting to kill individuals, and plotting an armed uprising to take over the federal government. For historical accounts of the Black Legion, see Peter H. Amann, "Vigilante Fascism: The Black Legion as an American Hybrid," *Comparative Studies in Society and History*, 25.3 (July 1983), 490–524; Michael S. Clinansmith, "The Black Legion: Hooded Americanism in Michigan," *Michigan History*, 55 (Fall 1971), 243–262; David J. Mauer, "The Black Legion: A Paramilitary Fascist Organization of the 1930s," in Frank Annunziata (ed.), *For the General Welfare: Essays in Honor of Robert H. Bremner* (New York: Peter Lang, 1989), 255–269.
63. "Whose Business is the Motion Picture," *Motion Picture Herald*, February 22, 1936, 15–16.
64. Harmon, memorandum commenting upon document entitled "CODE, EXTRA-CODE, AND INDUSTRY REGULATION IN MOTION PICTURES: A Study of the Production Code and its Administration upon the Type and Content of American Motion Pictures, and Certain Other Basic Industry Policies and Their Current Application." June 22, 1938.
65. Breen, June 22, 1938, MPPDA 1939 Production Code file.
66. Breen to Warner, 6-18-36, PCA *Black Legion* file.
67. Memo, June 19, 1936, PCA *Black Legion* file.
68. One source suggests that "Hunyak" was a derogatory term used by Germans to refer to people from the Banat area, now comprising western Romania, eastern Serbia, and southeastern Hungary, with Timoşoara as its historical capital. It also appears to be a surname of Polish or Ukrainian origin. http://archiver.rootsweb.ancestry.com/th/read/BANAT/2004-09/1095646080 (accessed March 2015).
69. Showmen's Reviews, *Motion Picture Herald*, January 9, 1937, 44.
70. *Night and Day*, July 8, 1937.
71. Dayton Dean, "Secrets of the Black Legion: The Black Legion Triggerman in the Killing of Charles Poole Tells All," *Official Detective Stories*, 2 (October 1936), 3–7, 36–37; Ralph Goll, "Ripping the Black Mask from Detroit's Black Legion," *Daring Detective* (August 1936); Kenneth Jackson, "I Was a Captain in the Black Legion," *True Detective*, 27 (January 1937), 26–29, 74–77; (February 1937), 54–55, 123–129; Charles Meehan, Jack Harvill, and Alfred E. Farrell, as told to W. St John, "Michigan's Black Legion Murder by the Detectives Who Cracked the Case," *Official Detective Stories*, 2 (September 1936), 3–7, 34–36; Henry W. Piel, as told to Weaver Little, "Secrets of the Black Legion," *Inside Detective* (September 1936), 22–27, 39–40.
72. *Motion Picture Herald*, June 26, 1937, 114.
73. Otis Ferguson's review in *New Republic*, for instance, complained that "There is no race angle, there is a simply implied class angle, there is no mutilation and the man escapes" (quoted in Wood 2009, 225). *New Masses* argued that without a depiction of the racial dimension, the picture inhibited "a complete understanding of the problem" (quoted in Giovacchini 2001, 67–68).
74. Breen to Jack L. Warner, January 30, 1937, PCA *They Won't Forget* file.
75. Easton Pennsylvania *Express*. The initial controversy about the picture was manufactured by Wanger's publicity director, but Catholic organizations subsequently denounced it as "a typical Communist deceit" (Bernstein 1994, 135).
76. Quoted in memo, Milliken and Harmon to Hays, September 20, 1938, MPPDA 1939 Production Code file (12-2045).
77. "Jurisdiction of Production Code Administration," August 31, 1938, MPPDA 1938 Production Code file (12-2057).
78. Quigley, January 10, 1939, quoted in Leff and Simmons 1990, 65; Breen to Warner, December 13, 1938, PCA *Confessions of a Nazi Spy* file.
79. Press clipping, no date, PCA *Confessions of a Nazi Spy* file.
80. Rosten 1941, 327, quoting *Time*, July 21, 1941, 73.
81. Jack Warner's inaccurate claim that the movie led to prison reform continues to be widely reproduced; in *The Rise of the American Film*, Lewis Jacobs describes *Fugitive* as having provoked such public indignation that *Hell's Highway* was "hurriedly made to counteract it" (Jacobs 1939, 522).
82. Kenneth Fearing, "The Screen: *Fury* – Anti-Lynch Film," *New Masses*, June 16, 1936, 28 (reprinted in Robé 2010, 166).
83. Study Guide to *The Big House* and *I Am a Fugitive from a Chain Gang*, Human Relations Series of Films Excerpted for Photoplays, Commission on Human Relations, Progressive Education Association, New York, 1939, 3.

References

Artaud, Antonin. (1958). *The Theater and Its Double*. New York: Grove Press.

Balio, Tino. (1993). *Grand Design: Hollywood as a Modern Business Enterprise, 1930–1939*. Vol. 5 of *History of the American Cinema*, ed. Charles Harpole. New York: Scribner's.

Baxter, Peter. (1993). *Just Watch! Sternberg, Paramount and America*. London: British Film Institute.

Beard, Charles Austin, & Beard, Mary Ritter. (1939). *America in Midpassage*. New York: Macmillan.

Behlmer, Rudy (ed.). (1986). *Inside Warner Bros. (1935–1951)*. London: Weidenfeld & Nicolson.

Bergman, Andrew. (1972). *We're in the Money: Depression America and Its Films*. New York: Harper Colophon Books.

Bernstein, Matthew H. (1994). *Walter Wanger: Hollywood Independent*. Berkeley: University of California Press.

Bernstein, Matthew H. (2009). *Screening a Lynching: The Leo Frank Case on Film and Television*. Athens: University of Georgia Press.

Burns, Robert E. (1997). *I Am a Fugitive from a Georgia Chain Gang!* Athens: University of Georgia Press. (Original work published 1932.)

Custen, George F. (1997). *Twentieth Century's Fox: Darryl F. Zanuck and the Culture of Hollywood*. New York: Basic Books.

Dickstein, Morris. (2009). *Dancing in the Dark: A Cultural History of the Great Depression*. New York: W. W. Norton.

Eldridge, David. (2008). *American Culture in the 1930s: Twentieth-Century American Culture*. Edinburgh: Edinburgh University Press.

Ferguson, Otis. (1971). *The Film Criticism of Otis Ferguson*, ed. Robert Wilson. Philadelphia: Temple University Press.

Giovacchini, Saverio. (2001). *Hollywood Modernism: Film and Politics in the Age of the New Deal*. Philadelphia: Temple University Press.

Hark, Ina Rae. (2007). *American Cinema of the 1930s: Themes and Variations*. New Brunswick: Rutgers University Press.

Herman, Felicia. (2001). "Hollywood, Nazism, and the Jews, 1933–41." *American Jewish History*, 89.1, 61–89.

Jacobs, Lewis. (1939). *The Rise of the American Film: A Critical History*. New York: Harcourt, Brace & Company.

Lacey, Robert. (1991). *Little Man: Meyer Lansky and the Gangster Life*. 1st edn. Boston: Little, Brown.

Leff, Leonard J., & Simmons, Jerold L. (1990). *The Dame in the Kimono: Hollywood, Censorship, and the Production Code from the 1920s to the 1960s*. New York: Grove Weidenfeld.

Levine, Lawrence W. (1993). *The Unpredictable Past: Explorations in American Cultural History*. New York: Oxford University Press.

Lichtenstein, Alex. (1995). "Georgia History in Fiction: Chain Gangs, Communism, and the 'Negro Question': John L. Spivak's *Georgia Nigger*." *Georgia Historical Quarterly*, 79.3 (Fall), 634–658.

Lugowski, David M. (1999). "Queering the (New) Deal: Lesbian and Gay Representation and the Depression-Era Cultural Politics of Hollywood's Production Code." *Cinema Journal*, 38.2, 3–35.

McElvaine, Robert S. (1984). *The Great Depression: America, 1929–1941*. New York: Times Books.

May, Lary. (2000). *The Big Tomorrow: Hollywood and the Politics of the American Way*. Chicago: University of Chicago Press.

Moran, Kathleen, & Rogin, Michael. (2000). "'What's the Matter with Capra?': *Sullivan's Travels* and the Popular Front Author(s)." *Representations*, 71 (Summer), 106–134.

Nugent, Frank. (1936). "'Fury,' a Dramatic Indictment of Lynch Law, Opens at the Capitol." *New York Times*, June 6, 21.

Nugent, Frank (1937). "The Screen; The Strand's 'Black Legion' Is an Eloquent Editorial On Americanism." *New York Times*, January 18, 21.

O'Connor, John E., & Balio, Tino (eds). (1981). *I Am a Fugitive from a Chain Gang: The Warner Brothers Screenplay*. Madison: University of Wisconsin Press.

Potamkin, Harry Alan. (1977). *The Compound Cinema: The Film Writings of Harry Alan Potamkin*, ed. Martin S. Dworkin. New York: Teachers College Press.

Robé, Chris. (2010). *Left of Hollywood: Cinema, Modernism, and the Emergence of U.S. Radical Film Culture*. 1st edn. Austin: University of Texas Press.

Roddick, Nick. (1983). *A New Deal in Entertainment: Warner Brothers in the 1930s*. London: British Film Institute.

Roffman, Peter, & Purdy, Jim. (1981). *The Hollywood Social Problem Film: Madness, Despair, and Politics from the Depression to the Fifties*. Bloomington: Indiana University Press.

Rosten, Leo C. (1941). *Hollywood: The Movie Colony, The Movie Makers*. New York: Harcourt, Brace & Company.

Schatz, Thomas. (1988). *The Genius of the System: Hollywood Filmmaking in the Studio Era*. New York: Pantheon Books.

Shindler, Colin. (1996). *Hollywood in Crisis: Cinema and American Society, 1929–1939*. London: Routledge.

Sklar, Robert. (1978). *Movie-Made America: A Cultural History of American Movies*. London: Chappell & Company/Elm Tree. (Original work published 1975.)

Smoodin, Eric Loren. (2004). *Regarding Frank Capra: Audience, Celebrity, and American Film Studies, 1930–1960*. Durham, NC: Duke University Press.

Sturtevant, Victoria. (2009). *A Great Big Girl Like Me: The Films of Marie Dressler*. Urbana: University of Illinois Press.

Thorp, Margaret Farrand. (1946). *America at the Movies*. London: Faber & Faber. (Original work published 1939.)

Tichi, Cecelia. (1987). *Shifting Gears: Technology, Literature, Culture in Modernist America*. Chapel Hill: University of North Carolina Press.

Vasey, Ruth. (1997). *The World According to Hollywood, 1919–1939*. Exeter: University of Exeter Press.

Wanger, Walter. (1939). "120,000 American Ambassadors." *Foreign Affairs*, 18.1, 45–59.

Wolfe, Charles. (1990). "Mr. Smith Goes to Washington: Democratic Forums and Representational Forms." In Peter Lehman (ed.), *Close Viewings: An Anthology of New Film Criticism* (pp. 300–332). Tallahassee: Florida State University Press.

Wood, Amy Louise. (2009). *Lynching and Spectacle: Witnessing Racial Violence in America, 1890–1940*. Chapel Hill: University of North Carolina Press.

12

Early American Avant-Garde Cinema

Jan-Christopher Horak
Director, UCLA Film & Television Archive, United States

Pre–World War II American avant-garde filmmakers, like their postwar successors, created films in opposition to commercial narrative cinema, yet unlike their successors who defined themselves as artists and filmmakers, these early filmmakers saw themselves as amateur lovers of cinema. Jan-Christopher Horak discusses numerous films, illustrating that, while European **modernist** influences always are present, the early American avant-garde expressed a **romantic** desire to represent nature. Urban mechanization either coexists with or stands in stark contrast to the natural world, as evident in **city symphony**-influenced films; films directly devoted to **natural subjects**, in which nature often is abstracted through an interplay of forms, shapes, light, shadow, and color; films focused on **the human body and its movement**; **animation**; unconventional **literary adaptations**; and even in **subjective/psychoanalytic portraits** and **surrealist/parodic films**. Horak provides discussions of **specific avant-garde filmmakers and their work**. His essay shares ground with Jared Rapfogel on American underground film in this volume and with Scott MacDonald on the contemporary avant-garde in Volume II.

Additional terms, names, and concepts: "little cinema," Film and Photo League, Amateur Cinema League, *cinéma pur*

Avant-garde film movements can only be historically circumscribed if they are constituted in terms of production, distribution, exhibition, and reception. Their place in the history of cinema should be gauged not only according to their individual aesthetic achievements, but also in terms of the myriad contexts of their reception. In addition to my own work, histories of the avant-garde by Paul Arthur, David James, and Scott MacDonald have employed such a strategy. In contrast, avant-garde film histories by P. Adams Sitney and Jonas Mekas have served polemical argument and the aesthetic legitimization of filmmakers enshrined in their canon, thus eliminating discontinuities and dead ends, which necessarily mark a film

American Film History: Selected Readings, Origins to 1960, First Edition. Edited by Cynthia Lucia, Roy Grundmann, and Art Simon.
© 2016 John Wiley & Sons, Inc. Published 2016 by John Wiley & Sons, Inc.

form based on individual modes of production. Contemporary reception of such work was sporadic, exhibition venues rising and falling – oftentimes victims of larger economic forces – while publications dedicated to the film avant-garde, too, appear more fragile than those catering to commercial markets.

A crucial difference to understanding the dynamics of the early American avant-garde in relation to its post–World War II successors involves the self-perceptions and material conditions of the two generations. Both defined themselves in opposition to commercial, classical narrative cinema, privileging the personal over the pecuniary. However, the 1950s avant-gardists proclaimed themselves to be independent filmmakers, actively engaged in the production of "art," while the earlier generation viewed themselves as cineastes, as lovers of cinema, as "amateurs" willing to work in any arena furthering the cause of film art, even if working for hire.

Lewis Jacobs, for example, then a member of a Philadelphia amateur film club, noted of his group: "Our club is composed of painters, dancers, and illustrators . . . . It is our aim to emphasize a direction that will result in cinematic form" (Gale 1928, 100). As a paradigmatic example of the contemporary 1920s cineaste one might fruitfully look at the career of Herman Weinberg: In the late 1920s, he worked as a manager for an art cinema in Baltimore, wrote film criticism for various magazines, and made avant-garde shorts. This plethora of activity in a variety of cinema-related endeavors was also economically determined, since no single effort offered a livelihood.

The first avant-garde defined itself not only aesthetically in opposition to the commercial industry, but also economically, producing films at minimal expense. Rather than involving large crews and expensive sets, avant-garde filmmakers worked with modest expenditures of money and materials, their budgets subject to the personal budgets of an amateur. When Slavko Vorkapich and Robert Florey completed *The Life and Death of 9413—A Hollywood Extra* (1928), the press continuously recalled that the film cost a mere $97.50. Florey's *The Love of Zero* (1928) was produced for only $200.00; Charles Vidor's *The Bridge* (1929) for approximately $250.00, plus sound work. Roman Freulich finished *Broken Earth* (1936) for $750.00, after earning a net profit of $200.00 on his first short, *The Prisoner* (1934).

Figure 12.1 "The Cinema Crafters of Philadelphia" (1929), including Louis Hirschman, Lewis Jacobs, and Jo Gerson. (Author's private collection.)

Early Avant-Garde Exhibition and Reception

Just as avant-garde film production created an alternative discourse on filmmaking, so too did the "little cinema" movement provide an exhibition outlet for avant-garde and European art films, frozen out of commercial cinema chains, dominated by major Hollywood studios. Not surprisingly, art cinema programs often paired American avant-garde films with European, especially German and Russian features. For example, *9413—A Hollywood Extra* played at the Philadelphia Motion Picture Guild with the German/Indian production *Die Leuchte Asiens* (1926), while Robert Florey's *Love of Zero* was billed at the Los Angeles Filmarte Theater with Gösta Ekman's *Kloven* (1927).

Art galleries were another potential site for avant-garde exhibitions. Strand and Sheeler's *Manhatta* (1921) was shown at Marius DeZayas's New York gallery, while Jay Leyda's *A Bronx Morning* (1931) was premiered at Julien Levy Gallery in New York, as was Lynn Rigg's *A Day in Santa Fe* (1931), Henwar Rodakiewicz's *Portrait of a Young Man* (1931), and Joseph Cornell's *Rose Hobart* (1936). After 1930 through mid-decade, the Film and Photo League, which was allied with the US Communist Party, provided another exhibition outlet. Apart from its film production and photography activities, the League also set up local and, in 1934, a national 16mm film distribution system. Presenting Soviet feature films, radical left-wing newsreels, as well as evenings of avant-garde films to its membership, the League was instrumental in developing an audience for art films. Undoubtedly, however, the most audience-rich center for the exhibition of avant-garde films was the Amateur Cinema League, which had local clubs in countless American cities. The League had begun to organize a lending library as early as 1927. The Amateur Cinema League's distribution catalog included *The Fall of the House of Usher*, *The Tell-Tale Heart*, *H_2O*, *Lot in Sodom*, *Mr. Motorboat's Last Stand*, among others, all of which were screened extensively throughout the United States.

Film magazines were another means of reception for avant-garde films. Dedicated to promoting art films, *Close-Up*, published in Switzerland in English, *Film Art*, published in London, *Experimental Film*, edited by Seymour Stern and Lewis Jacobs, and the *National Board of Review Magazine* all flourished briefly. The first three journals functioned as critical voices in the discourse around both European and American art film, while the last continued its battle for better films well into the postwar era.

Until recently, the first American avant-garde, if acknowledged at all, was characterized as essentially European in outlook, and derivative of 1920s European models. Avant-garde films made before the advent of Maya Deren were seemingly disqualified from serious consideration if they were seen as aping Expressionism, remaking Constructivist documentaries, or filming American versions of European avant-garde ideas.[1] While this particular critique has not held up under close scrutiny, it was the reception in the mid-1920s of German Expressionism and Soviet Constructivism that spurred American filmmakers to attempt independent productions outside the confines of Hollywood. In these American avant-garde films, as well as in the European films trickling over to the United States, film lovers perceived a clear alternative to the generic conventions of the domestic film industry. Yet, American films were unique products of American culture. The fact that they were born out of the *reception* of European avant-garde films *in America* inscribed their position: While often borrowing or quoting the formal techniques of the European avant-garde, they demonstrated a certain wild eclecticism, innovation, and at times naïveté, which was only possible for American filmmakers working far from Paris and Berlin – the centers of western high culture. Rather than denigrating American eclecticism, we now look at the early American avant-garde with a postmodern sensibility, appreciating the hodge-podge of styles (Expressionism, Cubism, Art Nouveau) and philosophical currents that make up the first American avant-garde.

Troubled Modernism and the First American Avant-Garde

Unlike the European avant-garde, the first American avant-garde, like the second post–World War II American film avant-garde, seems to have had an extremely contradictory relationship to the modernist project. Its use of modernist form in conjunction with the expression of highly romantic, even antimodernist sentiments is symptomatic of this ambivalence to modernism. A romanticism that manifests itself in the longing for (wo)man's reunification with nature informs the early American avant-garde's visualization of the natural environment and urban sprawl.[2] In European films nature is seen, at best, as an abstraction, as an ideal aesthetic construct, not as a primordial force from which human society has been forcibly separated. While the European avant-garde is defiantly modernist in its celebration of urbanism and the machine age, American avant-garde films are much more ambivalent, viewing the separation from nature with anxiety and sometimes dread. This romantic view not only separates the early American avant-garde from its European models but also connects it directly to the second American avant-garde, to filmmakers like Stan Brakhage, James Broughton, and Kenneth Anger.

Paul Strand and Charles Sheeler's *Manhatta* (1921) was not only the first avant-garde film produced in the United States and a model for subsequent "city films" in Europe and America, but also a highly contradictory, even romantic text.[3] On the one hand, *Manhatta* is central to film modernism's project of deconstructing Renaissance perspective in favor of multiple, reflexive points of view. On the other hand, its angled view of skyscrapers in lower Manhattan and its sunset-drenched views of the Hudson River are informed by metaphors of nature in Walt Whitman's poetry, quoted in the intertitles. Strand and Sheeler's work is thus mitigated by aesthetic concerns and philosophical premises that are archaic and antimodernist. In its conscious attempt to create an avant-garde, nonnarrative, and formally abstract cinematic experience in opposition to classical modes of address, *Manhatta*, however, never quite relinquishes those structures that manifest themselves most visibly in the tension between the image and verbal text, between its modernist perspectives and a romantic longing for a universe in which man remains in harmony with nature.

Robert Flaherty's *24 Dollar Island* (1926) is similarly inflected. The film begins with etchings of the Dutch buying Manhattan from the island's Native American inhabitants in 1624, then cuts to an aerial view of the city, taken three centuries later. The images that follow, often taken from a skyscraper's or a worm's-eye view, focus on construction and interplay between the city and the harbor. Quite a number of these images seem directly lifted from *Manhatta* with most of the film shot in the same lower Manhattan locations. Through the use of telephoto lenses and extreme camera angles, Flaherty collapses spaces, creating canyons of concrete and iron, giving the city a feeling of incredible density and power. The film presents urban civilization as completely overpowering and destructive of nature; a single, lone tree, for instance, is seen against a backdrop of the concrete jungle. The film suggests that the natural environment has been replaced by an artificially constructed, primordial environment devoid of humans.

Robert Florey's *Skyscraper Symphony* (1928) is even more abstract in its detachment from human images. By dissolving from one extremely high angle view of a skyscraper to another, or moving his camera across a building surface, Florey creates an abstract pattern of moving planes, whereby the indexical meaning of the image is obliterated. The play of light and shadow on concrete, the release of light through windows, and the shifting light of the sky transform real places into pure form; only a hint of clouds betrays the natural environment. Clearly indebted to *cinéma pur*, Florey's film privileges abstract visual poetry over documentary.

Jay Leyda's *A Bronx Morning* (1931) is much more celebratory of the city as a living space and more humanistic in its view of city dwellers. A tribute to photographer Eugene Atget, it is a lyrical look at Leyda's Bronx neighborhood. The film opens with moving camera shots, taken from an elevated train, that hark back to *Berlin: Symphony of a Great City* (1926), followed by images of storefronts, mannequins, and signs – many direct quotations of Atget's surrealistic photographs of Paris. After a montage of tenement windows, the film interestingly switches to what is essentially a feminine perspective – a world of children, pets, and cleaning – indicating that the street is a family space for social interaction. There are few images of men working, unlike in earlier city portraits, but the occasional image of a tree and a flight of pigeons that closes the film implies that nature is an absent presence.

Although it ends tragically, Lewis Jacobs's *Footnote to Fact* (1933) likewise portrays life on the street in a New York neighborhood, rather than focusing on its dehumanizing architecture. Beginning with a shot of a young woman, swaying to and fro, like Kiki in René Clair's *Entr'Acte* (1924), the film intercuts this recurring image with impressionistic, documentary shots of street life, signs, traffic. Shots of people picking through garbage, demonstrations of the unemployed, closed businesses, idle workers, and images of war introduce an explicitly political commentary on the Depression. The meaning of the woman's swaying action does not become clear until at the film's climax when we see her turn on the gas and commit suicide. This dark ending is reminiscent of Piel Jutzi's *Mutter Krausens Fahrt ins Gluck/Mother Krause's Journey to Happiness* (1929), and hardly in keeping with Jacobs's nominally optimistic leftist politics.

Another city portrait from the early 1930s was Irving Browning's *City of Contrasts* (1931). Released commercially with a superficial "comic" narration to improve its box office potential, the film nevertheless merits recognition in terms of its cinematography and sophisticated montage. Browning juxtaposes images both formally, through contrasting light, shadow, form, and use of extreme camera angles, and semantically, through contrasting various ethnic neighborhoods, skyscrapers and city parks, the wealthy at Riverside Drive and the shantytown of Hooverville on the Hudson. Contradictory social forces are accepted as endemic to urban life, rather than as a product of market forces.

Film historian Herman Weinberg produced *Autumn Fire* (1933), a city symphony that uses footage from his earlier film, *City Symphony* (1930). The film subjectively portrays two lovers who suffer through their separation when the man must go to the city for work. Employing the style of Soviet montage, Weinberg intercuts continually between the two, juxtaposing their environments by identifying the young woman symbolically with nature and the man with the city (New York). Their reunion in a train station is accompanied by an image orgy of flowing water, referencing Freud's symbol of female orgasm. Thus, the film mixes elements of the city film with a portrait of nature, expressing a romantic longing for man's lost connection with the wilderness. The longing lover, an object of the male gaze, is inscribed as "the waiting woman," consumed by emotional desire for the man. He, on the other hand, is identified with the rationalist construction of the city, while simultaneously subject to a sense of lack, expressed in views of slums and garbage.

American avant-garde films thematizing urbanity always seem to be about man and nature in the city. Such an ambivalent attitude toward urban spaces is nowhere as evident as in Willard Van Dyke, Henwar Rodakiewicz, and Ralph Steiner's government-sponsored documentary *The City* (1939). From the very beginning the film sets up a country/city dichotomy, juxtaposing the opening "New England" sequence with scenes of heavy industry. The metropolis is seen here as overcrowded, noisy, polluted, and unhealthy; images of smoke stacks, traffic jams, and substandard industrial housing predominate. Only in the latter half of the film is a new vision presented: a city without a cityscape, a city in harmony with the environment, a city replicating a small-town feeling, the urban jungle miraculously metamorphosed into suburbs.

Swiss-born photographer Rudy Burkhardt begins his *Seeing the World – Part One: A Visit to New York* (1937) with scenes of downtown skyscrapers and shots of the subway, while also clearly interested in spoofing travelogues with a humorous female narrator. Once "uptown" on Park Avenue, Burkhardt inserts a scene of a "blue blood" couple fighting over the placement of an abstract painting. Crossing Fifth, Sixth, and Seventh Avenues to Eleventh Avenue, we next enter a bar, reminiscent of a Parisian "Apache" café, where two bar flies nearly kill each other (one played by Joseph Cotten) before the narrator returns us downtown by subway. Ending on a bird's-eye view of Manhattan (the buildings are obviously models on a kitchen table), Burkhardt's intent is clearly satirical, treating the cinematic tourist to views of the high and low life of the city. In *The Pursuit of Happiness* (1940), Burkhardt's camera focuses on New York city crowds, showing their collective power through fast and slow motion, analyzing their individuality through close-up still photographs of faces. Much closer to *A Bronx Morning* or Helen Levitt's *In the Street* (1946), Burkhardt intercuts shots of shops, advertisements, and buildings, but these seem to be mere obstacles for the ever-moving urban pedestrians in their pursuit of happiness.

Surprisingly, then, most American "city films" seem to lack the unequivocal celebration of modernism and urbanism found in European city films such as *Rien que les heures/Nothing But Time* (1925), *Berlin: Symphony of a Great City*, and *Man with a Movie Camera* (1929), all of which rejoice in the urban environment's excitement, speed, and modernity, with few references to nature beyond its role in leisuretime activities for Sunday picnickers. The early American avant-garde, on the other hand, lament the urban separation from the countryside, a lament nowhere more evident than in their lyrical documentaries of nature.

Representations of Nature in the Early American Avant-Garde

If we theorize that many of the city films, constructed by the American avant-garde, present a mixture of modernist formal elements and romantic desires, then the avant-garde's depiction of nature seems to be a more direct expression of American romantic sensibilities. Certainly, the documentation of the natural environment seems to be almost completely absent from the European avant-garde, with its modernist fascination with speed, transportation, and the urban environment. What defines American avant-garde filmmakers as romantics is not only their interest in depicting nature, however abstracted, but also, and more importantly, their use of nature as a visual metaphor to express human (mostly male) subjectivity.

One of the earliest examples of this subgenre is Dudley Murphy's *Soul of Cypress* (1921). Shot on the California coast, the film opens with a young man communing with nature as he composes a song so enchanting to a dryad that she is released from her captivity in an old cypress. Shot in silhouette against a bright sky, she dances through the gnarled trees to his flute (with obvious sexual overtones), while violent waves crash against the rocky shore below. As he becomes aware of her presence, the young musician falls in love and eventually throws himself into the sea in order to be united with the wood nymph. As in so much romantic literature and art, woman is identified with nature, while man produces art in homage to nature.

Artkino's *Oil: A Symphony in Motion* (1933) postulates a radical synthesis of nature and technology by discovering the origins of the latter in the former. The film makes use of a first-person monologue in intertitles, spoken by the oil in the ground: "I am the pulse beat of green jungles stored in the ground beneath your farms." The monologue continues throughout the film, as "Oil" narrates its own rise to power as a driver of technology. Mostly framed in heroic high angles, with objects photographed against the open sky and strongly influenced by Soviet aesthetics, the film begins with a pastoral landscape of farms, cows, and farmers, slowly giving way (thankfully, since the soil is exhausted) to oil derricks. Yet these derricks are presented more as natural phenomena, as if willed into existence by the narrating oil, since they, too, are anthropomorphized. The final third of the film is a paean to technology and modern transportation as speed, as the filmmakers juxtapose antiquated horse-drawn buggies with quick motor cars, trains, and planes. A close-up of a rotating auto tire, superimpositions in crisscross patterns of fast-moving railroad cars, and high angle shots of the oil derrick silhouetted against the evening sky become metonymies for a technology functioning in harmony with nature. With its optimistic view of technology and, by extension, economic expansion, it is also very much an expression of male desire in the early twentieth century.

A much more abstract manifestation of this romantic impulse, Henwar Rodakiewicz's *Portrait of a Young Man* reflects the filmmaker's desire for union with nature. The young man of the title, in fact, never appears in the film, which, instead, presents a series of long takes of the sea, clouds, smoke, tree leaves – most held in extreme close-up to emphasize the abstract refraction of light and to dematerialize content. Divided into three movements, the film's construction and rhythm is modeled on that of a symphony: An adagio is layered between two faster-paced sequences. *Portrait of a Young Man* clearly owes a debt to Steiner's *H_2O*. Although it includes two brief sequences of abstracted moving machinery, it is indeed most concerned with subjectivity and emotional tonalities.

Ralph Steiner's *H_2O* is a 12-minute film of water, raindrops, pools, brooks, streams, rivers, and oceans, moving from very concrete images of water in all its manifestations to extremely abstract images of the way water reflects and refracts light. For Steiner, it is the camera's ability to capture the play of light in the water that becomes the film's actual text. These completely dematerialized images take on the quality of abstract art in motion. Similarly, Steiner's *Surf and Seaweed* (1930) is a montage of close-up images of the ocean, low angle shots of waves crashing against the rocks, and extreme close-ups of the swirling patterns of seaweed. The film's rhythm matches the endless to and fro of the surf, its images edited together abstractly according to formal rather than narrative or indexical criteria.

Subjectivity also informs Slavko Vorkapich and John Hoffman's *Moods of the Sea* (1942), a lyrical documentary using Felix Mendelssohn's "Fingal's Cave" as musical accompaniment. Opening with a view from a cave onto the ocean, the film orchestrates images of a powerful natural environment: Giant waves breaking on the shore, cliffs towering above the surf, a seagull in elegant flight, sea otters playing in the waves, gathering clouds above the ocean, a sunset on the horizon. The images, true to Vorkapich's interest in montage, are cut precisely to the music, each image sequence reaching a rhythmic crescendo with the melodies. The romanticism of Mendelssohn's music contributes to the film's overall romantic quality, but it is both the framed image from the cave entrance at the film's beginning and the constantly moving camera that emphasize the subjective nature of the camera's point of view. Thus, like Rodakiewicz's film, *Moods* refers not so much to nature as to the human observer's experience of nature, the subjectivity conjured up by a walk along the sea.

Slavko Vorkapich made a second nature film, *Forest Murmurs*, using Richard Wagner's eponymous musical piece, to illustrate woods and wildlife. Likewise, John Hoffman's *Prelude to Spring* (1946) presents a series of shots of mountains, woods, and brooks, as the snow slowly melts, spring arrives, and a storm comes and goes. Many of the images tend toward the abstract, especially the images of flowing water, an effect heightened by high-contrast printing. Unfortunately, the film is marred by the clichéd use of Sergei Prokofiev's "Peter and the Wolf" on the soundtrack, giving the film a literalness that undermines its oftentimes striking images.

Although framed as a lyrical documentary, Paul Burnford's *Storm* (1943) also is more concerned with the emotional value of its images of nature than with narrative content. Initially charting human preparations for a storm, especially through the use of scientific tools, Burnford's cloudscapes grow in intensity to gale force, revealing the power of nature against which civilization is ultimately powerless. The winter storm in particular, as well as its icy aftermath, occasions images of abstract beauty, while simultaneously conveying nature's destructive strength.

In reviewing the gamut of lyrical nature films, it seems evident that all of these experiments are motivated by a romantic subjectivity that seems at some level counter to the modernist project of the avant-garde, thus forcing us to reconsider our definitions. And as noted above, while images of nature are all but absent from the European avant-garde canon, they appear in overabundance in the early American avant-garde and will continue to be present in the work of the post–World War II generation. At the same time, the focus on reflected and refracted light in nature privileges the abstract and the purely subjective in these films, relating them to *cinéma pur* and abstract animation.

Light, Color, and Form as Subjects of the Early American Avant-Garde

Francis Bruguière's *Light Rhythms* (1930), made in collaboration with Oswald Blakeston, animates approximately 30 static forms solely through the manipulation of light. During its five-minute running time, the film presents a highly abstract meditation on the power of light to change perceptions of form. In this sense, the film can be compared to Moholy-Nagy's *Ein Lichtspiel schwarz weiss grau/ Lightplay: Black/White/Gray* (1930), except that in the latter film, light bounces off a moving object, while in this film the objects themselves never move. As in the case of similar European experiments, the impetus seems to be the creation of abstract painting in motion, here with black, white, and gray wavelike forms fluctuating and pulsating as light from a bright spot or spots passes over them.

Convinced of the formal possibilities of putting abstract, animated images to music, Mary Ellen Bute joined forces with Theodore Nemeth and Melville Webber to produce *Rhythm in Light* (1934), set to "Anitra's Dance" from Edvard Grieg's "Peer Gynt Suite." Through high-contrast lighting, extreme soft- and out-of-focus photography, and multiple exposures, abstract objects – whether circles, triangles, arrows, or more complex shapes like sparklers – appear to be moving through space in rhythm with Grieg's music. Bute and her collaborators thus produced an effective method of creating black-and-white animation in the third dimension, the length of the individual shots and their internal movement worked out with mathematical precision to visualize the accompanying music. Indeed, the stated goal was to visualize music, an objective that would continue in all of her future work, including *Synchromy No. 2* (1936), visualizing Wagner's "Song of the Evening Star," and *Synchromy No. 4: Escape* (1937), a color film using music from Bach's "Toccata and Fugue in D Minor," and, also in color, *Spook Sport* (1939), made in collaboration with Norman McLaren. Accompanying Saint-Saëns's "Danse Macabre," *Spook Sport* uses anthropomorphic forms, along with drawings of ghosts, bats, and skeletons.

Another pioneer of abstract animation, Francis Lee completed *1941* (1941), an emotionally powerful rendering of the Japanese attack on Pearl Harbor, presented as animated painting: An egg is smashed, red color dissolves over a globe floating in blue paint. Broken electric light bulbs litter the phantasmagoric landscape. Lee paints directly on glass, shooting from underneath to a light source above, giving the film's color a strong vibrancy, heightened by the extreme saturation of the colors and made possible through Kodachrome film stock. As the film progresses, the primary colors of the first images give way to grays, blacks, and browns, as the world is metaphorically turned into a desolate, ashen battlefield. While this description may seem to give the film a narrative dimension, Lee's films are essentially abstract, their effect based on the emotional quality of their colors and shapes, rather than any anthropomorphic reality. In *Le Bijou* (1946), Lee makes use of red, blue, and gold crystals, diamonds, and disks, which seemingly move through a barren landscape. The three-dimensional quality of the objects does tend to increase their anthropomorphic quality, however. Like *1941*, *Idyll* (1948) presents a phantasmagoric underwater landscape, using water and oil colors on glass. Here nature is abstracted, reducing animal and vegetable life to its spiritual essence, in which color, rather than shape, predominates. Unlike the earlier film, Lee's hues are closer to chalklike pastel colors, the whole underscored by romantic music.

Working contemporaneously to Lee, Douglass Crockwell began his own series of short color experiments, christened *Glens Falls Sequence* (1937–1946), which were produced by painting directly on glass or between two pieces of glass, then filming the results single frame. The early sequences are strangely anthropomorphic, resembling worms and flowers, in near monochrome, mutating later to moving landscapes with Christ-like figures and Mirò-like one-eyed creatures. Other sequences make use of cut paper and claymation.

Shortly after Lee and Crockwell, Dwinell Grant, an abstract painter since 1933, made his first film, *Composition 1 (Themis)* (1940), animating wood, glass, and paper forms with a stop-motion camera. The lines, circles, and squares vary in shape, movement, and color, mutating from shades of red to blue and yellow through the use of colored light. In many respects this work resembles a constructivist painting in motion, much as Oskar Fischinger would develop a similar tradition. Yet, while the film gives a sense of objects in motion (time), they move through a two-dimensional space, lacking the kinetic force of other abstract animation.

In *Composition 2 (Contrathemis)* (1941), Grant increases the sense of movement with pulsating lines that literally seem to breathe as they grow thick or thin and move in circular patterns. In his next two films, *Composition 3* (1942) and *Composition 4* (1945), Grant began exploring three-dimensional space, in the first film by using three-dimensional media like clay and wooden objects. In *Composition 4* he created this third dimension by developing a 3-D film that used a beam-splitter and Polaroid glasses for viewing.

It is no accident that a number of the avant-garde filmmakers discussed here were later accepted into the pantheon of the second American avant-garde. With the exception of Warren Newcombe and Bute, both of whom were perceived as tainted by commercialism because their work was shown in mainstream theaters, the work of these animators could be subsumed under the aesthetics of abstract expressionism. However, like their postwar epigones, these American filmmakers rarely shied away from a kind of anthropomorphism that was considered *gauche* in European art circles. And one can argue that even the abstract expressionism of latter-day painters had its romantic elements, in particular in its privileging of subjectivity.

Music, Movement, and Dance in Early Avant-Garde Film

It seems only a short step from abstract painting-in-motion to bodies-in-motion to express ideas through dance. *Danse Macabre* (1922), a collaboration between Francis Bruguière (lighting), Dudley Murphy (direction), F. A. A. Dahme (animation), and August Blom (choreography), visualizes in dance Saint-Saëns's music, opening with animated titles and a short animated sequence of Death playing a fiddle. We see the lovers (Blom and Ruth Page) dancing to celebrate their new-found love, suddenly threatened by the figure of Death, who appears superimposed with ever more frequency, playing and dancing. Just before Death grasps the girl in his huge hands, an animated cock crows, saving her from her fate.

Hands in motion seem to have been a popular trope of the period. In Berlin, American avant-garde filmmaker Stella Simon shot *Hands/Hände* (1927), subtitled "the life and loves of the gentler sex." Simon's film is a narrative of hands, as they dance through Expressionist-influenced miniature sets. The film opens with hands waving in front of black velvet, with these hands and arms standing in synecdoche for whole bodies. In the highly abstracted scenes that follow, male and female mate, a "coquette" entices a group of males, a wild party takes place, and a final reconciliation results in this story of a *ménage à trois*. Abstract sets reduced to constructivist triangles, squares, and circles, the film's spaces are further limited by numerous, variously shaped masks that focus its narrative attention. The film's abstract quality is further strengthened by Marc Blitzstein's 12-tone music. At the same time, the film presents a "melodrama" of female subjectivity and *Angst* as woman continually plays out masochistic fantasies of defeat and self-mutilation. The film's narrative closure, reproducing in its ballet of reunification a Hollywood ending, inscribes woman's desire for sexual harmony, and is indicative of Simon's romantic American origins.

Architect Norman Bel Geddes filmed Tilly Losch in *Dance of the Hands* (1930), his camera focusing on the famed Berlin dancer's hands, against a black background and her black dress, so that only her hands and face are highlighted. Unlike Simon's approach, the dance of hands here is purely abstract without any narrative elements. The interplay of the visible body as it contorts in front of a static camera signifies emotional states, its hands expressing that which is also reflected in the face.

Beginning much like the Bel Geddes film, *Hands* (1934), by Willard Van Dyke and Ralph Steiner, begins with close-ups of hands in motion in front of a black cloth, then presents a choreographed montage of close-ups, as hands work at every kind of profession – whether as painters, farmers, factory workers, carpenters, plumbers, or clerks. Made for Roosevelt's Works Progress Administration, the film continually intercuts these shots of hands with images of other hands exchanging money and checks, thus defining the relationship between labor and capital and implying that the economy will only move again through work.

While *Hands* can be classified as a dance film only in a wider sense, *Underground Printer* (1934) was more clearly a collaboration between filmmakers and dancers, although again with a strong political intent. Directed by Thomas Bouchard, in conjunction with the dancer John Bovington, the film was photographed and edited by Lewis Jacobs. Bovington's solo dance, which features grotesque movements, is broken up visually into essences, while Jacobs accents sound and image with percussion shocks, throwing into startling relief the gyrations of the dancer as he spins and whirls as Goebbels, explodes as Göring, and exults as the communist underground printer preparing his anti-Nazi leaflets.

Introspection (1941/1946), directed by Sara Arledge, illustrates another attempt at presenting individual body parts as dance. A series of multiple color exposures of male dancers, the film privileges heads, legs, arms, and bodies moving in layered images. In one sequence a body wrapped in rags much like a mummy moves in slow, dreamlike patterns around its own axis. These images are intercut with negative images of hands reaching out and with red-tinted images of a faceless body exercising. The repetition of movements, forms, and visual motifs makes the film almost structuralist in its concern with the cinema's formal applications. Unfortunately, as often the case with other avant-garde filmmakers, this beautifully conceived and mystical film was to remain Arledge's only completed film. A second film, *Phantasmagoria* (1946), shot on 16mm Kodachrome and "presenting some of the manifold possibilities of the motion picture as a medium for the dance," was apparently never completed (Arledge 1947, n.p.).

In 1933, painter Emlen Etting shot his first 16mm film, *Oramunde*, a visualization of the French symbolist play *Pelléas et Mélisande* by Maurice Maeterlinck, which became the basis for Claude Debussy's opera. Featuring Mary Binney Montgomery, the film opens on images of ocean waves breaking in the shore, then cuts to Mélisande, shrouded in white gauze, dancing through fields, her nearly naked body appearing and disappearing as she moves through the trees, over ocean cliffs, and in a grotto. Searching in vain for her lost ring, she crosses the Styx River in a rowboat, guided by a black-hooded figure. By eliminating the opera's other characters, Etting's film symbolizes woman's subjectivity, her desires for love, and her final sacrifice in death, framed in a natural environment identifying her with nature. Apart from its being a dance film, *Oramunde* illustrates the tendencies toward surrealistic imagery in those early American avant-garde films that create dreamlike states, or what P. Adams Sitney calls "the trance film," in reference to the postwar avant-garde. Certainly, the use of Freudian and psychoanalytic imagery would migrate from the European avant-garde in the 1920s to America, but American films would, as *Oramunde* demonstrates, continue to incorporate nature imagery in the mix.

Ironically, these early dance films, except for the work of Sara Arledge, failed to enter into the canon of the second American avant-garde – this despite the fact that the dance tradition would continue to have its supporters in the coming years, with many dancers like Maya Deren, Shirley Clarke, Kathy Rose, and Yvonne Rainer becoming avant-garde filmmakers.

Surrealist and Psychoanalytic Expressions in the Early Avant-Garde

The earliest known American experimental animated film, *The Enchanted City* (1922), is, like so much of the early avant-garde, informed by romantic and modernist discourses. Made by painter and set designer Warren Newcombe, the film treads an uneasy line between Hollywood kitsch and avant-garde abstraction. Seemingly archaic in its visual design and "romantic" story, its experimental use of animation and its fragmented Freudian narrative qualify the film as a modernist work. Newcombe animates a series of paintings by moving his camera over the surface of each, panning and tilting his camera, moving closer and further away, and creatively using irises and other cutouts to isolate parts of the image. Sandwiched between live-action images of a couple sitting at the seashore communing with nature, the animated dreamscapes reveal monumentalized spaces, devoid of human life, a primacy of the architectural over human form, while recalling the metaphysical paintings of De Chirico. Newcombe uses perspective, not for representational purposes but rather for purely evocative and emotional effect, privileging the imaginary over the real and a sense of mystery over concrete narrative flow. In its narrative of quest down a river through an enchanted city, the film inscribes a male spectator looking at woman while articulating man's anxieties in reference to woman. One of the earliest images of stairs, a tower, and a woman's face, references Freud's conception of the phallic woman and man's fear of castration. This fear is obsessively reworked in numerous other images – shots of phalluses and restrictive compositions creating tunnel-like vision – culminating in the image of the journeyman being engulfed in a giant waterfall. There is ultimately an irrationality to the sequencing of images, resulting in a narrative that does not so much resolve itself as come to a metaphysical halt, a formal *deus ex machina* dissolving the image of destruction into one of redemption.

Best known as a painter/sculptor, Joseph Cornell made *Rose Hobart* (1936), a 19-minute (at silent speed) reediting of Universal's *East of Borneo* (1931), with a few snippets from scientific instructional films thrown in. Cornell's film, like his famous collage boxes, is essentially a creation out of *objets trouvés*. Completely eliminating dialogue and any semblance of plot, Cornell's montage of the ostensible heroine, hero, and villain has them moving in slow motion through empty rooms, caressing curtains, reacting to unseen events, never meeting. Their looks lead nowhere; their erotic desires careen into a void, leaving the audience with a mystery, the film's purple-tinted eroticism masking unfulfilled desire. Cornell subverts not only the standard conventions of Hollywood filmmaking, but also the viewer's expectations of finding meaning. In keeping with the surrealist creed, *Rose Hobart* is ambiguously meaningful without meaning.

Jerome Hill began his career in the 1930s with *La Cartomancienne/The Fortune Teller*. True to the title, the film has mystical overtones, its narrative a product of psychoanalysis: A young woman hanging washing, a walk along the surf, a consultation with a gypsy fortune teller, a young man swimming – water is the great unifier. The film ends with the young man and woman coming together, the latter rising up out of the sea like Venus, wearing a garland of flowers she had previously woven. Inflected by Greek mythology, the film's images reference primordial fertility rites yet remain ambiguous – like an old gypsy's fortune visualized in the cards.

Emlen Etting's *Poem 8* (1933) opens with an off-kilter close-up of a woman's eyes and face, then cuts to images of nature and, like *Oramunde*, to Mary Binney Montgomery dancing in celebration of nature. It ends with the dancer shrouded in white. Woman's subjectivity and identification with nature is thus inscribed in the film's text from the first shot. In the sequences to follow, Etting cuts between various women and hand-held camera shots of an urban landscape filled with skyscrapers, fast-motion traveling in images shot from cars and trains, an ocean liner embarking, and the recurring trope of a small globe – all continuously emphasizing woman's point of view but also inserting symbolic shots that denote innocence, vanity, sexuality. Meanings in this surrealist visual poem likewise remain ambiguous.

Similarly, Christopher Baughman Young's first avant-garde film, *Object Lesson* (1941), begins with the statement: "Let us consider objects. For they tell the story of life. There is nothing without meaning – and the combination of things make new meanings that are too complicated to explain." The film opens with a series of natural landscapes, in which there appear various objects: the heads and masks of Greek statues, swords, shields, violins, and tennis rackets. These objects have been strewn about, out of place in the lush vegetation, creating a surrealist image of incongruence: nature littered with man's detritus. In the next sequence, Young presents documentary images of the Empire State Building, hydroelectric plants, and garbage, followed by a metaphorical rendering of war. There is no dialogue or commentary, just an array of sounds and musical excerpts, including liturgical music, industrial sounds, eastern European folksongs, and electronic music. Virtually all the images are static and carefully composed like photographs. The lack of motion or action within the individual shots heightens the film's surrealistic aspect, allowing the viewer to contemplate both the incongruence of the moment and the juxtaposition of images in a syntactical construction. Young's images must be read in two ways: as surrealist constructs (*sans raison*) and as metaphorical, poetic vision. At the same time, like so many other American avant-garde films, *Object Lesson* stresses the conflict between man and nature, and ultimately the belief in nature as a dominant and abiding force.

Lacking narrative cohesion, these seemingly diverse films nevertheless give evidence to authorial voices that foreground the subjectivity of the artist. In the works of Hill, Etting, and Young, there is a romantic urge to understand the mysteries of nature and, possibly, to escape into a universe in which a natural order once again holds sway. In such a world the role of the artist is productively defined; neither the artist nor his/her works are throwaway objects of civilization, as made clear in *Object Lesson*. Even Cornell's conscious deconstruction of narrative in the interest of subverting classical modes of address creates a new narrative out of the void, one in which the artist is central. The subtext in all of these surrealist films seems to be the avant-garde itself.

Other Artistic Influences within the Early Avant-Garde

Not all painters experimenting with avant-garde film made abstract animation or surrealist montages. Painter Boris Deutsch directed *Lullaby* (1925), which starred Deutsch's wife Riva and Michael Visaroff. Strongly influenced by both Soviet-style montage and German Expressionist set design, the film's narrative is situated in prerevolutionary Russia, opening on a painted Russian Orthodox church steeple that is composed diagonally, almost abstractly. The film cuts to the sitting room of a Russian kulak, drinking and eating happily, and a (Jewish?) maid rocking the family baby in a corner. The peasant patriarch mercilessly mistreats the maid, who suffers from horrible dream visions. After enduring a brutal beating, the maid flees into the night. In the last image she is happily lying in the arms of an accordion player who had earlier shown her a moment of kindness. This simple objective narrative is disrupted by flashes of interior vision consisting of Deutsch's abstract paintings spinning around their own axes and denoting the subjective state of the female protagonist. Later the maid sees cubistically influenced visages painted in stark black and white that mock her pain and drive her to contemplate killing the baby of her master. Given this narrative of repression and escape, the film's title can be read ironically: It refers to the baby, whose innocence contrasts so markedly with the cruelty of its parents, and is an ironic comment on the nightmare visions of the maid. Indeed, the stark abstraction and horrific anguish of the dreams create a narrative excess, which the film's final image of tranquility cannot contain.

If any film from the early American avant-garde was previously recognized as an experimental work, it was Robert Florey and Slavko Vorkapich's *The Life and Death of 9413—A Hollywood Extra* (1928). Purportedly made for under $100, the film uses mirrors to place actors in its miniature Expressionist sets, while high key lighting, black backgrounds, and a highly stylized acting further enhance its level of abstraction. A response to budgetary necessity, these forms would serve many future filmmakers. The film opens with multiple exposures of an urban landscape, intercut with the eager look of Mr Jones who wishes to become a motion picture actor. His letter of reference to "Mr Almighty" (himself reduced to the synecdoche of a pointed finger) gets him a job and a number on his forehead: 9413. The narrative proceeds in an extremely elliptical matter – the repeated shot of the actor running up an endless set of stairs becomes a trope for the inability of the "hero" to realize his dreams in this system of exploitation. Indeed, the film works almost exclusively with parts standing in for wholes: a face/mask for an actor, clapping hands for success, a silhouette of a sound stage for Hollywood, all of which culminate in the hand of the real "Almighty" wiping the number from the extra's forehead.

James Sibley Watson collaborated with Melville Webber on *The Fall of the House of Usher* (1928), possibly one of the most highly regarded amateur film productions of its day. Starring nonprofessional actors, including Hildegarde Watson and Melville Webber as the "mysterious stranger," *The Fall of the House of Usher* is virtually nonnarrative in its reimagining of Poe's short story. While critics have noted its indebtedness to German Expressionism, it is more radical in its construction of cinematic space; while Expressionism relies on painted sets, seen in medium and long shot to give some sense of an organic space, Watson and Webber's film has few recognizable sets and no recognizable geographic space, much like *Hollywood Extra*. It relies, rather, on a dazzling array of often distorted shots, multiple exposures, traveling mattes, and animated sequences that allow fragmented glimpses of characters in a purely cinematic space. Watson's high key, chiaroscuro lighting reveals and shrouds objects and characters, again giving audiences few visual cues to orient themselves in his spatial construction.

Watson and Webber's second avant-garde film, *Tomatos Another Day* (1930), on the other hand, is a unique example of Dadaist aesthetics in early sound cinema – a minimalist and virtually expressionless acting style is implemented on a claustrophobic set, the overtly melodramatic love triangle held in long takes and medium shots to accentuate the narrative's theatrical space. A husband surprises his wife *in flagrante* with her lover and shoots him. The actors verbalize their every action, ironically commenting on the oververbalization of early sound films and on the inane plots of post–silent era Hollywood productions. The Dadaist clash of low art melodrama and statically stylized body language was possibly too modernist and satirical for Watson's own taste; he considered the film a failure and suppressed its existence until it was recently discovered in the nitrate holdings of the estate.

Figure 12.2 Frame enlargement from 35mm print of director James Sibley Watson at the camera (1937). (Courtesy of George Eastman House, Motion Picture Department Collection.)

Collaborating again with Melville Webber, Watson also shot *Lot in Sodom* in his Prince Street studio in New York, using a home-made optical printer. While ostensibly based on the biblical story of Lot and his wife, who is turned into a pillar of salt while fleeing Sodom, the film is much more concerned with nonnarrative elements – the play of light and shadow, the balletic movement of bodies, multiple exposures and optical tricks, and lyrical visual symbolism. The film's imagery is also highly erotic in the scenes where Lot offers his daughter to the angel and homoerotic in its lightplay on semi-nude bodies of numerous young men. Working without dialogue and with sparse titles superimposed in English and Latin, the film features an atonal music track that underscores the film's modernist construction.

Ironically, Edgar Allan Poe was the inspiration for three major avant-garde works in 1928: "The Fall of the House of Usher" was adapted by both Watson and the French experimentalist Jean Epstein, while "The Tell-Tale Heart" was the literary source for Charles Klein's avant-garde short of the same name and was another very low-budget off-Hollywood production starring Otto Matieson, with camerawork by Leon Shamroy. Like *The Love of Zero*, Klein's *The*

Tell-Tale Heart featured expressionistically deformed sets, nineteenth-century Biedermeier costumes, and highly stylized acting. The film opens on a close-up of a pair of eyes superimposed over handwritten text from Poe's opening paragraph. Shot on one set, the film relates the story of an insane young man's murder of an old man and his eventual mental breakdown and confession to a pair of detectives questioning him. Two particularly interesting devices are the use of words burned into the image and the intercutting of single-frame images flashing back to the murder, capturing the subjective state of the protagonist. Another expressionist device is the extremely distorted close-up of the killer, as seen through a magnifying glass by the detectives, hoping to discover "guilt in his eyes." The close-up of the old man's eyes and the superimposition of a beating hammer become visual tropes for Poe's literary device of the victim's beating heart.

Charles Vidor's *The Bridge* (1931) is an adaptation of Ambrose Bierce's short story, "An Occurrence at Owl Creek Bridge." Although the story is set in the American South during the Civil War, Vidor's adaptation is set during World War I, somewhere in Austro-Hungary (based on the uniforms). Vidor uses both flashbacks and a flash-forward technique to visualize the escape fantasy of the protagonist condemned to hang as a spy. While the drum rolls, the spy remembers his mother and childhood, then as he falls and the noose snaps his neck, he fantasizes the rope breaking, allowing him to escape. As he runs joyously down a road, he sees his mother and himself as a child ahead, bringing flashback and flash-forward together with his realization that it is all a dream in the moment before death. The film's real locations, nonprofessional actors without makeup, and quick cutting style – creating a montage of fantasy and grim reality – effectively create a mixture of objectivity and subjectivity, stretching a few moments of story time into a one-reel film.

Adapted and edited by Seymour Stern, Josef Berne's *Dawn to Dawn* (1934) tells the story of a young farm girl who comes into conflict with her authoritarian father over a young drifter who spends the night at the isolated farm. In the morning the girl decides to flee with the boy but then tells him she cannot go through with it, not realizing that her father has died of a stroke in the next room. Presented in only a few scenes, with a cast of unknowns without makeup, and virtually silent except for a musical score, the film's strength is its lyrical realism, its explicit seduction scene, its pastoral scenes set on a real farm that do not suppress the harsh reality of American agriculture before the age of electricity and machinery. The film also employs strong diagonals in its composition, along with expressionist lighting effects in the final confrontation. Its central narrative conceit, the fear of strangers in a rural environment, touched deeply rooted chords in the American psyche, while almost self-consciously developing a realist aesthetic.

Finally, Hollywood stills photographer Roman Freulich directed his first short, *The Prisoner* (1934), now lost, followed by *Broken Earth* (1936). The later film relates the story of a black sharecropper whose son comes down with a fever and is miraculously revived through the father's fervent prayer. Shot in actual locations with nonprofessional actors (except for Clarence Muse), the film's early scenes focus in a highly realistic manner on the incredible hardship of black farmers – the plowing scenes similarly powerful to those in *Dawn to Dawn* – while the latter half demonstrates the centrality of the religious experience for a rural African-American population.

Parody and Metaphor in the Early Avant-Garde

It seems to be no coincidence that the experimental narratives discussed here were not only attempting to expand aesthetically beyond the confines of Hollywood classical narrative into an art cinema market, but also were produced by European-born or educated amateurs or film technicians who were on the fringes of the film industry. At the same time these films, like those of the Europhile James Sibley Watson, are not simply copies of European art films. Their thematic concerns are for the most part American, their stylistic sensibilities a mixture of sophistication and naïveté, and their aesthetics against the grain of Hollywood narrative. In contrast to these serious narratives, the first American avant-garde also developed a more satirical form of narrative. The 1930s avant-garde, in general, seemed to gravitate toward metaphor and parody, possibly a sign of the increasingly difficult times.

Robert Florey and William Cameron Menzies's *The Love of Zero* (1928) leans more toward parody, in this case of German Expressionism. Featuring Joseph Mari and costing only $200 according to the film's credits, the film alternates between campy stylization and earnest camera experiments. Visible in whole sets, heavily indebted to *The Cabinet of Dr. Caligari*, Zero is dressed in full Biedermeier regalia, the jerky acting a hyperbolic stylization of expressionist body movement. Reminding us of Méliès and anticipating Godard, Florey also uses jump cuts to have the hero hop around manically in an alley, after having fallen in love while playing trombone from a balcony. The painted flowers in the same scene will reappear in Menzies's design scheme for *The Wizard of Oz* (1939), for which he later won an Oscar. Zero is still playing trombone from his perch and his love listening adoringly when they learn that, by order of the Grand Vizier, she will never see him again. Zero offers love to a prostitute on the street, but she wants money, sending Zero to despair. In the dissolves that follow, Florey uses split screens to create a face from halves of the lovers' faces, along with multiple exposures to create subjective visions of horror until Zero seemingly goes insane.

Parody was the preferred genre of Theodore Huff, another prominent Amateur Cinema League member. Later known as a film historian and Chaplin biographer, Huff directed 16mm spoofs of Hollywood genre films in the early 1930s. His first two productions, *Hearts of the West* (1931) and *Little Geezer* (1932), starred children burlesquing the conventions of Westerns and gangster films. Shot under the pseudonym of D. W. DeReel, their stereotypical characters and plots referenced D. W. Griffith, Greta Garbo, and Warner Bros., but also employed Eisensteinian montage and hand-held camera techniques. The children emphasized that cinema was indeed in its infancy, but they also gave the films an ambiguous sexuality, implicating the subject in the director's slightly perverse gaze.

Mr. Motorboat's Last Stand (1933), Theodore Huff and John Florey's 16mm silent Depression comedy, is a much less self-conscious work, an ironic comment on America's inability to deal with the economic catastrophe of the 1930s. Telling the story of an unemployed African-American who lives in a junkyard, the film uses a garbage dump as a metaphor for capitalism's treatment of ordinary citizens. Living in an abandoned car which in fantasy is a limousine taking him to Wall Street where his business (an apple stand) is located, the hero suffers through the Crash of 1929 and the Depression to follow. *Motorboat* is, in fact, a humorous allegory on America's economic rise and fall, employing visual metaphor in the manner of medieval morality plays, where images communicate their meaning quite literally – the bursting bubble, for instance, refers to the "exploding prosperity bubble" of the 1920s.

Ralph Steiner contributed his own parody of American economic life with *Panther Woman of the Needle Trades, or the Lovely Life of Little Lisa* (1931), made in collaboration with John Florey. The film opens with Jehovah creating the world out of a test tube, then proceeds to present a short history of the universe before 1903, when Elizabeth Hawes, the real-life heroine of the film's title, is born. The film follows her career from childhood seamstress to Parisian designer of *haute couture* via a college education at Vassar.[4] Reminiscent of Florey's *Life and Death of 9413*, in terms of its art direction and elliptical narrative style, *Panther* is a parody of the all-American success story, a young woman's fantasy of a glamorous career in an age of diminishing possibilities.

Ralph Steiner collaborated on *Pie in the Sky* (1934) with Elia Kazan, Irving Lerner, and Molly Day Thatcher, in a film that parodies organized religion's efforts to convince the working classes that their day will come in heaven, making futile any struggle for social improvement on earth. Two working-class heroes embark on a quest through society – again represented as a garbage dump – to find something to fill their empty stomachs, but are served only slogans by various authority figures: A socialite charity person, a priest, and a welfare bureaucrat. The "piece of the pie" remains elusive as the heroes die of starvation and go to heaven, from where they encourage the audience to participate in a sing-a-long (a favorite Depression-era activity in movie theaters). Using polemical statements like just so many advertising campaign slogans, the film indicts the church, the state, and public figures, such as Father Coughlin, as apologists for ruling-class neglect of poverty.

While most avant-garde films discussed in this section are parodies of mainstream commercial cinema, two can be understood as parodies of the avant-garde itself. The first is William Vance's *The Hearts of Age* (1934), with a 19-year-old Orson Welles playing a number of male characters. According to Welles, the film was intended as a parody of *Blood of a Poet* (1930).

The film opens with a positive and negative image of a bell ringing. There follows a series of visual non sequiturs: an old woman sitting on a ringing bell, an angel carrying a globe, a Keystone cop, a Caligari-like figure repeatedly walking down stairs, a black man hanging, a hand beckoning from the grave. Like earlier avant-garde films, *Hearts* privileges obtuse camera angles, Expressionist-influenced makeup and lighting, and narrative ellipses – employing these avant-garde techniques both seriously and tongue-in-cheek.

Roger Barlow, Harry Hay, and LeRoy Robbins produced a parody of the film avant-garde and avant-garde filmmaking with *Even: As You and I* (1937). Playfully ironic, almost Dadaist in construction, the film narrates the attempts of three unemployed young men to earn a cash prize in an amateur film contest. After rejecting numerous "boy meets girl" script ideas, the three discover an article on surrealism and proceed to construct a film of random images. Their film within a film is an anarchistic montage, acknowledging its debt to surrealism, and directly quoting Eugene Atget, Donald Duck, *Un Chien Andalou* (1929), *Ghosts before Breakfast* (1928), *Entre'Acte*, and *Triumph des Willens* (1935), among numerous other avant-garde and nonnarrative films. Almost postmodern in its use of quotation, *Even: As You and I* also comments on the pressure of originality when a canon of avant-garde works has already been established.

Most of these satires have a political dimension – not surprising in a worldwide Depression – an implicit or explicit critique of social relations in American society and the inability of the economy to meet even the most basic needs of its constituency. Like their spiritual predecessor, *Entr'acte*, they also question the role of the artist and the intellectual in a society geared toward profit. But the Depression and World War II would upend the American film avant-garde, at least until a new generation arose in the late 1940s, a generation that would depict themselves as *sui generic*. Not until the end of the century would film historians discover what would once again be defined as the first American film avant-garde.

Notes

1. The 1950s avant-garde also acknowledged the reception of European models, e.g., through Museum of Modern Art film programs, in order to legitimize its own efforts.
2. I first articulated this notion in 1987, in "Modernist Perspectives and Romantic Desire: *Manhatta*," *Afterimage*, 15.4.
3. Virtually all the films discussed in this essay are available in the DVD box set *Unseen Cinema: Early American Avant-Garde Film 1894–1941* (2005), produced by Anthology Film Archives.
4. Elizabeth Hawes was in fact the first American *couturière* to have collections shown in Paris.

References

Arledge, Sara. (1947). Handwritten letter to Frank Stauffacher, August 25. "Art in Cinema" files, Pacific Film Archive, Berkeley, CA.

Arthur, Paul. (2005). *A Line of Sight: American Avant-Garde Film Since 1965*. Minneapolis: University of Minnesota Press.

Gale, Arthur L. (1928). "Amateur Clubs." *Amateur Movie Makers*, 3.2, 100.

Horak, Jan-Christopher (ed.). (1995). *Lovers of Cinema: The First American Film Avant-Garde 1919–1945*. Madison: University of Wisconsin Press.

James, David E. (2005). *The Most Typical Avant-Garde: History and Geography in Minor Cinemas in Los Angeles*. Berkeley: University of California Press.

MacDonald, Scott. (2002). *Cinema 16: Documents toward a History of the Film Society*. Philadelphia: Temple University Press.

Mekas, Jonas. (1972). *Movie Journal: The Rise of a New American Cinema*. New York: Collier Books.

Sitney, P. Adams. (1979). *Visionary Film: The American Avant-Garde 1943–1978*. New York: Oxford University Press.

Wasson, Haidee. (2005). *Museum Movies: The Museum of Modern Art and the Birth of Art Cinema*. Berkeley: University of California Press.

13

"Let 'Em Have It"

The Ironic Fate of the 1930s Hollywood Gangster

Ruth Vasey
Senior Lecturer, Flinders University, Australia

Percussive gunshots, explosions, fast cars, and ethnically inflected dialogue – gangster films produced between 1930 and 1932 took full advantage of new **sound technology** and advancing **realism**. But these aesthetic opportunities were trumped by Hollywood's concerns with public relations and keeping censors and social critics at bay. The result, as Ruth Vasey argues, was the "rapid effacement of the gangster's ethnic origins." Under continuous pressure from the **Production Code Administration**, working-class hoodlums were transformed into crime-fighting **G-Men** seeking to rid the nation of its **Prohibition-era** stains. The poor immigrant criminal was repackaged into a suave gentleman whose wits replaced his need for violence, the firepower now safely in the hands of federal agents. By decade's end, the Hollywood gangster film could not help but reflect on its **pre-Code** origins or turn toward **self-conscious parody**. Through extensive archival research, Vasey illustrates the gangster film trajectory as a case study of the studios' juggling box office demands, star personae, **Breen Office** interventions, and concerns about the reaction of foreign audiences to its Italian/Italian-American gangsters. Vasey's essay shares ground with Matthew H. Bernstein on the studio system and Richard Maltby on studio realism in this volume.

Additional terms, names, and concepts: Motion Picture Producers and Distributors of America (MPPDA), Edward G. Robinson, James Cagney, Joseph I. Breen

In the 1930s, the major Hollywood studios produced approximately 400 films per year. The vast majority of these faded from public memory almost immediately after their initial period of exhibition, but a small number have continued to resonate in the public imagination to the present day. Prominent amongst these is a spate of "gangster" films, including *Little Caesar* (Warner Bros., 1930), *The Public Enemy* (Warner Bros., 1931), and *Scarface: The Shame of a Nation* (Caddo, 1932), the majority of which were made in the production season of 1930/1931, when a grand total of 23 films revolving around "gang"

American Film History: Selected Readings, Origins to 1960, First Edition. Edited by Cynthia Lucia, Roy Grundmann, and Art Simon.
© 2016 John Wiley & Sons, Inc. Published 2016 by John Wiley & Sons, Inc.

themes were produced. This amounted to less than 6 percent of the industry's total annual output and from 1932 onwards the numbers of these movies dwindled, but the notoriety of a handful of the early films was perpetuated, particularly at Warner Bros., by the recirculation and reformulation of elements of the original gangster formula. This essay considers some of the factors that, while contributing to the popularity of the unreconstructed screen gangster in the early 1930s, also insured that he made an early exit from Hollywood's production schedules. It traces his subsequent reincarnations throughout the decade in forms that, while being engineered to constitute more socially benign entertainment, were nevertheless characterized by an increasingly complex, nuanced, and contradictory relationship with their audiences.

Like the "fallen women" movies that appeared at the same time, soon after the introduction of sound, the gangster movies provided a tangible focus for public disquiet about the cultural effect of screen entertainment and its perceived capacity to undermine middle-class values. Motion pictures were particularly vulnerable to attacks by conservative forces within the United States when they dealt with sex and crime, particularly in "sordid" situations, typically understood as the immigrant-dominated slums of the larger metropolises. The movies' offensiveness was exacerbated when the criminal or prostitute occupied the center of their narratives instead of being relegated to the margins. These sensitive factors converged in the gangster film, and the systematic distancing of the screen gangster from these environments during the 1930s reveals much about the Hollywood industry's attitudes to, and representations of, social class. At the same time, the Italian and Irish characterizations of the early gangsters, highlighted by the fact that newly disseminated sound technology allowed audiences to hear the dialogue spoken rather than reading it in intertitles, also made "mob" pictures particularly controversial, attracting the ire of both foreign and domestic critics of the industry. The rapid effacement of the gangster's ethnic origins throughout the decade constituted eloquent testimony to the on-screen compromises that were prerequisites for broad-scale distribution.

While the early gangster movies were conspicuous as a result of their centrality to public debates about the social and cultural impact of sound pictures, their enduring notoriety also had a more directly aesthetic dimension. The most prominent of the early gangster movies capitalized upon sound technology to create a sensational and innovative screen aesthetic featuring violent iconography and sound effects, organized around powerful central dramatic performances and overlaid upon traditionally melodramatic narrative structures. The extraordinary appeal of this aesthetic to young male audiences helps to account for both the short-term commercial success of the gangster movies and the strenuous efforts made by Hollywood's "organized industry" to suppress them in support of its long-term public relations interests.

Enter the All-Talking Gangster

The American screen has been attracted to movies about lower-class criminality virtually since its inception, from D. W. Griffith's early feature *The Musketeers of Pig Alley* (Biograph, 1912), which dealt with organized crime, to *Underworld* (Paramount, 1927) and *The Racket* (Caddo, 1928), which discussed official corruption. It was not until the production season of 1930–1931, however, following the widespread dissemination of sound technology, that underworld pictures began to be produced in sufficient numbers to constitute a "cycle," or a conspicuous production trend of movies resembling one another in theme and treatment. Tapping into topical discourses about juvenile delinquency, organized crime, and official corruption, the movies were loosely described as "gang pictures" within the industry; they have acquired their routine "gangster" tag and especially the notion that they belonged to a "gangster genre" only retrospectively. Set during the era of Prohibition, they were united by the brutality of their violence (especially gun-related violence), their evocation of metropolitan immigrant-dominated slums, and their thematic exploration of the notion of "success" as defined by the underworld rather than by conventional society.

It is not merely coincidental that the gangster cycle coincided with the widespread adoption of sound. Soundtracks introduced audiences to the gritty, "realistic" styles of representation that ambient sound made possible. Even in *The Lights of New York* (Warner Bros., 1928), the "first 100% talking picture," wailing sirens, squealing tires, and especially the sudden shock of gunfire showcased the discordant visceral impact of the new technology. In this sense, the gangster cycle was the obverse to the cycle of stage-based musicals that also capitalized on the introduction of sound. Where the musicals employed sound to invoke social harmony through the shared participation in song and dance, the gangster movies used it as an assault on the audience, invoking dissonance and social chaos. Where the musical constituted an optimistic and Utopian antidote to the Depression, the gangster movie reveled in the discordant and chaotic tenor of the times.

The public relations problems posed by the introduction of sound took considerably longer to solve than the technological challenges they presented. Silent movies with social problem themes had been able to gloss over sensitive subject matter using ambiguous visuals and vague or euphemistic intertitles; but with the introduction of a soundtrack containing dialogue, the movies were obliged to become more explicit. City conservatives, sections of rural American consumers, and significant areas of the foreign market, already concerned about the cultural impact of Hollywood, balked at the thought of contemporary social themes being discussed frankly in front of their children. The prospect of the movies drawing upon the Broadway stage for sophisticated dialogue-based subject matter was bad enough, but the "sordid realism" being brought to the treatment of criminal subjects was more alarming still. Despite the enthusiasm with which it was received by the majority of moviegoers, sound technology provided a new focus for criticism of Hollywood and called into question its suitability for general consumption.

Questions of taste and tone made the gangster pictures particularly vulnerable to middle-class condemnation. The American motion picture industry in 1930 was still trying to shake off the odium that attached to its already mythologized origins, in the crowded, lower-class immigrant areas of the largest cities. From its inception in 1922, the movie industry's trade association, the Motion Picture Producers and Distributors of America (MPPDA), had seen the solution to the industry's chronic public relations problems to be a matter of the gradual bourgeoisification of motion picture material. MPPDA head Will Hays had expended considerable time and effort trying to convince respectable middle-class organizations, from Daughters of the American Revolution to the Boy Scouts, to run campaigns to boost attendances at high-toned movies, in the hope that box office pressure would persuade producers that their best chance for profits lay in material that was tasteful, moral, and middle class. The gangster movies seemed to throw this entire hard-fought process into reverse. In the underworld settings of the gangster films, the movies returned to the lower-class urban environments from which they had being trying to free themselves for 20 years. The gangster was the antithesis of the upright bourgeois hero: Not only was he a criminal, but he was also typically a recent immigrant with vulgar taste in suits and ties. Instead of the movies fulfilling their great destiny in Americanizing their own domestic audiences (and thence the world), they threatened to teach their sons to speak in the bastardized Italianesque argot of Muni/Camonte and push grapefruits in the faces of their sisters at the dinner table in imitation of Cagney; and instead of teaching middle-class girls the virtues of modesty and womanliness, they showed them how to swagger and shimmer like Jean Harlow. Sound technology again exacerbated these issues, since it allowed the vernacular accents of the inner-city underworld to reach the screen for the first time, unmediated by literary titles. In a complete sense that had not been possible before, the personal style and vocabulary of the criminal or gangster were available for imitation, as was the drawl of his underdressed girlfriend.

In 1930, the year preceding the gangster cycle, the MPPDA had attempted to confront some of the public relations problems inherent in the sound film by introducing a codified set of standards to regulate aspects of Hollywood's representation, chiefly in the areas of sex and criminality. Titled a "Code to Maintain Social and Community Values in the Production of Synchronized and Talking Motion Pictures," or Production Code, and formulated in consultation with representatives of the Catholic Church, these standards superseded an existing set of guidelines (the "Don'ts and Be Carefuls"), which were themselves based upon analysis of the varying censorship standards that Hollywood had to contend with in foreign markets, US municipalities, and several US states. The Code was overtly introduced to appease the critics of the industry, but it also helped producers avoid "mutilation" of their products by censors – a much more expensive and difficult issue in the sound era than it had been throughout the 1920s. The MPPDA also strengthened earlier efforts to get producers to consult with the Association's own advisory committee, the Studio Relations Committee (later the Production Code Administration), during the preparation of scripts and later during the process of production; after October 8, 1931, the submission of scripts to the Studio Relations Committee was made compulsory.

While movies were still routinely marketed as "sensational," the well-publicized regulatory mechanisms of the MPPDA reassured their critics that they would not use their position of cultural centrality to undermine existing social structures. Although the movies' appeal was often in the way they showcased the material trappings of modernity – the latest products, fashions, and pastimes – the MPPDA's regulatory agencies worked tirelessly to insure that all this was packaged within apparently innocuous narrational frameworks with traditionally moral outcomes. As an agency of the motion picture companies themselves, the Studio Relations Committee (reconstituted in 1934 as the Production Code Administration) saw its job not as that of a censor but as that of a facilitating agency that could, through judicious advice and intervention, enable properties to be "picturized" without provoking damaging reactions from sensitive elements of the public. Its guidelines constitute a reliable index of the permissible limits of representation in movie narratives of the time, arising from the public anxieties that threatened the movie industry in the form of calls for censorship and legislative intervention. In this context, it is significant that, despite the fact that they were few in number, gangster movies constituted one of the MPPDA's greatest public relations concerns in the early 1930s, reflected in the disproportionate amount of time, correspondence, and revision required to bring these movies to the screen.

The Production Code responded to concerns that movies with underworld themes would act as "schools for crime" by limiting the representation of actions such as arson, safe-cracking, the "dynamiting of trains," and gambling. In the treatment of *Stolen Heaven* (Paramount, 1931), for example, the Studio Relations Committee advised the studio to shoot a gambling scene "so that the camera is just above the table line, leaving in the hands moving etc.," but excluding any details involving the exchange of money.[1] Such treatments were encouraged by censorship action: The New York Censor Board, for example, banned any scenes showing roulette wheels or the exchange of money in illegal gambling. Evasive strategies for representing crime were encouraged by the practical methods adopted by censor boards, whose members typically only saw a movie once, marking items for excision as they went along, resulting in a disproportionate emphasis upon concrete visual details.

While Hollywood's principal address was to its domestic customers, its products had to be capable of being distributed internationally, to a foreign market that consistently accounted for approximately 35 percent of its gross income between the world wars. The issue of stereotyping of foreign nationals, especially in criminal or comic roles, was taken very seriously by customer nations, which were apt to institute boycotts and bans in response to instances of offense. This was of particular relevance to gangster and underworld pictures, which typically depended upon colorful immigrant neighborhoods to populate their fictions. The Italian-American characters in the early 1930s gangster movies, including both *Little Caesar* and *Scarface*, incensed the vocal and powerful Italian contingent within the United States as well as the Italian government and led to protests from the Italian Embassy. Italy became so sensitive about representations of gangsters and Mafia figures that it banned *Star of Midnight* (RKO, 1935) on the strength of a reference to a Chicago gangster called Moroni, although the studio claimed that the villain was actually an Irishman named Maroney; the point was necessarily moot, since the character never actually appeared on-screen.

The most problematic public relations issue arising from the gangster movies was their tendency to publicize, if not to glorify, the exploits of criminal figures, especially those based on actual gangsters such as Al Capone. Parents and educators worried that children and other "impressionable" viewers (who comprised an imperfectly differentiated amalgam of illiterates, "morons," and immigrants) would be so impressed by the personalities on the screen that they would be inspired to imitate them; and while movies could be prevented from becoming "textbooks of crime" by the removal of the means of literal imitation, the prevention of the *desire* to imitate criminals was less straightforward. Stories with irreproachable moral resolutions were susceptible to subversive interpretations on the strength of the performances they contained, and a mandatory punishment for criminal or unconventional behavior did not necessarily cancel the appeal of a character's wildness or vitality.

Figure 13.1 In Mervyn LeRoy's *Little Caesar* (1930, producers Hal B. Wallis and Darryl F. Zanuck), the ambitions of Rico (Edward G. Robinson) are constrained by his class and ethnic origins, most conspicuously indicated by his fondness for flashy clothes and jewelry.

For example, *Are These Our Children?* (RKO, 1931), a story about drink and juvenile delinquency, was approved by the Studio Relations Committee as "a straight, realistic theme, pointing a very strong moral lesson,"[2] but the New York Censor Board subsequently rejected it on the grounds that its scenes of jazz parties and teenage dissipation, and especially its sympathetic teenage lead (Eddie Brand), would prove more attractive than cautionary to its young audiences.

Early 1930s Gangsters: *The Public Enemy, Little Caesar, and Scarface*

The Doorway to Hell (Warner Bros., 1930) was arguably the initiator of the gangster cycle, as its financial success was the first to suggest the viability of the gangster protagonist in the sound era. It is, however, *The Public Enemy*, *Little Caesar*, and *Scarface* that have come to represent the cycle in the popular imagination. All three are distinguished by the powerful performances of their central characters, played by James Cagney, Edward G. Robinson, and Paul Muni, respectively. These charismatic performances helped to make the films "movie dynamite" in the best and the most dangerous senses of the term.

Cagney as Tommy Powers in *Public Enemy* is probably the most well-known example of a performance that, despite the character's gruesome end, was celebrated and widely imitated among boys for its fidgety, streetwise edginess. That the gangster movies' appeal, especially those featuring Cagney, was overwhelmingly to an urban male audience is a fact widely attested in commentaries of the time. The trade journal *Variety* claimed in 1932 that Cagney's typical audience was "90% male," attracted by "the manner in which James handles his film women" and "the way he scraps" (*Variety* 1932). He certainly had a certain cocky charm, and his unmannered, rapid-fire vocal delivery and rather average looks made him a natural object of identification for metropolitan boys and men, who were also attracted by the movies' visceral effects associated with the performance of violence.

In *Little Caesar*, Robinson's Rico is a brutal but vain and ultimately tragic figure whose aspirations to become one of the suave "big boys" dominating gangland are doomed by his lower-class origins and sensibilities, as expressed by his dialogue ("It sure is good to see all you gents with your molls here") and his dress sense. His idea of success is to be able to afford fancy clothes and a jeweled tie-pin; he squirms uncomfortably when required to don a tuxedo to pay a visit to the higher-class "big boys" controlling the rackets. As played by Robinson, Rico is a habitual and unrepentant killer, but his small vanities and personal limitations also make him a sympathetic character, and when he is machine-gunned in cold blood by Flaherty, his policeman nemesis, at the end of the movie, there is little sense of moral triumph.

In *Scarface*, Muni's psychopathic Tony Camonte emerges from a working-class Italian neighborhood to rampage fearlessly through most of the movie with murderous mania and boundless self-confidence. While he ultimately follows the dictates of the Production Code and proves that crime does not pay, either losing his nerve and dying under police fire or being led to the gallows, depending on the version one encounters, this narrative resolution does little to dilute the striking impression of the previous scenes. The fact that aspects of his career were clearly based upon the exploits of Al Capone only exacerbated the perceived dangers in Muni's colorful performance.

Iconographically, the most objectionable feature of gangster movies was guns in the hands of criminals, as Stephen Prince discusses in detail in his *Classical Film Violence: Designing and Regulating Brutality in Hollywood Cinema, 1930–1968* (2003). The Studio Relations Committee worked hard to keep machine guns in particular off the screen. Yet even when shooting takes place offscreen or out of view, the importance of the soundtrack in creating an atmosphere of violence and menace cannot be overstated. In *Little Caesar* the opening shot merely shows two men entering a gas station in the middle distance at night in what is evidently a stick-up. No dialogue is audible, but when the lights are switched off shots ring out, announcing the first callous murder with a sense of shocking immediacy that was unachievable in silent film. In the versions of the movie that eventually went into release, Rico complies with the advice of the Studio Relations Committee by never actually using a machine gun himself, but this detail may have been lost upon audiences since the weapon still looms large in the action: Rico is the target of an attempted machine-gun hit by a rival mobster and is finally machine-gunned by the police at the movie's end.

In *The Public Enemy*, Tom Powers is also an exponent of the hand gun, although this in no way reduces his capacity for brutality. His execution of his former mentor Putty Nose is particularly chilling: The camera pans away just before the shots are heard, and the audience witnesses only the shocked reaction of Tommy's friend Matt (an unfortunate horse is purportedly killed in a similar manner). The atmosphere of violence and anarchy is ratcheted up by machine-gun attacks perpetrated by rival gangs, with a bomb lobbed into a bar for good measure; the images of these "gang war" sequences are married to the aural shocks on the soundtrack in a manner designed to elicit the maximum sensational impact upon an audience unaccustomed to synchronized effects.

Unlike *Little Caesar* and *Scarface*, *The Public Enemy* seeks to utilize sound to create a semi-documentary feel, especially in the opening "historical" footage of Tom's childhood environment. As Richard Maltby comments, the movie deliberately draws upon contemporary discussions of the influence of environment upon juvenile delinquency, especially the work of Chicago sociologist Frederic Thrasher, whose influential *The Gang: A Study of 1,313 Gangs in Chicago* was published in 1927 (Maltby 2005, 42–52). As described by Thrasher, gang membership was an adolescent or postadolescent phenomenon that acted as a kind of prelude to the mature criminality of the mobster, racketeer, or other professional criminal; thus, in Thrasher's terms, *The Public Enemy*, with its emphasis on Tommy Powers's boyhood and criminal education, is the "gangster" picture that goes most to the heart of contemporary notions of gangs.

Warner Bros., cognizant of the public relations problems inherent in juvenile delinquency themes, set out to justify the movie as an earnest, if entertaining, semi-sociological study of the kinds of social conditions that resulted in boys going off the rails. In case the audience missed the point, the movie was furnished with an explanatory foreword: "It is the ambition of the authors of 'The Public Enemy' to honestly depict an environment that exists today in a certain strata [*sic*] of American life, rather than glorify the hoodlum or the criminal ... " In the movie's early scenes the visuals of the working-class neighborhood are augmented by layered sound including ambient sounds of the street, a newspaper hawker, and a Salvation Army band. Despite some incongruously theatrical performances, notably from Donald Cook as Tom's brother Mike, the sense that the movie is grounded in "real" neighborhoods lends a palpable edge to the violence on the streets.

Both *Little Caesar* and *The Public Enemy* were produced by Warner Bros., which earned a reputation for relatively low-budget, gritty, crime-themed dramas that it brought out alongside its musicals and melodramas in the 1930s. *Scarface* was the odd movie out, having been produced by Howard Hughes's boutique studio, Caddo. Hughes was a man of strong opinions and with very little experience in conforming to the requirements of the "organized industry" as represented by the Studio Relations Committee. Not only was Tony Camonte a barely disguised version of Capone, but the movie was chock full of machine guns, including a scene in which Tony responds with gleeful enthusiasm when he comes into possession of a machine-gun cache. *Scarface* was held up in production for nearly two years while Caddo and the Studio Relations Committee struggled to reach a compromise over the nature of the script. Even in the highly compromised versions that were finally released (and there were several), the movie is a renegade for the time of its production and provides many of the most enduring images and sounds of the gangster cycle. Directed by Howard Hawks, it is extraordinarily fast-paced, its soundtrack laden with shots, explosions, screams, sirens, whistles, and machine-gun fire. Ironically, part of the Studio Relations Committee's strategy for releasing the picture involved turning it into a demonstration of the consequences of lax gun laws; in the process they managed to show just how sensational gun violence could be on the screen.

By the time *Scarface* was eventually released it was an anachronism; the original cycle of gangster movies was largely over. Motion picture cycles rarely lasted more than a couple of production seasons before they were supplanted by the next big thing. In the case of the gangster movie, however, there is no doubt that its phasing out was deliberately hastened by the intervention of the MPPDA. In April 1931, the Association had brought in a special resolution to stagger the release dates of underworld subjects, arguing that it was not good business practice to flood the nation's screens with movies based on a single theme, especially a controversial one. At the same time, in the short period since the introduction of sound, both the Studio Relations Committee and the studios themselves had rapidly become more practiced at handling problematic themes in ways that did not expose the industry to public disapprobation, and in the process the gangster theme had undergone a fundamental change. The new approach is illustrated in a 1932 letter from Jason Joy to MPPDA head Will Hays, concerning *The Mouthpiece* (Warner Bros., 1932):

> Another big question of the week was to do with a Warners story called *The Mouthpiece*, which in its original form was full of dynamite. It dealt with gangsters, a miscarriage of justice which sent the leading character off on the wrong track, and contained doubtful sex situations. First by attacking the theme itself, we were successful in taking the story altogether out of the gangster category and to substitute dramatic motivation which turned it into proper directions. By the time we had the second script we were in such position as to take up the lesser details and by almost casual suggestions even to correct such a policy matter as the character of a crooked banker, changing him into a stock broker. This latter had some significance as you will see in these precarious economic times when faith in banks is strained. This has been an interesting shaping of basic material which the Code makes possible.[3]

The movie concerned a lawyer who was disillusioned with the legal system and cynically manipulated it in order to defend underworld characters whom he knew to be guilty. In its final form, the lawyer not only recovered his confidence in American justice and underwent moral regeneration, but he also paid for his transgressions by being gunned down in the final sequence by his former underworld contacts.

The Post-Gangster Gangster Movie: *"G" Men* and *Bullets or Ballots*

In 1934 the Production Code was reaffirmed and strengthened with new financial sanctions available to be used against any instance of noncompliance. The Studio Relations Committee was reconstituted as the Production Code Administration (PCA) under the direction of Joseph I. Breen. While much has been made of Breen's function as a "new broom" to clean up motion picture content, in fact his approach to controversial material was the same as that employed by his predecessor Jason Joy: to render details of treatment sufficiently obscure for the audience to be responsible for their own conclusions, particularly in relation to sex and crime.

Some of the PCA's guidelines had a direct impact on narrative and character development, including the stricture that agents of law enforcement should not be shown dying at the hands of criminals. Mandates of this kind, introduced in order to avoid setting a bad example to impressionable and criminal elements, not only posed challenges for script development but also arguably worked in a manner contrary to their stated rationale: It is possible that, by making violent criminal acts less explicit and less consequential, they may have actually countered public alarm about armed criminality on the streets of America's cities. The guidelines also made it more difficult for the studios to characterize their criminals as utterly murderous. Under these conditions it was comparatively difficult to insure that criminals would not be viewed sympathetically, especially when they were inevitably doomed to be shot, executed, or incarcerated before the end of the picture. The solution devised by the studios in 1935, in a typically ingenious compromise, was to exploit "G-man" themes, in which a Justice Department operative with a cinematic license to kill, often acting undercover, could infiltrate the underworld and, in more ways than one, assume the role of a mobster.

As observed in many commentaries on the screen gangster, the G-man movies maintained a complex, more or less explicit, and frequently perverse relationship with the gangster movies that they replaced, expressed through both narrative references and, most obviously, casting and performance (see, for example, Munby 1999). In *"G" Men* (Warner Bros., 1935) James Cagney plays protagonist "Brick" Davis, who is an amalgamation of the iconic Tom Powers from *The Public Enemy* and other Cagney characterizations that built upon that movie's success, including Patsy Gargan in *The Mayor of Hell* (1933). Whereas Tom Powers's underprivileged upbringing on the mean streets of Chicago sees him live and die a gangster, Brick's underprivileged upbringing on the mean streets of New York persuades him to become a lawyer (albeit with his studies bankrolled by a well-meaning mobster), and ultimately to become a federal agent for the US Department of Justice, where his streetwise attitude and knowledge of mob life give him the skills he needs to track down a murderous gang. With the narrative trajectory safely contained within a moral framework, the work of the PCA was confined to insuring that nothing specifically objectionable occurred within the frame, or, in an interesting extension of the organization's earlier *modus operandi*, upon the soundtrack. Breen issued the following advice to Jack Warner:

> There should be no details of crime shown at any time. The action of the gangsters entering the bank, holding up the clerk and bashing him over the head with the revolver; slapping the girl; getting the money and running away; as well as the use of machine guns either by actual display or by inference from the soundtrack will have to be entirely deleted. We suggest that you indulge yourselves in this connection in a series of Vorkapich shots [i.e., a "Hollywood montage" sequence] merely suggesting the hold-up ... There should be no definite details of the hold-up at any time. Not only are the detailed methods of crime forbidden by our Code, but invariably they are deleted by censor boards everywhere – both in this country and abroad.[4]

In order for Tom Powers, the gangster, to reappear as Brick Davis, the G-man, it was necessary for the G-men themselves to undergo a transformation. The narrative is shaped around an historically based incident in which several government agents were gunned down by mobsters when transporting a federal prisoner, as a result of which early Federal Bureau of Investigation (FBI) agents gained the right to carry weapons. The inclusion of this scene in the movie not only allows it to replay the violent iconography and aural effects of the earlier gangster films, but also gives a narrative justification for licensing the G-Men, formerly the impotent victims of the mobs, to act with deadly force. By the end of the movie they are equipped to blaze away at their gangster foes in a prolonged shoot-out. It is during this exchange of fire that Cagney's performance of Davis is most strongly overlaid with his earlier performance of Powers: He enters the fray with his gun drawn and his coat collar turned up in a visual nod to the "I ain't so tough" shooting sequence near the end of *The Public Enemy*. This is the principal pay-off scene for the Cagney fans in the audience, in which the promise of the movie's tag line, "Hollywood's Most Famous Bad Man joins the 'G-MEN' and Halts the March of Crime!," is delivered in Cagney's simultaneous incarnation of the Famous Bad Man and his nemesis.

The casting of Hollywood stars in roles that echoed, developed, or inverted their previous box office successes was hardly unusual – indeed, it was fundamental to the varied interplay between narrative and performance that formed the basis of Hollywood genres. The character of Tom Powers in *The Public Enemy* had resonated so strongly in the public imagination that Cagney's subsequent roles were necessarily colored by the audience's awareness of that performance, even if it was only in his rapid vocal style or his habitual twitchiness (as in the 1933 Warner Bros. musical *Footlight Parade*, for example). In the case of the G-man movies, however, Hollywood's systems of regulation provided a systematic framework within which the studios negotiated characterization and performance.

By removing gangster antiheroes from the screen, the G-man movies were able to proclaim their own worthiness and, by extension, to insist upon the morally responsible stance of the Hollywood industry. The G-man movie *Let 'Em Have It* (Reliance/United Artists, 1935) provided a good deal of footage "given over to showing the care with which the Government selects these men, the period of training through which the men are put, and the intelligence with which later they proceed about their work," according to Joe Breen. He also noted that, "In all of these pictures there is a fine uplift, and the reaction we got last night after viewing the Reliance picture was most exhilarating."[5] Unfortunately, from the MPPDA's point of view, the trade-off for all this rectitude – the aesthetic of violence that had been the hallmark of the early gangster film – still tended to characterize the G-man variant, as the unreconstructed title of *Let 'Em Have It* suggests.

Breen still found reason to complain to producers about "details of crime, repeated scenes of vicious brutality, killings and the needless and excessive showing of guns and gunplay."[6] Uncomfortable with the sordid lower-class associations of stereotypical gangsters, he consistently attempted to modify their tone and milieu, and to discourage the representation of the "hard-looking, foul-speaking" type of gangster. Instead, he tried to promote a new kind of criminal who was "softly spoken and had the appearance of a gentleman": "Instead of showing an eagerness to kill, he is eager to avoid killing, preferring to use his wits to gain his ends rather than to use weapons, to resort to scheming rather than violence" (Martin 1937, 134). In relation to *Bullets or Ballots* (Warner Bros., 1936), Breen wrote to Jack Warner confirming the following strategy for representing racketeers:

> [Producer Lou] Edelman will keep away entirely from those incidents and details which are usually associated with "gangster pictures." … [T]he criminals engaged in the huge and highly profitable "rackets" will be of the suave, well-educated, well-dressed, polite type – more like successful bankers or businessmen than like gangsters. There will be no showing of guns, and no gun battles with police. The two sinister figures in the present synopsis, who are engaged as "killers," will not be shown in the new treatment; and where, for storyline, it is necessary to "bump off" two or three of our racketeers, this will be done either by suggestion or in dialogue, but not in any brutally murderous fashion.[7]

Breen's comments confirm the class-based objections that always underlay the MPPDA's objections to the gangster cycle: As long as the criminals were sufficiently polite and well dressed, and the movies avoided bad taste, vulgarity, and explicit violence, the problems associated with criminal/gangster themes would disappear.

Consciously or not, Breen's ideas echoed broader public perceptions about gangsters such as Al Capone as successful "criminal entrepreneurs" of the Prohibition era; as Thrasher put it, "They provide the organizing energy and business brains of crime; they are the so-called 'silk hat' gangsters who engineer the larger illegal enterprises" (Thrasher 1963, 286). Yet, in another of the many ironies adhering to the screen gangster, while the PCA wished to avoid the vulgar spectacle of lower-class criminality, it was even more averse to representation of the more elite levels of organized crime, beyond the wealthy "big boys" and "bankers" to whom the on-screen gangs answer. Breen's well-educated, well-dressed criminals were never, as a matter of industry policy, the corrupt politicians and municipal officials upon whom actual criminal gangs typically depended for protection and mutual profit.

In its finished form, *Bullets or Ballots* is probably the most extreme example of the complex evolution of the gangster picture into its more acceptable mid-1930s variant. The movie stars Edward G. Robinson of *Little Caesar* fame. In the mid-1930s Robinson was probably even more routinely identified with gangster themes than was Cagney, whose song-and-dance skills allowed him to inhabit a wider range of roles. As with Cagney in *"G" Men*, Robinson's appearance in *Bullets or Ballots* set up certain audience expectations about the aesthetic of violence that the movie would deliver. The striking thing about the movie is not so much that it delivers strongly negotiated and conditional versions of these rewards (as one would expect by 1936), but more the extent to which it incorporates an explicit discussion of its own constraints into the action on-screen.

The movie establishes its old-fashioned gangster credentials as early as the opening credits. The transitions between titles simulate the shattering of glass by machine-gun fire, an effect augmented by a snare drum in the accompanying music track. Instead of opening on an underworld scene, however, the movie begins with a shot that cranes down to a movie theater advertising the movies *Tomorrow* and *The Syndicate of Crime*. Two shifty-looking men ask the cashier what time the "crime picture" begins, then enter the cinema and take their seats. We soon learn, however, that the crime picture is far from a conventional shoot-'em-up gangster flick, as we might have expected. Rather, it is part of a series of short films "presented to the American public as a warning, to arouse them against a growing national menace, the modern racketeer." *The Syndicate of Crime* presents its audience(s) with figures, charts, and documentary footage to explain the extent of this social evil. This material serves the same purpose for the audience of *Bullets or Ballots* as the standard kind of prologue commonly used in Hollywood films to set up a rhetorical context for the action (as in the foreword to *The Public Enemy*, for example). By placing it in a film within a film, however, *Bullets or Ballots* is able to make the claim that the movies are part of the solution to social ills and not part of the problem. This moral claim applies particularly to "crime pictures" – the focus of so much recent criticism of the industry – such as *The Syndicate of Crime* and, by extension, *Bullets and Ballots*. The proposition is developed further when we learn that the two tough-guy moviegoers, Nick "Bugs" Fenner and Al Kruger, are racketeers who feel their operations are threatened by crusading newspaperman Ward Bryant, who is the producer of *The Syndicate of Crime*. In the next sequence arch-heavy Fenner (Humphrey Bogart) guns Bryant down because of the educative power of his movies, which he fears will cause the public to "wake up." Thus within five minutes of the opening credits, *Bullets and Ballots* has made a case for the potency of the motion picture industry as a "vice crusader" and has suggested that the making of crime pictures represents a principled and courageous public service.

When protagonist Johnny Blake (Robinson) is first introduced to the audience, his status within the narrative is ambiguous. The camera pulls back from a newspaper reporting Bryant's death to reveal the reader, in a big close-up of the unsmiling Robinson seated in a café. Given the audience's prior knowledge of Robinson's roles, he could as easily – or more easily – be a gangster than the veteran detective he turns out to be, and this ambiguity forms the crux of much of the plot, as Blake goes undercover to become racketeer and cop simultaneously. Is he a good cop gone bad? His friends and colleagues assume so, seeing him team up with the racketeers. The audience is left wondering until halfway through the film, when a secret meeting with the police commissioner reveals that he is engaged in a risky operation tracking down the corrupt bankers who control Al Kruger's mob.

In keeping with Breen's advice, Kruger and his gang operate out of a respectable office building: The sign on the door labels his operation as the "Metropolitan Business Improvement Association Inc." Kruger himself appears middle class, is not ethnically marked, and mostly behaves like a harried businessman. Although his gang still occupies a warehouse left over from the bootlegging days, they only use it for counting money; in other words, for accountancy. When members of the gang stand over cabaret owner Lee Morgan (Joan Blondell) and her friend Nellie LaFleur (Louise Beavers), trying to muscle in on their

Figure 13.2 In William Keighley's *Bullets or Ballots* (1936, producer Louis F. Edelman), the underworld lighting contradicts the respectable veneer of the Metropolitan Business Improvement Association Inc.

small-time numbers game, Nellie protests that, "You and no other gunmen's gonna tell us what to do." The response is, "You have us wrong, sister. We're businessmen. We don't carry guns . . . . We're just tellin' yer."

The characterization of the racketeers as "heavies" is partly achieved through their casting, as they are presented as the same generic mob of goons who populated the early gangster films, albeit more nattily dressed. In *Bullets or Ballots*, much of the menace of the mob is achieved through the manner in which they are lit, which anticipates the techniques of film noir with its backlighting and curling cigarette smoke (see Keating 2010 for an extended discussion of the expressiveness of lighting during this period). Although the racketeers inhabit modern offices with well-presented furniture and table lamps, the scenes in which they gather are as dark as their predecessors' pool halls and underworld dives. The lighting in these sequences is high contrast to the point of expressionism, with the racketeers' faces obscured by looming shadows and only Johnny's face clearly illuminated, both distinguishing him from the genuine mobsters and allowing the audience to enjoy the subtleties of his performance. While drafts of scripts were routinely subject to vetting by the PCA, meanings and overtones generated by performance, cinematography, and soundtrack only became apparent in the finished product, with the result that the look and feel of the final film could be considerably more semantically complex than was apparent in the script. Through lighting and other effects, an atmosphere of menace could be overlaid upon the most respectable milieu. Unlike conventional "lower-class" gangster iconography, overtones of this kind did not excite adverse public comment, were not subject to state or local censorship, and equally did not concern the regulatory agencies of the PCA.

Despite its efforts to cast itself in a more respectable mold – or because of them – *Bullets or Ballots* exhibits considerable nostalgia for the elements of explicit violence that had permeated the early gangster movies. As an old-fashioned cop with a history of punching out criminals, Johnny Blake is an anomaly in a new world of politically correct policing. In a strange sequence in which Blake and Kruger discuss Bryant's murder, they reminisce about the old days before crooks became businessmen – before Kruger had "a secretary and a chauffeur." As they sit chummily smoking in Kruger's office, they fondly recall the days when Blake used to rough Kruger up. Blake comments that Kruger will be a natural suspect in the murder case:

BLAKE They'll probably try to hang it on you.
KRUGER Well a couple of boys from headquarters were up here half an hour ago. They were very nice about it though.
BLAKE That's the trouble with them. They have to be.
KRUGER You'd have taken me around the corner and rolled up a newspaper.
BLAKE Yeah, I suppose I would. But I didn't get much out of you the last time I gave you a going-over.
KRUGER You came close to it.
BLAKE I wish I'd known it then. You'd have got some more. I wanted to get you on that rap.
KRUGER The good old days, eh Johnny?

There is a sense here in which not only the characters, but also the filmmaker (as well as the audience) yearn for those good old days when red-blooded action ruled the crime film. But Blake, unlike Kruger, has not really moved with the times. He retains his trademark style of resorting to his fists when people get in his way. He even lays out the police commissioner in one scene, and it is a genuine punch, even though it turns out to have been staged as part of his undercover strategy. His natural adversary in the movie is not Kruger, nor even the shadowy crime bosses from the bank, but Fenner, who is a hangover from the unreconstructed movies from 1931, as even his outmoded nickname "Bugs" suggests. Calling Fenner a "ten-cent thug," Kruger effectively accuses him of being in the wrong movie: "Fenner, some day you're going to get wise to the fact that that strong-arm gangster stuff went out with Prohibition. You're not running liquor any more. You're in big business!" Instead of focusing on profit generation, Fenner is motivated by old-fashioned malice; Kruger accuses him of "taking a chance of ruining a two-hundred-million-dollar goldmine to satisfy a grudge."

Although he stands condemned by the standards of the PCA and even by his fellow criminals, Fenner is a necessary ingredient of *Bullets or Ballots.* As the only racketeer prepared to use his gun, he provides not only the pivotal murder of Bryant, but also the climactic shoot-out with Blake, which leaves Fenner dead and Blake with only sufficient strength to stagger to the bank and engineer the capture of the master racketeers. Technically, Fenner's fatal shooting of Blake violates the PCA's guidelines, as it shows a law enforcement officer dying at the hands of a criminal; but Blake/Robinson's on-screen persona is so ambiguous that his death in the street from gunshot wounds (the classic gangster demise) proves too complex for the PCA's regulatory mechanisms to unpick. In any case, without Fenner the promise of traditional gangsterism inherent in the movie's title and credits would be unfulfilled and the audience cheated.

While *Bullets or Ballots* is novel in the way that it seeks to accommodate the mob within the more upmarket corporate environment of the racketeer, it is typical of the post-gangster movie of the mid- to late 1930s in the extent to which it is obliged to negotiate and ameliorate the problematic gangster archetype. Although it was no longer possible to make a naïvely unreconstructed gangster film in 1936, the appeal of gangster characters lingered amongst audiences; moreover, Warner Bros. still had Cagney and Robinson under contract, and it made economic sense to recycle aspects of characters that had made such an impression on the public imagination at the beginning of the decade. Most of Warners' late 1930s pictures with gangster elements feature Cagney or Robinson, often in combination with Bogart. Muni was again the odd one out: Although he was also a star at Warners after *Scarface*, he fulfilled a "great actor" role at the studio, in the second half of the 1930s specializing in prestigious biopics such as *The Story of Louis Pasteur* (1935), *The Life of Emile Zola* (1937), and *Juarez* (1939). Muni tended to submerge himself in his roles and did not carry with him a distinct, imitable set of mannerisms as did Cagney; in costume and makeup he also did not have a distinctive, instantly recognizable face, as did Robinson. Without a strongly marked persona that persisted from role to role, Muni's work was simply too varied to form the basis of generic recycling. While it is also true that his status at the studio gave him an unusual degree of control over his own casting, his performances did not lend themselves well to the production of character-centered intertextual meanings.

The repetitious casting of Cagney and Robinson meant that their successive roles operated in more or less explicit dialogue with those that had come before, in the process grappling with different aspects of the public relations problems inflamed by the original gangster cycle. *Angels With Dirty Faces* (Warner Bros., 1938) invokes a version of Cagney's *The Public Enemy* persona in a narrative built around the issue of juvenile delinquency. If the original Tom Powers was subject to criticism for showing kids how to act like tough guys, his alter ego in *Angels With Dirty Faces*, gangster Rocky Sullivan, not only shows that crime does not pay by being sent to the electric chair, but also demonstrates to them that beneath the surface tough guys are miserable cowards, by "turning yellow" and screaming for mercy as he enters the death chamber. The larger claim implicit here is that the movies themselves have been thoroughly reformed, and that far from glorifying criminals they function to strip them of their mystique. This imputation is, however, undercut by the suggestion that Rocky's uncharacteristic outburst is (unlike Tony Camonte's "yellow" performance in *Scarface*) actually an heroic deed staged at the behest of his friend, Father Jerry Connolly (Pat O'Brien), as a grand gesture to deter the delinquents in the movie from becoming career criminals. Consequently, as far as the boys in the audience are concerned, his death walk is rather more likely to enhance Sullivan's charismatic character than to undercut it. Like *Bullets and Ballots*, *Angels With Dirty Faces* is replete with ironies and contradictions as it contrives to walk the tightrope between high moral purpose and good box office.

When *Scarface* and *Little Caesar* had dramatized gun-running, Prohibition, and the exploits of Al Capone, they had been dealing with the events torn from the headlines. By the late 1930s, the same events could be treated at a remove, with the advantage of historical perspective. For example, *The Last Gangster* (1937) (starring Robinson, on loan to MGM) picks up the story of Joe Krozac, a Capone-inspired character, 10 years after his incarceration for tax evasion. By this time the aging gangster is more concerned about his role as absent father to his 10-year-old son than his role as a mobster. His gang history catches up with him and causes his demise by the end of the movie, while the virtue of clean living and family values – personified by James Stewart as journalist Paul North – are confirmed in the process.

The Roaring Twenties (Warner Bros., 1939) similarly treats its gangster subject in an historical framework, as is evident in the title and the tagline, "The land of the free gone wild! The heyday of the hotcha! The shock-crammed days G-men took ten whole years to lick!" Its original title, *The World Moves On*, was even more explicit about relegating the action to a previous era. The movie, featuring Cagney and Bogart, traces the rise and fall of the Depression-era gangster. Although it attempts to place the violent images and sounds of the earlier underworld movies in an historical context, it is still obliged to tread carefully to avoid the public relations pitfalls that had adhered to the originals. The studio wanted to insert a close-up of a machine gun in a montage sequence, "to show that this was a new and deadly innovation insofar as weapons were concerned, which has now gone out."[8] Breen advised them that he could make no exceptions to the stricture against showing machine guns, even though "it is true that your story, being a kind of 'museum piece' dealing with the history of an era now passed, might suggest something akin to extenuating circumstances,"[9] but in the end he relented, as machine guns are featured in an "historical montage" sequence halfway through the movie, with bombings, gunfire, and mayhem accompanied by the stentorian narration typical of newsreels: "1924 ... A new and horrible tool appears: the 'tommy,' a light, deadly, wasp-like machine gun, and murder henceforth is parceled out in wholesale lots." Although the effects of machine guns wielded by criminals are graphically shown in this sequence, the criminals themselves are either entirely hidden in the shadows or obscured within cars. The only characters clearly shown firing their "tommies" are a carload of police.

The Roaring Twenties' treatment of the Italian community also harks back to earlier concerns, and in the process demonstrates how hide-bound and inflexible many aspects of movie regulation had become by the end of the decade. Although the political situation arising from the coming war meant that Hollywood's official relations with Italy were distinctly frosty by the end of 1938 (Vasey 1997, 23), the PCA took the usual care to avoid causing offense to the Italian community by any implication that it had an association with the mob. The movie does not contain any mention of Italy or the Mafia, but the Anglo-looking gangster "Nick Brown" (Paul Kelly), who is part of a "syndicate that's running all the high-class [bootleg] merchandise that's being sold in this country," is shown to have a particular fondness for eating spaghetti.

The Post-Gangster Gangster Comedy

As Hollywood's best evidence for its determination to uphold "the highest standards of morality" in the 1930s, the Production Code was a very well-publicized document; thus audiences, understanding something of the ongoing negotiation that was taking place between the industry and its critics in the movies themselves, did not necessarily take the contradictory and sometimes downright puzzling representations that appeared on the screen at face value. Just as they could be depended upon to perceive the erotic implications behind apparently innocuous "romantic" exchanges that were constrained by the Code, it is reasonable to assume that many audience members were aware of the sophisticated game of obfuscation and subtext that was being played out between filmmakers, censors, the PCA, and themselves. As I have argued elsewhere, the experience of watching the regulated movies of the 1930s was often permeated with irony: What audiences saw was not always what they got (Vasey 1997, 206–219). This ironic dimension was the basis of the unique appeal of the screwball comedies of the late 1930s and early 1940s, in which sophisticated and sometimes outrageous humor was created by placing persistently innocent and well-meaning characters – often played by Cary Grant, Katharine Hepburn, Carole Lombard, or Irene Dunne – in a variety of sexually compromising situations.

In their transparent efforts to combine the demands of the Code with the demands of the audience, elements of the post-gangster dramas sometimes teetered on the brink of self-parody, as in the case of the spaghetti-munching, non-Italian, non-Mafia member Nick Brown, cited above. It was only a short step for an ironic sensibility to take over gangster themes completely, as they did in the curious subgenre of the post-gangster comedy. *A Slight Case of Murder* (Warner Bros., 1938) starts with a party marking the end of Prohibition, celebrated with the consumption of "the last keg of Prohibition beer in the house," representing the last Prohibition profits earned by bootlegger Remy Marko (Edward G. Robinson). The next scene shows Marko telling his gang of hoodlums that in the new post-Prohibition environment they will run a "business enterprise operated on a strictly legitimate basis – get me?" In a sequence designed to evoke the low-class gangster's standard transformation into more upmarket racketeer, he tells them to give up their guns, shave every day, and "lay off these striped silk shirts." He promises to give the place "a lot of class": "From now on everybody wears white shirts – get me? With clean collars." The joke is that Marko is not using legitimacy as a euphemism for better-dressed crime; to the consternation of his gang, he really does want to run a legal brewery. Unfortunately his beer is swill, and nobody will drink it now that they have a choice, which leads him to near-bankruptcy. The rest of the plot develops into a country-house farce involving a loose mixture of stolen loot, current and ex-criminals, a body in a cupboard, a streetwise juvenile delinquent, an ingenue (Remy's daughter), and a state trooper who is also her wealthy suitor. Much of the humor derives from the movie's mishmash of class signifiers, as old-fashioned movie hoods try to break free from their linguistic and sartorial stereotypes and mix with the middle and upper classes.

Robinson made something of a speciality of demonstrating the comic implications of the screen gangster's schizophrenic character in narratives that were also designed to showcase his versatility as a performer. He features as both an evil criminal and his middle-class, clean-living double in Columbia's 1935 comedy *The Whole Town's Talking*. Similarly, in *The Amazing Dr. Clitterhouse* (Warner Bros., 1938), released only three months after *A Slight Case of Murder*, he plays a scientist who is so determined to understand the criminal mind of the gangster that he decides to stage an experiment by becoming one himself. The movie pushes the crisis of identity that characterized Robinson in *Bullets or Ballots* in a more bizarre direction, with Robinson simultaneously being experimenter and experimental subject; educated scientist and underworld gang leader. The status of his personal identity is so convoluted that at the end of the movie the jury charged with considering his culpability in the murder of "Rocks" Valentine (Bogart) has no choice but to acquit him on grounds of insanity.

Brother Orchid (Warner Bros., 1940), again starring Robinson and featuring Bogart, is organized around a more direct discussion of the movie gangster and his relationship to class. The action begins with a gangster-film cliché: A door labeled "John Sarto Protective Association" dissolves to Sarto (Robinson) reading out the newspaper headline "Gangland and Guns Slay Rival Racketeer" to his assembled gang. Unexpectedly, however, he chides them for committing the murder, and the movie immediately establishes its comedy credentials through the mangled English of one of the gang ("Oh boss, you shouldn't take that altitude towards us … everybody thought you'd be glad to have that guy illuminated"). The main comic twist is that John Sarto, despite being the head of a protection racket, is a nice guy who hates bloodshed – the antithesis of the Little Caesar stereotype. He announces that he is "too sensitive" to stay in the racket, and intends to retire: "From now on I'm going after the two things I've always wanted most – good taste and refinement. I'm going to get what I was born to have – class." Sarto is Breen's polite and well-dressed gangster/racketeer pushed to his logical conclusion. Resolving to become a "world sportsman, socialite, and art student," Sarto dons his bowler hat and heads off to "London, Paris, and St Moritz, and with all the class that goes with them there joints." The rest of the movie is a lightly comic morality tale, demonstrating that indeed class is a matter of character and not money. In an echo of Rico's treatment by the "big boys" in *Little Caesar*, Sarto is cheated of his fortune in the capitals of Europe and his life is threatened by his own gang on his return. When he is taken in by an obscure monastic community, there is an opportunity for more comedy as his gangsterish behavior and language make him a classic fish out of water, but he eventually finds the true class that he has been searching for in the selfless life of the monks.

Conclusion

The gangster movie of the 1930–1931 production season had suggested a potent direction for the newly developed sound movie that maximized its visceral impact. It demonstrated a potential to combine gritty, documentary-style visuals with hair-raising sound effects to create a new kind of integrated realism that constituted a violent assault on the senses. The addition of sound to the existing crime film rendered it particularly disturbing because, unlike visuals that could be avoided by shutting one's eyes (or placing one's hat over the eyes of one's child), the sounds of the cinema could not be effectively avoided. Sound also enabled the cinema literally to speak in the accents of ethnic minorities and underworld characters. At the same time as musicals were exploring the potential of sound to create escapist, Utopian entertainments, the soundtracks of the gangster movies were experimenting with the evocation of "sordid" underworld environments that constituted a direct affront to the motion picture industry's efforts to portray itself as a safe, middle-class, and socially responsible institution. The movie industry's own regulatory agencies recognized the gangster movie as inimical to its broader economic and institutional objectives, and in the decade following the production season of 1930–1931 worked systematically to "redirect the energies" of Warner Bros., in particular, along less dangerous pathways. The success of these efforts can clearly be seen in the gradual bourgeoisification of the screen gangster, starting with his abandonment of the machine gun, moving through his period of employment as a G-man, and ending with his parodic enthusiasm for art school. Nevertheless, the casting of Cagney, Robinson, and Bogart in successive iterations of these "post-gangster" formulations kept shades of the original movies in the public consciousness far beyond their brief initial period of exhibition.

It is fascinating that Little Caesar, Scarface, and the public enemy Tommy Powers proved to be so difficult to kill. The particular circumstances surrounding Hollywood's cultural and institutional status in the 1930s required the gangsters to be suppressed, not only because they offended cultural conservatives but also because of their extraordinary appeal to young male audiences. In the postwar period the industry underwent radical industrial change, and as the power of the traditional studios waned the Production Code became less effective, with the result that comparatively explicit sex and violence began to return to the American screen. Criminal and gangster themes became staples of film noir, and by the time the Production Code was finally abandoned in favor of film ratings at the end of the 1960s, Hollywood was ready to embrace the unreconstructed gangster without reservation. When the *Godfather* movies made their triumphant appearance in the 1970s, male youths were the most important demographic sector in the Hollywood audience. The gangster movie again became a site in which, alongside the post-Code versions of the Western, the war movie, and the police drama, the motion picture was able to explore its extraordinary capacity to meld image, sound, characterization, and narrative in an aestheticized melange of violence, menace, and suspense.

Notes

1. Lamar Trotti, letter to Fingerlin, November 3, 1930, *Stolen Heaven* file, Production Code Administration Archive, Margaret Herrick Library, Academy of Motion Picture Arts and Sciences, Los Angeles (hereafter PCA Archive). Ironically, on a different level of obfuscation, Warner Bros. was advised to *introduce* gambling scenes into *Mandalay* (1933) to demonstrate that one of their locations (the Orient Cafe) was "more of a nightclub" than a brothel. James Wingate, letter to Jack Warner, October 20, 1933, *Mandalay* file, PCA Archive.
2. Jason Joy, résumé, June 29, 1931, *Are These Our Children?* file, PCA Archive.
3. Joy, letter to Hays, December 21, 1931, *The Man Who Talked Too Much* file, PCA Archive.
4. Joe Breen, letter to Jack Warner, February 14, 1935, *"G" Men* file, PCA Archive.
5. Breen, letter to Edward Small (Reliance), March 1, 1935, *Bullets or Ballots* file, PCA Archive.
6. Breen, letter to Edward Small (Reliance), March 1, 1935, *Bullets or Ballots* file, PCA Archive.
7. Breen to Jack Warner, December 20, 1935, *Bullets or Ballots* file, PCA Archive.
8. Sam Bischoff to Joe Breen, July 20, 1939, *The Roaring Twenties* file, PCA Archive.
9. Joe Breen to Walter MacEwen, August 9, 1939, *The Roaring Twenties* file, PCA Archive.

References

Keating, Patrick. (2010). *Hollywood Lighting from the Silent Era to Film Noir*. New York: Columbia University Press.

Maltby, Richard. (2005). "Why Boys Go Wrong: Gangsters, Hoodlums and the Natural History of Delinquent Careers." In Lee Grieveson, Esther Sonnet, & Peter Stanfield (eds), *Mob Culture: Hidden Histories of the American Gangster Film* (pp. 41–66). New Brunswick: Rutgers University Press.

Martin, Olga. (1937). *Hollywood's Movie Commandments: A Handbook for Motion Picture Writers and Reviewers*. New York: H. W. Wilson.

Munby, Jonathan. (1999). *Public Enemies, Public Heroes: Screening the Gangster from Little Caesar to Touch of Evil*. Chicago: University of Chicago Press.

Prince, Stephen. (2003). *Classical Film Violence: Designing and Regulating Brutality in Hollywood Cinema, 1930–1968*. New Brunswick: Rutgers University Press.

Production Code Administration (PCA) Archive. Margaret Herrick Library, Academy of Motion Picture Arts and Sciences, Beverly Hills, CA.

Thrasher, Frederic M. (1963). *The Gang: A Study of 1,313 Gangs in Chicago*. Abridged edn. Chicago: University of Chicago Press. (Original work published 1927.)

Variety. (1932). Review of *Taxi!*. January 12.

Vasey, Ruth. (1997). *The World According to Hollywood, 1918–1939*. Exeter: University of Exeter Press.

14

Landscapes of Fantasy, Gardens of Deceit
The Adventure Film between Colonialism and Tourism

Hans Jürgen Wulff[1]
Professor, Kiel University, Germany

The most flexible, diverse, and enduring of American film genres, the **adventure film** was a production staple of the **classical studio era**. Its invariably white, male protagonist might be a **swashbuckler**, an **Arthurian knight**, a **staunch individualist** as in ***Robin Hood*** films, a nobleman raised by apes as in ***Tarzan*** movies, or an **adventurer** happening upon mysterious, mythical places. Whatever the scenario, as Hans Jürgen Wulff argues, in these exoticist fantasies **colonialism** is central to encounters with the **Other**, staged to confirm the adventurer's cultural superiority and assert his economic and lawmaking control. Films like ***Red Dust*** and ***King Solomon's Mines*** simultaneously complicate and reinforce the implications of subordinating the Other or of "the adventurer's own transition into a world and life of Otherness." **Action** and **landscape** are central features, as they are in more recent, equally varied adventure films, from *Jaws* and the *Indiana Jones* series to *Dances with Wolves* and *The Piano*. Wulff's essay shares ground with Kirsten Moana Thompson on cel animation in this volume, with Bart Beaty on the blockbuster superhero in Volume II, and with Kevin L. Stoehr on the A-production Western in the hardcover/online edition.

Additional terms, names, and concepts: *aventiure*, cinematic spectacle, adventure parodies, prestige picture, Douglas Fairbanks, Sr and Jr and Errol Flynn as adventure film personae

The adventure film is one of film history's most expansive and heterogeneous genres. At its core is the exoticist adventure tale that frequently references and romanticizes the era of colonialism, but the genre also intersects with several partially overlapping subgenres, such as the medieval knight's tale, the pirate story and the high seas adventure, tales from the Arabian Nights, the swords-and-sandals epic, the cloak-and-dagger story, and the travelogue and discovery tale. The adventure film's themes and motives are drawn from popular adventure literature that peaked between the late eighteenth and late nineteenth centuries and frequently adopted a serial mode. The writings of authors such as Alexandre Dumas,

American Film History: Selected Readings, Origins to 1960, First Edition. Edited by Cynthia Lucia, Roy Grundmann, and Art Simon.
© 2016 John Wiley & Sons, Inc. Published 2016 by John Wiley & Sons, Inc.

Sir Walter Scott, H. Rider Haggard, Jules Verne, and, later, Jack London, Joseph Conrad, and Rudyard Kipling paved the way for the genre's cinematic success, though the literary motif of the *aventiure*[2] harks back to the legends of medieval knighthood. Likewise, the figure of the adventurer who sets out to distant shores to save the Holy Land, to conquer the Americas for the Spanish crown, or to liberate the Americas from the crown, who may be marooned on a distant island or become ruler of the jungle, has older roots and appears in many guises. But it was not until the nineteenth century that the specific tropes to which the genre has closely adhered – and which, it seems, still shape the stories of twentieth-century adventurers – began to crystallize. These adventurers may discover the North Pole, fight bounty hunters amidst the Pyramids or wildlife poachers in the jungle, run a plantation in colonial Indochina, fly postal planes across the Andes, or ferry passengers and cargo across treacherous South Pacific waters.

Reflecting the genre's anchoring in first-world patriarchal culture, the adventure hero is usually (though not always) a white male. His name may be Ivanhoe, Sir Lancelot, Robin Hood, the Scarlet Pimpernel, Ben-Hur, Zorro, D'Artagnan, Captain Nemo, Captain Horatio Hornblower, Phileas Fogg, Robinson Crusoe – and more recently, of course, Indiana Jones. One reason for the sustained lure of the white adventurer in exotic locales is the impact of colonialism – the conquering and linking of the whole world through the cultures of Europe – which went hand in hand with the emergence of an enduring experience of Otherness. It is no surprise, then, that the genre's cinematic heyday, lasting approximately from 1920 to 1960, comes to an end with the historical decline of the colonial empires in the early 1960s – which also coincides with the decline of the classical Hollywood studio system.

While many film industries the world over have produced adventure tales, Hollywood's particular combination of assets guaranteed its leadership in this genre since the 1910s. The industry's advantageous southern California location, its high technological standards, and its copious material resources enabled it to cultivate a product that, if not unique to the adventure film, is nonetheless crucial to it – cinematic spectacle. Directors such as D. W. Griffith, Fred Niblo, King Vidor, and Cecil B. DeMille spearheaded Hollywood's predilection for spectacular set pieces and exotic landscapes. In addition, the industry quickly learned to adopt a dual strategy for shaping its output: It produced B-movie serials modeled on and adapted from dime novels, but it also shrewdly catered to middle-class sensibilities by supplementing entertainment with a carefully infused dose of education (whether to garner cultural prestige or merely to placate the censors). This two-tiered approach accounts for the stratification not only of story materials, but also of budgets, production values, and marketing approaches. By the end of the silent era, many classic adventure heroes such as Tarzan (*Tarzan of the Apes*, 1918), Zorro (*The Mark of Zorro*, 1920), Ben-Hur (*Ben-Hur: A Tale of the Christ*, 1925), and Don Juan (*Don Juan*, 1926) had been introduced to the screen. For much of the 1930s and 1940s, adventure tales served as material for both Saturday afternoon matinee productions (such as the Tarzan films) and big-budget prestige films showcasing studio muscle and expertise (*The Adventures of Robin Hood*, Warner Bros., 1938). The industry retained its confidence in the adventure genre through the 1950s and early 1960s mainly because it remained a primary showcase for emerging technologies (such as the widescreen format) and a test case for new distribution and exhibition patterns (the roadshow engagement). On a smaller scale, the genre continued into a revisionist phase that might be called "the late adventure film" of the late 1960s and 1970s, during which time it reflected both politically and aesthetically on its own generic components, before experiencing a postmodern revival through the contemporary Hollywood blockbuster. Barring a few scattered precursors, critical treatment of the genre by film historians does not begin until the 1980s, triggered partially by a groundswell of interest in genre theory and history, but also, more specifically, by the widening impact of postcolonial studies, which came to support some of the methodological parameters for the genre's critical investigation.

Generic Configurations

The adventure film's generic boundaries are extremely blurred, mainly because the genre shares foundations with other similar genres, many of which feature odysseys of various kinds, revolve around treasures to be raided, and accord a role to nature and its vicissitudes. Countless Westerns and fantasy films are really adventure films, and adventures can be found in science fiction as well as in disaster and espionage films.[3] Urban locations, on the other hand, lack these multiple affinities to adventure, and relatively few melodramas incorporate adventure. The elasticity of generic relations makes it difficult to establish a historical chronology of the genre, and while it is more feasible to chart the respective histories of the genre's various subcycles, to do so in any comprehensive manner would exceed the parameters of this essay. A general observation that can be made is that each subgenre has its own peaks and troughs of prominence and popularity. The swords-and-sandals epic was popular during Hollywood's silent and early sound years, after which it entered a hiatus until the late 1940s, when it reappeared and remained popular until the mid-1960s. The knight's tale, the cloak-and-dagger adventure, and the high seas adventure (including the pirate film) were most prominent from the mid-1930s to the mid-1950s. Certain serials, such as the Tarzan films, remained popular throughout the classical studio era and even sparked television series. Others, such as the exoticist Jon Hall and Maria Montez adventure films (e.g., *Cobra Woman*, 1944), remained confined to the classical B-movie era. Exceptions pertain in almost all cases, however, and none of this begins to account for the generic life and popularity of adventure parodies, which began in the 1920s (with Buster Keaton's 1923 *Three Ages*, a parody of *Intolerance*), continued through the 1940s with the Bob Hope and Bing Crosby "Road to . . . " films and through the 1950s with such knight's tale parodies as Danny Kaye's *The Court Jester* (1955), into the 1960s and 1970s with auteur-driven, New Wave-influenced comedic extravaganzas such as *A Funny Thing Happened on the Way to the Forum* (1966), once again starring Buster Keaton, subtly ironic remakes of classics, such as *The Three Musketeers* (1973) and *The Four Musketeers* (1974), or lowbrow spoofs such as *Airplane* (1980).

Given this heterogeneity, a fruitful way to critically approach the genre is to investigate commonalities in its myths and story patterns by first exploring the very meaning of adventure and the mythological and narrative function of its protagonist and antagonist. The prototypical adventure film is a tale of heroes and scoundrels, trials and temptations, final rewards or failures. The narrative structure is ultimately simple and reminiscent of fairy tales: departure from home/adventure away from home/return home (cf. Klotz 1979, 44). Journeying, like no other activity, is thus linked to adventure. Those who sit at home will scarcely experience it. Leaving home on a trip that may span the globe and lead the traveler into regions where danger lurks is a necessary prerequisite for adventure. The hero must fulfill a given task – its abandonment never an option, the partial adventure is unthinkable, although in all adventure tales there are certain moments at which a return is possible. Such moments require decisions that affirm the irreversibility of the hero's adventure trajectory, even as they acknowledge the dangers that lie ahead.

Discussing the genre's heterogeneous plot motivations, Burckhardt Heer claims that "personal revenge, escape, a political mission, the hunt for treasures and happiness, exploration and discovery, though they figure prominently, are but a few of the imperatives" (1981, 6). At times, it is magical objects that are at stake – objects that serve humanity (a drug that prevents aging, as in *Medicine Man*, 1992; or the Holy Grail in *Indiana Jones and the Last Crusade*, 1989), or that help the hero gain power (as in *Excalibur*, 1981, or *Prince of Persia: The Sands of Time*, 2010). The story ends with the triumph of the hero (Cawelti 1976, 40), but this ending can only be reached if the hero masters the numerous trials and dangers held in store for him. Beyond the standard conventions of wrongs being righted, secrets unveiled, and spoils secured (Klotz 1979, 43), the hero, if all goes well, has had a learning experience and may even be rewarded with a princess.

Mandated by the formula of the fairy tale is the genre's happy ending. Bad endings – the hero's death or failure – are rare in the adventure film. Adventure stories are success stories in more than one sense: The adventure rarely consumes its heroes but instead enables them to grow, with honor and reward in store for them. If all effort is in vain, however, and death constitutes the wages of fear, what emerges is a melodramatic tension, a near-tragic effect.[4] Or the values that motivated the hero to plunge into adventure in the first place are now exposed as mere selfishness and naked materialism, as in *The Treasure of the Sierra Madre* (1948). In some films, delusions of power that lure the adventurer out into the world and give him free rein, however ephemeral, evaporate, as in *The Man Who Would Be King* (1975).

Finally, fate can also impose trials and tribulations upon the hero. A ship fails in the storm, with only one survivor. The test lasts 28 years and is mainly about adapting to a foreign environment. Robinson Crusoe stories are numerous and not always set on an island. Ships overturn (*The Poseidon Adventure*, 1972), planes crash into the jungle, into the desert (*The Flight of the Phoenix*, 1965), in undiscovered valleys (*Lost Horizon*, 1937), or near a tropical island (*Cast Away*, 2000). Small groups flee revolutions and wars (*The Inn of the Sixth Happiness*, 1958) or try to fight in them (*For Whom the Bell Tolls*, 1943; *55 Days at Peking*, 1963; *The Sand Pebbles*, 1966). Individuals face natural disasters (*The Rains Came*, 1939; *The Rains of Ranchipur*, 1955; *Earthquake*, 1974) or try to cope with man-made catastrophes (*The Towering Inferno*, 1974). Escape tales form their own subcycle of adventure stories. At stake is the protagonist's life or his liberty and dignity. The settings vary as widely as French Guyana (*Papillon*, 1973), Iran (*Not Without My Daughter*, 1991), or East Germany (*Night Crossing*, 1982).

Action and Movement, Spectacle and Performance, the Musical and Opera

In another approach to the genre, it is possible to identify adventure at the heart of action itself. The adventure film and the action film are next of kin, considered identical by some. Action is adventure's primary purpose, its *raison d'être*. It is within and for the sake of action that adventure is executed and experienced in the moment. The action sequence is undoubtedly the spectacular center of the film. This is particularly notable in the high seas adventure and its subgenre, the pirate film, as well as in the knight's tale and the cloak-and-dagger film. Action sequences often resemble the musical's organization into episodic climaxes. The perfect execution of fencing, for instance, as an athletic discipline, the elegance of the movements, the choreographed nature of the sequence, the way space is deployed and traversed – all are highly specific to how the players perform. It is not surprising that Gene Kelly's interpretation of the dueling D'Artagnan in the 1948 adaptation of *The Three Musketeers* is reminiscent in its wit, suppleness, and cocky physicality of his roles in musicals.[5] The classical duel opening acknowledges that it is staged for the viewer, its nature as spectacle frequently aided by its staging in front of a diegetic audience. Zorro (in the 1920 version) proceeds to humiliate the evil sergeant only after he has corralled the patrons of the inn into a corner from which they view the duel that unfolds *for* them. And the very first duel in the 1948 version of *The Three Musketeers* reveals how D'Artagnan, before dueling with Athos, first secures the attention of the duelists' seconds. When he is the only one left fighting and the other musketeers look on with amusement, he proceeds to fight with the oldest and most experienced of his opponents, turning it into a turbulent contest of skills, mocking and teasing the latter so as to make his humiliation complete.

The action sequence is a gymnastic intermezzo that possesses its own autonomous character. A specific temporal structure emerges that requires a periodic alternation between scenes that advance the narrative and those devoted to spectacle. In this respect also, adventure films recall the temporal structure and textual rhythm of musicals and opera. Because action is centrally determined by physicality, visuality, and concreteness, the characters' interior lives tend to play a secondary role, as do their internal conflicts, their motives, and their urges. Their personalities are located entirely in the realm of action and athletics. Few characters have embodied these features in such concentrated and comprehensive form as the swashbuckler. Originally describing a braggart, the term "swashbuckler" later served as a dramaturgical term for a kind of ruffian who is also a romantic love interest (Heer 1981, 12). He distinguishes himself through physical and athletic skills – he has no match when it comes to wrestling and boxing, riding and running, shooting and fencing. He is hands-on and quick on his feet, both physically and mentally. Highly stereotypical and stylized (as is his opponent) – a "type" more than a character – the swashbuckler is usually not designed with psychological depth.[6] The contrast between the flatness of the characters and the physical presence of the actors is central to the genre, which is precisely what makes the analysis of acting styles imperative.

That some variants of the adventure film have adapted and diversified the exaggerated expressive gestural play developed by folk burlesque and perfected in slapstick comedy is not surprising. Historically speaking, it has been certain actors who have shaped the look of the genre. These actors distinguish themselves through both the physical mode of their acting and their image that codes athleticism as a form of masculinity. Douglas Fairbanks, Sr was the actor who, around 1920, developed a cocky, boyish, agile persona that exploited scenic space to its full extent and conquered scenic height in particular. The performance standards he set for actors in adventure roles are still valid today. Several generations have superseded him – first Douglas Fairbanks, Jr and Errol Flynn, then Stewart Granger and Burt Lancaster, followed by Sean Connery and Steve McQueen, and, more recently, Mel Gibson, Russell Crowe, and Johnny Depp. What has remained, however, is the imperative that Fairbanks, Sr fulfilled like no other: Be self-confident and brash, welcoming every invitation to duel. Advertise your eroticism and enjoy action as such, with expansive movement and gesture. Embrace *Carpe Diem* – as a motto for life and for acting, though in an athletic rather than a hedonistic sense.

Personality versus Genre Hybridity: The Adventurer as Character

A swashbuckler film is always a generic hybrid that, as Heer points out, may be set in medieval England, in France at the time of the *ancien régime*, in the California of 1820 (then under Mexican rule), or in the Caribbean during the eighteenth century. Whatever the specifics of time and place, whatever the swashbuckler's status or provenance – whether a French citizen, an Anglo-Saxon bandit, an Oriental thief, an English pirate, or a Spanish nobleman – he is mainly an avenger who reestablishes justice (Heer 1981, 12). Few stories depart from this pattern, though justice is usually defined primarily in individual, familial, and moral terms. An exception is *Mutiny on the Bounty* (filmed in 1935 with Clark Gable and Charles Laughton and in 1962 with Marlon Brando and Trevor Howard),[7] a story in which adventure constitutes an escape from tyranny and enslavement, and the rebel adventurers must flee to the end of the world in order to avoid the wrath of the empire – and, in the process, enact a near-socialist utopia of equality and sexual freedom. Yet, stories with overt political overtones of utopian collectivity or socialist ideals are rare. Politicized worldviews are more likely expressed indirectly and invite allegorization in certain subgenres such as the knight's tale, the cloak-and-dagger film, or the pirate film. The knight's tale, which often centers on Richard the Lionheart and Ivanhoe, retelling with widely varying degrees of historical accuracy the conflict between Anglo-Saxons and Normans, has particular appeal for mythmaking machines like Hollywood. The tale can be transposed to numerous conflicts in American history ranging from the War of Independence to the Civil War and the conquest of the West (Hediger 2004, 46).

Indeed, for allegory to achieve success, history must not be too closely referenced and the hero, rather than being part of an explicitly identified political group, must remain a staunch individualist. This rule operated in close synergy with Hollywood's approach to manufacturing and deploying stars. Errol Flynn was one of the biggest male stars in the related subgenres of the knight's tale, the pirate and high seas adventure, and the cloak-and-dagger film. Like James Cagney, Flynn was a top male Warner Bros. star of the 1930s, though his fame came slightly later, in mid-decade, with a highly successful cycle of action adventure films. On the one hand, these films were somewhat atypical amidst the studio's output of gritty, contemporary urban dramas, melodramas, and gangster films; on the other hand, they formed a small and coherent subcycle of their own in the studio's production palette – all set in various colorfully embellished periods of England's past. Nick Roddick has dubbed this subcycle Warners' "Merrie England" films (1983, 235). Flynn stars in all of them and plays characters with similar traits. His hero is the "more or less persecuted and isolated defender of a legitimate, benevolent authority which is threatened with usurpation or subversion" (Roddick 1983, 236),[8] particularly true of *The Adventures of Robin Hood* (1938), in which Flynn as Robin is an outlaw seemingly fighting against his own country, temporarily ruled by a corrupt power elite. The rightness of his actions is never in doubt. In this sense, *Robin Hood* is exemplary of all Flynn's Warner Bros. vehicles that invariably call for the physical externalization of moral principles (Roddick 1983, 236).[9]

The Adventures of Robin Hood also exemplifies the adventure film as prestige picture. The film was both a commercial and critical triumph (Roddick 1983, 241) and is still seen as one of the high points of the classical studio-era mode of production (Hediger 2004, 46). As a high-gloss, high-budget product, it provides clear evidence of the well-oiled production machinery that, at the height of its efficiency, knew exactly how to please the public and how to use its talent to maximum effect (Roddick 1983, 241). Flynn's physical agility and bravado are at all times complemented by well-choreographed tracking and crane shots, swift editing, and a characteristic "combination of great sweeps of orchestrated movement with sudden stasis" (Roddick 1983, 241). As Roddick goes on to argue, the high production values, including technicolor cinematography and imposing sets, can in themselves be read within the context and as a sign of Warners' shift toward depoliticization in the second half of the 1930s, when the studio, at least at times, attempted to spruce up its production values to counterbalance the gritty urban look with which it was associated (1983, 242).

Warners' emulation of MGM product went hand in hand with what amounts to an ideological repurposing of the Robin Hood character. While Robin may be regarded as the "paradigmatic rebel with a cause," he is eager to relinquish his outlaw status as soon as law and order have been restored (Hediger 2004, 46). It is interesting to note that Cagney was initially cast as Robin, and it may have been only after Flynn was cast that Robin's class status was transformed from yeoman to nobleman.[10] Slightly more underscored by Flynn's than by Cagney's persona – not least because the latter was associated with a coterie of contemporary Depression-era heroes – the greater stress on Flynn's individualism is the clearest sign of Warners' conservative shift. If Flynn as a star became "the moral conscience of the Merrie England pictures, the embodiment of an action-based morality, which is that of the frontier adapted metaphorically to the political context of Roosevelt's second term" (Roddick 1983, 236), the hero's remolding as a noble outlaw plays into populism's more extremist tendencies, such as the adoration of a "quasi-superhuman champion": "Though right and wrong remain the same, the hero replaces the little man fighting for right" (Roddick 1983, 242).

Flynn also comfortably inhabited the world of the cloak-and-dagger film, and the impact of his physical bravura and braggadocio illustrates how Hollywood used the swashbuckler persona in both the cloak-and-dagger subgenre and the knight's tale (in which Robin Hood is anchored), notwithstanding the differences between those subgenres. Based partly on Sir Walter Scott's historical *Waverley* novels, but also drawing on the King Arthur myth (Hediger 2004, 47), the knight's tale is medieval not only in its semantic and syntactic elements, to use Rick Altman's concepts (1995), but also in terms of its ideology of featuring straightforward goals, moral clarity, limited patterns of behavior, and a quasi-utopian, counterfactual, transhistorical simplicity (Hediger 2004, 43). The cloak-and-dagger subgenre, by contrast, already looks toward certain aspects of modernity by virtue of its frame of reference in the Renaissance period (Midding 2004, 54). The semantic elements referenced in the genre's very name evoke an atmosphere of ambiguity, secrecy, and irony, as well as the tropes of disguise, deception, and performance. The implications of the cloak are very different from those of the knight's armor. The genre's most prominently featured dueling weapon is the épée rather than either the dagger, as suggested by its name, or the pistol, which, in actuality, had already eclipsed all blade weapons in popularity during the period (Midding 2004, 59). The épée carries a set of associations closely linked to the arts and to sports in which individuals can excel, unlike the sword, which references the sanguinary horrors of mass combat executed for the purpose of military warfare. The Renaissance swashbuckler is a versatile, sophisticated aesthete who dabbles in poetry and music and develops idiosyncratic cultural interests. His mannerisms mark him as a precursor of the dandy, albeit without the latter's melancholic predisposition (Midding 2004, 59).

Like the knight's tale, the cloak-and-dagger story concerns itself with the affairs of king and country, though more literally so. The syntactic structure of the genre differs from the knight's tale in that its romantically charged plots often revolve around illicit love affairs that could jeopardize a monarch's position and destabilize the political status quo, as is the case in *The Three Musketeers* (1948), in which the film's eponymous heroes and their new friend, D'Artagnan, must prevent the king's discovery of his wife's affair with the Duke of Buckingham (Midding 2004, 58). An outright lothario himself, the Renaissance swashbuckler still places all strategic maneuvering in the service of living up to his code of honor and, thus, frequently runs the risk of having his heart broken, as does D'Artagnan, who almost falls for the wicked Lady De Winter (Lana Turner). While Kelly's nimble, dancer persona seemed to make him

Figure 14.1 Robin (Errol Flynn) and Maid Marian (Olivia de Havilland) in William Keighley and Michael Curtiz's *The Adventures of Robin Hood* (1938, producers Hal B. Wallis, Henry Blanke, and Jack Warner).

an ideal fit for the role of the romantic swashbuckler, Flynn, at times, was able to temper his brash, priapic masculinity when called upon to suffer unrequited love or love that could not be declared unambiguously, as is true of *The Private Lives of Elizabeth and Essex* (1939) (Roddick 1983, 242). This flexibility enabled him to play romantic swashbuckler roles, such as in *The Adventures of Don Juan* (1948), even though Flynn's version was less successful than Warner Bros.' classic 1926 version (another prestige project pegged to the promotion of new technology, in this case, sound), and his appeal paled in comparison to Kelly's performance of D'Artagnan that same year. The Renaissance swashbuckler's less-than-fulfilled love life, which often forces him to forgo an aristocratic woman, thus also points to a similarity between knight's tale and cloak-and-dagger story that eclipses some of the differences between those subgenres: The hero's physical mobility must make up for his lack of social mobility. The persistence of this lack in most genre plots points to the fact that Hollywood opportunistically harnessed the rigidity of a class-based society, however fictionalized, to produce cinematic allegories that invariably advocated the preservation of the political status quo (Midding 2004, 64).[11]

If the swashbuckler is an outlaw, at least in a limited and ideologically safe sense, the ordinary traveler-adventurer is not a rebel to begin with. On the contrary, he is almost always a representative of established order – and these visions of order determine his notion of reality. His actions are never politically motivated, not even when his environment is marked by political interests and conflicts and when his own actions inevitably remain anchored in a broader political force field. To lure him into adventure requires a different set of desires and motivations. Some adventures arise from the temptation to attempt the impossible, which may come about with a wager (*Around the World in Eighty Days*, 1956) or a contest (in the 1965 *Those Magnificent Men in their Flying Machines* or the *Cannonball* films of the 1970s). There is the element of sport, an eagerness to test one's strength, not only against competitors but also against the odds imposed by the task itself – as if adventures are always individual high-performance tests.

Thus, even in contemporary narrative settings, the challenge of the adventure is closely linked to the audaciousness of the adventurer. The genre is informed by a notion of virtue present particularly in ordinary characters, whom fate pushes into a predicament they must master, forcing them to develop virtues they were unaware of possessing in their ordinary lives. In this respect, the disaster film also belongs to the adventure genre. Many adventure tales, therefore, are related to the novel of personal growth. They concern themselves with passages and transitions – new phases in life that draw blueprints of identity and test them in the field of action.

Colonialism and Its White Heroes

Colonialism frequently lies at the heart of the adventure genre. Conquering and controlling the world is part of the basic, inescapable destiny of the hero. Sometimes maps are shown with white "unknown regions." New areas must be explored or even conquered; insurgents must be quieted; the opposing power must be destabilized. It is no coincidence that a large number of Vietnam War films are adventure-like, as the framing interests hark back to the architecture of the great empires and the roles accorded their sunburned men. A basic colonialist or even imperialist tendency has long dominated the corpus. The western European finds himself in a foreign place, in the colonies, face to face with the colonized, who always harbor the threat of insurgence.

An encounter with Otherness almost always constitutes both high point and rupture within the adventure. What registers in this encounter is usually the experience of the power to control – in the form of political power and hermeneutic power or knowledge. At issue is the conquest, the political subordination, and the economic exploitation of the new territories, perhaps even their instrumentalization as tools to obtain spiritual, moral, or mystical values. The adventure film supplements the notion of adventure as an "unpredictable, fateful, chance-driven, hazardous scenario" (Hügel n.d., 2), with a depiction of the encounter between the self-controlled, self-confident merchant, who is intent on minimizing risk and maximizing profit, and the Otherness of the world out there. Whether he harbors or loathes mercantile interests, the adventurer approaches the colonial scenario as a conqueror, a representative of hegemonic European cultures. His life in the colonies helps him define his identity and discover certain virtues identified specifically as white, such as intelligence, courage, leadership, physical fitness, moral integrity, and the ability to adapt. In the course of dramatizing and showcasing these virtues, a certain contradiction emerges between the ambition to live up to civilized ideals and the attraction of erotic experience.

A prototypical example is *Red Dust*, a 1932 pre-Code MGM production that served as a star vehicle for Clark Gable and Jean Harlow and that, in certain ways, is exemplary of the contemporary exoticist adventure film set in the twentieth century. The film's opening establishes what is at stake: A bowl is tied to a tree and a hand reaches to pour the tree sap it has collected into a larger vessel. The camera travels back as the adventurer hero Dennis Carson – played by a youthful Clark Gable – steps onto the jungle stage of an Indochinese rubber plantation, checking the quality of the work. The tree was tapped too soon, as it turns out, and now it will be years before it can once again produce decent crude rubber. It is not until much later, when Carson shows a woman how the runny sap is turned into rubber mats that get shipped home to factories, that the film again depicts the harvesting process. The opening scene continues with Carson running to the next collection station, as if coursing a central park in which the crucial stages of production are condensed into a tight space. He drives a group of idling coolies back to work, calling them lazy. In the next scene a strong wind rises as a savage thunderstorm begins. The natives run for shelter, but the roof of a hut is about to blow off. Carson intervenes, ordering the coolies onto the roof. Agile and proactive, he throws heavy sacks on the roof to hold down its cover of palm leaves. By now one thing is evident: He is a European hero who creates order in the face of the natives' disaffection and inertia, who insures that production runs smoothly (and profits keep flowing), and who stays calm and knows how to act even during a crisis.

While Carson acquires a distinctive profile, the natives remain anonymous, nameless, none of them individualized as protagonists. They are reduced to helping hands that toil away in the background, that

Figure 14.2 The prostitute Vantine (Jean Harlow) and man of the jungle Dennis Carson (Clark Gable) in Victor Fleming's *Red Dust* (1932, producers Hunt Stromberg and Irving Thalberg).

hold a horse steady or perhaps unload crates from a supply ship calling on the plantation. The sole exception is the Chinese character, Hoy, who works as a cook and servant in the plantation's mansion. A Chinese national (played by Chinese-American actor Willie Fung), he, too, is an outsider on the plantation, but he acquires a presence as the giggling and grinning, ironically servile sidekick (the film even ends on a cutaway to his face). As is highly characteristic of the conventions of the adventure film, however, there is no engagement of the white masters with the film's geographic and ethnic Others. Carson and the other white plantation workers remain strangers in a foreign land, their smug and arrogant self-image as colonizers preempting any assimilation with the foreign country or its people. They act as slave masters of sorts to the coolies, who are not even allowed to bring their wives into the work camp – the women must remain behind in the villages.

The actual drama starts when Vantine "Lily" Jefferson (Jean Harlow), a prostitute from Saigon, steps off the boat. She has run into some trouble and has had to skip town. Prickly and stubborn, she defies everyone. Needless to say, Carson initially rejects her, but it doesn't take long for the two to start a sexually charged affair. A month later, disheartened that the relationship has gotten to her, Vantine decides to leave on the next boat – and, as she is leaving, Carson even offers to pay her for past sexual favors. He is a lone wolf who insists on remaining free and uncommitted, preferring to define sexual relations economically. But things change when the boat brings the genteel yet insecure land surveyor Gary Willis (Gene Raymond) and his refined wife Barbara (Mary Astor), who appeals to Carson precisely because of her European affectations and urbane pose. Although Carson is adamant about being a man of the jungle, he becomes obsessed with the otherworldly Barbara. In the end, he forestalls an affair with her that seemed inevitable, realizing that it has no future in the rough environment he has chosen to inhabit. He goes back to Vantine, who is very much at home with the local lifestyle (the film's most famous scene shrewdly exploits Harlow's earthy sex appeal by featuring Vantine taking a bath in a barrel, which offends the genteel Gary and Barbara).

Tension mounts and violence erupts (Barbara shoots Carson when she learns he wants to send her back to America), as do monsoon storms – elements that are among the classic conventions of the genre. At the same time, however, the film's romantic couplings and its dramatic exploitation of the cultural and ideological differences among the protagonists lend a psychological depth absent from the average adventure film. Ultimately, however, this overt psychologizing dimension supports yet another convention – the genre's characteristic, if rarely explicit, civilizational critique that regards the adventurer as an actualized ideal of masculinity who, at the same time, holds on to his lack of domestication. In this regard, Carson, the self-confident pragmatic, to whom social vanities, rituals, and status symbols are thoroughly alien, is no different from most other adventurers, whether Allan Quartermain (Stewart Granger), the hero of *King Solomon's Mines* (1950), to be discussed later, or, for that matter, many of the characters played by Clark Gable and other leading men in nearly three decades' worth of other adventure films.

The character constellation of *Red Dust* proved highly influential on subsequent Hollywood adaptations of life-in-the-colonies stories and was played out in a variety of ways. In *China Seas* (1935), another classic exoticist adventure tale, Gable plays Alan Gaskell, a hard-drinking sea captain whose rusty freighter is assigned an important money run for the British crown from Hong Kong to Singapore across pirate-infested, storm-tossed waters. Like Carson in *Red Dust*, Gaskell stands between two women, a lascivious blonde who goes by the name of "China Doll" – once again inimitably played by Jean Harlow – and a refined and genteel brunette, Sibyl, played by Rosalind Russell in the kind of role Mary Astor played in *Red Dust*. Confronted with the need to choose between the Dionysian blonde and the Apollonian brunette (Löser 2004, 167), Gable's character once again decides to stick with Harlow.[12] In *Congo Maisie* (1940), an actual remake of *Red Dust*, Ann Sothern plays the Jean Harlow part. She is the showgirl Maisie Ravier, who ends up in an African village with the attractive but hardboiled physician Michael Shane (John Carroll). Rita Johnson and Shepperd Strudwick play the outsider couple Kay and Dr John "Jock" McWade. The same story takes a more explicitly tourist-oriented turn in John Ford's 1953 adaptation *Mogambo*, which is set among wildlife hunters in Africa and features Clark Gable in his old role, this time named Victor Marswell, Ava Gardner in the Jean Harlow role as a dancer named Eloise Y. Kelly (known as "Honey Bear" Kelly), and Grace Kelly and Donald Sinden as the Nordleys, the troubled and repressed married couple. While *Red Dust* explicitly identifies the rigorous exploitation of natural resources by the American chemical industry as the reason for the existence of the plantation and the presence of the whites in the jungle, *Mogambo* rationalizes the presence of its white cast as employees of the leisure industry – they catch animals and deliver them to American zoos; they act in shows staged for tourists; and they work as zoologists who research the lives of mountain gorillas. The original economic conditions that had traditionally enabled adventure had, by 1953, been lost. What continues to remain, however, is the dynamic that renders the native population anonymous and faceless.

Tarzan

The perspective of the adventure tale is thus owned by the adventurer, the European, the civilized protagonist, who is engulfed by Otherness. Designating the adventurer as the tale's global focal point is an aesthetic strategy that systematically distorts the perception of the Other. The Other usually appears in the guise of a collective, not as an individual. Only the leaders are given an individual profile, though they do not sustain a coherent or nuanced identity. A rare case that inverts the perspective, turning the colonized into the righteous and the colonizer into the scoundrel, is the late, reflective adventure film *Burn!* (1969), directed by Gillo Pontecorvo and starring Marlon Brando. Equally rare, at least during the high phase of the genre, are stories told from the perspective of the colonized. They emerge only in the 1970s.[13] The overwhelming pattern that determines the history of the genre is that Otherness is always reproduced as just that – in the social, political, and economic sense – even when the adventurer rebels against the power relations and the ethical and moral codes of his European homeland.

Only the Tarzan films seem to constitute an exception. Tarzan, who already inhabited the jungle before the story begins, always helps white people who end up in the wilderness, but he often acts on the side of the jungle when the white intruders have selfish motives (such as searching for a long-lost treasure) or when they act against nature, catching animals that Tarzan has befriended, or shooting elephants for their ivory. As Richard Dyer has remarked, Tarzan is an environmentalist of sorts (1997, 157), who turns against the intruders when they act immorally. Yet, it is precisely this moral grounding that identifies him as a colonizer: "A lament for a loss of closeness to nature has run through a very great deal of white culture. With Tarzan, however, one can have colonial power and closeness to nature" (Dyer 1997, 157). Tarzan's whiteness is beyond doubt, even to those readers or viewers not familiar with Edgar Rice Burroughs's original story, in which the protagonist's aristocratic Scottish lineage functions prominently (not least for reasons of heredity). "Yet this white man is more in harmony with nature than the indigenous inhabitants. With Tarzan, the white man can be king of the jungle without loss of oneness with it" (Dyer 1997, 157). Although he is linked to colonial power by race only, he demonstrates the qualities ascribed to the colonizer.

If the condition of adventure is a test of the subject's ability to adapt and exercise control over nature and if the hero's calling is to search for "the extraordinary, the enormous, and the dangerous in order to prove his superiority over nature" (Dyer 1997, 157), then Tarzan is the adventure hero *par excellence*. And if one of the conditions of adventure fiction is its popularization through multiple episodic tales (literary or cinematic), then Tarzan's popularity is emblematic of the cultural triumph of the serial. Between his 1912 publication of the original story, *Tarzan of the Apes*, in *All-Story Magazine* and his death in 1950, Burroughs published 26 Tarzan novels; while not all of them were written by Burroughs himself, he authored the original character and his principal story. In 1922, Burroughs founded a licensing company, Edgar Rice Burroughs, Inc., which has authorized 44 Tarzan films to date and has overseen the character's expansion into photo novels, comic books, radio recordings (350 records of 15 minutes each), and a television series (Neumann 2004, 121). After the original film adaptation, *Tarzan of the Apes* (1918), became a considerable box office success, Hollywood went on to make Tarzan films more or less continuously for the next five decades.

The first Tarzan film adhered fairly closely to the novel in telling the story of the young Lord Greystoke, who, after his mother dies in childbirth and his father is killed by a gorilla, is raised by apes in the jungle. With the help of a knife he has found and some self-education (he learns to read from his father's books), Greystoke becomes ruler of the apes and lord of the jungle (Neumann 2004, 120). Subsequent films evince the most tenuous relation to the original story, and there is no narrative coherence through a sequel structure. For example, as Neumann notes, between 1921 and 1928, Tarzan gets married three times, twice to Jane (*Adventures of Tarzan*, 1921; *Tarzan and the Golden Lion*, 1927) and once to Mary (*Tarzan the Mighty*, 1928) (2004, 121). In some films he lives alone; in others he has a son. Tarzan has been played by 17 different actors to date, most famously and frequently by former Olympic swimming champion Johnny Weissmuller in six MGM films, made between 1932 and 1942, and six RKO productions, made between 1942 and 1948. While MGM's model for the Tarzan stories was predominantly that of the nuclear family consisting of Tarzan, Jane (played by Maureen O'Sullivan in several productions), their son Boy, and the chimpanzee Cheeta, later films placed him in varied settings, many of which were more mythical and fantasy-like (Neumann 2004, 122). As Neumann notes, Tarzan meets Amazons, Arabs, and Nazi agents, and the settings randomly reference widely varying cultural spheres, such as Polynesia, India, or Latin America (2004, 121). The depiction of flora and fauna, too, reflects the way in which the classical studio-era B-movie rigorously subordinated verisimilitude to fantasy and to dual projections of threat and lure: "The respective elements are mixed without any regard for Africa's factual vegetation, its cultures, and its animals: lions live next to tigers; gorillas become carnivorous monsters; Nomads' tents abut African straw huts, jungle abruptly gives way to the coast. All these details are interchangeable tools whose sole function is to narrativize adventure" (Neumann 2004, 121). Yet, two important epiphenomena must be noted: Whenever Tarzan is confronted with civilization, he is disappointed and returns to his tree house in the jungle – a sign that these films, for all their colonialist essentializing of nature, express an appealing pessimism about culture that brands civilization as a prison house (Neumann 2004, 121). Second, this romantic longing for the authenticity of nature may well account for the fact that all Tarzan films since 1957 have been shot in color and many on location, exchanging the synthetic world of the Hollywood backlot for actual rainforest surroundings (Neumann 2004, 122).

Landscape on Display

With the exception of the related Western, hardly any genre relies as heavily on the outside shot as the adventure genre. An adventure film that takes place indoors is unthinkable. Landscape is the space in which adventure unfolds, and landscape takes an active part in the unfolding plot. Extreme topography – jungle, sea, desert, mountains, polar ice – acts the part of the opponent, not only as challenging territory but as active antagonist that the hero must overcome. Each of these extreme landscapes has sprouted its own generic variants, its own tales, stars, and visual styles. In the adventure film, landscape is exhibited. Always. For its landscape cinematography, the adventure film draws on visual conventions that have guided the representation of landscape since the eighteenth century – a set of scenographic principles derived from landscape painting, dioramas, zoological and ethnological exhibitions – all of which are redeployed by the adventure film for the production and exhibition of exoticism.[14] The mode in which the exotic is exhibited follows the basic principle of presenting the foreign environment and its species on an imaginary stage[15] that goes back to the colonial era's ambition to offer a "living picture" of the colonies.[16] An important role in the dramatization of the experience of the foreign environment and of Otherness falls to the travelogue. Here, too, the European perspective is strictly maintained as the encounter with the Other is dramatized through a simple suspense dynamic that registers in phrases such as "scary moment," "ambush," and others.[17] The scenic mode of staging can also be traced to eighteenth-century landscaping – especially the English landscape garden, which seeks to explain, instruct, and entertain by staging landscapes as walkable displays of nature. The garden is a "dramatically conceived sequence of individual chapters or scenes that each harbor both surprise and information" (Trotha 2001, 31). Key points of the terrain are linked through meticulously calculated visual axes, and the swaths cut into the vegetation open up to highly limited views by blocking other perspectives (Trotha 2001, 31).[18]

At issue in the staging of exoticism is the selection of photographic perspectives, the array of objects in the deep space of the composition, the use of vegetation and plants that act like picture frames or vignettes that structure an embellishing view onto the surroundings. The camera subjects itself to the older and more basic principle of the "scenic view" and the "staging of the gaze."[19] In *King Solomon's Mines* (1950) – one of the classic adventure films based on a novel of the colonial era by English writer H. Rider Haggard – there is a sequence in which a walk around the Otherness on display is elevated to serve as the structuring principle of the scene. The group has left the savannah behind and has entered the jungle. The woman is fascinated by the foreign environment and takes it in with curiosity: "The jungle is beautiful!" Already there is a scenographic principle: A snake adorns the image in the foreground like a vine, and the guide explicitly points it out; a point-of-view sequence shows a monkey jumping from tree to tree. Then the group reaches a new scene, a "resting place." The woman sits down on a tree stump, and a negro servant emerges from the background to offer drinks and tobacco. The guide lectures on the jungle's Darwinist principles, ushering in a visual-instructional tour: There are maggots under the bark; a mamba slithers into the shrubs; there is a chameleon and there are "safari ants" that, we learn, attack in hordes and can eat a whole person; there is an armadillo. The tour is staged according to a list compiled through the act of showing and is realized via point-of-view shots drawn from archival footage whose role, from the 1950s on, became increasingly important to the adventure film's ambitions to authenticate its locales and displays.[20]

The combined and closely related approaches of touring the wilderness (which includes the option of resting and being served food) and showcasing the wilderness, as demonstrated in *King Solomon's Mines*, are based on a mode of appropriation that is still in practice today. The very act of showing repeatedly alternates between the viewers and what is presented for them, with the principle of display consistently palpable. A symbolic authority emerges that keeps the object of presentation at a distance from the viewer – and this visual rhetoric crucially facilitates the production of the Other as exotic. For example, the tribe of natives is exhibited primarily in a performative mode that, underscored by music, references a theatrical or show format. The foreign manifests itself as a performance of social acts whose meanings remain undisclosed, seemingly at no loss to the viewer, for to exhibit the rituals and dances of the "savages" on a natural stage is also part of tourism. It domesticates the Other without ever abandoning the position of the civilized observer.

The ideologically charged production of Otherness and the economy of gazes in *King Solomon's Mines* can be related to the history of the material and its two adaptations. Rider Haggard wrote the novel in 1885, the year in which Europe's colonial powers sealed the division of Africa at the "Congo Conference" in Berlin (Struck 2004, 222). A classic colonialist novel, *King Solomon's Mines* recasts imperialist expansion into two trivial, mass-cultural myths: the figure of the "white hunter" who tries to give meaning to his life by fleeing urban modernity and seeking the challenges of "savage" nature; and the related myth of the existence of a fabled secret that goes back to the distant past of one's own civilization but that has survived in a foreign, "virginal" land previously hidden from European eyes (Struck 2004, 222). The novel constructs its rationale around the search for a European who has gone missing in Africa while trying to find the gold mines of the Old Testament figure King Solomon. What unfolds are the adventures of a search expedition into the undiscovered regions of Africa, led by the crusty "white hunter" hero, Allan Quartermain. The first adaptation of the novel, an English production filmed in 1937, also prominently features another character, the outcast royal scion of an African tribe (Paul Robeson), who becomes crucial in aiding the expedition and, in turn, is helped by the white hunter in being rehabilitated by his tribe. Yet, as Struck writes, this quasi-Commonwealth *quid pro quo* barely conceals the colonialist nature of the enterprise, consisting of the conquest of a foreign territory through classic *divide et impera*, which secures mining rights, labor power, and provisions through the newly created indigenous ally. Robert Stevenson's adaptation features the diamond fields of Kimberley, South Africa, in a quasi-documentary sequence (Struck 2004, 223) and thus, not unlike *Red Dust*, fairly unselfconsciously acknowledges the exploitive motives of colonialism. The 1950 Hollywood remake, however, made at the beginning of the era of decolonization,[21] glosses over this motive by giving greater emphasis to the illicit love story between Quartermain (Stewart Granger) and the wife of the missing colonialist (Deborah Kerr), who hires him to find her husband. The search for the fabled treasure and its prehistory is downplayed in favor of the visual exploitation of the tour itself, impressively filmed by location director Andrew Marton (Struck 2004, 224). The dynamics of this showcasing of the wilderness proceeds by placing landscapes on display, as noted, which now facilitate the visual exploitation of Africa for a seemingly more "humane" postcolonialism and, thus, as in the case of *Red Dust*, function to obscure colonialism's historical-materialist foundations.

The Encounter with the Mythical and the Magical

As *King Solomon's Mines* demonstrates, adventure is a reflection of civilization's boundaries, which, in addition to nature and the Other, include a third area – the mythical, magical, and prehistoric. The adventurer comes upon mysterious places of bygone civilizations (such as Atlantis); he finds mythical treasures (the Holy Grail, King Solomon's diamonds, and so on); he discovers remnants of prehistoric life (from King Kong to dinosaur islands). Many of these stories are alternatively grouped together under the fantasy genre. A film like *The Ghost and the Darkness* (1996), which interjects elements of the horror film into the adventure tale, represents nature as a magical threat that demands absolute courage and commitment to conquer, as the adventurer simply cannot do so with his usual measured distance and rationality. Occasionally, adventures mediate between the mythical and the "real" present, due to the genre's border-crossing impulses and its tendencies to leave the civilized world behind, to travel to unmarked regions, to pursue mystery. However, the confrontation between humankind and nature often takes on a primal force. It runs through the genre from *Moby Dick* (1930, 1956) to *Jaws* (1976). In this conflict the adventurer's role is overdetermined – only one who can adapt to the environment and its risks can survive. The relationship to the Other – whether in the guise of nature, culture, or other peoples – can be divided into several radically diverse types, ranging from the subordination of the Other to the adventurer's own transition into a world and life of Otherness.

The adventurer's adaptation to the world of Otherness primarily constitutes an embracing of the Other as a sphere in which to live and act. This sometimes necessitates parting with the mother culture's way of doing things. Small details are revealing: In *King Solomon's Mines* (1950), the heroine renounces a corset and trims her own hair to a manageable length. Selecting the appropriate gear can turn into a serious concern, as evident in several scenes in *The Treasure of the Sierra Madre* (1948). In *Journey to the Center of the Earth* (1959), an expedition is robbed of its gear and cannot begin the trip. Foreign languages and rites of communication require study. The adventurer accepts foreign ways of greeting, of expressing gratitude and humbleness, and of presenting honors and gifts – even when these customs violate European rules. Her acceptance into a native tribe and the initiation rule by which the young woman in *Hatari!* (1962) becomes mother of the elephants is, at times, depicted as a crude joke. However, it does count as a form of de-Europeanization that constitutes a kind of cohesive force for the group of animal hunters beyond their work.

Scouts are part of adventure because they represent a measure of Otherness and indicate a magnitude of danger. In many Westerns and African adventures, the adventurer depends on a native guide who is familiar with the territory and is able to convey strategies of survival. In Nicholas Roeg's outback film *Walkabout* (1971), and similarly in the Kalahari film *A Far Off Place* (1993), a native boy's leadership skills are combined with erotic fascination. We catch a glimpse of an affective system that regards the Other as something natural, pure, and desirable, a system underscored by a force that causes civilization to open up from within. In general it is the European who is the center of this affective system. Only in this way can we understand a paradoxical reversal of perspectives: The Aborigine boy's encounter with civilization in *Walkabout* contaminates him and drives him to suicide.

The process of conversion goes beyond adaptation. Here the adventurer turns into an Other, leaves civilization, and crosses over to the other side. Familiarity with the Other evolves into merging with the Other, even at the cost of losing one's base identity. The eponymous protagonist of *A Man Called Horse* (1970) seemingly does turn into an Indian, and *Dances With Wolves* (1990) assumes an indeterminable cultural identity. What emerges is a subliminal cultural conflict that regards the Other as the better half of one's own self. Conversion is about transcending conventionality and tyranny, alienation and oppression, vanity and arrogance. In the same way as the noble savage stands in relation to civilized man, so the convert stands in relation to the past form of his own self. Conversions reflect processes of formation, of developing personality. On occasion, the converting or border-crossing hero bears a mark or stigma that signals his partial decivilization. Tattoos have, of late, especially been deployed in this function, surely pointing to the role of the body as a sign within cultural processes: In *Medicine Man* (1992), the woman receives a tattoo from an exotic medicine man long before her conversion.[22] In Jane Campion's *The Piano* (1993), the tattooed Harvey Keitel plays a man who, as a confidant of the Maori, assumes the position of cultural intermediary similar to that of the trapper in the Western (see, for example, Robert Aldrich's revisionist Western *Ulzana's Raid*, 1972). In *Papillon* (1973), tattoos alone signal membership in a certain layer of civilization. Sometimes the ultimate goal of the adventurer is the passage into a different state of mind. The "Kafiristan" of *The Man Who Would Be King* (1975) is a site not just of power but of meditation, where spiritual humility is obtained. (What is tragicomic about the story is that the adventurer is debunked as a con man and killed at the very moment when he is poised to convert to a higher state of mind.)

The considerable revisionist impulses of the films mentioned in this last section reflect the fact that the adventure film is not impervious to historical change. To determine generic specificity and the dynamics of generic evolution in the adventure film, however, is a difficult task given the overwhelming heterogeneity of the genre. Ultimately, what unites the chaotic diversity of stories and materials is the fact that the adventure genre is one of crossing borders. Conceived of as an adventure, this act of border crossing should be understood as a strategy to anchor a hero in his world rather than as representing a clear generic identity or a single narrative scheme. The adventure is a genre that is best grasped in its prototypes – not in its mythology, its stereotypical world order, or through any basic dramatic constellation.

Notes

1. Translated by Roy Grundmann.
2. As *aventiure* is a term that can be traced back to medieval knighthood tales, referring to the challenges that lie ahead, it bears a close relation to adventure. However, as Michael Nerlich writes (1990, 25–31), the shift from a medieval to a postmedieval connotation that no longer revolves around knights' tales but recounts the adventures of traveling merchants occurred in the thirteenth and fourteenth centuries. In this sense, the concept of adventure becomes closely linked culturally to the expansion of (mainly European) commerce, which finds its early high point in the fifteenth century. The basic design of the hero of adventure fiction must therefore be derived from the actual historical context of colonialism.
3. Consider the generic diversity of this list of only the most essential titles: *Tarzan of the Apes* (1918), *The Mark of Zorro* (1920), *Ben-Hur* (1925), *Don Juan* (1926), *Moby Dick* (1930, 1956), *Mr. Robinson Crusoe* (1932), *Red Dust* (1932), *King Kong* (1933), *The Scarlet Pimpernel* (1934), *China Seas* (1935), *The Crusades* (1935), *Mutiny on the Bounty* (1935, 1962), *Captain Blood* (1935), *Sinbad* (1936), *Lost Horizon* (1937), *The Adventures of Robin Hood* (1938), *The Rains Came* (1939), *Union Pacific* (1939), *The Four Feathers* (1939), *Only Angels Have Wings* (1939), *The Sea Hawk* (1940), *Congo Maisie* (1940), *The Jungle Book* (1942), *For Whom the Bell Tolls* (1943), *Ali Baba and the Forty Thieves* (1944), *Kismet* (1944), *To Have and Have Not* (1946), *The Treasure of the Sierra Madre* (1948), *The Three Musketeers* (1948), *King Solomon's Mines* (1950), *Pandora and the Flying Dutchman* (1950), *The African Queen* (1951), *The Big Sky* (1952), *The Wild North* (1952), *The Snows of Kilimanjaro* (1952), *Ivanhoe* (1952), *The Greatest Show on Earth* (1952), *Mogambo* (1953), *Knights of the Round Table* (1953), *Prince Valiant* (1954), *20,000 Leagues Under the Sea* (1954), *The High and the Mighty* (1954), *Land of the Pharaohs* (1955), *Blood Alley* (1955), *The Rains of Ranchipur* (1955), *Around the World in Eighty Days* (1956), *The Power and the Passion* (1957), *The Old Man and the Sea* (1958), *The Defiant Ones* (1958), *Ben-Hur* (1959), *Journey to the Center of the Earth* (1959, 2008), *The Magnificent Seven* (1960), *The Sundowners* (1961), *Hatari!* (1961), *El Cid* (1961), *Lawrence of Arabia* (1962), *The Guns of Navarone* (1962), *The Fall of the Roman Empire* (1963), *55 Days at Peking* (1963), *Lord Jim* (1964), *The Flight of the Phoenix* (1965), *Those Magnificent Men in their Flying Machines* (1965), *The Sand Pebbles* (1966), *Burn!* (1969), *Where Eagles Dare* (1967), *The Fantastic Voyage* (1967), *The Dirty Dozen* (1969), *The Wild Bunch* (1969), *A Man Called Horse* (1970), *The Poseidon Adventure* (1972), *Papillon* (1973), *The Three Musketeers: The Queen's Diamonds* (1973), *The Four Musketeers: Milady's Revenge* (1974), *The Wind and the Lion* (1975), *The Man Who Would Be King* (1975), *Robin and Marian* (1975), *Jaws* (1976), *Star Wars* (1977), *Sorcerer* (1977), *The Deep* (1977), *Apocalypse Now* (1979), *Alien* (1979), *Raiders of the Lost Ark* (1981), *Excalibur* (1981), *A Passage to India* (1984), *Romancing the Stone* (1984), *The Emerald Forest* (1984), *Silverado* (1985), *Legend* (1985), *Back to the Future* (1986), *Mosquito Coast* (1986), *Mission* (1986), *Empire of the Sun* (1987), *The Abyss* (1988), *Far and Away* (1992), *Terminator 2* (1992), *Jurassic Park* (1994), *Jumanji* (1995), *The Mask of Zorro* (1998), *The Mummy* (1999), *Gladiator* (2000), *Cast Away* (2000), *A.I. Artificial Intelligence* (2001), *The Lord of the Rings* (2001), *The Last Samurai* (2003), *Pirates of the Caribbean: The Curse of the Black Pearl* (2003), *Master and Commander: The Far Side of the World* (2003), *Prince of Persia: The Sands of Time* (2010).
4. Consider *Le Salaire de la Peur* (*The Wages of Fear*) (France/Italy, 1953, Henri-Georges Clouzot) and its American remake, *Sorcerer* (1977, William Friedkin).
5. This is also where the classical adventure film has since been superseded: Films such as *The Three Musketeers* achieved their ostentatious display of ballet-like qualities through the long take/long shot. In the modern adventure film, action is designed for speed and the scene is broken up into countless individual movements. The stagelike nature of the location is downplayed.
6. The concept of characterization is alien to the adventure novel, according to Best, and the adventurer is as devoid of character as Proteus, knowing no internal directives and acknowledging no external direction (Fritze et al. 1983, 40).
7. In addition to these Hollywood versions, there is a 1916 Australian version, *The Mutiny on the Bounty*, and a 1984 international coproduction, *The Bounty*, starring Mel Gibson, Anthony Hopkins, Laurence Olivier, Edward Fox, and Daniel Day-Lewis.

8. Flynn's other films in the cycle are *Captain Blood* (1935), *The Charge of the Light Brigade* (1936), *The Prince and the Pauper* (1937), *The Private Lives of Elizabeth and Essex* (1939), and *The Sea Hawk* (1940).
9. Roddick directly links these qualities to Flynn's star persona and his position in the studio's stable of stars: "Flynn becomes the least problematic embodiment of Warners' philosophy of individual morality, reflected more ambiguously in Paul Muni's biographical impersonations and James Cagney's contemporary struggles between selfishness and social conscience" (1983, 236).
10. Roddick cites Rudy Behlmer's speculation to this effect in his introduction to the published screenplay (Madison: University of Wisconsin Press, 1979), 18.
11. On the genre of the historical adventure film, see additionally Taves 1993.
12. In his discussion of the film, Claus Löser mentions that *China Seas* departs from the heavy-handed colonialist mentality of many adventure films. While the Asian passengers on board the freighter are represented as a faceless mass, their anonymity is relativized through the film's portrayal of piracy, which is not associated with the Other but, rather, becomes a ploy for the film to articulate an unmistakable skepticism toward the rule of the British empire. In addition, the only American is caricatured as a delirious Yankee (2004, 167).
13. Significantly, Jack Gold told the Robinson Crusoe tale from Friday's perspective in *Man Friday* (UK, 1975). See Jean Franco 1993, 90.
14. While the exotic has been exhibited as an object in various institutions since the beginning of the bourgeois era, botanical and zoological gardens, as well as the circus and the museum, are even older. But it is from the nineteenth century on that the exotic is explored systematically through a synergy of education and entertainment, so that it can be experienced by those who remained at home. Illustrations from travel literature as well as landscape photographs and postcards displayed the colonies to a European audience. The psychological-emotional landscapes of Romanticism, in which nature served as mirror and expression of internal tensions, likewise register as models.
15. This mode of staging, which came to dominate the classic exoticist adventure film, had already begun to evolve in various other media and modes of exhibition. An example is the pioneering approach of German animal merchant and zoo founder Carl Hagenbeck, who displayed animals according to species and in their natural habitat, a move that became a model for both the modern zoo and the staging of foreign worlds in miniature. A second narrative tendency in the staging of the exotic can be found in the scenarios of ethnographic and ethnological exhibitions, which Hagenbeck similarly influenced.
16. This type of exhibition offering a "living picture" of the colonies, facilitated through an immense spatialized exoticism, began in the seventeenth and eighteenth centuries, but its true popularity arrived in the heyday of colonialism in the late nineteenth century. On the history of ethnological exhibitions in Germany, see especially Goldmann 1988 (with regard to the relationship between Europeans and the "savage" Other); Thode-Arora 1989 (with regard to Carl Hagenbeck); and Thode-Arora 1997 (with regard to the impact of ethnological exhibits on German exoticist adventure films). Whereas in Germany ethnological exhibitions did not become popular until after 1870, in France they had been all the rage since around 1830 during the time of the empire. On the impact of zoological shows in Paris, see Allin 1998.
17. For a German-language volume that discusses the poetics of travel, see Ertzdorff-Kupffer 2000.
18. See also Trotha's book-length study of the English garden (1999).
19. Interestingly, the tendency to stage scenes and images is countered in the marketing of the films through statements that assure viewers of the authenticity of the images. With regard to Weimar cinema's images of India, see Brandlmeier 1997, 42. On the pseudo-authenticity of jungle films made by John Hagenbeck in Hamburg's Hagenbeck zoo, see Schöning 1997.
20. I have already mentioned the fact that, from the late 1950s on, most Tarzan films were shot on location. One also recalls the authenticating function of numerous anecdotes that were recounted around the shooting of Howard Hawks's animal adventure film *Hatari!* (1962).
21. Here one might think of decolonization also in terms of film history. This was a time when Hollywood found it harder to maintain its control over foreign markets, as some of those markets, including Britain, had begun to impose import tolls on American films.
22. See Jean Franco's analysis of *Medicine Man* in the context of the representation of tribal societies in feature films (1993).

References

Allin, Michael. (1998). *Zarafa: A Giraffe's True Story, from Deep in Africa to the Heart of Paris*. New York: Random House.

Altman, Rick. (1995). "A Semantic/Syntactic Approach to Film Genre." In Barry Keith Grant (ed.), *Film Genre Reader II* (pp. 26–40). Austin: University of Texas Press. (Original work published 1984.)

Best, Otto F. (1983). *Abenteuer – Wonnetraum aus Flucht und Ferne*. Frankfurt: Fischer.

Brandlmeier, Thomas. (1997). "Et ego fui in Arcadia. Die exotischen Spielfilme der 20er Jahre." In Jörg Schöning (ed.), *Triviale Tropen. Exotische Reise- und Abenteuerfilme aus Deutschland 1919–1939* (pp. 35–46). Munich: Cinegraph/Text + Kritik.

Cawelti, John G. (1976). *Adventure, Mystery, and Romance: Formula Stories as Art and Popular Culture*. Chicago: University of Chicago Press.

Dyer, Richard. (1997). *White*. London: Routledge.

Ertzdorff-Kupffer, Xenja von (ed.). (2000). *Beschreibung der Welt. Zur Poetik der Reise- und Länderberichte*. Amsterdam: Rodopi.

Franco, Jean. (1993). "The Representation of Tribal Societies in Feature Films." In John King, Ana M. Lopez, & Manuel Alvarando (eds), *Mediating Two Worlds: Cinematic Encounters in the Americas* (pp. 81–94). London: British Film Institute.

Fritze, Christoph, Seesslen, Georg, & Weil, Claudius. (1983). *Der Abenteurer. Geschichte und Mythologie des Abenteuer-Films*. Reinbek: Rowohlt.

Goldmann, Stefan. (1988). "Wilde in Europa. Aspekte und Orte ihrer Zurschaustellung." In Thomas Theye (ed.), *Wir und die Wilden. Einblicke in eine kannibalische Beziehung* (pp. 243–269). Reinbek: Rowohlt.

Hediger, Vinzenz. (2004). "Der Ritterfilm." In Bodo Traber & Hans J. Wulff, *Filmgenres. Abenteuerfilm* (pp. 42–54). Stuttgart: Reclam.

Heer, Burckhardt. (1981). *Der Abenteuerfilm. Eine Untersuchung*. Aachen: Bundesarbeitsgemeinschaft für Jugendfilmarbeit und Medienerziehung.

Hügel, Hans Otto. (n.d.). "Das Dilemma des Abenteurers. Zu einer Figur der Unterhaltungsliteratur." Unpublished manuscript. Hildesheim.

Klotz, Volker. (1979). *Abenteuer-Romane. Sue, Dumas, Ferry, Retcliffe, May, Verne*. Munich: Hanser.

Löser, Claus. (2004). "Abenteuer im Gelben Meer." In Bodo Traber & Hans J. Wulff, *Filmgenres. Abenteuerfilm* (pp. 164–168). Stuttgart: Reclam.

Midding, Gerhard. (2004). "Der Mantel-und-Degen-Film." In Bodo Traber & Hans J. Wulff, *Filmgenres. Abenteuerfilm* (pp. 54–66). Stuttgart: Reclam.

Nerlich, Michael. (1990). "Abenteur." In Hans Jörg Sandkühler (ed.), *Europäische Enzyklopädie zu Philosophie und Wissenschaften*, Vol. 1 (pp. 25–31). Hamburg: Meiner.

Neumann, Norbert. (2004). "Der Tarzan-Stoff." In Bodo Traber & Hans J. Wulff, *Filmgenres. Abenteuerfilm* (pp. 118–126). Stuttgart: Reclam.

Roddick, Nick. (1983). *A New Deal in Entertainment: Warner Brothers in the 1930s*. London: British Film Institute.

Schöning, Jörg. (1997). "Unternehmensgegenstand: Exotik. Der Produzent John Hagenbeck." In Jörg Schöning (ed.), *Triviale Tropen. Exotische Reise- und Abenteuerfilme aus Deutschland 1919–1939* (pp. 110–123). Munich: Cinegraph/Text + Kritik.

Struck, Wolfgang. (2004). "König Salomons Diamanten." In Bodo Traber & Hans J. Wulff, *Filmgenres. Abenteuerfilm* (pp. 222–225). Stuttgart: Reclam.

Taves, Brian. (1993). *The Romance of Adventure: The Genre of Historical Adventure Movies*. Jackson: University Press of Mississippi.

Thode-Arora, Hilke. (1989). *Für Fünfzig Pfennig um die Welt. Die Hagenbeckschen Völkerschauen*. Frankfurt: Campus.

Thode-Arora, Hilke. (1997). "Herbeigeholte Ferne. Völkerschauen als Vorläufer exotisier-ender Abenteuerfilme." In Jörg Schöning (ed.), *Triviale Tropen. Exotische Reise- und Abenteuerfilme aus Deutschland 1919–1939* (pp. 19–33). Munich: Cinegraph/Text + Kritik.

Trotha, Hans von. (1999). *Der englische Garten. Eine Reise durch seine Geschichte*. Berlin: Wagenbach.

Trotha, Hans von. (2001). "Utopie in Grün." *Die Zeit*, August 23, 31.

15

Cinema and the Modern Woman

Veronica Pravadelli
Professor, Roma Tre University, Italy

Breaking away from the Victorian ideal of **True Womanhood**, American cinema of the 1920s and early 1930s embraced **urban modernity**, and with it, the **New Woman** – an independent working- or middle-class female forging her way in various urban occupations, including prostitution, and asserting her sexual liberation with few negative consequences. As Veronica Pravadelli explains, however, these images of emancipation in films like ***Baby Face*** (1933), ***Glorifying the American Girl*** (1929), and ***Blonde Venus*** (1932), among others, would be plundered by ideologies touting female domesticity and masculine dominance in the mid-1930s, when censorship and other pressures kicked in. Pravadelli links 1920s and early 1930s cinematic tropes like the **urban dissolve** with larger thematic and ideological representations of women that challenged notions of female passivity. After 1934, the upper-class women of **screwball comedy** are among the few filmic females afforded such active agency. Pravadelli's essay shares ground with Shelley Stamp on women in silent film, David M. Lugowski on queer 1930s film images, and Roy Grundmann on *The Strange Love of Martha Ivers* in this volume, and with Lea Jacobs on the maternal melodrama and William Rothman on the screwball comedy in the hardcover/online edition.

Additional terms, names, and concepts: flapper film, serial queen, cinema of attraction, female exhibitionism

In American cinema of the 1930s the image of the modern woman and the trajectory of female desire present two different models. Between the end of the 1920s and the early 1930s, American cinema continued to focus on the image of the young, self-assertive, and sexy woman in her multiple facets: Working girls, gold diggers, flappers, show girls, and kept women inundated the talkies and perpetuated the cult of New Womanhood that emerged in the early years of the century. This tendency would wane as the decade progressed. From about the mid-1930s, the dominant narrative of female desire was tuned to the formation of the couple and to marriage while the figure of the emancipated woman became marginal. In this process

American Film History: Selected Readings, Origins to 1960, First Edition. Edited by Cynthia Lucia, Roy Grundmann, and Art Simon.
© 2016 John Wiley & Sons, Inc. Published 2016 by John Wiley & Sons, Inc.

the representation of class rise and upward mobility were also questioned and the heroine's social aspirations were more often thwarted than supported. One need only compare *Baby Face* (1933) and *Stella Dallas* (1937), both starring Barbara Stanwyck in the leading role, to realize how the convergence between gender and class changed dramatically in just a few years. In the second half of the 1930s, only the upper-class protagonists of screwball comedy enjoyed sexual freedom and independence, while working-class women were denied both upward mobility and gender equality.

This shift in the representation of gender identity was matched by a concomitant transformation in film style. In the early 1930s, American cinema extended the use of visual techniques developed during the silent period that we may consider in light of the "cinema of attractions." While such a cinema is overtly narrative, at specific moments (especially, but not only, in the opening episode), the film avoids both narrative articulation and dialogue and communicates merely through visual devices. Around 1934, the classical mode of representation, namely a rational and motivated mode of storytelling based on analytic editing and dialogue, became dominant, while visual attractions and techniques all but disappeared. If we look at the convergence between gender identities and film rhetoric in 1930s cinema we can assess the trajectory of the New Woman from her splendor in the "Age of Turbulence" to her demise in the "Age of Order" (Sklar 1994, 175–194).

Cinema, the New Woman, and Urban Modernity

In the last decades of the nineteenth century, industrial capitalism, urban modernity, and new forms of leisure time produced a watershed in women's lives. The impact of modernity on women's experience cannot be underestimated. While the new possibilities were not available to all, but mainly to unmarried young women working in urban areas, by the 1920s, young women of all classes living in big cities as well as small towns "claimed new sexual and romantic freedoms," and "found themselves with more money and more time to spend on themselves," while enjoying the same leisure culture as men. They also became avid media consumers. By 1929, "more than half of all single women were gainfully employed," and in large cities up to "one third of adult women workers lived alone in private apartments or boarding houses" and in the absence of parental supervision (Zeitz 2006, 29–31; see also Meyerowitz 1993, 43–71). Women left the rural areas in greater numbers than men in pursuit of better economic possibilities and in search of excitement. Overall, women's modern lifestyle was defined by financial independence and a whole new relation to work, leisure, and sex. While women had worked for wages throughout the Victorian Age, the cultural context now had changed. New jobs in department stores, large factories, restaurants, and offices provided alternatives to domestic service and sweatshops. The relationship between work and leisure also changed. In her groundbreaking study of working women and leisure in turn-of-the-century New York, historian Kathy Peiss claims that

> The perception of leisure as a separate sphere of independence, youthful pleasure, and mixed-sex fun, in opposition to the world of obligation and toil, was supported by women's experience in the workplace. (1986, 35)

Work did not inculcate "discipline and a desire for quiet evenings at home," since "earning a living" was both an economic necessity and "a cultural experience organizing and defining [women's] leisure activities" (Peiss 1986, 34–35). In this regard, the modern woman's trajectory may be understood in the broader context of the nation's economic growth and of "the changing attitudes that had focused on saving to focus on spending" (Cott 1987, 146).

The transition from the Victorian ideology of True Womanhood could not be more evident.[1] While married women's lives continued to center on the domestic sphere, single women forcefully entered the public sphere. Such a process spurred a "trend toward a pleasure-oriented culture" (Peiss 1986, 36–40) that defied the Victorian ethos toward domesticity and sexual purity (Welter 1978). In this process, media consumption, and especially moviegoing, represented a fundamental practice of women's everyday lives. While in the second half of the 1920s movie attendance continued to grow (Steinberg 1980, 46), the new mass consumption, which included a new standard of living in urban households, "portended a new level of standardization and uniformity of life." As Nancy Cott has argued,

> In the 1920s an American mass culture became possible, as the conjunction of mass production and marketing techniques with new technology added the radio and the movies to print media already crossing the nation. (1987, 147)

While mass media fed the tendency toward cultural uniformity and the creation of a specifically American modern way of life, "surveys reported that movie stars had replaced leaders in politics, business, or the arts as those admired by the young" (Cott 1987, 147).

In the transition years from silent film to sound, cinema was still the most effective form for representing modernity and urban life, as well as women's desire to emancipate. Surveys of the period and contemporary investigations in audience studies reveal that, in the 1920s and the early 1930s, women represented the majority of moviegoers. Working in this domain, Melvyn Stokes (1999) has noted that audience research studies at that time were rather impressionistic and that the data available are probably imprecise. Yet while estimates might be individually inaccurate, "collectively they suggest an impressive weight of evidence to buttress the idea of predominantly female audience" (43). Ultimately, whether women really formed a majority of the cinema audience was "less important than the fact that Hollywood itself assumed that, both through their own attendance and their ability to influence men, they were its primary market" (43–44). Such an assumption had a powerful effect on the industry. In the 1920s and the 1930s, Hollywood produced a vast number of films centered on women, often written by women scriptwriters. During the first half of the 1930s the woman's film made up a quarter of all movies on the "best lists," with 1931 as the year recording the highest number (Balio 1993, 237). In a similar way, one can read the greater success of female over male stars in those years as correlative to female moviegoing.

Women, of course, loved to see images of the New Woman, exemplified by such divas as Gloria Swanson, Colleen Moore, Clara Bow, and Joan Crawford. As Mary Ryan (1976) has pointed out, "the new movie woman exuded above all a sense of physical freedom – unrestrained movement . . . abounding energy – the antithesis of the controlled, quiet, tight-kneed poses of Griffith's heroines." She goes on to describe the "dashing spontaneity" with which "they rushed onto dance floors, leapt into swimming pools, and accepted any dare – to drink, to sport, to strip," as they moved into social, work, and higher education spheres (1976, 369–370).

In the 1920s, the flapper represented the most important image of the modern woman. Combining physical and behavioral features, the flapper had bobbed hair and short skirts, drank a lot, enjoyed partying, and followed loosened sexual standards. However, the key to her success was the contradictory status of her image since she was both sweet and wild, youthful and worldly, innocent and sexual (Ross 2000). While the flapper became a pivotal figure in all areas of American culture, from literature to fashion, from the popular press to advertising (Zeitz 2006), in cinema her status was assured by the genre of the flapper film, which developed roughly from 1922 to 1923 – with films such as *The Flapper* (1922) and *Flaming Youth* (1923) – to 1929, when Clara Bow played her last flapper role in Dorothy Arzner's *The Wild Party* (Ross 2000). In the following years female characters maintained the sexual openness and the frank assertiveness of the flapper, but most of them lacked her innocence and her girlish attitude. The new stars of the early 1930s tended to be slightly older[2] and often pushed their roles in a dramatic direction, true of Joan Crawford and Barbara Stanwyck. While a comedienne like Claudette Colbert, especially in the Oscar-winning hit *It Happened One Night* (1934), was a late example of the flapper, other stars such as Mae West and Marlene Dietrich revitalized the image of the strong and sexy woman by adding highly original traits.

The image of the New Woman in her different facets eclipsed the "cult of True Womanhood" by promoting a whole new set of gender attributes. As Barbara Welter has argued, the Victorian ethos prescribed for women a strict moral code based on four traits: domesticity, religiosity, sexual purity, and subordination to the male (1978, 313–333). In the films made for Griffith, Lillian Gish is the apotheosis of the Victorian heroine. Griffith's moral world focuses "upon woman's essential goodness and purity." The Griffith–Gish heroine was the epitome of innocence and Gish's face "expressed the artlessness and modest reserve of a virgin" (Higashi 1978, 3). As in nineteenth-century Victorian melodramas, the narrative tension resulted from the threats posed by the villain to the chastity of the female heroine. Similarly, as one can see in the opposing male characters in *Way Down East* (1920), "the city was the scene where rural values had gone to pot" and the sexual model of the film stands "in contrast to the freedom resulting from the urban, Jazz Age revolution in manners and morals" (Higashi 1978, 13).

The New Woman's trajectory, as Higashi implies, could only occur in the urban spaces of modernity. Indeed, in a vast number of films the heroine leaves her parochial birthplace and arrives in the big city to look for a job, as she does, for example, in *An American Tragedy* (1931), *Night Nurse* (1931), and *Baby Face*, among many others. In a similar fashion, the emergence of cinema itself was made possible by modernity. The "modernity thesis," as Ben Singer has suggested,

> stresses key formal and spectatorial similarities between cinema – as a medium of strong impressions, spatiotemporal fragmentation, abruptness, mobility – and the nature of metropolitan experience. Both are characterized by the prominence of fleeting, forceful visual attractions and contra-contemplative spectatorial distraction. (2001, 102)

Early cinema, as well as some narrative genres of the 1910s, may be seen as a formal expression of the modern subject's hyperstimulated experience in the metropolis. The serial-queen melodrama beautifully developed the theme of female heroism and was thus a paradigmatic example of the image of the New Woman:

> within a sensational action-adventure framework... serials gave narrative preeminence to an intrepid young heroine who exhibited a variety of traditionally "masculine" qualities: physical strength and endurance, self-reliance, courage, social authority, and freedom to explore novel experiences outside the domestic sphere. (2001, 221)

For Singer the serial-queen melodrama is an aesthetic version of everyday urban life, dominated by excessive visual sensations, in the sense that cinema duplicates, for the women in the audience, the female subject's urban experience.

One can test the changing institutional status of cinema as a form of entertainment as well as the trajectory of the modern woman by looking at how the representation of the New Woman changed throughout the first decades of the century. The masculine attitude of the silent serial queen was a product of the convergence of the social figure of the suffragette (Stamp 2000, 154–158) and the hero of stage sensational melodramas, while broadly, the serial thriller, best exemplified in the 1910s by the serial queen, is the clearest expression of the popular nature of early cinema. If the transition to the feature film is commonly assumed to be a staple in the transformation of cinema into a bourgeois form of entertainment, the female heroines of the 1920s and early 1930s also indicate a clear change in the social imaginary *vis-à-vis* the New Woman. In this regard we may seize both continuities and differences between the silent and the early sound period. While in the 1920s the flapper film became a production staple in all studios (Ross 2000, 112), as this image waned the figures of the working girl and of the performer (in her different guises as singer, chorus girl, comedian, etc.) became the most popular. If illicit sex was often a fundamental element of plot and character, women were defined, first of all, by their position in the working sphere. Between 1921 and 1930, Hollywood produced 46 films with domestic servants in minor roles, 49 with shop girls, 28 with stenographers, and 114 with secretaries (Ryan 1976, 374–375). What is also interesting was cinema's perspective in relation to class. In many cases, in fact, rich women were represented as uninteresting partners, or worse, as boring. Aristocrats and rich men, engaged or married to women of their class, frequently were shown to fall in love with women of a lower class who were livelier and funnier than their official partners. At times rich and independent women were also fun, as true of Ruth Chatterton's wonderful character in *Female* (1933) or Norma Shearer's Jerry Martin in *The Divorcée* (1930), but such women were definitely a rarity in those years. That dynamic would be reversed in the following years: The upper-class heroines of the screwball comedy would in fact inherit the glamour and the lively energy of the working girls who preceded them.

New Women and Visual Attractions

The modern metropolis as the site of change and transformation is beautifully exemplified in those films in which young women tried to improve their status through work or sex or both. The heroine's social rise did not simply involve a linear plot in the tradition of classical narratives based on cause and effect, however (Bordwell et al. 1985). Through formal devices drawn from the silent period, in the transition years to sound, American cinema expressed the New Woman's condition through visual spectacles that represented cinematically the ideas of movement and metamorphosis as well as the experience of excessive visual sensations typical of modernity. While the "urban dissolve" represented the most effective and radical case of this formal economy, such a tendency was also exemplified by location shooting in the streets, often with the camera positioned inside a car or a moving vehicle, or with the heroine framed while walking by glamorous shop windows as at the beginning of *Night Nurse* and *Red- Headed Woman* (1932), respectively.

In the early 1930s, cinema's mode of representation relied on a convergence between classical style and visual attractions, that is, between plots of emancipation and spectacular imagery. Tom Gunning (1990) has suggested that when the narrative form won out, the cinema of attractions did not disappear but went "underground, both into certain avant-garde practices and as a component of narrative films, more evident in some genres (e.g. the musical) than in others" (57). If we accept that the cinema of attractions represented an aesthetic solution to the condition of modernity, we must then historicize that concept and evaluate carefully the changing relation between attraction and narration. The cinema of the early 1930s is a fundamental episode in this trajectory since it calls for a *gendered reading* of the aesthetic concept of attraction. In the woman-centered films of the period, visual attractions rely on the image of the female body, while narratives focus on stories of female emancipation. The convergence between form and content around the woman's body is a very peculiar solution that deserves consideration.

The relation between woman and modernity found particular expression in two types of visual attractions – the "urban dissolve" and the exhibitionist display of the female body. The urban dissolve is a specific code of silent cinema, a rhetorical strategy developed in particular by the city symphony documentary in such films as Strand and Sheeler's *Manhatta* (1921), Ruttmann's *Berlin: Symphony of a Great City* (1927), and Vertov's *Man with a Movie Camera* (1929), but also used in narrative film, as in F. W. Murnau's American debut, *Sunrise* (1927). The urban dissolve is an extended dissolve, a series of superimpositions of images of urban life which amplifies "cinematically" the city's dynamism while also testing the spectator's perceptive skills. Shot in the most bustling areas of the metropolis, it shows masses of people walking or waiting, fast-moving lines of cars and trolleys, and other energized moments of everyday urban life. Far from being "realistic," the image loses its iconic properties via multiple and complex dissolves and constantly transforms itself to the extent that it may become pure movement and energy. While we are often unable to "read" the image, our perceptive experience registers endless movement and change as the main condition of city life. The urban dissolve is clearly antinarrative and contributes enormously to the opposition between narrative and spectacle that shaped American cinema in the early sound years.

Dissolves and visual polyphonies are often gendered, that is, related to the female body. Because they effectively exemplify the idea of metamorphosis, they are and were particularly fit to represent the modern woman's narrative of transformation. While this device was very common, it also could attain an unusual level of formal complexity and rhetorical force, as it did in *Glorifying the American Girl* (Millard Webb, 1929). A second strategy of attraction, female exhibitionist techniques, was also very common. The exhibition of the female body, especially in a performative context, preserved the impulse of early cinema as described by Gunning. As we see, for example, in *Rain* (Lewis Milestone, 1932), the display of the female body is an assault on the viewer, who is "forced" to experience the excessive sexual energy of the woman at the moment in which we see the protagonist introducing herself to the soldiers. I will analyze strategies of attraction in relationship to the female body by looking at the opening episode in *Glorifying the American Girl* and *What Price Hollywood?* (George Cukor, 1932) and by considering Joan Crawford's appearance in *Rain*. Antinarrative strategies are most commonly used at the beginning of the film before character and plot take up their role.

Glorifying the American Girl, produced by Monta Bell for Paramount, begins with a spectacular four-minute prologue composed of a series of complex superimpositions activating a vertiginous visual experience. The film tells the story of a young woman who

Figure 15.1 Millions of young women walk toward the urban areas: the opening dissolve in Millard Webb's *Glorifying the American Girl* (1929, producer Monta Bell).

wants to be in the Follies; in the meantime she works in a department store sheet-music section, where she sings the latest hits. She will become a successful performer on Broadway, but in the process she will break up with her boyfriend who is unable to cope with her career and who will marry a more "modest" girl. The prologue postpones the beginning of the narrative and visually "demonstrates" the relation between woman and modernity.

The first shot shows a map of the United States with long lines of young women walking on the American soil. Dressed in the same uniform, their movements design a series of serpentines occupying the whole national space. The women have a robot-like shape since they all look alike and the geometry of their movements resembles Busby Berkeley's dancing numbers in *42nd Street* (1933), *Gold Diggers of 1933* (1933), and *Footlight Parade* (1933). Then the shot slowly dissolves into the image of a young woman wearing a formal dress. Soon after, the image dissolves again into the figure of a Ziegfeld girl. On the lower part of the image the serpentines continue to walk on the map. The following shot frames a moving train while the serpentines are still superimposed, thus doubling the movement of the train itself. The prologue continues to develop along the same line: Dissolves as well as double or triple superimpositions will build up truly spectacular and dynamic visual effects on the theme of "women and the metropolis."

Neither the film's plot nor the revue format is highly original. One reviewer at the time wrote that the film presented "nothing . . . that has not been done in the talkies many times before" and another similarly said that "Its plot fairly reeks with familiarity" (quoted in Crafton 1997, 334). Yet the prologue, nevertheless, is quite stunning. While superimpositions and extended dissolves are indeed a typical trope of the period, this instance is certainly radical in relation to the usual use of the device. The visual imagery raises, in a very effective way, the question of female desire and emancipation. On the one hand, through multiple dissolves, the sequence suggests the idea of movement and transformation. On the other hand, such themes are clearly associated with a specific object, "the American girl." While a feminist ahistorical interpretation might take the film as the epitome of the representation of woman as commodity, "so that Gloria's middle-class occupation in the world of display showcases is a stepping-stone to the high-class showcase of the Ziegfeld revue" (Mizejewski 1999, 148), I believe, on the contrary, that the heroine's career as a Ziegfeld girl should be seen historically, namely, as a successful emancipation from the traps of Victorian America.

Though dominated by visual sensations, the prologue activates not merely a sensual experience but an intellectual process. As Francesco Casetti has pointed out, one of the challenges of modernity was precisely to reconcile the hyperstimulation of the senses – which defies meaning – with the possibility of making sense of everyday urban life. Cinema provides the means for negotiating such a duality (2008, 130–135). In the prologue of *Glorifying the American Girl*, all the human figures are female – better, the prologue alternates collective images with shots of individual subjects. The film seems to evoke in a rather precise fashion the historical condition of the modern American woman in the 1920s. In the same way that the title refers to any "American girl," the robot-like figures are devoid of any individualizing traits and connote a collective experience. The serpentines going toward the urban areas express quite literally the young women moving to the big cities in search of jobs. The robot-like figures walking on the map are, at the same time, anonymous and universal, recalling the thousands of stenographers and telephone operators, washerwomen and nurses, secretaries and sales clerks populating the workplace: According to historical research, these were the most common jobs held by American women in 1930 (Milkman 1979). Overall, the prologue makes a historical comment on the condition of the working woman by exploiting a typical formal device of the period, while the plot concentrates on the trajectory of the protagonist.

Engaged to Buddy, who thinks only of marrying her, Gloria (Mary Eaton) dreams of doing something important before settling down. While the young woman starts a career as a traveling performer and leaves her hometown, she remains in love with Buddy. Later Gloria returns to New York for an audition and gets the role. At this point realizing that she will not give up her career, Buddy begins to date Barbara, who dreams of marrying him. The film ends with Gloria's performance in the show "Glorifying the American Girl," as Buddy and Barbara sit in the audience. Between numbers when Gloria receives a telegram from the couple announcing their marriage, she begins to cry but changes to a new costume and returns to the stage for another number nevertheless: Overnight she becomes a Broadway star. Through the opposition between the two women, the film dramatizes the dialectic between New and True Womanhood, between the autonomy of the modern woman and the passivity of traditional femininity. While "female stardom means personal misery and sacrifice" (Mizejewski 1999, 148), women's newly acquired freedoms are a true conquest.

What Price Hollywood? tells a similar story – that of a young girl starting as a waitress and ending up as a Hollywood star. As in *Glorifying the American Girl*, the metamorphic trajectory of the heroine is anticipated in the opening sequence through a very effective use of dissolves and offscreen space. The first shots, all linked through lap dissolves, play around the dialectic between on-screen and offscreen space by hiding the heroine's face. By framing only the woman's torso, the sequence succeeds in negating her identity. At the same time, the film opens by producing an image of movement and change rather than representing an action. The first shot frames a fan magazine: A pair of hands are flipping through and reveal photos of glamorous divas. The image then dissolves into a pair of sexy legs: A woman's body is framed from the waist down while she puts on a pair of stockings. The relation between the two shots appears purely associative: The elegance of the woman's legs recalls the glamour of the film stars photographed in the magazine. The image dissolves again into the magazine: Offscreen hands continue to flip through. Further on the dissolve returns us to a female body: Now the woman, framed from the knees to the neck, perhaps the same one, is putting on a dress. Another dissolve leads to another frame of the magazine and, finally, to the detail of a woman's lips upon which, from the offscreen space, some invisible hands are putting on some lipstick. At this point a slow tracking shot reveals the woman's face. She continues to put on makeup by peeking at a magazine in order to imitate the style of her favorite stars. When we see a medium shot of the woman's whole body we realize that she is the same woman we saw in the previous shots: The dress is indeed the one we saw on the fragmented body.

At this point the film develops into a classical narrative: The young woman is getting dressed to go to work. She lives in a cheap room and works in a restaurant in Hollywood, hoping to get a chance to start a career in the movies. In the restaurant she will eventually meet a famous actor who will help her to get her first audition. While the episode is less elaborate than the opening sequence of *Glorifying the American Girl*, it relies on a similar rhetoric in suggesting the close association between female desire, change, and modernity. Like the earlier film, it also points to the collective thrust of its message: The woman we see getting dressed lacks any individualizing trait and can thus stand for all the young urban women moving to the big cities at the beginning of the century. While this image may be considered a paradigmatic example of female consumerism, it also shows how the construction of female identity occurs through a conscious and personal reworking of specific models and lifestyles – those of Hollywood's great divas. As an admirer of Greta Garbo, Constance Bennett is clearly a consumer of fan magazines. She does not passively imitate the glamorous stars she loves, but learns to construct her own identity through a process of negotiation between unconscious desires and a conscious understanding of the way the Dream Factory works (Berry 2000, 24–30).

In the same way as *Glorifying the American Girl* and *What Price Hollywood?*, Lewis Milestone's *Rain* begins with an explicitly antinarrative episode – a series of shots of heavy rain, storms, and running water, which clearly imitate Joris Ivens's experimental documentary *Regent Rain* (1929). While the sequence is indeed a spectacular episode, the most radical visual attractions of the film concern the sexual display of the female body. Through a truly exhibitionist technique that combines acting style, camerawork, and editing, Sadie Thompson (Joan Crawford) purposefully presents her body as an attraction. This performance is not a passive gesture, particularly if it is read in the overall context of the film, which supports Sadie's amoral behavior. Sadie is a prostitute who arrives on a boat in the Samoan village of Pago Pago, a somewhat "liberal" outpost where natives, American soldiers, and civilians live far away from the burden of civilization and religion. In Pago Pago having fun is the focus, and Sadie spends her time drinking and listening to music in the company of soldiers. Sadie catches the attention of Mr. Davidson, a missionary who has arrived on the same boat and who wants to reform her. At some point he seems to succeed: Sadie is enthralled by his preaching and begins a process of redemption. But the spell he has cast over Sadie sinks with Davidson when he mysteriously drowns in the ocean. In the end she goes back to her previous life and the whole island seemingly resumes its usual habits and routines. Throughout the film Sadie's sexual identity is registered on her body. Her sexy outfits give way to modest black dresses during her conversion, but, finally, after the spell wears off, she returns to her excessive wardrobe, heavy makeup, and flashy costume jewelry. The film supports Sadie's free lifestyle, condemns Davidson's excessive morality, and generally draws a clear association between Sadie's sexual freedom and the natives' savage life.

The most interesting visual attraction is related to Sadie's appearance when she is framed by a door and stands in front of the soldiers. Her exhibitionist performances occur twice, at the beginning of the film when she is first introduced, and at the end, when, after Davidson's death, she accepts Sergeant Tim O'Hara's courtship. Crawford's performance is not inscribed within the active male/passive female dichotomy that Laura Mulvey outlines in her seminal essay (1975). On the contrary, Sadie's appearance is quite literally an assault on the viewer and on the male protagonists, who are forced to experience Sadie's excessive sexuality. While the male look is part of the rhetorical construction of each performance scene, the active agency is Sadie's. It is possible, therefore, to interpret her show, the woman's sexual display, not "as a sign of male pathology" but as an indication of "female gratification" (Gaines & Herzog 1990, 5). While the two scenes are structured in the same way – Crawford emerges from an offscreen space to meet the boys' look – what is most striking is the choice to show her body by literally repeating the same five shots. Both episodes start with the male look, then present fragments of Sadie's body: her right hand adorned with jewels, her left hand, then her right foot, followed by the left, and, finally, Sadie's made-up face. If we look carefully at camera position and character's looks, it is clear that only the first of the five shots represents the subjective point of view of the diegetic male character. The scene is clearly shot and edited for the extra-diegetic spectator. Crawford's exhibition actively confronts the viewer rather than the diegetic characters. Through the use of close-ups the film "aggressively subjects the spectator to 'sensual or psychological impact'" (Gunning 1990, 58–59).

The exhibitionist dynamics of Crawford's interpretation in this film are elaborated in the many other films of the period focusing on female performers. Notwithstanding their different personalities and acting styles, Marlene Dietrich and Mae West represent the most radical examples of female exhibition of the body. In thinking about their performances, we may indeed apply Gunning's comment on early cinema. Like the cinema of attractions, their bodies "directly solicit spectator attention, inciting visual curiosity, and supplying pleasure through an exciting spectacle" (1990, 58). While Gunning "says very little about the way in which the female body functions as a main 'attraction' in the cinema of attraction" (Petro 2002, 171), it is clear that his ideas fit quite well the status of the female body in the early 1930s.

Blonde Venus (1932) is a peculiar case in the representation of female desire. The protagonist's trajectory evolves through a vertiginous and twisted plot where she plays a set of various roles, from affectionate mother and wife to glamorous singer and sexy kept woman, from runaway mother who must prostitute herself to support her child to famous singer performing in Paris. The film concentrates on the same body and the many options of female identity available at the time, but in so doing it undermines the dichotomies it plays out. While Helen Faraday (Marlene Dietrich) never gives up her maternal role, her unorthodox femininity is the result of coexisting antithetical images of female identity. As a sexually active woman, Helen challenges the convention of the sexless mother, a convention well respected by Hollywood cinema. While the film supports and reinforces the mother/child relation, it also undermines the function of the paternal role and of the nuclear family. Dietrich embodies varied images of female identity and desire and, as a result, becomes the very site of gender excess and queerness (Kuzniar 2007). In subverting the convention prescribing women to choose between motherhood and sexuality, she clearly emancipates herself from social norms and rules.

In this scenario, Dietrich's performances as a cabaret singer play a significant role. In the famous "Hot Voodoo" sequence the diva wears a monkey costume and sings to the sound of drums played by a band of "savages." This excessive performance makes an explicit comment on the relation between feminine sexuality, animalism, and primitivism. As Dietrich reveals her identity, stripping out of her excessively sexual costume, both the diegetic and the extra-diegetic audiences are caught by surprise and shocked by her outrageous performance. In relation to the look, it is Dietrich that attracts and elicits the audience's visual experience. Such a strategy is particularly evident in her last show in Paris at the end of the film. Helen appears on stage dressed in a white tuxedo like a Mannish Lesbian (Weiss 1992) and moves toward the audience, while the camera follows her movement in a long take. The camera lingers on her until she reaches her ex-lover, Nick Townsend (Cary Grant), who is watching the show. In an explicit reversal of the traditional paradigm proposed by Laura Mulvey, Marlene's body and performance control both the audience look and the camerawork. Even more explicitly than in the "Hot Voodoo" sequence, the episode is structured around female agency, namely, the performer's ability to reduce to passivity the male look.

In *I'm No Angel* (1933), Mae West's performance is choreographed in a similar fashion. Tira is a sensational attraction as a lion tamer who elicits her audience's curiosity. When she concludes the dangerous number by putting her head inside the lion's mouth, the audience is both greatly entertained and excited. Like Marlene's Helen, West's Tira is the active agent of her own performance and controls the look and the reaction of the paying customers. In a curious reenactment of early cinema's strategy of attractions, the New York socialites who have watched the show thank her because she has given them "a thrill," enabling them to experience a sensational and strong emotion. In the same way that the dynamic impulse of the (urban) dissolve is tuned to the emancipatory plot of the working girl, the exhibitionist displays of Joan Crawford, Marlene Dietrich, and Mae West are similarly related

Figure 15.2 Marlene Dietrich in a white tuxedo in *Blonde Venus* (1932, director and producer Josef von Sternberg).

to female sexual transgression. Both strategies also betray the persistence of preclassical formal ploys.

In *Three on a Match* (1932), the representation of gender and class identity in relation to female upward mobility has a peculiar force since the plot concentrates on the parallel trajectories of three young girls coming from different social backgrounds. Mary, Vivian, and Ruth attend the same public school in a New York City neighborhood. While Vivian and Ruth are quiet and behave properly, Mary is wild, smokes, and prefers the company of boys. As teenagers they follow their own inclinations: Mary (Joan Blondell) ends up in a reform school for women, Vivian (Ann Dvorak), the richest of the three, attends a boarding school for young ladies, and Ruth (Bette Davis) goes to the Metropolitan Business College. But the film's strength resides in its rhetorical strategies: Shots of the three girls are intertwined with superimpositions and dissolves of newspaper titles, city streets, sports events, and other episodes of urban modernity. The story of the three girls growing up in New York is framed within the context of modernity, from 1919 to 1930, through the use, once again, of the most modern filmic device, the urban dissolve. The newspaper titles announce several news items on the subject of modernity, such as women's suffrage, the advent of radio, the growth in beauty expenses, and so on. But the film also makes a comment on the relation between women, sex, and class in tune with the perspective we have discussed so far.

After losing track of one another, the three women meet again in a beauty parlor. Mary works in show business, Ruth is a white-collar girl, Vivian has married a rich lawyer and has a small boy. But Vivian is unhappy and will ruin her life by choosing drugs and alcohol in the company of a petty gangster. In the end, she will kill herself in order to save her child. On the contrary, Mary, who seemed destined to live a marginal life, will end up marrying Vivian's husband. And Ruth will work for the new family as a babysitter for their son. Mary's trajectory is particularly interesting since she is depicted as the most sexual and wild of the three. As in many other films of the period, frank sexual behavior is not the sign of moral corruption but the clearest symptom of women's force and emancipated status.

The Age of Order and the Demise of the New Woman

Sometime around 1933–1934 the dominant mode of female representation veers toward the convergence of normative forms of desire and strong narrative structures dominated by action and dialogue. While visual attractions tended to disappear, linearity and causality furthered a rational mode of storytelling which, in turn, supported traditional forms of identity and lifestyle, especially for women. Undoubtedly, in the latter half of the 1930s, antinarrative techniques and visual attractions tended to disappear, especially in relation to editing strategies. Bazin's argument is well known: We witnessed "the almost complete disappearance of optical effects such as superimpositions and even ... the close-up" (1967, 32), while analytic editing contributed to a tightening of narrative structure and stronger cause-and-effect construction. In relinquishing the ability to express meaning through its purely visual means, cinema, at that time, communicated primarily through actions and language. Yet, it was the combination of a purely invisible style with a new set of images concerning female and male desire that accounted for the shift in Hollywood's ideological project. What Robert Sklar (1994) has called the "Age of Order" implies a reversal *vis-à-vis* the gender discourse of the previous years. Transgressive sexual attitudes were no longer supported and women's working careers were similarly negated. The only trajectory available for women was marriage. More generally, while in the previous years cinema preferred to focus on their social rise, now women's experience was framed within marriage and the home. Emancipatory plots often had a negative outcome, while the formation of the heterosexual couple was the dominant mode of the period. The classical status of cinema, I would argue, does not simply involve formal and narrative techniques, but relies on a specific ideological project. In contrast to the earlier period, as well as to post–World War II cinema, classical cinema generally narrated plots of integration: That is why comedy is the key genre of the period. While it is true that the screwball heroine usually enjoys sexual and social freedom, the narrative nevertheless develops within the precincts of marriage or remarriage (Cavell 1984) in an upper-class scenario (see Pravadelli 2007).

In the same way as some screwball heroines are the heirs of the emancipated flapper of the 1920s, we will later see that this genre expressed Hollywood's only progressive position *vis-à-vis* female desire in the second part of the decade. The scenario had in fact dramatically changed in relation to the earlier years, both in the social and the filmic context. While women had dominated the industry on all levels – on the screen, at the box office, in the audience – now the values of masculinity and family came back with a vengeance. From the mid-1930s, the box office was topped by male stars, along with adolescent and child actors. The appeal of American traditional values is evident if we consider the major trends in moviegoing and public taste. Shirley Temple had a triumphant career and topped the box office for four straight years, from 1935 to 1938. In those same seasons, the virile Clark Gable was the most successful male star and was ranked second behind Temple. The most popular genres were adventure films – a typical male genre – and costume dramas, while another male genre – the biopic – was highly praised by critics and a favorite at the Oscars. Such genres were not only adequate to address the classical thrust for linear structures, but they all focused on male agency and relegated female characters to marginal roles. William Dieterle's biopics starring Paul Muni are particularly interesting in their support of the most traditional humanistic values. Dieterle's films were highly praised, and with *The Life of Emile Zola* (1937) the filmmaker became a hot commodity, especially for critics on the left struck by the antifascist stance of the film (Robé 2009).

Fred Astaire and Ginger Rogers were also key protagonists at the box office in the mid-1930s. The RKO musicals they starred in represented another paradigmatic case for testing the shift in the representation of gender identity. It is easy to see how the hyperbolic elements of Busby Berkeley's films, in relation to both female sexuality and film language, are totally tamed in the Astaire–Rogers films, where both the representation of the female body and the shooting and editing techniques follow classical precepts. While male genres and stars had a greater impact than their female counterparts, romantic couples and child actors developed the themes of marriage and family in a forceful way. In this scenario, it was not surprising that the trajectory of the independent woman usually had a negative outcome. In 1930s cinema strong women were often nasty, so that they could rightfully be punished. Bette Davis was the prototype of the "Hollywood Bitch." In several films she victimizes a weak man, but her behavior finally backfires on her, as in *Of Human Bondage* (1934), *Jezebel* (1938), *The Letter* (1940), and *The Little Foxes* (1941). Yet it is *Dark Victory* (1939) that most clearly reveals the dynamics at play during this period.

In that film Bette Davis plays Judith Traherne, a young Long Island socialite who spends her time horse riding and partying with her friends. She is rich and spoiled, but nice, amiable, and generous. Judith suffers from dizziness and headaches but ignores them, until she finds out that she is very seriously ill. Her illness triggers a deep rethinking of her lifestyle. As her very survival is suddenly in danger, Judith begins asking herself what it means to live. When she falls in love with her doctor, she believes she has found the answer to her existential query. The couple are engaged to be married and plan to leave the big city to settle in Vermont, where Frederick will continue his research on brain tumors. But while she packs his office, Judith finds her own file and discovers her illness is fatal. Believing Frederick wants to marry her out of pity, she breaks their engagement and resumes her former life. Later, she will return to him and the two will marry and move to Vermont. Judith will spend some very happy months with her husband, attending the house and the garden, and assisting him in his important work. After making sense of her life as a dutiful and passive wife, Judith will die alone in her bedroom while her husband is away at a conference. One can easily speculate that her early death is the direct effect of her modern lifestyle: Had she spent less time in having fun and paid more attention to her symptoms, Judith would still be alive. The wedding is a sort of redemption for her past "sins," the choice she should have made from the start. The change in lifestyle is complete and involves every aspect of her experience: Judith starts as a single, independent, and urban woman and ends as a married housewife in the countryside.

The shift in the representation of female desire is further evident if we look at Barbara Stanwyck's career throughout the decade (for a discussion of Stanwyck in the 1940s, see Roy Grundmann in this volume). Along with Joan Crawford, in the early 1930s Stanwyck had interpreted key roles as a young woman attempting to raise her social status through hard work and/or sex. Both actresses played working-class women who moved to the big city in search of a job, as well as playing a variety of fallen and/or redeemed women. Crawford also played some of the last significant flapper roles in *Our Dancing Daughters* (1928), *Our Modern Maidens* (1929), and *Our Blushing Brides* (1930). In the first two, Crawford is a society girl, but in the third she plays a working-class shop girl, a transition that prepares for the more dramatic roles she will later play (Ross 2000, 328–329). In *Paid* (1930), she is a shop girl sent to prison by her employer on false charges, and in *Possessed* (1931), she is a factory worker who becomes the mistress of a wealthy lawyer. In these same years, Stanwyck plays similar roles. In *Night Nurse* she is Lora Hart, a determined young woman who arrives in New York to look for a job. Lora begins to train as a nurse in a hospital and becomes close friends with B. Maloney (Joan Blondell), a more experienced nurse who helps get her adjusted to the new situation. The two women, who share a room in the hospital to save money, build a strong friendship and show little interest in men. In *Forbidden* (1932), Stanwyck has a married man's baby, and in *Shopworn* (1932), she is a hardworking waitress who falls in love with a college student. Her social rise will take place after several dramatic twists.

In *Baby Face*, one of her most famous roles, Stanwyck plays Lily Powers, a strong young woman who tries to cope with her abusive father, a violent man who runs a speakeasy where Lily serves drinks. A famous censorship case in pre-Code Hollywood (Jacobs 1997), the film contains among the most explicit of sexual contents during the period. Lily's father has prostituted his daughter to his customers for a few bucks since she was 14. Lily's life is miserable; her only comforts are Chico, the African-American maid who works for the family, and Mr Cragg, one of her father's customers. Mr Cragg is a cultivated man and is very fond of Lily. He urges her to leave the place and "go to some big city." Indirectly quoting Nietzsche's *Will to Power*, he tells her "to use men, not be used by them, to get things."[3] After her father accidentally dies, Lily and Chico leave Pittsburgh and go to New York. Lily will indeed follow Mr Cragg's suggestion *à la lettre* and use men to climb the social ladder. While the film resorts to a sentimental tone only at the very end, it provides a harsh and cynical representation of sexual relations in urban America. Yet it is far from criticizing Lily's behavior. On the contrary, *Baby Face* shows that sex is the only means a woman has to attract men's attention. Lily, in fact, is very good at her job, but it is only when her bosses realize she is pretty that they consider her for promotion. Similarly, when the new president of the bank she works for sees her in the Paris agency, he is very surprised to hear that her division has improved its business by 40 percent since he can only judge her by her good looks. But Lily is very capable at her job and is also a hard worker. If she needs powerful men to succeed, it is because women can, on their own, at best, be only secretaries.

In the following years Stanwyck continued to play characters whose desire for upward mobility would be repeatedly thwarted. In *The Bride Walks Out* (1936) she is Carolyn, a fashion model forced by her husband (Michael Martin) to quit her job after they get married. As she realizes that her husband's salary is not enough, Carolyn goes back to modeling. She keeps her work a secret to protect Michael's pride. But her decision will seriously jeopardize her marriage. Once her husband finds out about her job, he leaves her. After their divorce, Carolyn dates a rich man and is about to marry him when she learns that Michael has accepted a dangerous job in South America. In a comic ending, Carolyn will prevent her husband from taking the boat but in the process will get herself arrested. From inside the jeep, she promises Michael she will quit her job.

In the more well-known *Stella Dallas*, Barbara Stanwyck plays Stella Martin, an attractive young woman living with her working-class family in a factory town. Stella wishes to improve her social status and meets the rich Stephen Dallas, who manages the factory where Stella's brother works. Stephen, who has been forced to end his engagement, is lonely and appreciates Stella's company and lively manners. He falls in love and asks her to marry him. After their daughter Laurel is born, their marriage begins to crumble. Stephen seems to love Stella, but he cannot tolerate her uneducated manners and crude behavior. When Stephen is offered a better job in New York, Stella decides to stay in their house with Laurel, knowing that she'll never be a part of her husband's social circle. From then on, the two will lead separate lives. In New York Stephen meets his ex-fiancée, Helen Morrison, who is now a widow with three children. As Stephen and Laurel visit Helen's elegant house and parties, the film's discourse on class becomes clear. While Laurel is extremely attached to her mother and Stella cannot think of anything but pleasing her daughter, the film's heartbreaking narrative unfolds, making their relationship impossible. Stella is a loving mother, but she is also cheap and vulgar, most obviously in her choice of clothes and accessories. On the other hand, like her father and his new fiancée, Laurel is polite and understated in her behavior and mannerisms. The film's ideological project focuses precisely on taste. Stella's bad taste is the visible sign of her working-class status and is evidenced in her clothes, her home, and her raucous company. In the same way, Helen's proper behavior and controlled manners are reflective of her upper-class status, which is similarly evidenced in her clothing, her home, and her polite friends. When Stella realizes that Laurel will be better off in life without her, she sacrifices her love so that her daughter can attain the social status she once wished for herself.

A Notable Exception: Free Women and Screwball Comedies

While the demise of the New Woman was undeniable, the genre of screwball comedy represented a significant exception. If comedy's main ideological project aims at integrating the couple within the social structure through marriage, several comedies of the period presented radically progressive forms of sexual interaction and female desire. Moreover, in contrast to the sentimental tone of *It Happened One Night*, a rather traditional work in terms of gender relations, despite its promising beginning, films such as *Sylvia Scarlett* (1935), *The Awful Truth* (1937), *Bringing Up Baby* (1938), *The Women* (1939), *My Favorite Wife* (1940), *His Girl Friday* (1940), and *The Philadelphia*

Story (1940) expressed a deep understanding of the social nature of heterosexual love and of the unbridgeable gap between the sexual drive and the legal bond of marriage. In comedies of the late 1930s, two adults would generally decide to get married, not in order to form a family, but to satisfy their sexual impulses: Marriage was recognized as the institution that both contained *and* allowed the free expression of sexuality. The genre contributed to the symbolic production that gave voice to a new paradigm of sexual life and behavior that emerged at the beginning of the century. While it may have begun as a medical discourse produced by professionals, the debate around sexuality became part of the broader shift focused on the subject's experience in modernity and became a topic of discussion in various media, whether popular literature and press, women's magazines, or cinema. The change pointed toward acceptance of a sexual ethic that encouraged expressiveness rather than containment. While by the mid-1910s Freud's work was popularized to a larger audience in America, at that same time the writings of Havelock Ellis had a greater impact. Ellis advocated sexual gratification and claimed a distinctive sexual mode for each gender. Overall,

> the shift from a philosophy of continence to one that encouraged indulgence was but one aspect of a larger reorientation that was investing sexuality with a profoundly new importance. The modern regime of sexology was taking sex beyond a procreative framework... and, more commonly, theorists attributed to sexuality the power of individual self-definition. (D'Emilio & Freedman 1997, 225)

While such a discourse made possible a whole set of social dynamics, from the suffragette movement to the creation of radical and bohemian forms of living, it also explained the progressive and transgressive elements of plots in the screwball comedy. In *The Awful Truth*, for example, the female protagonist Lucy Warriner (Irene Dunne) has three male partners. Her promiscuous behavior, which causes some hilarious moments, especially when the three men are in her apartment, each unaware of the other two, can only be tamed by marriage. The viewer knows that Lucy loves only her ex-husband, Jerry (Cary Grant), and that she uses her lovers to make him jealous. It is also evident that their marriage ended because of their mutual betrayal. At the beginning of the film Jerry makes the point that in marriage each partner needs to trust the other. Marriage, in other words, is not based on fidelity *per se*, but on the lack of suspicions. In *My Favorite Wife* Cary Grant, as Nick Arden, and Irene Dunne, as Ellen Arden, ultimately choose to remarry, thus breaking up their triangular relation with Steve Burkett (Randolph Scott). But one clearly senses that the two are extremely attracted to Steve. Ellen has continued to have a long relationship with him since they were shipwrecked on a desert island. When she returns home, Nick, who believes her dead, is engaged to be married to his new fiancée. He is still in love with his wife but doesn't know how to handle the situation with his current partner. As he meets Steve, he is struck by his beautiful and athletic body and feels both inadequate and attracted to him. Both films solve, in a rational way, the problem of desire and sexuality: Marriage is a necessary institution if one wants to preserve the social order. In other films, sexuality is addressed in a different way. In *Bringing Up Baby*, for instance, Susan Vance (Katharine Hepburn) rescues her partner, David Huxley (played, once again, by Cary Grant), from a married life devoid of fun and sex. A serious paleontologist totally devoted to his work, David prepares to marry his prudish and boring assistant when Susan plunges into his life and drives him away from his plans. Susan is the epitome of the screwball heroine. She is funny, crazy, entertaining, extremely energetic, and contagious. Her desire to marry him is a true blessing for David: Susan will allow him to experience the joys of married life, especially sex.

In the screwball comedy the dynamics between male and female subtends a clear equality of the sexes in line with the model of companionate marriage that emerged in urban areas in the 1920s. In this new model of gender relations, a young man wanted a woman "he could sleep with and talk with too" and he wanted "it to be the same girl" (Trimberger 1983, 136). As in the new marital ideal, which "boosted marriage as more appealing than ever to women," in comedy sex is central: "the sexual adjustment and satisfaction of both partners [are] principal measures of marital harmony" and social order (Cott 1987, 156–157).

The comedy of the second half of the 1930s presented the most advanced and progressive model of gender relations of the period, one that continued the modern thrust toward female emancipation from Victorian passivity and domesticity. The convergence between gender and class identity was strikingly biased in favor of aristocratic and upper-class women. While in 1940 the genre produced some of its best examples, that same year a film like *Kitty Foyle* depicted, in a poignant fashion, the demise of the model of the New Woman for working girls. In that film, subtitled "The Natural History of a Woman," Kitty (Ginger Rogers) must choose between two men, and her choice is articulated along the lines of class difference (Doane 1987, 105). She will eventually choose a poor but idealistic doctor and refuse her aristocratic suitor. But the film begins with a nondiegetic prologue, the function of which is precisely to comment on the trajectory of women in the early decades of the century. The title announces that we are going to see the story of the white-collar girl, a novelty in American society. In the first scene, set in 1900, men in a crowded cable car rise to give their seat to a woman; we then see a courtship scene on a porch, and the same man who offered his seat asks the same young woman to marry him. In the following sequence a group of suffragettes protest and ask for equal rights. Then we are presented with its direct consequence: In a crowded cable car, nobody rises to offer his seat to the woman. The last title of the prologue states that men have gotten so accustomed to seeing women during the workday that, in 1940, white-collar women suffer from a new malady: "that five-thirty feeling" of not having a date for the evening, or a man waiting at home. At this point the prologue unfolds into the diegesis: This is the problem afflicting the young women working with Kitty in a luxurious boutique in New York. As the story develops, the relation between the prologue and the diegesis becomes clear: Kitty's problematic choice is the consequence of women's emancipation and working "careers."

The trajectory of the modern woman has thus ended miserably. If in the early 1930s class difference could be overcome and women's upward mobility (and sexual freedom) was one of Hollywood's favorite topics, in the following years working-class women were denied social rise, while spoiled aristocrats enjoyed romantic and sexual freedom. As Sam Wood's film sadly shows, at the end of the decade a girl of humble origins could not but marry a poor (and boring) doctor. But the viewer cannot forget that Kitty's only moments of happiness are those spent with Win, the charming Philadelphia aristocrat she could not have.

Notes

1. The cult of True Womanhood was the prevailing view on women's status and lifestyle in the Victorian era. According to this notion, upper- and middle-class white women had to embody perfect virtue, which they manifested, in particular, within the domestic sphere as nurturing mothers and obedient wives.
2. It is worth recalling one of F. Scott Fitzgerald's famous comments, that the ideal flapper was "lovely and expensive and about nineteen." On Fitzgerald and the flapper, see Higashi 1978 and Zeitz 2006.
3. Along with other scenes and dialogue these sentences would be cut in the theatrical release. For a comparison of the original version and the censored released version, see the DVD *Forbidden Hollywood* (vol. 2) released by TMC Archive.

References

Balio, Tino. (1993). *Grand Design: Hollywood as a Modern Business Enterprise, 1930–1939*. Berkeley: University of California Press.

Bazin, André. (1967). *What Is Cinema?*, trans. H. Gray. Berkeley: University of California Press. (Original work published 1958–1965.)

Berry, Sarah. (2000). *Screen Style: Fashion and Femininity in 1930s Hollywood*. Minneapolis: University of Minnesota Press.

Bordwell, David, Staiger, Janet, & Thompson, Kristin. (1985). *The Classical Hollywood Cinema: Film Style and Mode of Production to 1960*. New York: Columbia University Press.

Casetti, Francesco. (2008). *Eye of the Century: Film, Experience, Modernity*, trans. E. Larkin with J. Pranolo. New York: Columbia University Press. (Original work published 2005.)

Cavell, Stanley. (1984). *Pursuits of Happiness: The Hollywood Comedy of Remarriage*. Cambridge, MA: Harvard University Press.

Cott, Nancy F. (1987). *The Grounding of Modern Feminism*. New Haven: Yale University Press.

Crafton, Donald. (1997). *The Talkies: American Cinema's Transition to Sound, 1926–1931*. Berkeley: University of California Press.

D'Emilio, John, & Freedman, Estelle B. (1997). *Intimate Matters: A History of Sexuality in America*. 2nd edn. Chicago: University of Chicago Press.

Doane, Mary Ann. (1987). *The Desire to Desire: The Woman's Film of the '40s*. Bloomington: Indiana University Press.

Gaines, Jane, & Herzog, Charlotte (eds). (1990). *Fabrications: Costume and the Female Body*. New York: Routledge.

Gunning, Tom. (1990). "The Cinema of Attractions: Early Film, Its Spectator and the Avant-Garde." In Thomas Elsaesser (ed.), *Early Cinema: Space Frame Narrative* (pp. 56–62). London: British Film Institute.

Higashi, Sumiko. (1978). *Virgins, Vamps, and Flappers: The American Silent Movie Heroine*. Montreal: Eden Press Women's Publications.

Jacobs, Lea. (1997). *The Wages of Sin: Censorship and the Fallen Woman Film, 1928–1942*. Berkeley: University of California Press.

Kuzniar, Alice A. (2007). "'It's Not Often That I Want a Man': Reading for a Queer Marlene." In Gerd Gemünden & Mary R. Desjardins (eds), *Dietrich Icon* (pp. 239–258). Durham, NC: Duke University Press.

Meyerowitz, Joanne. (1993). "Sexual Geography and Gender Economy." In Barbara Melosh (ed.), *Gender and American History since 1890* (pp. 43–71). London: Routledge.

Milkman, Ruth. (1979). "Women's Work and the Economic Crisis." In Nancy F. Cott & Elizabeth H. Pleck (eds), *A Heritage of Her Own: Toward a New Social History of American Women* (pp. 507–541). New York: Simon & Schuster.

Mizejewski, Linda. (1999). *Ziegfeld Girl: Image and Icon in Culture and Cinema*. Durham, NC: Duke University Press.

Mulvey, Laura. (1975). "Visual Pleasure and Narrative Cinema." *Screen*, 16.3, 6–18.

Peiss, Kathy. (1986). *Cheap Amusements: Working Women and Leisure in Turn-of-the-Century New York*. Philadelphia: Temple University Press.

Petro, Patrice. (2002). *Aftershocks of the New: Feminism and Film History*. New Brunswick: Rutgers University Press.

Pravadelli, Veronica. (2007). *La grande Hollywood. Stili di vita e di regia nel cinema classico Americano*. [Classic Hollywood: Lifestyles and Film Styles in American Classical Cinema.] Venice: Marsilio.

Robé, Chris. (2009). "Taking Hollywood Back: The Historical Costume Drama, the Biopic, and Popular Front U.S. Film Criticism." *Cinema Journal*, 48.2, 70–87.

Ross, Sara. (2000). "Banking the Flames of Youth: The Hollywood Flapper, 1920–1930." PhD dissertation, University of Wisconsin-Madison.

Ryan, Mary P. (1976). "The Projection of a New Womanhood: The Movie Moderns in the 1920s." In Jean E. Friedman & William G. Shade (eds), *Our American Sisters: Women in American Life and Thought* (pp. 366–384). Boston: Allyn & Bacon.

Singer, Ben. (2001). *Melodrama and Modernity*. New York: Columbia University Press.

Sklar, Robert. (1994). *Movie-Made America: A Cultural History of American Movies*. Revised and updated. New York: Vintage Books.

Stamp, Shelley. (2000). *Movie-Struck Girls: Women and Motion Picture Culture after the Nickelodeon*. Princeton: Princeton University Press.

Steinberg, Cobbett S. (1980). *Film Facts*. New York: Facts on File.

Stokes, Melvyn. (1999). "Female Audiences of the 1920s and Early 1930s." In Melvyn Stokes & Richard Maltby (eds), *Identifying Hollywood's Audiences* (pp. 42–60). London: British Film Institute.

Trimberger, Ellen Kay. (1983). "Feminism, Men and Modern Love: Greenwich Village, 1900–1925." In Ann Snitow, Christine Stansell, & Sharon Thompson (eds), *Powers of Desire* (pp. 131–152). New York: Monthly Review Press.

Weiss, Andrea. (1992). *Vampires and Violets: Lesbians in Films*. New York: Penguin.

Welter, Barbara. (1978). "The Cult of True Womanhood: 1820–1860." In Mel Gordon (ed.), *The American Family in Social-Historical Perspective* (pp. 313–333). 2nd edn. New York: St Martin's Press.

Zeitz, Joshua. (2006). *Flapper: A Madcap Story of Sex, Style, Celebrity, and the Women Who Made America Modern*. New York: Three Rivers Press.

16

Queering the (New) Deal

David M. Lugowski
Professor, Manhattanville College, United States

In his comprehensive discussion of dozens of 1930s Hollywood films, both before and after the **Production Code** was vigorously enforced, David M. Lugowski illustrates that **queer images** were ubiquitous and irrepressible – whether in the form of characters like the **sissy**, the **pansy**, and the **"mannish" woman** or in terms of **cross-gendered** situations, costuming, and verbal references. His investigation of **Production Code Administration** files supports the Alexander Doty claim he quotes: "queerness . . . just might be the most pervasive sexual dynamic at work in mass culture production and reception." Lugowski contextualizes his study in Depression-era challenges to masculinity and PCA restrictions, which ironically tend to confirm Doty's claim in acknowledging the pervasive presence of queer content and in attempting, but ultimately failing, to restrict its admittedly implicit presence. While acknowledging the value of **Vito Russo's *Celluloid Closet*** interrogation, Lugowski recognizes empowerment in many representations that, for knowing viewers then and now, cleverly transcend confining stereotypes. Lugowski's essay shares ground with Veronica Pravadelli on cinema and the modern woman and Roy Grundmann on *The Strange Love of Martha Ivers* in this volume, and with Michael Bronski on queer cinema of the 1990s in Volume II.

Additional terms, names, and concepts: SRC (Studio Relations Committee), principle of deniability

Queerness and National Crisis

An extraordinary scene takes place near the beginning of *The Strange Love of Molly Louvain* (1932), directed by Warner Bros. ace Michael Curtiz. A small-time confidence trickster and his cronies are sitting inside a hotel lobby, staring out a window, betting on whether the next person passing will be a man or a woman. The con is on a winning streak, but when a man passing by tips his cigarette by flicking his wrist, the gang

American Film History: Selected Readings, Origins to 1960, First Edition. Edited by Cynthia Lucia, Roy Grundmann, and Art Simon.
© 1999 University of Texas Press. Published 2016 by John Wiley & Sons, Inc.

pauses before one says, "It's a man!" They try again; this time it's a woman, but the con protests his loss: "No, women in pants don't count."

This scene summarizes much of this essay. As cinema learned to talk, so did it also speak about gender roles so crucial to Hollywood. Far from giving viewers a "window" on reality, early sound films often "frame" their highly theatrical performativity. As with the betting game, these films came under scrutiny by producers and audiences alike, the former "shooting the works" in terms of titillating content, the latter less able to play the game with little money to spare. In the Depression's darkest days, every man felt that his winning streak could suddenly end. Many gender roles were out in the open, if only "in passing," with "women in pants" and effeminate men questioning the domain of the male breadwinner in the aftermath of the Crash, a moment of "lost bets."

Much has been written about how, as Robert McElvaine has argued, the Depression engendered a "'feminization' of American society. The self-centered, aggressive, competitive 'male' ethic of the 1920s was discredited. Men who lost their jobs became dependent in ways that women had been thought to be" (1984, 340). More women, married and single, had entered the workforce before the Depression than ever before, and women were in some ways less affected by the Depression insofar as the domain to which patriarchy had assigned them – the home – remained theirs ideologically, if not always literally. In fact, the domestic sphere needed their strength more than ever. And the cinema was patronized to a much larger extent than today by adult women (Shindler 1996). Meanwhile, 25 percent unemployment undermined men's status as breadwinners; men also experienced a shift from a "manly" production ethic to a "feminized" consumerism. Thus, they found their gender status, linked to notions of "work" and "value" promulgated by capitalism, in jeopardy. Indeed, even their status as consumers was threatened (Peiss 1986; Scharf 1980). Men who had internalized the American Dream's success myth – who had equated their manhood with material gain and their ability to provide – were now wondering about the feasibility of capitalism. They wondered about themselves too (Komarovsky 1940; Orwell 1937). Margaret McFadden writes that men "experienced their inability to provide adequate family support as a failure of masculinity" (1993, 119).

Suddenly, queer imagery in film – typically comical representations of gays, lesbians, and ambiguous sexuality – did not seem funny anymore, especially to those applying Hollywood's Production Code to film content. By "queer" imagery, I am focusing on situations, dialogue, and characters that represent behavior coded, according to common stereotypes, as cross-gendered. Played by such character actors as Franklin Pangborn, Edward Everett Horton, Grady Sutton, Erik Rhodes, Eric Blore, and Ernest Truex, queer men appear as two types. More subdued queers embody the dithering, asexual "sissy," befuddled, incompetent, and, if married, very henpecked (Horton), or fussy and officious (Pangborn). Pangborn, however, along with Tyrell Davis and Tyler Brooke, also played the more outrageous "pansy," an effeminate boulevardier sporting lipstick, rouge, a trim mustache and suit, complete with boutonniere.

Although many actors played such roles, one doesn't find many actresses whose personas seemed designed to connote lesbianism (the closest is Cecil Cunningham) (Barrios 2003, 155). Nonetheless, lesbian representation also occurs frequently, and in a greater range of gradations. At their most overt, lesbians were clad in a mannishly tailored suit (often a tuxedo), hair slicked back or bobbed. They sometimes sported a monocle and cigarette holder (or cigar!) and possessed deep voices and an aggressive attitude. Objections arose because they seemed to usurp male privilege; the pansy seemed to give it up.

If we need proof that the pansy was read as homosexual for 1930s spectators, George Chauncey demonstrates not only the conflation of then-new categories of sexuality with long-standing ideas about gender, but also just how visible pansies were outside the movie theater. Since a man's masculinity was not impugned as long as he maintained the "active" position sexually, rouged but not always cross-dressing fairy prostitutes did lively business. Gay bathhouses thrived, and hotels were open for sexual encounters and even romantic relationships (Chauncey 1994; White 1993). The "New Woman," meanwhile, included lesbians who found opportunities in expanded worlds of work, education, settlement houses, and feminist activism (Smith-Rosenberg 1985). Discourses about "intermediate" and "third sexes" dispersed widely, while disregard for many institutions resulted from the upheavals of urbanization and World War I. The post–World War I era, with its disillusioned veterans, feminist struggles, racial and ethnic migrations and shifts, and widespread contempt for Prohibition, was enabling for queerness. Vaudeville and burlesque, steeped in humor about the body, were fairgrounds for gender play, and Broadway first featured lesbian and gay characters in the 1920s (Allen 1985; Curtin 1987). These trends continued into the Depression, with nightclub "pansy" acts all the rage in New York in 1930–1931 and Los Angeles in 1932–1933. Queer characters were common in silent film, but presenting queerness in performance often rested on innuendo in dialogue and vocal intonation. Thus, when sound film emerged, urban audiences were particularly primed for pansies, sissies, and lesbians. Via mass dispersion and on-screen performance, sound gave queerness a new voice.

Using gender performance rather than sexual conduct as the arbiter of sexuality in the Depression manifests itself in film humor. The most famous example is Cary Grant, caught wearing a negligee in *Bringing Up Baby* (1938) and blurting out, "I just went *gay* all of a sudden!" As Chauncey notes, queer connotations emerge not because he had romantic feelings for a man, but because he was wearing a woman's nightgown. "The possibility of a more precisely sexual meaning would not have been lost on anyone familiar with fairy stereotypes" (1994, 18).

One finds such understandings of sexuality in the writings of Olga Martin, Production Code Administration (PCA) secretary, in 1937's *Hollywood's Movie Commandments*: "No hint of sex perversion may be introduced into a screen story . . . characterization of a man as effeminate, or a woman as grossly masculine would be absolutely forbidden . . . no comedy character may be introduced pantomiming a pervert" (42). Clearly, Martin had been acculturated by notions of what a contemporary song called "mannish-acting women and womanish-acting men": Gender performance for her was equivalent to sexual orientation.

Gay characters from this period evoke many stereotypical associations. One finds effeminate hairdressers, clothing designers, and tailors in films including *Manhattan Parade* (1932), *The Scarlet Empress* (1934), and *Hollywood Hotel* (1937). In *Winner Take All* (1932), two tailors shamelessly examine James Cagney's posterior while taking his measurements, while in *Child of Manhattan* (1932), the male "Madame Dulcy" tells Nancy Carroll not to see the "man" in him but only the "artist." Men working in theater and dance were often queer, like the tango instructor in gay director George Cukor's *Our Betters* (1933) or, in *Fast and Furious* (1939), the beauty pageant choreographer who teaches contestants how to walk. The men in 10-gallon hats and fringed chaps Joe E. Brown finds in *The Tenderfoot* (1932) reveal themselves as rouged chorus boys who acknowledge him with a flirtatious "Whoo!" Also memorable is the ballet instructor in *Stage Mother* (1933), whose exhortations to his girls to be ethereal – "We are fairies, we are elves!" – "out" his character to knowing audiences. This revelation is not lost on the eponymous character; in return for helping her daughter, she offers to find him new boyfriends (Barrios 1995, 432).

Butlers and other "man's men" also suggest queerness and even express same-sex desire. Although Charles Coleman in *First Love* (1939) proclaims, "Gay butlers are very rare," in *One Hour with You* (1932) he declares his eagerness to see his master in tights, and in *Diplomaniacs* (1933), he lisps and skips with abandon. One finds pansies, sissies, and fops in such unsurprising settings as a bathhouse, flirting with sailors (*Sailor's Luck*, 1933); at court (*Marie Antoinette*, 1938); and at the desk of a women's hotel (*Vivacious Lady*, 1938). One location whose same-sex environs enabled queerness was prison, whether comically (*Up the River*, 1930; *Betty Boop for President*, 1932), or in the social protest drama *Hell's Highway* (1932). The police lineup in *Who Killed Rover?* (1930), cast entirely with dogs, includes a pansy arrested while strolling (cruising?) in the park, and the killer in *The Herring Murder Case* (1930) is also queer. The best-known examples are the arm-in-arm prisoners Mae West dubs "the Cherry sisters" who share a cell in *She Done Him Wrong* (1933). Writing poetry feminized men in *The Warrior's Husband* (1933), as well as the title character of the animated *The Reluctant Dragon* (1941), and associating men with flowers (pansies, gardenias, lilies-of-the-valley, even the "dandelion/dandy lion" in *The Wizard of Oz*, 1939) could mark them as effeminate queers.

The title *The Warrior's Husband* might in itself connote queerness, if we assume that the "warrior" is a man. The film's warriors, however, are primarily women, and yet queerness remains because the women, including a butch queen, are Amazons, in a film in which genders are thoroughly inverted. Other women connote lesbianism by both cross-dressing and ruling. Recall Marlene Dietrich's masculinity as she ascends the throne in *The Scarlet Empress* and Greta Garbo as the monarch who kisses a lady-in-waiting and declares herself not an "old maid" but "a bachelor" in *Queen Christina* (1933). Other lesbians inhabit spaces that, as with the men, evoke queerness. Consider *Call Her Savage* (1932), in which lesbian couples sit alongside male couples while pansy entertainers, dressed as maids, perform in a Greenwich Village dive. Mannishly garbed barflies, sometimes wielding cigars, pal around with men, or confuse and emasculate them in *Lawyer Man* (1932), *Grand Slam* (1933), and *Blood Money* (1933).

Theaters and cabarets allow for female queerness too, as entertainers play with gender ambiguity in *Broadway Through a Keyhole* (1933) and, famously, *Morocco* (1930), in which a tuxedoed Dietrich kisses a woman on the mouth. Others associated with performance connote lesbianism too, as with the dance impresario in lesbian director Dorothy Arzner's *Dance, Girl, Dance* (1940). More spectacular, in Cecil B. DeMille's ancient Roman epic *The Sign of the Cross* (1932), is the lusty Ancaria who attempts to seduce the Christian heroine with her dance to "The Naked Moon." Lesbians also turn up in prison in *Ladies They Talk About* (1933).

Given the links between codes of gender and sexuality and the realm of work, women needed only to dress like men or hold down "male" jobs to seem queer. "I beg your pardon, old man," says the drunken filmmaker in *What Price Hollywood?* (1932) to a woman at a fashionable Hollywood restaurant, "Who's your tailor?" (Could this have been director George Cukor's sly reference to Arzner, daughter of a noted restaurateur?) Within other fields of work and across social classes, one finds that Aline MacMahon's rural mechanic in *Heat Lightning* (1934) and Jean Dixon's lawyer, dubbed a "new kind of woman," in gay director James Whale's *The Kiss Before the Mirror* (1933), also carry connotations of lesbianism.

While surveys like Vito Russo's *The Celluloid Closet* (1987) traversed similar ground, such representation is far more widespread than such studies suggest. I therefore have examined the responses of Hollywood's self-imposed content regulators at the PCA, reflecting on how and why attempts to eliminate queerness failed. Annette Kuhn (1988) argues that censors occupy the contradictory position of producing prohibition. This essay, therefore, is a historically specific case study shaped as a poststructuralist critique of the hypocrisies of censorship. In mobilizing extant censorship files, I use the homophobic attempts to eliminate such representations against the grain of their intention as evidence that these images were read queerly, thus anchoring my own readings of a nation whose crisis did not leave gender and sexuality unscathed. I argue that these images were read by 1930s spectators as queer and had the power to offend by their very presence, even though many seem to be "negative" stereotypes. Their popularity, however, suggests that many enjoyed these representations, possibly because they were stereotypes, but also because they were something more. The exceptionally common nature of these images – and the queer readings they entail – lend weight to Alexander Doty's contention that "queerness, not straightness, just might be the most pervasive sexual dynamic at work in mass culture production and reception" (1993, back cover). As even the preceding survey of a fraction of the films involved demonstrates, films with queer characters span every genre and studio. Even *Citizen Kane*'s (1941) brusque female librarian and the male guard teased by the reporter visiting the Thatcher Memorial as possibly being "Rosebud" – implicating Thatcher too – are sketched-in lesbian and gay stereotypes of the time (Lugowski 2006, 38–48). Indeed, although Russo claims that *Some Like It Hot* (1959) was "virtually the only female impersonation sustained throughout an entire film since the teens" (1987, 6–7), he overlooks two versions of the stage farce *Charley's Aunt* (featuring queerly coded Charles Ruggles and Jack Benny in the title roles), which, made in 1930 and 1941, neatly bracket the Depression years.

Reading the Code

Scholars have examined how the practices of Hollywood filmmaking and reception in the 1930s dovetail, *vis-à-vis* the industry's attempts at self-regulation, with other narrative and stylistic trends of the period, as well as with larger cultural currents of the Depression. Concerns about what movies were showing, for example, intensified. As Richard Maltby notes, "Movie content and the concern with content were symptoms of a moral panic about social behavior, induced by the economic collapse" (1993, 51). Concern over gender roles would occupy a central role in the ongoing struggle among studio profit motives, the varying demands of spectators, and what was seen as the need for "suitable" representation in light of the Depression's crisis of masculinity and the family.

The areas of largest attention have been gangster films and especially the "woman's film," specifically its "fallen woman" subgenre. Lea Jacobs (1992) and Maltby have shown that such films illustrate the work of Hollywood's PCA, part of Will Hays's Motion Picture Producers and Distributors of America (MPPDA), with respect to the narrative and discursive textuality of these films, as the PCA attempted to control topical "moral threats" like prostitution and ethnic criminality. They argue that the films of 1934 (the year the PCA was set up under Joseph Breen, replacing the weaker Studio Relations Committee, or SRC), while a "turning point" in the history of self-regulation, may not represent the mere "enforcement" of the Code, which was, to a large extent, already in place since 1930 and, indeed, one of the cautionary conventions dating from the 1920s.

The Production Code was notable for, among other things, the remarkable ways it attempted to regulate discourse in American film without baldly stating that certain elements were absolutely forbidden. Expressions including "should be avoided" and "should not suggest" were common. With several broad categories of representation, however, the Code did not equivocate. Clause six of section two on "Sex" states that "sex perversion or any inference to it is forbidden." And yet, as my survey above suggests, Depression-era cinema exhibits a surprising number of characters, generally in small parts and often used for comedy, who are codified and readable as queer. (While I would never admit to being a "size queen," notable exceptions to even this "bit part" tendency exist.) Furthermore, given that the SRC and the PCA were internal to the industry, shaping content so that films would not encounter problems during exhibition from local censors, queerness survived regulators or, ironically, they indirectly, indeed unwillingly, enabled it. I propose to examine historiographic models and conclusions reached by other scholars in light of this "boundary value" test case in order to queer the literature on the Code, but also, beyond that, to reconsider such paradigms so as to apply them to the roles that queerness in cinema played on the terrains of subversion, gender politics, and New Deal allegory.

When scholars talk about queer representations or discourse in films from this period, the word "subtext" invariably seems to "come out." Chon Noriega has helpfully shown how extra-textual film reviews could have cued audiences to the queerness censored from films based on queer Broadway plays. At one point, however, he cynically writes that critics tend to

> examine the film itself, and not . . . discursive acts that surround a film, . . . shaping its meaning(s). Contemporary . . . criticism [functions] . . . with the added limitation that . . . homosexual "images" either do not exist or were censored. Thus . . . to ensure "the survival of subcultural identity within an oppressive society," gay and lesbian . . . critics have employed . . . strategies to recuperate a history . . . The emphasis, therefore, has been on "subtexting" censored films . . . (1990, 20–21)

Noriega also claims that such reading strategies fail to distinguish that era's sensibilities and "cinematic codes" from today's. Such claims suggest that queerness is "absent" from film during this period; that censorship, which necessarily speaks that which it attempts to contain, is always completely successful; and that contemporary queer critics neither share nor can understand the sensibilities, codes, and oppressions of another era. Attending such charges are claims that critics are "reading too much into it" or "reading too hard." I, for one, am very interested in "hard" readings. As Richard Dyer notes, "Audiences cannot make media images mean anything they want to, but they can select from the complexity of the image the meanings and feelings, the variations, inflections and contradictions, that work for them" (1986, 5). Placing queer discourse in the untheorized netherworld of "subtext" is a policing of reading strategies and the limits of meaning, as if the text speaks only a self-evident discourse for all spectator-readers, in effect closeting both readers – historical and contemporary – and texts.

As for historical spectators, interview material that queerly reads older films, admittedly of a necessarily retrospective nature, does exist in places such as the Lesbian Herstory Archives. We also have another group of readers whose focus was on the films themselves, whose writings from the time exist and who, though hardly queer-identified, nonetheless did a great deal of queer reading, namely, our friends at the PCA! Censors, for example, were very concerned that *Dr. Monica* (1934) would be the story of three women: a nymphomaniac, an alcoholic, and a lesbian. Consider also an October 7, 1935 letter from Joseph Breen to RKO's B. B. Kahane regarding an all-male dance lesson Fred Astaire gives his buddies in *Follow the Fleet* (1936): "We are assuming of course that you will exercise your usual good taste in this scene of the sailors learning to dance. There will be no attempt to inject any 'pansy' humor into the scene."[1]

Censors not only saw queerness but also examined it as a boundary case. They were even defensive of the implications of reading queerness. Olga Martin writes:

> Smart alecks . . . hold that nothing artistic has come out . . . since the enforcement of the Code; that the Producers' Association and Mr. Breen are . . . fussy old maids, and . . . censoring pictures for grown-ups is an insulting and puerile undertaking. Yet it was only because of the PCA that the play, *The Children's Hour*, with its implications of sex perversion, was recast into a natural love story. (1937, 42)

How interesting that when Martin gives the most extreme example of what the PCA has "done" for Hollywood, she uses the censorship of queerness. (Times haven't changed much.) Even more striking is that censors – less intentionally – wanted to ward off queerness, not only from films, but also from the site of censorship (that is, the site of reading itself), so that Martin ends up defending PCA head Breen and other censors, mostly men, from the charge of being "fussy old maids."

Maltby seems to understand how reading opens up sites of queerness, however indirectly he says so, when he writes that the self-regulation that existed in certain conventions could operate "perversely" as an "enabling mechanism" as well as an instrument of repression (1993, 41). His charge, however, that only a very tiny and conventional canon of films, less than 1 percent of Hollywood's output from 1930 to 1934, challenged "traditional" values, cannot stand in light of the hundreds of examples of queerness I have found from this period. Nonetheless, he does call for symptomatic criticism that reads the era's crises through the refracting lenses of cinema, noting the frequent deaths of father figures, the inadequacy of such figures, and dysfunctional families as signs of crisis within capitalist patriarchy (1986, 25).

What is strange, though, is that scholars often confine themselves to films set in the contemporary 1930s as the ones that speak to Depression-era crisis, with the examples cited often limited to the gangster film and the "women's picture," genres that have dominated studies of the PCA. Criticism might locate both queer pleasures and social anxieties in queer genres, including frothy musicals, vaudeville-based comedies, and horror fantasies as well as in sober-minded drama (Benshoff & Griffin 2006). Furthermore, apart from some passing examples, scholars often ignore queerness and the responses it provoked. *Our Betters* has, for instance, been investigated in light of the SRC's concern over objections the British market might have had to its scenes in court and how South Americans would feel about the gigolo character, Pepi (Vasey 1997, 122). Understudied, however, is the brouhaha in censorship files surrounding the brightly flaming Ernest, who dominates the film's last reel with his tango lessons and gossipy repartee. Consideration of queerness is essential to understanding *both* the Code and patriarchal capitalism.

The Question of Subversion

Maltby's historiographic critique of a subversive canon debates with Robert Sklar's "Age of Turbulence/Age of Order" paradigm for the pre- and post-Code periods (1994, 175). (These terms, used by many, are decidedly inaccurate; "pre-PCA" and "post-PCA" would be better.) Sklar suggests that filmmakers "perpetrated" subversion, while Maltby, citing Hays, questions whether Hollywood was "fomenting" social disorder, arguing that, although ever-louder voices denounced Hollywood immorality, one could not say that cinema became more

> salacious or vicious between 1930 and 1934. With occasional exceptions, the reverse is the case, as . . . censors applied increasingly strict standards . . . the early '30s was a period of increasing moral conservatism [and Hollywood] failed to keep pace with "growing demand[s] for a return to decency" . . . The industry was pedaling backward as fast as it could, but not fast enough for its opponents. (Maltby 1993, 49, citing Hays, 1931 MPPDA report)

Perhaps both Sklar's and Maltby's choice of verbs, "perpetrating" and "fomenting," respectively, is a bit strong for an industry whose first imperative was, as Sklar notes, always a fast buck. Nonetheless, Sklar's distinction is useful for my historical, politicized symptomatology and my attendant textual analyses. After all, gangster films briefly became more provocative between 1930 and 1932 before being effectively banished. The women's picture sometimes supports the argument (compare the promiscuous Norma Shearer of *Strangers May Kiss* and *A Free Soul*, both 1931, with the demure Shearer of *Smilin' Through*, 1932), but abortion is alluded to more often in 1933–1934 than before. And we should not exclude the boldness, however ultimately compromised, of *The Story of Temple Drake* (1933), *Baby Face* (1933), and Shearer's *Riptide* (1934). Among neglected genres, the bullet-ridden zombies of *White Zombie* (1932), the synthetic flesh of *Dr. X* (1932), the vivisection of Charles Laughton in *Island of Lost Souls* (1932), the snake's attack of Lionel Atwill in *Murders in the Zoo* (1933), and the skinning alive of Boris Karloff in *The Black Cat* (1934) far outstrip the more genteel incidents and visual highlights of 1931's *Frankenstein* and *Dracula*. To take a different (but equally queer) genre, the salaciousness of Busby Berkeley's musical numbers "Pettin' in the Park" from *Gold Diggers of 1933* (1933), "By a Waterfall" in *Footlight Parade* (1933), and "Spin a Little Web of Dreams" in *Fashions of 1934* (1934) outstrips anything he had done before *42nd Street* (1933). Neither Maurice Chevalier's nor Eddie Cantor's material tones down entirely during this period; Wheeler and Woolsey act naughtier as they go along, and the downright raunchy series of "Baby Burlesks" that launched Shirley Temple appear in 1932–1933 (Jenkins 1992).

Consonant with these other transgressions, Hollywood is at its queerest from early 1932 to mid-1934, corresponding with the worst of the Depression. Not only do the number of queer incidents increase, but we also see more explicit references, longer scenes, and sometimes surprisingly substantial characterizations. Perhaps most important, pansies and lesbians remain, respectively, effeminate and mannish but become increasingly sexualized in 1933–1934. As the Depression continued, however, the need to establish "suitable" masculinities became important to moral watchdogs, paralleling the masculinist imagery of federally funded New Deal public art in the mid- and late 1930s (Melosh 1991). Thus there may be some virtue to arguments about Hollywood pushing the envelope, not in the interests of scholars writing histories of discrete, "before and after" turning points as in avoiding a uniform model, always properly functioning, of the so-called classical Hollywood cinema. Subversion of morality might not have been intended, but it might have resulted from the subversion or failure of industrial practices. Indeed, it might be wise to recall Dominick LaCapra's historiographic insight: "The apparent paradox is that texts hailed as perfections of a genre or a discursive practice may also test and contest its limits" (1985, 141).

Maltby himself notes Warner Bros.' lack of cooperation with the Code until the bitter end and how Paramount, cooperative under B. P. Schulberg, decided to be as daring as possible under Emmanuel Cohen in 1932–1933. At MGM, Irving Thalberg's resistance ended with his heart attack and journey abroad to recover in 1933. As James Wingate, Breen's SRC predecessor, put things that year:

> I wonder why companies... when we all desire to present pictures in conformity with the Code, continue to... present for approval material which, even after a great deal of work ..., must be close to the borderline. The fact that some of these are even submitted to us... indicates a degeneration on the part of the person or company responsible.[2]

Consider how, in 1934, Jack Warner did not respond to Breen's letter and phone calls about a scene openly expressing homoerotic desire in *Wonder Bar* (1934), in which a man interrupts a male–female couple on the dance floor with "May I cut in?" When the woman responds, "Why certainly," the man glares at her, opting to dance with the other man, leading witness Al Jolson to exclaim, "Boys will be boys. Whoo!" Breen wrote, "It is quite evident that the gentleman [Warner] is giving me the runaround. He evidently thinks that this is the smart thing to do."[3]

An even more remarkable example is RKO's handling of the SRC with respect to *Diplomaniacs*, which includes a scene where Wheeler and Woolsey, in bed together, are attended by a pansy butler before Woolsey helps Wheeler on with a negligee. As Wingate wrote to producer Merian C. Cooper on April 22, 1933, and to Will Hays on April 24, the film was premiered without informing SRC censors. RKO put off showing them the film until 11 days later, did not return phone calls, and claimed to have

Figure 16.1 A bug-eyed Al Jolson watches two men dance in Lloyd Bacon's *Wonder Bar* (1934, produced by Warner Bros. Entertainment).

left messages that were not received. When a meeting finally occurred almost two weeks later, Wingate observed that the scripts they had received while the film was in production never contained the offending scene. The studio, meanwhile, claimed that the film's negative had already been shipped to New York, that Wheeler and Woolsey were on a foreign tour, and that changing the sequence would disrupt continuity in the film's score. The scene remained in the film.

In light of such evidence, rather than suggest "pedaling backward" occurred between 1930 and 1934, I would contend that there was genuine resistance to the SRC on the part of Hollywood filmmakers. They attempted to replace one kind of "unsuitable" material with another, which may still have pushed at boundaries so as to attract the crucial sophisticated urban audience but was considered to be of less "dangerous" (to use a favorite word of Breen's) semiotic import. The violence of gangster films was used early on to attract audiences, and when that genre was clamped down upon, producers resorted to sex. As battles were waged over the "fallen woman" and "gold digger" films, producers tried to get away with making more raw their horror films and comedies, given that the more "unrealistic" nature of these genres made them less harmful to censors (Jacobs 1992, 82–83; Everson 1983). I thus find it also likely that filmmakers stepped up pansy humor, hoping that they could get away with scenes and characters aimed in that direction.

A good example is James Whale's *The Invisible Man* (1933), which, in monthly reports from the SRC to Hays, was generally categorized with horror films. While there was concern at early scripting stages about lines spoken by the power- and drug-crazed protagonist in which he plans to kill government officials, the film was later characterized in a report from Wingate to Hays as in a "highly fantastic and exoitc [*sic*] vein, and presents no particular censorship difficulties." This from a film in which the title character still spouts radical (if megalomaniacal) ideas, romps about naked (OK, so he's invisible), and indulges in pansy humor, skipping about to "Here we go gathering nuts in May." One can read society's invisible man as its homosexual man: effeminate, dangerous when naked, seeking a male partner in "crime," idolizing his abandoned fiancée rather than loving her, and becoming "visible" only when shot by the police, monitored by doctors, and heard regretting his sin against God (i.e., made into a statistic by the forces oppressing queers: the law, the medical establishment, and religious orthodoxy) (Lugowski 2005).

The Question of Difference

Antony Easthope (1990) sees the masculine ego as a defensive entity fearful of difference. Early talkies overflow with difference – difference based on sound. New cinematic universes create a dichotomy between talk and action, with talk taking over. With the final passing of the Old West in the teens seeming far away by the 1930s, the cowboy fades as the dominant American hero. So do the silent comedians, lost in oceans of talk, along with swashbucklers, whose acrobatics early talkies seem neither willing nor able to accommodate. The aviator briefly becomes important as an American hero, but his machines are at least as impressive as he is. He is frequently earthbound and stagebound for plot exposition, and the 1932 kidnapping of the Lindbergh baby seems to clip his wings. Indeed, given that the gangster does not have staying power, one of the dominant US heroes becomes the doctor, whose potency in film is based more on talk and skillful caregiving than on physical action. (One can add more overtly patriarchal figures – the judge, in the Andy Hardy films, for instance, which began in 1937, in which Andy's father saves the day with a wise word; and the priest, seen in *Boys Town* and *Angels With Dirty Faces*, both 1938.)[4]

While men had been able to dominate action scenes, they could not do so when it came to talking. The 1930s woman, continuing the trends of the 1920s in a greatly altered cinema, talked her way into six of the top 10 positions on the box office charts from 1931 through 1934. Even later, with the rise of screwball comedy, women were more present on the chart than they have been since – at present one finds one or two female stars, at most, among Hollywood's most bankable. Susan Ware connects women's speech and power when she writes: "Since women seem more autonomous the more they are allowed to talk on the screen, the heroines of... screwball comedies emerge as wonderful, if somewhat wacky, characters with brains of their own" (1982, 185). Elizabeth Kendall concurs that the "prideful femininity" of 1930s stars

> could not have surfaced... without the economic chaos of the thirties.... Poverty and uncertainty played havoc with people's assumptions about themselves.... Depression romantic comedies responded to their audience's loss of faith by making a virtue of traits usually thought of as feminine. (1990, preface)

When voices were heard, they were much more diverse than silent intertitles had managed via stereotypical written slang and dialect. Despite the heinous prejudices often inherent in media stereotyping, early talkies were uniquely heteroglossic, with the unabashedly Gallic and Latina innuendoes of Chevalier and Lupe Vélez; the Brooklyn sounds of Clara Bow, Barbara Stanwyck, and James Cagney; an English accent from Ronald Colman that boosted his stardom (as did the affectedly broad A's of Joan Crawford); and the Scandinavian intonations of Garbo and El Brendel, one of many dialect comedians, and one whose Latino-sounding stage name summed up the period's polyphony. Will Rogers's drawl was treasured, his slow delivery appropriate for Hollywood's biggest male star of 1933–1934, and Stepin Fetchit's even slower version of black vernacular helped him win a long-term contract. The stage-trained voices of Ruth Chatterton, Marie Dressler, and George Arliss helped them surmount Hollywood's age barriers, and attempts were made to feature the uniquely gender-bending pipes of Tallulah Bankhead as central to her star persona. And one should note the foreign-language productions shot simultaneously with their English counterparts on studio lots.

Given this explosion of voices that transcended barriers of age, race, gender, ethnicity, and class (John Barrymore always sounded aristocratic, Wallace Beery never did), it should perhaps not "sound" surprising that even barriers based on sexuality would not hold. Furthermore, if the power of the feminine – which had gathered momentum in the 1920s with women's suffrage and female executives, activists, and movie stars who doubled as their own producers – could be augmented via the voice, pansy characters, too, who flitted through the Jazz Age, could rise to the occasion.

Character actors such as Pangborn, Sutton, and Horton, who specialized in sissy roles, came to prominence during the later silent era and especially in talkies. Barrios contends that gay silent stars Ramón Novarro and William Haines were partially "outed" by talkies; they overcame the sound barrier until MGM dropped them by 1934 (1995, 289).

Audiences delighted in the flip, risqué repartee of pre-PCA queers as these "free radicals" flitted gaily through films, largely unburdened by plot or any recuperative strategies. Consider the effeminate man who opens *Palmy Days* (1931) by entering a bakery and requesting a pansy on the cake he orders. This curiosity about new voices, which so quickly turned to revulsion (e.g., think how many fewer Jews are found in post-PCA film compared to silent and pre-PCA days), was summed up in a brief scene from a 1931 Columbia mystery, *The Secret Witness*. Fluttery switchboard operator ZaSu Pitts is found reading Radclyffe Hall's best-selling lesbian novel, *The Well of Loneliness*, and trying to explain, over the phone, what it's really all about.

Lesbian Representation During a Masculinity Crisis

What lesbianism was "really all about" during the 1930s merits particular consideration. The lesbian of mainstream 1930s cinema was influenced by discourses on the working "New Woman" and the "aristocratic dyke" culture that found quintessential expression in Hall's novel. The most overt instantiation of the lesbian discussed earlier, with her severely tailored suit, monocle, and short hair, was, admittedly, less common than the pansy and was not a stock role for many character actors. Nonetheless, lesbianism was arguably more subtly pervasive than its male counterpart. Major stars could have mild lesbian connotations, albeit not called such and masked as strength or exoticism, accrue to their images (Ginger Rogers, Eleanor Powell, Marlene Dietrich, Katharine Hepburn, Clara Bow, Greta Garbo, Barbara Stanwyck, Ruth Chatterton). Furthermore, lesbian overtones, typically signified by tomboyishness, were sometimes portrayed and read more seriously in films: If the pansy was perceived as a failure, the lesbian could be seen as a threat.

Often, lesbian imagery suggests transgressions very different from gay maleness, insofar as lesbianism encompasses sexualities not predicated on men and thus is underrepresented because it threatens the very bounds of the representable. During an era of masculinity in crisis, such an immanent critique of heteropatriarchy, positing men as optional to sexuality, would be especially threatening. Olga Martin's reference to the rewriting of *The Children's Hour* for its first film version (*These Three*, 1936) was, significantly, a repression of overt lesbian representation. During this period, nonetheless, some of the extreme implications of the symbolic absence of men were dramatized. *It's Great to Be Alice* (1933), made during the Depression's worst year, literally has all the men on Earth (except one) die from a mysterious disease, and, as a result, some of the women "turn" to lesbianism.

Often, lesbian discourse does not exist apart from gay maleness; it is seen as part of a pervasive perversity. Lesbian representation existing alongside, and sometimes in dialogic relation to, pansy humor appears in the gay bar sequence in *Call Her Savage*, in *The Warrior's Husband*, in which the butch Amazon queen marries a pansy, and in *The Sign of the Cross*, *Paree Paree* (1934), *Sylvia Scarlett* (1936), *Stage Door* (1937), and *Turnabout* (1940). Although the huge PCA file on *Turnabout* suggests that industry regulators were most hysterical about a flirtatious scene between Franklin Pangborn and the male protagonist, who has magically switched bodies with his wife, lesbianism accompanies the male queerness, as the potentially threatening female takes up phallic cigars and takes over at the office. Lesbianism is thus significant for another reason, as the limitations of a binary, hierarchical gender system are opened for critique. When patriarchy admits only two genders, feminizing a man seems to require "masculinizing" a woman, and vice versa. Heterocentric oppression relies upon queerness to establish normalcy, yet that queerness only breeds other queernesses, undermining the system it means to bolster. In Cukor's *Our Betters* a previously unseen pansy dance instructor monopolizes the final reel, effects a reconciliation between the film's two primary female characters, and ends the film with a lesbian discourse-tinged line, "What an exquisite spectacle! Two ladies of title kissing one another!"

During the Depression, butch, powerful, cross-dressing, or simply intimate, affectionate women were often portrayed (and read) less as potentially lesbian than as shrews requiring taming. They were judged within the film to need a man, forgo a career, or stifle disruptive eccentricities. Consider Martin's remarks linking gender performance with sexuality: While male effeminacy is to be avoided completely, slightly mannish women are tolerated because tomboyishness may be useful (just don't be "grossly masculine," she says the Code warns). Such qualities may be manifested by strong women whose need to work was necessary during the Depression. With masculinity in crisis, though, the corresponding feminine qualities of male "perverts" are completely unacceptable. Thus, discourses about queer sexuality are never purely homophobic against men. They also have their basis in sexism against women, for it is the power of femininity, the "feminization" of 1930s culture, and the threat of working women "wearing the pants" that are the conditions being policed.

The metaphorical nature of a pants-wearing money-earner attaining independence from men connoted lesbianism as a break from the interwoven financial and sexual economies of patriarchy. If "clothes make the man," wearing pants in and of itself suggested a link to lesbianism that 1930s films simultaneously punish and offer as spectacle. Consider the lesbian puppet revealing her "nature" in a musical number set at the gates of Hell in *I Am Suzanne!* (1933). Asked to declare her identity, she states: "A woman, alas, by nature's plan / But I like to dress up like a man." The male devil responds that he "pulls the strings," in this case both figuratively and literally, as the puppet is cast into the flames, along with that undesirable 1930s male, the gangster, and a castrating mother-in-law. Sometimes, though, the independent career lesbian escapes unscathed. In James Whale's *The*

Kiss Before the Mirror, the career-oriented, mannishly garbed "New Woman" lawyer connotes slight copresent suggestions of heterosexuality that might have "protected" her. She does, however, offer a sardonic critique of heterosexism. Discussing a case in which a husband has murdered his wife, she offers an advantage to not marrying: "At least no one will ever murder me." She also responds to the question, "What are you? A lawyer, or a new kind of woman?" by noting "By day, I'm a lawyer. At night, well, you might be surprised." Despite her strong connotations of lesbianism or bisexuality, the SRC left her alone in her queer ambiguity.

Indeed, the most overt pansy representations in *Wonder Bar*, *Follow the Fleet*, and especially *Turnabout* and *So This Is Africa* (1933) provoked more outrage than the comparable lesbian scenes of the period. The PCA file on *Queen Christina* contains much more panic about the unwed Christina sharing a room and potentially having sex with a male diplomat than it does about her lesbian-coded relationship with her lady-in-waiting. Similarly, Sandra Shaw's quasi-dyke in *Blood Money* was not heavily criticized by the SRC, but more instances were mentioned and complained about from 1933 to 1936. Wheeler and Woolsey's *So This Is Africa*, by contrast, especially in its last reel, with the boys marrying two male natives, was edited to the point of creating glaring discontinuities. The possible circulation of *Turnabout* containing the aforementioned gay flirtation and the hero's climactic pregnancy brought a panicked flurry of telegrams desperately trying to halt the film's release. With lesbianism, though, the PCA saw the connection between vampirism and sexual desire in *Dracula's Daughter* (1936) but gave only brief warnings about possible queerness between the countess and her female victims. Promoting the film, Universal even played up this angle with the publicity catchphrase, "Save the women of London from Dracula's Daughter!"[5] Making women monsters – and simultaneously keeping them victims – could be accommodated quite comfortably by the Code. PCA files even refer to a Universal project entitled *The Loves of Women*, which correspondence frankly says deals with "lesbianism." The film appears not to have been made, but the very consideration of such a production is striking.

Cukor's *Sylvia Scarlett*, which caused a great deal of PCA consternation, is to some degree the exception to this tendency: The PCA was concerned about Katharine Hepburn's male disguise promoting lesbianism disguised as heterosexuality. But this film encompasses male queerness too, and heterosexuality that the characters suggest is rather gay (e.g., Brian Aherne's line to Hepburn: "I know what it is that gives me a queer feeling when I look at you"). Of course, censorship trends are historically specific. Ancaria's frottage-laden dance of lesbian seduction in *The Sign of the Cross* caused a storm of controversy and was deleted for post-PCA reissues of the film. Nonetheless, Cecil B. DeMille rammed his orgiastic vision of ancient Rome and his equally didactic portrait of early Christianity down the throats of thrill-seekers and prudes alike, and this hit played through the peak queer period of 1932–1933. When referring to different queernesses, the PCA usually managed to refer to "lesbianism" but seems to have had no word for gay male representation. It is usually referred to, in quotation marks, as "perversion," "that kind of humor," "effeminacy," "'pansy' humor," or "too 'pansy,'" ironically using words the PCA itself forbade in late 1933.

Figure 16.2 The lustful Ancaria (Joyzelle, right) tries to seduce virtuous Mercia (Elissa Landi) in *The Sign of the Cross* (1932, director and producer Cecil B. DeMille).

Establishing Masculinity

As the Depression continued, men's performances of gender became, to some extent, something that powerful sectors within US culture no longer felt could be ridiculed. Yet pansy and lesbian humor was evidently still seen as titillating to the sophisticated urban audiences so crucial to Depression-era revenues. Much scholarship on the PCA is strongest in explaining how the Code tried to at once repress and enable discourse to appeal to the broadest possible spectrum of viewers while offending the fewest. Ruth Vasey's useful expression is the "principle of deniability," whereby audiences were compelled to interpret "contradictory cinematic evidence" (1997, 128). The more potentially offensive the idea, the more vague its representation would be. Maltby, partly citing Jacobs, explains "deniability" further as

> indeterminacy that shifted responsibility for [interpreting films] away from the producer to the individual spectator. [Censor Jason] Joy recognized that if the Code was to remain effective, it had to allow… representational conventions "from which conclusions might be drawn by the sophisticated mind, but which would mean nothing to the unsophisticated … " [T]he Code was the mechanism [for] this multiplicity of viewing positions. (1993, 40)

This fits well with what happened to homosexuality during the late SRC and post-PCA periods. Producers sometimes attempted to use deniability to argue with content regulators about the interpretation of scenes. Consider a gag in *International House* (1933) where W. C. Fields, misinterpreting Franklin Pangborn's reference to "Wuhu" China as queer flirtation, denies the connotations of his own boutonniere, "Don't let the posy fool ya." The film's high innuendo content led censor Carl Milliken to write to Breen: "The dirty minded lout who put it in the picture knew perfectly well, however, what he was doing and undoubtedly felt he had gained something by getting away with it." A. M. Botsford of Paramount, however, wrote a denial to Wingate that "Fields' line… indicates merely a 'sissy' reaction. It would take an expert in abnormal psychology to wheedle out of that an inference of sex perversion."

Censorship trends are historically specific, and lesbianism could be both more and less controversial than queer male imagery, sometimes depending on the degree of same-sex desire represented. What needs emphasizing, though, if we don't want to flatten out changes between the two periods, is that more depends on the subtlety of interpretation, given that such words as "pansy," "fairy," and "lezzie" are banned completely. Furthermore, references to "lavender," as in *The Broadway Melody* (1929) or in *Hips, Hips, Hooray* (1934) (or, in the case of 1933's *Only Yesterday*, a mixture of blue and mauve!), though not outlawed by the PCA, disappear in the post-PCA period. The later Depression years from 1935 through 1941 are notable not only for a proliferation of child stars and male–female costarring teams, as Hollywood aggressively promotes innocence and heterosexuality, but also for its male-buddy teams (Clark Gable/Spencer Tracy, James Cagney/Pat O'Brien, Don Ameche/Tyrone Power, Bob Hope/Bing Crosby). Characters are less likely to be supporting pansies than stars who ironically indulge in queer banter to prove how manly they are. The best-known example is the relationship between Jeff (Cary Grant) and "The Kid" (Thomas Mitchell) in Howard Hawks's *Only Angels Have Wings* (1939) (Wood 1981, 182–183). Less sensitively drawn yet perhaps more prototypical is *Test Pilot* (1938), starring Clark Gable, Hollywood's most popular male star beginning almost immediately with the post-PCA period and a paradigm for a homophobic yet fully queer masculinity. In *Test Pilot,* he flirts with mechanic Tracy, who dies at the end, saying, "I love you," while simultaneously pleasing "perfect wife" Myrna Loy (that same year crowned Hollywood's "queen" to Gable's "king"). Normalcy is established by toying with, and resisting, queerness.

Even the word "gay," which had queer connotations even then, appears in fewer film titles after early 1935. Grant's aforementioned line in *Bringing Up Baby*, "I just went *gay* all of a sudden," was, as Russo notes, never in any official version of the script (1987, 47). Chauncey observes that the likewise ad-libbed line that follows, "I'm just sitting in the middle of 42nd Street waiting for a bus," if anything, clarifies the meaning of the "gay" line as it refers, in a pre–Christopher Street era, to what was New York's busiest gay cruising ground (1994, 18). While many 1930s Manhattanites would get the joke, few others would.

Getting rid of heavily denotative slang labels clearly wasn't enough, yet the "principle of deniability" was often exercised via coy behavioral tics suggesting effeminacy or, for that matter, ethnicities or political positions less welcome on American screens in post-PCA days. Maltby aptly notes that an increasingly nervous "Protestant provincial middle class sought to defend its cultural hegemony from the incursions of a modernist, metropolitan culture that provincials regarded as alien – a word often, but not always, a synonym for Jewish" (1993, 41). "Modernist," "metropolitan," and "alien" might also describe the intellectual, the leftist, and the homosexual. At least once the "alien" quality of the queer was made literal: In the science fiction musical *Just Imagine* (1930), an effeminate Martian standing by his planet's female ruler is characterized by Earthman El Brendel, "She's not the queen, he is!" This dialogue, and the Martian's reaction, according to SRC letters dated October 16 and November 16, 1930, "make it appear that he is 'queer'." And sometimes, more than two of these discourses overlap. To take an example from another realm of cultural production, painter Paul Cadmus's "sailors and foozies" trilogy (1933–1938), in which pansies are shown making liaisons with sailors, was criticized as the work of a "Communist Jew," when in fact Cadmus was neither.[6]

By terms like "alien," "Jew," and "queer," I refer not only to what people identified as but also to how they were perceived and represented, and how rabidly right-wing discourses of anti-Semitism and homophobia have intermingled in the history of oppression, perpetrated in the name of patriarchal nationalism. Such interrelated bigotries functioned not only in Nazi Germany, which centrally targeted Jews and also persecuted gays, but among right-wing discourses of US culture that differed in degree though perhaps not necessarily in kind (Mosse 1996; Black 1994). Other ethnicities and minorities are linked with queerness in Depression cinema (e.g., blacks in *So This Is Africa* and *Wonder Bar*; Italians in *Colleen*, 1936, *The Gay Divorcee*, 1934, and *Top Hat*, 1935). A public figure no less than Mussolini objected to the queers Erik Rhodes played in the latter two films, claiming they did not represent "true Italian manhood."[7] The Jewish–queer link in modernity, however, is especially pronounced (Boyarin et al. 2003). The most prominent filmic example is Eddie Cantor's 1930s star persona, but there is also the Jewish pansy choreographer Max Mefoofsky, played by Gregory Ratoff in *Broadway Through a Keyhole*. Ratoff also plays Pinkowitz in *I'm No Angel* (1933), whose name Mae West spells as beginning with "P . . . as in pansy." In the post-PCA period, visible markers of ethnicity diminish in American film, and yet a notable elision occurs in *The Life of Emile Zola* (1937). Admittedly fairly bold in addressing anti-Semitism by dramatizing the Dreyfus affair, the film nonetheless never mentions the word "Jew"; Zola does, however, call the case "queer."

The incursions of queer culture entailed a backlash as the Depression led America in increasingly conservative directions. The stronger enforcing of the Code was only part of the era's construction of what would be, by the 1940s and 1950s, firmly built as "the closet" (Chauncey 1994). Studios often failed to heed suggestions or insistences from industry regulators, however, or compromised only slightly, making trims to pacify the PCA but leaving queerness intact. RKO producer Pandro Berman was evasive about a scene Breen wanted removed from *Top Hat* in which Rhodes apologizes to Edward Everett Horton by kissing him on both cheeks, with witness Helen Broderick quipping, "Go right ahead, boys, don't mind me." The studio trimmed Broderick's reaction shot slightly, but left the scene otherwise intact.

As the 1930s progressed, activity readable as queer by "sophisticated" audiences was more actively contained, contradicted, or even punished within a film. In the musicals starring Ginger Rogers and Fred Astaire, for instance, which seemed (to the PCA as well as to later historians) among the queerest films of the post-PCA period, the sissy is given a wife or contends for Rogers's hand. We also see queer byplay in the elevator between songwriters George Murphy and Hugh Herbert in *Top of the Town* (1937) as they try out prospective titles for romantic ditties on each other while the heroine (Doris Nolan) misunderstands their conversation as gay. She later pointedly asks about their antics, only to have their activity explained to her. Most violently, we witness the death of the lesbian vampire in *Dracula's Daughter* at the hands of her "pimp" when he symbolically rapes her with a phallic wooden shaft through the heart at the film's climax.

Readers, too, are policed by discourses surrounding the cinema. Horton's role in *Holiday* (1938) is praised by the *New York Times* as one in which his on-screen wife actually respects him. The article plays up his early stage days as a romantic lead before speaking of "a certain muliebrity of manner" in his 1930s films that has caused "the more captious among filmgoers to accuse him of effeminacy," suggesting just how common queer readings of Horton must have been.[8] As if the threat of being labeled "captious" weren't enough, studios sometimes insured the status of their contract players via physical threats: "Call Franklin Pangborn a sissy offstage and he'll plant five hard knuckles on your proboscis," stated RKO press releases for their Ginger Rogers vehicle, *Professional Sweetheart* (1933).[9]

Policing strategies such as these, whether within or surrounding films, nonetheless failed to eliminate queerness. It was both too entertaining and sometimes too necessary to the ideological value of many films, including *The Big Noise* (1936), a routine, 56-minute Warner Bros. film relying structurally upon queerness in allegorizing a New Deal saga. Its story centers on the embodiment of American Dream individualism – the small business owner. Honestly committed to quality, Trent (Guy Kibbee) has built his garment manufacturing business from scratch, but with the Depression, his profits are slipping. A member of his board of directors, Andrews (William B. Davidson), engineers a takeover in which a cheaper but less durable synthetic fabric, Woolex (dubbed "a new deal for the Trent mills"), will be used to make a flashier product. The designer of this line is pansyish Mr Rosewater (Andre Beranger, credited as Berenger), who replaces Trent's blue serge with robin's egg blue, seaweed green, and oyster gray and his "honest tweed" with "powder-puff texture." Trent tries retirement, but after talking with a fellow senior citizen about the importance of being active (i.e., a man), starts over again. He teams up with an enterprising young inventor (Warren Hull) in running a dry-cleaning store. Before long, Trent makes a success of his business and defeats gangsters who have been pressuring businesses for "protection" money. Woolex, meanwhile, has provoked complaints among sellers and customers alike. Rosewater cannot understand how buyers can quibble about durability when his color schemes are just "too divine." Andrews is booted out, and Trent regains his company, his "values" having won out. Even this short description of the film should make obvious that Rosewater, whose color, fabric, and fashion obsessions are completely impractical (read: feminine), exemplifies the overtly queer pansies more prevalent in pre-PCA days. He is linked with the excesses of the 1920s via the recurrent mention of "powder-puff" styles, the description recalling the names Rudolph Valentino was called when his persona led some to question his masculinity (Hansen 1991, 254–268; Lawrence 2010, 96–105).

Rosewater and Andrews stand in for all those superficial, grab-for-a-buck values that the opportunistic 1920s promoted and for which people during the Depression were "paying the price." A name like Rosewater suggests all the perfumed affectations that symbolize failed masculinity, whose ultimate expression was homosexuality, for which effeminacy stood in both metonymically and allegorically. Indeed, Rosewater's status as a man is questioned once Trent is out of work. (The temporary nature of his status is important; this is, after all, a Depression-era success fable.) Trent describes Rosewater to his elderly friend as "a man – or something – back in my factory." During one of Trent's tirades about what's wrong with "his" company, Rosewater is framed in the background, a visual pointer for precisely those values Trent is indicting.

In an early script – significantly, *Big Business*, its working title, was the more allegorically clear – more time was devoted to Rosewater's pansy humor. At one point, Rosewater, never far from his "powder-puff" shades and unnatural textures, misplaces his "Pussy willow Weave." He also wears one of his creations, sashaying about, hand on hip, like a (female) model. Later, he must also endure the scorn of a burly factory worker who totes his bolts of fabric, calling him "Mr Rosepetal" and recalling the rosewater that (feminizing) mothers put in their sons' hair. Rosewater even expresses a gushy attraction to the scornful Trent, remarking, "Isn't he dynamic?"[10]

Breen, reviewing one script in a February 12, 1936 letter, called attention to two points that could be "dangerous if not rightly treated." One was the gangster flavor of the racketeers; recommendations were made that gun battles occur offscreen. The other ultimately more problematic matter was that "whenever Rosewater appears, neither dialogue nor action must lend a pansy flavor to his character. Anything savoring of 'pansy' is, as you know, quite definitely objectionable."

Two weeks later, the PCA found a revised script "basically satisfactory," but a month after that, the film, as shot, still posed problems. The gun battle was "now satisfactory" even if a shot of a bomb being thrown was frowned upon. More difficult, however, was the minor figure of Rosewater. Breen wrote Jack Warner on March 24 that "we reviewed for a second time... *Big Business* and regret to inform you that we shall withhold the certificate of the

Association until certain changes, requested in our letters upon the script, shall have been made." The final film displays several jump cuts, typically around the figure of Rosewater. One cut, during one of Rosewater's speeches about his beloved fabrics, indicates that, as originally written and shot, his character was pushing at the boundaries of how much queerness filmmakers could get away with in the less friendly climate of 1936.

Given Rosewater's completely dispensable role in the narrative, one wonders why his troublesome part remains in the film at all. (Equally striking is Warner Bros. still trying to get away with briefly glimpsed pansy designers in *Hollywood Hotel* and *Talent Scout* in 1937.) Rosewater does appear in the key boardroom sequence, so editing him out might have entailed costly reshooting. He also exists to provide levity to a hackneyed script too serious for its own good. Guy Kibbee, typically cast as comical sugar daddies, blowhards, blunderers, and Babbitts, is very unamusingly crotchety as the lead of this "B" film. (His illness during production and workdays of up to twelve and a half hours might have contributed to this.) More importantly, though, Rosewater serves as an ideal for Trent – and by extension, audiences – to find distasteful. The remasculinization that the New Deal hoped to effect via federally funded art and confidence-building speeches also found expression in films closely linked to government and business policies. (Warner Bros. was the studio that most overtly sucked up to Roosevelt, but the tone of many post-PCA/New Deal films infiltrates the entire studio system.) The film ends with Trent surrounded by his loving family. His winning back his business is linked to the heterosexual coupling of his daughter and the inventor. Trent speaks of his planned first action back on the job, and his response is the last line spoken by a human in the film: "Fire Mr Rosewater." Thus, the film's ideological project comes to fruition. Old-fashioned values are back after America has paid for its sinful excesses (e.g., the Florida land boom of the late 1920s). The honest man has used his own wits to regain control over his life, and does so by excising frivolous affectation, reinstating systems where "men are men." In *The Big Noise*, queerness is shown so that it can be eliminated. Titillating but regulated, queerness contrasts with and indeed props up heterosexual masculinity and the dominance and business success that it signifies.

The film, though, also suggests nagging doubts that the lengthy Depression had, by then, firmly engendered in American culture. A running gag throughout the film is the gab spouted by the mascot parrot of the dry-cleaning business. Immediately after Trent speaks the last "human" dialogue, there is one more line. The parrot gets the last word, repeating his appellation for the cranky Trent, "Nice old man," which causes the film's hero to pull a comically disapproving face as the end title appears. The parrot, whose high-pitched delivery sounds effeminate, thus leaves some doubt about the Depression-era man's credibility. It suggests that while the ideal might be a "man," he is also getting "old" and is potentially "nice." This word suggests that he might be a bit "soft," much like Rosewater; it also sardonically questions the brusque actions of a New Deal hero who ruthlessly tricks gangsters into killing each other.

Conclusion

I have argued that queer imagery, exemplified primarily by effeminate "pansies" or fussy "sissified" men and mannish "New Women," was more common in Depression cinema than has been previously cataloged. Queerness exists in hundreds of Hollywood films produced between the 1929 stock market crash and the US entry into World War II. Furthermore, this imagery was read *as such* by people at the time. Yet the stereotypical nature of many of these representations was not enough to make them "desirable" or "safe" for many viewers. Indeed, many were offended; the very existence of these images outweighed their often negative connotations. Beyond that, queer imagery serves as a refraction of the widespread gender crisis brought about by the Depression. Pansy and sissy representations suggest and were read as a symbolic emasculation of US patriarchy resulting from socioeconomic crisis, while "mannish" women embodied the threat of unmarried and/or working women. With pansy humor directly, and lesbian representation indirectly, negative reactions constituted a sexist response to notions of "weakness" often labeled "effeminacy" and coded as feminine.

What such stereotyping fitfully attempted to mask was that values culturally associated with women (keeping families together, care for the needy, collective support, modesty, pursuing romance and other "sincere" leisure activities, gentleness combined with unheralded endurance) came to the fore during the Depression. Simultaneously, a masculinist ethos of the 1920s (emphasizing individualism, competition, material gain) fell apart. In the eyes of the PCA (and conservative religious and women's groups), queerness evoked the excesses and "sins" of contested 1920s culture and immoral money-grubbing mainstream entertainment. In a bigoted manner, it is also linked explicitly with urbanites and ethnic and political minorities (especially Jews and communists), labeling members of certain groups "unmanly," "decadent," or "anarchistic." Nonetheless, queerness survives even amid industry self-regulation because of the necessary role it plays in entertainment, indeed within the institutionalization of heterosexuality and patriarchy, whether as close bonding or as weakness and perversion that must be shown in order to be ridiculed and rejected.

As Robert Sklar has noted, "The historiographic issues of gender definition within specific societies and past cultural formations have barely been touched" (1992, 17). I want to conclude by suggesting the value of these images beyond what they tell us about gender during the Depression, or about the ironies and hypocrisies of censorship and homophobia. Cinema of the 1930s refracts, however indirectly, and certainly through the prism of homophobia, what queernesses must have been like then. Of course Vito Russo is right to label Hollywood and US culture itself as homophobic. Real-life queers of the Depression viewed images that were largely caricatures, in which gays and lesbians were often ridiculed and scorned.

Yet not all of these images were homophobic, at least not completely so. While one should not equate fiction with reality, some queer characters critique heterosexism, or are treated with affection and respect by other characters. Also, characters otherwise coded as non-queer (e.g., Wheeler and Woolsey) enjoy performing queerness. Even more important is what 1930s queer audiences might have made of such moments, how they honed their reading practices (a skill of life-and-death importance in meeting other gays) on these images. Perhaps they laughed at such representations with a healthy critical distance or found comforting identification with them. However the two men dancing together in *Wonder Bar* may have made closeted gay men in small towns feel once Al Jolson made the requisite wisecrack, that scene suggested that such people did exist. Andrea Weiss writes that for people "striving toward self-knowledge, Hollywood stars became important models in the foundation of gay identity" (1991, 288).

Furthermore, we must not write off, in the name of a Russoesque righteous anger, the lived behaviorisms and self-identifying gestures of earlier queers. Russo claimed not to mind sissyness in gay men, yet his stomach for it in cinema seems limited. If, as Jamie Gough (1989) argues, gay men became more "masculinized" in performing gender with the increased mainstreaming of gay culture in the post-Stonewall era, one might look at cinema to bolster historical, sociological, and literary studies of how queer men were perhaps more "feminine"-acting before that time (Marshall 1981). Chauncey (1994) has made explicit for queer history that the most visible modern gay man was the obviously effeminate one. Lillian Faderman (1991), writing about twentieth-century lesbianism, explores the wide range from women's "romantic friendships" to butch transvestites who sometimes passed for men. Such claims broadly characterize an era and a "type" of queer that was actually "types," but we must admit the historical, culturally specific nature of subjectivity. I prefer this approach to those that theorize, often via ahistorical psychoanalysis, opposite gender-identified identities; some of these analyses suggest that gender is fluid and then stop there. If we seek continuities – and disjunctures – it might be better to place them fully within the contexts of social production and reception, the interpsychic, and the historico-political.

Historical studies of periods paralleling our own reveal continuities as we see how queer representation, then and now, is at once "safe" in providing "harmless" laughs involving, say, cross-dressing comedians, yet also a boundary case when it comes to censorship. The government and the military use queerness with respect to awarding NEA grants, placing art in – or removing it from – the National Portrait Gallery, and determining eligibility to serve in the armed forces. (Indeed, the military demonstrates how regulating queerness has been understood to constitute national identity.) In his 1998 essay "No Sex, Please. We're Gay," Richard Goldstein refers to the 1930s when he notes that the "celluloid closet has [recently] become a room with a view... Gay characters are nearly as ubiquitous as aliens at the cineplex, and for the most part, they are lovable, even noble souls." But, he adds, there was and is quite a price for respectability, namely, that such queer "figments of the Hollywood imagination have no sex lives." Of Hollywood films of the 1990s, he points out that "gays are about as chaste as Franklin Pangborn was" (1998, 51).

While I agree with Goldstein's evaluation of the limitations of contemporary Hollywood's liberalism, I demur against his contention that the queers of yore were presented, or read, as chaste and "harmless." This reading projects contemporary notions of sexual orientation onto an era when gender behavior rather than object choice was the marker of queerness. But even with respect to desire, one need only see Pangborn with an on-screen boyfriend in *Only Yesterday*, disconcerting a homophobic businessman yet bonding with the man's butch wife in *Turnabout*, or admiring Johnny Weissmuller's chest in *Stage Door Canteen* (1943) to realize that Pangborn's persona was far from chaste and had the power to offend. In the cinema, where fantasies meet realities on the horizon of the sociopolitical, Pangborn and company were clearly/queerly many things to many people.

Notes

An earlier version of this essay appeared as David M. Lugowski, "Queering the (New) Deal: Lesbian and Gay Representation and the Depression-Era Cultural Politics of Hollywood's Production Code," *Cinema Journal*, 38.2 (1999), 3–35.

1. All PCA letters cited are from files, named after each film mentioned, in Special Collections, Academy of Motion Picture Arts and Sciences (AMPAS).
2. PCA file, *Nana* (1934); also quoted in Sklar 1991, 129–134. Note the queer connotations, ones that existed in the 1930s, of something being "degenerate."
3. Also quoted in Leff and Simmons 1990, 44.
4. My thanks to Bill Everson for these insights.
5. Press book, *Dracula's Daughter*, Billy Rose Theater Collection, Lincoln Center Library.
6. Interview, Cadmus, in documentary *Paul Cadmus: Enfant Terrible at 80* (David Sutherland, PBS, 1984).
7. Interview, Rhodes, in documentary *Hollywood: The Golden Years* (BBC TV, 1987).
8. "Hailing a new Horton," *New York Times*, June 19, 1938.
9. Clippings file, "Franklin Pangborn," AMPAS. Also quoted in Russo 1987, 34.
10. Scripts and production records, *The Big Noise*, Warner Bros. Archive, USC.

References

Allen, Robert. (1985). *Horrible Prettiness: Burlesque and American Culture*. Chapel Hill: University of North Carolina Press.

Barrios, Richard. (1995). *A Song in the Dark: The Birth of the Musical Film*. New York: Oxford University Press.

Barrios, Richard. (2003). *Screened Out: Playing Gay in Hollywood from Edison to Stonewall*. New York: Routledge.

Benshoff, Harry, & Griffin, Sean. (2006). *Queer Images: A History of Gay and Lesbian Film in America*. Lanham, MD: Rowman & Littlefield.

Black, Gregory. (1994). *Hollywood Censored: Morality Codes, Catholics, and the Movies*. New York: Cambridge University Press.

Boyarin, Daniel, Itzkovitz, Daniel, & Pellegrini, Ann (eds). (2003). *Queer Theory and the Jewish Question*. New York: Columbia University Press.

Chauncey, Jr, George. (1994). *Gay New York: Gender, Urban Culture, and the Making of the Gay Male World, 1890–1940*. New York: Basic Books.

Curtin, Kaier. (1987). *"We Can Always Call Them Bulgarians": The Emergence of Lesbians and Gay Men on the American Stage*. Boston: Alyson Publications.

Doty, Alexander. (1993). *Making Things Perfectly Queer: Interpreting Mass Culture*. Minneapolis: University of Minnesota Press.

Dyer, Richard. (1986). *Heavenly Bodies: Film Stars and Society*. New York: St Martin's Press.

Easthope, Antony. (1990). *What a Man's Gotta Do: The Masculine Myth in Popular Culture*. Boston: Unwin Hyman.

Everson, William K. (1983). "Screwball Comedy: A Reappraisal." *Films in Review*, December, 578–584.

Faderman, Lillian. (1991). *Odd Girls and Twilight Lovers: A History of Lesbian Life in Twentieth-Century America*. New York: Columbia University Press.

Goldstein, Richard. (1998). "'No Sex, Please. We're Gay': The Bad Bargain of Liberal Homophobia in Hollywood and the Media." *Village Voice*, March 31, 51.

Gough, Jamie. (1989). "Theories of Sexual Identity and the Masculinization of the Gay Man." In Simon Shepherd & Mick Wallis (eds), *Coming On Strong: Gay Politics and Culture* (pp. 119–136). London: Unwin Hyman.

Hansen, Miriam. (1991). *Babel and Babylon: Spectatorship in American Silent Film*. Cambridge, MA: Harvard University Press.

Jacobs, Lea. (1992). *The Wages of Sin: Censorship and the Fallen Woman Film, 1928–1942*. Madison: University of Wisconsin Press.

Jenkins, Henry. (1992). *What Made Pistachio Nuts? Early Sound Comedy and the Vaudeville Aesthetic*. New York: Columbia University Press.

Kendall, Elizabeth. (1990). *The Runaway Bride: Hollywood Romantic Comedy of the 1930s*. New York: Anchor Books/Doubleday.

Komarovsky, Mirra. (1940). *The Unemployed Man and His Family: The Effect of Unemployment Upon the Status of the Man in 59 Families*. New York: Octagon.

Kuhn, Annette. (1988). *Cinema, Censorship and Sexuality, 1909–25*. New York: Routledge.

LaCapra, Dominick. (1985). *History and Criticism*. Ithaca: Cornell University Press.

Lawrence, Amy. (2010). "Rudolph Valentino: Italian American." In Patrice Petro (ed.), *Idols of Modernity: Movie Stars of the 1920s* (pp. 87–107). New Brunswick: Rutgers University Press.

Leff, Leonard J., & Simmons, Jerold L. (1990). *The Dame in the Kimono: Hollywood, Censorship and the Production Code from the 1920s to the 1960s*. New York: Doubleday.

Lugowski, David M. (2005). "James Whale." *Senses of Cinema*, 37, October–December, at http://sensesofcinema.com/2005/great-directors/whale/ (accessed March 2015).

Lugowski, David M. (2006). "Queering *Citizen Kane*." In Kylo-Patrick Hart (ed.), *Film and Sexual Politics* (pp. 38–48). Newcastle upon Tyne: Cambridge Scholars Press.

McElvaine, Robert S. (1984). *The Great Depression: America 1929–1941*. New York: Times Books/Random House.

McFadden, Margaret T. (1993). "'America's Boy Friend Who Couldn't Get a Date': Gender, Race and the Cultural Work of the Jack Benny Program 1932–1946." *Journal of American History*, 80.1, 113–134.

Maltby, Richard. (1986). "Baby Face, or How Joe Breen Made Barbara Stanwyck Atone for Causing the Wall Street Crash." *Screen*, 27.2, 22–45.

Maltby, Richard. (1993). "The Production Code and the Hays Office." In Tino Balio, *Grand Design: Hollywood as a Modern Business Industry, 1930–1939* (pp. 37–72). New York: Charles Scribner's Sons.

Marshall, John. (1981). "Pansies, Perverts and Macho Men: Changing Conceptions of Male Homosexuality." In Kenneth Plummer (ed.), *The Making of the Modern Homosexual* (pp. 133–154). Totowa, NJ: Barnes & Noble.

Martin, Olga J. (1937). *Hollywood's Movie Commandments*. New York: H. M. Wilson.

Melosh, Barbara. (1991). *Engendering Culture: Manhood and Womanhood in New Deal Public Art and Theater*. Washington, DC: Smithsonian Institution Press.

Mosse, George. (1996). *The Image of Man: The Creation of Modern Masculinity*. New York: Oxford University Press.

Noriega, Chon. (1990). "Something's Missing Here! Homosexuality and Film Reviews During the Production Code Era, 1934–62." *Cinema Journal*, 30.1, 20–41.

Orwell, George. (1937). *The Road to Wigan Pier*. London: Victor Gollancz.

Peiss, Kathy. (1986). *Cheap Amusements: Working Women and Leisure in Turn-of-the-Century New York*. Philadelphia: Temple University Press.

Russo, Vito. (1987). *The Celluloid Closet: Homosexuality in the Movies*. Revised edn. New York: Harper & Row. (Original work published 1981.)

Scharf, Lois. (1980). *To Work and to Wed: Female Unemployment, Feminism, and the Great Depression*. Westport, CT: Greenwood Press.

Shindler, Colin. (1996). *Hollywood in Crisis: Cinema and American Society 1929–1939*. New York: Routledge.

Sklar, Robert. (1991). "'I Never Want to See That Factory Again': Hollywood's Banned Films in Comparative Context." In Giuliana Muscio (ed.), *Prima del codici 2. Alle porte di Hays* (pp. 129–134). Venice: Biennale di Venezia/Fabri Editori.

Sklar, Robert. (1992). *City Boys: Cagney, Bogart, Garfield*. Princeton: Princeton University Press.

Sklar, Robert. (1994). *Movie-Made America: A Cultural History of American Movies*. Revised and updated. New York: Vintage Books.

Smith-Rosenberg, Carroll. (1985). *Disorderly Conduct: Visions of Gender in Victorian America*. New York: Alfred A. Knopf.

Vasey, Ruth. (1997). *The World According to Hollywood 1918–1939*. Madison: University of Wisconsin Press.

Ware, Susan. (1982). *Holding Their Own: American Women in the 1930s*. New York: Twayne.

Weiss, Andrea. (1991). "'A Queer Feeling When I Look at You': Hollywood Stars and Lesbian Spectatorship in the 1930s." In Christine Gledhill (ed.), *Stardom: Industry of Desire* (pp. 287–304). London: Routledge.

White, Kevin. (1993). *The First Sexual Revolution: The Emergence of Male Heterosexuality in Modern America*. New York: New York University Press.

Wood, Robin. (1981). *Howard Hawks*. Revised edn. London: British Film Institute.

17

There's No Place Like Home
The Hollywood Folk Musical

Desirée J. Garcia
Assistant Professor, Arizona State University, United States

Unlike **show musicals** of the late 1920s and early 1930s, **folk musicals** of the World War II era seamlessly **integrated** story, song, and dance. They replaced earlier themes of aspiration aimed at "putting on a show" and achieving social acceptance with politically conservative themes of "making a home" and preserving already tightly knit families and communities. Desirée J. Garcia explores the paradoxical attitudes concerning rural tradition, **urban migration**, and **modernity** that define the period and inform folk musicals – particularly those produced by **Arthur Freed** at **MGM**, which included ***The Wizard of Oz***, ***Babes in Arms***, and ***Meet Me in St. Louis***. With its nostalgic representation of "a time before the troubling effects of modernity," its cautionary attitude against migration from hearth and home, and its romanticizing of America's cultural traditions, the folk musical became an apt vehicle for promoting American values, as the government's **Office of War Information** clearly understood. Garcia's essay shares ground with Veronica Pravadelli on cinema and the modern woman and Kirsten Moana Thompson on animation and World War II in this volume, and with Kevin L. Stoehr on the A-production Western in the hardcover/online edition.

Additional terms, names, and concepts: Bureau of Motion Pictures (BMP), Motion Picture Producers and Distributors of America (MPPDA), vaudeville, minstrelsy

Commenting to the *New York Times* in 1959, MGM producer Arthur Freed emphasized the importance of portraying the past, with its associations of tranquility, grace, and charm, in the making of successful musical films, saying that "the period musical can capture a charm that many people long for today. It lets us enjoy, for a while, a more easy [*sic*] and more gracious way of life than exists in our now everyday life."[1]

He argued that such images held an immense appeal for audiences who were weary of the fast and often bewildering modern world. The Hollywood musical could transport viewers to a safe place that remains

American Film History: Selected Readings, Origins to 1960, First Edition. Edited by Cynthia Lucia, Roy Grundmann, and Art Simon.
© 2016 John Wiley & Sons, Inc. Published 2016 by John Wiley & Sons, Inc.

intact and impervious to the fragmentation of the present day.

"Period musicals," he asserted, were popular among audiences for their "once upon a time quality."[2] His films, *The Wizard of Oz* (1939), *Babes in Arms* (1939), and *Meet Me in St. Louis* (1944), take place in rural and small-town settings that harbor strong families and insular communities, celebrate ordinary "folk," and express emotion with musical numbers that rise in an organic, integrated fashion from the narrative. These "folk musicals," as Rick Altman (1987, 274) would later describe them, create utopias of community and family life that react against the social atomization of the modern world. In particular, the folk musical reflects the social concerns of one of modernity's most glaring effects – migration. By glorifying family and home life, the folk musical privileges a premigratory existence in which confraternity and familial love triumph in the face of any actual or threatened journeys away from home. In this way, the folk musical reflects a central paradox of modernity that is experienced alternately as individual progress and social deterioration. While the films hark back to a "more easy and gracious way of life," that way of life still remains situated within the modern era – such as the experience of riding a trolley or going to the World's Fair in turn-of-the-century St Louis. While the films do not disavow the progress and conveniences of modern life, of which the cinema itself is an integral product, they do attenuate the destabilizing effects of mobility and migration as experienced by many Americans in the 1930s and 1940s.

By extension, just as the films reveal the paradox of modernity, they also reveal the paradox of "America." As the destination of the migrant's journey, America continues to be a promised land that offers opportunity and a better way of life. Upholding this ideal, the folk musical situates itself in the communities of rural Kansas or turn-of-the-century towns that, at least indirectly, are identified as destinations for migrants. Yet the films also persist in favoring a premigratory state in which staying home, deciding not to migrate, proves to be the better option for the sake of the individual and the family. As in *The Wizard of Oz*, Dorothy longs for a life "over the rainbow," but once there, she realizes that "there's no place like home." Folk musicals like *The Wizard of Oz*, *Babes in Arms*, and *Meet Me in St. Louis* hold these paradoxes of modern life in balance – to migrate and thus affirm the American ideal or to stay home and admit that what is lost in America is too great a cost. The genre is able to depict both sides of the migration experience in this way – a journey is always taken all the while the experience of staying/returning home is achieved. Producers like Freed used home as a powerful weapon to be wielded against the forces of change, namely, geographic mobility and the challenging of traditional values. The folk musical explores the processes of making home, leaving home, and staying home that were used to reflect and attenuate, if temporarily, the social fissures that were present in American society at large.

This essay traces the entry and the adoption of the folk format in the Hollywood musical of the World War II era. During the 1930s, when "race" films employing the folk format such as *Georgia Rose* (1930), *Mayne Yidishe Mame* (1930), and *Allá en el Rancho Grande* (1936) entertained diasporic audiences of African-Americans, Jews, and Mexicans, Hollywood devoted the majority of its musical productions to stories about show business and Broadway. By contrast, when producers did embrace the folk, such as with *Hallelujah!* (1929), *Hearts in Dixie* (1929), and *Fiesta* (1943), the narratives took place far from the world of the stage and featured communities of African-Americans and Mexicans. These films show how Hollywood producers considered the folk to be the realm of peoples of color whose inclination for song and dance was deemed premodern, authentic, and natural, rendering them a cohesive, if segregated, community. Highly romanticized and rooted in racial and ethnic stereotypes, these films limited the range of representation available to peoples of color in mainstream American film.

Hollywood did not create folk musicals for a mainstream (white) audience until the eve of World War II. The genre embraced many of the most potent elements of race cinemas such as sentimentality, melodrama, the exaltation of the home and family, and the joy of cultural identification through communal song and dance. The breakup of families, unprecedented entry of women in the workplace, and stark xenophobia marked the World War II era and made nostalgic portrayals of American home life particularly resonant with cinematic audiences. Hollywood producers such as Freed came to recognize the potency of the folk format, with its ability to wield and soothe the stresses of modern life through its formal integrated structure and nostalgic depictions of home. An analysis of the process by which the folk migrated to the dominant cinema reveals the complexity involved in the production of the Hollywood integrated musical and, more importantly, the influence of marginalized communities on mainstream American culture.

Genre and Modernity

As MGM producer Freed also noted in an article on the history of the musical, "a revolutionary change" occurred within the genre in the late 1930s. Freed remembered: "Gone were the gigantic production numbers, the trick camera angles, the dances and songs that stopped the plot cold until the last chorine waved her last ostrich feather in the camera's focus."[3] Instead, the musical's song and dance numbers became integral parts of the narrative and the plot turned to sentimental themes that procured emotional appeals from the audience. The films produced by Freed's unit at MGM, including *The Wizard of Oz*, *Babes in Arms*, and *Meet Me in St. Louis*, reflect this shift in form and content. The folk musical is that strain of the genre that is most well known among current audiences for its characters who can move seamlessly into song, managing to achieve the spontaneous performance of community where "everyone is a neighbor, where each season's rituals bring the entire population together" (Altman 1987, 274). Integration, social cohesion, ritual, and tradition are the folk musical's driving forces.

By contrast, the show musical revolves around the world of the stage and efforts of individual performers to achieve success. This was the form that dominated the musical film since the genre's inception with *The Jazz Singer* (1927). Such stories legitimize their musical numbers by restraining them to rehearsal and performance sequences on a stage (*42nd Street*, 1933; the *Gold Diggers* films of 1933, 1935, and 1937), casting its characters as performers themselves (such as Fred Astaire's characters in *Flying Down to Rio*, 1933; *The Gay Divorcee*, 1934; *Follow the Fleet*, 1936), or creating scenarios of imaginative fantasy wherein anything can happen (such as the Jeannette MacDonald and Nelson Eddy operettas). The show musical, as Jane Feuer has argued, is inherently self-reflexive in that it valorizes entertainment itself (2002, 31).

Yet the show and folk formats not only represent technical distinctions in form, they indicate the different social functions of the musical as well. The show format positions the performers of the screen as outsiders "performing" their way into social acceptance by the (potentially hostile) film's audience of insiders. The need for the contextualization of each musical number within the boundaries of a proscenium arch and the primary role that the audience has in critiquing the entertainment make the show musical a self-conscious, insecure strain of the genre. It operates from the assumption that the entertainment, the success of the show, may or may not be well received by the audience. The dramatic tension of the film hinges on this potentiality and the film ends happily only when the audience has sanctioned the "good" performance. This was the preferred form of the musical film by the genre's producers in Hollywood, themselves eastern European immigrant Jews and their descendants. As outsiders in control of a mainstream, American industry, studio executives like Harry Warner and Louis B. Mayer sanctioned their position as arbiters of entertainment through the self-reflexive show musical.

Conversely, the folk musical creates an on-screen community that mirrors the (friendly) community of the film's audience. It does so by breaking down the barrier between performer and audience in order to achieve social harmony and cultural solidarity through song and dance. Transcending the insider/outsider dynamic in American life, the folk musical envelopes the audience and performer in shared communal experiences through universal themes of familial love and loss and the musical expression of emotion. While the show musical occasionally featured integrated musical numbers that arise organically from the story and advance the narrative action – such as in the Fred Astaire and Ginger Rogers vehicles at RKO – the integrated form became more closely associated with the MGM folk musical in the late 1930s and 1940s (Mueller 1984).

Through its very formal structure, the integrated musical joins together the film's diegetic world – its characters, plot, and mise-en-scène – in such a way that it fills the void left by the disintegration of modern life. It produces social integration through its very formal structure of uniting music, community, and narrative. The genre achieves utopia by addressing inadequacies in American society such as scarcity, exhaustion from labor, dreariness of monotonous days, manipulation, and fragmentation and displacement. The "temporary answers" to these problems posed by the musical's abundance, energy, and formation of community unsettle and complicate a genre that is criticized for its vapidity (Dyer 2002). Escapism in the musical is a function of its quest for utopia, the alleviation of very real concerns felt by marginalized, often ethnoracialized audiences. It calls attention to the dissatisfaction that certain groups felt with modern American life, unsettling the notion of America as a promised land and, instead, presenting it as a place from which one needs to escape. This was a common feature of Yiddish, African-American, and Mexican cinemas of the 1930s that used the integrated, folk format in order to reflect and respond to the process of migrating to and within the United States. With formal and narrative conventions, producers of these cinemas crafted images of belonging in order to counter the experience of being an outsider in American society – a reality experienced by successive waves of im/migrants throughout the twentieth century.

Dual products of modernity, cinema and migration had a dialogic relationship throughout this period. This dynamic is further complicated by the immigrant heritage of the Hollywood studio executives. These men operated in a time when assimilation demanded the suppression of ethnicity on the screen. Yet, as Mark Winokur explains, this only led to the presence of a "disguised ethnicity" that was transposed onto the forms and conventions of film genres like antic and screwball comedy (1996, 14).

Similarly, a migrant sensibility pervades the narrative and formal structure of the folk musical. Though it is never mentioned in his biographies, including what is considered the authoritative work by Hugh Fordin (1975, reprinted 1996), Freed's parents were part of the immigration of eastern European Jews at the turn of the twentieth century. Freed's Jewishness, like the relationship of the Hollywood studio heads to their own Jewish background, was repressed in his public career but everywhere inscribed onto his craft. Fundamental to Freed's style was his own faith in the malleability of the folk:

> American folk music, plus the folk lore [*sic*] that goes with it, yields the most universally appealing, interesting and satisfying musical. It is material known by and beloved of the whole population, and its values are not transient ... [4]

Freed's position as an immigrant outsider and his own desire to assimilate led him to make such optimistic statements about the folk musical's universal appeal. As a result, the experiences of the dispossessed, and the basic struggle between insider/outsider status in society, became displaced onto the formal elements of the Hollywood musical.[5]

While this type of engagement with the migrant experience is subtle and indirect, it nevertheless demonstrates the historical role that cinema has had in being a part of and responding to modernity and its effects. As a form of popular culture, cinema is a polysemic entertainment that reflects the dynamic and diverse sociocultural environment in which it was born. The musical's basic formal features catered to this desire for excitement by emphasizing motion through elaborate choreography and quickly changing camera angles, and by offering sensorial stimuli with vibrant color and dramatic lighting. In particular, the use of Technicolor, a highly saturated film-coloring process, gave musicals a stunning effect by producing a hyperrealistic visual world.

Nevertheless, scholarly accounts of the history of moviegoing reveal that the experience could also attenuate the alienating effects of modernity. These accounts show how going to the movies was very much a social activity in the first decades of motion picture exhibition.[6] With its performances of communal song and dance, the folk musical preserved the social function of the early moviegoing experience. Just as the movies were an outgrowth and reflection of modernity, providing spectators with examples of technological progress and visual stimulus, the movies could also provide an experience of soothing modernity's harsher effects such as alienation, migration, and the separation from home and loved ones. The choreography in musicals, though exciting, was also well ordered and graceful and served to bring communities together, not to separate them. The "sound" of such films is one of voices singing in harmony, not in chaotic opposition. Thus, being involved in going to the movies was a paradox that at once reflected modernity's marvels, of which the cinema was an integral part, and offered spectators the ability to hold onto what had been lost in modern life.

In particular, the folk musical serves this reactionary function and stands in stark contrast to the other films that came out of Hollywood in the 1930s and 1940s, including *The Life of Emile Zola* (1937), *Angels with*

Dirty Faces (1938), and *Citizen Kane* (1941), which addressed the social realities of vice, injustice, and poverty.[7] While these films are critically and artistically significant, it is important to understand why musical films were so much more popular amongst audiences. Musicals were the most expensive genre to make, but studios invested in them because they also yielded the highest revenue.[8] Their appeal to moviegoers, I argue, stems from the musical's ability to place dual valences on mobility and stasis. The images that the folk musical offers are of cohesive communities who are ultimately impervious to the harsh effects of migration. With their integrated formal structure, in which musical numbers arise organically and are performed collectively, the films ease the disintegration that characterized contemporary American society.

The Hollywood Musical and Wartime America

It is no coincidence that producers and audiences embraced the more socially inclusive folk musical during the late 1930s and 1940s. Demands for unity on the home front, while American troops fought the war abroad, were codified into official Hollywood procedure through the collaborative efforts of the studios and the Bureau of Motion Pictures (BMP) of the Office of War Information (OWI). As a result, Hollywood released extremely patriotic pictures that strongly emitted a sense of duty to and sacrifice for the country, family, and home. The coalition between Hollywood and Washington meant little interference with production and, more importantly, the sanctioned approval of the motion picture industry. It also meant that the industry would not have to undergo the war conversion experienced by the steel, auto manufacturing, and construction industries.[9]

Hollywood producers and representatives of the OWI believed that, since American films were superior in both production quality and appeal, they were best suited to be exported around the world. As head of the BMP, Francis S. Harmon declared that the movie industry "recognizes its responsibility to the free society of which it is both a part and a symbol."[10] In this context, the Motion Picture Producers and Distributors of America (MPPDA), the movie industry's self-regulatory organization, became the "silent salesman" of American life. As Ruth Vasey has found, the MPPDA actively "encouraged the perception of the [film] medium as universal, capable of transcending cultural boundaries" (1997, 44), in order to secure American cinema the broadest appeal and revenue possible. In order to create this perception, producers had to make films that appealed widely to a diversity of peoples both at home and abroad. The MPPDA's self-censoring agency, the Production Code Administration (PCA), facilitated this project, as its officers worked closely with producers to foster textual ambiguity and multivalence in its films. Since the advent of sound, the PCA and Hollywood producers labored to create levels of interpretation for the audience that enabled spectators to "read through the action on the screen to identify deliberately displaced meanings" (Vasey 1997, 105), depending on the spectator's willingness and experience. This strategy minimized potential offense and maximized the film's relevance to a diverse audience.

The folk musical was one of Hollywood's primary vehicles of this sentiment because it suggested a time before the troubling effects of modernity. It offered viewers a palliative that removes elements of difference most blatantly suggested by the presence of immigrants and peoples of color from a homogeneous and white, middle-class community of Americans. As such, the folk musical spoke to the concerns of the majority. The destabilizing effects of wartime included the separation of family members as men went to war and left their families behind. Higher rates of marriage between young couples about to be separated by the war and the immediate desire to create families at war's end were the primary means by which Americans dealt with an uncertain future (May 1988). Images of secure and stable home life, wherein able fathers supported their wives and children and mothers preserved the sanctity of the domestic sphere, abounded from the Hollywood studios and worked to reinforce and sanctify the middle-class ideal.

In this period, the folk musical took form and gained acclaim for its ability to alleviate the concerns of a diverse range of peoples with nostalgia, song, and dance. At the center of such imagery was the powerful symbol of home. The following analysis of three folk musicals, *The Wizard of Oz*, *Babes in Arms*, and *Meet Me in St. Louis*, shows how such films have elements of fantasy, homogeneity, and wholesomeness, but they also bespeak the experience of modernity on the levels of form and content.

The Wizard of Oz (1939)

The phrase "there's no place like home" permeates one of Hollywood's most beloved musicals, *The Wizard of Oz*. While the film contains a substantial dose of fantasy, which prompts Rick Altman (1987) to categorize it as one of Hollywood's fantasy musicals, I argue for its consideration as a folk musical. Combining sepiatone photography with brilliant Technicolor, *The Wizard of Oz* tells the story of Dorothy, a young girl from Kansas, who dreams of a better life "over the rainbow." That dream comes true when a violent tornado picks up her farmhouse and deposits it in the magical world of Oz. Her journey through Oz is a bewildering and at times dangerous one. But, in the end, it is her profound desire to return to Kansas that eventually reunites Dorothy with her family on the farm. The trip to Oz forces her to realize that, in producer Arthur Freed's words, "What we often strive for so earnestly has been ours all the time, but we have been unable to see it."[11] As clearly expressed by the film's narrative and musical score, the real dream is about familiarity, family, and home. Dorothy, the migrant, realizes that the fulfillment of her dreams is not to be found over the rainbow, but in her own backyard.

Why is home so important in this film and why is there no place like it? The construction of "home" in the folk musical is a crucial project for its makers. It is the center around which the narrative turns and provides the physical place that serves as the symbol of belonging, safety, and familiarity. The palliative in the folk musical resides in the image of home as a stable and recognizable, if imagined, place. This place is often depicted in a richly nostalgic fashion with the narrative set in the past and/or in a rural, precosmopolitan setting – a Kansas farm in *The Wizard of Oz*, small-town America in *Babes in Arms*, and St Louis on the cusp of modernity in *Meet Me in St. Louis*. These places themselves carry dual connotations such as the simultaneous invocations of agricultural plenty and Dust Bowl migration that the depiction of Kansas might conjure. Such films also cast the utopian world of "home" as a universal one onto which diverse audiences could project their own specific experiences. In the folk musical's diegetic world (its narrative, characters, and mise-en-scène), the paradox of modernity – progress versus deterioration, gain versus loss – is encoded so that a simultaneous engagement with and attenuation of the reality of migration can occur. The films take the audience on a journey, but they ultimately return them safely home again.

In *The Wizard of Oz* Freed injected the primary theme of home, the process of leaving it and the desire to return to it, into Frank Baum's story (Harmetz 1989, 91). The phrase "there's no place like home" is a thematic addition by the film's producers. Consequently, the theme prompted scriptwriters to elaborate on the Kansas sequences. Whereas Baum's book devotes only two pages at the beginning and nine lines at the end to the Kansas sections, the film elaborates on Dorothy's relationship to her family (Uncle Henry and Auntie Em), friends (Zeke, Hunk, and Hickory), and foes (Miss Gulch) (Rushdie 1992, 14). In this way, Dorothy's home makes up a larger part of the story.

While it is Dorothy's home, the Kansas farm is also marked by the economic plight and material scarcity that characterized Depression-era agricultural communities. Filmed in nostalgic sepia tone, the house in which she lives is a humble, wooden structure that seems vulnerable on the vastness of the farm property. From the outset, the farm seems in jeopardy as Auntie Em and Uncle Henry scramble to fix the incubator in which they keep the farm's chicks. Similarly, the film invokes the region's susceptibility to environmental disasters such as the Dust Bowl with the catastrophe wrought by the twister on Dorothy's home. The Kansas sequence, therefore, is meant to be a realistic portrait of Midwestern farm life that is cast into harsh relief by the vibrant and plentiful land of Oz.

One way in which the film makes Kansas a "home" is in the sympathetic portrayal of the three farmhands, played by Ray Bolger, Jack Haley, and Bert Lahr, who reappear in Oz as the Scarecrow, the Tin Man, and the Cowardly Lion, respectively. In Oz, they become Dorothy's fellow migrants in search of what they too are missing. While at first glance the Scarecrow, Tin Man, and Cowardly Lion appear to be premodern characters (due to their associations with the farm and nature), they are revealed in the Oz sequence to be products of modernity. The Scarecrow is missing brains. He is a rube who does not know anything and is bewildered and confused by everything he encounters. Like the shock with which urbanity confronts

Figure 17.1 Dorothy (Judy Garland), in Norman Taurog, King Vidor, Victor Fleming, Mervyn LeRoy, and George Cukor's *The Wizard of Oz* (1939, producers Mervyn LeRoy and Arthur Freed), realizes that her adventure in Oz was merely a dream and she is safe at home.

the rural dweller, the wonders of Oz and the Emerald City mystify and assault the Scarecrow. Similarly, the Tin Man is a hollow man made of metal. He has lost his heart, that which makes him human and able to feel. Born of industry, the Tin Man is adrift from the natural world of living things. Lastly, the Cowardly Lion cannot be king of the forest because of his timidity and effeminacy. Even the wild beasts of the forest have become overcivilized by modern society to the point that they cannot fulfill their natural function as rulers and predators. In his solo performance, the Lion sings, "I'm just a dandy lion, a fate I don't deserve!"

Yet, it is Dorothy's concern, her yearning for home, that drives the film's narrative and musical score. Early on in the production process, composer/arranger Roger Edens wrote a lyric that would not be used, although it assisted the many others who wrote and composed for the film. Edens wrote the following as a song for Dorothy to sing while in Oz:

> Mid pleasures and palaces,
> In London, Paris, and Rome,
> There is no place quite like Kansas
> Any my little Kansas home-sweet-home.[12]

The song emphasizes what would become the "there's no place like home" theme in the film with its assertions of the singular place that is Kansas precisely because it is "home." Contributing to the same theme, composer Herbert Stothart used instrumental versions of "Home Sweet Home" and a children's nursery song, "My Castle's in the Courtyard," to undergird the action (Fricke 1993).

Much attention has been paid to the film's most famous song, "Over the Rainbow." Written by Harold Arlen and E. Y. "Yip" Harburg, both sons of Jewish immigrants, the song expresses the desire to leave, a common desire among im/migrants who look elsewhere for a better life. Yet as the film's score and narrative prove, the desire to return home again is more palpable in the film. The journey turns into a nightmare for Dorothy, from the first violent act of being caught in a tornado to being pursued by the Wicked Witch. Desperate to return home once she learns what lies beyond the rainbow, Dorothy reenacts the common experience felt by im/migrants who realize that America is not the land of promise that they had hoped it would be.

Dorothy returns to find the family intact just as she left it. Miss Gulch, who first threatened Dorothy's dog, Toto, seems to have been removed as a menace, leaving the self-sufficient American family strong in the face of external perils. With such an illustration of home and family life, the producers of *The Wizard of Oz* prove their commitment to the concept of home as an indestructible bulwark that remains and assists the im/migrant in the face of changes in modern uncertainties. Seen in this way, the film is not merely about escape but, rather, about the implied positives and negatives of staying home (stasis) versus leaving home (mobility).

Babes in Arms (1939)

The Wizard of Oz was Arthur Freed's first producing job at MGM. Mayer and Freed developed a symbiotic relationship in the late 1930s that would last until the studio changed hands in 1948. They were both sentimental men who loved music, family, and the depiction of stable homes and communities on the screen. The musical film, as the most popular and successful genre at MGM, fulfilled Mayer's vision largely through the efforts of Arthur Freed, who idolized the concepts of home, morality, and family (Fordin 1996, 10).

The film *Babes in Arms* privileges the values embraced by the Freed unit. In Hollywood, the film took on a drastically different tone than it had as a Broadway show two years earlier. Although the show's original composer/lyricist team of Richard Rodgers and Lorenz Hart contributed to the film, all but two of the original songs ("Babes in Arms" and "Where or When") were cut and several new ones, written by Freed himself, were added. Andrea Most (2004) notes that the original *Babes in Arms* was a complex work that introduced and grappled with such issues as political activism, ambivalence about New Deal legislation, and race relations.

In the Broadway version, the story revolves around the efforts of children, whose parents are ex-vaudevillians, to keep from being sent to a New Deal "work farm" while their parents are away working for the Works Progress Administration (WPA). The "babes" in the story represent a variety of characters including intellectuals, lawyers, members of the working class, and two black hoofers played by Fayard and Harold Nicholas of the Nicholas Brothers tap dancing team. The characters put on a show, in the hopes of raising money to keep them off of the work farm.

In Freed's hands, the show takes on quite different meaning. Much like he pressed for "home" to be the central theme in *The Wizard of Oz*, Freed placed at the foreground of the film the struggle between parents and children and what it means to have to leave home as a result of modern dislocation. In the case of the folk musical, for both Freed and Hollywood, leaving home was a far more evocative and universally relevant theme in that it raises issues of filial piety, the differences between old world and new, and the struggle to hold on to one's roots in a changing society.

Babes in Arms, the film version, begins with a montage sequence that highlights the stars of vaudeville in the early twentieth century. Joe Moran, one of vaudeville's greats, has just finished his act at the Palace Theatre and is informed by a stagehand that his wife has given birth to a son. He announces his happy news to the audience and they applaud enthusiastically for his growing family. With this opening scene, the film establishes the marriage of vaudeville entertainment with family and community. While toasting to the birth of his son, Joe gives a speech to his fellow vaudevillians:

> Vaudeville is the greatest entertainment in the world. It made me what I am today, a papa! And it's pretty nice, I tell ya. Having that little home down there on Long Island where ya can take the wife and kiddies. Where ya can lay off all summer long in the country, instead of a crowded boarding house in the roaring forties where there's nothing but streets to play in like I had when I was a kid. What other business is like that, I ask ya? There ain't none! Vaudeville, boy, you're something!

Vaudeville has allowed for Joe's success in his personal life and the world of popular entertainment.

As the Morans' children get older, they are woven into their parents' act. The film continues with a montage sequence that shows the children with their first pair of tap shoes, hats, and canes. Such a recasting of vaudeville as a family-building entertainment revises the historical record in which this itinerant form of entertainment broke up families rather than built them.

Nevertheless, the central concern in *Babes* is the imminent death of vaudeville due to the rising popularity of the movies. This new technological advancement, with its mechanical nature and its impersonality, threatens to wipe out this more family-based entertainment. In setting up vaudeville's association with parents and the more "Old World" associations of confraternity, with its groupings of family and friends all held together by their common lifestyle, values, and desires as performers, the film suggests that the new generation is in danger of losing all that their parents hold dear.

The headlines "Talkies Arrive!" – "Talkies Top Vaudeville!" – and "Vaudeville is Doomed!" flash upon the screen. In the next scene, Joe Moran is despairing about the death of vaudeville to his family in their comfortable Long Island home. The children, Mickey and Molly, are now teenagers and both are aspiring to a career in show business. But Joe tries to discourage them. Once an advocate for show business, Joe is now disillusioned by a life in the theater. In a fit of frustration, he declares, "Mickey had better learn a trade and give up show business or he'll end up like me!" His family urges him to give vaudeville one more try and he organizes their town of ex-vaudevillians into a road show. When the children ask to go along, the parents argue that entertainment is too unstable a career for them. The children, the parents admonish, should get an education to become doctors and lawyers, not performers.

With the parents away, a social worker, Martha Steele, played by Margaret Hamilton, harasses the "babes." Similar to many social and settlement house workers who attempted to alleviate the problems of urban slums at the turn of the century, Miss Steele does not understand the needs and concerns of this community. Instead, she believes the kids will become hooligans if someone does not intervene. Like her role as the Wicked Witch in *The Wizard of Oz*, Hamilton's character in *Babes* poses a threat to the migrant in search of home. She takes the kids to court, but ultimately, Mickey wins the judge's sympathy by tearfully imploring:

> I'm so worried about my family, Judge, I'm sick inside me! We're not her kind of people or yours either. We belong in show business … I'm not sayin' I hate her, but why can't people leave other people alone?

Mickey makes a case for show people and a society that is more tolerant of difference. He tries to explain that Miss Steele and the Judge do not understand show people and should not be allowed to impose their will and standards of living on them.

In the name of holding their family together and proving that they have chosen a valid and successful career in the theater, the kids put on a show. If the show is a failure, the welfare of their families and their town is in jeopardy. This lends a great degree of urgency to the film's first major musical number, "Babes in Arms." Just after being instructed that they are not to accompany their parents on the road, the kids commit to putting on a show "in the barn." One boy begins the song – "They call us babes in arms, but we are babes in armor" – as the others march behind them through their town. Boys and girls join from neighboring houses until all are joined as a unified community. Directed by Busby Berkeley, this number takes on a militant tone as the kids finish their song by stoking a large bonfire. Yet, instead of a political protest, as occurs in the Broadway version, the number is a sung commitment to their homes, families, and each other in the film.

The show that the kids put on in the barn is, in fact, a celebration of vaudeville, that form of entertainment that made their parents' careers. As a celebration of the past, the show within the film, also called "Babes in Arms," demonstrates that the kids have an appreciation for their parents' values and contributions to the business. These include sentimentality and the showing of emotion as well as an homage to past entertainment forms such as minstrelsy. In fact, much of the show "Babes in Arms" as it is revealed in the film is a minstrel show. With the lead characters Mickey (played by Mickey Rooney) and Patsy (Judy Garland) at the forefront, the cast wears blackface and sings such classic minstrel numbers as "I'm Just Wild About Harry" and "Mr Bones" and sentimental, period tunes like "Ida" and "On Moonlight

Bay." Patsy begins this sequence with a dedication to her forefathers in entertainment:

> Gee, I'd like to be a minstrel man
> I'd like to black my face, put on a stove
> pipe hat
> Get out an old banjo and go once again
> down memory lane
> With that old-fashioned minstrel show!

Against a plantation-scene backdrop and with the exaggerated eye-rolling, gestures, and dialect of minstrelsy, the kids celebrate an "old-fashioned minstrel show" of "daddy's" generation. The film does not include African-Americans in the cast in contrast to the Broadway show. Instead of exploring African-Americans' right to entertain as the Broadway version does with the Nicholas Brothers routines, the film references black culture in a reactionary, nostalgic fashion. The heritage of black musical entertainment is woven into the film's celebration of minstrelsy, but it is just as much a celebration of the appropriation of that entertainment for the pleasure of a white audience. In this way, the film reflects Eric Lott's (1995) assertions about minstrelsy in American culture. This particular form of entertainment essentializes African-Americans to the level of derogatory stereotype (eye-rolling, chicken stealing), while it places black culture at the center of an idyllic, more simplistic past that is untainted by modernity.

By invoking this minstrel tradition, the kids in *Babes in Arms* engage in the "love and theft" of black culture in order to foreground the film's central message, which is the importance of family (Lott 1995, 4–6). Blackface minstrelsy also becomes part of the larger project of *Babes in Arms*, which is a celebration of past entertainment forms for their perceived wholesomeness and simplicity ("go once again down memory lane") and their association with a time that valued sentimentality and familial values ("My Daddy was a minstrel man"). Nevertheless, such themes are also often part of the nostalgic mystification of racial oppression.[13]

In addition, if one considers that Hollywood films such as *Hallelujah!* and *Hearts in Dixie* were integrationist folk musicals rather than vaudeville-like show musicals, then this instance of minstrelsy in *Babes in Arms* also ignores the formation of the musical film as a genre. The film's elision of this more recent form of black film performance constitutes a form of generic blackface: It denies the reality of the black experience in musical film and prefers the atavistic. In other words, it replicates on the level of genre history what blackface does through semiotics.

The film justifies this atavistic use of black music when the minstrel number gains the attention of a theatrical producer who decides to take "Babes in Arms" to Broadway. He declares his commitment to past forms of entertainment by declaring, "old-fashioned sentiment isn't taboo anymore." But Mickey refuses to go without his parents, who have failed with their road show. Colluding with the producer, Mickey secures his father work with the show so that Joe will feel needed and valued once more. What was once at stake in leaving home has been sidestepped, as Mickey proves that not only can you secure home, you can take it with you as well. The kids' show on Broadway saves the community from financial ruin and the pestering of Miss Steele, and preserves the family with an act of filial gratitude. At the same time, entertainment such as vaudeville, and, by extension, the *Babes in Arms* film that privileges vaudeville, is commemorated as being a major contribution to American culture.

Just as the film's first scenes associate vaudeville with family, so does its finale identify vaudeville's inheritor, the movie musical, with the virtue of family and the American people. In this way, the film draws upon the show musical format. It makes a plea for entertainment, the movies, and movies' use as an ambassador of Americanism. Coming on the heels of the Nazi invasion of Poland and on the cusp of the US entry into war, *Babes in Arms* ends with the song "God's Country," written by Harold Arlen and "Yip" Harburg as a patriotic salute to the United States, the diversity of its peoples, and the freedom to live one's life in happiness:

> Hi there, neighbor / Goin' my way
> East or West on the Lincoln Highway?
> Hi there, Yankee, Give out with a great big thankee,
> You're in God's Country.

The kids perform this number by walking through the rows of the theater's audience and the audience joins in singing with them. The song invokes such modern symbols as the Lincoln Highway that ran the length of the United States from Times Square in

New York City to Lincoln Park in San Francisco. Uniting the East and West Coasts, this "Main Street across America," as it was popularly called, signified the progress of modern life and its capacity to foment social unity and democracy rather then disunity and fragmentation (Wallis & Williamson 2007). Furthermore, the "God's Country" lyric references figures of popular entertainment, including George Jessel, Al Jolson, Greta Garbo, and Norma Shearer, as representative of America's strengths for its ability to impart tolerance and social inclusion ("We've got no duce, we've got no fuhrer, / But we've got Garbo and Norma Shearer"). Mickey clarifies the film's integrationist message when he exclaims, "Gee, it's bigger than just a show. It's everybody in the country!"

Meet Me in St. Louis (1944)

The prospect of leaving home takes a much darker turn in Freed's *Meet Me in St. Louis.* Set in St Louis in the year before the 1904 World's Fair and based on the story by Sally Benson, this film follows the activities of the Smith family from their most menial concerns such as ketchup-making to making major decisions, such as whether to move to New York City. Vincente Minnelli brought his eye for color and period detail to the film as director, and Judy Garland stars as the Smith daughter who falls in love with the "boy next door." The home in St Louis is a perfect one. Grandpa, Mr and Mrs Smith, and their children Rose, Esther, Lon, Agnes, and Tootie plus Katy, their maid, make up this household. According to Gerald Kaufman (1994), screenwriters Fred Finkelhoffe and Irving Brecher wanted to create a "unity of place" by basing most of the action in and around the Smith home. Toward this aim, they eliminated scenes that had been planned that took place at Princeton University, the Smiths' grandparents' home in Wisconsin, and Mr Smith's office.

The community that the film evokes – St Louis of 1903 – is one of safety, cohesion, and permanency. The first scene of the film shows as much when the title song, "Meet Me in St. Louis," gets passed from Agnes, the young daughter walking up the staircase, to Grandpa in the washroom, to Esther (played by Judy Garland), to an elder sister, Rose, just arriving home in a horse and buggy. The number demonstrates how the family is intertwined by a set of emotions portrayed by the song, conveying hope and expectation for the coming of the fair and the glory of St Louis. The spontaneous and natural way in which the various members of the family carry the verse demonstrates the family's unity. Other numbers in which the family shows its solidarity include "Under the Bamboo Tree," "Skip to My Lou," and "The Trolley Song." These numbers perform and establish community in the film, and the nostalgia for real period tunes, such as "Meet Me in St. Louis" and "Skip to My Lou," give the film's audience a means of identifying with the community on the screen.

While the real city of St Louis was a bustling metropolis in 1903, which made it a prime candidate to host the World's Fair, Freed recasts it in more comforting terms. The evidence of modern life is present, but it is contained and woven into the film's overall project of crafting social and familial unity. In an early scene, the family eats dinner together in anticipation of a phone call from Rose's boyfriend. She hopes that he is calling to propose. The boyfriend does call, but he does not ask the hoped-for question. To Rose's embarrassment, the entire family has witnessed the conversation. By placing such a modern invention as the telephone in the dining room, Freed and Minnelli integrate modernity into the family's daily life in a way that is nonthreatening. While it causes Rose some discomfort, the family shares in the use of the telephone just as it shares in everything else. The coming of the telephone has not produced the fracturing of society.

The film handles the streetcar trolley in the same fashion. At the turn of the century, such a contraption was a source of stress, noise, and, not infrequently, physical harm. It was an object of fear and fascination and embodied the shocking and jolting experience of the modern city. Contemporary newspapers reported in sensational terms the many accidents, injuries, and deaths of pedestrians at the hands of the streetcar (Singer 2001). As part of the "shock effect" of urban life that Walter Benjamin (1968) identified, the trolley altered not only the visual experience of the city, but also the aural and physical experience. Such an impression is not reflected in *Meet Me in St. Louis.* Instead, "The Trolley Song" is a rollicking and blissful ride the young people take to see the fairgrounds. Judy Garland sings the song along with her many friends as she rides the rolling trolley. While the lyrics suggest the new aural dimension of urban life ("Clang, clang, clang went the trolley / Ding, ding, ding went the bell"), they place it within the context of a comforting and fun experience of comradeship and romance ("Zing, zing, zing went my heartstrings / From the moment I saw him I fell ... "). In this way, the folk musical could ease the "shock effect" of modernity by weaving it into the musical's formal structure and enlisting it toward the project of social integration.

Yet, this harmony is threatened when Papa brings news of his imminent transfer to a law firm in New York City. The position will be an advancement for his career and will, he hopes, mean a better life for the family. But the family treats his news as a catastrophe. The Smiths go from having a pleasant celebration on Halloween to despair and sadness:

MR SMITH: It's all settled. We're moving to New York!

MRS SMITH: I must say, you're being very calm about the way you pack us off lock, stock, and barrel.

MR SMITH: I've got the future to think about. The future for all of us. I've got to worry about where the money is coming from with Lon off to Princeton and Rose off to college.

ESTHER: I can't move to New York, I just can't!

AGNES: I'm taking my cat. Lady Baby goes wherever I go.

KATY: Where ya goin' to keep her? Cooped up in a tenement?

AGNES: For pity's sake, don't they have houses in New York?

ROSE: Rich people have houses. People like us live in flats, hundreds of flats in one building.

TOOTIE: I'd rather be poor if we could only stay here! I'd rather go with the orphaluns, at the orphaluns home!

As this dialogue suggests, New York City in 1903 was an immigrant city. In the diegesis of the film, St Louis is cast as a small town, even though in reality it was a major urban center ("New York is a big city. Not that St Louis isn't big, but it just doesn't seem very big out here where we live"). In order to make a stark contrast between modern New York and the home of the Smith family, such a reinvention was necessary. Tenements, buck stoves, and cramped space were realities for many of the immigrants who lived and worked in New York. The Smiths fear that theirs will be the immigrants' experience, that not only their living space will change, but their familial makeup will be in jeopardy. Will Katy and Grandpa be able to live with them now that there will be space constraints? What will happen to the budding romances of Rose and Esther? And will Tootie be able to grow up in a safe and healthy environment similar to the one she enjoys in St Louis? These are all concerns to be considered by the immigrant in search of a better life. Producer Arthur Freed, his own family constantly disrupted by displacements, declared that New York should be "the villain" in this film. By contrast, the original Benson story devotes only three pages to the New York episode (Kaufman 1994, 15).

As the family leaves the dinner table in despair, only Mr and Mrs Smith remain. Mrs Smith goes to the piano, a symbol of family coherence and middle-class status. She begins to play the song, "You and I," which was written by Freed for the film:

Time goes by
But we'll be together
You and I.

As she sings, Mr Smith joins her (his voice is dubbed by Freed), and, one by one, the family members return to the room to listen to their parents. "You and I" is an assertion that the family will not be separated and that the love between them will bind them together no matter what happens.

In a subsequent scene, however, the terror of leaving is made real through the perspective of the youngest Smith, Tootie. Played by child actress Margaret O'Brien with great emotional hysteria, Tootie grows despondent while listening to Esther singing "Have Yourself a Merry Little Christmas." Written for the film by Ralph Blane and Hugh Martin, this song expresses the hope that the family might be united sometime in the future though they may be separated for the time being. Initially, however, the song's lyric reflected a disillusioned and even sinister vision for the family: "Have yourself a merry little Christmas, it may be your last / Next year we may all be living in the past." In a 2006 interview with Terry Gross on NPR, Martin referred to the original lyric as "so lugubrious that Judy Garland refused to sing it." Other phrases of the original referred to "Faithful friends who were dear to us will be near to us no more" and "No good times like the olden days,

Figure 17.2 The Smith family, in Vincente Minnelli's *Meet Me in St. Louis* (1944, producer Arthur Freed), rejoices at the news that they will not move to New York after all.

happy golden days of yore." Garland told Martin, "If I sing that to little Margaret O'Brien, they'll think I'm a monster." Upon Garland's request, Martin altered the lyric to be lighter and more hopeful in tone. In the completed film, Garland sings, "Have yourself a merry little Christmas, / Let your heart be light." And instead of separating the Smiths from their "faithful friends," the final lyric promises that they "will be near to us once more."[14]

The two versions of this song reflect the paradox of modernity that exists in the Freed folk musicals. The earlier version admits the shocks and jolts of migration, a reality of modern life that affected a range of peoples. It admits that when the migrant leaves home, it is not a happy process even while it is a necessary one ("Next year we may all be living in the past"). It also suggests the impossibility of returning home ("No good times like the olden days, happy golden days of yore"). Furthermore, the song indicates that the social integration of home is one of the key comforts that will be lost in the process of migration ("Faithful friends who were dear to us will be near to us no more").

The second and official version of the song attenuates these harsh effects. It provides a utopian vision of home as something that remains intact and can even be brought with the migrant. The folk musical achieves this function with its narrative, such as in the final lyric of "Have Yourself a Merry Little Christmas" ("Some day soon we all will be together"), as well as *in the act* of watching the film itself. Within the context of the movie theater, the past could be brought into the present, thus easing the shock of migration. In the process, the musical film conceals itself as a cultural product that is synecdochic of modern life. The folk musical held the positive and negative aspects of migration in precarious balance by suggesting that the future will be bright ("Next year all our troubles will be miles away") while it admits to the pain, however much in attenuated form, associated with having to migrate in the first place ("Until then, we'll have to muddle through somehow").

Despite the gentle and hopeful sentiment, the song propels Tootie into a fitful rage. She runs into the cold, snowy night and begins to knock down the heads and bodies of the snowmen that the family had made earlier that day. She screams to Esther, "Nobody's gonna have them, not if we're going to New York. I'd rather kill them if we can't take them with us!" Clearly for Tootie, what is being left behind far outweighs any merit that their "better life" in New York City promises.

Tootie's hysterical outburst is what prompts Mr Smith to change his mind about the move. The prospect of leaving proves to be too painful for all involved. The film's happy ending occurs when Mr Smith realizes that he has made a mistake and announces that the family will stay in St Louis. Mr Smith walks through his house and observes the bare walls and packed boxes on Christmas Eve. Suddenly, while he is about to light his pipe, the glow of the burning match illuminates his face and, as though by divine inspiration, he realizes the importance of remaining at home.

He calls the family to his side and, in a joyous scene, they embrace around the Christmas tree and form the supreme image of familial unity. It is only after Mr Smith announces his decision that Rose's long-awaited marriage proposal occurs. The resolution means the family will get to see the fair, Esther and Rose may pursue their love interests, the children can go on with their familiar games, and most important of all, the family will remain together in St Louis (Kaufman 1994, 13). As the *Variety* reviewer noted, the film's theme is that "'getting ahead and going to New York' isn't everything."[15] The film confirms that an appreciation of home and its gifts is of paramount importance.

Conclusion

The change that the musical underwent in the late 1930s and 1940s reflected more than a mere change in form. As "putting on a show" gave way to "making a home," the musical shifted its function from being a vehicle for securing the acceptance of an audience of outsiders to forming an inclusive community of understanding and appreciation. Some of the most well-known "Freed unit" musicals reflect this shift, including *The Wizard of Oz*, *Babes in Arms*, and *Meet Me in St. Louis*. Spanning the "golden age" of filmmaking at MGM, during the period in which Louis B. Mayer remained at the helm of the industry and World War II fostered a supportive environment for the studios, these folk musicals featured integrated song and dance numbers in order to amplify the strength of their diegetic communities. In the process, the genre enfolds the audience into its idyllic world of home and home-making. A Kansas farm, a small town on Long Island, and turn-of-the-century St Louis are places that evoke a simpler, more conducive era for making home, raising families, and forming community.

Producers like Arthur Freed believed that the folk musical could resonate across cultures and communicate "universal values" of cherishing family and home. During the war, government officials advanced this function of the movies to include Allied aims abroad as well. The communities pictured in folk musicals have, as Freed desired, that "once upon a time quality" that, if it did not reflect America as it was in the present, portrayed an America that should be in the future. The past in the folk musical harbors a home that existed before the migration of modern life altered society. Preserving that home, returning there, and staying there, the films suggest, are goals that all the world's migrants share.

Notes

1. Arthur Freed quoted in Murray Schumach, "Hollywood Musicals, Producer Arthur Freed Sings Their Praises," *New York Times*, April 26, 1959, Sunday Section, X7.
2. Ibid.
3. Arthur Freed, "Making Musicals," *Films and Filming*, January 1956, 30.
4. Arthur Freed quoted in William R. Weaver, "Folk Lore and Folk Music Basic Freed Formula for Musicals," *Motion Picture Herald*, September 7, 1946, 33.
5. In the show musical, the insider/outsider dynamic finds expression in the relationship between performer and audience, structurally demarcated by stage space versus audience space. In the folk musical, outsider insecurities are attenuated by depictions of resilient, insular communities and the visual and aural ways in which the communities are linked by song and dance.
6. For example, see Carbine 1996.
7. See Giovacchini 2001, 47, 127.

8. *Meet Me in St. Louis*, for example, cost $1,707,561.14 and grossed over $7 million on its initial release, while *Citizen Kane* lost a substantial amount of its $800,000 investment (Fordin 1996, 118; Schatz 1999, 94).
9. Revenues in this period soared from $20 million in 1940 to $35 million in 1941 and skyrocketed to $60 million for the remainder of the war (Schatz 1999, 131, 139, 203).
10. Francis S. Harmon, "The Motion Picture and the World Community," Address on Radio Forum: "The World of Sight and Sound." Broadcast nationally by NBC, July 31, 1943. For the transcript of this address see Harmon 1944, 34–36.
11. Arthur Freed interview. Clippings Files, Margaret Herrick Library, Academy of Motion Picture Arts and Sciences, Los Angeles, California.
12. Lyric by Roger Edens in Fricke 1993, 16.
13. Though minstrelsy was on the wane in American theater, it nevertheless persisted in the Hollywood musical. World War II proved a watershed moment for Hollywood blackface due to the democratic rhetoric that dominated America in wartime and the burgeoning Civil Rights Movement that criticized and censured such depictions. An example of this transformation can be seen in the Paramount Pictures films *Holiday Inn* (1942), in which Bing Crosby performs in blackface, and its sequel *White Christmas* one decade later. This latter film has a minstrel number, but the producers chose to forgo blackface altogether. Instead, Bing Crosby, Danny Kaye, Rosemary Clooney, and Vera-Ellen perform the traditional "Mr Bones" skit in elegant, evening attire.
14. Hugh Martin, Interview with Terry Gross, Fresh Air/NPR, December 22, 2006. The original "Have Yourself a Merry Little Christmas" lyric is quoted at length in Kaufman 1994, 9. In addition to the NPR interview, Martin recounts this story in the *Meet Me in St. Louis* DVD, Warner Home Video, Inc., 2004.
15. Abel, "Meet Me in St. Louis (Technicolor; Songs)," *Variety*, November 1, 1944, 10.

References

Altman, Rick. (1987). *The American Film Musical*. Bloomington: Indiana University Press.

Benjamin, Walter. (1968). "The Work of Art in the Age of Mechanical Reproduction." In Hannah Arendt (ed.), *Illuminations* (pp. 217–251). New York: Schocken Books.

Carbine, Mary. (1996). "'The Finest Outside the Loop': Motion Picture Exhibition in Chicago's Black Metropolis, 1905–1928." In Richard Abel (ed.), *Silent Film* (pp. 234–262). New Brunswick: Rutgers University Press.

Dyer, Richard. (2002). "Entertainment and Utopia." In Steven Cohan (ed.), *Hollywood Musicals: The Film Reader* (pp. 19–30). London: Routledge.

Feuer, Jane. (2002). "The Self-Reflexive Musical and the Myth of Entertainment." In Steven Cohan (ed.), *Hollywood Musicals: The Film Reader* (pp. 31–40). London: Routledge.

Fordin, Hugh. (1996). *The World of Entertainment: Hollywood's Greatest Musicals*. New York: Da Capo. (Original work published 1975.)

Fricke, John. (1993). *The Ultimate Oz: The Definitive Collector's Edition*. Santa Monica: MGM/UA Home Video.

Giovacchini, Saverio. (2001). *Hollywood Modernism: Film and Politics in the Age of the New Deal*. Philadelphia: Temple University Press.

Harmetz, Aljean. (1989). *The Making of the Wizard of Oz*. New York: Pavilion Books.

Harmon, Francis S. (1944). *The Command Is Forward: Selections from Addresses on the Motion Picture Industry in War and Peace*. New York: North River Press.

Kaufman, Gerald. (1994). *Meet Me in St. Louis*. London: British Film Institute.

Lott, Eric. (1995). *Love and Theft: Blackface Minstrelsy and the American Working Class*. New York: Oxford University Press.

May, Elaine Tyler. (1988). *Homeward Bound: American Families in the Cold War Era*. New York: Basic Books.

Most, Andrea. (2004). *Making Americans: Jews and the Broadway Musical*. Cambridge, MA: Harvard University Press.

Mueller, John. (1984). "Fred Astaire and the Integrated Musical." *Cinema Journal*, 24.1, 28–40.

Rushdie, Salman. (1992). *The Wizard of Oz*. London: British Film Institute.

Schatz, Thomas. (1999). *Boom and Bust: The American Cinema in the 1940s*. Berkeley: University of California Press.

Singer, Ben. (2001). *Melodrama and Modernity: Early Sensational Cinema and its Contexts*. New York: Columbia University Press.

Vasey, Ruth. (1997). *The World According to Hollywood, 1918–1939*. Madison: University of Wisconsin Press.

Wallis, Michael, & Williamson, Michael S. (2007). *The Lincoln Highway: Coast to Coast from Times Square to the Golden Gate*. New York: W. W. Norton.

Winokur, Mark. (1996). *American Laughter: Immigrants, Ethnicity, and 1930s Hollywood Film Comedy*. New York: St Martin's Press.

18

The Magician
Orson Welles and Film Style

James Naremore
Chancellors' Professor Emeritus, Indiana University, United States

James Naremore challenges generally accepted arguments claiming **realism** as the primary attribute of Orson Welles's films, grounded in **long take**, **deep focus** visual aesthetics by inviting readers to consider the very meaning of cinematic "realism." Through detailed analysis of image, sound, editing, and acting in selected scenes from *Citizen Kane* and *The Magnificent Ambersons*, Naremore argues that Welles radically departs from Hollywood conventions, not on the basis of heightened realism, as French film theorist André Bazin most famously argued, but rather on the basis of excess. Naremore claims that Welles presents viewers with "ostentatious distortions of the natural world . . . as if he were trying to break down a visual frontier." A seminal Welles scholar, Naremore illustrates the ways in which the filmmaker contests Hollywood studio conventions – narrative chronology, seamless editing, minimal acting – to provide, instead, "an almost shrill acting style and a mise-en-scène distinguished not so much by its ambiguity [as Bazin suggested] as by its density and multiplicity." Naremore's essay shares ground with Matthew H. Bernstein on the studio system in this volume.

Additional terms, names, and concepts: wide angle lens, in-the-camera treatment of perspective, shot-reverse shot editing

According to John Houseman, Orson Welles was "at heart a magician whose particular talent lies not so much in his creative imagination (which is considerable) as in his proven ability to stretch the familiar elements of theatrical effect far beyond their normal point of tension" (1972, 495). Left-handed as the compliment may seem, Welles was in fact a magician, and watching his movies is sometimes like attending a performance by Blackstone or Sorcar. In *Citizen Kane* (1941), for example, there is a famous shot where the camera moves in to a close-up of a group photograph of the *Chronicle* staff while Kane talks about what good men they are; suddenly Kane walks right into the photo, and as the camera pulls back from the assembled journalists we find ourselves at an *Inquirer* party six years later. Near the beginning of *The*

American Film History: Selected Readings, Origins to 1960, First Edition. Edited by Cynthia Lucia, Roy Grundmann, and Art Simon.
© 1989 James Naremore. Published 2016 by John Wiley & Sons, Inc.

Magnificent Ambersons (1942) Welles reads Booth Tarkington offscreen while the house across the street from the Amberson mansion is shown in long shot; slowly the sky darkens, a moon appears, and the house is festooned with lanterns – as if by magic, a winter day is transformed into a summer night. Moments like these are not merely functional; they also draw upon a cinema of illusionism as old as Méliès. Even if we were to disregard such obvious showpieces of movie trickery, Welles's films would still seem flamboyant, filled with magic and "theatrical effect."

Most people are attracted to Welles's work because of this spectacular quality, despite the fact that he liked to think of himself as a man of ideas. Before considering any of his films as narratives or philosophic statements, therefore, let us look at their surfaces – scenes within a given film. For at this level Welles's handling of the medium constitutes an idiolect, a personal style with as many historical, cultural, and psychological implications as his more public ideas or themes.

The obvious place to begin is with *Kane*, and within that film a logical starting point is the wide angle, deep focus photography that became one of the most distinctive features of Welles's style. His methods were to change somewhat, growing more fluid, various, and in some ways more daring as he gained experience and encountered other cameramen after Toland; in fact he seldom returned to a really elaborate depth of field – as in those grotesque shots where a giant head only a few inches from the screen is in equally sharp focus with a figure that seems to be standing a mile away.[1] Nevertheless, the principle of exaggerated perspective was suited to his temperament, and remained an essential quality of his work. Like much of the acting in his films, it creates a slightly hallucinatory effect, marking him from the beginning of his career as anything but a purely representational or conventional artist. Indeed in every feature of his early work – from the photography, to the sound, to the acting – Welles's style is mildly unorthodox, implicitly rebellious against the norm. These points will become clearer, however, after we have examined a few scenes.

Deep Focus and Realism

One of the best-known and most written about moments in Welles's first movie is the boardinghouse segment, where we meet Kane in his youth. The camera pans slowly across a handwritten line of Thatcher's memoirs – "I first met Charles Foster Kane in 1871" – and then, accompanied by Bernard Herrmann's lilting "Rosebud" theme, the image dissolves from the white margin of the page into an unreal land of snow where Charlie frolics with his sled. At first the black dot against pure white echoes the manuscript we have been looking at, but it swoops across the screen counter to the direction the camera has been moving, in conflict with the stiff, prissy banker's handwriting, suggesting the conflict between Kane and Thatcher that runs through the early parts of the movie. The camera moves in closer, and an insert establishes the setting when one of the boy's snowballs strikes the sign over Mrs Kane's boardinghouse. Following this shot is a single, characteristically Wellesian, long take. The camera retreats from the boy, and moves through the window where his mother stands admonishing him not to catch cold; she turns, accompanied first by Thatcher and then her husband, walking the full length of the parlor, the camera tracking with her until it frames the whole room. She and Thatcher sit at a table in the foreground, and the camera holds relatively stationary for the rest of the scene. By this means Welles deliberately avoids conventional editing techniques and lets each element – the actors and the decor of the home – reveal itself successively, until everything is placed in a highly symbolic composition.

Toland's photography is of course much sharper than this reproduction of a frame can indicate. The deep focus enables us to see everything at once, and the wide angle lens slightly enlarges the foreground, giving it dramatic impact. As is typical in *Kane*, the camera views the action in terms of three planes of interest: In the foreground at the lower right, Mrs Kane and the banker sit negotiating the child's future; in the middle distance, Mr Kane makes agitated pacing movements back and forth, whining and complaining to his wife; far away, framed in the square of the window as if in the light at the end of a tunnel, Charlie plays in the snow. While the parents and banker converse inside, the sound of the boy's play can be heard through the window, which Mrs Kane has insisted must be left open. According to the RKO cutting continuity, the boy's shouts are "indistinct," but if you listen closely you will hear some of his lines. As his mother prepares to sign him over to a guardian and thus dissolve her family, the boy shouts, "The Union forever! The Union forever!"

Figure 18.1 As the child Kane plays outside in the snow in *Citizen Kane* (1941, director and producer Orson Welles), his mother signs him over to Thatcher and his agitated father looks on. (Corbis.)

Undoubtedly Welles's theatrical experience led him to conceive movie images in this way; the *Julius Caesar* stage sets had been designed to allow for just this sort of in-depth composition. Actually, however, Welles's long takes are in some way less conventionally theatrical than the typical dialogue scene in a Hollywood feature, which does nothing more than establish a setting and cut back and forth between close-ups of the actors. Hollywood cinema was basically a "star" medium, designed to highlight faces and words, whereas Welles tried to introduce a sense of visual conflict and directorial presence, even in the absence of cutting. In the scene at hand, the three planes of interest have been as carefully "reconstructed" as any montage, and they function in a roughly similar way. One important difference is that the spectator has an immediate impression of the whole, of several conflicting elements presented not in sequential fashion, but simultaneously. The movies, after all, are not an exclusively linear medium; if the director wishes to preserve the temporal continuity, he has a second dimension – depth – along which fragments of an idea can coexist. Thus while the story of *Kane* moves briskly forward, we occasionally have the sense of slicing through a cross-section of a moment, looking down a corridor of images and overlapping events.

Welles designs the boardinghouse scene in such a way that we cannot help looking down Mrs Kane's parlor to the window that neatly frames and encloses the boy's play, seeming to trap him at the very moment when he feels most free. At virtually the same time we are aware of Mrs Kane seated with the banker in the foreground, her face the image of stern puritanical sacrifice; Thatcher hovers over officiously, while in the middle distance, caught between son and mother, the weak, irresponsible Mr Kane keeps saying he doesn't like turning the boy over to a "gardeen." The faces, clothing, and postures of the actors contrast with one another, just as the slightly blurred, limitless world of snow outside the window contrasts with the sharply focused, gray interior. Clearly, the shot was meticulously organized in order to stress these conflicts; in fact it took Welles and Toland four days to complete the sequence, because everything had to be timed with clockwork precision. As a result *Kane* has a somewhat authoritarian effect; Welles may not be so Pavlovian a director as Eisenstein, but neither is he quite willing to let the spectator choose what he will see. He keeps the actors and the audience under fairly rigid control, just as the characters in this scene seem under the control of Fate.

Abetted by Toland's extreme-depth photography, Welles uses the long takes in *Citizen Kane* in highly expressive ways. As in the shot described above, the actors often take unnatural positions, their figures arrayed in a slanting line that runs out in front of the camera, so that characters in the extreme foreground or in the distance become subjects for the director's visual commentary. Actors seldom confront one another face to face, as they do in the shot-reverse shot editing of the ordinary film. The communications scientists would say that the positions of figures on the screen are "sociofugal," or not conducive to direct human interaction, and this slight physical suggestion of an inability to communicate is fully appropriate to the theme of social alienation which is implicit in the film.

Space in the conventional Hollywood film – especially in action genres like the gangster movie or the Western, which used a sharp, relatively "deep" photography – had been freer, more mobile, and certainly less symbolic than this. Oddly, however, Welles's long takes have frequently been praised for their heightened "realism." For example, in the course of his fine early essay on *Kane*, David Bordwell has written that the boardinghouse scene demonstrates the self-effacing quality of Welles's direction: "Despite the complexity of set-ups, we gain a sense of a reality – actual, unmanipulated, all of a piece."[2] He remarks that key features of Welles's technique are designed to create the illusion of a "real world." "The spatial and temporal unity of the deep-focus, the simultaneous dialogue, the reflections and chiaroscuro, the detached use of the moving camera, the intrusion of sounds from outside the frame – all increase the objectively realistic effect" (Gottesman 1976, 118).

Bordwell's notions about technique seem to derive, with some modification, from André Bazin, whose famous essay "The Evolution of Film Language" has been a major influence on Welles's critics. Indeed Bazin's commentary on *Kane* raises so many interesting questions that no study of Welles's deep focus compositions can afford not to give it a brief review. Summarized, his argument runs as follows: Between 1920 and 1940, there had been two kinds of filmmakers – "those who put their faith in the image and those who put their faith in reality" (1967, 24). By the "image" Bazin meant "very broadly speaking, everything that the representation on the screen adds to the object there represented"; by "reality" he was referring to an unmanipulated phenomenal world spread out in front of the camera, a world that he believed could leave its essential imprint on the film emulsion. According to Bazin, a director had two ways of adding to the object represented and thereby diluting the "reality." He could manipulate the "plastics" of the medium – the lighting, the sets, the makeup, the framing of the shot, etc. – or he could employ montage, which would create "a meaning not proper to the images themselves but derived exclusively from their juxtaposition" (1967, 25). Around 1940, according to Bazin, the principle of "adding" to the reality was challenged by directors like Jean Renoir, William Wyler, and Orson Welles. Thanks to the depth of field in *Kane*, Bazin wrote, "whole scenes are covered in one take . . . . Dramatic effects for which we had formerly relied on montage were created out of the movements of the actors within a fixed framework" (1967, 33). In Welles and in his predecessor Renoir, Bazin saw "a respect for the continuity of dramatic space and, of course, its duration" (1967, 34). Indeed, he said, the alternation of expressive montage and long takes in *Kane* was like a shifting back and forth between two tenses, or between two modes of telling a story.

Because the many deep focus shots in *Kane* eliminated the need for excessive cutting within a scene, because they theoretically acted as a window upon what Bazin regarded as the ambiguous phenomenal world, he praised the film as a step forward in movie "realism." Furthermore, he argued that the deep focus style was appropriate to ideas expressed in the script. "Montage by its very nature rules out ambiguity of expression," he wrote, and therefore "*Citizen Kane* is unthinkable shot in any other way but in depth. The uncertainty in which we find ourselves as to the spiritual key or the interpretation we should put on the film is built into the very design of the image" (1967, 36).

Bazin was certainly correct in describing *Kane* as an ambiguous film, and as a departure from Hollywood convention; nevertheless in his arguments about "realism" he underemphasized several important facts. For example, if in some scenes Welles avoided using montage to "add to the object represented," this left him all the more free to add in another way – through what Bazin had called "plastics." Interestingly, some of the deep focus shots in the film were made not by simple photography but by a literal montage, an overlaying of images in a complicated optical printing process that created the impression of a single shot. *Kane* is one of the most obviously stylized movies ever made; the RKO art department's contribution is so great, Welles's design of every image so constricting, that at times the picture looks like an animated cartoon. Indeed this very artificiality is part of the meaning – especially in sequences like the election rally and the surreal picnic in the Xanadu swamplands. Technically speaking, Welles has made the ultimate studio film; there is hardly a sequence that does not make us aware of the cleverness of various workmen – makeup artists, set designers, lighting crews, and perhaps most of all Orson Welles. Critics as diverse as Otis Ferguson, Paul Rotha, and Charles Higham have complained that *Kane* calls attention to its style, making the audience aware that they are watching a movie. Even François Truffaut and Joseph McBride, who are strongly influenced by Bazin's aesthetics, seem to prefer Welles's less obtrusive films – *Ambersons*, say, or *Falstaff* (1965). "When a director matures," McBride says, "his work becomes more lucid, more direct, allowing room for deeper audience response; as Truffaut has put it, what is in front of the camera is more important" (1972, 180). Behind this axiom one can feel the whole weight of Bazin's theories, although to McBride's credit he acknowledges a flaw in the argument. When he met Welles, he asked about the relative simplicity of the later European films: "I asked him why, in recent years, his movies have had less and less of the razzle-dazzle of his youth. Could it be a kind of growing serenity? 'No, the explanation is simple,' he said. 'All the great technicians are dead or dying'" (1972, 154).

Yet the statements of both Welles and Toland, in other contexts, seem to foreshadow or confirm Bazin's notions about realism. Toland has claimed that Welles's idea was to shoot the picture in such a way that "the technique of filming should never be evident to the audience,"[3] and in his well-known *American Cinematographer* article, we repeatedly encounter comments such as the following: "The attainment of approximate human-eye focus was one of our fundamental aims" (Gottesman 1971, 74); "The *Citizen Kane* sets have ceilings because we wanted reality, and we felt it would be easier to believe a room was a room if its ceiling could be seen" (Gottesman 1971, 75); "In my opinion, the day of highly stylized cinematography is passing, and being superseded by a candid, realistic technique" (Gottesman 1971, 77). The last statement finds an echo in Bazin's notion that *Kane* is part of a general movement, a "vast stirring in the geological bed of cinema," which will restore to the screen the "*continuum* of reality" and the "ambiguity of reality" (1967, 37). The same general argument can be heard in Welles's own remarks. In an interview with Peter Bogdanovich, he was asked why he used so much deep focus. "Well," he replied, "in life you see everything at the same time, so why not in the movies?" (Gottesman 1971, 46).

One should remember that the term "realism" (often used in opposition to "tradition") nearly always contains a hidden ideological appeal, and that the word has been appropriated to justify nearly every variety of revolution in the arts. But if "realism" is intended simply to mean "verisimilitude," then Welles, Toland, and Bazin are at best half right. It is true that deep focus can preserve what Bazin called the "continuum" of reality, and that three-dimensional effects on the screen (which owe considerably to Welles's blocking and Toland's skillful lighting) can give the spectator the impression of looking into a "real" space. Nevertheless Welles and Toland are inaccurate when they imply that the human eye sees everything in focus, and Bazin is wrong to suggest that either reality or human perception is somehow "ambiguous." On the contrary, human vision is exactly the opposite of depth photography, because humans are incapable of keeping both the extreme foreground and the extreme distance in focus at the same time. The crucial difference between a camera and the human eye is that the camera is non-selective; even when we are watching the deep focus composition in *Kane* we do not see everything in the frame at once. We are aware of an overall composition that exists simultaneously, but, as Bazin has noted, the spectator is required to make certain choices, scanning the various objects in the picture selectively. Welles seems instinctively aware of this fact, because he has designed his images quite rigidly, sometimes blacking out whole sections of the composition or guiding our attention with movement and frames within the frame. Welles's movies make relatively greater intellectual demands upon the audience, giving them *more* to look at, but the information that is crowded on the screen has been as carefully manipulated and controlled as in any montage.

Still another and perhaps more important factor needs to be taken into account in any discussion of the phenomenal "realism" of Welles's technique. Toland claimed that he was approximating the human eye when he stopped down his camera to increase the depth of field, but what he and most other commentators on the technique do not emphasize is that he also used a wide angle lens to distort perspective. *Kane* was photographed chiefly with a 25mm lens, which means that figures in the extreme foreground are elongated or slightly ballooned out, while in the distance the lines formed by the edge of a room converge sharply toward the horizon. Thus if Toland gave the spectator more to see, he also gave the world a highly unnatural appearance. In fact Welles's unusual images fundamentally alter the relationship between time and space, calling into question some aspects of Bazin's arguments about duration. Here, for example, is an extract from an interview with the British cameraman/director C. M. Pennington-Richards:

> Of course using wide angle lenses the time-space factor is different. If you've got a wide angle lens, for instance a 1″ lens or an 18mm, you can walk from three-quarter length to a close-up in say four paces. If you put a 6″ lens on [i.e., a telephoto], to walk from three-quarter length to close-up would take you twenty paces. This is the difference: During a scene if someone walks away and then comes back for drama, they come back fast, they become big fast. There is no substitute for this – you only can do it with the perspective of a wide angle lens. It's the same with painting; if you want to dramatize anything, you force the perspective, and using wide angle lenses is in fact forcing it.[4]

These comments signal the direction that any discussion of photography in *Kane* should take. But while there has been a great deal of theoretical discussion about depth of field in the film, rather little has been said about forced depth of perspective, which is the *sine qua non* of Welles's style, and which accounts for a great deal of the speed and energy of his work. And the technique is effective precisely because it lacks verisimilitude. Most directors operate on the principle that the motion picture image should approximate some kind of human perception; the virtue of Welles's films, however, is that they work in a different direction, creating what the Russian formalist critic Victor Shklovsky (1998) would call a poetic "defamiliarization."

There were, of course, several purely practical advantages to Toland's use of this special lens. It increased the playing area, not only in depth but also in width, allowing the director to integrate characters and decor. Although it made panning movements somewhat ugly by Hollywood standards (there are relatively few in *Kane*), it greatly enhanced the dramatic power of tracking shots, giving impact to any movement forward or backward, whether by the camera or by the players. Indeed the values of this technique were so many that a 35mm lens, once considered extreme, is now standard, and much shorter lenses are used regularly in horror films. (On television these lenses are used frequently, partly because they compensate for the small screen. One problem, however, is that TV directors use dual purpose lenses; to save time and money, they zoom in on details instead of tracking, thereby losing the dramatic shearing away of space that is produced by wide angle camera movement.)

In retrospect, what was really innovative about Toland and Welles was not their sharp focus but their in-the-camera treatment of perspective. Depth of field was less unusual than Toland and later historians have made it seem; like the photographing of ceilings, it was at least as old as Griffith and Bitzer – indeed there are beautiful examples of it in Chaplin's *The Gold Rush* (1925). A certain "normality" of spatial relationships, however, had been adhered to throughout the studio years, with only an occasional photographer or director behaving differently; filmmakers used a variety of lenses, but they usually sought to conceal optical distortions by means of set design, camera placement, or compensatory blocking of actors. When Welles and Toland deliberately manipulated perspective, they foreshadowed the jazzy quirks of movement and space that were to become almost commonplace during the 1960s and 1970s.[5]

Not that wide angle perspectives were new when *Kane* was made. Welles's favorite director, John Ford, had used them extensively in *Young Mr. Lincoln* and *Stagecoach* (both 1939), and Toland had made some interesting experiments with them in *The Long Voyage Home* (1940), sharing a title card with Ford. In 1941, the same year as *Kane*, Arthur Edeson photographed *The Maltese Falcon* at Warner Bros. using a 21mm lens, which, at least theoretically, distorted space even more than in Welles's film. It is instructive, however, to contrast the effect of *Falcon* with that of *Kane*. The space in the John Huston film, far from seeming exaggerated, seems cramped; nearly the whole action is played out in a series of little rooms with the actors gathered in tight, three-figured compositions. Huston, like most other Hollywood directors, stayed within the limits of studio conventions, underplaying Edeson's offbeat photography. Welles, on the other hand, used the lens distortion openly, as an adjunct to the meaning of the story; in fact the peculiar exaggeration of perspective in *Kane* is equivalent to effects one sees everywhere in German Expressionist cinema, where sets are usually built in tunnel-like designs. Toland's wide angle photography is therefore made to contribute to the "horror movie" feeling of the film, and is the perfect visual equivalent to Welles's earlier theatrical productions. In *Kane*, space becomes demonic, oppressive; ceilings are unnaturally low, as if they were about to squash the characters; or, conversely, at Xanadu rooms become so large that people shrink, comically yet terrifyingly dwarfed by their possessions. (This effect is enhanced by set design. At one point Kane walks over to a huge fireplace and seems to become a doll, warming himself before logs as big as whole trees: "Our home is here, Susan," he says, absurdly playing the role of paterfamilias.)

Again and again Welles uses deep focus not as a "realistic" mode of perception but as a way of suggesting a conflict between the characters' instinctual needs and the social or material world that determines their fate. He continued this practice, fantastically exaggerating space in his later films (*Touch of Evil* was shot largely with an 18.5mm lens), making exaggeration a key feature of his style. The short focal length of the lens enabled him to express the psychology of his characters, to comment upon the relation between character and environment, and also to create a sense of barely contained, almost manic energy, as if the camera, like one of his heroes, were overreaching.[6]

This highly charged, nervous dynamism of imagery and action can be found everywhere in *Kane*, and is produced by other techniques besides photography. Fairly often Welles will stage important moments of his story against some counterpointing piece of business, as if he were trying to energize the plot by throwing as much material as possible onto the screen. One of the most obvious examples is the party sequence in the *Inquirer* offices, where Leland and Bernstein debate about Kane's character. Here again the shot establishes three planes that are set in conflict with one another. To the left is Leland, a young, handsome, fastidious WASP a little like the "New England schoolmarm" Kane will later call him. To the right and slightly nearer is Bernstein – slight, ugly, Jewish, and as loyal as a puppy. Leland is bareheaded, but Bernstein wears a Rough Rider's hat as a sign of his allegiance to Kane's war in Cuba. The contrast is further emphasized by the dialogue: Throughout the scene Leland refers to Kane as "Charlie," implicitly recognizing that they belong to the same class, whereas Bernstein always refers to his boss as "Mr Kane." (Incidentally, we have just heard a song about Kane. Charles Bennett, the entertainer at the head of the chorus line, asks, "What is his name?" The chorus girls sing, "It's Mr Kane!" The whole crowd joins in, singing, "He doesn't like that Mister / He likes good old Charlie Kane!")

The brief conversation in this scene is important because it underlines Leland's growing disillusionment and Kane's increasing ambitions. In the original Mankiewicz–Welles script, the dialogue was played at an interlude in the party, while various members of the newspaper staff danced with the chorus girls. By the time of the actual filming, however, Welles had decided to stage the conversation simultaneously with Kane's dance. Leland and Bernstein literally have to shout to be heard over the raucous sounds of the orchestra and chorus, and our eyes are continually pulled away from them toward the antics in the background. Even when Welles cuts to a reverse angle, we can still see Kane and one of the girls reflected in the glass of a window.

This shot contains an echo of the composition in the boardinghouse; once again Kane is supposed to be at play, and once again a window frame seems to mock his apparent freedom. The violent overlapping and baroque contrasts of space are used here not only on the visual level, but also on the soundtrack. Welles did not invent overlapping dialogue any more than he and Toland invented deep focus, but the complex, hurried speech in *Kane* and the various levels of sound within a scene are especially effective corollaries of the complex photographic style. To complement what Toland had publicized as "pan focus," Welles devised a sort of "pan sound," drawing on his years in radio, where he had gained a reputation as an experimenter. Indeed this reputation is alluded to in a biographical profile for the *Saturday Evening Post*, written before the idea of *Kane* was conceived, when Alva Johnson and Fred Smith comment on the powers of Welles's "auditory nerve":

> Recently he was in a restaurant with some people who became interested in the dialogue at the table on the left; they eavesdropped eagerly, but without catching more than an occasional word. Welles then gave a full account of the discussion at the table on the left and threw in for good measure the substance of the discussion at the table on the right ... Welles insisted that the triple-eavesdropping faculty could be acquired by anyone who practiced earnestly. (Johnson & Smith 1940)

Welles probably believed that a complex soundtrack like the one at the *Inquirer* party is more "real," more true to the welter of conversations in life; we know from testimony of people like John Houseman that Welles's radio dramas had gone to extraordinary lengths to achieve documentary-like speech or sound effects. Here again, however, the technique is in fact an expressive device. Despite Welles's demonstration in the restaurant, the listening ear doesn't make sense of overlapping speech or the chaos of sounds in the environment. Like the eye, it is highly selective, and needs to screen out unwanted noises. The microphone, on the other hand, is as nonselective as the camera – that is why the sounds in *Kane*, like the images, have been carefully orchestrated to blot out unwanted distractions and to serve symbolic functions, even while they overheat the spectacle and make the spectator work to decipher it.

Critics have often pointed to the "radio" sound in *Citizen Kane*. (In fact, the first words that Welles speaks in the film, after the whispered "Rosebud," are a reference to his Mars broadcast: "Don't believe everything you hear on the radio," he chuckles.) As evidence of Welles's expertise with sound, commentators always mention the "lightning mixes" – scenes in which one character's speech will be cut off abruptly, only to be completed by another character in another time and place. These charming tricks, however, are a logical extension of the Vorkapich montages Hollywood used so often in the 1930s, and there is nothing especially original about them; one finds similar transitions in *Trouble in Paradise* (1932) and *Gold Diggers of 1935* (1935). What is more interesting and perhaps more "radio-like" is the degree to which music and sound in Welles's films become natural adjuncts to the "layered" principles of deep focus. The best example of the technique, it seems to me, is not in *Kane* but in the snow scene in *The Magnificent Ambersons*, where jingling sleigh music is first alternated and then intertwined with the dissonant squeaking of an automobile handcrank. These sounds are subtly combined with the excited chatter of six characters (all of them, as in the earlier ballroom sequence in the same film, postsynchronized by RKO technicians), creating a true montage of conflicts and reinforcing a major theme. Similar effects are at work in a modest way in the boardinghouse episode and the *Inquirer* party in *Kane*, where the sound in the background is meant to contrast with the sound in the foreground. In the climactic moments of *Touch of Evil* (1958), the technique can be seen in its most radically expressive form, as if Welles's work were evolving toward greater, not less, stylization.

There are, of course, other moments in Welles's movies when the dialogue and incidental sound have been made deliberately and "realistically" chaotic, because the director has been willing to sacrifice clarity for pure speed. By the middle 1930s, a fast-talking, breezy manner had become virtually the norm for American movies, and Hiram Sherman, one of the stars of the 1938 Mercury stage production of *Shoemaker's Holiday*, recalls that Welles was particularly fond of the technique:

> He loved you to bite the cue. Everything had to mesh, go together. You didn't finish a speech that someone else wasn't on top of you. All the time. This kind of repartee

> was very effective in *Shoemaker*. It was going lickety-split all the time. We didn't even have an intermission. We tried it for one preview, but Orson decided to cut that out and plow right on.[7]

Sherman's emphasis on how "everything had to mesh, go together," is an important key to the overall style of a movie like *Kane*, where so much depends on superimposition and simultaneity, one scene dissolving into the next, one account of Kane's life slightly overlapping the succeeding account, one actor biting the other's cue. In its first half, the film is as rapidly paced as a Howard Hawks comedy, but not so much for the sake of realism as for the sheer thrill of the zesty atmosphere.

Furthermore, this sense of pace and energy depends more on cutting than is usually noted. Even Bazin, who was interested chiefly in the long take, recognized that "superimpositions" were characteristic of Welles's work. What Bazin did not emphasize, as Brian Henderson has pointed out, is that "the long take rarely appears in its pure state." In fact, Henderson notes, "the cut which ends a long take – how it ends and where – determines or affects the nature of the shot itself" (1971, 6).

For example, toward the end of the scene in Mrs Kane's boardinghouse, Agnes Moorehead rises and walks back toward the window, the camera slowly following her. She pauses, and Welles cuts to a reverse angle, looking past her face toward the opposite side of the room. The scene as a whole is not a long take but a shot-reverse shot combination that is fundamental to narrative movies. There are, however, some interesting differences between this particular editing style and standard Hollywood practice: For one thing, the rhythm of the cutting is not keyed to the rhythm of the dialogue – instead it imposes a structure on the narrative, holding off the crucial close-up until the most effective moment. Equally important, the editing of shots such as this one, photographed with a wide angle lens, creates a slightly more violent effect than the editing of normal perspectives, and makes the audience more aware of the cutting process. The exaggeration of space gives the reverse angle an unusual force, as if we had been jerked into a radically different viewpoint. Thus Mrs Kane's face looms up in the foreground, and the impact of this image is reinforced by having her call loudly out the window to Charles. The cut emphasizes the mother's pain and her pivotal role; behind her, we can see the figures of the father and the banker standing awkwardly in the distance, dwarfed by the size of her head.

Because of the many wide angle views in *Kane*, shot-reverse shot editing takes on new dramatic possibilities. Consider, for example, the scenes of Kane and Susan separated by the vast halls of Xanadu, where a simple over-the-shoulder editing style becomes a powerful and witty statement about alienation and loneliness. Earlier, in the newspaper office, a reverse angle is used to convey Kane's anger at Leland: Leland emerges from a drunken stupor and stands at the door of his office, looking out toward where Kane is composing a review of Susan's opera debut; we cut to a reverse shot composed in extreme depth (so deep, in fact, that it was created by the optical printing I have mentioned), showing Kane's massive head at the left of the screen and Leland stepping out of the door in the far distance. Simultaneous with this violent change of perspective, Kane pushes back the typewriter carriage with a loud slam; the sound of the typewriter, which was tiny in the previous shot, suddenly becomes close up and frightening.

Elsewhere in the film, Welles avoids reverse views altogether, playing out whole scenes in one take and "editing" by revealing successive playing areas. In some of his more elaborate montages he will throw a brief wide angle shot on the screen with stunning effect, as in the *Inquirer* party, where a distorted close-up of a smiling black man coincides with a blast of music. In many other scenes, however, he uses an ordinary shot-reverse shot style and even an ordinary lens – consider the argument between the young Kane and Carter in the newspaper office, or the meeting between Kane and Susan in her apartment. Ultimately, therefore, it might be said that the chief difference between *Kane* and the standard film has less to do with an unusual editing style than with the size and relative perspective of the shots Welles puts on the screen, plus his tendency to animate the space around the actors. Generally he keeps the camera at a distance, using the wide angle lens to increase the playing area, so that he can draw out the individual shots and fill them with detail. Although there are far more close-ups in *Kane* than Welles himself remembered, we seldom see an actor's face isolated on the screen. Welles wanted the audience to "read" a complex imagery, wanted them to appreciate his skill at rapid manipulation of the magic-show qualities of the medium. In

Figure 18.2 Exaggerated perspective dwarfs Thatcher and Mr Kane, as Mrs Kane dominates the frame in *Citizen Kane* (1941, director and producer Orson Welles). (Corbis.)

other words, his work ran somewhat against the grain of classic studio movies, which encouraged the audience to forget technique and identify with the players.

The acting in Welles's early films is determined by similar principles, being slightly overwrought and at times self-consciously inflated. George Coulouris, who played Thatcher in *Kane*, has remarked on this quality:

> I made many films after *Kane* and one thing I've noticed is its intensity and power – more than would be tolerable in many films. The scene in which we argue back and forth in the newspaper office is not conventional movie acting. With other actors or another director, it would have been "brought down" a lot and lost a good deal.[8]

In fact the argument between Kane and Thatcher – and virtually the entire Thatcher section of the film – is a foreshadowing of a technique that would become increasingly evident in Welles's later work; the players "project" their lines to a greater degree than in the ordinary movie, as if they were oblivious to the idea that acting for a camera ought to be low-key and naturalistic. The Thatcher section is a subtle, deliberate echo of Victorian melodramatics, but even the later episodes are particularly high-pitched, creating a sort of repressed hysteria. Agnes Moorehead, Ray Collins, and Dorothy Comingore are a bit more wide-eyed and loud than they need to be; Collins, for example, underplays the villainy of Jim Gettys, but he stays in one's mind as a vivid portrait largely because he handles the quieter lines of dialogue almost like a stage actor, preserving the illusion of calm while he speaks at a high volume. Later, in the scene where Susan attacks Kane for allowing Leland to write a negative review of her singing, the sound technicians seem to have added an extra decibel to her already piercing voice: "What's that?" she shouts as Kane opens a letter from Leland. "A declaration of principles," he says, almost to himself. "*What?*" she screams, the sound cutting at the audience's ears and making Kane flinch as if from a whiplash.

Welles's own remarkable performance in the central role is in keeping with this stylized quality. The resonant, declamatory voice speaks its lines very rapidly, almost throwing away whole phrases but then pausing to linger over a word, like a pastiche of ordinary excited speech. A masterful stealer of scenes, Welles also knows that if he glances away from the person to whom he is speaking he will capture the audience's attention. His slightly distracted look, plus the gauzy photography he prefers for his own close-ups, gives his acting what François Truffaut calls a "softly hallucinated" tone, something of a counterpoint to the more nightmarish mood of the rest of the movie.[9] (At this point, however, one should note that Welles's screen persona and some of his directorial mannerisms may have developed less out of taste or theory than out of necessity, because he always disliked his own body. A massive, fascinating presence, he was nevertheless somewhat flatfooted and graceless in movement, and his best performances were in the roles of very old men. As the young Kane he is usually photographed sitting down; when he does move – as in the dance at the *Inquirer* party or in the scene where he destroys Susan Alexander's room – his stilted, robot-like behavior is acceptable because it is in keeping with the highly deterministic quality of the script and the visuals.)

Keenly aware of his acting range, Welles has designed every shot in *Kane* to accommodate his physical limitations; partly as a result of this habit, he has also been very fussy about the choreography of the other actors, who, as we have seen, are locked into rigidly structured patterns. Unlike Hawks, Ford, or any of the "action" directors of the time, he gives us very few moments when the camera sits passively by and allows an actor's body its own natural freedom. Yet in Welles's first two films there are individual scenes that go beyond artifice and bring an extraordinarily truthful, unmannered quality to the acting. In both cases – Kane's rage in Susan's bedroom and Aunt Fanny's hysterical outburst near the end of *Ambersons* – the emotions seem to rise out of a sexual frustration that has been building throughout the plot, and in both cases the actors are no longer quite pretending. (After the bedroom scenes Welles is rumored to have remarked, "I really felt it." Aunt Fanny's collapse, on the other hand, was reshot dozens of times, until Agnes Moorehead was literally shedding tears of exhaustion.) On the screen, these moments feel so authentic that they almost break through the fictional context, but in their own way they are as unconventional as the otherwise slightly exaggerated, artful playacting. By the early 1940s American movies had developed a slick, understated acting style that avoided behavior extremes; when characters cried, their tears seemed real but never really disturbing. Among the chief performers of the decade, only James Stewart was able to convey psychic breakdowns with an intensity comparable to the ones in *Kane* and *Ambersons*, but his anguish was usually softened by Frank Capra's sentimental, optimistic stories. Welles's films were slightly different; they made the audience conscious of psychological pain – and also of the art of acting – in a way that was more common to the theater. Hence a movie like *Citizen Kane* may have been a dreamworld, a wondershow, but it was also capable of touching upon important emotional realities.

Faust or Quixote?

Welles was slightly unorthodox and special, but of course he had been assisted by the RKO staff and learned most of what he knew from watching the films of his Hollywood predecessors, including Ford, Lubitsch, Sternberg, and Murnau. In fact Murnau's *Sunrise* (1927) contains nearly all the essential ingredients of Welles's visuals, down to a sharply focused shot that modestly prefigures the famous attempted suicide in *Kane*: In the foreground is a glass containing a spoon; in the middle distance a woman reclines on a bed; in the far distance we can see activity outside a window. In turn, Welles's own work was to influence American cinema throughout the 1940s: stylish melodramas such as Edgar Ulmer's *Ruthless* (1948) and John Farrow's *The Big Clock* (1948), to cite only two examples, are filled with flashbacks, elaborate tracking shots, long takes, compositions in depth, and even set designs that are vaguely reminiscent of *Kane*.

Nevertheless, if the "classic" studio cinema ever existed (and by "classic" I mean movies that used chronological narrative, invisible editing, minimal acting, and a muted photographic expressionism – everything designed to immerse the audience in "content" and make them forget the manipulations of style), then Welles's individualism was a challenge to the system. Furthermore, whatever the derivation or influence of Welles's techniques, the peculiarities of his cinema seem to me to consist of different elements from the ones emphasized by Bazin. *Citizen Kane* has a crisp, three-dimensional photography, an accurate sense of period manners and decor, and a depiction of social caste almost as vivid as Eisenstein's. To these ostensibly "realistic" qualities it adds an almost shrill acting style and a mise-en-scène distinguished not so much by its ambiguity as by its density and multiplicity. Thus Welles's movies contrast with others of the period because they contain such a fine frenzy of performance and information; the overriding quality of his work is not its phenomenal realism but its distortion and excess. And the progress of his American films was to be a fairly steady movement away from the conventions of cinematic reality toward the bizarre and surreal.

Most of his later pictures, made under severe contractual restraints and without the Mercury company, are characterized by a sort of dazzling aesthetic unrestraint, and are contemptuous of naturalism, reason, and decorum. The images he projects on the screen are ostentatious distortions of the natural world, lacking the orderly planes of classical expression, as if he were trying to break down a visual frontier by dramatically emphasizing any movement forward or backward along the tunnel of space in front of the camera. In this regard he becomes the exact opposite of an equally ostentatious but popular director like Hitchcock, whose films have several parallels with his own, but whose imagery is always lucid and orderly. (Interestingly, Hitchcock once told students at the American Film Institute that he disliked deep focus compositions as a rule, and that he thought the wide angle lens caused too much exaggeration.) Like Hitchcock, Welles inherited certain mannerisms from the Germans: an authoritarian blocking of actors; heavy, dramatic lighting; and a fondness for shooting from radical angles. But when these attributes are added to the forced perspective of his imagery and the unusually crowded, intense effect of his action and dialogue, the result is an impression of a romantic temperament gone completely unchecked. In fact the very density and bravado of this style may have helped RKO executives to fuel the myth of extravagance that still surrounds Welles's life and work. Welles never went drastically over budget and was never responsible for a true financial disaster; nonetheless the idea persisted that he was a waster of studio money. This, together with his satiric vision of America and his lack of box office success, severely limited his ability to work in Hollywood.

Welles's artistic flamboyance and unrestrained power also had a somewhat paradoxical effect on the films themselves, because from the beginning of his career his leading themes were the dangers of radical individualism and unlimited power. Most of his films are about tyrannical egotists, men who try to imitate God. His major characters usually try to live above the law, in contempt of ordinary human restraint, and as a result they cut themselves off from their community, becoming prisoners of guilt, self-delusion, and old age. Nevertheless, Welles's own public philosophy was consistently humanistic and liberal, and nearly all his Hollywood films were grounded in social commentary. The question naturally arises, then, whether there was not a tension or contradiction between Welles's philosophic stance and the personality that is implicit in his style.

Clearly there was such a tension, and it is echoed in other aspects of Welles's work, especially in the nest of conflicts and oppositions in *Citizen Kane*. For example, Welles's typical way of dealing with a film story was to begin at the level of social satire and then to become preoccupied with "tragic" issues, so that he seemed to be responding to two distinct urges. His preference for the Gothic or "expressionist" mode is a further sign of an emotional dualism: Gothic writers have typically been political rebels of a sort, trying to depict the corruption and degeneracy of an entrenched order; even so, as Leslie Fiedler has noted, there is a contradiction between the "liberal uses and demonic implications, the enlightened principles and reactionary nostalgia of the tale of terror" (1966, 138). Thus the tyrants at the center of Welles's films are usually more fascinating and sympathetic than the naïve, commonplace figures around them – this in spite of the fact that Welles puts many of his own political sentiments into the mouths of "starry-eyed idealists" like Jed Leland, Michael O'Hara, and Mike Vargas. Actually, the demonic, obsessive drives of the tyrant begin to take on a sort of moral purity, as if egomania and self-delusion were partly a reaction against a sickness in the society at large.

Welles never attributed the sickness to any clear systemic causes: In fact he was more given to explaining his sympathetic tyrants in terms of neurotic sexual obsessions, or to contrasting the madness of America with momentary glimpses of pre-industrial "innocence." But the stylistic quality I have been describing above – the density of manic extremism of Welles's typical scenes – is perfectly expressive of the displaced libidinal urges that cause his protagonists to launch their frustrated drives for power. And even though Welles was critical of these Faustian types, they had something deeply in common with the personality of the director himself, as it is suggested in the gorgeous excess of his style. According to his friend Maurice Bessy, Welles lamented the fact that he was "made to follow in the footsteps of the Byronic adventurer, even though I detest this sort of man and everything he stands for."[10] Such a remark suggests an extraordinary division in Welles's own character, and may help explain why he often portrayed the romantic egotist as a driven and deeply interesting person; certainly his ironic treatment of Kane or the Ambersons did not conceal his sympathy, his fascination with their absurd grandeur. His overreachers tend to be tyrants in spite of themselves, pathetically trying to determine their own fate even while they are doomed by their childhood and victimized by a society beyond their control. As Bessy has pointed out, the Wellesian tyrant, for all his destructiveness, is a wielder of sham power: Kane tries to construct his own world at Xanadu; George Minafer thinks he can become a "yachtsman"; Macbeth believes he is a king; Mr Arkadin imagines he can eradicate the past; Mr Clay attempts to gain immortality. The ambitions of these men are at once awesome and laughable, much like the young Welles himself. None of them is really in control, and most of them are naïvely, ludicrously out of touch with reality, motivated by sexual urges they never fully understand. Therefore the Faustian protofascist in a Welles movie usually turns into a sort of perverse Don Quixote, a man in tragicomic rebellion against a world that conspires to inhibit his dream of autonomy and control.

When Welles's films are viewed in this way, the connection between his heated, sometimes outrageous style and his rather philosophic subject matter becomes more apparent. In one sense Welles was critical of romantic egotism – that is why he often combined German Expressionism with the sort of absurdist comedy that has always been at the heart of the American Gothic. At the same time, however, the Orson Welles who tried to master Hollywood was himself a victim of his childhood and his romantic character. While intellectually Welles may have been a liberal, emotionally he was something of a radical; his fascination with passing time and human mortality, his preoccupation with characters who are slightly out of step, his interest in a past when everything was somehow better than it is now – all these things indicate that at one level he was both a rebel and, in one sense, a reactionary. Thus John Houseman was right to say that Welles pushed "theatrical effect" far beyond its "normal point of tension." In this way, Welles's films suggest how much he had in common with his characters, to say nothing of what he had in common with the romantic agony that runs throughout American literature. It is precisely this quality of his style that made his career in American movies so difficult, and that made his own life seem to imitate that of one of the protagonists of his stories.

Notes

An earlier version of this essay appeared in James Naremore, *The Magic World of Orson Welles*, new and rev. edn (Dallas: Southern Methodist Press, 1989).

1. My arguments on deep focus photography and motion picture soundtracks were influenced by Burch 1973. Burch is also important to my understanding of "self-reflexive cinema."
2. Bordwell 1971, reprinted in Gottesman 1976, 116.
3. Toland 1941, 55, reprinted in Gottesman 1976, 74.
4. Reprinted in Naremore 2004, 131.
5. A useful reference on optical printing and other techniques of motion picture photography is Campbell 1970.
6. For an "orthodox" view of how lenses should be used in the classic Hollywood movie, see Donohue 1966.
7. Hiram Sherman is quoted in Richard France's "*The Shoemaker's Holiday* at the Mercury Theatre," in *Theatre Survey*, November 1975, reprinted in France 1977, 139.
8. George Coulouris's remarks appear in an interview with Ted Gilling in *Sight and Sound* (Summer 1973).
9. François Truffaut's comments on Welles's acting are taken from the official program of the American Film Institute "life award" ceremony honoring Welles.

10. Welles is originally quoted in an interview with André Bazin, Charles Bitsch, and Jean Domarchi (Bazin et al. 1958), reprinted in English in Mark W. Estrin (ed.), *Orson Welles: Interviews* (Oxford, MS: University Press of Mississippi, 2002), 57.

References

Bazin, André. (1967). *What Is Cinema?*, vol. 1. Berkeley: University of California Press.

Bazin, André, Bitsch, Charles, & Domarchi, Jean. (1958). "Entretien avec Orson Welles." *Cahiers du Cinéma*, 84, 1–13.

Bogdanovich, Peter. (1972). "The Kane Mutiny." *Esquire Magazine*, October, 99–105, 180–190.

Bordwell, David. (1971). "*Citizen Kane*." *Film Comment*, 7.2, 38–47.

Burch, Noël. (1973). *Theory of Film Practice*. New York: Praeger.

Campbell, Russell (ed.). (1970). *Practical Motion Picture Photography*. Cranbury, NJ: A. S. Barnes.

Donohue, Jay. (1966). "Focal Length and Creative Perspective." *American Cinematographer*, July.

Fiedler, Leslie. (1966). *Love and Death in the American Novel*. New York: Stein & Day.

France, Richard. (1977). *The Theatre of Orson Welles*. Lewisburg, PA: Bucknell University Press.

Gottesman, Ronald. (1971). *Focus on Citizen Kane*. Englewood Cliffs, NJ: Prentice Hall.

Gottesman, Ronald (ed.). (1976). *Focus on Orson Welles*. Englewood Cliffs, NJ: Prentice Hall.

Henderson, Brian. (1971). "The Long Take." *Film Comment*, 7.2, 6–11.

Houseman, John. (1972). *Run-Through*. New York: Simon & Schuster.

Johnson, Alva, & Smith, Fred. (1940). "How to Raise a Child." *Saturday Evening Post*, January 20, 9–11, 94–96; January 27, 24–25, 51–54; February 3, 27, 38, 40, 45.

McBride, Joseph. (1972). *Orson Welles*. New York: Da Capo.

McBride, Joseph. (2006). *What Ever Happened to Orson Welles? A Portrait of an Independent Career*. Lexington: University Press of Kentucky.

Naremore, James. (2004). *Orson Welles's Citizen Kane: A Casebook*. New York: Oxford University Press.

Shklovsky, Victor. (1998). "Art as Technique." In Julie Rivkin & Michael Ryan (eds), *Literary Theory: An Anthology*. Oxford: Blackwell.

Toland, Gregg, ASC. (1941). "How I Broke the Rules in *Citizen Kane*." *Popular Photography Magazine*, 8, June.

19

Classical Cel Animation, World War II, and *Bambi*

Kirsten Moana Thompson
Professor, Victoria University of Wellington, New Zealand

Kirsten Moana Thompson provides a concise history of **film animation** from its origins through World War II, including its precursors dating back to cave drawings; its developing techniques and technology, from the **rotoscope** and **storyboarding** processes to **cel animation**; its evolving themes and genres; and its practitioners, both within and outside the **Hollywood studio system**. Thompson discusses the contribution of animated features, shorts, and **cartoons** to the war effort as both **instructional** and **propaganda films** for home-front and military audiences. **Disney**, especially, produced work that served the war effort, both directly in shorts like *Thunderstorms*, commissioned by the Bureau of Aeronautics, and indirectly in the classic ***Bambi***, a ***Bildungsroman*** story inscribing issues of danger, death, and dread. *Bambi* crucially refined **anthropomorphic characterization** and **stylized realism** in representations of animals and their natural habitats, as well as the role of **diegetic sound** and **nondiegetic music** as narrative enhancements. Thompson's essay shares ground with Desirée J. Garcia on the folk musical and Charles Wolfe on the Capra *Why We Fight* series in this volume, and with Krin Gabbard on Friz Freleng's animation and music in the hardcover/online edition.

Additional terms, names, and concepts: stop-motion photography, reflexive self-figuration, rubber hosing, squash and stretch, three-strip Technicolor, SNAFU, mickey-mouse musical scoring

The word animation derives from *anima*, meaning "breath" or "soul," and *animare*, "to give life to." Animation creates the *illusion of life*, and it does this through movement. There are two distinguishing characteristics: First, the image is photographed on film frame by frame, and second, in consequence the illusion of motion is *created* cinematically rather than recorded. In animation, a special camera is used that can photograph one frame at a time. Between exposures, the animator incrementally moves an object: It may be cels, puppets, clay, sand, or paper cutouts, but the basic principle is that the illusion of motion is

American Film History: Selected Readings, Origins to 1960, First Edition. Edited by Cynthia Lucia, Roy Grundmann, and Art Simon.
© 2016 John Wiley & Sons, Inc. Published 2016 by John Wiley & Sons, Inc.

constructed *cinematically*. That is, rather than photographing something that is already moving, movement is created *in the camera* through stop-motion photography, or the photographing of an object frame by frame (Solomon 1994, 5, 9–12).

Just as drawings in flip-books also seem to move when we flip the pages, we perceive motion in a succession of rapidly projected still images. Nineteenth-century curiosity items and optical toys like praxinoscopes, thaumatropes, and zoetropes[1] were the product of this fascination with the novelty of motion, and were the precursors of animated film. Early filmmakers like Albert E. Smith (*The Humpty Dumpty Circus*, 1898?), James Stuart Blackton (*The Haunted Hotel*, 1907), and Edwin S. Porter (*Fun in a Bakery Shop*, 1902) created "trick" films with stop-motion photography, which seemed to make simple props and objects move.

Genre and Mode of Production

Animation comes in many possible styles and modes, as it can be lyrical, abstract, poetic, experimental, or nonnarrative. It can be in short or feature-length form, and be made by large studios or by independent and experimental artists, like Canadian-American Caroline Leaf (1946–), who "paints with sand," or German Lotte Reiniger (1899–1981), who animated extraordinarily delicate paper cutouts or silhouettes, or the American twin brothers Quay (1947–), who work with strange dolls, puppets, and found objects. Animation has drawn upon oral folklore and fairy tales, in the rich puppet animation of Poland, Russia, and the former Yugoslavia and Czechoslovakia. Japanese manga (graphic novels) are the source for anime feature films like *Akira* (Otomo, 1988) and *Ghost in the Shell* (Oshii, 1995). Although animation also includes pinscreen[2] animation, stop-motion animation, direct or scratch-on-film, and 3-D puppet and clay animation, by the 1910s cel and paper animation already dominated the form (Furniss 2008, 16). Cel animation (today largely displaced by computer animation) is so called because animators draw objects, subjects, and backgrounds on separate sheets of transparent celluloid acetate sheets called cels (patented by Earl Hurd and J. R. Bray in 1915), which are laid on top of one another in order to save time in an extraordinarily labor-intensive medium (one second of film can equal 12–24 individual drawings).

Animation's precursors date back to the earliest examples of human art in the cave paintings of Lascaux and Altamira, which suggested motion through the segmentation and duplication of animal limbs in prehistoric cave paintings of hunters and prey. Animation also has links to Egyptian hieroglyphics, which created meaning through sequential drawings. Perhaps its strongest roots are in the eighteenth-century graphic tradition of illustration, caricature, and satire of British artists like Thomas Rowlandson (1756–1827), William Hogarth (1697–1764), James Gillray (1757–1815), and George Cruikshank (1792–1878), and nineteenth-century artists like John Tenniel (1820–1915), who illustrated Lewis Carroll's *Alice in Wonderland*, and Wilhelm Busch (1832–1908), a German graphic artist and poet whose *Max und Moritz* (1865) series directly influenced Rudolph Dirks's *Katzenjammer* comic strip and Hearst's later animated film series. Many early animators like John Randolph Bray, Winsor McCay, and Max Fleischer were newspaper cartoonists or commercial illustrators. Animated cartoons in the teens and twenties were gag-based, and drew from graphic conventions of the comic strip and political cartoon with speech bubbles, dotted point-of-view lines, and simple symbols like a light bulb for an idea, or footprints for motion. Some of the earliest animated films like James Stuart Blackton's *Enchanted Drawing* (1900) and *Humorous Phases of Funny Faces* (1906), or Winsor McCay's *Gertie the Dinosaur* (1914) were influenced by vaudeville or traveling fairs in which the artist quickly created drawings on paper or blackboard called "lightning sketches." Many animated cartoons capitalized on the popularity of preexisting comic-strip characters, like Winsor McCay's Little Nemo, E. C. Segar's Popeye, Bud Fisher's Mutt and Jeff, Andy Capp's Li'l Abner, or George Herriman's Krazy Kat and Ignatz Mouse. Capitalizing on this popularity, the newspaper publishing magnate William Randolph Hearst (1863–1951) established an animation department as part of his film studio, International Film Service, in 1915, and converted many of his comic strips into animated cartoon series. The relationship also works the other way: For example, Disney's Mickey, Warner Bros.' Bugs Bunny, Daffy Duck, and Porky Pig, and Otto Messmer's Felix the Cat all became popular comic-book characters as a result of their initial theatrical success.

As the film industry shifted to an industrialized assembly-line system in the teens, so too did animation. As Donald Crafton has shown, the labor-intensive nature of animation (at sound speed of 24 fps, generally 12 drawings, each photographed twice, are used to produce one second on-screen) meant that 720 individual drawings (60 × 12) were needed to produce one minute on-screen. This meant that pioneer artisans like Émile Cohl in France, McCay in the United States, and Ladislas Starevich in Russia were replaced by animation studios created by Bray, Hearst, and French-Canadian Raoul Barré, whose mass-production requirements necessitated division and specialization of labor (Crafton 1982, 137–168). In 1914, Bray established the first animation studio, and Barré created the first animated cartoon series with *Colonel Heeza Liar in Africa* (1913) (Beck 2004, 89–90). Early inventions like Hurd's cels simplified and streamlined the production process, because, unlike paper, they were more durable and could be reused. Barré's development of a "peg and punch" system aided the precise registration of thousands of drawings (preventing the image from wavering), and his "slash and tear" method was a competing time-saver method to Hurd's cels, using a paper cutout that also reduced the need to redraw backgrounds. Animating on "twos" or "threes," or rephotographing every second or third drawing, reduced the total number of individual drawings by a third to a half (thus 480 or 720 drawings created one minute of action). All of these devices were labor-saving techniques designed to aid the animator in an assembly-line system.

Kristin Thompson suggests that with the decline of live-action films' novelty value beginning around 1907, cartoons replaced them in this function. Whereas live-action moved toward an emphasis on stars, narrative, genre, and ever-greater realism, animation stressed the cinema's magical qualities. Many cartoons self-reflexively foregrounded the process of their own creation, or what Crafton calls "self-figuration" (1982, 347), with cartoon studios of the teens and twenties developing cartoons that mixed live-action and animated forms – Walter Lantz's *Dinky Doodle* series showed animator Lantz interacting with Dinky, while the Fleischer Bros.' *Out of the Inkwell* (1919–1926) series began with Koko the Clown leaping out of a bottle of ink to play pranks on a live-action Max Fleischer. By contrast, Walt Disney's Alice series (1924–1927) featured a live-action girl interacting with an animated universe.

For much of the history of cel animation in the United States, comedy has been the dominant genre with the gag, metamorphosis, and slapstick predominating in the early silent and classical sound eras. By 1914, with Winsor McCay's Gertie, personality animation emerged and, by the 1930s, led by Disney, story would increasingly replace episodic gags, although formulae like the chase continued to be important. Pioneers in personality animation included Messmer (Felix the Cat) and the Fleischer Bros.' Koko the Clown and Bimbo. With the coming of sound to the film industry, musical cartoon series featuring popular musical forms like jazz, swing, the rumba, and samba proliferated in the early 1930s and included the Silly Symphonies (Disney), Looney Tunes and Merrie Melodies (Warner Bros.), Happy Harmonies (MGM), and the Swing Symphonies (Universal/Walter Lantz) series.

Disney's Impact on the Art Form

Disney's third Mickey Mouse cartoon, *Steamboat Willie* (1928), has often claimed the title of first synchronized sound cartoon, although this rightfully belonged to the Fleischer Bros.' first Song Car-Tune *Oh Mabel!* (1924). The Fleischer Bros.' *36 Song Car-Tunes* (1924–1927), including 19 De Forest sound-on-film cartoons first called Ko-Ko Song Car-Tunes, created a moving ball that bounced over the lyrics of a popular song, with which the audience was invited to sing along (these were renamed in 1929 as the "Screen Song" series). The Fleischers continued to innovate with the Betty Boop cartoons of the 1930s, featuring musical songs sung by their eponymous heroine, with guest stars like Cab Calloway in *Minnie the Moocher* (1932), *Snow White* (1933), and *The Old Man of the Mountain* (1933), and Louis Armstrong in *I'll Be Glad When You're Dead, You Rascal You* (1932). The Fleischers recorded their soundtracks after the animation whereas the Disney studios created the soundtrack first. Disney's character Oswald the Rabbit (1927–1928), and the first (silent) Mickey cartoon *Plane Crazy* (1928), as well as *Steamboat Willie*, were all animated by Ub Iwerks, who was one of his most important creative collaborators and who also animated the first Silly Symphony *Skeleton Dance* (1929).

Although Disney was not the pioneer in sound or color it has often claimed to be, the studio was a leader in using these new elements. It also pioneered the use of storyboards (the first form of a visual script to break down and plan action) in the early Mickey Mouse cartoons. Meanwhile at Warner Bros., Rudolf Ising and Hugh Harman developed a pilot sound cartoon, *Bosko the Talk-ink Kid* (1929/1930), which led to a contract with Leon Schlesinger to provide cartoons to Warner Bros. *Sinkin' in the Bathtub* (Harman/Ising, 1930) launched the Looney Tunes series, and the Merrie Melodies series followed in 1931, both designed to promote the Warner Bros. sound catalog.

Among Disney's most important competitors were the Fleischer Bros. The technical inventions of Max Fleischer included the rotoscope (1915, patented 1917), which involved the tracing of live-action photography onto cels to capture realistic motion (used extensively in their first feature, *Gulliver's Travels*, 1939), and the stereopticon, or setback (1933), a device to enhance three-dimensionality. This enabled the insertion of cels in front of, or into, a 3-D model set, which could be rotated on a turntable, and it was used extensively in the Popeye featurettes of the late 1930s (*Popeye the Sailor Meets Sindbad the Sailor*, 1936). European animators like Lotte Reiniger, however, had preceded the Americans in experimenting with depth.[3] Meanwhile at Disney, a team led by William Garity conducted early tests with the multiplane camera in *Three Orphan Kitties* (1935), and then *The Old Mill* (1937) (Smith 1987). The multiplane camera was a vertical (and later horizontal) camera system that allowed the camera to track downward past layers of paintings on sheets of glass that could move independently toward or away from the camera, in order to create the illusion of depth. It would later be used to masterly effect in features like *Snow White and the Seven Dwarfs* (1937), *Pinocchio* (1940), and *Bambi* (1942).

Where Disney was known for its bucolic and pastoral mise-en-scène, Fleischer cartoons of the 1930s and 1940s (and later those of Warner Bros. and MGM) were brashly urban, with stories set in factories, skyscrapers, nightclubs, and bars. The approach to storytelling varied as well, with Disney favoring a childlike innocence that was mocked in cartoons like Warner Bros.' *A Corny Concerto* (1943), which parodied *Fantasia* (1940), or MGM's *Swing Shift Cinderella* (1945), which made fun of Disney's earnest adaptations of fairy tales. The Fleischer Bros.' Betty Boop series addressed adult viewers, alluding to sexual desire, prohibition, and homosexuality. Even the death penalty was a pretext for a gag with the electric chair in *Betty Boop for President* (1932). Fleischer cartoons articulated social anxieties around sex, prostitution, unemployment, gambling, and vice, and would influence the adult humor of Warner Bros.' animation of the 1940s.

By the 1930s, Disney was pioneering a shift away from the dominant aesthetic of the 1920s, called *rubber hosing* (in which bodies and limbs of characters were like balloons or rubber hoses and could expand and contract at will), and toward a new technique called *squash and stretch*, in which characters had three-dimensionality and consistent volume and weight. The other major technological and formal innovations of the 1930s were the introduction of sound and three-strip Technicolor. While Bray had led the field with the earliest cartoon in color with *The Debut of Thomas the Cat* (1920) in the Brewster Color process, a British puppet cartoon, *In GollywogLand* (F. Martin Thornton, 1912/1916), made in Kinemacolor, has also been claimed as the first color cartoon.[4] With an exclusive three-year agreement with Herbert and Nathalie Kalmus's Technicolor Corporation, Disney introduced three-strip Technicolor (which combined red, green, and blue) in its Academy Award-winning short *Flowers and Trees* (1932), while the other studios had to content themselves with two-strip Technicolor (red and green) until 1934. Disney's first animated feature, *Snow White and the Seven Dwarfs*, featured a more discreet palette compared to the later *Fantasia*. Whereas, until the 1960s, color in live-action cinema was largely confined to travelogues, musicals, and costume and fantasy pictures like *The Adventures of Robin Hood* (1938), the animation industry led the way in color's generic association with fantasy.

Changes in the 1940s Cartoon: Speed and Sex

One of the major changes by the 1940s was the introduction of the screwball character (Woody Woodpecker, Bugs Bunny, Screwy Squirrel) and the extraordinary acceleration in narrative pacing and comedic speed pioneered by Tex Avery, first at Warner Bros., and then at MGM, where he moved in 1941. Animators like Avery, Bob Clampett, and Frank Tashlin at Warner Bros., and William Hanna and Joseph Barbera at MGM, made cartoons that were self-reflexive, hyperbolic, and full of sexual innuendos, and their hallmarks were absurdity and speed. Avery's cartoons were known for their direct address to the viewer, with characters who held up signs that commented on the action, or other characters with phrases like "Silly, isn't he?" Fred "Tex" Avery was an enormously influential animator. As Avery noted: "I found out that the eye can register an action in five frames of film. . . . Five frames of film at twenty-four a second, so it's roughly a fifth of a second to register something, from the screen to your eye to the brain" (Maltin 1987, 296). Avery's insight into the speed with which spectators can understand and process visual information shows he was a pioneer for the subliminal editing and breakneck narrative strategies that are the norm today. Humor and cynical sophistication were also hallmarks of Avery's work. World War II led to a partial relaxation of the Production Code, or Hollywood's self-censorship system, with more sexual jokes in cartoons, especially in those made exclusively for soldiers. However, even for the homefront audience, cartoons became more risqué. Avery's Woolfy and Showgirl series at MGM featured the sexual chases of a "Wolf" who exhibits various exaggerated expressions of sexual desire and appreciation for a showgirl (animated by Preston Blair), including erection jokes, such as the Wolf turning into a torpedo or a stiff cardboard figure, or hitting himself on the head with a mallet in his sexual excitement. In the Wolf series, Avery took reaction shots (called takes or extremes) further than any other animator, beginning with *Red Hot Riding Hood* (1943), followed by *Swing Shift Cinderella*, *Wild and Woolfy* (1945), and *Little Rural Riding Hood* (1949). Avery's influence is evident in a Tom and Jerry cartoon *Mouse Cleaning* (William Hanna and Joseph Barbera, 1948) where Tom's eyeballs disconnect from his head in an exaggerated take. Avery's satiric reinventions of traditional children's fairy tales as adult tales of male desire run amok, together with his hyperbolic formal experimentation and direct address, have influenced films like *The Mask* (1994) and *Who Framed Roger Rabbit* (1988), and contemporary animation like *South Park* and *The Simpsons*.

Animation and War

Propaganda, according to Webster's dictionary definition, is "the spreading of ideas, information, or rumor for the purpose of helping or injuring an institution, cause, or person." In other words, propaganda is always *tactical and strategic*, that is, it has specific goals. Like the rest of the film industry, animation studios soon shifted production toward the war effort after the United States declared war on Japan and Germany in December 1941. Hollywood features, newsreels, cartoons, and other shorts promoted a number of specific goals. These included: (1) clarifying why Americans were fighting, through a contrast between democracy and fascism; (2) promoting patriotism and solidarity with American allies, especially the British and French; (3) instilling a hatred of the enemy and challenging lingering currents of isolationism; and (4) encouraging Americans to do specific things – pay their taxes (*The New Spirit* and *Spirit of '43*, both Disney); buy war bonds (*Any Bonds Today*, Warner Bros.; *Seven Wise Dwarfs*, Disney); ration food (*Point Rationing of Foods*, Warner Bros.); recycle (*Weakly Reporter*, Warner Bros.); grow vegetables in "victory" gardens (*Barney Bear's Victory Garden*, MGM; *Ration Fer the Duration*, Fleischer Bros.); watch for spies and avoid gossip (*Spies* and *Rumors*, both Warner Bros.); and support the first peacetime draft initiated in 1940 (*Draftee Daffy* and *Draft Horse*, both Warner Bros.). While men were away at war, women took over traditional male jobs from driving taxis to factory work, and many cartoons acknowledged these social changes or used them as gags. For example, Tex Avery's modernized fairy tale *Swing Shift Cinderella* ends with Cinderella as a Bette Davis caricature catching the bus to the "Lockweed 12 o'clock aircraft shift."

Created in 1942, the First Motion Picture Unit (FMPU, known as "Fumpoo") or 18th Air Force Base was led by Rudolf Ising and was based at Culver City (Solomon 1994, 113). Like the Signal Corps unit in Dayton, Ohio, with 150 photo retouchers, FMPU's staff of 125–150 men combined limited animation, recycled cartoons, and live-action photography as cheap strategies to increase production and churn out training and propaganda films. For example, *The Thrifty Pig* (1941) was a recycled version of *The Three Little Pigs* (1933) with a Nazi wolf trying to blow down a brick house reinforced with war bonds.

Disney's production increased an extraordinary amount: from 37,000 feet before the war to 204,000 feet at the end of the fiscal year 1942–1943, with 95 percent dedicated to the war effort (and this with a third of Disney's original staff drafted) (Solomon 1994, 119). Actors like James Stewart and Clark Gable volunteered for the Air Force or Army, and so did animators. In addition to FMPU and the major animation studios (Warners, Disney, Fleischers, MGM, Columbia, etc.), independent animation contractors like former Disney animator Mel Shaw and former MGM director Hugh Harman also competed for war contracts. By the mid-1940s, major studios were devoting most of their workloads to projects for the US Army, Navy, and Air Force.

Like the rest of Hollywood, animation studios turned over some of their physical plant for War Department needs and devoted production to war-related matters. The Army billeted men in the Disney studios and stored ammunition for the defense of the California coastline there. Disney animators designed free cartoon logos for 1,400 civilian and military units, with many of them featuring Disney characters – the most popular of which was Donald, who appeared on 25 percent of the logos (Solomon 1994, 117–119). Walter Lantz studios did the same with logos featuring their stars Andy Panda and Woody Woodpecker.

Wartime animation was of two principal types: either the explicit propaganda short or those animated films that made incidental or passing references to the war. Disney led the first category with earnest propaganda cartoons, including *Education for Death: The Making of a Nazi* (Clyde Geronimi, 1943) – a *Bildungsroman* of a young German boy, Fritz, growing up, becoming indoctrinated, and joining the Nazi war machine. Also directed by Clyde Geronimi in 1943 was *Chicken Little*, a barnyard parable about a fox, Foxy Loxy, who wants to get into the henhouse. He reads from a "Psychology" book (originally titled *Mein Kampf*), quoting: "If you tell 'em a lie, don't tell a little one, tell a big one." Indeed, animal allegories like Warner Bros.' *The Ducktators* (1942) were among the simplest ways to refashion fables or fairy tales (which already contained moral lessons or warnings) with wartime messages about the threat of fascism or demagogues. Parables in cartoons had also appeared before the United States joined the war, the most notable of which was MGM's Academy Award-nominated *Peace on Earth* (Hugh Harman, 1939), a Christmas fable in which Grandpa Squirrel tells his grandchildren how human beings ended up wiping themselves out through endless war. This allegory about the human proclivity for violence and destruction would be picked up more obliquely in the ominous figure of "Man" in *Bambi*, as we will discuss below.

The second category of cartoons, or those which made passing or incidental references to the war, included many allusions to blackouts, "no unnecessary travel," and the rationing of meat and other luxuries, as with Bob Clampett's *Coal Black and de Sebben Dwarfs* (Warner Bros., 1943), a parody of Disney's feature *Snow White and the Seven Dwarfs*, which replaces the film's white characters with black racial caricatures. In Clampett's version, the "Wicked Queenie" is rich in scarce wartime goods: white-walled tires, coffee, and sugar. She hires Murder, Inc. to "black out So White," and their van has the racial sight "gag" "We rub out anyone, $1. 1/2 price midgets. Japs free."

Although films like *Peace on Earth* and *Education for Death* adopted a serious tone, many more propaganda cartoons used comedy as a strategy to disarm audiences. Donald Duck in *Der Führer's Face* (1943) dreams he lives in Nazi Germany and is an assembly-line worker in a munitions factory. Like Chaplin in *Modern Times* (1936), Donald can't keep up with his workload. As he struggles to keep saluting ("Heil Hitler! Heil Hitler!" he quacks repeatedly to Hitler's portrait) while simultaneously screwing on the tops of bombs, he eventually becomes entangled in the production line. All the while, anthropomorphized fascist loudspeakers yell at Donald to work faster or to take an enforced (20-second) vacation. *Der Führer's Face* featured marvelous surreal sequences which, like the earlier "Pink Elephants" sequence in *Dumbo* (1941) and the riotous musical climaxes in *Saludos Amigos* (1943) and *Three Caballeros* (1945), were rare departures from Disney's dominant aesthetic of verisimilitude.

Many wartime cartoons used language as a comedic device, exaggerating the speech patterns of Adolf Hitler who speaks a pseudo-German (as in Tex Avery's *Blitz Wolf*, 1942), just as Charlie Chaplin parodied Hitler with a spluttering Adenoid Hynkel in *The Great Dictator* (1940). Caricatures of enemy leaders like Hitler, Benito "Il Duce" Mussolini, or Emperor Hirohito, or political or military figures like Hideki Tojo, Joseph Goebbels, or Hermann Göring,

Figure 19.1 Donald Duck dreams he is a Nazi worker in Jack Kinney's *Der Führer's Face* (1943, producer Walt Disney). (Image enlargement.)

frequently appeared with exaggerated physical features, implying negative character traits (Goebbels was often small, weasel-like, and green, Mussolini was a burly buffoon and a braggart).

Racist attitudes and stereotypes also shaped differences in caricaturing the enemy, with the Italians and Germans being treated quite differently from the Japanese. Thus, Mussolini and Hitler were usually shown as buffoons speaking a nonsensical Italian ("tutti-frutti") or German in *The Ducktators*, a barnyard parable with Hitler, Tojo, and Mussolini as ducks, but the Japanese were repeatedly caricatured in racial terms, often with large glasses and protruding teeth; as Popeye describes them, they are "slant-eyed, buck-toothed, yellow-skinned Japansies" in *You're a Sap Mr. Jap* (1942), and appear in similar fashion in *Tokio Jokio* (1943). *Bugs Bunny Nips the Nips* (1944) is typical of deeply embedded white American racial attitudes. Bugs washes up on a Pacific Island and finds Japanese soldiers quartered there. Pretending to be a Good Humor ice cream salesman, he hands out grenades to them disguised as popsicles, saying "here's yours, bowlegs, here's one for you monkey face . . . Here ya are slant eyes."

In other words, animation was a disarming and deceptively entertaining system to convey specific dominant ideologies, whether in the form of demeaning racial caricatures or to exercise control and manipulation of the GI and the home front. Animation was especially useful in training soldiers in particular skills and had already been used in World War I.[5] And while many training films were largely in live-action, the use of animation for select sequences was a visually simple way to communicate highly technical, yet vitally important, information (because it could save lives), often to soldiers with limited education and literacy skills. It gave advice on the care and maintenance of weaponry (*Gas, Fighting Tools*), suggested survival strategies for the battlefield, explained how to identify enemy warplanes or boats, and warned GIs about booby traps (*Booby Traps*) and Axis spies (*Plane Daffy, Spies*). It stressed the importance of keeping one's gun clean and one's mouth shut (*Spies*, *Rumors*), and taking one's malaria shot (*The Winged Scourge, Private Snafu vs. Malaria Mike*). A training film like *How to Fly a Lazy Eight* stressed the importance of pilots turning slowly when flying a figure eight (or else the plane would stall, leading to a potentially fatal situation), and FMPU used Mae West's voice and caricature to convey the message with humor and sexual innuendo. Disney made over 200 training films in the course of World War II, such as *Stop That Tank* (1942), which taught soldiers through a mixture of animated and live-action sequences how to use a particular antitank weapon. It opened with an animated Hitler speaking the usual comedic German (spluttering words like "sauerkraut") in a little tank. The effectiveness of the antitank gun eventually sends Hitler down to hell, where he throws tantrums, and the Devil mockingly tells us, "he says he's being oppressed." Adopting the sexual allusions of many wartime cartoons, the cartoon ends showing a silhouetted soldier holding his rifle in his tent, observing that a rifle is like a woman – "It must be caressed and nourished." *Thunderstorms*, a black-and-white Disney training film commissioned by the Bureau of Aeronautics, showed pilots when they could fly into thunderstorms, and when they should fly around them. As always, these were quick, cheap productions, with Disney recycling weather sequences from *Bambi* in *Thunderstorms*.

Warner Bros. (through Leon Schlesinger Productions) made 26 cartoons between 1943 and 1945 featuring a GI character named SNAFU (an acronym, "situation normal – all fucked up") for the *Army-Navy Screen Magazine* film series for soldiers. These cartoons educated through comedy. Frequently, the stupidity of the series' protagonist, Private Snafu, led to his premature death or imprisonment in a POW camp, because he does not take appropriate precautions (*Booby Traps*). A number of the cartoons (*Gripes*, *Spies*, *Rumors*) were written by Theodor Geisel (Dr Seuss) and featured his distinctive rhyming schemes. Warner Bros. also made a similar Capt. Hook series for the Navy.

Many wartime cartoons featured cartoon stars like Donald and Daffy Duck as enlisted soldiers. Daffy Duck is terrified of a visit from the persistent little man from the Draft Board in *Draftee Daffy* (1945); Donald is grouchy about training marches in *Fall Out, Fall In* (1943); Pluto wants to join up in *The Army Mascot* (1942); while Popeye is a wartime sailor in *The Mighty Navy* (1941). Popeye and his can of spinach (a Fleischer addition to the Segar comic strip) was a metaphor for the industrial strength of wartime America, and the Superman series showed the superhero fighting against industrial sabotage, Axis spies, and fifth columnists in Fleischer cartoons like *Japoteurs* (1942) and *Secret Agent* (1943). Using stars like Bugs, Daffy, and Popeye suggested that they embodied vital wartime virtues like toughness, persistence, and determination; further, that these were uniquely American values, as with the wisecracking coolness of Bugs Bunny, who is slow to anger but who also means business when he declares in his Brooklyn accent, "This means war!" (using Groucho Marx's famous phrase). Bugs suggests in *Super Rabbit* (1943) that citizen soldiers are the real heroes. He enters a phone booth, saying, "this is a job for a real superman," and exits dressed as a Marine. Historian Steve Schneider suggests that "Bugs Bunny has been loved for over a quarter of a century now, but he has never been loved the way he was during the war years.... [He] was a symbol of America's resistance to Hitler and the fascist powers ... and it is most difficult now to comprehend the tremendous emotional impact Bugs Bunny exerted on the audience then" (1988, 181).

As for Daffy Duck, in his earliest incarnations in *Porky's Duck Hunt* (1937) and *The Daffy Doc* (1938), he was a screwball rather than a cantankerous character. Schneider suggests that Daffy's screwiness and impetuosity were ideologically useful:

> the character became heroic, a blaze of unstoppable spirit useable for patriotic ends ... If the duck's lack of restraint permits him to do anything, let him do it against the enemy. (1988, 156)

For example, *Plane Daffy* (1944) spoofs the World War I fighter pilot genre and the classic femme fatale spy Mata Hari. Daffy Duck plays a courier pilot with a "military secret" who is determined to withstand the sexual wiles of "Hatta Mari, a gal who's a spy for the enemy Axis." We know she is a Nazi spy because in quick succession we see three rapid zoom-ins on swastika earrings, a swastika garter belt, and a swastika brooch on her shoes. The sequence is hilarious precisely because the swastikas are such overt signifiers. Hatta Mari has been responsible for the death of many a fighter pilot, including the unfortunate Homer Pigeon, who was easily seduced by her wiles. Determined to fight the Nazi femme fatale, Daffy says, "I'm the squadron woman hater! She won't get to first base, this Hatta Mari tomater!" Frank Tashlin humorously plays with abrupt changes in pace between extremely fast and very slow movement when Daffy speeds away from Hatta Mari, then leisurely climbs some steps (mickey-moused with single piano notes), then resumes his dash (with a smear of paint for blurred motion). The military secret turns out to be a piece of paper that says "Hitler is a stinker," and then caricatures of Göring and Goebbels pop up to say, "Ja, everybody knows that."

Cartoons were not always subtle in their ideological approach. The US Treasury commissioned Disney to make *The New Spirit* (1942) in order to explain why a massive expansion of taxation under Roosevelt was necessary to fight the war. It spawned a sequel, *The Spirit of '43*, in which Donald Duck is confronted by his good angel, a Scottish-accented figure who advises him to save his money and "fight the Axis by paying his taxes," but Donald also has a bad zoot-suit-wearing devil who encourages his spendthrift nature. The cartoon warns Donald and the audience that they need to remember the following dates (March 15, June 15, September 15, December 15), "when" as the cartoon's voiceover portentously announces, "every American should pay his or her income taxes, gladly and proudly." It demands of the audience: "Will you have enough money on hand to pay your taxes when they fall due?" It urges: "Spend for the Axis, or save for taxes!" Warner Bros. was particularly dedicated to the antifascist fight and was the first studio to make anti-Nazi live-action films like *Confessions of a Nazi Spy* (1939), after a Jewish employee was beaten to death in 1936 in Berlin. Their cartoon *Russian Rhapsody* (1944) promoted solidarity with the Soviets, with a comical Hitler, speaking pseudo-German, going off in a plane to bomb Moscow. He is soon sabotaged by Russian gremlins who sing: "We are the gremlins from the Kremlin" (to the tune of a Russian folksong, "Orchechornya"). Hitler crashes his plane after the gremlins frighten him by wearing a mask of Joseph Stalin.

Disney first turned to feature film production for economic reasons. With the introduction of color and sound, his animated shorts became increasingly expensive, with costs outweighing profit. In addition, a shift to features allowed for greater character and story development and away from the limitations of gag-based comedy. Let's take a look now at a representative example of Disney's feature work with *Bambi*. Although Disney first conceived of *Bambi* as far back as 1935, even as he began work on his first feature-length animated film *Snow White and the Seven Dwarfs*, *Bambi* took five years to make.[6] Delayed partially by the 1941 studio strike and the onset of war, it was preceded by the release of *Pinocchio* (1940), *Fantasia*, *The Reluctant Dragon* (1941), and *Dumbo*.

Bambi

Promoted in its trailers as "the world's greatest love story," *Bambi* premiered on August 8, 1942, and received three Academy Award nominations: Best Song ("Love is a Song"), Best Sound, and Best Musical Score. It lost money on its initial release, leading Disney to re-release *Snow White and the Seven Dwarfs* in 1944, but by 1947 with a re-release, it began to recoup its $2 million cost.[7] After *Snow White*, Disney wanted to make a feature entirely with animal characters. He once observed, "I'm a lover of nature. I respect nature very much.... I feel that observing the habits of the creatures of nature, man can learn a lot."[8] The film was based on Austrian Felix Salten's 1923 novel *Bambi: Ein Leben im Walde/A Life in the Woods*,[9] and the central character's name was derived from the Italian word *bambino*, "little one." The innovations of this film were in two principal areas: (1) the stylized naturalism of the landscape backgrounds, with the environment of the forest and the meadow based on the impressionist paintings of inspirational artist Tyrus Wong; and (2) the stylized anatomical verisimilitude of the animal designs and motion. A strong believer in improving his animators' draftsmanship, Disney had paid his animators to attend the Chouinard Art Institute a decade earlier, and in 1932, he began studio art classes led by Don Graham. As part of Disney's educational training programs, animators also attended the lectures of Rico LeBrun, a painter who specialized in animals.

The animators initially drew from real deer, skunk, and rabbit models, but as these studio models rapidly became domesticated, the animators also turned to studying Maurice Day's documentary footage of animals and foliage in Maine and made trips to the Los Angeles Zoo. Drawing deer presented certain challenges, with their eyes on either side of the face, small chins, and the wide gap between eyes and mouth – the latter two elements being key ways to express personality in animation. Bambi's head is stylized, rounder than a real deer's head, and the eyes are exaggeratedly large to aid expression. The original deer of Salten's novel were changed from European roe deer to American white-tailed deer, and the character of Thumper was a Disney addition. Other innovations included complex establishing shots created with the multiplane camera, giving an extraordinary sense of depth to the forest mise-en-scène in expository establishing shots and specific sequences like "April Showers." Disney also sent two cameramen to Katahdin State Forest in Maine to shoot model footage of the deer and foliage for the animators (Grant 1987, 197), and David Whitely has also suggested that Yosemite National Park and its landmarks provided another important visual referent for the film (2008, 65–68).

Anthropomorphism and the Cycle of Life

Snow White and the Seven Dwarfs and the features that followed in the 1940s established a recurrent Disney theme: the separation, orphanage, or isolation of child from parent, whether it be Dumbo, who loses his mother to the circus, or Pinocchio, who is imprisoned by Stromboli and later taken to a Dickensian Pleasure Island where little boys are turned into donkeys. Similarly, Snow White has no mother, and her wicked stepmother the Queen seeks her death. When she flees into the forest, she discovers the Seven Dwarfs' cottage, which she initially assumes to belong to children, because their furniture is so small. She wonders if, like her, they have no parents; in turn, she becomes a mother for them, cleaning house and making the dwarfs wash their hands before dinner.

Sharing with the other features a theme of childhood loss, *Bambi* is a *Bildungsroman*, a portrait of the eponymous hero's physical and emotional growth to adulthood (including mating and reproduction), which includes his two anthropomorphized friends, Thumper Rabbit and Flower the skunk.

Part of this maturation process is the experience of loss and death, and one of the film's most powerful and traumatic scenes is the tragic loss of Bambi's mother (voiced by Paula Winslowe), who is shot in the meadow by "Man" the hunter. Original plans that included Bambi returning to find his mother dying in a pool of blood were scrapped as too gruesome, yet the mother's offscreen death nonetheless remains an emotionally devastating scene. The immensity of Bambi's loss is accentuated through acoustic and visual strategies: As Bambi searches for her, repeatedly crying "Mother," we hear a nondiegetic choir humming. The reality of Bambi's now permanent isolation is intensified by the special effects of snow falling ever more densely in the foreground, which also softens the entrance of Bambi's father, as he delivers the dreadful words: "Your mother can't be with you anymore."

Bambi continued Disney's pioneering development of the animation of weather effects, expanding on techniques that he first experimented with in the 1937 Silly Symphony *The Old Mill*, with rain, wind, thunder, and lightning. When Disney shifted into features, he developed a new animation department called special effects, in which animators specialized in animating water or light or shadows. These artists created the striking shadows and subtle candlelight that mimicked live-action chiaroscuro cinematography, when the Wicked Queen transforms into an old hag in *Snow White*. They pioneered the realistic animation of water in the underwater scenes with Monstro the Whale in *Pinocchio*. In *Bambi* the pastoral mise-en-scène is the setting against which the characters grow and mature, and the special effects department created the extraordinary detail needed for the seasonal transitions from spring to winter, and expanded on water and light effects with innovations in the representation of snow and fire.

Another pioneering technique used in *Bambi* was the voice talent, which included actual children's voices for the animals: Bambi (voiced by four different actors at different ages, including Bobby Stewart, Donnie Dunagan, Hardie Albright, and John Sutherland), Thumper (Peter Behn and the adult voices of Sam Edwards and Tim Davis), and Flower (Stan Alexander, and the adults Sterling Holloway and Tim Davis). Most famously, the distinctive voice of Thumper Rabbit was that of Peter Behn, a very young child whose comedic charm led to an

Figure 19.2 Anthropomorphized *Bildungsroman*: Thumper, Bambi, and Flower grow up together as friends in David Hand's *Bambi* (1942, producer Walt Disney). (Image enlargement.)

expansion of Disney's anthropomorphic addition to the Salten story. Thumper is essentially a precocious, rambunctious little boy, whose name and tendency to thump his rabbit foot in excitement suggest his personality. His vivid character was a striking example of the studio's development of personality animation, which used subtle physical and facial details to convey individuality.

For example, when Thumper mocks Bambi's spindly attempts to walk as a young fawn, his mother intervenes. "Thumper!," comes a stern voice from off-frame. The camera pans left to reveal Mrs Rabbit. Like a contrite child, Thumper responds, "Yes, Mama." She sternly asks him, "What did your father tell you this morning?" Clearly, he has done this before (and not so long ago at that). With his eyes closed, Thumper recites as if from an oft-repeated lesson he has learned by heart, "If you can't say something nice . . . " (He then pauses, almost forgetting the next part.) Taking a deep breath, with a twitch of the nose, he then recovers the thread, "don't say nothing at all." Physical behavior conveys a character's thought process and personality. As Thumper speaks, he goes slightly pink, puts his paws behind his back, and his ears go back. He starts to rotate his left foot in concentration, expands his chest as he pauses, and then opens his eyes and looks to his mother for approval at the end of his speech. These physical details help suggest a succession of emotions – the recalcitrance, embarrassment, contrition, and restlessness typical of a young child. As Milt Kahl, one of the four supervisors, noted in a lecture on this scene, "Peter Behn had trouble remembering the lines, so the animators used the hesitation, to suggest a similar one in the character: the main thing is that in this case you have fairly subtle ideas, but the changes of mood he goes through are strong enough to be successful" (Canemaker 2001, 141). Like human children, Thumper also doesn't like to eat his vegetables. He tells Bambi how much he loves eating blossoms, in preference to clover. Just as he is about to bite a blossom, Thumper's Mother again scolds. "What did your father tell you about eating the blossoms and leaving the greens?" As we hear these lines, Ollie Johnston enhances the comedy with a "hold" or freeze, with Thumper poised with his mouth wide open over his favorite blossoms.

Bambi's growth to adulthood, along with that of his friends, structures the narrative: He experiences the natural world with all its wonders (a rainstorm); he sees his reflection for the first time (which startles him); he goes ice-skating with Thumper in winter; and he meets Faline, with whom he will eventually mate. A major rite of passage in this pastoral *Bildungsroman* is the "Twitterpated" sequence where Bambi, Flower, and Thumper learn about springtime mating and the necessity to avoid it from Friend Owl (voiced by Bill Wright), who warns them: "nearly everyone gets twitterpated in the spring time." Despite the warnings, Flower falls in love with a female skunk, and a subtle erection joke follows. After she kisses him, Flower turns red, then stiff as a board, and falls over. A similar scenario develops with Thumper, who spots Miss Bunny, the future Mrs Thumper. Here anthropomorphic details of her primping and preening, stroking her ears as if they were hair, plumping her cheeks, chest, and tail as if they were clothing (all the while humming to herself), transform the rabbit's behavior into recognizable human actions. Staging of the shots or the arrangement of the character in the space also accentuates certain details. Disney's shots mimic live-action editing, as we cut between reaction shots of a stunned Thumper and Miss Bunny, as she walks closer and closer to the (implied) camera, until her giant blue eyes dominate the frame, underscoring her mesmerizing quality. Thumper's arousal is an intense thumping of his foot, and again a subtle sexual pun follows where Miss Bunny touches his nose, and he collapses. Meanwhile, Bambi turns away in disgust, only to run smack dab into Faline, who now has matured into a young doe, and for whom he too becomes "twitterpated."

Dread and Death

Yet, lighthearted sequences like springtime mating alternate with scenes of dread in *Bambi*. The violence, death, and social displacement that Man the Hunter brings in the form of a forest fire could not but have reminded audiences of the world war then raging. Initially premiered in London in August 1942, *Bambi*'s release in New York had been delayed by over a month with the extended run of another wartime melodrama, *Mrs. Miniver*, which, like *Bambi*, deals with the loss and suffering that war brings.

Bambi links a strong sense of dread with a specific space: the meadow that tempts the young deer with its openness and plenitude. Bambi's mother's quiet-spoken yet intensely serious voice helps establish this sense of dread, which prompts Bambi to slink back into the grass, ears back in fear, as she warns:

> "You must never rush out on the meadow. There might be danger. Out there we are unprotected. The meadow is wide and open and there are no trees or bushes to hide us so we have to be very careful. Wait here. I'll go out first and if the meadow's safe, I'll call you."

To heighten the tension at this moment there is no nondiegetic score, and then strings and woodwinds play slow, isolated phrases that start and stop, mimicking the cautious actions of Bambi's mother as she advances into the meadow, ears cocked for signs of danger.

The meadow scene emphasizes that nature is not only a playground for the adventurous young Bambi and Thumper, but also dangerous and foreboding, and this dread comes largely from "Man," an ominous figure who is much talked of but never shown full-frame. Largely because of his success in evading Man, Bambi's father is noble; his longevity brings him respect and communal status. As Bambi's mother says, "of all the deer in the forest, not one has lived half so long. That's why he's known as the Great Prince of the Forest." Hence, Bambi's family is an aristocracy of survival, and Bambi's own birth at the beginning of the narrative marks him as a celebrity, just as the birth of the adult Bambi's two baby fawns, which concludes the film, suggests that a new "circle of life" begins again (a theme renewed 50 years later in *The Lion King*).

As the "young Prince," Bambi must survive in order to mature, whether a battle with Ronno for his mate Faline, or a gunshot wound which, unlike his mother, he can overcome ("get up Bambi," urges his father). To survive, one must be extraordinarily cautious (skills taught by his mother), and even then, this does not guarantee life. Coolness under fire is required, and a scene with a quail shows the consequences of fear. When Man returns to hunt, the quail becomes hysterical with the tension, shrieking, "I can't stand it anymore!" Despite the other animals' warnings, she flies up and is shot. This scene intensifies the sense of dread we feel every time Man is spoken of ("Man – was in the forest"), for when the animals speak of him, it is in abstracting, emphatic terms – and we only see him metonymically as arms or feet. When Bambi grows into an adolescent, his father takes over his instruction. A large hunting party has arrived, and Bambi's father warns, "It is Man. HE is here again. There are many this time. We must go deep into the forest – Hurry!"

Wise counsel, because Man once again brings death, and Bambi must rescue Faline, who has been cornered by Man's hunting dogs. Man's carelessness with his fire leads to the inferno that sweeps the forest. A wide shot of the valley reveals the spreading forest fire, with crows circling in the sky. Panic follows, with all the animals (rabbits, chipmunks, squirrels, birds, deer) fleeing and seeking refuge on an island in the middle of a lake. We see anthropomorphized refugee mice, birds, raccoons, and possums with their offspring coming ashore, backlit against the blazing fire. For the audiences of the day, images of flames and refugees could not but remind them of the Blitz and wartime bombing, and those fleeing Nazi Germany.

The Musical and Domesticated World of Nature

Ted Sears, who worked on *Bambi* in story development, said: "I think we should get away from the book. I think we should look at it as a symphony based on the story of Bambi."[10] So far, we have seen that *Bambi* typifies Disney's binary representation of nature as either terrifying, haunted, and violent or benign, domesticated, and anthropomorphic. One is a violent nightmare, where Man is in the forest and brings sudden death and fire; the other is a cozy playground of anthropomorphic animals who frolic in play and mating rituals among beds of flowers. Disney's 75 Silly Symphony cartoon shorts, made between 1929 and 1939, established this close relationship of the pastoral and the musical, as we see in *Winter* (1930) raccoons and rams go ice-skating, while a mouse plays icicles as if they were a xylophone. Flowers and fish dance to Pan's music in *Playful Pan* (1930), and in *Summer* (1930), caterpillars, dragonflies, and stick insects dance and play. As in *Steamboat Willie*, animals become musical instruments, playing one another as if they were drums or pianos.

In other words, if nature is sometimes cozily bucolic, with friendly rabbits and chipmunks who help Snow White with her domestic tasks ("Whistle While You Work"), it is always musical, and the domestic and the pastoral are frequently conjoined through the expository and atmospheric use of classical music. In *Bambi*, a symphonic structure narrates a film in which there is limited dialogue, introducing the deer community and the Great Prince. Through Bambi's eyes, we see and hear the herd on the meadow for the first time, as the nondiegetic score by Frank Churchill and Edward Plumb mimics the tempo and physical movement of the characters. String instruments mickey-mouse, or precisely mimic, the tempo, "shape," and rhythm of the playful prancing of the deer, and then Bambi also imitates their movement. French horns mark the magisterial entrance of Bambi's father. The symphonic score can also express dramatic conflict: As Bambi fights Ronno for Faline, the clash of percussion is an analogue to the expressionistic rim lighting depicting the battling deer.

The "April Showers" song sequence musically narrates Bambi's first experience of rain. It starts with mickey-moused clarinet notes paralleling isolated drops of rain that accelerate in tempo, to which a triangle joins. A vocal accompaniment then joins in, singing, "drip drip drop, little April showers." *Bambi* was one of the few features in which all the songs (written by Churchill and Larry Morey) are nondiegetic rather than sung by characters. Dramatic attention is on the beautifully detailed water effects and the various animal families scurrying for shelter (quails, birds, squirrels), beautifully animated by Sylvia Holland. A field mouse that darts from mushroom to mushroom becomes our focal point for a time, comically sheltering beneath a mother pheasant's tail. Three-dimensionality is enhanced by foreground elements of branches and leaves, as the multiplane camera pans to follow the rivulets of water that pour down in the middle field of action. The dramatic midpoint of the song is marked by a slow pan upward to the tops of trees as lightning begins, and we cut back to Bambi, who now hides beneath his mother, terrified of the alternating flashes of light and dark that simulate a lightning effect. The vocal and instrumental score accelerates as edits quicken, cutting to a low angle shot of the treetops and a backlit shot of a family of rabbits looking out from a cave. Like the flashes of lightning in *The Mad Doctor* (1933) and *Snow White*, lightning illuminates as if it were an X-ray, showing the veins of the leaves. At last, the musical and visual tempo slows with the diminishing raindrops, and a track out with the camera takes us through a thick forest of leaves, concluding with a tilt down to raindrops slowly dripping on a reflection of the dramatic orange sky. And so we move musically through the seasons, which score Bambi's growth and experience. From facing his first rainstorm to delighting in flowers and butterflies, or negotiating a frozen lake in winter and seeing his first snow, Bambi grows and matures, and at every step Disney's musical score shapes our perception of the narrative and emotional significance of these events.

After the enormous success of *Snow White*, the features of the wartime years like *Bambi*, *Dumbo*, and *Fantasia* were financial disappointments, partly due to the higher production costs and loss of the European markets caused by World War II. In response to these serious financial constraints that threatened the company's existence, Disney adopted money-saving strategies for the remainder of the decade. Feature films became partially live-action, like *The Reluctant Dragon* and *Victory Through Air Power* (1943), or were anthologies of shorter cartoons. Strung together with animated transitions linked by characters like Donald Duck, these anthology or package features would include *Make Mine Music* in 1946 (which featured "Peter and the Wolf"), *Fun and Fancy Free* (1947) with "Mickey and the Beanstalk," and *Melody Time* (1948) with "Little Toot" and "Johnny Appleseed." Even the Latin American package films *Saludos Amigos* and *The Three Caballeros* were underwritten by Nelson Rockefeller's Office of the Coordinator of Inter-American Affairs (CIAA), as part of its "Good Neighbor" policy, which sponsored visits of Disney animators to research and produce South American-themed shorts and was designed to shore up Latin American countries like Brazil, Argentina, Chile, Paraguay, and Peru against fascist influence. More importantly for Disney, this financial support became an opportunity to cultivate a new market to replace the European one he had lost during the war. After *Bambi*, Disney would make seven of these anthology feature films, and it was not until *Cinderella* in 1950 that the company would return to making a feature-length animated story. Today, *Bambi* is a key film in the Disney canon. With its iconic characters Bambi and Thumper, its lyrical depiction of natural landscape and seasonal change, its skillful blend of documentary-like observation of animal movement and comedic anthropomorphism, and its emotionally powerful and manipulative depiction of pastoral life, *Bambi* would influence many Disney features to follow.

Notes

1. First called a Daedalum when it was invented by William Horner in 1834, the zoetrope was given its name by Pierre Desvignes. The device was a cylinder with slits on the side, through which one could view drawings on a strip of paper. When rotated, the images seemed to move. A praxinoscope was a similar device that used mirrors instead of slits. A thaumatrope was a card with a different picture on each side attached to two strings, which, when rapidly rotated, seemed to combine the two images (e.g., a bird and a cage appear to be superimposed as a bird in a cage).
2. Pinscreen animation, developed by husband-and-wife animators Alexandre Alexeieff and Claire Parker, uses a screen of movable pins, which can be moved in or out by pressing an object onto the screen. The screen is lit from different angles so that the pins cast shadows to form images, which are photographed.
3. Disney and Fleischer were not the first to develop the illusion of three-dimensionality, as Lotte Reiniger had used a version of the multiplane camera in 1926 on *The Adventures of Prince Achmed*, as had Berthold Bartosch in 1930 for *The Idea* (Crafton 1982, 245).
4. Additive color processes, such as Kinemacolor (1906), could reproduce a specific color by adding and then mixing red and green through filters in the printing and projection process. Subtractive processes such as the Brewster method (1913), and later two-strip Technicolor (1922), split red and green light waves onto separate negatives, which were then recombined and printed. Three-strip Technicolor added blue to this process, for a result that combined red, green, and blue.
5. J. R. Bray's studio was the first company to produce military training films for the US government in World War I, with Max Fleischer supervising production at

Fort Sill in Oklahoma in 1918 (Beck 2004, 90). There were also war-themed cartoons with the *Colonel Heeza Liar* and *Mutt and Jeff* series (Shull & Wilt 1987, 12), and cartoons that mimicked newsreels, like Winsor McCay's *The Sinking of the Lusitania* (1918).

6. Four of the "Nine Old Men" (Milt Kahl, Eric Larson, Frank Thomas, and Ollie Johnston), or the leading animators in Disney's shift to feature production in the 1940s, worked part-time on the film. However, *Bambi* differed from the earlier features in that animators worked on specific sequences of the film rather than having sole responsibility for a character (Barrier 2003, 315).
7. Internet Movie Database, at http://www.imdb.com (accessed March 2015).
8. "The Magic Behind the Masterpiece," *Bambi*, two-disc CAV Laserdisc, 55th Anniversary Edition (1997). Also available on "The Making of Bambi," two-disc Special Platinum DVD Edition (2005). In 2011, Disney released a two-disc DVD/BluRay Diamond Edition with two deleted scenes and one deleted song previously not released.
9. Salten was a pseudonym for Austrian Jew Siegmund Salzmann, who was born in Budapest and later moved to Vienna. Initially published in 1923, *Bambi* was translated into English in 1928, and later became a Book of the Month selection. Disney purchased the rights to the story from Sidney A. Franklin for $1,000 in 1937. Franklin initially conceived of a live-action film, but realizing the practical difficulties approached Disney to make an animated version instead. Twin Books, a company that bought the rights to the novel from Salten's son-in-law, sued Disney for copyright infringement, arguing it was entitled to greater royalties (Disney's film and related publications were highly profitable). Copyright had originally been secured in 1926, and renewed by Salten's daughter Anna in 1954, but Disney successfully argued that the book had in fact been published in 1923 without copyright, and so in effect had passed into the public domain. This was reversed by an appeals court in 1996. See Paul Schons, "Bambi, the Austrian Deer," originally published by the Germanic-American Institute in September 2000, at http://courseweb.stthomas.edu/paschons/language_http/essays/salten.html (accessed February 2, 2009).
10. "Inside Walt's Story Meetings," Platinum DVD Edition, 2005.

References

Barrier, Michael. (2003). *Hollywood Cartoons: American Animation in its Golden Age*. New York: Oxford University Press.

Beck, Jerry. (2004). *Animation Art: From Pencil to Pixel, the History of Cartoon, Anime and CGI*. New York: Harper Design.

Canemaker, John. (2001). *Walt Disney's Nine Old Men and the Art of Animation*. New York: Disney Edition.

Crafton, Donald. (1982). *Before Mickey*. Cambridge, MA: MIT Press.

Furniss, Maureen. (2008). *Art in Motion: Animation Aesthetics*. Revised edn. New York: John Libbey.

Grant, John. (1987). *The Encyclopedia of Walt Disney's Animated Characters*. London: Hamlyn.

Maltin, Leonard. (1987). *Of Mice and Magic: A History of American Animated Cartoons*. Revised edn. New York: Plume.

Schneider, Steve (ed.). (1988). *That's All Folks! The Art of Warner Bros. Animation*. New York: Henry Holt.

Shull, Michael S., & Wilt, David. (1987). *Doing Their Bit: Wartime American Animated Short Films, 1939–1945*. Jefferson, NC: McFarland.

Smith, David. (1987). "New Dimensions – Beginnings of the Disney Multiplane Camera." In John Canemaker (ed.), *The Art of the Animated Image* (pp. 36–49). Los Angeles: American Film Institute.

Solomon, Charles. (1994). *The History of Animation: Enchanted Drawings*. Revised edn. New York: Random House.

Thompson, Kristin. (1980). "Implications of the Cel Animation Technique." In Teresa Lauretis & Stephen Heath (eds), *The Cinematic Apparatus* (pp. 106–120). New York: St Martin's Press.

Whitely, David. (2008). *The Idea of Nature in Disney Animation*. Aldershot: Ashgate.

20

Mapping *Why We Fight*

Frank Capra and the US Army Orientation Film in World War II

Charles Wolfe

Professor, University of California, Santa Barbara, United States

Charles Wolfe skillfully combines political history and close textual analysis in discussing the ***Why We Fight*** **documentaries**, produced as a seven-part series to explain America's involvement in World War II. He situates the project within an account of the government's wartime objectives and military bureaucracy, suggesting that, at the heart of this project supervised by **Frank Capra**, was a **rhetoric of mapping** that used the cinema's entire visual field, including **Disney animation**, to explain the geo-military, diplomatic, and civilian imperatives of the war effort. Tapping into traditions of socially engaged 1930s documentaries, *Why We Fight* was deployed as a teaching tool for soldiers headed overseas and for civilians on the home front. Wolfe claims that, while occasionally simplifying the conflict as an **"us" versus "them"** struggle, the series remained generally sensitive to the globally diverse cultures called upon to unite in defeating Germany and Japan. Wolfe illustrates how both **narrational style** and **editing tropes** contributed to educating a nation that, prior to **Pearl Harbor**, had been deeply wary of involvement in the world crisis. Wolfe's essay shares ground with Kirsten Moana Thompson on animation and Saverio Giovacchini on the Hollywood Left and World War II in this volume.

Additional terms, names, and concepts: "fireside chat," Film Section/Army's Special Services Division

In a "fireside chat" delivered over national radio on Washington's Birthday, February 23, 1942, President Franklin Delano Roosevelt offered an expansive account of the conflict in which the United States was now engaged, the scope of which extended far beyond Pearl Harbor and the events that had propelled US entry into the war 11 weeks before. The oceans of the world, Roosevelt stressed, were no longer buffers but battlefields and vital thoroughfares for communication and logistical supplies. "It is warfare in terms of every continent, every island, every sea, every air lane in the world," he explained. "That is the reason why I have asked you to take out and spread before you the map of the whole earth, and to

American Film History: Selected Readings, Origins to 1960, First Edition. Edited by Cynthia Lucia, Roy Grundmann, and Art Simon.
© 2016 John Wiley & Sons, Inc. Published 2016 by John Wiley & Sons, Inc.

follow with me in the references which I shall make to the world-encircling battle lines of this war." Referring repeatedly to the listener's map – "I ask you to look at your map again ... " – Roosevelt identified various continents, subcontinents, and nations where America's Allies were embattled: China and Russia, the British Isles, Australia and New Zealand, the Dutch Indies, India, the Near East, and Africa. "Look too at North America, Central America, and South America," he advised, and contemplate the consequences "if all these great reservoirs of power were cut off from each other either by enemy action or self-imposed isolation." Taking pains to dispel rumors that the US Pacific fleet had been completely destroyed at Pearl Harbor, Roosevelt insisted that topography was of greater consequence than surprise in the success of Japan's attack. Here, too, a world map revealed the true source of the challenge the Allies faced – Japan's complete domination of the islands between Hawaii and the Philippines. Yet the Axis Powers should take no comfort in this advantage, Roosevelt assured his listeners, for "Germany, Italy, and Japan are very close to the maximum output of planes, guns, tanks, and ships." The task for Americans now was to build up production "so that the United Nations can maintain control of the seas and attain control of the air."[1]

Roosevelt's address came at a crucial moment in the early conduct of the war. Negotiations with Churchill in the weeks following Pearl Harbor yielded their common commitment to an "Atlantic-first" strategy, but a series of early, dramatic losses in the Pacific led to mounting public sentiment that Japan rather than Germany should be the immediate focal point of the war effort. Roosevelt also was mindful of the calls from prewar isolationists for a quick, negotiated peace and of criticism from Republican opponents in Congress that the administration was using the circumscribed event of Pearl Harbor as an opportunity to expand executive authority and advance New Deal principles at home and abroad. In his radio talk, Roosevelt countered these criticisms by detailing the contours of a "new kind of war," situating the attack on Pearl Harbor within a broader historical narrative in which peaceable nations were pitted against aggressors and democratic institutions were threatened around the globe (Dallek 1979, 317–334).

Roosevelt's argument had taken shape over the course of a series of foreign policy pronouncements following Germany's invasion of Poland in September 1939, but the government's case for a multilateral war assumed its most intimate form in Roosevelt's fireside chats, in which he drew upon the conversational style and rhetoric of national crisis and commitment that informed his radio talks from the beginning of his presidency. Contending that US interests were inextricably bound up in distant conflicts, Roosevelt invited listeners to join him in visualizing their relation to world events in new ways. "Let us sit down together again, you and I, to consider our own pressing problems that confront us," Roosevelt proposed at the beginning of his May 26, 1940 fireside chat, and then explained how news from abroad had shattered the illusion, for whatever reason held, that "we are remote and isolated and, therefore, secure against the dangers from which no other land is free."[2] In a radio address announcing an Unlimited National Emergency, delivered live before the Governing Board of the Pan-American Union on May 27, 1941, he painted a striking picture of shadows lengthening across the European continent, Britain fighting valiantly along a "far-flung battle line," and Nazi forces parceling out the world to puppet regimes along the length of the Mediterranean and coastal Africa, only to extend their reach still further to Iceland and Greenland, which were but "stepping stones" to Canada and the islands of the North and South Atlantic. "Anyone with an atlas, anyone with a reasonable knowledge of the sudden striking force of modern war," Roosevelt concluded, "knows that it is stupid to wait until a probable enemy has gained a foothold from which to attack."[3]

Capitalizing on the geographic specificity of this earlier imagery, Roosevelt's fireside chat on Washington's Birthday, 1942, placed the national security argument in the framework of an international alliance. To his by now well-honed theme of defense against Axis aggression, he added a new metaphor. It was the task, not of the United States alone, but of a community of nations to exercise control over the seas and the air. Fought along many fronts, over many continents, the war in progress was only winnable in partnership with the "United Nations," a term proposed by Roosevelt during his negotiations with Churchill at the White House in December 1941, and incorporated into their Joint Declaration of the United Nations, released on January 1, 1942, accompanied by the signatures of 26 nations. The document affirmed the principles of the Anglo-American Atlantic Charter of August 1941, which called for the disarmament of aggressors and the self-determination of nations. Explaining the war as a defense of "life, liberty, independence, and religious freedom," the new document echoed language in the preamble to the US Declaration of Independence and Roosevelt's assertion of four essential human rights – freedom of speech and worship, freedom from want and fear – in his State of the Union address of January 1941. The signatories pledged to employ their full resources in the defeat of the Axis Powers and to make no separate peace with enemies, apart from the action of the coalition. The "United Nations" became Roosevelt's favored term for the Allies in his subsequent public statements and radio talks.

Meanwhile, behind the scenes, Army Chief of Staff Gen. George C. Marshall was developing plans for a fuller visualization of national defense aims. During the week prior to Roosevelt's Washington's Birthday address, on Marshall's approval, Hollywood director Frank Capra was commissioned a Major in the Signal Corps and appointed head of a new Film Section in the Army's Special Services Division.[4] The Film Section was the brainchild of Brig. Gen. Fredrick H. Osborn, an anthropologist, management consultant, and national defense adviser to the Roosevelt administration, whom Marshall had recruited to serve as Chief of the Army's Morale Branch in September 1941. Bringing a civilian perspective to bear on military bureaucracy, Osborn carved out space for Capra's fledgling film unit in the Morale Branch, or, as it was known by the time of Capra's appointment, the Division of Special Services (Culbert 1983, 174–175).[5] Capra reported not to the Signal Corps Photographic Center, where Army training films conventionally were produced, but to the Division's director of film, radio, and publication, Col. Edward L. Munson, Jr, who had served previously as the Army's representative to a blue-ribbon, civilian Committee for National Morale in 1940–1941.[6] Two weeks later, Marshall summoned Capra and Osborn to his office and requested that Capra immediately begin production on a series of orientation films explaining the causes and events of US entry into the war. A lecture series on this topic had been prepared by Col. Herman Beukema, an expert in German geopolitical philosophy at the US Military Academy, but Marshall thought the talks were uninspiring and had been unevenly presented.[7] With the active support of Osborn and Munson, Marshall now gambled that a film series produced by Capra – an Academy Award-winning director at the top of his profession – would provide the remedy.

Energized by the assignment, Capra temporarily resettled in Washington. With the aid of a civilian assistant, Edgar Peterson, and Russian-born Hollywood director Anatole Litvak, he began collecting and reviewing war-related films, including commercial newsreels, documentaries from Allied embassies and news bureaus, footage held by the Library of Congress and National Archives, and confiscated films from Germany, Italy, and Japan. Iris Barry of the Museum of Modern Art made available material from the Museum's Film Library, and arranged for a special screening of Leni Riefenstahl's *Triumph of the Will* at the National Archives in Washington.[8] In July 1942, Capra persuaded authorities to move his new Special Service film unit to Los Angeles, where he set up shop at the old Fox lot on Western Avenue, close to the resources of the major film studios. During the spring and summer months, scripts for a seven-part orientation series – collectively labeled *Why We Fight* – were completed and production on the first four films began. Related projects were also assigned to Capra's unit, including a six-part *Know Your Ally/Know Your Enemy* series, for soldiers entering the territory of combatant nations, and a biweekly *Army-Navy Screen Magazine* for recreational screening at military posts.[9] According to Capra's estimate at the time, by the fall of 1942 the film unit employed 15–20 officers and 55 enlisted men, with top talent from the studios also volunteering on specific projects.[10]

The *Why We Fight* films exemplified a new kind of Signal Corps documentary, one in which the historical and psychological conditions of combat took precedence over a narrow technical or tactical approach. In testimony before the Army Inspector General, whose office in the fall of 1942 investigated the possible redundancy and impropriety of the Signal Corps' ties to Hollywood, Capra drew a firm distinction between the US Army training films produced by the Signal Corps Photographic Center and the series to which his unit had been assigned, which focused on the causes and events of the war.[11] The distinction was no less sharply drawn on the other side by officials of the Photographic Center, who, during the course of the same investigation, contended that "morale films" of the kind that Capra's unit was producing were of secondary value to the military and recommended that the "Army restrict its motion picture activities to films for use by and within the Army for military operations, training, and engineering."[12] Marshall, however, deemed the morale films of immense importance. In a memo to Osborn in October 1942, he argued that "the insistence of the military mind on precision" in presenting technical topics impeded the ability of Signal Corps instructors to present material in an "impressive manner."[13] In what proved to be a deft bureaucratic move, Marshall also initially withheld information concerning the development of the *Why We Fight* series from both Secretary of War Henry Stimson and the president and his advisers, so as to prevent bureaucratic meddling that might slow down or block the launching of the series.[14] Among the writers assigned to *Why We Fight*, Eric Knight, Anthony Veiller, and Robert Heller played formative roles in shaping the plotline of the series. Scripts were approved by Munson, Osborn, and State Department officials; completed films were also reviewed by Marshall, Stimson, and the Army's Director of the Bureau of Public Relations, Maj. Gen. Alexander D. Surles.[15]

From the outset of planning the *Why We Fight* series, Marshall had a wider audience in mind than simply new Army recruits. In a memo to Roosevelt in September 1941, Marshall expressed concern about the narrow worldview not only of soldiers, but of their parents and home communities as well. The problem of morale, he suggested, involved the citizenry as a whole.[16] In August 1942, after viewing a rough cut of the first film in the series, *Prelude to War*, Marshall began at once to press for its public release. Political turf wars in Washington and Hollywood, however, complicated the effort. Lowell Mellett, head of the newly formed Bureau of Motion Pictures (BMP) of the Office of War Information (OWI), objected to the film's emotionally charged characterization of the enemy, argued that government pressure on exhibitors would undermine a distribution agreement that his office had worked out with the motion picture industry, and warned of Congressional backlash to the theatrical distribution of films that advanced the administration's war aims (Steele 1979, 232; McBride 1992, 475–479). Mellett's last point gained additional credence when, following a preview of *Prelude to War* for members of the American Legion, Senator Rufus C. Holman (R-Oregon) complained on the Senate floor that references to war and oppression in *Prelude to War* served as "window dressing and stage scenery for cleverly organized campaign material" in support of Roosevelt's reelection. In assuming full responsibility for the *Why We Fight* series, however, Marshall was able to counter criticism that the film was election propaganda. Responding to Holman, Marshall noted that Roosevelt had been unaware of preparations for the film until after its screening "to probably a million troops," and that, in ordering the making of the film, his paramount concern had been the effective conduct of the war.[17] Meanwhile, in Los Angeles, Capra joined in the campaign for the film's theatrical release, soliciting support from industry leaders and arranging, over Mellett's objections, for screenings of *Prelude to War* to studio personnel.[18] In March 1943, the Academy of Motion Picture Arts and Sciences bestowed an Academy Award on *Prelude to War*, among other Allied wartime documentaries, boosting the case for its theatrical distribution. On May 13, 1943, *Prelude to War* finally premiered at the Strand Theater in New York. Two weeks later, 250 prints were made available free of charge to theaters nationwide.[19]

Although resistance from the domestic branch of the OWI would continue throughout the war years, two other films in the *Why We Fight* series, *The Battle of Russia* (1943) and *War Comes to America* (1945), also received theatrical release.[20] Required viewing for Army recruits, the series was screened on a voluntary basis to other military personnel, and to workers in the war industries, with recreation halls, cafeterias, locker rooms, and other makeshift theaters at times appropriated for this purpose.[21] In December 1943, the New York Film Critics voted a special award to the series, granting it further public recognition.[22] Osborn arranged with Robert Riskin, chief of the OWI Overseas Motion Picture Bureau (and a former screenwriter for Capra), for distribution of the first three of the *Why We Fight* films to theaters in England, Australia, South Africa, and New Zealand, and later to liberated areas of Europe in the wake of the Normandy campaign.[23] *The Battle of Britain* (1943) was shown to civilian audiences in Great Britain, accompanied by a prologue by Winston Churchill. *The Battle of Russia* circulated throughout the Soviet Union, with Joseph Stalin providing an introduction, and was admired and studied by Soviet filmmakers, especially for its editing (Leyda 1969, 58). With the exception of *The Battle of China* (1944), soundtracks for the *Why We Fight* films were prepared in Spanish and Portuguese for distribution in South America through the Office of the Coordinator for Inter-American Affairs (Bohn 1977, 107–108). The series also was the subject of social scientific research on the effectiveness of film propaganda, including an experiment in which *The Nazis Strike* (1943) was screened to German POWs as part of a far-fetched plan to reeducate 380,000 captured German soldiers imprisoned in the United States (Smoodin 2004, 178–182).

In the remarks below, I examine how the *Why We Fight* films map and explain a dispersed, worldwide conflict, and the implications of these strategies for postwar documentary cinema. Roosevelt's radio addresses serve as a touchstone to this discussion. A former councilor of the American Geographical Society and Assistant Secretary of the Navy, Roosevelt paid close attention to the work of professional geographers in the US State Department and took a particular interest in articulating war aims to the public in fresh geographic terms. In his wartime fireside chats, he asked listeners to envision a world outside the realm of their routine perceptions and experiences, a shrinking globe in which boundaries between nation-states had been fractured and violent conflicts proliferated in interconnected ways. It is unlikely many members of his radio audience, on the evening of February 23, 1942, had readily at hand a map or atlas of sufficient scope and detail to allow them to follow along with the president's entire commentary. But the efficacy of the talk's central motif perhaps depended less on the availability of any printed map of the "whole earth" than on the rhetorical appeal of Roosevelt's empirical, cartographic references in support of an account of unfolding events around the globe that ran counter to entrenched isolationist sentiments. As his political opponents no doubt recognized, Roosevelt's "world map" was a surface upon which a narrative of international crisis, obligation, and realignment could be inscribed.

Maps were reproduced in different formats during World War II to serve a variety of military, diplomatic, and civilian functions, but the geographic argument for US intervention found its most dramatic and widely viewed expression in the *Why We Fight* series, produced by Hollywood-trained personnel within and against the boundaries of War Department practices, policies, and hierarchies. In ways to which Roosevelt could only allude in his radio talks, the films interwove accounts of the causes and effects of specific battles with an expressive treatment of the experience of warfare and its consequences. How might a world in such flux be charted or plotted? From what vantage point did such a world cohere? Rendering palpable a sense of physical and psychological dislocation and displacement, the films traded in a particular capacity of motion pictures to construct complex battlescapes defined by sudden shifts in scale, perspective, and time. In doing so, the series also amplified tensions in the administration's foreign policy pronouncements, especially as the war unfolded and postwar planning emerged as a central political concern.

Where We Fight

"Causes and events leading up to our entry into the war," voiceover narrator Walter Huston announces, emphatically and drily, at the outset of *Prelude to War*, over footage of soldiers parading in review. "Well, what are the causes? Why are we Americans on the march?" His didactic tone then acquires dramatic urgency. Accompanied by the sounds of bombs and gunfire, fighter planes and rolling tanks, over scenes of combat and military occupations around the world, he ticks off the names of hot spots in the news – Pearl Harbor, Britain, France, China, Czechoslovakia, Norway, Poland, Holland, Greece, Belgium, Albania, Yugoslavia, Russia – each a possible answer to the question of why the United States was now at war. For the next 50 minutes, *Prelude to War* then mounts the argument that the enemy comes from no single direction, nor is defined by a single regime or territory, sketching in quick, broad strokes a global narrative that subsequent films in the series explore on a regional scale. Exhorting viewers to abandon the illusion that the North American continent is a safe haven buffered by two oceans, *Prelude to War* depicts a world riven by a high-stakes struggle between free and slave states, the latter led by the Axis despots with a coordinated plan for global control.

The seventh and final *Why We Fight* film, *War Comes to America*, similarly opens with the naming and depiction of remote war zones. Over footage of distant combat, Huston announces:

> In the jungles of New Guinea, on the barren shores of the Aleutians, in the tropic heat of the Pacific Islands, in the

> subzero cold of the skies over Germany, in Burma, and Iceland, the Philippines, and Iran, France, in China, and Italy – Americans, fighting, fighting over an area extending seven-eighths of the way around the world.

Note, however, that American soldiers are now themselves combatants, no longer recruits in need of training, and the varied locations they inhabit are backdrops to their common labor. The settings are also described in more evocative language, as if experienced directly through the senses, "tropic heat" to "subzero cold." Following this preamble, as in *Prelude to War*, prewar events are recounted, but again in a more poetic voice. The US Army, we are told, was forged of recruits from the "green hills" of New England, the "sun-baked plains" of the Middle West, the "cotton fields" of the South, the "close-packed streets" of Manhattan and Chicago, the "teeming factories" of Detroit and Los Angeles, and the "endlessly stretching distances" of the Southwest. Reaching back further in time, *War Comes to America* then offers a patriotic account of US history, illustrated with scenes borrowed in part from New Deal-era documentaries, and concluding with a detailed reconstruction of the process by which isolationist sentiment in America gave way to military preparedness during the interwar years. Retelling the story of Japan's plan to conquer Asia and join forces with the Nazis, *War Comes to America* then concludes abruptly with the bombing of Pearl Harbor, bringing the *Why We Fight* series full circle.

Framed by these two films, the middle five focus on macro-regional conflicts: the German annexation of Austria and the Sudetenland and invasion of Czechoslovakia and Poland, in *The Nazis Strike*; the German *Blitzkrieg* across northern Europe in *Divide and Conquer* (1943); and the defense of three Allied nations from Axis attack in *The Battle of Britain*, *The Battle of Russia*, and *The Battle of China*. The time structure often folds back on itself, both within and across episodes. *Divide and Conquer* foregrounds Nazi conquest as experienced by its Danish, Dutch, Belgian, and French victims, all of whom, we are told, "will never forget." *The Battle of China* begins with the bombing of Shanghai in 1937, backtracks to sketch the history of modern China and Japan, and highlights Japan's invasion of Manchuria and "rape of Nanking," before replaying footage from the opening battle. Only in this fuller historical context, the film suggests, can the traumatic violation of Shanghai be comprehended and its significance teased out. Throughout the series, moreover, tight editing allows for temporal and geographic compression, identifying historical patterns in what might at first seem disparate, small-scale political events. In a summary passage of *Prelude to War*, narrator Huston observes that while it may be hard to convince an Iowa farm boy, a London bus driver, or a Parisian waiter of the significance of an incident in a mud hut in Manchuria in the early 1930s, a line can be drawn directly from that event and the worldwide conflict in which their nations were now engaged. Understanding the war thus required a new way of thinking about both geography and causality, and an appreciation of the deeper course of history running beneath the surface of daily news reports.

Seams dividing the seven films also are cross-stitched. *The Nazis Strike* refers back to plotlines laid out in *Prelude to War*, and sets up the story of the German occupation of Norway, Holland, Belgium, and France in *Divide and Conquer*. *The Battle of Britain* recapitulates the fall of northern European countries, before fixing squarely on the London blitz. *The Battle of Russia* offers a similar recap of events in eastern Europe and the Balkans. In *The Battle of China*, the failed defense of Shanghai is compared and contrasted with that of London and Moscow. Commentary at the conclusion to *The Battle of China*, narrated by Anthony Veiller, provides the template for the opening remarks by Huston in *War Comes to America* cited above. *War Comes to America* then draws on images and commentary from all of the previous films, as it juxtaposes violence overseas with activities and debates among Americans at home. Beyond serving as the closing frame to the series, *War Comes to America* thus recapitulates the overarching narrative of *Why We Fight*, ending with the retelling of the events leading up to Pearl Harbor, the founding trauma the series labors repeatedly to explain.

Combining excerpts from newsreels, documentaries, and stock footage with historical fiction and staged reenactments, the *Why We Fight* films assemble heterogeneous material in ways that draw out fresh implications. Crucial to the film's editorial approach is a kind of documentary *jiu jitsu* in which the apparent meaning of enemy propaganda films is turned against itself. Although responsibility for anchoring these new interpretations is principally placed in the vocal commentary, in the most memorable passage in *Prelude to*

War the commentator remains silent while the images evoke, through editing and music, the global menace of fascist regimentation and discipline. Parallel scenes of conscripted youth in Germany, Italy, and Japan are interwoven, as boys are molded into vast armies of men, their lockstep movements matched by the sound of drum rolls and cymbals, the repetition and amplification of which contribute to the passage's chilling power. Noting the "virtuoso job of selection and cutting" in the sequence, reviewer James Agee declared it "the grimmest image of fascism I have seen on screen" (1943, 844). Manny Farber praised the style of storytelling in the film overall for "compressing incidents to their barest essentials and then overlapping or double-exposing them." The pace of the film, he observed, had been "adapted to the explosiveness of blitz warfare" (1943, 743). In this way the cutting of *Prelude to War* was likened to modern combat itself.

Throughout the *Why We Fight* series animated maps of various kinds serve to orient and guide the viewer to and through this barrage of images. Some maps serve a *tactical* or *strategic* function, highlighting environmental features that determine military maneuvers, or delineating the broader trajectory of a campaign of which a specific line of attack or defense is but a part. In *Divide and Conquer* animated maps illustrate how Norwegian fjords shelter German U-Boats and how the Ardennes Forest functions as a hidden shield, in contrast to the conspicuous Maginot Line. In *The Battle of Russia* the beginning of the siege of Leningrad is illustrated by a map of the city's encirclement by Nazi forces, and the tactical opportunity for surviving the siege over the course of the bitter winter months by maps that chart the construction of a supply line across the frozen surface of Lake Ladoga.

Other maps offer a *historical* perspective, as when an outline of the 13 US colonies in *War Comes to America* builds out across the continent to encompass all 48 states. These maps tend to delineate the "natural" contours of territories, so as to distinguish the integrity of nation-states from the efforts of fascist forces to achieve unbounded, global political control. *The Battle of Russia* and *The Battle of China* in particular take a "national geographic" approach, devoting considerable attention to the topography, natural resources, and cultural characteristics of these nations before providing a graphic account of the battles that have scarred the land. National maps also measure size. The vast expanses of Russia and China are contrasted graphically with the more reduced size of the United States, North America, and Continental Europe.

In *The Battle of China* the Japanese are said to be capable of imagining the conquest of their "outsized neighbor" because the latter is culturally fragmented like "a jigsaw puzzle," an image easily visualized through motion graphics. Unification of China, the film goes on to propose, requires the development of a modern infrastructure, including the building of railroads and highways, and a system for the extraction and distribution of raw materials on a national scale. Stock footage illustrates these nation-building activities, while maps outline the bigger picture.

Maps also frequently take on the quality of pictorial *caricature*. The vividness of such imagery is attributable to the Disney Studio, with whom the Signal Corps contracted for work on this and other US Army documentaries. Not simply diagrammatic, these maps are dynamic and expressive, at times even darkly playful. In *Prelude to War* the geographical borders of Germany, Japan, and Italy inspire the transfiguration of each nation into an iconic image: a swastika, dragon, and fasces, respectively. In *The Nazis Strike* swastikas drip blood. In *Divide and Conquer* they morph into insects and scurry across the face of Europe. In the same film, invading phalanxes of Nazi forces, mounting a "pincer" attack on Norway, turn into crustacean claws. Roosevelt's account of Hitler's master plan is at times explicitly visualized through such animations. At the outset of *The Battle of Britain*, the elongated shadow of a Nazi soldier falls across northern France in the direction of the English Channel; black ink then spreads across the British Isles as Hitler's plan for the conquest is described. In keeping with Roosevelt's effort to map the encroachment of Nazi forces into the Western Hemisphere, in *War Comes to America* black ink spreads across Iceland and Greenland, and newly vulnerable islands off the coast of North and South America are identified by name – Miquelon, Martinique, Curaçao, and French and Dutch Guiana.

Military navigators and strategists employed mechanical tools to divide the curved surface of the earth into mercatorial quadrants, with distances between land masses mathematically scaled, and elevations quantified and charted across three dimensions, so as to rationalize zones of combat on land, in the air, and at sea. In contrast, the animated maps in the *Why We Fight* films are malleable, at times more

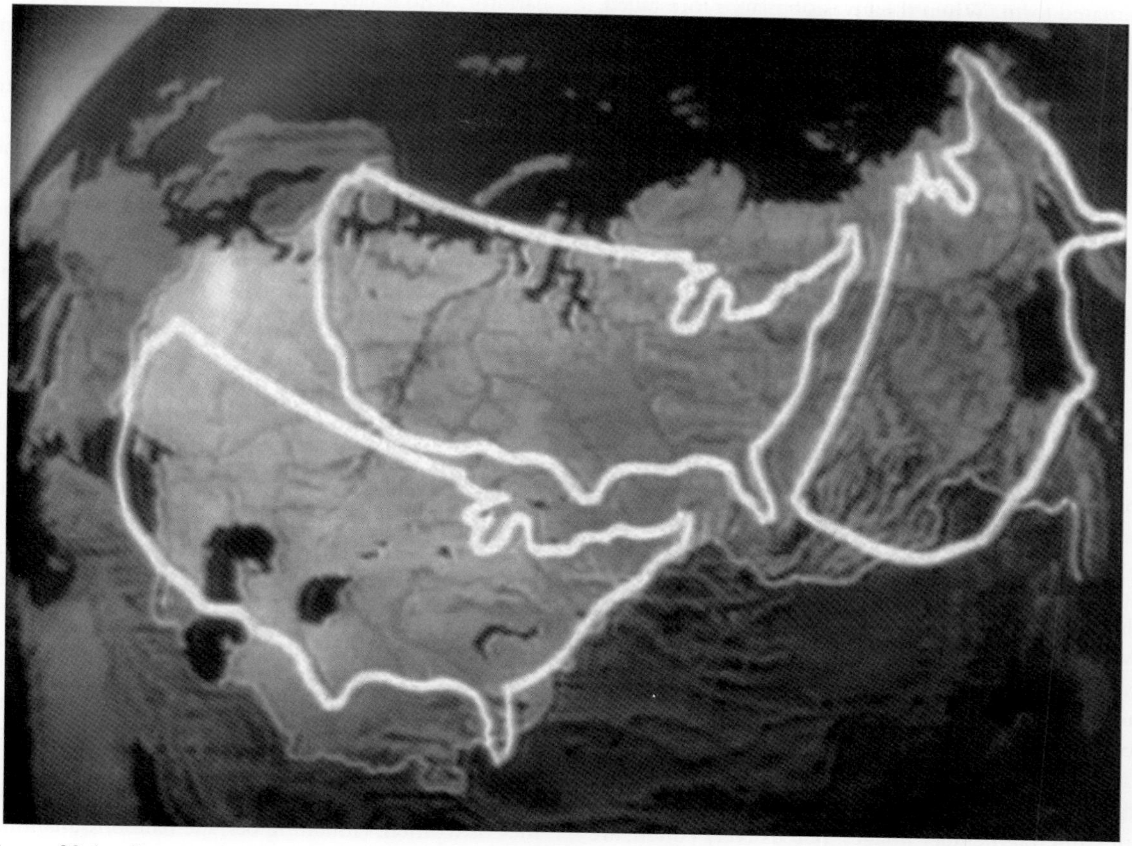

Figure 20.1 Comparative size: the United States and the USSR as represented in Anatole Litvak and Frank Capra's *The Battle of Russia* (1943, producer US War Department).

choreographic than cartographic, orchestrating visual elements in ways that register rising tensions, dynamic conflict, and the reconfiguration of opposing forces. Beyond the tutorial functions of the animated map – the drawing of national boundaries across seemingly borderless terrain, or the charting of the movement of armed forces and munitions in advance or in retreat – the appeal here is to a geographic imagination, inviting viewers to envision how the unleashing of mechanized, military power across the surface of the earth has led to a perilous state of affairs.

To the extent that they represent contested terrain, maps are available for appropriation no less than other kinds of images. Emblematic of tactical and strategic planning more broadly construed, acts of map reading serve to personify, and sometimes vilify, those engaged in such plotting. In *Divide and Conquer* German military leader Hermann Göring looks up from a map and wrings his hands excitedly just prior to scenes of the Nazi assault on France. *The Nazis Strike* showcases the Munich Institut für Geopolitik, established under the direction of geographer Karl Haushofer, and explains how theories incubated there gave shape to Hitler's imperial longings. After Hitler consults his map, we see him stand at a dock as Nazi agents fan out around the world. His generals then join him in more map reading, and an attack on eastern Europe is launched. Another version of this trope appears early in *The Battle of Britain*, when Hitler peers through tourist binoculars across the English Channel, occupying the precise place, the narrator informs us, where Napoleon stood 100 years before. Cut to stock shots of Dover, and of the waters from which its white cliffs rise, then to a map of the British Isles ("smaller," the narrator informs us, "than the state of Wyoming"). Hitler's master plan is then recapped in animated form. When the invasion plan is forestalled, Hitler and Göring, huddling over a map, select their next target, the city of London, to be attacked by air, and the survival of which serves as the principal focus of the remainder of the film. Allied leaders, too, are on occasion shown consulting war maps in preparation for combat. In *The Battle of China* a resistance leader gestures toward a wall map outlining a plan for tactical withdrawal, as fellow officers seated around a table listen and look on. Later, Japanese leaders lift their heads wearily from a table map, aware that a key phase of their battle plan has gone awry. In *The Battle of Russia* the parallel plotting of opposing map readers is juxtaposed even more directly, by way of a simultaneous, split-screen effect.

If military maps turn land and cityscapes into abstract planning documents, in *Why We Fight* they also serve as entry points to scenes of physical and psychological disturbance. Imagining the subjective elements of life in combat zones, the *Why We Fight* films rework available footage to explore an affective dimension to the story. Toward this end, Capra and his team of editors, led by William Hornbeck, quickly absorbed stylistic strategies found in partisan documentaries from war fronts in Europe and Asia. Faces of combatants and victims are incorporated into fabricated point-of-view sequences. Camera vibrations and fragmentary images, percussively edited, are accompanied by the sounds of the machinery of warfare. During the course of an attack, the wailing of sirens may be followed by the cries of the wounded and grief-stricken. Mid-battle, spatial relations are often fragile and sometimes entirely uncertain, as the delineation of geographical boundaries yields to the orchestration of emotional effects. Impressionistic collages register the impact of an attack on the ground, amid more distant shots and aerial overviews. This constitutes yet another kind of mapping, requiring the viewer to integrate multiple, changing perspectives, some of which can only be assimilated by reference to generic displays of military force. We see, in various combinations, another aerial flyover, another blown-out window, another helmeted artilleryman, another plane spiraling downward, another infant corpse, another grieving mother. Are we in Warsaw or in London? In Leningrad or Nanking? The specificity of a battle may fade amid these recurring, compound montage effects. Hence the periodic need to return to a conventional map, or to the voice of the narrator, who is rarely very far from our ear, prepared to name, describe, and assess the significance of a given encounter in relation to a wider campaign.

Across the *Why We Fight* films, this authority to explain events vocally is distributed in varied ways. Although the lead voices are those of Huston and Veiller, the distinctive speech of other narrators is heard in *Divide and Conquer*, *The Battle of Britain*, and *War Comes to America*. Typically the narrators trade off, so as to vary the tonality and rhythm of the spoken commentary. *The Battle of Britain* even features an implied colloquy between the narrators. Military experts on occasion appear on-screen to clarify details. In *Divide and Conquer* the narrator instructs us to "watch the map" as an intelligence officer, pointer in hand, explains the technical aspects of Germany's rout of Allied defenses in France. Later he returns to describe the German attack along the Maginot Line. From behind a desk, military attaché Col. William Mayer in *The Battle of China* describes the diplomatic exchange leading up to Japan's invasion of China in 1937, then briefly speaks over combat footage and animated maps documenting the attack. In *The Battle of Britain* authority is briefly vested in the postsynchronized voices of fabricated "characters" located amid the action. "We're in this too," a woman asserts, before describing the defense activities of women: launching barrage balloons, manning anti-aircraft guns, running the railroads, ferrying planes, and running dispatches, among other tasks. Night wardens and RAF pilots exchange communication in the dark. An elderly woman enumerates the various kinds of bombs with which she has become familiar before insisting, resiliently, "but we will stick it." In *The Battle of China* the postsynchronized voices of assailants and victims alike are scripted into dramatic accounts of Japan's assaults on Nanking and Chunking.

In the two framing films, the relationship between vocal authority and political power is most fully explored. US noninterventionist policy in the 1930s is presented in *Prelude to War* as a reflection of the opinions of "John Q. Public," views authentically held and freely expressed, however uninformed. In counterpoint, Roosevelt is introduced as "one among many elected leaders who warned us of danger," as he stands before a bank of radio microphones, condemning Italy's invasion of Ethiopia in 1935. The peoples of the Axis nations, in contrast, are depicted as

Figure 20.2 Visualizing radio waves in Frank Capra's *Prelude to War* (1942, producer US War Department).

wholly at the mercy of imperious leaders who demand ideological purity and fealty, ban and burn books, and ruthlessly dictate wartime policy from the top. In the fascist state, narrator Huston asserts prior to the montage of conscripted children, "the Head of State is the voice of God." German radio propagandists demand "*Lebensraum* – living room," a concept key to Haushofer's *Geopolitik*. In a Disney map, radio waves bearing propaganda spread outward in concentric circles from broadcast towers in Berlin, Rome, and Tokyo, disseminating lies intended to soften up the enemy, as the signals penetrate the airspace of adjacent nations around the globe.

War Comes to America returns to this theme in even more pointed fashion, presenting Hitler as Roosevelt's rival at the microphone. In a newsreel excerpt, Hitler addresses the German Reichstag, reading aloud with mockery, and to mounting laughter from those assembled, the names of independent nations that Roosevelt had declared off-limits to the Germans. In contrast, *War Comes to America* explains changes in US foreign policy as a deliberative and public process, involving many different voices. State Department officials speak out: Cordell Hull on hemispheric unity, Dean Acheson on exporting munitions to Japan, Adolph Berle on the Tripartite Agreement signed by the Axis Powers. Americans seated by their radios listen to H. V. Kaltenborn describe the fall of France. Radio newsman William L. Shirer reports on the French Armistice from the Compiègne Forest, and Edward R. Murrow on the blitz from London. Contrasting sentiments concerning the fate of Britain are offered by isolationist Charles Lindbergh and internationalist Wendell Willkie, seen in newsreel excerpts.

Congressional debates are echoed by street corner talk, popular public discourse that, in turn, shapes the new legislation Congress adopts. "Man on the street" interviews function as a recurring motif, selected to illustrate the gradual public acceptance of US involvement in the Allied war effort, while Gallup polls serve as another index to the "voice of the people." *War Comes to America*, in short, treats the development of a global worldview by US citizens as a mediated, democratic process, involving instruction, polling, radio broadcasts, movies, newsreels, newspapers, and public debate. Roosevelt at times guides but does not dictate the outcome of these discussions. At the film's conclusion, he simply gives voice to the inevitable endpoint to this story. In an excerpt from a speech to Congress, broadcast to the nation, and to be replayed many times over in years to come, Roosevelt pronounces December 7 as a "date which will live in infamy," the preamble to a request for a declaration of war, the full compass of which remained to be defined.

Why We Fight and the Postwar World

In an essay entitled "The Global Film," first published in English in *Hollywood Quarterly* in July 1947, Russian director Vsevolod Pudovkin cited *Prelude to War* as the prime example of a new kind of documentary that had acquired definition during the war years. Feature-length productions, these films employed methods of montage editing in ways that invested actuality footage with abstract ideas and hence could be considered "a phenomenon of high art." *Prelude to War* was a global film, Pudovkin contended, in two related ways. Visual fragments photographed in locations spanning half the globe were linked together to establish core assertions about the rise and impact of fascism in Germany, Italy, and Japan. At the same time, the film resolved a problem that had confronted filmmakers since the arrival of theatrically styled "talkies" – language barriers that diminished cinema's international character. *Prelude to War*, in contrast, was "fully international," its commentary capable of being translated into any language with no loss to the integrity of the film. The strength of the basic form of the global film followed from its capacity to present cultures *relationally*. This was vital because the "real truth about a people cannot be shown in separate and partial examples, localized to one or another place. It must be allowed to tell itself on a broad scale, revealing, as a principle, the historical essence of each phenomenon." In this way the global film promised to bridge different groups of peoples, a factor of increasing importance in the postwar period (Pudovkin 2002, 332).

In grounding his assessment of the global film in the potential translatability of the medium, Pudovkin evinced nostalgia for the now faded art of the silent cinema, whose capacity to transcend language barriers had once been touted by critics and practitioners. But Pudovkin's commentary also pointed decisively toward a utopian future. As signaled by its publication in *Hollywood Quarterly*, a politically oriented journal, Pudovkin's essay reflected mainstream progressive thought concerning documentary filmmaking as a socially responsive endeavor, about which robust critical discussion had emerged in the 1930s and early 1940s (Smoodin & Martin 2002, xi–xxiii; Doherty 1999; Wolfe 1993). As Erik Barnouw notes, potential opposition from civil libertarians to government propaganda during the war years likely was mitigated in the case of *Why We Fight* by its overtly liberal stance with respect to isolationism, the Spanish Civil War, and US relations with the Soviet Union (1983, 162). Well into the early Cold War years, moreover, the *Why We Fight* series was singled out as one among a very few wartime government films to capitalize on a tradition of engaged social documentary filmmaking – "propaganda for progressive ideas and actions," in the phrase of Richard Griffith (1952, 358), who had regularly worked for the Capra Unit as a researcher in the Museum of Modern Art film library in New York (Katz & Katz 1948, 426; Gallez 1955, 125).

Although not versed in the traditions of documentary cinema, George C. Marshall also came to think of the *Why We Fight* films as a model for a new form of historical writing and pedagogy, with wide application outside of military circles. Marshall had long held the view that an effective morale program required attention to winning the peace as well as the war, and to the place of the individual soldier within democratic processes and historical traditions. Upon viewing the finished version of *Prelude to War* in October 1942, Marshall expressed his belief that Capra had developed a new educational tool, the far-reaching effects of which would only be realized after the war's end.[24] Marshall again cited the value of Capra's wartime work in an address to the Maryland Historical Society in June 1945, in which he proposed that knowledge of world history had been tested in the last war and found alarmingly deficient. Discussions under way in San Francisco concerning the charter of the United Nations as a constituted body highlighted further the importance of understanding different viewpoints in the conduct of international affairs. "We urgently need a more effective system of instruction," he asserted, "and I am sure the motion picture medium can be of much assistance."[25] At a dinner at Capra's home in March 1946, Marshall also expressed strong interest in using documentary films on US political institutions as a tool in "democratizing" China, which he was about to visit as an envoy of President Truman, and solicited Capra's advice on how best to proceed with such a program.[26]

Marshall's subsequent role as public spokesperson for the European Recovery Program (colloquially, the "Marshall Plan"), following his appointment as secretary of state in 1947, highlights the degree to which this international planning was bound up in economic questions. In this regard the mapping of the world in the *Why We Fight* series is congruent with twentieth-century conceptualizations of American globalization, based not on territorial expansion but on pan-global markets, economic spheres of influence, and permeable state boundaries. Between 1939 and 1945 Roosevelt's leading geographer, Isaiah Bowman, spearheaded an effort to redefine geographic concepts in accord with the changing role of the United States on the world stage. As geography scholar Neil Smith details, Bowman's "philosophy of gradual change" became the cornerstone of liberal internationalism in the war and postwar periods, a middle stage between Woodrow Wilson's failed "moral geography" of 1919 and the accelerated economic globalism of the 1980s and 1990s. As the war drew to a close, according to Smith, government planners endeavored to devise a "postwar political economy that simultaneously fixed postwar political geography and constructed the requisite institutions to regulate transborder fluidity of goods, raw materials, capital and people, ideals and technology" (2003, 20–21). In its excoriating critique of fascist territorial conquest, in its embrace of the rationale for war set forth in the Joint Declaration by the United Nations, in its comparative analysis of patterns of economic and political development in specific contexts around the globe, and in its dynamic and sometimes dizzying cutting among countries and continents at different levels of scale, the *Why We Fight* series gave expressive form to the idea, at the center of the work of government geographers, that historical forces were shaping the world anew.

At the same time, the international scope of the *Why We Fight* series complicates the forms of address the films adopt. Taking a cue from the title of Cleveland Amory's article in the June 1941 *Atlantic Monthly*, "What We Fight For," the series employs the collective "we" in an effort to identify and define the shared aspirations of American citizens, including but not limited to military inductees. Over the course of the series, however, the "we" invoked in *Why We Fight* increasingly becomes intertwined with the goals and experiences of other members of the "United Nations." David Culbert argues plausibly that "the *Why We Fight* films defined American war objectives to military civilian audiences throughout the world in a way Roosevelt's Four Freedoms never could" (1983, 189). In attempting to do so, however, the films also confronted ambiguities in the administration's foreign policy pronouncements, which Roosevelt himself could skirt in the more intimate fireside chats. In his Washington's Birthday address, for example, Roosevelt finessed the question of affiliation among the designated United Nations by focusing on the common enemy. "We and the other United Nations," he asserted, "are committed to the destruction of the militarism of Japan and Germany.... Soon, we and not our enemies will have the offensive; we, not they, will win the final battles; and we, not they, will make the final peace." Relations among the nations of the world here are reduced to a simple binary – "we" and "they" – a reduction the *Why We Fight* films on occasion does adopt, as when the films depict a world cleaved into two parts, one slave, one free. As historical documentaries, however, the *Why We Fight* films were obliged to provide a fuller sense of the nature of these wartime alliances, attending to the diversity of cultures bound up in a common cause.

The distribution of the films to international audiences no doubt complicated matters further. At the very least, writers in the Capra Unit were required to depict all Allies in a positive and unthreatening light. The strain here is most apparent in *The Battle of Russia* and *The Battle of China*. Treating the Soviet Union and China as full partners with the capitalist democracies involved necessary simplifications and evasions. Tellingly, the role of communist politics, in either its statist or revolutionary form, is conspicuously elided from these accounts. Instead, both films strive to establish close connections between the political and cultural histories of the Russian and Chinese people and that of US citizens. In *The Battle of Russia* the history of the Soviet republics is likened to that of the American states, and viewers are invited to imagine themselves as Russians engaged in battle, as "if *you* were a soldier." In *The Battle of China* the mass migration of 30 million Chinese is recast as an American Western narrative, "driven by epic impulse." The Chinese people, we learn, have already secured two of Roosevelt's "four freedoms" – that of speech and worship. "China's war is our war," the narrator asserts, over images of Chinese soldiers in US Army uniforms, training in the Southwest United States, indistinguishable from American recruits. "Now her millions," the narrator concludes, "belong not only to a united China but also to the United Nations." At the close of *The Battle of Russia* viewers are similarly informed that Russia's enemies "will be attacked, and attacked, and attacked by these united people of these United Nations," a declaration capped by a musical tribute to the United Nations, over an animated parade of flags, with the US flag leading the way, and the Soviet hammer and sickle close behind.

Political tensions, suppressed during the war years, would soon resurface, however, to render both films unsuitable as postwar propaganda. Criticized by officials in the War Department at the time of its making, *The Battle of China* only had limited circulation in 1944 and was quickly withdrawn; subsequent versions were distributed with a disclaimer that the film bore no relation to current US policy. Although it enjoyed modest critical success when released theatrically in 1943, *The Battle of Russia* was classified "restricted" in 1947, despite the Army's recognition that it would be impossible to recover all of the prints of the film given their wide distribution to libraries by the OWI.[27] Capra would face personal repercussions as well. The target of Army intelligence investigations as early as 1942, he found his association with *The Battle of Russia* a source of embarrassment and apprehension during the postwar Red Scare, and continued to downplay his role in the making of the film on into his later years (Capra 1971, 347–348; McBride 1992, 462, 486–489, 600–602). In contrast, *War Comes to America*, trimmed down from 65 to 50 minutes and relabeled *War Came to America*, was selected by the Army for ongoing distribution to schools and civic organizations beginning in June 1947.[28] Missing what was originally intended to be a second part, covering life in America during the war years, *War Came to America* secured a place in Cold War American culture as a publically circulated civics text. Sidestepping the fate of native peoples, the enslavement of African-Americans, and the internal crisis of the Civil War, the film's highly selective history of US continental expansion emphasizes instead the legacy of freedom vouchsafed to immigrants, and their harmonious contributions to the growth of the nation. Public debate during the prewar years then serves as a model of democratic deliberation concerning international affairs, with the closing images of the attack on Pearl Harbor marking a decisive turning point in US history, when national security was dramatically breached and isolationist illusions shattered.

Produced under wartime government sponsorship, the *Why We Fight* series was designed to "orient" US soldiers and civilians alike to remote events in an embattled world. In an effort to counter, and appropriate the power of, fascist propaganda, the series argued for the virtues of liberal political traditions – the exercise of reason and free speech, the defense of cultural diversity and religious tolerance – while also demonizing the enemy and at times reducing the complex political coordinates of the conflict to a Manichaean struggle between slave and free states. Detailing the horrifying consequences of violent aggression – devastation, death, despair – it also affirmed the assertion of overwhelming, countervailing military power. Presenting a world of nation-states in flux, open to be pictured in new ways, the series in composite projected what might be thought of as an Allied imaginary, with the United States at its center, within a widening sphere of mediated political images and ideas. Modern technologies of transportation, communication, and warfare, the films proposed, had altered modern conceptions of the geography of the globe. The implicit, corollary point was that motion picture technology was capable of representing such a world, rendering visceral the effects of violent political upheaval, extracting abstract ideas from photographic and written evidence, and circulating a partisan interpretation of these events far and wide. Above and beyond the specific battles recounted, the *Why We Fight* series thus made evident the affinities between the mobility and power of "global film" and the consciousness required to fight a global war.

Notes

1. Roosevelt Fireside Chat, February 23, 1942, John T. Woolley and Gerhard Peters, *The American Presidency Project*, at http://www.presidency.ucsb.edu/ws/?pid=16224 (accessed March 2015).
2. Roosevelt Fireside Chat, May 26, 1940, John T. Woolley and Gerhard Peters, *The American Presidency Project*, at http://www.presidency.ucsb.edu/ws/?pid=15959 (accessed March 2015).
3. Roosevelt Radio Address, May 27, 1941, John T. Woolley and Gerhard Peters, *The American Presidency Project*, at http://www.presidency.ucsb.edu/ws/?pid=16120 (accessed March 2015).
4. Capra testimony to Maj. John H. Amen, Los Angeles, November 25, 1943, in Culbert 1990a, 450.
5. Marshall memo to Stimson, April 28, 1941, #2-434, *The Papers of George Catlett Marshall*, ed. Larry I. Bland, Sharon Ritenour Stevens, and Clarence E. Wunderlin, Jr, at http:// marshallfoundation.org (accessed March 2015).
6. Munson to Chief, Planning and Research Division, July 7, 1941, in Culbert 1990b, 33–35.
7. Capra testimony to Amen, in Culbert 1990a, 451; Osborn to Chief, Administrative Service, April 23, 1942, in Culbert 1990b, 99–102; Munson to Robert Cutler, August 18, 1945, in Culbert 1990b, 85; Marshall memo to Osborn, October 1942, #3-381, Marshall Papers; Marshall memo to FDR, November 23, 1942, #3-421, Marshall Papers; *George C. Marshall: Interviews and Reminiscences for Forrest C. Pogue*, rev. edn (Lexington, VA: George C. Marshall Foundation, 1991), 463–464, Marshall Papers.
8. Osborn to Chief, Administrative Services, in Culbert 1990b, 99–100.
9. Capra to Osborn and Munson, August 19, 1942, in Culbert 1990b, 146–148; Richard T. Schlosberg to Chief Signal Officer and Chief of Special Services, July 1, 1942, in Culbert 1990b, 118–120; "Objectives of Orientation and Information Films to Be Produced by Special Services," July 2, 1942, in Culbert 1990b, 121–126.
10. Capra testimony to Amen, in Culbert 1990a, 461.
11. Capra testimony to Amen, in Culbert 1990a, 451.
12. Fredrick W. Hoorn, "Memo for the Record," December 21, 1942, in Culbert 1990a, 382.
13. Marshall to Osborn, October 25, 1942, #3-381, Marshall Papers.
14. *Marshall: Interviews and Reminiscences*, 91.
15. Munson to Cutler, in Culbert 1990b, 87–88.
16. Marshall to FDR, #2-544, September 6, 1941, Marshall Papers.
17. Congressional Record, 78th Congress, 1st Session, February 8, 1943, 674–676; Marshall to Rufus C. Holman, #3-506, February 9, 1943, Marshall Papers.
18. Osborn to Mellett, November 21, 1942, in Culbert 1990b, 162.
19. Bosley Crowther, "'Prelude to War' Shown to Public," *New York Times*, May 14, 1943, 23.
20. Bosley Crowther, "New Film Surveys Soviet Role in War," *New York Times*, November 15, 1943, 23; "Screen News," *New York Times*, June 14, 1945, 23.
21. Philip K. Scheuer, "'Why We Fight' Goes Right to Warworker," *Los Angeles Times*, June 25, 1944, C1, 6.
22. "'Watch on Rhine' Voted Best Film," *New York Times*, December 29, 1943, 19.
23. "Of Local Origins," *New York Times*, March 13, 1943, 9; Thomas M. Pryor, "The OWI Reports," *New York Times*, December 24, 1944, 33.
24. Marshall to Osborn, October 25, 1943, #3-381, Marshall Papers.
25. Speech to the Maryland Historical Society, Baltimore, Maryland, June 11, 1945, #5-160, Marshall Papers.
26. Notes of Frank McCarthy, March 1946, #5-428, Marshall Papers. Marshall's former aide, and by now an executive at Twentieth Century-Fox, Frank McCarthy arranged the dinner. According to these notes, he and Capra proposed to form a nonprofit company to produce the films for Marshall, but the project never came to pass.
27. Felix Johnson, Director of Public Relations, to Assistant to the Secretary of Defense, December 1947, in Suid 1991, 3–4.
28. Stuart Palmer, Acting Chief, Pictorial Section, to Chief, Army Pictorial Service, June 17, 1947, in Suid 1991, 8–11.

References

Agee, James. (1943). "Films." *The Nation*, 156.24 (June), 844–845.

Amory, Cleveland. (1941). "What We Fight For." *Atlantic Monthly*, June, 687–689.

Barnouw, Eric. (1983). *Documentary: A History of the Non-Fiction Film*. Revised edn. Oxford: Oxford University Press.

Beukema, Herman. (1942). "Introduction." In Andreas Dorpelan, *The World of General Haushofer: Geopolitics in Action*. New York: Farrar & Reinhardt.

Bohn, Thomas. (1977). *An Historical and Descriptive Analysis of the "Why We Fight" Series*. New York: Arno.

Capra, Frank. (1971). *The Name Above the Title: An Autobiography*. New York: Macmillan.

Culbert, David. (1983). "'Why We Fight': Social Engineering for a Democratic Society at War." In Ken Short (ed.), *Film and Propaganda in World War II* (pp. 173–191). Knoxville: University of Tennessee Press.

Culbert, David (ed.). (1990a). *Film and Propaganda in America: A Documentary History. Vol. 2: World War II, Part 1*. New York: Greenwood Press.

Culbert, David (ed.). (1990b). *Film and Propaganda in America: A Documentary History. Vol. 3: World War II, Part 2*. New York: Greenwood Press.

Dallek, Robert. (1979). *Franklin D. Roosevelt and American Foreign Policy, 1932–1945*. New York: Oxford University Press.

Doherty, Thomas. (1999). "Documenting the 1940s." In Thomas Schatz (ed.), *Boom and Bust: American Cinema in the 1940s* (pp. 397–421). Berkeley: University of California Press.

Farber, Manny. (1943). "Education for War." *New Republic*, 108.22 (May 31), 734.

Gallez, Douglas. (1955). "Patterns in Wartime Documentaries." *Quarterly Review of Film, Radio, and Television*, 10.2 (Winter), 125–135.

Griffith, Richard. (1952). "The Use of Films by the U.S. Armed Services." In Paul Rotha, *Documentary Film: The Use of the Film Medium to Interpret Creatively and in Social Terms the Life of the People as it Exists in Reality* (pp. 344–358). 3rd edn. London: Faber & Faber.

Katz, Robert, & Katz, Nancy. (1948). "Documentary in Transition, Part I: The United States." *Hollywood Quarterly*, 3.4, 425–433.

Leyda, Jay. (1969). *Films Beget Films: A Study of the Compilation Film*. New York: Hill & Wang.

McBride, Joseph. (1992). *Frank Capra: The Catastrophe of Success*. New York: Simon & Schuster.

Pudovkin, Vsevolod. (2002). "The Global Film." In Eric Smoodin & Ann Martin (eds), *Hollywood Quarterly: Film Culture in Postwar America, 1945–1957* (pp. 327–333). Berkeley: University of California Press.

Smith, Neil. (2003). *American Empire: Roosevelt's Geographer and the Prelude to Globalization*. Berkeley: University of California Press.

Smoodin, Eric. (2004). *Regarding Frank Capra: Audience, Celebrity and American Film Studies, 1930–1960*. Durham, NC: Duke University Press.

Smoodin, Eric, & Martin, Ann. (eds). (2002). *Hollywood Quarterly: Film Culture in Postwar America, 1945–1957*. Berkeley: University of California Press.

Steele, Richard W. (1979). "'The Greatest Gangster Movie Ever Filmed': *Prelude to War*." *Prologue: The Journal of the National Archives*, 11.4 (Winter), 221–235.

Suid, Lawrence H. (ed.). (1991). *Film and Propaganda in America. Vol. 4: 1945 and After*. New York: Greenwood Press.

Wolfe, Charles. (1993). "The Poetics and Politics of Nonfiction: Documentary Film." In Tino Balio, *Grand Design: Hollywood as Modern Business Enterprise, 1930–1939* (pp. 251–286). New York: Charles Scribner's Sons.

21

A Victory "Uneasy with Its Contrasts"

The Hollywood Left Fights World War II

Saverio Giovacchini

Associate Professor, University of Maryland College Park, United States

Saverio Giovacchini examines the intersection of wartime Hollywood and the professional and political commitments of artists on the **left**, many of whom advocated for films taking an **antifascist** stance well before America's involvement in World War II. Upon US entry into the war, the Hollywood Left's socially engaged impulses moved from the margins to the center as the film industry, in partnership with the government, took up the cause. One result is what Giovacchini calls a **cinema of presence**, bridging the geographical and psychological distance between moviegoers and the war. Giovacchini discusses Hollywood conventions informing wartime documentaries, also examining **combat films** like ***Bataan*** and the treatment of race by liberal filmmakers. Although wartime cinema with its **documentary style** and educational orientation marked a breakthrough, it was eclipsed by the **anticommunist** storm that would come to mark peacetime cinema. Giovacchini's essay shares ground with Richard Maltby on 1930s social realist cinema and Charles Wolfe on Capra's *Why We Fight* documentaries in this volume, and with Larry Ceplair on Hollywood unions and blacklists in the hardcover/online edition.

Additional terms, names, and concepts: Hollywood Anti-Nazi League, "democratic tradition," Office of War Information's Bureau of Motion Pictures, Production Code Administration, semi-documentary mode/techniques

Introduction: The Promise of a Bloodbath

In 1941, screenwriter Paul Jarrico was elated to leave his hometown, Los Angeles, to join the Merchant Marine. The urgency of the war made his work as a screenwriter at MGM pale. "We are getting a little tired of telling ourselves that the greatest contribution to the war we can make is right at our desks," he wrote to friend and comrade Michael Wilson, himself then serving with the Marines. "The tendons of conscience grow taut," he went on to observe (Ceplair 2007, 69).

American Film History: Selected Readings, Origins to 1960, First Edition. Edited by Cynthia Lucia, Roy Grundmann, and Art Simon.
© 2016 John Wiley & Sons, Inc. Published 2016 by John Wiley & Sons, Inc.

He was finally assigned to serve in the Merchant Marine on a Liberty ship bound for Naples, Italy. He was on it for three and half months. "The voyage was wonderful, everything I wanted, the smartest thing I ever did," Jarrico wrote Wilson (Ceplair 2007, 71). He would enlist again in 1945. Many Hollywood leftists shared Jarrico's enthusiasm. At its onset the war seemed a great opportunity to defend their country in uniform. The war effort also seemed to swing Hollywood in the direction leftists had long supported.

Jarrico was a communist, but his experience was similar to that of those progressive members of the Hollywood film industry who had never been members of the party. After all, the success of the Hollywood Left was contingent on its ability to be a coalition of communists, fellow travelers, and liberal New Dealers who shared certain goals, among them the commitment to antifascism and to the politicization of Hollywood films. Philip Dunne, for example, was a liberal New Yorker who had come to Hollywood in 1930. Irish Catholic Dunne had endorsed Franklin Delano Roosevelt throughout the 1930s and even visited the president at the White House. In addition to his support for the New Deal, like other Hollywood progressives, Dunne was invested in the project of making Hollywood cinema responsive to contemporary problems, in particular American poverty and the rise of fascism and Nazism. An early member of the Hollywood Anti-Nazi League, founded in 1936 by a coalition of American liberals and radicals and European antifascist refugees (Giovacchini 2001, 81–86), Dunne had penned the script for *Lancer Spy* (Gregory Ratoff, 1937), which, after the famous 1934–1936 Congressional hearings on World War I profiteering and the mid-1930s Neutrality Acts, dared to remind Americans of German espionage during World War I. After the United States entered the war, Dunne, like Jarrico, wanted to enlist. In April 1943, he wrote – to no avail – to Frank G. Andrews of the Civil Aeronautics Administration to ask about "qualifying under Navy's program" as a pilot.[1] Dunne then tried to enlist in the Army and was rejected on the basis of his too-liberal political background. Barred from active service, Dunne worked in Nelson Rockefeller's Office of the Coordinator on Inter-American Affairs (CIAA). Rumors of his political liability followed him, even after he left the CIAA, displeased with the way the billionaire New Dealer ran the agency. In 1943, Dunne asked Rockefeller to dispel the gossip that he had been fired from the CIAA for being a "dangerous radical."[2] Dunne finally found a niche in the Office of War Information, where he wrote films for the liberated areas, in particular Jean Renoir's *Salute to France* (1944).

The Nazi–Soviet Non-Aggression Pact of August 1939 briefly created a cleft between communists and the other noncommunist liberal and radical New Dealers who made up the Hollywood Left. In September 1939, Dunne had broken ties with all his communist friends. Later in his life Dunne argued that the Communist Party's inane policies had beheaded a thriving American left and, in so doing, gave the party a "share of the responsibility for postwar McCarthyism and Nixonism" (1992, 114). In some sense, however, the rift was not serious. The Communist Party core of the Hollywood Anti-Nazi League (HANL) had indeed hijacked the League after the Pact, toed the party line, and turned the League's name into the Hollywood League for Democratic Action, but the shameful deed had been done somewhat half-heartedly by the famously independent communist cell in Hollywood, which, according to Gerald Horne, was thought of as "one of the least sectarian units of the organization nationally" (2001, 63). Indeed, the behavior of the Hollywood communist left seems to confirm the direction of the new scholarship that underscores the existence of "the many worlds of American communism." If the Communist Party of the United States of America (CPUSA) leadership inhabited the world of the Kremlin, its base was often immersed in a web of local alliances and political relationships that placed it at odds with the national leadership (Cherny 2002). When the upper echelons of the party endorsed the new Soviet policy, the Hollywood chapter paid only lip service to the directive. Abraham Polonsky at that time saw the Eastern cadres as "the fools in New York," adding that "the cultural leadership obviously didn't know what they were talking about." The screenwriter remembers that, "We ignored them out here, and we did a lot of wonderful things despite them" (Buhle & McGilligan 1997, 494).

Polonsky's attitude was not surprising. Nazism was the enemy the left had been spoiling to fight for a long time. Hollywood communists and fellow travelers had immediately and vehemently supported the HANL in 1936 and many of them had written the few "premature" antifascist films that Hollywood produced before the war broke out, including *Blockade* (1939) – directed by progressive, German-born William Dieterle and scripted by one of the future Hollywood Ten, John Howard Lawson – and *Confessions of a Nazi Spy* (Anatole Litvak, 1939), which involved the collaboration of many Hollywood progressives with the numerous anti-Nazi refugees working in the Los Angeles ateliers (Giovacchini 1999, 212–213). Communists and fellow travelers had been behind the theatrical production of *Meet the People*, the first Los Angeles-produced show to travel eastward, rather than westward, to New York's Broadway. Premiering on Christmas Day 1939, the piece directly satirized Stalin and Hitler. "Hitler is mimicked a few times," noted *Variety*, "as are Chamberlain and Stalin."[3]

As a matter of fact, several of the antifascist films that Hollywood did produce before Pearl Harbor were penned by communists or fellow travelers.[4] In 1940, communist Lawson wrote *Four Sons*; Sam Ornitz and Bernard Vorhaus – both future blacklistees – scripted *Three Faces West*; and fellow traveler Howard Koch wrote the anti-Nazi parable *The Sea Hawk*, using Elizabethan England to spin a tale of anti-Hitler resistance. The first year of the war produced a discrepancy between the Hollywood leftists' work and their public statements. In 1941, the screenwriter of *Stagecoach* (1939), Dudley Nichols, signed "In Defense of Culture," the communist-sponsored antiwar manifesto of the Fourth American Writers' Congress.[5] The same year, however, Nichols worked with antifascist refugee Fritz Lang on the script of the anti-Nazi film *Man Hunt* (1941). By January 1941, part of the script was almost finished and was good enough for Lang to declare himself "in love" with it.[6] Another signatory of "In Defense of Culture," Lillian Hellman, wrote the anti-Nazi play *Watch on the Rhine* about a member of the German resistance who kills a Nazi infiltrator.[7]

Party film critics – usually closer to the official CPUSA national leadership – had to sweat bullets to explain away the call for militant anti-Nazism evident in the work of their Hollywood comrades. Writing in the philo-communist folio *The Clipper*, Wolfe Kaufman was left to hope that Jack Lawson's script for *Four Sons* had been rewritten by the studio. Too bad that the *New York Times* commented that "Mr. Lawson writes like a man whose heart is in what he's doing."[8] *New Masses* praised the intentions of Lillian Hellman's *Watch on the Rhine*, but argued that the play, which was soon to be made into a film, was flawed and could be "misused by those who would like to whip us or cajole us into imperialist war under the banner of fighting Fascism in Germany."[9]

Along with a commitment to unionism and to more realistic pictures, antifascism had been part of the glue that had kept the Hollywood Cultural Front together in the 1930s. Even after the 1939 Pact, Hollywood communists and fellow travelers tried to balance directives coming from the national party leadership with a local, grassroots tradition of cooperation that called for internationalism and political collaboration. The twist in the CPUSA line momentarily reestablished a gap between the spheres of work and politics, but soon enough the Nazi invasion of the Soviet Union and the Japanese attack on Pearl Harbor mended the rift. In their history of the Hollywood Left, Paul Buhle and Dave Wagner argue that in 1941, "the Left's Hollywood moment had come. The politically shaded films on international themes that had been impossible to make as late as 1938–39 became barely possible in 1940, and sometimes wildly popular as well as wildly admired by 1941–42" (2002, 209–210).

The "Democratic Tradition" Comes to Hollywood

After Pearl Harbor, Hollywood seemed, finally, to be doing what the Hollywood Left had asked the studios to do throughout the 1930s. In 1934, *New Theater* critic Robert Gessner argued that all revolutionary artists "must, in order to be at this time effectively heard, consider seriously the question of working through Hollywood."[10] Gessner and other left-leaning film and theater critics argued that, to be sure, Hollywood films still possessed a tendency toward escapism, but progressives in the industry could inject the antidote of socially and politically conscious themes through plot, characterization, and film style. A good movie would, in fact, promote the social engagement of its audience by tackling the issues of the day in a semi-documentary style and by proposing progressive solutions (Giovacchini 2003, 426). In the first issue of the short-lived periodical *Films*, Philip Sterling noted that this had actually been done since the beginning of Hollywood cinema. "We can assume," he wrote, "that, from the invention of the Kinetoscope to the last Academy dinner, there has also existed a tradition of protest, of the urge of social change." In its first 40 years Hollywood had produced not only "a fond, uncritical defense of the *status quo*," but also a "democratic tradition" which progressive filmmakers were to expand. As examples of this tradition, Sterling pointed to D. W. Griffith's *A Corner in Wheat* (1909), Ernst Lubitsch's *Broken Lullaby* (1932), and William Wellman's *Wild Boys of the Road* (1933).[11]

This "democratic tradition" had seemingly culminated in *Confessions of a Nazi Spy*, the first anti-Nazi film produced by a major studio. In February 1939, when *Confessions* was finally put into production at Warners' Burbank soundstages, many progressives had volunteered their services (Giovacchini 2001, 93–98). The result was encouraging. *Confessions* was unmistakably about Nazism – parading swastikas and Hitler's images – prompting an apprehensive studio head, Hal Wallis, to write to producer Robert Lord that "we are using too many pictures of Hitler in our picture ... I am afraid we are heaping it on too thick."[12] *Confessions* also rejected the Hollywood lightness of touch and mixed newsreels with reenactments and fictional scenes. Possibly the film's more radical modification was the downplaying of the protagonist's role. Edward G. Robinson's character Edward "Ed" Renard, based on real-life FBI agent Leon G. Turrou, enters the film only in the middle. "Perhaps the smartest stunt of the film's direction was the careful underplaying of Robinson as the G-Man," *Variety* noted. The film "is a group's job."[13]

Fairly weak at the box office, *Confessions* performed strongly among American leftist intellectuals. Reviewing the film, *New Masses* noted how *Confessions* proved the New York political and aesthetic avant-garde had made it to Hollywood: "The fruitful experiments of men like Joris Ivens and Herbert Kline, and neglected bands like Frontier Films have at last reached Hollywood."[14] For Manfred George, the editor of *Aufbau*, the preeminent periodical of the community of anti-Nazi refugees, *Confessions* was "evidence" of Hollywood's overcoming the "commercial instincts" of its producers and of its intent to fulfill its "moral and cultural possibilities of Enlightenment and Progress" (1939, 4). In contrast, writing for *Commentary* in 1947, in the context of the incipient Cold War and the anti-Hollywood intellectual climate of postwar America, cultural critic Robert Warshow derided the culture of the 1930s as a "disastrous vulgarization of intellectual life" in which "Father Divine rode in the May Day parade ... *The Grapes of Wrath* was a great novel ... *Confessions of a Nazi Spy* was a serious movie, and 'Ballad for Americans' was an inspired song" (2001, 4).

Confessions did not immediately trigger a cycle of anti-Nazi films. Germany had sabotaged the European distribution of the film and in the face of ostensible American neutrality, studios had become "jittery" about film treatment of Nazism since, in *Variety*'s words, "there is no way of telling which way the diplomatic cat will jump."[15] In October 1939, Jack Warner had announced that "America is neutral and we are Americans. Our policy is 100% neutrality. There will be no propaganda pictures from Warner Brothers" (quoted in Dick 1985, 87). Pearl Harbor, however, changed all this, making the anti-Nazism of *Confessions* the norm rather than the exception. More importantly, *Confessions* and its aesthetics were now endorsed by the administration and the main propaganda agencies. Established in June 1942 by Franklin Delano Roosevelt to coordinate all government agencies devoted to the production of war propaganda, the Office of War Information (OWI) had a branch devoted to film, the Bureau of Motion Pictures (BMP), headed by Lowell Mellett. OWI's power to restrain and direct the Hollywood studios was undefined, but Ulric Bell, the representative of the OWI's Overseas Branch in the Bureau, could hit Hollywood where it hurt by hampering the foreign distribution of a movie he deemed detrimental to the war effort. As Clayton R. Koppes and Gregory D. Black have extensively documented in their *Hollywood Goes to War* (1990), relations between OWI and Hollywood studio executives were often strained. Studio heads were resentful of the authority of OWI and accused its representatives of incompetence. As a matter of fact, neither Lowell Mellett nor Ulric Bell had much direct experience of making motion pictures. However, OWI was soon to draw its staff from the industry itself. In 1945, the War Activities Committee calculated that 7,000 Hollywood studio employees worked for military agencies at some point during the conflict (Doherty 1993, 60).

Hollywood leftists volunteered to work for the organization. Leonardo Bercovici, one of the highest-paid writers in Hollywood, remembers the work he did for OWI as the only work that had "political content" (Buhle & McGilligan 1997, 42). Condemned by many contemporary conservative politicians as a refuge for liberal and radical New Deal intellectuals (Blum 1976, 39–76), OWI is indeed depicted as a place of masculine, martial virtues in many of the autobiographies of Hollywood figures. OWI was "a no nonsense, no frills, no glamour" agency where the willingness to do one's part counted more than one's politics, recalls Dunne (Blum 1976, 165).

Many of the OWI's directives mirrored the demands that Hollywood progressives had insisted upon during the previous five years. At the center of the first government manual to the motion picture industry issued by the Roosevelt administration on June 2, 1942 stood a program for motion pictures that closely resembled what the Hollywood Left had demanded of the studios in the 1930s. Hollywood was to cease being mere entertainment and embrace the higher cause of the political education of the American masses. Thus, the war was to be represented as a "people's war," both outside and inside the United States. Stressing the democratic health of the American people, Hollywood films were also to differentiate between the peoples of the countries the United States was fighting and their dictatorial leaders. The manual also expressed faith in Hollywood cinema as a possible channel of political and factual communication, the precondition for informed public opinion and for a democratic war. "We believe," the manual argued, "that mass opinion is intelligent and will support an intelligent program – *if informed*" (Short 1983, 174). Cinema therefore was to inform the public about all aspects of the war and the manual focused specific sections on six: "The Issues" of the war, "The Enemy," "The United Nations and Peoples," "Work and Production," "The Home Front," and "The Fighting Forces" (Short 1983, 174–180).[16]

In fact, a comparison between the 1942 government manual and the Hollywood Production Code reveals the changes in public perception of cinema, from an institution dedicated to the private accumulation of profits to one with an increasingly public role. The 1930 Code, which the Production Code Administration (PCA) enforced after 1934, stated explicitly that its authors "regarded the function of cinema primarily as entertainment without any explicit purpose of teaching and propaganda."[17] For the government as well as for Hollywood progressives, the war pictures had a public function – that of informing and educating the masses about the issues of the day. They were, in other words, to be a solution to what a liberal producer like Walter Wanger called "the problem of motion pictures and mass enlightenment" (quoted in Bernstein 1994, 74).

What this meant was that in 1942, the "democratic tradition" of the center-left Hollywood coalition had moved from the margins to the heart of the public discourse about cinema. Not surprisingly, some directly referred to *Confessions of a Nazi Spy* as the model of the "correct" war film. In 1945, Walter Wanger was asked to write an essay on the movie industry during the war for a collection that was to be titled "How We Did Our Own Specific Jobs." Wanger, who had been a protagonist of progressive Hollywood in the 1930s, identified *Confessions of a Nazi Spy* ("a monumental film") as the precursor for the kind of Hollywood war film OWI demanded: "An intelligent blending of entertainment and ideas."[18]

A Cinema of Presence

The antifascist war represented the crowning of several deeply felt political choices, and missing it meant for many in the Hollywood Left that they had been unable to live up to their ideals. The style of the films that Hollywood leftists concocted during World War II reflected this participatory élan and leaned toward what I would call a "deontology of presence." In other words, it gestured toward a political aesthetics that pivoted on the notion that being physically present in the war effort was a moral and aesthetic duty for the progressive filmmaker because the camera's proximity to the action made for a more engaging and more politically effective cinema.

At one level, war cinema was to make the war concrete to potentially distracted American audiences that had not experienced the shame of invasion and the horrors of air raids. "We suffer – we vaguely realize – a unique and constantly intensifying schizophrenia which threatens no other nation involved in this war. Geography is the core of the disease," wrote James Agee in *The Nation* in October 1943 (2005, 71). Cinema's realism was to erase the boundaries between the theater and the war front, making adherence to war necessities urgent to Americans. On another, more personal level, the call for presence was about film artists' own desire to have a visible place in the world struggle for democracy. For the antifascist filmmaker to be absent from the place where the antifascist struggle was unfolding was a contradiction. The very presence of the filmmaker on the antifascist battle front was, instead, a moment of personal glory, an event to be commemorated in writing and represented in images. Behind or before the camera, their performances often stressed and emphasized their own "presence" and participation in the conflict.

Hollywood celebrated its "presence" in the war effort in films like *Hollywood Canteen* (1944), directed and scripted by liberal Delmer Daves, frequent collaborator of communist screenwriter Albert Maltz, and featuring the work of many Hollywood progressives, from John Garfield to lyricist Yip Harburg ("you can always tell a Yank ... by the way he fights for the Bill of Rights"). Participating in the war was often an exercise in self-styling, a way of reinventing oneself. Like soldiers, Hollywood performers trimmed their bodies according to military needs. Famously, Veronica Lake abandoned her peek-a-boo hairstyle to sport a more martial haircut. In speeches he delivered during the conflict, actor Edward G. Robinson constructed a complicated and fascinating dialogue between himself and his most famous screen character. In these performances the legacy of the gangster Rico, a.k.a. "Little Caesar," was both called upon and exorcised. In one speech he delivered to soldiers at an army base, Robinson's evocation of his 1931 star-making role allowed the wealthy, refined actor, who had not been able to enlist because of his age, to relate to the violence of the soldiers' experience and their social status, which was so different from his own. In the course of the performance Robinson suddenly took a sub-machine gun out of a violin case and shouted, "Pipe down, you mugs, or I'll let you have it.... This is the Kid himself talking – Little Caesar, remember?" He then proceeded to relate the war experiences of his gangster alter ego. Rico wanted to enlist but was given a 4F by the draft board. "'As far as we are concerned,'" the doctors had told him, "'you'll never be Edward G.I. Robinson.'" But contrary to the board's recommendations, Little Caesar had gone to war anyway and killed himself some Nazis. Robinson finally switched back to speaking as himself, telling the soldiers that this is the "most privileged moment of my life ... I have seen the men who are defeating Hitler."[19]

Others in Hollywood simply refused to represent their enemy on-screen. According to Hans Kafka, who reported from Hollywood for the refugee magazine *Aufbau*, Francis Lederer, the Czech star of *Confessions* and an early member of the HANL, withdrew from Paramount's *Hostages* (Frank Tuttle, 1943) so as not to play a Czech quisling.[20] Thomas Mitchell did the same when asked to play a collaborator in Fritz Lang's *Hangmen Also Die!* (1943).[21] In many cases, leftist performers could finally project on-screen more of their political and cultural identity. In the 1930s, progressive actors in particular had often kept their two "bodies" – the real one and the image on the screen – separate, disconnected by the relative implausibility of Hollywood films and, for some of them, by their scarce investment in the roles they were allowed to play. There had been instances when the two bodies almost coincided, as in the case of *Confessions of a Nazi Spy*, in which many of the participants were acting out their real political and social beliefs. Following that film, however, its anti-Nazi star Edward G. Robinson went back to playing a gangster in *Brother Orchid* (1940). For Hollywood progressives the war represented an opportunity to reunite their screen personae with their antifascist selves. On the screen, if not in real life, Hollywood progressives and refugees could get the antifascist job done.

Nothing, however, could beat the real thing. As hard as they worked in anti-Nazi productions and as satisfying as they characterized their experience in the OWI to have been, most of the Hollywood progressives wanted to serve. For future blacklistee screenwriter John Sanford, who briefly worked for the famous 834th Signal Service Photographic Detachment Unit, headed by Frank Capra, a military uniform was "the only clothes (aside from overalls) that the day recognizes as respectable" (quoted in McBride 1993, 463). His case was a sad one as Capra dismissed him for political reasons after a few weeks (McBride 1993, 459–460). Peter Viertel, the son of Salka Viertel, the host of the most important Modernist salon in Los Angeles, went through the gruesome Marine boot camp (1969, 262). The first 11 months of his service had been so bad that he suspected there was "a secret file against him." Rather than throwing in the towel, the young writer decided to stick it out: "The true Marine that he is, he wants to go after the invisible enemy," his mother wrote Ernst Lubitsch, not without pride.[22]

Sanford was not the only Hollywood radical to be barred from the Army because of his political views. Screenwriter John Bright – 33 years of age, a communist, and in good health at the time of Pearl Harbor – immediately volunteered for active service only to be turned down because of his radical politics. Eventually Bright made it into the Coast Guard (Bright 1991, 25). Edward Dmytryk was rejected because of his "premature antifascism" (Dmytryk 1996, 4), and so were the Epstein brothers and Jerome Chodorov, all of them progressive Hollywood talent from New York or the East Coast, whom Frank Capra had originally selected for his unit (McBride 1993, 457–465). Others did not make it because of their health or their age. At 47, Walter Wanger was too old (Bernstein 1994, 174). Thirty-year-old Nicholas Ray tried to enlist but was given a 4F deferral because he had lost the sight in his right eye as a result of a car accident (Kreidl 1977, 24). John Garfield applied for the Army but was designated 4F because of a congenital heart murmur (Hoopes 1994, 169). If they made it into the armed forces, their service was to be celebrated. In their biographies, articles, films, and letters, the Hollywood talent who did experience service and combat reveled in the details and in the hardships they shared with the ordinary American boys. The 1945 volume of the *Screenwriter*, the Screen Writers Guild (SWG) magazine edited by Dalton Trumbo, is replete with "reports from a GI typewriter," memoirs written from the front by Hollywood progressives and commemorating the experience of the war.[23]

Those Hollywood progressives who took active part in the conflict also provided a visual representation not only of the war, but also of their own presence in it. Progressive screenwriter-turned-director John Huston enlisted in the Signal Corps in April 1942 and was sent into the inhospitable subpolar climate of the Aleutian Islands to shoot a documentary about American aerial attacks on the Japanese base of Kisca. In his autobiography *An Open Book*, Huston emphasizes that on Kisca he was not treated any differently from the other soldiers, living in a tent in the cold "along with the rest of the personnel" (1980, 88). Huston's men were not Hollywood professionals but common men. Huston remembers Sergeant Hermann Crabtree, for instance, as a giant Li'l Abner with enormous eyes: "He was strong as an ox too. We'd load him up with the equipment … to take out to the planes. I could've jumped onto his back too, and I swear, he wouldn't have known the difference" (1980, 90). The movie that came out of the experience, *Report from the Aleutians* (1943), was both a committed tribute to the common Americans living and dying in the armed forces and a celebration of those in the Hollywood industry present on the scene – much like Joris Ivens's *Action Stations!* (completed in February 1943 for the Royal Canadian Navy), Huston's *The Battle of San Pietro* (1944), William Wyler's *Memphis Belle* (1944), or John Ford's *The Battle of Midway* (1942).[24]

The first reels of *Report from the Aleutians* are dedicated to identifying the soldier as a common American. The Army was the successful melting pot, blending "men from Brooklyn, or from Texas" and "bookkeepers, farmers, college men" into the new common identity of "soldier," a democratic community where – as Huston's commentary notes over images of soldiers informally saluting superior officers – "there is little room for formal discipline." At the same time, it erases the protagonist role to give space to the teamwork.

The rest of *Report* made sure the spectators knew that Huston and his crew were active members of this democratic community, present in the conflict, and actively participating in the combat. The long, protracted aerial assault on Kisca of the last two reels constructs, in fact, an aesthetic of authenticity based on the "presence" of the filmmaker aboard the ship. Shot from one of the planes, the mission over Kisca situates itself within the Hollywood narrative tradition. It is what John Howard Lawson would call the "obligatory scene," the climax of the film "which the audience foresees and desires and the absence of which it may with reason resent" (1936, 18–19). At the same time, the realism of the scene is markedly colored by the "presence" of the filmmaker next to the bomber's crew. When the aircraft is shot at by the enemy, the camera bounces, at times losing a clear focus, while the commentary stops and is replaced by frantic exchanges over an intercom and the booming sound of the battle.

Progressive critics took notice. *New Masses*' Joseph Foster noted that "by the ingenious use of the camera you become witness to every last detail of [the] action."[25] In *The Nation*, James Agee remarked upon the "vigorous and pitiful sense of the presence, danger, skill, and hope of several human beings" and commented that "everything is seen, done, and experienced as if from inside one or another of the men in the plane." Comparing William Wyler's *Memphis Belle* to the British *Desert Victory* (1943), Agee wrote that the former finally compared favorably with the British documentaries (2005, 108).

Through their bouncing cameras, liberal and radical filmmakers like Huston, Wyler, John Ford, and Joris Ivens implicitly inserted in their films a self-portrait that represented them as soldiers, ordinary Americans fighting and risking their lives amidst ordinary men. These films focused on the Army as a stand-in for the American people imagined as a predominantly male, interclass, and interethnic construct governed by internal solidarity against the enemy. Nonsoldiers and diplomats are, if present at all, ironically juxtaposed to the fighting forces with whom the sympathy of the director lies. In *Memphis Belle*, Wyler's final reel captures the incongruous visit of the British royal family to the base immediately after the mission has been completed. Huston routinely clashed with the upper echelons of the Army, recalling that the military brass disliked *The Battle of San Pietro* and the film was saved only through the intercession of George C. Marshall. His 1946 documentary *Let There Be Light*, a poignant portrait of shell-shocked veterans in a Long Island hospital, was too controversial for the Army and deemed unfit for general distribution until 1980 (Huston 1980, 126).

The narrative style of these films had its conventions, among which was a profound respect for reality itself and the potential of cinema to capture it. The long, unedited sequences of Huston's and Wyler's documentaries emphasized the intrinsic value of original footage where, as Hermine Rich Isaacs put it in *Theater Arts*, "the combat photographer is forced by the circumstances of his profession to speak his piece in pictures" (1944, 345). But it is problematic to position these films outside the Hollywood tradition. As a matter of fact, these documentaries reflect the political aesthetics of 1930s Hollywood progressives, which demanded the combination of newsreel techniques and Hollywood narrative tradition in order to achieve a powerful realism, while emphasizing American democracy. They were, as Gary Edgerton has pointed out, "traditional in film form and style" (1993, 34). Wyler, Ford, Huston, and Ivens employed Hollywood narrative style in their war documentaries, most obviously in the reenactments that occupy most of the footage of John Ford's and Gregg Toland's *December 7th* (1943) or Joris Ivens's *Action Stations!* ("Sounds like Hollywood," the communist Dutch filmmaker commented in a lecture he gave at USC in June 1943), or in *Memphis Belle*'s ad lib intercom dialogue between the bomber crewmen. Hollywood is also visible in the editing of these documentaries, which builds to the climax of the last-reel battle, heightens the suspense of the return, and leads to the eventual happy ending.[26]

Bringing the War into the Hollywood Film

In an interview with British documentarian Midge Mackenzie, John Huston once argued that he never saw any difference between a good feature film and a documentary (Mackenzie 1998). The attempt to graft the issues of the day onto Hollywood narratives had been *the* project of the Hollywood Left in the 1930s. During the war the semi-documentary mode became somewhat popular in Hollywood, especially because the style now had the imprimatur of the OWI and of American intellectuals. *Wake Island*, released in September 1942, was an early semi-documentary, its credits listing half a dozen military advisers and informing the public that the film was drawn entirely "from the records of the U.S. Marine Corps." Reviewing the film, *New Republic* critic Manny Farber declared that "finally – and it's about time – Hollywood has gone to war," and hoped it would "mar[k] the start of a new attitude."[27] Lewis Seiler's *Guadalcanal Diary* (1943) was based on the contemporaneously published diary of Marine Richard Tregaskis. The film's titles readily acknowledge production assistance from the Marine Corps. The film avoids any trace of an easy, happy ending and serves up newsreel footage and brutal images of *mano a mano* combat with the Japanese. Released in October 1943, *Guadalcanal Diary* features images of Marines lying dead on a Solomon Islands beach, explicitly echoing George Strock's famous images of the dead Marines on Buna Beach in New Guinea that *Life* had just published in September 1943 (Roeder 1993, 14). Like those pictures, *Guadalcanal Diary* rejects a protagonist-driven narrative and strives for the kind of communal protagonist featured in *Confessions*. Moreover, the group of soldiers at the center of the film forms what Horace Kallen would have called "a democracy of nationalities" (1915, 220). The Jew sings Catholic hymns next to the Irish Catholic, and the Latino character – played by Anthony Quinn – reads aloud letters in Spanish from his many girlfriends. The film does its job in making the war present to the audiences at home. The audience at the Roxy, wrote Bosley Crowther in the *New York Times*, was "visibly stirred and ... no doubt had the impression that it was witnessing the battle of Guadalcanal."[28] In *New Masses*, Daniel Prentiss called the film a "deeply affecting exposition of the character of American fighting men."[29] Crowther praised the film's first part as "almost documentary real." If anything, the film was not documentary enough, because the filmmakers had "rigged up a patent fiction to fit the pattern of a film."[30]

In the films that OWI considered successful examples of the Hollywood contribution to the war effort, narrative choices endorsed such a strategy. The realism of *Air Force* (1943) was approved by almost everybody. OWI liked the film, which was directed by Howard Hawks, scripted by Dudley Nichols, and cast with a mixture of professional and semi-professional actors led by John Garfield. The *Daily Worker* called it a "remarkably good movie."[31] The military even sent Jack Warner several letters congratulating him.[32] The reason was the film's realism. *Air Force*, concluded the *Daily Mirror*, was a "screen document" of the war, exactly communicating its experience. Therefore, "women should see such things, [as] they can't live them."[33] In February 1943, publisher Nelson Poynter wrote to Warner: "Several members of our staff saw *Air Force* this week and are as enthusiastic about it as I am." Bell agreed. He recommended *Air Force* for "its use overseas," and called the film "a fine contribution to the war effort."[34]

The film's pursuit of realism and the Hollywood stars' commitment to the war effort even modified the way the notorious Hollywood pecking order was presented in the film's screen credits. As Robert Sklar has noted, the credits of *Air Force* disregarded the relative box office appeal of its cast and – recalling the example set in 1939 by the credits of *Confessions* – listed the actors according to their military rank (1992, 143). Moreover, drafts of the screenplay show that since the initial treatment, Dudley Nichols had replaced Hollywood glamour with wartime rigor. The opening was to show only

> faces, instruments, making us feel the excitement of this difficult work. We don't tell what it is about. The men have oxygen tubes protruding from their masks. We can cut in on the "intercom" ... and get the "feel" of what it is like to be on a bombing mission.[35]

A production note from Warner Bros. remarked that "only 20 percent of the footage of *Air Force* has dialogue; ordinarily there is twice that much conversation ... [and] the average number of close-ups per foot of film has been reduced by ninety percent, thus heightening the speed and tempo tremendously."[36] James Agee noted in *The Nation* the "gladdening effort to get away from the movie faces and to give the men diverse and authentic speech" (Agee 2005, 41). Much of the film's realism resulted from materials, faces, and imprimaturs provided by the military, which dispatched two technical advisers to the set, Captain Sam Triffy and Captain Theron Coulter. In exchange, the Pentagon demanded the film be subjected "to review by the War Department prior to any showing (sneak preview, press, or sales screenings) or public release."[37] The studio – conservative producers and progressives alike – complied. After Pearl Harbor, Jack Warner had affixed placards all over the Burbank sound stages to inform his employees of a "ban on conversing in any foreign language" (Hough 1942, 7). Director Hawks and 10 others, including principals in the cast, were required to take an oath that they would maintain the secrecy of official military information necessary for the filming.[38] "Christ, he [General Henry H. "Hap" Arnold] even made me a general for a week," Hawks dryly commented (McBride 1982, 90).

Narrative modifications to conventional Hollywood form also heightened realism. In a postwar essay, a frequent collaborator of the Hollywood Left, director Fritz Lang, railed against the Hollywood convention of the happy ending that prevented Hollywood cinema from achieving realism (Lang 1948). Yet, many World War II movies resisted this Hollywood convention. One of Lang's own war films, *Hangmen Also Die!* (1943), dealt with the massacre of Lidice at the hands of the Nazis in retaliation for the assassination of the deputy *Reichsprotektor* of Bohemia and Moravia, Reinhard Heydrich. There was not much happiness to be found in this story of murder and massacre, and the treatment by Bertolt Brecht and Fritz Lang, as well as the script, written by Brecht (uncredited) and American communist John Wexley, reflect this.[39] Scholars have long debated how the original cut of the film ended and Ehrhard Bahr has succinctly summarized this debate in his *Weimar on the Pacific* (2007, 145). DVD and VHS copies of *Hangmen* do not show the mass graves of hostages or the actual execution of the resistance hero Professor Novotny. Citing the film as an example of a non-conventional happy ending, however, in 1948 Lang wrote that he "ended [*Hangmen Also Die!*] with the anti-fascist professor going to his death along with the other Czechoslovakian hostages" (Lang 1948, 27). Whether or not Lang's memory of the film's original cut is correct, even the copies of the film in current circulation unambiguously show the costs of resisting the Nazi war machine. Though the Nazis cannot find the real assassin, Lang shows the audience that hostages are executed. The film – "America's finest artistic comment on the war," according to *New Masses* (Davidman 1943, 28)[40] – rejected any sense of a happy ending or of narrative closure, its concluding frame pushing the struggle forward by reading, "Not the end." OWI was not worried, and Ulric Bell applauded the film as "probably the most gripping war picture yet to come from Hollywood."[41] United Artists sent exhibitors ad packages that stressed the "realism" of the film as one of its selling points.[42]

As in Lidice, Hollywood made some effort to stick to the realities of the war and not rewrite history. Reflecting the early defeats of the American troops at the hands of the Japanese, *Corregidor* (1943) ended with the surrender of the American troops to the armies of the Rising Sun. The final reel of one of the most famous and most praised of the Hollywood war films, Tay Garnett's *Bataan* (1943), showed Robert Taylor shooting at the advancing Japanese from a grave, surrounded by the freshly dug graves of the other members of his platoon, who have all been killed by the "Japs."

Race, the Hollywood Left, and the War Film

Some scholars have noted the timidity with which Hollywood war films tackled the issue of American racism at home and in the military, as well as Hollywood's unfair and racist representation of Japanese soldiers ("the beast in the jungle") in comparison to representations of Italian and German combatants (Koppes & Black 1990, 248; Roeder 1993, 56–58). In their account of leftist activities in Hollywood, Paul Buhle and Dave Wagner argue that the Hollywood Left was also in the forefront of antiracism, and Hollywood's dismal record was mainly due to "forces beyond [the] control" of the left: the myopia of the studios and the timidity of the government (2002, 187–192). The question, however, remains relevant: If with Pearl Harbor "the Left's Hollywood moment had come," what was the effect of this leftist surge on the representation of race in American film? In other words, if the left was so engaged and effective in pursuing its Hollywood project, why is Hollywood's record so checkered when it comes to race?

Before discussing Hollywood's shortcomings, it is fair to note that the Hollywood film was ahead of, and not behind, the majority of white America in its attitude toward race. "The main barrier to equal treatment of blacks in the combat film," notes Thomas Doherty, "was the unequal treatment of blacks in the military services" (1993, 211). When Robert Andrews and the other filmmakers involved in the making of *Bataan* showed a *de facto* racially integrated platoon, they were five years ahead of the American military, which integrated its troops in 1948 only after President Harry Truman's executive order. "The roll call with which *Bataan* begins represents a fictive or imaginary American community," writes Richard Slotkin. "The *Bataan* platoon represents a military unit that could not have existed in the American army as it was then constituted" (2001, 479).

Slotkin has suggested that *Bataan* marked a defining moment in the cinematic representations of race because the film evidenced "the shift from the myth of America as essentially a white man's country, to that of a multi-ethnic, multi-racial democracy" (2001, 470). Andrews, the former Chicago journalist turned screenwriter, wanted his script to be a document of what was really happening on the war front so as "to wake the good citizens to what they were up against" (quoted in May 2000, 147). The film is violent, dark, and, for the time, realistic. As far as race relations go, however, *Bataan* sins in the direction of wishful thinking. *Bataan*'s platoon is represented through what Slotkin terms the "'melting pot' roll call," the

Figure 21.1 *Minimus inter pares* – or "the least of his peers." Kenneth Spencer as Private Epps and Desi Arnaz as Felix Ramirez in Tay Garnett's *Bataan* (1943, producer Irving Starr).

multiethnic and multiracial nature of the unit revealed by the aural and visual apparatuses of the film that stress non–Anglo Saxon names and accents, as well as nonwhite complexions. The film features stoic black Private Epps (Kenneth Spencer), feisty Latino Private Felix Ramirez (Desi Arnaz), heroic Filipino soldiers Yankee Salazar and Corp. Juan Katigbak (Alex Havier and Roque Espiritu), along with Polish-American private F. X. Matowski (Barry Nelson) and Jewish-American Corp. Jake Feingold (Thomas Mitchell).

To be sure, the racial and ethnic integration of *Bataan*'s platoon is contradictory in its representation. The ethnic characters of the film represent what Slotkin calls "patronizing stereotypes" that imprison the soldiers within their own ethnic clichés, while they are treated with condescension by the commanding officers, all of whom sport solid white Anglo-Saxon names like Capt. Henry Lassiter (Lee Bowman), Lt Steve Bentley (George Murphy), and Sgt Bill Dane (Robert Taylor) (2001, 480). This taxonomy also locates the black character in something of a liminal position – *in* the platoon but somehow not *of* the platoon. Private Epps's contested belonging to this "band of brothers" is put into question visually by his not wearing a uniform for most of the movie, his racialized status made clearer by the opening shot that represents him shirtless, doing the platoon's laundry and singing a spiritual.

Filipinos do better than blacks in *Bataan*. Dressed in their full uniforms, heroic, and even allowed to play baseball, Filipinos are allotted two spots out of the platoon's nine. This, however, should not surprise, as the United States was trying to counteract Japanese accusations of racial imperialism with promises of postwar Filipino independence. OWI applauded the film's choices and noted that the "Philippines angle is treated very nicely."[43] The Filipino issue was of course thorny, as American soldiers had died at the hands of insurgents during the bloody war of conquest that had ushered the Philippines into the small group of American colonial possessions where they remained until the Japanese invaded the islands in 1941. American films dealt with the conundrum of a somewhat repentant colonial power in splendidly contradictory fashion, celebrating the courage of the Filipinos as well as the benefits of American colonization. In *Back to Bataan* (1945), scripted by communist screenwriter Ben Barzman and directed by future (though temporary) blacklistee Edward Dmytryk, Anthony Quinn impersonates the grandson of the legendary Filipino guerrilla Andrés Bonifacio. Unable to solve the obvious inconsistency between the American past and the current promises of freedom and democracy, the film cites them side by side, projected against the future of United States-granted Filipino independence. One school kid eulogizes the anti-American resistance of the Filipino guerrillas ("Americans cannot beat Filipinos!"), while more authoritative characters (the martyred Filipino school principal and the American schoolteacher) go to great lengths to praise America for teaching Filipinos the meaning of freedom (and even Spain, for giving Christianity to the archipelago!).

Racism, of course, contributes to the repulsive representation of the Japanese in *Bataan*, where Japanese troops are relentlessly termed "rats." And racism also prompts the unfounded accusations of espionage leveled against the Japanese community in Hawaii in *Air Force*. Even when this unfair treatment concerned American citizens, OWI seemed not to care all that much. It strongly protested the most outlandish accusations against Japanese-Americans, like those in *Little Tokyo, USA* (1942), which celebrates the relocation of the Los Angeles Japanese community and a nonchalant police attitude toward the Bill of Rights (Koppes & Black 1990, 72–76). But, like most of the personnel in the Roosevelt administration (Robinson 2001), the outrage was moderate and administered with an eye to the possibility of embarrassing anti-Japanese domestic riots. In fact, Waterson Rothacker sheepishly praised *Bataan*'s producers to Ulric Bell for agreeing "to delete a line in which the Japs are referred to as 'the little yellow rats,' leaving out 'yellow.'"[44]

OWI's timidity is telling, and archival digging has yet to unearth evidence that the Hollywood Left consistently resisted anti-Japanese depictions in film. It may be argued that one of the most glaring shortcomings of the Hollywood war film reflected, at least in part, one of the weak points of American leftist vision. Yet, at the same time, Hollywood's attitude toward African-Americans did change during the war and often in films that bore the mark of the Hollywood Left, like *In This Our Life* (1942), directed by John Huston and scripted by Howard Koch, in which an earnest African-American man is unjustly accused of a homicide committed by a Southern matron, played by Bette Davis; or *Sahara* (1943), scripted by John Howard Lawson and featuring Rex Ingram's righteous beating of a Nazi *Übermensch* (Kurt Kreuger).

Archival evidence also shows that the Hollywood Left's most forward attempts to put race at the center of the American film were chastised by more powerful external forces. Lillian Hellman's original script for *The Negro Soldier* (Stuart Heisler, 1944) was rejected by the Army. The treatment that Hellman had originally prepared for William Wyler centered on a conversation on the 80th anniversary of the Emancipation Proclamation between John, a black soldier, and Chris, a dissatisfied African-American youth. It directly referred to lynching, Jim Crow, and black poverty, even though it affirmed the final necessity of African-Americans to fight for the United States.[45] Capra rejected the idea, and when William Wyler balked, he assigned the project to director Stuart Heisler. He also commissioned African-American playwright and Orson Welles alumnus Carlton Moss to write a new story line, which he accepted after toning down its "angry fervor," as Capra writes in his autobiography (1971, 358). The final result was, it is fair to say, one step backward and two forward. A film unthinkable during the previous world war, *The Negro Soldier* was, however, progress fraught with contradictions. As Thomas Cripps has written, it showed that "*some* change of collective mind had taken place, but not enough to cheer about" (1993, 125, author's emphasis). After a prologue in a black church, a breathtaking montage combines excerpts from *America*, D. W. Griffith's 1920 epic on the War of Independence, with newsreel clips from Joe Louis's bouts and clips from Tuskegee football games in order to recount the first 200 years of the African-American experience – all without mentioning slavery, lynching, or Jim Crow. The spending of public moneys

Figure 21.2 *Primus inter pares* – or "the first among his peers." Randolph Scott as Col. Thorwald in Ray Enright's *Gung Ho!* (1943, producer Walter Wanger).

on a documentary about black soldiers, which was then commercially distributed and made mandatory viewing for black and white GIs, meant that change was occurring. *The Negro Soldier* was one of the milestones in the cinematic representation of blacks in America, even though it was probably not the most radical.

To recognize that *The Negro Soldier* or *Bataan* were achievements should not obscure the tensions and unresolved contradictions that mark Hollywood work in the matter of race in these and other films. Lary May has argued that the entire crop of films produced during World War II contains a conservative "conversion narrative" that silences all kinds of nonmainstream ethnic, racial, and political identities and sensibilities. Thus, he writes, the racial and ethnic "pluralism [of the World War II film] bore a striking resemblance to the older ethos of assimilation defined by Anglo-Saxon opinion makers" (2000, 144). Ready to effectively lobby the studios for important changes in terms of themes and style, the Hollywood Left may have not been as firm in demanding that the American combat film tackle the many forms of American racism in a time of war. Even sympathetic observers like Buhle and Wagner recognize that left-wingers were not "entirely innocent in this atmosphere" (2002, 192).

The films the left admired, in fact, were not much better than the rest when it came to the Japanese. The "sizzling war film"[46] and Evan Carlson vehicle *Gung Ho!* (1943) celebrates the teamwork and democratic spirit of the Marine raiders ("We are going to be more than officers and men in this. We are going to be comrades . . . . We will fight and endure and win together") and features a striking plotline devoid of any real protagonist.

In the 15-minute-long opening scene, audiences watched reenacted interviews with Marine grunts. The raiders are shown as a socially mixed group with varied motivations for enlisting. Some want to serve to prove that they are worth something. Some want to enlist because they had already fought fascism in China and Spain. But some just want to "kill Japs," and that seems a good enough reason for the filmmakers and for *New Masses*, which called the film an "effective picturization" of Major Carlson's Marine raiders' heroic efforts.[47] Although low-level employees of the OWI took issue with the narrative of Japanese-American treason in *Air Force*, both Ulric

Bell and Nelson Poynter ignored the criticism and praised the film as "a most wonderful contribution [to the war effort]."[48]

The timidity of the government's policies and the backward response of white American audiences aside, the roots of this blindness, of this soft, ugly side of the American World War II film, perhaps travel back to the 1930s and touch the core of the liberal and radical New Deal imaginaries, which could not or did not introduce into the political debate issues of ethnic – or, for that matter, racial or gender – equality. Since ethnic and racial issues had been effectively marginalized since the 1920s, Gary Gerstle writes that American 1930s liberal intelligentsia found it "easy – remarkably easy – to exclude ethnics and blacks from their representations of the critical New Deal constituencies" (1994, 1068). Though the national cohesion requested by the war allowed for the representation of ethnic types, the tentativeness of these films' representation of racial issues may be as much imposed on the left from the outside as it was subscribed to by the leftists themselves.

In the 1930s, most black and white American progressives, in fact, disagreed with W. E. B. Du Bois's insistence that race still mattered, surmising that racism would disappear with class oppression. Young black politicians like Ralph Bunche, or young black intellectuals like sociologist Franklin Frazier and economist Abram Harris, tended to downplay race in an effort to establish "an alliance with the resurgent labor movement under the leadership of the CIO" (Singh 2004, 71). As for white liberals, after Pearl Harbor American racism may have gone down a further notch in their priorities, as they now subscribed to the urgency of unity and defeat of American enemies. Progressives at the OWI or in Hollywood noted racism, but they were essentially willing to exchange the anti-Japanese racism of the war film for a renewed emphasis on realism and teamwork. The truncated narrative of *The Negro Soldier* was indeed applauded by the left, with only a few, including *The Nation*'s James Agee, remarking upon the mildness of the film ("pitifully, painfully mild") (2005, 98). And there is no archival evidence of leftist mobilization in favor of Lillian Helman's script. As he lectured at USC in 1943, Dutch progressive director Joris Ivens, who was then working in Hollywood and for OWI, made clear that *Air Force*, also, was among the recent American films that most clearly evidenced the positive changes the war was producing in Hollywood.[49]

Conclusion

Contradictions took their toll and by the end of the war many on the Hollywood Left, who had entered the war so hopefully, were assessing the result of their participation. On the surface things had gone fairly well. In 1945, Joseph Foster wrote in *New Masses* that "it was once the universal custom to dissolve in uncontrollable belly laughter at the mere mention of the word Hollywood." The atmosphere, however, had radically changed in Hollywood, and at a meeting Foster attended, the filmmakers "were making the kind of speeches that I once heard only at the most advanced political gatherings." Foster had to pinch himself to make sure that "it was all happening" (quoted in Horne 2001, 59). A few months later, however, one of the keenest minds at the OWI, Dorothy Jones, noted the checkered result of four intense years of moviemaking. Evaluating the Hollywood war effort in 1945 for the progressive magazine *Hollywood Quarterly*, Jones argued that many of the Hollywood war films had failed to make any positive contribution to the conflict. Of the 1,313 films released during the war, 374 had been war films. And most of these films reflected business as usual. By Jones's count, only "approximately 4% of the film output of these three years, or about one out of every ten war pictures, made such contribution" (1945, 12).

Interestingly, positions not dissimilar from Jones's were expressed by some in the Hollywood industry like Preston Sturges, for instance, who had long rejected the idea of making Hollywood pictures *à la Confessions of a Nazi Spy*. The semi-documentary message movie simply did not interest the director. In 1943, Sturges envisioned the credits of his antimilitaristic comedy *Hail the Conquering Hero* as a put-down of Hollywood semi-documentary style. "During the main titles," he wrote,

> we have seen some heroic stuff of fighting marines, preferably jungle fighting, if available some official War [*sic*] footage. To a great screaming of sirens, we see the Newsreel stuff of the debarkation of the Guadalcanal Marines. The last shot is a walking INSERT of the blue diamond bearing the big one with GUADALCANAL written on it, surrounded by the Constellation of the Southern Cross.[50]

But doubts about the ultimate outcome of the war effort on the Hollywood film were creeping into circles identifiable with the left or traditionally close to it. Already in 1943, anti-Nazi refugee Billy Wilder told *Aufbau* that he had no idea about the direction Hollywood films would take after the conflict. The war cycle was going to end as American audiences were showing signs of being tired of the "issues of the day." The way producers would choose to go was anyone's guess.[51] The turning point in the left's optimism may be dated to October 1943, at the Hollywood Writers' Mobilization (HWM) Congress at UCLA. The Congress was the creature of the leftist HWM and the left wing of the UCLA faculty. Its Advisory Committee included members of different political creeds: moderate Jack Warner, liberals Dore Schary and Walter Wanger, and radicals Sidney Buchman and Dudley Nichols.[52] The congress was a success. Later, Ulric Bell, the chief of the Overseas Branch of the OWI's Bureau of Motion Pictures and the real power in OWI after the Congressional cuts of 1943, was in the HWM Advisory Committee. Dorothy Jones was in the Seminar Committee. UCLA theater professor Ralph Freud was the cochairman of the Congress along with screenwriter Mark Connelly. UC President Robert G. Sproul, along with the National Association for the Advancement of Colored People's Walter White, the Director of OWI's Pacific Operations in San Francisco, Owen Lattimore, and Lt Col. Evans Carlson of the Marine Corps, welcomed the Congress.[53]

In its lineup the Congress offered the same image of unity encouraged by the war and by the multifaceted nature of the Hollywood Left. The Congress reiterated the faith in the possibility of grafting documentary techniques and progressive messages onto the fictional film. James Wong Howe, the director of photography of *Air Force*, spoke of the technological changes the war was bringing to Hollywood, including the use of 16mm cameras, and "documentary style."[54] Participants also attacked "the artificial distinction between film with social content and films designed for entertainment."[55] Under the surface of enthusiasm, however, a certain degree of disillusionment was detectable. America seemed to resist reform. Those on the left who, like screenwriter Dalton Trumbo, were most sensitive to racism, were flustered that, in the middle of a war against fascism and racism, racial relations remained the American dilemma. In his intervention at the Congress, Trumbo thundered against Hollywood's almost complete opposition to a realistic and dignified representation of African-Americans.[56] If the racial situation remained unresolved within and without the United States, anthropologist Harry Hoijer reminded Congress that the Allies' "victory will avail us nothing."[57]

Participation in the war revealed the limits of Hollywood and of the classical Hollywood narrative. The feasibility of mixing political messages with Hollywood films was questioned by some. "[P]ure fiction-film production methods have not proved well suited to the documentary field," radical Dutch filmmaker Joris Ivens wistfully noted, while acknowledging the contribution of the "many Hollywood directors, writers, cameramen, editors, technicians" to the field.[58] Ivens was soon to leave southern California for Europe, and thence for Asia, and his move was more than geographical: He advocated the resurrection of a political and aesthetic avant-garde with separate styles and audiences – a challenge to the realist paradigm that had seen the possibility of using Hollywood appeal to bring progressive politics and radical aesthetics to the masses.

The semi-documentary style was supposed to blur the boundaries of the screen and make the war "present" to Americans. But Americans at home apparently were not demanding "presence." On the contrary, they craved distance from the war. American exhibitors were making clear that "the preponderant demand is for entertainment and entertainment of the sort that puts aside the cares of these war worn days" (Doherty 1993, 181). Arthur Mayer, the progressive manager of the New York Rialto, reported at the HWM Congress that Americans seemed to dislike entertainment laced with references to the reality of war, and those of the Hollywood films that followed the semi-documentary model were not doing well at the box office. Mayer proposed to alter the mixture of entertainment and politics by increasing the ratio of the former. *Confessions of a Nazi Spy* did "a great job," insofar as it was a "fictional fil[m] of topical themes." In the film, Mayer argued, "the fundamentals of showmanship" were not ignored.[59]

Since American audiences at that time were not as receptive to the semi-documentary style as leftists had imagined, Hollywood producers saw no reason for promoting it. In a long letter dated July 30, 1942 to OWI's Gardner Cowles, the head of the Office's Domestic Branch, Walter Wanger, expressed his enthusiasm about the possibility of enlisting Hollywood in the war effort: The town was full of antifascists and was just waiting for the government's call. "I feel strongly that the government has not used Hollywood to its full potentialities in the war effort," he wrote Cowles.[60] But writing in 1945, Wanger mournfully noted that "the motion picture industry has been somewhat remiss in its responsibility to keep to the truth and keep to realism."[61]

Hollywood's production, so unified during the war, had not yet found the ability to respond to the mutated condition of peace. Backed by the government and spurred on by its numerous antifascist practitioners, the American commercial film had launched a great campaign to remake itself into a medium of democratic education. Semi-documentary techniques, nonprofessional actors, lighter and more movable cameras, had all made inroads into the mainstream of American cinema. The welcoming reception among the most intellectual of American filmgoers of postwar realist trends in world cinema (Lughi 1989, 58) undoubtedly had its roots in the changes brought about by World War II in American cinema. The moment of the left had indeed arrived. If elements of its program had become a "known quantity" to the average American moviegoer, however, they had not become popular. Like many changes brought about by the war – one can think of the heightened role of women in the economy or the changes in the governmental attitude toward civil rights (Blum 1976, 182–220) – these transformations were fraught with inconsistency and contradiction. Considering the future of Hollywood two months after the war, progressive screenwriter Albert Maltz noted in the *New York Times* that the situation in both the United States and Hollywood did not lend itself to linear interpretations. It was, on the contrary, "uneasy with its contrasts" (1945, X3). The "moment" of the American Hollywood Left had come and, perhaps, it was already gone in what seemed to some an uncertain victory.

Notes

1. Dunne to Frank G. Andrews, Civil Aeronautics Administration, April 14, 1943, Box 5, Folder: Correspondence 1943–1944, Dunne Papers, University of Southern California Cinema-Television Library (USC-CTL).
2. Philip Dunne to T. H. Westerman, 1943, Box 5, Folder: Correspondence 1943–1944, Dunne Papers, USC-CTL.
3. *Variety*, January 31, 1940, n.p. "Meet the People" Clipping File, New York Public Library-Billy Rose Collection.
4. A list of anti-Nazi films released in the United States before Pearl Harbor includes: *Arise My Love* (October 17, 1939), directed by Mitchell Leisen and scripted by Billy Wilder and Charles Brackett; *The Mortal Storm* (June 21, 1940), directed by Frank Borzage, scripted by Georg Froeschel, Claudine West, and Andersen Ellis; *Three Faces West* (August 19, 1940), directed by communist Bernard Vorhaus and scripted by Sam Ornitz, Joseph Moncure March, and Hugh Herbert; *Four Sons* (June 16, 1940), directed by Archie Mayo and scripted by John Howard Lawson; *The Man I Married* (August 7, 1940), directed by liberal Irving Pichel and scripted by Oliver H. P. Garrett; *Underground* (June 28, 1941), directed by Vincent Sherman, an instructor at the radical People's Education Center in Los Angeles; *Escape to Glory* (November 10, 1940), directed by German refugee John Brahm and scripted by P. J. Wolfson; *Foreign Correspondent* (August 29, 1940), directed by Alfred Hitchcock and scripted by Charles Bennett, Joan Harrison, James Hilton, and Robert Benchley; *The Great Dictator* (October 15, 1940), written, directed, and produced by Charles Chaplin; *Escape* (November 12, 1940), directed by Mervyn LeRoy and scripted by Arch Oboler.
5. See the list of the signers of the call in "Fourth American Writers' Congress," *The Clipper*, 2, June 1941, 3.
6. Fritz Lang to Nichols, January 30, 1941, Box 8, Folder N, Lang Papers, American Film Institute, Los Angeles.
7. The play premiered at the Martin Beck Theater in New York, April 1, 1941. *Watch on the Rhine* is included in Lillian Hellman, *Four Plays* (New York: Modern Library, 1942). Filmed by Warner Bros. during the conflict, *Watch on the Rhine* is unmistakably a call for action: "Too much talk," says one character, "by this time all of us know where we are and what we have to do."
8. Wolfe Kaufman, "War, Propaganda, and Hollywood," *The Clipper*, 1, August 1940, 27–30. *New York Times*, June 8, 1940, quoted in Gary Carr, *The Left Side of Paradise* (Ann Arbor: UMI Research Press, 1984), 81.
9. See *New Masses*, April 15, 1941, 27. See also the mixed review by Ralph Warner in *Daily Worker*, April 4, 1941, 7, which surmises that a "fabric of omissions" hangs over the play.
10. See Robert Gessner, "Massacre in Hollywood," *New Theater*, 1, March 1934, 17. In 1935, his enthusiasm had, however, cooled off a little. See also Robert Gessner, "Movies About Us," *New Theater*, 2, June 1935, 12. See also Giovacchini 2003.
11. Philip Sterling, "A Channel for Democratic Thought," *Films*, 1, Spring 1940, 7.

12. Memo from Hal Wallis to Robert Lord, February 14, 1939. "Confessions" Picture File, Warner Brothers Archives, University of Southern California (USC-WB).
13. *Variety*, May 3, 1939, 16. See also Louella Parsons's review in *The Examiner*, May 5, 1939.
14. *New Masses*, May 9, 1939, 27–28.
15. *Variety*, May 17, 1939, 1.
16. The manual also repeated the caveats typical of Hollywood progressives concerning the necessity to attenuate the excessively protagonist-centered drive of American films. Hollywood war films should not indulge in narrative excesses of individual heroism. On the contrary, films should make an effort to celebrate the collective aspects of the war and the least glamorous elements of the fighting forces: It was "easy to dramatize the more spectacular services of the Army. It is a more difficult but necessary job to dramatize ... the service of Supply" (Short 1983, 179).
17. Association of Motion Picture Producers, Inc., and Motion Picture Producers and Distributors of America, "The Production Code," reprinted in John Belton (ed.), *Movies and Mass Culture* (New Brunswick: Rutgers University Press, 1996), 138.
18. The unpublished, uncorrected draft of the essay is in the Walter Wanger Collection, Box 36, Folder 57, University of Wisconsin, Madison.
19. Edward G. Robinson, speech dated June 16, 1944, Box 30, Folder 2, Robinson Papers, USC-CTL.
20. *Aufbau*, February 19, 1943, 15.
21. "Tell Lang – no – I wouldn't play a Quisling for all the tea in China," wrote Mitchell to Johnnie Maccio. T. W. Baumfeld to Lang, September 3, 1942, *Hangmen Also Die!* file, Lang Papers, USC-CTL.
22. Salka Viertel to Lube [Ernst Lubitsch?], December 20, 1943, Viertel Nachlass, Schiller National Museum, Deutsches Literaturarchiv, Marbach am Neckar, Germany.
23. Harold Medford, "Report from a GI Typewriter," *Screenwriter*, 1, June 1945, 15–22; Lester Koenig, "Back from the War," *Screenwriter*, 1, August 1945, 23–28; Robert R. Presnell, "The Great Parenthesis," *Screenwriter*, 1, September 1945, 12–16; Dalton Trumbo, "Notes on a Summer Vacation," *Screenwriter*, 1, September 1945, 17–41; Sidney Buchman, "A Writer in VIP Clothing," *Screenwriter*, 1, October 1945, 17–31; Thomas Spencer Jones, "Can They Still Look Back?," *Screenwriter*, 1, December 1945, 31–35.
24. Between his film crew and the crew of the Canadian Corvette hunting U-Boats in the Atlantic, Ivens told an anonymous interviewer in 1944: "There was a kind of comraderie [*sic*] with jokes about how the movie people were not fast enough" (Ivens, "Interview" 1944, untitled and undated, Folder 4, Joris Ivens–Herman Shumlin Collection, Margaret Herrick Library, Academy of Motion Picture Arts and Sciences [AMPAS]).
25. *New Masses*, May 2, 1944, 28.
26. Joris Ivens, "Notes on Documentary Film," June 11, 1943, Folder 14, Joris Ivens–Herman Shumlin Papers, AMPAS.
27. *New Republic*, September 7, 1942, 283.
28. *New York Times*, November 18, 1943, 29.
29. *New Masses*, December 7, 1943, 27.
30. *New York Times*, November 18, 1943, 29.
31. Nelson Poynter to Warner, February 4, 1943, and Ulric Bell to Warner, February 6, 1943, *Air Force* Production File, USC-WB; *Daily Worker*, February 10, 1943, 7, *Air Force* Clipping File, USC-WB.
32. Jack Warner to General H. H. Arnold, April 7, 1943, *Air Force* Production File, USC-WB.
33. *Daily Mirror*, February 4, 1943, 31.
34. Nelson Poynter to Warner, February 4, 1943, and Ulric Bell to Warner, February 6, 1943, *Air Force* Production File, USC-WB.
35. Dudley Nichols, Treatment for *Air Force*, n.d., *Air Force* Script File, USC-WB.
36. *Air Force* Production Sheet, no author, n.d., *Air Force* Production File, USC-WB.
37. W. M. Wright to Jack Warner, May 22, 1942, *Air Force* Production Files, USC-WB.
38. *Air Force* "Production Notes," n.d., *Air Force* Production Files, USC-WB.
39. Wexley received sole credit for the script, Lang's protests notwithstanding. On the thorny issue of Brecht's relative authorship of the film's script see Bahr 2007, 133–147. See also the archive-based interpretation contained in Rolf Aurich, Wolfgang Jacobsen, and Cornelius Schnauber (eds), *Fritz Lang. Leben und Werk. Bilder und Dokumente* (Berlin: Deutsche Kinemathek, 2001), 352–358.
40. See also David Platt's column "Film Front," *Daily Worker*, May 9, 1943.
41. Bell to Robert Riskin, February 23, 1943, *Hangmen Also Die!* File, Office of War Information Records, RG 208, National Archives, College Park, Maryland. The less famous film on the same episode, *The Hangman* (1943), also directed by a refugee from Nazi Germany, Douglas Sirk, and partly scripted by an erstwhile communist, Melvin Levy, from a story by two refugees, Emil Ludwig and Albrecht Joseph, also dispatched any good news. *The Hangman* ends even more bleakly than *Hangmen Also Die!*, with all the villagers shot by the Nazis under the marble eyes of the statue of the patron saint of Lidice. OWI had reservations about showing Czech collaborators, but loved that "Nazi

methods of suppression are graphically demonstrated in the mass execution of Lidice men," and Ulric Bell greenlighted the film for overseas distribution. OWI review of release print of *The Hangman*, January 22, 1943, unsigned. Ulric Bell to Waterson Rothacker, January 29, 1943, *The Hangman* File, Office of War Information Records, RG 208, National Archives, College Park, Maryland.

42. See *Hangmen Also Die!*, Publicity File, AMPAS.
43. Bell to William B. Cherin (Associate Director Commonwealth of Philippines Office of Special Services, Washington, DC), *Bataan* File, Office of War Information Records, RG 208, National Archives, College Park, Maryland.
44. Waterson Rothacker to Ulric Bell, March 19, 1943, *Bataan* File, Office of War Information Records, RG 208, National Archives, College Park, Maryland.
45. Lillian Hellman's script is in Box 10, Folder 1, Stuart Heisler Collection, UCLA Special Collections (UCLA-SC). For another example see communist Alvah Bessie's protests against producer Jessie Wald's anti-Japanese revision of Bessie's script for *Objective Burma* (1945) in Koppes and Black 1990, 263.
46. *New York Times*, January 26, 1944, at http://www.nytimes.com/movie/review?res=9F07EFDD153DE13BBC4E51DFB766838F659EDE (accessed March 2015).
47. *New Masses*, February 15, 1944, 29.
48. The anti-Japanese racism was also denounced by several observers, among them R. M. Mac Iver from Columbia University's Department of Sociology and Lawrence Jaffa of the YMCA. Mac Iver to Warner, April 30, 1943; Jaffa to Warner, May 3, 1943, *Air Force* Production Files, USC-WB. Poynter to Warner February 4, 1943, and Bell to Warner, February 6, 1943, *Air Force* Production File, USC-WB.
49. In his cycle of lectures at USC, the Dutch director singled out *Air Force* and *Wake Island* as the latest evidence of Hollywood's "good" side, its documentary tradition, along with *The Grapes of Wrath*, *Dead End*, *Fury*, *They Won't Forget*, *Our Daily Bread*, and *I Am a Fugitive from a Chain Gang*. Joris Ivens, Lecture, March 24, 1943, Folder 14, Ivens–Shumlin Papers, AMPAS.
50. Preston Sturges, *Hail the Conquering Hero*, temporary script, June 13, 1943, Box 8, Folder 11, Preston Sturges Papers, UCLA-SC.
51. K. H., "Hollywood nach dem Krieg. Ein Interview mit Billy Wilder," *Aufbau*, May 7, 1943, 10.
52. Box 3, Folder "Appendix," Writers' Congress Papers, UCLA-SC.
53. *Los Angeles Times*, October 2, 1943, n.p. Writers' Congress Papers, Clipping File, UCLA University Archives. That the Congress embodied uncharted possibilities for the collaboration between Hollywood progressives on one side, and the local and national intellectual community on the other, was well understood by California Senator Jack Tenney, a showman turned politician and the chairman of the Joint Fact Finding Committee on Un-American Activities of California legislature. Tenney combined a suspicion of foreigners and intellectuals with a deeply felt hatred for the Hollywood leftists whom he accused of having ousted him from the presidency of the Local 47 of the American Federation of Musicians. In his attacks against the Congress, Tenney attempted to separate the HWM from UCLA, repeatedly asking President Sproul and Dean Gordon S. Watkins to disentangle the university from the event. Sproul, however, did not change his mind and addressed the Congress. After all, the gathering had the blessing of the government, the military, and FDR himself, who sent a telegram to the gathering. Los Angeles *Evening Herald-Express*, September 29, 1943, n.p., Writers' Congress, Clipping File, UCLA University Archives. On Tenney, see Ingrid Scobie Winther, "Jack B. Tenney: Molder of Anti-Communist Legislation in California 1940–49" (PhD dissertation, University of Wisconsin, 1970). See also Jack B. Tenney, *Oral History*, 2 vols (Los Angeles: Oral History Program, University of California-Los Angeles, 1969), vol. 1, *passim*.
54. James Wong Howe, "Documentary Films and Hollywood Techniques," Box 1, Folder "The Documentary Film," Writers' Congress Papers, UCLA-SC.
55. "Notes on the Discussion," Box 1, Folder "The American Scene," Writers' Congress Papers, UCLA-SC.
56. Dalton Trumbo, "Minorities and the Screen," Box 1, Folder "Minority Groups," Writers' Congress Papers, UCLA-SC. See also Writers' Congress, "A Declaration of Principles to the American Entertainment Industry," Box 1, Folder "Resolutions," Writers' Congress Papers, UCLA-SC.
57. Harry Hoijer, "Statement of the Problem," Box 1, Folder "Minority Groups," Writers' Congress Papers, UCLA-SC.
58. Joris Ivens, "Notes on Documentary Film," June 11, 1943, Folder 13, Ivens–Shumlin Papers, AMPAS; and "The Documentary Film and Morale," Box 1, Folder "The Documentary Film," Writers' Congress Papers, UCLA-SC.
59. Arthur L. Mayer, "Documentary Film and Box Office," Box 1, Folder "The Documentary Film," Writers' Congress Papers, UCLA-SC.
60. Walter Wanger to Gardner Cowles, Jr, July 30, 1942, Office of War Information Records, RG 208, Records of the Office of the Director, National Archives, College Park, Maryland.

61. Wanger, "How We Did Our Own Specific Jobs: The Movies," uncorrected draft, 1945, Walter Wanger Collection, Box 36, Folder 57, University of Wisconsin, Madison.

References

Agee, James. (2005). *Film Writing and Selected Journalism*. New York: Library of America.

Bahr, Ehrhard. (2007). *Weimar on the Pacific: German Exile Culture in Los Angeles and the Crisis of Modernism*. Berkeley: University of California Press.

Bernstein, Matthew. (1994). *Walter Wanger, Hollywood Independent*. Berkeley: University of California Press.

Blum, John Morton. (1976). *V Was for Victory*. New York: Harcourt.

Bright, John. (1991). *John Bright*. Interviewed by Larry Ceplair. Los Angeles: University of California Oral History Project.

Buhle, Paul, & McGilligan, Patrick. (1997). *Tender Comrades*. New York: St Martin's Press.

Buhle, Paul, & Wagner, Dave. (2002). *Radical Hollywood: The Untold Story behind America's Favorite Movies*. Berkeley: University of California Press.

Capra, Frank. (1971). *The Name Above the Title*. New York: Macmillan.

Ceplair, Larry. (2007). *The Marxist and the Movies*. Louisville: University Press of Kentucky.

Cherny, Robert W. (2002). "Prelude to the Popular Front: The Communist Party in California, 1931–1935." *American Communist History*, 1.1, 5–42.

Cripps, Thomas. (1993). *Making Movies Black*. New York: Oxford University Press.

Davidman, Joy. (1943). "*Hangmen Also Die!*" *New Masses*, May 4, 28.

Dick, Bernard K. (1985). *The Star-Spangled Screen: The American World War II Film*. Lexington: University Press of Kentucky.

Dmytryk, Edward. (1996). *Odd Man Out*. Carbondale: Southern Illinois University Press.

Doherty, Thomas. (1993). *Projections of War*. New York: Columbia University Press.

Dunne, Philip. (1992). *A Life in Movies and Politics*. Updated edn. New York: Limelight.

Edgerton, Gary. (1993). "Revisiting the Recordings of War Past: Remembering the Documentary Trilogy of John Huston." In Gaylyn Studlar & David Desser (eds), *Reflections in a Male Eye* (pp. 33–61). Washington, DC: Smithsonian Institution Press.

George, Manfred. (1939). "Hollywood's Politische Probe." *Aufbau*, July 1, 4.

Gerstle, Gary. (1994). "The Protean Form of American Liberalism." *American Historical Review*, 99.4, 1043–1073.

Giovacchini, Saverio. (1999). "Negotiated Confessions: The Making of *Confessions of a Nazi Spy*." In Bianca Maria Tedeschini Lalli & Maurizio Vaudagna (eds), *Brave New Words. America in the '30s: Languages between Ideology and Experimentation*. Amsterdam: VU University Press.

Giovacchini, Saverio. (2001). *Hollywood Modernism*. Philadelphia: Temple University Press.

Giovacchini, Saverio. (2003). "'Hollywood is a State of Mind': New York Film Culture and the Lure of Los Angeles from 1930 to the Present." In David Halle (ed.), *New York and Los Angeles: Politics, Society and Culture: A Comparative View* (pp. 423–447). Chicago: University of Chicago Press.

Hoopes, Roy. (1994). *When the Stars Went to War*. New York: Random House.

Horne, Gerald. (2001). *Class Struggle in Hollywood 1930–1950: Moguls, Mobsters, Stars, Reds, and Trade Unionists*. Austin: University of Texas Press.

Hough, Donald. (1942). "War is Changing the Movies." *Los Angeles Times Magazine*, March 15, 7.

Huston, John. (1980). *An Open Book*. New York: Knopf.

Isaacs, Hermine Rich. (1944). "War Front and Film Fronts." *Theater Arts*, June 28, 345.

Jones, Dorothy. (1945). "The Hollywood War Film, 1942–1944." *Hollywood Quarterly*, 1.1, 1–20.

Kallen, Horace. (1915). "Democracy versus the Melting Pot." *The Nation*, February 18, 190–194; February 25, 217–220.

Koppes, Clayton R., & Black, Gregory D. (1990). *Hollywood Goes to War: How Politics, Profits, and Propaganda Shaped World War Two Movies*. New York: Free Press.

Kreidl, John Francis. (1977). *Nicholas Ray*. Boston: Twayne.

Lang, Fritz. (1948). "Happily Ever After." *Penguin Film Review*, 5, 22–29.

Lawson, John Howard. (1936). "The Obligatory Scene." *New Theater*, 3, March, 18–19.

Lughi, Paolo. (1989). "Il neorealismo in sala. Anteprime di gala e teniture di massa." In Alberto Farassino (ed.), *Neorealismo. Cinema Italiano 1945–49* (pp. 53–59). Turin: E.D.T.

McBride, Joseph. (1982). *Hawks on Hawks*. Los Angeles: University of California Press.

McBride, Joseph. (1993). *Frank Capra*. New York: Simon & Schuster.

Mackenzie, Midge (dir.). (1998). *John Huston War Stories*. Barnsbury Productions, UK.

Maltz, Albert. (1945). "War Film Quality." *New York Times*, August 19, X3.

May, Lary. (2000). *The Big Tomorrow*. Chicago: Chicago University Press.

Robinson, Greg. (2001). *By Order of the President*. Cambridge, MA: Harvard University Press.

Roeder, George. (1993). *The Censored War*. New Haven: Yale University Press.

Short, K. R. M. (1983). "Washington's Information Manual for Hollywood, 1942." *Historical Journal of Film, Radio and Television*, 3.2, 171–180.

Singh, Nikhil Pal. (2004). *Black is a Country*. Cambridge, MA: Harvard University Press.

Sklar, Robert. (1992). *City Boys*. Princeton: Princeton University Press.

Slotkin, Richard. (2001). "Unit Pride: Ethnic Platoons and the Myths of American Nationality." *American Literary History*, 13.3, 469–498.

Viertel, Salka. (1969). *The Kindness of Strangers*. New York: Holt, Rinehart & Winston.

Warshow, Robert. (2001). *The Immediate Experience: Movies, Comics, Theatre and Other Aspects of Popular Culture*. Enlarged edn. Cambridge, MA: Harvard University Press.

Writers' Congress. (1944). *The Proceedings of the Conference Held in October 1943 under the Sponsorship of the Hollywood Writers' Mobilization and the University of California*. Berkeley: University of California Press.

22

Hollywood as Historian, 1929–1945

J. E. Smyth
Reader, University of Warwick, United Kingdom

J. E. Smyth challenges long-standing arguments about the movie industry as interpreter of the past, taking to task scholars of the "**classical Hollywood system**" for their narrow definition of the period 1929–1945 and their contention that the classical era was characterized by "**genre templates**, **film conventions**, and **enduring ideologies**." Smyth counters this one-dimensional portrait with a discussion of **the historical film**, tracing its trajectory from the silent to the sound era and identifying it as cutting across genres and dominating production during the 1930s. Smyth's extensive archival research uncovers the work process for writers like **Howard Estabrook (*Cimarron*)** and **Dalton Trumbo (*Kitty Foyle*)**, highlighting also the prominent roles played by **female novelists**, whose books were adapted to the screen, and by **female screenwriters** in Hollywood. Smyth defines the historical film less as a tribute to great men than as a multifaceted vehicle involving female audiences, **prestige studio production**, and women as frequently the driving force behind history. Smyth's essay shares ground with Shelley Stamp on women in the silent era, Veronica Pravadelli on cinema and the modern woman, and Desirée J. Garcia on the Hollywood folk musical in this volume.

Additional terms, names, and concepts: historical film, historiography, dominant ideologies, biopic

While American filmmakers' preoccupation with visualizing the past is nearly as old as the cinematic medium itself, large-scale historical filmmaking truly emerged as a substantial component of production with the successes of European historical epics (*Cabiria*, 1914), biblical dramas (*Judith of Bethulia*, 1914), Westerns (*The Battle of Elderbush Gulch*, 1913), adaptations of popular historical literature (*A Tale of Two Cities*, 1917), biopics (*Joan the Woman*, 1916), the success of *Gettysburg* (1913), and the notoriety of D. W. Griffith's *The Birth of a Nation* (1915). History – predominantly European and American – was reconstructed and enjoyed in a wide variety of formats, adaptations, and emerging film genres during

American Film History: Selected Readings, Origins to 1960, First Edition. Edited by Cynthia Lucia, Roy Grundmann, and Art Simon.
© 2016 John Wiley & Sons, Inc. Published 2016 by John Wiley & Sons, Inc.

the silent era. There was no distinct "historical" genre; rather, historical dramas, lives, and perspectives formed a small but prestigious component of silent film production. Though biographies of "great" men and dramatic political and military events featured prominently, filmmakers also represented the history of Native Americans (*The Red Man's View*, 1909; *The Vanishing American*, 1925), women (*Janice Meredith*, 1924; *So Big*, 1924; *Glorious Betsy*, 1928), African-Americans (*Uncle Tom's Cabin*, 1927), and the working class (*Oliver Twist*, 1922; *Down to the Sea in Ships*, 1923). By 1927, American filmgoers could expect half a dozen major historical films and a cluster of shorts and serials in theaters each year. But by the early 1930s, what had once been an occasional, expensive practice became the Industry's "most innovative, prestigious, and controversial form of feature filmmaking" (Smyth 2006, 6). Although the historical film did not exist as a traditional genre, Hollywood's obsession with projecting the past was the dominant production trend from the early sound era through the mid-1940s, impacting every form of feature filmmaking, from musicals to literary adaptations to biopics to war films, Westerns, and gangster pictures.

In many ways, Hollywood was simply tapping into a widespread and eclectic revival of interest in social and cultural history. The post–World War I trends in disillusioned war memoirs (Hervey Allen's *Toward the Flame*, 1925; Robert Graves's *Goodbye to All That*, 1929), "debunking" biographies (Rupert Hughes's *George Washington: The Human Being and the Hero*, 1926), and historical relativism were followed by popular interest in the lives of forgotten men and women (Allen 2000; Brackman 1983). The historical climate in America was lively, diverse, and often critical, ranging from the best-selling historical fiction of Edna Ferber (*So Big*, 1924; *Cimarron*, 1929) and Walter D. Edmonds (*Drums Along the Mohawk*, 1936; *Chad Hanna*, 1940) to the historiography of Matthew Josephson (*The Robber Barons*, 1934), Angie Debo (*The Rise and Fall of the Choctaw Republic*, 1934), and W. E. B. Du Bois (*Black Reconstruction*, 1935). Hollywood's commitment to representing history is certainly tied to American historian Carl Becker's belief, expressed in 1931, that "Everyman" was a potential historian and that history was more than printed words on an unread academic page (Becker 1932, 221–236).[1]

Hollywood's golden age of historical filmmaking occurred between 1929 and 1945. During that time, the studios rethought the mechanics of historical filmmaking, developed concepts of studio research and screenwriting, and made serious efforts to connect their historical work with similar trends in American popular culture, historiography, biography, and historical fiction. Production units – and in one major case, whole studios – pivoted around the production of historical films. Though film historian George Custen has pointed out Hollywood's investment in traditional forms of history "through standardization of the great man narrative," masculine biopics from *Disraeli* (1929) to *Captain Eddie* (1945) were only one strand of the studios' investment in historical filmmaking (Custen 1992, 22). Popular history – especially historical fiction – became Hollywood's main market for historical cinema. Many of Hollywood's most popular historical films, though set within a recognizable era, starred "fictional" protagonists.[2] The adaptation of women's history dominated the genre. Much of the historical material purchased by the studios in the 1930s and 1940s was not only about, but authored by, women. Using this material, Hollywood writers and producers developed a cast of controversial mavericks who often rebelled against traditional racial, ethnic, class, and gender roles (*A Woman Rebels*, 1936; *Show Boat*, 1936; *Jezebel*, 1938; *Gone With the Wind*, 1939; *Kitty Foyle*, 1940; *Saratoga Trunk*, 1945; *Duel in the Sun*, 1946). There was a strong element of historical revisionism within these narratives, and it operated as a corrective to the frequently eulogistic portrayals of dead, white men in more traditional Hollywood biopics.

This essay challenges many long-standing critical assumptions about Hollywood's historical filmmaking in the studio era. Traditional genre frameworks, an exclusive focus on masculine biopics, and an under-reliance on screenwriting and other aspects of studio archival research have limited previous assessments of Hollywood's projection of history during the so-called "classical" era. I begin by exploring the legacy of classical Hollywood's historical genre within film studies and history, the alleged conflicts between the discourses of visual and textual history and genre, and recent critical interventions in the field. I then examine the historical and technological factors contributing to the rise of historical filmmaking in the early 1930s, I focus on the development of historical film production and screenwriting by the major studios, and I analyze several key films that define the genre's engagement with the past, including *Cimarron* (1931), *Show Boat* (1936), *Gone With the Wind* (1939), *Kitty Foyle* (1940), *Citizen Kane* (1941), and *Saratoga Trunk* (1945). Instead of selling standardized, conservative, dead-white-male history during the studio era, Hollywood filmmakers often invested in controversy. The most powerful historical current in Hollywood between 1929 and 1945 was not Darryl F. Zanuck's set of masculine biopics but the representation of women's history.

Film versus History?

In the past, both academic and popular work on studio-era Hollywood dismissed filmmakers' explorations of history as inaccurate, uncritical reflections of national myths and conservative capitalist ideologies. While more recently historians and film critics have acknowledged that certain European auteurs (Luchino Visconti, Rainer Werner Fassbinder, Andrei Tarkovsky) and post-1968 Hollywood-financed "mavericks" (Alex Cox, Ridley Scott, Oliver Stone) constructed unusual visual interventions in the understanding of the past, many film historians and cultural critics still resist or deride the idea of "classical" Hollywood cinema producing a critical, nuanced form of cinematic historiography. In most circumstances, one could expect an article entitled "Hollywood as Historian" to follow a set template about lack of accuracy or "floating signifiers," popular myths, censorship, racism, and financially determined needs for stock romance and well-worn action sequences. It has been perhaps too easy for different generations of film historians and cultural critics to fall back upon Hortense Powdermaker's epithet, the "Hollywood Dream Factory." Despite the "grand design" of studio-era Hollywood film practice and "geniuses of the system" like Irving Thalberg, Darryl F. Zanuck, and David O. Selznick, the prevailing view is of a "classical Hollywood cinema" comprised of powerful genre templates, film conventions, and enduring ideologies (Bordwell et al. 1985; Ray 1985; Vasey 1998). The roots of classicism convey a grandeur supported by resistance to criticism, irony, and change. This view of the American film industry has had unusually insidious implications for the critical assessment of historical films made during the studio era, since historians like to believe that dreams and myths are antithetical to traditional historical practice. Similarly, factories, even dream factories, are not ivory towers. Although, over the years, many have commented upon the polarization in film history between historians and film studies scholars, both camps tend to agree upon studio-era Hollywood's inadequacy as a historical interpreter.

Yet, the persistent belief in Hollywood's incapacity for historical narrative and argument has been supported by an old-fashioned, narrowly defined view of what constituted history. Historians did not simply view textual and visual forms of history as "separate but equal," but denied visual history's ability to comment upon and render aspects of the past (Smyth 2006, 2011). Film theory and criticism's impact was more far-reaching and complex. On the one hand, traditional film criticism from Robert Warshow and André Bazin focused upon studio-era Hollywood as the creator of genres. Stable, structured, unchanging set pieces – Hollywood genres, whether Westerns (for example, *Stagecoach*, 1939) or gangster films (*The Public Enemy*, 1931) – were defined in the language of myth. Myths, though often originally inspired by historical events, do not operate with the complexity, detail, and criticism supposedly part of western definitions of historical writing. This view gave license to genre studies, which marginalized films' historical content and focused instead on films' distinct patterns and structures. The work on Westerns by Jim Kitses, Will Wright, and John Cawelti followed the prescriptive brand of structuralism, despite the obvious historical resonances of the Western genre. Western history and the impressive rhetoric of the Frontier Thesis have always thrived on performance (George Armstrong Custer, Buffalo Bill, Annie Oakley) and their own nationalist myth. Yet narratives of white masculine conquest, whether written or filmed, often seemed impervious to change, irony, or critique. Although the New Western History of the 1980s and 1990s had not yet punctured the historical certainties of traditional "frontier" historiography, film historians easily adapted to the structuralist critiques of Hollywood's oldest genre. Yet one of the most striking ironies of the period from 1929 to 1945 is that film historians tend to view the 1930s as the "empty decade" in which Western filmmaking withered (Stanfield 2001; Schatz 2003). Following the failure of *The Big Trail*

(1930), major Westerns allegedly disappeared until the release of Ford's *Stagecoach*, when the time-honored traditions of the genre returned. Yet film critics and Western historians, in editing *Cimarron* (1931), *Silver Dollar* (1932), *The Mighty Barnum* (1934), *Sutter's Gold* (1935), *Annie Oakley* (1935), *The Plainsman* (1936), *Come and Get It* (1936), *Ramona* (1936), *Robin Hood of El Dorado* (1936), *The Cowboy and the Lady* (1938), *Union Pacific* (1939), and *Jesse James* (1939) from standard histories of the Western, were practicing their equivalent of genre cleansing, for during this period, history reinvigorated Westerns and the genre expanded its borders. Biographies, adaptations of popular literature, Mexican frontier dramas, sprawling "national" epics, and modern-day explorations of the cowboy all became part of the West.

Work on Hollywood genres also complemented more popular sociological studies by Powdermaker, emphasizing Hollywood's mechanistic production of "culture." Hollywood regained a measure of critical respect following European critics' creation of director "auteurs" in the 1950s. However, when the criticism of François Truffaut, Jean-Luc Godard, and Andrew Sarris infused Hollywood film criticism with eulogies to auteurs like John Ford and Orson Welles, history was sidelined as merely an artistic tool of the director. Auteurist criticism worked hand-in-glove with structuralist and Frankfurt School/Marxist-derived film criticism of the 1970s.

This was particularly true of the seminal work of the editors of *Cahiers du Cinéma* on *Young Mr. Lincoln*, published in 1970. Building upon the work of Jean Louis Comolli, the editors claimed that while most Hollywood films merely reflected the dominant ideology, a handful of films – including *Young Mr. Lincoln* – were capable of resisting or even subverting the capitalist order. *Young Mr. Lincoln*, they argued, was not just a conventional eulogy to a great man and a mythic reflection of American history. Director John Ford revealed the repressiveness of the Lincoln figure in several key sequences, showing him to be doom-ridden, dark, and excessively intimidating. However, this "resistance" was not a conscious action of Ford's, but an unconscious expression revealed only by *Cahiers*' analysis. Despite raising the tantalizing possibility of a major Hollywood film being ideologically subversive, the interpretation perpetuated the myth of Hollywood's passive discourses and denied the possibility of filmmakers projecting independent historical perspectives or critiques. This was film studies' way of saying that Hollywood films, even one directed by John Ford, lacked the capacity to project a self-conscious argument, and therefore could never rise above mythic status. At best, *Young Mr. Lincoln* and other Hollywood films reflected their own era's dominant cultural or ideological beliefs; at worst, they were patriotic propaganda. This perspective dominated work on Hollywood's history films for the next 30 years. Only American cultural historian Warren Susman defended studio-era Hollywood's ability to interpret history, arguing in 1985: "John Ford is perhaps the most influential *historian* of the United States in the twentieth century" (1985, 31). Sadly, neither film scholars nor historians pursued Susman's work. The most prominent scholars writing about historical films usually ignore Hollywood's studio era altogether. Robert Rosenstone, Marcia Landy, Robert Burgoyne, William Guynn, and Robert Brent Toplin continue to find post–studio-era Hollywood more interesting.[3]

However, John E. O'Connor and Martin Jackson's *American History/American Film: Interpreting the Hollywood Image* (1979) contains several perspectives on studio-era historical films such as *Drums Along the Mohawk* (1939) that evaluated the films as more than passive expressions of mainstream historical discourse. Using textual analysis, reviews, and broad comparisons with the films' contemporary contexts and more recent historical views, the approach became a template for studies of Hollywood's historical films. But ensuing anthologies about aspects of US or European history tend to dismiss or ignore the studio era's interest in history (Carnes 1995; Ellwood 2000; Landy 2001). Robert Brent Toplin's work on *Sergeant York* is symptomatic of traditional approaches to the Hollywood historical film that condemn studio-era productions for their inaccuracy, inanity, and service to conservative propaganda. *Sergeant York* could be a good historical film only if it passed a textbook litmus test for historical accuracy. Yet studies of Hollywood production, including Thomas Schatz's *The Genius of the System*, Tino Balio's history of 1930s Hollywood film production, *Grand Design*, and Tom Stempel's work on screenwriters Nunnally Johnson and Philip Dunne, contributed to a growing understanding of Hollywood's investment in prestigious historical productions and the many ways in which film could visualize history.

George F. Custen's *Bio/Pics: How Hollywood Constructed Public History* (1992) and *Twentieth Century's Fox: Darryl F. Zanuck and the Culture of Hollywood* (1997) were the first major attempts to take seriously studio-era Hollywood's interest in filming history, without necessarily arguing for its complexity. Custen believed all forms of history to be subjective cultural productions, and therefore saw filmmakers and more traditional historians engaged in the same process of manufacturing conservative attitudes toward the past. Film historian Robert Sklar is one of the few major figures in either film studies or history to discuss mainstream cinema's potential for "resisting" dominant ideologies, but even he has argued that Hollywood's historical films should not be judged with the same criteria as historiography: "By what authority does an academic historian assert power over how filmmakers interpret history? Isn't it just as likely that the history film and 'traditional scholarship' in history are two entirely different domains, with their own rules and discourses?" (Sklar 1997, 347). Robert Rosenstone and Roberta Pearson concur, arguing for a separate but equal status for film and historiography, while I have argued elsewhere that a filmic writing of history occurred during the classical Hollywood era when filmmakers self-consciously appropriated aspects of traditional historiography and incorporated them within an emerging cycle of prestigious historical filmmaking (Pearson 1998; Rosenstone 2004). The work of Leger Grindon and David Eldridge offers another compromise between text and image and the ideologies of historians and film scholars. Grindon sees historical cinema, even films of Hollywood's studio era, as a genre responding to not only its own sets of codes and conventions but also wider cultural arguments about the past. In practice, however, Grindon tends to see romance and spectacle driving studio-era narratives rather than historical arguments and controversy. David Eldridge's ambitious study of 1950s historical films acknowledges that not every Hollywood history film "would impart an enhanced understanding of historical reality," but he argues that some did and were directly tied to mainstream historiographic trends in social, political, and intellectual history (2006, 2).

Custen and Eldridge both provide a more general assessment of American and European historical films. In my own work, I have examined studio-era Hollywood's interest in American history from the early sound era to the beginning of World War II (Smyth 2006). While I discuss many of the more traditional historical films and masculine biopics, I also explore the studios' interest in modern history (*The Public Enemy*; *Scarface*) and the history of women and mixed-race Americans (*Annie Oakley*; *Ramona*; *Gone With the Wind*). While traditional approaches to Hollywood's historical films tend to ignore or denigrate their representation of race and gender, within the past few years several major studies have appeared revising traditional critical perspectives on sound-era Hollywood. In addition to Lauren Berlant's work on *Show Boat*, Linda Williams's *Playing the Race Card: Melodramas of Black and White from Uncle Tom to O.J. Simpson* (2001) examines Hollywood and the media's representation of African-Americans and the ambiguities of visualizing race. Williams's discussions of *Show Boat* (1936) and *Gone With the Wind* (1939) are particularly relevant for studies of Hollywood's complex attitude toward history. M. Elise Marubbio's *Killing the Indian Maiden* (2006) explores the mostly sexualized images of Native American women in Hollywood cinema, while I look at the more ambivalent images of mixed-race Native American and African-American women in historical fiction and film. While studio-era Hollywood's war genre remains one of the liveliest areas of research on issues of film and history, there is less attention paid to the ways in which the studios historicized World Wars I and II between 1929 and 1945. The notable exceptions to this are, of course, Michael Isenberg's pioneering *War on Film* (1981), John Whiteclay Chambers's work on *All Quiet on the Western Front* (1996), and John E. O'Connor and Peter Rollins's *Why We Fought* (2008). Ironically, there has been surprisingly little attention paid to Hollywood's historical representation of class in America and abroad, despite ample archival evidence that filmmakers focused on these issues. While masculine class dramas often focused on modern material that linked the working class with violence (*Heroes For Sale*, 1933; *Dead End*, 1937; *Black Legion*, 1937), films about women sometimes addressed the history of work in a more positive light (*Kitty Foyle*, 1940; *A Tree Grows in Brooklyn*, 1945).

One of the major problems with research on studio-era Hollywood is that despite the pioneering archival work of Thomas Schatz, Robert Sklar, Rudy Behlmer, and Tino Balio, until recently only a handful of historians and critics writing about historical films consulted studio archives with any thoroughness. Historians and film scholars writing about "historical" cinema have tended to employ traditional textual analysis, occasionally supplemented by secondary social and cultural historiography, film reviews, and widely circulated publicity. However, they often sidelined the piles of memos, script drafts, censorship records, and financial analyses available in the major studio archives. In consequence, Hollywood's complex attitudes toward the production of history were simply ignored in favor of convenient arguments about streamlined production values, recycled narratives, and conservative history.[4] To be fair, unless a film historian was enterprising or well connected, access to studio archives was fairly limited until the early 1990s. The Academy of Motion Picture Arts and Sciences Library (Beverly Hills, CA), the University of Southern California's Cinema-Television Archive, the Warner Bros. Archive attached to USC, the University of California-Los Angeles's Arts Special Collections, the United Artists Collection deposited at the State Historical Society in Madison, Wisconsin, the National Archives in Washington, DC, the Library of Congress, and university collections at Wesleyan, Brigham Young, Wyoming, Yale, Harvard, and Boston continue to be the main archival resources for studying studio-era Hollywood's historical practices. As more and more scholars consult their massive collections, scholars and the public may adjust their attitudes toward studio-era Hollywood's filmic writing of history.

A Hollywood Cavalcade

Between 1929 and 1945, filmmakers produced an unprecedented array of sprawling, multistarred historical epics, biopics, period musicals, and adaptations of classic literature, often courting critical acclaim and public controversy as well as big box office returns.[5] Screenwriters, directors, and producers created a new form of historical narration in the sound era, one that borrowed from both conventional textual history and the more ambiguous vocabulary of visual history. Genres set in the distant and not-so-distant past, such as the Western and gangster film, well known to audiences from the early silent era, were given the "prestige" treatment – researched screenplays, elaborate text forewords, historical settings and protagonists, liberal production budgets, and targeted publicity (Smyth 2006, 57–114). Biopics capitalized on trends in popular history and the American public's growing appetite for unconventional "heroes," adding new dimensions to star personas, whether it was Paul Muni playing Al Capone (*Scarface*, 1932) or Benito Juarez (*Juarez*, 1939), or Bette Davis playing an unconventional Southern belle (*Jezebel*, 1938) or an equally unconventional British monarch (*The Private Lives of Elizabeth and Essex*, 1939).[6]

Often lavishly produced and financially risky, historical films nonetheless dominated American filmmaking during the Great Depression. Studios such as Warner Bros. and MGM had thriving historical short departments, which produced a series of military vignettes and "great man" biopics ranging from *The Romance of Robert Burns* (Crane Wilbur, 1937) to a biopic of African-American doctor George Washington Carver (*The Story of Doctor Carver*, Fred Zinnemann, 1938) to *Sons of Liberty* (Michael Curtiz, 1939), which told the story of Jewish-American patriot Haym Salomon. Hollywood even made a studio-wide, feature-length tribute to its historical filmmaking for the 1939 World's Fair, *Land of Liberty*, which used clips from two decades of films about the history of the United States (Behlmer 1991; Palmer 1993; Smyth 2006, 307–317). By 1940, over half of the A-budget feature films were based upon historical material, an astonishing figure considering the diversity of Hollywood film production (*Film Daily* 1940, 1941).

Though remakes of major classics of historical literature were common during the silent era (*Ramona*, 1910, 1916, 1928; *The Last of the Mohicans*, 1909, 1920; *The Spoilers*, 1905, 1914, 1923), studios like Twentieth Century-Fox and MGM became so historically savvy that they remade their own period films on a more lavish scale (*Frontier Marshall*, Fox, 1933, 1939; *Waterloo Bridge*, MGM, 1931, 1940; *Smilin' Through*, MGM, 1932, 1941). Fox and MGM also bought successful historical properties from the smaller RKO and Universal when they went into receivership. Fox remade Universal's *Destry Rides Again* (1932) on a grander scale in 1939, and MGM purchased the rights to the adaptations of Fannie Hurst's *Back Street* (RKO, 1932) and Edna Ferber's *Cimarron* (RKO, 1931) and *Show Boat* (Universal, 1929, 1936) for future remakes. MGM mogul Louis B. Mayer also bought percentages of *Gone With the*

Wind's future profits from a financially straitened David O. Selznick and allegedly offered to purchase all rights to *Citizen Kane* for the sole purpose of burning the negative (Balio 1996, 209). By the end of the 1930s, historical filmmaking had become a competitive market, with studios rushing to corner the rights to historical novels and major and less-known historical and biographical areas of research. Even the demands of wartime production could not entirely eclipse the genre, although the number, variety, and box office returns of major historical films declined between 1941 and 1945.[7]

Historical films about America and Americans dominated the genre, and some historians have argued that the overwhelming crisis of the Great Depression caused many filmmakers, artists, and public figures to focus upon the grandeur and problems within the national past (Pauly 1974; Shindler 1996). But this usable past, whether a familiar collective comfort, a revisionist critique of traditional values, or a source of national mediation, was most widely realized by historians in Hollywood. American history was more familiar than Europe's and potentially engaged American filmgoers on many levels. While American critics and audiences might watch the lavish historical inanities of *Madame Du Barry* (1934) or *Pride and Prejudice* (1940) with uncritical enjoyment, they would be less apt to praise a blatantly unrealistic biopic of Lincoln or an "inaccurate" adaptation of Margaret Mitchell's *Gone With the Wind*. Studio production records reveal that screenwriters and producers treated national history with more accuracy, nuance, and insight. While working on the script of *The Littlest Rebel* (1936), Twentieth Century-Fox production chief Darryl Zanuck warned an adventurous scriptwriter: "If you even suggest that Shirley Temple was the inspiration for the Gettysburg Address, they'll throw rocks at us" (Zanuck 1935). But he was less particular about suggesting creative changes to European history. During a story conference on *Cardinal Richelieu* (1935), writer Nunnally Johnson recalled Zanuck growling at one outraged historical expert: "Aw, the hell with you. Nine out of ten people are going to think he's Rasputin, anyway" (Stempel 1980, 60).

While studio publicity for European historical dramas focused on the accuracy of costumes, wigs, and sets, many American historical films were marketed and reviewed for their unique historical arguments and ways in which they exploited the incompleteness or inaccuracy of traditional historiography (*Marie Antoinette* Press Book 1938; *Adventures of Robin Hood* Press Book 1938). As film critic Thornton Delahanty remarked, *The Prisoner of Shark Island* (1936), a biography of alleged Lincoln assassin Samuel Mudd, "drags up an unsavoury episode in American history and treats it with compelling honesty, helping thereby to vindicate the memory of a man to whom was done an irreparable wrong by a public whose sense of patriotism ran amok ... The picture goes outside the history books." *The Prisoner of Shark Island* exposes the shortcomings of traditional historiography while still maintaining allegiances to objectivity and accuracy. However, historical filmmakers like David O. Selznick often used historical ambiguity to their advantage in foreign historical contexts. In Selznick's 1937 production of *The Prisoner of Zenda*, the narrative is ostensibly based on an unproven, mysterious rumor about a romance between an Englishman and a European queen at the end of the nineteenth century. This sort of history would never have been written down, and the narrative progresses through the visual identification and misrecognition of the protagonist (Ronald Colman) as a double for the king. The authenticity of the face, rather than any mundane written document, becomes the most important historical "evidence" in the narrative. Colman's star image is the basis of the film's alternative historical narrative.

Despite the dominance of American narratives, Hollywood filmmakers maintained a serious interest in global history, projecting major A-budget feature films on Central and South America (*Captain Blood*, 1936; *Juarez*, 1939), Russia (*Rasputin and the Empress*, 1930; *A Royal Scandal*, 1945), France (*The Life of Emile Zola*, 1937; *All This and Heaven Too*, 1940), Great Britain (*Cavalcade*, 1933; *The White Cliffs of Dover*, 1944), Germany (*All Quiet on the Western Front*, 1930; *Lancer Spy*, 1937), Canada (*Hudson's Bay*, 1940), Egypt (*Suez*, 1938), India (*Clive of India*, 1935; *Gunga Din*, 1939), China (*The Adventures of Marco Polo*, 1937), and the Philippines (*The Real Glory*, 1939). These "foreign" historical films often lured audiences with exotic locales, color, and larger-than-life protagonists, but were supported by studio research and publicity. Studio publicity often associated filmmakers with the historical genre, and while Zanuck, Nunnally Johnson, Lamar Trotti, Bette Davis (*Jezebel*, 1938; *The Sisters*, 1938; *Mr. Skeffington*, 1944;

The Corn is Green, 1945), and Cecil B. DeMille (*The Plainsman*, 1936; *The Buccaneer*, 1938; *Union Pacific*, 1939; *Reap the Wild Wind*, 1942) were often linked to American historical productions and roles, publicists emphasized links between actors Edward G. Robinson (*Dr. Ehrlich's Magic Bullet*, 1940) and Paul Muni (*The Story of Louis Pasteur*, 1936) and European history. George Custen has argued that German-born William Dieterle, as Warner Bros.' premier biopic director (*The Story of Louis Pasteur*, 1936; *The Life of Emile Zola*, 1937; *Juarez*, 1939; *Dr. Ehrlich's Magic Bullet*, 1940), was "one of the few directors in 1930s Hollywood to exercise complete control on a film" (1992, 66–67; Elsaesser 1986). During this period, Greta Garbo turned increasingly to the prestige associated with period films (*Queen Christina*, 1933; *Anna Karenina*, 1935; *Camille*, 1936; *Conquest*, 1937), while her rarefied brand of stardom and demands for distance from the public complemented her career as MGM's premier star of historical productions.

British history was a particular favorite of Hollywood producers from the early sound era through World War II. A thriving expatriate film community, time-tested historical literature by the likes of Charles Dickens and the Brontës, and, as World War II loomed, shared fascist enemies insured the powerful alliance of British and American history, culture, and prestige (Cull 1996; Glancy 1999). Stars such as British George Arliss (*Disraeli*, 1929; *Alexander Hamilton*, 1931) and Leslie Howard (*Berkeley Square*, 1933; *Gone With the Wind*, 1939), the Anglo-Irish Greer Garson (*Goodbye, Mr. Chips*, 1939; *Pride and Prejudice*, 1940; *Random Harvest*, 1942; *Blossoms in the Dust*, 1941; *Madame Curie*, 1943), Tasmanian-born Errol Flynn (*Captain Blood*, 1936; *The Adventures of Robin Hood*, 1938; *Dodge City*, 1939; *They Died With Their Boots On*, 1941), and director-producer Frank Lloyd (*Cavalcade*, 1933; *Wells Fargo*, 1937) often crossed the borders between British and American history.

Hollywood's Historians in the Sound Era

The normalization of sound technologies was perhaps the most decisive factor in developing Hollywood's projection of history. Although hearing the blade of the guillotine fall in *A Tale of Two Cities* (1935) or the echoes of Jesse James's bullets (*Jesse James*, 1939) certainly brought history to life in ways that traditional historiography could not, sound technologies changed filmmaking – and historical filmmaking in particular – even before the start of shooting. Sound film enabled screenwriters to write history in the manner of more traditional academic and popular historians. Introductions to the period, narrative structure, the use of primary and secondary sources in dialogue and staging, all had to be worked out in greater written and oral complexity, detail, and accuracy. With the advent of sound, it is more difficult for academic criticism to argue for filmed history's "separate but equal status" with traditional historiography (i.e., that filmmakers produced visual history while historians generated the more venerable textual history) (Ferro 1988, 161–163; Rosenstone 2004, 29–33; Smyth 2006, 18–19).

For the first time, Hollywood's writers of history achieved a measure of autonomy and prestige in the filmmaking hierarchy. While, during the silent era, screenwriters were rarely accorded recognition or respect as the writers of filmed history, by the early 1930s they dominated the production of historical films. In his history of American screenwriting, Stempel (2000) focuses on several key writers, including Lamar Trotti, Nunnally Johnson, Preston Sturges, Herman Mankiewicz, Sarah Mason, Victor Heerman, John Balderston, Sonya Levien, Ben Hecht, Casey Robinson, and Dudley Nichols. All of these writers made their reputations with historical films. It was no accident that writers were treated best at Twentieth Century-Fox; the production chief, Darryl F. Zanuck, had started out as a writer for Warner Bros. Zanuck and Selznick, another young producer to form his own studio in the mid-1930s, worked closely with individual writers on historical projects, supported by impressive research libraries and professional researchers. During the silent era, the only books and literary material the studios retained were individual copies of best sellers purchased for the story department to vet for potential production. Studio research libraries did not exist. But beginning in the 1930s, the studios developed their research libraries, sometimes on a massive scale, as in the case of Warner Bros., Fox, and Paramount. Mainstream historical journals such as the *North American Review*, *Library Journal*, and the *Wilson Bulletin for Librarians* carried articles featuring the likes of Herman Lissauer,

Warner Bros.' research library director, and Frances Richardson, director of Twentieth Century-Fox's library, praising their meticulous craft (Carter 1939, 404–407; Smyth 2006, 101–103).

Screenwriters not only read old scripts and popular literature but also supplemented their work with traditional and revisionist historiography. Often writers sought out unresolved historical controversies as potential material (*I Am a Fugitive from a Chain Gang*, 1932; *The Life of Emile Zola*, 1937), added their own perspective on more traditional events and figures (Lamar Trotti, *Young Mr. Lincoln*, 1939; Mark Hellinger, *The Roaring Twenties*, 1939), and even beat their ivory-tower equivalents to the field of postwar twentieth-century events and people (*The Public Enemy*, 1931; *Scarface*, 1932; *Mata Hari*, 1932; *Lancer Spy*, 1937; *The Roaring Twenties*, 1939). Writers, particularly those at Twentieth Century-Fox, RKO, and Warner Bros., began to feature prominently in contemporary reviews and publicity. Even when material was based on classic literature or runaway best sellers such as Wister's *The Virginian* (1902, 1929), Ferber's *Cimarron* (1929, 1931), Hope's *The Prisoner of Zenda* (1899, 1937), Mitchell's *Gone With the Wind* (1936, 1939), or Steinbeck's *The Grapes of Wrath* (1939, 1940), screenwriters still headlined the credits and publicity, often obtaining a separate credit title. Howard Estabrook and Nunnally Johnson, possibly the two most powerful writers of this era, would go on to combine their interests in writing screen histories with producing. Preston Sturges's career writing unconventional biographies of fictional "historical" figures was particularly unusual. *The Power and the Glory* (1933) was the first script to earn a writer a percentage of the film gross, and with *The Great McGinty* (1940), Sturges became the first writer in the sound era to direct and maintain creative control over his work (Dooley 1981, 126–127).

But the advent of sound also changed the way screenwriters, cinematographers, and directors projected history. While the metaphor of shot to word or shot to sentence is well known from the work of Pudovkin, Eisenstein, and semiotics of the 1970s, and it is tempting to see a film editor's job in the same terms as a historian's assemblage of argument, evidence, and emphasis (what to include and leave out), sound film fundamentally enabled screenwriters to construct a new form of historiography that bridged the discourse of traditional historiography and the new challenges of visual history, or as Hayden White put it in 1988, "historiophoty." While silent film all but vanished from screens after 1929, intertitles (projected text) did not disappear. During the sound era, filmmakers projected text on screen as a single intertitle or series of titles, as document inserts, or as superimpositions over an image or montage of images. Beginning in the 1930s, text figured most prominently in historical cinema and even today is the preeminent visual and verbal marker of the historical film. During the silent era, titles were of course an indispensable means of conveying dialogue, setting, and the passage of time – and sometimes, as in the case of Griffith's *The Birth of a Nation*, were used self-consciously to convey historical arguments. Although talking pictures had effectively rendered intertitles obsolete, "historical films retained and embellished their textual content as a means of lending their narratives historical credibility and prestige" (Smyth 2006, 7). Screenwriters and other filmmakers reinforced the historical script's connection to written history, referring to the opening intertitles as "forewords." Text inserts placed throughout the film narrative often functioned as footnotes or "chapterization." Superimposed dates and text forewords were primarily nondiegetic historical tools, enabling filmmakers to foreground a particular historical perspective, but document and photographic inserts (and even references to them) functioned diegetically, often connecting supposedly fictional characters to a recognizable historical era (or demonstrating their resistance to and contempt for mainstream attitudes).

For instance, one sequence in William Wellman's *The Public Enemy* (1931) begins with "1917" superimposed over the screen. Protagonists Tom Powers and Matt Doyle fail to understand the paperboys as they shout news headlines about America's entry into World War I. Here, scriptwriter Harvey Thew and director William Wellman emphasize the heroes' isolation from mainstream American concerns like patriotism and sacrifice. Tom and Matt have other bootlegging battles to fight at home. *The Public Enemy*, long considered a modern gangster film reflecting Depression-era conflicts about masculinity and success (Clarens 1980; Munby 1999), nonetheless uses the tools of historical filmmaking (superimposed dates, text inserts, references to historical events) to historicize the lives of fictional gangsters. Recognition of the widespread use of these historical matters (or semantic genre elements) has prompted some to rethink the historical discourse of many early gangster films (Maltby 1993; Smyth 2004).

Some filmmakers during this period – perhaps most prominently Cecil B. DeMille – continued to use text forewords and projected text in the traditional manner of silent intertitles. DeMille's particular brand of progressive, triumphant, patriotic, white man-made history has come to symbolize many historians' beliefs about the conservative historical discourse of Hollywood cinema (Birchard 2004; Marubbio 2006, 106). However, many other historical filmmakers of the sound era did more than simply use text as a means of setting an appropriate historical tone or reinforcing the dominant, usually traditional viewpoint. On one level, the self-conscious use of text in the sound era deliberately drew audience attention to the constructed nature of the film. Historical films, though often appealing to emotional or nationalistic responses, were not constructed as seamless studio fantasies or "realistic" historical enactments. Often filmmakers played with the notion of textual authority and authenticity, setting text in opposition to or in conjunction with ensuing historical images. Two of the more remarkable examples from this era are Howard Estabrook's *Cimarron* (RKO, 1931) and Herman Mankiewicz and Orson Welles's *Citizen Kane* (RKO, 1941). They highlight not only the use of text, but also historical production practices and concerns that would predominate in the studio era.[8]

Estabrook's script, adapted from the number one best seller of 1929, Edna Ferber's historical novel, was the first major historical epic of the era to use text in a variety of forms throughout the narrative. Text and image work in counterpoint throughout the earliest versions of the script and, remarkably, none of Estabrook's text inserts were cut from the final print. Estabrook began his script with an impressive two-shot intertitle intoning the core of progressive Western history: "A nation rising to greatness through the work of men and women ... new country opening ... raw land blossoming ... crude towns growing into cities." *Cimarron* appears to be a traditional nation-making epic, reflecting the frontier rhetoric of historians Theodore Roosevelt and Frederick Jackson Turner. But the first images following the titles show a white trader lashing out at some Native Americans shortly before the 1889 land run in the Oklahoma territory. The trader's "get out" reveals the other side of the frontier story, and *Cimarron*'s fictional narrative of Yancey and Sabra Cravat reveals other facets of revisionist social history still at the margins of mainstream writing in the 1930s. Yancey or "Cimarron" (Richard Dix) is a mixed-blood Cherokee, not the traditional white hunter-hero of the American Western. Sabra (Irene Dunne) is the true focus of the narrative, and it is she who runs the papers and determines how the West will be read and remembered.

Though doomed Native American heroes and shrinking Prairie Madonnas were not unknown in the silent cinematic West (*The Covered Wagon*, 1923; *The Vanishing American*, 1925), tough mixed-bloods and articulate women were new to American history. The critical Western social and cultural histories of Mari Sandoz and Angie Debo had yet to be published, but Estabrook's research bibliography reveals that he was looking at the work of future Indian Bureau leader John Collier and less well-known Native American historians (Estabrook 1930). *Cimarron*'s revisionism, though unique, would influence other Hollywood filmmakers to test the boundaries of the American frontier, and women's Westerns – occasionally with mixed-blooded historical characters – became an important part of film production during the era (*Laughing Boy*, 1934; *Annie Oakley*, 1935; *The Plainsman*, 1936; *Ramona*, 1936; *Robin Hood of El Dorado*, 1936; *Drums Along the Mohawk*, 1939; *Arizona*, 1940; *Belle Starr*, 1941; *Duel in the Sun*, 1946).

Estabrook's practice of annotating the main historical source (in this case, Ferber's novel) for narrative construction, dates, and dialogue would become the norm. His papers at the Academy of Motion Picture Arts and Sciences Library still contain the writer's research bibliography, notes, and series of scripts. The extent of the bibliography reveals the seriousness with which Estabrook took not only the writing of frontier history, but also his interest in new research on Native Americans and other aspects of social history neglected by traditional Western historians and producers of cowboy-and-Indian "horse operas." Many of the books were taken from the Los Angeles Public Library, but several were evidently studio copies, and as time went on, RKO, like the other majors, acquired an impressive research library of newspaper clippings, journal articles, image references, and books. The research libraries were run as separate units, and grew out of necessity. Although studios were not known for freely cooperating with one another, it was standard practice for filmmakers to use other studios' textual and visual archives.[9]

For the studios, history was synonymous with prestige, and prestige needed credentials. Research provided credentials. At Universal it was not unknown for researchers to chase down the present location of a painting of the French–Indian War for production designers of *The Last of the Mohicans* (1936), or for Sonya Levien and Lamar Trotti to visit the Huntington Library in San Marino, or for MGM designers to track down authentic eighteenth-century French furniture for *Marie Antoinette* (1938) through the assistance of researchers. The screenwriter was always the first and the most thorough library customer, although at Warner Bros. Herman Lissauer's team of researchers supplied a question-and-answer service to screenwriters at later stages of production (e.g., "What were women's hat styles like in 1860?" or "Who was Mary Stuart's principal foreign minister?"). However, Warner Bros. researchers also provided a "bible" for each historical film, sometimes over 100 pages long, which included period photographs, drawings, and advertisements, excerpts of memoirs and major histories, and portraits of the protagonists. These "bibles" could then be checked out by the director and by the set or costume designers. But research departments also served the studio publicity departments. Press books for historical films always contained several articles about the amount of research in the film, how many costumes were designed, what priceless artifact was featured, how many books were consulted. The studios advised exhibitors to create historical tie-ins for the first-runs of major historical films: book displays, essay contests, costume parties, special tickets for school children and teachers. When new war pictures premiered, theaters gave US veterans free tickets; the Daughters of the American Revolution were summoned to premieres of "nation-making" pictures; and much of the historical literature adapted for major historical films became part of high school reading lists across the country.

Filmmakers Herman Mankiewicz and Orson Welles were not interested in this kind of publicity. In 1940, they began to work on a script about the life of a living "great man" – media magnate William Randolph Hearst. *Citizen Kane* used many of the historical components developed by Estabrook in *Cimarron*, including the extensive use of projected text, the importance of documents within the narrative, and the use of a controversial newspaperman protagonist. But the film also capitalized on the trend in biopics. Sound biopics had accelerated in popularity since George Arliss's success reprising his stage role in *Disraeli* (Warner Bros., 1929), but early in the 1930s, even gangsters like Frankie Lake, Terry Druggan, Jack Lingle, and Al Capone were subjects of film biographies (*Little Caesar*, 1931; *The Public Enemy*, 1931; *The Finger Points*, 1931; *Scarface*, 1932). The Production Code had reacted violently to the biographical material and overt historical elements like projected text, dates, and inserted news headlines in both *The Public Enemy* and *Scarface*. Putting modern racketeers in the same biographical categories as statesmen, bankers, and war heroes meant a radical rethinking of modern history and the cult of celebrity. Many filmmakers had been struggling to put contemporary or postwar history into perspective. Hollywood grappled with the adaptation of Erich Maria Remarque's *All Quiet on the Western Front* (1930) and Ernest Hemingway's *A Farewell to Arms* (1932), but even more harrowing than these tales of wartime disillusionment was the aftermath of decline. Robert Burns's *I Am a Fugitive from a Chain Gang* (1932) and *Heroes for Sale* (1933) were especially powerful and controversial views of the 1920s. Hollywood courted material about "forgotten" men and women and those who were by profession or temperament outside the traditional canon of biography. But in choosing Hearst as a subject, Mankiewicz and Welles had to do what so many other filmmakers were forced to do in the past: rename their protagonist ("Capone" became "Camonte" in *Scarface*). It was not just fear of censorship that prompted the creation of "Charles Foster Kane," but worries about lawsuits.

As the studios found out, dead historical subjects were "safe" from lawsuits. Warner Bros. could say anything they liked (within the strictures of the 1934 Production Code) about Elizabeth I, but the living subjects of biography could sue and win. The novelty of constructing powerful modern history on-screen had its risks. But even then, screenwriters and studios were not always immune from charges of libel and plagiarism. Frequently, legal offices were handling multiple letters of complaint from popular historians charging that the studios had plagiarized their work. Hearst biographer Ferdinand Lundberg did just this to Mankiewicz following the release of *Citizen Kane*, alleging that the screenwriter had copied Lundberg's

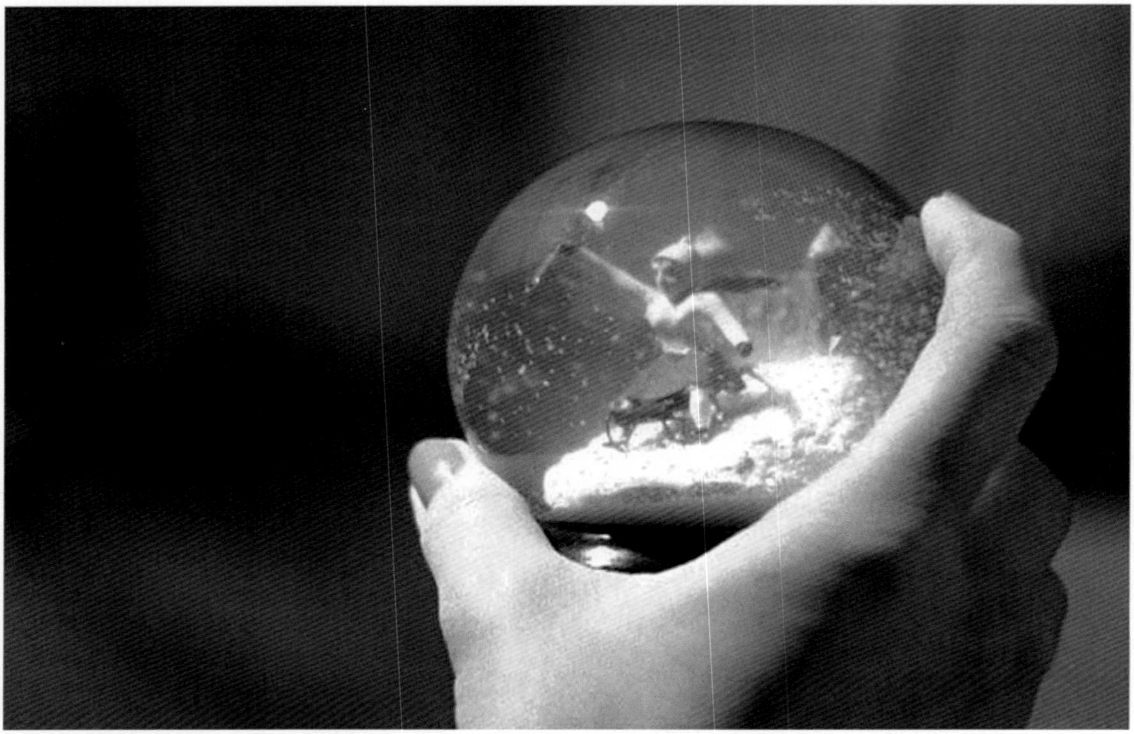

Figure 22.1 The snow globe in Sam Wood's *Kitty Foyle* (1940, producer David Hempstead).

critical historical perspective and arguments about Hearst (Carringer 1985; Gottesman 1996; Street 1996). Several years before, Warner Bros.' critical look at the Georgia penal system in *Fugitive* caught them in another lawsuit. But historical filmmakers realized that their original historical material had an advantage – even over adaptations of historical novels like *Anthony Adverse* (1936) and *All This and Heaven Too* (1940): History cost nothing to option, and historical material was in the public domain. If historians' unique arguments were protected by copyright, then Hollywood simply had to create its own perspectives. Zanuck was perhaps the most astute cultivator of the "original" historical screenplay, and Nunnally Johnson's work on *The Prisoner of Shark Island* (1936) and *Slave Ship* (1937) and Lamar Trotti's original research for *Young Mr. Lincoln* (1939) became some of the most respected historical films of the era.

Welles and Mankiewicz played carefully with the developments in biopics and historical cinema, using the traditional hallmarks of the genre but vastly expanding the vocabulary of filmic history. Borrowing from Preston Sturges's work on *The Power and the Glory* (1933), they used nonchronological flashbacks, undercutting traditional linear historiography, its sense of biographical and historical progression, and traditional values of success. Kane's life was presented in fragments by various biased sources, and historical knowledge, like objectivity, was limited. Though historical filmmaking frequently used documentary techniques such as archival footage, text inserts, and voiceover narration (*The Public Enemy*, 1931; *The World Changes*, 1933; *The Roaring Twenties*, 1939), these were still "fictional" films. *Citizen Kane*'s famous "News on the March" film biography confronts the arbitrary boundary separating fiction from nonfiction film, and history from fiction. The use of a pompous, bombastic voiceover often counteracts the authority of the images, and Kane's own voice is surprisingly rendered with a silent intertitle. Kane's great-man biopic gets only a raspberry from an audience of reporters. The succeeding personal story might be regarded as the social and cultural history that so often

Figure 22.2 Needlepoint intertitle from Sam Wood's *Kitty Foyle* (1940, producer David Hempstead).

is missing from traditional biographies, or the "outtakes" from a traditional biopic. Thompson's search for the meaning in Kane's life ironically begins in an archive where he confronts the handwritten diaries about Kane's early life out West. Thompson literally reads himself back into the romantic completeness of America and Kane's frontier past. In one of American cinema's most famous sequences, words fade into the image of Charlie clutching Rosebud and cheering, "The Union forever!" Text and image work in counterpoint to create a new form of film historiography. Although many critics have attempted to see *Citizen Kane* as an aberration in classical Hollywood cinema, it was written and shot within the historical film genre tradition (Smyth 2006, 317–336). Even Kane's snow globe, the petrified image of a frontier childhood, was borrowed from two other historical films of the previous year: a nineteenth-century French love triangle starring Charles Boyer and Bette Davis, *All This and Heaven Too* (1940), and RKO's star vehicle for Ginger Rogers, *Kitty Foyle* (1940), marketed as the "natural history of the American woman."

History, Prestige, and Women Audiences

Citizen Kane borrowed more than its snow globe motif from the two films. Ironically, while both *Kitty Foyle* and *All This and Heaven Too* have been overshadowed by the reputation of Welles and Mankiewicz's unconventional masculine biopic, they were also biographies of unconventional women that challenged traditional methods of narrating history onscreen. In some ways, they were more radical than *Citizen Kane*. Warner Bros.' production of Rachel Field's 1938 best seller did not use significant textual inserts to narrate the life of French governess Henriette Deluzy Desportes. Rather than associating Henriette's story with the more rigid textual discourse of traditional history or the authoritative masculine narration of Kane's "News on the March," screenwriters used flashbacks and her voiceover as historical tools. Though women's voices in 1940s cinema sometimes conveyed the insidiously constructed paranoia of period noir melodrama, more frequently women's voices were authorities on their own lives and the lives of other women (*Rebecca*, 1940; *I Married a Witch*, 1942; *So Proudly We Hail*, 1943; *I Remember Mama*, 1948; *Cheaper By the Dozen*, 1949).

Similarly, at RKO, Dalton Trumbo also preserved much of Sheridan Morley's working-class Philadelphia protagonist's story by structuring *Kitty Foyle* as a series of personally narrated flashbacks. These memories did not emerge in an unchallenged, nostalgic haze but were constantly questioned and critiqued by the older Kitty/narrator as she wryly stares at her reflection in her bedroom mirror. This ongoing dialogue between ironic narrator and the constructed, mass-marketed images of childhood, young womanhood, and working life formed most of the structure of the film. Kitty's snow globe may have contained a petrified image of a joyous young girl on a sled, but Trumbo's Kitty challenges that untroubled image and its conventional romantic aftermath. However, the screenwriter also playfully connected *Kitty Foyle* to the masculine biopic cycle by preserving author Sheridan Morley's historical subtitle and by opening the film with a brief documentary – narrated at one point with needlepoint intertitles – of the white-collar working woman from 1900 to 1939 (Trumbo 1940a, 1940b, 1940c). Significantly, this mini-biopic of an average young woman, wife, mother, and suffragette shows her returning to the workforce *after* marriage rather than simply abandoning work upon her marriage. Her descendant, Citizen Kitty, may be another fictional Hollywood heroine, but this woman of the people emerged from the twin histories of early twentieth-century women's liberation and of the historical film genre.

Through the historical genre, Hollywood had a uniquely interconnected market of readers and viewers, and this period witnessed a growing alliance between studios and major publishing houses. A successful historical novel had the advantage over new material in that it was "presold" twice (the historical material and the novel); the studios already had an informed market waiting for the film adaptation. That audience was overwhelmingly female. Women had been America's main reading population since the nineteenth century and were undoubtedly Hollywood's mainstay during the studio era (Baym 1978, 277; Douglas 1988). Steven Neale has pointed out that producers believed, sometimes in the absence of any market research, that "women constituted an important, even dominant sector of the viewing population" (2000, 194). Arguably, Robert and Helen Lynd's 1929 sociological study of the average American town, *Middletown* (Muncie, Indiana), provided the necessary proof that women of all classes still dominated the nation's reading market and other cultural venues (1929, 231–239). Women were reading not only movie magazines but also historical fiction, whether it was the work of Fannie Hurst, Edna Ferber, or Margaret Mitchell. In May 1929, Jason Joy, head of the Studio Relations Committee of the Motion Picture Producers and Distributors of America (MPPDA), addressed the General Federation of Women's Clubs, arguing that women were Hollywood's greatest asset in determining prestige picture trends. "We come to you because you are a trained group ... You have many interests but they all reach back to the same roots, which are promotion of culture." Joy proposed a closer relationship between filmmakers and female audiences – not only the Daughters of the American Revolution, but also the American Association of University Women!

In his history of American cinema during the 1930s, Tino Balio notes the connection between female audiences and prestige filmmaking, focusing on the most famous historical film of this era, *Gone With the Wind* (1939): "That the era's most successful production was targeted at women and employed a woman's perspective provides a starting point for an understanding of production trends during the thirties" (1996, 1). Balio, however, does not make the link between historical cinema, prestige filmmaking, and female audiences. Though Mitchell and *Gone With the Wind* are key to understanding Hollywood's historical cycle, they represent only a fraction of Hollywood's commitment to making women's history. In adapting the work of writers Edna Ferber (*Show Boat*, 1926, 1936; *Cimarron*, 1929, 1931), Helen Hunt Jackson (*Ramona*, 1884, 1936), Jane Austen (*Pride and Prejudice*, 1814, 1940), Emily Brontë (*Wuthering Heights*, 1848, 1939), Louisa May Alcott (*Little Women*, 1865, 1933), and Margaret Mitchell (*Gone With the Wind*, 1936, 1939), Hollywood connected women's history and female audiences with prestige filmmaking and the broader discourse of "national" history (Smyth 2009).

During the studio era, Hollywood producers purchased a wide variety of material for their historical films, ranging from popular biographies and history to best sellers and widely read articles in major journals like the *Saturday Evening Post* and the *Ladies' Home Journal*. Although a surprising number of women worked as top-earning screenwriters throughout the silent and early sound eras – such as Lillian Hellman (*The Little Foxes*, 1941), Anita Loos (*San Francisco*, 1936), Frances Marion (*Camille*, 1937), and Jeanie Macpherson (*The Plainsman*, 1936) – even more women sold their historical fiction to the studios. In the 1930s, Hollywood bought the work of writers such as Fannie Hurst (*Imitation of Life*, Universal, 1934, 1959 and *Back Street*, Universal, 1931, 1941), Elizabeth Madox Roberts (*The Great Meadow*, MGM, 1931), Edith Wharton (*The Age of Innocence*, RKO, 1934), Rachel Field (*All This and Heaven Too*, Warner Bros., 1940), and Margaret Mitchell (*Gone With the Wind*, Selznick, 1939). In the 1940s, writers such as Ethel Vance (*Escape*, MGM, 1940), Jan Struther (*Mrs. Miniver*, MGM, 1942), Betty Smith (*A Tree Grows in Brooklyn*, Twentieth Century-Fox, 1945), Marcia Davenport (*Valley of Decision*, MGM, 1945), Kathleen Winsor (*Forever Amber*, Twentieth Century-Fox, 1947), and Marjorie Kinnan Rawlins (*The Yearling*, Twentieth Century-Fox, 1946) all made lucrative studio deals.

Until recently, critical appraisals of classical Hollywood's historical genre concurred that on-screen, national history was dead, white, and male and reflected an old-fashioned, heroic view of the past (O'Connor & Jackson 1979; Custen 1992; Toplin 1996). Although a majority of biopics released during the classical era focused on the exploits of conventional heroes (*Disraeli*, 1929; *Abraham Lincoln*, 1930; *Silver Dollar*, 1932; *Voltaire*, 1933; *Svengali*, 1934; *Diamond Jim*, 1935; *The Life of Emile Zola*, 1937; *Sergeant York*, 1941; *Buffalo Bill*, 1944; *The Adventures of Mark Twain*, 1944; *Wilson*, 1944, to name only a handful), unconventional women dominated Hollywood's adaptation of historical fiction. Perhaps more than any other author, Edna Ferber's work was responsible for making women and minorities an integral part of Hollywood's projection of history (*Cimarron*, 1931; *So Big*, 1932; *Show Boat*, 1936; *Saratoga Trunk*, 1945). Ferber's conception of American history was not a celebration of masculine ingenuity, strength, and hard work. Instead, it was American women who dominated her narratives, making decisions, overcoming romantic disappointment and social prejudice, achieving public fame. Women drove the course of American history.

Many of these female historical protagonists were also of mixed ethnic and racial backgrounds, and much of Ferber's historical fiction focused on the ambiguities of visualizing racial difference and femininity. Ferber's heroines of *Show Boat* (1936), Julie and Magnolia, are romantic doubles, each struggling with the ambiguities of race and romance in nineteenth-century America. Julie, a mixed-race African-American actress (played by Helen Morgan), is expelled from the showboat troupe when it is discovered she has violated the miscegenation laws in marrying a white performer. Blackness does not "show" in her skin color; musical knowledge betrays her in part, but it is a musical knowledge Magnolia (Irene Dunne) shares. *Show Boat* was the first musical to deal seriously with the existence of America's two major subaltern classes – women and African-Americans – and throughout the 1930s, historical films more than any other genre addressed the ambiguities of race and gender, even in the face of Production Code censorship of interracial romance.[10] Jill Watts has argued that Mae West's musical performances and star persona in period films of the 1930s addressed similar racial and sexual ambiguities in American culture. Bette Davis played a rebellious Southern belle in *Jezebel* (1938), and through cinematography, filmmakers were able to hint at her racial as well as gendered aberrance. She is the only belle to wear a "colored" dress at New Orleans' Olympus Ball. Her peers wear white, and because *Jezebel* was made in black and white, Julie's red dress becomes black. These stark color-coded images were used heavily in publicity. Something similar happened when cinematographer Ernest Haller shot Scarlett (Vivien Leigh) returning home through war-devastated Georgia in *Gone With the Wind*. Shooting into the sun, Scarlett literally turns black, and with frizzled black hair and a hoopless dress, the famously transgressive, unfeminine belle breaks racial boundaries (Smyth 2006, 157–162).

Hollywood's censors, the Production Code Administration, only read scripts; visual arguments escaped their notice, and frequently historical filmmakers exploited their advantage through cinematography. But on the production of the immensely successful *Saratoga Trunk* (1945), Warner Bros. director Sam Wood and screenwriter Casey Robinson worked to preserve the mixed-race identity of Edna Ferber's heroine, Clio Dulaine (Ingrid Bergman). Clio was part African-American, and though Bergman wore a black wig for the role, the filmmakers struggled to keep dialogue references to her ambiguous heritage. Their solution was to add short sequences during shooting, bypassing even the final script. So Clio's leading man, Clint Maroon (Gary Cooper), mischievously alludes to her highly powdered complexion while they lunch in a stylish New Orleans restaurant: "You look kinda funny with all that white stuff on your face" (Robinson 1942, 1943). Joseph Breen was outwitted; only the cutting continuities contained this potentially controversial remark. For perhaps the first time, Hollywood screens challenged the image of the tragic mulatto, showing a mixed African-American woman appear in whiteface, defy her enemies and post–Civil War segregation, and become rich and famous. Warner Bros. publicity also used elements from *Jezebel*'s production to highlight Clio's racial heritage. In all publicity posters and advertising, Bergman appears completely in black, while her leading man, Gary Cooper, stands opposite her in white Stetson and suit.

Although many critics of classical Hollywood cinema have dismissed studio films as racist reinforcements of dominant racial stereotypes and historical attitudes, fearful of racial mixing and mixed-race characters, Bergman's role belongs to a surprisingly large genre of classical Hollywood films with mixed-race female protagonists – many of them adapted from works by women (Smyth 2008). But *Saratoga Trunk* was the first of several postwar films with mixed-race protagonists, including Selznick's *Duel in the Sun* (1946), starring Jennifer Jones, and Twentieth Century-Fox's *Pinky* (1949), with postwar star Jeanne Crain in the title role. Audiences loved *Saratoga Trunk*. It was the number two box office hit in Hollywood's most successful year, 1946, grossing over $5 million in its initial run. Ironically, another major production with a mixed-race heroine, Selznick's *Duel in the Sun* (planned 1943–1945; released 1946), remains the second-highest-grossing Western of the 1940s (Coyne 1998, 42). Women's history, race, and controversy sold well.

Filmmakers undoubtedly courted women viewers with prestigious historical work by the likes of Ferber and Mitchell, but as M. Alison Kibler admits, women brought cultural respectability at a price: "Critics throughout the twentieth century have used femininity to symbolize the passivity and decay they identify in mass culture" (1999, 12). Beneath much of the contemporary critical respect for prestigious women's pictures was an undercurrent of highbrow derision that would increase in the second half of the 1940s. Though Ginger Rogers won the Best Actress Oscar for *Kitty Foyle*, the "Natural History of a Woman" did not receive the prestigious reception of contemporaneous historical films. *Saratoga Trunk* is another case in point. While many film critics admired Bergman's performance and noted the film's drawing power, they dismissed it as "gaudy junk," "trashy," and "a complete women's film" (Cameron 1945; Crowther 1945; Parsons 1946). Throughout her career, Ferber had successfully marketed women's history as material for prestigious historical films, but increasingly in the 1940s, critics described historical films about women as colorful melodramas, or, in the words of Bosley Crowther, "high romantic polish and maddening emptiness underneath." In addition, while filmmakers courted prestige and box office via women's history, academic film critics and historians generally ignore the presence of women in studio-era Hollywood's historical narratives, preferring to classify them as women's melodramas, musicals, or swashbucklers. But arguably, this derision is part of a more general critical disdain for Hollywood's historical genre.

Film studies scholars are often contemptuous of historical studies of films, arguing that historians' litmus tests of historical accuracy merely condemned Hollywood cinema and kept studies of historical cinema at a limited intellectual level (Pearson 1998, 197–198). To a certain extent these claims are valid. Often films reveal as much about their own production eras as the historical era they are attempting to recreate. Yet merely calling historical figures in film "floating signifiers" and abandoning questions of authenticity, revisionist historiography, objectivity, and the lures of textual representation also abandons what studio-era filmmakers actually cared about. Historical research, prestige, even the participation in revisionist historical perspectives and controversies mattered to filmmakers like David O. Selznick, Howard Estabrook, Darryl F. Zanuck, William Dieterle, and Orson Welles. Often their critiques of traditional historical arguments and concepts of heroism, race, and gender anticipate the work of mainstream historians writing in the late twentieth century. The diversity of historical work projected between 1929 and 1945 is even more impressive in comparison with contemporary Hollywood's revival of historical films. Westerns (*Unforgiven*, 1992; *No Country For Old Men*, 2008), gangster films (*The Departed*, 2006; *Public Enemies*, 2008), and biopics of famous men (*Ray*, 2005; *W*, 2008) still dominate critical and box office polls, but biopics of famous women and adaptations of women's historical literature (with the exception of the ubiquitous Jane Austen) are far more rare today than they were in 1939.

Studio-era filmmaking is allegedly built upon unchanging, classical structures of filmmaking, but in responding to history, Hollywood did not merely replay standard narratives in a self-enclosed world. As Rick Altman has argued, in many senses the traditional concept of film genre is antithetical to history and its emphasis on changing contexts. Perhaps that is why it has been notoriously hard for critics and historians to define Hollywood's attitudes toward history as a finite genre. Biopics, costume dramas, melodramas, Americana, prestige pictures, women's pictures, war films, period musicals, adaptations of literature – Hollywood's historical interests knew no generic boundaries in the studio era, and it is only within the past few years that scholars have begun to understand how little historical filmmaking insured "production simplicity, standardization, and economy" or a conservative masculine-driven historiography (Altman 1999, 38).

Notes

1. For studies of the rise of 1930s social history, see Strout 1958; and Des Jardins 2003.
2. Some of the more famous examples are *The Virginian* (1929), *All Quiet on the Western Front* (1930), *The Public Enemy* (1931), *The Power and the Glory* (1933), *She Done Him Wrong* (1933), *The Merry Widow* (1934), *Anna Karenina* (1935), *Captain Blood* (1936), *San Francisco* (1936), *The Prisoner of Zenda* (1937), *A Star is Born* (1937), *Jezebel* (1938), *Gone With the Wind* (1939), *The Sea Hawk* (1940), *Citizen Kane* (1941), *Meet Me in St. Louis* (1944), and *Saratoga Trunk* (1945).
3. See also McCrisken and Pepper 2005; and Hughes-Warrington 2009.
4. Bordwell et al. and Ray's perspectives on the studio era (1985) reinforce these assumptions. See also Carnes 1995; Toplin 1996; Ellwood 2000. The notable exception to this form of textual analysis and film history in the 1980s is the well-connected Thomas Schatz, whose work on *Hollywood Genres* (1981) and *The Genius of the System* (1988) contained a mine of archival work.
5. Among the major historical epics, see *The Sign of the Cross* (1932), *The Gorgeous Hussy* (1936), *In Old Chicago* (1938), *The Roaring Twenties* (1939), and *Gone With the Wind* (1939). For biopics, see *Disraeli* (1929), *Scarface* (1932), *Voltaire* (1933), *Annie Oakley* (1935), *Marie Antoinette* (1938), *Young Mr. Lincoln* (1939), *Citizen Kane* (1941), and *Blossoms in the Dust* (1941). Among the most successful of Hollywood's musicals from this period are *The Merry Widow* (1934), *Sweet Adeline* (1935), *Naughty Marietta* (1935), *Show Boat* (1936), *San Francisco* (1936), *The Story of Vernon and Irene Castle* (1939), and *Meet Me in St. Louis* (1944). Some of the studios' prestige literary adaptations are *The Age of Innocence* (1934), *David Copperfield* (1935), *Ramona* (1936), *The Last of the Mohicans* (1936), *The Adventures of Tom Sawyer* (1938), *Pride and Prejudice* (1940), and *Jane Eyre* (1944).
6. See Nevins 1939 and Wecter 1941 for a broader study of biography and hero-worship during this period. George Custen 1992, 61–63, examines Muni's star status; Schatz 1995 and Smyth 2006, 154–157, look at Bette Davis's historical star personae.
7. Major prestige history films such as *Tennessee Johnson* (1942), *Wilson* (1944), and *The Adventures of Mark Twain* (1944) were notable box office failures. See Knock 1976 and Schatz 1997, 227. On *Tennessee Johnson*, see Koppes and Black 2000, 139.
8. *Cimarron* in particular was used as an industry-wide historical touchstone. In 1939, MGM advertised its historical Western, *Stand Up and Fight*, as "the grandest adventure-romance since *Cimarron* stormed the screen!" *Motion Picture*, 57.1, February 1939, 4.
9. For instance, while in preproduction for *Duel in the Sun* in 1945, David O. Selznick's researchers copied DeMille's expensive image archive at Paramount for *Union Pacific* (1939) on the building of the transcontinental railroad. *Duel in the Sun* Research Files, King Vidor Collection, UCLA Special Collections.
10. The 1929 version cut all mention of miscegenation from the narrative. See Berlant 2008, 69–106.

References

Adventures of Robin Hood. (1938). Press Book. Warner Bros. Warner Bros. Archive, University of Southern California.

Allen, Frederick Lewis. (2000). *Only Yesterday: An Informal History of the 1920s*. New York: HarperCollins.

Altman, Rick. (1999). *Film/Genre*. London: British Film Institute.

Balio, Tino. (1996). *Grand Design: Hollywood as a Modern Business Enterprise, 1930–1939*. Los Angeles: University of California Press.

Baym, Nina. (1978). *Women's Fiction: A Guide to Novels by and about Women in America, 1829–1870*. Ithaca: Cornell University Press.

Bazin, André. (1967). *What Is Cinema?*, vol. 1. Berkeley: University of California Press.

Becker, Carl. (1932). "Everyman His Own Historian." *American Historical Review*, 37, 221–236.

Behlmer, Rudy (ed.). (1972). *Memo from David O. Selznick*. New York: Viking Press.

Behlmer, Rudy. (1991). "Land of Liberty, a Conglomerate." *American Cinematographer*, 72 (March), 34–40.

Behlmer, Rudy. (1993). *Memo from Darryl F. Zanuck*. New York: Grove.

Berlant, Lauren. (2008). *The Female Complaint*. Chicago: University of Chicago Press.

Birchard, Robert S. (2004). *Cecil B. DeMille's Hollywood*. Lexington: University Press of Kentucky.

Bordwell, David, Staiger, Janet, & Thompson, Kristin. (1985). *The Classical Hollywood Cinema: Film Style and Mode of Production to 1960*. New York: Columbia University Press.

Brackman, Harold. (1983). "'Biography Yanked Down Out of Olympus': Beard, Woodward, and Debunking Biography." *Pacific Historical Review*, 52.4, 403–427.

Burgoyne, Robert. (1997). *Film Nation*. Minneapolis: University of Minnesota Press.

Burgoyne, Robert. (2008). *The Hollywood Historical Film*. Oxford: Blackwell.

Cameron, Kate. (1945). "*Saratoga Trunk*." *New York Daily News*, November 22.

Carnes, Mark (ed.). (1995). *Past Imperfect: History According to the Movies*. New York: Henry Holt.

Carringer, Robert. (1985). *The Making of Citizen Kane*. Berkeley: University of California Press.

Carter, Mary Duncan. (1939). "Film Research Libraries." *Library Journal*, May 15, 404–407.

Cawelti, John. (1984). *Six-Gun Mystique*. Bowling Green, OH: Bowling Green State University Popular Press.

Chambers, John Whiteclay. (1996). "*All Quiet on the Western Front*: The Antiwar Film and the Image of Modern War." In John Whiteclay Chambers & David Culbert (eds), *World War II, Film and History* (pp. 13–30). Oxford: Oxford University Press.

Clarens, Carlos. (1980). *Crime Movies*. New York: W. W Norton.

Coyne, Michael. (1998). *The Crowded Prairie: American National Identity in the Hollywood Western*. London: I. B. Tauris.

Crowther, Bosley. (1945). "*Saratoga Trunk*." *New York Times*, November 22.

Cull, Nick. (1996). *Selling War: The British Campaign Against American "Neutrality" in World War II*. Oxford: Oxford University Press.

Custen, George F. (1992). *Bio/Pics: How Hollywood Constructed Public History*. New Brunswick: Rutgers University Press.

Custen, George F. (1997). *Twentieth Century's Fox: Darryl F. Zanuck and the Culture of Hollywood*. New York: Basic Books.

Delahanty, Thornton. (1936). "Warner Baxter and Others in a Rugged Historical Drama." *New York Post*, February 13.

Des Jardins, Julie. (2003). *Women and the Historical Enterprise in America*. Chapel Hill: University of North Carolina Press.

Dooley, Roger. (1981). *From Scarface to Scarlett: American Films of the 1930s*. New York: Harcourt Brace Jovanovich.

Douglas, Ann. (1988). *The Feminization of American Culture*. New York: Doubleday.

Editors of *Cahiers du Cinéma*. (1986). "John Ford's *Young Mr. Lincoln*." In Philip Rosen (ed.), *Narrative/Apparatus/Ideology* (pp. 444–482). New York: Columbia University Press.

Eldridge, David. (2006). *Hollywood's History Films*. London: I. B. Tauris.

Ellwood, David (ed.). (2000). *The Movies as History: Visions of the Twentieth Century*. Stroud: Sutton Publishing.

Elsaesser, Thomas. (1986). "Film History as Social History: The Dieterle/Warner Brothers Bio-Pic." *Wide Angle*, 8.2, 15–31.

Estabrook, Howard. (1930). Research Bibliography, *Cimarron*. Howard Estabrook Papers, Academy of Motion Picture Arts and Sciences Library, Beverly Hills, CA.

Ferro, Marc. (1988). *Film and History*. Detroit: Wayne State University Press.

Film Daily. (1940). New York: *The Film Daily*.

Film Daily. (1941). New York: *The Film Daily*.

Glancy Mark. (1999). *When Hollywood Loved Britain: The Hollywood "British" Film, 1939–45*. Manchester: Manchester University Press.

Gottesman, Ronald (ed.). (1996). *Perspectives on Citizen Kane*. New York: G. K. Hall.

Grindon, Leger. (1994). *Shadows on the Past: Studies in the Historical Fiction Film*. Philadelphia: Temple University Press.

Guynn, William. (2008). *Writing History in Film*. London: Routledge.

Hughes-Warrington, Marnie (ed.). (2009). *The History on Film Reader*. London: Routledge.

Isenberg, Michael T. (1981). *War on Film*. Rutherford: Fairleigh Dickinson University Press.

Joy, Jason. (1929). "Introducing – A Shopping Guide to the Movies." Los Angeles: MPPDA. Crawford Collection, Yale University.

Kibler, M. Alison. (1999). *Rank Ladies: Gender and Cultural Hierarchy in American Vaudeville*. Chapel Hill: University of North Carolina Press.

Kitses, Jim. (2004). *Horizons West*. Revised and updated. London: British Film Institute.

Knock, Thomas J. (1976). "'History with Lightning': The Forgotten Film *Wilson*." *American Quarterly*, 28.5 (Winter), 523–543.

Koppes, Clayton, & Black, Gregory. (2000). "Blacks, Loyalty, and Motion Picture Propaganda in World War II." In Matthew Bernstein (ed.), *Controlling Hollywood*. New Brunswick: Rutgers University Press.

Landy, Marcia. (1996). *Cinematic Uses of the Past*. Minneapolis: University of Minnesota Press.

Landy, Marcia (ed.). (2001). *The Historical Film: History and Memory in Media*. New Brunswick: Rutgers University Press.

Lynd, Robert, & Lynd, Helen. (1929). *Middletown*. New York: Harcourt Brace.

McCrisken, Trevor, & Pepper, Andrew. (2005). *American History and Contemporary Hollywood Film*. Edinburgh: Edinburgh University Press.

Maltby, Richard. (1993). "Grief in the Limelight: Al Capone, Howard Hughes, the Hays Code, and the Politics of the Unstable Text." In James Combs (ed.), *Movies and Politics* (pp. 133–181). New York: Garland.

Marie Antoinette. (1938). Press Book. MGM. Academy of Motion Picture Arts and Sciences Library, Beverly Hills, CA.

Marubbio, M. Elise. (2006). *Killing the Indian Maiden*. Lexington: University Press of Kentucky.

Munby, Jonathan. (1999). *Public Enemies/Public Heroes*. Chicago: University of Chicago Press.

Neale, Steven. (2000). *Hollywood and Genre*. London: Routledge.

Nevins, Allan. (1939). "What's the Matter with History?" *Saturday Review of Literature*, 19, February 4, 3–4, 16.

O'Connor, John E., & Jackson, Martin (eds). (1979). *American History/American Film: Interpreting the Hollywood Image*. New York: Ungar.

O'Connor, John E., & Rollins, Peter (eds). (2008). *Why We Fought: Hollywood's Wars in History and Film*. Lexington: University Press of Kentucky.

Palmer, A. W. (1993). "Cecil B. DeMille Writes America's History for the 1939 World's Fair." *Film History*, 5.1 (March), 36–48.

Parsons, Louella. (1946). "*Saratoga* a Woman's Film." *Los Angeles Examiner*, March 9.

Pauly, Thomas. (1974). "*Gone With the Wind* and *The Grapes of Wrath* as Hollywood Histories of the Great Depression." *Journal of Popular Film*, 3.3, 202–218.

Pearson, Roberta. (1998). "The Twelve Custers or Video History." In Edward Buscombe & Roberta Pearson (eds), *Back in the Saddle Again: New Essays on the Western* (pp. 197–213). London: British Film Institute.

Pearson, Roberta, & Urricchio, Williams. (1993). *Reframing Culture: The Case of the Vitagraph Quality Films*. Princeton: Princeton University Press.

Powdermaker, Hortense. (1950). *Hollywood – The Dream Factory*. Boston: Little, Brown.

Ray, Robert. (1985). *A Certain Tendency of the Hollywood Cinema*. Princeton: Princeton University Press.

Robinson, Casey. (1942). *Saratoga Trunk*. Final Script. September 30. Story files. Warner Bros. Archive, University of Southern California.

Robinson, Casey. (1943). *Saratoga Trunk*. Second Revised Final Script. February 23. Story files. Warner Bros. Archive, University of Southern California.

Rosenstone, Robert. (1995a). *Revisioning History: Film and the Construction of a New Past*. Princeton: Princeton University Press.

Rosenstone, Robert. (1995b). *Visions of the Past*. Cambridge, MA: Harvard University Press.

Rosenstone, Robert. (2004). "Inventing Historical Truth on the Silver Screen." *Cineaste*, 29.2, 29–33.

Schatz, Thomas. (1981). *Hollywood Genres*. New York: McGraw-Hill.

Schatz, Thomas. (1988). *The Genius of the System*. New York: Pantheon.

Schatz, Thomas. (1995). "A Triumph of Bitchery: Warner Bros., Bette Davis, and *Jezebel*." In Janet Staiger (ed.), *The Studio System* (pp. 74–92). New Brunswick: Rutgers University Press.

Schatz, Thomas. (1997). *Boom and Bust: American Cinema in the 1940s*. Los Angeles: University of California Press.

Schatz, Thomas. (2003). "*Stagecoach* and the Regeneration of the Hollywood Western." In Barry Keith Grant (ed.), *John Ford's Stagecoach*. Cambridge: Cambridge University Press.

Shindler, Colin. (1996). *Hollywood in Crisis: Cinema and American Society, 1929–1939*. London: Routledge.

Sklar, Robert. (1994). *Movie-Made America: A Cultural History of American Movies*. Revised and updated. New York: Random House.

Sklar, Robert. (1997). "Scofflaws and the Historical Cop." *Reviews in American History*, 25, 346–350.

Sklar, Robert, & Musser, Charles (eds). (1990). *Resisting Images*. Philadelphia: Temple University Press.

Smyth, J. E. (2004). "Revisioning Modern History in the Age of *Scarface*." *Historical Journal of Film, Radio and Television*, 24.4 (October), 535–563.

Smyth, J. E. (2006). *Reconstructing American Historical Cinema from Cimarron to Citizen Kane*. Lexington: University Press of Kentucky.

Smyth, J. E. (2008). "Hollywood's Filmic Writing of Interracial History, 1931–1939." In Mary Beltran & Camilla Fojas (eds), *Mixed Race Hollywood* (pp. 23–44). New York: New York University Press.

Smyth, J. E. (2009). *Edna Ferber's Hollywood: American Fictions of Gender, Race, and History*. Austin: University of Texas Press.

Smyth, J. E. (ed.). (2011). *Hollywood and the American Historical Film*. London: Palgrave Macmillan.

Stanfield, Peter. (2001). *The Lost Trail*. Exeter: University of Exeter Press.

Stempel, Tom. (1980). *Screenwriter: The Life and Times of Nunnally Johnson*. San Diego: A. S. Barnes.

Stempel, Tom. (2000). *Framework: A History of Screenwriting in the American Film*. Syracuse: Syracuse University Press.

Street, Sarah. (1996). "*Citizen Kane*." *History Today*, 46.3 (March), 48–52.

Strout, Cushing. (1958). *The Pragmatic Revolt*. New Haven: Yale University Press.

Susman, Warren. (1985). "Film and History: Artifact and Experience." *Film and History*, 26–36.

Toplin, Robert Brent. (1996). *History By Hollywood: The Use and Abuse of the American Past*. Urbana: University of Illinois Press.

Toplin, Robert Brent. (2002). *Reel History: In Defense of Hollywood*. Lawrence: University Press of Kansas.

Trumbo, Dalton. (1940a). *Kitty Foyle*. First Draft Continuity. June 1. Box S719, RKO Collection, UCLA Arts Special Collections.

Trumbo, Dalton. (1940b). *Kitty Foyle*. July 10. Box S719, RKO Collection, UCLA Arts Special Collections.

Trumbo, Dalton. (1940c). *Kitty Foyle*. Final Script. August 13. Box S719, RKO Collection, UCLA Arts Special Collections.

Vasey, Ruth. (1998). *The World According to Hollywood*. Madison: University of Wisconsin Press.

Warshow, Robert. (1962). *The Immediate Experience*. Garden City, NY: Doubleday.

Watts, Jill. (2000). *Mae West: An Icon in Black and White*. Oxford: Oxford University Press.

Wecter, Dixon. (1941). *The Hero in America: A Chronicle of Hero Worship*. New York: Charles Scribner's.

White, Hayden. (1988). "Historiography and Historiophoty." *American Historical Review*, 93.5 (December), 1193–1199.

Williams, Linda. (2001). *Playing the Race Card: Melodramas of Black and White from Uncle Tom to O.J. Simpson*. Princeton: Princeton University Press.

Wright, Will. (1975). *Six Guns and Society: A Structural Study of the Western*. Berkeley: University of California Press.

Zanuck, Darryl F. to Raymond Griffith. (1935). August 8. Twentieth Century-Fox Papers, Cinema-Television Library, University of Southern California.

Part III

1945–1960

23

Setting the Stage
American Film History, 1945–1960

In 1949, Nicholas Ray directed *In a Lonely Place* (1950), the second film produced by Santana, Humphrey Bogart's production company. Bogart plays Dixon Steele, a cynical Hollywood screenwriter at a desperate point in his career, whose romance with a beautiful neighbor, Laurel Grey (Gloria Grahame), restores not only his creativity but also his passion for life. *In a Lonely Place*, however, is not a story of revival but one of self-destruction. Wrongly accused of a murder but displaying the kind of wild mood swings and violent tendencies that make him a likely suspect, Steele frightens Laurel into mistrust. His paranoia and violence strangle their love just as Steele almost strangles Laurel in the closing scene. After a few weeks of intense love and work, the protagonist finds himself no better, and perhaps much worse, than he was before, still confined in a lonely place.

Ray's film makes an excellent starting place for a history of American film in the post–World War II period. Indeed, resonating to a remarkable degree through *In a Lonely Place* are some of the central issues that would define this era, even up to 1975. Like so many protagonists of the postwar cinema, Dix Steele finds his agency circumscribed by conditions beyond his control and his self-destructive impulses a powerful roadblock to his goals. From Chuck Tatum in *Ace in the Hole* (1951) to Eddie Felson in *The Hustler* (1963), from Joe Buck in *Midnight Cowboy* (1969) to Harry Caul in *The Conversation* (1974), Hollywood would redirect the optimism of the classical era through characters whose best-laid plans go tragically astray. And like Steele, so many of them would be centered on the returned veteran. Across genres, in films such as *Till the End of Time* (1946), *Crossfire* (1947), *Suddenly* (1954), *Five Against the House* (1955), *Blackboard Jungle* (1955), *The Phenix City Story* (1955), *The Searchers* (1956), *The Manchurian Candidate* (1963), *Cool Hand Luke* (1967), and *Taxi Driver* (1974), to name just a few throughout this period, American cinema would consider the problem of the returning veteran – whether from World War II, Korea, or Vietnam – and his reintegration into postwar life. *In a Lonely Place* would project the ambiguity of guilt and innocence, as well as the dark cynicism of film noir, and would end with the failure rather than the consummation of the romantic ideal that had been so firmly conventionalized in pre–World War II cinema. And in its portrayal of an unkind movie business, the fragile egos, box office sensibilities, and near contempt for the average moviegoer (after all, wide-eyed movie fan Mildred Atkinson [Martha Stewart] is mocked by Steele, then murdered shortly after), Ray's film would take its place within a cycle that offered a biting critique of the movie business – sharing

American Film History: Selected Readings, Origins to 1960, First Edition. Edited by Cynthia Lucia, Roy Grundmann, and Art Simon.
© 2016 John Wiley & Sons, Inc. Published 2016 by John Wiley & Sons, Inc.

ground with films like *Sunset Boulevard* (1950), *The Bad and The Beautiful* (1952), *The Star* (1952), *A Star is Born* (1954), *The Big Knife* (1955), and *Two Weeks in Another Town* (1962). This cycle of critically reflexive films was produced during, and perhaps made possible by, a period of profound reorganization and realignment within the Hollywood studios. Here, too, *In a Lonely Place* sharply exemplifies a movement toward independent production that resulted from significant shifts in the way Hollywood did business.

In stark contrast to the era of classical studio sound production, the 30 years after World War II were marked by profound instability as the movie industry was buffeted by the economic, demographic, and political changes of postwar society. It is difficult to prioritize these changes and their effects. Perhaps the most significant was the dramatic acceleration of a prewar trend, the flight of millions of Americans from city centers to the suburbs – a movement fueled by unprecedented postwar prosperity. The issue was not simply about the numbers of Americans who were fleeing to the suburbs, but, as significantly, about those who were doing so. While urban centers increased in population between 1940 and 1950, it was the loss of white-collar, middle-class residents that shifted general movie consumption away from the great first-run theater cities, as the Hollywood studios might have defined them. Having earned and saved during the war, Americans became consumers like never before, turning their long-pent-up buying desires toward expensive investments like houses and automobiles. The baby boom – and all that went with it in recreational terms – that would define the late 1940s and 1950s also directed disposable income in new ways. As a result, the movies that had served as a perfect pastime for Depression and wartime audiences suffered marked reductions at the box office. In just three years, total studio profits fell from an all-time high in 1946 of just under $120 million to $33.5 million in 1949 (Schatz 1999, 465). As a result, between 1947 and 1963 nearly one half of all four-wall (or non-drive-in) theaters closed (Maltby 2003, 163).

Just as many Americans were relocating away from urban movie screens, they were introduced to what would become the most transformative cultural force of the second half of the twentieth century and beyond – television. In 1947, when the decline in box office receipts began, there were approximately 14,000 television sets in America's homes. Just seven years later, there were 32 million and by 1960, 90 percent of homes had at least one television (Balio 1976, 315). The relationship between television and the movies would be complex. Television domesticated the moving image, fracturing the audience from large crowds into small units that could now watch movies or other programming while attending to activities at home. In response to the ease of television consumption, and its small, black-and-white image, the studios worked to remind audiences how big the movies could be. In the 1950s, several studios turned to various widescreen formats, most successfully CinemaScope, expanding the aspect ratio of the projected image. This format, adapted primarily to epics, Westerns, and some musicals, enhanced the cinematic spectacle, especially when wedded to the increased use of color. In 1949, when Eastman Kodak introduced a new, less expensive color film – one more amenable than Technicolor to standard movie cameras – the studios increased considerably their number of color productions. By 1953, roughly half of all features were made in color (Izod 1988, 138). While the revival of the biblical epic and other spectacle films set in ancient times, in their widescreen and colorful sweep, may have been relatively short-lived, they were immensely profitable. Advertising itself as the first movie on the "New Miracle Curved Screen," *The Robe* (1950), along with *The Ten Commandments* (1956) and *Ben-Hur* (1959), ranked among the top 10 moneymakers of the decade. It was not until the early 1960s that the disappointing returns of *The Fall of the Roman Empire* (1964) and the huge losses of the grotesquely expensive *Cleopatra* (1963) curbed Hollywood's enthusiasm for such super-productions.

Television and the Movies

But from the earliest days of television, as Michele Hilmes makes clear in Volume II of this series, and indeed from the earliest days of broadcast radio, Hollywood partnered with emerging mediums in search of mutually enhancing relationships, both artistic and commercial. Warner Bros. and Paramount purchased radio stations in the 1930s and almost all of the studios used radio either to promote films or locate talent. As television emerged, Paramount moved quickly to be involved, gaining ownership of four of the first nine stations in the country (Wasko 2003, 128). The

Supreme Court's ruling in the Paramount Case curtailed studio efforts to secure a greater stake in TV, but antitrust law could not stop the movie industry from establishing a deeply reciprocal relationship with the new medium. Television became a training ground for new big screen talent and a destination for its veterans. During the 1950s, television production relocated from New York to Hollywood, and over the course of the decade – as studios divorced themselves from theaters and the profitability of television production became clearer – the major studios became increasingly involved in producing shows for the small screen. By mid-decade, the studios recognized the potential profits sitting on their shelves in the form of old movies and began selling their pre-1948 films for exhibition on television. Selling their libraries to syndication companies or creating their own television distribution subsidiaries, the studios, starting with RKO in 1955, began providing many local stations with hundreds of hours of programming. But the broadcasting of feature motion pictures would not become a prime-time event until the 1960s. While the afternoon matinee movie and the "late show" were certainly staples for many TV viewers, when ABC broadcast *The Bridge on the River Kwai* in September of 1966 (the film had been released in 1957), an estimated 60 million viewers tuned in. Historians have rightly argued that the movies and television, far from being adversaries, operated as partners, eventually being folded together into even larger entertainment conglomerates. But it would be wrong to conclude that television's effect on the cinematic experience was totally benign. The exhibition of feature films on TV forever altered the reception, and perhaps even the meaning of movies. Although it downsized the screen, redefining the visual expectations of subsequent generations of moviewatchers, it greatly expanded the catalog of movies the average spectator could see, educating an entire generation of baby boomers, some of whom would go on to become noted filmmakers. Television also turned the art form, for many, from a communal to a private experience.

The Paramount Case and HUAC

Coinciding with these changes in the economics and demographics of movie consumption was a one-two punch to the film industry from the United States government. The first came from the judicial branch, the second from the legislative. The judicial blow came in May 1948, when the Supreme Court ruled in the decade-long antitrust suit that has come to be known as the Paramount Case. The court found the vertically integrated business structure of the five major studios and the trade practices that had long sustained their operation to be in violation of antitrust law. RKO and Paramount signed the earliest consent decrees, beginning a process whereby each company would divest itself of its theater holdings. Warners, Loew's, and Fox stalled their day of reckoning with various legal maneuvers, but by 1953, all had been forced to divorce production–distribution from exhibition. It was the end of an era and of the studio system as it had operated for more than a generation. Now a season's worth of production had to be sold on a film-by-film basis, and theaters were not locked into block booking. The profits that had been guaranteed by the old system were no longer assured, and the tremendous overhead costs of the studios had to be reduced. Short films were largely phased out, cartoons migrated to television, and B-films lost their spot at the lower half of the double bill, now becoming stand-alone features in the growing numbers of drive-in theaters and in second- and third-run houses. Indeed, whereas the Big Five had released 153 films in 1950, by 1956 – the last year of significant production for RKO before it closed – that figure had fallen to 116. And by 1960, the total number of films released by all the formerly integrated majors plus Columbia, Universal, and United Artists stood at 184 (Lev 2003, 303).

One result of theater divorcement was that studios devoted greater resources to fewer projects, banking on the profitability of prestige pictures in anticipation of a blockbuster strategy that would come to dominate the industry over the next decade. Another outcome was that independent production became an essential part of the business. Often incorporated for the making of a single picture, independent productions were frequently developed by the increasingly powerful talent agencies, capable of bringing together star, director, and screenwriter into a package. Still, such independence was predicated on obtaining a distribution deal. As Richard Maltby, among others, has suggested, in their capacity as major distributors, the studios remained key players in this arrangement, helping both with financing and with providing production facilities to artists now permitted to work under semi-autonomous terms (2003, 171).

In 1947, the House Un-American Activities Committee (HUAC), a Congressional Committee fueled by Cold War anticommunism, turned its campaign of political persecution on Hollywood. Nourished by its support from studio bosses and various high-profile friendly witnesses, HUAC sought to vilify left-wing and liberal artists in Hollywood, many of whom had taken part in either radical or progressive activities during the 1930s – the struggle against fascism, the formation of trade unions, membership in the American Communist Party, or the support of FDR's New Deal. The now famous Hollywood Ten – seven screenwriters, two directors, and one producer – defied the Committee by insisting on their First Amendment rights, constitutional guarantees which, they argued, protected them from the Committee's inquisition into their political and religious backgrounds, as well as its infringement on their freedom of artistic expression. All 10 (John Howard Lawson, Albert Maltz, Dalton Trumbo, Ring Lardner, Jr., Lester Cole, Herbert Biberman, Alvah Bessie, Adrian Scott, Edward Dmytryk, Samuel Ornitz) were cited for contempt of Congress, found guilty in 1948, and – after the failure of their appeals – served prison terms of between six months and one year.

On the same day as contempt citations were announced for the Ten, studio executives met at the Waldorf-Astoria Hotel in New York City to decide how to handle the brewing political imbroglio. The next day they issued what has come to be known as the "Waldorf Statement" – a full condemnation of the Ten and a pledge to "not knowingly employ a Communist or a member of any party or group which advocates the overthrow of the Government of the United States by force or by any illegal or unconstitutional means" (Cogley 1956, 22). The Statement concluded with the industry's assertion that no investigation could mar Hollywood's record with respect to its invaluable support of the government in peace and war. As the founding document for the notorious blacklist to follow, the Waldorf Statement carried a particularly cruel irony with respect to the Hollywood Ten, for several of the studio's most potent wartime films had been scripted by several of the very artists who were now summarily dismissed as un-American: *Destination Tokyo* (1943) and *Pride of the Marines* (1945), by Albert Maltz; *A Guy Named Joe* (1943) and *Thirty Seconds Over Tokyo* (1944), by Dalton Trumbo; *Objective, Burma!* (1945), by Lester Cole; and *Sahara* (1943) and *Action in the North Atlantic* (1943), by John Howard Lawson.

As Larry Ceplair has pointed out in the hardcover/online edition and elsewhere, red-baiting and blacklisting in Hollywood at this time were not confined to the high-profile cases of the Hollywood Ten. Former members of the Conference of Studio Unions – a group founded in 1941 that challenged the authority of the dominant and fiercely anticommunist International Alliance of Theatrical and Stage Employees (IATSE) – would be blacklisted by both IATSE and the studios in the early 1950s. HUAC returned to investigate Hollywood again in 1951 and left in its wake a decade-long blacklist far more sweeping than the Waldorf firing of 10 artists. A climate of fear, intimidation, and secrecy issued from HUAC's investigation, and the split between those who named names and those victimized by the witch hunt would remain a defining feature of the era. Many among Hollywood's talent, particularly screenwriters, sought to escape the witch hunt by migrating to Europe or New York, where they continued their work under various guises, including the use of so-called fronts.

The blacklist also generated *Salt of the Earth* (1954) – one of the most well-known independent films in American film history. Directed by Biberman after his release from prison, produced with the help of numerous blacklisted Hollywood professionals, and sponsored by the International Union of Mine, Mill, and Smelter Workers, *Salt of the Earth* tells the gripping story of a labor struggle between Mexican-American zinc miners and a mining company that attempts to crush their efforts to organize and fight for equal pay with Anglo workers. The film was aggressively boycotted by the industry and suffered a scattered initial release, but has long since become a classic.

Postwar Hollywood Genres and Auteurs

It is difficult to assess the impact of the blacklist and the Paramount decision on the content and quality of Hollywood films from the 1950s. The absence of Jules Dassin, Abraham Polonsky, Albert Maltz, and their comrades within the Hollywood Left created a silence that can never be measured. But the era's changing landscape of production and exhibition seems to compound the tragedy. Here were artists for whom the new conditions could have been exceedingly amenable. Had they been granted access to the mechanisms of 1950s independent production, free from political intimidation, the short-lived social problem film of the late 1940s – with its focus on racism (*Home of the Brave*, 1949; *Pinky*, 1949; *Intruder in the Dust*, 1949), anti-Semitism (*Crossfire*, 1947; *Gentleman's Agreement*, 1947), and the corrosiveness of capitalism (*Body and Soul*, 1947; *Force of Evil*, 1948) – might have been extended and sharpened through the decade. To be sure, the HUAC inquisition forced out many of the industry's most socially engaged artists, but the social problem film, as it has come to be known, still emerged in this period as an important subgenre of drama. Elia Kazan was perhaps its most skilled practitioner. The former left-winger and star director of the American stage turned HUAC sympathizer tackled racism in *Pinky*, anti-Semitism in *Gentleman's Agreement*, working-class struggles in *A Tree Grows in Brooklyn* (1945), and the power of celebrity in *A Face in the Crowd* (1957).

Whereas Hollywood invested in the social problem film, especially in the first five or six years after the war, production of the social documentary waned dramatically. Cold War anticommunism was largely to blame for this, as blacklisting and intimidation of activist artists deterred the production of critical films and forced many such artists into commercially sponsored nonfiction filmmaking. In addition to nontheatricals promoting some aspect of corporate activity – the auto industry, oil and chemical companies – nonfiction filmmakers devoted their energies to educational films sponsored by business and nonprofits. Religious and civic advocacy groups such as the National Conference of Christians and Jews, National Urban League, and the American Jewish Committee sponsored, and in some cases oversaw, the production of films promoting racial and religious tolerance, a subgenre known at the time as the human relations film.

These films were not totally shorn of political content, however. In *Brotherhood of Man*, a 1946 animated film produced by the UAW-CIO, with script contributions from Ring Lardner, Jr. and John Hubley, the commonalities of humanity and the imperative to peacefully coexist in the postwar world were promoted. In *Make Way for Youth* (1947), one of the most widely circulated social problem pictures produced beyond the walls of the studios, youth divided by race and religion channel their energies into civic participation and learn there is strength in tolerance. And in *A City Decides* (1956), Charles Guggenheim, with financing from The Fund for the Republic, depicted the integration of the St. Louis public schools. Unlike documentaries that focused on Great Depression struggles, the human relations documentary generally avoided radical rhetoric and form, often combining voiceover narration, nonprofessional actors, and fictionalized illustrations of real social problems. It would be wrong, therefore, to see the 1950s as a period in which committed filmmakers left the scene entirely. Left-leaning artists such as Ben Maddow, Willard Van Dyke, Leo Seltzer, Irving Lerner, and George Stoney continued to work, contributing to socially minded projects across genres throughout the decade. Beyond the human relations documentary are two noteworthy documentaries of the period – the Disney film *The Living Desert* (1953), which earned an Oscar for Best Documentary Feature and initiated a series of wildlife documentaries to follow, by both Disney and other sources, and *Jazz on a Summer's Day* (1960), a feature-length concert film about the 1958 Newport Jazz Festival, shot by up-and-coming advertising and society photographer Bert Stern in direct cinema style.

The 1950s also saw significantly increased activities in the areas of avant-garde cinema and independent film. In the late 1940s, San Francisco became the center of the postwar West Coast experimental scene that produced such notable filmmakers as Kenneth Anger, Curtis Harrington, Sidney Peterson, and James Broughton, all of whom made films with a notable queer sensibility. On the East Coast, Willard Maas, Marie Menken, and Stan Brakhage began to develop their own carefully wrought aesthetic languages. Both groups were united by Amos Vogel, whose "Cinema 16" screening series begun on the East Coast in the early 1950s exposed a weekly audience in the hundreds to the work of filmmakers from both locations. Vogel's series also showcased classics of European art cinema, as well as contemporary documentaries and independent films, such as John Cassavetes's *Shadows* (1959), Robert Frank and Alfred Leslie's *Pull My Daisy* (1959), and Ron Rice's *The*

Figure 23.1 In *The Lady from Shanghai* (1948, producer Columbia Pictures Corporation and Mercury Productions) Orson Welles fractures the film frame, capturing layers of deception as femme fatale Elsa Bannister (Rita Hayworth) confronts the confused Michael O'Hara (Welles).

Flower Thief (1960). The latter two films are expressions of the Beat sensibility, which emerged in the mid-1950s as an important literary movement, before being mainstreamed as a fashionable lifestyle and cannibalized by Hollywood. Jack Kerouac wrote the *Daisy* screenplay, adapted from his stage play *The Beat Generation*, while Rice set his film in San Francisco's North Beach area and featured Beat poets in supporting roles. In contrast to mainstream cinema, those independent films made in association with the Beat scene had a barebones, improvisational, and essayistic quality that blurred the boundary between fiction and documentary. This approach, as Ted Barron points out in the hardcover/online edition, would become highly influential in the 1960s, but was first exemplified by two late 1950s "docu-dramas," *The Savage Eye* (1959), co-directed by Sidney Meyers, Joseph Strick, and Ben Maddow, and *On the Bowery* (1958), directed by Lionel Rogosin. Both films deploy fictional stories to expose the poverty and despair at the margins of postwar American society. The brittleness of the American Dream was most crushingly exposed, however, in Kent MacKenzie's 1961 drama, *The Exiles*, which follows the lives of Native Americans who escape their stunted existence on the reservation and move to Los Angeles' Bunker Hill district, where they exist as a subculture barely noticed by an uncaring, sometimes hostile society.

If several genres of the 1950s hinted at social and political uneasiness just beyond the façade of a homogeneous era of good feeling, perhaps none did so with the consistency of film noir – a cycle often dated from 1944 with *Double Indemnity* (although its literary antecedents emerged in the previous decade) to 1958 with *Touch of Evil*. As precursors to the social problem film, films noir only ambiguously expressed anxiety with the social fabric, rarely naming the "problems" or imagining solutions. But as a body of work, noir offered up a rather despairing portrait of urban life and a population suffering from an acute set of symptoms – alienation, guilt, and fatalism. Many noir films center on a protagonist who is drawn into some unseemly situation, compelled to cross a moral boundary into a criminal or darkly marginal world from which he cannot escape. Whether it is Walter Neff in *Double Indemnity*, The Swede in *The Killers* (1948), or Michael O'Hara in *The Lady from Shanghai* (1948), the men of noir get caught up in webs of deceit and criminality that either kill them or leave permanent scars. As Christine Noll Brinckmann discusses in her essay on *Force of Evil* (1948) in this volume, noir would expose the corrupting core of capitalism and, in this case, its devastating effect on two brothers. The femmes fatales of these films are seductive figures whose desire for men or for money often threatens the very stability of male identity and agency. These figures registered anxiety not only about the growing independence of women in the postwar era, but also about difficulties faced by returning veterans negotiating an uneasy reintegration into family and the workforce. As Paul Arthur argues in the hardcover/online edition, a series of films noir express the anxieties of white-collar, mid-level workers caught in the mundane, hierarchical corporate structure. But noir was more a state of being than a set of plot points and that state was tied directly to nocturnal urban life – its dark alleyways, its lounges and bars, its fleabag apartments and hotel rooms. Through its chiaroscuro lighting, canted angles, and claustrophobic spaces, film noir made clear the dark romanticism of a hard-boiled resistance to the emerging demographic of suburban sprawl and its happy families represented on television. The denizens of noir are damaged figures at the margins of society, desperate for an end to loneliness and tempted to chase after one last score.

Fritz Lang continued to work in a variety of genres during this period – among them the war film (*American Guerrilla in the Philippines*, 1950), the Western (*Rancho Notorious*, 1952), the adventure-thriller (*Cloak and Dagger*, 1946), notably written by Albert Maltz and Ring Lardner, Jr., who later would be blacklisted. By far, however, Lang is most recognized for his many contributions to the film noir cycle: *The Woman in the Window* (1944), *Scarlet Street* (1945), *Secret Beyond the Door* (1947), *House by the River* (1950), *Clash by Night* (1952), *The Blue Gardenia* (1953), *The Big Heat* (1953), *Human Desire* (1954), *While the City Sleeps* (1956), and *Beyond a Reasonable Doubt* (1956). Noiresque themes in these films – the ambiguous line between guilt and innocence, characters wrongly accused of crimes, driven or nearly driven to criminality as a result, corrupt or potentially corruptible institutions, including the police and the media – and the films' murky urban landscapes with spaces that variously entrap or dwarf confused, lost characters, all become extensions of Lang's thematic concerns and visual style in his earlier work, grounded in German Expressionism. In *Secret Beyond the Door*, starring Joan Bennett, Lang creates a modern version of the Bluebeard tale, with its woman-in-peril theme infusing the film with elements of the female Gothic. Two other notable collaborations with Joan Bennett and Edward G. Robinson – *The Woman in the Window* and *Scarlet Street* – explore tropes of impaired masculinity and the femme fatale so common to the noir cycle. In both films Robinson plays a weak man, in the throes of mid-life crisis, drawn to the younger, beautiful Bennett onto whom he projects his fantasies and desires, blind to her duplicitous nature – in the former it all turns out to be nothing but a bad dream, but in the latter it is all too real, with the defeated, dissipated Robinson wandering the streets aimlessly at film's end.

Perhaps the most disturbing of Lang's films noir is *The Big Heat*, his first of two collaborations with actors Glenn Ford and Gloria Grahame (followed by *Human Desire* in 1954, one of the few films of the period to reference the Korean War). In *The Big Heat* Ford plays Dave Bannion, a forthright cop and family man with a loving wife and daughter. As he investigates the death of a fellow officer, he encounters intractable obstructions to justice in the form of a corrupt police commissioner and a mob boss who owns the commissioner and the entire department. After Bannion's wife is killed by a car bomb meant for him, he leaves the department in order to conduct his own investigation, leading him into a morass of criminality that threatens to destroy and discredit him as he obsessively seeks revenge. It is only through the sympathetic bond he gradually develops with mobster Vince Stone's girlfriend (Grahame), after Stone (Lee Marvin) sadistically disfigures her, that Bannion comes to his senses. Through the help of a newly reformed police lieutenant, Bannion defeats the mob and exposes corruption without crossing the line. Although seemingly a positive, if not joyful, ending, when Bannion returns to his desk in the police department, Lang's stark mise-en-scène is a haunting reminder of irretrievable loss, emotional isolation, and the fragility of individual integrity. This somber skepticism informs much of Lang's film noir work.

Other notable émigré directors from Germany and Austria who shaped film noir in Hollywood were Robert Siodmak, Edgar G. Ulmer, and Max Ophuls, the latter having made several films merging film noir with the woman's film. Ophuls's last American film, *The Reckless Moment* (1949), about a housewife who covers up a killing, exposes yet another feature of film noir – not only can the genre be seen as an antidote to post–World War II optimism, but some films specifically attack this optimism as rooted in the American suburbs, as Roy Grundmann points out in this volume. Accomplished American-born filmmaker Robert Aldrich, who worked in a variety of genres including the Western and the melodrama, directed the highly unconventional *Kiss Me Deadly* (1955), a film noir adaptation of Mickey Spillane's detective novel. The film's treatment of noir conventions, in some scenes bordering on parody, often is regarded as a self-conscious statement signaling a cycle that not only had reached maturity but also was entering its final phase. Sam Fuller, Joseph H. Lewis, and Phil Karlson – 1950s Hollywood independents – produced work that would cut across multiple genres, including the gangster and war films, occasionally adopting a noirish atmosphere, as Haden Guest points out in the hardcover/online edition.

In his 1946 Western *My Darling Clementine*, about the legendary gunfight at the O.K. Corral between Marshal Wyatt Earp and the Clanton family outlaws, John Ford arranges all elements of his Western mythology in near-classical balance. *Clementine*'s juxtaposition of wilderness vs. civilization is thematically richer and far less racist than Ford's earlier, already celebrated *Stagecoach* (1939). At the same time, the film remains more positive about the settlement of the West than Ford's later, much darker, Westerns. The film's classical genre structure is matched by a carefully calibrated mise-en-scène that combines the hallmarks of realism (including long takes, long shots, and deep focus) with crisp, high-contrast cinematography that, particularly in scenes involving Doc Holliday, evince a noirish quality. In his earlier adaptation of John Steinbeck's *The Grapes of Wrath* (1940), Ford, along with cinematographer Gregg Toland, strongly anticipates the chiaroscuro aesthetics of film noir in several scenes, sometimes with the light source limited to one or two flickering candles.

Rarely shown but often indirectly referenced in film noir, the suburban home of the future, to which many Americans fled after the war, would be stocked with the consumer goods of a new technological frontier. Hollywood matched that with representations of another frontier, one with its own new threats, heroes, and mechanized accouterments. While science fiction tended to be a B-production genre, it nonetheless reflected an era of postwar prosperity through its fascination with the technological imagination. Historians have stressed the connection between 1950s science fiction and Cold War fears of the atomic age and the threat of communism. These fears took the form of invading aliens and creatures transformed by radiation and can be found in such films as *The Day the Earth Stood Still* (1951), *Invasion of the Body Snatchers* (1956), and *Them!* (1954). In contrast to earlier sci-fi cycles, the genre's postwar representation of other worlds more technologically advanced than our own also reflected the period's economy of consumption. Although sci-fi as a genre did not migrate to television until the 1960s, the television set, itself, is surely the most potent symbol of this phenomenon. The wonder of new machines and gadgets was central to advertising during this era in marketing automobiles, washers, vacuum cleaners, and the entire catalog of products now available to the postwar consumer. While technology produced miracles of convenience in the domestic space of the home, it posed unimaginable threats in sci-fi on the big screen.

Inscriptions of television in various film genres suggested that the small screen could be a degrading force if not a sinister presence. Billy Wilder treats this with some humor in *The Apartment* (1960) as C. C. Baxter (Jack Lemmon) enthusiastically awaits the broadcast of *Grand Hotel*, only to be frustrated by commercial interruptions. *A Face in the Crowd* and *Ace in the Hole* (1951), among other Hollywood films of the period, elevate the cinema by casting television, not as an artistic medium, but as a tool for the seduction of gullible masses. But the small screen makes perhaps its most disheartening appearance in Douglas Sirk's *All That Heaven Allows* (1955). Here, the children of an affluent widow see a TV set as an appropriate gift for their mother whose empty days will be filled and whose libido will be quelled by the parade of images beaming through her living room. The domestic melodrama, a genre that has fascinated film scholars for decades, was frequently built around a mise-en-scène of bold primary colors and elaborate decor that masked the repressed emotions lurking beneath bourgeois respectability. The melodrama also often pivoted around weak or absent fathers or children whose search for independence ignited a clash of generations. Sirk was the master of the form and in this film, as in *Magnificent Obsession* (1954), *Written on the Wind* (1956), and *Imitation of Life* (1959), he channeled the genre's overheated emotions – desire, jealousy, and insecurity – into a subtle yet nonetheless searing critique of middle-class America at mid-century. Sirk's stylized interiors, enhanced in five of his films by Russell Metty's cinematography, feature deep shadows and reflections from mirrors and screens. *There's Always Tomorrow* (1956) and *The Tarnished Angels* (1957) demonstrate that he was just as adept at working in black-and-white.

The melodrama was also central to the work of Nicholas Ray and Vincente Minnelli. Ray's *Bigger Than Life* (1956) projected the crisis of patriarchy through a cortisone-addicted father played by James Mason. But it was Ray's *Rebel Without a Cause* (1955) that depicted the quintessential weak father (Jim Backus) who is unable to give his troubled son (James Dean) the strong role model he desperately craves. Minnelli's melodramas – *The Bad and the Beautiful* (1952), *The Cobweb* (1955), and *Two Weeks in Another Town* (1962) – on the other hand, were decidedly centered on adults. In *Some Came Running* (1959), Minnelli told the story of Dave Hirsh (Frank Sinatra), a veteran who finds himself back in his Midwestern hometown torn between two postwar paths – the well-mannered literary life with the middle-class Gwen (Martha Hyer) or the ill-mannered gambling life with the working-class Ginnie (Shirley MacLaine). Each choice both attracts and repulses him. *Some Came Running* projected anything but a postwar optimism with its small-town life marked by the social artifice and familial hypocrisy of Dave's brother Frank (Arthur Kennedy). Much more attractive is Bama (Dean Martin), a local gambler, whose lack of middle-class pretense makes him a suitable companion to Dave's brutal honesty. Caught between these worlds, Dave's decision is made for him when fate takes over in the form of Ginnie's jealous suitor. Aiming for Dave, he fatally shoots Ginnie, killing the most innocent among them. Minnelli's film expresses directly what many films in the genre implied, that the melodrama was about much more than tears, that the Oedipal excesses and unhappy marriages mobilized a critique of 1950s America and its most cherished ideal – the stable acquisitive family.

While the melodrama and film noir raised doubts about the ideological stability of the postwar years, one of Hollywood's most enduring genres, the musical, largely maintained its affirmative posture. Problems could still be resolved through song and dance, even though plenty of scores made room for sadness. During the 1950s, the genre followed three distinct paths. The first is distinguished by some of the finest pieces of entertainment made by the industry, vehicles that were unit produced, such as those overseen by Arthur Freed at MGM, that integrated song, dance, and story featuring stars nurtured and often solely identified with the movie musical. *An American in Paris* (1951), *Singin' in the Rain* (1952), *Royal Wedding* (1951), and *The Band Wagon* (1953), to name just a few, enjoyed robust budgets and box office-tested talent in Gene Kelly and Fred Astaire. The second trajectory of the genre was propelled by a significant number of Broadway adaptations often featuring talent better known for their stage work. *Oklahoma!* (1955), *The King and I* (1956), *Carousel* (1956), *Damn Yankees!* (1958), and *South Pacific* (1958) had been tremendous hits on stage and their widescreen treatment allowed moviegoers across the country to see what New York theatergoers had been raving about. While the Broadway adaptation would survive the end of the 1950s in *My Fair Lady* (1964), *West Side Story* (1961), and later *Oliver!* (1968) and *Fiddler on the Roof* (1971), as Karen Backstein argues in Volume II, the musical waned toward the end of the 1960s as the studio system waned. Its finest talent aged, its production infrastructure underwent a major transition, and, perhaps just as importantly, the nation's musical tastes shifted.

This shift in tastes points toward the third path for the musical, one carried largely on the shoulders (hips and voice) of Elvis Presley, whose film career began in the 1950s but who became far more prolific in the 1960s. Like Bing Crosby and Frank Sinatra before him, Presley came to the movies via the recording industry, but his national celebrity had been solidified through the power of television, especially after two

Figure 23.2 Sheriff John T. Chance (John Wayne) in the jailhouse with his loyal deputies Dude (Dean Martin) and Stumpy (Walter Brennan) in *Rio Bravo* (1959, director and producer Howard Hawks).

appearances on Milton Berle's show in 1956. That same year he signed a contract with Paramount and, remarkably, between 1956 (*Love Me Tender*) and 1969 (*Change of Habit*), he starred in 31 films. While the majority of Presley's film career belongs to the 1960s, his work in the 1950s started the process by which the cinema softened Presley's image, muting his sexual charge and, in many films, turning him into a non-threatening orphan in search of love and maybe even family.

In the postwar period the Western – for decades a foundational genre for Hollywood – underwent a critical reassessment. With the heroic cowboy an emerging fixture on television, his big-screen counterpart began to show his age as an increasing number of films worked to scratch the luster off his legend. In *The Gunfighter* (1950) Jimmy Ringo (Gregory Peck) finds himself trapped by his own myth as fastest gun. Having returned to the town of Cayenne to see his son and former lover in the hopes of starting life over, he becomes the target and eventually the victim of a new generation of Westerners looking to make their own reputations. In several key films of the period, the West becomes a space of last stands and in films such as *The Gunfighter*, *High Noon* (1952), and *Rio Bravo* (1959), the plot stresses the hero's stasis rather than mobility. Many 1950s Westerns offer a stage for a generation of figures headed toward retirement in one form or another. In *The Searchers* (1956), certainly among the most celebrated of postwar Westerns, Ethan Edwards (John Wayne) succeeds in freeing his niece Debbie from Indian captivity, but there is no place for him within home and family at film's end. At the end of *High Noon*, Will Kane (Gary Cooper) dispatches the Miller gang, only to quit his job as marshal and leave the town that refused to help him.

Ford's *She Wore a Yellow Ribbon* (1949) centers precisely on the issue of retirement with the story of Captain Nathan Brittles's (John Wayne) last days with the US cavalry.

But whereas *The Gunfighter* and *Rio Bravo* confine their heroes to just one town and very few locations within it, thereby eliminating shots of the majestic landscape, Ford's Westerns retained the desert Southwest as the sublime attraction of the genre. Whether in the painted buttes and skies of *She Wore a Yellow Ribbon*, the black-and-white outcroppings of *Wagon Master* (1950), or the long-shot vistas of Budd Boetticher's films, including *Seven Men from Now* (1956), *The Tall T* (1957), or *Ride Lonesome* (1959), the West as rugged and beautiful open space remained essential to the theatrical form of the genre in a way not available to its television kin. To this, the genre added a dimension of psychological complexity, as core issues such as violence, masculinity, and race could no longer be treated unproblematically. This tendency began, perhaps, during the wartime period with *The Ox-Bow Incident* (1943), in which mob justice, fueled by explicit references to upholding manhood, leads to the hanging of three innocent men. In the films of Anthony Mann, overland treks are frequently accompanied by the Westerner's emotional journey. In five of his films Mann cast James Stewart, the classical-era star most associated with psychological struggle during the 1950s, a persona sharpened through the actor's work with Alfred Hitchcock.

Howard Hawks continued to work across genres during this period, returning to the Western in the postwar era with the visually stunning *Red River* (1948). Foregrounding the homosocial and Oedipal aspects of the genre as films of the period began to do, *Red River* helped initiate the cycle of revisionist Westerns to follow, in which themes of generational conflict and frontier violence would take on a newly critical dimension. Its most breathtaking sequence hinges on a series of shots from slightly odd low angles (typical of Westerns when shooting men on horseback but here somewhat off-kilter) and tight close-ups, heightening the sense of tension and anticipation as cattle drivers prepare to begin a dangerous journey from Texas to Kansas with their herd. Rapid-fire editing, typical of Hawks's screwball comedies, especially, makes palpable the pressure of the moment. Hawks's earlier adventure-romance *To Have and Have Not* (1944), in which he cast cover girl Lauren Bacall in her first movie role, initiated her admirable movie career and ignited her legendary romance with co-star Humphrey Bogart. The two would go on to co-star in Hawks's film noir *The Big Sleep* (1946), in which the director – somewhat against the noir mode – would place much of the dialogue-centered action in the domestic space of an ornate home, evoking a steamy claustrophobia in its greenhouse sitting room. That Bacall's androgynous appearance appealed to Hawks is an expression of a distinct theme in his oeuvre, as earlier noted: his creation of masculine codes of honor, friendship, and professionalism in male-centered narratives.

Returning successfully to comedy, after having been so influential in the screwball tradition of the 1930s and 1940s, Hawks directed *I Was a Male War Bride* (1949), *Monkey Business* (1952), and the musical comedy *Gentlemen Prefer Blondes* (1953), two of which playfully invert gender boundaries and roles. In *War Bride* Cary Grant appears in drag, echoing his famous fur-trimmed satin robe scene in Hawks's *Bringing up Baby* (1938). In *Gentlemen Prefer Blondes* the two female leads, played by Marilyn Monroe and Jane Russell, manipulate the strings of power, with men depicted as not very bright and sexually objectified in a manner usually reserved for women in films of the period. As Russell sings "Ain't There Anyone Here for Love," she strolls, playfully twirling her tennis racket, through rows of male Olympic swimming team members, dressed in skin tight, flesh-colored trunks, who train at poolside, touching their toes, with their asses in the air. And even though the movie ends with a double wedding, in the final frame only the two women appear, implying that the true marriage, the genuine bond, exists between them – with husbands literally placed to the side.

The most honored musical composer of the studio era, at least by industry standards, was Alfred Newman. Nominated for 45 Oscars and awarded nine over a career in the movies that spanned four decades, Newman left his imprint, as either conductor or composer, on over 200 films. Arriving in Hollywood at the age of 29, having already worked with the biggest names on Broadway including Irving Berlin and Richard Rogers, Newman conducted or scored films for the Goldwyn Studio, Paramount, and RKO before spending 20 years at Twentieth Century-Fox.

Figure 23.3 Alfred Hitchcock's *Vertigo*'s love scene (1958, producers Herbert Coleman and Alfred Hitchcock) appears artificial and overwrought – precisely because it is. Scottie (James Stewart) is enthralled with an illusion – a woman (Kim Novak) sculpted precisely to arouse his fetishistic desires.

Remarkable for his versatility, he composed music for such varied films as *Wuthering Heights* (1939), *Gentleman's Agreement* (1947), and *How to Marry a Millionaire* (1953). He brought tense rhythms to film noir in *Cry of the City* (1948) and a sweeping, monumental score to *How the West Was Won* (1962). He was perhaps just as gifted as an adapter and conductor and in these roles brought life to compositions by virtually every major figure in musical theater and film. He also composed the dramatic fanfare that accompanies the searchlights over the Twentieth Century-Fox logo at the beginning of every film from that studio.

Hollywood Realism and a New Method of Acting

If postwar cinema is characterized by a new accent on realism, be it the working-class stories of *Marty* (1955) and *The Catered Affair* (1956) or the on-the-streets cinematography of *The Naked City* (1948) and *The Sweet Smell of Success* (1957), it also can be defined by the pursuit of psychological realism. For many in Hollywood this meant a new direction in acting. A generation of Method actors emerged, many of whom trained at the Actors Studio. As the widespread publicity around the Method insisted, acting required work and could be refined in a laboratory environment in which actors took risks in experimenting with their craft. This was a far cry from an earlier era in which acting talent was taken as a natural gift, an ineffable quality of the star, as Cynthia Baron and Beckett Warren point out in this volume. Those trained in the Method were understood to achieve a new level of authenticity, primarily by creating, rather than just "acting," the emotions or thought processes of a character. James Dean brought the Method to the melodrama, and his teaming with Natalie Wood in *Rebel Without a Cause* juxtaposed the era's two divergent approaches to acting. As Cynthia Lucia discusses in this volume, Wood had literally grown up in the movies and would be, arguably, the last studio-made star. Dean's career would come to a tragic early end but his generation of Method performers, including Marlon Brando, Rod Steiger, Eva Marie Saint, Montgomery Clift, and Karl Malden, would offer some of the most emotionally penetrating performances of the decade. As filmmakers left the studios in search of authentic locales – as many did during the 1950s – the Method appeared an appropriate companion to this search for realism.

But no one explored the darker realities of the human psyche more entertainingly than Alfred Hitchcock. Hitchcock's career is distinguished by the remarkable compatibility he found between studio resources – the support of producer David O. Selznick; stars like Cary Grant, Grace Kelly, and James Stewart; the cinematography of Robert Burks; the musical scores of Bernard Herrmann – and personal obsessions with criminal psychology, repressed sexual desire, and voyeurism. For Hitchcock, suspense mattered more than violence, arousal more than consummation, blondes more than brunettes. At the same time as he appeared to fetishize the blonde, however, he also, to some degree, exposed the patriarchal traditions and male-centered attitudes behind such fetishization – no more powerfully than in *Rear Window* (1954), *Vertigo* (1958), *The Birds* (1963), and *Marnie* (1964). And since his subject was the psychological realm, his visual style was permitted gestures that were unconventional – the Salvador Dali-designed dream sequence in *Spellbound* (1945), Scottie's pulsating animated nightmare in *Vertigo*, and the shower murder montage in *Psycho* (1960). Even beyond these tour de force moments, Hitchcock's canted angles, reflective surfaces, and narratives that only superficially appear to provide closure can be understood simultaneously as apt renderings of his characters' psychological dilemmas and his own personal artistic flourishes and thematic obsessions.

Hitchcock's artistic achievements made a particularly strong impact on a generation of young European filmgoers, the now famous cineastes who took up film criticism in France and England during the 1950s and who would go on to become the leading forces behind the various New Waves of postwar European cinema. In the pages of the *Cahiers du Cinéma*, Hitchcock, John Ford, Howard Hawks, Nicholas Ray, Fritz Lang, Orson Welles, and Vincente Minnelli, to name perhaps the top tier, would be enshrined in the canon of American directors, those deserving of the title "auteur." When they turned to making their own films, of course, the New Wave directors hardly created a cinema in the tradition of these Hollywood masters. But the films they did create, and the international community of cinephiles that emerged at this time, had a profound impact on the American film scene, fueling, by the late 1960s, what some deemed a renaissance.

The Studio Era in Transition

Like every period in film history, the one running from the end of the studio era to the rise of the so-called New Hollywood in the late 1960s is marked by contradictions. If box office popularity were the sole index, the 1950s would appear as conservative as the conventional myth that for too long has characterized the Eisenhower years. Of the top 10 moneymakers of the decade, four were Disney features, three were biblical epics, one was an adaptation of a Broadway musical, and two were widescreen extravaganzas. In fact, Disney would place three films in the top 10 during the 1960s as well.

But to focus on box office figures is only to overlook Hollywood's response to the significant shifts in temper and morality taking place during the 1950s. Sexuality, as public social science and subject of mass culture, informed the 1950s unlike in any previous decade, and the movies would eventually lead, after initially following, the slow revolution in American morals. While John Wayne, Doris Day, and Rock Hudson were among the era's most popular and well-paid stars, the appeal of Marilyn Monroe, Marlon Brando, Kim Novak, and James Dean pointed toward a cinematic body that rested on the erotic and not merely the romantic. Indeed, it was the 1950s that witnessed the erosion of the once firm Production Code. Part of the pressure came from the importation of foreign films. Responding to the shrinking number of studio releases, many urban theaters began to exhibit the work of a revived European postwar film industry and many of these films presented themes of sexuality and politics with a maturity, indeed a frankness, not found in their American counterparts.

But the studios themselves had begun to chafe under the restrictions of the Code well before Otto Preminger's *The Moon is Blue* (1953) and *The Man with the Golden Arm* (1955) were released without a PCA seal of approval. In a 1947 memo, producer Jerry Wald expressed his frustration to Steven Trilling, Jack Warner's executive assistant, over the PCA's objections to the script for *Key Largo* (1948): "The Breen office today goes by a production code that was written in 1930. Many important events have taken place since the code was written. Is it possible that the code is dated? Certainly a re-examination is due" (Behlmer 1985, 293). Nine years after Wald's memo, the Motion Picture Association of America (MPAA) announced it was revising the Code, liberalizing its restrictions on the representation of abortion and drug abuse and dropping any mention of the representation of miscegenation (Lev 2003, 93). It would only be a half dozen more years before the Code would become obsolete. It is worth recalling that industry self-regulation had originally been established to preempt state and local censorship boards. But in 1952, the Supreme Court handed down a ruling in a case involving Roberto Rossellini's short film *The Miracle* (1948), about a young woman who claimed to have been made pregnant by St. Joseph. Banned by the New York State Board of Regents, *The Miracle* was returned to exhibition after the high court reversed its findings in the 1915 Mutual case and declared that movies were now protected by the First Amendment's guarantee of free speech. While this by no means ended the debate over film and obscenity, it did make local censorship of the movies much more difficult.

As the movie industry adapted itself to a new social environment and also to the business changes wrought by the Paramount Case and the waning of the Code, it entered what Robert Sklar has called "a new era of seriousness and responsibility" (Sklar 1994, 280). This is not to suggest that it abandoned its pursuit of light entertainment. The immensely popular team of Dean Martin and Jerry Lewis in the 1950s extended the lineage of male comedy teams in the late 1920s and 1930s, such as Stan Laurel and Oliver Hardy, and in the 1940s of Bud Abbott and Lou Costello, and Bob Hope and Bing Crosby. But the change to independent production, the maturing of studio-era directors, and the cinema's new role within mass culture once television had established itself, produced a shift in genre sensibility. Whereas the accent had earlier been on subtle variations within the successful formulas of the musical, Western, and melodrama, even directors such as Howard Hawks, John Ford, and Vincente Minnelli now placed more emphasis on character and a self-conscious attention to convention.

The shift being suggested here was by no means across the board and in some cases involved only subtle changes in approach. But as the studio era began to wane, several of its most accomplished directors struck an elegiac tone. In Hawks's *Rio Bravo*, for example, the violent West has largely been eclipsed by a study in camaraderie, the emotional rehabilitation of Dude (Dean Martin), and his competition with Colorado (Ricky Nelson) as right-hand man to Sheriff John Chance (John Wayne). In Hitchcock's *Vertigo*, high-pitched suspense gives way to a temporality that slowly reveals Scottie's complicated fixations and desire. Ford's *The Searchers*, punctuated by moments of traditional violence, distills the genre down to traversing the desert landscape in winter and summer, developing the complex relationship between Ethan Edwards and Martin Pauley and ultimately exposing Ethan's profound alienation from the world around him. Minnelli's *The Band Wagon* is most explicit in this regard as it acknowledges a new era in which no one bids on the famous top hat and cane once used by faded star Tony Hunter (Fred Astaire), as Gilberto Perez observes in the hardcover/online edition. The film centers precisely on the anxiety of age and whether Tony can be paired with a younger woman and return to the stage after the decline of his Hollywood career. In the final years of the studio era, some of its most important artists took an accounting. Close-ups of stars now displayed faces etched with the lines of age. Stories played out in the shadows of mortality. *The Searchers*, *Sunset Boulevard* (1950), *Limelight* (1952), *The Man Who Shot Liberty Valance* (1962), *Vertigo*, *Touch of Evil*, *Clash by Night* (1952), *High Noon*, and *Ride the High Country* (1962) all featured actors who had begun their careers at the beginning of the sound era, if not earlier, in films that now pivoted around aging, a sense of loss, and isolation.

The End of the Classical Era

In 1960, as the classical era was drawing to a close, the Motion Picture Academy honored as the best picture of the year Billy Wilder's *The Apartment*. It now reads as a fascinating transitional work, one that points both back to the studio era and forward to a new American cinema. Wilder had been working in Hollywood since the mid-1930s and had come of age in that golden season of 1939–1940 with the screenplay for *Ninotchka*. The story construction and studio sets for *The Apartment*, especially the monumental office of Consolidated Life, draw on the best traditions of

Hollywood's heyday. Independently produced by the Mirisch Company, the film was part of a trend that had emerged in the 1950s and that would become a central feature of film production in the United States in the 1960s and beyond. It starred one actor (Fred MacMurray) whose career dated back to the mid-1930s, and two (Jack Lemmon and Shirley MacLaine) who would become major players for the next several decades.

But the story of *The Apartment* looked forward, as Robert Sklar argues in this volume, with subject matter unacceptable to the decaying Production Code and a complex emotional tone that would be found in many films of the later New Hollywood. Nice guy C. C. Baxter lends the eponymous apartment to his corporate superiors and in the process moves up the occupational ladder. But when he learns that personnel director Jeff Sheldrake (MacMurray) is using his place for trysts with Fran Kubelik (MacLaine), the woman Baxter has come to adore, the schlemiel becomes a mensch and closes the door on both his boss and his job at Consolidated. Baxter is no budding 1960s revolutionary, but he reclaims his integrity by turning his back on the corporate elevator. Like so many of the New Hollywood heroes to come, Baxter, at film's end, is ready to hit the road, either to a new city or, at least, a new apartment. In a nod to the traditional happy ending perhaps, Baxter wins the girl for his actions, but not before the film has dealt in a serious way with adultery and suicide, integrated with scenes of light comedy. In exposing sexism and hypocrisy within the workplace, and giving agency to Fran Kubelik to abandon the heel and reach for someone better, the film anticipated feminist impulses in later films. The studio era was drawing to an end, but American film would, in less than a generation, be informed by a renaissance, and inhabit, however briefly, yet another golden age.

References

Balio, Tino (ed.). (1976). *The American Film Industry*. Madison: University of Wisconsin Press.

Behlmer, Rudy. (1985). *Inside Warner Bros*. New York: Viking.

Cogley, John. (1956). *Report on Blacklisting: I Movies*. New York: The Fund for the Republic.

Izod, John. (1988). *Hollywood and the Box Office: 1895–1986*. New York: Columbia University Press.

Lev, Peter. (2003). *The Fifties: Transforming the Screen 1950–1959*. Berkeley: University of California Press.

Maltby, Richard. (2003). *Hollywood Cinema*. 2nd edn. Oxford: Blackwell Publishing.

Schatz, Thomas. (1999). *Boom and Bust: American Cinema in the 1940s*. Berkeley: University of California Press. (Original work published 1997.)

Sklar, Robert. (1994). *Movie-Made America: A Cultural History of American Movies*. Revised and updated. New York: Vintage Books.

Wasko, Janet. (2003). "Hollywood and Television in the 1950s: The Roots of Diversification." In Peter Lev (ed.), *The Fifties: Transforming the Screen 1950–1959* (pp. 127–146). Berkeley: University of California Press.

24

Taking Stock at War's End

Gender, Genre, and Hollywood Labor in *The Strange Love of Martha Ivers*

Roy Grundmann
Associate Professor, Boston University, United States

Appearing in 1946, *The Strange Love of Martha Ivers* allegorically inscribes Hollywood's transition from wartime to postwar conditions – whether in its **hybrid** status as a **crime melodrama**, heavily inflected with elements of the **female Gothic** and **film noir**; its narrative centered on class tensions, political maneuverings, and female empowerment; or its casting of **Barbara Stanwyck** and **Van Heflin**, whose lives and screen personae add further resonance. Roy Grundmann examines the film's mediation of multiple cultural anxieties, including a growing **anticommunist paranoia** and the increasingly incendiary negotiations between **Hollywood labor unions** and studios. He further uncovers struggles among right- and left-leaning unions, themselves – all at a time when **HUAC** and the **blacklist** were on the horizon. Grundmann's essay shares ground with Saverio Giovacchini on the Hollywood Left and World War II, Richard Maltby on studio realism, and Christine Noll Brinckmann on *Force of Evil* in this volume, and with Larry Ceplair on Hollywood unions and blacklists in the hardcover/online edition.

Additional terms, names, and concepts: Conference of Studio Unions (CSU), International Alliance of Theatrical Stage Employees (IATSE), exaggerated woman, the woman's film, femme fatale/femme noir, Motion Picture Alliance for the Preservation of American Ideals (MPAPAI), Hollywood Independent Citizens Committee of Arts, Sciences, and Professions (HICCASP), Screen Writers Guild

At the end of World War II, America found itself at one of the most profound junctures in its history. War had not only transformed the national economy, but had ushered in significant social and cultural change, much of which was set in motion before the United States entered the war but would be irreversible in large part as a result of it. Although the transition to a peacetime economy presented broad-based opportunities, the end of the war also created numerous challenges, dilemmas, and hardships that had not been anticipated. As large sectors of production had to be modernized and retooled for the manufacture of

American Film History: Selected Readings, Origins to 1960, First Edition. Edited by Cynthia Lucia, Roy Grundmann, and Art Simon.
© 2016 John Wiley & Sons, Inc. Published 2016 by John Wiley & Sons, Inc.

consumer goods, the daunting task of reorganizing the national workforce was further complicated by the need to absorb the massive influx of returning veterans seeking jobs – some of which no longer existed in the peacetime economy, while others were now possibly taken by women. It would not be long before the vicissitudes of industrial reorganization and postwar economic retrenchment, therefore, would ignite conflicts between labor and industry. To be sure, some of these conflicts stemmed from the years of the Great Depression, but their New Deal legacy took on a new status in the post–World War II political climate.

Although fascism had been defeated, worries about the rising influence of communism abroad and at home quickly filtered down from government and civic institutions to the average citizen. And while concerns over Soviet imperialism were legitimate, the domestic orchestration of fear established a climate of paranoia that both supported and thrived on authoritarianism. The anticommunist witch hunt also threw into relief America's long-standing ambivalence toward the state, whose increasing reach and power in the postwar period were at once secretly furthered and publicly denied. Calls to reform the top-down administrational mode of the war years clearly echoed the lingering resentments of conservatives against the political legacy of the New Deal. Yet, the postwar security state waged war not against big government – it *was* big government – but against the lower rungs of its infrastructure and socioeconomic liaisons, first among them organized labor. At the same time, however, unions found themselves battling not only with business leaders and politicians, but also with one another. Their tenacious vying for governance revealed a much broader divide stemming from the days of the Popular Front, when labor issues had become linked to a cluster of ideologically charged causes including immigrant protection, racial equality, free speech, and other civil rights-related issues. These causes now represented political baggage, making the left vulnerable to right-wing attacks and, more specifically, to redbaiting. Labor issues also were central in reshaping gender relations. The influx of returning veterans reduced the high numbers of women in the workforce and drastically reversed the broader, sociocultural promotion of female self-reliance that had begun in the 1920s and that was supported by government and industry during the war.

The film industry was a microcosm of many of these developments. The decade's "momentous reversals" (Schatz 1997, 2) had an immediate and sustained impact on the studio system, affecting not only the ways Hollywood designed, produced, and advertised its product, but also the manner in which the studios treated their labor force and responded to labor conflicts. The government had marshaled Hollywood into supporting the war effort with morale-boosting entertainment, information, and propaganda films. In turn, it had allowed the industry to retain autonomy over its own affairs, granting it vital economic protection that insured the studios' most profitable five-year period in history. When the war was over, the government markedly reversed its position in relation to the industry. It resumed several prewar investigations and legal disputes whose outcomes would have profound implications for Hollywood's economic and artistic future: The antitrust suit would force the studio system to dismantle its vertically integrated structure and would help to weaken and eventually eliminate the Production Code. The suspicions against communist infiltration of the industry, which had prompted scattered investigations in 1941 but had waned with Nazi Germany's invasion of the Soviet Union, now reemerged with the advent of the Cold War. The resulting blacklist, as Robert Sklar has pointed out, led Hollywood to devour its most valuable talent and enter a path of artistic self-destruction (1994, 249–250). But Hollywood had not exactly been usurped by anticommunist witch hunters. It had invited them in, partially out of fear and inexperience and partially because the moguls resented the labor unrest that had erupted at the beginning of 1945, when MGM refused to recognize the left-liberal Conference of Studio Unions (CSU) as an alternative to the politically conservative and industry-loyal International Alliance of Theatrical Stage Employees (IATSE). The protracted war between these two unions prompted studio management to drop its paternalistic protection of the base that might otherwise have blocked the reach of redbaiters. It propelled the company town into a period of paranoia fueled by intrigues, smear campaigns, and behind-the-scenes power struggles that resulted, among other things, in strained loyalties and rapidly shifting alliances. In what must be the most cynical of historical and ideological reversals, prewar Popular Front credentials and wartime patriotic support for America and its Allies suddenly were reinterpreted as evidence of communist conspiracy.

Layered and multifaceted as they were, the political and sociocultural conflagrations that marked the postwar period often were directly or indirectly related to labor struggles. Thus, when we assess the decade's many historical shifts and reversals, we should do so with the labor issue in mind. Remembering that labor issues have not only a complex history but a specific historical arc will help us place the period's key phenomena within a broader, more heterogeneous context in which, as it turns out, dominant events existed side by side – and, at times, intersected with – more submerged occurrences that constituted latent, long-term trends of their own. For historians, as Dana Polan argues, this means resisting the temptation to let the war's momentous impact overdetermine the structure of historical accounts of the period and, instead, to discern "continuities across time" (1986, 16). Considering the Republican opposition to the war effort, the sputtering and stalling of the war bond drive, and the various strikes and Congressional investigations that plagued Hollywood even during the war (Sklar 1994, 249–250), it is undeniable that layers of dissent – many of which were labor-related – existed beneath the sheen of ideological cohesion and hegemony of the war years. In turn, it would be equally misguided to characterize the postwar years as driven solely by social conflict that tends to emerge in periods of political decentralization and economic privatization. Any such tendencies were offset by a reconsolidation of authority on the level of the state and civic institutions. The fact that putatively emancipatory bodies like labor organizations adopted the same dynamics of power and paranoia (to borrow Polan's phrase) that pummeled them at this historical moment – despite their general claim of valuing democratic decision-making, transparency, and respect for the base – is a measure of the era's shift toward authoritarianism (Polan 1986, 1–20).

The complexity of the postwar moment, as Polan goes on to argue, imposed special needs on American representation (1986, 8). Hollywood adopted an astoundingly comprehensive slate of strategies concerning how best to acknowledge the war and its aftermath. It did so by drawing on the ability of genre cinema to both reference real-life conflicts and displace them through the various realms of fiction and fantasy. Approaches ranged from the escapist, though often direct address, of musical revues to the indirect wartime or Cold War messages of Westerns and adventure films, and from the unambiguous patriotism of homefront films to the ideological ambiguities of a range of dramas frequently featuring crime plots. This last group of films is particularly intriguing because it "managed to convey a range of wartime conditions – working women, absent husbands, housing shortages – without invoking the war," as Thomas Schatz has pointed out with reference to *Mildred Pierce* (1945) (1997, 202).

Usually featuring strong female protagonists who, when left to fend for themselves, achieve a measure of independence and success, which nevertheless forces them to make sacrifices or brings them into conflict with the law and other male-dominated value systems, such films implicitly identified women as the most significant domestic audience during the war years. While rarely placing work at front-and-center of the narratives, many films of this type either directly or indirectly reference issues relating to some form of female labor – domestic labor, wartime labor, the struggle to obtain labor, the conflict between family and labor, and so on. The introduction of crime plots into these narratives shows how Hollywood deftly drew on the principles of genre hybridity in order to maximize audience appeal. Combining crime plots with emotionally oriented dramas and branding them as "crime dramas" or "crime melodramas," Hollywood's genre hybrids demonstrated a unique capacity for sponsoring – both within a single film and across several genres – a range of viewer identifications, some consummate and exclusive, others partial, ambivalent, and contradictory.

Although not nearly as large in number as other Hollywood genres, 1940s crime melodramas had a signature character, their narratives filled with plot twists and suffused with paranoia, both indexing and mediating the decade's seismic historical shifts, social changes, and cultural anxieties. Their obsession with the past flew in the face of American culture's official resolve to leave the war behind, betraying an awareness of unresolved problems and latent, long-term dysfunctions. While often rote and recycled, crime melodramas nonetheless reflected very real sociocultural conflicts, of which the upheaval in gender relations was the most prominent. And their casts, notwithstanding heavy stereotyping, evinced a surprising degree of nuance.

Constructing a Hollywood Prestige Film

Issues of genre, gender, and spectatorial address are thus central to the case study of this analysis, which focuses on a classic representative of the 1940s crime melodrama, *The Strange Love of Martha Ivers* (1946). Made in the fall of 1945 by Hal B. Wallis, one of the industry's most seasoned and powerful producers, and released by Paramount Pictures in 1946, *The Strange Love of Martha Ivers* is a classic example of a Hollywood prestige production, whose hallmarks in the 1940s – star casting, increased length, complex plot, psychological nuance, and genre hybridity – are discussed below. The film boasted a crew of top industry talent (including director Lewis Milestone, screenwriter Robert Rossen, cinematographer Victor Milner, and costume designer Edith Head), established stars (Barbara Stanwyck, Van Heflin), and a musical score by Miklos Rozsa, one of the industry's most prominent composers. Jack Patrick, who wrote the story on which the screenplay is based, received a 1947 Oscar nomination for Best Writing, Original Story, and in the same year the film was entered into competition at Cannes.[1] The film received an elaborate marketing campaign and considerable industry buildup as "quality entertainment." Just under two hours in length, it features a cast of well-developed male and female characters grouped around the central female protagonist. The title announces Martha as an exaggerated woman – a term coined by Jeanine Basinger to describe female characters of the period who, although potentially selfish, haughty, and emotionally overwrought, endure by developing spunk, shrewdness, and stoicism, particularly when forced to renounce or defy men (Basinger 1993, 17).[2] The film's title also links the heroine with the theme of love, thus signaling its generic provenance as a woman's film. Yet, the qualification of this love as "strange" indicates the existence of a negative force in the heroine's life, pushing the film in the direction of the female Gothic – a subcycle of 1940s film noir that, combined with the hard-boiled detective thriller, revolved around issues of sexual difference and gender identity, subsuming crime under concerns with family and interpersonal relationships (Schatz 1997, 236). The female Gothic presented a duality of worlds depicted – worlds that were seemingly ordered, secure, and removed from poverty but that evoked an ominous sense of claustrophobia and threat. The historical trajectory of the female Gothic registers increasing female awareness of patriarchal oppression. Yet, while the postwar female Gothic notably problematized women's recent reconfinement to the home, narrative resolutions simultaneously endorsed it (Williams 1988, 25).

Martha Ivers begins with a prologue in which we see young Martha (Janis Wilson) growing up in the mansion of her cold, rigid aunt (Judith Anderson). She despises her aunt, who repeatedly foils Martha's attempts to escape Iverstown, the industrial community founded around the Ivers family factory. Martha, whose deceased mother is implied to be an Ivers, is forced to endure her aunt's wrath and disparaging remarks about her dead father, a working-class drunk whose name was Smith, and whom the aunt fears Martha will emulate. When she sees her aunt hitting her kitten with a cane atop the mansion staircase, Martha, in a moment of uncontrolled rage, wrests the cane from her aunt, strikes her, and causes her to fall to her death. The killing is witnessed by young Walter O'Neill (Mickey Kuhn), the obsequious son of Martha's private tutor, Mr O'Neill[3] (Roman Bohnen), also a sycophant attempting to sway the old lady to pay for Walter's college education. After the aunt's death, Mr O'Neill sees the path to his dream: He strategically accepts Martha and Walter's account that the aunt was killed by a burglar who fled the scene, thus deflecting Martha's role in the events and setting her on a course to become the town's high-powered magnate and benefactor, who will later see to it that an innocent man hangs for her crime.

The main narrative picks up 18 years after the killing, with Walter (Kirk Douglas, in his screen debut) and Martha now married, representing Iverstown's marriage of big business and political power (Walter, now a lawyer, is running for D.A.). Walter has become a paranoid, guilt-ridden alcoholic. When Martha's old sweetheart, Sam Masterson (Van Heflin) – with whom she had tried to flee on the night of Mrs Ivers's killing – returns to town, Walter believes that the past has caught up with them. Although Walter assumes that Sam also had witnessed the aunt's death and that he now intends to blackmail them, a scene before the killing shows Sam running toward the front door when he hears the aunt's voice – a crucial detail the narrative suppresses or at least renders ambiguous until the very end. It is not entirely clear exactly what Sam has or has not witnessed – the prologue ends with Martha and Walter telling Walter's father about the mysterious man who killed her aunt, and looking in the direction of the wide open door.

The main narrative, in many instances as elliptical as the prologue, has Sam enter town by chance as a result of car trouble. He is reintroduced to Martha when he hears her voice on the radio (announcing that her husband will not appear at a campaign event as scheduled), and he is reintroduced to Walter through his image on a campaign poster. On the same evening Sam meets and finds himself attracted to Toni (Lizabeth Scott), just as she is about to leave Iverstown. The narrative thus constructs triangles of love and jealousy involving Toni, Martha, and Sam, as well as Walter, Sam, and Martha. The film climaxes with an argument at the mansion involving Martha, Walter, and Sam, echoing the earlier prologue – it is now Walter who drunkenly falls down the stairs, with Martha begging Sam to kill him while he remains unconscious. Sam refuses, prompting Martha now to turn a gun on Sam. Daring Martha to shoot and seeing that she is unable to, Sam walks out the door, as he had so many years earlier – this time to flee Iverstown with Toni. Having regained consciousness, Walter now points the gun at Martha, who helps him pull the trigger, killing herself. To complete the double suicide, Walter shoots himself.

The elaborate prologue, exploring the relationship between Martha and Sam, the teenage object of her love, is the foundation for the film's melodrama and crime hybridity, for it culminates in Martha's killing her aunt – a fateful act in several ways: It places her at the helm of the Ivers business empire, but it also separates her from Sam, who flees the scene. Sam drifts back into town to find Martha unhappily married to Walter, who has not only become a corrupt politician, but is now also acting as the paranoid custodian of Martha's dark past. Reflecting the conventions of the woman's film, the narrative builds around the question of whether Martha and Sam's love can be rekindled – indeed, whether love can be restored at all to the life of this professionally powerful yet personally unhappy and guilt-ridden heroine. Yet the film also is guided by conventions of the female Gothic that make the question of love inseparable from propositions of betrayal and murder – as does film noir, with which the female Gothic often overlaps. As typical of noir with its display of moral anxiety in the face of weakness, vice, and depravity (Cook 1981, 467–468, cited in Schatz 1997, 235), *Martha Ivers* adopts a general sense of fear, paranoia, and spatial and psychological entrapment (Sklar 1994, 253, cited in Schatz 1997, 235).

Like so much of film noir, *Martha Ivers* mediates postwar gender anxieties. The weakened Walter is in some ways typical of the film noir male – a middle-class character who, torn away from his values, registers a sense of crisis experienced by so many returning veterans. However, he never elicits sympathy as the typical noir hero does. The film reserves this function for Sam who, like the returning veteran, seems deracinated but with none of the veteran's physical or psychological scars. *Martha Ivers* further complicates the film noir formula that typically divides its female characters along two lines – the sexually independent woman of power who often is defined as duplicitous when pursuing her own desires and ambitions, and the innocent, attractive, though sexually neutral female who is defined as nurturing and supportive of her man as he pursues his own desires and ambitions. Martha becomes a purely evil femme fatale only at the end, and Toni's innocence is not unambiguous, nor is she rendered sexually neutral. Despite these complications, *Martha Ivers* – like film noir and the female Gothic – uses gender to mediate cultural anxieties concerning women's roles and the push toward a return to prewar "normalcy."

The casting of Barbara Stanwyck was of central importance in the intersection of genre, gender, and ideological struggle in the postwar era. She was at the height of her popularity in the late 1930s and early 1940s, when she played the eponymous heroine in the classic maternal melodrama *Stella Dallas* (1937), the female lead in Cecil B. DeMille's big-budget historical Western *Union Pacific* (1939), and the feisty femme in a string of successful romantic comedies including such classics as *Remember the Night* (1940), *The Lady Eve* (1941), and *Ball of Fire* (1941). By then, well past the age of playing ingénues, Stanwyck would have been poised for decline had it not been for the onset of World War II. The war caused a shift in the demographic of domestic moviegoers, which led to the resurgence of the woman's film and extended or revived the careers of some of the biggest female stars of the 1930s who were in Stanwyck's age bracket. Like Bette Davis, Claudette Colbert, Ginger Rogers, and Joan Crawford, Stanwyck began to play a menagerie of mature, independent heroines in their late thirties and forties to a devoted audience of rapidly maturing, increasingly independent home-front women. Many of the characters played by Stanwyck and her peers were exaggerated women, roles Basinger links to the loss of sex appeal and romantic lead caliber on the part of female stars who played the type (1993, 167–169). Certainly, Stanwyck's enduring success (in 1944 she was America's highest-paid actress) was due mainly to her reputation as a dramatic actress who only occasionally played sexpots and frequently toned down the sexual aspects of her own roles (Lugowski 2010). Yet, most of the parts she played during the 1940s still involved romance and pivoted on her glamour and desirability.

Stanwyck's roles can also be related to the evolution of the female Gothic. Her acting was ideally suited to this type of material. Her slightly feline face with its high cheekbones and expressive mouth could convey calculating coldness and emotional breakdowns with equal conviction. She commanded the range of emotional registers that lay between these extremes and would move among them with great alacrity. It is the very introduction of the female Gothic into her career that may be read as an indication of growing patriarchal anxieties. As the decade progressed, her characters' ambitions became increasingly subject to punishment. Further, while the duality of victim and victimizer, as typical of the female Gothic, had been part of her persona from the beginning, it became infused with violent hyperbole when crime melodramas and hard-boiled noirs began to eclipse the share of classic woman's pictures and light comedies in her repertoire. While her role as Phyllis Dietrichson in *Double Indemnity* (1944) is commonly billed as the high-water mark of female cunning, the film's classic comeuppance logic is fairly predictable and has a self-containing effect. From an ideological perspective, Stanwyck's post–Phyllis Dietrichson parts were arguably more complex, but also more questionable, because they gradually shifted the balance from victimizer to victim and increasingly pathologized their respective female protagonists.[4] *Martha Ivers* marks the beginning of this trend. But while its ending turns the heroine into a frenzied Lady Macbeth, the film surpasses many of Stanwyck's later films in complexity. This in part is due to the way in which the film suspends its heroine between conventions of noir and the woman's film. But another factor is that Stanwyck's performance of the exaggerated woman shapes viewer affect and, thus, ultimately transcends the character binary of victim and victimizer. As I will argue below, in its discursive management of this binary, *Martha Ivers*'s portrayal of its heroine as a powerful but emotionally scarred female professional *disables* rather than *enables* a historically concrete analysis of women's hegemonic status as both oppressors and oppressed.

The *Martha Ivers* Marketing Campaign

Clearly Stanwyck was central to Paramount's marketing campaign for *Martha Ivers*. In its marketing of the film, Paramount systematically exploited the film's double appeal as a crime melodrama. Its core component is an elaborate press book that includes posters, lobby cards, photo mats, and other exploitation materials, as well as plot synopses, prefabricated reviews, and background stories about the film's stars – a type of marketing, as Mary Beth Haralovich has pointed out, that was practiced by every major studio throughout the classical era (1997, 196). Targeting moviegoers, reviewers, and theater owners, this strategy gave each film a specific generic identity and positioned it within a field of consumer expectations. Briefly consulting Haralovich's findings in her study of the marketing of *Mildred Pierce* is relevant to our discussion – for both its correspondences to and differences from the *Martha Ivers* publicity strategies. A female Gothic and woman's film/film noir hybrid about a frustrated but successful businesswoman wrongly accused of murdering her husband, *Mildred Pierce* has been established as a scholarly paradigm of sorts for the study of films like *Martha Ivers*. Released in 1945 just around the same time *Martha Ivers* went into production, *Mildred Pierce*, like *Martha Ivers*, indirectly references women's wartime experiences, but also casts these in the context of a crime plot that subjects female activities to male interrogation and judgment. Launching what one may call a process of taking stock, each film centers on its heroine's past activities, investigating in close conjunction her moral probity and the legitimacy of her professional success. Each film sensationalizes its heroine in its marketing campaign, defining her as an alluring but also fiercely independent and rather domineering woman. Perhaps not surprisingly, the part of Mildred Pierce had initially been offered to Stanwyck, before Joan Crawford, who had tenaciously pursued it, was able to claim the role by impressing director Michael Curtiz with a screen test.[5]

Paramount's promotion of *Martha Ivers* slightly differs from Warner Bros.' marketing of *Mildred Pierce*. While clearly attempting to capitalize on the success of the *Double Indemnity* formula, the campaign for *Martha Ivers* presents the film's generic components – the hard-boiled noir and the female Gothic – relatively evenly across the publicity materials. The press book contains assorted poster designs for print ads and marquee display intended to give publicists, editors, and theater owners a maximum of flexibility in selecting the generic spin most appealing to their region and demographic. One version plays up the film's hard-boiled aspect. It features a drawing of the protagonists, Martha and Sam, locked in passionate embrace. The image codes Martha as a sexually aggressive femme fatale – her lips are lustfully parted, her fingers stretch out across Sam's cheek to hold him like an object[6] – with Sam as the ensnared yet wary-looking hard-boiled hero. The pleading face of a younger-looking woman is positioned directly beneath Sam's head, her folded hands identifying her as the virtuous future wife Toni. The polarized effect of this hard-boiled rhetoric is reinforced by two tag lines. The more prominent line exclaims in large type and capital letters, "FATE DREW THEM TOGETHER AND ONLY MURDER COULD PART THEM," and is placed beneath Martha and Sam, clearly aiming to evoke associations with *Double Indemnity*'s murderous couple, Walter Neff and Phyllis Dietrichson. This impression is cemented by the contrasting rhetoric of the other, less conspicuous tag line associated with the younger woman – "There's a tender side to this drama, too, and lovely Lizabeth Scott is it!"[7]

By contrast, a second poster foregrounds the film's female Gothic angle. Martha's head in profile dominates as she faces Sam, who is positioned on the right margin. Both have their eyes closed, shifting the nature of their attraction slightly away from pure lust and toward romance. This image depicts Martha less as a villainess and more as an overemotional, psychologically fragile woman. She appears regal yet still volatile in profile. The effect is underscored by a different tag line, with its first half, "In the Strange Shadows of her Mind . . . ," set in large type, and its resolution, "desire and hate fused in one consuming passion," printed in smaller type below. Martha's fragile state of mind is further suggested by a drawing of the ostentatious staircase that seemingly spirals out of Martha's head to the bottom of the image. In addition to implying the female protagonist's great wealth (conjuring the interior of a heritage mansion), the staircase symbolizes her troubled, tortured psyche. In postwar American culture, and particularly in the female Gothic, the staircase has been linked to mental instability and to the discovery of horrific secrets. The drawing includes a lifeless male body at the bottom of the stairs, suggesting a crime has been committed that may possibly be linked to the heroine. She may have committed it herself, though perhaps less out of sheer evil than in a fit of rage, as a crime of passion. The tag line aims to convey the woman's excitability and irrationality, thus underscoring her dual status as victim and victimizer. Correspondingly, the face of Lizabeth Scott's character Toni, positioned literally behind Martha's back, looks less innocent and more hardened and calculating, suggesting she may possess a tinge of noiresque duplicity herself.[8]

Like the poster art, the studio's prefabricated reviews for *Martha Ivers* use a shifting combination of female Gothic and hard-boiled noir elements. Most of the reviews draw parallels to Stanwyck's femme fatale stardom, asserting she has a "more-evil-than 'Double Indemnity' type of role" and calling her "doubly as devilish." One article claims Stanwyck will soon be known as "the screen's most bloodthirsty woman"; another is headlined "Barbara Stanwyck Revels in Menace" (Paramount Pictures 1946, 5–9).[9] In contrast to *Double Indemnity*, however, the campaign for *Martha Ivers* downplays the femme fatale's physical allure in favor of the twin qualities of sartorial glamour and psychological volatility.[10] Several press book items clearly echo the female Gothic's binary definition of the exaggerated woman. One description focuses on the character's dual identity as victim and victimizer, calling her a "murderess who is gradually trapped by her own obsession of guilt"; another builds on the Gothic cycle's intimations of sadomasochism, characterizing her as an overbearing wife who is crushed by unrequited love for another man and "twice tries to murder the one man she is

Figure 24.1 Poster art promoting the hard-boiled angle of Lewis Milestone's *The Strange Love of Martha Ivers* (1946, producer Hal B. Wallis).

Figure 24.2 Poster art promoting the female Gothic angle of Lewis Milestone's *The Strange Love of Martha Ivers* (1946, producer Hal B. Wallis).

capable of honestly loving" (Paramount Pictures 1946, 5–6).

This other man, Sam, is unmistakably the hard-boiled hero, described in the press book as "no angel," but nevertheless "able to deal with [Martha] and her weakling husband" (Paramount Pictures 1946, 6). The tag line's description of the male characters/cast members indicates that film noir's rendition of masculinity in crisis is not automatically at variance with Hollywood's reactionary affirmation of dominant gender roles. *Martha Ivers* effectively channels this crisis by limiting certain taboo qualities, most notably male weakness, to the character of Walter. Sam, by contrast, is labeled "rugged," comprising patriarchy's classic trifecta of virility, intelligence, and moral authority. Describing him as "a worldly wise gambler" and as "the man who untangles the mess," the press book romanticizes his freedom and lack of attachment, yet asserts that he is able to discern what really matters (Paramount Pictures 1946, 6). Unlike Fred MacMurray's Walter Neff in *Double Indemnity*, Sam remains untarnished by the decay that engulfs him, able to disentangle himself from the ensnaring power of the femme fatale, "finally overcoming her and yielding to the finer love of Lizabeth Scott" (Paramount Pictures 1946, 6).

Sam's ability to triumph implies that he possesses the moral authority to probe the femme fatale's virtue by investigating her past. But on what exactly is Sam's moral authority founded? Numerous male-centered noirs from the mid- to late 1940s depict their male protagonist as disillusioned drifters perfectly willing to be a femme fatale's partner in crime. At the same time, these treatments typically ennobled the hard-boiled hero, using his returning veteran status to rationalize his unanchored existence.

Although references to this effect were often fleeting or indirect, they strongly resonated with postwar audiences, not the least because Hollywood publicized the return of many of its own stars from the war. The returning veteran performed several rhetorical functions: It helped film noir narratives account for the hero's prolonged absence and forestalled any second-guessing about his own past, while turning his years in the service into a moral badge that entitled him to judge others. The *Martha Ivers* press campaign references Van Heflin's returning veteran status only indirectly,[11] perhaps because the studio publicist could expect the print media and radio to disseminate the news of Heflin's return. The *New York Times* review of the film promptly mentions that the part of Sam was Heflin's first since he was discharged from the Army, adding that "he brings to it the quality of rugged integrity and certainty of action that is characteristic of Spencer Tracy's acting."[12]

The comparison to Tracy reinforces the link between military service and moral authority that underscored polarized gender themes of 1940s crime melodramas. It also indicates the ideological stakes of "taking stock" and assessing America's wartime experience. But if the patriarchal logic behind the act of taking stock posited women as alluring criminals with dark pasts, the studios' marketing campaigns at least partially offset this logic through "interactive" forms of pop culture consumption. Some materials in the press book instruct theater owners and magazine editors to engage viewers and interested fans through gossip, confession, and other rituals and social practices. They shift the emphasis from criminalizing the woman's past and its secrets to questions of guilt, sacrifice, punishment, and social stigmatization, drawing on those same themes central to the woman's film. For instance, a photo mat titled "How My Strange Secret Destroyed Me!" reframes six scenes from *Martha Ivers* to represent the consequences of her teenage crime from Martha's point of view. Martha's confession functions not only as a warning, but also as a tale with which to identify.[13]

The poster design also includes an "interactive" element that spurs audience interest in the heroine. Inserted in all versions of the design directly under the film's title is a parenthetical tag line that reads, "whisper her name … " The line alludes to a painful aspect of Martha's past – the status of her biological father who was never to become part of the Ivers dynasty. In characteristic woman's fiction mode, Martha, struggling to find her identity, must confront her family's traumatic history. She suffers from the effect of larger social forces – orphanhood, disrupted lineage, and oppressively rigid family rules – that have put a curse on her own existence, rendering her an outsider even among kin and forcing her to rely on herself alone. While moviegoers who had yet to see the film would have been unaware of these details (unless filled in by word-of-mouth), the tag line does suggest that there is something disturbing about Martha's family name. The poster initiates a dynamic of viewer engagement defined by curiosity, speculation, and gossip that the film furthers rather than limits and that at least implicitly encourages empathy for the heroine's predicament.

Film Noir's Male-Centered Narrative Arc

The complex conjuncture of generic elements taken from male- and female-centered crime melodramas is not limited to the marketing campaign of *Martha Ivers*. It also informs the film's construction of its dramatis personae – that is, the manner in which the film introduces and builds its characters, places them in the frame, makes them into figures of identification, and imbues them with historical connotations. By drawing on the woman's film at least as much as it draws on film noir, *Martha Ivers* enables audiences to empathize with Martha until late in the narrative – when it defines her as an evil femme fatale, as noted, who receives nothing more than Sam's pity. As we shall see, it is the film's visual and melodramatic aspects that temporarily maintain the female point of view against the male perspective, although these aspects eventually are subordinated to the male-centered conventions of the narrative arc.

The film's prologue opens with the teenage Sam hurrying across train tracks at night, preparing to skip town with Martha, his sweetheart. It closes by showing him leaving town without her upon his fleeing the mansion. Eighteen years later, when Sam finds himself back in Iverstown after an accident has forced him to interrupt his odyssey, the town sign he crashes into is a kind of siren call that sets him on a new course – film noir's classic narrative of disintegration.[14] In this case, however, the crisis is but temporary. After resolving a mystery relating to his past that forces him to wade into crime and moral decay, he leaves his childhood sweetheart behind once again (this time to her own death) to resume his journey with a new woman. Around Toni the film devises a subplot that feeds the female mystery quotient by briefly questioning her loyalty to Sam. Seemingly set up by Toni, Sam is roughed up by Walter's thugs. Dumped outside town, Sam, in typical noir manner, is a bit like Walter Neff in *Double Indemnity*, and like so many other noir males. As Neff says – after a murder *he* committed – "I couldn't hear my own footsteps – it was the walk of a dead man."[15] Such male abjection in film noir often results from relationships with women. Sam is now forced to investigate two women – either (or both) of whom may be responsible for his suffering, and either (or both) of whom may be bent on destroying him. What we soon learn, however, is that Walter has bullied Toni into helping him get to Sam.

The revelation of Toni's victim status is a step toward the film's polarization of "good" and "bad" women – Toni is ultimately "good"; Martha is ultimately "bad." The film carries this polarization forward in a scene in which Martha pays a surprise visit to Sam and Toni in their hotel room. As in most Hollywood films, costuming underscores character. Toni is dressed in a midriff-revealing blouse and a removable skirt, with white shorts under the skirt – all conferring a fresh, youthful look. Martha, huddled in an ornately patterned, hooded dress that lends an elegance, though decidedly foreboding, has the look of the exaggerated woman. Quite simply, Toni's clothes convey her straightforwardness and her restored innocence, while Martha's costume signals her potential as a spider woman, entrapping her victims in her web (not incidentally, she owns the hotel in which Sam and Toni are staying and has access to all rooms).

The scene also reflects the film noir convention of the powerful femme fatale's luring the hard-boiled hero away from his honest and pure girlfriend, who, powerless though she is, resigns herself to awaiting his uncertain return, thus restoring her power within the limits of patriarchy. As typical of male-centered noir, Sam's momentary decision to attend to Martha rather than Toni appears neither irrational nor immoral – the male investigator alternately investigates the mystery woman and makes love to her. In fact, it is the latter that allows him to do the former: Sexual intimacy gives him access to her past. After a romantic evening of dining and dancing, Martha and Sam drive to a campsite atop a hill overlooking Iverstown, a place they used to visit during their youth. Assuming she can trust Sam, Martha asks him why he didn't prevent her from killing her aunt, to which Sam replies that he never saw what happened that night at the mansion. Feeling exposed by his revelation, Martha attacks Sam with a burning log but then yields to his passionate embrace (clever ellipsis in the classic Hollywood Production Code fashion strongly implies that they have sex).

While Martha's expression of remorse about her past actions enables viewer empathy with her conflicting feelings of guilt, shame, and desire, these complex dynamics are nonetheless framed and guided by noir's male-centered logic. Although devoid of male voiceover narration and male-authored flashbacks – tropes typical of many films noir – the narrative enables Sam to plead ignorance of the crime by referencing the prologue's elliptical climax. Though in the beginning of the main narrative the film clearly shows that Sam gets stranded in Iverstown by accident and only gradually grows suspicious of Martha and Walter, up until this scene it withholds any explicit information, as noted, about the extent of Sam's knowledge of the crime. Given that the story's central conflict turns on Walter's paranoid misassumptions about Sam, triggering the provocations and recriminations that follow, the narrative's reticence about Sam's status, on one level, is simply a dramaturgical device to propel the story forward. Nevertheless, it produces gender imbalance. By presenting Martha's confession as seemingly unforced (even though Sam provoked it strategically), the film strengthens Sam's status as a moral authority entitled to interrogate and judge her.

While the campfire scene continues the process of transforming Martha from exaggerated woman to murderous villain, her remorse, despair, and melodramatic excess still keep Sam, the investigator, uncertain about her moral status. The film does not transform her, finally, into a murderous femme fatale until the final scene at the mansion, when Sam confronts both Walter and Martha about their record of corruption and crime. In the course of their increasingly tense confrontation, Walter reveals that Martha, although she was initially manipulated by his father into

Figure 24.3 "Now, Sam. Do it now!" Martha exclaims, in Lewis Milestone's *The Strange Love of Martha Ivers* (1946, producer Hal B. Wallis).

keeping the crime a secret, soon took advantage of her new-found power and security. She allowed an innocent man to pay with his life for her crime. At this point, the more outlandish components of the female Gothic devolve into heavy-handed noir melodrama. Martha righteously rejects Sam's plea to turn herself in to the police. When Walter, drunk and exhausted, falls down the mansion's grand staircase and Martha suddenly switches registers, seductively pleading with Sam to kill Walter, the scene reinforces her image as a crazed and volatile Lady Macbeth whose manic behavior is foiled by the hero's rationality and mercy. What follows reinforces Sam's moral authority further, when he walks out on the couple after daring Martha to shoot him. Once outside the house, he not only is cleared of his association with them and their past, but, as it turns out, is also unable to prevent the couple's suicidal demise.

Crime, Gendered Perspective, and the Woman's Film

The femme noir is a victimizer who only pretends to be a victim. The exaggerated woman in a female Gothic or other kinds of woman's films genuinely combines both qualities. In *Martha Ivers* these qualities are clearly established in the film's prologue and are held in balance for much of the film. The fairy-tale aspects of Martha's girlhood – she is caged, feels unloved, and her role models are rejected by the powers that be – are signature qualities of the woman's film in which, as Molly Haskell has noted, "All women begin as victims" (1974, 161). Although Martha deliberately falsifies the circumstances of her aunt's death, the killing itself is an unpremeditated act. The casting of Judith Anderson in the role of Martha's stern aunt immediately places the film within the female Gothic, yet, as with her role as Mrs Danvers in Alfred Hitchcock's *Rebecca* (1940), Anderson gives a nuanced performance that, like Stanwyck's, enhances the character's complexity.[16] Janis Wilson is similarly well cast in the role of young Martha. For all of her hatred of the old lady and for all of her vulnerability and ambition to escape her reach, young Martha already looks like a teenage version of her aunt. Like her aunt, Martha will come to share the fate of a certain type of heroine of women's fiction – one who finds that her solitude, partially incurred as a price for her independence, is harder to negotiate than she was prepared to admit.

In the woman's film the victimizer/victim duality can also play itself out on a smaller, less intense scale, though the heroine's volatile behavior may cause her predicament to escalate at any moment. Heightened emotionality is thus the defining feature of the exaggerated woman. It typically embroils the heroine in a string of bizarre events with life-long repercussions. But this same emotionality also gives her poise, making her an ideal vehicle for the dramatization of disappointment, frustration, and anger. The spectacular quality of the exaggerated woman is underscored by a particular narrative convention – her drawn-out, eagerly anticipated first-time introduction to the audience. The appearance of Barbara Stanwyck – the film's major star – does not occur for at least 15 minutes, given the lengthy prologue and the main narrative's first, rather long sequence of Sam's return to Iverstown and first meeting with Toni. As Basinger has pointed out with reference to Bette Davis in *Now Voyager* (1942), this buildup raises audience expectations and triggers a set of questions easily adapted to a discussion of *Martha Ivers*: Is Stanwyck really playing Martha? How will she look (both as a star and in character)? Who is Martha Ivers and what is her story? As Basinger goes on to say, several classic woman's films execute the star's visual introduction in pieces, initially revealing only parts of her body, such as gloved hands or feet (1993, 16). By contrast, when the adult Martha finally appears, she is shown in full, with a sweeping entrance through the front door of her mansion from the pouring rain – as if moving onto a stage. Unlike in film noir, however, where the first view of the woman usually belongs to a man and is framed by male voiceover, *Martha Ivers* provides the audience direct access to the female protagonist.

Yet, the film does not fully diverge from the piecemeal mode of delivery. There is one part of Martha – her voice – that is presented before we see her in the radio address Sam first hears in the garage. The film's deployment of voice is rather complex: While film sound lends itself less easily to cinematic suturing than do images, the introduction of Martha's voice is analogous to film noir's visual introduction of the femme fatale. Her first "appearance" clearly frames Martha as the focus of male attention. In accordance with the conventions of the woman's film, however, the film endows Martha's voice with an air of power.[17] It gives her a sense of ubiquity normally associated with men (underscored by Stanwyck's masculine voice), while also indicating that much of this power has been deployed on behalf of men (the purpose of her address, as noted, is to fabricate an excuse for her husband's cancellation of a campaign appearance). The film thus associates sound with a male-centered power structure, which it uses to dramatize Martha's struggle to find her own voice. This logic is brought full circle in the scene of her death, when Martha, in response to an ethereal offscreen voice whispering "Ivers! Ivers! Ivers," speaks her last words: "No, my name is Smith" (recalling her father's name). This response is consistent with the ideology of women's fiction that affirms female independence "within limits" (that is, as long as this independence does not violate patriarchy). Martha's attempt to appropriate patrilineage for the purpose of self-determination certainly helps foreground gender, but it does not politicize it. The film's ending conveys a clear sense that taking stock at the historical moment into which the film was released involved a decidedly gendered perspective; but instead of letting history enter its fiction, the film converts the act of taking stock into a moral judgment performed by a man.

It would be incorrect, however, to read *Martha Ivers* as a simple reflection of male systems of meaning; it would be just as specious, at the same time, to read the film as a feminist text. *Martha Ivers* simultaneously enacts and displaces the process of taking stock that so heavily defined the immediate postwar moment. The film *enacts* the process by showing Martha as a successful female professional; it *displaces* it through narrative ellipsis that both implies that killing her aunt was the primary cause of her success and represses the actual work she performed in transforming the family business into a powerful corporate entity (much of which would have transpired during wartime). The conventions of crime melodrama sanction the film's representation of what Linda Williams, in discussing *Mildred Pierce*, calls "the otherwise unrepresentable exhilarations of matriarchal power,"[18] which ultimately are repressed (1988, 24), lest female agency suddenly appear intrinsically meritorious and women's independence a reality of history rather than a cultural fantasy. Williams argues that 1940s woman's films discursively "manage" (1988, 24) women's wartime experience in the sense that they at once reflect and repress this experience.

Martha Ivers makes this no more prominent than in its dual representation of the staircase as a means to access and deflect from the past. This is where the heroine learns certain things about herself – where she loses her innocence and forfeits her happiness. It is on the staircase where the teenage Martha quickly realizes that she is capable of turning her aunt's death to her own advantage in order to cement her position of power, even if her action has criminal implications. It is on the same staircase where the adult Martha, in a more cruel and premeditated manner, attempts to cover up the crimes she had formerly committed in order to preserve her position of power. Hence, the killings Martha commits or contemplates committing on the staircase lock her life into a static pattern, forcing her to remain in Iverstown, to continually live out the repercussions of her past. Notwithstanding its grand, dynamic design connoting power and privilege, what the staircase in *Martha Ivers* elicits, then, is the rigid and entrapping space that joins the female Gothic with the film noir aesthetic.

Martha's and Sam's respective accounts of the past are characterized by a basic asymmetry that, as Andrea Walsh has pointed out, reflects patriarchal society's gender-specific designation of morality. According to this logic, women's moral sense is meant to revolve around conflicting responsibilities, while for men it arises from competing rights (Walsh 1984, 75–79). The film only very briefly alludes to Sam's decorated war record. But, as noted, this fleeting reference suffices to anchor the character in actual history. And despite the fact that this reference conflates Sam's years in the service with his peripatetic gambler existence (we don't know when exactly the former ended and the latter began), it functions to endow him with moral probity. It matters little that Sam's attempt to own a menagerie of circus animals misfired, that he chose to flee the situation rather than face it, just as he had fled the scene of the killing and, by writer's fiat, escapes the scene of the double suicide. There is little need for the narrative to downplay (or embellish) Sam's consistent lack of commitment. Society is likely to forgive men for such behavior, because, as Walsh rightly claims, it defines male gender roles in terms of entitlement, not responsibility.

The script gives Martha several opportunities to explicitly chastise Sam for his lack of commitment. When Sam tells her that his stay is temporary, she responds by saying, "That's the way you've always been!" Notwithstanding its acuity, however, this observation is eclipsed by Sam's negative comment on Martha's dining room, which he finds "crowded." It is the hero's prerogative to judge the heroine and, given the fact that the room, like everything else in the house, functions as an extension of Martha herself, this judgment also refers directly to Martha or, more specifically, to her crowded mind. Realizing that she and Walter fear him for reasons he has yet to fully understand, Sam baits Martha in her office, by demanding "half of everything" she owns. We are, again, encouraged to empathize with her response: "You ran out of here a dirty little kid once before! That can happen again! I don't have to give you anything if I don't want to!" This exchange, it would seem, rather favorably compares Martha's dedication to entrepreneurship to Sam's flight from responsibility. Indeed, the prologue's date, 1928, locates Martha's taking charge of the family business within the time frame of the 1930s, implicitly making her a Depression-era heroine. Yet, the script does not allow Martha to capitalize on this aspect. It relativizes her independence by suggesting that she is personally unfulfilled. To Martha's assertion, "I don't have to give you anything if I don't want to!" Sam replies, "but you do want to," suggesting that for the heroine of a woman's film, neither her wealth nor her profession substitute for a man in her life (Basinger 1993, 20). In the absence of even so much as a brief montage of work footage, Martha's assertions about her work-filled past sound overly defensive. Before completing this process of historical repression with the climactic scene on the staircase, during which Martha is fully transformed from an exaggerated woman to an evil criminal, the film applies one additional, rather bold rhetorical strategy – it redefines the act of taking responsibility as an act of self-absorption.

Figure 24.4 Martha evokes the biblical image of Lot's wife, in Lewis Milestone's *The Strange Love of Martha Ivers* (1946, producer Hal B. Wallis).

The scene between Martha and Sam at the campfire begins with a shot of them arriving by car at the hilltop overlooking Iverstown. As Sam stops the car, Martha looks back over her shoulder, taking in the scenic view of the town. Her ornate dress and the hood she wears give her a vaguely "biblical" look. This impression is promptly underscored by Sam's comment: "You know what happened to Lot's wife when she looked back, don't you?" The association with Lot's wife suggests that Martha is "materialist" – that is, she is enamored with the accumulation of earthly wealth. To Sam the site of this wealth does not look real; to Martha, as she explains, "it is very real – owning it gives you a sense of power. You'd know what I meant if you had it." Sam gives Martha a disapproving look, as her entranced gaze wanders across the nocturnal city. True to the film's nature as a generic hybrid, this moment deploys the logic of the woman's film (women are incapable of maintaining critical distance) to prepare viewers for the climactic scene on the staircase, which partakes in the logic of film noir, defining female narcissism as evil.

The hilltop scene closely exemplifies the discursive management of the female experience in the immediate postwar years as analyzed by Williams: No doubt, Martha's impulse to "look back" at the fruit of her labor spoke to American women at war's end, reflecting their own impulse to take stock of their homefront accomplishments. But to characterize the female protagonist as feminist is to ignore the massive work of repression *Martha Ivers* performs on another level – work that prevents the film from acquiring more direct relevance for female viewers. The woman's film denies its heroines entry into the public sphere (even Martha, the powerful business woman, dies inside her house); it recasts her professional pride as a form of narcissism; it anchors her ambitions and ideals within a male frame of reference; and it reduces all assessments of her character to a moral level. It should be acknowledged that recent work on melodrama has convincingly argued that melodrama, while basically Manichaean in nature, is far from simplistic or crude (Williams 2001). Due to its uncanny capacity for presenting more than one moral position with equal conviction, melodrama has been able to offer to a heterogeneous audience of complexly structured modern subjects a pool of stories in which they see themselves represented, however partially and/or obliquely. Yet, while melodrama, and indeed the crime melodrama, reflects to audiences their existence in the world, it represses the concrete circumstances of this existence.

Company Town

The last part of this essay shifts the analysis of *Martha Ivers* to another phenomenon that characterizes the historical moment of the film's release – Hollywood labor relations and their dramatic escalation into a class struggle. In performing this shift, I do not mean to abandon an analysis of gender and its relation to genre but, rather, to illuminate the position of gender within a larger historical context. To do so, it is important to consider yet another aspect of the film's generic identity – its claim to provide "socially responsible" entertainment. Films like *Martha Ivers* that depict their characters at the intersection of power, social privilege, and crime were made by a specific group within Hollywood – left-wing producers, directors, and screenwriters who found themselves at the epicenter of the labor struggle. In certain instances, these artists presented crime as a metaphor for larger social ills that reflected not only their own increasingly precarious position as Hollywood's creative labor force, but also a bitter ideological war that was soon to grip all of postwar America.

The plot descriptions and prefabricated reviews in the press book for *Martha Ivers* construct an image that clearly corresponds to the thematic concerns of what has since become known as film noir.[19] One review brands the film "a grimly realistic story of real people, unsavory as they are"; a second characterizes it as a "gripping tale about cold and heartless people who are motivated by an avaricious lust for money and power, and by uninhibited passions that lead to murder, blackmail and deceit" (Paramount Pictures 1946, 5). Although several studio-authored reviews of the film invoke the word "realistic," the suggested link between wealth and moral decay primarily is aimed at sensationalizing the generic ingredients of crime and melodrama so as to promote the film's entertainment value. It appears that critics who reviewed the film upon its release bought into this approach. The *New York Herald Tribune* praised what it perceived as the film's "tough realism," and summarized the film as "essentially a clinical case history of a supposedly successful homicide."[20] Describing the female protagonist, Martha, as "ruthless and fabulously wealthy," the *New York Times* called the film an "at times harrowing exposition of moral and, to a somewhat lesser extent, physical decay."[21] Yet the review stopped short of assessing just how representative this moral decay may have been of American life in the late war and postwar years.

Critics' and studio publicists' simultaneous acknowledgment and disavowal of *Martha Ivers*'s topicality exemplify the problems encountered by film historians in assessing the status of movies as social barometers. Film noir has been at the center of this debate for some time, and for good reason. If examined as a group, the period's crime melodramas, brimming as they are with criminals, cynics, and amoral drifters, certainly seem to point to a larger crisis in postwar American society, which appeared to have fallen into a moral vacuum and was besieged by coldness and materialism. But while many films noir express skepticism about the possibility that justice can ultimately prevail, the deployment of crime as a metaphor for larger social ills was as apt to neutralize social critique as it was to facilitate it. In the case of *Martha Ivers*, the Breen Office, as Brian Neve points out, was more concerned with "elements of illicit sex" that were "treated without proper compensating moral values" (2007, 191) than with what Breen might have perceived as a hard-hitting political indictment of American society. The double suicide of Martha and Walter – which represents the twin demise of big business and political corruption – constitutes sufficient evidence that all human relationships, which Neve claims are reduced in film noir to "alienated, contractual relationships" (1992, 139), had no chance of survival in America. This notwithstanding the fact that Sam, upon leaving Iverstown, once again conjures the image of Lot's wife when he warns his future wife Toni not to turn around and look at what a roadside placard advertises as "America's Fastest Growing Industrial City."

When the Motion Picture Alliance for the Preservation of American Ideals (MPAPAI), Hollywood's most prominent right-wing lobbying group, cited *The Strange Love of Martha Ivers* as a film that contained "sizeable doses of Communist propaganda" (quoted in Neve 1992, 140), it did not reference specific scenes as evidence of red content but, instead, took the political leanings of director Lewis Milestone and, in particular, scriptwriter Robert Rossen as sufficient evidence that such content existed. Milestone was not actually a member of the Communist Party, though he did have a noted track record as a director of left-liberal, antiwar, and antifascist dramas. Rossen was a member of the Communist Party from 1937 to 1947 (Neve 2007, 184) and had previously collaborated with Milestone on *Edge of Darkness* (1943), a drama about the Norwegian resistance to the Nazi occupation, and *A Walk in the Sun* (1945), a gritty combat picture about the costly 1943 American invasion of Italy. A highly visible, politically active Hollywood leftist, Rossen, until 1944, chaired the Hollywood Writers Mobilization, an organization that coordinated screenwriters' contributions to the war effort that had been established by the left-leaning Screen Writers Guild (Neve 2007, 188). He also was on the executive board of the Hollywood Independent Citizens Committee of the Arts, Sciences, and Professions (HICCASP), Hollywood's most high-profile Popular Front alliance of liberals and radicals (Ceplair & Englund 1979, 218).[22]

Rossen's collaboration with Warner Bros. earlier in his career must likewise be given due consideration in order to fully assess *Martha Ivers*'s implications as a social critique of America. Several of the film's thematic and stylistic elements resonate with the films Rossen wrote for Warners between 1936 and 1944, films that were representative of the studio's prewar output of gritty, contemporary dramas with social implications as well as its slate of wartime films directly or indirectly engaging the war. *Martha Ivers*'s opening sequence, in which a teenage Sam is heading across the train tracks to plan his boxcar escape with Martha, is reminiscent of the studio's Depression-era juvenile delinquency films, such as *Wild Boys of the Road* (1933) and the opening montage of *Angels With Dirty Faces* (1938). The motive of discontented youth on the run was also central to Rossen's unrealized project, *Marked Children*, about a 14-year-old girl who runs away from her grandparents in search of her mother working in a war plant. In light of this project, it is not difficult to see why Jack Patrick's short story, *The Strange Love of Martha Ivers*, appealed to Rossen, especially since the short story mainly deals with the young Martha, providing Rossen the opportunity to invent what would become the film's main narrative (Neve 2007, 189), in which Walter is portrayed as a corrupt and autocratic ruler. Rossen had already explored this theme more directly in his screenplay for Warners' adaptation of Jack London's *The Sea Wolf* (1941). Through the tyrannical protagonist, played by Edward G. Robinson, "a Nazi in everything but name" (Robinson & Spigelgass 1973, 218, cited in Neve 2007, 187), Rossen was able to examine the psychology of fascism.

Above and beyond any specific theme, however, the quality that inhered most notably in Rossen's Warner Bros. films and that translated most lastingly to his postwar films was a particular kind of realism – not an "in-the-streets" realism of slavish mimetic accuracy, but a realism marked by a certain aesthetic heterogeneity that, as Richard Maltby (2012) notes, was cultivated by the studio as a way to meet perceived audience demands. At issue was what Saverio Giovacchini has characterized as the "realistic paradigm" (2001, 132), in which, as Maltby goes on to say, "contradictory notions of 'realism' and 'social value' could cohabit in an aesthetic coalition as broad and as imprecisely defined as the 'complex, contradictory, and discordant *ensemble*' of social forces that traveled under the banner of the Popular Front" (2012, 92). Thus, while postwar Hollywood's mode of production was undoubtedly rejuvenated by the combination of lightweight equipment, on-location shooting, and less expensive, more innovative scripts that marked the ultra-realist look of films like *The Naked City* (1948), genre cinema's popularity continued to endure mostly by virtue of a more fragmented realism, whose self-contradictory representations proffered a more traditional, displaced frame of reference. This was the approach taken by crime melodramas like *Martha Ivers*, whose social implications were far from clear-cut and which, as noted, may be said to reflect as well as repress salient issues. It is within these terms that we have to read Martha's admission, at one point in the film, that "owning" Iverstown gives her a

Figure 24.5 Toni's "United Nations blouse," in Lewis Milestone's *The Strange Love of Martha Ivers* (1946, producer Hal B. Wallis).

sense of power. Within these terms we also must consider the nature of her defensive rationalization of the murder of her aunt: "Look what I've done with what she left me – I've given to charity, built schools, hospitals – I've given thousands of people work – What was she?" These lines further exemplify the film's repression of women's actual homefront achievements; at the same time, they illustrate Rossen's indictment of the phony rhetoric of social responsibility that is the mark of the political right but is not gender-specific.

That Rossen was able to infuse *Martha Ivers* with certain political concerns dear to him significantly owed to the fact that the film was produced by Hal B. Wallis, Rossen's former boss at Warner Bros., who had since set up his own company (Hal Wallis Productions) and who gave the Rossen–Milestone team relative freedom in filming the script. What *did* get cut from this script indicates even more clearly what Rossen was after. In a line dropped from the film, Walter, for instance, says to Martha: "You are my father's estate. His gift to me. He brought me up to believe that it's a son's duty to protect his inheritance" (Neve 2007, 191). This line is consistent with a remark Walter later makes to Martha, included in the film, about "the power and the riches that you'd learned to love so much, and that I'd learned to love too." Neve is, of course, correct in claiming that these lines strongly indicate Rossen's desire to use the film to mount a critique of the false values of postwar America, which Sam and Toni fight in their roles as little people on the street who sleep in dingy hotels, travel on buses, or let people hitch rides in their car, and who – in best grassroots manner – use the newspaper archive for their sleuth work centered on the innocently hanged man. *Martha Ivers* further conveys this grassroots mentality through its use of fashion, particularly in the scene when Martha looks up Sam and Toni in their hotel room.

Martha's heavy, old-fashioned, and foreboding dress signifies hidebound isolationism, which stands in contrast to Toni's midriff-revealing blouse that features a vivid pattern of flags of assorted nations. This pattern could be seen to symbolize the United Nations, whose founding was met with skepticism by American conservatives. Toni is thus positioned in contrast with Martha's conservative values, but the blouse also, more broadly, could be seen to symbolize the heterogeneity of the Popular Front alliance as it was recently reinvigorated by the Hollywood Independent Citizens Committee of which Rossen was a prominent member. The symbolic implications of the hotel confrontation are additionally underscored by the fact that HICCASP's conservative counterpart and nemesis was the MPAPAI, which included among its founding members none other than Barbara Stanwyck.

The fact that Toni's "UN blouse" can be related to Hollywood's Popular Front and can, even more specifically, be read as a banner for HICCASP suggests that *Martha Ivers* may be about something more specific than the broad ideological conflict between progressive and conservative forces that was sweeping America. Iverstown, America's fastest-growing industrial city, not only is a symbol of the corrosive forces of capitalism, but also is a stand-in for another company town – Hollywood. The battle between Sam, Martha, and Walter can be related to the increasing climate of animosity, suspicion, and paranoia that characterized Hollywood in the late war and postwar years. The crucial year in this context is 1945, the year *Martha Ivers* was written and filmed, the year the war came to an end, and the year, too, that saw the beginning of a protracted battle between the two rival unions – a battle that would prove fatal for Hollywood's left. IATSE, Hollywood's biggest, most established, and most hierarchized labor organization, maintained its pro-studio status by brokering sweetheart deals with the moguls. Yet IATSE's status had been weakened by a scandal that exposed its leaders' lack of financial integrity. In the course of this crisis, a rival emerged to challenge IATSE's hegemony, the CSU, which was smaller than IATSE and catered to crafts people.

Generally not considered communist (though some of its members were), the CSU was nonetheless disliked by studio brass because of its militant bargaining politics. In early 1945, the two unions became involved in an internal jurisdictional dispute around the recognition of a local, erupting in an eight-month strike in which the studios first yielded to the CSU, only to lash back at it with the help of IATSE in the years to come – among other things, by agreeing to cooperate with HUAC (Schatz 1997, 305; Ceplair & Englund 1979, 217; Horne 2001, 160). A consideration of the leaders of each union, who became figureheads in the class struggle that gripped Hollywood, reveals that *Martha Ivers* reflects key elements of this struggle.[23]

When IATSE in early 1945 was threatened to be eclipsed by the CSU, it received a new West Coast manager, Roy Brewer, who had no history of racketeering and was considered a new-generation bureaucrat. But Brewer's leadership turned out to be just as questionable as that of his predecessors. He brokered secret negotiations with studio heads and labor groups and launched illicit investigations of his opponents (especially his CSU counterpart, Herb Sorrell) to discredit them and insure studio loyalty. As Thomas Schatz explains: "as the labor strike intensified, Brewer took advantage of the anti-Communist climate through two related tactics: flagrant redbaiting of the CSU, with Herb Sorrell as his primary (and admittedly vulnerable) target; and appeals on behalf of IATSE to the studios and the guilds to form an anti-Communist coalition" (Schatz 1997, 306). When writing *Martha Ivers*, Rossen inscribed a good deal of Brewer into the part of Walter. The first thing we learn about Walter is that he has no opponents in his campaign for D.A. The film portrays him as a shifty player who creates a climate of internal subversion and mistrust. Rossen links these qualities to issues of class. Neither hailing from the upper class, for whom Walter's father worked as a private teacher, nor belonging to the likes of Sam's class, Walter represents the historical ambition of the middle class to play both opposing ends of the class spectrum against each other to its own advantage. He is literally in bed with power, while presenting himself as from the people and for the people. Central to Walter's cunning is his ability to create negative projections of Sam that turn Martha against Sam – a parallel to Brewer who launched a sustained redbaiting campaign against CSU leader Sorrell and who actually started his career as a projectionist (a craft that was exclusively represented by IATSE). Walter speaks in visual images and ambiguous metaphors. Realizing that Sam is going to expose his and Martha's past record, he asks Sam to help him determine what to do about the three of them: "It sounds like a poem – if it would rhyme, it would rhyme in murder."

Rossen then juxtaposes what Brian Neve calls Walter and Martha's "personal fascism" to the Popular Front values of antifascism, internationalism, and working-class solidarity embodied by Sam and Toni. Sam's hard-boiled hero personality, which enables him to stand up against the corrupt excesses of business and power, is reminiscent of CSU leader Herb Sorrell's reputation as a hard-boiled labor leader. Like Sorrell, Sam becomes the target of slander. Not a communist, Sorrell was considered someone who was "totally apolitical and totally lacked leftist grounding" (Horne 2001, 17), qualities clearly reflected in Sam's rugged individualism. The hard-boiled hero of film noir is scarcely meek, but the film's depiction of Sam as a natural fighter is meant to allude more specifically to Sorrell's public image as hypermasculine pugilist who, even in younger years, was not afraid to use violence (Horne 2001, 16). Despite his ability to defend himself, however, film noir's hard-boiled hero frequently gets beaten up by bands of anonymous goons working for secret syndicates. This happens to Sam in *Martha Ivers* and it also happened to Sorrell – but Rossen reinforces the parallel by modeling Sam's abjection fairly closely on Sorrell's. Sorrell once stated that during a studio lockout of CSU workers, he was captured, beaten, and subjected to a process whereby they "drag you out into the desert and leave you out there" (Horne 2001, 19). This is exactly what happens to Sam in *Martha Ivers*. He is beaten unconscious in a back alley and taken far outside city limits, where he is dumped in a dried-up river bed.

It would seem, then, that Rossen uses Sam to carry the torch in *Martha Ivers*'s allegorical depiction of the class struggle in Hollywood. And yet, the picture is considerably more complicated, for there is something profoundly ambiguous about the film's portrayal of Sam. This ambiguity is a sign of considerable ambivalence among many in the industry, including Rossen, toward Sorrell. Many of Sorrell's negative qualities – his nativism and racism, his brutishness, and his lack of union organizing skills – would have been difficult for Rossen to write into the script. What Rossen does reference – even if only indirectly – is Sorrell's profound ignorance about Hollywood as an industry. It was this ignorance that moved Sorrell to lead the CSU into a strike that many in the industry perceived more as gratuitous provocation than well-thought-out strategy. The communists vehemently opposed the strike, first, because they saw it as weakening Hollywood's antifascist efforts in the still ongoing war; second, because it gave studio bosses the impression that the gauntlet had been thrown down; and third, because it gave Brewer and IATSE an excuse for intensified redbaiting. Looking at the conflict in this way, it could be argued that Sam, rather than picking up Walter's gauntlet, is the one who, in fact, throws it down by fueling Walter's suspicions and causing both Walter and Martha to believe that he wants to blackmail her. In the thickening plot, Martha is positioned in the middle, just as the studios were positioned between the two rival unions headed by Sorrell and Brewer. Sam's counterintuitive behavior can be read as Rossen's commentary on just how irresponsible and questionable a leader Sorrell really was.

Sorrell never denied that there were certain oddities about his career as a labor leader. "I would have voted for Hoover when he ran in 1928," he admitted, "but I happened to be a little bit filthy rich and I had hit the stock market, and my wife and I were on tour" (Horne 2001, 19). In the same statement, however, he went on to emphasize that, thereafter, he always voted for Roosevelt. This statement must have resonated with Rossen, who showed young Sam leaving Iverstown by going "on tour" with the circus. While it remained unrealized, Rossen's original intention was to have this scene end with a shot of campaign posters for Hoover, followed by a shot of posters for Roosevelt that marked the beginning of the film's main narrative when Sam returns to Iverstown (Neve 2007, 190). If historians' descriptions of the class conflict in Hollywood are accurate, one senses that many in the industry, and communists in particular, may have felt that Sorrell's leadership of the CSU was as problematic as Brewer's leadership of IATSE. This impression is reinforced in *Martha Ivers* when the film suggests that Sam and Walter are, in fact, mirror images of each other. The first time Sam encounters the image of the adult Walter is on the campaign poster hanging in the garage where he drops off his damaged car. Surprised to learn from the attendant that Walter and Martha are the town's power couple, Sam recalls Walter as a "scared little kid who used to live

Figure 24.6 The reflection of political ambiguity in Lewis Milestone's *The Strange Love of Martha Ivers* (1946, producer Hal B. Wallis).

on Sycamore Street." He walks up to the campaign poster and repeats the comment just as the camera tilts below the poster to reveal Sam's reflection in a mirror. The only detail of the poster that remains inside the film frame is the phrase "District Attorney." The film thus likens Sam with Walter – they are unified under the designation "District Attorney," which Rossen used as a decidedly ambiguous trope throughout his work (Neve 2007, 187); and they are linked visually by the mirror shot, which alludes to the symmetry Rossen accorded them in their offices and political roles.

How does Martha fit into this scheme of associations? Her relationship with Walter – which is primarily a business partnership – identifies her both diegetically and allegorically as the industrial establishment. In the narrative, she is Walter's prized asset and, as indicated by the words Rossen put in Walter's mouth about "the power and the riches that you'd learned to love so much," Martha's assets are also dear to her. Her upper-class status is consistent with construction of class privilege (or, in some cases, upward mobility) in the woman's film that appealed to its predominantly middle-class female audience. But Martha is also the prized asset of the film itself. Her character functions as a vehicle for one of the period's major stars, and while Stanwyck was not exclusively bound to one particular studio during this period, her star status still signified all the power and prestige of studio filmmaking. To insiders, who were able to decode the film's male characters as players in another drama – Hollywood's labor struggle – Stanwyck was more than the wealthy Missus positioned atop the sweeping staircase of a grand studio set. She embodied the very powers that owned this grand studio. She stood for the "bad employer" around whom the labor struggle ultimately revolved.[24]

But because Stanwyck was also a vocal Hollywood conservative, her casting in the lead role of *Martha Ivers* resonated even more strongly within Hollywood.[25] As a founding member of the MPAPAI, Stanwyck significantly contributed to the consolidation of Hollywood's right wing. Even before war's end, she and her husband, Robert Taylor, began campaigning against what they perceived as the manipulation of Hollywood movie content by left-wing artists and, in particular, screenwriters. On March 7, 1944, the MPAPAI wrote a letter to the arch-conservative North Carolina Democrat Robert R. Reynolds, encouraging him to launch a Congressional investigation of communism in the film industry (Ceplair & Englund 1979, 212; Madsen 2001, 213). While the MPAPAI went over the heads of studio bosses in inviting HUAC, the labor struggle that unfolded the following year would alienate studio heads so much that they would eventually cooperate with HUAC.

While Stanwyck was by no means alone in her anticommunist stance, I do not mean to suggest that her conservatism was representative of the political outlook of most American women during and after the war. Nor were Stanwyck's political views representative of female Hollywood stars in general. For every Stanwyck there was a Katharine Hepburn, for every Ginger Rogers a Lauren Bacall. What makes Stanwyck's biography instructive in the context of a discussion of Hollywood and gender is not her political conservatism. It is the fact that neither she nor anyone else read her success as a woman as an inspiration to politicize the position of women in Hollywood or elsewhere, or even so much as to ponder the question of female solidarity. Like many of the heroines she created on-screen, Stanwyck very much saw herself as a free player, with the difference that she would not accept punishment for her ambitions and achievements. Her "I-did-it-all-by-myself" attitude may have been overly self-righteous (Madsen 2001, 212), but her life-long propagation of the doctrine of self-reliance points to a more pervasive cultural phenomenon. It is connected with the atomizing aspects of social hegemony that tend to undermine most forms of political collectivism – including feminism.

While Stanwyck's political conservatism is relevant to a discussion of *Martha Ivers* as a preblacklist allegory of the Hollywood class struggle, it is Stanwyck's individualist interpretation of her relative social privilege, coupled with her embrace of traditional values and established powers, that connects her screen characters to the wartime and postwar female audiences who identified with them. These two aspects of Stanwyck's persona came together when, during the shooting of *Martha Ivers* in October 1945, Stanwyck became a scab. The ongoing tensions between the CSU and IATSE had led to a march on Warner Bros. in Burbank, where 800 CSU members attempted to keep IATSE workers from going onto the studio lot. After days of bloody fighting, overturned cars, and 80 injured, the CSU workers were beaten back by IATSE, Warner Bros. guards, and police, but several groups of picketers made it over to the Paramount lot where *Martha Ivers* was shooting (Madsen 2001, 235). As Kirk Douglas is quoted as saying, "We continued to shoot, but it meant we were locked in at the studio – if we went out, we couldn't get back in" (Douglas 1988, 136, quoted in Madsen 2001, 235). Because the script had been completed, Rossen was not on the set. As an adamant leftist, Milestone favored the CSU strikers. According to Douglas's account, Milestone left the set of *Martha Ivers* and went to a café across the street to talk to the strike supporters, which meant he promptly got locked out. As Douglas states, "For a while, the picture was directed by Byron Haskin. I felt guilty. What was I supposed to do? Barbara Stanwyck was working" (Douglas 1988, 136, quoted in Madsen 2001, 235).

The work of scabs is traditionally defined as a rejection of solidarity with a collective for the obtainment of personal gains. It is further understood as a transgressive spatial move that literally crosses a line. That Stanwyck's scabbing violated this pattern – she simply stayed put – may, on one level, be strictly circumstantial. In the context of the spatial metaphors of the film Stanwyck was in the process of shooting, however, her sedentary status is not without irony. Deciding to guard the Paramount lot by staying on the studio-built set of the Ivers mansion, Stanwyck moved closer to the character she was playing. Considering Stanwyck's attitude to and position within the studio system, this lot must have meant more to her than did Paramount, the studio that owned it. Stanwyck's free player status in the studio system had won her a nonexclusive contract with Paramount. Over the years, she worked for many studios in Hollywood. Her loyalty was neither to Paramount nor to any other studio. Her loyalty was to the studio *system*. She felt wedded to a specific mode of industrial production, including its assets, its lots, and its value system. Her scabbing put her in a place that stunningly foregrounds this double position. Faced with the decision to either leave the lot, stop working, and, thus, alienate the system that had given her security, a home, and a career, or to remain secluded inside its walls that suddenly, in this new era, seemed tarnished, Stanwyck decided to stay.

Because the motivation behind her action was not simply the securing of her privilege but also constituted a politically righteous fight against the forces that tried to destabilize the status quo, her decision might well appear to have been guided by a sense of responsibility, not entitlement. Under patriarchy, entitlement is something that is usually associated with the consequences of spatial mobility – as many films noir demonstrate, it is claimed by roamers and occupiers. By contrast, responsibility is associated with staying put, standing by, and taking charge after others have left. This is what Stanwyck did by installing herself as the custodian of the dominant powers – though it is important to point out that Stanwyck's decision did not reflect the classic association of responsibility with women who remain confined. In fact, her decision apparently compelled her younger, much less experienced colleague, Kirk Douglas, to do the same. The actor's comment, "I felt guilty. What was I supposed to do? Barbara Stanwyck was working" (Madsen 2001, 235), poignantly foregrounds the effeminacy of his fictional character, Walter, by invoking the traditional feminine rhetoric of there-was-really-nothing-I-could-do, the classic defense of those who claim to be caught in the middle. Stanwyck's resolve and steadfastness indicate she had no interest in having her sense of responsibility defined by this rhetoric. Like many others during the time, she would claim that what she did was the only responsible thing to do – just as it was responsible to keep the system going through these turbulent times. She had no intention of jeopardizing her hard-won career. So she did her bit – as an industry professional, a political conservative, and a woman who had made it in a man's world – to insure that Hollywood production kept going and quality films were being made. In so doing, she undermined those who did not think as she did. More specifically, her actions undermined the class struggle of her left-wing colleagues, many of whom were women and many of whom would get blacklisted just a few years later by testimony from friendly witnesses like her real-life husband.

Her fervent conservatism, it would seem, might have compelled Stanwyck to refuse working with left-wing artists in the wake of the 1947 hearings. This, however, was not the case. She, like the industry as a whole, knew all too well about the artistic skills of people such as Dalton Trumbo, Clifford Odets, and Lewis Milestone. So Stanwyck, like the rest of the industry, hypocritically continued to work with them (Madsen 2001, 254). Stanwyck controlled her emotions, developed a sense of pragmatism, and did what for so many at the time seemed the responsible thing to do – kept Sodom going.

Notes

1. Jack Patrick (usually billed as John Patrick) went on to write the screenplays for such notable films as *Three Coins in the Fountain* (1954), *High Society* (1956), *The Teahouse of the August Moon* (1956), *Some Came Running* (1958), *The World of Suzie Wong* (1960), and *The Shoes of the Fisherman* (1968).
2. The type of the exaggerated woman overlaps with Haskell's description of the "extraordinary" woman (1974, 16), but Haskell stresses these women's projection of sexual emancipation and independence over their neuroticism and eventual humiliation and containment.
3. Although there is some variation in sources concerning the spelling of "O'Neill," the film's press book spells it as listed here.
4. While *The Two Mrs. Carrolls* (1947) and *Cry Wolf* (1947) are still traditional female Gothics in which Stanwyck's characters have to prove their mettle (increasingly struggling against the odds), *Sorry, Wrong Number!* (1948) punishes her for both her wealth and her neurosis that paralyzes her and, thus, keeps her from escaping her killer. Even her melodramas increasingly became infused with the theme of illness. In *The Other Love* (1947) she plays a concert pianist who dies of tuberculosis (not, though, before being allowed a final taste of love); in *The Lady Gambles* (1949) she plays a woman with a gambling addiction. See Lugowski 2010 for a detailed discussion of this trend.
5. Stanwyck eagerly accepted the part after Bette Davis, Ann Sheridan, and Rosalind Russell had turned it down

and was deeply disappointed when Crawford took it away from her (Madsen 2001, 222–223).

6. The tag line in another poster version further implies Martha's overbearing personality: "For her demands ... a man had but two answers ... Complete Surrender or Death!"
7. This constellation is supported in the design for the theater lobby cards for the film. One design that plays up the hard-boiled aspects of the noir formula features Sam sparring with another man who is holding a gun. The female characters are again positioned according to their respective roles as femme fatale and virtuous future wife. The femme fatale (recognizable as Stanwyck, who is given a scheming face and claw-like fingernails) is placed above the scene of the fighting men, suggesting that she may have caused the fight. The other woman is placed below the two men. Her subordinate position, her youth, and her pleading face suggest her virtue and her nurturing function.
8. An alternative version of this design crucially manipulates two details to build up a rather different set of expectations about the female characters. It replaces Scott's noir-looking face with her virginal pose from the other design and positions it underneath rather than behind Martha's head. Tellingly, this version of the ad replaces the word "passion" in the tag line with the word "frenzy." The implication is that Martha's violent passions can be unleashed even without the trigger of female competition (this version once again identifies Scott's character as an innocuous virgin who is now not positioned behind Martha's back but beneath her). Overall, it is notable that a slight shift in the definition of Stanwyck's character necessitates a much more radical redefinition of Lizabeth Scott's character. Women are thus forced to occupy one of two opposing stereotypes, guileless virgin or shrewd (and possibly similarly hardened) competitor. The second version is played up even further in yet another lobby card, in which Scott's character Toni is drawn in full, is given the pose of a loose woman or prostitute, and is positioned above the more neutral-looking faces of Sam and Martha (the latter now looking more wistful and suffering).
9. The prefabricated summaries link the femme fatale with the spectacle of violence: "Before the story has run its course, Barbara [Stanwyck] is guilty of braining her old aunt to death, sending an innocent man to the gallows for the deed, attempting mayhem twice on the person of Van Heflin and in turn suggesting to Heflin that he kill Kirk Douglas, who portrays her unwanted mate" (Paramount Pictures 1946, 7).
10. These components did, of course, come to define most exaggerated woman parts played by Davis, Stanwyck, and Crawford from the 1940s onward. But case-by-case assessments reveal the operation of a complex cultural dialectic in which one studio's near-contradictory construction of femininity, wrought by internal creative struggle between director and producer, becomes another studio's integrated marketing approach. The fact that Twentieth Century-Fox undermined the sex appeal of *Double Indemnity*'s femme fatale by forcing her to wear a cheap blonde wig that made her look slightly grotesque apparently all but inspired Warner Bros., the studio that produced *Mildred Pierce*, to tote the seductive qualities of a frustrated cake-baking mother approaching middle age. Thus, while tag lines read, "She's the kind of woman men want ... but shouldn't have!" and "Mildred! ... she had more to offer a man in a glance than most women give in a lifetime!," poster graphics shrewdly withhold Crawford from public view, displaying her in silhouette only (Haralovich 1997, 199–200). By contrast, Paramount's posters for *Martha Ivers* – Stanwyck's femme fatale follow-up to *Double Indemnity* – openly display Stanwyck in character, but with tag lines that replace sexual seductiveness with traits evoking the "exaggerated woman" and more broadly defined glamour.
11. An anecdote in the press book (Paramount Pictures 1946, 7) quotes Stanwyck claiming in jest that her acting assignments require home rehearsals of all her evil parts with her husband, Robert Taylor, who thus gets to use his combat training. Yet the anecdote is laid out with a photo of Stanwyck with Heflin, not Taylor, extending the military allusion to the actor who played Sam.
12. *New York Times*, July 25, 1946, n.p.
13. Another section of the exploitation page provides guiding questions for local gazettes: "HAVE YOU EVER KEPT A STRANGE SECRET?" and "WOULD YOU MARRY A WOMAN WITH A PAST AS WALTER O'NEILL DID IN THE STRANGE LOVE OF MARTHA IVERS?" These questions would have resonated strongly in the war and postwar years, when many Americans accumulated experiences they might have been hesitant to disclose later.
14. See Paul Arthur's essay in Volume III of the hardcover/online edition and his unpublished doctoral dissertation, New York University, on the subject (Arthur 1985).
15. The list of films that feature male protagonists in a state of abjection is too long to be quoted here. The best-known examples include *Double Indemnity*, *Lost Weekend* (1945), *D.O.A.* (1947), *Dark Passage* (1947), and *Where the Sidewalk Ends* (1950).
16. The script effectively shades her role through dialogue that suits the deep-voiced Anderson's angular performance. While the aunt is cold and stern toward Martha, she is not ignorant of the girl's qualities and talents, astutely professing that "Martha will be alright

anywhere." She hits the kitten as much out of fright as outrage, and while she does seem to possess a sadistic streak, she is also lonely and needy, commanding Walter's father to keep her company despite the fact that she sees right through his kowtowing on behalf of his son's education.

17. As Axel Madsen has noted of Stanwyck: "In her teens her voice was already deep and husky and made her sound like someone with a secret. Her alto was all-business, and it deepened over the years into a voice whose throaty undertone warned of the scam to come" (2001, 3).
18. It should be noted that Williams's definition of matriarchal power decidedly goes beyond the notion of woman as mother. For Williams, it means more broadly women's feeling of independence in the absence of men, as was the case during World War II for many women. Williams makes specific reference to *Mildred Pierce*'s depiction of Mildred's career and of Mildred's and Ida's financial success (1988, 23).
19. It was not until after the war that critics, who in the 1950s would write for the influential French film journal *Cahiers du Cinéma*, coined the term to designate a new dark tendency they recognized in American cinema, particularly those films adapted from the hard-boiled detective fiction of writers such as Dashiell Hammett, Raymond Chandler, James M. Cain, and Cornell Woolrich.
20. *New York Herald Tribune*, July 25, 1946, n.p.
21. *New York Times*, July 25, 1946, n.p.
22. In 1947, Rossen and Milestone became part of the Hollywood Nineteen, the "unfriendly" witnesses subpoenaed by the House Un-American Activities Committee (HUAC) to appear at the Washington hearings (though neither had to testify before the hearings were called off). Rossen appeared to have terminated his membership in the Communist Party that same year and went on to make several films, now also as a director, the most significant of which were the 1947 John Garfield boxing drama *Body and Soul*, and the 1949 prestige political drama *All the King's Men*, adapted from Robert Penn Warren's novel. However, while shooting on location in Mexico for Columbia's *The Brave Bulls* (1951), Rossen was named by friendly witnesses as a communist, upon which Columbia Pictures terminated its contract with him (Neve 1992, 139). During HUAC's second wave of hearings beginning in 1951, Rossen testified that he no longer was a communist; however, as Neve states, "unable to get his passport renewed he appeared the second time as a cooperative witness, providing – or more precisely confirming – the names of fifty-three Communists" (Neve 2007, 197).
23. See also Broe 2010 for a comprehensive discussion of this issue.
24. One might object to this view by pointing out that stars were just one more part of the labor force and that this part, as had become clear through a few acts of rebellion by female stars in particular, was just as much at the mercy of their employer as were, say, the writers, painters, and set builders. While certainly not wrong, this observation begs qualification. As the industry's main asset, stars were at the top of Hollywood's labor hierarchy. Their contracts were more favorable than those of any other workers in Hollywood. Their union, the Screen Actors Guild (SAG), had a much more accommodating relationship with the studios than had the Screen Writers Guild (SWG) or the CSU. In fact, SAG and IATSE were closely aligned in their centrist-conservative political predisposition and in their loyalty to their employer. Thus, while I don't mean to deny the existence of a basic labor hierarchy in Hollywood, my point is that this view of Hollywood's labor force is too broad and needs to be supplemented by an understanding of the internal hierarchies and political fault lines that ran among Hollywood workers. As such, it must be acknowledged that the history of unionism is determined not only by heroic rebellions and hard-won achievements, but also by internal factionalism and purges, as well as by accommodation and acquiescence.
25. It is important to note that Stanwyck rarely played foreigners or even historical characters, instead portraying contemporary American women who connoted ordinariness and identifiability (Lugowski 2010). These qualities closely tied in with Stanwyck's offscreen image as a patriot. On a postwar trip to Paris, she affronted French fashion designers by refusing to buy anything, stating: "I think American designers did a terrific job during the war with inferior material." On her return voyage she angrily defended the shipboard service on the SS *America* to complaining European travelers: "When American troops were going overseas not so long ago, we didn't hear any of you complaining about American service. You were pretty damn happy to see those GIs when they liberated Paris. You were pretty damn happy to get American food and supplies from the American Red Cross" (quoted in Madsen 2001, 241–242).

References

Arthur, Paul. (1985). "Shadows on the Mirror: Film Noir and Cold War America, 1945–1957." Unpublished doctoral dissertation, New York University.

Basinger, Jeanine. (1993). *A Woman's View: How Hollywood Spoke to Women, 1930–1960*. New York: Alfred A. Knopf.

Broe, Dennis. (2010). *Film Noir, American Workers, and Postwar Hollywood*. Gainesville: University Press of Florida.

Ceplair, Larry, & Englund, Steven. (1979). *The Inquisition in Hollywood: Politics in the Film Community, 1930–1960*. Berkeley: University of California Press.

Cook, David. (1981). *A History of Narrative Film*. 2nd edn. New York: W. W. Norton.

Douglas, Kirk. (1988). *The Ragman's Son: An Autobiography*. New York: Simon & Schuster.

Giovacchini, Saverio. (2001). *Hollywood Modernism: Film and Politics in the Age of the New Deal*. Philadelphia: Temple University Press.

Haralovich, Mary Beth. (1997). "Selling *Mildred Pierce*: A Case Study." In Thomas Schatz, *Boom and Bust: American Cinema in the 1940s* (pp. 196–202). Berkeley: University of California Press.

Haskell, Molly. (1974). *From Reverence to Rape: The Treatment of Women in the Movies*. Baltimore: Penguin.

Horne, Gerald. (2001). *Class Struggle in Hollywood, 1930–1950: Moguls, Mobsters, Stars, Reds, and Trade Unionists*. Austin: University of Texas Press.

Lugowski, David M. (2010). "Claudette Colbert, Ginger Rogers, and Barbara Stanwyck: The American Homefront Women." In Sean Griffin (ed.), *What Dreams Were Made Of: Movie Stars of the 1940s*. New Brunswick: Rutgers University Press.

Madsen, Axel. (2001). *Stanwyck*. San Jose: iUniverse.com, Inc.

Maltby, Richard. (2012). "'As Close to Real Life As Hollywood Ever Gets': Headline Pictures, Topical Movies, Editorial Cinema, and Studio Realism in the 1930s." In Cynthia Lucia, Roy Grundmann, & Art Simon (eds), *The Wiley-Blackwell History of American Film. Vol. 2: 1929 to 1945* (pp. 76–111). Oxford: Wiley-Blackwell.

Neve, Brian. (1992). *Film and Politics in America: A Social Tradition*. New York: Routledge.

Neve, Brian. (2007). "Red Hollywood in Transition: The Case of Robert Rossen." In Frank Krutnik, Steve Neale, Brian Neve, & Peter Stanfield (eds), *"Un-American" Hollywood: Politics and Film in the Blacklist Era* (pp. 184–197). New Brunswick: Rutgers University Press.

Paramount Pictures. (1946). *The Strange Love of Martha Ivers: Press Book*. Los Angeles.

Polan, Dana. (1986). *Power and Paranoia: History, Narrative, and the American Cinema, 1940–1950*. New York: Columbia University Press.

Robinson, Edward G., & Spigelgass, Leonard. (1973). *All My Yesterdays*. New York: Hawthorn.

Schatz, Thomas. (1997). *Boom and Bust: American Cinema in the 1940s*. Berkeley: University of California Press.

Sklar, Robert. (1994). *Movie-Made America: A Cultural History of American Movies*. Revised and updated. New York: Vintage Books. (Original work published 1975.)

Walsh, Andrea S. (1984). *Women's Film and Female Experience, 1940–1950*. New York: Praeger.

Williams, Linda. (1988). "Feminist Film Theory: *Mildred Pierce* and the Second World War." In Deirdre Pribram (ed.), *Female Spectators: Looking at Film and Television* (pp. 12–30). London: Verso.

Williams, Linda. (2001). *Playing the Race Card: Melodramas of Black and White from Uncle Tom to O.J. Simpson*. Princeton: Princeton University Press.

25

Natalie Wood
Studio Stardom and Hollywood in Transition

Cynthia Lucia
Professor, Rider University, United States

As the last child actor emerging into adult stardom from the **Hollywood studio system**, **Natalie Wood** allegorizes the decline of an industry and era, as her roles in ***Rebel Without a Cause*** and ***Inside Daisy Clover***, and as censorship battles over ***Splendor in the Grass*** signify. Cynthia Lucia explores Wood's career trajectory in the thriving studio system that gave birth to "Natalie Wood," shaping her star image and regulating her on-screen sexuality, a matter complicated as the system declined and Wood matured. As an established "star," Wood struggled to be recognized as a serious "actress" in the **New Hollywood**, at a time when publicity surrounding **Method acting** created a division between the two – a dichotomy adding further resonance to the evolving conception of what "Hollywood" would come to mean. Lucia's essay shares ground with Mark Lynn Anderson on the star system, Matthew H. Bernstein on the studio system, and Cynthia Baron and Beckett Warren on the Actors Studio in this volume, and with Derek Nystrom on the New Hollywood in Volume II.

Additional terms, names, and concepts: Production Code Administration, Catholic Legion of Decency, identity crisis, momism, the Kinsey Report

A 1963 *Look* magazine article asks about 24-year-old actress Natalie Wood, "How long does it take to grow up in the movies?" Born in 1938, Wood was raised and schooled mostly on studio lots, having worked steadily in film from the age of six. She made a successful transition from child actor to teenage idol in 1955, opposite James Dean in *Rebel Without a Cause*, and came of age as an adult star in the early 1960s, just as the system (as it had existed in the previous three decades) had all but vanished. If not *the* very last star to emerge from the studio system, Wood was certainly the last to have done so as a child of the system. The title of the article, "Natalie Wood: Child of Change" (*Look* 1963, 91), succinctly establishes two qualities that were crucial to defining the star: Natalie-as-child would never completely fade from her adult star image – whether in Hollywood publicity or in the press – and "change" would become a lingering part

American Film History: Selected Readings, Origins to 1960, First Edition. Edited by Cynthia Lucia, Roy Grundmann, and Art Simon.
© 2016 John Wiley & Sons, Inc. Published 2016 by John Wiley & Sons, Inc.

of that image. A third defining quality – her Russian heritage – would find frequent though less consistent expression in press accounts and indirect expression in several roles that defined her as ethnically or racially "other."

In the most obvious sense, Wood's on-screen maturation, both physically and in increasingly adult roles, was an unambiguous marker of change. But even more significantly, in her time, place, and circumstances, Wood embodied a Hollywood in transition, on the cusp of significant change. If it is true, as David James argues, that every film is an allegory of its own mode of production (1989, 12), then the roles Wood played and aspects of her personal life, both real and as molded by studio publicity and the press, can be seen to allegorize the very pressures enacted within and on the studio system in transition. Whether in the call for greater realism in story content, style, and performance, or in the demand for more open representations of sexuality in the face of a weakening, though nevertheless meticulously enforced Production Code, Wood's films allegorize not only transition, but also the efforts of adjustment and correction that transition often triggers. Her films dramatize these corrective impulses in their representation of American culture and society, with its patriarchal prerogatives and crises, at a point when the culture itself was on the verge of far-reaching change. As a commodity operating within an industry in decline, Natalie Wood – her star persona, her films, and their marketing – allegorizes the industry's response to its own crisis, revealing something about how Hollywood, in the 1950s and 1960s, wished to see itself, whether in the fictional and publicity department representations it manufactured of its past, or in its refashioning of those images in anticipation of its future.

As far into her career as 1965 – when she was 26 and had made some 38 films – a Warner Bros. press release announcing her title role in *Inside Daisy Clover* observed that

> in Natalie today there is a haunting resemblance to the little girl who appeared in such films as "No Sad Songs For Me" and "Happyland." But she has acquired additional depth, charm and beauty with the years, plus a marked technical skill in acting.

Promoting the image of Wood as a maturing and skilled actress – not merely as a movie star – the release attempts to shape the image of a new kind of Hollywood, one that can be said to appreciate and respect acting more than stardom, and one able to produce a self-reflexive and self-critical movie such as *Daisy Clover*, in which the industry simultaneously purports to represent and revise its own history. Elaborating upon (or perhaps exploiting) the idea of change as it had accrued to her image, the release quotes Wood as saying, "Life is change. To try to stem the years is foolish and tragic. I didn't mind growing up personally and on the screen." About her childhood acting she says, "I never had to carry a film, like Shirley Temple or Jane Withers," a factor she sees as contributing to her successful transition into adult stardom:

> I had no "image" . . . The public didn't have a set idea of what I looked like, how I should behave. Consequently, when I started to grow up and change they didn't resent me, as they had no preconceived idea of what I should look like and remain.

Wood was invited to ponder this subject very likely because *Daisy Clover* is about the rising but short-lived stardom of its title character whose career begins when she is a teenager and is washed up well before she reaches 20. With prescient insight into the workings of Hollywood stardom and her own position as a former child actor, Wood comments that "child stars bring out the mother–father–brother–sister aspects of fans . . . . When an adored child star grows up this makes the fans feel older themselves." Referring to how families often try to keep their youngest child "young beyond its years," she sees it as "mostly to help themselves ignore the passing of time, a foolish effort to drink from the fountain of youth."[1] Her words, insofar as they are her own, grow out of lived experience it would seem, given that in her early teenage years, movie and TV studios did precisely this – they attempted to keep her young beyond her years.

Coming of Age in Hollywood

Born to Russian parents as Natalia Zakharenko, Wood began her career in the movies at the age of four, with a nonspeaking role in Irving Pichel's *Happy Land* (released in 1943). Her father, a carpenter plagued by alcoholism, changed the family name to Gurdin in the hope of more favorable placement on job lists during the Depression (Finstad 2001, 18). He eventually would be employed in constructing Hollywood studio sets. Her mother, a former amateur ballet dancer and/or actress, depending on the source you read, devoted herself to promoting Natalie's career. Biographer Suzanne Finstad reports that the actress's career was of such intense and immediate importance to the mother that she moved her family from Santa Rosa to Hollywood, despite their having almost no money – with only the hope of shopping little Natalia around to the studios and especially to Pichel (2001, 29). Studio press releases, on the other hand, typically state that Pichel "sent for" Natalia. Whatever the case, from the time he met the little girl when directing *Happy Land*, Pichel took a strong interest in Natalia – whether to make her a star, as publicity claims, or to protect her, as Finstad reports, from the deforming effects of life as a child actor that he witnessed her mother so aggressively pursuing. Pichel, in fact, offered to adopt her. Finstad believes that Natasha (as she preferred to be called) "felt an oppressive burden, at five, to be a success in Hollywood, thinking she was responsible for the family's upheaval" (2001, 33). In pursuing her own goals, her mother found that her persistence *did* pay off, for at the age of seven Natasha Gurdin was christened yet again, this time as "Natalie Wood," by producers at International Pictures, where she played her first speaking role as an Austrian refugee – required to speak German and to speak English with a proper German accent – alongside Orson Welles and Claudette Colbert in Pichel's *Tomorrow Is Forever* (1946) (Finstad 2001, 36–39). Her childhood career took hold with her performance as the mature-beyond-her-years Susan who resists belief in Santa Claus in *Miracle on 34th Street* (1947). After that film Natalie worked steadily, making several movies a year, until offers slowed a bit during her early adolescence. But even then she appeared in television roles, more often in pigtails and frilly dresses than in costumes more appropriate to her age.

Her role as Judy in *Rebel Without a Cause*, released in 1955 when she had turned 17, established Wood in the public mind as no longer a little girl, but as a beautiful, restless teenager and burgeoning young woman. Privately – and something the fanzines only hinted at – her experience far exceeded her years. As a 16-year-old, before getting the role in *Rebel*, she had an affair (beginning around January 1955) with its 43-year-old director, Nicholas Ray, who remained reluctant to cast her in the film, saying (without apparent irony) that her "little girl" image would be too difficult to erase in the public mind (Finstad 2001, 165–179). The story goes that, after a February 1955 car crash involving alcohol and with her teenage friend Dennis Hopper (also cast in *Rebel*) at the wheel, Wood called Nick Ray – not her parents – to her hospital bedside and made her plea: "They called me a goddamn juvenile delinquent! *Now* do I get the part?" (quoted in Finstad 2001, 176).[2] Natalie clearly had absorbed her mother's ambition. In a March 1, 1955 memo from Nicholas Ray to *Rebel* producer David Weisbart on casting the female lead after dozens were tested, Ray wrote:

> there is only one girl who has shown the capacity to play Judy, and she is Natalie Wood... Although there has been talk of Debbie Reynolds for this part, especially from an exploitation standpoint, I think the studio might develop a star of its own with Natalie Wood.[3]

Once cast in *Rebel*, Wood signed a seven-year contract with Warner Bros., and both she and the studio worked hard at countering her little girl image, while at the same time hoping to preserve enough of it to keep the public invested in the idea of a maturing "girl" whose sexual innocence was a fragile matter, to be sure. A 1957 issue of *Look* ran a story on Wood titled "Teen-age Tiger," with the subhead "Hollywood's number one cut-up girl delights rebellious teen-agers." The article begins with "Natalie Wood, 18... makes it crystal-clear that she is a 'wild girl,' 1957 teenage style. Once, she was an angelic child actress. Then she played James Dean's delinquent girl friend... and her life became exciting." Natalie is dubbed the "favorite rebel of many teenagers." Yet, we are told that "beneath her giddy exterior, she is an actress who is... [very] ambitious." The article takes care to note that she lives with her parents in her "own private suite." We hear that although she avoids household chores, "she has been working since she was six and never plans to stop" (*Look* 1957, 96). While the public image of the teenage and young adult Natalie Wood is carefully crafted to create a persona appealing to youth audiences of the day, she is nevertheless presented as a "safe" rebel – apolitical, sexy but not actively sexual, and generally nonthreatening to the parents who will likely fund the moviegoing habits of their teens. Both in her

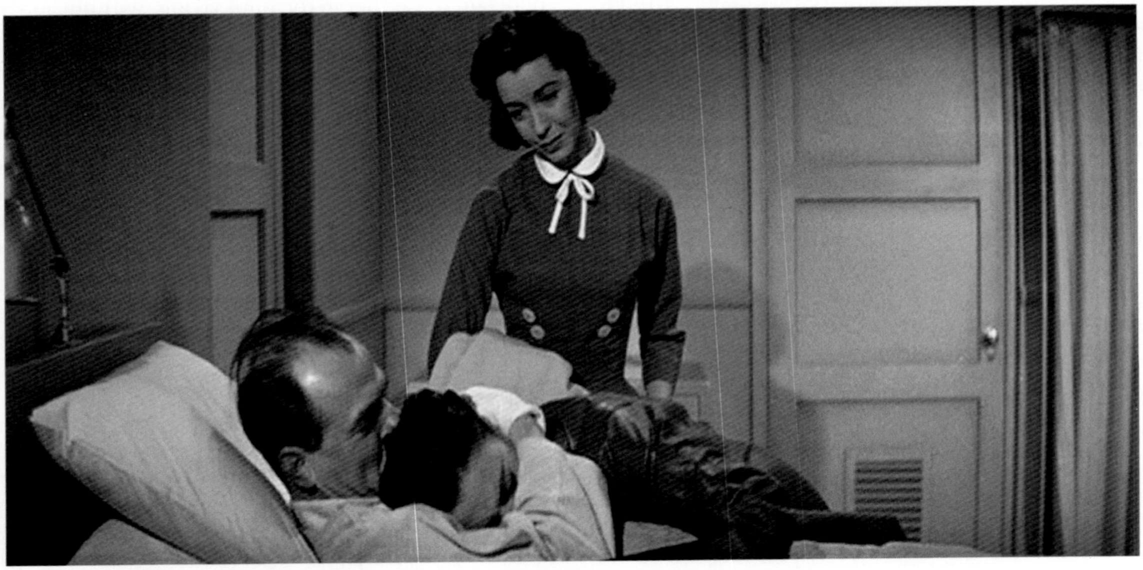

Figure 25.1 The image of reconciliation between father and daughter literalizes the family drama in Gordon Douglas's *Bombers B-52* (1957, producer Richard Whorf).

star image and in the roles she played, Wood was being shaped to conform to the postwar, 1950s ideal, as Elaine Tyler May defines it: "Sexy women who became devoted sweethearts or wives would contribute to the goodness of life; those who used their sexuality for power or greed would destroy men, families, and even society" (1988, 63). Natalie Wood consistently is represented as the former, both in the roles she plays and in the press.

Reflecting tensions between the desire and repression at play in cultural anxieties centered on female sexuality – especially where a "daughter" growing to womanhood is concerned – many of Natalie Wood's more adult roles continued to center on themes of maturation, including *Marjorie Morningstar* (1958, when she was 20), *Cash McCall* (1960), *Splendor in the Grass* and *West Side Story* (both 1961, when she was 23 and played a teenager), *Gypsy* (1962), *Love with the Proper Stranger* (1963), *Inside Daisy Clover* (1965, when, at 27, she was cast as a 15-year-old), and *This Property Is Condemned* (1966). Each narrative, in one way or another, revolves around her sexual status. *Gypsy*, *Inside Daisy Clover*, and *This Property Is Condemned* explicitly construct her as a commodity on the entertainment and/or sexual market (much, one might say, as her mother, first, and the Hollywood industry later had done). The developing sexuality of the characters she plays, sometimes inflected by questions of race or ethnicity, form the narrative focus, with plots centered on her virginity and the (potential) consequences of its loss. Even among several of the earlier films this is true, including *Rebel Without a Cause*, *Bombers B-52* (1957), *Kings Go Forth* (1958), and two 1956 films, *The Searchers* and *A Cry in the Night*, both of which cast her as a kidnapping victim, though in very different narrative contexts.

Although not a child in these roles, she often plays something of a child struggling against parental control in order to grow up – sometimes in conflict with a father who, in the classic psychoanalytic sense, is both jealous and fearful of her emerging sexuality; sometimes with a mother who, with a tinge of underlying envy, preaches to her daughter about what "nice girls" should and should not do on dates – very much in line with 1950s ideology, as May defines it. In *Bombers B-52*, for instance, Wood plays the young adult Lois whose father (Karl Malden), an Air Force mechanic, strongly disapproves of her dating a pilot (Efrem Zimbalist, Jr), higher in rank than himself. The conflict prompts her to pack her bags with plans to leave home, until she learns that her father has been injured. The Oedipal implications abound in the hospital room reconciliation between father and daughter.

Shot composition establishes the classic Freudian family drama, with Lois taking the place of her mother (Marsha Hunt), as her mother looks on, followed by the father and daughter, alone, embracing in an image clearly evoking underlying desire at the core of the family drama.

The final lines Wood's character speaks to her father neatly capture the typical interplay between resistance and reconciliation in the narrative of transition, with words that can just as easily be directed toward viewers who may have watched Wood grow up on the screen: "Dad, I know that when you look at me, you think I'm a little kid climbing a tree. But I'm not a kid anymore, Dad. I'm grown up – I'm all grown up . . . "

In so many films, as in this one, Wood's character struggles for independence but always safely within acceptable bourgeois (Production Code) limits, keeping the family (if not always her own implicit virginity) intact. In this film, Lois's father admits his mistake in having misjudged the pilot and gives his blessing to his daughter and their relationship. Yet tensions present themselves in contradictory directions – whether between patriarchal desire and control or filial devotion and rebellion. Here, the family drama is an overt plot element, and it is at play in a number of Natalie Wood films, whether directly or indirectly. That drama, however, is often reconfigured. In *Bombers B-52* the father at first jealously rejects the younger though, not incidentally, higher-ranking pilot, followed by his eventual acceptance and even identification with the younger man (Chodorow 2004, 471) – particularly after he had saved the father's life. It is the father who now must identify with the "son," a reversal of the Freudian model. This reconfiguration has allegorical implications, perhaps expressing the industry's need (in spite of initial resistance) to embrace less rigid top-down, patriarchal models of management and to consider new, more flexible codes of representation in order to appeal to the tastes of a younger audience seeking something new that a seemingly outmoded industry could not deliver.

In *A Cry in the Night* (1956), Wood's police captain father (Edmond O'Brien) is something of an exaggerated hysterical male – both when he thinks his daughter is out too long on a date with a "boy" he disapproves of, and later, when he finds she's been kidnapped on the lover's lane where she and the boy, her future fiancé, were parking. Though we should be cautious about too literally applying the terms of the Freudian family drama, which itself has been challenged, it is possible to suggest that, in a general way, many of the films invite viewers, already familiar with Wood as a child, to play and replay the family drama in various configurations around her on-screen presence. Wood's own analogy between her having grown up on-screen and family relations in general perceptively taps into this idea. At the same time, Hollywood itself can be seen to stand in for the (nurturing) family through the narratives and mise-en-scène it delivers, "safely" positioning the former little-girl star within a dominant value system. This strategy seems aimed at asserting traditional industry "values" as superior to the more openly sexual subject matter in films from foreign markets, at the same time as it exposes the attitude of repression that fostered turbulence both in the industry and in the culture.

This is especially true of *Rebel Without a Cause*, a film that "stages" Wood's transition into adult stardom. *Rebel* is a significant film for Wood in ways that play out allegorically in the interlocking contexts of her own career – American film history and mid-1950s preoccupations with masculinity, female sexuality, and identity – all within the context of family dynamics. As in *Bombers B-52* and so many of her films to follow, narrative complications involving Wood's character arise from both the exposure and the repression of erotic dynamics within the family – all with multiple self-reflexive and allegorical implications. The film also is among the first to target a newly acknowledged and profitable teen audience[4] – in part through the casting of James Dean and Sal Mineo, both Method actors who brought a highly publicized and popularized "new" realism to screen performance.

The repressed sexual dimension of the "family drama" in *Rebel Without a Cause* is central to the narrative strand involving Wood's character Judy. Her womanly, maturing physical presence poses a conflict for her father (William Hopper), who no longer wants to kiss or show affection to his "glamour puss," as he calls her (this is one small unsettling detail among many in the movie hinting at deep-rooted psychic conflict). He reprimands her harshly when she attempts to kiss him as she always had as a child: "What's the matter with you? You're getting too old for that kind of stuff, kiddo . . . ," he says. "Girls your

Figure 25.2 In Nicholas Ray's *Rebel Without a Cause* (1955, producer David Weisbart), the womanly teenager Judy craves the affection her father had conferred more openly when she was a child.

age don't do things like that. Do you need an explanation?" he scolds, in response to her own words expressing confusion about this sudden change: "I guess I just don't understand anything." She is naïve to the sexual charge her physical maturation generates – especially for her father. As in *Bombers B-52* and conforming to psychoanalytic readings of the family drama, the mother passively recedes into the background, functioning mainly as mediator and as substitute object for the father's repressed desire – something made clear when, after Judy expresses her confusion, her father, troubled and aggravated, proclaims, "I'm tired. I'd like to change the subject," addressing his words not to Judy but to his wife. As this scene opens, an image rife with erotic tension places Judy in profile, emphasizing her sexualized figure as her father walks by.[5] Composition and costuming capture the mixture of womanly attraction and girlish vulnerability Wood embodies, while the cinemascope frame heightens tension by emphasizing tokens of masculine dominance – even in the family dining room, male athletic trophies and phallic swords decorate the space. Yet these props call attention to themselves as just that – adornments that prop up an unsteady masculine authority.

Questions of masculine dominance, how it should be asserted, and what it means to be a man, are central to the film's narrative. In contrast to Judy's father, and the phallic props that surround him, is the father of James Dean's Jim Stark. Dressed in a woman's apron and doing domestic chores in more than one scene, Jim's father (Jim Backus) finds it impossible to assert himself or to give his son guidance or advice. Jim's rebellion is prompted by his need to restore conventional patriarchal order to his own family, where the father is consistently dominated and overruled by his wife and his mother, who lives with them. While cast as teenage rebels, Jim, Judy, and the very childlike Plato (Sal Mineo) want nothing more than a conventionally stable, loving family with parents who are honest and "sincere" – a word spoken more than once in the film. Yet, just as sexual tensions and repression rock the dynamics within Judy's family, they also underlie the more perfect surrogate family that Jim and Judy as "parents" form with Plato as "child," but with an interesting alteration – Plato's desire is directed toward Jim as surrogate father rather than toward Judy as surrogate mother.[6] The homoerotic charge resulting – on the one hand, from overidentification with Jim as "the father" and, on the other hand, from desire for him as potential lover – is undeniable and can perhaps be understood as a commentary on Hollywood's "coded" representations of sexuality, and particularly in its suppression of public knowledge about the sexual orientation of its gay or bisexual male stars, like Dean and Mineo, among so many others.[7] While on the surface working within those codes, the reconfigured family here hints at multiple directions

Figure 25.3 Initiating the "chickie run," Natalie Wood as Judy in Nicholas Ray's *Rebel Without a Cause* appears as a star stepping onto the stage for the first time (1955, producer David Weisbart).

of desire at play, articulated powerfully in the performances of Mineo and Dean – most poignantly when Plato tenderly holds and brushes his lips against Jim's jacket after Jim offers it to him.

In a tender love scene between Judy and Jim, again "coded" by narrative elision, with a dissolve implying that some form of sexual intimacy has occurred, they talk about what a man should be: "Gentle and sweet, like you are. And someone who doesn't run away when you want them, like being Plato's friend when nobody else liked him. That's being strong," says Judy, presenting an alternative version of manhood from that embodied by her father, by Jim's father, or by the violent gang out to get Jim. Her words further imply the need for more stable, responsible families than their own – misshapen by overly assertive, castrating mothers who undermine their husbands and sons (as in Jim's family), by mothers who are too passive and asexual to counter the erotic charge their daughters unwittingly ignite (as in Judy's family), or by parents involved in their own separate pursuits and pleasures, consigning the care of their children to "hired help" (as Plato's wealthy, divorced parents have done). The film's politics thus waver between a critique of the older generation against which the teens rebel and a conservative reassertion of the importance of family and the centrality of "proper" expression of patriarchal control within the family – again with allegorical resonance, as the weakening studio system negotiates new ways to survive and preserve some fragment of its own diminishing dominance.

Through its narrative centered on Jim's searching for a new way to "be a man" and in its "staging" of Natalie Wood's coming of age as a new teenage star, *Rebel* allegorically merges underlying cultural tensions with the "staging" of Hollywood's own transition – perhaps into a second period of adolescence, as it now may seem in retrospect. Born out of dramatically diminished box office returns, in part because of television and other competing forms of leisure entertainment, the industry would be forced to redefine itself. The movies would need to find a newly appealing identity, whether through color and new widescreen productions or through the increasingly popular drive-in theater that would provide a more "private" venue for movie viewing outside the home (Lev 2003, 80, 212).

Allegorically staging Wood's emergence into stardom is the image of Judy signaling the beginning of the "chickie run" – in which Buzz has challenged Jim to see who is least chicken (most manly) by remaining longest in the stolen cars they race toward the edge of a cliff. The mise-en-scène echoes that of the paradigmatic star narrative – with car headlights standing in for theatrical footlights, thus recreating the "big" stage on which an inexperienced but talented actress first sets foot. By extension, of course, the mise-en-scène signifies the power of the theatrical establishment that has placed her there – and, moreover, of the film industry that represents it on-screen. Wood captures the excitement, defiance, and danger involved when the new performer (child actress) asserts her presence on stage (screen) for the first time (as a mature actress) – all of which resonates, at the same time, with Judy's rebellion against her father, whose rejection prompted her to flee from the house to seek out this thrill instead. At the same time, a second, very distant high angle shot emphasizes her vulnerability, tying the teenage star with her past as a child actor, and implying the need for a protective (better) family to counter Judy's misguided, short-sighted rebellion.

Rebel's overt attention to family and the complicated place of the adolescent within it not only reflexively identifies and addresses Hollywood's newly "discovered" teenage demographic, but it also defines the teenage period as a discrete developmental stage, as it was just coming to be regarded in postwar America. *Rebel* taps into the popularized discourse emerging from the work of psychoanalyst Erik Erikson and others, who linked individual psychic development not only with the family but also with other social institutions. In his 1950 book, *Childhood and Society*, Erikson identified adolescence as "the pivotal phase of ego development," according to Mark Poster in his discussion of Erikson (1988, 66).

During this period of "identity crisis," central to "an individual's sense of coherence" (Poster 1988, 66), the role of the family could not be underestimated. Erikson saw ego formation as crucial to "a sense of... being one's self, of being all right, and of being on the way to becoming what other people, at their kindest, take one to be" (quoted in Poster 1988, 65). The film also taps into public discourse on "momism," a term popularized by Philip Wylie in his 1942 book, *Generation of Vipers*. "Momism" describes the destructive potential of overly dominant mothers, "frustrated women who smothered their children with overprotection and overaffection, making their sons in particular weak and passive" (May 1988, 74) – an apt description of both Jim's mother and grandmother. At the same time, weak mothers or those discouraging the healthy (socially acceptable) sexual development of their daughters were likewise considered a threat to the balanced family and to ego formation – a circumstance indirectly expressed in Judy's family but, as we shall see, more dramatically expressed in the family dynamic of *Splendor in the Grass*.

In her films of the period concerned with the formation of a coherent identity and the recuperation and/or redefinition of masculinity, Natalie Wood – the "girl men hold tenderly, not passionately," as *Look* magazine described her (1963, 94) – seemed perfectly positioned as an agent both to expose masculine crisis and to restore a degree of masculine stability. Her role as the kidnapped daughter in *A Cry in the Night*, for instance, casts her as a perceptive, intelligent young woman who negotiates with her dangerously disturbed yet emotionally fragile kidnapper (Raymond Burr) far more effectively than her police captain father is able to. Extending this image beyond the screen, the *Look* article suggests that she is the kind of person men would want to marry: womanly, wise, and sexually attractive, while also girlish, vulnerable, and genuine in manner – nonthreatening but nevertheless capable of demanding and bringing out the best in the men who possess her.

Sex and the Single Girl

In his study of charisma, a quality he claims some but not all stars possess, Richard Dyer argues that the charisma of Marilyn Monroe "has to be situated in the flux of ideas about morality and sexuality that characterised the fifties," fueled by the publication of the Kinsey Report (*Sexual Behavior in the Human Male*, 1948, and *Sexual Behavior in the Human Female*, 1953) and of Betty Friedan's *The Feminine Mystique* (1963), as well as the growing popular awareness of psychoanalysis. Monroe's "combination of sexuality and innocence," Dyer claims, is "part of that flux" so that "she seemed to 'be' the very tensions tha[t] ran through the ideological life of fifties America" (1991, 58–59). While a comparable sense of flux is central to Natalie Wood's image, with its similar interplay of sexuality and innocence, a brief look at the different manifestations in Wood's persona is instructive.

The challenge in the case of Monroe was to temper her sexuality with a girlish, kittenish, girl-next-door vulnerability – transforming her from the femme fatale she played in *Niagara* (1953) to a woman whose "sexual allure contribute[s] to men's power and enjoyment," as Elaine Tyler May explains (1988, 63). The challenge, on the other hand, in Natalie Wood's case, was to temper her girlish innocence with a heightened womanly sexuality, while at the same time to reassert her girlishness, thus reassuring the public that she was still, in many ways, the child they had known for a decade in the movies. Whereas Monroe's sexualized body – her breasts, legs, and buttocks – were featured prominently in film and photographic images, Wood's face, and particularly her eyes – often described as deep, dark, sincere – were most prominently featured. A 1962 *Newsweek* cover story, for instance, describes her "large brown eyes [that] fire off silent bursts of emotion" (*Newsweek* 1962, 54). When her body is remarked upon, it is often to emphasize her small, pixieish frame and slender form. The *Newsweek* article, written when Wood was 23 and rehearsing for her role in *Gypsy*, asserts that "she is tiny, young, and her very eagerness makes her seem vulnerable" (1962, 54), thus maintaining the idea of the girl inside the woman – particularly interesting here, in an article about her role as the famous stripper. Indeed, *Gypsy* allegorically stages Wood's flowering from child performer (very much in supporting roles, as her character Louise is) to sexualized star – all under the supervision of a mother who both exploits her and tries to manage her morals. And even though Wood plays an accomplished sexologist in *Sex and the Single Girl* (1964), the film builds its narrative around the does-she-or-doesn't-she, did-she-or-didn't-she question, despite her character's (academic) expertise and her eponymous best-selling book on the subject.[8] This process of layering innocence with sexuality reveals much about the smoldering preoccupation with sexuality in the 1950s, and the reluctance, indeed the prohibition in the context of the movies, to confront it head-on. More closely aligned with the overt values and underlying tensions of middle-class life than was Monroe, Wood embodied not only those tensions but also, and more significantly, the very real struggle involved in acknowledging and coping with them.

Expressing some (albeit playful) anxiety concerning her sexual activity, a photo caption of Wood and actor Rad Fulton in *Motion Picture* (circa 1957) asks, "Is Natalie Wood dating too much? Some say yes."[9] Another 1957 article in *Modern Screen*, titled "How Natalie Handles Boys and Older Men," asserts that unlike Liz Taylor who "marries at eighteen, divorces at nineteen ... Natalie Wood is still fresh-eyed ... She can handle her job, her fun, her men, with grace and judgment" (1957, 50). Speculating about her relationships with a range of men, including James Dean, Sal Mineo, Tab Hunter, Nick Adams, Elvis Presley, and Raymond Burr, among others, the article points out that "she attracts and is attracted to as wide a range of beaux as you could count on a couple hundred fingers," but assures readers that "she instinctively knows just what to do to keep a wolf from her door" (1957, 51). Actor Nick Adams is quoted as saying, "I don't know any man who has ever had a bad word to say about Natalie ... She's like a little puppy" (1957, 69). Her real mother, as her screen parents often do, mediates her daughter's sexuality and is quoted as saying, "This easy freedom that young girls have in working and playing with boys gives them an opportunity to know men better than we ever did in my day," adding at another point in the article, "I'm afraid Natalie won't ever consider marrying anyone who isn't working in some phase of the theatre." We hear that Natalie continues to live with her parents, as *Modern Screen* puts it, "because a family can furnish advice as needed and love enough to keep a girl from doing anything foolish out of loneliness" (1957, 70). In tune with the image presented in her films, Wood remains firmly enfolded within family. The *Newsweek* story (1962) includes a picture of the 23-year-old Natalie with her mother, above the caption: "Star and mother: Filiarchy since 6," referring to Natalie as the family's primary breadwinner from a young age, but also to a certain degree of stage-motherish exploitation and obsession.

The complications of mother–daughter relations in many of Wood's film roles – very prominently present in *Gypsy* and *This Property Is Condemned* – are most powerfully expressed in *Splendor in the Grass*, a film disparaging of a mother and very much in tune with residual attitudes of momism. But *Splendor* also extends its critique to a father as well, showing the damaging effect that parents, in general, can have on their children. In the end, the younger generation must resign itself to the way things are – a bittersweet resolution the film seems both to support and condemn. Lines from the William Wordsworth poem, "Ode: Intimations of Immortality from Recollections of Early Childhood," not only give the film its title but also capture this sense of resignation, longing, and nostalgia for what has been lost with the passing of youth. As the film closes and Wood's character leaves the home of the man she loves, after they have been forced to go their separate ways, she speaks Wordsworth's lines in voiceover: "Though nothing can bring back the hour / Of splendour in the grass, of glory in the flower; / We will grieve not, rather find / Strength in what remains behind."[10]

Set in rural Kansas in 1928, when the stock market was soaring before imminent collapse, *Splendor in the Grass* tells the story of two high school seniors, Bud Stamper (Warren Beatty) and Deanie Loomis (Natalie Wood), who are deeply in love and longing for the sexual intimacy that society and Deanie's mores – unrelentingly inculcated by her puritanical mother (Audrey Christie) – firmly prohibit. Bud's wealthy father (Pat Hingle), an oil mogul, is far more permissive, advising Bud to go out with a "different kind" of girl for sex. Yet in his tyrannical bearing, his father fails to listen to Bud or understand the emotional pain he would (and does) experience in "substituting" anyone else for Deanie. Bud announces his decision to marry Deanie, as so many of his 1920s generation and the early 1960s film-viewing population would likely have done in negotiating the prevailing taboo against premarital sex. Elaine Tyler May points out that early marriage was part of a "sexual containment ideology," fueled by "the preoccupation with female 'promiscuity'" generally in place from the 1920s to the (early) 1960s (1988, 116–117). Bud's father, however, insists that Bud first attend Yale, despite his son's lack of interest in academics and his desire to attend agricultural school and take over his father's ranch.

The film extends little sympathy either to Bud's father or to Deanie's mother. Mrs Loomis consistently preaches that "no nice girl does" have feelings like those that confuse and frustrate Deanie, and Bud's father insists that a New York chorus girl who looks like Deanie is the "same damned thing." Mr Stamper's pervasive sexism, even as it extends to his wife and daughter, is shown to be vulgar, as are his attempts to buy people off with his wealth – until the stock market crashes, bringing financial ruin and, with it, his suicide. The damaging effects of his attitude are made clear through the behavior of Bud's older sister Ginny, a liberated "flapper" (played wonderfully by independent filmmaker Barbara Loden, who would go on to direct and star in *Wanda*, 1970). Ginny is perceptive, misunderstood, and impulsive, with longings for fulfillment that are stunted by her father's intolerance. She wants to study art, she says, to which he crudely retorts, "Art who?"

When she kisses her father at a New Year's Eve celebration (much as Judy kisses her father in *Rebel Without a Cause*), he violently and publicly humiliates her, setting off her drunken flirtations with a host of men that end in a gang rape. Ginny is the "kind of girl" his father encourages Bud to "use." And although the film exposes the decisive role her father plays in Ginny's self-destructive choices, it nevertheless seems to confirm that she is a "type." Likewise, when Deanie's mother gossips earlier that Ginny had been "in a family way" and had to have "one of those awful operations," this cautionary tale positions Mrs Loomis as destructively moralistic, while at the same time confirming that there are, indeed, two kinds of girls. After Ginny's rape, Bud breaks up with Deanie, confused and fearing his own desires as much as he worries about preserving her "good girl" status. Adult hypocrisy and repressive sexual mores are exposed as misguided, at best, or highly damaging, if not tragic, at their worst (Ginny is killed in a car accident, we hear; Deanie attempts suicide and is hospitalized for more than two years after the breakup with Bud, who attends and flunks out of Yale; Deanie and Bud eventually will marry others they undeniably care for but do not love in the way they once did each other).

Just as the film's subject and the character she plays resonate strongly with and contribute further to Natalie Wood's public persona, so too does its historical moment provide rich opportunities for allegorical readings.[11] Had the main action of the film not been set in the late 1920s but rather in its contemporaneous period, it might arguably have triggered more stringent opposition from the Production Code Administration (PCA) – and, somewhat ironically, may have been less well received by the public and critics, a few of whom, even at the time of its release, found the story of repressed teenage sexuality outmoded and/or overwrought.[12] The professional and personal resonance for Natalie Wood – as an actress of 23 playing a repressed 17-year-old – is powerful in the light of studio promotion and publicity that, as noted, continued to present her as a developing woman, indeed a star, who nevertheless remained partly a girl, and as an obedient daughter who, in spite of rebellious moments, ultimately resigned herself to a larger structure of parental (and studio) rule. In a dispute with Warner Bros., Wood had been suspended shortly after her marriage to actor Robert Wagner in 1958, when she demanded to make outside films, given the spate of very weak pictures her contract with Warners had forced upon her (Davidson 1962, 36). She renegotiated a contract in 1959, with the role of Deanie in mind (Finstad 2001, 247–250). For Hollywood, still constrained by the Production Code, the allegorical implications abound – much as the older generation is policing the lives and sexual expression of their teenage children in the story, so, too, the old Hollywood was policing the narratives and modes of representation an emerging new Hollywood was struggling to create.

The Warner Bros. archive reveals more than a few censorship struggles over this film – with its very "frank" discussion of sexuality. In an April 6, 1960 letter from Geoffrey M. Shurlock, the director of the PCA, to director Elia Kazan in response to the script, for example, a line of dialogue concerning one of the more willing girls at school with whom Bud would eventually have sex is deemed "unacceptable."

"Juanita's the only girl in the whole school who knows what it's for" is an instance of "excessively blunt language by young people which is proving extremely offensive to our audiences," according to Shurlock, who also reminds Kazan that, in the opening scene when Deanie and Bud are necking, "This should not be a scene of excessive passion. Furthermore, the Code specifically prohibits open-mouth kissing."[13] An earlier letter from Shurlock to Kazan, dated September 15, 1958, states, "Any suggestion that Deanie is having an orgasm would be unacceptable. The same is to be said with reference to Bud … It has already been pointed out that using an oil well as a symbol in this context would be unacceptable."[14] Clearly, the negotiations were detailed, tedious, and unrelenting – even at a time when restrictions were beginning to relax. In the film's final version Juanita is "the only girl … who knows what it's all about"; there is no oil well used symbolically, although several rapidly paced montage sequences of a surging waterfall stand in for the characters' overflowing sexual desire. And while Deanie never has an orgasm, she does, in desperation, induce what seems like a brief dreamlike trance of erotic longing after an argument with Bud, almost as a way of complying with Bud's (and her own) desire and at the same time deflecting responsibility for whatever may happen. In this nuanced scene capturing the overheated push and pull of desire and frustration, Bud pushes Deanie to her knees as they are necking and she has asked him to "stop." Confused and cruel, Bud commands: "At my feet, slave – tell me you love me, tell me you can't live without me." Immediately realizing how he has hurt her, Bud apologizes, claiming he was only joking. She responds first in tears and then in a kind of self-induced orgiastic state, repeating that she would do anything for Bud. Now he is the one who refrains, uncertain and perplexed.

As if playing out the film's own story in this struggle for control and sexual independence, the producers introduced test screenings by referring to *Splendor* screenwriter William Inge, whose previous work as a playwright and screenwriter included *Bus Stop* and *Picnic*, with comments aimed at combating potential Production Code and Catholic Legion of Decency objections:

> Most of the [Inge's] plays were of adult nature, realistic and honestly portrayed. Yet, believe it or not, such great plays or books about real people and real situations are in jeopardy. In jeopardy insofar as the possibility of their ever being made into motion pictures.
>
> The reason is simple. There has been a great deal of pressure against adult films fomented by just a few small pressure groups who shout long and loud. Most of them, believe it or not, do not even see the pictures they yell about. And strangely enough, the great number of people that flock by the thousands to such fine foreign pictures as "Room at the Top," "La Dolce Vita" … are never heard from, their voices are still. Consequently, studios such as Warner Bros., because of these small pressure groups, will find themselves by nice-nelly censorship forced to make only pap … But if we are to compete with such fine foreign pictures which have none of the restrictions that U.S. pictures have, then we cannot be held back in the buying of adult books and plays, nor can such men as Elia Kazan and William Inge be held back from giving us the kind of pictures that they are best suited to write and direct.[15]

The introduction ends by reiterating the restriction that anyone under 16 must be accompanied by an adult for admittance to the movie – a restriction the filmmakers agreed to adopt by request of both the Catholic Legion of Decency and the PCA, in order to avoid slashing the film's content (and one that anticipates the emergence of the rating system

Figure 25.4 The push and pull between desire and frustration troubles Bud and Deanie in *Splendor in the Grass* (1961, director and producer Elia Kazan).

seven years later). The reference to foreign films and their serious, adult content directly acknowledges a key box office competitor of the day (not unlike the role the other "kind of girl" plays in the film). The "nice-nelly censorship" seems an indirect reference to the Catholic Legion of Decency, which in some instances was a more formidable force than the Code, especially as the Code was relaxing (and may be read as a reference to what women like Deanie's mother would insist upon).[16] The use of the word "realistic" to describe Inge's plays, in their typical brand of personal/psychological drama, often in the context of repressive social mores, and the repeated use of the word "real" to describe films like *Splendor*, echo a growing call for greater realism among some critics and audiences. Here centered on "real people" – on the characters and the actors who play them – the words evoke thoughts of the much publicized Method that purported to train actors in getting at the deeper, psychological "truth" of the characters they played. With Elia Kazan – one of the founding members of the Actors Studio, the training ground for actors in the Method – as director of *Splendor*, it seems no accident that this would be a main point of interest in promoting the film to test audiences.

In foregrounding the names of Kazan and of Inge, both of whom were perceived as cutting-edge artists, the test-screening remarks also indirectly recall censorship problems Kazan, particularly, had confronted in the past, most notably with his film adaptation of *A Streetcar Named Desire* (1951), in which he was forced to alter the ending of the Tennessee Williams play. Very likely because he had worked with Kazan on *Streetcar*, studio chief Jack Warner questioned and exerted some degree of pressure on Kazan in regard to the content of *Splendor*. In a January 1961 letter to Warner and studio aide Benjamin Kalmenson (who would eventually become executive vice president at Warner Bros.), in response to their request that the gang rape of Ginny be eliminated, Kazan gingerly refuses, explaining that the rape provides crucial motivation for understanding Bud's breakup with Deanie: "the boy, still sexually innocent, is so shocked by what his sister brings on herself in the parking lot, that he is frightened to give expression or even a chance to his own sexual impulses." Kazan goes on to assure, "I can make the audience feel the horror and sin of what his sister has brought onto herself. And I did. I did not want to make what was going on glamorous . . . I made it look ugly and cheap and brutal." What is fascinating here is that, in defending the film against censorship, Kazan expresses attitudes almost as moralistic as those who would censor him, particularly insofar as Ginny bringing it "on herself" is concerned. Perhaps his words reflect his genuine attitude; perhaps he chooses them strategically in keeping with his own knowledge of what he thinks the studio would like to hear, or perhaps his language reflects a fusion of the two.[17] Whatever the case, the film's own contradictory impulses are registered here. Kazan goes on to defend the scene by saying that he had already made cuts and that "I'm going to have her say in a low voice: 'Get away from me. I don't want you.' From my experience, I know how much this will help with [Jack] Vizzard and [Geoffrey] Shurlock [of the PCA]."[18]

Another controversial scene for Kazan in negotiation with Warner and Kalmenson – and the most poignant scene of the film, often held up also as a high-point in Wood's career and as testimony to the fact that she was emerging as a serious actress – is one between Deanie and her mother. Deanie soaks in a hot bathtub, seeking solace from the pain and confusion of Bud's suddenly (and, to her, inexplicably) breaking off their relationship. Her mother enters, trying to offer comfort that nevertheless falls short – more centered on asserting normalcy than on truly helping her daughter. "Do you feel better, dear?" she asks – this, a short time after Deanie has confessed that she wants to die. Quite the opposite of her words – "Oh yes, oh yes, yes . . . I'm sorry I've troubled you . . . I didn't want to worry you, I didn't want to worry anyone" – Deanie's emotional fragility is apparent through Wood's thin vocal register, turbulent repetition of lines, and distant, detached manner. As she reclines in the tub, Wood strikes an iconic movie star pose, but here in a very different, disquieting context. As her mother begins to question Deanie more directly about what has been bothering her ("Is it all on account of, because of Bud, because he doesn't call for you anymore?"), Deanie's underlying distress surfaces through Wood's increasingly agitated, though carefully controlled, movements: "I don't know, I don't know, Mom." Two moments drive Deanie to levels of increasingly panic-stricken despair: the first when her mother facetiously proffers help ("I have a mind to call that boy and tell him . . . "), prompting Deanie frantically to interrupt, repeating the words, "Don't you dare, don't you dare, Mom . . . Mom, if you do something like that, I'll do something desperate. I will. I will, Mom. I will." Wood's vocal quality and a jarring guttural sound she emits – half scream/half cry – reveals that Deanie is on the edge of emotional collapse. Deanie's second, far more anguished reaction is to her mother's very pointed question: "How serious have you and Bud become? I mean, now you know what I mean . . . Did he spoil you?" Deanie lets out a hauntingly hollow laugh as she repeats, "Spoil? Did he spoil me?" She submerges her head under water as if to drown herself (foreshadowing her later suicide attempt by swimming toward a waterfall), then stands up naked before her mother screaming, "No, no Mom. I'm not spoiled. I'm not spoiled, Mom. I'm just as fresh and I'm virginal like the day I was born, Mom. I'm a lovely virginal creature . . . I'm a good little girl, Mom, a good little, good little, good little girl. I've always done everything daddy and mommy always told me," and ending as she runs out of the bathroom screaming repeatedly, "I hate you, I hate you." From her bedroom she screams the muffled lines, "I'm not spoiled, I'm not spoiled, Mom." Beyond Wood's moving performance and editing rhythms that convey the heightening levels of panic Deanie is experiencing, lines of dialogue stressing the word "Mom" work to amplify her vulnerability and despair in attempting to assert her own identity, let alone her desires. Dialogue also implies the same "terrible web of dependency" as Robert Wagner says was present in Wood's relationship with her own mother, who was "afraid to let Natalie out of her sight, because Natalie was the breadwinner" (Wagner with Eyman 2008, 105).[19]

One can easily guess that Warner and Kalmenson questioned the figure of a naked Natalie Wood – if only shown from the waist up and from behind, using highly fractured editing patterns. Asserting that

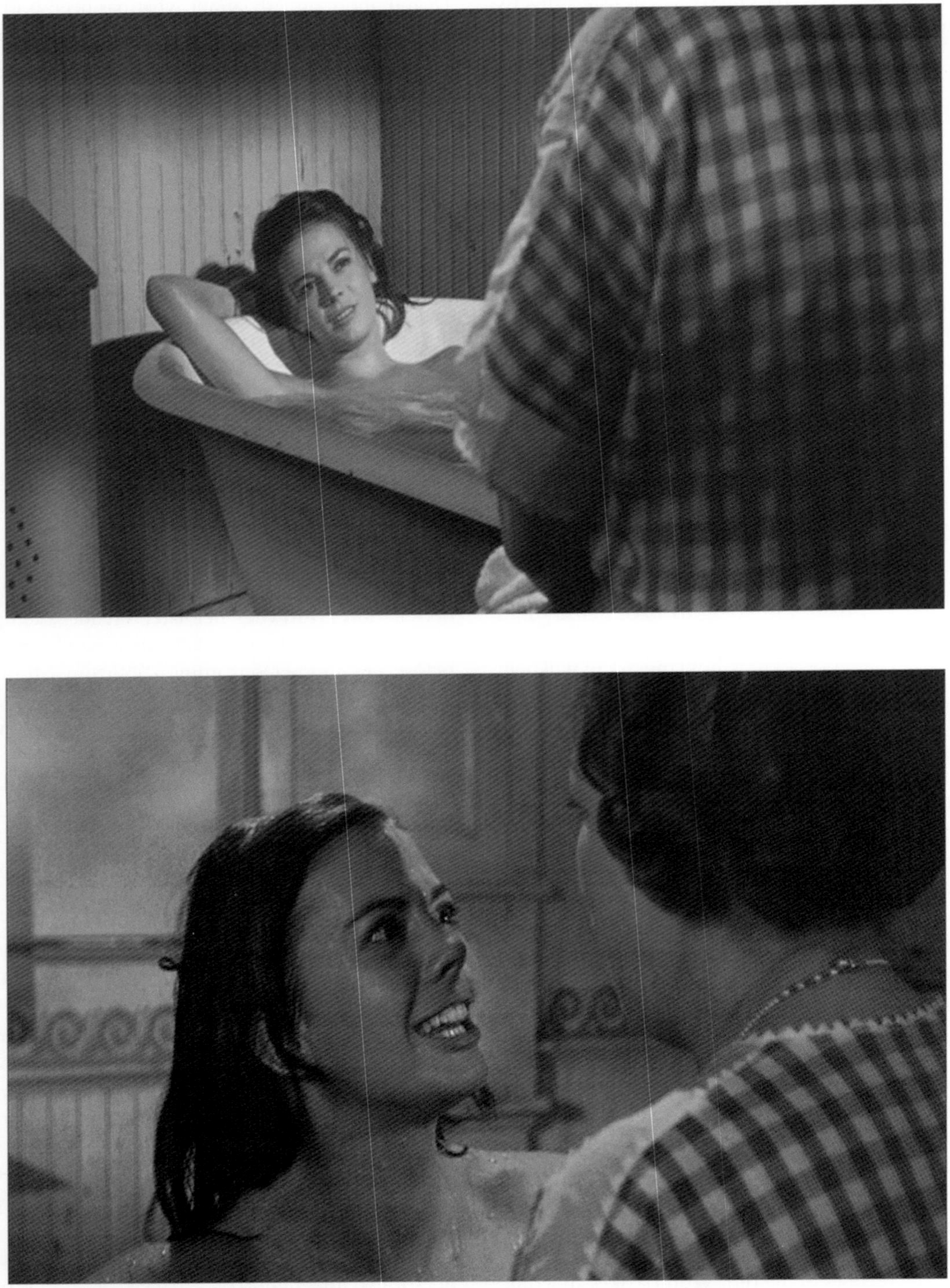

Figure 25.5 Deanie, on the edge of emotional collapse, confronts her repressive mother in one of the most powerful moments of *Splendor in the Grass* (1961, director and producer Elia Kazan), considered one of the finest acting moments in Natalie Wood's career.

"I don't want censor problems," Kazan nevertheless holds his ground in his letter, saying,

> when something is absolutely legitimate and harmless and pure like that four-foot cut of the naked girl (with her boy's body) in an extreme long shot running from the bathroom into her bedroom – well why pull it out before anyone has even objected?... If I were showing her naked form in order to bring a sensational element to the film ... I would have been much closer and would have dwelt on the shot ... it is pure and clean and innocent.[20]

Kazan's notion that Wood has a "boy's body" – though he is probably exaggerating to make his point – reflects the generally held sense of her as a child/woman whom one embraces "tenderly, not passionately." The repetition of "pure" further suggests his possibly choosing words in accordance with what he imagines the studio would like to hear.

Despite the censorship struggles, *Splendor in the Grass* is generally held as a film indicative of the Code's erosion. Paul Monaco claims this is so because the film "dealt with the story of two young lovers who paid no price for their sexual indiscretion and who suffered emotionally by having denied their sexual impulses" (2001, 57). While Monaco admits that the denial of their desire results in suffering, he fails to see how that suffering might be understood as a punishment for desire itself, since Bud and Deanie never do actually engage in sexual indiscretion. He also fails to recognize that the most flagrant sexual indiscretions – those of Ginny – are most certainly punished. At the same time, however, Monaco correctly points out that *Splendor*'s having been granted the seal of approval is a sign of change. Quoting actor John Wayne as saying that the film is "too disgusting for discussion," Monaco points out that "few American adults appeared to agree" (2001, 57). Box office figures corroborate: Box Office Report.com ranks *Splendor* as eighteenth among top box office films in the years 1960–1962; during the same period, *West Side Story*, also starring Wood, ranks second.[21]

Identity Crisis and Transition: Star and Actor

Splendor in the Grass invites additional allegorical readings of Hollywood in transition if considered in the context of Natalie Wood's position as a studio-trained actress in a film directed by Kazan, a cofounder of the Actors Studio, at a time when the Method was very much in vogue. The Method represented apparent change both for Hollywood and for Natalie Wood – though, in retrospect, it may have been a less radical departure from the past than was generally held, whether in public or critical perceptions of the time (see Baron and Warren's essay in this volume). Those perceptions were in place, however, and left Wood conflicted. She embraced her career and wanted to be understood as a serious actress of this perceived "new" era, but she also embraced her identity as a "star," manufactured by and representative of the "old" Hollywood – even as it was eroding. Suddenly, the two seemed dichotomous, something that had not been the case, according to Baron, until the late 1950s when "the labor expended by film actors and actresses came into view," and "the 'new breed' of movie stars were presented as individuals who studied their craft and developed their skills." This stood in marked contrast to earlier decades when studio publicity "occluded the labor expended by the men and women whose images appeared on screen." Publicity emphasized the "expert makeup and publicity men" behind the creation of actresses, "while actors played themselves" (Baron 1998, 90). Baron argues that a new interest in acting emerged as a result of performances like those of Marlon Brando in *A Streetcar Named Desire* and *On the Waterfront* (1954) – both also directed by Kazan – with his "gestures, postures, and vocal mannerisms" considered paradigmatic of "the Method 'style.'" At the same time, however, Brando himself cited studio actors like Spencer Tracy, Paul Muni, Cary Grant, and James Cagney as models for his own work (Baron 1998, 94). The demise of the studio system and its contractual employment of actors "led to the closing of studio drama schools, and the decline of institutions such as the Pasadena Playhouse and the American Academy of Dramatic Art which served as training grounds for actors bound for Hollywood." As Baron points out, the Method's New York-based Actors Studio became "one of the few growing institutions of actor training" (1998, 101).

In her 1998 essay, Baron cites a 1957 *Life* article about Natalie Wood and her "dedication to acting" (1998, 92; *Life* 1957, 96).[22] The article refers to Wood's close study of her favorite film performance – Vivien Leigh's in *A Streetcar Named Desire* – as one aspect of her rigorous "new" training. Baron believes this is possibly "one of the first times that aspect of actor training was represented in the popular press," although studio training programs had often included the close study of other actors' performances in films (1998, 93). Primarily a photo essay, the *Life* piece shows Wood engaged in acting exercises with fellow actors Dennis Hopper and Nick Adams. The trio rehearses both in private and in public, where they observe everyday people in everyday situations, an approach Robert Brustein, in a 1959 *Film Quarterly* article, associates with a new realism that had come to dominate Hollywood, primarily through the influence of "New York naturalistic theater schools like the Actors' Studio" (1959, 26). Founding director of the Yale and American Repertory Theaters, Brustein places this new realism in opposition to older Hollywood formulas featuring "colossal screen glamor" and "giantism," observing that the new realism involves "an increasing tendency to deglamorize the Hollywood star," with "new actors [who] attract attention by their intensity of feeling, rather than by physical attractiveness" (1959, 24, 26), thus reinforcing the dichotomy between actor and star. Yet, for all of this, Brustein assesses this brand of realism as "more akin to Zola naturalism – dedicated to a purely surface authenticity" (1959, 25). It appeals to teenage audiences because "it offers a youthful, rather than a mature picture of the world" (1959, 31), and to adult audiences because of its "*distance* from everyday life," given that American prosperity allowed middle-class audiences "to be indulgent toward grubbiness and poverty" so that they could "regard the torn T-shirt, the dirty fingernails, and the cluttered sink as the 'truth about existence'" (1959, 30).

Wood expressed her ambition to traverse the star/actor divide in an (unsourced) interview cited by Finstad: "Stardom is only a by-product of acting. I feel that it's possible to be a star yet be a good actor." While she admits "it would be foolish of me to say I don't want to be a star," she also adds, "If I didn't believe in what I'm doing, I'd rather go to work in a dime store" (2001, 206). Robert Wagner claims that Wood saw New York "as a sort of acting promised land" (Wagner with Eyman 2008, 115). Yet, in parallel with Hollywood's conflicted identity during this period of transition, Wood's idealized attraction to Method performers (Finstad 2001, 183; Wagner with Eyman 2008, 115) caused her to feel "embarrassed by her child star past" and "inferior to anyone with [Actors] Studio training" (Finstad 2001, 183, 184). On the other hand, in a 1957 *Los Angeles Times* article, Hedda Hopper quotes Wood as saying that she was "an observer" at the Actors Studio and attended several Lee Strasberg classes held outside the Studio, and "as far as I could tell, this is the way I'd always worked" (Hopper 1957).[23] Although she would repeat this impression in future interviews, her ambivalence is nevertheless apparent.

The tension between old mores and new in *Splendor*, then, allegorizes not only that of Hollywood in transition but that of Wood, who would come to be perceived either as too tied to old, outmoded expressions of Hollywood stardom, both in her self-presentation and acting, or as continually in transition, still finding her way but never fully identified with the new.[24] Although the 1957 *Life* article positions her as a figure heralding the new, two 1962 articles express uncertainty about how to regard Natalie Wood – at a time when she was at the apex of her career, with an Academy Award nomination for her performance in *Splendor* and critical acclaim for her performance in *West Side Story*. Bill Davidson's *Saturday Evening Post* article, titled "Hollywood Throwback," refers to Wood's "anachronistic appeal," while admitting her "top-caliber acting performances" in both films (1962, 32). Davidson interviews Kazan, who speaks of his initial reluctance to cast her in *Splendor* because "she had made so many lousy pictures and she was getting worse and worse." But later he was impressed with her "intuitive" qualities, saying, "She's bright as hell about things that count to her as an actress" (1962, 36). Davidson, however, does not seem fully convinced: "In this day of drab, earnest method actresses . . . nothing fazes her in her relentless campaign to be recognized as a movie star in the old flamboyant tradition" (1962, 32).

In an article appearing in *Show* a month earlier, Murray Kempton calls Wood "entirely Hollywood's child" who "applies the word 'star' to herself as though it were a job description."[25] She is, he claims, at minimum, "the best young actress we have who has never had the association of a live audience." Embedded here is an obvious critique of the insular Hollywood system and the charge of inferior artistry for having never worked in live theater (as so many trained at Actors Studio had). He explains that "the circumstances which made her a star seem contrived when one recollects them; in the beginning . . . she was talked about more than observed" (1962, 51).

Kempton nevertheless claims that, "Having been a star, she is becoming an actress. She is rising from pretense – a gift – to illusion – a conquest" (1962, 50). Kempton speculates that a childhood in the industry "does mean the consumption of emotional capital; the Actors' Studio may seem irrelevant to Miss Wood because the resources it taps were exhausted long ago" (1962, 52). Although Wood's remarks to Kempton concerning the Actors Studio echo those she had made to Hedda Hopper, it is evident that neither the Method nor the actor/star dichotomy it initiated were irrelevant to her – something Christopher Plummer, who costarred with Wood in *Inside Daisy Clover*, recalls: "She underrated herself... She was truly a 'beautiful Hollywood star' – in quotes. And she wasn't ashamed of it... But she did once say to me... 'Oh God, I'm just a trustworthy pro. I wish I could be more than that'" (Porton 2009, 15–16).

Identity Crisis and Transition: Hollywood Old and New

A film about the process of manufacturing a star in Hollywood's heyday, *Inside Daisy Clover* provides a self-reflexive look at the industry and, at the same time, allegorizes its own production context in the mid-1960s. Wood's title character is both truculent and acquiescent, much as Wood herself, who wavered between independence as an actor and compliance as a star tied to a nearly extinct system. Kempton reports: "To her the new star's role is the assertion of independence: 'None of them would have thought of fighting the studio,'" she says in their interview (1962, 52). While Daisy fights the system impulsively, having neither power nor autonomy, Wood did so more categorically, most dramatically in 1966 – a year after *Daisy Clover* – by paying Warner Bros. $175,000 to terminate her contract after a string of critical failures (including *Inside Daisy Clover*, *The Great Race*, 1965, *This Property Is Condemned*, and *Penelope*, 1966) (Finstad 2001, 316). She would not make another movie until 1969, when she starred, as part of an ensemble cast, in the very successful *Bob & Carol & Ted & Alice* – her last movie hit. *Inside Daisy Clover*, produced by Alan J. Pakula and directed by Robert Mulligan, is based on the eponymous novel by Gavin Lambert, who also wrote the screenplay. In his biography of Wood, Lambert quotes her as saying, "I want to do things on my own," and he claims that "1965 was the year that she would come as close as she would ever get to realizing [that] ambition" (2005, 222). Even though the film was shot at the Warner Bros. Burbank studio, it was considered an "outside film" for Wood, since her contract was with Park Place, the independent production company formed by Pakula and Mulligan (Lambert 2005, 221–222).

Although primarily a star narrative, *Daisy Clover* is also, in part, a mother/daughter narrative as disquieting as that of *Splendor in the Grass*, though for very different reasons. Daisy is a mature-beyond-her-years 15-year-old who shares a seaside shack with her sweet but batty mother (Ruth Gordon) in Angel Beach, California (Santa Monica Pier was the shooting location). Daisy's father left them seven years earlier and, as the film opens, Mrs Clover reports him missing – "I only started to miss him this morning," she says to a befuddled police officer. The story begins on August 24, 1936, Daisy's birthday, and covers two years – from the time she is "discovered" as a star until the day she walks out on that career. Her mother is in a world of her own, with Daisy very much in charge – cooking for her own birthday and imploring her mother to "concentrate" when decisions must be made or events out of the ordinary occur. When he first met with Wood to discuss the script, Lambert was impressed with what he saw as her "very acute, very personal comment": "'At every important moment of Daisy's life, she's alone. No one to turn to, no one she can really trust'" (2005, 220). Her mother's benign neglect leaves Daisy largely on her own to run a concession stand selling publicity glossies of Hollywood stars, complete with the autographs she forges. Her negligible income from the stars only ironically hints at her desire to become one. Her tomboy bearing and rough manners capture nothing of what Hollywood stardom required of its women in that era – an exaggerated commentary, it would seem, on the contemporaneous "deglamorization" of stars like Natalie Wood herself – complete with the torn T-shirt and dirty fingernails – that Brustein associates with the new Hollywood realism. In off-handed, yet nevertheless determined pursuit of stardom, she sends a sample recording of her voice to Swan Studios as part of a talent contest. Summoned by mogul Raymond Swan (Christopher Plummer), who is impressed with what he hears, Daisy passes a screen test, and Swan transforms her into a new star – "America's Little Valentine," an obvious reference to the first of the studio-manufactured stars, Mary Pickford, whose sobriquet, "America's Sweetheart," *Clover* producers had wanted to use but were forced to revise when Pickford refused to grant them her permission.[26]

On the one hand, the film presents a self-consciously "knowing" critique of the studio system and in so doing obliquely positions the new Hollywood and its greater authenticity as superior to the old, thus eliding the very notion of decline. The concrete industrial exterior of the Swan studios is both dwarfing and dehumanizing when Daisy is first escorted there, and its cavernous interior evokes a vampiric, horror film atmosphere hyperbolizing the film's negative appraisal of the old studio system. Plummer's performance as Swan – with clipped dialogue and sardonic stance – broadens commentary on the hegemonic, patriarchal system that turns people into property. Even though at one point he becomes her (married) lover (tantamount to incest, given his role as father figure – once again referencing and refiguring the family drama), Swan's concern for Daisy extends only to the point of protecting his investment. In the film's exaggerated terms, her becoming a star is akin to her making a pact with the "Prince of Darkness," as matinee idol Wade Lewis (Robert Redford) calls Swan. In league with her husband, Swan's wife Melora (Katharine Bard), as her name implies, offers the "golden apple" of stardom to hungry young hopefuls. Immediately, the bargain Daisy unwittingly strikes for stardom forces her to sacrifice her mother – something that deeply distresses her and sours her journey from the start. With the help of Daisy's opportunistic older sister Gloria (Betty Harford), Swan has Mrs Clover committed to a rest home in order to bury her from public view, insisting that Daisy must claim both her parents are dead. As a result, Daisy never takes much pleasure in stardom; her only source of genuine pleasure is in singing, in performing – echoing terms of the star/actor divide. Swan announces to Daisy that, "Incredible as it may seem I'm going to make something out of you." When she wonders what that may be, he replies bluntly, "Money." He goes on:

> There's a certain mixture of orphan and clown that always packs them in. It's got a dirty face, a heart of gold, and it sings. It doesn't smoke or bite its fingernails or cut its hair without permission. It becomes America's little Valentine.

His choice of pronouns, of course, could not be more revealing.

Within the film's reflexive critique a corrective is implied – just as Daisy asserts her independence in the end, so does the film present itself as a response to the system it condemns, thus registering the emerging trend in the 1960s toward independent productions and stars independently contracted to appear in them. Yet, the film fails to acknowledge the dependence of both on the former system, most literally, in this case, with a film shot in a Warner Bros. studio, distributed by Warners, dependent on the Warners publicity machinery, and featuring a star who is the product of that studio and of the system in general.

Allegorical readings abound in two films "produced" and screened within the film – the first an extravagant musical short designed to introduce Daisy to the world and promote her talent; the second a documentary short titled "Meet Daisy Clover," purporting to present fans with Daisy's biographical background, almost all of which is egregiously fabricated. Her ancestors were "early Pennsylvania settlers," the narrator intones; she was a "lonesome child" whose "father was killed in a railroad accident" and whose "mother, too, died during a flu epidemic." The documentary references and parodies Hollywood newsreels and also makes commentary on the old studio approach to typecasting and serial production – Daisy is always seemingly cast as a ragamuffin in a series of films including "The Dime Store Kid," "The Back Lot Kid," and the "Big Top Kid." And in an apparent attempt to reshape her image as more adult and implicitly sexual, the bio-doc announces that her new film will be "The Duke and the Ballerina."

More interesting for its allegorical implications, however, is the musical promo, presented at a lavish Christmas Eve party hosted by the Swans. While the level of excess registers a (laughable) critique of the old Hollywood, it does, at the same time, dazzle – first by presenting a montage of iconic Hollywood stars, among them Myrna Loy and Fred Astaire, and second, by drawing attention to visual effects that were possible to achieve only through 1960s film technology. The sheer excess in the use of effects that merge animation with live-action as Daisy sings "You're Gonna Hear from Me," while dancing through the cosmos, simultaneously draws attention to the artificiality of old Hollywood, while celebrating the power of the new Hollywood both to produce and to parody such

Figure 25.6 Robert Mulligan's *Inside Daisy Clover* employs 1960s film technology in its parody of 1930s Hollywood artificiality and excess (1965, producer Alan J. Pakula).

fantastic artifice through sophisticated, cutting-edge effects. In many ways this display of excess through technology allegorizes Hollywood's own identity crisis at this time of transition. While presenting a critique of the old Hollywood – its artificiality, its deforming danger to the stars it manufactures – the film, in asserting its separation from and superiority to that system, nevertheless reveals its dependence on it as a marker of its own legitimacy, something the film seems reluctant to acknowledge.

In this regard, studio press releases for *Inside Daisy Clover* are especially telling. They celebrate the film's meticulously constructed period details, the luxurious locations scouted for the Swan mansion, and the effects used within the "promotional" film. One release tells us that

> Natalie Wood is flying high today. Literally. Natalie wings off into the heavens, skirts Saturn, slides down the shaving of a new moon, taps along the Milky Way and from her vantage point in the heavens looks down on planet Earth. These celestial peregrinations have nothing to do with rockets – it's all movie magic, pointed to make one of the most elaborate musical production numbers ever filmed...

Wood is quoted as saying, "All sorts of trick effects are used... to get that effect of casual magic." Placing this new Hollywood film in the context of Space Age technology, the release quips in its closing line: "In some ways Natalie has it rougher than John Glenn. HE didn't have to sing and dance while exploring the heavens." At the same time the release situates this sequence and the larger film in the context of "the lavish type of song and dance routine popular in films three decades ago by Warner Bros., the studio that pioneered with such celluloid extravaganzas as 'The Gold Diggers of Broadway,' '42nd Street,' and 'Footlight Parade."' We hear from choreographer Herbert Ross, who claims, "We aren't imitating them... we are just approximating the mood and manner and spirit of the numbers that were such hits with the fans of the period."[27] Pakula, as producer, is quoted in another press release as saying, "We're recreating dramatic Hollywood of three decades ago with candor and editorial comment... Gavin Lambert's screenplay has the bite which distinguished his best-selling novel." He goes on to assure the public that "there are always fresh facets, new approaches, to a motion picture about motion pictures."[28] The words of both Ross and Pakula convey the way the film simultaneously embraces and denies its own position in what was increasingly perceived as an outmoded system.

The casting of Natalie Wood is strategic, of course, for the public had witnessed her own emergence first as a teen and then as an adult star. One press release stresses her background in movies, along with that of former child star Roddy McDowall, also in the film.[29] And another release reminds viewers of her small, girlish (or tomboyish, for this role) frame: "Natalie's normal weight is an even 100 pounds. But rehearsing her strenuous dance routines . . . brought the scales tilting down to 95."[30] And although Wood is cast as a tomboy "kid," Daisy is not an innocent, nor is her virginity a centerpiece of narrative concern as it had been in *Splendor* and many of her earlier films – in part because Wood herself was older, in part because her tomboy looks somehow neutralize the anxiety surrounding female promiscuity, to paraphrase May, and also because the PCA had continued to relax its standards (however inconsistently), as the larger culture itself had. When she returns to her beach shack in the early morning hours after her birthday, we can only infer that Daisy has spent the night with a boy whom we have seen pursuing her. (In a bizarrely uneven trail of correspondence – one that speaks volumes about Hollywood's "identity crisis" at the time – the PCA forced Mulligan to cut a scene in which Daisy is seen knocking on the boy's door at night, knowing that his parents are away.)[31]

One scene in *Daisy Clover* metaphorically links Wood's (and Daisy's) transition from child star to mature (and sexually experienced) woman in an instant – implicitly critiquing Hollywood's former tendency to cast child actors in parts that are young beyond their years, to paraphrase Wood. The sequence also purports to critique old PCA prohibitions, while at the same time narrative elision affirms that such prohibitions remain (rather weakly) in effect. The movie star Wade Lewis, with whom Daisy has had a one-night fling, turns up on her movie set after having left her with only a note on the morning of his departure, and having then disappeared for months afterward. She is wearing an infantile rag doll costume, and Wade approaches her, tenderly removing her clownish white makeup and yellow pigtailed wig. A cut immediately returns them to the same yacht on which they spent their first night, as they embrace on the deck with Daisy wrapped only in a blanket. Later, Wade (whose real name is Lewis Wade) repeats his performance, this time deserting Daisy after their wedding night.

Daisy learns from a drunken Melora Swan – who confesses her own affair with Wade and her suicide attempt when he left her – that Wade would certainly abandon Daisy, for "your husband never could resist a charming boy," a line that lends new meaning to the strangely embittered response of Swan's assistant Baines (Roddy McDowall) when Wade announces his plans to marry Daisy. The note Wade left for Daisy on their first night now gathers greater resonance as a critique of the system that forced him to hide his identity: "I apologize for the behavior of Mr. Wade Lewis last night. He is an imposter. I hate him. [signed] Lewis Wade."

Now, 10 years after *Rebel Without a Cause*, *Inside Daisy Clover* could more directly reveal Wade's sexual orientation, but in many ways adopted just as rigidly limited an attitude. Unlike the powerfully sympathetic treatment of Plato and Jim, whose homoerotic attraction was only hinted at, neither Wade nor Baines is a sympathetic figure. While the film appears to deride the ethically bankrupt system that would require a star like Wade to uphold an unambiguously masculine, heterosexual image, its treatment of Wade as an unscrupulous charmer reflects nearly as repressive a position. Wade is most sympathetic in his absence, his note to Daisy his only genuine expression of sincerity. As for Daisy, her sexual relationships are continually fraught.

Swan seals his "property rights" in seducing a vulnerable Daisy, their affair paving the way for her mother's release from the rest home and for the two to live together again in a seaside cottage. Upon returning home to discover her mother dead one night, Daisy suffers a breakdown – represented in a sequence that recalls the bathtub scene in *Splendor*. Inside a studio sound booth while post-synching a song for her latest film, Daisy struggles to retain composure. Fragmented editing patterns and an eerie silence when the camera is positioned outside the booth, as she stands inside singing, powerfully convey her fractured, fragile identity. She spends weeks in bed recuperating, until Swan pronounces her cured and orders her to work – delay will cost him money. Her first impulse is to kill herself by breathing in gas from the kitchen oven – a suicide attempt played mostly for humor as she is continually interrupted, several times by the ringing telephone and once by the buzzing doorbell (one among several missteps within the film). Exasperated, she demonstrates new resolve – this time to live and to assert her independence. Turning on the gas full blast, she leaves the house with a cup of coffee and walks along the beach until the house explodes – an explosion that liberates her from her short-lived career as a star and one that can be seen as perhaps a wistful statement about the demise of the old Hollywood system – one that might better have ended with a bang than the protracted whimper still reverberating.

At this point, it seems important to return to Wood's career but now from a more personal perspective, in light of the particular resonance she felt with Daisy Clover that Lambert remarks upon. Wood was encouraged in her "star" identity by her mother's relentlessly ambitious "star-driven regime," as Finstad aptly phrases it (2001, 206), a regime as ambitious and profit-driven as Swan's, it would seem.[32] Wood also was encouraged by her two-time husband Robert Wagner, who, eight years her senior, had begun his career as a matinee idol and continued to embrace the system that supported him. Although he befriended and respected some of those associated with the emerging new Hollywood (as he most certainly had Kazan), Wagner felt more comfortable with those of the old Hollywood, as his autobiography suggests. Quite possibly he felt threatened by "Natalie's fascination ... with young Method actors, guys who played the same brooding notes as Brando and Monty Clift but didn't actually have their talent," as he expresses it (Wagner with Eyman 2008, 115). Wagner explains that, as a couple during their first marriage, he and Wood "didn't exactly integrate [their] very different social circles" and that primarily "we started associating with Frank Sinatra and his circle and the rest of my friends" (2008, 112). Lambert recalls that Wagner "seemed to belong to an earlier era," and felt "alien" on the set of *Splendor* with Natalie, who, having worked with Nicholas Ray and others in the past, was comfortable in that sort of company (2005, 159). Natalie's mother, Wagner believes, approved their relationship because "from her point of view ... I was better than any of the alternatives ... I was successful, famous, presentable, well connected ... I was legitimate" (2008, 107).

Although caution is always advisable when drawing parallels that too closely align an actor's life with her roles, it is worth noting that several factors are generally cited in biographical speculation concerning the breakup of the first Wood/Wagner marriage in 1962: career pressures (her career was at its height with great promise for the future; his was in the doldrums), her increasingly unsteady emotional state (it was after *Splendor* that she first sought therapy, something Wagner questioned and possibly felt threatened by), and Wagner's possible bisexuality. It is rumored that Wood found Wagner "in a compromising position with another man," according to Finstad's sources (2001, 272). Whether true or not, those rumors, of which she was certainly aware, along with professional tensions she had lived through, very likely were factors attracting her to the role in *Inside Daisy Clover* (a "dream project" Wood fought for; Warner Bros. had forced her to star in *The Great Race* with the role of Daisy Clover as her reward; Finstad 2001, 298, 295).

Wood's desire to hone her art and craft as an actress was intensified, as we have seen, by actors like James Dean, Dennis Hopper, and Nick Adams when they worked together on *Rebel Without a Cause*, by her work with Kazan on *Splendor*, and by her careful study and deep admiration for other actors not associated with the Method like Vivien Leigh and Laurence Olivier (with whom she and Wagner acted in a 1976 television production of *Cat on a Hot Tin Roof*, directed by Olivier). Following a self-imposed hiatus from acting in order to give her attention to family and motherhood – lasting from about 1970 to 1978, during which time her work in film and television was infrequent – Wood made a concerted effort to return to the screen in the late 1970s and early 1980s.[33] At that time, although public attention to the Method had faded, as had its undiluted influence on acting methodology, the same star/actor conflict seemed to resurface, possibly heightened by the conflicting demands of motherhood and career, both of which she had now dedicated herself to pursuing. Her desire to work seriously in her career and on her craft was arguably reignited by actor Christopher Walken, with whom she costarred in her final film, *Brainstorm* (1981, released 1983), and with whom she and Wagner spent the November 1981 weekend aboard their yacht that would be her last – a weekend when she would inexplicably drown. Wagner admits that Walken "began talking about his 'total pursuit of a career' and that Natalie should live like that too ... He also said it was obvious that I didn't share his point of view, which was an understatement" (2008, 255).

The star/actor conflict that in some part defined Natalie Wood's life also may have contributed to the turbulence of her last hours when the three, but particularly Wagner and Walken, debated, indeed argued about, this very issue. Quoting a close friend of Wood's, Lambert writes: "'Natalie had been fired by Walken's talk of freedom and dedication to art . . . he represented a new, independent generation like Robert de Niro and Al Pacino . . . she was looking for a way to bust out'" (2005, 304). Whether this professional attraction resulted in emotional or sexual infidelity is a subject of speculation, as is the subject of what exactly happened on the yacht and to Natalie Wood during that fateful Thanksgiving weekend (see Finstad 2001; Lambert 2005; Wagner with Eyman 2008). Whatever the circumstances, until the very end, Wood embodied both aspiration and transition. By the late 1970s, the industry had completed its navigation – for better or worse – through its own unsettling period of transition to arrive at the "next" Hollywood, both characterized and enlivened by fragmentation and contradiction. Having been offered the female title role in *Bonnie and Clyde* – one of the truly significant, defining films of that new era – Wood turned it down, both for personal reasons and because "she felt . . . that she would not be convincing as a girl from the Texas backwoods" (Lambert 2005, 235–236). In retrospect, her decision captures her very essence as Hollywood's "child of change." She stood as an emblem of transition who would define those crucial years when Hollywood was forced to seek a new identity. As a child actor shaped so fundamentally by that system, however – and so much like her film *Inside Daisy Clover*, in which she performed so compellingly – Natalie Wood could not quite "convincingly" play a part in the Hollywood that was about to emerge.

Notes

I would like to express my gratitude to Rider University for providing a summer research grant that helped make this essay possible. I also want to thank Ned Comstock, Jonathan Auxier, Sandra Joy Lee, and Sandra Garcia-Myers of the USC Warner Bros. archives and the USC Cinematic Arts Library for their invaluable help in accessing the Natalie Wood archives, and to Jacque Rogers who assisted me in my early stages of research.

1. USC (University of Southern California) Warner Bros. Archive, *Inside Daisy Clover* Publicity Folder, 630, # F000565.
2. Quoted from Nicolas Ray's biography, *Nicolas Ray: An American Journey* (Faber & Faber, 1996), by Bernard Eisenschitz.
3. USC Cinematic Arts Library, Natalie Wood, Box 1 of 1, *Rebel Without a Cause* Folder, 1955. Also cited by Finstad 2001, 178.
4. Peter Lev explains that it was not until the mid-1950s that Hollywood began to see that "teenagers were the backbone of the film audience, and therefore teen-oriented movies would be good investments." Lev points to the success of *Blackboard Jungle* (released in March 1955) and *Rebel Without a Cause* (released in October of the same year), along with the popular embrace of rock and roll, as "events that catalyzed these rather tardy realizations" (2003, 244).
5. Finstad's biography notes that padding was necessary in fashioning the womanly curves on the very petite and rather undeveloped Natalie, who was 16 when the film was shot (2001, 179).
6. Wood biographer Gavin Lambert (also a novelist and screenwriter) refers to Mineo's offscreen attraction to Dean, pointing out that "both Dean and Nick [Ray] were aware of it; and Nick, who was also aware of Dean's bisexuality, asked him to 'use' it in their scenes together" (2005, 98).
7. Even after his death, the mythology surrounding James Dean cast him as heterosexual – a *Modern Screen* article about Natalie Wood's dating life tells readers that "once there was a boy she loved . . . . That boy was Jimmy Dean" (1957, 50). At the same time, the article tip-toes around his sexuality: "They weren't a romance in the usual sense of the word, and many girls adored Dean . . . . Natalie, however, achieved what many girls did not. A real understanding of a boy who often preferred to be misunderstood" (1957, 68).
8. For an excellent discussion of attitudes concerning virginity in the postwar era through the early 1960s, as it plays out around Natalie Wood and particularly the character she plays in *Marjorie Morningstar*, see Sullivan 2010.
9. This article is part of the Constance McCormick Photo Collection on Natalie Wood in the USC Cinematic Arts Library. Full citation information is unavailable.
10. The lines as quoted in the film are here taken from Perkins 1967.
11. In an early 1980s interview with Dick (Dickie) Moore concerning her role in *Splendor*, Natalie Wood reflected, "I always had a bit of inner resistance to doing that part, because I felt that in order to play some of those scenes I would have to open doors and relive a lot

of feelings that I had put the lid on" (1984, 228). In her biography of Wood, Finstad infers that these words are a reference to her mother's having forced Natalie to end the relationship with her first love, Jimmy Williams, the son of a dairy farmer, whom she had met when she was in the eighth grade and got to know better in high school during one of her several brief experiences in public schools outside of the studio (2001, 92, 122). Interestingly, and perhaps in somewhat overdetermined ways, Finstad describes Jimmy in terms that strongly echo Jim Stark in *Rebel Without a Cause* (2001, 120–121).

In her interview with Moore, Wood gave no specific details but admitted that her role in *Splendor* "did open up a lot of wounds and led to the marriage [the first marriage to Robert Wagner] breaking up. Then I knew I had to get to a doctor" (1984, 228) – extending into her own life, it would seem, the narrative of her character Deanie. Although her parents wanted her to return home after the marriage ended, Wood says, "I knew I needed to be independent," which, for her, meant staying with friends because "I was still terrified to be alone," a fear she attributes, in part, to "having welfare workers always hovering [required by law for child actors who spent many hours each day in the studio], and directors to tell me what to do. It was as though there was some great danger in being independent" (Moore 1984, 228). Whether Finstad's theory is correct or not, it is clear that her role in *Splendor* triggered deeply personal and emotional associations for Wood.

12. Critical response was largely positive, however, and the film garnered a 1962 Academy Award for William Inge for its screenplay and an Academy nomination for Natalie Wood as Best Actress in a Leading Role.

    Yet, in an essay on *Marjorie Morningstar*, Rebecca Sullivan notes that in 1962 – one year after the release of *Splendor* – "Gloria Steinem argued that virginity had ceased to be a major issue for young women." She quotes Steinem as saying that, while the eponymous 1951 novel, on which the 1958 movie starring Natalie Wood was based, may have been "taken seriously enough . . . [it] is now regarded as a . . . *Much Ado about Nothing* in modern dress" (2010, 71). This view of the issue certainly accounts for a similar reception, among some, of *Splendor*. And depending upon how widely we believe that Steinem's words reflect the dominant thinking of the time (an issue of genuine debate, I believe, for I'm not sure they do), they nevertheless hint at how seriously Hollywood was lagging behind the changing attitudes and mores of America.
13. USC Warner Bros. Archive, *Splendor in the Grass*, 1961, Bar Code B00397, "Memos and Correspondence" folder, # 2274.
14. USC Cinematic Arts Library, Natalie Wood, *Splendor in the Grass*, "Kazan Correspondence," Folder 6.
15. USC Warner Bros. Archive, *Splendor in the Grass*, 1961, Bar Code B00397, Folder # 696, "Publicity 1 of 2 Misc." Along with the index cards on which the introductory remarks are typed are two questionnaires – one for adults and one for teenagers of 16 and older.
16. A letter from studio aide Benjamin Kalmenson to Reverend Patrick J. Sullivan of the National Legion of Decency, in fact, assures the priest that "the changes you saw yesterday in reel # 2 of 'SPLENDOR IN THE GRASS' plus the other change that was made in the line-up scene when Mr. [Jack] Vizzard [from the PCA] was here will prevail in the prints that will be used everywhere in the world" (a compromise made by Kazan who tried to argue for a less censored version of the film for foreign markets).

    "In our advertising . . . all ads will say that no one under sixteen years will be permitted unless accompanied by an adult" (n.d., USC Warner Bros. Archive, *Splendor in the Grass*, Folder 16749A LEGAL, Bar Code B00397).
17. During heated censorship battles over *A Streetcar Named Desire* – involving Stanley Kowalski's rape of Blanche DuBois, among other issues – Kazan is quoted as saying about the magnetism of Brando in the role of Stanley: "you can understand a woman *playing* affectionately with an animal that's going to kill her . . . She protests how vulgar and corrupted he is, but she also finds the vulgarity and corruption attractive . . . . I saw Blanche as [playwright Tennessee] Williams, an ambivalent figure who is attracted to the harshness and vulgarity around him at the same time that he fears it, because it threatens his life" (Ciment 1973, 71). (My gratitude to my colleague Roy Grundmann for sharing this material with me.)

    Although not an ambivalent figure in quite the sense that Williams, as a gay man, was at the time, Ginny is nevertheless longing for the opportunities and sexual freedom reserved for (straight) men. She is frustrated, angry, and rebellious when denied these ambitions and longings, and is further hurt when facing harsh social judgment for pursuing them. Like Blanche, she is strongly attracted to the men who have what she yearns to possess, and in her sexual contact with them somehow feels able to capture some small part of it – if only vicariously and self-destructively, given the larger culture within which she must negotiate such desires.

    Does Kazan extend sympathy to Ginny (as the film seems to suggest) or does he blame her (as the words of his letter suggest)? It is an interesting question that brings us back to Kazan's favored word, "ambivalence" – a word he uses again and again in interviews to discuss the nature of acting and of human interaction, and a word he calls upon to explain his refusal to use storyboards when shooting films – because such rigid preplanning will not allow for the unexpected, the spontaneous, the more truthful human and ambivalent emotions and reactions that may emerge (*A Streetcar Named Desire*, DVD, Disc 2 Special Features, "Censorship and Desire," 2006, Warner Home Video, Inc.).

18. USC Warner Bros. Archive, *Splendor in the Grass*, Folder # 2953, Bar Code F000566. Letter from Elia Kazan to Messrs Jack Warner and Benjamin Kalmenson, January 4, 1961, p. 2 of 4.
19. Wagner discusses the irrational fear of being alone instilled in Natalie by her mother Maria from an early age (2008, 105), one fear among a catalog of others that haunted Wood even into adulthood and that Finstad also attributes to her mother (2001, 43). Most striking was her mother's obsessive fear of drowning in "dark water," as a fortune teller predicted she would (Finstad 2001, 20), a fate that hauntingly would end the life not of the mother but of the daughter through whom she had lived so vicariously.

    According to Wagner – with similar information also presented in Finstad's biography – her mother "wanted to control Natalie's money and control her parts. She wanted to control who could be at one of Natalie's parties, control who Natalie dated, control everything" (2008, 106).
20. USC Warner Bros. Archive, *Splendor in the Grass*, Folder # 2953, Bar Code F000566. Letter from Elia Kazan to Messrs Jack Warner and Benjamin Kalmenson, January 4, 1961, pp. 2–3 of 4.
21. See http://www.boxofficereport.com/database/1961.shtml (accessed May 2011).
22. My gratitude to Cynthia Baron for so generously sharing both her own 1998 essay and the 1957 *Life* article with me.
23. This article is part of the Constance McCormick Collection. "*Natalie Wood*, Volume I," USC Cinematic Arts Library.
24. Within two months in 1965 she was given the Golden Globe Award as World Film Favorite, an award Finstad sees as "illustrating that her stardom had eclipsed the perception of Natalie as a serious actress," and was voted the Worst Actress of Last Year, This Year and Next by the *Harvard Lampoon*, an award she accepted with good humor (Finstad 2001, 314; Lambert 2005, 234).
25. My gratitude to my colleague Art Simon for sharing this article with me.
26. USC Warner Bros. Archive, *Inside Daisy Clover*, Folder # 2007, Bar Code B00212. Letter from Mary Pickford to Jack Warner, February 25, 1965.
27. Ibid., Folder # 630, Bar Code B00212. Press release dated June 4, 1965.
28. Ibid., Folder # 630, Bar Code B00212. Press release dated April 9, 1965.
29. Ibid., Folder # 630, Bar Code B00212. Press release dated March 24, 1965.
30. Ibid., Folder # 630, Bar Code B00212. Press release dated May 13, 1965.
31. Ibid., Folder # 2001, Bar Code B00212. Letter to Jack Warner from Geoffrey Shurlock, dated February 15, 1965.
32. The mother's ambition and, indeed, exploitation are best exemplified by an incident that occurred when Natalie was 10 and suffered a broken wrist during an accident on the set of *The Green Promise* (1949). Fearful that the studio (RKO) would replace her daughter – or that there would be other repercussions – her mother never reported the injury nor had it tended to. Wood was forever self-conscious of her misshapen left wrist that had healed improperly. She always wore a cuff bracelet to cover it in her films and public appearances, one accessory (along with what many critics observed as her excessive plying on of makeup, even as a teen) in creating what she later came to call "the badge" – the public, performative "Natalie Wood" (Finstad 2001, 78, 151) – a manufactured (studio) entity she saw as somehow separate from herself.
33. After having divorced Robert Wagner in 1962, she married British movie agent Richard Gregson and gave birth to her first child, Natasha, in 1970; she divorced Gregson in 1971, upon discovering that he was having an affair, and she remarried Wagner in 1972, and gave birth to their daughter Courtney in 1974 (Finstad 2001, 328–342).

References

Baron, Cynthia. (1998). "The Method Moment: Situating the Rise of Method Acting in the 1950s." *Popular Culture Review*, 9.2, August, 89–106.

Brustein, Robert. (1959). "The New Hollywood: Myth and Anti-Myth." *Film Quarterly*, 12.3, Spring, 23–31.

Chodorow, Nancy. (2004). "Pre-Oedipal Gender Configurations." In Julie Rivkin and Michael Ryan (eds), *Literary Theory: An Anthology* (pp. 470–486). Oxford: Blackwell. (Extract from Nancy Chodorow, *The Reproduction of Mothering*. Berkeley: University of California Press, 1978.)

Ciment, Michel. (1973). *Kazan on Kazan*. London: Secker & Warburg.

Davidson, Bill. (1962). "Hollywood Throwback: Academy Award Candidate Natalie Wood – a Screen Queen in the Old Flamboyant Tradition." *Saturday Evening Post*, 235.14, April 4, 32–36.

Dyer, Richard. (1991). "Charisma." In Christine Gledhill (ed.), *Stardom: Industry of Desire* (pp. 57–59). London: Routledge.

Finstad, Suzanne. (2001). *Natasha: The Biography of Natalie Wood*. New York: Three Rivers Press.

Hopper, Hedda. (1957). "Natalie's Career Enters Adult Stage." *Los Angeles Times*, April 4.

James, David. (1989). *Allegories of Cinema: American Film in the Sixties*. Princeton: Princeton University Press.

Kempton, Murray. (1962). "Natalie Wood: Mother, Men, and the Muse (the Dilemma of the Girl Next Door)." *Show*, 2.3, March, 50–53.

Lambert, Gavin. (2005). *Natalie Wood: A Life*. New York: Back Stage Books.

Lev, Peter. (2003). *The Fifties: Transforming the Screen 1950–1959*. Vol. 7 of Charles Harpole (gen. ed.), *History of the American Cinema*. Berkeley: University of California Press.

Life. (1957). "Strange Doings of Actress at Practice." January 28, 96–100.

Look. (1957). "Teen-age Tiger." 21, June 25, 96f.

Look. (1963). "Natalie Wood: Child of Change." 27.16, August 13, 91–94.

May, Elaine Tyler. (1988). *Homeward Bound: American Families in the Cold War Era*. New York: Basic Books.

Modern Screen. (1957). "How Natalie Handles Boys and Older Men." February, 50–51, 68–70.

Monaco, Paul. (2001). *The Sixties*. Vol. 8 of Charles Harpole (gen. ed.), *History of the American Cinema*. Berkeley: University of California Press.

Moore, Dick. (1984). *Twinkle, Twinkle, Little Star (But Don't Have Sex or Take the Car)*. New York: Harper & Row.

Newsweek. (1962). "Movie Star into Actress: The Story of Natalie Wood." February 26, 54–57.

Perkins, David (ed.). (1967). *English Romantic Writers*. New York: Harcourt, Brace, & World.

Porton, Richard. (2009). "Acting in the Grand Manner: An Interview with Christopher Plummer." *Cineaste*, 34.3, Summer, 12–17.

Poster, Mark. (1988). *Critical Theory of the Family*. New York: Continuum, at http://www.humanities.uci.edu/mposter/CTF (accessed March 2015). (Original work published 1978.)

Sullivan, Rebecca. (2010). "Postwar Virginity and the 'Marjorie' Phenomenon." In Tamar Keffers McDonald (ed.), *Virgin Territory: Sexual Inexperience in Film* (pp. 68–82). Detroit: Wayne State University Press.

Wagner, Robert J., with Scott Eyman. (2008). *Pieces of My Heart: A Life*. New York: Harper Entertainment.

26

The Politics of *Force of Evil*

An Analysis of Abraham Polonsky's Preblacklist Film

Christine Noll Brinckmann
Professor Emerita, University of Zurich, Switzerland

Christine Noll Brinckmann argues that the menace in the **film noir/gangster hybrid**, ***Force of Evil***, should be understood not as eternal or inescapable but as a set of economic forces undeniably at play. She integrates specific historical and film industrial contexts, illustrating the film's blending of **studio style** and **personal statement**. Director **Abraham Polonsky** worked, however briefly, as an **auteur** enjoying creative independence at **Enterprise Productions**, where political conscience and artistic vision coalesced around a handful of films. Brinckmann examines Polonsky's visual style in the context of **genre**, placing *Force of Evil* in counterpoint to prevailing **1940s gangster film** patterns. She argues that, although at times "too restrained, too terse, too symbolical, and too open-ended to involve the audience emotionally," the film is, nevertheless, "a rare work of art," at once popular and poetic. Brinckmann's essay shares ground with Ruth Vasey on the gangster film, Richard Maltby on studio realism, Roy Grundmann on *The Strange Love of Martha Ivers*, and Cynthia Baron and Beckett Warren on the Actors Studio in this volume.

Additional terms, names, and concepts: blacklist, House Un-American Activities Committee (HUAC), John Garfield persona

Introduction

Force of Evil was the first film Abraham Polonsky directed, and it is not without structural flaws. It is, however, a rare work of art in that it is poetic, popular, and political at the same time. Unlike other political art in which the balance between message and aesthetic form is usually uneven and the difficulties the artist had in creating an imaginative framework around his or her statement can be felt throughout, *Force of Evil* shows no seams. Although revealing the corruption of the capitalist system, the information it gives cannot be subtracted from its fictional, emotional impact, and although its effect on the viewer is agitational, there is no proposition for practical action.

American Film History: Selected Readings, Origins to 1960, First Edition. Edited by Cynthia Lucia, Roy Grundmann, and Art Simon.
© 1981 Cambridge University Press. Published 2016 by John Wiley & Sons, Inc.

The reasons for this unique blend are probably to be found in the fact that the filmmakers were less alienated from their work than other Hollywood artists. Instead of catering to other people – the producers, the masses, the critics – they made a film that first of all was to comply with their own tastes and political beliefs, even though it was subject to a number of practical and economic restrictions.

The mentality out of which *Force of Evil* evolved was that of creative intellectuals who had worked within the movie industry but whose independent spirit and leftist political awareness did not fit into the Hollywood system.[1] This is not to say that they looked down upon popular art – there was no elitist or puritanical distaste for the movies and no cynical contempt for mass audiences. On the other hand, there was no overall didactic impulse to enlighten the masses either.

The filmmakers did not perceive themselves as missionaries of political ideas, and they knew they had to make money in order to survive. Even though the film is original and bold, it also employs popular movie patterns, and it contains nothing to offend the censors. And even though Polonsky was closely in touch with the political situation and knew that he might not get another chance at directing a film,[2] the production of *Force of Evil* implied no acts of personal martyrdom; the time of the blacklist was close but had not yet begun. The production history of *Force of Evil* is thus not to be compared to that of *Salt of the Earth*.[3] But it is not the usual Hollywood story either.

Force of Evil was an independent production, produced by the newly established Enterprise studios. Independent production companies, which had been a marginal phenomenon during the 1930s and 1940s, suddenly started to burgeon after World War II. In 1946, the economic prospects of the movie industry looked highly promising. Audience attendance had reached its peak. It was before television had made its significant impact and before the postwar baby boom began to keep young couples at home. The antitrust suit had not yet forced the studios to divest themselves of monopoly holdings and to break up their vertical integration with movie theaters. The British market was still intact. It was therefore little wonder that movies were considered a particularly safe investment and that it was comparatively easy to find the money necessary for a new film project.[4]

Independent production companies could thus spring up and become an alternative to the Hollywood establishment. They were, however, mostly funded by the same type of investors and, therefore, basically controlled by the same free-enterprise ideology as the big studios. They also had to use the same channels of distribution and to show their films at the same theaters to audiences shaped by, and accustomed to, Hollywood. While it was thus rather unlikely that independent productions would differ drastically from the usual Hollywood fare, they did provide a slight opening for divergent, innovative talent. Things could be handled on a more personal basis and with less rigidity than in the big studios, and there was also some ambition to avoid stale patterns and be at least moderately experimental (and it made commercial sense, too).

Enterprise Productions went into business in 1946 and soon merged with Roberts Productions, an independent studio founded by the producer Bob Roberts and the actor John Garfield.[5] One of Enterprise's first releases, and its most successful, was *Body and Soul* (1947), directed by Robert Rossen, written by Abraham Polonsky, photographed by James Wong Howe, and starring John Garfield and Lilli Palmer. Though not a particularly expensive production, its credits include a number of well-known names. Moreover, the film tapped a popular genre and made use of the narrative patterns and visual style of its day. *Body and Soul* is a prizefight picture, told in first-person flashbacks and set and photographed in the dark, expressionist-realist tones of film noir. It is the story of a ghetto hero who has made his way up only to realize that in boxing he has to face the same corrupt and corruptive forces he had set out to avoid. After sacrificing personal happiness and moral values for fame and material wealth, he finally acknowledges that he has sold himself and walks out on his oppressors.

The social criticism contained in this story is more detailed and consistent than in comparable films. Although never obtrusive enough to occupy center stage, the information conveyed about commercialism in prizefighting and the moral stance taken by the protagonist tend to affect us in more than a superficial way. Apart from its underlying message, *Body and Soul* is also memorable for employing a black actor in a fairly important character role. In other respects, however, the film is more or less conventional and not even altogether successfully so. Lilli Palmer's acting is wooden, the dialogue is sometimes stilted and sentimental, some of the scenes move clumsily, and the film seems too long.

Body and Soul immediately became a big hit, reaping substantial profits and winning an Academy Award for editing. As the laws of the market demanded, Enterprise decided to repeat its success with another, relatively similar film. John Garfield, as one of the cofounders and investors of the production company, as well as one of its chief assets as an actor, planned to star in a comparable role. Again Abraham Polonsky wrote the script, but this time he was to direct the film as well. Because Polonsky had been on the set during the entire production of *Body and Soul*, working closely with the movie crew and especially with Garfield, assisting (and fruitfully contradicting) the director (Pasternak & Howton 1976; Pechter 1976, 390f), he seemed well qualified for the job.

Abraham Polonsky was brought up in New York, in a socialist Jewish milieu (Talbot & Zheutlin 1978, 55f; Pechter 1976, 391f). He attended City College in the 1930s – when it was a center of political and ideological controversy – joined a number of Marxist discussion groups, and taught classes in English literature. Having graduated from Columbia Law School and earning his living as a lawyer, he soon began to write fiction as well. He gave up law for radio writing in 1939, and at the same time became involved in union work for the Communist Party. During the war, Polonsky joined the Office of Strategic Services and was sent to Europe. Before his departure, he had signed a contract with Paramount Studios to become a screenwriter. After moving to Hollywood, Polonsky worked on several scripts – none of which were filmed in the form in which they were written (Talbot & Zheutlin 1978, 66f), became an editor of the critical journal *The Hollywood Quarterly*, and again took part in radical politics and union struggles. It was only after he had moved to Enterprise Productions that his career as a creative screen artist finally got under way, and it was only then that he could combine his political and artistic identities in his film work.

At Paramount, Polonsky's original talents and political energies had gone unnoticed. But within the small Enterprise group of dedicated movie workers with their dynamic esprit de corps, he suddenly came into his own. His friendship with John Garfield, another New York Jew who held similar, if intellectually less articulate, political beliefs (Polonsky 1975, 8), proved especially constructive, but Bob Roberts, the producer, also defended the project against the other, less enthusiastic financiers. Polonsky soon obtained almost total control over the production of *Force of Evil*: He rewrote the script (originally written by Ira Wolfert after his novel *Tucker's People*; see Pechter 1976, 391f), selected the locations, influenced the camera style, lighting, and music score, and supervised the editing.[6] *Force of Evil* is thus one of the few films of the 1940s that can rightfully be called the work of an auteur. As Polonsky's own comments on the film show, he always considered it to be *his* film, a work of art that evolved out of a complex set of personal and political decisions.[7]

When *Force of Evil* was released in December 1948, the fate of Enterprise Productions was already sealed. Consequently, the film did not receive proper publicity. It was distributed by MGM in an inexpensive, listless way and advertised as another gangster thriller.[8] Although a few critics mentioned it favorably,[9] *Force of Evil* soon disappeared from the screen. It did not reach its audience until it was rediscovered by television in the 1950s, but it has remained a kind of intellectual cult movie ever since.

Abraham Polonsky wrote one more script, *I Can Get It for You Wholesale* (1951), before he was blacklisted. As an avowed Marxist, a member of the Communist Party, and one of the most active participants in Hollywood's radical efforts, he was named by several "friendly witnesses" and summoned before the House Un-American Activities Committee (HUAC).[10] Realizing that he could no longer find work in the film industry, Polonsky moved back to New York. He started to write for television under a pseudonym and eventually resumed his work as a screenwriter, using other writers' names as fronts (as neither Polonsky himself nor the writers concerned have disclosed which films he wrote, this part of his career remains to be discovered).[11] It was not until 1968 that Polonsky's name was allowed to appear on the screen again (in *Madigan*, directed by Don Siegel), and not until 1970 that he got another chance at directing a film (*Tell Them Willie Boy Is Here*).[12]

Strangely enough, but in accordance with the usual practice of HUAC and the studios, Polonsky was not blacklisted on account of *Force of Evil*. Inconspicuous, commercially unsuccessful, and not to be categorized as pro-Russian, the film did not arouse the interest

Figure 26.1 View from the office in Abraham Polonsky's *Force of Evil* (1948, producer Bob Roberts). (Reproduced courtesy of MGM.)

of the Committee (Polonsky 1970, 45). Stranger still, but probably because of its poor distribution, *Force of Evil* was not recognized as a radical film by scholars of the blacklisting period either. John Cogley mentions Abraham Polonsky only as the writer of *Body and Soul*, and Dorothy B. Jones, in her extensively researched content analysis of postwar films, "Communism and the Movies," does not mention him or *Force of Evil* at all.[13] Obviously, the film had not begun to reach its audience by 1956.

Close Description

It is difficult to convey an impression of *Force of Evil* by summarizing its plot, as so much depends on the way images and sound coexist, function on their own, or are dialectically set against each other.

One has to imagine sets and locations photographed in what Polonsky wanted to be the equivalent of Edward Hopper's style in painting: "Third Avenue, cafeterias, all that backlight, and those empty streets. Even when people are there, you don't see them, somehow the environments dominate the people" (Sherman 1970, 20). City architecture and the empty clarity of the 1940s interiors are depicted with a predominance of rectangular planes and a clear distribution of masses, resulting in a simple sense of perspective. Each scene has a precise iconic identity, rich in symbolic overtones. An overall gloomy, stark style rather than a glossy visual one imparts an atmosphere of anxiety, reinforced by the claustrophobic quality of some of the sets and a film noir taste for

Figure 26.2 The city at night in Abraham Polonsky's *Force of Evil* (producer Bob Roberts). (Reproduced courtesy of MGM.)

shadows, almost total darkness, and the nervous flicker of neon signs.[14] This was not the usual style of the cinematographer, George Barnes, who was famous for the romantic glow of his pictures.

The clarity and poetic economy of the images are matched by the soundtrack, which, although highly complex, is equally lucid and expressive. It consists of three separate strands: the music score, the dialogue and noises connected with the action, and a voiceover narration commenting on and sometimes poeticizing the scenes. Poetry is, however, not limited to the voiceover – it is as much a quality of the dialogue, in fact one of the most original and most beautiful features of the film. As Polonsky has said in an interview, "the language almost obeyed my intention to play an equal role with the actor and visual image and not run along as illustration, information, and mere verbal gesture" (Pechter 1976, 391). And it is the poetry of the language as applied to the Wall Street locale or the sordid atmosphere of betting offices, courtrooms, taxicabs, and bars that gives the film its intensity.

Force of Evil tells the story of Joe Morse, a young lawyer who has made his way up from the Jewish ghetto to a Wall Street office. He is played by John Garfield and endowed with the inimitable Garfield personality –dynamically virile, persevering, hotheaded, tough, yet strangely sensitive.[15] Joe Morse is a character destined to undergo radical changes. One is immediately made aware of this by the two functions he has in the film: as a fictional character, blindly and ruthlessly involved in the action, and as a voice, commenting on the action as if it had happened long ago and to a much younger, less mature person. But in spite of the spiritual distance, there is a strong support between the voice and the character on the screen, and the voiceover somehow manages to emphasize the emotional sensitivity of Garfield's face.

The opening scenes show Joe Morse on the eve of the Fourth of July, contriving a scheme to destroy all the betting offices or "banks" connected with the numbers racket. By manipulating the results at the racetrack, the number 776 will be made to come up, and all the bettors who have traditionally chosen this number will consequently win – enough to make the numbers banks go bankrupt and to give Joe Morse's boss, Tucker (Roy Roberts), full control over the racket.

During the planning and execution of this scheme, one sees Joe functioning as a shyster lawyer, energetically trying to come to grips with the intricacies of the racket, on the one hand, and the law, on the other. But whereas he is highly successful in pulling the necessary strings, he fails to save his brother, one of the "bankers" involved. Leo Morse (Thomas Gomez), a rigidly moral person, runs his numbers bank like a benign patriarch, suppressing the fact that the nature of his business connects him inescapably with illegality and crime. Consequently, he considers Joe's proposition morally contaminating and refuses to play the part that would save him. This is emotionally taxing for Joe, for Leo has sacrificed his own career in order to put him through law school.

In the course of the action, Joe has Leo's betting office raided by the police. This event thoroughly upsets Leo's patriarchal enclave – his young secretary, Doris (Beatrice Pearson), quits her job, and his bookkeeper (Howard Chamberlain) becomes an informer, both to the police and to Tucker's men. Aware of the pressures Leo's stance puts on Joe and of the security risk involved, Tucker tries to double-cross Joe. He has Joe's phone tapped by Hall, the special prosecutor and a mysterious figure looming in the wings of the plot. But Joe has been warned. He clears out his safe and deserts his law office, never to return. Tucker's response to this is the attempt to have Leo kidnapped, using the bookkeeper as a decoy. In an ill-fated assault, the bookkeeper gets shot and Leo, too sick to endure the shock, dies of heart failure. Dismayed by his brother's death, for which he holds himself responsible, Joe takes revenge on Tucker and Tucker's Mafia partner Fico. In a dramatic shoot-out conducted in Tucker's office, he kills both men.

The scenes leading up to this final confrontation differ widely in tone. The encounters with Tucker's racket are crisp and fast, showing Joe in full control of the situation. The meetings of the two brothers are gloomy and slow, Leo Morse presenting himself as an insurmountable obstacle whose irrationality resists every argument. Emphasizing this difference, Tucker's environment looks pompously expensive, while Leo's office is depicted as a dark, narrow trap. Even Leo's physical appearance expresses his painful intractability – he is fat, unhealthy, elderly, and seedy. But most of all it is his traditionally Jewish rhetoric of futility, guilt, and victimization that characterizes the scenes between the brothers and makes it clear to us from the beginning that Joe will be unable to save Leo.

There is, however, a third kind of scene that is set in still another tone and reveals another aspect of Joe's character. During the first confrontation with Leo, Joe meets Doris, his brother's gentle, innocent secretary. It is through Doris, who is fascinated by him yet terrified at becoming contaminated, that Joe begins to see himself in a new light. Their encounters oscillate between romance and disillusionment, attraction and repulsion, hope and despair. And although their relationship is dissonant and dynamic in its own right, it serves as a mellow, almost peaceful counterpoint to the aggressiveness and speed of the main plot. Images of flowers, jewelry, softly swinging dresses, and domestic paraphernalia characterize most of the scenes with Doris, and her pure, intensely serious voice, even when talking about Joe's world, seems to come from an entirely different place. But Doris is not a weak character, and her firmness runs parallel to Joe's energetic rashness and enforces the sense of determination the film conveys. It is thus significant for the final breakthrough (as well as romantically appropriate) that Doris follows Joe after the shoot-out to find his brother's body.

The shoot-out is the climax and ending of Joe's involvement with the numbers racket, but it is neither the climax of his emotional development nor the end of his ideological struggles. Although his belief in his career as Tucker's lawyer has been shaken, Joe's decision to disappear with the money is dictated by egotism and practical necessity rather than by moral disgust. And his final turning against Tucker is shown as the outcome of his grief rather than the result of a mature analysis of the situation. The film defers Joe's full change until the very last, separating it from the scenes of violent action by images of pure symbolic movement and lyrical intensity. Joe is seen running

Figure 26.3 Joe (John Garfield) and his brother Leo (Thomas Gomez) in Abraham Polonsky's *Force of Evil* (producer Bob Roberts). (Reproduced courtesy of MGM.)

down Wall Street, descending to the bank of the Hudson River at the first rays of dawn. It is now that the metaphors of ascent and descent, and of day and night, that have been recurring throughout the film acquire full significance. Joe is forced to sink to depths deeper than the slum from which he came and to endure a night as dark as hell so that he may undergo purification and attain a new, dynamically positive personality.

The final voiceover, spoken while Joe turns back from his brother's body and starts walking up again toward the city with Doris, expresses the flow of energy from grief to future action:

> I found my brother's body at the bottom there, like an old dirty rag nobody wants. He was dead and I felt that I had killed him. I turned back to give myself up to Hall. Because if a man's life can be lived so long and come out this way, like rubbish, it's something that is horrible and has to be ended one way or another. And I decided to help.

Combining the Personal and the Political

In his review of *Odd Man Out* (Carol Reed, 1947), Polonsky states that the film is

> actually a stereotype of realism and the literary form of melodrama. Its content, as differentiated from its mechanical form, is essentially anti-realistic, a consideration of a metaphysical and not a social struggle. In treating social events it is necessary to know their precise historical conditions in order to evaluate the operation of moral choices. (Polonsky 1947)

Figure 26.4 Joe in search of his brother's body in Abraham Polonsky's *Force of Evil* (producer Bob Roberts). (Reproduced courtesy of MGM.)

What Polonsky resents is that images with an intensely realistic impact are used to depict a story only vaguely rooted in reality. One does not know the "object of the terror, the suspense, the suffering, the meanness," as one gets no information about the organization for which the protagonist is fighting; and "we do not know in what sense it represents the population or some part of it. We do not know why the police must suppress it" (Polonsky 1947). For Polonsky, it is not sufficient to show that a fictional character is seriously engaged in a conflict of some sort. The audience has to be put into a position to judge whether this conflict is meaningful in its own right as well.

Applied to his own film, Polonsky's theory makes a lot of sense. The lives of Joe and Leo Morse and of Doris and other characters are explained in terms of socioeconomic struggles. Public and private affairs, the characters' business identities and their personal lives, merge into each other. All situations and relationships are permeated by the same central conflict: the question of whether it is possible to be financially successful without becoming corrupt. Essentially a moral issue, this question has as much bearing on personal decisions as it has on the evaluation of the structure of society.

Polonsky's strategy of combining the personal and the political is especially evident in the scenes between Joe and Doris. Traditionally limited to the expression of personal feeling, love scenes in gangster movies usually function as moments of emotional relief. Without denying the romantic aspects of love, Polonsky breaks with this tradition by placing Doris within the arena of racket decisions and police raids. The conversations between Joe and Doris revolve around Joe's part in the numbers scheme, moving swiftly back and forth between lovemaking and ideological conflict, until one becomes inseparably entwined with the other. Joe and Doris are alternately seen in business locales and romantic places, using offices and courtrooms for passionate conversations and the steps of Trinity Church or Doris's kitchen for discussions of corruption and contamination.

Sometimes the atmosphere of the setting is transformed by purely visual means, as in the scene at the courthouse, when the profiles of Joe and Doris appear as romantic silhouettes on the translucent panes of the door. Totally out of keeping with the bleak environment, this image is "the complete opposite of the milieu. As if to say that you can still hold on to something beautiful and delicious despite everything." As Polonsky further points out, the image expresses Joe's point of view: "Garfield still thinks so, because he is not finished yet" (Sherman 1970, 22). While combining the worlds of sordid business and romantic love, the image also comments on the futility of fleeing from one into the other.

If one of the strategies of the film is to show how the protagonists are personally affected by the system, another one is to keep their antagonists as impersonal, unsympathetic, and static as possible. Tucker in particular, the boss of the racket, remains a cipher. Portrayed by Roy Roberts as more like a business executive than a gangster, he lacks the charisma that usually distinguishes the villain of a plot. As we learn nothing about his past and are never allowed to participate in his decisions, we never get inside the character. Consequently, Tucker comes to stand for the system that motivates him, or as Polonsky puts it, "the more shadowy Tucker is, the more omnipresent the feeling of what he represents" (Sherman 1970, 14).

One of the achievements of the film is to emphasize the fact that the real source of conflict transcends the characters – that the "force of evil" cannot be personalized in the usual, fictional way. The audience has to accept the socioeconomic system instead of the racketeer Tucker as the main antagonist of the plot. Spectators are thus asked to think about the part this system plays in their own lives. But Polonsky's strategy could, of course, have the reverse effect as well: As an antagonistic force in a fictional plot, the system could be divested of its connection to the real and become part of the fiction. It could play the traditional role of fate, of evil in general, or stand for an overall sense of inevitability, uncontrollability, or obstruction. In each case the political impact of the film would be weakened.

One of the main devices used to prevent this effect is to set the film in authentic locations. Contrary to the prevailing Hollywood style, the exteriors of *Force of Evil* were shot in New York City.[16] Wall Street, Trinity Church, the bank of the Hudson River, and other locales are allowed to play themselves, as it were, and give a documentary touch to the film. Their monumentality and symbolic connotations – as the site of the Stock Exchange and the leading banks of the western world – already signify to the audience the spirit of free enterprise. Authenticity is thus "naturally" accompanied by symbolic significance, the symbols depicted being part of the audience's reality.

Another, related feature of the film is the numbers racket, a lottery that was, and to some degree still is, immensely popular with the lower classes. By using the numbers game as one of the pivotal points of the plot, Polonsky introduced a commonplace phenomenon with which everybody was familiar, although it did have a smack of the illegal and mysterious.[17] It was, therefore, possible to let the numbers banks play two simultaneous roles: as the natural place where the numbers business would be conducted and, metonymically, as representative of the real banks, "establishments for the custody, loan, exchange, or issue of money" (Webster's New Collegiate Dictionary).[18] The Wall Street environment, then, serves several purposes. While it sets the action in locations that are at the same time realistically authentic and authentically symbolic, it also enforces the duplicitous use of the word "bank." Again, fictional world and reality are fused in an intricate way.

Considerations of Genre

It is typical of Abraham Polonsky's work to cut across the traditional distinctions between fiction and factual information, fantasy and politics, entertainment and serious art. Considered in this light, one of the most relevant features of *Force of Evil* is that it uses the framework of the gangster genre as a foil for its divergent content. It would not be correct, however, to maintain that Polonsky started out with a political message

Figure 26.5 Joe and Doris (Beatrice Pearson) in conversation in Abraham Polonsky's *Force of Evil* (producer Bob Roberts). (Reproduced courtesy of MGM.)

that he then tried to disguise as popular fiction. As the production history shows, his assignment was to create a popular movie (with progressive overtones), and the more radical content of the film only materialized as he went along. But even if the choice of a popular genre was a given, it did not run contrary to Polonsky's style and inclinations. His other scripts and films are characterized by the same strategy of employing fictional patterns in order to undercut their conventional structures, though *Force of Evil* remains the most explicit example. The documentary, or semi-documentary, is not a mode of expression Polonsky has attempted.

The gangster qualities of *Force of Evil* are prominent enough to have induced several film historians to classify it as a prime example of the genre. Jack Shadoian in his *Dreams and Dead Ends: The American Gangster/Crime Film* and Stanley J. Solomon in his *Beyond Formula: American Film Genres* have both used it to illustrate the development of the gangster film in the 1940s. But *Force of Evil* does not "fit comfortably into the genre," as Shadoian has it (1977, 134); nor does it portray evil as "one of the pervasive elements of modern life, its source seeming to lie *within* man," as Solomon claims (1976, 178). The way Polonsky makes us aware of the corrupting influence of the system rather than the corrupt nature of individual people already serves to contradict Solomon, and the way the personal and the political are combined in the main characters is another instance of deviating from the usual pattern. There is, however, further evidence on this point, which will also help to explain how Polonsky avoids the pitfall of fictionalizing the social forces he depicts.

Figure 26.6 The courthouse door: Joe and Doris in Abraham Polonsky's *Force of Evil* (producer Bob Roberts). (Reproduced courtesy of MGM.)

In his seminal article "The Gangster as Tragic Hero" (written in 1948, the year *Force of Evil* was made), Robert Warshow traces several basic qualities of the American gangster film. One of them concerns the nature and filmic depiction of the gangster's criminal activity, which are reflected in its function for the audience:

> The gangster's activity is actually a form of rational enterprise, involving fairly definite goals and various techniques for achieving them. But this rationality is usually no more than a vague background: we know, perhaps, that the gangster sells liquor or that he operates a numbers racket; often we are not given even that much information. So his activity becomes a kind of pure criminality: he hurts people. Certainly our response to the gangster film is most consistently and most universally a response to sadism; we gain the double satisfaction of participating vicariously in the gangster's sadism and then seeing it turned against the gangster himself. (Warshow 1972, 131f)

Force of Evil is, however, not at all vague about the particulars of the criminal setup. Much time is occupied with pointing out how the numbers banks work and how their bankruptcy is to be engineered. Although the film is not repetitious – it is in fact so terse that audiences are sometimes at a loss – many scenes or parts of scenes are dedicated to minor details: We are told about betting habits, about the way police detectives spy on numbers banks dressed up as bus supervisors, or how incriminating objects should be dropped before the police enter, as they cannot serve as evidence unless found in the defendant's hands. The audience is confronted with relentless

Figure 26.7 Trinity Church, downtown Manhattan, in Abraham Polonsky's *Force of Evil* (producer Bob Roberts). (Reproduced courtesy of MGM.)

explanations that often transcend the dramaturgical necessities of the plot.

Force of Evil deviates from the typical gangster picture also in that it does not supply sadism in the way Warshow describes it. Neither Joe Morse nor Tucker is presented as sadistically inclined, and the physical violence that does occur on the screen – the police raid of Leo's office, the kidnapping scene in which the bookkeeper is shot – has masochistic overtones rather than sadistic ones. In each case we see how a group of more or less anonymous men assault defenseless people; and in each case we sympathize with the assaulted, although we also feel that their pain and misery are to some degree self-inflicted or, in Leo's case, even sought. As for the final shoot-out in Tucker's office, which could have provided a scene of grim violence, its crucial moments take place in almost complete darkness. There is no way of knowing who fires at whom with what success, and consequently, no way of experiencing vicarious sadistic pleasure.

Apart from its avoidance of sadism, *Force of Evil* also refrains from presenting the typical, significant gangster career. As Warshow points out,

> we are always conscious that the whole meaning of this career is a strive for success: the typical gangster film presents a steady upward progress followed by a very precipitate fall. Thus brutality itself becomes at once the means to success and the content of success – a success that is defined in its most general terms, not as accomplishment or specific gain, but simply as the unlimited possibility of aggression. (1972, 132)

In *Force of Evil*, the action begins at a point where the "steady upward progress" has already reached its climax. Thematically, the myth of the American dream is present throughout the entire film, but experientially it is almost absent. If Joe Morse is still seen as fighting against all odds, his fight no longer leads him upward. While he succeeds in engineering the numbers scheme, this success is accompanied by the failure to persuade and save his brother. And while he manages to kill his adversaries, he loses or gives up all he has achieved during his career as a gangster lawyer. The film is thus not a story of economic, material success, and it does not end with a "very precipitate fall."

One could, of course, argue that Warshow's categories do not fit every gangster film and, in fact, do not have to do so – that it is their very "archetypicality" that makes them an inappropriate tool for the analysis and classification of *individual* works. Further, Warshow only speaks about films in which the gangster is the hero, whereas the term "gangster film" includes all kinds of pictures in which gangsters appear. It is true that Joe Morse is not even presented as a genuine gangster – he is a gangster's lawyer – and that the real gangster of the story is the shadowy, marginal figure of Tucker. But the plot of the film is continuously, if dialectically, evocative of Warshow's gangster syndrome, as is the character of Joe Morse. The battle for material success and power is the model *against* which the film is set, as sadism is the attitude one expects but never sees. The typical career of the gangster hero, from the slums to the lonely summit of a powerful syndicate, is the career Joe renounces.[19]

In an interview with Pasternak and Howton, Polonsky commented on the significance of film genres and their transformation in art:

> I think genres, like other social habits, speak for us in terms of summaries of the way we see life. We live out the myths and rituals, because that's the way we systematize our relationship to society and our relationship to other people. I think anthropologically speaking it has very deep connections with the role of religion in life. I would assume that I am essentially a religious person of some sort, at least in the sense that I try to make things signify as if there were some ultimate significance all the time – the ultimate significance being something that's not so ultimate after all ... I don't think that the development of genres in the art forms are [*sic*] accidents. I think they're fundamental to the way art operates in our life ... So in the long run, they're inescapable. Now, always, of course, as art advances, what you do is destroy the genre in one form or another, and reconstruct it in some other form, ultimately. (Pasternak & Howton 1976, 25f)

Apart from being a convenient vehicle for telling a story and attracting a mass audience, a film genre is, then, a way of structuring the world. And it supplies the artist with a presystematized framework that can be further paraphrased, transformed, or used as a foil for a dissident perception of reality. In *Force of Evil*, Polonsky has made use of the genre in all these ways, reemphasizing some of the established gangster film statements about society, modifying others, and evoking a number of traditional patterns without fulfilling them, transferring the energies they carry to a different cause.

Highly aware of his own strategies, Polonsky has commented on several subtle ways in which he has transformed the genre. One of these involves the use of music. In the kidnapping scene, we hear a kind of religious dirge instead of the usual musical equivalent for violence and aggression, introducing a "note of disruption" that alienates us from the images as well as from our sense of expectation. Polonsky chose this way of presenting the scene in order to "create a sense of general anxiety. When you do a thing like that, what you do is utilize the *familiar* as a way of calling attention to the fact that it's not so familiar after all" (Sherman 1970, 12).

In the same interview Polonsky explains the significance of the telephone in *Force of Evil*. A mode of communication that figures large in most gangster films, the telephone usually emphasizes the technological ease with which the racket network functions, and expresses the isolation and refrainment from personal, emotional contact it involves. By using a specially made oversize telephone, which sits in the foreground of some images like an enormous black contraption, Polonsky at once acknowledges the symbolic convention and takes it to obtrusive extremes.

At the same time, he exploits the (visual) anonymity and functional sameness of the people engaged in telephone conversations in order to indicate a sense of identity between them. When Joe Morse speaks first with his boss, then with the police, there seems to be a "direct parallel between Tucker and the Law on the other end of the telephone" (Sherman 1970, 14). Or, as Polonsky further elaborates, "The people live in a lane, and on both sides of this lane are vast, empty places. On one side, it says LAW, and on the other, it says CRIME. But, in fact, you can't tell one from the other" (Sherman 1970, 14).

Figure 26.8 Joe picks up the telephone in Abraham Polonsky's *Force of Evil* (producer Bob Roberts). (Reproduced courtesy of MGM.)

Again, one of the traditional metaphorical devices of the gangster genre is used in a more salient, ideologically more pointed way. The equation of crime with business in general, of the criminal world with society, or of gangsterism with Americanism becomes the equation of crime with the established countermeasure directed against it, the law itself.

The Story of Cain and Abel

Whereas the gangster features of *Force of Evil* are evident in the factual setup of the plot, in most of the personnel involved, and in the iconography of many scenes, the dramatic core of the film goes back to a much older, almost timeless mythical source. It is the archetypal conflict between Cain and Abel, the story of how one brother turns against the other or, more generally, of how men are unable to understand and tolerate each other. Like the myth of Cain and Abel, the film revolves around egotism, distrust, and discordance, ending in the death of one of the brothers.

Cain and Abel are, however, one-dimensional characters who represent evil and good, respectively – the provocation inherent in Abel's priggish righteousness is not in the foreground of the biblical fable, and Cain has to bear the full punishment for the deed. Contrary to this, the film incriminates both brothers (Sherman 1970, 19). Although Joe resembles Cain in that he is violent, selfish, and irreverent, and Leo resembles Abel in his gentleness and morality, Joe is also characterized as responsible, repentant, and able to reform, whereas Leo is rigid, irrational, and despairing and tries to put the blame on his brother. It is as much Leo's rigidity and eagerness to victimize himself as it is Joe's involvement in the racket that finally results in Leo's death. Moreover, Joe wishes to help his brother, and this desire increases until it becomes the primary motive of all his actions. That his reform comes too late to save his brother is a tragic coincidence. Joe's sense of guilt is, therefore, gratuitous to some degree, and it functions as a redeeming quality. Purified rather than contaminated, Joe is now able to dedicate himself to the fight against the forces that caused his own corruption and his brother's death.

The myth of Cain and Abel thus does not provide the skeleton of the plot, because the deviations from it are more significant than the similarities. Again, Polonsky has drawn from a well-known pattern without following its implications, and again the film profits from the strategy. For one thing, the familiarity with the myth sets up audience expectations. For another, it furnishes a moral framework within which the characters can be evaluated. Joe and Leo themselves often conjure up the specter of fratricide, adding emotional intensity to their discordance. But, most of all, the biblical connotations of the myth give an aura of seriousness, dignity, and weight to the film.

The deviation from the myth also serves to save *Force of Evil* from the danger of becoming "melodramatic" in Polonsky's sense of the word. For the Cain and Abel story could have provided the same kind of metaphysically oriented, eternally humanitarian, nonconcrete, nonrealistic thrust Polonsky criticized in his review of *Odd Man Out*. As it is, however, *Force of Evil* does not allow such an interpretation. Apart from its significantly different ending, which alone would make a metaphysical reading somewhat difficult, and apart from the way Joe and Leo Morse differ from Cain and Abel, the film shows how the brothers have been shaped by their environment. Because the economic system rather than some innate moral deficiency has to be held responsible for their mistakes, *Force of Evil* is not about the evil eternally and inescapably present in the human race.

But the pattern of the two discordant brothers does have some allegorical overtones, and their being brothers is more than a neat coincidence of the plot. Not a very convincing pair of siblings, their family resemblance showing neither physically nor spiritually, Joe and Leo Morse represent two alternatives, two almost complementary ways of being. This is evident in their characters, as well as in their attitudes and their ability to adjust to the system.

Joe has decided to use his education and intelligence in order to make as much money as possible, no matter how immoral the means. "I had not enough strength to resist corruption, but I was strong enough to fight for a piece of it," he tells Doris. No longer able to see the difference between being a gangster's lawyer and doing a gangster's business, he is on the verge of becoming a gangster himself. Leo, on the other hand, has no education and is not as smart as his younger brother. He tried very hard to earn his living honestly but was forced by bitter circumstances to go into the numbers business. Looking back on his life, he too is no longer able to discriminate between legality and illegality:

> I've been a businessman all my life, and honest, I don't know what a business is ... Real estate business, living from mortgage to mortgage, stealing credit like a thief. And the garage, that was a business. Three cents overcharge on every gallon of gas – two cents for the chauffeur, and a penny for me. A penny for one thief, two cents for the other.

The brothers demonstrate that whatever you do, you get caught in the mesh of corruption (Pasternak & Howton 1976, 27). Dramatically opposed in all important respects, they represent a wide range of contamination, and their being brothers only adds to the sense of totality conveyed. The generality inherent in the motif of the two brothers has thus been employed to express a political statement.

Spectatorial Affect

The discussion so far has concentrated on Polonsky's attempts to render a critical analysis of the capitalist system. By focusing on concrete details, by introducing authentic materials, or by transforming the genre or myth employed, *Force of Evil* disrupts the fictional conventions and succeeds in drawing a detailed and manifold picture of the system. All these strategies appeal to, and depend on, the mental capacity of the audience to grasp the meaning of the deviations and understand their bearing on reality. But the film is not an essay on capitalism, and nothing would be achieved if the audience could not respond emotionally as well. In a work of fiction, the analytical insights have to be aligned with the emotional impact of the story – or the story will appear stale and ultimately unconvincing. Although stories have a strong tendency to absorb all kinds of material, they suffer easily from being didactically overloaded. It is, therefore, as necessary to keep the emotional experience of the audience intact as it is to protect the political message from being smothered in the magic of fiction.

Polonsky's strategy to achieve the right balance consists first of all in shifting the main emotional impact from the story to what could be called the "spiritual intensity" of the film – intensity of character, feeling, atmosphere, or poetic presentation in general. As has been indicated before, the plot itself does not fulfill the requirements of a gangster story (or of other genre fiction, for that matter): It does not portray the rise and fall of a criminal hero; it does not focus on personal violence; it refrains from melodrama; it shows little dramatic interaction between the protagonist and his antagonists; and the love story is neither supplementary nor pathos-ridden, nor does it furnish the pivotal point of the action. Although tightly knit and determining each scene logically, the plot of *Force of Evil* is also too restrained, too terse, too symbolical, and too open-ended to involve the audience emotionally. Instead of participating in the actual incidents of the story, one is induced to watch them from a detached point of view.

This detachment is, however, counterbalanced by the high emotional intensity that characterizes the film. For one thing, *Force of Evil* is permeated by an overall sense of anxiety present even in its most romantic scenes. Visually, this anxiety is expressed through the narrowness, darkness, and bleakness of most of the locales – much of the film takes place at night, in confined interior spaces or in Leo's office, to which daylight is not permitted. But claustrophobia is not only expressed through the images (as it is in many a film noir of the period).[20] One of the characters actually suffers from it, and it can thus be vicariously experienced by the audience. When one of Leo's employees explains to the police how he was trapped in his car after it had been pushed off the road into the river, they insist nonetheless that he ride in the narrow back of the van. His reaction is extreme, providing the film with one of its most agonizing moments.

Other scenes also impart a sense of acute physical discomfort – for example, when the police burst the door of Leo's bank open, regardless of the group of people crowded behind it; or when Leo's heart condition manifests itself, so that his weight and hysterical irritation are felt as a constant threat to his life; or when Joe gets so drunk at the nightclub that he is hardly able to speak. All these scenes have a harrowing, anxiety-raising quality, because one is forced to experience empathetically what it feels like to be physically hampered or disabled.

Another way in which the film raises anxiety is by repeatedly introducing situations of frustration and impotence. A frequent instance of this is provided by the telephone, through its threatening capacity to exert remote control over people and through its constant liability of being tapped. It is mostly the main character who experiences – and conveys – this anxiety, for his impatience and dynamic agility make him all the more prone to frustration. In spite of all his bustling activity and dreamlike presence of mind, Joe is not able to control what is going on. His actions are almost inevitably reactions, and he is always either just in time to forestall greater loss or already too late to prevent disaster. Consequently, the audience feels a growing sense of uneasiness and nervous urgency, and it is only at the end that one is able to breathe freely again.

Polonsky attributes this climate of anxiety to the prevailing political experience of the period in which the film was made. *Force of Evil* can be considered an expression of the fear that spread in the leftist movement as American policy changed in the postwar years, and of the traumatic insight that the movement was to be curbed and destroyed (Polonsky 1970, 44f). But the anxiety in the film is not only a reflection of the historical situation. It also serves to emphasize the general sense of alienation and impotence inflicted by a dehumanized and corrupt economic system. Anxiety is thus part of the basis of the film and, therefore, a particularly appropriate sensation to be imparted to the audience in order to keep it in a state of emotional agitation.

Anxiety is, however, not the only intense emotion the film evokes. For one thing, *Force of Evil* is steeped in melancholy that is both painful and sweet. It is the feeling that accompanies the remembrance of things past, especially memories of one's youth, and it is created by the voiceover, on the one hand, and Joe Morse's youthful enthusiasm, on the other. As the voiceover is spoken from a vantage point

Figure 26.9 The stairs leading up to the numbers bank in Abraham Polonsky's *Force of Evil* (producer Bob Roberts). (Reproduced courtesy of MGM.)

above the film and sufficiently removed temporally to allow a contemplative stance, the scenes presented become less imminent and the situation appears no longer hopeless: If the main character has survived and matured into a person capable of narrating his own story with feeling and insight into its general significance, we may be reassured that anxiety, frustration, and dismay can be overcome.

For another thing, the aesthetic structure of the film serves to suspend our anxiety. The poetry of the language, as well as the beautiful texture of the images, heightens the feeling of reassurance, while both add overtones of lyrical assonance and the excitement of intense compression and expressiveness. Through the mythical symmetry of the motif of the two brothers, the recurrent patterns of descent and ascent, and the metaphorical framework of day, night, and morning, the film conveys a sense of aesthetic control strong enough to counterbalance the experience of being at the mercy of a hostile, uncontrollable system.[21] In a way, the voiceover is a manifestation of this control, too. Free-floating, capable of entering the film at any given moment, divested of a visible source and omniscient in its understanding, the voice is as much that of the filmmaker as it is that of Joe Morse. A creative authority, it is able to conjure up forces and counterforces, to cope with dismay and passion, and to explain the significance of it all as far as it is explicable.

The Ending

Apart from the highly charged atmosphere of *Force of Evil*, it is chiefly the spiritual energy of the protagonist that keeps the audience involved, and like the emotions of anxiety and reassurance it contributes to the effectiveness of the statement the film makes, Joe Morse's personality comes across equally strong in romantic scenes and in business encounters – even in brief moments of trivial occupation, like climbing stairs or opening a door. As portrayed by John Garfield, the character of Joe Morse is endowed with a depth and swiftness of feeling irresistibly attractive and with emotional and physical energies bound to make the audience identify with him. Polonsky was well aware of Garfield's powers: "Garfield was the darling of romantic rebels – beautiful, enthusiastic, rich with the know-how of street intelligence. He had passion and a lyrical sadness that was the essence of the role he created as it was created for him" (Polonsky 1975, 8).

Although empathetic identification with the main character (and a glamorous star at that) is a phenomenon usually connected with escapist Hollywood movies, it can be put to different uses as well. What Polonsky attempted to achieve through his star was different already in that it was to function in a differently structured film: As has been indicated before, the Garfield character serves as a center of emotional intensity in a rigorously condensed plot loaded with thought and information. But it also serves to give an emotionally and, to some degree, politically satisfactory ending to *Force of Evil*.

Again the device of the voiceover is responsible for the way in which the main character is experienced. Garfield's split identity, the fact that he exists in the present as well as the past, serves to disentangle him from the events on the screen. For the voiceover makes it quite clear that what we see is the past, which has to be lived through and overcome, and that the point we are to reach is a point at the end of the film, or even outside it. Although this does not drain Joe's screen activities of their dynamic quality, they seem to occur on a plane once removed from the central awareness of the film. Joe's energy is thus not completely integrated into, and at the disposal of, the plot. He has a kind of surplus power that, together with his invulnerability (also guaranteed by the voiceover) and his charisma, makes him a hero figure who can continue after the plot of the film has exhausted itself.

The ending of *Force of Evil* is bound to disappoint those who pay too much attention to the plot, ignoring its functional, almost allegorical character and not acknowledging the implications of the voiceover. David Talbot and Barbara Zheutlin give evidence of this fallacy in their comment on Joe Morse's descent to the bank of the river: "His descent is so long and steep, and the sight of his dead brother so terribly final that it is evident Morse will never fully regain his humanity – despite his declared intention of turning himself in to the district attorney" (1978, 81).

But how can he "never fully regain his humanity" and at the same time be capable of telling his story the way he does? And isn't it precisely the steepness and length (and pace) of his descent that give him the energy to turn around and make a new beginning? There is, moreover, the metaphor of night and morning used again and again, visually as well as verbally, to characterize Joe's moral awakening. The finality of his brother's death cannot interfere with the tremendous energy he gains in the course of this experience, especially as it is the price he has to pay for his purification. It is, then, certainly a strategy of Polonsky's to invest Joe Morse with more spiritual intensity than the plot requires. Joe is set up as a contagious center of energy, a kind of energizing spirit of revolt who bursts the fetters of the system to prove that it is possible to live outside it. And his experience could not be conveyed effectively if the powers of the protagonist were limited to the self-contained fictionality of a story.

In his review of *The Best Years of Our Lives* (William Wyler, 1946) Abraham Polonsky finds fault with the ending of that progressive and in many respects exemplary film:

> Unfortunately, in the *Best Years*, as in most social-problem fiction, the artist falls into the trap of trying to find local solutions in existence for the social conflicts, instead of solving them in feeling. This is, of course, the industry's demand for happy endings …
>
> Fascism is solved with a punch; a bad marriage by the easy disappearance of a wife; the profound emotional adjustment of a handless veteran by a fine girl; the itchy conscience of a banker by too many drinks. The future is not to be predicted out of such formulas. (Polonsky 1946–1947, 258–259)

Polonsky objects to the way the picture first "exposes the fraud of America's promises to its soldiers," then finds cheap and – at best – individually convincing solutions for their problems. In his own film, Polonsky has avoided covering up unsolvable problems with happy endings; in fact, he does not offer any solutions or practical suggestions at all. The shooting of the two racketeers will clearly not make a difference to the system; Leo's death is shown as inevitable, no matter what Joe might have done; and Leo's life proves that there was no way of escaping corruption. Reality is thus depicted as endlessly frustrating, but it is the explosive power of pent-up frustrations that may ultimately lead to relief. The only "solution" or positive experience *Force of Evil* offers is a "solution in feeling," that is, a solution that makes the audience aware of its own anger and the potential to break free and strive for change, in spite of the all but utopian chances to win.[22]

Minor Imperfections

If this interpretation sounds overenthusiastic, it is because the weaknesses of the film have not been discussed. *Force of Evil* is not all it could have been – wrong casting of some of the minor characters (especially Marie Windsor as Tucker's wife) and a few scenes that are too sparse or too sketchy to fulfill their aesthetic functions are shortcomings that could have been avoided. But they are probably due to the small budget of the film, and they do not seriously detract from its merits. There are, however, a few points that concern the political effect of *Force of Evil*, and these have to be raised.

For one thing, *Force of Evil* has an over-terseness that makes it difficult to grasp the film's full meaning at first viewing. In the light of its intended political impact, this could be detrimental, and one can argue that Polonsky sacrificed some of the agitational effect of his film in an effort to achieve aesthetic perfection. Instead of making music, words, and images work together, one repeating and elaborating on the message the others convey, he has made his film say different things on different levels simultaneously. Moreover, all of the scenes are short, and nothing is said twice – a policy of communication appropriate for poetry or philosophical discourse, perhaps, but not for a motion picture aimed at an audience accustomed to the redundancy of Hollywood movies and in the habit of seeing a film only once.

A related problem is Polonsky's strategy of using a popular fictional pattern as a vehicle for political content. As the box office figures indicate, *Force of Evil* did, in fact, alienate its audience, and it is quite conceivable that its mixture of popular appeal and poetic sophistication is responsible for its failure. In the mood for escapist entertainment and expecting to see a gangster movie, the audience may have felt cheated, and many people may have been less inclined to engage themselves in aesthetic subtleties and ideological analysis.

With a running time of only 78 minutes, *Force of Evil* is also at the lower end of the usual scale. This is partly the result of a few substantial cuts Polonsky made in the course of shooting the film, and partly aesthetically motivated. In a letter he wrote to me,[23] Polonsky commented on his omissions from the original script and his reasons for making them. I shall quote from this letter extensively because it touches on a number of questions raised throughout this essay, and also because it refers to a flaw in the film that I shall subsequently discuss:

> Originally, the screenplay began and ended with a court trial. After I shot the first half of the court scene which would then in narrative sequence lead to the present film, the original script returned to the court for the conclusion.
>
> Naturally in shooting the courtroom scenes they were scheduled to be shot together. I did the first part of a good section of it as I recall and when I saw the rushes decided this would destroy the entire film so I just junked the whole concept.
>
> My reasons for doing this were aesthetic and political. Aesthetically, it destroyed the continuing sense of the present which I wanted to be the feel of the film. The voice-over took the place of the original mechanical flashback technique and gave the sense of Morse meditating upon the nature of what he was living through, rather than supplying mere narrative elements in the story.
>
> Politically, I didn't want Joe Morse to be co-operating with the police and the law in any way or to be seen doing so. What he was doing was co-operating with what was suppressed in his own nature and in the society in which he found himself. There is just enough dubious hinting for the censors to believe it might be the law of the land he was talking about, but for me, it was the law of history he meant.
>
> Naturally, I had no practical suggestions in the film for political organizations since even now as we search, we still don't find.
>
> Of course the elimination of two courtroom scenes made the film shorter. But you must also remember that in those days, films that were an hour or more long were

> considered long enough and it's only now that the habit of making much longer films has become a feature of the feature film. A feature film, like a novel, should be long enough, but after that, it's either long enough or too long, and the question is aesthetic. I assume that your question means perhaps that you would feel more fulfilled if the film were longer.
>
> I made two other cuts in it. One dealt with the bookkeeper's home life with his wife. I shot that but it seemed extraneous when I edited the film and I left it out. The second part I cut out was a very long sequence between Doris and Joe which was a kind of monologue on his part filled with prophecy underlined with personal loneliness. I liked it well enough but in the three or four times I showed the film to audiences, they seemed to find this a place to be very restless. In the end I reduced it to a minimum so that it served merely a narrative function.
>
> While these things shortened the film, I intended not too long a film in the beginning. It was basic to the style and verbal relation with the images. But I did not deliberately make it as short as it became, originally. That happened to it. But it seemed to be all that it had to be, so there I paused.

Two kinds of shortcoming have to be distinguished in *Force of Evil*: its inability to reach the masses, on the one hand, and its intrinsic imperfections, on the other. Although not reaching the audience it was initially made for is a serious deficiency, it can be attributed to Polonsky's lack of experience with movie audiences outside New York and Los Angeles or outside his own political environment. The film has meanwhile proved to have a strong appeal to more sophisticated audiences, and its terseness, experimental nature, and ideological commitment are precisely the qualities responsible for its success.

The film contains, however, one major inconsistency that is bound to weaken its political impact. It is the ambiguity or contradictoriness with which the law and Joe Morse's attitude toward it are treated. On the one hand, the film insinuates that the law is a kind of mirror image of the racket – as impersonal (using the telephone to assert itself), as threatening, and probably as corrupt. On the other, there is no unmistakable evidence of this. Hall, the special prosecutor, never appears on the screen in person, and we have no way of knowing what his real intentions are. It is, however, ideologically inconceivable not to consider the law as part of the "system": Either the law would appear to be so weak as not to deserve anybody's respect, or the system would be a minor problem indeed. If Joe decides to cooperate with the law, his decision implies an acknowledgment of the system and, therefore, a denial of all for which his own purification and liberation stand.

Abraham Polonsky's statement that he had to compromise in order to pass the censors is an honest and acceptable explanation of this inconsistency. But his additional remark that what he actually meant was the "law of history" is, of course, irrelevant for the audience.[24] Joe Morse's final words, in which he informs us that he "turned back to give myself up to Hall," are much too explicit to be taken metaphorically.

Conclusion

I shall conclude this essay with a review that appeared in *Variety* after *Force of Evil* was released in 1948. The mouthpiece of the movie industry, *Variety* puts its finger on the film's most salient deviations from the usual Hollywood fare, pointing them out as artistic shortcomings instead of political strategies. This may prove how seismographically the response of the audience could be predicted. But it also proves to what degree a critic faithful to the standards of the industry could renounce his or her perceptions, evaluating them contrary to the film's intentions as if the review had been written with tongue in cheek:

> *Force of Evil* fails to develop the excitement hinted at in the title. It's a missout for solid melodramatic entertainment, and will have to depend upon exceptionally strong exploitation and the value of the John Garfield name for box office. Makers apparently couldn't decide on the best way to present an exposé of the numbers racket, winding up with neither fish nor fowl as far as hard-hitting racketeer meller is concerned. A poetic, almost allegorical interpretation keeps intruding on the tougher elements of the plot. This factor adds no distinction and only makes the going tougher.[25]

Notes

An earlier version of this essay appeared as Christine Noll Brinckmann, "The Politics of *Force of Evil*: An Analysis of Abraham Polonsky's Preblacklist Film," *Prospects*, 6 (1981), 357–386.

1. As Dorothy B. Jones's study on "Communism and the Movies" has shown, it was practically impossible to smuggle Marxist ideas into movies produced by the big studios: "The very nature of the film-making process which divides creative responsibility among a number of different people and which keeps ultimate control on content in the hands of top studio executives; the habitual caution of moviemakers with respect to film content; and the self-regulating practices of the motion picture industry as carried on by the Motion Picture Association, prevented such propaganda from reaching the screen in all but possibly rare instances" (1956, 197). For Polonsky's views on the problematic, see especially Polonsky 1970, 43f.
2. See Polonsky's interview with J. D. Pasternak and F. W. Howton, especially pp. 22ff, in Henderson 1971.
3. See the book *Salt of the Earth*, which contains Michael Wilson's screenplay and an extensive commentary on the background and making of the film by Deborah Silverton Rosenfelt (Wilson 1978).
4. For a more thorough analysis of the economic situation of Hollywood in the 1940s, see Sklar 1976, part 4.
5. Clayton M. Steinman has compiled a short history of Enterprise Productions in his dissertation; see Steinman 1979, 268–282.
6. See Polonsky's interview with Jim Cook and Kingsley Canham in Cook & Canham 1970. *Tucker's People* was published in 1943.
7. Still interested in his early work, Polonsky has been one of his own most acute critics. He is generous in granting interviews and answering questions, and all the interviews published abound with valuable bits of information, aphorisms, and sympathetic and critical insights on the merits and failures of *Force of Evil*. Polonsky was kind enough to see me in April 1979, and I also have a letter he wrote to me, answering a number of questions I submitted to him.
8. Promotion materials (issued in 1949; filed at Lincoln Center Library) characterized *Force of Evil* with the following slogans: "Sensational story of a numbers king whose number was up!" "He wouldn't live within the law – or without love." "He fought with the woman he loved and made love to the woman he hated." At the same time, the publicity experts advised exhibitors not to stress the controversial contents of the film: "When you exploit *Force of Evil*, don't take a controversial attitude on the perils of local gambling. Don't crusade for better local conditions or improvements, unless such a drive is already underway at the time of your play dates; then play safe and merely cash-in with picture tie-ins. Spearheading such a drive, or participating aggressively, might have unpleasant repercussions for your theater. You can, however, institute a campaign for city-wide endorsement of your engagement by enlisting the support of influential people." The pressbook also suggests valuable promotion ideas: "CRIME DOESN'T PAY. *Force of Evil* is a thriller-diller example of the fact that crime doesn't pay; so seize every opportunity to bring it to the attention of the public – at sports events, in bowling alleys and pool-rooms, recreation centers, with spot announcements at end of radio crime programs &c." Also: "STOP THESE MEN! Prepare 40 × 60 lobby board containing tough-looking heads of John Garfield and other male members of the cast, under above headline and describe under each head the manner in which that person is a 'menace' to society. Finish up with picture billing and play date announcement. Strong stuff for patrons who like their pictures hard-boiled and exciting."
9. Bosley Crowther, in the *New York Times*, called the film "a dynamic crime-and-punishment drama, brilliantly and broadly realized ... a sizzling piece of work," and he considered Polonsky "a real new talent in the medium ... a man of imagination and unquestioned craftsmanship" (Crowther 1948). Perhaps the first critic to recognize the genuinely political implications of *Force of Evil* was the British director Lindsay Anderson in "Last Sequence of *On the Waterfront*" (1955).
10. See Bentley 1971. Other materials on HUAC and Hollywood blacklisting include Kahn 1948; Cogley 1956; and the special double issue of *Film Culture* on Hollywood blacklisting, nos 50–51 (Fall and Winter), 1970.
11. In *Film Culture*, Polonsky gives his reasons for not disclosing which films he wrote during the blacklist period: "It might not be damaging today to name the films I worked on during the blacklist period, but I think it's up to the persons who lent their real names to this purpose to name the films, not me. I don't see why they should do so. There would probably not be any harm, except to them personally perhaps. I mean, it's a very difficult thing to be a writer who's writing, and occasionally someone else writes something but your name is on it. That's the greatest sacrifice you can demand of a friend. And to say later, 'I want to distinguish between this and that' seems to be absurd, because I don't think there are any great major works of art now going under false pretenses." He goes on: "But perhaps as history the exact credits are important. If the situation were reversed, I don't know what I would do. I wouldn't do anything, I guess, unless I felt it was a bad thing that I was keeping something from someone, but that's because I'm an old Puritan. But in general I don't think the inaccuracies of these credits, due to the blacklisting, is a bad thing. I think it's better to let the past be the way it is. And instead let us writers make our usual claims that we wrote all the good pictures and

everyone else wrote all the bad ones. In that way the guerilla warfare continues" (Polonsky 1970, 42).

12. Naturally, Polonsky commented widely on his blacklisting experiences. His most detailed accounts are the interview with Cook and Canham in *Screen* and the *Film Culture* article, both 1970.
13. See note 1 above.
14. For a perceptive description of film noir style, see Place & Peterson 1974.
15. Garfield's personality and career have been described by Howard Gelman, *The Films of John Garfield*, with an introduction by Abraham Polonsky (1975), and by George Morris, *John Garfield* (1977).
16. *Force of Evil* is, however, not the only film of the period to be filmed on authentic locations. During World War II many Hollywood filmmakers had been involved in combat photography or the production of training films and other documentary materials. After the war some of them tried to apply documentary effects and techniques to feature films.
17. Like many features of *Force of Evil*, this goes back to the novel it was adapted from, *Tucker's People*. The novel is, however, set in Harlem, adding another problematic to its analysis of capitalism.
18. Jack Shadoian points out that the word "business" plays a similar role in *Force of Evil*: "Business is the American way of life, and because it is ingrained, legal, and philosophically supportable, its destructiveness remains unnoticed until an analysis is made of it" (1977, 138f).
19. Other gangster films of the time also tend to move away from Warshow's pattern. But instead of evoking it as *Force of Evil* does, they drop it altogether in favor of a different type of story and a different hero personality. In pictures like *Kiss of Death* (Henry Hathaway, 1947), *They Live by Night* (Nicholas Ray, 1948), or *Side Street* (Anthony Mann, 1949), the protagonist is a simple, basically innocent young man who got involved in crime only because he was too weak to extricate himself from bad influences or to resist the temptation of the moment.
20. In a paper delivered at the College Art Association National Conference in 1976, "Le Film Noir: The Political Space of America in the Cold War," Paul S. Arthur analyzed the relationship of film noir claustrophobia and other visual motifs with the political climate of the period.
21. Simon O. Lesser holds that it is one of the major functions of form to relieve free-floating anxiety: "The highest achievements of form, it may be conjectured, are due to the double requirement of having to subdue the quotient of anxiety which is always with us as well as the anxiety which may be aroused by the subject matter of a particular story." Through our positive response to form, "we are paying homage to the superego, not simply attempting to deceive or conciliate it, but asseverating our devotion and our unqualified acceptance of its demands" (1957, 129, 130).
22. Whether Polonsky's political strategies in *Force of Evil* can be considered to constitute a Marxist film aesthetics, I do not know. It is a question raised in one way or another by most of his critics and interviewers. Polonsky himself has commented on what the attitude of the Hollywood Left was in respect to a Marxist aesthetics: "Their attitudes (about film) reflected – to a certain extent – what was going on in the Soviet Union, which had destroyed the dynamic aesthetic movement of its late 1920s. So they thought of aesthetics in terms of social content. To them, the social content of a film *was* its aesthetic. If the Party line of progressive social ideas or progressive subjects were treated in a film – *that* was communist aesthetics" (Talbot & Zheutlin 1978, 83). Polonsky clearly dissociates himself from this attitude, and justly so, as I hope to have demonstrated.
23. Letter from Abraham Polonsky to author, dated March 7, 1979.
24. In his interview with Sherman (1970), Polonsky attempted to explain the ending in a slightly different way: "It was partly a cop-out. It was saying to the censor, 'Look. It's ok. Don't worry about it. He had a change of heart.' But that was *completely* on the surface. I didn't mean it at all. What I really meant were all those words at the end of all those images: 'Down, down, down.'" He goes on: "At the end of the picture, in Garfield's case, it's like being left back in school. I remember in Thomas Mann's *The Magic Mountain*, when he talks about Hans Castorp's youth. Hans is in school, and he gets left back – and what a *relief* it was to get left back! Because *then* you don't have to get ahead anymore. A kind of liberation and freedom comes from failure. What I tried to do there was to get the feeling of that, having reached the absolute moral bottom of commitment, there's nothing left to do but commit yourself. There's no longer a problem of identity when you have no identity left at all. So, in your very next step, you must become something."
25. *Variety*, December 24, 1948 (signed "Brog").

References

Anderson, Lindsay. (1955). "Last Sequence of *On the Waterfront*." *Sight and Sound*, March, 130.

Arthur, Paul S. (1976). "Le Film Noir: The Political Space of America in the Cold War." Paper delivered at College Art Association National Conference.

Bentley, Eric. (1971). *Thirty Years of Treason: Excerpts from Hearings before the House Committee on Un-American Activities, 1938–1968*. New York: Viking Press.

"Brog." (1948). "Review of *Force of Evil*." *Variety*, December 24, n.p.

Cogley, John. (1956). *Report on Blacklisting I: The Movies*. New York: Fund for the Republic.

Cook, Jim, & Canham, Kingsley. (1970). Interview with Abraham Polonsky. *Screen*, 2, Fall, 68–70.

Crowther, Bosley. (1948). "*Force of Evil*." *New York Times*, December 27.

Gelman, Howard. (1975). *The Films of John Garfield*. Secaucus, NJ: Citadel.

Henderson, Ron (ed.). (1971). *The Image Maker*. Richmond, VA: John Knox Press.

Jones, Dorothy B. (1956). "Communism and the Movies: A Study of Film Content." In John Cogley, *Report on Blacklisting I: The Movies*. New York: Fund for the Republic.

Kahn, Gordon. (1948). *Hollywood on Trial*. New York: Boni & Gaer.

Lesser, Simon O. (1957). *Fiction and the Unconscious*. New York: Vintage.

Morris, George. (1977). *John Garfield*. New York: Jove.

Pasternak, James D., & Howton, F. William. (1976). "Interview with Abraham Polonsky." In Andrew Sarris (ed.), *Hollywood Voices: Interviews with Film Directors* (pp. 21–23). New York: Avon.

Pechter, William. (1976). "Interview with Abraham Polonsky." In Andrew Sarris (ed.), *Hollywood Voices: Interviews with Film Directors* (pp. 390–392). New York: Avon.

Place, J. A., & Peterson, L. S. (1974). "Some Visual Motifs of Film Noir." *Film Comment*, 10.1, January–February, 30–32.

Polonsky, Abraham. (1946–1947). "'The Best Years of Our Lives': A Review." *Hollywood Quarterly*, 2, 258–259.

Polonsky, Abraham. (1947). "'Odd Man Out' and 'Monsieur Verdoux.'" *Hollywood Quarterly*, 2, July, 403.

Polonsky, Abraham. (1970). "How the Blacklist Worked." *Film Culture*, 50–51, Fall/Winter, 41–48.

Polonsky, Abraham. (1975). "Introduction." In Howard Gelman, *The Films of John Garfield*. Secaucus, NJ: Citadel.

Shadoian, Jack. (1977). *Dreams and Dead Ends: The American Gangster/Crime Film*. Cambridge, MA: MIT Press.

Sherman, Eric. (1970). "Interview with Abraham Polonsky." In Eric Sherman & Martin Rubin (eds), *The Director's Event: Interviews with Five American Filmmakers* (pp. 3–37). New York: Atheneum.

Sklar, Robert. (1976). *Movie-Made America*. New York: Vintage.

Solomon, Stanley J. (1976). *Beyond Formula: American Film Genres*. New York: Harcourt Brace Jovanovich.

Steinman, Clayton M. (1979). "Hollywood Dialectic: *Force of Evil* and the Frankfurt School's Critique of the Culture Industry." PhD dissertation, New York University.

Talbot, David, & Zheutlin, Barbara. (1978). *Creative Differences: Profiles of Hollywood Dissidents*. Boston: South End Press.

Warshow, Robert. (1972). *The Immediate Experience*. New York: Atheneum.

Wilson, Michael. (1978). *Salt of the Earth*. New York: Feminist Press.

Wolfert, Ira. (1943). *Tucker's People*. New York: Popular Library.

27

The Actors Studio in the Early Cold War

Cynthia Baron & Beckett Warren
Professor, Bowling Green State University, United States
Independent scholar

Cynthia Baron and Beckett Warren critically interrogate widely popularized understandings of the **Actors Studio** and its "**Method**" approach to acting. The Studio's claims of producing a "new breed" of actors embodying "'American' authenticity and expressivity," in spite of its Russian, **Stanislavskian roots**, ironically meshed with America's 1950s **Cold War** agenda. Such **Group Theater** luminaries as **Stella Adler** and stage influences as **Lunt–Fontanne** were cast as inferior, despite the fact that recognized "Method" actors **Marlon Brando** and **Montgomery Clift** cite these and other classical Hollywood actors as their primary influences – far above those of Actors Studio cofounder **Elia Kazan** or instructor **Lee Strasberg**. The Actors Studio and Kazan – who "named names" at **anticommunist HUAC** hearings – emerged as the winners during **blacklist** proceedings and beyond. Even today "the Method" carries a mystique that Baron and Warren instructively demystify. Their essay shares ground with Cynthia Lucia on Natalie Wood and Roy Grundmann on *The Strange Love of Martha Ivers* in this volume, and with Larry Ceplair on Hollywood unions and blacklists in the hardcover/online edition.

Additional terms, names, and concepts: Actors' Laboratory, International Alliance of Theatrical Stage Employees (IATSE), Conference of Studio Unions (CSU), Waldorf Statement, Hollywood Ten, affective memory, melodrama and masculinity

The Actors Studio has come to be identified as "the home of the American Method," which is often seen not "merely as an approach [or] the locus of American acting since the late forties [but also] the goal toward which serious American acting was striving" (Vineberg 1991, 1, 20). In many accounts of film acting, the formation of the Actors Studio is described as a watershed, with productions emblematic of nineteenth-century theatrical realism and work by the Group Theatre in the 1930s framed as developments that led toward the kind of modern American acting that finally became fully realized because of

American Film History: Selected Readings, Origins to 1960, First Edition. Edited by Cynthia Lucia, Roy Grundmann, and Art Simon.
© 2016 John Wiley & Sons, Inc. Published 2016 by John Wiley & Sons, Inc.

acting techniques formulated by Lee Strasberg. However, in theater and performance studies, it is well known that actor training "did not begin and end with Lee Strasberg, the Method, and Marlon Brando" (Watson 2001, 61, 70) and that practitioners have been rejecting the "domination of the Method" since the 1960s, to the point that in universities and professional schools "Method acting has fallen out of favor" (Krasner 2000, 6).

Yet in film studies and the popular press, Strasberg, the Method, and the Actors Studio are still associated with serious, modern acting, while other teachers, approaches, and institutions are not. In addition, references to "American" traits and temperaments often figure into accounts of Method acting, with some arguing that the Method "is a natural dramatic expression of the way Americans understand and define themselves" (Vineberg 1991, xii). However, Strasberg's Method, with its focus on affective memory, and the Method style that is well suited to portrayals of characters defined by their psychological rather than social dilemmas need not be linked to some abstract quality of American national identity. Instead, our lasting misperceptions about the uniqueness of the Studio's serious approach, the widespread use of Strasberg's primary technique, and the inherent superiority of the Method style have likely been shaped by historically specific cultural and material developments integral to the early years of the Cold War and of Hollywood's post-studio period.

The era's wave of publicity about Strasberg's top secret invention and Method actors' solemn but mysterious psychological labor need not be taken as transparent evidence of new developments in acting, but instead can be seen as reflections of the same cultural politics that led highbrow critics and the popular press to value and promote abstract expressionism for its perceived expressive freedom, vitality, and authentic virility. Rather than regarding the Actors Studio, Strasberg's Method, and the Method style as the apex of some natural, evolutionary process, the emerging image of the film actor as an author who draws on personal experiences to create performances can be considered a correlative to stars' increasingly important economic role in the new system of "independent" film production that the studios created in response to the Paramount Decrees, the rising influence of agents like Lew Wasserman, and the emergence of television.

The quickly widening influence of the Actors Studio in the late 1940s and early 1950s can also be understood as a by-product of the anticommunists' success in using allegations of communist influence to control postwar labor unrest in Hollywood and, by extension, the country at large. For when the Actors Studio in New York opened its doors in 1947, it stepped into a vacuum created by anticommunists' successful efforts to discredit the Actors' Laboratory in Hollywood. The Actors' Lab had been a theater company and acting school since 1941, and as Actors Studio historian David Garfield points out, the Lab was "the first large-scale introduction of the Method on the West Coast" (1984, 256). Guided by former Group Theatre members Roman (Bud) Bohnen, J. Edward Bromberg, Morris Carnovsky, and Phoebe Brand, and housed in two ramshackle buildings behind Schwab's drugstore between 1943 and 1949, the Lab had mounted small-scale productions and provided acting classes for studio contract players throughout the 1940s. While Lab members were respected but generally unknown character actors, there were times when they received national recognition. In 1945 the Lab was the subject of a *Life* magazine article that told readers, "some of the most skillful acting in the United States today is being done in Hollywood by some part-time refugees from the movies" (Actors' Laboratory Collection). Subsequent press coverage would focus on the Lab's alleged status as a communist front. Thus, the Actors Studio, and not the Actors' Lab, was able to lay claim to the Group Theatre legacy.

In the highly polemical environment of the Cold War era, publicity surrounding the Actors Studio also eclipsed the work of former Group Theatre members Stella Adler, Sanford Meisner, and Robert (Bobby) Lewis, as well as the teachings of Russian émigrés Michael Chekhov, Maria Ouspenskaya, and Richard Boleslawski. The stance that modern acting had been invented at the Actors Studio also concealed the modern dimension of programs at the American Academy of Dramatic Art, the Pasadena Playhouse, and the various drama schools established by the Hollywood studios in the 1930s. Rhetoric that sanctioned the Actors Studio's institutional approach to actor training effectively discredited the apprenticeship system that allowed actors like Montgomery Clift to learn a "naturalistic" style and attention to craft from experienced players like Alfred Lunt and Lynn Fontanne. It also occluded the reality that from the 1930s forward, stage and screen actors have worked individually with coaches, sometimes the same coach for major portions of their careers, as, for instance, Montgomery Clift worked with Mira Rostova.

Cold War Winners (the Actors Studio) and Losers (the Actors' Lab)

The cessation of war in Europe on May 8, 1945 and in the Pacific on August 14, 1945 had powerful consequences for many Americans whose income depended on the war economy. By the winter of 1945–1946, 25 percent of war workers had lost their jobs and in the 12 months following the victory over Japan, there were more strikes than in any other comparable period in American history. Self-appointed critics of the labor unrest sweeping America in the late 1940s consistently stressed the idea that communists were instigating strikes as part of a larger plan to install a Bolshevik regime in the United States. While such a scenario was entirely unlikely, the strategy did work to insure labor would be weakened going forward. By April 1947, 61 percent of Americans responding to a Gallup Poll supported the outlawing of the Communist Party. By February 1948, 35 percent of the American public believed that the Communist Party "was getting stronger and ... already in control of important elements in the economy," while 10 percent "thought the Communist Party was reaching the point where it could dominate the nation" (Reeves 1997, 209).

In Hollywood the studios and the studio-sanctioned union, the International Alliance of Theatrical Stage Employees (IATSE), had, since the 1930s, attributed strikes and labor demands to communist influence. During the war, the formation of the rival Conference of Studio Unions (CSU), its strike against Disney in 1941, and its jurisdictional dispute with IATSE that began in 1943, disrupted operations. The dispute also called attention to the unfair labor practices of the Association of Motion Picture Producers (AMPP) headed by Pat Casey, the often overlooked labor relations entity conjoined to the studios' highly visible public relations entity, the Motion Picture Producers and Distributors Association (MPPDA) led by Will Hays. For in February 1945, the federal War Labor Board ruled in favor of the CSU, but the AMPP refused to comply and simply continued to support IATSE's jurisdictional claims. (In 1945, the MPPDA became the Motion Picture Association of America, MPAA; in 1964 the AMPP became the Association of Motion Picture and Television Producers, AMPTP, and in 1982 the Alliance of Motion Picture and Television Producers.)

The AMPP's decision to ignore the Labor Board finding led the CSU to strike in March 1945. However, their opponents were ready. The ongoing disturbance to the smooth operation of the studio system had led established industry figures like Sam Wood, Cecil B. DeMille, Walt Disney, Lela Rogers, Hedda Hopper, Borden Chase, Rupert Hughes, Morrie Ryskind, and Roy Brewer, the West Coast head of IATSE, to form the Motion Picture Alliance for the Preservation of American Ideals (MPAPAI) in February 1944. By March they had already started to lobby for government assistance to combat "communist influence" in the film industry. With the 1945 CSU strike underway, their request was granted. In July 1945, Congressman John Rankin announced that the House Un-American Activities Committee (HUAC) would investigate the individuals and organizations in Hollywood bent on "the destruction of the Constitution and the American way of life" (Barrett 1951, 30). Those investigations led to closed hearings in Los Angeles in May 1947; subpoenas to friendly and unfriendly witnesses in September 1947; the widely publicized hearings chaired by J. Parnell Thomas in Washington, DC in October 1947; the blacklist policy established by the studios' Waldorf Statement in November 1947; the imprisonment of the Hollywood Ten in 1950; the wave of HUAC hearings chaired by John S. Wood in 1951 and 1952; and the sporadic hearings chaired by Congressmen Harold H. Velde and Francis E. Walter that began in 1953 and wound to a close in 1956. The Actors' Laboratory was one of many institutions of interest to HUAC. Its support of the CSU strike in October 1945 led Jack Warner and other studio executives to see it as an organization that threatened the American way of life. Allegations to sustain that view began to appear in November 1945, when the *Hollywood Reporter* told the film community that "people of repute" determined that the Lab was dominated by individuals who were "as red as a burlesque queen's garters" (Actors' Laboratory Collection). In

February 1948, the California Fact-Finding Committee on Un-American Activities led by State Senator Jack B. Tenney essentially sealed the Lab's fate when he held hearings that allowed him to put into public record the charge that the Lab's primary function was "to draw ambitious young actors and actresses into the orbit of Communist front organizations" (Tenney 1948, 104). In the fall of 1948, columnist Hedda Hopper added her voice of condemnation by censuring the Lab for holding a racially integrated fundraiser on Labor Day. Warning that the event could have incited race riots, Hopper declared that Hollywood "was shocked at this public display on the part of the Actors' Lab" (Actors' Laboratory Collection). That same month, the *Los Angeles Examiner* ran a story entitled "Justice Department Labels Actors Lab Theatre a Communist Front" (Barrett 1951, 365).

In sharp contrast to the increasingly embattled and weakened position of the Actors' Lab in the late 1940s, when the Actors Studio held its first session in October 1947, a few weeks before HUAC opened its hearings on communist influence in the motion picture industry, Elia Kazan, the driving force behind the Studio, was the most powerful alumnus of the Group Theatre; more successful than Harold Clurman, Lee Strasberg, and Cheryl Crawford, who had founded the Group Theatre; more visible than Stella Adler, Sanford Meisner, and Bobby Lewis, who had all continued to work primarily in theater; and in a far more secure professional position than Lab members Phoebe Brand, Morris Carnovsky, J. Edward Bromberg, and Roman Bohnen, who, in contrast to Kazan, had joined the Group as actors affiliated with the highly respected Theatre Guild. At this distance, it may be difficult to appreciate Kazan's singular position in American theater and film during the 1940s. His Broadway productions included Thornton Wilder's Pulitzer Prize-winning *The Skin of Our Teeth* (1942), with Tallulah Bankhead, Fredric March, and Montgomery Clift; and Arthur Miller's *All My Sons* (1947), with Ed Begley, Arthur Kennedy, and Karl Malden, which received Tony Awards for Best Play and Best Direction. Kazan had directed the critically acclaimed films *A Tree Grows in Brooklyn* (1945), *Boomerang!* (1947), and *Gentleman's Agreement* (1947), which in 1948 would go on to win Oscars for Best Picture, Best Direction, and Best Supporting Actress (Celeste Holm). In addition to directing these films for Twentieth Century-Fox, Kazan had also been hired by MGM to direct *Sea of Grass* (1947), starring Spencer Tracy and Katharine Hepburn.

Buoyed up by this string of stage and screen productions, Kazan had started rehearsals for *A Streetcar Named Desire* starring Marlon Brando the same week the Actors Studio opened for business. Clearly in a position to continue moving ahead without assistance from senior colleagues, Kazan never envisioned the Studio as a venue for recreating the dynamics of the Group Theatre. In the period leading up to the Studio, Kazan had conveyed his disinterest in working with the more experienced members of the Group Theatre. Clurman was the person "who first suggested the idea of a studio to Kazan [but he was subsequently closed out of the venture] because Kazan felt a certain intellectual and emotional rivalry with his former teacher" (Garfield 1984, 46). Kazan appears to have felt the same rivalry with the founders of the Actors' Lab, for while they could have easily filled bit parts in the films he directed and even though he had expressed an interest in working with actors who shared his vocabulary, throughout the 1940s, whether working in theater or film, Kazan never opted to create that production environment by hiring Bohnen, Brand, Bromberg, Carnovsky, or other people who had come into the Group Theatre as established actors. Instead, in 1947, Kazan decided that he would "cultivate a new crop of performers trained in the techniques he had learned in the Group" (Garfield 1984, 46). As a consequence, for young actors especially, Studio membership was a valuable commodity, for it meant belonging to "a 'pool' or 'stable' of actors for Kazan's productions" (Garfield 1984, 46).

Even after he was no longer directly involved in the Actors Studio, Kazan would advance his career by making choices that echoed the sense of rivalry implied by his earlier dealings with senior members of the Group Theatre. His 1952 testimony for the HUAC insured that the Actors' Laboratory in Hollywood would continue to be seen as a communist front throughout and beyond the blacklist period. Kazan told HUAC that he had brought Lab member Phoebe Brand into the Communist Party and that he had worked in a CP unit with Lab members J. Edward Bromberg and Morris Carnovsky when they were part of the Group Theatre. Kazan also provided HUAC with a version of opposing factions within the Group Theatre that effectively cordoned off the Actors Studio from HUAC scrutiny. For while

Kazan identified five former Group colleagues – Art Smith, Toby Kraber, Lewis Leverett, Clifford Odets, and Paula Miller – as members of the Communist Party, he assured the committee that the Group Theatre had never been in danger of falling under the control of the Communist Party because its founders, which included Cheryl Crawford, the Studio's long-time business manager, and Lee Strasberg, the Studio's artistic director, were staunch anticommunists. Kazan also told the committee that he believed Paula Miller (who married Lee Strasberg in 1934) had, under the guidance of her wise husband, long ago given up her affiliation with the Communist Party (US Congress, 1951). Some contend that Kazan's testimony was not designed to influence the trajectory of his career or to impact the lives of others. Yet because personal motivations are impossible to determine fully, examining the chronology of events to locate likely points of causation is a more viable option. Taking that approach, it is clear that Kazan's testimony is one factor contributing to the Studio's gaining prominence, while the Actors' Lab was sinking into obscurity.

The Actors Studio and Method Acting: From Kazan to Strasberg

When the Actors Studio held its first meeting on October 5, 1947, the participants included a group of 52 established actors who had been invited to join the workshop to be led by Bobby Lewis. The others were 26 young actors Kazan had selected from the hundreds who auditioned to join his beginning class. Even though Kazan and Lewis were both former members of the Group Theatre, their classes were quite different. Kazan introduced exercises designed to develop young actors' imagination and concentration. He emphasized action exercises that focused the actors' attention and imagination on "the character's objective in a scene: what the character wants and why he wants it" (Garfield 1984, 58). By comparison, Lewis's workshop gave established actors an opportunity to work on roles distinct from ones in which they were often cast. Marlon Brando, for example, worked on a scene from *Reunion in Vienna* to recreate the role of the Hapsburg archduke made famous by Alfred Lunt.

Interestingly, the framework set up in October lasted only a few months. By December 1947, Kazan and Lewis had disinvited 19 of the established actors. By the spring of 1948, other experienced actors, including Montgomery Clift, had withdrawn from Lewis's workshop. On August 4, 1948, Lewis announced his resignation from the Studio after Kazan had edged him out of a directing assignment. By the summer of 1948, Kazan had turned his class for young actors over to Martin Ritt, and between 1948 and 1951 classes at the Actors Studio were taught by a series of people that included Lee Strasberg. In fall 1951, Kazan and business manager Cheryl Crawford "decided it was time to put an end to the coming and going of various interim teachers and to consolidate all the acting classes under a single instructor" (Garfield 1984, 76). Although Kazan "had reservations about some aspects of Strasberg's teaching – especially about the emphasis put on the actor's personal experiences as tapped by means of affective-memory exercises," Strasberg was put in charge of teaching at the Studio (Garfield 1984, 80).

Since the 1930s, Strasberg's reliance on Evgeny Vakhtangov's idea "that it is the actor's life, and not necessarily the role, that inspires" had put him at odds with other proponents of the Method (Krasner 2000, 29). Once he was artistic director of the Actors Studio, Strasberg set out to "show everyone that they knew nothing about the Method" (Garfield 1984, 82). With Lewis out of the picture, Strasberg could sidestep his objections to "the value of emotional memory exercises," and so he began by challenging Kazan's emphasis on characters' objectives in a scene, focusing instead on the idea that an actor's "remembered sensations and emotions [that parallel the character's experience could] color his or her behavior and vocal expression in ways that both the actor and the audience experience as viscerally real and exciting" (Bosworth 1978, 84; Garfield 1984, 16). That focus was diametrically opposed to the approach used by another interpreter of Stanislavsky, Michael Chekhov, who explored and developed roles "by experimenting with the shape and quality of the character's movement and rearrangements of his body size" (Gordon 1985, 15). As Mel Gordon points out, Chekhov's work represented "a kind of imaginative training totally alien from Lee Strasberg's interpretations of Stanislavsky and Vakhtangov [and it] provided the strongest intellectual counterweight to Strasberg's much criticized Method" (1985, 17).

Strasberg's techniques for preparation, character development, and performance were also quite different from those formulated by leading teachers of Method acting like Stella Adler and Sanford Meisner (Barton 2006; Krasner 2000). Describing their distinct approaches in the simplest terms, Strasberg popularized the use of affective memory and the substitution of actors' personal experience for characters' circumstances and objectives. Adler emphasized creative use of imagination, careful study of the fictional world disclosed by the script, and research into the historical circumstances referenced by the script. Meisner shared Adler's opposition to Strasberg's emphasis on the actor's personal emotion and developed his own unique exercises to help actors establish and maintain deep connections with each other during performance (Baron & Carnicke 2008).

While all three variations of the Method differ from the system that Stanislavsky developed over the course of his life, Strasberg's emphasis on affective memory is distinctly at odds with Stanislavsky's focus on the actor's duality of consciousness and on playable actions. What Strasberg viewed as primary, Stanislavsky had discarded after early experimentation. In addition, Strasberg moved key elements of Stanislavsky's system from the actor's to the director's control by having actors modify Stanislavsky's question, "What would I do if I were in the character's circumstances?" to a less analytical and more personal question, "What in my own life would make me behave as the character?" Strasberg's restated question generates a "personal substitution" from the actor's life, rather than the imaginative flight into the character's world that Stanislavsky's question encourages. Once a personal substitution has been identified, the actor simply relives that remembered emotional life in front of the director, audience, or camera. An actor need not think or feel like his or her character as long as the content of the actor's thought leads to the performance that the director desires. In addition, for Strasberg, unlike for Stanislavsky, the cast need not necessarily share a common understanding of the characters and story, since each actor can draw on different personal substitutions to generate the performance required.

Acting teachers in the Hollywood studio era actually taught techniques that were more compatible with the central principles of Stanislavsky's system. For example, they argued for the value of training the body and the voice because they saw actors' minds and bodies as unified, organic wholes. They believed that the script provided the blueprint for building characters and that preparation made it possible to integrate directorial suggestions and interact effectively with other actors. Studio-era practitioners also emphasized the dispassionate execution of performance that was facilitated by concentration on the character's circumstances, goals, and actions.[1] These ideas also underlie the work of Broadway stars Alfred Lunt and Lynn Fontanne, whose performances from the 1920s forward established their reputation as "the arch perfectionists of the theatre" (Funke & Booth 1961, 41). Known for their use of life study, exhaustive script analysis, extensive rehearsal, and "naturalistic" performance choices that included dovetailing dialogue and Lunt's signature gesture of turning his back to the audience during scenes of high emotion, they explained that while they did not adhere to any one method, they sought to "act with as much reality" as possible, and thus were "heading for the same place" as Method actors (Funke & Booth 1961, 46, 49).

Still, it would be the Actors Studio that became associated with modern American acting and Lee Strasberg who would become the most recognized acting teacher in the country. In addition, the name, "Method acting," gave Strasberg's teachings an aura of scientific validity because Strasberg had a *method* actors could learn and apply to their work. The scientific aura surrounding the label attached to Strasberg's teaching at the Studio made him an expert at a time when American culture had come to valorize experts. As Warren Susman points out, "consciousness of living in a new machine age, the Depression (and to a lesser extent World War II)" had generated insecurities in American culture that led to an emerging reliance on experts (1973, 9). Strasberg became a valuable expert because he had a scientific method for managing one of the more mysterious aspects of social interaction – performance. While others had tinkered with passing along bits and pieces of folklore, Strasberg had finally come up with something that was comprehensive, tangible, and concrete. Strasberg's method also became a topic for the press and the public because the closed-door policy at the Actors Studio shrouded the Method in veils of secrecy. Sharon Carnicke points out that a sometimes "prurient interest" in what Stanislavsky's interpreters were doing "climaxed during the 1950s, ironically piqued by

Figure 27.1 Broadway star Alfred Lunt in Sidney Franklin and Harold S. Bucquet's *The Guardsman* (1931, producer Albert Lewin) – an important influence on subsequent "Method actors."

Strasberg's adamant attempts to protect his actors from the gaze of observers" (2009, 10). As a consequence, Strasberg's Method became a fixture of popular discourse in the 1950s not only because the name gave his teachings unparalleled concreteness. The "policies" of the Studio also generated intrigue and helped make those teachings *top secret*.

Publicity versus Reality

In the 1930s and 1940s, publicity generated by the studios presented readers with a very specific picture of film acting that occluded the labor expended by the men and women whose images appeared onscreen. To naturalize the star system's effacement of actors' labor, studio publicity tapped the longstanding assumption that film acting did not involve skill or training, and it circulated images that conformed to prevailing representations of gender distinctions. For example, magazines such as *Collier's*, *Ladies' Home Journal*, *Life*, and the *Saturday Evening Post* would publish articles that purported to demystify stardom, while still telling the public that actresses were manufactured by Hollywood's expert makeup artists, and actors played themselves and learned the tricks of the trade. Drama schools received little attention throughout the 1930s and 1940s; when the press covered them, the angle confirmed the view that film stars created performances by relying on their personalities and attractive appearances.[2]

In the post-studio era, the press began to circulate a rather different image of what it meant to act in film. Movie stars of the "new breed" were presented as individuals who studied their craft and developed their skills. Accounts emphasized that actors' training reflected a rigorous, if eccentric, plan, and that their performances depended on the application of a conscious methodology. Whereas reports about actors' training and preparation were at odds with institutional practices in place until the 1950s, when transformations in the Hollywood system opened a space for a new image of the film actor to emerge, behind-the-scenes coverage of actors practicing their craft became not only plausible but newsworthy as well.

Once the Actors Studio and Strasberg's Method became part of popular discourse, even film acting could be considered not only a craft but an art as well. Carnicke notes that Strasberg publicly "marveled at the phenomenal public interest" of the general audience; offering his own unique account of theater history, he proposed: "this is the first time in the history of theatre ... that general people – the barbershop and beauty parlor attendants – are discussing the work of the Actors Studio, and talking about whether it is too realistic" (2009, 9, 10). The public's sudden interest in acting depended on a constellation of converging factors. It was, in part, an effect of the work of actors such as Montgomery Clift and Marlon Brando, who presented audiences with a style of performance suited to the aesthetic demands initiated by new forms of domestic drama and location shooting. Clift's performances in *The Search* (1948), *Red River* (1948), and *From Here to Eternity* (1953), Brando's portrayals in *A Streetcar Named Desire* (1951), *The Wild One* (1953), and *On the Waterfront* (1954), and James Dean's appearances in *East of Eden* (1955) and *Rebel Without a Cause* (1955) captured public imagination so completely that the Method style came to be defined largely in terms of the gestures, postures, and vocal mannerisms used to represent the characters in these films.

While these performances included choices that were different from many of those found in films of the Hollywood studio era, they were not radically different from some performances in the 1940s, for example, Burt Lancaster's work in *The Killers* (1946) or Robert Mitchum's performance in *Out of the Past* (1947). Moreover, they were not a studied departure from work in the studio era. Talking about Spencer Tracy, James Cagney, Paul Muni, and Cary Grant as actors whose work he studied, Brando describes his interest in the way Tracy "holds back, *holds* back – then darts in to make his point, darts back" (Capote 1973, 127), and in Cagney as "a self-made actor [who] believed he was the character and made audiences believe it" (Brando 1994, 206).

In fact, while Brando was often featured in the Actors Studio's fundraising and publicity campaigns, he never trained with Strasberg and instead participated only in workshops led by Bobby Lewis and others. His primary teacher was former Group Theatre member Stella Adler, who opposed Strasberg's interpretation of Stanislavsky, especially after she met with Stanislavsky in 1934. In contrast to the unnamed adaptations of Stanislavsky taught by Adler, Meisner, Chekhov, and others, Brando believed that "'Method Acting' was a term popularized, bastardized and misused by Lee Strasberg," and throughout his career, he championed Adler's work because he felt it did not lend itself "to vulgar exploitations, as some other well-known so-called methods have done" (Brando 1994, 81; Adler 1988, 1).

Montgomery Clift also opposed Strasberg's approach, valuing instead what he had learned from people whose reputations were established long before the formation of the Actors Studio. Working with Alfred Lunt and his wife Lynn Fontanne, Clift increased his ability to use script analysis and rehearsals to create "the thought processes, the specific character needs," and subtexts that would color each moment of a performance (Bosworth 1978, 77). Clift's first appearance on Broadway was in 1935 at the age of 14. His 1938 portrayal in *Dame Nature* marked the beginning of his success; as Patricia Bosworth explains:

> Days after the opening his name went up in lights at the Booth Theatre, and Leland Hayward, the most prestigious agent of the time, signed him up. Word spread quickly around Broadway that Montgomery Clift's performance was special, unorthodox, and it had to be seen. (1978, 67)

In 1939, Lunt cast Clift as the idealistic resistance fighter in Robert E. Sherwood's timely play, *There Shall Be No Night*, and for the next two and a half years and 1,400 performances Clift apprenticed with the Lunts. Bosworth notes that when the Lunts talked about Clift, "they implied that he was their best disciple [and that with work] he could carry on in their tradition" (1978, 79). Clift credits Alfred Lunt especially "for his development as an actor," for it was Lunt who talked most with him about "the artist's dedication to craft" and showed him how to create performances through the "accumulation of subtle details" (Bosworth 1978, 83, 84; see 101).

Lunt would provide a model for Clift throughout his career, and explicitly so in Clift's performance in *The Skin of Our Teeth*, which opened on

Broadway in November 1942. During the run of the play, Clift sometimes "fell back into Lunt mannerisms"; it is reported that on opening night Clift "sounded exactly like Alfred Lunt [who was known for his] Midwestern drawl, combined with an English accent" (Bosworth 1978, 94). That Clift's portrayal reflected stylistic choices suggested by Lunt's body of work – rather than decisions made by director Elia Kazan – is significant, for it reveals that accounts of modern American acting need to include reference not only to Elia Kazan and the Actors Studio but also to Broadway stars like Alfred Lunt.

Clift's extensive, individual work on each of his roles with acting coach Mira Rostova is the other factor central to his performances. Clift first met Rostova in 1942 when they were both cast in an experimental production directed by Bobby Lewis. Rostova, a Russian émigré and student of Lewis, worked with Clift on his part for the play; the two "discussed Vakhtangov, Bolesla[w]ski, Michael Chekhov, and Stanislavski together and talked about how the truth of an actor's art is in imagination" (Bosworth 1978, 86). Recognizing that "no one could dissect a role as shrewdly as Mira," Clift worked with Rostova to develop his characterizations for *Foxhole in the Parlor* (1945) and *You Touched Me!* (1945) (Bosworth 1978, 106). His performance in *You Touched Me!* led Howard Hawks to ask Clift to play Matt Garth in the film *Red River*, which wrapped in December 1946 but was not released until September 1948. As Clift moved into film, he continued to work with Rostova; in fact, for the next film, *The Search*, directed by Fred Zinnemann, Clift put Rostova on salary as his coach and, working with her at night, he not only rehearsed but also rewrote all of his scenes (see Bosworth 1978, 126–130). While Clift's script revisions led to battles with producer Lazar Wechsler, Clift would later describe this film, which completed production on October 2, 1947, "as the most fulfilling artistic experience of his life" (Bosworth 1978, 131). Referring to Rostova as his "artistic conscience," Clift collaborated with her to work out "every beat in every scene in restrained and poignant detail" in all of his films in the early 1950s, including *From Here to Eternity* (1953), when she worked with Clift and Frank Sinatra (Bosworth 1978, 165, 182; see 249).

With the release of *The Search* on March 3, 1948, Clift became "a new hero to postwar audiences" and his performance was seen as "a new kind of acting – almost documentary in approach" (Bosworth 1978, 137, 138). This "new kind of acting" has been consistently attributed to the Method, Lee Strasberg, and the Actors Studio. For instance, in a chapter on Clift and Brando that opens with a quote from Strasberg, Steve Vineberg uses *The Search* as evidence that Clift "was the first member of the Actors Studio generation to become a movie star" (1991, 143). However, the films that established Clift as a star, *The Search* and *Red River*, had been shot before the Actors Studio opened on October 5, 1947, and the people who shaped Clift's performances in these films are Zinnemann, Hawks, and most particularly Rostova, as noted.

Moreover, as Garfield points out, Clift's "relationship to the Studio was tenuous at best" (1984, 65). He had been invited to join Lewis's workshop, but his participation was limited to the period between fall 1947 and spring 1948. Thus, Clift never actively sought membership in the Studio and had left the Studio before Strasberg started teaching in fall 1948. In addition, Bosworth explains that Clift "was never truly a 'Method' actor," in that he never used Strasberg's central technique (1978, 133). From Clift's perspective, a lot of Method actors "never created characters [and] instead merely played variations of themselves" (Bosworth 1978, 133). Knowing this, it appears that Clift's few months in Lewis's workshop did not involve exposure to new methods, for he had already worked with Lewis in 1942. It is likely he was killing time, waiting to see how his writing and performance efforts in *The Search* would be received. The wave of positive reviews in spring 1948 was the first part of his news; a year later, he was nominated for Best Actor, Zinnemann for Best Director, and the script that included his uncredited revisions won an Oscar for Best Motion Picture Story and a Golden Globe Award for Best Screenplay.

The Method Acting Style and Cold War Conceptions of Character

The Method style that became dominant in the 1950s has been thought to represent an evolution from a "theatrical" to a "realistic" film acting style and to be based on a progression from an unschooled, instinctive approach to one informed by training and technique. The observable change in the repertoire of gestures, expressions, poses, and line readings actors used to portray characters has been linked to Strasberg's emphasis on affective memory. The new style has also been associated with a younger generation of actors who, in contrast to unschooled actors working in theater and film during the Depression and World War II, were seriously dedicated to their art and, for the first time in history, equipped with a scientific approach to acting called "the Method."

However, as the details of Clift's career suggest, changes in American acting need not be attributed exclusively to the Actors Studio. Instead, what is seen as a Method style is difficult to ascribe to any set of individuals, for it seems to be best understood as a reflection of changes in the conception of character that actors used as the basis for their performances. For while many of the characters in Depression and World War II films were to some degree identifiable social types, psychological character types appear during the war, in films like *Random Harvest* (1942) and *Spellbound* (1945), and become increasingly dominant after the early years of the Cold War and Hollywood blacklist period. Method style's growing importance can also be linked to changing cinematic conventions for conveying emotion, particularly the emotion of central male characters. For whereas films in the 1950s often disperse affect so that intense or "unmanly" emotional responses are conveyed by the performances of minor characters, in 1950s male melodramas, actors from Montgomery Clift, Marlon Brando, and James Dean to James Stewart (*The Naked Spur*, 1953), Henry Fonda (*The Wrong Man*, 1956), and James Mason (*Bigger Than Life*, 1956) take center stage in films that use the performances of the lead actors to communicate the characters' conflicting emotions. While there are scores of exceptions to these general assessments about character type and cinematic convention, actors and directors have long recognized that acting choices must be keyed to narrative design and filmic conventions. Comparative studies of films produced in different time periods and national cinemas reveal connections between acting choices and filmic choices (Baron & Carnicke 2008). Comparative analysis can also illuminate the various factors that surround the shift to the Method style, which was well suited to "divided parts based on unresolved tension between an outer social mask and an inner reality of frustration that usually has a sexual basis" (Atkins 1975, 114). The transformation in conception of character, cinematic convention, and acting style that distinguishes studio-era performances from ones associated with Strasberg's Method is visible in the contrast between two prestige pictures about military men: William Wyler's *The Best Years of Our Lives* (1946) and Fred Zinnemann's *From Here to Eternity*.

Whereas the three central characters in Wyler's film (played by Fredric March, Dana Andrews, and non-actor Harold Russell) are distinguished by the social markers of class, age, and military branch, Zinnemann's film is a psychological drama about the conflicting drives of Robert E. Lee Prewitt (Montgomery Clift) to be a good soldier and a man true to his own code of honor. Additionally, in Wyler's film, the performances of actors in minor roles often convey the fraught emotional experiences of the main characters, in this case, the returning veterans. In one instance, through the swell of emotion in his voice as he reads a letter of commendation, Roman Bohnen, who plays the ineffectual father of Air Force veteran Fred Derry (Andrews), communicates the private suffering his son experienced not only in combat but also as a grown man whose only marketable skill is being a soda jerk. In another instance, musician Hoagy Carmichael, cast as the uncle of Navy veteran Homer Parrish (Russell), gives expression to Homer's longing for acceptance through the gentle way he plays "Lazy River" and the soft, wistful tone of his voice, especially when he advises Homer not to worry too much about his family's initial response to his war injuries, since in the next war everyone will be blown to bits on the first day.

By comparison, the narrative design and filmic choices in Zinnemann's film require Clift's performance to communicate the confusion, frustration, and despair that Prewitt works to hide from the company of men around him. Zinnemann places Clift at the center of the story and the frame beginning with the film's opening shot, a long take in which Clift moves from extreme long shot, toward the camera/audience, and into a low angle, medium close-up that highlights the quiet determination conveyed by Clift's physical choices, his easy but measured gait that is accompanied by his calm, open-eyed but set facial expression. This moment of emotional repose is transitory, of course, for in subsequent scenes, including ones that feature Prewitt/Clift bugling,

Clift's performance is what conveys Prewitt's inner turmoil.

Near the end of the film, the death of Maggio (Frank Sinatra) leads to Prewitt's public display of grief, which is conveyed largely by the tears that stream down Clift's face as he plays a bugle into the loudspeaker at the base, an image that is supported by the clear, mournful sound of taps (dubbed, though Clift could play the bugle). Earlier, in the wake of Pvt Prewitt's score-settling fist fight with Sgt Galovitch, Prewitt joins two other soldiers in an earthy rendition of "Re-enlistment Blues." Framed by Zinnemann so that Clift is centered, upstage, and the focus of attention, the languid quality of Clift's pose as he reclines on the bench conveys Prewitt's satisfaction in besting Galovitch. At the same time, the strong, bound quality in Clift's shoulders when he leans forward to play – and that colors the way he grips the bugle mouthpiece he uses as an instrument – suggests the simmering frustration Prewitt still feels in response to Capt. Holmes's demand that he violate his ethical choice to quit boxing after he'd blinded a friend in a fight.

Even the first time we see Prewitt play a bugle, Zinnemann frames Clift's performance so that his acting choices, rather than those of a secondary player, express the character's unspoken, inner experience. In this instance, Prewitt is out drinking with his buddies, on a pass for the first time in six weeks. Through his firm voice, direct glare, and forceful motions as he slaps the top of his beer mug, grinds it into the table, and stabs out a cigarette, Clift reveals that Prewitt wholly rejects a fellow soldier's argument that he has a right to complain about the rough treatment he has gotten at the base. However, Clift's performance also makes Prewitt's underlying frustration visible. Grabbing a bugle from a soldier sitting next to him, Clift throws himself into an impassioned impromptu performance of "Chattanooga Choo Choo." As Clift rises from his chair and unfurls himself to his full height, the rage and self-declaration of defiance suggested by his gesture are heightened by Zinnemann's staging, framing, and editing choices: Clift is not only the literal center of attention for the men in the bar, he is placed at the center of a medium long shot and his entire performance is covered in a long take that is interrupted only by a quick cut away to Sgt Warden (Burt Lancaster) and an officer looking on with admiration.

With a film like *From Here to Eternity* featuring such moments of bravura performance, it is little wonder that this film would draw attention to the qualities that distinguished Clift's performance. Significantly, however, the increased emphasis on Clift's display of psychological conflict seems to correspond to the film's tendency to elide socially significant content; Production Code requirements forced the elimination or bowdlerization of various incidents. Whereas a pre–Cold War film like *The Best Years of Our Lives* was allowed to present some degree of social critique in its look at the plight of returning veterans, *From Here to Eternity* was forced to direct attention to Prewitt's personal, ethical dilemma rather than to the more representative, historically specific challenges faced by the returning veterans. Zinnemann's film touches on the social reality of the years leading to World War II when men joined and reenlisted in the armed services for economic rather than patriotic reasons, yet its focus on characters' psychological rather than social problems is indicative of films produced during the blacklist period. Its depiction of the soldiers' valiant but makeshift response to the Japanese attack on Pearl Harbor also tacitly reinforces the Cold War stricture that Americans be ever vigilant about threats on their home ground. As to the question of acting style and conception of character, it may be that the Method style is well suited not only to portrayals of characters distinguished by psychology but also to dramatic art produced during the Cold War when any reference to social facts could be seen as un-American.

Polemics and Cultural Context

For James Naremore, Method acting is best understood in relation to "stylistic or ideological leaning within fifties culture" (1988, 200). Gregg Rickman argues that the Method's emphasis on psychology made it a more or less calculated response to the Cold War. He explains that the increased attention given to Method acting "at the same time that its originators were either being blacklisted or cooperating, like Kazan, with anti-Communist authority" reflects a larger "cultural move from ideology to psychology demanded by the Cold War" (1992, 43). Putting that in more specific terms, the rhetorical strategies that helped secure a popular and critical following for the

Figure 27.2 Montgomery Clift in Fred Zinnemann's *From Here to Eternity* (1953, producer Buddy Adler) – soft-pedaling Cold War tensions by keeping the focus on characters' psychosexual desires.

Studio and Kazan's naturalistic film and theater productions were drawn from some entrenched rivalries that acquired special saliency in the early Cold War period. Using a strategy well suited to its cultural moment, Kazan and Strasberg made "restrained," "contrived," "artificial" British acting a target for their attack on existing traditions on Broadway and in Hollywood.

For decades, British acting traditions had shaped American theater, for "just as America imported its social and economic institutions from England, so it imported English drama and English professional players" (Cole & Chinoy 1970, 536). Theatrical production in the colonial period depended on a repertory that included Shakespeare, Cibber, Congreve, Fielding, Garrick, and others. The long-standing British influence in American theater carried over to film practice. In the 1920s, Hollywood was interested in stage-trained British actors because they were "legitimate" actors respected by the press, and "respectable" actors who could be called on to improve Hollywood's tarnished image. After the transition to sound, British actors became even more valuable, for as Sheridan Morley points out, they "possessed something of remarkable commercial and artistic worth, a clearly intelligible speaking voice, often stage-trained, readily understandable to American audiences" (1983, 9).[3] Strasberg, however, proclaimed that the English style was outdated and British acting came to be seen as "external, cultivated, and manicured, like a well-tended English garden" (Hirsh 1984, 220). British acting was considered too formal and overly articulate, while Method acting was "American" – spontaneous, intense, physically active, and filled with defiant emotionality.

Importantly, the connection between Method acting and "native" American expression provided a way for the Actors Studio to finesse its interest in Russian theater. As Kazan explained it, Method actors embraced the model suggested by the Moscow Art Theatre rather than the performances of British actors in Hollywood and on Broadway only because the

"Russian idea of the profound soul of the inconspicuous person also fits the American temperament" (Vineberg 1991, 113). Kazan would add: "We have not got the burden that everyone should be noble or behave heroically, that the English used to have" (Vineberg 1991, 113). Thus, the Studio's attack on British acting created a safe, politically expedient way to borrow from "known communists." It made Strasberg's use of Stanislavsky appear to be a sign of patriotism rather than communism, and the working-class heroes in the productions associated with Kazan and the Studio seem like American heroes rather than agents of class rebellion.

To some degree, Strasberg's and Kazan's opposition to British actors played on cultural tensions that had emerged 100 years earlier. By the mid-nineteenth century, there were separate theaters for working- and upper-class audiences. In New York, the Bowery and Broadway theaters were for unsophisticated audiences who championed the vigorous style of American actor Edwin Forrest, while the Park Theatre and Astor Place Opera House were for those refined enough to appreciate a British star like William Charles Macready, whose cerebral style and aristocratic demeanor made him the darling of American gentry. Forrest had become the first American actor to challenge England's domination of the American theater, and the much discussed Forrest–Macready rivalry came to symbolize a collection of strongly felt antithetical aesthetic and cultural values. These class antagonisms tied to pro- and anti-British sentiments broke out on May 10, 1849, in the Astor Place Riot, when the National Guard fired point blank into the throng of some 20,000 people who had surrounded the Astor Place Opera House to protest Macready's performance (Cliff 2007).

Anti-British sentiments also bubbled up during the Cold War period and the open opposition of the Actors Studio to British acting dovetailed with the anti-British rhetoric of other Cold War cultural artifacts. Analyzing the complex role that anti-British depictions play in *The Ten Commandments* (1956) and *Ben-Hur* (1959), Melani McAlister notes the heroic Hebrews and Christians are played by American actors, whereas the powerful characters in the villainous empires of Rome and Egypt are portrayed by non-American, especially British actors. Reckoning with the curious reality that even though the United Kingdom was a close Cold War ally and member of NATO, it also represented an imperial past that must be abandoned, McAlister argues that the films use "differences in accents and personal carriage of the actors … as signifiers of imperial versus democratic values" (2005, 65). Identifying the same Cold War pattern that allowed the Studio to equate British acting and un-American acting, McAlister observes that in the biblical epics, the danger posed to American interests by exhausted British imperialism becomes tacitly linked to the danger represented by Soviet totalitarianism. Making an important point about that strange conflation, she explains: "In the context of the 1950s, it would not have seemed incongruous for Rome and ancient Egypt to simultaneously suggest the failures of the British Empire and the Soviet Union" (2005, 67).

Considered as a component of Cold War culture, the narratives of the biblical epics make it possible for America to emerge as an alternative to the moribund empire and communist state insofar as it is associated with the new societies depicted in the films that are not only individualistic but also "politically, morally, and sexually superior" (McAlister 2005, 65). In addition, their rhetorical strategies are comparable to those of Kazan and Strasberg. In the case of the Actors Studio, the attack on British acting helped to establish the Method's association with "American" authenticity and expressivity. The challenge to established, confining, British acting traditions bolstered the image of the Studio as a bastion of American artistic and political freedom. Importantly, these types of contrasts were not confined to the world of theater and film. Just as Method acting was held up as a model of American freedom and personal expression, in the 1950s abstract expressionist painters were "promoted into the official spotlight, as exemplars of American liberty" (Wollen 2008, 101).

Cold War commentary about American fine art also constructed an opposition between, on the one hand, American freedom and exuberance and, on the other, European constraint and totalitarianism. In the 1940s, a number of American artists had turned away from the "craft traditions and the politicized craft ethos of WPA civic art" and, drawing on disparate European modern art traditions, became associated with what would come to be seen as the New York School (Taylor 1999, 20). Writing about this new American modernism, Clement Greenberg championed work by Jackson Pollock and others that could be linked to cubist abstractionism. Describing the remarkable critical and commercial success of abstract expressionism, Greg Taylor observes that critics like Greenberg were able to promote "seemingly nonfunctional, inaccessible *unpopular* art on the basis of its expression of personal liberty and vitality" (1999, 21).

Establishing a contrast between Soviet censorship of modern art and American artists' "expressive freedom," critics and curators in the United States argued that "America's natural vitality" made it the ideal country to "pick up the modernist torch" (Taylor 1999, 21). With abstract expressionism heralded as art that was "expressive of both liberal democracy and authentic virility," in the 1950s the work of Jackson Pollock "garnered national, then international fame and prestige, and created a huge American constituency for expressive painting, sculpture, dance, theater, and music" (Taylor 1999, 21, 26). As Taylor observes: "Once the province of a marginal avant-garde, aesthetic liberty and vitality," in the Cold War period, high art thought to be imbued with these values was "distributed to an unprecedented audience, and on an unprecedented scale" (1999, 26).

However, from the standpoint of earlier avant-garde artists, American abstract expressionism represented nothing more than "a weak mishmash of European ideas thrown together with some heroic bluster and marketing panache" (Taylor 1999, 26). That observation could likely be made about Method acting, especially if one considers the eclectic collection of "Russian" ideas woven into the rhetoric Kazan and Strasberg used to promote the Actors Studio as the home of modern American acting. Colored by Cold War polemics, the acting style and acting techniques associated with the Actors Studio acquired a kind of legitimacy not extended to the work of established stage and screen actors. In the Cold War moment, distinctions between styles and theories of acting came to be seen in black-and-white terms. According to the Actors Studio, acting styles were either American or implicitly un-American. In Strasberg's view, actors either built their characters the right way, the American way, from the "inside out," or the wrong way, the implicitly un-American way, from the "outside in." Actors who worked from the "inside out" created authentic, realistic, American performances; people working from the "outside in" produced portrayals that were conventional, false, and perhaps even worthy of suspicion. Speaking from the bully pulpit of the Studio, Strasberg argued that actors belonged either to his enlightened, scientific, American era or to a dark age when some actors worked instinctively toward the authenticity his Method made possible.

Looking back, it is possible to see that the cultural climate of the Cold War years advanced the careers of individuals associated with the Actors Studio but insured that the careers of those suspected as communists, like the members of the Actors' Lab, would not advance. Reflecting on Cold War developments that affected high and low art, Peter Wollen identifies the fickle operation of cultural criticism and political hit jobs, as he points out that while high art critics were busy building Pollock up into "a monument of American freedom," they ignored "the purges taking place in the movie industry" and the decision of film and theater artists like Brecht, Chaplin, Huston, Losey, and Welles to leave for Europe (2008, 101). Wollen attributes this disinterest in anticommunists' success in the Hollywood film business with high art critics' "political drift to the right" and deep-seated "dislike for the popular arts" (2008, 101). That disregard for lowbrow art and commerce seems to have been widespread, for Pollock and other fine artists were never blacklisted, even though they belonged to a generation of painters who "had been involved in the Popular Front and the Artists' Union, just as a generation of scriptwriters, actors and stage directors had been involved in parallel organizations" (Wollen 2008, 101). As if cordoned off from anticommunist challenges, the abstract expressionists and the Actors Studio were championed as exemplars of American art, with Greenberg's interest in the "violence, exasperation, and stridency" of Pollock's paintings echoed in commentaries about the new style of Method acting, and Greenberg's assessment that Pollock's art dwelt "entirely in the lonely jungle of immediate sensations, impulses and notions" repeated in observations about the performances of Method actors (O'Brian 1986, 166). And so while in the early Cold War years the American public learned to value the work of Studio actors and abstract expressionists for its uniquely "American" qualities, perhaps by now it is possible for accounts of modernism and American acting to mention the work of people sidelined by Cold War polemics, from Broadway star Alfred Lunt to drama coach Mira Rostova to the members of the Actors' Lab in Hollywood.

Notes

1. The group of studio drama coaches includes Sophie Rosenstein, Florence Enright, Lillian Burns (Sidney), Phyllis Loughton (Seaton), Lela Rogers, Lillian Albertson, Josephine Hutchinson, and Estelle Harmon (see Baron 1999).
2. For a more complete picture of how the press covered actor training in the studio era see Baron 1998.
3. In addition to stars like Laurence Olivier, Cary Grant, and Ronald Colman, British actors such as George Arliss, Cedric Hardwicke, C. Aubrey Smith, Leslie Howard, Herbert Marshall, Robert Donat, and Ray Milland were an integral part of the studio era.

References

Actors' Laboratory Collection. *Special Collections Department*, University of California, Los Angeles, Boxes 1–19.

Adler, Stella. (1988). *The Technique of Acting*. New York: Bantam.

Atkins, Thomas R. (1975). "Troubled Sexuality in the Popular Hollywood Feature." In Thomas R. Atkins (ed.), *Sexuality in the Movies*. New York: Da Capo.

Baron, Cynthia. (1998). "The Method Moment: Situating the Rise of Method Acting in the 1950s." *Popular Culture Review*, 9.2, 89–106.

Baron, Cynthia. (1999). "Crafting Film Performances: Acting in the Hollywood Studio Era." In Alan Lovell & Peter Krämer (eds), *Screen Acting*. London: Routledge.

Baron, Cynthia, & Carnicke, Sharon Marie. (2008). *Reframing Screen Performance*. Ann Arbor: University of Michigan Press.

Barrett, Edward L., Jr (1951). *The Tenney Committee: Legislative Investigation of Subversive Activities in California*. Ithaca, NY: Cornell University Press.

Barton, Robert. (2006). *Acting Onstage and Off*. 4th edn. Belmont, CA: Thompson.

Bosworth, Patricia. (1978). *Montgomery Clift: A Biography*. New York: Harcourt Brace Jovanovich.

Brando, Marlon. (1994). *Songs My Mother Taught Me*. New York: Random House.

Capote, Truman. (1973). "Brando by Capote." *McCalls*, 90, 123–129. (Originally published 1957.)

Carnicke, Sharon Marie. (2009). *Stanislavsky in Focus*. 2nd edn. New York: Routledge.

Cliff, Nigel. (2007). *The Shakespeare Riots*. New York: Random House.

Cole, Toby, & Chinoy, Helen Krich (eds). (1970). *Actors on Acting*. New York: Crown.

Funke, Lewis, & Booth, John E. (1961). *Actors Talk about Acting*. London: Thames & Hudson.

Garfield, David. (1984). *The Actors Studio*. New York: Macmillan.

Gordon, Mel. (1985). "Introduction." In Michael Chekhov, *Lessons for the Professional Actor* (pp. 11–18). New York: Performing Arts Journal Publications.

Hirsh, Foster. (1984). *A Method to Their Madness*. New York: Da Capo.

Krasner, David. (2000). "I Hate Strasberg: Method Bashing in the Academy." In David Krasner (ed.), *Method Acting Reconsidered* (pp. 3–39). New York: St Martin's.

McAlister, Melani. (2005). *Epic Encounters: Culture, Media, and U.S. Interests in the Middle East since 1945*. Berkeley: University of California Press.

Morley, Sheridan. (1983). *Tales from the Hollywood Raj: The British, the Movies and Tinseltown*. New York: Viking Press.

Naremore, James. (1988). *Acting in the Cinema*. Berkeley: University of California Press.

O'Brian, John (ed.). (1986). *Clement Greenberg: The Collected Essays and Criticism. Volume 1: Perceptions and Judgments, 1939–1944*. Chicago: University of Chicago Press.

Reeves, Thomas C. (1997). *The Life and Times of Joe McCarthy*. New York: Madison.

Rickman, Gregg. (1992). Review of *Three Generations of Film Actors*. *Film Quarterly*, 46.1, 43–44.

Susman, Warren. (1973). *Culture and Commitment*. New York: Braziller.

Taylor, Greg. (1999). *Artists in the Audience: Cults, Camp, and American Film Criticism*. Princeton: Princeton University Press.

Tenney, Jack B. (1948). *Fourth Report of the Senate Fact-Finding Committee on Un-American Activities, 1948: Communist Front Organizations*. Sacramento: California Legislature.

US Congress, House Committee on Un-American Activities. (1951). *Communist Infiltration of Hollywood Motion-Picture Industry*. Washington, DC: United States Government Printing Office, at https://archive.org/details/communistinfiltr07unit (accessed March 2015).

Vineberg, Steve. (1991). *Method Actors: Three Generations of an American Acting Tradition*. New York: Schirmer.

Watson, Ian. (2001). "Actor Training in the United States: Past, Present and Future (?)." In Ian Watson (ed.), *Performer Training: Developments across Cultures* (pp. 61–82). Amsterdam: Harwood.

Wollen, Peter. (2008). *Raiding the Icebox: Reflections on Twentieth-Century Culture*. New York: Verso.

28

Authorship and Billy Wilder

Robert Sklar
Late Professor Emeritus, New York University, United States

Robert Sklar instructively complicates notions of **film authorship** in the larger context of American film history. He outlines the French, American, and British definitions of the **auteur** – from **François Truffaut**, **Andrew Sarris**, and **Peter Wollen** to French theorists **Roland Barthes** and **Michel Foucault**. Sklar eventually arrives at **Stephen Crofts** as the most viable model. Using American **émigré** film director **Billy Wilder** as a case study, Sklar proposes his own argument that collaborative efforts (between Wilder and his co-screenwriters **Charles Brackett** and **I. A. L. Diamond**, for instance) must always be taken into account. Originally eschewed by Sarris and **Jean-Luc Godard**, Wilder's films prevailed in the popular consciousness, in Oscar award nominations, and to this day in academic film studies. Through close analysis of two popular Wilder movies, ***Double Indemnity*** and ***The Apartment***, and two box office failures, ***Ace in the Hole*** (since critically lauded) and ***Kiss Me, Stupid***, Sklar compellingly invites us to reconsider approaches to film authorship. Sklar's essay shares ground with his own discussion of film historiography in Volume II of this series and with James Naremore on Orson Welles in this volume.

Additional terms, names, and concepts: *La politique des auteurs*, *Cahiers du Cinéma*, the auteur theory

The thirty years' war over authorship in film culture, fought from the 1950s through the 1980s, may seem as remote in retrospect as the original Thirty Years' War of the seventeenth century. Who were its partisans? What was at stake? Did anyone win or lose, or did it just peter out from exhaustion or from some sort of truce? And does any of it still matter?

One way to respond to such broad questions is to do as the movies do, narrow them down, make them personal, tie them to an individual's fate. For our purposes, let that individual be Billy Wilder (1906–2002), a European émigré who left Nazi Germany in the 1930s and who wrote and directed (and latterly produced) some 25 feature films in Hollywood

American Film History: Selected Readings, Origins to 1960, First Edition. Edited by Cynthia Lucia, Roy Grundmann, and Art Simon.
© 2016 John Wiley & Sons, Inc. Published 2016 by John Wiley & Sons, Inc.

from 1942 to 1981. Not himself a participant in the authorship war – although that statement may need reexamination – he was nonetheless targeted as one of its primary victims, in the sense that in the struggle over who was or was not to be certified as a film author he was ignored or actively derided, judgments with the potential irrevocably to harm his historical reputation. Decades later, however, we're still talking about Wilder, in fact more than ever, so the questions with which we began aptly may be addressed through the prism of one more: What does it mean to speak of Billy Wilder as author of the films that bear his name?

Perhaps the idea of an authorship *war* smacks of hyperbole, when "controversy" or "debate" or even a peaceful word like "concept" might serve as well. But it's important to convey the atmosphere of militancy in which the advocacy of authorship was launched, the aggression, the strong feelings and hard words (one pertinent example: Jean-Luc Godard in 1956 referring to "that sucker Wilder" (1972, 35)). Something serious definitely was thought to be at stake and what that was changed over several phases of the authorship conflict. Much of this history is widely known, yet it requires a certain recapitulation both for newcomers to the story and to see what new perspectives, both from greater distance and in the specific Wilder context, may emerge.

To begin with, authorship was alternatively a negligible or a flexible concept during the first half century of movies. Who originates or gives existence to a motion picture? In the framework of American film history, some individual filmmakers laid claim to authorship because as artists they also owned the means of production; Charlie Chaplin, studio boss, producer, writer, director, star – also editor, and when sound arrived, composer – was the *ne plus ultra* of film authors. Almost every other commercial fiction film, however, was made differently. A movie company's story department acquired a property (novel, play, treatment, etc.) and assigned multiple staff writers to prepare a screenplay. Other departments developed budgets, built sets, made costumes, hired casts, and picked a director from a studio's contract roster. Often the director would join a project when all the other preparation was complete and leave it even before postproduction work began. Who was the author in this setup? To film historian Thomas Schatz, borrowing a phrase from French critic André Bazin for a book title, what gave existence to a motion picture was *The Genius of the System* (Schatz 1988).

Newspaper reviewers during the studio era invariably described movie companies as the originators of films' style and content; focusing on stars and genres, they sometimes failed to mention the director's name at all. Nevertheless, even as studio employees, directors began to gain recognition from both industry peers and critics. Best director prizes were among the Academy Awards from their beginning in 1927/1928, and the New York Film Critics Circle also named an annual best director when its awards were launched in 1935; John Ford became the dominant figure of the period with three Oscars and four New York film critics' accolades between 1935 and 1941. In later years Wilder benefited as much as any other director from the industry awards regime. Of the 14 films he made between 1944 and 1960, no fewer than eight gained best director nominations from the Academy and he won twice, for *The Lost Weekend* (1945) and *The Apartment* (1960), both of which were also named best picture. (As well, the New York critics gave those two films best picture and best director awards.) Ironically, Wilder's prizes from both critics and the industry held negative value in nearly all phases of the authorship war.

La politique des auteurs

Phase One of the authorship war began in France. A new film journal, *Cahiers du Cinéma*, was founded in 1951. Among its staff were young writers – François Truffaut, for example, born 1932, was not yet 20 years old – who wished to become filmmakers; besides Truffaut, they included Godard, Claude Chabrol, Jacques Rivette, and others who a decade later emerged as the star directors of the French New Wave. But in the beginning they perceived barriers to opportunity and they used their critical platform to break down the walls. Truffaut's famous 1954 polemic, "A Certain Tendency of the French Cinema," attacked what he called the "Tradition of Quality" in contemporary French filmmaking, which in his view valorized unwieldy literary screenplays to which directors merely added pictures. What doesn't appear in the article's English translation (Truffaut 1976) is the French phrase that would become *Cahier*'s critical touchstone: *la politique des auteurs*, or a policy that favored directors who functioned as *auteurs*, who made *cinema* rather than, as Truffaut alleged, filmed literature.

Truffaut's concern in his article was with France, but even earlier *Cahiers* critics were discovering auteurs among the often overlooked ranks of Hollywood studio directors. What they were looking for was exemplified by the term mise-en-scène: In basic definition, it represented a director's technique for visualizing scenes that conveyed the specific character of a work. And where they found such technique most prominently was in the films of Howard Hawks, Alfred Hitchcock, and Nicholas Ray. Half a century and more later we might yawn and say, well of course. But at the time these were startling and even controversial valuations; in Hollywood's terms these men were, to be sure, respected professionals, but not ranked in the prize-winning category, among the elite: Ray was never nominated for a best director Academy Award, Hawks only once, and Hitchcock several times, but never a winner (the New York critics did name Hitchcock best director back in 1938 for a film he made in Britain, *The Lady Vanishes*). It is fair to say that they owe their present high reputations, in the first instance, to *Cahiers du Cinéma*. A number of other Hollywood directors came in for praise in the journal, or disparagement, but aside from being the target of a rare offhand attack ("that sucker . . . "), Billy Wilder was one of those, in the words of a later *Cahiers* critic, simply "thrown out of the club" (Comolli et al. 1986, 200).

Auteur Theory

By the time the *Cahiers* critics had established themselves as directors the authorship war had crossed the Atlantic and entered its second phase. A New York film critic and journalist, Andrew Sarris, championed *la politique des auteurs*, translating and transforming it into what he called "the *auteur* theory." (It also leapt the English Channel to Britain, where it was engaged by the film journal *Movie*.) If *la politique* in *Cahiers*' pages was often couched in windy rhetoric, Sarris's formulations tended to be even more indistinct. His "theory" of authorship had three parts. First came the familiar notion of technique; second was "the distinguishable personality of the director as a criterion of value"; and third was "interior meaning," or "*élan* of the soul" (1974, 512–513). However vague these terms, they provided enormous opportunity for Sarris to evaluate directors' personalities and assert his views of filmmakers' "souls," and he was nothing if not confident in those capacities.

By his 1968 book *The American Cinema: Directors and Directions, 1929–1968* "the *auteur* theory" had expanded into a "theory of film history" and Sarris offered thumbnail appraisals of some 200 directors in 11 different categories, from "pantheon" to sub-basement in his judgment of worthiness (see Sarris 1985). From its inception in the early 1960s "the *auteur* theory" was the subject of heated polemics in American film journals, with film critic Pauline Kael most implacably in opposition. Nevertheless, *The American Cinema* became an indispensable reference for fledgling cinephiles aspiring to knowledge of American film history, and Sarris's rankings exerted enormous influence.

Where stood Wilder on Sarris's ladder of assessment? Already in a 1962 article proclaiming the auteur theory he had pegged Wilder as an example "of writer-directors without technical mastery" (1974, 513). In *The American Cinema* he spoke of "the superficial nastiness of [Wilder's] personality," and as for his "soul," as it were, the verdict was that he was "hardly likely to make a film on the human condition" (1985, 166). Sarris placed Wilder, after some 60 or so higher names, in his fifth category, "Less Than Meets the Eye," directors whose "personal signatures to their films were written with invisible ink" (1985, 155). In subsequent years perhaps no other of Sarris's decrees was so frequently called into question as his dismissal of Wilder.

Phase Three of the authorship war was inaugurated with the expansion of academic cinema studies in the 1970s amid the pervasive influence of current European theories grouped under such labels as semiotics, structuralism, and poststructuralism. One impetus was to aim at establishing *auteurism* on a more rigorous basis, to supplant the flights of rhetoric of both the *Cahiers* critics and Sarris with a more systematic, quasi-scientific form of analysis. A writer associated with this approach was Peter Wollen in his 1969 *Signs and Meaning in the Cinema*, although Wollen originally placed emphasis on a director's motifs rather than on style. In a 1972 postscript, Wollen also drew on psychoanalytic terminology as he shifted focus away from individual creativity toward an analysis of film structure. "The structure is associated with a single director, an individual, not because he has played the role of an artist, expressing himself or his own vision in the film," Wollen wrote, "but because it is through the force of his preoccupations that an unconscious, unintended meaning can be decoded in the film, usually to the surprise of the individual involved" (1981, 146). He was perhaps recasting his assessment of the "*auteur* theory" in the framework of an emerging thesis that proposed discarding the concept of authorship entirely.

Two essays by eminent French theorists propounded the anti-authorship argument: "The Death of the Author" by Roland Barthes and "What Is an Author?" by Michel Foucault, published respectively in 1968 and 1969, at the same time as Sarris's and Wollen's books. Barthes's characteristically brief, allusive commentary questions the possibility of originality or self-expression: "a text is made up of multiple writings, drawn from many cultures and entering into mutual relations of dialogue, parody, contestation ... a text's unity lies not in its origin but in its destination." A reader, not an author, "holds together in a single field all the traces by which the written text is constituted" (1977, 148). Foucault's emphasis was on what he called the "author-function":

> under what conditions and through what forms can an entity like the subject [read: author] appear in the order of discourse ... In short, the subject (and its substitutes) must be stripped of its creative role and analyzed as a complex and variable function of discourse. (1977, 137–138)

Whatever is left of the author in the frame of Barthes's notion of writing and Foucault's of discourse, "personality" and "soul" play no part at all.

Following these negations, film theorist Stephen Crofts assessed the state of the authorship war in a 1983 article "Authorship and Hollywood." He usefully summarized four conceptions of the film author: "1. Author as expressive individual. 2. Author as constructed from the film or films." (Further broken down into different manners of construction, such as reading off thematic and stylistic properties, or a set of structures.) "3. Author as social and sexual subject. 4. Author as author-name, as function of the circulation of the film or films" (1983, 17). Each of these conceptions comes in for critique by Crofts for its inadequacies. Ultimately he calls for a historical analysis of the concept of film authorship itself, a form of metacritique or even self-critique that decenters the putative film author in favor of investigating the historical and cultural circumstances in which a film is made (with numerous potential contributions to authorship) and received by critics and spectators. "This article clearly points to the necessity of abandoning any theory of authorship modeled on an interpersonal theory of communication," Crofts writes, "whereby meaning is somehow transferred from author to reader." Textual "meaning" will vary over time, "as will that of the author-name which may be attached to it" (1983, 21).

Crofts's summary and evaluation of the authorship war signaled that a truce was imminent, or that exhaustion had set in. As studio archives became available to researchers around this time, historical analysis of many elements of filmmaking became possible, and scholars could detail the processes of production in which directors collaborated not only with writers, producers, and performers but with cinematographers, editors, designers, composers, and others – the complex panoply of art and craft and power out of which films were created. Authorship became not a dead letter but an inevitably incomplete project yielding valuable new insights that eschewed the impressionistic and moralistic judgments that launched the concept a generation previously.

It was perhaps in this spirit that Andrew Sarris returned to the subject of Billy Wilder in his long-awaited 1998 study of the American sound film up until 1949. The book remained true to Sarris's original methodology. After short segments on studios and genres, its central section consists of essays on individual directors, 21 in total, of whom Wilder was one. "I must concede that seemingly I have grossly underrated Billy Wilder," Sarris writes, "perhaps more so than any other American director." How did that come to pass? "Somehow," Sarris asserts, "I managed to let people talk me out of my instinctive enthusiasm for his films" (1998, 324). Wilder is elevated from the fifth circle of indifference all the way up to the top, Sarris's Pantheon. Yet what is striking in reading through the essay is not that Sarris's critical perspective on the films has changed – he finds them no less cynical and nasty than they appeared to him three decades earlier – so much as the critic's willingness to excuse them and to assert that all along he rather ambivalently admired them.

Sarris's views earlier had begun to change when he praised several of Wilder's otherwise undervalued 1970s films. The director was asked about the critic's more positive appraisals in a 1979 interview. His reply took in not only Sarris but also any and all other detractors: "They just don't feel like kicking an elderly man in the ass any more" (McBride & McCarthy 2001, 159).

Vienna, Berlin, Hollywood

Wilder was born in 1906 into a German-speaking Jewish family living in a village outside Krakow in an area of Poland then part of the Austro-Hungarian Empire. The family moved during World War I to Vienna, seat of the soon-to-expire empire, and it was there in postwar Austria that Billie, as he was then known, while still in his teens began to write for newspapers. Barely 20, he moved on to a more cosmopolitan city, Berlin, capital of Germany, where he continued as a journalist and began writing screenplays. In 1929 he received his first screen credit for *Der Teufelsreporter* (literally "The Devil Reporter," with several other English-language variations in standard sources) and also took part with the future Hollywood filmmakers Robert and Curt Siodmak, Edgar G. Ulmer, and Fred Zinnemann in making the documentary-fiction film *Menschen am Sonntag* (*People on Sunday*). He gained credit for collaborating on screenplays for nearly a dozen more films made in Germany between 1931 and 1933.

Following the Nazi seizure of power, Wilder left for Paris. There he worked as codirector with Alexander Esway on a 1934 film, *Mauvaise Graine* (*Bad Seed*), and also collaborated in the writing. Before its release he had embarked for the United States with a ticket paid by Columbia Pictures and a writing contract awaiting him at the studio arranged by an émigré who preceded him, director-producer Joe May. Wilder biographer Ed Sikov rightly speculates on whether this offer was actually for future writing or a pretext for a rescue; apparently May didn't tell Columbia that Wilder knew little or no English (1998, 104). Soon Wilder was unemployed and required to leave the country – in his case, to Mexico – in order to apply for reentry and permanent resident status. Achieving that, he returned to Hollywood and set out to learn a new language.

The émigrés tried to take care of their own. Now at Fox, May was working with Erich Pommer, producer of numerous Weimar-era German classics, and they gave Wilder writing work. On another Fox project Wilder collaborated with two other screenwriters from Berlin, Franz Schulz and Hanns Schwarz; according to Sikov, they turned in a script in German and the studio had to have it translated (1998, 109–110). This couldn't last. After a return to Vienna to visit his mother, Wilder appears to have made an effort to work with writers whose birth language was English. In 1936 at Paramount, an executive teamed him with Charles Brackett.

The Brackett–Wilder collaboration, which lasted from 1936 to 1950, has been a subject of extensive commentary over the years, but it has been considerably one-sided. There are many biographies and critical studies dealing with Wilder, none concerning Brackett; Wilder gave innumerable interviews in which their work together was obviously a topic on which he expressed his views; Brackett (1892–1969), who died before Hollywood history emerged as a subject of strong scholarly and cultural interest, addressed it in public barely at all. (However, Brackett's handwritten diaries are now housed at the Academy of Motion Picture Arts and Sciences library, and as they are transcribed and studied by researchers, new perspectives on the relationship may emerge.)

In the meantime, a story of opposites persists. Brackett had genteel upstate New York origins, attended Williams College and Harvard Law School, and served overseas in noncombat roles during World War I. After the war he worked in his father's law firm and then broke away to write novels as well as drama reviews for the *New Yorker*. Hollywood scooped him up as a writer for talkies, and in the early 1930s he garnered nearly a dozen credits, none distinguished or particularly memorable. It seemed that he needed someone like Wilder as much as Wilder needed someone like him, and their first assignment together was a significant challenge and step up for both – a screenplay for a major director, Ernst Lubitsch, which became the 1938 film *Bluebeard's Eighth Wife*.

Much is invariably made about how much Brackett and Wilder fought with one another, but what writing collaborators don't? It's less important that they bickered –few commentators can escape a marriage metaphor – than that they stayed together so productively so long. They wrote 13 films together, occasionally with additional collaborators. Their first seven, for other directors, included the classic *Ninotchka* (1939), directed by Lubitsch, *Midnight* (1939), directed by Mitchell Leisen, and *Ball of Fire* (1941), directed by Howard Hawks. They wrote six of the first seven films that Wilder directed, five of which Brackett produced: *The Major and the Minor* (1942, the only one with a different producer), *Five Graves to Cairo* (1943), *The Lost Weekend* (1945), *The Emperor Waltz* (1948), *A Foreign Affair* (1948), and *Sunset Boulevard* (1950). Wilder ended the partnership, to Brackett's dismay; among whatever other motives, the director wanted thenceforward to be his own producer. This essay will not go further into the Brackett–Wilder collaboration, but its current status as a closed story in which Wilder invariably has the upper hand is ripe for further exploration and revision.

Wilder, as has been noted, was well aware of the case against him. That critical negativity may have provided one motivation for his willingness to grant extensive interviews to journalists, biographers, and admiring fellow filmmakers like Cameron Crowe (Wilder & Crowe 1999) and Volker Schlöndorff (Schlöndorff & Grischow 2006). He outlived nearly all of his coworkers, in some cases by decades, and that circumstance gave him the last, and lasting, word. He was an entertaining raconteur and his self-created legend is full of anecdotes that his admirers prize too much to question. Can the subject of Wilder and authorship be approached in a more historical manner, superseding judgmental auteurism and the filmmaker's beguiling biographical tales? This essay considers the question by focusing on four Wilder films – two major successes, *Double Indemnity* (1944) and *The Apartment* (1960), and two controversial box office flops, *Ace in the Hole* (1951) and *Kiss Me, Stupid* (1964) – in the context of his career and its changing cultural context.

Double Indemnity

Wilder's third film, *Double Indemnity*, made his name as a major director, but without detracting from his achievement one could say also that it was a film significantly "authored" by its historical conjuncture. The Production Code Administration had preemptively blackballed James M. Cain's original story from studio consideration back in the 1930s, but its book publication during World War II provided an opportunity to relent. As film historian Sheri Chinen Biesen has noted, wartime conditions gave rise – particularly among millions of servicemen – to a craving for "red meat" pictures offering more candid representations of sex and violence than the Production Code allowed (Biesen 2005). Paramount came up with a treatment of Cain's tale that the PCA surprisingly approved; the film's forceful linkage of illicit sexual desire and murderous intent went on to set a template for the emerging film noir movement. Wilder did not work with Brackett on the screenplay and he is the only source for accounts of Brackett's unwillingness to participate. The studio brought in crime novelist (but novice screenwriter) Raymond Chandler as substitute collaborator.

If Wilder's working relationship with Brackett was contentious, he reached new heights of incompatibility and mutual hostility with Chandler. Yet the outcome was an extraordinary screenplay, for which no commentator has been able convincingly to apportion credit. In auteurist mode, many take for granted that the work has a single author – a form of rhetoric that assumes not only that Wilder alone wrote the words but also cast the actors and designed and built the sets, while the studio, producer, cowriter, art director, even the carpenters recede from view. Let us assume that Chandler did his share, while granting that it is only an assumption. "Chandler was instrumental (albeit grossly underpaid and perhaps underacknowledged) for his keen contribution to the moody descriptions and dialogue of the film," Biesen claims, but does not provide a word of evidence to support this view (2005, 105). In *Raymond Chandler and Film*, William Luhr draws the necessary conclusion: "Chandler's specific contribution to the film is difficult to isolate and can only be discussed tentatively because of the collaborative nature of the project" (1991, 32).

Double Indemnity's voiceover/flashback narrative structure was among the most notable in an era in which both devices were frequently utilized. The film opens in Los Angeles at night with a careening automobile arriving at the offices of Pacific All Risk Insurance Company. The driver, insurance salesman Walter Neff (Fred MacMurray), blood spreading on

Figure 28.1 Phyllis Dietrichson (Barbara Stanwyck) and Walter Neff (Fred MacMurray) begin the flirtation that leads to adultery and murder in Billy Wilder's *Double Indemnity* (1944, producer Paramount Pictures).

his jacket from a wound in his left shoulder, his brow perspiring, enters his office and begins speaking a confession into a Dictaphone machine. The addressee is his colleague, claims manager Barton Keyes (Edward G. Robinson). Growing weaker through the film, Neff recounts and we see in flashback the events leading up to what will be his dying moment.

Neff sets the date as 1938, as the writers seek to distance peacetime crime from wartime valor and signal why a healthy single man in his thirties is not in uniform. He tells Keyes of his visit to an auto policy client on Los Feliz. There he encounters the customer's wife, Phyllis Dietrichson (Barbara Stanwyck), viewed from below, fresh from taking a "sun bath," wrapped in a towel with, we are to assume, nothing on underneath. A flirtation immediately commences, with MacMurray's facial expressions displaying lascivious intent rarely seen in a Hollywood film since Erich von Stroheim's continental rakes of the silent era. Their brazenly metaphorical dialogue is an often-quoted gem of studio screenwriting.

Soon the lovers are plotting the husband's murder and an insurance scam that will gain them twice the policy's value (double indemnity, if they can make the crime appear as an accidental death). We see only Phyllis's impassive face as Neff strangles the man in the car seat beside her. Neff then impersonates the dead man on a train ride as they succeed in making it appear that he has accidently fallen off and been killed. Keyes, whose job is to uncover insurance fraud, is suspicious but doesn't connect the scheme to his colleague Neff, who lights his cigars and several times speaks their ripe intimacy with the words, "I love you, too." Nevertheless, the scam unravels through various stages of the lovers' self-disgust and mutual capacity for betrayal; they satisfy the Production Code by shooting each other, with Neff surviving long enough to tell Keyes and us the story.

Double Indemnity served as a model for future noir films in visual style as well as narrative form. Cinematographer John Seitz's exceptionally dark palate was partly shaped by wartime lighting restrictions, particularly in outdoor night scenes, but it also helped to establish the horizontal Venetian blind as the sine qua non for shaping interior light patterns in noir imagery. Yet overall the film is more a triumph of scriptwriting than of mise-en-scène – perhaps a reason Wilder did not rate in the *politique des auteurs*. Another telling aspect of the film's reception in France was voiced in Raymond Borde and Etienne Chaumeton's path-breaking 1955 *Panorama du film noir américain*. The authors dislike the "perfidious sensuality" and "tortuous intrigue" of Barbara Stanwyck's character. "It's rare to find a lady as dubious as this in everyday life," they write, "and *Double Indemnity* remains, due to its very improbability, extremely remote from us." They greatly prefer Lana Turner's character in a later Cain adaptation, *The Postman Always Rings Twice* (1946), whose avarice, adultery, and crime of murder seem to them "perfectly legitimate" and "not at all sinister." The difference has something to do with her white clothing and "the movement of her hips" (Borde & Chaumeton 2002, 69). But, Turner's allure aside, the judgment struck an ominous note that Sarris later was to echo, concerning what appeared to some to be excesses of candor or ardor in depicting malice, duplicity, and other unsavory character traits in the protagonists of Wilder's films.

Double Indemnity received seven Academy Award nominations, including best picture, direction, screenplay, cinematography, and music, along with Stanwyck for best actress, but won none. The best picture, director, and writing awards went to another Paramount film which the studio was said to favor, Leo McCarey's *Going My Way*. As happens sometimes with the Oscars, voters the following year offered rectification to the loser by giving awards for a lesser work: in this case Wilder's 1945 *The Lost Weekend*, which won best picture, direction, and screenplay (Brackett back with Wilder), as well as best actor for Ray Milland. (There were nominations also for cinematography, editing, and music.) Wilder then spent a period of time in postwar Germany working with US occupation forces. His next film, *The Emperor Waltz* (1948), was something of an anomaly, a musical comedy confection for Bing Crosby set in a fantasy European kingdom, followed by a work of considerably greater realism, *A Foreign Affair* (also 1948), which takes place in contemporary war-ravaged Berlin. The decade, as well as the collaboration, ended for Brackett and Wilder with their greatest film together, *Sunset Boulevard* (1950), an undoubted classic of American cinema; it won the writers (along with a third collaborator, D. M. Marshman, Jr) another screenplay Oscar, but lost best picture and direction to Joseph L. Mankiewicz and *All About Eve*.[1]

Ace in the Hole

Wilder became his own producer with *Ace in the Hole*, a status he was able to maintain for a majority of films during the remainder of his career. Asked about this new role by French critic Michel Ciment in a 1980 filmed interview, he spoke disparagingly of "studio producers." "Since they cannot write, since they cannot direct, since they cannot act, since they cannot compose, they become the head of everything," Wilder said. "That was the ultimate control. It was a question not of power but of ultimately having it as close on the screen to what you first imagined" (Tresgot & Ciment, 1982). This comment ignores the fact that, as noted earlier, his producer on five of his first seven films had been none other than his writing partner, who clearly had a hand in what was "first imagined" and would presumably have wanted as much as Wilder to see it realized on the screen. So perhaps it was a question of power after all.

Being his own producer was still not the same as having ultimate control. Just before *Ace in the Hole* was to be released, Paramount arbitrarily and against Wilder's wishes changed the film's title to *The Big Carnival*, perhaps hoping to mitigate a looming box office disaster. The dual titles served to cloud the film's posterity, but its circle of admirers has gradually expanded over the decades and under its original title, *Ace in the Hole* has gained recognition as one of the more bleak and downbeat – and culturally prescient – works in American film history.

Ace in the Hole offers an early portrait of social and cultural pathologies with which we have grown increasingly familiar since the film was made: cynical media manipulation of private pathos, goading a jaded and bored populace into morbid curiosity that quickly transforms itself into a wild circus bordering on mass hysteria. Its narrative stems from an idea proposed by a new writing collaborator, Walter Newman, based on the story of Floyd Collins, who became pinned by a rock while exploring a cave in Kentucky in 1925. A local reporter kept in contact with Collins, feeding accounts of the rescue effort to newspapers across the country whose screaming front-page headlines drew inquisitive crowds to the site. After 18 days underground, Collins died. The Collins saga remained vivid for many years thereafter, a harbinger of the media's power to activate mass emotions.

With Newman and a third writer, Lesser Samuels, Wilder used the Collins story as a template, bringing the action into the present and relocating it in New Mexico, which offered the opportunity for a more complex ethnic mix than the original Collins tale, taking in the western state's Native American and Hispanic cultures. More significantly, they shifted the emphasis from the victim to the media manipulator. Portraying this central character, Charles "Chuck" Tatum, a defrocked big-city reporter, Kirk Douglas gives Wilder's worldly skepticism a cold, misanthropic desperation, denying spectators any haven in illusion or hope. Jan Sterling as Lorraine Minosa, embittered wife of the trapped man, Leo, matches his brilliantly caustic characterization.

The film begins in a comic, ironic mode, with Tatum arriving in Albuquerque insouciantly behind the wheel of a convertible being pulled by a tow truck. He lands a job at the *Sun-Bulletin* newspaper and bemuses the staid denizens of its newsroom with his sly innuendos and city slicker frustrations, while a darker melody of his self-destructiveness plays beneath them. Driving with a young photographer into the barren hinterlands on a mundane reporting assignment, Tatum notices a commotion outside a dreary, dust-caked curio shop. Leo Minosa has been pinned by falling debris while hunting in ancient Indian burial caves for new curios to sell in his roadside store. Tatum knows about Floyd Collins. This could be his ticket back to the big time.

A superstitious remark gives Tatum his clue on how to hype the story: "Ancient Curse Entombs Man" reads the head over his byline. A further undertone is a mordant portrait of the modern American West, New Mexico style, with a native past producing both souvenirs and curses, a Hispanic present represented by Leo's devoutly Catholic but ineffectual parents, and forward-looking Anglos, rapacious, immoral, and self-absorbed. Tatum persuades Lorraine to playact as the devoted wife and teams up with a complaisant sheriff to prolong the rescue effort so the story will last longer and give him the leverage to regain his big-city career.

This tragedy in the making unfolds along two main thematic lines, beyond the psychopathologies of Wilder's major and minor characters. The first and most obvious one, as previously noted, is media manipulation and its social consequences. Leo Minosa's story starts out as a newspaper event, as was the case with Floyd Collins, but Wilder and his cowriters also bring into play newer media that didn't figure in the 1920s frenzy: radio, television, and, crucially if obliquely, the movie medium itself. Within the narrative, in particular, live radio transmissions from the scene give voice to bystanders and pose a potential, though containable, challenge to Tatum's orchestration of events through the press. Television takes on a token role, limited by the then state of its technology to a more distant, less mobile position suited mostly for official pronouncements.

What is most intriguing about the film's representation of media is what is implied about the role of the film medium itself. As the bleak plain between Minosa's curio shop and the Indian caves becomes transformed into a carnival site, the thought may occur that Wilder is putting into question his own role as filmmaking instigator and ours as at least vicarious spectators of this burgeoning mass hysteria. As crowds swell, prices go up and amusements appear; traffic snarls and a special train disgorges hordes of fresh onlookers running to become part of the scene. With public fervor growing in intensity, not one but four large trucks pass from right to left across the scene, each labeled "The Great S&M Amusement Corp." They give ample notice that the sadomasochistic enjoyment of Leo's plight by the on-site revelers is something that the film industry promotes and produces for the theater-bound viewer as well.

The second principal theme harks back to *Double Indemnity*. A little family arrives by car to become the first curiosity-seekers at the site; the father identifies himself (to a radio interviewer) as an employee of Pacific All Risk, the insurance company in the

Figure 28.2 Alighting from a train, new onlookers rush to join the carnival atmosphere surrounding the attempted rescue of a man trapped in a cave in *Ace in the Hole* (1951, director and producer Billy Wilder).

earlier film. This is a signal that *risk* is one of the film's central subjects. If its principal characters are invariably deceivers or transgressors, what are the risks involved? The *Sun-Bulletin*'s cautious editor wears a belt and also suspenders, no risk of his pants falling down, and Tatum at first emulates him. But Leo's hazardous curio hunting, against both the putative ancient curse and the present reality of rotting timbers and falling rock, serves to reactivate Tatum's recklessness. He ostentatiously removes his apparently redundant suspenders but he has failed to calculate the risk both to Leo and to himself.

As it becomes clear to Tatum that his forcing a change of tactics has ruined Leo's chance of rescue, he forges a dual identity with the doomed man: both have taken a chance, both have misunderstood the odds, both are trapped in a hole, real or metaphorical. Tatum's similar fate becomes the logical necessity of the narrative. He becomes Leo's surrogate, not as passive victim but as resentful avenger, forcing Lorraine to put on a cheesy fur stole Leo bought her for the couple's anniversary, choking her with it until, defending her life, she gives him a fatal stab wound with a pair of scissors. In the film's final shot, his lifeless body drops toward the camera, turning the screen black. There's no ray of light left for the spectator, no moral redemption, no better future for someone, anyone – only the drifting crowds departing in clouds of dust, until the next media sensation unites them into morbid momentary community.[2]

Ace in the Hole presented a viewpoint on contemporary media and society that few in the United States of 1951 wanted to hear, or agreed with. Wilder's first major setback in his Hollywood career left him chastened. He was too secure a figure to have seriously damaged his livelihood, but the lesson he learned – as in different circumstances many others in that conformist era were made to realize – was to be more cautious and circumspect. The less daring he became, ironically or perhaps logically, the more honor the industry granted him. Wilder's 1950s proceeded with a string of mostly pleasant films none of which ranks among his most significant: *Stalag 17* (1953), *Sabrina* (1954), *The Seven Year Itch* (1955), *The Spirit of St. Louis*, *Love in the Afternoon*, *Witness for the Prosecution* (all 1957). Yet for half of these prudent works – *Stalag 17*, *Sabrina*, and *Witness for the Prosecution* – he received Academy Award nominations for best director, a sign, as we have earlier seen, of the growing gap between Hollywood's self-estimation in that era and the new way of assessing the achievements of American cinema that the *politique des auteurs* had begun to expound.

The 1950s era also marked Wilder's search for new writing collaborators. He had eight different credited cowriters on the six films released from 1953 to 1957, none more than once. One of them was to return, however, and to become Wilder's sole writing partner on all 11 films that he made until the end of his career. This was I. A. L. Diamond (1920–1988). Born in Romania, he came to the United States as a child with his family, grew up in Brooklyn, and graduated from Columbia University. In a dozen years as a writer in Hollywood he had earned about the same number of credits, nearly all nondescript, until Wilder took him on to cowrite *Love in the Afternoon*. Differently from Brackett (or Chandler), now Wilder was the senior partner in age as well as status, and they shared a European background and a bred-in-the-bone Jewish wit. The films with Diamond as collaborator make an intriguing comparison with the Brackett years. Some of Wilder's critics regard Brackett's sensibility as a restraining counterweight to his partner's predilection toward cynicism and malice, while in this view Diamond was too junior and too alike to prevent the producer-director-writer from carrying his impertinence to a self-defeating extreme.

Their second collaboration, which established their permanent connection, seemed to strike a near-perfect balance between impudence and reassurance, sexual taboo and imaginative possibility, satire and romance. This was the 1959 classic *Some Like It Hot*, which the writers based rather more than they acknowledged on a 1951 West German film *Fanfaren der Liebe*, itself drawn from a 1935 French work, *Fanfare d'amour*. What Wilder and Diamond added most crucially to this tale of unemployed male musicians who dress up as women to perform in an all-girl orchestra was the past tense: a 1920s Chicago gangland setting already mythologized to excess in movies, a surfeit of clichés and fantasies that could be parodied but also subtly – or outrageously – extended into transgressive realms through playfulness, comedy, and innuendo. Basically, whatever 1950s moral authority might have regarded as improper or unsuitable in the film could be excused because it was happening in a nowhere time and place that was Hollywood's Roaring Twenties. The movie industry was sufficiently both enamored with and cautious toward the film that among its six Academy Award nominations, including screenplay and director but not best picture, it won only for costume design. In recent years, as the subjects of gender and performance – and the performance of gender – have grown increasingly important in film studies, *Some Like It Hot* has gained considerable critical attention; I focus here on the film that followed it in the Wilder–Diamond collaboration, *The Apartment* (1960).

The Apartment

The Apartment's transgressions in the sphere of sexuality were more familiar and conventional than those of *Some Like It Hot*, and the film may have benefited from a compensatory vote at the Academy Awards, as it appeared that *The Lost Weekend* had gained support the year after *Double Indemnity*. *The Apartment* received 10 nominations and won five Oscars, including best picture, director, original screenplay, editing, and art direction. (The New York Film Critics Circle also honored it with a best screenplay award and a tie for best picture and director.) It was, tellingly, the first Wilder screenplay since *Ace in the Hole* not based on another source, and also, perhaps equally significant, its public setting, like *Double Indemnity*, was the offices of an insurance company. This one was in New York, however, so it was called Consolidated Life instead of Pacific All Risk. As a voiceover at the beginning tells us, the company had over 30,000 employees and, in a design triumph by art director Alexander Trauner, an enormous floor of identical desks with men and women toiling at calculators, extending as if to infinity.

The speaker is C. C. Baxter (Jack Lemmon), whose ambition to rise up out of calculator-punching

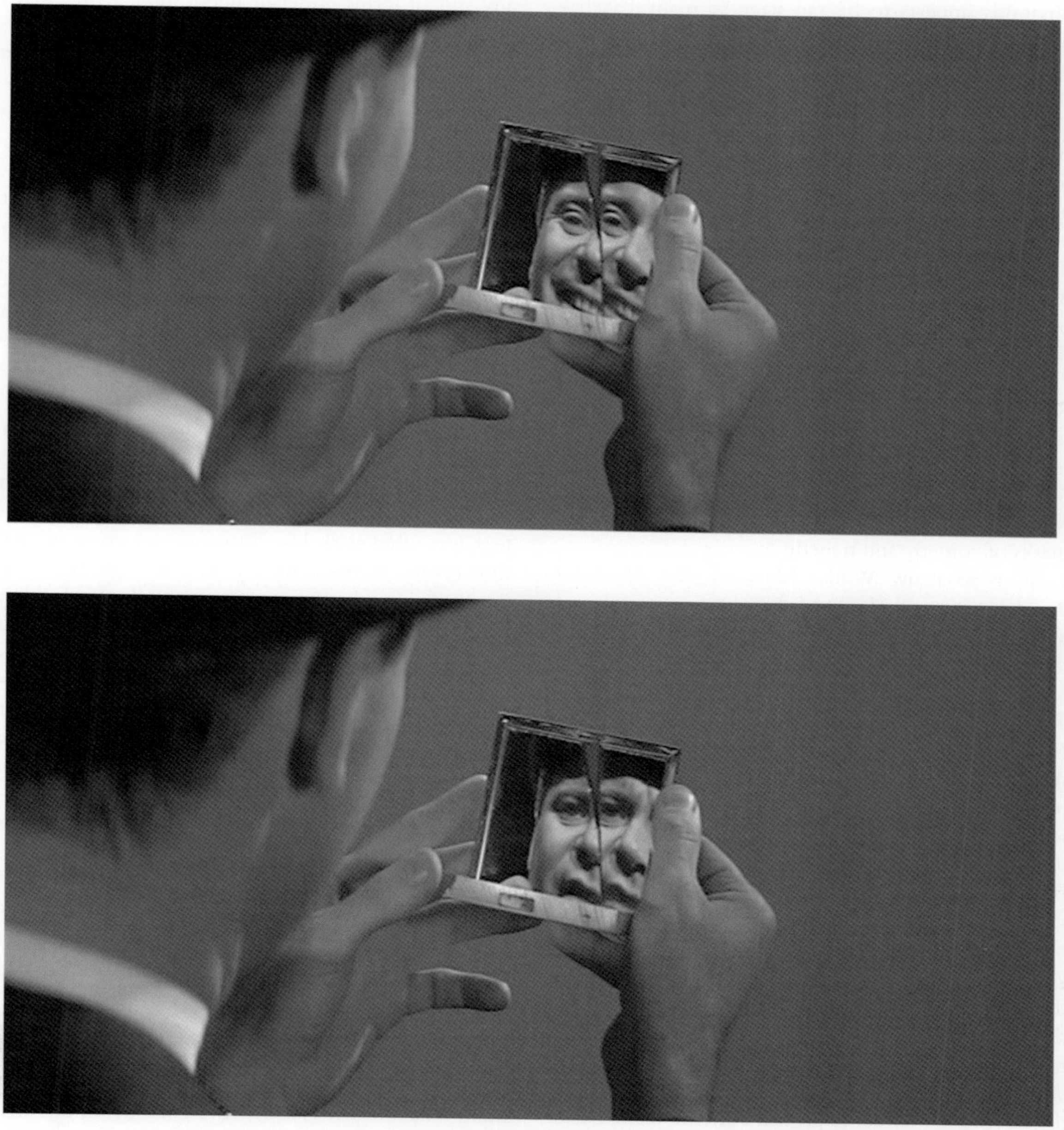

Figure 28.3 C. C. Baxter (Jack Lemmon) veers from joy to heartbreak as he realizes, through her broken compact mirror, that the woman he desires is the mistress of his boss, in *The Apartment* (1960, director and producer Billy Wilder).

anonymity toward the perks of a junior executive has led him to acquiesce in the amorous intrigues of his bosses: He lends them the key to his West Side apartment so they can conduct extramarital affairs with the company's female underlings, from secretaries to switchboard operators. The apartment hosts so many assignations – while Baxter works late at the office or catches cold on a park bench – that his landlady and next-door neighbors, who are Jewish, cannot comprehend how such a "schmuck" and "nebbish" as he obviously appears to be can stage so many bacchanals. Baxter gains his promotion after he gives the key to the head of personnel, Sheldrake (Fred MacMurray), who is seeking to rekindle his illicit affair with an elevator operator, Fran Kubelik (Shirley MacLaine). Baxter is himself enamored of Miss Kubelik, and the screenplay shapes a brilliant device to drive home the pathos of this unequal triangle. He finds a makeup compact with a broken mirror left behind by Sheldrake's lover in his apartment. When he returns it to Sheldrake, the executive opens it and complacently observes in the mirror the two-faced image of his duplicity (he lets Baxter know that the relationship is "just for laughs"). Later, when Baxter seeks to court Kubelik, she hands him her compact so he can see in its mirror how he looks in a new hat. As he realizes from the broken mirror that she was the woman with Sheldrake in his apartment, his face turns from smile to despair, enacting in a single gesture the theatrical masks of comedy and tragedy.

As in so many Wilder films, in *The Apartment* deception is a central trait of character motivation and behavior. In different works deception takes different forms: the insurance scam in *Double Indemnity*, Norma Desmond's self-deception in *Sunset Boulevard*, Chuck Tatum's deception for ambition's sake in *Ace in the Hole*. Here deception is performance in the private sphere. Sheldrake performs the role of an unhappy husband in a crumbling marriage to hold on to his serial girlfriends, who hope for some connection more than casual. The break comes for Kubelik when, in Baxter's apartment on Christmas Eve, harried by his split obligations, Sheldrake's act falters and he pulls a bill out of his wallet, saying, "Here's $100. Go buy yourself something." Crushed, and then left alone in the apartment, Kubelik takes an overdose of Baxter's sleeping pills. When Baxter arrives in time to save her, calling on his neighbor Dr Dreyfuss for help, the young man chooses to maintain his performance as a dissolute roué in order to protect both the woman and his boss.

The doctor (Jack Kruschen, who was nominated for a supporting actor Oscar, along with Lemmon and MacLaine for best actor and actress) urges Baxter to "be a mensch," while his wife (Naomi Stevens), bringing chicken soup to the recovering woman, berates Baxter as "Max the Knife," a "beatnik" for using paper towels as napkins, and "King Farouk" for any and all forms of debauchery. Some writers have criticized an excess of Jewish shtick in these scenes, but a key to the film's achievement lies in its capacity to meld comedy and pathos through language, particularly with isolated nuggets of slang or contemporary reference that lighten and energize the text.

The Apartment succeeds above all on the foundation of its writing. Sikov quotes Diamond saying that Wilder first thought of developing the concept into a play, but opted for film instead because of the difficulty of realizing both the mammoth office and intimate apartment on a stage (1998, 431). Yet mammoth office aside, the film retains the character of a stage work, or perhaps one might think of the *kammerspiel* (chamber play) genre of Weimar-era German cinema. Even within Trauner's extraordinary settings – Baxter's apartment as well as the insurance offices – Wilder, his cinematographer Joseph LaShelle, and editor Daniel Mandell appear content too often with big close-ups and conventional shot-reverse shot continuity with a single figure in the Panavision widescreen frame (Hollywood didn't complain: Mandell won the Oscar for editing, as did Trauner along with Edward G. Boyle for art direction/set decoration; LaShelle was nominated for cinematography and Gordon Sawyer for sound). Wilder may have been making a joke about his own stylistic proclivities when he shows Baxter surfing channels on his television set and viewing snippets of exciting, fast-paced mobile camera Western action scenes: Indians chasing a coach in *Stagecoach*; the US cavalry charging, from *Fort Apache*; and a wild saloon brawl.

Wilder's next film, *One, Two, Three* (1961), suffered from bad timing: A comedy about East–West relations in divided Berlin, it was partly completed before but released after East Germany put up the Berlin Wall, which rendered the subject considerably less amusing. His following picture, however, was in every way a success. Reuniting MacLaine and Lemmon, *Irma la Douce* (1963) was a comedy set in Paris, in which the former plays a streetwalker and the latter an uptight policeman who falls for the prostitute, becomes her pimp, and then disguises himself as a client to keep her away from other men. A marker of Hollywood's easing moral stricture – and no doubt made more palatable by its fanciful foreign setting in which two recognizably American actors seem to be playacting at wicked sophistication – the film was one of Wilder's major box office triumphs. Even Godard liked it:

> Thanks to the keenness and delicacy of its Panavision, thanks to the limpidity of the acting of Jack and Shirley, thanks to the delicacy of the colours of LaShelle and Trauner, sweet Irma, as I say, sets a wonderful seal on a twin ascension to box-office and to art. The outcome: a combination of qualities peculiarly sufficient to turn a gentleman-in-waiting into a film-maker arrived. (1972, 204)

Wilder, an *auteur* at last!

Kiss Me, Stupid

And then he blew it. That at least is one way to look at the more-or-less disaster of *Kiss Me, Stupid* (1964). Once again, the issue may have been timing, but it was not an external circumstance like the Berlin Wall that mattered, it was more a matter of gauging the nature and velocity of cultural transformation. At the top of his game, acclaimed both commercially and as an artist, Wilder may have let his antenna down. Perhaps it was a simple matter of hubris. A man who, however likable, was frequently described by coworkers as calculating, ruthless, imperious – no doubt all prerequisites for a successful career as a Hollywood director – was about to get his comeuppance.

Wilder and Diamond based *Kiss Me, Stupid* on an Italian stage farce. In their version, it also becomes a self-reflexive commentary on creative collaboration, Wilder's way of writing movies. In the crudely named fictional town of Climax, a dusty, out-of-the-way hamlet in the Nevada desert, an aspiring songwriting team, Orville (Ray Walston), a piano teacher, and Barney (Cliff Osmond), an auto mechanic, have been perennial failures in gaining the attention of producers or vocalists for their tunes (which, in one of the film's jokes, are in fact drawn from the songbook of George and Ira Gershwin). By happenstance the Las Vegas crooner Dino (Dean Martin, in a game self-parody) drives through town. Barney seizes the chance to present their songs to a possible buyer by disabling Dino's car to make him stay overnight, and then promotes a scheme to entertain the fabled ladies' man by offering him Orville's wife for his comfort. Only they'll substitute a local bargirl/prostitute, Polly the Pistol (Kim Novak), for the wife, so matrimonial fidelity would not be compromised.

Kiss Me, Stupid opens with farce at full throttle and rarely lets up. One problem with the film lies in its casting. The character of Orville was to be played by Peter Sellers, who had demonstrated in *Dr. Strangelove* and many other films the shape-shifting range to portray a wimpy piano teacher absurdly but groundlessly jealous of his beautiful wife Zelda (Felicia Farr) yet also capable of risking his marriage by acquiescing in Barney's plan as "a business promotion." Sellers actually began work on the film, but tensions with Wilder may have contributed to a medical crisis that almost cost the actor his life and led to his leaving the project. Brought in as substitute, Walston, dependable as a character actor in films and the star of a television science fiction comedy, *My Favorite Martian*, fell significantly short of Sellers's comic capacity to be ingratiating even when behaving bizarrely. Nor did it help that Barney's machinations, as Osmond plays him, appear less wacky than malevolent. But it is not appropriate to blame the actors for the sour, unsubtle tone undoubtedly set by the producer-director-writer.

For spectators who didn't walk out in the middle – a phenomenon that several reviewers noted – the last act is actually quite tender in its way, though an egregious affront to conventional morality. Orville refuses to pimp his surrogate spouse to Dino and ends up in bed with Polly; Zelda, sleeping off a lonely drunk in Polly's trailer, finds unexpected solace when the randy singer mistakes her for the prostitute (these consummations are signaled with a closing door and a fade to black). All four participants draw satisfaction from these dual adulteries, which produce only positive outcomes, against every stricture of the crumbling Production Code.

If the Code had become toothless and moribund, the Roman Catholic Legion of Decency still attempted to impose its moral standards on films, while offering injunctions and prohibitions to parishioners. It objected more strenuously to *Kiss Me, Stupid* than to any other film in years and succeeded in forcing some changes (an alternate editing of the encounter between Zelda and Dino exists as an added feature on DVD, but it is unclear which version was in the original release print). Reviewers, however, did not need the Legion's prompting to register their

Figure 28.4 Polly the Pistol (Kim Novak) and Zelda Spooner (Felicia Farr) after a night of switched roles, as wife and prostitute, in *Kiss Me, Stupid* (1964, director and producer Billy Wilder).

distaste. At the mainstream end of the critical spectrum, Thomas Thompson in *Life* wrote,

> What [Wilder] put on the screen can be compared with one of those dirty jokes that somebody tells at a sedate party. *Kiss Me, Stupid* is a titanic dirty joke, an embarrassment to audiences, the performers and the industry which produced it. (1965, 51)

At the opposite film buff end, *Films in Review*, journal of the erstwhile censorship organization National Board of Review, was if anything even more scathing, regarding the film as an attack on the nation's virtue and Wilder as an alien interloper. "*Kiss Me, Stupid* comes out of Wilder and I. A. L. Diamond['s] heads, not out of American life, and its situation and action are far from US reality," Adelaide Comerford asserted. "Americans ultimately tire of having the hand that feeds bitten" (1965, 118).

From a perspective looking back, it is difficult to imagine the United States circa 1965 as akin to a "sedate party" or "US reality" as proper as Comerford implies. *Kiss Me, Stupid* is in many ways a failure but it deserves attention as an index to the confusions of mind both of its maker and the nation at large at a historical moment of fundamental change. Wilder was not again to play so significant a role in representing American values and mores on screen, even though he continued to work through the early 1980s, completing six more films, nearly a quarter of his total corpus as director: *The Fortune Cookie* (1966), *The Private Life of Sherlock Holmes* (1970), *Avanti!* (1972), *The Front Page* (1974), *Fedora* (1978), and *Buddy Buddy* (1981). The first of these gained Wilder (with Diamond) his final Oscar nomination, for screenplay. The prizes after that came in the form of lifetime achievement awards.

What does it mean to speak of Billy Wilder as author of the films that bear his name, was a question posed at the beginning of this essay. As it happens, film theorist C. Paul Sellors asks a similar question at the beginning of his insightful reflections on the authorship wars, *Film Authorship: Auteurs and Other Myths*. Sellors opens his book by describing a scene from *Sunset Boulevard* and then listing some of the creative personnel who contributed to shaping it. "Who is the author of *Sunset Blvd.*?" Sellors inquires.

> The answer "Billy Wilder" may come to mind because he is the director of the film. Given the significant contributions from others working on the film, and the extent that it incorporates existing material, this answer does not seem entirely justified. (2010, 2)

We have come a long way from the *politique des auteurs* and the "*auteur* theory." If Sellors is calling Wilder's authorship into question, it is not because the director lacked technique or possessed a cynical soul; it is because authorship in cinema rarely can be attributed to a single individual. Determining actual responsibility, or creativity, is a task for historical research. In the case of Wilder the controversy over his status as an auteur – he was neither the lone author nor the mere studio craftsman, as admirers and detractors, respectively, have pictured him – has hampered assessment of his career. From the days when, with other émigré artists, he submitted a screenplay in German, to his fortuitous teaming with Charles Brackett and beyond to his mature years as producer-director, out of necessity and then out of wisdom, he made a principle of choosing skilled and sympathetic partners, as he sought also to fashion films as expressions of his own unique voice. If creativity in the American movie industry is almost invariably achieved through collaboration, then Billy Wilder, auteur or not, should be recognized as one of the consummate practitioners of Hollywood's form of art.

Notes

1. In the confines of this essay I've chosen for this juncture in Wilder's career not to write about this well-known film but on its successor, the neglected 1951 *Ace in the Hole*; for my extensive discussion of *Sunset Boulevard* in a different context see Sklar 2011.
2. The discussion of *Ace in the Hole* draws on material from my review of the Criterion Collection DVD in *Cineaste*, 33.2 (2008), 67–69.

References

Barthes, Roland. (1977). "The Death of the Author." In *Image-Music-Text*, trans. Stephen Heath (pp. 142–148). New York: Hill & Wang.

Biesen, Sheri Chinen. (2005). *Blackout: World War II and the Origins of Film Noir*. Baltimore: Johns Hopkins University Press.

Borde, Raymond, & Chaumeton, Etienne. (2002). *A Panorama of American Film Noir, 1941–1953*, trans. Paul Hammond. San Francisco: City Lights. (Originally published as *Panorama du film noir américain*, 1955.)

Comerford, Adelaide. (1965). "*Kiss Me, Stupid*." *Films in Review*, 16.2, 118.

Comolli, Jean-Louis, et al. (1986). "Twenty Years On: A Discussion about American Cinema and the *politique des auteurs*." In Jim Hillier (ed.), *Cahiers du Cinéma, 1960–1968: New Wave, New Cinema, Reevaluating Hollywood* (pp. 196–209). Cambridge, MA: Harvard University Press. (Originally published as "Vingt ans après. Le cinéma américain et la politique des auteurs," *Cahiers du Cinéma*, 172, November, 1965.)

Crofts, Stephen. (1983). "Authorship and Hollywood." *Wide Angle*, 5.3, 16–22.

Foucault, Michel. (1977). "What Is an Author?" In *Language, Counter-Memory, Practice: Selected Essays and Interviews*, trans. Donald F. Bouchard & Sherry Simon (pp. 113–138). Ithaca: Cornell University Press.

Godard, Jean-Luc. (1972). *Godard on Godard*, ed. and trans. Tom Milne. New York: Da Capo Press.

Luhr, William. (1991). *Raymond Chandler and Film*. 2nd edn. Tallahassee: Florida State University Press. (Original work published 1982.)

McBride, Joseph, & McCarthy, Todd. (2001). "Going for Extra Innings." In Robert Horton (ed.), *Billy Wilder Interviews* (pp. 140–160). Jackson: University Press of Mississippi. (Originally published in *Film Comment*, January–February 1979.)

Sarris, Andrew. (1974). "Notes on the Auteur Theory in 1962." In Gerald Mast & Marshall Cohen (eds), *Film Theory and Criticism: Introductory Readings* (pp. 500–515). New York: Oxford University Press. (Originally published in *Film Culture*, 27, Winter 1962–1963.)

Sarris, Andrew. (1985). *The American Cinema: Directors and Directions, 1929–1968*. Chicago: University of Chicago Press. (Original work published 1968.)

Sarris, Andrew. (1998). *"You Ain't Heard Nothin' Yet": The American Talking Film, History and Memory, 1927–1949*. New York: Oxford University Press.

Schatz, Thomas. (1988). *The Genius of the System: Hollywood Filmmaking in the Studio Era*. New York: Pantheon.

Schlöndorff, Volker, & Grischow, Gisela (dirs). (2006). *Billy Wilder Speaks*. Documentary film.

Sellors, C. Paul. (2010). *Film Authorship: Auteurs and Other Myths*. London: Wallflower.

Sikov, Ed. (1998). *On Sunset Boulevard: The Life and Times of Billy Wilder*. New York: Hyperion.

Sklar, Robert. (2011). "Hollywood about Hollywood: Genre as Historiography." In J. E. Smyth (ed.), *American Historical Film* (pp. 71–93). London: Palgrave.

Thompson, Thomas. (1965). "Wilder's Dirty-Joke Film Stirs a Furor." *Life*, January 15, 51.

Tresgot, Annie, & Ciment, Michel (dirs). (1982). *Portrait of a "60% Perfect Man": Billy Wilder*. Documentary film.

Truffaut, François. (1976). "A Certain Tendency of the French Cinema." In Bill Nichols (ed.), *Movies and Methods: An Anthology* (pp. 224–237). Berkeley: University of California Press. (Originally published as "Une certaine tendance du cinéma français," *Cahiers du Cinéma,* 31, January 1954.)

Wilder, Billy, & Crowe, Cameron. (1999). *Conversations with Wilder.* New York: Knopf.

Wollen, Peter. (1981). "The Auteur Theory" (extract). In John Caughie (ed.), *Theories of Authorship: A Reader* (pp. 138–151). London: Routledge & Kegan Paul. (Originally published in Peter Wollen, *Signs and Meanings in the Cinema,* 1969.)

29

Cold War Thrillers

R. Barton Palmer
Professor, Clemson University, United States

R. Barton Palmer examines the **Cold War thriller** in the context of anticommunist political rhetoric and actions in the post–World War II era, including the **Truman Doctrine**, responses to the **Korean War**, **HUAC**, and the **Senate Permanent Subcommittee on Investigations** chaired by **Joseph McCarthy**. Numerous Hollywood and newly independent productions of the period both explicitly and implicitly register not only **anticommunist paranoia** but also – more gingerly in light of the **blacklist** – threats posed by authoritarian governmental suspicion and surveillance. Palmer deftly surveys dozens of films, from those lesser-known like *The Big Lift*, *Invasion U.S.A.*, *I Was a Communist for the FBI*, and *The Atomic City* to the more recognized, sometime classics like *The Steel Helmet*, *Fail-Safe*, *The Iron Curtain*, *Pickup on South Street*, and *The Manchurian Candidate*. Palmer's essay shares ground with Roy Grundmann on *The Strange Love of Martha Ivers*, Christine Noll Brinckmann on *Force of Evil*, and Cynthia Baron and Beckett Warren on the Actors Studio in this volume, and with Larry Ceplair on Hollywood unions and blacklists in the hardcover/online edition.

Additional terms, names, and concepts: George F. Kennan and "diplomatic victory," containment, "city confidential" films, film noir, semi-documentary form

A Diplomatic Victory?

A forceful and articulate analyst with unusually extensive diplomatic experience, George F. Kennan became the chief strategic architect of national policy during what became known as the Cold War, that long period of hostility, rivalry, and proxy conflicts that characterized the relationship between the United States and the USSR and their clients from the late 1940s to the fall of the Soviet Union in 1991. In the famous 1946 "Long Telegram" that he sent from Moscow to the State Department,

American Film History: Selected Readings, Origins to 1960, First Edition. Edited by Cynthia Lucia, Roy Grundmann, and Art Simon.
© 2016 John Wiley & Sons, Inc. Published 2016 by John Wiley & Sons, Inc.

Kennan's main argument was that the Soviet Union, by the logic of Marxist-Leninism, was driven toward an expansionist foreign policy that treated the outside world

> as evil, hostile and menacing, but as bearing within itself germs of creeping disease and destined to be wracked with growing internal convulsions until it is given [the] final *Coup de grace* by [the] rising power of socialism and yields to [a] new and better world. (Kennan 1947)

The United States, so Kennan advised, should in response devote its main energies toward resolving such explosive domestic issues as institutionalized racism and class inequality. The object was to improve the image of the nation abroad and reassure the American people in a time of growing uncertainty. Here was a public relations project of epic proportions that the Hollywood film industry soon found itself engaging, if unofficially and of its own accord. No call for action issued from Washington, but none was needed. Studio heads, as well as the independent producers then beginning to shape decisively the industry's product, were eager to turn out films that dramatized that stance. A cinematic series – the Cold War thriller in its various forms – was the result. Whether these films contributed to the "diplomatic victory" Kennan hoped for is a question that is impossible to answer. Cold War thrillers were often embarrassingly chauvinistic and obviously propagandistic, but they regularly proved at least moderately successful with audiences. In treating those films released during the years 1945–1965, I will place a special emphasis on lesser-known releases that are most useful for illuminating the politics of the period, both national and cinematic.

Neurotic and Paranoid Views of World Affairs

In the early postwar period, the terms of this informally organized program of cinematic representation were set by the evolving nature of the conflict itself, which was waged abroad and also, if surreptitiously for the most part, in the American public sphere. Like many in the Truman administration, George Kennan believed that opposition to Soviet designs on an increased sphere of influence and the spread of communism more generally should be proactive: "the main element of any United States policy toward the Soviet Union must be a long-term, patient but vigilant containment of Russian expansive tendencies" (Kennan 1947).

Kennan's strategy of containment would become the main principle of the Truman Doctrine, promulgated in March 1947, according to which US policy should be directed toward thwarting Soviet (indeed, any communist) initiatives abroad. It was in this atmosphere of heightening military threat that American statesman and dedicated internationalist Bernard Baruch dubbed the East/West rivalry the "Cold War." While thus acknowledging the proxy, indirect nature of the conflict, Baruch and others recognized that this ideological struggle could break out into actual fighting on any number of barely foreseeable fronts. It was thus not much of a surprise that the North Korean invasion of South Korea in 1950 signaled the advent of a proxy war that dominated world politics for three years, especially after Communist China "unofficially" entered the conflict.

The Hollywood response to the conflict in Korea and its disappointing inconclusion (despite more than 36,000 American battlefield deaths) was in large measure to produce the kind of morale-boosting war films that had been such a staple of industry production during World War II. At least two films, however, were exceptions to this rule, exploring in some depth the ideological nature of the conflict. In Samuel Fuller's *The Steel Helmet*, released in 1951 by Lippert Studios, a captured North Korean officer attempts to convince the African-American and Japanese-American members of the platoon escorting him back to base that the system they live under not only fails to live up to its official Jeffersonianism, but is also committed officially to perpetuating a violent and destructive racism. Unusual for a Hollywood film of the period, *The Steel Helmet* offers frank and disturbing (if brief) discussion of the lynching of blacks in the South and the daily insult of segregated facilities; attention is also called to the unconstitutional internment of Japanese-Americans during World War II. The soldiers in question, however, remain loyal to their country, accepting its promise of a just society and rejecting as empty and unrealizable the Marxist platitudes spouted by the enemy officer. The importance of the current war against communism is underlined by the fact that one of the members of the platoon had been a conscientious objector during

World War II. In the midst of this current life and death ideological struggle, he finds such idealism no longer tenable. Even the squad's medic removes his Red Cross armband to man a machine gun when the group seems about to be overrun by a human wave attack of fanatic North Koreans.

Andrew Marton's *Prisoner of War*, released by MGM in 1954, demonizes the enemy by dramatizing the then widespread (and largely factual) charges by the United Nations forces that the enemy were mistreating prisoners of war, including the use of torture and psychological techniques (popularly known as "brainwashing"). Ronald Reagan stars as an army officer, Capt. Web Sloane, who allows himself to be taken prisoner simply to learn the truth about these brutal allegations. He becomes part of a death march in which only 211 of the original group of 718 prisoners survive, and then witnesses the collusion of Russian officers as they plan and execute brutal methods of "behavior modification." In calling attention to the enemy's undoubtedly abusive treatment of POWs, the film, true to its propagandistic intentions, has nothing to say about the widespread and horrific retribution exacted by South Korean military forces, sometimes under US direction, from suspected communist sympathizers. Even with these strategic exclusions, *Prisoner of War* presents a persuasive case that the Cold War rivalry is a deadly struggle, ideological and military, in which quarter will neither be expected nor given. *The Steel Helmet* suggests much the same, beginning as it does with the aftermath of a North Korean slaughter of American prisoners that seems based on the carefully documented POW shootings that took place early in the war on Hills 312 and 303 around the Pusan perimeter.

Could the Korean War have been avoided had a Cold War mentality not taken hold in Washington? As the 1940s had drawn to a close, Kennan, supported by influential pundits like journalist Walter Lippmann, himself began to argue for the opening of discussions with the Soviets in order to solve or at least mitigate outstanding disagreements and differences of vision about the nature of the postwar world. Ironically, he was quickly marginalized within the State Department by advocates of black-and-white ideological thinking, particularly Secretary of State Dean Acheson. These influential supporters of the Truman Doctrine, so Kennan opined years later, distorted his advocacy of containment, which was initially meant to be largely economic and political. Instead, Acheson and company "pursued it exclusively as a military concept; and I think that that, as much as any other cause, led to [the] 40 years of unnecessary, fearfully expensive and disoriented process of the Cold War" (Kennan 1996).

One consequence was that the Cold War soon turned into a nuclear arms race that threatened destruction on a global scale. In consequence, more Americans found themselves adopting positions similar to those of Lippmann and Kennan, questioning the staunch anticommunism that had become the cornerstone of national foreign policy. From the late 1950s, moreover, there was a growing belief among many in the US that a vigorous anticommunism was counterproductive in terms of winning hearts and minds, chiefly because US support was often lent to authoritarian, repressive regimes whose one necessary virtue was that they opposed Russian or so-called communist initiatives. Joseph L. Mankiewicz's *The Quiet American*, released by United Artists in 1958, dramatizes this conflicting attitude in the tragic story of an idealistic young American diplomat (memorably played by World War II war hero Audie Murphy) who is murdered because he cannot understand how Vietnamese nationalism, though taking for strategic reasons a communist form, threatens no American interests.

Until the end of the Korean War, however, such productions would never have come from Hollywood. Those in the industry would have been pilloried as pinkos or fellow travelers for even suggesting that some communists might pose no threat to US interests; blacklisting and thus career ruin would have been a real possibility. But as the 1950s drew to a close, the national mood did shift decisively. In 1960, voters rejected, if barely, Richard Nixon's bid to continue Eisenhower's foreign policies; Nixon had staked his career on a vigorous opposition to communism. The outbreak of nuclear war, and its inevitable horrific aftermath, was a grim possibility that Hollywood had already begun to explore. Stanley Kramer's *On the Beach*, released in 1959 by United Artists, examined how the world might end after a mutually destructive nuclear war between the superpowers. Civilization, indeed life on earth itself, grinds slowly to a halt in an Australia inexorably engulfed by fallout. The last survivors of the human race commit suicide rather than face a horrible death from radiation poisoning, in perhaps the bleakest finale ever of any Hollywood release.

An even grimmer outcome of East/West rivalry is dramatized in 1964's *Fail-Safe*, a Columbia release directed by Sidney Lumet. Here mechanical failure results in a flight of long-range bombers dispatched toward Russia. Efforts at recall fail, as the president of the United States (Henry Fonda) and his Russian counterpart desperately struggle to avoid the worst, ironically discovering *in extremis* a basis for trust and cooperation that had previously eluded them. Moscow is wiped off the map, and the president is forced to make history's most disagreeable decision: ordering a nuclear bomb to be dropped on New York City, where he knows his wife is visiting, in order to satisfy the demands of *lex talionis* (an eye for an eye) and thereby avert an even costlier retaliation from the Soviets. John Frankenheimer's *Seven Days in May*, a 1964 Paramount release, similarly meditates on what might be the self-destructive consequences of Cold War fears. In this political thriller, a liberal president (Fredric March) follows the path then advocated by Kennan and Lippmann, offering to open negotiations with the Russians about nuclear arms reduction or elimination. The country's more right-wing military leaders, including the head of the Joint Chiefs of Staff, a ramrod stiff Air Force general (Burt Lancaster), find this diplomatic initiative threatening enough to plot a military coup, which is foiled only by the quick thinking and reflex patriotism of a junior officer (Kirk Douglas). Lancaster's swaggering performance heightens the script's all-too-obvious references to Air Force General Curtis LeMay, who had strongly argued in October 1961 for a preemptive nuclear strike on Cuba. *Seven Days in May* carried a powerful message about the danger, foreseen by the Founding Fathers, that is posed to civilian government by the kind of powerful professional military the Cold War required.

Even when they avoid imagining the unimaginable, other Cold War films of this later era, such as Martin Ritt's *The Spy Who Came In From the Cold* (released in 1965 by Paramount), routinely construe the superpower rivalry as pointlessly destructive.

This point, of course, had been made even earlier and most memorably by Stanley Kubrick in his black comedy *Dr. Strangelove, or How I Learned to Stop Worrying and Love the Bomb*, released by Columbia in early 1964. Kubrick's psychotic or cold-hearted military leaders seemed cut from the same mold as the most ardent supporters of Barry Goldwater, the extremist Republican trounced by Johnson in the 1964 presidential election. In the film's poetically just finale, US headquarters, along with the rest of the world, is destroyed by a "Doomsday device" that the Russians trigger in retaliation for a nuclear bomber strike ordered by a psychotic Air Force commander. The world ends in a mushroom cloud.

Fortress America?

In the first decade or so of the postwar era, however, Hollywood offered no trenchant criticism of the containment strategy and the inevitable, distasteful political compromises such a policy entailed simply on the basis of the strategic principle that the enemy of my enemy is my friend. Events such as the reluctance of the Eisenhower administration to support with more than words the Hungarian Revolt of 1956, widely perceived in the US as a betrayal of the Truman Doctrine (*Time* magazine featured "the Hungarian freedom fighter" as its "man of the year"), did not find representation on the silver screen. At least in terms of its releases, the film industry also strongly supported for almost a decade the domestic struggle against enemy espionage and infiltration. The threat from domestic communists and Soviet agents, which was real enough but on a rather small scale, began to be imagined by many as more pervasive, as a clear and present danger demanding action.

One national response was investigatory. The House Un-American Activities Committee (HUAC), which became a permanent committee in 1945, and the Senate Permanent Subcommittee on Investigations in the early 1950s, chaired by the soon notorious Joseph McCarthy, conducted widely publicized inquiries into the supposed communist connections of key figures within the government and the media, most notoriously in the film, radio, and television industries, as well as in the Army. Unsurprisingly, it is this aspect of the Cold War, rather than international rivalries of various kinds, that received the most substantial treatment from Hollywood.

These films, however, present the domestic threat posed by communism in radically different ways. Americans, Kennan had argued, should not feel powerless, even if they had good reason to fear an ever watchful enemy. Americans were living in a free and prosperous society whose system of government (unlike that of the Soviet Union) had stood the test of time. The Soviet Union, Kennan presciently believed, might just collapse from the dead weight of its own economic unworkability, especially when the linked benefits of capitalism and participatory democracy became known to those who found themselves trapped behind the Iron Curtain.

Interestingly, one of the earliest films of the Cold War cycle, William Wellman's *The Iron Curtain*, released by Fox in 1948, examines just that feature of the postwar Russian *mentalité*. The film dramatizes the inherently self-destructive energies and incapacities of the Soviet system, avoiding the black and white thinking abhorred by Kennan, which became, unfortunately, the apparent guiding principle of most later Hollywood productions. *The Iron Curtain* is based on the actual experiences of Igor Gouzenko, a Soviet code clerk who is dispatched during the closing days of World War II to his nation's embassy in Ottawa. Establishing a life in Canada with his wife, Anna (Gene Tierney), and newborn son, Gouzenko (Dana Andrews) rapidly loses his commitment to the espionage duties he has been assigned once the ostensible enemy turns out not to fit what he had been taught about capitalist exploiters. A trusted colleague, who is a decorated veteran, betrays to Igor his own profound doubts about the morality of the system he has been sworn to support, openly confronts the station chief with the party's hypocrisy, and resigns himself to immediate liquidation upon his return home.

Living in democratic Canada and watching their neighbors go about their business with no interference from the government, the Gouzenkos, moreover, begin to resent the constant surveillance they find themselves under from their ostensible colleagues. In a short time, the couple become thoroughly Westernized. With his term of duty about to expire, Igor decides to seek political asylum as a defector. He steals from the embassy files the documents that detail the extensive Soviet spy network in the country, which, as the film dramatizes, has found success obtaining information about the Canadian contribution to atomic weapons research. In contrast to those in his own embassy, who are dominated by distrust and paranoia, the Ottawa officials to whom he shows the documents do not at first take Gouzenko seriously. The truth, so the film's narrator proclaims, is simply "too big, too incredible." Gouzenko, however, puts his faith in an institution whose function in a free society he has only recently come to realize: the press. Only when he goes to a leading newspaper does he find one reporter willing to believe what he says and help Gouzenko get his information to the proper authorities. Resettled in a remote part of Canada, Gouzenko must live out the rest of his life in fear that Soviet agents will find and kill him; a detail of protecting police can never leave his side, an ironic comment on the fact that the refugees now live in a free country.

The Iron Curtain reveals the substantial threat of Soviet spy networks, whose most dangerous members are committed native communists. John Grubb (Berry Kroeger), head of the Canadian Communist Party, is a smarmy yet effective seducer of the intellectually gullible who manages to "turn" both a high-ranking Air Force officer and also a scientist with access to atomic secrets (a character clearly based on the notorious Alan Nunn May, who served 10 years for espionage). In his mistaken liberalism, this scientist supports the "people's war" against fascism and is convinced by Grubb that only if Russia also possesses the bomb will there be an end to global conflict. It turns out that these efforts to subvert the West are undone not by the Canadian authorities but by a man of conscience within the spy ring itself, who is persuaded to betray his country by nothing more dramatic than the evidence of his own experience.

Its exteriors shot in Ottawa, *The Iron Curtain* adopts a thoroughly deglamorized and unsensationalized realist style (there are no action sequences to speak of) in order to deliver a sobering yet uplifting message: Only when the struggle against communism is won will those in the West be able to enjoy full freedom. In a finely conceived ironic touch, the great orchestral classics of Soviet composers from Shostakovich to Prokofiev and Miskovsky play continually in the embassy decoding room in order to drown out the conspiratorial conversation of the spymasters in the adjoining suite. But these same beautiful themes are heard in other sequences as a musical accompaniment to the dramatic encounters of the characters. The score is especially prominent in the film's closing sequences, as Gouzenko and his family effect their escape, abandoning for good their national identity. By refusing to demonize the enemy, *The Iron*

Curtain brilliantly walks a fine line between condemning the Soviet system, on the one hand, and, on the other, showing a deserved respect for Russian culture and the Russian people.

Foreign Intrigues

Other films of the late 1940s and early 1950s offer a glimpse (usually somewhat sympathetic) into what was thought to be going on in the lives of ordinary people living behind the Iron Curtain. Like *The Iron Curtain*, Felix Feist's *Guilty of Treason* (released by the British Eagle-Lion in 1950) also offers a thinly fictionalized version of Soviet and eastern European experience, using the arrest and trial of Hungary's Catholic primate, Cardinal Mindszenty, as a framework for exploring the growing disillusionment of Soviet subjects with the system. Mindszenty (Charles Bickford) heroically resists an inexpertly organized attempt to paint him as a traitor because of his public criticism of the continuing Soviet occupation; the film grimly details the various forms of torture, both psychological and physical, to which the cardinal is subjected and over which, in the end, he is perceived as having triumphed despite an obviously drug-induced "repudiation" of "past errors." *Guilty of Treason*, however, is most effective in dramatizing the growing rift over the Mindszenty affair that soured relations between Russia and its erstwhile client state. The cardinal's arrest fatally strains the romantic relationship between Hungarian artist Stephanie Varna (Bonita Granville) and Russian colonel Alex Melnikov (Richard Derr), who works for the occupation force. Varna, who fought with the French resistance during the war against Hitler, finds herself persuaded of the cardinal's innocence and puts herself in danger by speaking out against his arrest. Her lover tries to spirit her out of the country, but she refuses to abandon Hungary. Agonizing over his affection for the beautiful woman (which, if revealed to his superiors, could end up destroying him), Melnikov decides to remain faithful to his political beliefs and eventually gives Varna up to the secret police, who then torture her to death in a failed attempt to extract a confession.

Brokenhearted, Melnikov returns to their lovenest, where he is discovered by the secret police and killed. American journalist Tom Kelly (Paul Kelly), who has been sent to Budapest to get the "real story" of the Mindszenty affair, functions as the film's moral center. He tells Melnikov he is supporting a system that is just as evil as the Nazism he struggled so valiantly in a defensive war to resist, in effect simply exchanging one tyrant (Stalin) for another (Hitler). Badly beaten by a gang of former Hungarian Nazis turned Communist thugs, Kelly leaves Budapest after Mindszenty is predictably found guilty at the end of his show trial. If he returns to the safety of Paris, however, it is to deliver a stirring address to the Overseas Press Club. Kelly reminds his fellow members of the "free world" that the countries behind the Iron Curtain are not surrendering meekly to Soviet overlordship and that "liberty is everybody's business." Kelly is certain that the Russian domination of eastern European countries will continue to be resisted; the film presciently anticipates the dissatisfaction that would break out into widespread social unrest and work stoppages through East Germany in 1953 and then, soon afterward in 1956, into open revolt in Hungary. In such circumstances, the American role, Kelly proclaims, is to support the restoration of political freedom, especially by making sure the truth about the emerging Soviet system continues to be made known throughout the free world.

In his *The Big Lift* (released by Fox in 1950), George Seaton treats these same themes in a somewhat different key. In part, the film pays an extended tribute to the heroic efforts of the Army Air Corps to keep West Berlin supplied with food, medicine, and fuel when the Russians unexpectedly closed down land and water routes to the city in June 1948 and kept them closed until the following May in the first part of an attempt, it later emerged, to force the Allies out of occupied Germany. Seaton emphasizes how the round-the-clock flights sustained a population already suffering from the after-effects of the war (in a city that had experienced near total destruction), but the film otherwise has little to say about Soviet motives or communist ideology. Instead, *The Big Lift* concerns itself with postwar American attitudes toward the West Germans, recently a deadly enemy and now become necessary allies in the opposition to Russian expansionism. In the manner of the Italian Neorealists, Seaton uses the developing relationship between an American flyer, Danny MacCullough (Montgomery Clift), and a German widow, Frederica Burkhardt (Cornell Borchers), to explore the city (all exteriors were shot on location) and the lives of its inhabitants, who are shown struggling with the destruction caused by the war as they attempt to create a new culture under the watchful eyes of the Allies, who have taken responsibility for their welfare. Pursued at one point by the police, the couple manage to melt away into the crowd when they enter a traffic circle over which all four occupying powers claim sovereignty, if limited and hard to fix precisely. Their pursuers become too concerned with the question of proper jurisdiction to pay proper attention to the fugitives, a humorous development that speaks volumes about the fate of ordinary people in a postwar Europe increasingly dominated by petty rivalries among the victors.

Danny's sympathy for the Germans contrasts with the hatred felt by his flying partner Hank Kowalski (Paul Douglas), who, during his time in a prisoner-of-war camp, had been treated harshly and disrespectfully by his captors. One day, Hank comes across one of the guards who had mistreated him, but finds himself unable to take the kind of vengeance on that man that he had dreamed about. Despite these deep anti-German feelings, Kowalski develops, like Danny, a relationship with one of the city's numerous "schatzies" (dames), a young woman named Gerda (Bruni Löbel), who is eager to go to America one day and is spending all her free time studying the American system of government. Part of Hank's frustration with Gerda is that she asks him to explain the principles of democracy, a task he finds himself ill-equipped to do, though he is challenged by her irrepressible interest and learns from her the virtues of the system he lives under.

The film's treatment of its "sympathetic" Germans, however, is by no means simple. It turns out that Frederica has lied about her past. Her father was not a professor imprisoned for speaking out against National Socialism, and thus she has no connections to any resistance to Hitler. On the contrary, her husband had served in the Waffen SS and was thus a party member. Danny is eager that they should be married in any case, but, thanks to the watchfulness of one of her neighbors, Frederica is soon exposed as an opportunist eager to exploit marriage to Danny in order to gain US citizenship. Her intention is to divorce Danny once they have entered the country. She will then rejoin her German lover, who is already living in the States. At this point, it is announced that the Russian blockade has been lifted. Danny's unit returns home, but Kowalski decides to stay on and help with the Marshall Plan reconstruction of the country, exemplifying the change in heart toward the Germans that, in part because of the Cold War, had become official US policy.

Several less artistically successful productions of the early postwar period also treat, with different degrees of political depth and detail, the various difficulties of a Continental culture caught in the trap of ideological conflict as the political, social, and physical wreckage of civilization's most destructive war still waited to be cleared. George Sidney's *The Red Danube*, released by MGM in 1949, an otherwise unengaging melodrama, is notable for tackling the issue of what agreements should be kept with the Russians. Charged with carrying out the Allied commitment to repatriate Russian citizens living in Vienna's British zone, Colonel Michael Nicobar (Walter Pidgeon) finds himself aiding the escape to the West of a beautiful ballerina (Janet Leigh) after discovering how brutally the Russians treat returning displaced persons. *Diplomatic Courier*, directed by Henry Hathaway and released by Fox in 1952, offers a dark, suspenseful tale of postwar espionage in the divided city of Trieste. The film ends with the improbable, if ideologically satisfying, conversion of the beautiful Russian agent (Hildegarde Neff) to democratic principles as well as a romantic commitment to her handsome American counterpart (Tyrone Power). Victor Saville's *Conspirator*, released by MGM in 1950, updates the threatening-husband Gothic romance popularized by Hitchcock's *Rebecca* (1940) and George Cukor's *Gaslight* (1944) by providing it with political relevance. Starry-eyed newlywed Melinda Curragh (Elizabeth Taylor) slowly comes to realize that her handsome but maddeningly remote husband, Michael (Robert Taylor), a British major entrusted with sensitive intelligence work, is actually funneling state secrets to Russian agents. The film's political content is strikingly thin and certainly politically incorrect by current standards. Somewhat shockingly, it is revealed that Michael Curragh's motive for treason has little to do with the Cold War, but instead is the standard motive provided British traitors in World War II dramas. Curragh, we learn, is Irish, which seems to be all the explanation necessary to account for his conversion to communism and subsequent betrayal of the government he had fought and bled for during the German war.

Domestic Discontents

Hollywood's films dealing with the various European developments and foreign intrigues of Cold War politics nicely demonstrate that no thoroughgoing "fatalism" as such, despite Kennan's worries, is present in Hollywood's initial response to the Cold War. And this was true even though the social problem film anatomized the deficiencies of American society, particularly its pervasive racism, albeit from a positive, progressive perspective, in a cycle that became increasingly prominent in the early postwar years. And so, despite the persistence of the cliché, the films of this early era only sporadically exemplify anything like a collective hysteria over a supposed "Red Scare." Even those productions that can be viewed as somewhat paranoid in their treatment of the Soviet threat to American safety tend to conclude quite positively.

Most notably, Alfred Green's "B" programmer *Invasion U.S.A.* (released in 1952 by Columbia) ignores the strength of the containment strategy and makes the dubious case that American culture has again fallen into an isolationism that marks it as easy prey to Soviet aggression. Much of the film is an unconvincing pastiche of World War II combat footage and ineffectually staged action scenes (in which the "Russian" soldiers, in a bizarre move that reflects the film's minuscule budget, wear US uniforms and carry American weapons as a supposed "disguise"). *Invasion* delivers its message through the too-late conversion to political activism of four strangers (a businessman, Congressman, reporter, and industrialist) who find themselves in a New York bar when news comes through that the Russians have begun an air assault on Alaska. This attack is soon followed, implausibly enough from the viewpoint of military realities, by a massive ground invasion. At first, the war goes disastrously for the American side, with principal US cities destroyed by atomic bombs, until finally New York City falls. But all is not as it seems. As the film draws to a conclusion, it turns out that the "war" is simply a collective delusion induced by the fifth member of the group, a magician with seemingly occult powers who is eager to relieve his erstwhile companions of their nationally destructive self-involvement. Now "awakened" to supposed geopolitical realities, the four characters, in the manner of Scrooges who have internalized the bleak significance of Christmas future, resolve to support both an active policy of resistance to Russian encroachments and a thoroughgoing rearmament of the military.

Perhaps a more plausible danger was subversion of the American system from within, as diversions from domestic discontents of various kinds grew into an ever growing support for communism as a political philosophy. R. G. Springsteen's *Red Menace*, released by Republic in 1949, traces how an ex-serviceman, Bill Jones (Robert Rockwell), comes to flirt with communism after he becomes disenchanted with government attempts to recover money embezzled by a crooked home builder who is exploiting the recently instituted housing provisions of the G.I. Bill of Rights. Bill's fiancée deserts him after they are bilked of their down-payment, putting an end to his dreams of postwar middle-class respectability. At the Veterans Service Center, Bill is approached by Jack Tyler (William J. Lally), a member of the local Communist Party who hangs out there in order to prey on the disgruntled. In an attempt to complete this seduction, Tyler introduces Bill to a beautiful woman, Mollie O'Flaherty (Barbra Fuller), who quickly beds him. Bill, escorted by Mollie, soon meets up at party headquarters with a stereotypical gallery of other disgruntled citizens: a Jewish poet/intellectual, Henry Solomon (Shepard Menken), a Negro writer, Sam Wright (Duke Williams), and a Russian party leader now resident in the US, Nina Petrovka (Hanne Axman).

In just a few weeks, Bill witnesses the thorough disillusionment of this group with Soviet-style ideological rigidity and its inclination toward violence. Solomon publishes a poem that calls attention to Marx's expression of long-held ideals within Western culture about emancipation from tyranny. But party officials will not allow that Marx belongs to any tradition at all save that of the system he invented, and Solomon is asked to recant. He refuses and, after denouncing local leaders as perverting the real nature of Marx's thought, Solomon is condemned as a Trotskyite. Shunned by the group, Solomon soon commits suicide, leaping to his death through the party office window. Nina and Sam Wright are appalled that party leaders order a young student named Reachi (Norman Budd) to be beaten to death after he questions the validity of their criticism of the American system at a public rally. Sam's father eventually welcomes his son back into mainstream society, emphasizing how communists are manipulating the dissatisfaction of black Americans facing racial discrimination as a means to achieve their cynical ends. There are more slaves in communist countries, his father suggests, than there ever existed in the US. Approached by her priest and her mother, Mollie too is persuaded to give up her political allegiance to Stalinism. Dramatically reentering her parish church, she suddenly rediscovers the deeper meaning of religious faith and undergoes a sudden conversion from political activism.

Bill and Nina, meanwhile, have become lovers and decide to leave the party. Believing they need to flee, they drive furiously across the country until they end up exhausted in a small Texas town, whose kindly sheriff patiently explains that they live in a free country and therefore have nothing to fear since they have committed no crime. As they leave the sheriff's office, a little boy informs them that the man is known in town as "Uncle Sam." Reviewing the film in the *New York Times*, Bosley Crowther was moved to comment that "if the local comrades are as corny as they act in this film, then their only likely potential would seem to be to make us laugh ourselves to death" (1949).

Establishing the Industry's Bona Fides

Hollywood's Cold War films demonstrate a greater variety and political depth than might ordinarily have been expected. In part, this was because the industry had good reasons of its own for strongly supporting, with timely productions, the vigorously anticommunist policies of first the Truman and then the Eisenhower administrations. The 1947 HUAC investigations of the industry resulted in 10 from the filmmaking community being designated as "unfriendly witnesses" and subsequently convicted on contempt citations, leading to their imprisonment. This widely publicized episode proved unexpectedly harmful and embarrassing, as the industry, its studios headed by some of the nation's most successful and prominent Jewish businessmen, fell under a cloud of suspicion that was never far from tapping into the deep anti-Semitism long latent in American culture. Ironically, a special difficulty was raised by Hollywood's participation in government propaganda efforts during World War II, when the Soviet Union had become a de facto ally.

It did not seem to matter to the HUAC investigators that the World War II pro-Russian films had been made with government approval and encouragement. Roosevelt's Office of War Information had been eager to justify to the American public the huge investment in Lend-Lease to the Russian army, and the industry had accommodated the wishes of the administration. In the early years of the Cold War, Hollywood took pains to deny that legacy, with every studio, major and minor (Universal alone excepted), producing at least one anticommunist spy thriller or melodrama. Industry conservatives (including actors John Wayne, Ronald Reagan, and director King Vidor) even founded the Motion Picture Alliance for the Preservation of American Ideals, with novelist Ayn Rand penning *A Screen Guide for Americans*. This short list of general principles was meant to serve the industry as an informal "production code" shaping its anticommunist policies.

With its self-consciously realist approach to crime, celebrating the virtues and power of law enforcement and of civil institutions more generally, the noir semi-documentary proved an especially useful subgenre for establishing the industry's political bona fides, as we have seen in the case of *The Iron Curtain*. A "secular" parallel can be glimpsed in one of the most popular subtypes of film noir, the "city confidential" films of the era. A notable example is Robert Wise's *The Captive City*, released by United Artists in 1952, which traces the heroic attempts of a newspaper reporter to uncover the workings of a crime syndicate that has seized control of local politics. Senator Estes Kefauver, who in the 1950s headed a Senate committee investigating small-town corruption, appears in the film preaching the need to defeat this menace threatening the American way of life. A significant and popular group of anticommunist films of that era collectively make up a kind of "national confidential" meant to inform the American public of the deadly conspiracy operating just beneath the apparently benign surfaces of everyday life.

A number of these noirish exposés, to be sure, are only barely politicized, using anticommunist themes merely as an attempt to breathe life into narratives and themes that threatened to become overly conventional. Robert Aldrich's *Kiss Me Deadly*, released in 1955 by United Artists, sinks private detective Mike Hammer (Ralph Meeker) into an ever more threatening whirlpool of intrigue involving a gang of criminals eager to obtain a briefcase (dubbed "the great whatsit" by Hammer's secretary Velda (Maxine Cooper)) that contains, as it turns out, radionuclide material. In the final scene, the briefcase is opened, revealing its true nature as a Pandora's box that explodes, with the result (only in the film's original theatrical release ending) that something like a world-ending nuclear apocalypse occurs. Aldrich's original notion, later restored in the DVD release, was less earth-shattering, a house fire from which Hammer and Velda escape to apparent safety in the nearby ocean.

In *Pickup on South Street*, directed by Samuel Fuller and released by Fox in 1953, a small-time pickpocket (Richard Widmark) accidentally steals microfilm of secret US government plans stolen by a communist spy ring. Though the film has become a cult classic because of Fuller's brash visual style and provocative representations of violence and sexuality, *Pickup on South Street* does not deal in any depth with Cold War themes and ideology. Its spies seem no different from ordinary gangsters.

So superficial is the anticommunist material, in fact, that when the film was released in France and its politics needed to be sanitized, it proved easy enough to eliminate all reference to the gangsters as spies, converting them instead to drug dealers. An artfully scripted updating of the pre-noir thriller *The Petrified Forest* (1936), *Split Second*, directed by Dick Powell and released by RKO in 1953, also minimally engages Cold War themes. The film explores the reactions under pressure of a diverse group of hostages held by escaped criminals in a ghost town. The only connection to contemporary politics is that the nuclear age provides its ticking clock source of suspense, as the town is the designated site for an upcoming nuclear test, from which the group escapes with barely a minute to spare.

Columbia's 1959 release *City of Fear*, directed by Irving Lerner, only minimally engages global realities. Like Elia Kazan's more justly famous *Panic in the Streets* (1950), this thriller traces the police pursuit of a man evading capture in a large metropolitan area (here Los Angeles rather than New Orleans) who is unwittingly in the process exposing his fellow citizens to great danger (now the radioactive material he has stolen rather than the bubonic plague). An extended pursuit, artfully managed, also forms the centerpiece of *The Atomic City*, directed by Jerry Hopper and released by Universal in 1952. Despite the elaborate security precautions taken with the personnel at Los Alamos involved in nuclear weapons research, Russian agents manage to kidnap the young son of one of the program's most important scientists, Dr Frank Addison (Gene Barry), with a view to extorting vital information from him. Though it begins in full semi-documentary style (a stern voiceover plays over actual footage of the semi-industrial New Mexico complex), *The Atomic City* soon abandons any pretense at political relevance; the Russian agents seem little different from standard noir heavies out to collect a ransom rather than a scientific formula.

The interesting entries in the national confidential series treat Cold War themes in more depth and detail. An ideal pattern for this series was found in an early postwar release that treated domestic espionage during World War II. The 1945 production of *The House on 92nd Street* (directed by Henry Hathaway and produced by Louis de Rochemont) was based on an actual case: the FBI's roundup of German spies belonging to the so-called Duquesne spy ring, to this day the largest arrest and subsequent conviction of foreign agents in US history. Many sequences were filmed on the streets of New York, while FBI files were made available to the screenwriters. Sequences shot silent are explained by the self-assured and omniscient narrator (Reed Hadley, in a role he would reprise several times, including in notable anticommunist films such as *The Iron Curtain*). Though *House* approaches its subject from the perspective of the FBI (whose functioning as the guardian of national security is lavishly praised), its focus is uneasily split between the Nazi agents, those fascinating perpetrators of an unfathomable and perverse evil, and their pursuers, whose unalloyed and rather flat virtue proves much less appealing, even though they naturally emerge victorious in a finale that celebrates the invincibility of national institutions.

Albert L. Werker's *He Walked by Night*, released by Eagle-Lion in 1948, also offered the barely fictionalized recounting of a true story: the pursuit and eventual capture of a sociopathic thief and murderer who has mastered police procedures and uses his quick wits to evade detection and capture. The film is structured around the same split in focus between the criminal and the police as proved effective in *The House on 92nd Street*. Werker virtually remade *He Walked by Night* as an anticommunist spy thriller entitled *Walk East on Beacon!*, released by Louis de Rochemont in 1952. Here too the narrative focus is divided equally between the villains (Russian spies and their American

Figure 29.1 An apprehensive but confident group of law enforcement officials considers the insidious threat posed by communist infiltration and espionage in Alfred L. Werker's *Walk East on Beacon!* (1952, producer Louis de Rochemont).

operatives eager to blackmail a scientist into surrendering important defense secrets) and the heroic FBI agents who, tipped to the suspicious activities of one of the spies, immediately discover the man's connection to a "sleeper" whom the Bureau had had under surveillance since the late 1930s. Working undercover, the Feds soon discover that the master spy is an experienced Russian also well known to the FBI. The Russian confronts the scientist with the information that his son is being held by Soviet police in East Berlin and will only be released unharmed if the man gives vital information about the project he is working on for the government. At this point, agent James Belden (George Murphy) persuades the scientist to hand over false information to the Russians. Setting up an elaborate sting operation, Belden is able to make sure that the scientist's son is rescued from his captors. The spy network is then quickly rolled up.

If in *He Walked by Night* the sociopathic criminal is truly an intellectual match for the Los Angeles police, the spies in *Walk East on Beacon!* are a fairly pathetic lot, easily disposed of by the FBI despite their elaborate and careful plotting. Obviously, one challenge of the "national confidential" film was to make the communist threat fearful enough to energize the narrative, while, at the same time, establishing that the Russians actually pose little challenge to their American counterparts. The imbalance between the two opposing forces finds an unintentionally humorous reflex in the film's narrative climax, in which the spies attempt to flee Boston harbor in a yacht but are quickly foiled by Belden aboard a huge Navy cruiser.

The problem of imbalance is artfully avoided in the most artistically successful of the national confidential films: *Walk a Crooked Mile*, directed by Gordon Douglas and released by Columbia in 1948. The daring murder of an FBI agent who is trailing a suspicious foreigner named Radchek in Lakeview, California (where an important weapons research facility is located) alerts his superior, Daniel O'Hara

(Dennis O'Keefe), that something sinister may indeed be afoot. Radchek is trailed to San Francisco, where he is murdered despite 24-hour surveillance. O'Keefe is at this point introduced to British MI5 agent Philip Grayson (Louis Hayward), who has come to the States in order to investigate how a painting shipped from there to London has had ingeniously inscribed beneath the paint a secret formula only recently developed at the Lakeview facility.

The two agents join forces in an investigation that eventually reveals how the most strenuous security precautions have failed to prevent not only this formula, but a continuous series from being transmitted to the painter, who is a member of a communist spy ring. Suspicion then falls on the five scientists involved in the project. Only the persistence, endurance, and courage of the two detectives (rather than the impersonal workings of a vast enforcement agency) lead to the eventual discovery of the culprit; in an interesting twist, he is not one of the two "foreign" members of the group but its American-born leader, Dr Romer Allen (Charles Evans), who, it is revealed, is the scion of a prominent Boston family with deep roots in American society. In accordance with the noir semi-documentary formula, much of *Walk a Crooked Mile* takes place entirely in the transitory social spaces of the nighttime underworld from which everyday society and family life have been completely banished: seedy gyms, dark alleys, cheap apartments, and underground railroad tracks, where a complex shootout is effectively staged. Even O'Hara's office is glimpsed only late at night when empty of other agents and personnel. Instead of the customary chest-thumping portrayal of its huge force of trained functionaries, even the FBI gets the sinister noir chiaroscuro treatment.

Besides being European aesthetes (who else would have conceived the plan to smuggle out vital information copied onto an oil painting?), the communist operatives in *Walk a Crooked Mile* seem little different from typical noir criminal "masterminds." And, as in *The Atomic City*, they are served by seemingly brainless thugs who differ not at all from conventional noir heavies (and are played by actors prominent in that series, such as Raymond Burr, the conscienceless killer in *Walk a Crooked Mile*, who is made to look more "foreign" by a pasted-on goatee). The film's most political moment comes when a rooming house domestic, just arrived in the country from eastern Europe, takes a bullet meant for O'Hara and dies happy, so she admits, because she has played a role in the defeat of this plot to undermine her newly adopted country.

Though it otherwise follows closely the same formulae, Gordon Douglas's *I Was a Communist for the FBI* (released by Warner Bros. in 1951), based on the "real-life" experiences of Matt Cvetic (played by Frank Lovejoy), more interestingly explores the supposed political activities and domestic subversion practiced by American communists in the industrial center of Pittsburgh. One highly placed party member, Jim Blandon (James Millican), works in the personnel office of a local steel mill and makes sure that key positions are filled by fellow communists. At one point Blandon arranges for the local union to strike at the plant and then for hired thugs to attack them using steel pipes covered in copies of the local Yiddish-language newspaper, hoping to incite an anti-Semitic reaction among the general public that the party can manipulate and exploit.

The communists, it is revealed, customarily use both the discontents of minorities and prejudice against them in order to create civil unrest. At one party meeting, the party's legal support of the Scottsboro boys – a group of young black men accused, falsely as it turns out, of raping two white prostitutes – is cynically discussed as an inexpensive way of making international news out of American racism. The party's infiltration of the educational system is also emphasized. Just returned to Pittsburgh, Cvetic is approached by Eve Merrick (Dorothy Hart), a local schoolteacher who has been sent by party leaders to check on his movements. An idealist seduced by the promise of communism to deliver social justice, Merrick is soon thoroughly disillusioned by the party's conscienceless exploitation of social prejudice. She and Cvetic eventually become lovers when she realizes that he is working for the FBI; only with difficulty do they escape from the party thugs sent to eliminate them. Rejected by his family for his supposed embrace of communism, Cvetic is finally exonerated when he testifies for the government at the HUAC meeting in which the Pittsburgh party operatives are revealed as dangerous subversives. His true patriotism revealed, the erstwhile true believer reconciles with his son and brother, who had for years become thoroughly disgusted by what they thought was Matt's traitorous behavior. The "adventures" of this double agent (now known as Herb Philbrick) were continued, first on radio and then on television, in one of the most popular series of the era: *I Led Three Lives*.

Given Hollywood's fearful experience with their investigations, it is perhaps not surprising that stern and patriotic members of HUAC play a heroic role in *I Was a Communist for the FBI* (interestingly enough, the film also "earned" an Academy Award Best Picture nomination even though it is clearly not an "A" production and undoubtedly stood no chance of actually winning). Even more supportive of HUAC, however, is *Big Jim McLain*, directed by Edward Ludwig and released by Warners in 1953. After a brief prologue in which the voice of a ghostly, and deeply worried, Daniel Webster inquires if all is well in the country, the film opens with a HUAC meeting in which an obviously guilty communist (the viewer knows that because he is a shifty-eyed man with a foreign accent) pleads Fifth Amendment protection when asked if he is a communist. Apparently hampered by the freedoms afforded citizens in the Bill of Rights, the committee must turn to less formal (that is, strong-arm) methods of getting at the truth. Two massive and hulking investigators, Jim McLain and Mal Baxter (played by John Wayne and James Arness respectively), are dispatched to Hawaii, where they are to identify local members of the party in order to foil the subversive activities in which it is suspected they are involved.

Like Matt Cvetic, McLain hooks up almost immediately with a local female member of the party, Nancy Vallon (Nancy Olson), who also by film's end becomes disillusioned with the party's tactics. In his attempts to first identify local communist leaders and then to discover who has murdered Baxter, McLain makes his way through something like the dangerous noir underworld (including a brassy but harmless landlady memorably played by Veda Ann Borg). The only difference is that the lowlifes McLain runs into are largely now disillusioned ex-communists who, formerly taken in by the party's appeal to unionism and egalitarianism, have now realized that its real aim is the destruction of the American way of life. The seriousness of their plotting emerges when, having kidnapped Baxter, the communists accidentally kill him with an overdose of truth serum. With the help of the political converts, McLain is finally able to make sure that Baxter's murderers (including the group's cold-blooded leader, Sturak, played superbly by Alan Napier) are brought successfully to justice. But the others, not implicated in any specific act of lawbreaking, only find themselves testifying before a special session of HUAC. They too "plead the fifth" and must be released from custody. McLain's righteous indignation at this cynical exploitation of American freedoms is assuaged somewhat by his witnessing, at film's end, an Army unit parading through the refurbished docks of Pearl Harbor. This sequence completes the patriotic tour of the base that had begun earlier with a heartrending visit to the memorial to the battleship *Arizona*, sunk during the Japanese attack on Pearl Harbor. At film's end, the narrator is thus able to answer Webster's question about the state of the republic with a resounding proclamation that all is well.

We Will Not Be Driven by Fear into an Age of Unreason

As *Big Jim McLain* and these other films suggest, Hollywood easily adapted the noir semi-documentary to anticommunist themes, adding just enough political content to provide a topical flavor. Committed to hard-boiled dialogue and action, these releases lack the deeper engagement of less generic productions such as *The Iron Curtain* and *Guilty of Treason* with the difficult social and ideological questions raised by the growth of East–West rivalry, the formation of the Eastern bloc, and the contrast in economic and social promise of liberal democratic capitalism, on the one hand, and state socialism based on Marxist theory, on the other. This is true as well of the several crime melodramas of the early postwar period that emphasize communist themes, usually in a fairly superficial or predictable fashion. Political commitment and its lasting consequences for an attempted "fresh start" are the focus in *The Woman on Pier 13* (also released under the more provocative title *I Married a Communist*), directed by Robert Stevenson and released by RKO in 1949. Brad Collins (Robert Ryan), a well-placed executive in a San Francisco shipping company, is actually Frank Johnson, a former dockworker and member of the Communist Party. On his honeymoon, Collins runs into an old girlfriend, Christine (Janis Carter), who, still an active member of the Communist Party, tells the party boss, Vanning

(Thomas Gomez), that Collins could easily be blackmailed through threats to expose his past, especially since he had, as Johnson, been embroiled in a murder. Approached by Christine, Collins tells her that he has put the foolish political commitments of his youth behind him – and that he also wants nothing to do with her. The blackmail eventually succeeds, however, as Collins cooperates for a time with party thugs in order to shut down the waterfront. Realizing his error as his wife finds herself in danger, Collins turns on Vanning and kills him, but is fatally wounded in the process. Before dying, the repentant former communist tells his wife he met her too late to begin a new life.

In *The Woman on Pier 13*, the fear that the vast communist conspiracy can manifest itself anywhere at anytime expresses itself through the noir theme of the "dark past." Like many a noir fellow traveler, Brad Collins finds himself trapped between times and between different versions of himself. Such instability renders impossible his coupling with a good woman and the everyday respectability he now eagerly pursues. The noir theme of the dark underside of everyday life figures prominently in another notable crime melodrama of the period with a communist theme: the oddly titled *The Whip Hand*, directed by William Cameron Menzies and released by RKO in 1951. The film opens with a meeting of the Russian military chiefs in Moscow, at which it is most improbably decided that the plan to cripple American society by spreading a killer virus is best served by making a home base in the backwoods community of Winnoga, Wisconsin. A vacationing journalist, Matt Corbin (Elliott Reid), foils the plot when he becomes suspicious that much of the property in the area has been bought up by a group of foreigners (who, somewhat stupidly, are proudly displaying on a bookshelf in the local lodge several books by their leader, a notorious former Nazi criminal scientist, Dr Wilhelm Bucholtz). Bucholtz, it turns out, is living in Winnoga under an assumed name, and he is served by the usual gang of noirish thugs (the reliable heavy Raymond Burr is chief among them). With the aid of the local authorities, Corbin manages to prevent Bucholtz from poisoning Chicago's water supply.

In the early postwar era, such narratives had a persistent appeal, even as the political climate began to change. For example, in *The Fearmakers*, directed by Jacques Tourneur and released by United Artists in 1958, Alan Eaton (Dana Andrews) returns home from the Korean War to find that his business partner has mysteriously died. The firm has passed into new hands, a blustery man named McGinnis (Dick Foran), who has moved it into a quite different area of business: conducting public polls to support certain "special interest" groups. It soon becomes apparent to Eaton that McGinnis is running a communist front organization whose purpose is to influence public opinion, particularly on the issue of banning nuclear weapons. Despite recurrent flashbacks from the brainwashing he suffered as a North Korean prisoner of war, Eaton manages to collect enough evidence for the police to take action. That communists need to be routed from places of influence by the actions of heroic individuals is a theme that appears also in *The Trial*, directed by Mark Robson for MGM and released in 1955. Only by outing a young Mexican boy's trial lawyer as a communist eager to see his client martyred for the "cause" does David Blake (Glenn Ford) come to see the "truth" about prominent liberal organizations supposedly dedicated to social justice (the film's target seems to be a quite thinly disguised American Civil Liberties Union). Blake saves the boy from an unjust sentence with an effective appeal to the very community that had seemed so desperate to see him executed (a lynching is barely averted as the boy awaits arraignment). The film thus makes two related points: that the party does not have the best interests of the poor and downtrodden at heart, despite appearances; and that, properly informed and led, the American people will act justly, showing that the system does work even when strained by prejudice and unreason.

On March 9, 1954, famed journalist Edward R. Murrow treated the television audience of his popular show *See It Now* to a lesson about anticommunism in general and the seemingly unending investigations of Senator Joseph McCarthy in particular. In arguing that a free society must distinguish dissent from disloyalty, Murrow famously remarked: "We will not be driven by fear into an age of unreason." The journalist was echoing George Kennan, as he undoubtedly knew, in this plea to his fellow countrymen to avoid compromising or abandoning the very freedoms that distinguished American society from its communist counterparts. By the end of the early postwar period, some films had begun to explore that age of unreason and the forms it might take. *Three Brave Men*, directed by Philip Dunne and released by Twentieth Century-Fox in 1957, dramatizes what happens to a loyal Naval Department employee, Bernie Goldsmith (Ernest Borgnine), whose behavior is deemed suspicious enough to trigger an investigation into his political affiliations. Detectives are dispatched from Washington to interview Goldsmith's neighbors, and on the unsupported accusation of two of these (who, it turns out, have personal reasons not to like him), the man is fired from his job. Goldsmith becomes a pariah through no fault of his own as the news spreads through the town. However, he is eventually rehabilitated through the strenuous efforts of his lawyer and also the cooperation of the government attorney, who, ordering another investigation, discovers the fatal flaws of the first. For all its traditional Hollywood support of the status quo (including the bona fides of government officials), *Three Brave Men* uneasily probes the difficulties involved in loyalty testing and the terrible consequences that follow when an innocent man is mistakenly branded as a traitor. Directed by Daniel Taradash and released by Columbia in 1956, *Storm Center* explores a related issue: the intolerance of ideas thought threatening to a free society. Small-town librarian Alicia Hull (Bette Davis) refuses to remove volumes about Marxism from the shelves when local officials demand it. She is fired when town officials learn that she belonged to several Russian relief agencies during the war. The townspeople realize their error only after one of Alicia's favorite young students, confused by what he has heard about her, accidentally burns down the library. Realizing that she should have struggled harder to keep her job, Alicia agrees to stay in town and supervise the rebuilding of what once had been the pride of the town and the center of its intellectual life.

Life in Cold War America, however, was hardly that simple. Based on Richard Condon's controversial novel, John Frankenheimer's *The Manchurian Candidate* (released in 1962 by United Artists) captures the political complexities of the period, of which it wisely never attempts to make sense. No doubt, the film is the most artistically successful of the Cold War films, precisely because, adapting an ideologically paradoxical, bitterly sardonic, and darkly humorous source, it notably exceeds the usual self-imposed limits of the genre. A platoon of GIs in Korea is led into an ambush, captured, drugged, and then flown to Manchuria, where a noted Russian behavioral psychologist subjects them to an intense form of brainwashing. One of the group, Raymond Shaw (Laurence Harvey), is conditioned to become a conscienceless assassin, while the others, including their leader Bennett Marco (Frank Sinatra), are conditioned to misremember their "training" as a combat operation in which Shaw performs with incredible heroism (while in fact he simply "practices" his technique on his erstwhile comrades). Returned to American society, where he is welcomed as a Medal of Honor winner, Shaw unconsciously assumes the deep cover of his previous identity. His stepfather is a senator, an obvious version of Joseph McCarthy, who, instructed by his wife, has begun an intimidating campaign against those government officials he accuses of being communists. In reality, his wife is a Soviet agent, and he her unwitting tool, soon to be nominated as his party's vice-presidential candidate. Shaw's Russian handlers "test" their pawn by having him murder both his father-in-law and his own wife. Meanwhile, Marco's conditioning begins to break down, as he realizes the dim outlines of what happened to him and the others in the platoon. In the film's suspenseful climax, Marco races to find Shaw at the convention hall, where his stepfather is about to be nominated. He fears correctly that Shaw has been programmed to assassinate the presidential candidate, allowing the stepfather to become the party's nominee. But Shaw's conditioning has also deteriorated, and instead of his intended target he guns down both his stepfather and his mother before killing himself. In a radical and unexpected twist, the brainwashed Shaw transforms himself from an ersatz to a genuine hero by preventing a military coup in which he has unwittingly played a major role. But to save his country he must murder his own mother and stepfather. He thus wills himself into becoming the worst kind of pariah, paradoxically carrying out the kind of self-destructive act that his communist brainwashers had intended him to perform, yet, because chance and his own strength of mind permit, doing so to achieve the opposite of their intentions. If, having shot down his parents, he finds it necessary to turn the rifle on himself and blow out his brains as well, the viewer is asked to understand this extreme finale as not only heroic, but life-affirming.

But this final sequence, driven by a suspense that is founded on those false assumptions, is preceded by a moving scene in which Frankenheimer allows us to

Figure 29.2 Captain Bennett Marco (Frank Sinatra) and Sergeant Raymond Shaw (Laurence Harvey) are two members of an American patrol kidnapped during the Korean War by Russian agents and then subjected to a terrifying brainwashing designed to transform Shaw into an automaton-assassin in John Frankenheimer's *The Manchurian Candidate* (1962, producers George Axelrod and John Frankenheimer).

see how Shaw is now prodded by the increasing horror of the infamy that, robot-like, he has coolly perpetrated upon command. Weeping confusedly, sensing the hitherto unfathomed horror of all he has done, Shaw begins to come to himself (as the clichéd phrase has it) in a phone call to Marco. The irony, of course, is that such a return, because it requires the commission of what, in some sense, is just as evil as what he has done, can hardly be salvific. In his own view, these final murders, the only ones he intends to commit, are self-damning. Arguably, these deaths must be paid for by the forfeit of his life, so completely do they violate the most deeply rooted of all taboos. And yet these killings also hold out the possibility of redemption because, in their punishment of the guilty and their partial remediation of the damage caused by their depredations, they restore the moral order Shaw has violated. In a turn of cosmic irony, this act both affirms and denies the transformation effected by his communist handlers. Shaw becomes the effective assassin they trained him to be, but, Samson-like, destroys both the elaborately conceived plans he was meant to serve and those close to him who were intending to benefit from his dehumanization.

All the bewildered killer can utter, before finally putting the muzzle under his chin and pulling the trigger, is a desperate, inchoate plea: "Oh, God, Ben." It is Marco who correctly interprets and passes the final judgment on Shaw's actions, imagining the kind of conventionally unconventional citation that the man should have received were his deed one that could be publicly acknowledged.

In an interpretive gesture that probably overreaches, historian Michael Rogin suggests that in the larger history of "American demonology" films of the Cold War not only detail "the rise of the national-security state," but also explore the discontents of a persistent national theme, "the simultaneous glorification and fear of maternal influence within the family" (1987, 238). What a popular cultural critic of the era, Philip Wylie, calls "momism" is beyond doubt an element of the dark underside of American life that film noir more generally, and some Cold War thrillers in particular, explore in the period (cf. Alfred Hitchcock's *Strangers on a Train*, 1950). But as this chapter has demonstrated, the Cold War thriller in general is more concerned with political than domestic discontents; the fear that this series of Hollywood films treats is that of the threatening other who, to our unending terror, may also be found within. It is that paradoxical truth, the signature element of the era's paranoia, that this film is most interested in exploring, not the creepiness of Shaw's imprisonment by and subsequent severing of his primary attachment.

The Manchurian Candidate is both an indictment of the self-serving fabulations of McCarthyism about some supposed widespread communist infiltration of the federal government and a terrifying dramatization of how, in fact, a sophisticated conspiracy, directed by Moscow, might plausibly decapitate American society. Cinematically, the film looks forward to how, in the course of the 1960s and 1970s, the notion of "conspiracy" in American life would come to be expressed, particularly in popular culture, as a gaming of the system from within by those who, lacking any scruples, would do whatever might be necessary to seize and maintain power. For American filmmaking, the legacy of the Cold War cinema is the political thriller writ large, a narrative form with seemingly endless appeal devoted to exposing the unexpectedly sinister inner workings of a society which, as film after film continues to suggest, is never what it seems to (or should) be.

References

Crowther, Bosley. (1949). "*The Red Menace*." *New York Times*, June 27, at http://www.nytimes.com/movie/review?res=940DE5DE113CE23BBC4F51DFB0668382659EDE (accessed March 2015).

Kennan, George F. (1947). "The Sources of Soviet Conduct." *Foreign Affairs*, at http://www.foreignaffairs.com/articles/23331/x/the-sources-of-soviet-conduct (accessed March 2015).

Kennan, George F. (1996). "An Interview with George Kennan." CNN, at http://www.johndclare.net/cold_war7_Kennan_interview.htm (accessed March 2015).

Rogin, Michael. (1987). *Ronald Reagan: The Movie*. Berkeley: University of California Press.

30

American Underground Film

Jared Rapfogel
Programmer, Anthology Film Archives, United States

Although most closely associated with the 1960s, **American underground film** acknowledged its influences in the 1930s with **Joseph Cornell**'s *Rose Hobart*, and found its roots in the 1940s with **Maya Deren**'s *Meshes of the Afternoon*, **Curtis Harrington**'s *Fragment of Seeking*, and **Kenneth Anger**'s *Fireworks*; and in the 1950s with **Stan Brakhage**'s *Reflections on Black*, **Alfred Leslie** and **Robert Frank**'s *Pull My Daisy* and its **Beat** milieu, and with the work of **Jonas Mekas** as filmmaker and exhibitor. In his transitional essay to Volume II of this series, Jared Rapfogel discusses these influences, along with central works of 1960s underground cinema, including the films of **Bruce Conner**, **Jack Smith**, **Andy Warhol**, **Gregory Markopoulos**, **Ken Jacobs**, **Ron Rice**, **Harry Smith**, **Marie Menken**, **Bruce Baillie**, Anger, Brakhage, and Mekas, among others. Variously referred to as avant-garde, experimental, or nonnarrative, the work of these filmmakers – including their publications and film clubs – created an "underground" movement devoted to liberating cinema from mainstream stylistic norms and "prudish, self-censoring restrictions." Rapfogel's essay shares ground with Jan-Christopher Horak on early avant-garde cinema in this volume, with Eric Schaefer on low-budget exploitation and Scott MacDonald on the contemporary avant-garde in Volume II of this series, and with Michael Zryd on cinephilia in the hardcover/online edition.

Additional terms, names, and concepts: Film-Makers' Cooperative, New American Cinema, Cinema 16, trance film, mythopoeic film, lyrical film

The first step in introducing the vast, but often neglected, topic of American Underground Cinema is to clarify what is meant by "underground." In the field of noncommercial, independent cinema, descriptive terms and definitions are endlessly debated, as cases are made for and against labeling various (and inevitably ambiguous and overlapping) categories of films as "avant-garde," "experimental," "nonnarrative," and so on. "Underground" is very much a part of this disputed flock, a term that is

American Film History: Selected Readings, Origins to 1960, First Edition. Edited by Cynthia Lucia, Roy Grundmann, and Art Simon.
© 2016 John Wiley & Sons, Inc. Published 2016 by John Wiley & Sons, Inc.

sometimes understood as more or less synonymous with "avant-garde" or "experimental," and at other times applied to films that push the boundaries of sex, violence, or simply good taste. In still other contexts "underground" is used more precisely to identify a specific period in the history of noncommercial American filmmaking, from the late 1950s to the mid-1960s – a period that saw an explosion of personal, independently made and produced films; the formation of cohesive communities of independent filmmakers; and the establishment of structures for the exhibition, distribution, and promotion of these films. This period, one of social and cultural transformation and upheaval throughout America, saw the alternative cinema coalesce into a vigorous movement, achieving an unprecedented cultural prominence.

Defining "Underground Cinema"

In its broadest sense, Underground Film represents an alternative to commercial filmmaking, a form of cinema in which personal expression is freed from the conventions and structures of the movie industry. But this opposition to older models varies dramatically, encompassing, at one extreme, films like John Cassavetes's *Shadows* (1959) and Shirley Clarke's *The Connection* (1962), which radically reconfigure narrative conventions but by no means reject them; at the other extreme lie films like Stan Brakhage's *Text of Light* (1974), a 70-minute study of the effects of light refracted through a glass ashtray. Both *Shadows* and *Text of Light* can be identified as "underground," but only by making use of a very broad, and even contradictory, definition of the term.

Nevertheless, in the context of a national cinema in which one, strictly limited form of moviemaking – the Hollywood model of narrative fiction, with its strict conventions regarding acting, editing, and mise-en-scène, its endorsement of traditional moral and social values, and its embodiment of an industrial mode of production – has attained such a profound dominance, the various kinds of films that have attempted to explore other forms and methods have inevitably formed a unity. However distinct they may be from one another stylistically or formally, these films are suffused with a conviction that the mainstream cinema has neglected the greater part of the medium's vast spectrum of possibilities, that the cinema is capable of far more than simply telling stories by means of an established, codified narrative language. The filmmakers of the underground were devoted to asserting the cinema's potential as an art form, and they worked to develop means of cinematic expression reflective of such forms as painting, poetry, dance, and music, rather than that of traditional Hollywood storytelling.

Moreover, the filmmakers who made up the underground were generally convinced that their attempts to liberate the cinema from mainstream norms were further expressions of the larger transformations occurring throughout American culture and society. Many of them shared the increasing revulsion, felt by so many at this time, at what they saw as a complacent, arrogant, and corrupt society. Writing in 1962, in his magazine *Film Culture*, Jonas Mekas, the central proselytizer of the underground movement, declared that in a period when

> governments are encroaching upon [one's] personal being with the huge machinery of bureaucracy, war and mass communications, [the American artist] feels that the only way to preserve man is to encourage his sense of rebellion, his sense of disobedience, even at the cost of open anarchy and nihilism. (1962, 14)

It was in the context of such attitudes that the underground filmmakers devoted their energies to forging a new cinema, one that would offer an alternative to the dominant culture. Mekas called this movement "existential" and would go on to define it primarily as "an ethical movement, a human act," rather than an aesthetic movement. "Even when our films seem to be utterly detached from reality," he contended, "they come from a dissatisfaction with the static, outdated concepts of life and art. One could say that there is a *morality in the new*" (1962, 14). This was the quality which the filmmakers of the underground prized above all others – their methods were often radically different, but the goal they sought, both aesthetically and culturally, was a new freedom of expression liberated from inherited, conventional mores and forms.

J. Hoberman, David E. James, and others have defined the Underground Film movement in precise terms. In his indispensable study of 1960s American independent filmmaking, *Allegories of Cinema*, James identifies its specific historical moment as extending from the appearance of *Pull My Daisy* in 1959 to the uptown New York City theatrical run of *The Chelsea Girls* in 1966, which he called "the last and the most scandalous of a series of dramatic eruptions of the underground into the attention of the general public" (1989, 94). Hoberman, in his chapter on "The Underground" in *Midnight Movies*, notes that, "Throughout the 1960s, 'underground movies' were synonymous with all avant-garde or 'experimental' films," but like James he clarifies his use of the term as concentrating on

> a group of filmmakers who emerged in New York City during the early sixties and whose work was distinguished from ... the earlier avant-garde by a combination of willful primitivism, taboo-breaking sexuality, and obsessive ambivalence toward American popular culture (mainly Hollywood). (Hoberman & Rosenbaum 1991, 40)

This narrower definition more closely reflects the connotations suggested by the term "underground" – the shadowy, subversive qualities embodied by Jack Smith's *Flaming Creatures* (1963), Ken Jacobs's *Blonde Cobra* (1959–1963), and Kenneth Anger's *Scorpio Rising* (1963), among others. And indeed, it was primarily these films, with their rejection of prudish and self-censoring restrictions, and their determination to push boundaries, both social and aesthetic, that exploded into the cultural consciousness in the late 1950s and early 1960s. Films like *Flaming Creatures* and *Scorpio Rising* truly seemed to emerge from underground – from regions of consciousness and experience that had been banished from the screen thus far, while *Pull My Daisy* (1959) and much of Warhol's early work introduced the Beat and Factory subcultures to the public at large. These films became an authentic cultural force, triggering endless discussion in the alternative and mainstream press, eventually even making their way into "respectable" movie theaters, and ultimately triggering much-publicized censorship battles with the government. They posed a challenge, and a perceived threat, to much more than cinematic practice, embodying the profound and widespread social upheaval that rocked the entire American cultural landscape in the late 1950s and into the 1960s.

Roots of the Underground Movement

The movement that burst forth so dramatically in this period was rooted in a broader, more varied one that was forming simultaneously, a rapidly developing network of relationships and structures independent of mainstream culture. The epicenter of both dimensions was the editor, critic, and filmmaker Jonas Mekas, a dynamic, volcanically energetic Lithuanian émigré who was largely responsible for creating the infrastructure that made the New American Cinema (his own term for the emerging movement) possible. The extent to which this independent filmmaking activity emerged as a cohesive movement was thanks in large part to the passionate – even evangelical – promotion Mekas practiced in its behalf in *Film Culture*, the journal he and his brother Adolfas founded in 1954, and – even more publicly – in his weekly *Village Voice* column, "Movie Journal." Mekas would soon extend his activities even further, organizing the Film-Makers' Cinematheque and the Film-Makers' Cooperative. The former, a roving screening series following in the footsteps of Amos Vogel's pioneering exhibition and distribution organization, Cinema 16, showcased the challenging new work that was emerging at an increasingly remarkable rate. The Coop, founded by Mekas in concert with a number of other filmmakers comprising the New American Cinema of the period, was (and remains) an artist-run cooperative distribution outlet, open to any and all filmmakers wishing to submit work. The Coop became invaluable to the developing community of underground filmmakers, providing not only a means of distribution, but a kind of home-base: "A crowded loft, filled with floor-to-ceiling metal film racks, projectors, screens, editing equipment, and a couch for homeless filmmakers (or, more often, Mekas himself) to crash on, the Coop became a twenty-four-hour-a-day nerve center for the underground" (Hoberman & Rosenbaum 1991, 52).

This multifront initiative – with structures in place for the exhibition, promotion, and distribution of independent films – insured the viability of the new, alternative film practice, creating practical possibilities that had not existed up until that point, as well as a cohesive community that provided support of a less tangible but equally important kind, whether in the form of encouragement or shared values and ideas. This self-sustaining community was to be crucial to a movement that was always about much more than sexually explicit content, censorship battles, or countercultural cachet. Many of its films did indeed transgress social and sexual boundaries, but they were equally dedicated to reconceiving the forms and functions of the cinema, transforming a medium that had become almost purely commercial into a tool for unmitigated personal expression.

The filmmakers of the underground movement were bound too by their shared roots, their films evolving out of the work of an earlier generation of pioneering artists who heroically had forged a tradition of filmmaking apart from Hollywood. Though themselves influenced by the European avant-garde tradition of the 1920s – as embodied in films like Luis Buñuel and Salvador Dalí's *Un Chien Andalou* (1929), Jean Cocteau's *Blood of a Poet* (1930), and René Clair and Francis Picabia's *Entr'acte* (1924) – these filmmakers were largely *sui generis*, striving to create a cinema of personal artistic expression when such a concept barely existed within American culture. Among the most crucial figures of this earlier generation were Maya Deren, Joseph Cornell, Sidney Peterson, and the young Kenneth Anger.

Maya Deren and Her Influence

The importance of Maya Deren in particular can hardly be overstated – *Meshes of the Afternoon* (1943) is arguably the founding work of the movement-to-be, an evocative, haunting exercise in dream-logic that uses frank symbolism, trick photography, and discontinuous editing to narrate a woman's interior psychological journey. *Meshes* was overwhelmingly influential in the short term, giving rise to the "trance film" – a term coined by P. Adams Sitney in his seminal survey of the cinematic avant-garde, *Visionary Film* – a veritable genre of films, more or less explicitly couched in the form of a dream, in which the protagonist (often the filmmaker him- or herself) moves through a surreal landscape of symbolic and psychological significance (Sitney 2002, 87). This new form would dominate the avant-garde of the late 1940s and early 1950s, encompassing many of the period's key works, from Curtis Harrington's *Fragment of Seeking* (1946) to Anger's *Fireworks* (1947) and Brakhage's *Reflections on Black* (1955).

But Deren's influence may be even greater in practical terms, thanks to her role in setting into motion the formation of the avant-garde community and its infrastructure. She tirelessly promoted the cause of independent cinema in *Film Culture* and elsewhere, while the screenings she organized in 1946 at New York's Provincetown Playhouse demonstrated the hunger for new forms of filmmaking and inspired Amos Vogel to create Cinema 16. This organization and its West Coast counterpart, the San Francisco-based Art in Cinema series, were integral to the development of the American avant-garde cinema and were the primary forerunners to the various other organizations at the heart of the underground movement, such as the Film-Makers' Cinematheque and Cooperative, and, in San Francisco, Canyon Cinema.

Despite the enormous importance of Deren's work, both filmic and infrastructural, the 1950s marked a transition in underground film away from the literary, psychodramatic approach of Deren, Curtis Harrington, and the young Brakhage. According to Sitney, "the 1950s were quiet years within the American avantgarde cinema ... [with no] significant influx of new artists until the very end of the decade" (2002, 156). His account anticipates the emergence of the mature Brakhage as one of the dominant figures of the next phase of the movement's history, but it also suggests the quiet before the erupting storm represented by *Pull My Daisy*, *Shadows*, and the Beat and underground films, which were to mark a departure from much of the avant-garde cinema of the 1940s. While Sitney's narrative sees the trance film as developing into a form concerned with ritual and myth (the "mythopoeic" film) (2002, 109) – an evolution that culminates in indisputably underground films like Anger's *Inauguration of the Pleasure Dome* (1966) and *Scorpio Rising*, and in Brakhage's *Dog Star Man* (1961–1964) – there is scant precedent in Deren, Harrington, or Peterson for the social and cultural provocations of *Scorpio Rising*, or its use of ideologically charged found footage, or for the extreme cultural complexity and optical investigations of *Dog Star Man*. And the emerging Beat films, from *Pull My Daisy* to the films of Ron Rice, owe a debt to Peterson, and certainly to Christopher Maclaine's *The End* (1953), but less so to the trance or mythopoeic film.

Kenneth Anger's *Fireworks* and Joseph Cornell's *Rose Hobart*

From the perspective of the late 1950s and early 1960s, the two most significant early American avant-garde films are Anger's *Fireworks* and Joseph Cornell's *Rose Hobart* (1936). These two films, the products of profoundly different artistic sensibilities, contain the seeds of much of the later avant-garde. Both films, moreover, are particularly influential on one of the underground's key figures, Jack Smith.

Fireworks stands as the strongest bridge between the trance films of Deren and her successors and the sexually and socially transgressive, defiantly countercultural works of the underground movement at its height. Although the film adheres to Sitney's prerequisites for the trance film, Anger invests the form with a vision entirely his own, a sadomasochistic, unapologetically (homo)sexual content that is entirely new. *Fireworks* is a fever-dream of a home movie, in which a young man drifts through a world transfigured by fantasy and nightmare. Beaten by muscular sailors and cut open to reveal a gas-meter heart, the protagonist's vision culminates with the spectacle of a roman-candle penis set ablaze, triumphantly spewing sparks as it spins – an explosive and liberating image. *Fireworks* borrows the radical, innovative cinematic language of Deren, but uses it to portray experiences, dreams, and desires that were at that time taboo in the culture at large and would not find their way to American screens again, even via the underground, for at least another decade.

Cornell, a famously solitary artist known primarily for his idiosyncratic, eccentric, and deeply evocative box constructions, demonstrated an abiding interest in filmmaking throughout his life, working in the late 1950s in collaboration with the young Brakhage, Larry Jordan, and Rudy Burckhardt, each of whom photographed a number of films for him. Two decades earlier he had made several films on his own, entirely constructed from found footage, most likely the first films to be made in this manner. Most of these were left unfinished until the 1960s, but he did complete *Rose Hobart* in 1936. Although he was reluctant for many years to show it, *Rose Hobart* ultimately became one of the most cherished of all American avant-garde films, even if its influence was not to be directly felt for many years.

Cornell's box constructions took ordinary, ubiquitous, leftover materials – worn-out toys, newspaper clippings, dime-store objects – and made of them something strange, mysterious, and beautiful, creating through a process of both preservation and transformation self-enclosed worlds that penetrated directly to the evocative, nostalgic power inherent in a culture's detritus. In making *Rose Hobart*, Cornell enacted an analogous transformation of a cinematic artifact, an unremarkable Hollywood picture called *East of Borneo* (1931), starring the actress Rose Hobart. By radically reediting and condensing the original film (*Rose Hobart* runs 20 minutes) and replacing its soundtrack with two Brazilian pop songs, Cornell frees the imagery from the derivative and formulaic narrative of the feature film, obscuring the logical, banal meaning of the original, while unleashing a whole host of possible new meanings, more elusive but infinitely richer and more evocative, lying dormant in the original material.

The profoundly private, intimate method through which Cornell created *Rose Hobart* laid the groundwork for filmmakers like Brakhage and others. His use of found footage would eventually inspire a whole host of artists, including Anger (*Scorpio Rising*), Ken Jacobs (*Star Spangled to Death, Tom, Tom, the Piper's Son*, and *Perfect Film*), and Arthur Lipsett (*Very Nice, Very Nice* and *21–87*), as well as later filmmakers from Hollis Frampton (*Works and Days*) and Ernie Gehr (*Eureka*) to the contemporary master of the form, Craig Baldwin (*Tribulation 99* and *Spectres of the Spectrum*). But the genre's most famous practitioner would be Bruce Conner, a collage artist, who was to make several masterpieces of the form, most notably *A Movie* (1957), which makes use of varied footage – including excerpts from movies, newsreels, and advertisements – to formulate an increasingly disturbing commentary on American culture. Conner, like Cornell, strips away the intended narrative logic of the original material, removing each fragment from its original context and forcing it into collision with other fragments – an approach that reveals new connections and ideas, and ultimately aims to uncover

Figure 30.1 One of the many "creatures" cavorting through the legendary – and famously banned – underground classic *Flaming Creatures* (1963, director and producer Jack Smith).

the deeper, but hidden, meanings embedded in pop-cultural refuse. As Conner would declare,

> Anything which was taken for granted as not serious, not art, just things that are thrown away, were exactly what I paid attention to ... if you want to know what's going on in a culture, look at what everybody takes for granted. (Wees 1993, 79)

Jack Smith: His Work and His Influence

Cornell's sensitivity to the surrealism and illogical power at the heart of even the most derivative Hollywood product points as well toward the work of Jack Smith. Just as Cornell "rescued" Rose Hobart from *East of Borneo*, so Smith tirelessly extolled the virtues of the much-maligned Hollywood actress Maria Montez, whose roles in a series of costume-adventure films won her the title, "Queen of Technicolor." Smith expressed his allegiance to Montez in "The Perfect Filmic Appositeness of Maria Montez," an article he published in *Film Culture* in 1962, and his films, most notably *Flaming Creatures*, embody the ideas articulated there.

Flaming Creatures (1963) is perhaps the underground film par excellence, a movie born of Hollywood – insofar as it reflects Smith's preoccupation with the fragile glamour of Montez and the ornate visual splendor of Josef von Sternberg – but also as far from a mainstream narrative film as one can imagine: in format (at 45 minutes, it's neither feature nor short film), visual texture (shot on out-of-date film stock, the image is hazy and unstable, sometimes washed-out almost to the point of illegibility), cast of characters (a group of flamboyantly dressed or, to varying degrees, undressed figures, many in drag), structure (the "narrative" amounts to no more than a succession of disconnected situations and episodes taking place within a single setting), and sexual content (a quasi-orgy of writhing, fondling, assaulting, and masturbation).

Flaming Creatures courted controversy from the beginning, with theaters at first pressured and ultimately forced to cancel engagements. Ultimately, Mekas and Ken Jacobs were arrested and convicted for exhibiting the film, triggering a legal battle that would wind its way to the US Supreme Court (where five of the nine justices would vote not to hear the case, allowing the original conviction to stand) (Hoberman 2001, 47). Despite these scandals, the most radical aspect of *Flaming Creatures* is not its nudity or its depiction of gay and transvestite culture, but rather its total rejection of Hollywood professionalism – an attack less on the content of Hollywood filmmaking than on its basic premises. In his *Film Culture* article, "Belated Appreciation of V.S." (using language that embodies his philosophy of imperfection), Smith identifies a disconnection, even an opposition, in von Sternberg's films between their preposterous, often exaggeratedly absurd plots and their images. People, according to Smith,

> have to have explanations for themselves and others. So Von Sternberg's movies had to have plots even tho they already had them inherent in the images . . . . The explanations . . . [had] nothing to do with what he did (& did well), the *visuals* of his films. (1963–1964, 4)

In *Flaming Creatures*, and its successor *Normal Love* (1963–1964), which adds vibrant color and outdoor settings to the mix, Smith puts his theories into action, taking von Sternberg's instincts (as he understands them) further than von Sternberg ever could have, and liberating the visual dimension from the stories the earlier films concocted (however peremptorily).

Dispensing almost entirely with a narrative, *Flaming Creatures* simply creates a space (an unapologetically unrealistic set) in which its cast of flamboyant, elaborately costumed characters (Smith called them his "creatures") enact a collective make-believe fantasy, performing for each other and displaying themselves for the camera in their adopted guises. These guises are transparently artificial, but the conviction that fuels Smith's art is that, paradoxically, they reveal a truth that Hollywood illusionism stifles, since they represent an expression of each performer's sensibility. In his *Film Culture* article on von Sternberg, Smith writes that "a bad actor is rich, unique, idiosyncratic, revealing of himself not of the bad script" and that such an actor can provide "a visual revelation very appropriate to the complex of ideas and sets of qualities that make up your film" (1963–1964, 5). Smith uses "bad" acting or filmmaking to open a breach in fictional illusionism, a breach that allows reality – the unique personalities of his "creatures," the immediacy of the filmmaking process, the existence of the desire for the fantastic – to flood in, but without causing the fantasy to collapse. This celebration of the "bad," the amateurish, is the foundation of Smith's approach to cinema, a conviction that amateurishness communicates much more than a slick, well-crafted illusionism. As Smith famously said of Maria Montez: "One of her atrocious acting sighs suffused a thousand tons of dead plaster with imaginative life and a truth" (1962, 28). The truth Jack Smith is after is not the truth of verisimilitude – a surface truth, a persuasive fiction – but the truth that comes from men and women revealing their souls, their imaginative lives and desires, to the camera.

Smith's attitudes toward role-playing and identity are strikingly mirrored by an observation of Kenneth Anger. Referring to Rio de Janeiro's Carnival celebrations (as part of a discussion of *Scorpio Rising*), Anger contends that many of the city's shanty town residents "save up all year for the fab costume that they will wear . . . [and] when they're all dressed up, that's really them, it's not them when they are working, sweeping the street or doing somebody's washing" (quoted in Sitney 2002, 101). Both Smith and Anger see fantasy and role-playing as ways of expressing identities far more authentic and personal than the predetermined ones imposed by society. In this context, *Scorpio Rising* is Anger's most important film – a portrait of a particular subculture, the world of motorcycle gangs, and its specific rituals, customs, codes, and subtexts – and has a great deal in common with *Flaming Creatures*, which is, in its way, a portrait of a subcultural community. But at the same time the differences in the two films are striking. Smith is very much a participant in the ritual represented in *Flaming Creatures*, his film a celebration and an example of the liberating potential of fantasy. Anger, on the other hand, is an outsider within the subculture he portrays, and adopts an ironic and often critical distance from the bikers. *Scorpio Rising* is a study, rather than an expression, of the creation of identity. And as such, its structure, mode, and texture are entirely different from those of *Flaming Creatures* – multi-layered where Smith's film is straightforward, technically polished and fluid rather than intentionally amateurish, and tonally much darker and more disturbing, as Anger's own "creatures" come increasingly to embody forces of death, power, violence, and self-destruction.

Anger's command of the medium throughout *Scorpio Rising* is astonishing – structured as a series of episodes and scored to a progression of then-current pop songs (brilliantly mixed with sound effects), the film is a visually dense and rhythmically complex web of highly stylized, sensuously lit sequences, of spontaneously captured documentary-like material, and of found footage (from Brando's *The Wild One* and a dramatization of the life of Jesus), edited together into a disorienting but always perfectly coherent whole. The opening sequences find Anger, through his precise camerawork and expressive lighting, eroticizing the bikers (in a manner familiar from *Fireworks*), transforming them into fetish objects in an expression both of Anger's desire and of the bikers' narcissism. But before long, the emphasis changes from observation, however stylized, to an investigation into the bikers' desires and the ideals to which they aspire. In contrast to *Flaming Creatures*, in *Scorpio Rising* the projection of identity increasingly takes on a sinister flavor. The footage of Brando and images of James Dean suggest that the bikers' concept of rebellion is a superficial one, their identity adopted from popular culture. Anger intercuts footage of the bikers roaming the streets with found footage depicting Jesus and his disciples trekking through the desert, while on the soundtrack Little Peggy March sings, "I will follow him wherever he will go." As if this cue does not suffice, the appearance of Nazi paraphernalia makes it clear that what the bikers seek (in Anger's portrayal, at least) is not the flaming creatures' desire for sexual liberation and personal freedom, but rather power and control.

Jack Smith's contribution to the underground movement extends well beyond the (sadly) few films he completed, or those he left unfinished. His distinctive sensibility also dominates the films to which he lent his extraordinary presence, especially Rice's exquisite *Chumlum* (1964) and a number of works by Ken Jacobs. *Chumlum* in particular is an extension of Smith's body of work, a remarkable visual chamber piece filmed in Smith's apartment during the preparations for and the filming of *Normal Love*. That *Chumlum* feels very much a part of Jack Smith's universe (with its focus on performance and, visually, on decor and costume), while also displaying the intricate visual layering and breathtaking command of composition, color, and light of filmmakers like Brakhage, Baillie, and Markopoulos, illustrates the profound fluidity between the various cinematic approaches that characterized the underground in this period. Gregory Markopoulos and Ken Jacobs, two of the underground's most protean figures, best exemplify this fluidity, each occupying a point at which various approaches intersect.

Gregory Markopoulos and Ken Jacobs

Markopoulos began making films in the late 1940s in the trance-film tradition, and throughout the 1950s and 1960s he made a number of short and feature-length narrative works (including *Swain*, 1950; *Serenity*, 1961; *Twice a Man*, 1963; and *The Illiac Passion*, 1964–1967), most adapted from literary or mythological sources. With these films, Markopoulos, perhaps more than any other underground filmmaker in the mid- to late 1960s, kept alive the literary, explicitly symbolic cinematic legacy of the trance film and of the earlier European work of Buñuel and Cocteau. But starting in 1966, a new dimension appeared in Markopoulos's cinema, and developed in parallel to his quasi-narrative films. These gem-like short works, screened alone or grouped together into feature-length compendia, consisted of portraits – of people (*Galaxie*, 1966; *Political Portraits*, 1969) or places (*Ming Green*, 1966; *Bliss*, 1967; *Sorrows*, 1969) – and were edited entirely in-camera, a seemingly miraculous fact given their rhythmical complexity and stunning use of juxtaposition. The product of an extraordinary perfection of technique – by which Markopoulos would run the film back and forth within the camera and add additional layers of imagery with each pass – these remarkable films document particular people and places while collapsing time into multiple visual and temporal layers, achieving a plastic beauty undreamed of by conventional narrative cinema.

Ken Jacobs's early films were made in collaboration with Jack Smith, and most of them showcase Smith's genius as a performer. *Little Stabs at Happiness* (1959–1963), as well as the short films collected together as *The Whirled* (1956–1963), are celebrations of spontaneity, improvisation, and unbridled energy, in the emerging tradition of *Pull My Daisy* and Rice's *The Flower Thief* (1960), but with even less of a narrative framework than either of those works. His early films embody the underground's newfound cinematic freedom, the willful disregard for stifling seriousness, technical polish, and narrative consistency. While they do not suggest a particularly ambitious formal approach, during this period Jacobs was also at work on a magnum opus (one which would remain perpetually unfinished until the early 2000s), entitled *Star Spangled to Death* (1957–2004), which reveals a new dimension of his sensibility, intermixing familiar, *Little Stabs*-like footage of Smith and Jerry Sims with a whole host of found footage, much of it presented in such large, uninterrupted chunks that the film becomes less a collage than an archive, a compendium of cultural artifacts. *Star Spangled* unveiled not only Jacobs's formal ambition and structural boldness, but also his passionate rebellion against the social and cultural status quo, a protest expressed on multiple levels: The filmed footage in which Smith dominates, for instance, represents the liberated, unbound creativity missing from mainstream culture, while the various pieces of found footage (including Nixon's famous "Checkers" speech and a documentary about scientific testing inflicted on monkeys) form a remarkably revealing, damning (self-)portrait of the culture.

Jacobs's fascination with found material would surface in other films as well, including *Blonde Cobra*, which he constructed out of footage (featuring Smith) shot by Bob Fleischner for a failed project, and *Perfect Film* (1985), which is a kind of cinematic readymade: a reel consisting of news footage on the assassination of Malcolm X which Jacobs discovered on the street and found to be so perfect as to demand no modification. But his fascination with found footage would reach its most ambitious manifestation with *Tom, Tom, the Piper's Son* (1969), a feature-length analysis of an early Billy Bitzer one-reeler, which Jacobs rephotographed – stretching it out to feature length by slowing the projection, at times nearly to a halt, repeating passages over and over, and zooming in on various details. The tension between the actuality represented (the men, women, and settings being recorded) and the photographic medium (made manifest by the magnification of the film grain) heralded both an approach Jacobs would return to throughout his career and his embrace of the structuralist currents that would dominate the cinematic avant-garde in the late 1960s into the 1970s.

Pull My Daisy and Beat Cinema

The spontaneity, roughness, and imperfection found in Smith's and Jacobs's work became more culturally conspicuous with the appearance of *Pull My Daisy* in 1959. Based on the third act of an unpublished play by Jack Kerouac, the film was a collaboration between the painter Alfred Leslie and the photographer Robert Frank, who would shortly achieve fame with the publication of his book *The Americans*. Both play and film were inspired by an incident that occurred at the California home of the Beat poet Neal Cassady and his wife, when the couple arranged an ill-advised meeting between a Catholic minister and Kerouac (along with Allen Ginsberg and Peter Orlovsky). *Pull My Daisy* transposes the incident to a New York City loft, and features Ginsberg and Orlovsky as versions of themselves, as well as Gregory Corso as Kerouac's stand-in, Larry Rivers as a version of Cassady, and in other roles, the artist Alice Neel and the actress Delphine Seyrig (then married to the painter Jack Youngerman). Given these countercultural, and specifically Beat, bona fides, it's no wonder *Pull My Daisy* demonstrates a radical approach to narrative filmmaking – ragged, anarchic, and apparently spontaneous, its style partakes of the same subversive, uninhibited spirit its characters inflict on the hapless minister, sending him and his bewildered mother and aunt into premature flight. Its boldest and most distinctive strategy is its decision to devote the soundtrack to Kerouac's narration, which he improvised while watching the edited film (though the final track is compiled from three separate takes) – a tour-de-force of punning, mimicry, and invention which acts in dynamic and often comic counterpoint to the imagery. While the film's seemingly spontaneous camerawork suggests home movie or cinéma vérité filmmaking, the narration exists on its own level, outside the moment of creation and commenting on the action from a distance, calling attention to the process of crafting the final work. Ironically, it is the narration that is largely improvised, while the rest of the process, according to Leslie, was carried out in a far more traditional manner than it appears – scripted, rehearsed, and blocked out in advance.

However premeditated the filming of *Pull My Daisy* may have been, the impression of spontaneity it exudes was hugely influential on the underground, suggesting an energy that stood in stark contrast to the frozen, rigid conventions of Hollywood moviemaking. And it would not be long before other filmmakers would advance further down this path, making of spontaneity not only a quality to be expressed but a method of production. The underground celebrated improvisation as an indispensable means of throwing off inherited, conventional forms and of engaging with reality in as unmediated a manner as possible. Mekas, in his "Notes on the New American Cinema," would give perhaps the clearest and most passionate statement of this philosophy, calling improvisation

> the highest form of concentration, of awareness, of intuitive knowledge, when the imagination begins to dismiss the pre-arranged, the contrived mental structures, and goes directly to the depths of the matter ... it is not a method at all, it is, rather, a state of being necessary for any inspired creation. (1962, 15)

Ron Rice's *The Flower Thief*, made in full allegiance to the new ethos of improvisation, is one of the defining works of the Beat cinema and a key film from the West Coast school of underground film, a tradition pioneered by Deren, Peterson, Anger, Markopoulos, Harrington, and Maclaine. The West Coast underground was in full swing by the mid-1960s, thanks to the work of Rice, Baillie, Conner, Robert Nelson, Wallace Berman, and others. Shot on the streets of San Francisco and in an abandoned factory, *The Flower Thief* is a vehicle for the great Taylor Mead, a coffeehouse poet blessed with a clown-like physiognomy and a gift for physical comedy, whose remarkable abilities as a performer and camera subject were soon to make him a ubiquitous presence in the underground cinema. *The Flower Thief* anticipates *Flaming Creatures* in its subordination of plot, technique, and structure to a confrontation with the sensibilities of its performers – but here the focus is on a single figure let loose on the world at large. The structure of the film is simply the string of incidents that occur as Mead's Flower Thief – an impossibly innocent, free-spirited figure, and an embodiment of the Beat rebellion against civilized, "mature" society – roams through San Francisco, his encounters with other people and places allowing the fiction and the filmmaking process to closely reflect each other. Mead, recounting Rice's method, has observed that he

> just picked locations, and let us do whatever we wanted to, just spontaneous ideas [that] came to us.... We didn't really bother with plots, just locations, that's all Ron was interested in ... Wonderful locations and people and to me that's about everything a director can do. (Sargeant 2008, 82, 84)

The Cinema of Andy Warhol

No other filmmaker was to take Rice's and Jack Smith's methods so much to heart as Andy Warhol. Warhol went even further than Rice and Smith in dispensing with plot in order to focus his attention on a group of remarkable, charismatic personalities, and in conceiving of his own role as merely to observe and record. He subscribed wholeheartedly both to Smith's philosophy of "bad" acting and filmmaking and to his preoccupation with the glamour and the mythos of Hollywood. Like Smith, Warhol's goal was not to deny the glamour of Hollywood cinema, but to claim that glamour for himself and his performers – to reconcile the glamorous with the everyday.

But Warhol's project departs in crucial respects from those of Smith and Rice. The performances in *Flaming Creatures* and *The Flower Thief* are collaborations between performer and director. A great deal of Smith's work involved the crafting of the actors' costumes, as well as the sets and decor; as a filmmaker his presence is felt in every gesture of the camera, every incident or detail it picks out. And while Rice may be behind the camera as Mead stands before it, they seem to be equal participants. But Warhol's stance is one of extreme detachment and impassivity – his camera purely an instrument for recording, a blank

Figure 30.2 The clown prince of underground film, Taylor Mead, in the seminal Beat film *The Flower Thief* (1960, director and producer Ron Rice).

screen onto which his performers project their identities. Just as Warhol's famous screenprints of Campbell Soup cans, celebrity publicity portraits, and newspaper imagery radically de-emphasized the hand of the artist, so his directorial stance was one of minimal involvement, of conception more than of craft or execution.

There is a difference in emphasis between Smith's and Warhol's conceptions of the nature of performance, as well. For Smith, the amateurish, patently artificial performances he prizes so highly are valuable insofar as they reveal a kind of truth, a revelation of the actors' innermost fantasies and desires. Warhol's emphasis, however, is on the elusiveness of truth, the existential significance of acting. Smith's "creatures" or the figures in Rice's films engage in a kind of play-acting, dressing up and acting out their fantasies for the film. But the impression Warhol's films provide is that his actors are perpetually acting, that performance has become a way of life for them, the theme of their existence. For Warhol, acting *is* the truth, there is nothing to reveal except the instinct to perform, to assert an identity. And if his "superstars" fabricate and project their own identities more explicitly than most, their performances are only magnifications of the same process we all take part in. This dimension is less conspicuous in his earliest and most minimal films, most of which involve the simplest of activities, observed with a painstaking degree of attention and patience. *Eat* (1963), for instance, is a 45-minute document of the artist Robert Indiana consuming a mushroom; the six-hour-long *Sleep* (1963) observes the poet John Giorno sleeping, while the numerous *Screen Tests* remove any pretext of activity, consisting simply of three-minute-long confrontations between camera and subject. The figures in these films are not performing in any conventional sense at all, but the impassive, implacable gaze of the camera highlights their self-consciousness, provoking a need to act, rather than simply to be. James identifies the existential undercurrent when he writes, "The camera is a presence in whose regard and against whose silence the sitter must construct himself. As it makes performance inevitable, it constitutes being as performance" (James 1989, 69). The *Screen Tests* demonstrate this aspect of Warhol's cinema at its purest – in each of them, Warhol does little more than simply provide each subject with three minutes of screen time, within which the subject becomes the author of his or her own portrait.

Warhol's later films would tend more and more toward narrative, as he began collaborating with the playwright Ronald Tavel (soon to found the Theatre of the Ridiculous), who furnished scenarios for films such as *Harlot* (1964), *The Life of Juanita Castro* (1965), *Vinyl* (1965) (an adaptation of Anthony Burgess's *The Clockwork Orange*), and *Kitchen* (1965). But the loosely structured narratives are only a pretext, a nod to the Hollywood model – they serve mainly to call attention to Warhol's own radical approach, which continues to feature a fixed camera, a near total lack of editing, and amateurish, anti-illusionist acting. *Vinyl*, for instance, uses a single camera setup, the actors crowded claustrophobically within the tight frame; and while it may be best known for introducing Edie Sedgwick to the screen, she remains, despite her conspicuous presence in the forefront of the composition, entirely silent throughout, almost as if her *Screen Test* were encompassed within the larger film.

Warhol would continue to focus on performance and identity-projection throughout the 1960s, above all in two of his most ambitious films, *Outer and Inner Space* (1966) and *The Chelsea Girls* (1966), both of which represent remarkable experiments with double-screen filmmaking. *Outer and Inner Space* is technically a two-screen film, with two 16mm images projected side by side. Each image finds Sedgwick confronting her own (prerecorded) image on a video monitor, doubling the already doubled screen, and amplifying Warhol's fascination with the process of identity projection, as Sedgwick contends with both the camera and her own image. In *The Chelsea Girls*, the effect is not a doubling of essentially the same image but rather a counterpoint between two largely unrelated ones, glimpses into two different rooms within New York's Chelsea Hotel and the activities taking place therein. The (unedited) individual reels bear a great deal in common with Warhol's earlier films, observing from a detached perspective the attempts of a series of Warhol's superstars to assert themselves through their performances. With two reels projected simultaneously side by side, however, our perspective is rendered even more detached, each scene competing with the neighboring one, an element in a larger ensemble rather than the focus of attention. And since the soundtrack is played on only one projector at a time, one scene in each pair is silenced, the performers denied a crucial means of expression. The counterpoint is exhilarating, the eye free to focus on one or the other screen, and the soundtrack of the one fusing with the image of the other to create a strange hybrid, a whole greater than the sum of its parts.

Underground Narrative Filmmaking

The radical amateurishness of Rice, Jack Smith, and Warhol was an extreme example of an approach practiced more guardedly by other filmmakers, who chose to engage with narrative filmmaking on their own terms. *Shadows* is the best-known example, partly because of John Cassavetes's later fame and partly because its departures from narrative conventions are relatively gentle, at least in its final cut, which is substantially different from the hour-long version[1] that premiered alongside *Pull My Daisy* in late 1959, and that was celebrated by Mekas and others but never again shown publicly (Hoberman 1992, 101). But aside from Cassavetes, the underground included a number of filmmakers who were determined to create a new narrative form, one truer to the times they lived in. Striving to breathe life into a tradition which, they felt, had grown perilously out of touch in Hollywood's hands, they sought to recast the form into one that would reflect the social and cultural conditions brewing as the 1950s gave way to a new decade (one soon to prove so cataclysmic). Shirley Clarke, Lionel Rogosin, Robert Frank, Robert Downey, Sr, and even Jonas Mekas himself, who soon turned to making feature films, with *Guns of the Trees* (1961) and *The Brig* (1964) (before embracing the diary-film form he was to pioneer), all attempted to develop new narrative approaches, styles, and languages, embedding fictional stories in a wealth of what was essentially documentary footage, as in Rogosin's *On the Bowery*

(1956) and *Come Back, Africa* (1959), and Clarke's *The Cool World* (1963). The filmmakers mined the actors' lives and ideas for dramatic material (*Guns of the Trees*) or transformed low-budget conditions into a formal principle by telling a story via still images (Downey's *Chafed Elbows*, 1966), among many other strategies.

If these experiments in narrative filmmaking are less radical than the work of Smith, Anger, Warhol, and the other filmmakers discussed previously, they share a dedication to the stripping away of illusionism, a belief in the reinvigoration that comes from breaking down the walls of well-polished technique – the signifier of "quality" in the commercial cinema. All these films celebrate, in one way or another, roughness, instability, improvisation, and hand-craftedness. This elevation of amateurishness applies to the even more radical work of filmmakers like Stan Brakhage, Marie Menken, and Bruce Baillie, whose films stand at the opposite end of the spectrum from the innovations in narrative filmmaking pioneered by Rogosin, Clarke, and Mekas. The amateurishness of Brakhage, Baillie, and Menken is different, more complete. Their films are not amateurish in the sense of being made without care or technique – indeed, these are among the most finely crafted, technically elaborate, and perfectly formed films in existence – but in the more literal sense of a direct, solitary relationship between the artist and the material of his or her medium, a relationship unmediated by crews, sets, or even actors.

Experimental Animation: Harry Smith

The films of Menken, Brakhage, Baillie, Harry Smith, and Robert Breer, as well as Markopoulos's in-camera-edited short films, represent the furthest the underground has gone in exploring the cinema's potential as a purely (or primarily) visual medium – one free from storytelling, drama, and language. These films have their roots in what Sitney has termed the graphic cinema, the generally abstract and/or animated films issuing from the European avant-garde movement of the 1920s and 1930s (from filmmakers such as Hans Richter, Viking Eggeling, Oscar Fischinger, and Marcel Duchamp), from the nascent American experimental film movement that followed shortly thereafter (in the work of Len Lye, John and James Whitney, and Mary Ellen Bute), and from the contemporary work of the Austrian filmmaker Peter Kubelka in the late 1950s. Even when these films were photographed rather than animated, they were generally graphic in nature, concerned predominantly with shape, rhythm, and composition, in contrast to the work of Menken, Brakhage, and Baillie which was concerned with the qualities of light or the nature of perception. As such, the first wave of personal, non-narrative filmmaking was to prove influential more in terms of its mode of production than in its precise formal and aesthetic qualities. But this tradition does have an American legacy, in the painter turned filmmaker Robert Breer, and especially in the person of Harry Smith, one of the most gifted, idiosyncratic, and protean figures of the American avant-garde.

Harry Smith, like Cornell, was an underground filmmaker in the truest sense of the word, an artist working not only outside the conventions and structures of mainstream filmmaking, but to a large extent outside the stream of any tradition. Raised in a family of Theosophists, Smith developed a set of interests that encompassed the occult, Native American rituals and customs, and rural American folk music (his major claim to fame is as the compiler/editor of the *Anthology of American Folk Music*, a collection of folk recordings that was to exert a major influence on American popular music). His films, on which he labored practically in secret throughout the 1940s and 1950s, and which were to gain little or no notice until the underground movement was in full swing in the mid-1960s, are, like Cornell's boxes, made in an idiom almost entirely of his own invention. The earliest works are abstract, animated films, made using a variety of techniques. Later, he was to experiment with collage (*Mirror Animations*, 1957; *Heaven and Earth Magic*, 1957–1962) and superimposed photography (*Late Superimpositions*, 1964), often adding colored filters and other elements during projection. And at his death, he left unfinished the elaborate, contrapuntal, four-screen spectacle that is the unfinished *Mahagonny* (1970–1980). All of his films conjure up a world of uncanny, mysterious, deeply private imagery and associations, a world transfigured by the imagination into something strange, highly suggestive, but ultimately impenetrable. Most famous is *Heaven and Earth Magic*, a nearly hour-long, black-and-white animation, a stark collage in which various figures and objects interact and undergo a series of transformations. Sitney places *Heaven and Earth Magic* into the category of mythopoeia (2002, 109), and if its imagery seems too elusive to qualify as myth, there is no question that Smith's films exude a sense of a mysterious ritual. Though entirely different in technique and texture, they are closely connected to Anger's later work, with their immersion in a world of obscure symbols, cosmic imagery, and uncanny implications.

Adventures in Perception: Marie Menken, Stan Brakhage, and Bruce Baillie

The more immediate precursors to Marie Menken's later films, and to the work of Brakhage and Baillie, are to be found in the work of Menken's husband, Willard Maas, especially *Geography of the Body* (1943), a short film consisting of shots of the human body, magnified to the point of abstraction, and in Menken's own first film, *Visual Variations on Noguchi* (1945), an impressionistic, fragmented study of sculptures by the Japanese-American artist Isamu Noguchi. Though both films seem at first, in the tradition of the earlier graphic cinema, to tend toward abstraction, here the photographed objects are not reduced to two-dimensional shapes and surfaces, but rather observed so closely, with such a fresh perspective, that they reveal qualities we are not accustomed to perceiving. The goal is to sharpen perception, to liberate the eye from the conventions of preconditioned visual interpretation.

Though Menken was not to produce another film until 1957, with *Glimpse of the Garden*, that film took up where she had left off – in it, she trains her eye on a friend's garden, recording her impressions of light, color, and form with utmost directness, spontaneity, and simplicity. *Glimpse of the Garden*, as well as Menken's *Notebook* (1940–1962) and *Lights* (1964–1966), among many others, demonstrate one of the underground movement's most fecund and distinctive new forms, which Sitney calls "the lyrical film" and credits Stan Brakhage with pioneering. According to Sitney, "the lyrical film postulates the film-maker behind the camera as the first-person protagonist of the film," with the imagery filmed "in such a way that we never forget his presence and know how he is reacting to his vision" (2002, 160). Sitney goes on to assert: "In the lyrical form there is no longer a hero; instead the screen is filled with movement, and that movement, both of the camera and the editing, reverberates with the idea of a person looking" (2002, 160).

Menken's films are certainly lyrical – the fleet, blissful, careening camerawork of *Glimpse of the Garden* expressing her sensibility with a directness unique to avant-garde film. But in Menken's work, the emphasis is on the object of sight, the environment to which she turns her attention. In the mature films of Stan Brakhage, one of the towering figures of the avant-garde cinema, on the other hand, the emphasis shifts to the process of seeing. His filmmaking, as much as Menken's, is founded on his engagement with the external world and its phenomena, but this world is transfigured by his dedication to "untutored" or even "closed eye" vision, his conception of perception an increasingly metaphysical one. This preoccupation with the relationship between the external world and the process of seeing would become Stan Brakhage's life work, a project embodied in his prolific filmmaking, as well as in his book *Metaphors on Vision*.

The first phase of Brakhage's filmmaking was in the tradition of the trance film, but the direction of his work was soon to change. In Sitney's model, Brakhage moved increasingly toward the mythic, or more precisely, the "mythopoeic" – the "often attempted and seldom achieved result of making a myth new or making a new myth" (Sitney, introduction to Brakhage 1963). Certainly Brakhage was fully committed to self-mythologizing, characterizing his work as more than simply a contribution to the art of cinema, but as a project of the most profound intellectual and cultural import. *Metaphors on Vision* is the source of Brakhage's famous declaration of his determination to steer film toward a new investigation into the nature and untapped possibilities of perception, a project for which the cinema would seem to be uniquely suited, but which few filmmakers had thus far pursued:

> Imagine an eye unruled by man-made laws of perspective, an eye unprejudiced by compositional logic, an eye which does not respond to the name of everything but which must know each object encountered in life through an adventure of perception. How many colors are there in a field of grass to the crawling baby unaware of "Green"? How many rainbows can light create for the untutored eye?

> Imagine a world alive with incomprehensible objects and shimmering with an endless variety of movement and innumerable gradations of color. Imagine a world before the "beginning was the word." ... I suggest that there is a pursuit of knowledge foreign to language and founded upon visual communication, demanding a development of the optical mind, and dependent upon perception in the original and deepest sense of the word. (Brakhage 1963)

This passage identifies the nature of Brakhage's project, his determination to develop a radically new cinematic language that would privilege optical perception, imparting a pure experience of light, color, and motion unmediated by cultural conditioning. This new language dispensed with many of the commercial cinema's most cherished standards of quality – stable focus, fluid and motivated camera movement, comprehensible imagery, easily assimilated editing – instead transforming the camera into a finely tuned, sensitive, and intuitive instrument of vision. Brakhage's mature films not only convey, but demand, an unfamiliar, heightened, and challenging level of attention and comprehension.

Metaphors on Vision also suggests Brakhage's conviction that his project extends beyond cinematic, artistic significance to represent an advance in human awareness and understanding. *Dog Star Man*, the first major embodiment of his perceived mission, is certainly mythopoeic, insofar as it dramatizes this pursuit of a new level of perception. Its five parts demonstrate the full spectrum of Brakhage's radically new cinematic language – a densely edited and rhythmically complex combination of abstract fields of color, found footage of both cosmic and microscopic phenomena, and scratches made directly on the surface of the film. The various parts are unified not only by their style but also by the presence of the Dog Star Man, a figure (embodied by Brakhage himself) whose actions (chopping wood, struggling to uproot a tree, and laboriously climbing a hill) reflect an allegorical representation of Brakhage's own struggle to forge a new way of seeing, and a new way of capturing perception cinematically.

If the Dog Star Man represents a mythic embodiment of Brakhage's project, his later films, in keeping with Sitney's characterization of the lyrical film, dispense with any form of protagonist, even an allegorical one, attempting something like the direct transmission of visual perception, utilizing the camera as a conduit between filmmaker and viewer. Brakhage would explore this notion of the function of cinema in many different contexts, applying his radically subjective method to the documentation of objective events, both personal (the birth of his children in *Window Water Baby Moving*, 1959, and *Thigh Line Lyre Triangular*, 1961), and public (the work of Pittsburgh's police, hospital, and morgue workers in his *Pittsburgh Trilogy*, 1971), as well as to the investigation of totally abstract visual phenomena (as in *Text of Light*, a feature-length study of the play of light, shadow, and color produced by filming through a glass ashtray). He would gradually eschew photography altogether, devoting himself to producing films by scratching or painting directly on the filmstrip, circumventing the photographic process in his attempts to inspire a mode of vision free of accepted forms and categories. By positioning his films as part of a grand, visionary project, and by building a body of work marked by epic-length statements or multifilm series, Brakhage's own identity looms large over his films, both as subjective conduit and as self-mythologizing creator.

Bruce Baillie is generally considered an important follower of Brakhage's innovations, though his early films are reminiscent more of Menken's simple, unaffected observations of her environment than of Brakhage's visionary adventures in superperception. Baillie would, however, eventually produce three longer-form, more ambitious films – *Mass for the Dakota Sioux* (1963–1964), *Quixote* (1964–1968), and *Quick Billy* (1967–1970) – which would find him working very much in Brakhage's mature mode, documenting his own life and his interactions with his environment and employing a camera-eye of great sensitivity and freedom. All three of these films combine Brakhage's optical investigations with a political awareness and engagement distinctive to Baillie, an expansion of Brakhage's approach into new areas.

While these are Baillie's most ambitious undertakings, his greatest single film may be *Castro Street* (1966), a short study of a trainyard, which boasts a visual and rhythmic complexity equaled only by Markopoulos's portrait films. *Castro Street* may be more modest in its goals than *Quixote* or *Quick Billy*, or than Brakhage's work, but it is a perfect illustration of the cinematic potentialities unveiled by the American avant-garde in this period, a revelation of the possibilities of superimposition, composition, editing, and rhythm that attains a visual sophistication analogous to the very greatest achievements in music, and compared to which most narrative films appear paltry and barren.

Conclusion

Although Hoberman, James, and others may date the end of the underground movement to the commercial success of *The Chelsea Girls* in 1966, the larger American avant-garde movement, of which the underground represented only a phase – albeit a crucial one, encompassing the formation of a cohesive, lasting, and vigorous community, a remarkable convergence of energies and institutions – was in no danger of being eclipsed. Nevertheless, the mid-1960s ushered in an unmistakable transition in the approaches and goals of many experimental filmmakers, no less than did the mid-1950s. The changes were already being glimpsed in the work of Brakhage, Warhol, and Baillie, all of whom used flash-frames, black leader, sprocket holes, and other explicit elements of the material aspect of the medium. And they were especially evident in the trajectory of Ken Jacobs's work, from *Blonde Cobra*'s bold structural use of black leader to *Tom, Tom, the Piper's Son*'s transformation of a short silent film into a study of the texture and grain of exposed celluloid. These filmmakers would be joined by a new wave of artists – including Hollis Frampton, Michael Snow, George Landow (a.k.a. Owen Land), and Standish Lawder in the United States, along with Malcolm Le Grice, Kurt Kren, and Brigit and Wilhelm Hein in Europe – who would go even further in investigating the formal and material properties of film and in stripping the medium down to its essential characteristics in an attempt to declare its independence from other art forms.

Some have seen the rise of structuralism, the term applied to the new direction taken by the experimental cinema, as the ultimate step in the avant-garde's rejection of narrative conventions and its focus on strictly cinematic concerns. But this turn inward, this focus on film as film, also represented a retreat from the social engagement, or socially motivated disengagement, reflected by much of the underground of the late 1950s/early 1960s. David E. James has most astutely identified this shift, observing in *Allegories of Cinema* a splitting off within independent American filmmaking, a division between the avant-garde, which moved increasingly toward the art world and its predominantly formal concerns, and radical political filmmaking, which took the form of a proliferation of collective Newsreel organizations. While these Newsreel organizations remained aware of the formal dimension of filmmaking, they were focused on political engagement (James 1989, 164–165). It is difficult to argue that the period's remarkable eruption of energies and possibilities, of intertwined political dissent and aesthetic innovation, has not cooled in the intervening decades. The explicitly political cinema declined as the social energies erupting in the 1960s and 1970s lost momentum, and underground film has yet to regain the relative cultural prominence it briefly achieved in the first part of the 1960s. But, while the underground may have retreated back underground, the alternative cinema pioneered by Maya Deren and others, and consolidated by Jonas Mekas and the host of filmmakers who made up the underground, New American Cinema, or experimental film movements, remains a vital, if underappreciated dimension of American film culture, continuing to explore the myriad potentialities of the medium that the commercial cinema persists in neglecting.

Note

1. The two versions share only about a half-hour's worth of footage.

References

Brakhage, Stan. (1963). *Metaphors on Vision*. New York: Film Culture Inc.

Hoberman, J. (1992). "The Forest and *The Trees*." In David E. James (ed.), *To Free the Cinema: Jonas Mekas and the New York Underground* (pp. 100–120). Princeton: Princeton University Press.

Hoberman, J. (2001). *On Jack Smith's Flaming Creatures (and Other Secret-Flix of Cinemaroc)*. New York: Granary Books/Hips Road.

Hoberman, J., & Rosenbaum, J. (1991). *Midnight Movies*. New York: Da Capo Press. (Original work published 1983.)

James, David E. (1989). *Allegories of Cinema: American Film in the Sixties*. Princeton: Princeton University Press.

Mekas, Jonas. (1962). "Notes on the New American Cinema." *Film Culture*, 24, 6–16.

Sargeant, Jack. (2008). *Naked Lens: Beat Cinema*. Berkeley: Soft Skull Press. (Original work published 1997.)

Sitney, P. Adams. (2002). *Visionary Film: The American Avant-Garde 1943–2000*. 3rd edn. Oxford: Oxford University Press. (Original work published 1974.)

Smith, Jack. (1962). "The Perfect Filmic Appositeness of Maria Montez." *Film Culture*, 27, 28–32.

Smith, Jack. (1963–1964). "Belated Appreciation of V.S." *Film Culture*, 31, 4–5.

Wees, William C. (1993). *Recycled Images: The Art and Politics of Found Footage Films*. New York: Anthology Film Archives.

Index

Entries for film titles are in italics, followed by the date of release in brackets, e.g. *Walk a Crooked Mile* (1948). Page references for illustrations are also in italics.

American Film History: Selected Readings, Origins to 1960, First Edition. Edited by Cynthia Lucia, Roy Grundmann, and Art Simon.
© 2016 John Wiley & Sons, Inc. Published 2016 by John Wiley & Sons, Inc.